NATIONAL GEOGRAPHIC | U.S. HISTORY

AMERICA
THROUGH THE LENS

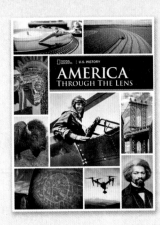

Clockwise from center:

- American aviator Amelia Earhart poses in the cockpit of her autogyro in 1931 after setting an altitude record for female pilots.

- Completed in 1909, the Manhattan Bridge spans the East River in New York City, connecting Lower Manhattan to Brooklyn.

- Frederick Douglass was born around 1818, escaped from slavery, sought an education, and became an abolitionist and activist.

- A drone hovers mid-air, capturing footage of rain clouds with its camera.

- Rock art, or petroglyphs, carved by the ancestral Puebloans cover a rock formation near Blanding, Utah.

- An American icon—a bison—enjoys the safety of the Maxwell Wildlife Refuge in Canton, Kansas.

- The work of artist Rosalia Torres-Weiner is part of an exhibition called *Gateways/ Portales,* which explores the experiences of Latino immigrants and migrants in four U.S. cities with growing Latino populations.

- The vinyl record player evolved from the phonograph, which was invented by Thomas Edison in the 1870s.

- Alfalfa, a hay crop commonly used to feed cattle, is harvested by a farmer in Kansas.

Back Cover:

American company SpaceX successfully launches the Falcon Heavy rocket into deep space on February 6, 2018 from Cape Canaveral in Florida.

This book is dedicated to Jeanine Childs, a beloved member of the National Geographic Learning family.

Acknowledgments

Grateful acknowledgment is given to the authors, artists, photographers, museums, publishers, and agents for permission to reprint copyrighted material. Every effort has been made to secure the appropriate permission. If any omissions have been made or if corrections are required, please contact the Publisher.

Credits

Front Cover: (tl) Tetra Images/Getty Images. (tr) Andy Sacks/ Getty Images. (cl) ©Rosalia Torres/Brandon Torres-Weiner. (c) ©Bettmann/Getty Images. (cr) pidjoe/Getty Images. (bl1) Joel Sartore/National Geographic Creative. (bl2) David Hiser/ National Geographic Creative. (bc) Amos Chapple/Getty Images. (br) Library of Congress, LC-DIG-ds-07422.

Back Cover: SpaceX.

Acknowledgments and credits continue on page R93.

For product information and technology assistance, contact us at Customer & Sales Support, 888-915-3276

For permission to use material from this text or product, submit all requests online at **www.cengage.com/permissions**

Further permissions questions can be emailed to **permissionrequest@cengage.com**

National Geographic Learning | Cengage
1 N. State Street, Suite 900
Chicago, IL 60602

Cengage is a leading provider of customized learning solutions with office locations around the globe, including Singapore, the United Kingdom, Australia, Mexico, Brazil, and Japan. Locate your local office at **www.cengage.com/global.**

Visit National Geographic Learning online at **NGL.Cengage.com/school**

Visit our corporate website at **www.cengage.com**

ISBN: 978-133-711-191-1

Printed in the United States of America.

Print Number: 05
Print Year: 2022

SENIOR CONSULTANTS

FREDRIK HIEBERT

Fred Hiebert is National Geographic's Archaeologist-in-Residence. He has led archaeological expeditions at ancient Silk Roads sites across Asia. Hiebert was curator of National Geographic's exhibition "Afghanistan: Hidden Treasures from the National Museum, Kabul," and its more recent exhibition, "The Greeks: Agamemnon to Alexander the Great."

PEGGY ALTOFF

Peggy Altoff's career includes teaching middle school and high school students, supervising teachers, and serving as adjunct university faculty. Altoff served as a state social studies specialist in Maryland and as a K–12 coordinator in Colorado Springs. She is a past president of the National Council for the Social Studies (NCSS) and served on the task force for the 2012 NCSS National Curriculum Standards.

FRITZ FISCHER

Fritz Fischer is a professor and Director of History Education at the University of Northern Colorado, where he teaches U.S. History and Social Studies Education courses. Fischer is also Chair Emeritus of the Board of Trustees of the National Council for History Education (NCHE), the largest national membership organization focusing on history education at the K–12 level.

PROGRAM CONSULTANTS

KATHRYN KEANE
Vice President, National
Geographic Exhibitions

ROBERT REID
Travel Writer

National Geographic
Digital Nomad

WILLIAM PARKINSON
Associate Curator of Anthropology,
Field Museum of Natural History

National Geographic Explorer

ANDRÉS RUZO
Geothermal Scientist

National Geographic Explorer

NATIONAL GEOGRAPHIC TEACHER REVIEWERS

National Geographic works with teachers at all grade levels from across the country.
The following teachers reviewed chapters in *U.S. History: America Through the Lens.*

CRYSTAL CULP
McCracken Regional
School
Paducah, KY

KAREN DAVIS
St. Joseph School
Conway, AR

NICOLE ESHELMAN
Manheim Township High
School
Lancaster, PA

KIMBERLY HENDRICKS
Park Hill South High
School
Kansas City, MO

MARY JANZEN
Duncan High School
Fresno, CA

SYLVIA MCBRIDE
Castle Park High School
Chula Vista, CA

NATALIE WOJINSKI
West Contra Costa USD
Richmond, CA

NATIONAL GEOGRAPHIC SOCIETY

The National Geographic Society contributed significantly to *U.S. History: America Through the Lens.* Our collaboration with each of the following has been a pleasure and a privilege: National Geographic Maps, National Geographic Education and Children's Media, and National Geographic Missions programs. We thank the Society for its guidance and support.

NATIONAL GEOGRAPHIC

NATIONAL GEOGRAPHIC EXPLORATION

National Geographic supports the work of a host of anthropologists, archaeologists, adventurers, biologists, educators, writers, and photographers across the world. The individuals below each contributed substantially to *U.S. History: America Through the Lens*.

SAM ABELL
National Geographic
Photographer

ROBERT BALLARD
National Geographic
Explorer-in-Residence

ARI BESER
Fulbright–National
Geographic Fellow

KEVIN CRISMAN
National Geographic
Explorer

JASON DE LEÓN
National Geographic
Explorer

LESLIE DEWAN
National Geographic
Explorer

KEVIN HAND
National Geographic
Explorer

BILL KELSO
National Geographic
Explorer

SARAH PARCAK
National Geographic
Fellow

SANDRA POSTEL
National Geographic
Freshwater Fellow
(2009–2015)

TRISTRAM STUART
National Geographic
Explorer

THROUGH THE LENS PHOTOGRAPHERS

The work of the National Geographic photographers below helps tell the story of America in striking, image-focused lessons.

LYNSEY ADDARIO   **JIMMY CHIN**   **JEFFREY GUSKY**   **DAVID GUTTENFELDER**   **MICHAEL NICHOLS**   **PAUL NICKLEN**

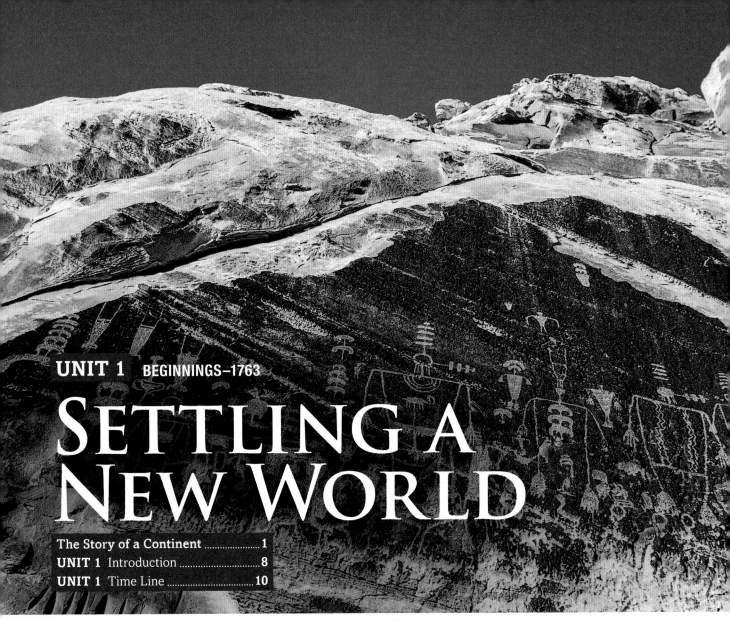

UNIT 1 BEGINNINGS–1763

SETTLING A NEW WORLD

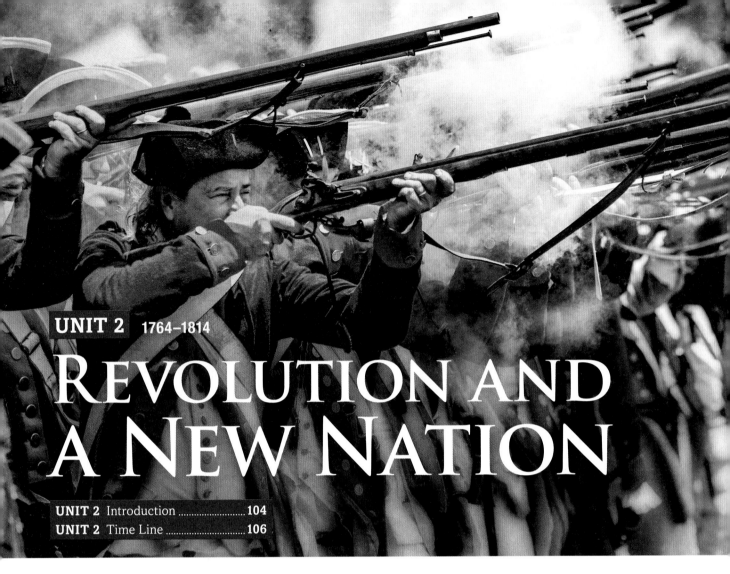

UNIT 2 1764–1814

REVOLUTION AND A NEW NATION

UNIT 3 1814–1854

EXPANDING THE NEW NATION

ARCHAEOLOGY AND U.S. HISTORY

Dr. Fredrik Hiebert

Archaeologist-In-Residence,
National Geographic Society **342**

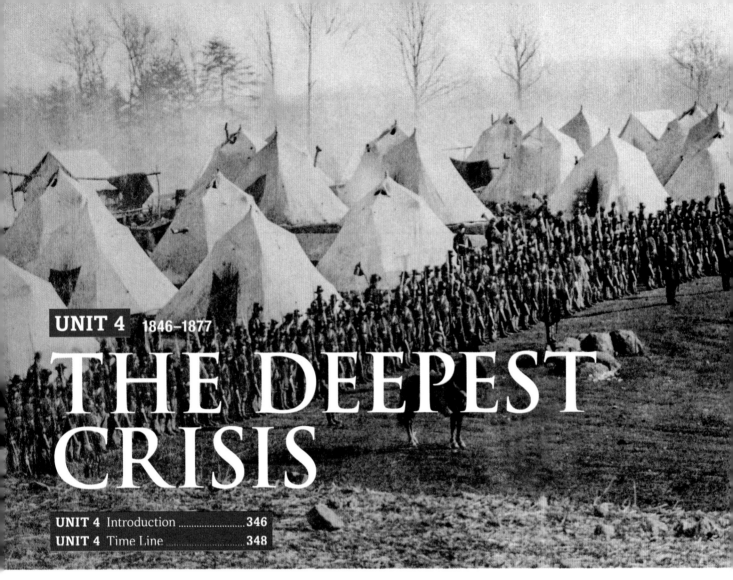

UNIT 4 1846–1877
THE DEEPEST CRISIS

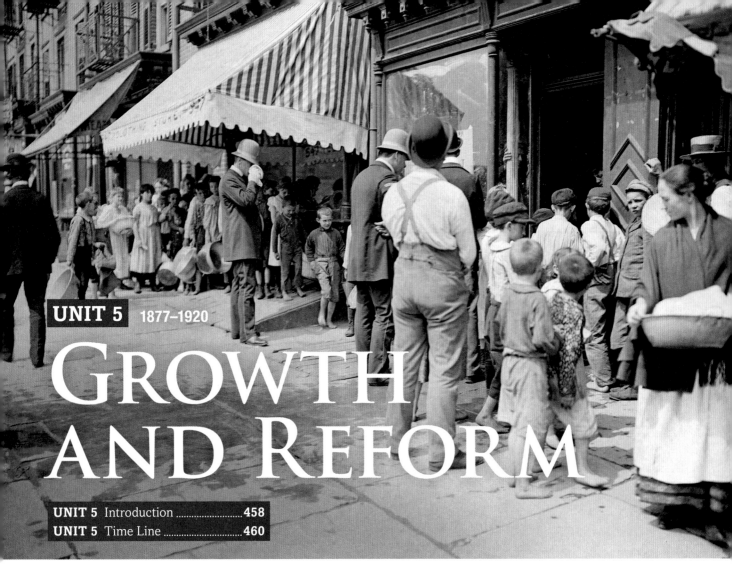

UNIT 5 1877–1920

GROWTH AND REFORM

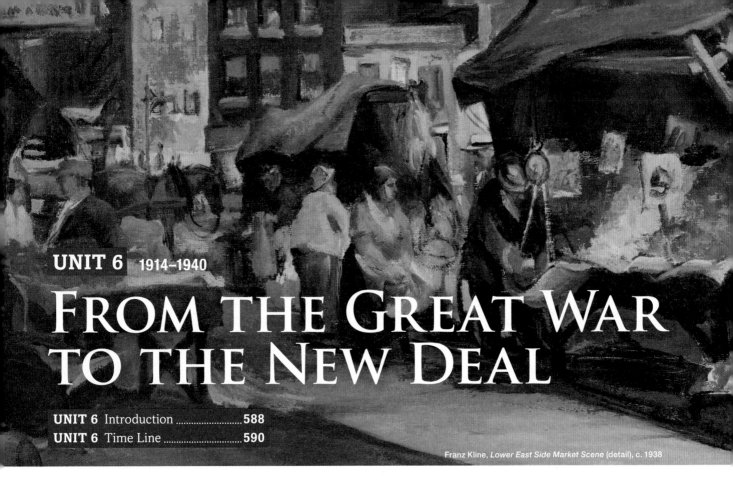

UNIT 6 1914–1940
FROM THE GREAT WAR TO THE NEW DEAL

Franz Kline, *Lower East Side Market Scene* (detail), c. 1938

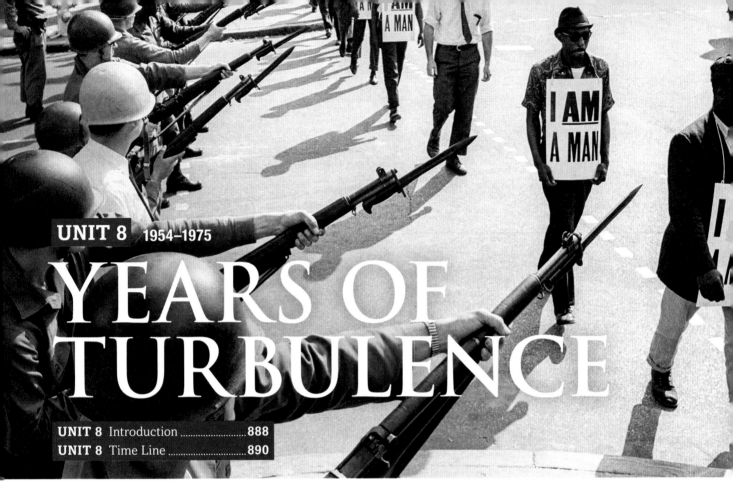

UNIT 8 1954–1975

YEARS OF TURBULENCE

UNIT 9 1968–PRESENT
CHALLENGES OF A NEW CENTURY

NATIONAL GEOGRAPHIC FEATURES

Maps

National Geographic Contributors

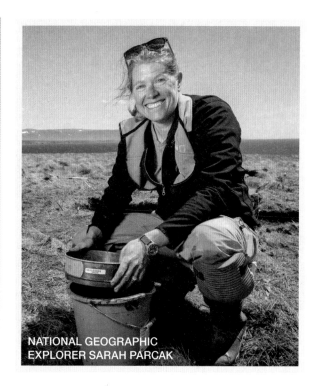

NATIONAL GEOGRAPHIC
EXPLORER SARAH PARCAK

Curating History

Document-Based Questions

GREENSBORO SIT-IN, 1960

SAILORS ON THE DECK OF THE USS MONITOR, 1864

American Stories

American Stories Online

American Galleries Online

Student Handbooks

Geology in History

American Voices Biographies

SEQUOIA NATIONAL PARK

HARRIET TUBMAN

Through The Lens Features

Featured Themes

Featured Photographers

Featured American Places

THE STORY OF A CONTINENT

BY DR. WILLIAM PARKINSON
National Geographic Explorer
Associate Curator of Anthropology
Field Museum of Natural History

CRITICAL VIEWING This artist's rendering shows the Laurentide Ice Sheet, which, at times, covered large parts of North America during the Pleistocene epoch. Present-day glaciers, particularly in Canada, are remnants of this ice sheet. What does the image reveal about this glacial period?

EARTH'S TIME LINE ⎯⎯ 100 Million Years

Earth Forms
4.5 Billion Years Ago

First Life Appears on Earth
3.8 Billion Years Ago

Close your eyes for a minute and try to imagine the United States without any of the familiar trappings of 21st-century life—no smartphones, hoverboards, or tablets. No iTunes, YouTube, or video games.

Imagine traveling from place to place without paved roads to follow—in fact, with no roads at all, and no wheeled vehicles or even horses to carry you. Instead of strip malls, fast-food chains, and electric streetlights, there are lush, dark forests, pristine rivers and streams, and abundant plant and animal life as far as your eye can see.

Take a deep breath while we travel back to the earliest history of North America, from the beginnings of civilization and even further back to a time when mammoths and mastodons, saber-toothed cats, and giant ground sloths roamed the lands of North America. It was a time when your own species, *Homo sapiens*, evolved and spread throughout the world.

This is the moment in a play just before the main curtain rises on North America—a continent with a story much longer than you may think.

GEOLOGY AND LANDSCAPE

North America is geologically dramatic, featuring towering mountains, vast deserts, sandy beaches, and rolling hills. But the landscape that Europeans like Christopher Columbus encountered when they arrived in the "New World" just a few hundred years ago was profoundly different from the world that the earliest humans experienced when they first came to North America.

Let's go way back in time to when the first modern humans arrived in North America. It was at the end of a more than 2-million-year period that geologists refer to as the **Pleistocene epoch** (PLEIS-to-seen EH-puhk). During this period, the climate and ecology of North America was completely different from the climate and ecology of today and included supersized animals and plants that no longer exist. During the Pleistocene epoch, modern humans across the world honed their skills in hunting, created early artwork, developed fire, and began to use language.

Many people think the climate during the Pleistocene was always cold when, in fact, there were dramatic fluctuations in temperature over relatively short periods of time. At some points, the climate during the Pleistocene was about the same as it is today. During **glacial periods**, or **ice ages**, when glaciers expanded across Earth's surface, the global average annual temperature was significantly colder.

During the Pleistocene epoch, there were more than 20 cycles of glacial periods in which the movement of ice and water changed the landscape and shorelines of the continents drastically, especially around the edges of the Arctic Circle and in present-day North America, Europe, and Asia.

In North America, ice sheets extended as far south as the Missouri and Ohio rivers and covered nearly all of Canada and much of the northern Great Plains, the Midwest, and the northeastern United States. Some recognizable bodies of water and landforms created by glacial movement include the Great Lakes, Cape Cod in Massachusetts, Long Island in New York, and Glacier National Park in Montana. When the glaciers retreated about 10,000 years ago, the North American landscape looked much like it does today.

◀ 2.6 MILLION YEARS AGO

TODAY ▶

PLEISTOCENE EPOCH
2.6 Million to 11,700 Years Ago

⊦————⊦ 100 Thousand Years

People Arrive in North America 18–12,000 Years Ago

Modern Humans Evolve 75,000 Years Ago

HOLOCENE EPOCH
11,700 Years Ago to Today

North America Splits from Pangea
200 Million Years Ago

TODAY ▶

BRIDGING THE CONTINENTS

In Europe, Asia, and Africa, modern humans evolved between 75,000 and 35,000 years ago—long before they arrived in North America. By the end of the Pleistocene, about 12,000 years ago, the only surviving hominid species was modern humans.

Scientists love debates, and one of the biggest debates in archaeology centers around the arrival of the earliest modern humans in North America. We know that when the Pleistocene ended, there were modern human societies living throughout the continent. The debate revolves around pinpointing when during the Pleistocene the first people migrated to the Americas and whether they came by boat or walked. Yes, it was possible for people to have *walked* from Europe and Asia to the Americas! Yes! But the continents are separated by oceans!

Today, the continents are separated by oceans, but during the Pleistocene, there were glacial periods when ice sheets covered the continents. In addition, the oceans contained less water, and the coastlines of the continents were much larger. After the last major glacial period, about 20,000 years ago, the two ice sheets that covered northern North America began to melt, leaving North America temporarily connected to Asia by a large stretch of land between modern-day Alaska and Siberia that scientists call the **Bering Land Bridge**. About 11,000 to 12,000 years ago, the land bridge disappeared as the ice melted, the oceans filled with the water, and the coastlines receded.

A team of paleontologists from the University of Michigan recovered this mastodon skull and more than 60 percent of the animal's skeleton in October 2016. Mastodons are extinct relatives of the elephant.

MAN   ELEPHANT   MAMMOTH   MASTODON

ENORMOUS ANIMALS

About 12,000 years ago, we entered the Holocene (HO-luh-seen) epoch, which we are still in today. Many animals that lived during the Pleistocene went extinct around the beginning of the Holocene, including many species of large animals, or megafauna, such as mammoths, mastodons, and saber-toothed cats. Along with other oversize animals, like giant sloths, giant beavers, and American lions, horses also lived in North America until the end of the Pleistocene but were reintroduced by Europeans a few hundred years ago. They became a critical aspect of Native American culture, especially on the Great Plains. This was the incredible environment the earliest humans encountered when they first arrived in North America at the end of the Pleistocene.

THE GREAT DEBATE

Until recently, scientists believed that the earliest people to arrive in the Americas just before the land bridge disappeared were **hunter-gatherers** who specialized in hunting large herd animals that migrated back and forth across the continent. Archaeologists call them the Clovis Culture, based on a kind of stone tool—a Clovis point—that people made at that time.

But there is growing evidence that other groups may have reached the Americas before the Clovis Culture. Sites in Chile and Pennsylvania suggest that there was a pre-Clovis occupation of North America, and some scientists even speculate that people may have arrived by boats earlier in the Pleistocene, perhaps from Europe rather than Asia.

By the end of the Pleistocene, the climate began to stabilize, and modern humans spread throughout the Americas. They were specialized, mobile hunters and gatherers like their contemporaries elsewhere in the world, and they used the same technology— Clovis points—to hunt. These points have been found throughout North America, and similar ones have appeared as far south as Venezuela. People began to settle in different regions of the North American continent that can be distinguished according to the specialized stone tools that were made and used in the Holocene.

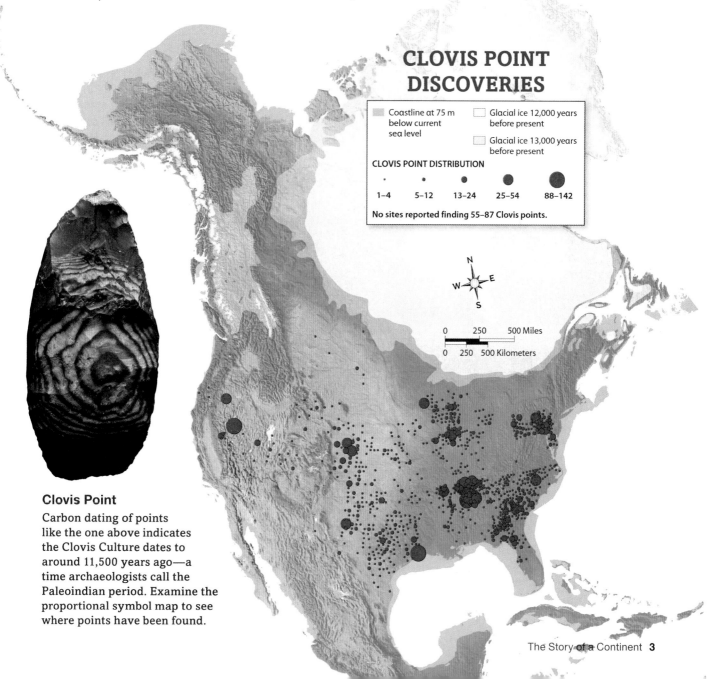

CLOVIS POINT DISCOVERIES

- Coastline at 75 m below current sea level
- Glacial ice 12,000 years before present
- Glacial ice 13,000 years before present

CLOVIS POINT DISTRIBUTION

1–4 5–12 13–24 25–54 88–142

No sites reported finding 55–87 Clovis points.

0   250   500 Miles
0   250   500 Kilometers

Clovis Point

Carbon dating of points like the one above indicates the Clovis Culture dates to around 11,500 years ago—a time archaeologists call the Paleoindian period. Examine the proportional symbol map to see where points have been found.

THE AGRICULTURAL REVOLUTION

For several thousand years during the Holocene, people continued to live in small groups and move frequently throughout the year, but everything changed when some groups of mobile hunters and gatherers started to experiment with planting their own crops. This transition from relying on gathering wild plants and hunting animals to planting crops and raising animals is called the **Agricultural Revolution**.

The practice of bringing plants and animals under human control is called **domestication**. Almost all the foods we eat today are domesticated instead of wild, which means they have been modified from their wild forms and are to some extent reliant upon humans for their existence. Corn, for example, is the domesticated form of a plant called *teosinte* (TAY-oh-SIN-tay), and cows are the domestic form of a wild herd animal called an *aurochs* (OR-auks). Domestication had a dramatic impact on society and actually transformed human life as people settled down and became reliant upon domestic plants and animals.

Out of all the plants domesticated in North America thousands of years ago, the real game changer was corn. The hunters and gatherers who began experimenting with the domestication of corn had no idea of the impact their little experiment would have on the world in the years to come. Corn is now grown almost everywhere in the world and tied to almost everything Americans eat and many things Americans produce, such as toothpaste and gasoline. But the biggest impact corn had in North America was its unparalleled ability to feed large populations.

This copper plate, discovered in 1906 near Malden, Missouri, provides evidence of Mississippian cultures outside of Cahokia.

SETTLING DOWN

It took a while for corn to be adopted and widely used in North America. In eastern North America, for example, it wasn't a major part of the human diet until about 1,000 years ago. Growing crops like corn and remaining in one location allowed social groups to grow larger and develop more complex political systems. In some places, these groups built massive cities and had extensive trade networks that moved goods across the continent.

One of these cities was located in present-day Illinois along the Mississippi River near the city of St. Louis, Missouri. Founded around A.D. 800, Cahokia would come to be the capital of a large community called a **chiefdom**. By A.D. 1250, Cahokia was a thriving community that controlled a massive geographic area at the confluence of three rivers (the Missouri, Illinois, and Mississippi), and at its height may have had a population of about 15,000 people. It is considered the most sophisticated prehistoric native civilization north of Mexico.

Since the fertile soil of Cahokia was easy to farm and was well suited to growing corn, people farmed more and hunted less. And archaeological evidence unearthed from the site indicates the people of Cahokia ate well.

Although Cahokia and other similar sites in the southeastern United States were heavily dependent upon domestic crops like corn, communities in other parts of North America were not. They continued to hunt and gather wild resources as a major part of their diet.

CORN EVOLVES

Corn's wild ancestor, a grass called *teosinte*, doesn't look much like corn but has a very similar genetic makeup. After corn was introduced to North America 6,000 to 10,000 years ago, it spread from Mexico into the American Southwest and across the continent. Early farmers learned to grow types of corn with preferred qualities such as resistance to pests and the ability to grow in different types of soil, which led to a great diversity of species.

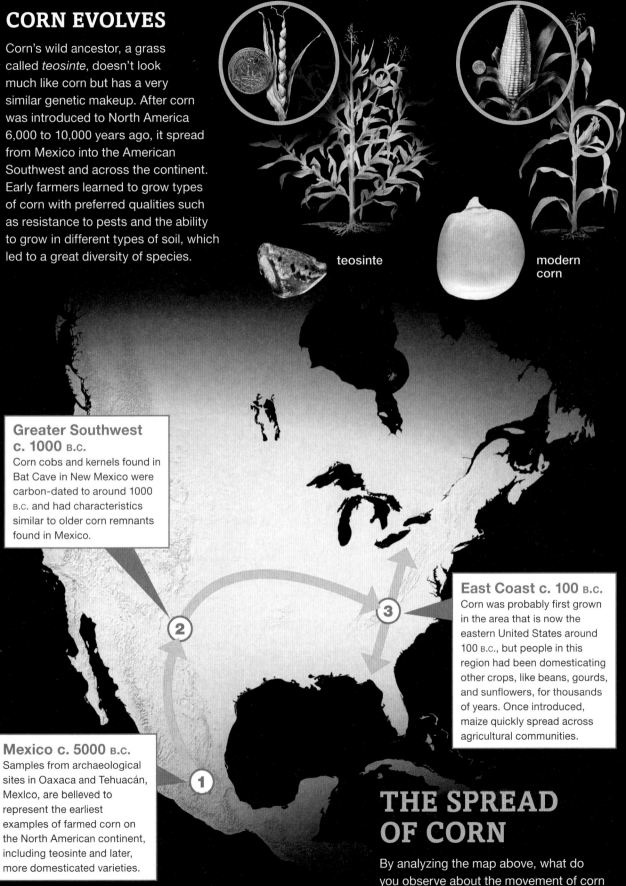

teosinte

modern corn

Greater Southwest c. 1000 B.C.
Corn cobs and kernels found in Bat Cave in New Mexico were carbon-dated to around 1000 B.C. and had characteristics similar to older corn remnants found in Mexico.

East Coast c. 100 B.C.
Corn was probably first grown in the area that is now the eastern United States around 100 B.C., but people in this region had been domesticating other crops, like beans, gourds, and sunflowers, for thousands of years. Once introduced, maize quickly spread across agricultural communities.

Mexico c. 5000 B.C.
Samples from archaeological sites in Oaxaca and Tehuacán, Mexico, are believed to represent the earliest examples of farmed corn on the North American continent, including teosinte and later, more domesticated varieties.

THE SPREAD OF CORN

By analyzing the map above, what do you observe about the movement of corn across the North American continent?

A CULTURAL MOSAIC

Before the 1500s, the Americas, Europe, and Africa had been isolated from one another, but as Europeans began looking beyond their shores for riches and resources, Africa's mighty empires wanted to show their strength. Both continents were on a collision course with the Americas, but the Europeans got there first.

When the Europeans arrived in the "New World," they experienced a mosaic of diverse cultures and landscapes. From the hierarchical chiefdoms of Florida to the more mobile, less hierarchical groups of the Great Basin, the cultures of North America made up a patchwork quilt of societies with distinct languages, economic practices, political systems, and traditions as varied as the landscape.

These petroglyphs in California's Chidago Canyon are thought to be the visions of ancient Paiute shamans.

Everyone has a personal American story to tell, and those stories often reflect the diversity of our cultural mosaic. It's not always easy to build consensus or get everyone "on the same page," but that diversity is one of the best things about life in the United States. With so many options and perspectives and our persistent American drive, we have the potential to develop amazingly creative solutions to 21st-century issues.

So raise the curtain on this incredibly rich and varied landscape, well equipped to sustain and nurture the promise of a unique new country and a vibrant people. The action and the drama are just about to begin.

THINK ABOUT IT

What does the fact that these diverse cultures all expressed themselves through art suggest about early humans?

This two-chambered pigment bowl in the form of a bird was found in the Pacific Northwest region of North America.

NORTHWEST

PLATEAU

BASIN

CALIFORNIA

SOUTHWEST

Believed to be 1,000 years old, the Pilling Figurines from the Fremont group in Utah were named for the rancher who discovered them in 1950.

Like other groups in the Southwest, the Hohokam of southern Arizona created pottery painted with elaborate designs.

ARCTIC

SUBARCTIC

PLAINS

NORTHEAST

SOUTHEAST

In the Woodlands culture, a bird stone like this one found in Jefferson County, New York, was used to properly weight a throwing stick, or atlatl.

A Hopewell artist created this pipe in the form of a toad between 300 B.C. and A.D. 500.

Created by a Great Plains craftsman around 1720, this necklace is made of leather and bear teeth.

The ruins of more than 600 cliff dwellings where the ancient Pueblo lived between 500 and c. 1300 can be seen at Mesa Verde National Park in Colorado.

This Mississippian vessel with a human face dates to between 1300 and 1500.

CRITICAL VIEWING Petroglyphs, or rock carvings, created by ancient
Native American artists can be found throughout the Southwest. The
petroglyphs in this photo by National Geographic photographer Paul
Chesley include many different figures. Describe some of the figures
you see. What types of activities or events might they represent?

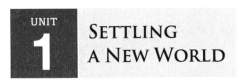

THE AMERICANS

1492
Christopher Columbus arrives in the Americas to search for gold and other precious items to take back to Spain. *(model of Columbus's ship, the* Santa Maria, *the largest of the three ships he used in 1492)*

1607
English settlers found the colony of Jamestown in Virginia. *(key to a sea chest belonging to a passenger who sailed to Jamestown)*

Early 1600s
The first enslaved Africans arrive in the American colonies of Virginia and Maryland to work on tobacco farms.

1600

1500s
Spanish explorers conduct expeditions in the Americas, conquer native peoples, and claim their lands.

1500

THE WORLD

1517 EUROPE
Martin Luther nails his 95 Theses to a church door in Germany, sparking the Reformation and giving rise to Protestantism.

1588 EUROPE
The British defeat the Spanish Armada, which leads to the establishment of colonies in North America by the English, Dutch, and French.

1603 ASIA
Tokugawa Ieyasu establishes a shogunate in Japan. *(photo of the Imperial Palace in Tokyo, which stands on the site of the castle built by the Tokugawa shogunate)*

1675
Native American chief Metacom, also known as King Philip, leads a bloody uprising against colonists in New England. *(engraved portrait of Metacom)*

HISTORICAL THINKING

DETERMINE CHRONOLOGY Which events in the Americas and the world resulted in revolts by African-American slaves and Native Americans?

1763
The French and Indian War ends, and the Treaty of Paris is signed. *(pistol used by the British in the war)*

1730s
A religious revival, known as the Great Awakening, sweeps through the colonies.

1692
Young women in the village of Salem, Massachusetts, accuse their neighbors of witchcraft, resulting in trials and executions.

1712
Slaves in New York stage a revolt, killing nine white colonists.

1800

1700

1757 ASIA
The British East India Company, a powerful trading company, effectively rules India.

1762 EUROPE
Catherine the Great begins her reign of Russia as an enlightened despot. *(portrait of Catherine the Great)*

1650 AFRICA
More than 40 trading posts on Africa's west coast send slaves to the Americas. *(photo of Ghana's Elmina Castle, a trading post where African slaves were held before being shipped across the Atlantic)*

11

THE ATLANTIC WORLD
Beginnings–1550

HISTORICAL THINKING What impact did European exploration have on the cultures of North America and Africa?

During its 100th anniversary in 2006, Mesa Verde National Park lit up Cliff Palace, Colorado's largest ancient cliff dwelling. From this image, it is possible to imagine a firelit evening among the ancient Pueblo people, who lived in the region more than 700 years ago. Cliff Palace has about 150 rooms and more than 20 kivas, or rooms for religious rituals.

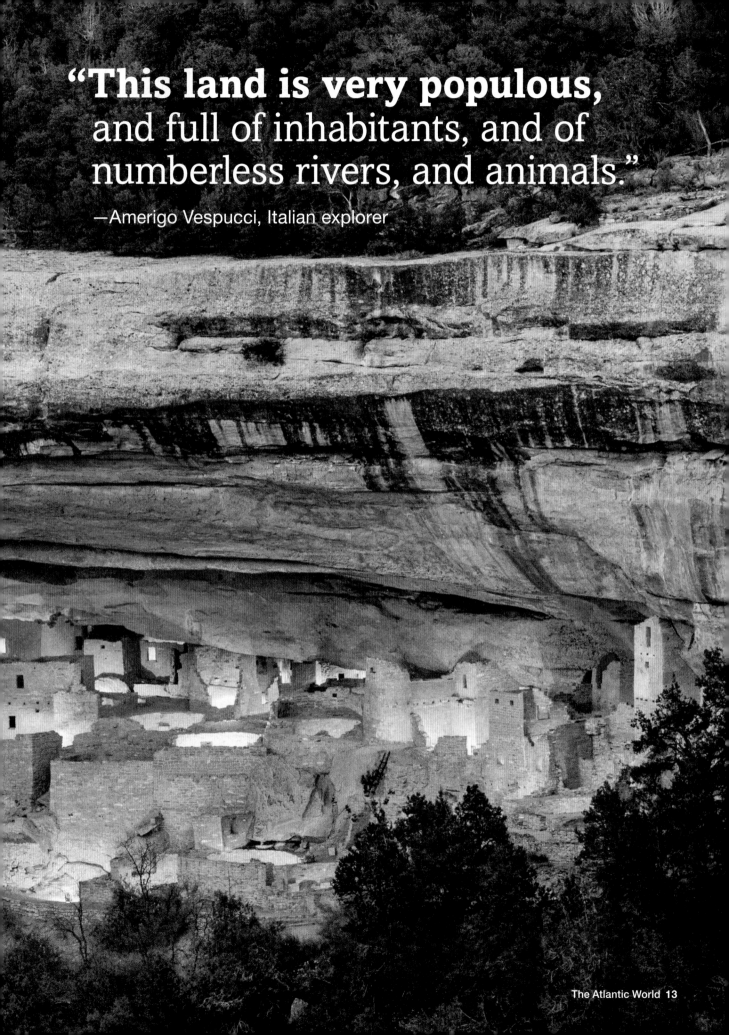

"**This land is very populous,** and full of inhabitants, and of numberless rivers, and animals."

—Amerigo Vespucci, Italian explorer

CULTURES OF THE AMERICAS

Imagine if you could travel back in time to the year 1492 and fly over the Western Hemisphere. You would see thousands of villages, cities, and even a sprawling empire or two. These vibrant cultures were unaware of the change that was coming, but their traditions and ways of life would soon alter the world.

A LARGE AND DIVERSE POPULATION

Archaeologists, scientists who study human history through the excavation and analysis of artifacts and other remains, generally believe the first humans to populate the Americas began arriving some 15,000 to 20,000 years ago. Many came in waves into the northern part of North America from Asia. Others came from Europe, traveling from island to island in the North Atlantic until they reached the continent. As small bands spread across the Americas, they found an abundant and challenging land. They faced frozen regions, grasslands, mountain ranges, deserts, and rain forests. In time, the migrants' languages, customs, and cultures became as different as their locations.

Historians don't know for sure how many people lived throughout North and South America in 1492, but their estimates range from 54 to 100 million. Trading networks crisscrossed North and South America, bringing items such as maize, or corn, from what is now Central America as far north and east as present-day Georgia. Ancient arrow and spear points made of obsidian, a hard, sharp stone quarried in northwestern Wyoming, have been unearthed in the Ohio River Valley, more than 1,600 miles to the east. Various cultures, traditions, and ways of life also traveled along these routes. Unfortunately, so did disease, which devastated the populations of both continents soon after their first contact with Europeans.

Native American groups of the Northwest Coast often wore masks during healing rituals, feasts, performances, or secret society meetings. This mask, most likely created by a Tsimshian (SHIHM-shee-uhn) artist, was made with wood, copper, paint, and shells.

THE FAR NORTH AND PACIFIC COAST

To the far north of North America, other Native American cultures thrived in the harsh climate of what is now Alaska and northwestern Canada. The Inuit (IH-noo-wit) were one of the largest Native American groups in this region. They lived in small communities along the northernmost coast of North America and inland on the flat, frozen **tundra**. The tundra's frozen ground made farming impossible, so the Inuit depended on fishing and hunting. They took to the sea in light boats called kayaks, made of wood and the hides of seal or walruses. Their hunting economy expanded when East Asian traders arrived. The Inuit traded furs and walrus ivory for Asian steel knives, hooks, and spear points. They could now hunt larger whales. As a result, they began using whale bones to build their houses. By the 1300s, the Inuit had spread across Canada and onto the island of Greenland, where they traded with the Vikings—European seafarers and warriors from Scandinavia—for iron tools and weapons.

The moderate climate farther south along the Pacific Coast made some farming possible and ensured that a greater variety of fish and game was available to those who settled the forests and coastal areas from present-day British Columbia to Baja California. The Kwakiutl (kwah-kee-YOO-tuhl) are one tribe that flourished along the

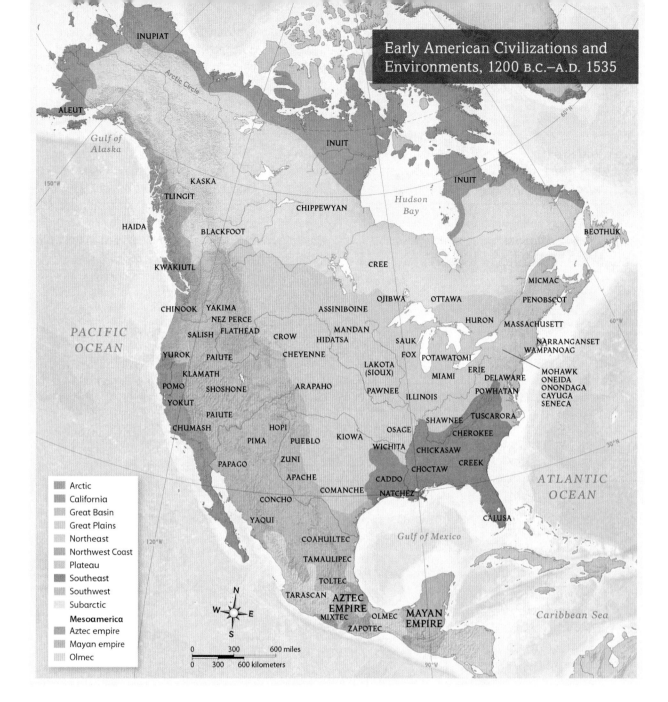

Early American Civilizations and Environments, 1200 B.C.–A.D. 1535

Legend:
- Arctic
- California
- Great Basin
- Great Plains
- Northeast
- Northwest Coast
- Plateau
- Southeast
- Southwest
- Subarctic
- **Mesoamerica**
  - Aztec empire
  - Mayan empire
  - Olmec

Northwest Coast. To show their status and wealth, Kwakiutl families periodically held **potlatches**, or lavish feasts. Over several days they fasted, prayed, danced, and bestowed generous gifts on guests.

THE DESERTS AND THE PLAINS

Farming in the deserts that characterize the American southwest might seem an unlikely prospect. But the **ancient Pueblo** (PWAY-bloh) and the **Hohokam** (ho-ho-KOM) people made the most of their sparse water sources, which included only a few major rivers. They developed a series of canals to irrigate, or supply the fields with water, and produce abundant crops. Through trade, the people acquired maize from Mesoamerica. By adding maize to the number of plants they **domesticated**, or grew

themselves, such as squash, beans, and cotton, they developed a diverse agricultural economy.

To house their growing populations, both groups built large adobe houses of sun-dried clay and straw in complexes that resembled modern-day apartment buildings. Many of these were tucked into cliffs on the edges of desert mesas, possibly as a defense against enemy attacks. It appears that these once-thriving communities were abandoned around A.D. 1200, perhaps due to warfare or **drought**, a prolonged period of little or no rainfall.

Northeast of the deserts were vast grasslands extending from the Mississippi River to the foot of the Rocky Mountains and north into Canada. Today this region is called the Great Plains. Many Native American nations flourished here. In the western Great Plains, **nomadic** tribes such as the Blackfoot traveled the land following herds of game, particularly bison. The bison, or buffalo, was the center of their way of life, providing food, sinew for making thread, bones for making tools, and hides for clothing and shelter. Portable tents covered in hide, or tepees, could easily be packed up and moved over distances of hundreds of miles. On the eastern plains, Native Americans such as the Mandan and Pawnee lived more settled lives and farmed the land. They lived in villages of earthen lodges, some of which provided shelter for thousands of inhabitants.

THE MOUND BUILDERS

Around 1000 B.C., two hunter-gatherer cultures, the Adena and Hopewell, began building mounds across the upper and lower Midwest into present-day southern Ohio and Pennsylvania. Archaeologists refer to these cultures, which constructed the mounds along with the cities surrounding them, as **Mound Builders**. Built in a variety of shapes and sizes, the earthen mounds had different purposes, including as burial sites, temples, or ceremonial centers. The Serpent Mound in Ohio is one of the largest, winding more than 1,300 feet across the land. Seen from above, it appears to be a serpent holding an egg or jewel in its mouth. The mound may have been used as a burial site.

Beginning about A.D. 700, a new mound-building culture known as the Mississippians spread from present-day Georgia to Minnesota. Unlike the Adena and Hopewell, the Mississippians lived as settled farmers and could support large populations. Their capital, Cahokia (kuh-HO-kee-yuh), was built around a group of mounds in what is now southern Illinois. Between A.D. 1000 and 1100, Cahokia's population exceeded 15,000 people. At its center was Monks Mound, the largest human-made structure north of modern Mexico. About 100 feet high, its base is larger than Egypt's Great Pyramid of Giza. Some historians think Cahokia's population collapsed from the effects of a huge flood in about 1200. When Europeans first passed through the area, the city was gone.

THE EASTERN WOODLANDS

The land east from the Mississippi to the Atlantic Ocean and south to the Gulf of Mexico was covered with dense forests. Native Americans cleared portions of the woodlands to farm crops similar to those cultivated in the southwest: corn, beans, squash, and pumpkins. **Slash-and-burn agriculture**, the practice of cutting brush and burning trees to clear land for planting crops, forced the people to move their farms periodically to allow the soil to renew.

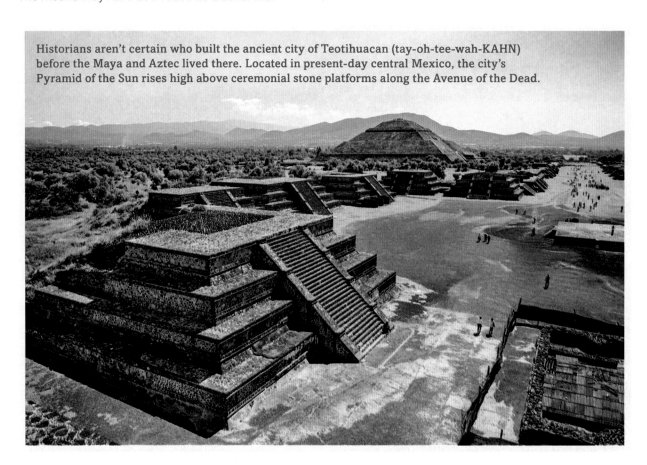

Historians aren't certain who built the ancient city of Teotihuacan (tay-oh-tee-wah-KAHN) before the Maya and Aztec lived there. Located in present-day central Mexico, the city's Pyramid of the Sun rises high above ceremonial stone platforms along the Avenue of the Dead.

Plentiful crops meant large populations. In the south, these included the Cherokee, Chickasaw, and Choctaw, among others, who farmed the land surrounding their permanent villages. In the north and throughout much of the region, most tribes belonged to either the Algonquian (al-GAHN-kwee-uhn) or Iroquois (IHR-uh-kwoy) language group. The Algonquian speakers lived mainly along the Atlantic coast and to the foot of the Appalachian Mountains. The Iroquois-speaking nations lived mainly in the central part of present-day New York State and throughout the eastern Great Lakes region. They lived in longhouses, dwellings built of wood and bark that were large enough to house extended families. Although their ways of life were similar, Algonquians and Iroquois were usually enemies.

MESOAMERICAN EMPIRES

Mesoamerica once covered what is now southern Mexico and parts of Central America. Its fertile lands supported several civilizations, or complex societies. Among the best known are the **Olmec, Maya,** and **Aztecs**, civilizations that flourished in the region at different times from around 1200 B.C. to A.D. 1520. The oldest of these three, the Olmec settled along the coast of the Gulf of Mexico. They had an extensive trade network throughout Mesoamerica and greatly influenced the Maya, who thrived to their south. Visitors to Guatemala and the Yucatán (yoo-kuh-TAN) can still see the Maya's huge temple complexes and step pyramids, images of their solar and lunar calendars, and examples of their hieroglyphic, or picture-based, writing form.

The last Mesoamerican empire, the Aztec Empire, arose about A.D. 1200 in what is now central Mexico. At its height, nearly 6 million people lived under Aztec rule. The empire consisted of city-states controlled by the emperor, his council, and a strong military. Conquered city-states were allowed to govern themselves, but they were required to pay tribute, or bring rare and expensive gifts, to the emperor.

By the 1500s, the Aztecs' capital city of Tenochtitlán (tay-nohch-teet-LAHN) was one of the largest in the world. Built on small islands in a lake, the city grew rapidly. To increase its land, the Aztecs constructed artificial islands over the lake and nearby marshes to house lavish temples and palaces. The empire had plenty of food and developed a robust economy. But it also had a darker side: To appease their gods, the Aztecs sacrificed thousands of people each year. The army periodically raided nearby communities to keep the capital supplied with human victims.

This gold bee is one of many artifacts crafted by the Nasca people in ancient Peru.

Museo Larco, Lima – Perú

A SOUTH AMERICAN EMPIRE

Further to the south and west, the Inca developed an impressive civilization high in the Andes Mountains. The Inca rose to power in the 12th century, around the same period as the Aztecs, and built the largest empire on Earth at that time. Its boundaries ran 2,500 miles, from what is now Ecuador to central Chile, and boasted a population of around 10 million.

Inca engineers and architects created an **infrastructure**, or a series of connecting systems necessary for a society, that serves as an example of human planning even today. They developed terraced fields for agriculture and built miles of roadways and bridges to link all parts of their kingdom. Their stonework in the cities of Cusco (KOOS-koh) and Machu Picchu (MAH-choo PEE-choo) is so precise that not even a knife blade will fit between any two adjoining stones. The Inca adorned their cities with gold mined from the Andes. They amassed gold, silver, and gems for use in clothing, decorations, and jewelry, and their empire became the wealthiest and most powerful in the Americas.

HISTORICAL THINKING

1. **READING CHECK** How did present-day North and South America first become populated?

2. **ANALYZE CAUSE AND EFFECT** What made it possible for ancient Pueblo and Hohokam communities to grow crops?

3. **MAKE INFERENCES** What does the presence of a large trading network throughout North America imply about the different groups of people who lived on the continent?

4. **INTERPRET MAPS** What benefits did the Inuit and Aleut derive from their geographic locations?

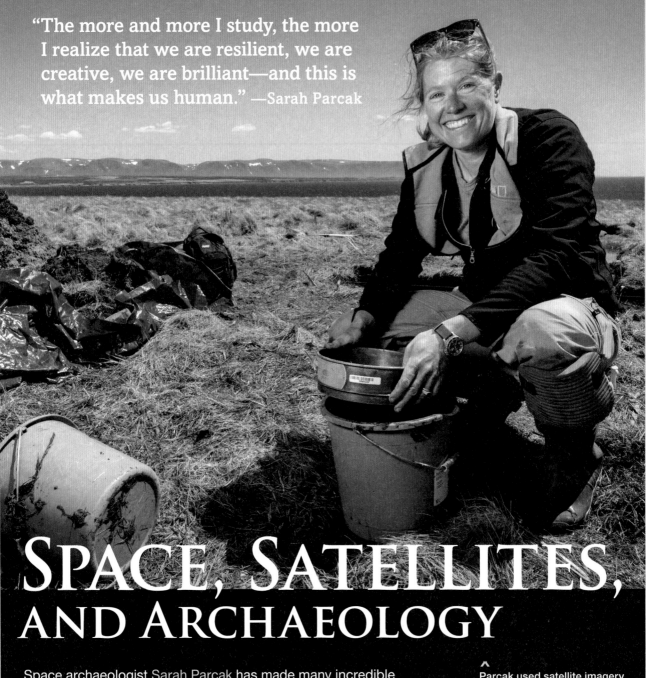

"The more and more I study, the more I realize that we are resilient, we are creative, we are brilliant—and this is what makes us human." —Sarah Parcak

Space, Satellites,
and Archaeology

Space archaeologist Sarah Parcak has made many incredible discoveries, including 17 possible pyramids in Egypt, 3,100 missing settlements, and 1,000 lost tombs. She uses modern tools, like space satellites, to unlock these ancient, hidden worlds. "Literally everywhere we look, we don't know what we are going to find," she explains. Parcak's work has taken her to rain forests in Peru, deserts in Egypt, and to the Canadian coast in search of Viking settlements. Sometimes, her searches leave her empty-handed, but that's just part of the scientific process. Recently, Parcak has set a lofty goal. She's using satellites to detect looting at archaeological sites in order to help preserve the integrity and history of each site.

^
Parcak used satellite imagery to look for evidence of settlement at Point Rosee, a narrow peninsula stretching from southern Newfoundland into the Gulf of St. Lawrence. In this location, her team discovered a stone hearth used for working iron.

MAIN IDEA Sarah Parcak, space archaeologist, uses satellite technology to discover civilizations that have been lost for thousands of years and look for signs of looting.

To find evidence of looting in Egypt, Parcak compares current satellite images like this one to older satellite images. The winner of the 2016 TED Prize, she is funding a project in the Middle East that includes identifying and protecting archaeological sites through the use of satellite imagery.

THE SPACE ARCHAEOLOGIST

When you picture an archaeologist, what comes to mind? Maybe someone wearing khaki-colored clothing and a large-brimmed hat, painstakingly brushing away the dirt that surrounds an artifact? That may be the typical image of an archaeologist, but Sarah Parcak doesn't fit this description. Instead of using brushes and shovels, this space archaeologist is more likely to use satellites and other remote sensing tools to locate and study ancient settlements.

One tool in Parcak's high-tech toolbox is a form of remote sensing called LIDAR, which stands for Light Detection and Ranging. LIDAR is used to collect data from an airplane, helicopter, or drone. It sends laser pulses down to ground level and records the rate at which the pulses return to build a map of the landscape below. But Parcak primarily uses satellite imagery to search areas of Peruvian rain forest or portions of the Egyptian desert for lost civilizations. As a result, more often than not, you'll find her in the lab. "We don't just grab an image, flip it into the computer, and press a button," she says. "I've spent more than 10,000 hours of my life staring at satellite imagery to understand what I'm seeing."

With satellite technology, Parcak has discovered ancient ruins—and sometimes entire civilizations— that have been hidden underground for tens to hundreds of thousands of years. "Satellite imagery is a powerful new tool that gives us eyes in the sky," explains Parcak. "We can process images captured from space in a way that lets us see patterns in the vegetation and the soil that might signal a man-made feature, hidden from view."

VIKINGS IN NORTH AMERICA?

One of Parcak's satellite imagery projects has taken place in North America. After studying the Canadian coastlines from above, one site—Point Rosee—stood out to Parcak as a place where humans might have lived long ago. During a June 2015 excavation of this site, which is hundreds of miles south of the only known Viking settlement in North America, Parcak's team discovered an ancient iron hearth and bits of iron ore. The presence of the iron as well as other structures on the site pointed to a possible second Viking settlement in North America—a discovery that, if proven true, would shake the archaeological world to its core and potentially rewrite some of the history of the Americas.

Parcak was skeptical, and the discovery raised many questions—where the Norse people sailed, how they lived, and how long they settled in one region. Parcak and her team returned to Point Rosee in March 2016 to get some answers, but the dig did not turn up artifacts that reinforced the possibility of a second Viking settlement. For now, those questions remain unanswered, but Point Rosee will continue to be explored. "It's just the nature of science," says Parcak. "I think ultimately we just have to let the science speak for itself."

HISTORICAL THINKING

1. **READING CHECK** How does Sarah Parcak use satellite technology in the field of archaeology?

2. **SUMMARIZE** How could Parcak's research reshape the history of North America?

3. **FORM AND SUPPORT OPINIONS** If you were an archaeologist, would you embrace tools like LIDAR or stick with more traditional methods? Explain.

15TH-CENTURY EUROPE

Have you ever felt as if everything in your life was changing? During the 1400s, people in medieval Europe experienced such an upheaval. New ideas overturned centuries of traditional beliefs, sparking the creative rebirth of Europe.

THE MIDDLE AGES

The **Middle Ages** began with the fall of the Roman Empire in about A.D. 500 and lasted until the end of the 15th century. The western part of the empire split into several Germanic kingdoms, all warring against one another. To keep their lands and to protect their people, the Germanic kings developed a system known as **feudalism**. Under this system, the king granted land to the nobles, known as lords, who in turn gave land to lesser noblemen, called **vassals**. In exchange for a lord's protection, vassals paid taxes and pledged their military service.

Feudalism created a stable social structure organized like a pyramid. The king ruled at the top, lords were directly beneath him, and vassals beneath the lords. However, most people, including peasants and serfs, formed the broad base of the pyramid. Many were bound to a noble's land under the **manor system**. This system was a way of life in which peasants paid a landowner for his military protection through labor and with the agricultural goods they produced. They could buy their freedom, but few could earn the funds to do so. The majority of people, and their children after them, remained in bondage to the landowner.

PLAGUE SWEEPS EUROPE

From 1347 to 1351, the bubonic plague killed about 25 million people in Europe. Known as the Black Death because of the black spots that appeared on its victims' skin, the infection struck with frightening speed. People who went to bed healthy could be dead by morning. Symptoms began with swellings in the groin or armpits. Within hours, victims were racked by fever, chills, vomiting, and terrible pain until, finally, death came.

Today, antibiotics make the rare case of plague treatable, but in the Middle Ages, no one knew how the disease spread or how to fight it. One doctor speculated, "instantaneous death occurs when the aerial [air-borne] spirit escaping from the eyes of the sick man strikes the healthy person standing near." Other physicians, such as the French doctor who developed the "protective" uniform (shown here)in the 1600s, believed the plague was spread by bad air or odors. Doctors relied on their usual practices, such as bloodletting, burning aromatic herbs, and giving rosewater or vinegar baths. Nothing worked.

Christianity became another stabilizing force during the Middle Ages. The Roman Catholic Church unified medieval Europe under its spiritual and political authority. In the 11th century, the Church called on monarchs to launch the **Crusades**, a series of religious wars meant to battle the rise of **Islam** and regain the Holy Land—Jerusalem and the surrounding area. The followers of Islam, called **Muslims**, had captured the Holy Land and attacked the Christian Byzantine Empire, which had been the eastern half of the Roman Empire.

Although the Crusades ultimately failed, they enabled European monarchs to claim some lands in the east and establish trade routes between Europe and the Middle East. As trade increased, Europe began to prosper, encouraging the growth of towns and cities where merchants could sell their trade goods.

Trade routes also opened the continent to a terrifying threat. In October 1347, the bubonic plague, or Black Death, arrived in Italy on ships from the East. Spread by rats and the bite of infected fleas, the plague swept across Europe. Within two years, it had killed nearly a third of the population and left many towns and cities in need of workers. People lucky enough to survive

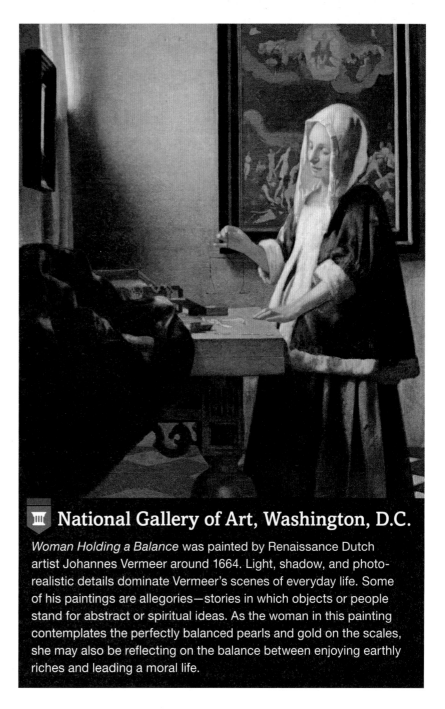

🏛 **National Gallery of Art, Washington, D.C.**

Woman Holding a Balance was painted by Renaissance Dutch artist Johannes Vermeer around 1664. Light, shadow, and photo-realistic details dominate Vermeer's scenes of everyday life. Some of his paintings are allegories—stories in which objects or people stand for abstract or spiritual ideas. As the woman in this painting contemplates the perfectly balanced pearls and gold on the scales, she may also be reflecting on the balance between enjoying earthly riches and leading a moral life.

left the manors for these jobs. The steady exodus, or departure, of people from the manors weakened the feudal system and helped end the Middle Ages. By the 1400s, Europe was ripe for change.

THE RENAISSANCE

In the years of conquest before the Crusades, Muslim scholars had acquired and preserved many ancient Greek and Roman texts and works of art. Returning crusaders and other travelers brought translations of classical thinkers such as Aristotle, Euclid, and Ptolemy back to their homes. In time, this knowledge inspired a cultural revolution in the royal courts, towns, and universities of Europe.

By the 1400s, Europeans were making new advances in the arts, sciences, and technology. Historians call this era the **Renaissance**, or "rebirth." The Renaissance began in Italy and spread to many parts of Europe. The movement was founded on Greek and Roman ideas and on the philosophy of **humanism**. Humanists focused on individuality and encouraged critical thinking and the development of new ideas.

The Renaissance influenced all aspects of European culture. The revival of the arch and column, for instance, allowed architects to build in ways that seemed new, but that hadn't been used in nearly 1,500 years. New ideas regarding democracy and representative government made their way into intellectual circles. In the arts, the detailed study of human anatomy and perspective, a technique used to give the illusion of depth and distance, inspired the great artists of the Renaissance. Michelangelo, Raphael, and Leonardo da Vinci portrayed the human body realistically in their paintings and sculptures, even in their portraits of God. Today the term "Renaissance man" or "Renaissance woman" defines anyone who has many exceptional talents. **Leonardo da Vinci** may be the best example, excelling as an artist, inventor, scientist, engineer, and architect.

The Renaissance period also saw a steady rise in literacy, or the ability to read and write. Around 1452, **Johann Gutenberg** invented a printing press that used moveable type to set up pages of text. This invention allowed people to mass-produce and distribute commentary and literature, including classical and humanistic literary works. With more printed materials available, more people learned to read. Gutenberg's printed Bible allowed many Europeans to read Christianity's holy book for themselves, rather than having its contents interpreted for them by a priest. The combination of printing and increased literacy helped spread Renaissance ideas rapidly throughout Europe.

In the Middle Ages, scholars generally studied nature by reading what others had written about a topic. During the Renaissance, however, scholars preferred to find out for themselves through direct observation and experiments. One of the greatest Renaissance scientists, the Polish astronomer Nicolaus Copernicus, used mathematical calculations to show that Earth was not the center of the universe. Instead, it was only one of several planets revolving around the Sun. His work sent shock waves through Europe and opened the door to further discoveries.

Among the social changes taking place during the Renaissance was the rise of a wealthy merchant and financial class. The Medici (MEH-dee-chee) and Borgia (BOR-juh) families of Italy became more powerful than many European kings.

Members of the Medici family were bankers for the Roman Catholic pope and held government jobs. Some of the men became popes and some of the women became queens of France. As famous patrons of the arts, the Medici commissioned paintings, sculptures, buildings, and even their own mausoleums, or burial sites.

THE REFORMATION

By the time of the Renaissance, the Roman Catholic Church was beginning to lose some of its political power. The pope had once been the true ruler of Europe, commanding the loyalty of monarchs and clan leaders. But corruption often grows out of such widespread power, and as the Church's influence diminished, some Europeans began to speak out against several of its practices. The Renaissance humanist movement encouraged people to be more critical of the Church.

In 1517, German clergyman and university professor **Martin Luther** called for the Church to reject its corrupt practices. He singled out the selling of **indulgences**, or official forgiveness of sins. Luther believed that salvation for Christians was a gift from God in return for their faith, and it could not be bought. He wrote his ideas in a list of **95 Theses**, or statements of belief, and according to legend, nailed it to a church door.

Printed with movable type in 1455, this copy of Gutenberg's Bible features traditional hand-painted illustrations characteristic of earlier illustrated, or "illuminated," manuscripts. Fewer than 50 years after Gutenberg printed his Bible, print shops opened in more than 200 cities across Europe.

Luther didn't stop there. He challenged the Church's tight control over the Bible, which had been translated into Latin. Luther argued that Christians should be able to read the word of God themselves. He translated the Bible into German and used the printing press to distribute his translation widely.

In response to Luther's actions, the Church excommunicated, or ejected, him. But it was too late to stop the spread of Luther's ideas. Many rulers and their subjects sided with Luther and broke from the Church in a movement known as the **Protestant Reformation**. The word *protestant* referred to "protests" against the Catholic Church. However, reasons for leaving the Church were as much political as religious. A number of monarchs and nobles resented the power of the pope. By creating their own local churches, they could further weaken the Church's authority.

In Germany, some princes welcomed Luther's teachings and formed the new Lutheran Church. The spread of Lutheranism in northern Europe inspired other critics of the Catholic Church to offer their own Protestant doctrines. The most influential was **John Calvin**, a native of France. In the early 1530s, he attempted to create a model Christian society in Geneva, Switzerland. Calvin believed in predestination, or the idea that God had already decided who would go to heaven. People could not save themselves through faith or good works. Calvin's followers established churches in what became known as the Reformed tradition.

The pope and his allies, however, were equally determined to maintain control in Europe. Not surprisingly, the split between Catholics and Protestants led to a series of religious wars fought during the 1500s and 1600s.

NATIONS AND TRADE

By the 15th century, the political map of Europe was rapidly changing. Smaller kingdoms merged into larger **nation-states**, which united people who shared a common culture or language. The nation-states eventually organized into established nations, similar to modern-day countries. England, France, and Spain emerged as Europe's most powerful nations.

Their rise inspired a fierce competition for trade. As nations developed their own national economies, trade became crucial to their wealth. A growing merchant class expanded Europe's overland routes into the Middle East, Africa, and East Asia, where they traded European goods for salt, gold, silk, and exotic spices. Most countries adopted the practice

Thanks to the printing press, Luther's 95 Theses were quickly distributed throughout Germany after he posted them on the door of All Saints' Church in Wittenberg. The theses below express some of Luther's thoughts about the selling of indulgences. Purgatory is where souls go after death to repent and make amends for their sins in life.

32. *Those who believe that they can be certain of their salvation because they have indulgence letters will be eternally damned, together with their teachers.*

35. *They who teach that contrition [repentance and regret] is not necessary on the part of those who intend to buy souls out of purgatory or to buy confessional privileges preach unchristian doctrine.*

36. *Any truly repentant Christian has a right to full remission [reduction] of penalty and guilt, even without indulgence letters.*

of **mercantilism**, or government protection and encouragement of trade, based on the theory that such businesses create wealth. Under this system, nations tried to export more goods than they imported and fought to control the best trade routes.

But the best overland trade routes were becoming too costly to use. In 1453, the Turks of the Middle Eastern Ottoman Empire captured the city of Constantinople, which linked Europe and Asia, and gained absolute control of overland trade routes. They charged Europeans steep prices for Asian goods. European countries knew the only way to re-establish direct trade with Asia was by sea. This triggered a race to find the best sea route to East Asia and ultimately led to the exploration of the Americas. The winner of the race could become the wealthiest country in Europe.

HISTORICAL THINKING

1. **READING CHECK** What was the role of peasants in the manor system?

2. **ANALYZE WORD MEANING** Why do you think the word Renaissance was applied to artistic and intellectual changes of the 15th century?

3. **COMPARE AND CONTRAST** What were the main differences between the beliefs of Martin Luther and John Calvin?

4. **ANALYZE CAUSE AND EFFECT** How did the rise of powerful nations result in the development of mercantilism?

WEST AFRICAN KINGDOMS

In the 800s, Arab traders were telling Europeans about a "land of gold" in West Africa. In this great kingdom, they said, even the dogs wore collars of gold. Those tales turned out to be true.

GEOGRAPHY AND TRADE

On the map, West Africa seems an unlikely place for great kingdoms to arise. To the north lie the semi-arid Atlas Mountains, forming a geographic barrier to the Mediterranean Sea and Europe beyond. The world's largest desert, the **Sahara**, stretches from the Atlantic Ocean to the Red Sea, covering most of northern Africa. South of the Sahara lies the Sahel, a region of **steppes**, or grasslands with few trees and moderate rainfall. The Guinean Forests lie south of the Sahel. These lush rain forests support more than a quarter of all African mammals.

You might think the vast Sahara would be an insurmountable barrier to trade, but by the early Middle Ages, West Africa had become a major hub of commerce, trading primarily with North Africa and the Middle East. What were they trading? The big-ticket items were gold and salt. Beneath the southern

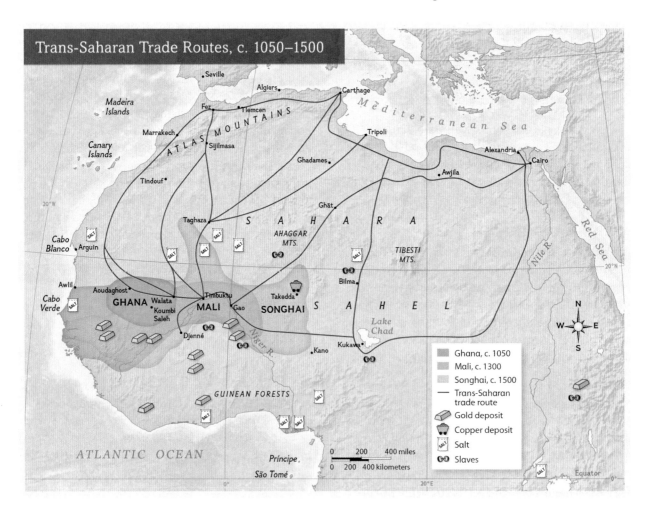

Trans-Saharan Trade Routes, c. 1050–1500

As they have for centuries, camel caravans carry salt slabs cut from Lake Assale's dry seabeds in Ethiopia to distant market towns. A valuable commodity, salt provides the salt miners and camel keepers with a livelihood. But technology and big companies pose a threat to traditional salt harvesting and transportation methods.

forests lay huge deposits of gold, while the Sahara had an abundant supply of salt. Vital for preserving foods, salt had been a form of currency in parts of the ancient world and was extremely valuable.

To transport these goods across the desert, traders established **trans-Saharan** trade routes. They crisscrossed the Sahara, extending from the Sahel and West Africa north to the shores of the Mediterranean Sea and as far east as Alexandria in Egypt. Camels made crossing the desert possible and profitable. These animals can walk nearly 100 miles without stopping for water, carrying heavy loads across the sands in scorching heat. Traders organized **caravans**, or groups of merchants traveling together, to carry their goods across the desert. Trans-Saharan trading fostered the development of market towns and, eventually, the rise of three West African empires—Ghana, Mali, and Songhai.

THE KINGDOM OF GHANA

The kingdom of **Ghana** began as a group of farming villages south of the Sahara that gradually banded together to form one state. By A.D. 500, Ghana had become the first great trading empire in West Africa. Its capital city, Koumbi-Saleh (KUHM-bee SAHL-uh), stood midway between the gold trade flowing north from Ghana's mines and the salt trade flowing south from the Sahara.

Ghana's kings grew rich by levying taxes on goods moving into and out of their empire. They also controlled the price of gold, decreeing that all nuggets belonged to the king and only gold dust could be traded. This made the supply of gold scarce and kept its price high. By the ninth century, Ghana

had become wealthy and powerful. The kingdom was structured according to a feudal system. Although Ghana appeared stable, outside forces gradually began to weaken it.

One such force was Islam. As early as the 700s, Arab traders began to introduce the religion's scriptures and laws to the region. Literacy rose as people learned to speak, read, and write Arabic. Before that time, no West African culture had had a written language. Then, around 1050, an Islamic group known as the Almoravids attacked Ghana and tried to force its royal families and other leaders to convert, or change their religion. The Ghanians resisted, but were overpowered. The Almoravids captured Koumbi-Saleh in 1076.

Environmental changes also contributed to the demise of Ghana. Centuries of farming had exhausted the soil, and it could no longer support the population. By the early 1200s, Ghana's traders and farmers were leaving for better opportunities and more fertile lands to the south and west. The kingdom of Ghana gradually came to an end. Yet this "land of gold" had played a major role in developing West Africa's trade and culture.

THE KINGDOM OF MALI

After Ghana, the kingdom of **Mali** emerged as the new ruling power in West Africa, seizing control of the gold and salt commerce. The kingdom was fortunate in its geography and in its early leaders. Mali's land consisted largely of **savanna**, fertile grasslands where abundant rains fell. The soil was ideal for growing rice, millet, and other grains. Surplus crops allowed Mali to expand trade, support the development of art, and

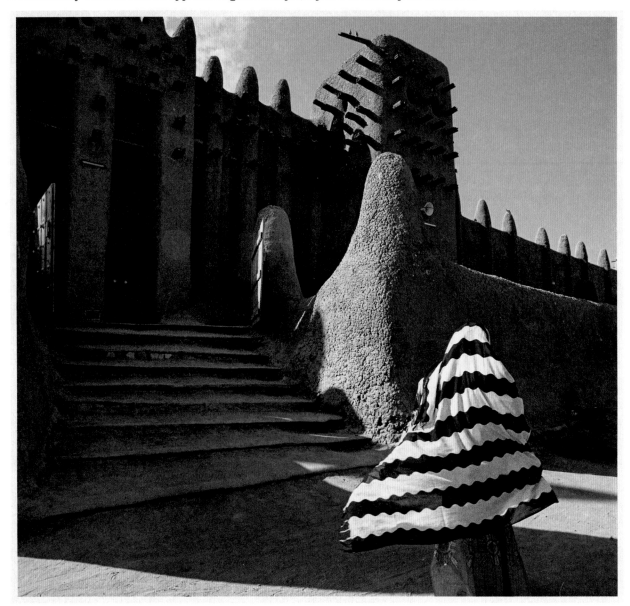

Built of mud, the Great Mosque of Djenné is an architectural wonder located in the ancient city of Djenné, Mali. National Geographic photographer Jimmy Chin captured this image of a colorfully dressed Malian approaching the mosque, a place of worship for Muslims.

construct impressive buildings. With its population of nearly 40 million people, Mali became one of the largest empires in West African history.

Unlike Ghana's original rulers, Mali's kings were Muslim. The kingdom's founder, Sundiata Keita (sun-JAHT-ah KAY-tah) brought peace, tolerance, and the rule of law to his diverse empire. In 1324, Sundiata's most famous descendent, **Mansa Musa**, expanded the empire and made a legendary pilgrimage to Islam's holy city of Mecca, in what is today Saudi Arabia, to fulfill his religious duty. His caravan is said to have included more than 60,000 servants and 80 camels loaded with gold. He distributed gold and lavish gifts to people along the way, and his generosity is credited with expanding Mali's trade network farther into the Middle East.

When Mansa Musa returned from Mecca, he laid the groundwork for making the trading city of Timbuktu a major center of Islamic learning and the arts. His finest achievements included the construction of the Great Mosque and the Sankara Madrassa, the largest library in Africa at the time. Weaker leaders followed Mansa Musa, however, and eventually their poor management allowed the empire to fragment into smaller kingdoms. One of these new kingdoms grew to surpass Mali in size and splendor.

THE KINGDOM OF SONGHAI

That kingdom was **Songhai**, the largest of the West African empires, extending some 2,500 miles from the Atlantic Ocean to the central Sahara. In the early 1300s, Mali, fearful of Songhai's growing power, attacked the kingdom and captured its capital city, Gao. About 50 years later, Songhai rebelled, retaking Gao, attacking the weakened Mali kingdom, and capturing Timbuktu. Now that it controlled the region's gold and salt trades, Songhai accumulated enough wealth to build its own empire. The walled city of Gao became a multicultural marketplace that attracted traders from northern Africa, the Middle East, and Europe.

One of Songhai's greatest rulers, Askia Muhammad (ahs-KEE-ah moh-HA-muhd), built alliances, or agreements, with other Muslim states and reformed the government, banking, and education systems for the entire empire. But later Songhai rulers fought over control of the empire, leaving it vulnerable to envious neighbors. In 1591, Morocco seized Timbuktu and Gao, ending the Songhai empire.

BENIN AND KONGO

Two other African kingdoms, **Benin** (buh-NEEN) and **Kongo** (KAHNG-goh), established important trading networks in the 1400s. The kingdom of Benin dominated the forested region that covered the Niger River delta. Benin was known for its skilled artisans, or craftspeople, who created impressive ivory and wood carvings as well as bronze and brass objects.

The densely populated kingdom of Kongo arose in west-central Africa, south of the Congo River. It began as a loose partnership of smaller kingdoms that gradually banded together. By the mid-1500s, Kongo was a unified kingdom that had established a wide and well-organized trading network with other parts of the African continent.

Both Benin and Kongo were located along the coast, and as Portuguese mariners began exploring the sea routes surrounding Africa, they made contact with the people and kingdoms of the western part of the continent. For example, the Portuguese arrived in Kongo in 1483 and began a robust trade. They sent their missionaries and teachers to Kongo in exchange for goods such as ivory, salt, copper, and textiles. They also established a slave trade with both Kongo and Benin.

Slavery is a social system in which human beings are owned and completely controlled by other humans, usually as a source of forced labor. The practice had existed in West Africa and throughout most of the Eastern Hemisphere for centuries before the Portuguese began trading for slaves with the West African kingdoms. In fact, slavery existed in most civilizations throughout the world, including in the Americas. Up until the late 15th century, enslaved

PRIMARY SOURCE

Famous medieval traveler Ibn Battuta visited Mali on one of his many journeys through the Middle East, Europe, and Africa in the 14th century. While in Mali, he witnessed the sultan, Mansa Suleyman, enter his palace garden to hold court.

On certain days the sultan holds audiences in the palace yard, where there is a platform under a tree. The sultan comes out of a door in a corner of the palace, carrying a bow in his hand and quiver on his back. His usual dress is a velvety red tunic, made of the European fabrics called "mutanfas." The sultan is preceded by his musicians, who carry gold and silver guimbris [two-stringed guitars] and behind him come three hundred armed slaves. He walks in a leisurely fashion. As he takes his seat the drums, trumpets, and bugles are sounded.

—from *Travels in Asia and Africa*, by Ibn Battuta, 1325–1354

What detail in Battuta's description leads you to understand the extent of Mali's world trade?

people were usually prisoners who had been captured in war or people punished for committing a crime. Some had bonded themselves into slavery to pay off debts or to have food to eat and a roof over their heads. They were often able to buy or work off their bondage, and they sometimes had certain rights as slaves, even though they were not free. Their enslavement was not attached to their race, and their children were not automatically born into bondage. The Portuguese entry into the West African slave trade changed the very definition of slavery and expanded this new practice of slavery across the Atlantic Ocean and throughout the Western Hemisphere, triggering the greatest transfer of enslaved people in the history of the world.

HISTORICAL THINKING

1. **READING CHECK** What two valuable trade goods helped build the wealth and size of the West African kingdoms?

2. **INTERPRET MAPS** How did Ghana's location help it rise to power?

3. **DETERMINE CHRONOLOGY** Identify in order the rise and fall of the major West African empires.

4. **ANALYZE CAUSE AND EFFECT** How was West Africa important to the African continent and the known world in the late 15th century?

OPENING UP THE OCEAN WORLD

"Gold, Glory, and God!" Desire for wealth, national power, and the spread of Christianity drove the European explorers and their patrons. Success would bring power and wealth to many of them. To Europe and the Americas, it would bring catastrophic change.

EARLY EXPLORATION

As you have read, the Turks controlled overland trade routes to Asia, and they charged high tolls for European merchants to use them. In the 1400s, science, technology, and trade converged to help Europe establish ocean routes to the regions with which its countries traded. **Prince Henry of Portugal**, called "the Navigator," promoted and funded these efforts. He hoped to increase Portugal's political and mercantile power by claiming territory in different parts of the world where Portugal traded, promoting trade along the coast of Africa, and gaining converts to Christianity. But by around 1420, **cartographers**, or mapmakers, had charted only about 1,900 miles—or nearly one-fifth—of West Africa's coast. The true length and breadth of Africa were unknown.

Improvements in navigation and ship design during the 15th century made long sea voyages possible. The Portuguese had developed a small but sturdy ship called a **caravel**, whose triangular sails allowed it to maneuver more accurately at sea. As the Portuguese sailed southward along the western coast of Africa, they discovered just how large the continent was, and as far as they were concerned, most of it was theirs. In 1455, the pope had resolved a

dispute between Portugal and Spain over trade in West Africa by giving the Portuguese sole rights to coastal West Africa. In 1488, the Portuguese explorer **Bartholomeu Dias** sailed around the Cape of Good Hope at the southern tip of Africa. This voyage proved that a sea route around Africa to India was possible. Finally, in 1498, another Portuguese explorer, **Vasco da Gama,** and his crew became the first Europeans to reach India by sea.

This statue of Prince Henry the Navigator stands in Tomar, Portugal, where he was thought to have developed his plans for expanding the Portuguese empire.

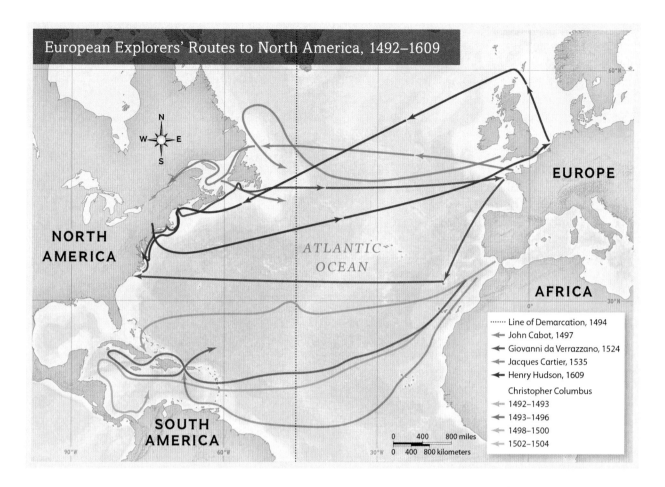

European Explorers' Routes to North America, 1492–1609

Legend:
- Line of Demarcation, 1494
- John Cabot, 1497
- Giovanni da Verrazzano, 1524
- Jacques Cartier, 1535
- Henry Hudson, 1609
- Christopher Columbus
  - 1492–1493
  - 1493–1496
  - 1498–1500
  - 1502–1504

COLUMBUS SETS SAIL

In the meantime, Ferdinand and Isabella, king and queen of Spain, had decided to sponsor **Christopher Columbus** in his search for a sea route to Asia. The devoutly Catholic monarchs wanted to find trading partners and establish colonies to increase their power, exploit colonial wealth, and spread Christianity. Columbus, a native of Genoa, Italy, was an experienced sailor and navigator. He believed that a European fleet could reach Asia by sailing west across the Atlantic Ocean. Like most Europeans, however, he supposed the Atlantic was far smaller and Asia far closer than either turned out to be.

In August 1492, Columbus and his men set sail from the Canary Islands, Spanish-ruled islands located in the Atlantic off the coast of northern Africa, with two caravels—the *Niña* and the *Pinta*—and the larger *Santa Maria*. Upon reaching land two months later—probably at present-day San Salvador Island in the Bahamas—Columbus thought they had arrived off the coast of China. Hoping to establish trade networks, they sailed southward to Cuba and then to Hispaniola, the island consisting of present-day Haiti and the Dominican Republic. There Columbus encountered the Taino (TIE-noh) people, who traded their gold trinkets for goods Columbus had brought.

The Spanish crew took timbers from one of their ships, which had wrecked nearby, and built the first Spanish fort in the Americas. Columbus left a portion of his crew at the fort and set sail for Spain.

On Columbus's return trip, a storm forced him to seek shelter in Portugal, and his reports of his voyage immediately set off another dispute between Spain and Portugal. Portuguese leaders refused to believe that Columbus had reached Asia. They insisted that those lands lay within Portugal's domain. Isabella and Ferdinand objected. In 1494, the pope negotiated the **Treaty of Tordesillas**, which established a north-south boundary—called the **Line of Demarcation**—that passed vertically through the Atlantic and present-day Brazil. The treaty gave Spain permission to colonize all land west of the line and gave Portugal a portion of land to the east of the line. It affirmed Portugal's right to the African sea route to India and its control of the Atlantic slave trade. This agreement would shape the political, economic, and cultural future of the Western Hemisphere.

Columbus returned to the Americas in 1493 with an even larger fleet, only to discover that the Taino had killed his men and destroyed the fort. He made two more voyages to the Americas, continuing to explore Caribbean islands and the South and Central

American coasts. Although he did not find the riches he hoped for, his voyages produced more accurate maps of the region than had ever before been available. While other explorers began to realize that two continents lay between Europe and Asia, Columbus himself refused to accept that idea. He died in 1506, poor and disgraced, still believing he had discovered a western route to Asia.

EXPLORATION CONTINUES

Between 1493 and 1529, Portugal and Spain sent many expeditions to the Western Hemisphere in search of gold. The Spanish found little on Hispaniola but assumed the Taino had obtained their supply of the precious metal from nearby islands or even from the mainland. European explorers obsessed with finding the source of the Taino gold began charting new lands in the Americas.

Other nations also searched for a western trade route to Asia. Italian sea captain **Amerigo Vespucci** made two separate voyages, one for Spain in 1499 and one for Portugal in 1501. His maps and charts revealed that South America was a huge landmass that had to be **circumnavigated**, or sailed around, to reach Asia. In recognition of his insight, a German mapmaker applied Vespucci's first name to the newly discovered continents, which became known as North America and South America.

England and France also entered the race. Ignoring the Treaty of Tordesillas, they searched for a northwest passage to Asia through North America. In 1497, Italian explorer **John Cabot**, sailing for England, arrived at Newfoundland and Nova Scotia. Like Columbus, he believed he had reached China. One of the most famous English explorers, **Henry Hudson**, made four voyages across the North Atlantic to what is now the northeastern United States. Hudson never found a passage to Asia, but some of the places he visited bear his name, including the Hudson River and Hudson Bay. Later, England used these voyages to reinforce its claims to land in North America.

In 1524, France sent another Italian mariner, **Giovanni da Verrazzano**, to look for the elusive northwest passage. Verrazzano sailed along the Atlantic coast to Newfoundland but found no waterway through the continent. French explorer **Jacques Cartier** tried in vain to locate the passage in 1534 and 1535, sailing into and down the St. Lawrence River. Although neither explorer found a passage to Asia, their voyages established France's claim to that region of the continent.

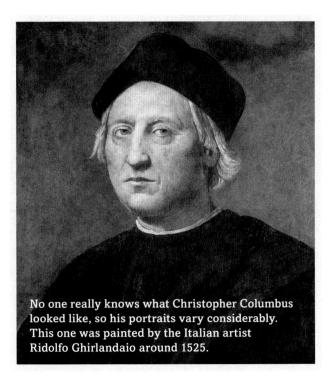

No one really knows what Christopher Columbus looked like, so his portraits vary considerably. This one was painted by the Italian artist Ridolfo Ghirlandaio around 1525.

GROWTH OF THE SLAVE TRADE

As Europeans began to establish colonies in the Americas, they needed laborers to work on their farms, plantations, and settlements. Spanish settlers initially enslaved Native Americans, mostly to work as forced labor in the sugarcane fields Spain had cultivated on Caribbean islands. But many Native Americans died, either from disease or from the brutal treatment they received. Although slavery and forced servitude had existed for centuries among civilizations in the Western Hemisphere, the practice grew under the Spanish and pitted tribe against tribe. The Spanish paid Native Americans for bringing them slaves, and this encouraged warfare as some tribes raided others to take prisoners to sell into slavery. Then Queen Isabella forbade the enslavement of Native Americans. Isabella's decision partly had a religious basis, but that did not stop Spain from turning to the African slave market.

The Atlantic slave trade began in the 1440s, with numbers of enslaved Africans being sent to Spain. Over the next four centuries, Africa lost more than 10 million people to bondage. Portugal, as you have read, was one of the first European nations to engage in the slave trade, and it dominated this harsh enterprise for almost 200 years. Once other European nations and the Americas became heavily involved, the enslavement of Africans only grew crueler. Unlike slavery in Africa, which was regarded as a temporary condition, the institution of **chattel slavery** that developed in Europe and the Americas required permanent bondage.

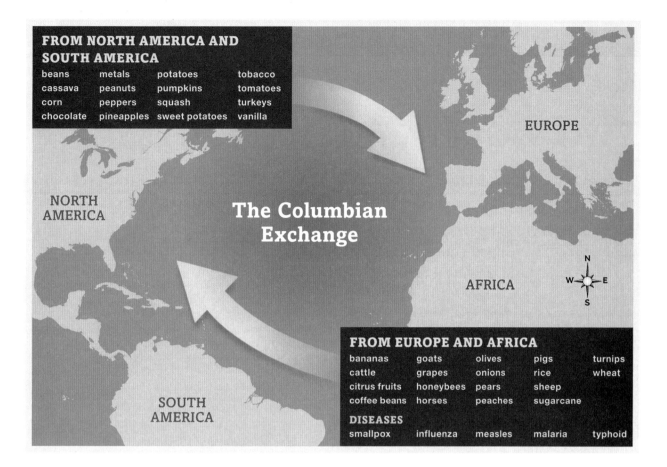

FROM NORTH AMERICA AND SOUTH AMERICA

beans	metals	potatoes	tobacco
cassava	peanuts	pumpkins	tomatoes
corn	peppers	squash	turkeys
chocolate	pineapples	sweet potatoes	vanilla

The Columbian Exchange

NORTH AMERICA

EUROPE

AFRICA

SOUTH AMERICA

FROM EUROPE AND AFRICA

bananas	goats	olives	pigs	turnips
cattle	grapes	onions	rice	wheat
citrus fruits	honeybees	pears	sheep	
coffee beans	horses	peaches	sugarcane	

DISEASES

smallpox	influenza	measles	malaria	typhoid

Chattel means "personal property." Under this system, the people enslaved lost all human rights and, as property, they and their children could be bought and sold at the enslaver's whim. At the time, Europeans believed their civilization was superior to others—enough to justify depriving other human beings of liberty and often of life itself. Nearly 600 years later, the legacy of slavery still influences the social, economic, and political life of the Americas, particularly in the United States.

THE COLUMBIAN EXCHANGE

From the first voyage of Columbus, the transfer of goods and culture between Europe and the Americas began to fundamentally transform world society. This process, known as the **Columbian Exchange**, led to an exchange of crops, animals, technology, and medicines across the Atlantic. Food crops such as corn, potatoes, tomatoes, chocolate, and peppers were shipped to Europe while wheat, rice, olives, bananas, and onions arrived in the Americas. Horses, brought to the Western Hemisphere by the Spanish, radically changed the lives of Native Americans.

Not all parts of the exchange were beneficial. Native Americans had no immunity to European diseases such as smallpox, typhoid, measles, chickenpox, and influenza. It is estimated that within three centuries after Columbus arrived, epidemic diseases had killed up to 90 percent of the native population. As disease devastated Native Americans, **quinine**, a new medicine made from the bark of a South American tree, was developed in the 1600s. For three centuries, it was the only effective treatment for malaria, a disease carried by mosquitoes.

In part, the Columbian Exchange had a positive effect on all societies. For example, the availability of a greater variety of foods led to improved nutrition. But Native Americans experienced the worst negative effects, particularly through the decimation of their communities from European-introduced diseases and the resulting loss of Native American knowledge in areas such as agriculture and medicine.

HISTORICAL THINKING

1. **READING CHECK** What prompted Columbus to take his first voyage west?

2. **ANALYZE CAUSE AND EFFECT** What caused the practice of slavery to change in the late 1400s?

3. **INTERPRET MAPS** According to the sea routes on the explorers' map, which European nations sent explorers to North America?

4. **INTERPRET VISUALS** What lasting effects has the Columbian Exchange had on the Americas and the rest of the world?

TWO WORLDS MEET

When Europeans and Native Americans first encountered each other, they experienced people and cultures completely unknown to them. Their languages, clothing, tools, and customs were all extremely different. In some ways, it was like meeting someone from another planet.

Over the years, European and American artists and illustrators have depicted these encounters as meetings between civilized Europeans and primitive Native Americans. We now know that this interpretation is not accurate. In reality, Native Americans often thought the Europeans lacked a basic understanding of what many Native Americans believed to be the best, most productive ways to live.

Long after the age of exploration, these misconceptions often grew even more pronounced. In 1846, the famous printing company of Currier and Ives produced this hand-colored lithograph, *The Landing of Columbus Oct. 11th 1492.*

CRITICAL VIEWING How do you think the artist wanted Columbus to be portrayed, and what details in the painting might help represent him that way?

DOCUMENT ONE

Primary Source: Diary
from *The Diary of Christopher Columbus's First Voyage to America, 1492–1493*

Christopher Columbus and his crew had been at sea for two months when they first spotted the islands of the Caribbean. Convinced they were near mainland China, the men waded ashore, eager to make contact with the people of "Asia."

CONSTRUCTED RESPONSE How is Columbus's view of the Taino formed by his own beliefs and assumptions?

October 12, 1492: To some of them I gave red caps, and glass beads which they put on their chests, and many other things of small value in which they took so much pleasure and became so much our friends that it was a marvel. But it seemed to me that they were a people very poor in everything. They should be good and intelligent servants, for I see that they say very quickly everything that is said to them; and I believe that they would become Christians very easily, for it seemed to me that they had no religion.

DOCUMENT TWO

Primary Source: Speech
from a Native American leader after meeting Columbus, c. 1500

The Native Americans first encountered by Europeans did not have written languages. The only records of their words come from reports written by Europeans. The following speech by a Native American to Columbus was reported by Peter Martyr D'Anghera (MAR-tur dahn-GEHR-uh), an Italian historian in the service of Spain. Martyr did not witness the speech himself. He published the first volume of his account, *De Orbe Novo (On the New World)*, in 1516.

CONSTRUCTED RESPONSE What was one reaction Native Americans had to Europeans?

It is reported to us that you have visited all these countries . . . formerly unknown to you, and have inspired the inhabitants with great fear. Now I tell and warn you, . . . that the soul, when it quits the body, follows one of two courses; the first is dark and dreadful, and is reserved for the enemies and the tyrants of the human race; joyous and delectable is the second, which is reserved for those who . . . have promoted the peace and tranquility of others. If, therefore, you are a mortal, and believe that each one will meet the fate he deserves, you will harm no one.

DOCUMENT THREE

Primary Source: Retold Story
from a Wampanoag legend about the European arrival, c. 1700

Native Americans often passed down their history and culture through an oral tradition. Many of the stories told were fables or myths not meant to be taken literally. Instead, they were used to teach a lesson or to reflect a tribe's point of view. British settlers heard Wampanoag (wahm-puh-NOH-ag) legends about a giant named Maushop and recorded them in journals and letters as early as 1643.

CONSTRUCTED RESPONSE What does the change in Maushop's behavior convey about the Wampanoag's reaction to the arrival of Europeans?

On the west end of [present-day Martha's Vineyard] is a hill with a large cavity. A local Indian tradition says the deity Maushop lived there before the Europeans came to America. Maushop often invited Indians to share his meals. Once, to show their gratitude, they offered Maushop all the tobacco that grew on the island in one season. It barely filled his great pipe, but he . . . turned out the ashes into the sea, which formed Nantucket island. Upon the Europeans' arrival in America, Maushop retired in disgust, and has never since been seen.

SYNTHESIZE & WRITE

1. **REVIEW** Review what you have learned about the impressions and reactions of Native Americans and Europeans toward one another.

2. **RECALL** List the main ideas expressed in each document.

3. **CONSTRUCT** Construct a topic sentence that answers this question: How did Native Americans and Europeans view one another during the time of exploration?

4. **WRITE** Using evidence from the chapter and documents, write an informative paragraph that supports your topic sentence in Step 3.

VOCABULARY

Use each of the following vocabulary terms in a sentence that shows an understanding of the term's meaning.

1. infrastructure
   The Inca built an infrastructure of terraced fields and mountain roads and bridges.

2. domesticate

3. feudalism

4. humanism

5. mercantilism

6. nation-state

7. trans-Saharan

8. cartographer

9. chattel slavery

10. Columbian Exchange

READING STRATEGY
ANALYZE CAUSE AND EFFECT

Complete the following graphic organizer to show the major effects of European nations seeking to expand and claim global trade routes. Then answer the question.

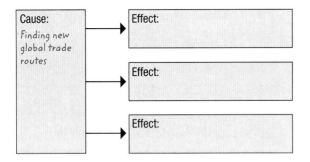

Cause:
Finding new global trade routes

Effect:

Effect:

Effect:

11. How did the expansion of global trade lead to a new view of the world for people on four continents?

MAIN IDEAS

Answer the following questions. Support your answers with evidence from the chapter.

12. How did geography influence early Native American cultures? **LESSON 1.1**

13. How was life in Europe changing by the 1400s and early 1500s? **LESSON 1.3**

14. Why did Martin Luther call for reform in the Roman Catholic Church? **LESSON 1.3**

15. What were the sources of wealth for three major kingdoms in West Africa? **LESSON 1.4**

16. How did European voyages of discovery change life for Native Americans and Africans? **LESSON 2.1**

HISTORICAL THINKING

Answer the following questions. Support your answers with evidence from the chapter.

17. **MAKE INFERENCES** What do structures such as the Great Serpent Mound reveal about ancient Native American cultures?

18. **IDENTIFY PROBLEMS AND SOLUTIONS** How did adopting the policy of mercantilism help strengthen some nations' economies?

19. **ANALYZE LANGUAGE USE** Why was the word *humanism* chosen to describe the philosophy that promotes individuality, critical thinking, and new ideas?

20. **DRAW CONCLUSIONS** Did Christopher Columbus's voyages confirm his ideas about world geography? Cite evidence from the text to support your conclusion.

21. **FORM AND SUPPORT OPINIONS** Should Native Americans have feared European explorers? Explain your answer.

22. **COMPARE AND CONTRAST** In what ways did Native American farming methods differ across North America?

This detail of West Africa from a medieval map illustrates aspects of the region's culture, as well as the famous ruler of Mali, Mansa Musa. Study the map details and answer the questions.

23. What details on the map reveal which figure is Mansa Musa?

24. What do the other illustrations on the map tell you about medieval trading in West Africa?

Jacques Cartier was unsuccessful in finding a northwestern water route to Asia, but he did learn much about the geography of the region he explored. He also frequently interacted with many Native American people during his voyages. This excerpt from the log of his first voyage in 1534 describes one such meeting. Read the passage and answer the question.

> Next day, having good weather, we sailed till noon. But, as we perceived there was no passage, we coasted along, and as we sailed saw some savages on the shores of a lake. The savages approached us and brought us pieces of cooked seal, which they placed on pieces of wood and then retired, giving us to understand that they gave them to us. We sent men ashore with hatchets, knives, chaplets [beads], and other articles, in which the savages took great delight, and they came all at once in their canoes to the shore where we were, bringing skins and other things they had to exchange for our articles, and there were more than three hundred of them— men, women, and children.

25. What words in Cartier's description help you understand how he regards this group of Native Americans?

26. **ARGUMENT** Columbus Day was established to honor Christopher Columbus's landing in America. Some people want the United States to stop celebrating this holiday because of what we know about Columbus's treatment of Native Americans. Do you agree? If so, whom might you honor instead? Write a letter to the editor of a newspaper explaining your views. Support your argument with evidence.

TIPS

• State your position about whether your city or state should celebrate Columbus Day.

• Use information from the chapter and your own ideas to support your argument.

• Research to learn more about both sides of the controversy.

• Address any counterarguments.

• Use two or three key vocabulary terms from the chapter in your letter.

• Conclude your letter with a sentence summarizing your position.

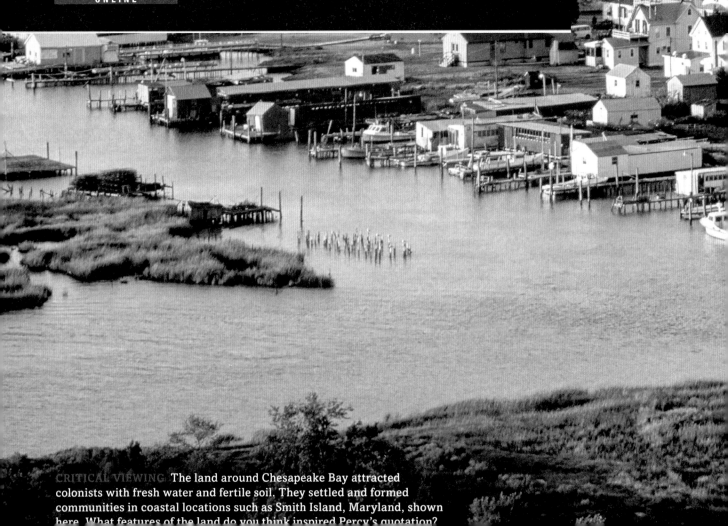

CHAPTER 2

COLONIZING NORTH AMERICA

1513–1752

HISTORICAL THINKING How were the North American colonies shaped by their geography and by the people who settled them?

AMERICAN STORIES The Colony of Jamestown

SECTION 1 **Spain in North America**

SECTION 2 **Colonization on the Atlantic Coast**

SECTION 3 **Middle Colonies and Southern Colonies**

AMERICAN GALLERY ONLINE Southern Plantations

CRITICAL VIEWING The land around Chesapeake Bay attracted colonists with fresh water and fertile soil. They settled and formed communities in coastal locations such as Smith Island, Maryland, shown here. What features of the land do you think inspired Percy's quotation?

"We entered into
the Bay of [Chesapeake]
. . . I was almost ravished
at the first sight thereof."
—George Percy, early Virginia colonist

CRITICAL VIEWING This aerial photograph of the Jamestown excavation site shows one corner of the triangular fort. Archaeologists have identified bulwarks, which were used to store artillery, at each of the fort's corners. What other details does this photo reveal about the site?

THE COLONY OF
JAMESTOWN

For many Americans, the names John Smith, John Rolfe, and Pocahontas have been familiar since childhood. And so the basic outlines of early Jamestown are generally well known: In 1607, a group of English colonists established a settlement in a land they called Virginia—the rest was history.

This American Story is a deeper look at aspects of the well-known tale of Jamestown. It's an opportunity to explore the colonists' motivations and struggles and learn about their encounters—sometimes friendly, often hostile—with Native Americans. It also explores the ways the colonists irrevocably changed the land and its inhabitants by ultimately driving out most of the native groups.

GENTLEMAN COLONISTS

If you were planning an expedition to uncharted territory, knowing that you were months away from any possibility of resupply, whom would you choose to bring with you? Farmers, hunters, or others who could enable the expedition to live off the land? You might not bring many people who present themselves with the job description of "gentleman."

The first Jamestown expedition had a slightly different notion about necessary personnel. The list of names of the first 104 colonists includes 29 "gentlemen," a ruling council of 6 men, and 13 "labourers." There were also 6 carpenters and a handful of other craftsmen to round out the number of settlers with practical skills.

This ratio of useful workers to men who would hesitate to get their hands dirty seems frighteningly impractical to the modern-day mind. The Virginia Company, however, was certain the settlers could obtain most or all of their food from the local Indians, who were described as "generally very loving and gentle" by one writer in 1609. In the meantime, the settlers could occupy themselves searching for the gold and silver that they were certain existed in abundance in North America.

A historical interpreter leaves the gate of the re-created James Fort in 2007, the 400th anniversary of the founding of Jamestown. The festivities for the anniversary included the launch of a replica of the *Godspeed*, one of the three ships that carried the original settlers from England.

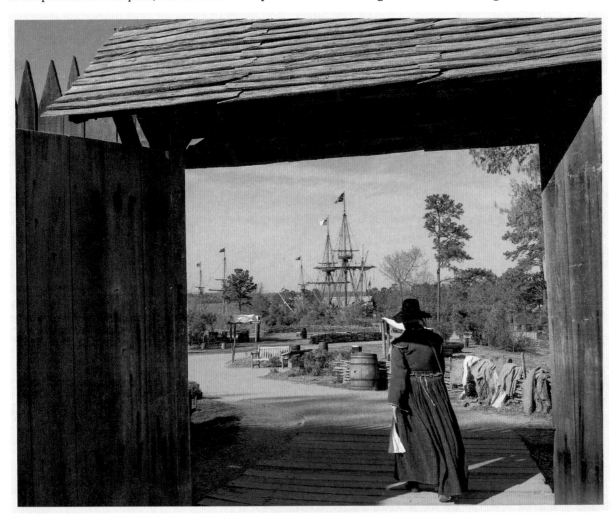

This breezy confidence proved to be a dangerous miscalculation. While they did trade with Jamestown to some extent, the Native Americans were either unable or unwilling to entirely support the colony. Starvation loomed, but the colony survived its first year, partly thanks to the leadership of John Smith, who decreed, "He that will not work shall not eat."

The overabundance of gentlemen was not the sole reason that only 38 colonists survived the first 9 months of Jamestown's existence. The colony had been established on a marshy plot of land with a tainted drinking water source. Archaeologists have also recently discovered evidence that many of the colonists worked very hard at fishing, woodworking, and other enterprises. Still, some testimony indicates that the work ethic of at least a few was an ongoing concern. One governor of Jamestown, arriving in 1611, was dismayed to find the inhabitants "bowling in the streets" rather than working in the few gardens they had planted.

PIGS, GERMS, AND TOBACCO

In Jamestown's earliest years, the region experienced a drought. While Native American groups seemed to manage, the colony teetered on the edge of disaster, saved only by the regular influx of additional settlers. Why, then, did the English prevail over the Native Americans in a relatively short time? Author Charles C. Mann, in a 2007 article for *National Geographic*, proposed an ecological explanation, noting that the colonists brought with them several organisms that were new to North America and destructive to the Native Americans' way of life.

Before 1607, there were few domestic animals in North America. Pigs, goats, cows, and horses all arrived with the Europeans, and when these animals wandered away from their enclosures,

POCAHONTAS, DIPLOMAT

The famous American legend tells that Pocahontas, the daughter of Chief Powhatan, rushed in just as John Smith was about to be executed by the chief's warriors and saved him from that terrible fate. It's an exciting story, but historians agree that Smith either made up the whole event years later, or misunderstood the Native American ceremony he witnessed. The tale of Pocahontas is correct, however, in recounting that she married John Rolfe in 1614.

It is less well known that the Jamestown colonists kidnapped her in 1613 to compel her father's cooperation and that during her time in captivity she converted to Christianity. In a 1614 letter to Sir Thomas Dale, the governor of Virginia, Rolfe claimed to feel "affection" for Pocahontas and added that she gave "a great appearance of love" in return. He also insisted that his chief purpose in wanting to marry Pocahontas was "for the good of this plantation, for the honour of our countrie, for the glory of God, for my owne salvation, and for the converting to the true knowledge of God and Jesus Christ, an unbeleeving creature." The wedding may have been as much an act of diplomacy as a union of souls, as it initiated a truce between colonists and Indians that lasted until 1622.

Sadly, the truce lived longer than Pocahontas herself. She died in 1617, at the end of a trip to England with her husband and young son.

Even though it contains historical inaccuracies, this 18-foot-tall bronze statue of Pocahontas is one of the most famous features of Jamestown Island. The statue's hands are worn to a bright copper color due to the number of visitors who have held them while posing for pictures.

they wreaked havoc on the Native Americans' fields. Pigs were especially destructive, with their huge appetites, willingness to eat most anything, and ability to dig up roots and tubers.

The English settlers also carried a tiny, but no less powerful, import in their blood: the parasite that causes malaria, a disease that can sicken and weaken an individual for years. Some researchers theorize that malaria reached Virginia and infected the Native Americans in the early 1600s. It's even possible that malaria was responsible for the seeming laziness—or actual illness-related fatigue—of early colonists who failed to farm for food.

Tobacco was not an import to North America, but the Native Americans had never grown it in large quantities. As noted by scientist Leanne DuBois, "Tobacco has an almost unique ability to suck the life out of soil." To feed England's growing appetite for the crop, the colonists cleared acres of forest and left behind mostly depleted open lands. Mann sums up the results of the changes introduced by the English with a blunt conclusion: "Four centuries ago, the English didn't discover a New World—they created one."

A strain of sweet South American tobacco seed, brought to Jamestown by settler John Rolfe in 1610, quickly became Virginia's major cash crop and number one export.

THINK ABOUT IT

In what ways did the English create their own world in Virginia, rather than fitting into the existing environment and societies?

THE LIVELY TALE OF JOHN SMITH

Americans remember John Smith principally for his leadership of the Jamestown colony and his part in the Pocahontas legend. In fact, settling Jamestown was not Smith's first—or even his most exciting—adventure.

John Smith was born in 1580 and left home at 16 to become a soldier, joining a group in France that was fighting to free Holland from Spain's control. Later, he served as a sailor on a merchant ship and fought with Austrian troops against Turkey. In 1602, he was wounded and captured during a battle in present-day Romania and then sold into slavery. The Turk who bought Smith sent him as a gift to a woman he admired. Smith later claimed that the woman fell in love with him and arranged for him to train as a soldier in the Turkish army. He escaped and spent time in Europe and North Africa before returning to England in 1604 or 1605. Considering Smith's retelling of his encounter with Powhatan and Pocahontas, we might conclude that his greatness as an adventurer was matched by his brilliance as a storyteller.

A bronze statue of John Smith stands within the outlines of the original James Fort. The inscription on the base reads "John Smith, Governor of Virginia, 1608" and features Smith's coat of arms and motto, *vincere est vivere* ("to live is to conquer").

THE NOT SO DISTANT PAST

Smith and Rolfe, Pocahontas and Powhatan—these names often seem to belong to a remote, untouchable past. Modern-day research and archaeology, however, have helped to reveal the Jamestown colonists and Native Americans of the region as living, relatable people. Over several years of patient digging, researchers have unearthed the walls of the original fort and other buildings at Jamestown, as well as artifacts that allow valuable glimpses into the inhabitants' everyday lives.

The site is preserved within Historic Jamestowne Park, which is operated by the National Park Service and an organization called Preservation Virginia. At Historic Jamestowne, exhibits, tours, and costumed interpreters help visitors experience Jamestown as a real community that is not lost in distant history.

Glass wine bottles

Men's tooth and ear picker

Iron caltrops were laid on the ground to injure enemies and prevent attacks.

PRIMARY SOURCE

In 1609, a pamphlet called "Nova Britannia" ("New Britain") appeared in England to promote the colony in Virginia to investors and potential colonists. At this point, Jamestown was still engaged in a desperate struggle against starvation and disease.

The country itself is large and great assuredly, though as yet, no exact discovery can be made of all. It is also commendable and hopeful in every way, the air and climate most sweet and wholesome, much warmer than England, and very agreeable to our natures. . . . the land naturally yields . . . [an] abundance of fish, both scale and shell; an infinite store of both land and water fowl.

There are valleys and plains streaming with sweet springs, like veins in a natural body; there are hills and mountains making an offer of hidden treasure, never yet searched; the land is full of minerals, plenty of woods (the wants of England).

—from "Nova Britannia," 1609

NOVA BRITANNIA.

OFFRING MOST Excellent fruites by Planting in VIRGINIA.

Exciting all such as be well affected to further the same.

LONDON
Printed for SAMVEL MACHAM, and are to be sold at his Shop in Pauls Church-yard, at the Signe of the Bul-head.
1609.

CREATING THE SPANISH EMPIRE

Legend has it that Hernán Cortés told the Aztec, "We Spanish have a disease of the heart that can only be cured by gold." Native Americans might have thought Cortés was speaking literally, judging by Spanish conduct toward them.

CORTÉS AND THE AZTEC

For several decades after they settled in the Americas, the Spanish faced little competition from other European powers. This allowed them to explore large parts of North and South America. Between 1513 and 1598, **conquistadors**, or Spanish soldiers and adventurers, set out from their settlements in the Caribbean bound for the mainland to claim more land and riches for Spain.

One of the most famous of the conquistadors was **Hernán Cortés**. Cortés journeyed to the Caribbean in 1504 and took part in the Spanish conquest of the island of Cuba in 1511. In 1519, he sailed to the mainland of North America, leading an army of fewer than 600 soldiers deep into the Aztec Empire. The army carried firearms and rode horses, neither of which the Native Americans had seen before. Along the way, the Spanish recruited allies from smaller Native American

Cortés displays his military strength to impress Moctezuma's ambassadors in this painting, *The Arrival of Cortés in Vera Cruz*. It was created in the late 17th century by an unknown artist and is one in a series of scenes of the conquistador's visit.

tribes that had been conquered and enslaved by the Aztec. These new soldiers spoke local languages and helped Cortés communicate with his now-diverse army.

Cortés and his men arrived in Tenochtitlán (tay-nohch-teet-LAHN), the Aztec capital, without opposition. The Aztec ruler, Moctezuma (mahk-tuh-ZOO-muh), received them warily but peacefully. This proved to be a mistake. The Spaniards quickly seized Moctezuma and took control of the city and empire through him. Cortés's men demanded gold and attacked the Aztec during a religious ceremony. The Aztec rebelled and, during the battle, many people lost their lives, including Moctezuma and a third of the Spanish troops. The Spanish retreated from the city and attempted to **beseige** it, cutting off its access to supplies and reinforcements.

The Aztec victory was short-lived, however. About a year later, the siege, coupled with an epidemic of European diseases, had weakened the Aztecs' ability to defend Tenochtitlán, and Cortés and his troops attacked and conquered the city. After that, Spain quickly took charge of Mexico and began its large-scale colonization, claiming new territories for itself outside of its national borders. The Spanish also began enslaving native populations. They called their lands in the Americas "New Spain."

PIZARRO AND THE INCA

Spanish conquistador Francisco Pizarro arrived in the Americas in 1502. By 1520, he was living prosperously in Central America, in what is now Panama, but he had greater ambitions. Over the years, Pizarro had heard stories of cities to the south that were constructed of gold and silver. Pizarro led exploratory voyages down the Pacific coast of South America, where he and his companions found convincing evidence of a wealthy civilization in the Andes Mountains, the **Inca Empire**. Pizarro set out in January 1531 with about 180 men and a small number of horses to conquer the land we know as Peru on behalf of Spain.

Fortunately for Pizarro, the Inca's powerful emperor had died around 1527. Historians believe he died of **smallpox**, a deadly, infectious disease introduced by Europeans that was spreading throughout the empire. Without their emperor, the Inca fell into a civil war. The epidemic and the war had greatly weakened the Inca before Pizarro arrived.

When Pizarro visited the city of Cajamarca (kah-hah-MAHR-kah) in 1532, an Inca leader named **Atahualpa** (ah-tah-WAHL-pah) agreed to a peaceful meeting. Atahualpa arrived at the meeting accompanied by 3,000 unarmed soldiers. He hoped his show of force would discourage the Spaniard from attacking. Much like Moctezuma before him, Atahualpa was wrong to trust the Spanish.

After a brief discussion in the city square, Pizarro's men opened fire, killing many of Atahualpa's soldiers. The Spanish took Atahualpa prisoner and held him for ransom, demanding a massive amount of gold and silver. The Inca complied, but the Spanish killed Atahualpa anyway. Then they installed a puppet leader at the Inca capital of **Cusco** (KOOZ-koh), which sparked a rebellion that continued for decades. The Spanish did not achieve full control of Peru until 1572.

How was it possible for so few Spanish soldiers to bring down such huge empires as the Inca and the Aztec? The Spanish had a number of advantages over Native Americans. They had firearms, cannons, armor, and horses, which made their armies more effective in battle. Aztec and Inca weapons were no match for them. The Spanish were masterful at forming alliances with Native American groups. They recognized that both empires consisted of conquered peoples who were not loyal to the Inca or the Aztec. They also realized that the organization of the Inca government allowed for one leader to replace another quite easily. Much like the leadership of the U.S. government today, Inca leadership could change and not directly affect commerce or the lives of its citizens.

The biggest factor contributing to Spain's success, however, was disease. Smallpox and other European illnesses killed or weakened many thousands of Native Americans throughout the Americas, and these epidemics aided the Spanish in their conquests. Smallpox eventually killed about half of all the Inca. Throw in a little luck, military skill, and utter ruthlessness, and the conquistadors' achievements begin to make a little more sense.

HISTORICAL THINKING

1. **READING CHECK** What error did both Moctezuma and Atahualpa make upon first encountering the Spanish?

2. **IDENTIFY MAIN IDEAS AND DETAILS** What factors led to the Spanish conquests in the Americas?

3. **MAKE GENERALIZATIONS** How did the Spanish desire for gold affect the people of Central and South America?

MAIN IDEA Spanish explorers in Central America pushed deeper into North America in search of new territories and riches, bringing their rigid political and class systems with them.

SPANISH RULE OF NORTH AMERICA

You've probably heard the old saying that fortune favors the bold. Spain's expeditions into North America were both bold and very dangerous, but if the explorers survived, fortune might be theirs. The same was not true of the people they encountered on their journeys.

SPANISH EXPEDITIONS MOVE NORTH

As Cortés and Pizarro were conquering Mexico and Peru, Spanish explorers undertook several expeditions farther to the north, entering parts of what would become the United States. **Juan Ponce de León** (PAWN-say day lay-OHN) was the first European to set foot in Florida. In 1513, he landed near modern-day St. Augustine before sailing south through the Florida Keys.

More than two decades later, in 1539, **Hernando de Soto**, the Spanish governor of Cuba, landed in Florida and led a three-year expedition through what is now the southeastern region of the United States to claim land and search for treasure. The explorers trekked as far north as the Tennessee River Valley. On their way back, they destroyed Native American villages and killed or enslaved the inhabitants. De Soto died of a fever on the trail in 1542.

Álvar Núñez (NOO-nyehz) **Cabeza de Vaca** became the first European to cross the American West. In 1528, his expedition shipwrecked on the Gulf Coast of what is now Texas. He and a few survivors lived among Native Americans for four years before they traveled across present-day Texas, New Mexico, and Arizona to reach other Spaniards in northern Mexico. Cabeza de Vaca published an account of his remarkable journey and worked to change Spain's policies toward Native Americans.

From 1540 to 1542, **Francisco Vásquez de Coronado** led a large military expedition from Mexico to explore what is now California and parts of the Southwest. Spanish authorities sent Coronado in search of the Seven Cities of Cíbola (SEE-boh-lah), a wealthy kingdom rumored to be located north of Mexico. Expecting to discover silver, gold, and other riches, Coronado only found Native Americans hostile to Spanish rule.

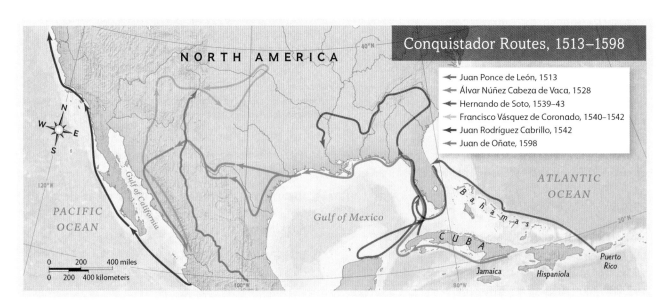

Conquistador Routes, 1513–1598

- Juan Ponce de León, 1513
- Álvar Núñez Cabeza de Vaca, 1528
- Hernando de Soto, 1539–43
- Francisco Vásquez de Coronado, 1540–1542
- Juan Rodríguez Cabrillo, 1542
- Juan de Oñate, 1598

As Coronado's expedition wound down, **Juan Rodríguez Cabrillo** (kuh-BREE-yoh) sailed up the Pacific coastline in search of a northern water route connecting the Pacific and Atlantic oceans. His ships may have traveled as far as the Pacific Northwest before turning back, but Cabrillo never returned to Mexico. He was injured during a battle with Native Americans in 1543 and died of his wound.

In early 1598, **Juan de Oñate** (oh-NYAH-tay) headed north from Mexico on a mission of colonization. His party of soldiers, settlers, and Franciscan friars (Catholic missionaries) established a colony in what is now Santa Fe, New Mexico. From there, Oñate journeyed as far as present-day Kansas and the Gulf of California seeking riches, but, like Coronado, he came back empty-handed.

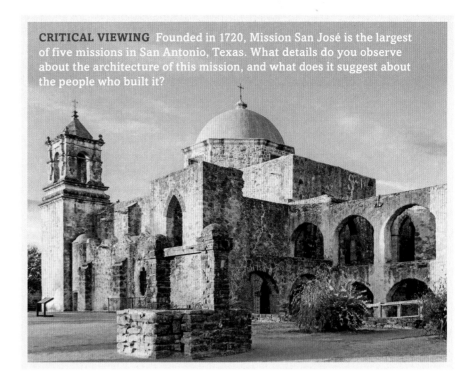

CRITICAL VIEWING Founded in 1720, Mission San José is the largest of five missions in San Antonio, Texas. What details do you observe about the architecture of this mission, and what does it suggest about the people who built it?

Franciscan friars, such as those who accompanied Oñate, played a big part in colonizing New Spain. They established missions where they provided Native Americans with food and shelter in exchange for labor and attempted to convert them to Christianity. By 1629, more than 25 churches existed in New Mexico. Friars also built missions from Florida west to the Gulf Coast and north into present-day southeast Georgia.

THE SPANISH SYSTEM

By 1650, the Spanish colonies in the Americas stretched from New Mexico and Florida in the north to Chile in the south. How was it possible for the Spanish crown to control this huge overseas empire?

The king of Spain was the ultimate authority. He was aided by the Council of the Indies, a group of advisors who regulated trade, appointed officials, and made laws in the colonies. Beginning in the 16th century, Spain's colonies in the Americas were divided into two **viceroyalties**: New Spain and Peru. New Spain included portions of Central and North America. Peru covered portions of South America. Each viceroyalty was ruled by a viceroy, who reported to the king.

This hierarchical system existed to expand the power and wealth of the Spanish crown, in part by enriching Spanish settlers. To exploit the labor of the Native Americans and to profit from the natural wealth of the Americas, the Spanish king granted conquistadors large tracts of farmland called **haciendas** (hah-see-EHN-dahz). A hacienda included a second grant, or **encomienda** (ehn-koh-mee-EHN-duh), that allowed owners to enslave a certain number of Native Americans to work the land. However, so many Native Americans died under the harsh conditions of the encomienda system that the Spanish began to import enslaved African people to replace them, though the Portuguese dominated the slave trade.

Spain dominated colonization in the Americas until 1588, when the British defeated the **Spanish Armada**, a fleet of warships sent by Spain to attack Britain. As a result, Spain's reputation as a major political power in the world diminished. Britain and other European countries took advantage of this change to start their own colonies in the Americas.

HISTORICAL THINKING

1. **READING CHECK** What was Spain's ultimate goal in devising the viceroyalty and encomienda systems?

2. **DRAW CONCLUSIONS** Why do you think the Spanish were constantly exploring and attempting to colonize new areas?

3. **ANALYZE CAUSE AND EFFECT** How did the defeat of the Spanish Armada affect the colonization of the Western Hemisphere?

TRIANGULAR TRADE

Frederick Douglass, a former slave, once said, "No man can put a chain about the ankle of his fellow man without at last finding the other end fastened about his own neck." Those who benefited from the booming American slave trade, however, saw only wealth, not consequences.

THE PORTUGUESE SLAVE TRADE

To capitalize on the farms in the West Indies, hacienda owners forced enslaved Native Americans to work long hours under grueling conditions. Many of these Native Americans died. As a result, owners turned to slave traders from Portugal, who had been transporting kidnapped Africans since the 1440s.

For the Portuguese, the slave trade had been profitable since the 1480s. So many Africans were captured, traders had to build large forts along the West African coast to house them until they could be transported by ship. Slavery began on the islands of the Caribbean Sea around 1518. By the time the first documented enslaved African set foot on the mainland of North America, more than a million people were already in bondage throughout the European colonies of the Western Hemisphere.

Meanwhile, in some areas of West Africa, the income generated from slavery rivaled that of other **commodities**, or products, of the region, including salt and gold. The demand for slaves required more traders to enter the business. Their raiders attacked villages in the African interior, marching their captives in chains to the slave forts. The trek was brutal, and only about half of those captured survived. From there, the enslaved were loaded onto ships bound for the Americas.

TRIANGULAR TRADE

As European colonies in the Americas began exporting resources and commodities across the Atlantic, a three-part trading route developed. Under this **triangular trade** system, ships exchanged goods from different continents and used the profits to fund the next leg of the journey. On the first leg, European ships carried textiles, firearms, gunpowder, iron, and brass to West Africa, where the items were sold to fund the purchase of enslaved Africans.

This diagram of the lower deck of the British slave ship *Brookes* illustrates how 292 enslaved people were stowed, some under shelves, during their journey on the Middle Passage.

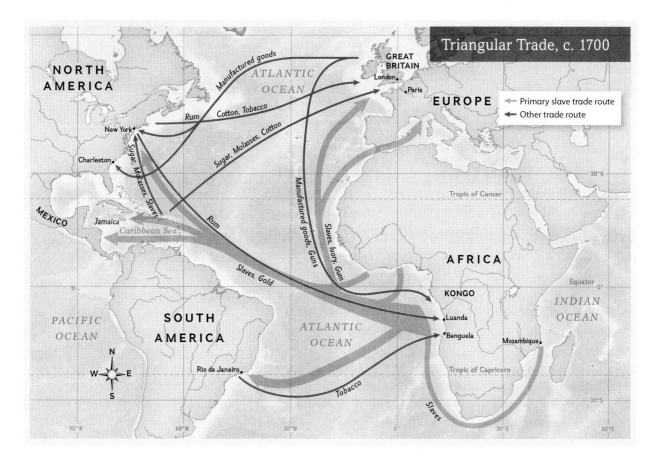

Triangular Trade, c. 1700

NORTH AMERICA
ATLANTIC OCEAN
GREAT BRITAIN
London
Paris
EUROPE

Primary slave trade route
Other trade route

Manufactured goods
Rum
Cotton, Tobacco
Sugar, Molasses, Cotton
New York
Charleston
Sugar, Molasses, Slaves
MEXICO
Jamaica
Caribbean Sea
Rum
Manufactured goods, Guns
Slaves, Ivory, Gum
Tropic of Cancer
30°N
AFRICA
KONGO
Luanda
Benguela
Mozambique
Equator 0°
INDIAN OCEAN
PACIFIC OCEAN
SOUTH AMERICA
ATLANTIC OCEAN
Slaves, Gold
Rio de Janeiro
Tobacco
Tropic of Capricorn
Slaves
30°S
90°W   60°W   30°W   0°   30°E   60°E

The second leg of the route, the infamous **Middle Passage**, transported captive Africans to the Americas. As the North American slave trade increased, slave ships shifted their primary ports from Central and South America to the West Indies. From there, enslaved people were transported to the English colonies on the mainland. Profits from North American slave markets were used to purchase goods to export to Europe—items that often depended on slave labor to produce. Once these goods reached Europe, the process began again.

As you can see from the map, trade across the oceans was not limited to this system. But for centuries, the main trade followed the triangular route that fueled it.

THE MIDDLE PASSAGE

The Middle Passage is referred to as "infamous" for good reason. The ships on that leg of the triangular trade route carried captives more than 5,000 miles from their homes and families. They had to survive brutal living conditions and starvation. The captives were chained to each other and to a floor of the hold below deck during the voyage. With 300 to 400 people crowded into a hold with only about three feet of headroom, there was little space to move. Ventilation was limited, and few ships were equipped to deal with human waste. Illnesses broke out often.

Approximately 10 percent of the captives who began the Middle Passage died of disease or despair before reaching the Americas.

During the four centuries of active Atlantic slave trading, ships carried more than 10 million people to the Western Hemisphere. Today, the removal of so many Africans from their homeland to the Americas is known as the **African diaspora**. The displaced Africans brought with them many traditions, which became the basis of a resilient culture that defied enslavement. Such spreading of traditions from one place to another is called **cultural diffusion**. Folktales such as the stories of Brer Rabbit and musical styles such as merengue are two examples of African traditions brought to the Americas and adapted by the descendants of the enslaved.

HISTORICAL THINKING

1. **READING CHECK** Why was the leg of the triangular trade route that transported slaves to the Americas called the Middle Passage?

2. **INTERPRET MAPS** What goods were exported from North America to Europe as part of the triangular trade system?

3. **DETERMINE CHRONOLOGY** How did the slave trade expand from Portugal, Spain, and their territories to the rest of the world?

THE ENGLISH IN VIRGINIA

England soon followed Spain to the Americas. Hungry for gold, the first English colonists were blind to the true wealth of North America. In the end, it was the sale of tobacco, not precious metals, that filled the pockets of investors.

THE FOUNDING OF JAMESTOWN

During the late 15th and 16th centuries, England could not compete with Spain and Portugal in overseas exploration and colony building. The nation's attention was devoted to wars abroad and internal struggles. By the end of the 16th century, England had expanding agricultural and mining industries, land shortages, and an increasingly mobile population. These factors set the stage for England to challenge its rivals in the Americas.

England's first colonial venture in North America, a settlement on Roanoke Island in what would become North Carolina, took place in 1585. With the blessing of Queen Elizabeth I, English adventurer **Sir Walter Raleigh** sent about 100 settlers to Roanoke, but the settlers quickly realized that they lacked farming and fishing knowledge and returned to England. Raleigh organized a second attempt in 1587, but that colony was also abandoned.

In 1606, King James I awarded a **charter**, or a written grant of rights and privileges, to the Virginia Company to start a colony in North America. The Virginia Company was a **joint-stock company**, a business in which wealthy individuals pooled their money together and shared ownership. The company's investors hoped to find silver and gold and a viable trade route to Asia.

On April 26, 1607, three ships carrying about 105 colonists arrived at Chesapeake Bay on the mid-Atlantic coast of North America. The group's leaders established a fort on an unoccupied peninsula at the mouth of what is now the James River. The swampy site had no spring to provide fresh water, and the surrounding river water was brackish, or salty. But here the colonists built Jamestown, England's first permanent settlement in the Americas. They named the surrounding land Virginia.

From the beginning, the colony was unstable. Relations with the local Native Americans, the Powhatan, were tense. The Powhatan resented the English intrusion on their territory, so they were not always interested in trading food with the settlers. Some of the early colonists did not have experience hunting, fishing, or farming, so they were often in need of supplies. Poor leadership, disease, and famine also kept the colony on the brink of failure.

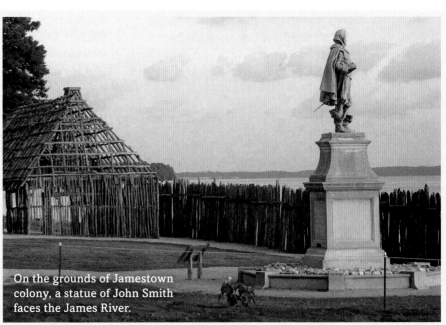

On the grounds of Jamestown colony, a statue of John Smith faces the James River.

THE COLONY GAINS A FOOTING

In late 1608, Captain **John Smith** became leader of the colony, and circumstances began to improve. Smith had struck up a friendship with **Pocahontas**, the daughter of the Powhatan chief. This alliance helped Smith broker peace between the settlers and the Powhatan, who supplied food to Jamestown for the winter. Smith also required regular work, military training, and discipline for all the colonists. A year later, Smith was injured and, unfortunately for the colony, returned to England for good.

After Smith's departure, the Powhatan refused to supply food to Jamestown and attacked colonists who dared to leave the fort to hunt or forage. During the "starving time" in the winter of 1609–1610, the settlement's food ran out. When help from England finally came the following spring, only 60 of 500 colonists remained.

In the wake of Jamestown's almost total failure, a new leader, Thomas West, Lord Delaware, helped put the colony back on track. Just as important, the marriage of colonist **John Rolfe** and Pocahontas signaled a period of peace between the English and the Powhatan. Rolfe was a planter who had brought a new strain of tobacco to Virginia from the West Indies. The new tobacco sold well because of its sweet taste. In 1617, the colony shipped nearly 20,000 pounds of tobacco to England, stoking a demand in Europe. Rolfe's enterprise helped to raise the profits that Jamestown's English investors so desperately sought.

With a popular cash crop to back it up, the Virginia Company began to offer land in the colony to landless English farmers. The need for labor skyrocketed. The Virginia Company and then the planters themselves began to bring **indentured servants**, people who pledged to work for a period of four to seven years in exchange for ocean passage and necessities, to the colony.

The year 1619 brought two major institutions to Jamestown: slavery and a formal government. The colony's first slaves were African captives taken from a Portuguese ship by English raiders. That same year, the Virginia Company established the **House of Burgesses**, an assembly of elected delegates, or representatives, to help govern the colony. It was not a democracy. Only landowners could vote for delegates, a governor appointed by the English monarch could veto delegates' ordinances, and the Virginia Company chose more than a fifth of the delegates. The House of Burgesses was, however, the first form of representative government in English North America.

Ætatis suæ 21. Aº. 1616.

🏛 The National Portrait Gallery Washington, D.C.

In her portrait, Pocahontas wears the high lace collar and ornate clothing that was the fashion in England during the early 17th century. The painting was made while she and her husband visited England in 1616. Her clothing choice and the English name she took, Lady Rebecca Rolfe, indicate a desire to conform to European culture.

In March 1622, a surprise attack by Native Americans killed nearly one-third of the 1,240 Jamestown settlers in one day. In response, King James put the colony under direct British rule. Although its success as a business venture was decidedly mixed and it bears the stain of early slavery, the Jamestown colony is important as the first, lasting foothold of England in North America.

HISTORICAL THINKING

1. **READING CHECK** What disadvantages did the Jamestown colony have to overcome?

2. **IDENTIFY PROBLEMS AND SOLUTIONS** What difficulties plagued Jamestown settlers in the early years, and how could they have been avoided?

3. **COMPARE AND CONTRAST** How were English and Spanish colonies in the Americas similar and different?

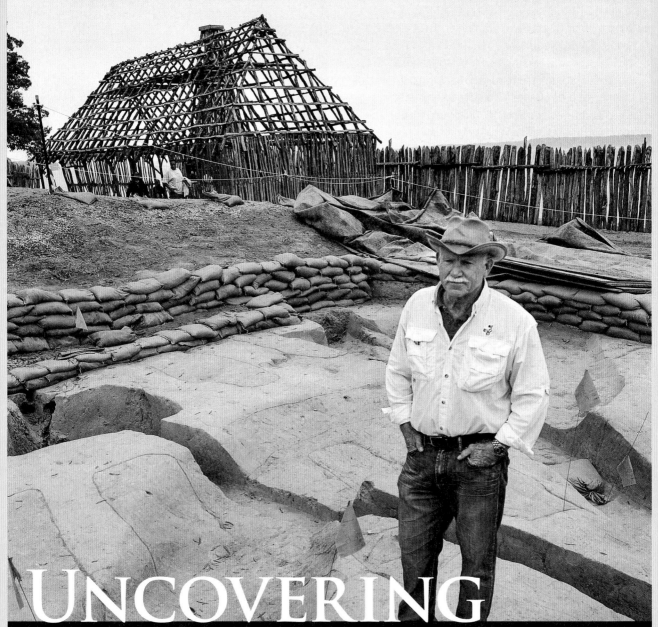

UNCOVERING
AMERICA'S BIRTHPLACE

"The American dream was born on the banks of the
James River." — William Kelso

For years, most experts believed James Fort, the original fort built
by the Jamestown colonists in 1607, had been washed away by the
James River. But archaeologist William Kelso had his doubts. In 1994,
he set out alone with his shovel to find signs of the triangular fort. After
digging for just a few hours, he discovered an old trash pit containing
glass beads, brass buttons, pottery shards, and copper scraps. His
quest for Jamestown's buried truths was just beginning.

^
Kelso stands on the spot in
the Jamestown church where
Pocahontas, the daughter of
Algonquian chief Powhatan,
wed John Rolfe. According to
Kelso, the church was the first
major English church in the
United States.

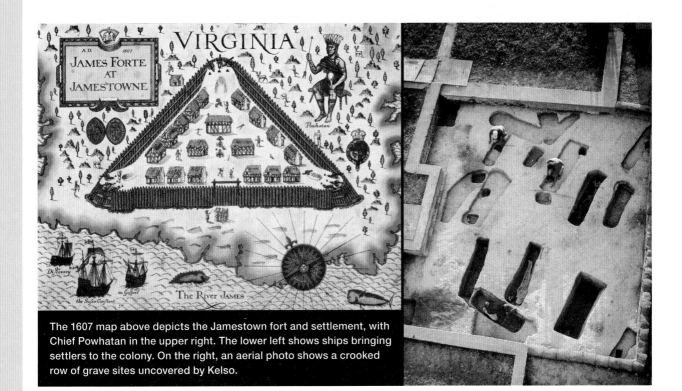

The 1607 map above depicts the Jamestown fort and settlement, with Chief Powhatan in the upper right. The lower left shows ships bringing settlers to the colony. On the right, an aerial photo shows a crooked row of grave sites uncovered by Kelso.

MAIN IDEA National Geographic Explorer William Kelso discovered evidence that has changed people's ideas about the Jamestown settlers.

EUREKA MOMENTS

Following his discovery, Kelso formed a team to excavate the Jamestown site. Within two years, they found evidence of a fort wall—earth stained dark by wooden posts that had decayed long ago. Kelso called that discovery "eureka moment number one."

Many more eureka moments followed. For more than 20 years, Kelso and his team have been excavating the site. They have identified evidence of all but one corner of the fort's structure. They also have discovered interior buildings, the settlement's first church, a well, several dump sites, and graves with human skeletons. The uncovered artifacts number more than a million.

REWRITING HISTORY

Kelso's discoveries have changed historical views of the Jamestown settlers. Some historians had portrayed the settlers as English noblemen who were unaccustomed to hard work. However, while reconstructing the fort using the kinds of materials and tools available to the settlers, Kelso discovered just how hard they had worked. He uncovered plenty of fishhooks and weapons as well as woodworking and glassmaking equipment. According to Kelso, "All of this flies in the face of conventional wisdom, which

says that the colonists were underfunded and ill-equipped, that they didn't have the means to survive, let alone prosper. What we have found here suggests that just isn't the case."

During the winter of 1609–1610, called the "starving time," all but 60 of the 500 settlers died from starvation and disease. They resorted to eating rats, snakes, dogs, and shoe leather. But Kelso points out that a major drought occurred at that time, which would have dried up water supplies and killed crops.

Kelso hopes to uncover more about Jamestown. However, the sea level around Jamestown Island is rising. The river didn't wash away James Fort, but it's possible ocean water might. And Kelso believes the site is worth saving. He credits the settlers for developing a new form of government there when they organized a representative assembly about 1619. As Kelso says, "That's when liberty got out of the bag, and nobody could stuff it back in." Jamestown, Kelso insists, "is where America began."

HISTORICAL THINKING

1. **READING CHECK** What evidence has William Kelso uncovered on Jamestown Island?

2. **IDENTIFY MAIN IDEAS AND DETAILS** How has Kelso's work changed historians' views of the Jamestown settlers?

3. **DRAW CONCLUSIONS** How did the Jamestown settlers contribute to the development of American constitutional democracy?

FRENCH AND DUTCH COLONIES

Nobody likes to feel left out. At the turn of the 16th century, Spain and Portugal were far ahead of most other nations in exploration and colonization. When England got into the game, France and the Netherlands wanted in, too.

THE FRENCH FUR TRADE

While the English were turning their first North American colony into a large-scale agricultural settlement, French activity in the Americas focused on trading with Native Americans—especially in furs. This angle was virtually assured in 1582 when a French ship returned from North America with a cargo of furs that earned a 1,500 percent profit. More ships quickly followed.

In 1608, **Samuel de Champlain** established a base at Quebec, which means "the place where the river narrows" in Algonquian. As it turned out, Quebec was an ideal location for controlling what would become the Canadian interior. For almost 20 years, Champlain went about his business, acquiring furs and establishing good relationships with his Native American trading partners. He even went so far as to fight personally alongside France's Algonquian and Huron allies in conflicts with their enemies. His actions helped cement alliances between **New France** and various Native American nations. These alliances, in turn, earned the French access to valuable fur sources much farther to the west.

Quebec was still essentially a trading post with only a few hundred French inhabitants in 1627. In that year, the Company of New France, a joint-stock company, was established with Champlain as a member. The company's royal charter included total control of trade in the Americas, a requirement that 200 to 300 settlers be brought over each year, and the exclusion of Huguenots, a sect of French Protestants. As the ruler of a Roman Catholic nation, the French king frowned on Protestants, whom he considered to be heretics. **Heretics** are people who disagree with the established teachings or beliefs of a particular religion.

French and Dutch Colonies, 1605–1630

Area of Dutch settlement
Area of English settlement
Area of French settlement

NEW FRANCE
Québec 1608
Montréal 1642
St. Lawrence R.
45°N
Lake Champlain
Lake Ontario
NEW NETHERLAND
Hudson R.
Connecticut R.
NEW ENGLAND
MASSACHUSETTS BAY COLONY
PLYMOUTH COLONY
Delaware R.
New Amsterdam 1626
40°N
ATLANTIC OCEAN
VIRGINIA
Chesapeake Bay
Jamestown 1607
75°W
70°W
0 100 200 miles
0 100 200 kilometers

The city of Montreal, about 140 miles inland from Quebec along the St. Lawrence River, was founded in 1642, but the population of this settlement was also very slow to increase. The French king only allowed Catholics to settle there, and land distribution policies required most colonists to work for landowners instead of becoming landowners themselves. Consequently, peasants living in France saw little chance of improving their lives by moving to North America. France also sent missionaries to Native American villages in New France to learn their languages and traditions in hopes of converting them to Catholicism.

In 1663, when the crown dissolved the company, New France had only 2,500 inhabitants. However, it boasted a well-organized administration, along with schools and hospitals. The fur trade brought French colonists west into the Great Lakes region of New France, where their interactions with Native Americans were mostly friendly. The French set up trading posts and missions on the Upper Peninsula of Michigan. From there in 1673, Frenchmen Louis Jolliet and Jacques Marquette explored parts of Wisconsin and Illinois and navigated the Mississippi River as far south as present-day Arkansas.

NEW NETHERLAND

During the 16th century, the Netherlands had become an economic powerhouse. The Dutch—the people of the Netherlands—based their economy on the fishing and shipping industries. In 1609, the Dutch East India Company hired English seafarer Henry Hudson to search for the elusive northwestern route to Asia. Upon reaching the shore of North America, Hudson sailed 150 miles up what is now the Hudson River to present-day Albany, New York. Along the way, he traded for furs with local Native Americans. Trading was so lucrative that the Dutch established a post in the area, called Fort Nassau, in 1614.

In 1621, the Dutch government chartered the Dutch West India Company to trade and set up colonies in North America. In 1624, the company established **New Netherland** on Governors Island, just off the tip of what the Lenape—the Native American inhabitants of the region—called Manna-hata Island. The Dutch originally thought the tiny island would be easier for settlers to manage than the much larger Manna-hata. Soon, however, they were ready to expand.

A legend claims New Netherland leader Peter Minuit purchased Manna-hata, which we now know as Manhattan, in 1626 for $24 (60 Dutch guilders). The purchase, however, is not well documented. True or

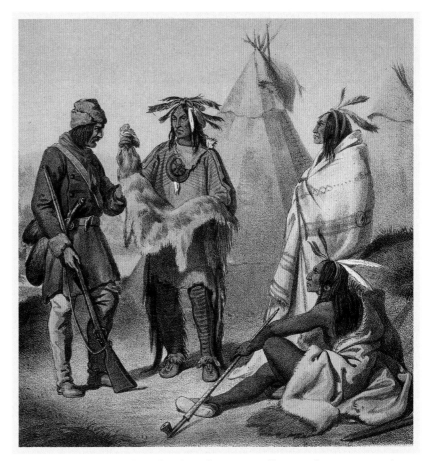

CRITICAL VIEWING A Native American man offers a pelt to a trapper in this print made by Jean-Adolphe Boquin in the 1870s. What does this print suggest about the relationship between these individuals?

not, the result was plagued with misunderstanding. While the Dutch may have believed they owned the island outright, the Lenape believed they had only sold the Dutch the rights to share the land. Several years later the misunderstanding erupted into war.

Nevertheless, the colony's capital, **New Amsterdam** (present-day New York City), was built on this island. In the following years, food and lumber production and the fur trade aided in expanding the economy, and Dutch colonists began to move north and settle in the Hudson River Valley.

HISTORICAL THINKING

1. **READING CHECK** How did Samuel de Champlain prove himself to France's Native American allies?

2. **FORM AND SUPPORT OPINIONS** Why do you think the French were successful in their commercial ventures in North America?

3. **INTERPRET MAPS** How many years separated the founding of Quebec, Jamestown, and New Amsterdam?

NEW ENGLAND

Have you ever felt so fed up with a situation that you just wanted to walk away and leave it all behind? Throughout their persecution by the English authorities and the Church of England, the Puritans held fast to their beliefs—even to the point of leaving their homes forever.

THE PLYMOUTH COLONY

While Jamestown was an almost purely commercial endeavor, the founding of New England had an added motivation: religious freedom. After King Henry VIII broke from the Roman Catholic Church and established the Church of England in 1534, different types of Christian worship became an increasingly troubling issue in England. The Church of England retained many elements of Catholicism. Puritanism, a Protestant movement in England in the late 16th and

17th centuries, sought to "purify" Christian worship by deleting these practices. Because of their beliefs and active opposition to the Church of England, Puritans were considered religious **dissenters**, or rebels. As such, they faced government persecution, including fines and imprisonment.

One group of Puritan dissenters, whom we now refer to as the Pilgrims, were **separatists** who believed that leaving England and its official church behind

AMERICAN PLACES
Plimoth Plantation

Founded in 1947, Plimoth Plantation is a living museum in Plymouth, Massachusetts, that provides an experience of life in colonial America in 1620. Interpreters in period clothing answer visitors' questions and demonstrate how the colonists lived.

was their only option. In September 1620, about 100 men, women, and children set sail for Virginia on the *Mayflower*. The voyage went astray, however, and the ship landed near what today is **Plymouth**, Massachusetts, more than 200 miles north of the original destination. Once they decided to found their colony there, the Pilgrims drafted the **Mayflower Compact**, a pledge signed by all of the adult males to establish a government and obey the laws and regulations that were subsequently enacted.

Pilgrim Hall Museum Plymouth, Massachusetts

Exhibits in Pilgrim Hall, the nation's oldest continuously operating public museum, tell the founding story of the United States. This wooden sculpture of Squanto from the 19th century forms part of the museum's collection. It shows what one artist imagined the Native American guide might have looked like.

The colonists chose as a settlement site a Native American village abandoned by the Pawtuxet after a recent epidemic had killed most of the inhabitants. There, the Pilgrims endured their first winter, which only about half of them survived. **Squanto**, an English-speaking Pawtuxet, translated for the Pilgrims and helped them plant crops the following year. Historians believe Squanto had been kidnapped as a youth by English seafarers and taken to England, where he learned the language. He returned to North America years later. The colonists commemorated the 1621 harvest with three days of celebration shared with the area's Pokanoket people, with whom Squanto lived.

Governor **William Bradford** and military leader Myles Standish helped establish the Plymouth colony, maintaining order and keeping peace with the Pokanoket. Bradford served as governor for 30 years. He championed democratic institutions and acted as a stabilizing influence for the community. This stability, coupled with the colonists' hard work and thrift, helped the colony become self-sustaining by 1624. Although the Plymouth colony's success continued and its population reached about 2,000 by the mid-1640s, it remained separate from the other English dissenter colonies that soon began to spring up in New England.

THE MASSACHUSETTS BAY COLONY

Another group of dissenting Puritans arrived in 1630 and established the **Massachusetts Bay Colony**. Unlike the separatist Pilgrims, this colony's leaders sought to reform the church through their pious example, which they hoped would one day be taken up back in England. In the words of leader **John Winthrop**, the colony would be "as a Citty upon a Hill, the Eyes of all people are uppon us . . . wee shall be made a story and a byword through the world."

The Massachusetts Bay Company obtained a charter from King Charles I that specified the colony's government and boundaries. The charter called for a governor, a deputy governor, and an executive board of 18 delegates to be elected by freemen, or company stockholders. Together, they would meet in a legislative body called the General Court to make laws and regulations, appoint lower officials, grant lands, and punish lawbreakers. The colony's leaders changed the rules, however, to allow all male church members, not just stockholders, to become freemen. In theory, every freeman would be a member of the General Court. But as the population grew and towns formed quickly, freemen voted in town meetings for representatives to the assembly.

According to their religious beliefs, the colony's founders thought if they maintained a moral society, God would help the colony prosper. To promote this end, church leaders dominated the government and took steps to guarantee their power. Laws required residents to attend Puritan church services, and, even though the Puritans were themselves dissenters from the Church of England, dissenters from Puritan beliefs were punished, often quite harshly.

Following English tradition, Puritan society in New England was strictly hierarchical. In the family, a husband was superior to his wife, and the children obeyed their parents. In general, Puritan women saw themselves not as individuals with rights equal

The Fundamental Orders of Connecticut in 1639 was based on a sermon given by Thomas Hooker. The order joined together three settlements along the Connecticut River under one government. This document is essentially the first written constitution in North America. This excerpt includes 5 of the 11 orders presented in the document.

1. It is Ordered . . . that there shall be yearly two General Assemblies or Courts.

4. It is Ordered . . . that no person be chosen governor above once in two years.

5. It is Ordered . . . that to the aforesaid Court of Election the several Towns shall send their deputies.

7. It is Ordered . . . that . . . the Constable or Constables of each Town shall . . . give notice distinctly to the inhabitants of the same.

10. It is Ordered . . . that every General Court . . . shall consist of the Governor . . . and four other Magistrates.

to those of men, but as part of a community and a family, with duties determined by their gender and age. Aside from raising children, women's duties were many and important: keeping the house and garden; preserving fruits and vegetables; making cider, cheese, and butter; tending livestock; making cloth and sewing clothes; and more. The role of Puritan women in the church, where they were expected simply to listen and keep quiet, was indicative of their place in society. But they also were expected to administer a religious education to their children, and in that way, they were the spiritual equals of men.

CONNECTICUT AND RHODE ISLAND

By the mid-1640s, the Massachusetts Bay Colony had grown to more than 20,000 inhabitants, but not all of these residents were content with the colony's strict religious principles. In 1633, Puritan preacher **Thomas Hooker** arrived in Massachusetts Bay Colony and became a minister in the town of Newtown (later Cambridge). Hooker and his congregation weren't comfortable under the established Puritan leadership and migrated to the Connecticut River Valley to establish the town of Hartford. In 1639, prominent Hartford residents drafted a government framework called the **Fundamental Orders of Connecticut**. This influential document did not require church membership for voting and empowered voters

to elect both the legislature and the governor. Most important to the residents, it helped cement Connecticut's status as its own colony, independent of the authorities in the Massachusetts Bay Colony.

The founding of Rhode Island, too, resulted from unhappiness with the way the Massachusetts Bay Colony was governed. Minister **Roger Williams** arrived in Massachusetts in 1631. Williams's beliefs led him to openly criticize the Puritan establishment. First, he claimed that the colony rested on stolen property because the English king had no right to give away land that already belonged to Native Americans. Next, he attacked laws requiring church attendance as well as those that granted tax support for Puritan churches.

For his subversive, or rebellious, views, Williams was banished from Massachusetts Bay. In 1636, he established the settlement of Providence on land purchased from the Narragansett people. His settlement's policies of separation of church and government and religious tolerance, or allowing all people to freely practice their religion or beliefs, made Providence a destination for a variety of Christian dissenters.

One of these dissenters, **Anne Hutchinson**, accused Massachusetts Bay ministers of straying from accepted Puritan theology. She challenged the idea that understanding the Bible required the interpretation of ministers. This dispute was all the more serious to colony leadership because it came from a woman. Like Williams, Hutchinson was banished from Massachusetts Bay. With Williams's help, she and a group of supporters established a settlement they named Portsmouth on Narragansett Bay. Eventually, these settlements secured a charter, and Portsmouth and Providence united with nearby communities at Newport and Warwick to form the colony of Rhode Island.

CONFLICTS WITH NATIVE AMERICANS

During the 1600s, the colonial population grew, and settler communities spread across New England. As colonists sought to control and exploit an expanding share of territory and resources, Native Americans resented being pushed off their lands. The **Pequot War** of 1636–1637 was fought between the Pequot nation and an allied force of English colonists and other Native Americans. Throughout the war, colonists sold captured Pequot as slaves to other Native American tribes or to plantation owners in the West Indies. The largest battle involved a massacre of the Pequot, including women, children, and old men. The treaty to end the conflict led to the downfall of the Pequot nation.

CRITICAL VIEWING This woodcut of a Native American fort served as an attack plan in the final battle of the Pequot War in May 1637. What does this artwork reveal about this historical event?

In the decades that followed the Pequot War, an uneasy peace prevailed between Native Americans and European colonists in New England. More than 50,000 Europeans settled in the region, occupying hunting, fishing, and agricultural lands of Native Americans. Resentments soon resurfaced. In 1671, colonists forced the Wampanoag nation to surrender its guns. Killings and retaliations followed. Wampanoag leader **Metacom** (known as King Philip in English) assembled raiding parties of Wampanoag and their Algonquian allies and attacked towns throughout New England. Colonial troops responded in kind. They also took this opportunity to attack their longtime allies, the Narragansett, whose land they sought to acquire. These battles came to be called **King Philip's War**.

In the end, about 600 colonial soldiers died in the conflict. Seventeen colonial towns were destroyed (including Providence, Rhode Island, which burned in 1676), and roughly 50 more communities were seriously damaged. For the Native Americans of southern New England, the war was a calamity. Thousands died, and many others were captured and enslaved. Even groups that supported the English lost out. When the war was over, all Native Americans in the area either fled or stayed and lost their independence under English rule.

HISTORICAL THINKING

1. **READING CHECK** How did the Pilgrims and the founders of Massachusetts Bay differ in their views on the Church of England?

2. **COMPARE AND CONTRAST** How was the role of religion different in New England than in New France?

3. **DRAW CONCLUSIONS** In what ways did Native American tribes aligned with the colonists suffer as a result of King Philip's War?

MIDDLE COLONIES

What's important to you when you think about places you'd like to live one day? A mild climate? Job opportunities? Tolerance and diversity? The Middle Colonies fit all those requirements. In fact, one of them was even founded on the principle of tolerance.

FROM NEW AMSTERDAM TO NEW YORK

The English **Middle Colonies** along the mid-Atlantic coast of North America were comprised of Delaware, New Jersey, Pennsylvania, and New York. In addition to the Dutch communities that were established there as part of New Netherland, the area attracted settlers from many other European countries who were searching for economic opportunities and religious freedom.

At first, to continue its lucrative fur trade, New Netherland maintained good relations with local Native Americans. But as you have read, in the Lower Hudson River Valley in the late 1630s and early 1640s, land disputes led to local wars between the Dutch colonists and Native Americans. In spite of this, by the 1650s, New Netherland was thriving.

Even so, New Netherland did not remain for long on the colonial map. The growing rivalry for sea power and trade dominance between England and the Netherlands ended up being the colony's undoing. King Charles II of England granted his brother, James, Duke of York, vast tracts of land in North America—including New Netherland. In 1664, a large English fleet arrived that vastly outnumbered the Dutch. The English took the colony without so much as a struggle. New Netherland was renamed New York, New Amsterdam became New York City, and the official Dutch presence on the mainland of North America came to an end.

PENNSYLVANIA

In 1681, King Charles II granted a charter for a colony to **William Penn**, in part on lands seized from the Dutch. Penn was a **Quaker**, a member of a religious group also called the Society of Friends. Quakers believe in a direct experience of God without need

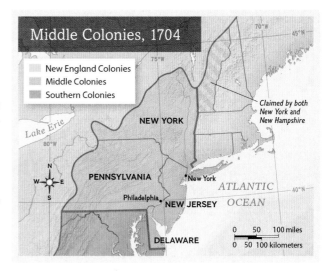

Middle Colonies, 1704

New England Colonies
Middle Colonies
Southern Colonies

Claimed by both New York and New Hampshire

NEW YORK

Lake Erie

PENNSYLVANIA   New York   ATLANTIC

Philadelphia   NEW JERSEY   OCEAN

0   50   100 miles
0   50 100 kilometers

DELAWARE

for traditional church hierarchies. In addition, they practice equality, simplicity, and pacifism. **Pacifism** is the belief that war is morally wrong.

William Penn had an ambitious plan for the colony. First, he wanted to make Pennsylvania a refuge for Quakers, who had been persecuted for years in England and in other colonies. Several unrepentant Quakers were even hanged for their beliefs in the Massachusetts Bay Colony.

Next, Penn wanted to guarantee freedom of conscience, or the right to hold different religious convictions than others, in the colony. But he believed in freedom *of* religion, not freedom *from* religion. Quakers tolerated diversity in beliefs, but still required Pennsylvanians to "acknowledge one almighty God to be the creator, upholder, and ruler of the world." Penn also supported fair treatment for Native Americans, and his policies translated into a long period of peaceful relations between Pennsylvania's settlers and Native Americans.

William Penn (center) stands with Delaware Indians after signing a treaty that finalized the sale of Pennsylvania. This carving is housed in the U.S. Capitol building.

Penn's plans for government, too, were forward-thinking. His Frame of Government of 1682, a written plan for the government of Pennsylvania, included an elected General Assembly, and succeeding amendments increased the power of the voters in instituting public policy.

When Penn's policies were enacted, the colony became an attractive destination for people of many faiths and nationalities. Pennsylvania's diversity included large numbers of Amish and Mennonite believers from Germany and Switzerland. There were also Irish Catholics, French Huguenots, Spanish Jews, English Methodists—groups who felt a fresh start in a new land that, more or less, tolerated their religion was worth the risk of leaving their homeland.

Pennsylvania's harmonious society attracted hardworking people who were ready and able to cultivate its fertile lands. The agricultural output of the region surpassed local consumption, meaning there were surpluses of corn, wheat, rye, hemp, and flax to export. The port of Philadelphia became the trading hub through which agricultural and other exports flowed. Lumber, iron production, papermaking, and printing businesses flourished.

The colony's early economic success was in part due to enslaved labor. Though they would be known eventually for their antislavery views, Quakers owned slaves and were involved in the Philadelphia slave trade early in Pennsylvania's history.

NEW JERSEY AND DELAWARE

The colonies that existed on the land now known as New Jersey were a part of New Netherland. When the British took over, the land was divided between two British royal subjects, Lord Carteret and Lord Berkeley, and renamed New Jersey. In 1681, Penn and other Quakers bought the section owned by the Carteret family and incorporated it into Pennsylvania. The rest remained New Jersey.

In 1682, the king gave Penn three "lower" counties south of Philadelphia. Despite Penn's efforts to create an ideal colony, the non-English European settlers who lived in these counties were not happy being a part of Pennsylvania and at times clashed with colonial authority. Penn tried unsuccessfully to unite the English and the other Europeans. In 1704, after two decades of difficulties, he allowed the counties to split off. They joined together under the common name of Delaware and formed a government assembly.

HISTORICAL THINKING

1. **READING CHECK** Identify two reasons why William Penn was able to acquire the land that would eventually become Pennsylvania.

2. **DRAW CONCLUSIONS** In what ways were some Quaker beliefs reflected in the founding ideas of Pennsylvania?

3. **INTERPRET MAPS** Why might it have been easy for settlers in the lower counties of Pennsylvania to break away and form Delaware?

SOUTHERN COLONIES

The Southern Colonies were a bit of a mixed bag—new and old, poor and rich, Protestant and Catholic. The one thing that eventually unified them was a plantation economy and a heavy reliance on enslaved Africans for labor.

CHESAPEAKE BAY COLONY

George Calvert, the first **Lord Baltimore**, wanted to find a haven for English Catholics in North America. King Charles I granted a charter for a new colony called Maryland in June 1632. It was to be located north of Virginia. However, the charter did not arrive in time for Calvert, who had died in April, to take control. Instead, his son Cecilius, the second Lord Baltimore, became the **proprietor**, or owner of the colony. The first ships sailed through Chesapeake Bay in March 1634 with 17 landowning families and about 200 others who had come to work. Most were indentured servants.

The leaders of the settlement were determined not to repeat the mistakes of Virginia. They made sure to purchase land from the local Yaocomico (YAH-oh-com-ih-koh) people and establish friendly relations with them. They also set up farms and trading posts. Initially, most of the labor fell to indentured servants. Later, the owners of plantations began to purchase enslaved Africans to work their lands.

Maryland's charter was based on outdated feudal principles. The proprietor had sweeping civil and military powers and, like a medieval lord, could even confer titles. Maryland's first governor was Cecilius's younger brother Leonard, but it was not long before pressure from small landholders and local Protestants forced a colonial assembly to convene. Then, in 1638, the assembly established its right to initiate colonial legislation. This change brought the colony in line with legislative practices in England, where Parliament had the ability to propose laws. One of Maryland's better-known laws is the Religious Toleration Act, passed in 1649, which guaranteed freedom of worship, but only for Christians.

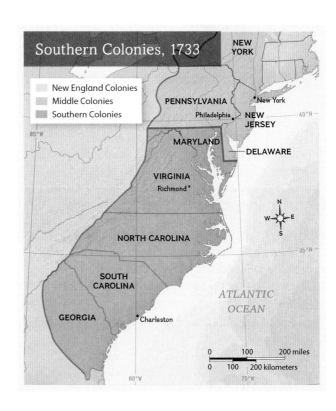

Southern Colonies, 1733

- New England Colonies
- Middle Colonies
- Southern Colonies

Maryland's status as a Catholic colony was a source of persistent problems. A Protestant rebellion, started by a Virginia trader named William Claiborne, forced the governor to briefly flee the colony in 1644. In 1650, spurred by the triumph of Puritans back home in the English Civil War, a successful Puritan revolt in Maryland led to more political upheaval. The new government revoked the Religious Toleration Act and essentially outlawed both Catholicism and Anglicanism—or membership in the Church of England. But in November 1657, England's Puritan leader, Oliver Cromwell, restored Lord Baltimore's proprietorship of Maryland along with the Religious Toleration Act. In the years that followed, the population of Maryland grew steadily, from about 8,000 in 1660 to about 16,000 by 1676.

The Rackliffe House near Berlin, Maryland, has stood on a ridge overlooking Sinepuxent Bay and Assateague Island since Captain Charles Rackliffe built it in the 1740s. Today it serves as a museum dedicated to preserving the culture of 18th-century Maryland colonists.

BACON'S REBELLION

Twenty years after Maryland's religious tensions began, civil rebellion erupted in the Virginia Colony. This conflict, which began in 1676 and came to be known as **Bacon's Rebellion**, did not involve religion. Instead, it arose out of disputes with Native Americans, echoing battles farther north, such as the Pequot War and King Philip's War.

The tension was caused in part by a treaty signed in 1646 between the Virginia government and the Powhatan, which set aside territory north of the York River for the Powhatan. In the years following the treaty, Virginia's population continued to grow, and land available to farm tobacco became scarcer. Landless freemen grew resentful of the Powhatan

and other local Native Americans and began to covet their land. As planters pushed into the frontier, the Native Americans pushed back.

Throughout the early 1670s, a cycle of raids and reprisals took place. When the frontier planters, led by Nathaniel Bacon, demanded permission to remove the Native American threat by any means they deemed necessary, Virginia's governor, William Berkeley, opted instead for a peaceful policy that would protect both the Native Americans and the colony's profitable fur trade with them.

Bacon, an ambitious 29-year-old councilman, saw an opportunity to challenge Berkeley's leadership. He stoked the hostility that many landless men and small farmers felt toward Berkeley and other substantial landowners. Bacon and a large group of armed supporters attacked Native American villages and then quickly turned their aggression on the authorities in Jamestown itself.

Berkeley submitted to the rebels' demands, permitting their war against the Native Americans, but that was not enough for Bacon. He went a step further, attempting to overthrow Berkeley and take control of the colony. A full-scale rebellion followed. Berkeley fled Jamestown. Bacon and his followers continued killing Native Americans, and, in September 1676, they set much of Jamestown on fire. A month later, however, Bacon was dead, possibly the victim of dysentery, and the energy that fueled his rebellion died with him.

Bacon's Rebellion marked a serious defeat for the area's Native Americans. Many were killed, and the protections of the 1646 treaty were no longer enforced. The landless freemen, for their part, found the rebellion to be a largely empty victory. Rather than opening up Virginia society to better opportunities, the freemen's revolt spurred landowners to replace them and their labor with enslaved Africans.

SETTLING THE CAROLINAS

After the English Civil War, the monarchy was re-established, and Charles II ascended the throne in 1660. However, the king had a serious problem. The upheavals of the previous 12 years had left the royal treasury empty, and there were large debts outstanding. By granting colonial lands to some creditors, he was able to both repay debts and bolster England's commerce and power.

In 1663, King Charles granted land south of the Virginia colony to prominent supporters, including Virginia governor William Berkeley and royalist politician Anthony Ashley Cooper. Cooper organized the colony of **Carolina** with the port of **Charles Town** as its major city that same year. The original Carolina charter was similar to Maryland's, and from it, the wealthy proprietors drew up the Fundamental Constitutions of Carolina to run the colony. But this document was complicated and feudal in nature—it even included a hierarchy of nobles and lords—and was soundly rejected by the colony's ordinary settlers.

By 1691, two colonies had developed out of the Carolina land grant. Small planters from Virginia moved into the first, which later became North Carolina. As early as 1653, people had settled on the shores of Albemarle Sound, where they raised tobacco, corn, and livestock. The Albemarle settlement, which remained poor, had been a haven for pirates and difficult to govern. Nevertheless, the population grew so large that eventually the proprietors appointed a governor.

The second colony attracted planters from the West Indian island of Barbados. Land on the island had become scarce, so a number of planters sailed to the mainland with enslaved Africans and bought large tracts of land on which they developed plantations. The region where they settled became South Carolina. At first, they shipped the goods they produced, such as food, livestock, firewood, and wooden planks for making barrels, back to Barbados. But the colony's plantation economy soon came to be dominated by such valuable cash crops as rice

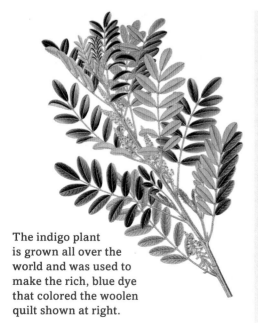

The indigo plant is grown all over the world and was used to make the rich, blue dye that colored the woolen quilt shown at right.

and indigo (a natural source of deep blue fabric dye). A cash crop is produce grown to be sold for profit rather than for use by an individual farmer.

THE FOUNDING OF GEORGIA

The last British mainland colony, Georgia, received its charter from its namesake, King George II, in 1732. Enlightenment principles of human progress and freedom drove the colony's founders, **James Oglethorpe** and John Viscount Percival, to secure the charter. They envisioned Georgia as a place where the poor of England could get a fresh start in life. The idea attracted German, Scottish, and Scots-Irish settlers, too. Georgia would also serve as a shield between South Carolina and Spanish colonial Florida.

George II placed the colony in the hands of **trustees**, or managers who could neither receive financial benefits from the colony nor own land within its boundaries. The trustees, led by Oglethorpe, intended to create a peaceful, moral society of small farmers in which all except indentured servants worked for themselves. To this end, the trustees prohibited both rum and slaveholding and limited each landholder to 500 or fewer acres. Each free male immigrant was granted land at no charge, but no one could buy or sell land, and only men could inherit it. The prohibition on slavery and the limitations on landholding existed to prevent South Carolina's plantation culture and its use of slave labor from taking hold in Georgia.

In February 1733, the first settlers arrived and built the colony's first town, **Savannah**, on a high bluff overlooking the river of the same name. Oglethorpe purchased land from the Native Americans and went on to establish alliances with the Lower Creek, Cherokee, and Chickasaw nations against Spanish Florida. As more settlers arrived, the prohibitions on liquor, slavery, and land sales grew increasingly unpopular. Without hard liquor, Georgians could not engage in the rum trade with the West Indies, which would have been a ready market for Georgia's lumber. And the prohibition on creating plantations rankled some who aspired to the opulent lifestyle of the wealthiest plantation owners in South Carolina.

The settlers were powerless to make changes, however, because the colony lacked a representative assembly. As a result, many settlers chose to leave

The statue of James Oglethorpe in Savannah, Georgia, faces south in memory of the threat the Spanish settlers in Florida posed during Georgia's early years.

almost as soon as they arrived, which slowed the population growth of Georgia. Facing rising discontent and a fleeing population, the trustees eventually reversed course, allowing the importation of rum in 1742 and land sales and slavery in 1750. As they had feared, plantation agriculture, focused on rice, indigo, and sugar and powered by enslaved Africans, became common. Georgia's population swelled, but ownership of the colony transferred back to England in 1752. Oglethorpe's experiment had failed.

HISTORICAL THINKING

1. **READING CHECK** What issues in Virginia society helped lead to Bacon's Rebellion?

2. **COMPARE AND CONTRAST** In what way were the settlers of Maryland similar to the settlers of Massachusetts Bay?

3. **EVALUATE** How did differences in settlement patterns lead to distinct economic developments in North and South Carolina?

The Expansion of Slavery in the Americas

To be enslaved was to be treated as less than human. Enslaved African Americans could be bought and sold as property, worked beyond endurance, and thoughtlessly ripped away from their families. Yet it was their labor that produced much of the wealth of the American colonies.

CASH CROPS ARE KING

In many ways, cotton, tobacco, indigo, and rice were responsible for the success of colonial North America. As you have read, the economy of the Southern Colonies shifted from selling goods strictly to buyers in the West Indies to producing large amounts of cash crops to sell in the other colonies and across the Atlantic Ocean. The humid climate and fertile land of Maryland and Virginia were ideal for growing tobacco. The swampy coasts of South Carolina and Georgia were well suited for growing rice.

The trouble with growing rice in the Southern Colonies, however, was that colonists were not familiar with the delicate process of successful rice cultivation. To grow rice, farmers must flood the fields where it is grown in a controlled way. Proper harvesting of the grain requires a lot of backbreaking labor. The plants must be cut down and beaten to release the grains. Then the grains must be tossed to separate their parts and pounded to remove their hard covering. The colonists had to rely on enslaved laborers, many of whom came from rice-producing areas of Africa, to teach them how to grow enough

Enslaved women in Georgia use a tool called a pestle to grind rice in a vessel called a mortar.

Mortars and pestles can be made from many materials, including stone, metal, or ceramic. This set is carved from wood.

rice to make their plantations profitable. The demand for labor caused by the expansion of rice and other cash crops initiated a boom in the slave trade.

Because of knowledgeable enslaved people, landowners in the Southern Colonies became wealthy, and even more landowners moved to the area to cash in. Rice plantations popped up along the region's rivers, which provided both the water necessary for growing the rice and a convenient way to transport the harvested and processed crops. Because rice cultivation took up so much land, plantations were enormous and the owners' homes were separated by large distances. Thus, many wealthy landowners moved to the bustling port city of Charles Town (known today as Charleston) for part of the year to escape the isolation. And as the demand for enslaved labor increased in the colonies, Charles Town and its slave markets became an important center of the North American slave trade.

SLAVE CODES

As slavery took hold, especially in the Southern Colonies, it became written into law in ways that deprived a whole group of people of their basic human rights. Before 1660, the status of black laborers in Virginia varied. Some were locked in their lives of enslavement, some were working in bondage until they paid off a debt, and a few were free. After 1660, however, Virginia enacted laws that defined enslavement in the South for African Americans and instituted the practice of chattel slavery. By law, an enslaved person's bondage lasted for his or her entire lifetime and passed from mother to child. This became the normal status of the majority of Africans from Africa and African Americans who were born in the colonies.

Slave codes, or racist laws passed by the governments of Virginia and Maryland during this period, codified severe discrimination based solely on skin color. The Virginia assembly, for example, ruled that an owner who killed a slave during punishment could not be charged with a felony. Further, slave codes banned interracial marriage and criminalized the freeing of slaves, except under certain conditions. As the codes evolved, enslaved people could no longer travel without permission, own property, testify against white people in court, or even gather in groups. Eventually, the other English colonies adopted aspects of these codes, with differing degrees of severity based on geography and slave population. For example, colonies in New England had relatively moderate codes, but South Carolina's were extremely harsh.

The labor extracted from enslaved people varied by region. In the Chesapeake Bay and Carolina regions, most toiled in the plantation fields, tending to the cash crops. Some men and women were assigned domestic, or household, duties, and others became artisans, learning skilled trades. In the middle and northern colonies, farms that raised corn and wheat required fewer field hands, but many colonists still purchased enslaved people to work as servants in their households. Regardless of duties or region, one fact never changed: To be enslaved meant that someone else controlled your destiny.

Enslaved Africans who had lost their homelands and families found comfort by establishing new families and friendships in the colonies. They all knew, however, that their owners could destroy these relationships by selling them or their loved ones. This cruel and dehumanizing situation led to resistance during the 1700s, which you will read about in the next chapter.

HISTORICAL THINKING

1. **READING CHECK** How did enslaved people help establish the cultivation of rice in South Carolina?

2. **DRAW CONCLUSIONS** Why do you think slave codes contained differing levels of severity in different parts of the American colonies?

3. **MAKE PREDICTIONS** Predict the ways in which you think enslaved Africans and African Americans will resist control and servitude.

4. **MAKE INFERENCES** In the end, why could it be considered nearly irrelevant that some slave codes were not as harsh as others?

VOCABULARY

Use each of the terms below in a sentence that expresses an understanding about an event or topic from the chapter.

1. conquistador

   Conquistadors, such as Cortés, were the first Europeans to encounter many Native American groups.

2. indentured servant

3. commodity

4. viceroyalty

5. slave code

6. dissenter

7. joint-stock company

8. charter

9. heretic

READING STRATEGY
DRAW CONCLUSIONS

Drawing conclusions can help you make connections and better understand the text. Complete the following chart to draw conclusions about religion in the early American colonies. Then answer the question.

Text Clues	What I Know	My Conclusions

10. How great a role did religion play in the settlement of England's American colonies?

MAIN IDEAS

Answer the following questions. Support your answers with evidence from the chapter.

11. Why did the Aztecs' past military success actually make them more vulnerable to attack from an outside group such as the Spanish? **LESSON 1.1**

12. How did Catholic friars play a part in helping to broaden the Spanish empire in the Americas? **LESSON 1.2**

13. Why was the Middle Passage a dangerous journey for enslaved Africans? **LESSON 1.3**

14. What important role did John Rolfe play in the economy of Jamestown? **LESSON 2.1**

15. What religious issue hampered the development of the New France settlements along the St. Lawrence River? **LESSON 2.3**

16. What are two serious criticisms that Roger Williams leveled at the leaders of the Massachusetts Bay Colony? **LESSON 2.4**

17. What common disagreement between settlers and Native Americans was a contributing cause of both the Pequot War and King Philip's War? **LESSON 2.4**

18. What conflict helped England acquire New Netherland from the Dutch? **LESSON 3.1**

19. In what ways were Maryland's first settlers better equipped to start a colony than Virginia's first settlers? **LESSON 3.2**

20. How did Georgia's founder, James Oglethorpe, bolster the colony's standing as a barrier against Spanish Florida? **LESSON 3.2**

21. How did the slave codes fundamentally alter the status of Africans and African Americans in the colonies? **LESSON 3.3**

Answer the following questions. Support your answers with evidence from the chapter.

22. **COMPARE AND CONTRAST** How were the initial settlements of Massachusetts Bay and Georgia similar and different?

23. **ANALYZE CAUSE AND EFFECT** How did the large-scale adoption of slave labor in England's North American colonies affect global trade?

24. **IDENTIFY** Which two issues sparked Bacon's Rebellion?

25. **DRAW CONCLUSIONS** How and why were Native Americans' relations with New France and New England different?

INTERPRET MAPS

Look closely at the map below. Use information from the chapter and the map to answer the questions that follow.

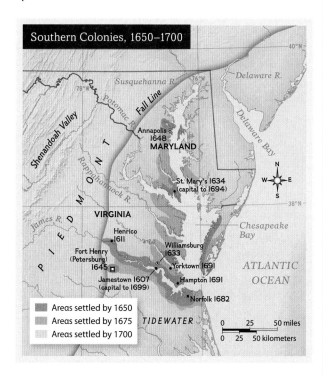

26. What possible effects of Bacon's Rebellion can be seen on the map?

27. Using what you have learned in the chapter, what reasonable relationship can be drawn between the information on the map and levels of slave ownership in the Chesapeake region?

ANALYZE SOURCES

In September 1620, after their ship sailed off course, the Pilgrims arrived on the shore of Massachusetts. Before they disembarked from the ship, they wrote an agreement called the Mayflower Compact. Read the excerpt below and answer the question.

> [We] doe . . . covenant [agree] and combine ourselves together into a civill body politick, for our better ordering and preservation, and furtherance of the ends aforesaid; and by virtue hereof to enacte, constitute, and frame such just and equall laws, ordinances, acts, constitutions and offices, from time to time, as shall be thought most meete [correct] and convenient for the generall good of the Colonie.

28. Why did the Pilgrims write the Mayflower Compact?

CONNECT TO YOUR LIFE

29. **EXPLANATORY** The discovery that there were two large continents—North and South America—that previously had been unknown to them changed the way Europeans viewed the world. In the past 30 years, advances in digital communications and computing have changed the way people perceive the world, as well. Review what you learned about the growth of the American colonies and find parallels between that development and the digital revolution. How do these modern parallels affect people's daily lives?

TIPS

• Use textual evidence from the chapter to support your explanation.

• Look for parallels between positive and negative aspects of the American colonies and the digital revolution.

• Focus on how people's lives changed in each instance and if people have truly benefited from the changes.

CHAPTER 3

THE COLONIES MATURE

1675–1765

HISTORICAL THINKING As the colonies matured, how did the colonists' identities evolve?

CRITICAL VIEWING In this photograph, the white spire of the Maryland State House rises above Annapolis, the state's capital. First opened in 1772, the building is the oldest U.S. state capitol in continuous legislative use. Each of the colonies developed its own government, whose representatives often met in a state house. The colonies also had their own constitution and flag. Why do you think the colonists chose to establish their own governments and state houses?

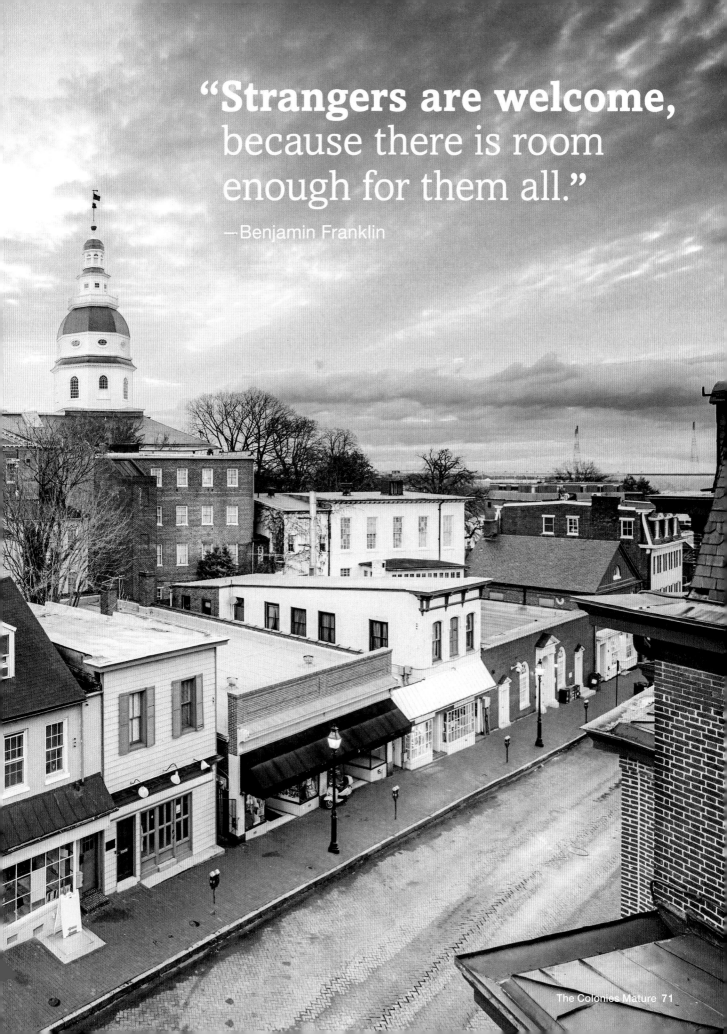

"**Strangers are welcome,** because there is room enough for them all."

—Benjamin Franklin

MAIN IDEA As New England's economy grew through industry and trade, its Puritan society began to undergo change.

NEW ENGLAND'S ECONOMY AND SOCIETY

When people settle in a new place, they learn to take advantage of what it offers. In the 17th century, New Englanders learned to harvest both the land and the sea.

ECONOMIC ACTIVITIES

Most New England colonists were farmers, but farming in the region was a challenging occupation. New England's long, cold winters made for a short growing season. In addition, farms were often located on rocky soil amid thick forests, which made clearing the land difficult. Farming involved an entire family, with all members helping to plant and harvest crops and take care of the farm animals. These families practiced **subsistence farming**. This means that farmers produced only enough food to provide for their family with little, if any, left over to sell or trade. Many New England farm families raised livestock and grew wheat, rye, corn, and fruit.

The Atlantic Ocean provided more profitable economic opportunities for New Englanders, and fishing and whaling became important industries during the 17th century. Fishers sold their catches to London merchants in return for manufactured goods such as shoes, textiles, glass, and metal products. Colonial whalers hunted their prey along the coasts as well as in deeper waters. They sold and exported most parts of the huge creatures, including the whale meat, oil, bones, and blubber. Blubber is whale fat, and it was used to light oil lamps and make candles. These **maritime**, or seafaring, activities led to the development of a thriving shipbuilding industry. Forests in the region supplied plentiful lumber for the ships. In addition to the shipyards where the vessels were built, iron foundries and sawmills sprang up to meet the demand for ships, employing many workers.

CENTER OF TRADE

As a result of all this economic activity, New England found itself at the center of colonial trade. Merchants in the region traded with other colonies and exchanged goods directly with Europe. In the early 1700s, merchants in Boston and other port cities in Massachusetts and Rhode Island dominated colonial trade. In time, however, trade expanded across the Atlantic through the triangular trade routes. As you have read, these routes connected merchants in North America, Europe, and Africa. New England merchants sold such colonial goods as cotton and rum to Europe. In return, they received fruit and salt from Africa and sugar and dyes from the Caribbean. After 1750, the increased trade led to the growth of new port cities, including New York and Philadelphia in the Middle Colonies, and Charleston in the Southern Colonies.

To pass free time at sea, crew members on whaling ships often practiced scrimshaw, the art of carving whale teeth and bones. A sailor likely carved this whale's tooth with an intricate design of a ship either for his own amusement or for loved ones at home. The whalers also used whale parts to make practical tools for use on the ship.

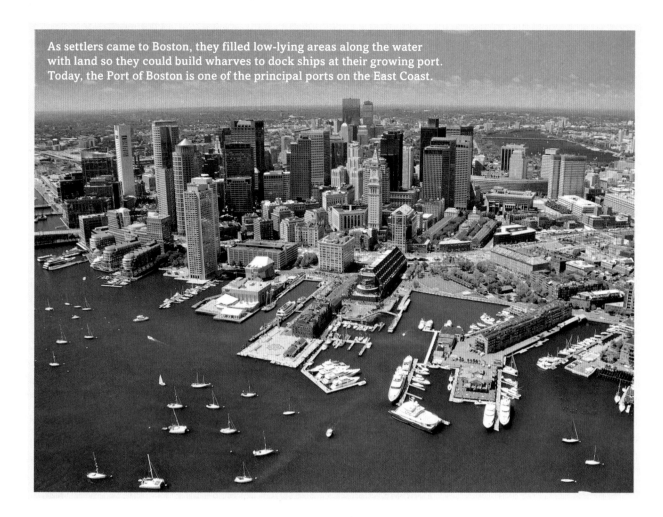

As settlers came to Boston, they filled low-lying areas along the water with land so they could build wharves to dock ships at their growing port. Today, the Port of Boston is one of the principal ports on the East Coast.

As trade in New England grew, British leaders decided they were entitled to their share of the profits. Beginning in 1651, Britain passed a series of laws called the **Navigation Acts**. The acts required that all goods brought to Britain or its colonies be transported on British or colonial-made ships. And colonial products, including tobacco, sugar, cotton, and dyes, could only be sold to Britain and its colonies.

The acts also allowed Britain to control and tax all trade to and from the American colonies. For example, all European products destined for the colonies had to go to a British port first. These products were then loaded onto British or colonial-made ships that carried the goods to colonial ports where additional taxes were levied on the imports. British authorities also taxed any colonial goods that were not shipped to Britain. The colonists, of course, resented the additional charges on both imports and exports. This led some to turn to smuggling, or trading goods illegally, a practice the British found hard to control.

PURITANISM DECLINES

When industry and trade developed in New England, Puritan leaders objected to the emergence of a merchant class in the region. They feared that making money would become more important to New Englanders than their religion. And, in fact, membership in the Puritan church began to decline around 1650. The Puritans also perceived other Protestant groups, including Quakers and Baptists, as threats to their authority. To maintain control, the Puritans only gave Puritan men the right to vote and hold office. Meanwhile, they punished those who voiced conflicting religious views. They even hanged some Quaker missionaries. However, after British king Charles II sent a letter forbidding the execution of Quakers, both Quaker and Baptist communities began to flourish in New England.

Still, Puritan leaders continued to overstep royal authority in religious and economic matters. As punishment, Charles II revoked the Massachusetts Bay Colony's charter in 1684. His successor, James II, further strengthened British control over Massachusetts. As of 1686, the king had combined Massachusetts, New Hampshire, Connecticut, the disputed Narragansett territory of Rhode Island, and the present-day state of Maine to form the **Dominion of New England**. Eventually, the Dominion was extended to include New York and New Jersey. The creation of the Dominion angered colonists, who felt they'd lost the rights and freedoms they'd enjoyed under their own colonial charters. Their resentment grew when James II appointed **Sir Edmund Andros** to be the Dominion's governor in 1686.

In April 1689, after news reached Boston that James II had been deposed, colonists overthrew the Dominion government and imprisoned Andros. With the Dominion gone, many of the colonies reactivated their charters. But Massachusetts, whose charter had been canceled under Charles II, was issued a new one by Britain's reigning king and queen, William and Mary. The 1691 Massachusetts charter guaranteed religious freedom for all Protestants and forbade religious restrictions on voting. The new charter greatly increased the number of voters in New England and caused Puritanism to decline even further.

NEW ENGLAND SOCIETY

Even as the Puritans lost some of their authority, they continued to influence colonial life—particularly in the realm of education. Puritans wanted children to learn to read so they could learn about God. In the 1640s, Massachusetts set up **common schools**, or elementary schools, which focused on instruction in the Bible and moral behavior. The colony also established secondary schools called Latin grammar schools. Neighboring colonies followed suit, and soon more people could read in New England than in any other region. Many children learned skills they would use later in life. Colonial boys often served as apprentices, living with a master craftsman to learn a trade, such as carpentry. Colonial girls typically stayed at home to learn cooking, sewing, and other skills necessary to run a household from their mothers.

The Puritans also founded colleges, including Harvard in Massachusetts in 1636 and Yale in Connecticut in 1701. Both colleges instructed only male students, most of whom planned to become members of the clergy. Today, Harvard and Yale are modern institutions that offer classes to both men and women in a broad range of subjects and the opportunity to earn a variety of different degrees.

Some of the people in New England society were not free to attend school or learn the trade of their choosing. Enslaved African Americans made up about 2 or 3 percent of the region's population. The percentage was small because most New England farmers either didn't need or couldn't afford to buy enslaved workers. The slaves who did come

THE SALEM WITCH TRIALS

In 1689, British rulers William and Mary started a war with France that spilled into the American colonies, particularly the northern part of New York. Some of the colonists who fled the war ended up in Salem Village in the Massachusetts Bay Colony. These colonists put a strain on the village's resources and further heightened the existing tensions between its leading families. The quarrels that erupted were believed by many to be the work of the devil. This atmosphere of fear led Salem authorities to accuse three women of being witches in February 1692. All three were jailed, and soon villagers started accusing many others of witchcraft.

In all, nearly 200 women and men were accused and brought to trial for witchcraft. "Evidence" consisted largely of gossip. Twenty of the accused were put to death, most by hanging. Eventually the hysteria ran its course. In May 1693, Governor William Phips pardoned those still imprisoned and returned not-guilty verdicts in the remaining cases. About 200 years later, artist Joseph E. Baker created the engraving above called *The Witch No. 1*. In this fanciful take on the Salem witch trials, lightning breaks the chains that had bound the hands of the accused and strikes one of her questioners, knocking him to the floor.

AMERICAN PLACES
Yale University, New Haven, Connecticut

The college was officially named Yale in 1718 in honor of Welsh merchant Elihu Yale. He had given 417 books, money from the sale of goods, and a portrait of Britain's king George I to the college. The first planned college campus in the United States, Yale became a university after it added multiple schools with instruction in many subjects. The aerial photo below shows the extent of the university today, which has produced five presidents among its graduates.

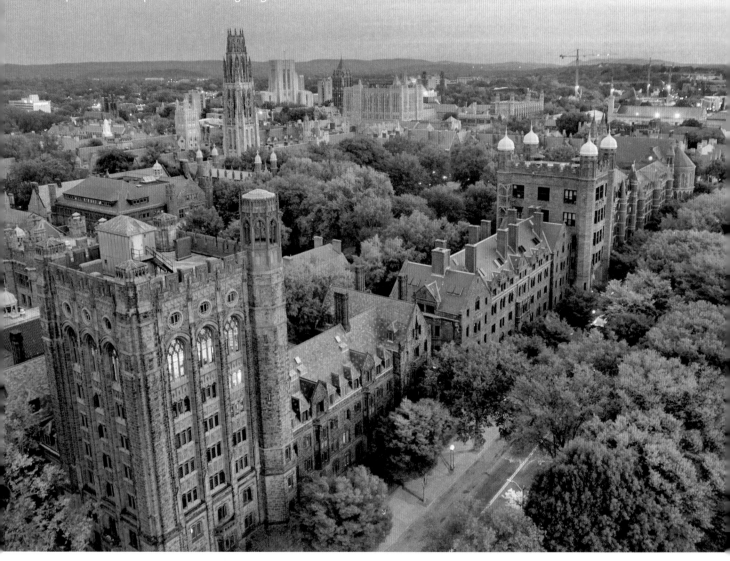

to New England usually worked as household servants, artisans, and laborers. In port cities, enslaved persons sometimes labored alongside their masters in the shipyards and as fishers, whalers, and shipbuilders. Free African Americans, many of whom had spent part of their lives as slaves, also lived in the New England colonies. Although they had some legal rights, they did not always receive equal treatment. A Massachusetts law, for instance, required all African Americans to remain indoors after 9 p.m. unless their owners had sent them out on business.

HISTORICAL THINKING

1. **READING CHECK** What were the major economic activities in 17th-century New England?

2. **EVALUATE** What role did geography play in the number of enslaved workers in New England?

3. **MAKE INFERENCES** How do you think some colonists viewed British authority after the passage of the Navigation Acts and the formation of the Dominion of New England?

4. **SUMMARIZE** Why did Puritanism decline?

The Colonies Mature 75

THE PROSPEROUS MIDDLE COLONIES

A strong economy is a desirable characteristic in any location. But people also want to share the same rights and privileges. In the Middle Colonies, some people enjoyed equal treatment, but others did not.

BOOMING ECONOMY

The Middle Colonies were similar to New England colonies in some respects. Like New England, the Middle Colonies had access to wide, navigable rivers and to the Atlantic Coast, which provided lucrative, or moneymaking, trade and seafaring opportunities. Bustling port cities such as New York City and Philadelphia became centers of maritime trade in the Middle Colonies. This trade boosted shipbuilding and rope- and sail-manufacturing industries and created large numbers of jobs for dock workers and sailors.

Unlike New England, the Middle Colonies had a milder climate and fertile soil, which allowed the region to develop a profitable agricultural industry. Farmers in the Middle Colonies raised livestock and crops such as rye, barley, potatoes, oats, and wheat, the region's most important cash crop. In fact, wheat was the most popular grain in colonial America. By the early 1700s, more than 350,000 bushels of wheat and 18,000 tons of wheat flour flowed out of Middle Colony ports, bound for other colonies, Europe, and the Caribbean. Because of their production of wheat and other grains, the Middle Colonies became known as the "breadbasket of the colonies."

Through the wealth generated by the region's thriving economy, Middle Colony port cities attracted a variety of talented people. As a result, New York and Philadelphia also became leading cultural centers. A young man who would become one of Philadelphia's most famous residents, **Benjamin Franklin**, arrived in the city in 1723 at the age of 17. Franklin had left his hometown of Boston to seek a fresh start in a new city. Within five years, he owned a printing shop and published newspapers and *Poor Richard's Almanack*. An almanac is a publication that contains many types of information. Franklin's almanac included calendars, information on the weather and planting, and witty proverbs, such as "Three may keep a secret, if two of them are dead." The yearly volume was always a best seller. As you have read,

GRISTMILL

Middle Colony farmers often took their grain to a gristmill, a building that housed machinery for grinding grain. Colonial gristmills were usually built near a river so that its water could be used to power a waterwheel set outside the mill. The moving waterwheel turned gears inside the building that then rotated the top stone and bedstone. These worked together to crack the hard outer layers of the grain as it flowed through the hopper, grinding it into soft flour. Grinding flour at gristmills was an important industry in many communities in the Middle Colonies.

grain   hopper   top stone   bedstone   gears   waterwheel

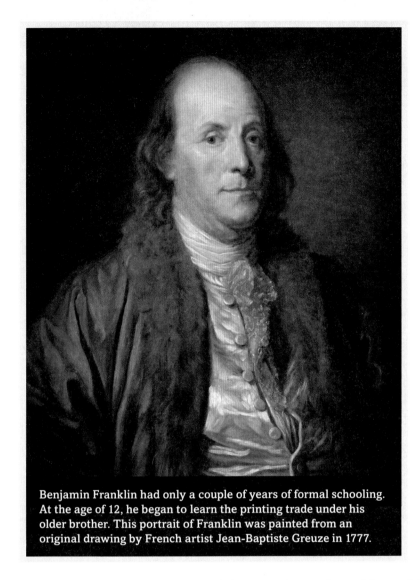

Benjamin Franklin had only a couple of years of formal schooling. At the age of 12, he began to learn the printing trade under his older brother. This portrait of Franklin was painted from an original drawing by French artist Jean-Baptiste Greuze in 1777.

Unfortunately, not everyone in the Middle Colonies extended a tolerance for diversity to African Americans. Most African Americans in the region lived in New York City, where about 40 percent of white families owned at least one slave by 1711. Many enslaved people were skilled artisans who worked for colonial craftsmen and manufacturers.

Enslaved African Americans in New York City often searched for paid work on their own when slaveholders had none available. But seeing many unaccompanied African Americans on the city streets frightened some white people. As a result, a law was passed that required all hiring of slaves to take place at a designated slave market. Of course, African Americans resented this further restriction on their lives.

Their resentment finally erupted on the night of April 6, 1712, when about 20 African Americans set fire to a building and attacked those who tried to extinguish it. In this first major slave rebellion in colonial America, nine whites were killed. The incident raised the fear that others

the literacy rate in the colonies was rising around this time, creating a big demand for newspapers and books—and almanacs.

TOLERANCE AND TENSION

You have read that William Penn encouraged tolerance of other religions when he founded Pennsylvania. This acceptance of others extended through much of the Middle Colonies and was due, in part, to the legacy of the original Dutch settlers. In the Netherlands, the Dutch had welcomed Jews and many Protestant groups. They carried their practice of religious tolerance with them when they founded New Netherland. In addition to different religions, the Dutch settlers embraced people from Sweden, Finland, and Norway. This diversity, or wide variety of people, in the Middle Colonies set them apart from the other American colonies.

The Quakers not only accepted people of different faiths, but they also believed that all people were equal before God. They were the first group in America to speak out against slaveholding.

would soon follow. To discourage new uprisings and punish those involved in the New York revolt, locals took revenge on the African-American community. Thirteen slaves were hanged, three were burned at the stake, and two others were tortured or starved to death. Although some whites questioned the morality of slavery and others opposed it out of fear of more revolts, the institution would be part of American life for more than 150 years. And even today, long after slavery's abolition, its legacy continues to have an impact on African Americans.

HISTORICAL THINKING

1. **READING CHECK** What factors accounted for the economic growth of the Middle Colonies?

2. **COMPARE AND CONTRAST** How were New England and the Middle Colonies similar economically and culturally, and how did they differ?

3. **SUMMARIZE** What was life like for African Americans in the Middle Colonies in general and in New York City in particular?

IMMIGRATION AND GROWTH IN THE MIDDLE COLONIES

Think about what you might look for in a new home. If you wanted to live in a place with a strong economy, developing cities, and a history of tolerance, you might have chosen the Middle Colonies.

IMMIGRANTS

After the English took over the Middle Colonies, most of the region's new immigrants came from England and Germany. Between 1683 and 1783, more than 100,000 Germans immigrated to the region. Many of these immigrants fled religious persecution and other forms of oppression for the promise of religious freedom in the Middle Colonies. German immigrants were particularly diverse in their religious beliefs and brought Lutheran, Amish, and Mennonite traditions to the region. Other German immigrants looked to the Middle Colonies as a place of economic opportunity. They had heard about the region's arable, or fertile, and inexpensive land.

The majority of German immigrants settled in the backcountry of Pennsylvania to farm. The **backcountry** stretched along the Appalachian Mountains from Pennsylvania south through the Shenandoah Valley to the Carolinas. This region included the rich soil, rolling hills, and deep forests of the **Piedmont**, a relatively flat area between the mountains and the coastal plain.

The German farmers introduced new techniques to the region. For example, they built shelters for their animals in the winter. Germans also developed the Pennsylvania long rifle for hunting

and designed the **Conestoga wagon**, a heavy covered wagon usually pulled by horses or oxen. The wagon could carry up to four tons of cargo. Few German farmers used slaves to work in their fields. As their land became more productive, many farmers were able to sell more of their harvest as cash

🏛 National Museum of American History, Washington, D.C.

Four to six horses were needed to pull a fully loaded Conestoga wagon. As the wagon bumped along the trails, its curved shape prevented the cargo from shifting. Its white canvas cover protected the goods against bad weather. From about 1750 to 1850, Conestoga wagons, like the one shown here, hauled farm products and manufactured goods on three-to four-week trips between rural areas and cities.

crops and sell and export their livestock. German immigrants also settled in New York and other Middle Colony cities. There, some German artisans became ironworkers while others made glass, furniture, and kitchenware. By the 1740s, German artists were also creating distinctive house ornaments and elaborately illustrated documents.

In 1654, the first Jewish settlers arrived in Dutch New Amsterdam. Like many German immigrants, the Jews were fleeing religious persecution. Most of these early Jewish immigrants came from Spanish or Portuguese territories in South America and the Caribbean. But by the mid-1660s, the majority of them had left New Amsterdam. Other Jews returned to the site, which was then New York, in the early 1680s, and this time the settlers stayed. By 1685, about 100 Jews lived in New York City. By the late 1720s, that number had doubled. These immigrants built a synagogue—a Jewish place of worship—and established schools where religious subjects were taught as well as reading, writing, and arithmetic.

GROWING CITIES

Immigration from foreign countries and from other American colonies resulted in tremendous population growth in the cities of the Middle Colonies. Philadelphia was founded in 1681 as a village along the Delaware River and became the fastest-growing city in the colonies. Its population numbered more than 2,000 in 1700 and jumped to about 23,000 by 1760. At that time, more people lived in Philadelphia than in either New York City or Boston. Crops and trade made Philadelphia thrive. The city was also an attractive place to live. William Penn had envisioned Philadelphia as a large "green country town." As the city grew, planners built wide streets set in a grid pattern, public parks, and houses made of brick.

New York City also expanded. After it was acquired by the English in 1664, New York merchants maintained ties with the Netherlands and its colony, the Dutch West Indies. Trade goods continued to be shipped between New York and Amsterdam. As a result of these ties, the population of New York more than doubled between 1720 and 1760. The Dutch influence on New York could be seen in its architecture. The brick houses with low-sloping roofs that lined the city's streets strongly resembled those found in many Dutch towns. The English, however, soon put their stamp on New York by building houses made of brick and wood in their own style.

Although the economy in Middle Colony cities was booming, not everyone shared in the wealth. While rich merchants lived in mansions, many other city

Francis Daniel Pastorius was a German immigrant to the colony of Pennsylvania. In 1683, he founded the city of Germantown, north of Philadelphia. In the 1690s, Pastorius wrote a description of this city and surrounding land, hoping to attract more Germans to immigrate and settle there.

On October 24, 1683, I, Francis Daniel Pastorius, with the good will of the governor, laid out another new city of the name of German-ton, or Germanopolis, at a distance of two hours' walk from Philadelphia, where there are a good black fertile soil, and many fresh wholesome springs of water, many oak, walnut, and chestnut trees, and also good pasturage for cattle. The first settlement consisted of only twelve families of forty-one persons, the greater part High German mechanics and wavers [weavers], because I had ascertained [learned] that linen cloth would be indispensable.

—from Francis Daniel Pastorius, 1690s

dwellers shared crowded quarters and scraped by, working for low wages. And the burgeoning, or expanding, cities lacked sanitation, putting those who lived in close quarters at particular risk from the spread of disease. These poorer inhabitants had little legal opportunity to improve their lives. Throughout the colonies, only white men who owned property had the right to vote. There were exceptions to that rule, however. Landowning men who were Catholic or Jewish were often denied voting rights.

Life was hard for women as well as men in the cities. Married women cared for their children and the household. Wealthier wives employed servants or used enslaved persons to perform domestic chores. In less wealthy urban families, some women worked alongside their husbands in shops and businesses. Women could also serve as midwives, helping to deliver babies and provide other medical care. The legal rights of women in the Middle Colonies were the same as those in other regions. They did not have the right to vote or manage their property once they married.

HISTORICAL THINKING

1. **READING CHECK** What attracted immigrants to the Middle Colonies?

2. **MAKE INFERENCES** How did the Middle Colonies probably benefit from the influx of immigrants?

3. **SUMMARIZE** Describe life for the rich and the poor in Middle Colony cities.

AN AGRICULTURAL SOCIETY

Unlike the economies of New England and the Middle Colonies, the economy of the Southern Colonies relied almost entirely on agriculture. The economy also rested on the unfortunate shoulders of an enslaved labor force.

SOUTHERN CROPS

As you have read, the fertile soil and mild climate of the Southern Colonies allowed farmers to grow such cash crops as cotton, tobacco, indigo, and rice. Tobacco flourished in the humid climates of Virginia and coastal Maryland. Rice grew well in the lowland swamps and tidewater areas of the Carolinas' coastal rivers. However, southern farmers had little experience with growing rice. Enslaved people who were brought from rice-growing regions in West Africa to the Southern Colonies shared their knowledge of rice cultivation with southern farmers, and rice yields increased dramatically. As the crop took hold, exports of rice from the Carolinas reached 1.5 million pounds per year by 1710 and nearly 20 million pounds by 1730. The chief markets for rice were Europe and the West Indies.

Among the Southern Colonies, North Carolina ranked third in tobacco production after Virginia and Maryland. Most of North Carolina's tobacco plantations were located along the coastal plain or near Virginia's border. In this photo taken in 2009, migrant workers from Mexico harvest tobacco leaves by hand in North Carolina.

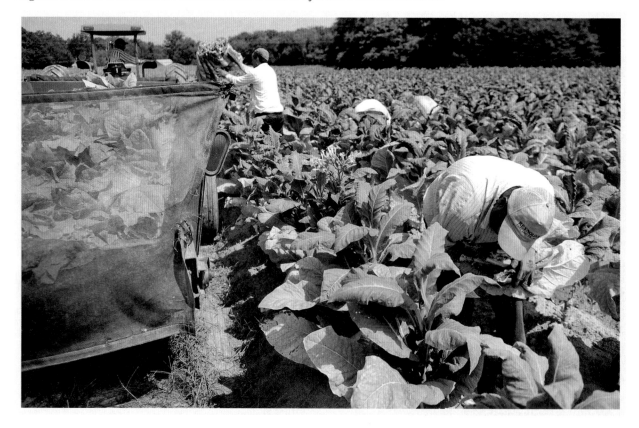

Rice plantations sprang up along rivers in the Carolinas. Ships could sail up tributaries of the Chesapeake Bay to dock at the plantations and pick up the goods. The vessels then transported the exports to various markets. As a result, port cities did not emerge in the Southern Colonies as they had in the colonies to the north. The one exception was the busy port that developed in Charles Town (now known as Charleston, South Carolina). Wealthy plantation owners and merchants lived in Charles Town part of the year, and the city prospered through the export of rice and other crops. Charles Town became the fourth-largest city in the colonies, after Philadelphia, Boston, and New York.

SOUTHERN SOCIETY

As the plantation system in Maryland, Virginia, and the Carolinas became more entrenched, a distinct hierarchy of social classes developed in southern society. Wealthy plantation owners, also known as the southern gentry, were at the top of the social ladder. They lived like European nobles in their lavish mansions. With their armies of enslaved Africans, they enjoyed a leisurely lifestyle. Although relatively few in number, these rich landowners wielded tremendous political and economic power.

Below the southern gentry came farmers who owned much smaller portions of land. These farmers lived in modest houses and generally owned few, if any, slaves. They also struggled to compete with the large plantations. In fact, wealthy plantation owners often expanded their holdings by buying more land from small farmers. Colonists who rented rather than owned the land they farmed came next in the hierarchy. These farmers rarely owned enslaved workers. Some families could afford livestock, such as cows, pigs, and horses, as well as basic farming tools and equipment. Often, however, they secured these items on credit from wealthy merchant-planters to whom they could become indebted for a lifetime.

Enslaved men and women were at the bottom of the social hierarchy. They worked long hours in the fields planting, weeding, and harvesting crops. They usually labored until their **overseer**, or supervisor, allowed them to stop—often long after nightfall. Overseers and plantation owners sometimes used whips and other violent measures to make slaves work harder or to punish them for failing to obey orders. The development of rice cultivation significantly increased the slaves' workload. Work in a plantation owner's home was sometimes less brutal. Household slaves cooked, cleaned, and worked in the garden. Women

This ornately engraved silver mug, which was made in London around 1740, belonged to a wealthy plantation owner. Members of the southern gentry filled their homes with fine furniture, paintings, and silver. They also adopted the sports of English aristocrats, including horse racing and fox hunting.

often took care of the owners' children, and some served as nurses and weavers. Enslaved men were sometimes allowed to become artisans.

The immigrants who settled in the Piedmont area of the backcountry were also part of the society of the Southern Colonies. In the early 1700s, many of those who moved to the backcountry were Scots-Irish immigrants from the north of Ireland. They carved their farmland out of the forests and used the timber to build small log cabins. Land in the backcountry was not suited for large plantations. Instead, backcountry farmers hunted and raised only enough crops and livestock to feed their families. Women took part in every aspect of farm life. They worked in the home, in the fields, and in the forests, where they often hunted along with the men. Self-sufficient and determined, the farmers living in the backcountry did not rely on enslaved labor.

HISTORICAL THINKING

1. **READING CHECK** How did the Southern Colonies' geography and climate support their main crops?

2. **IDENTIFY MAIN IDEAS AND DETAILS** What social classes developed in the Southern Colonies?

3. **EVALUATE** How did the southern gentry perpetuate the social hierarchy of the Southern Colonies?

MAIN IDEA As increasing numbers of enslaved Africans were brought to the Southern Colonies, they tried to hold onto their traditions and cope with their living and working conditions.

LIFE UNDER SLAVERY

People do what they can to cope in dire circumstances. It is almost impossible for us to imagine the conditions under which enslaved people lived. That makes their efforts to survive and preserve their identity all the more remarkable.

LIVING CONDITIONS

You may remember that planters in the Southern Colonies originally hired white indentured servants to farm their land. That changed in 1698 when English merchants were allowed to engage in the slave trade. Many of the enslaved people were sold in the American colonies. Southern plantation owners took full advantage of this new labor force.

These owners included planters who lived in the **Chesapeake**, the settled land around the Chesapeake Bay. The slave trade greatly increased the African population of the Chesapeake. In 1660, only 900 Africans lived there, some of whom were free of bondage. By 1720, Africans and African Americans made up one-fifth of the Chesapeake's population. Their population in Virginia and the Carolinas also soared. By 1750, African Americans were 40 percent of Virginia's population and more than half of South Carolina's. Nearly all of the African Americans in the Southern Colonies were enslaved.

Enslaved people were powerfully impacted by their slavery, but they were not entirely defined by their circumstances. Enslaved men and women often lived in the one-room cabins they had to build for themselves. They supplemented the meager amount of food the slave owners provided by planting vegetable gardens, raising hogs and chickens, and hunting and fishing. They also created a resilient and life-affirming culture through religion, music, food, and oral folktales.

Many of these cultural traditions found their way into colonial America. For example, enslaved Africans contributed words to the English language. Because slaves from different parts of West Africa frequently lived together on plantations, they sometimes used a mixture of African languages and English to communicate. As a result, words such as *yam*, *goober* (peanut), and *tote* were introduced to the colonists. Also, the rhythms of African music influenced colonists' music and dances and would later form the roots of jazz and the blues. African designs decorated the musical instruments, pottery, and baskets made by slaves. Enslaved Africans also contributed to the food culture of the colonies by popularizing okra, melons, and bananas.

SLAVE RESISTANCE

Enslaved people resisted the efforts of their enslavers to reduce them to commodities in both revolutionary and everyday ways. Some resisted by disrupting

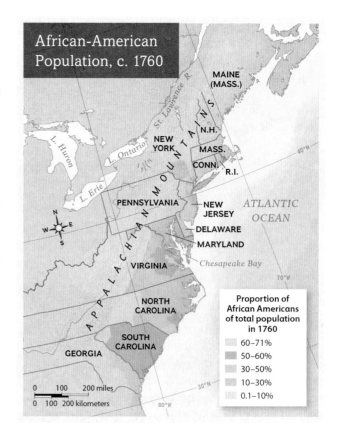

African-American Population, c. 1760

Proportion of African Americans of total population in 1760
60–71%
50–60%
30–50%
10–30%
0.1–10%

farm production. They slowed down their work, faked illness, and secretly destroyed crops and tools. Theft was another common form of resistance. Slaves stole food, livestock, tobacco, and money from their owners. In addition, slaves sometimes ran away. A few enslaved people turned to violence, killing plantation owners or setting fire to their fields and homes.

You've read about the slave uprising in the American colonies that occurred in New York in 1712. As you may recall, white colonists at that time feared more slaves would stage a revolt. That's just what happened in 1739, near the Stono River in South Carolina. A group of more than 50 enslaved people raided a firearms store and then killed 20 whites as they marched south. Their leader was a literate slave named Jemmy (also known as Cato) whose owner had taught him to read and write. By morning, armed white planters had killed nearly half the participants of the **Stono Rebellion**. The others managed to escape. Their goal was to reach St. Augustine, Florida, where Spanish authorities offered freedom and land

This West African drum traveled with enslaved people to Virginia in the 1700s.

to fugitive slaves from the British colonies, but few reached that destination. Most of the rebels were eventually captured and executed.

To prevent future revolts in South Carolina, the colony's legislature passed a new slave code in 1740. The code decreed that all slaves, their children, and later generations would remain permanently enslaved. In addition, it prohibited anyone from teaching an enslaved person to read or write. The code remained in force until 1865. In spite of such laws, some African-American slaves did learn to read and write. They employed their literacy to tell their stories and inform the world about the horrors of slavery.

HISTORICAL THINKING

1. **READING CHECK** How did the slave trade affect the populations of the Southern Colonies?

2. **MAKE INFERENCES** Why do you think enslaved people tried to keep their African culture alive?

3. **SUMMARIZE** In what ways did enslaved African Americans rebel against their bondage?

An enslaved person performs a traditional African stick dance, accompanied by a banjo player and drummer, in this late-1700s watercolor painting titled *The Old Plantation*.

OLAUDAH EQUIANO 1745–1797

"I believe there are a few events in my life which have
  not happened to many."—Olaudah Equiano

The quotation above is quite an understatement, coming as it does from Olaudah Equiano (oh-LOW-duh ehk-wee-AHN-oh), a man who was repeatedly bought and sold as a slave, took part in an expedition to the Arctic, and wrote a best-selling autobiography—among many other episodes in an eventful life. The quote introduces his autobiographical work, *The Interesting Narrative of the Life of Olaudah Equiano, or Gustavus Vassa, the African*. Most of what is known about Equiano comes from this book.

CONTROVERSIAL BEGINNINGS

Equiano begins his autobiography with descriptions of life in the West African province of Eboe, an area in present-day southern Nigeria, where he says he was born. The enslavement of Africans by other Africans was part of the culture of the region and, indeed, of much of the continent. In fact, according to Equiano, his own family had slaves. His parents tried to protect their children from abduction, but one day Equiano was kidnapped and taken from his home. Before long, the 11-year-old boy was sold to European slave traders.

The traders took Equiano to the coast and the slave ship that would carry him to the Americas. Equiano says it was the first time he had ever seen white people, and his astonishment changed to terror as the slavers dragged him on board. As Equiano writes in his autobiography, "I was now persuaded that I had got into a world of bad spirits, and that they were going to kill me."

Olaudah Equiano,
or
GUSTAVUS VASSA,
the African

Published March 1 1789 by G. Vassa

CRITICAL VIEWING This engraving of Equiano appears opposite the title page in his narrative. In the portrait, Equiano looks directly at his readers and is dressed in the elegant clothes of an English gentleman. He holds a Bible open to a passage whose subject is central to his narrative: salvation. Why do you think Equiano chose to be portrayed in this manner?

When he was brought below decks where the captured Africans were quartered, the awful stench of the place made him sick. The suffocating heat, the numbers of people crammed into the space, and the chains used to bind them "rendered the whole a scene of horror almost inconceivable." Many of the captives died on the Middle Passage to the Caribbean island of Barbados—some by suicide—but Equiano survived the journey.

His moving account of the conditions and suffering on the slave ship creates a vivid, unforgettable picture, but Equiano may not have actually experienced what he describes. In Vincent Carretta's 2005 biography of Equiano, the American writer revealed that he had found two documents that indicated his subject had been born in South Carolina, not Africa. The findings resulted in a fierce debate over Equiano's birthplace, which continues today. However, Equiano wrote his autobiography to inform readers about the brutal reality of slavery. Some historians believe he felt his narrative had to include a description of his abduction and the Middle Passage, whether it was based on his own experiences or those of others he'd heard or read about.

ABOLITIONIST AND WRITER

While Equiano's discussion of his early life has raised questions, Carretta and others have found evidence that backs up most of his story. In 1756, British naval officer Michael Pascal purchased Equiano in Virginia and gave him the name Gustavus Vassa. For about seven years, Equiano served and traveled with Pascal and became a seasoned sailor. When Britain was drawn into war, Equiano fought in battles alongside his owner. During this time, Pascal also sent Equiano to England, where he learned to read and write and converted to Christianity. After 1763, he was sold to other slaveholders who set him to work on trading ships. By engaging in some trading of his own, Equiano was able to buy his freedom in 1766.

But Equiano soon discovered that, as a free man, he lived "in constant alarm for [his] liberty." Several times, he was pursued by men who tried to capture him and return him to slavery. In part to escape from being seized, Equiano took to the seas again and worked in trade. He also joined an expedition in 1773 to find the Northwest Passage, a westward sea route that would connect the northern Atlantic and Pacific oceans by way of the Arctic Ocean. Explorers had been searching for such a route since the 15th century.

In 1777, Equiano returned to England where he became involved in the abolitionist, or antislavery, movement. He toured Britain and spoke out against

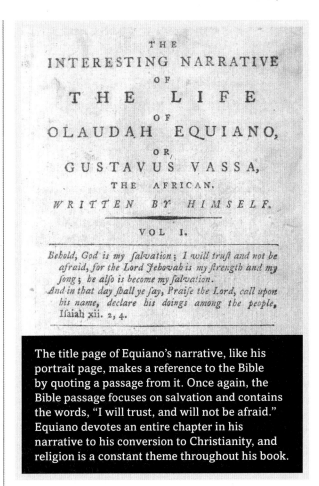

The title page of Equiano's narrative, like his portrait page, makes a reference to the Bible by quoting a passage from it. Once again, the Bible passage focuses on salvation and contains the words, "I will trust, and will not be afraid." Equiano devotes an entire chapter in his narrative to his conversion to Christianity, and religion is a constant theme throughout his book.

the cruelty of slaveholders, which he had witnessed firsthand. Urged to write about what he had seen, Equiano published his autobiography in 1789. The book was translated into several languages and became a best-seller. Sales of the book made Equiano a wealthy man.

He continued his work as an abolitionist, helping poor blacks in London and campaigning for an end to slavery. In his autobiography, Equiano writes, "I hope to have the satisfaction of seeing the renovation [renewal] of liberty and justice, resting on the British government, to vindicate [redeem] the honor of our common nature." Slavery was finally abolished in Britain in 1807, but Equiano did not live to see it. He had died 10 years earlier.

HISTORICAL THINKING

1. **READING CHECK** How does Equiano help his readers envision the horrors of the Middle Passage?

2. **MAKE INFERENCES** What characteristics helped Equiano survive life as a slave?

3. **FORM AND SUPPORT OPINIONS** If historians determined conclusively that Equiano was born in America, do you think that fact would discredit his entire story? Explain why or why not.

THE WHITNEY PLANTATION WALLACE, LOUISIANA

Set on land where enslaved people labored for more than 100 years, the Whitney Plantation is the first museum dedicated exclusively to telling the story of slavery in the United States. More than 350 enslaved people worked on the plantation between 1752 and 1867, bringing great prosperity to its owners, a German immigrant family named the Haydels.

The Whitney Plantation employed one of the largest slave forces in Louisiana. Today, the names of those enslaved workers are etched in granite on the Wall of Honor at the plantation. Their stories and those of other slaves are told through the museum's restored buildings, artwork, exhibits, and hundreds of first-person narratives.

Slave Quarters

The Whitney Plantation has seven slave cabins that were acquired and moved there from nearby plantations. Before the Civil War, the Haydel plantation had 22 slave cabins, but most were torn down in the 1970s.

The number of enslaved workers on the plantation varied, but in 1819, there were 61 enslaved men and women. A sizeable labor force was required for the production and processing of sugarcane. Enslaved workers boiled sugarcane juice in large iron kettles like those shown in front of the cabins.

Inside a Slave Cabin

This photograph shows the sparse, simple furnishings of a slave cabin. A two-room wooden shack on the Whitney Plantation might have housed two families, with as many as six people sharing a single room. People slept on simple beds like the one shown here or on pallets on the floor. In the hot summers, they might move their pallets to the porch and sleep outside.

Cabins contained a fireplace to provide heat and a place to cook, though cooking was also done on outside fires. Weekly food rations typically included cornmeal and bacon.

Plantation Kitchen

Enslaved cooks prepared meals for the master's family in this kitchen, which was located in a building separate from the large plantation house. Because they were hot, smoky, and smelly, kitchens were often detached from the main house. The loft above this kitchen served as a *pigeonnier*, a nesting place for pigeons that were a source of food and fertilizer.

Based on what you observe of these kitchen tools, how might plantation kitchens have been a challenging place to work?

Slave Jail

At slave markets in New Orleans, enslaved people were locked up in jails similar to this one to await sale at auctions. The interior walls of the jail have small cutouts for attaching a slave's chains.

Posted near the jail at Whitney Plantation is a list of slaves and the prices for which they were bought and sold. Runaway slaves were also punished by being kept in these kinds of jails. The steel jails became like hot ovens in the summer. This jail was brought to Whitney Plantation to demonstrate the kind of brutal treatment slaves typically endured.

THE ENLIGHTENMENT

Ideas can be liberating, but they can be dangerous, too. They may be especially threatening when they question traditionally held beliefs and those in authority. Once such ideas take hold, they can be very hard to stop.

THE LIGHT OF HUMAN REASON

Around the mid-1600s, many European thinkers began to challenge the traditional religious ideas taught by the Catholic Church. The thinkers believed people should use reason and ask questions to help them understand the physical world and their place in it. The intellectual movement these thinkers sparked is called the **Enlightenment.** Rather than simply accept what religious and political figures had to say, Enlightenment thinkers encouraged others to employ logic and experience to gain knowledge and shatter the "darkness" of ignorance.

This movement was influenced, in part, by the Scientific Revolution, which began in Europe around 1550. Scientists applied the scientific method to conduct research and answer their questions. This step-by-step method involves identifying a problem; constructing a hypothesis, or a proposed solution to a problem; and collecting data through observation and experiments to test the hypothesis. English scientist **Isaac Newton** used the scientific method to investigate the natural world. By 1700, he had discovered the universal laws that predictably govern gravity, the natural bodies visible in the sky, and the ebb and flow of tides. Newton's work demonstrated that the universe operates according to fixed principles humans are capable of detecting and understanding. His findings and those of other scientists of the time challenged the idea that God was responsible for the placement and workings of the universe.

The 17th-century English philosopher **John Locke** developed Enlightenment thought by applying a logical approach to questions about society and government. In 1689, Locke published *An Essay Concerning Human Understanding*, in which he argued that people were not born with ideas implanted by God, but rather were "clean slates." He claimed humans had the ability to learn for themselves and to use their acquired knowledge to benefit society. That same year, in *Two Treatises of Government,* Locke declared that humans were born free and equal with natural rights, including life and liberty. He asserted that people should join together in what

PRIMARY SOURCE

John Locke published the radical ideas expressed in his *Two Treatises* anonymously. The excerpt below is from his second treatise, which contends that government should only exist by the consent of the people.

For no government can have a right to obedience from a people who have not freely consented to it; which they can never be supposed to do, till either they are put in a full state of liberty to chuse [choose] their government and governors, or at least till they have such standing laws, to which they have by themselves or their representatives given their free consent.

—from *Two Treatises of Government,* by John Locke, 1689

he called a "social contract" to form governments that would guarantee those rights. If a state failed in its obligation, the people had the duty to rebel and establish a new government. French Enlightenment philosopher **Jean-Jacques Rousseau** (roo-SOH) agreed with Locke and expressed his contempt for economic and political oppression and inequality. In *The Social Contract*, written in 1762, Rousseau maintained that the good of a community or society as a whole should have priority over the interests of individual citizens. He believed that only a government freely elected by the people had the authority to enact laws or constraints.

INFLUENCE ON THE COLONIES

The Enlightenment ideas of Locke, Rousseau, and others spread to the colonies in the 1700s. These ideas helped shape colonial thought. Benjamin Franklin became an important American Enlightenment leader.

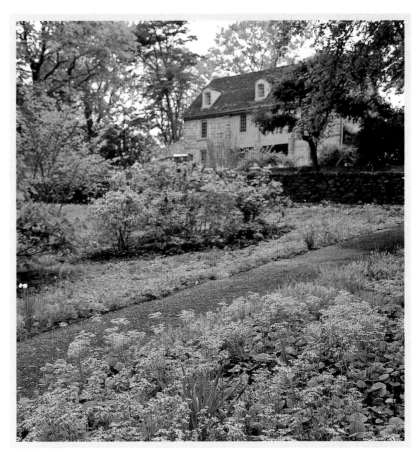

When John Bartram purchased a 102-acre farm in Philadelphia in 1728 and dedicated it to the cultivation of native North American plants, he founded America's first garden. For more than 50 years, Bartram and his sons collected and studied the plants. He also built the stone house shown in this photo of the garden. In 1963, Bartram's Garden was designated a National Historic Landmark.

You've learned that Franklin was a printer, but he was also a writer, inventor, and scientist. As a scientist, he was influenced by the Scientific Revolution. For example, he used the scientific method to study the nature of electricity, and his findings brought him international fame.

In 1743, Franklin founded the American Philosophical Society in Philadelphia to promote "useful knowledge." He got the idea for the society from his friend, **John Bartram**, a naturalist and explorer. Bartram, who is considered the "father of American botany" for his exhaustive study of plants, had proposed forming a group of men to discuss nature, arts, and sciences. With the goal of using intellectual inquiry to further the common good, Franklin drew members from across the colonies to join his association and share new ideas and technologies. He also encouraged communication with members of similar associations in Europe. Soon philosophical societies began to spring up in other colonies. The books and newspaper articles on the Enlightenment penned by the members of some of these societies helped introduce the movement to colonial America. In addition, literacy rates increased as interest in the ideas grew.

Franklin would soon dedicate himself to public service. In fact, it is as a statesman that he is best known and honored. Enlightenment ideas influenced Franklin and other leaders who represented the colonists against British authority. Inspired by Locke's ideas on the role of rulers, Franklin and many other American Founders would eventually start to demand rights and freedoms for the colonies.

HISTORICAL THINKING

1. **READING CHECK** What were some of the ideas advanced by Enlightenment thinkers?

2. **MAKE CONNECTIONS** What type of government best reflects Locke's and Rousseau's ideas on the role of rulers?

3. **MAKE INFERENCES** Why do you think Franklin and others inspired by the Enlightenment began to be more critical of British authority?

THE GREAT AWAKENING

Are you persuaded by a message that appeals to your emotions, or are you more convinced by logic and reason? In the 18th century, emotional appeals persuaded colonists to adjust their ideas about religion, themselves, and the world.

RELIGIOUS REVIVAL

Enlightenment ideas gained popularity among some Protestant colonial ministers who believed God had created humans as rational beings so they could use reason to determine right from wrong. However, other religious leaders pushed back against the Enlightenment. They feared that colonists were abandoning Christianity and losing sight of the importance of God in their lives.

As you know, many of the first colonists who settled in North America came seeking religious freedom. After they had gained that freedom, however, some of their earlier religious fervor died down. By the early 1700s, colonists had shifted their focus from religion to work and the attainment of material goods. Some even stopped attending church regularly. To revive religious life, many Protestant ministers began delivering stirring and emotional sermons during a series of religious revivals known as the **Great Awakening**. From about 1720 to the 1750s, these ministers sought to reconnect people with God and persuade them to recommit to their spiritual beliefs.

The revival began in western Europe in the late 17th and early 18th centuries and then spread to the colonies. In colonial America, the revival took hold primarily among members of the Dutch Reformed Church, which was established by the Dutch settlers in New Netherland; Congregationalists; Presbyterians; Baptists; and some Anglicans. They challenged the rationalism and emphasis on ritual and doctrine practiced by other Protestant denominations. The revivalists favored a more emotional and personal religious experience and preached that all people were equal before God. This spiritual equality appealed to African Americans in the Southern Colonies. Many of them began to move away from traditional African religions and embrace Christianity. Some southern whites began allowing African Americans into their churches.

One of the most effective preachers of the Great Awakening was the minister **Jonathan Edwards** of Massachusetts. In 1734, he began preaching fiery sermons on **salvation**, or the deliverance from sin through the acceptance of Jesus Christ. Edwards drew large crowds for his sermons. He spoke calmly and made few movements, but his words had a dramatic effect on his listeners, who often wept and moaned aloud.

George Whitefield, an Anglican minister from England, was another important figure in the movement. Whitefield visited North America several times between 1739 and 1770 and preached

PRIMARY SOURCE

Jonathan Edwards delivered his most famous sermon, "Sinners in the Hands of an Angry God," in 1741 to a congregation in Connecticut. In the sermon, he described the fiery fate he believed was in store for those who failed to seek salvation.

The God that holds you over the pit of hell, much as one holds a spider, or some loathsome insect over the fire, abhors [hates] you, and is dreadfully provoked: his wrath [anger] towards you burns like fire; he looks upon you as worthy of nothing else, but to be cast into the fire; he is of purer eyes than to bear to have you in his sight. You have offended him infinitely more than ever a stubborn rebel did his prince; and yet it is nothing but his hand that holds you from falling into the fire every moment.

—from "Sinners in the Hands of an Angry God," by Jonathan Edwards, 1741

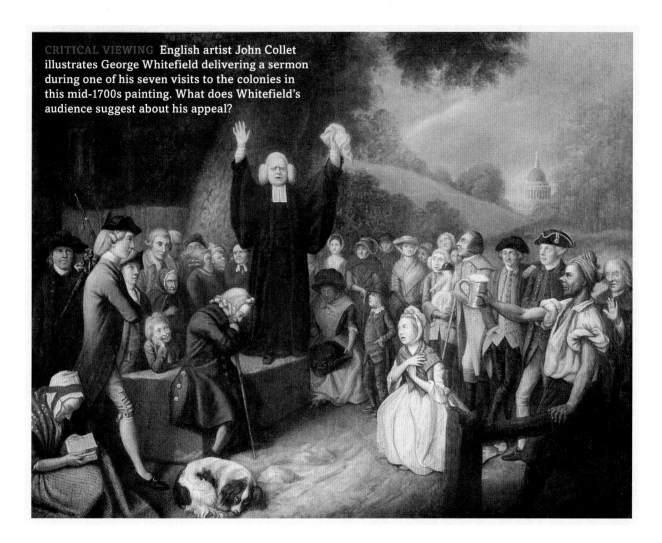

CRITICAL VIEWING English artist John Collet illustrates George Whitefield delivering a sermon during one of his seven visits to the colonies in this mid-1700s painting. What does Whitefield's audience suggest about his appeal?

throughout the colonies. Because so many people wanted to hear him, his meetings were held in open fields. Unlike Edwards, Whitefield used dramatic gestures and varied the pitch of his voice for increased effect. It worked. Some listeners sobbed and even fainted during his sermons. Like Edwards, Whitefield called on his congregations to accept Jesus Christ. He claimed that by doing so, they would experience a "new birth."

IMPACT ON THE COLONIES

The Great Awakening profoundly affected the social and religious lives of the colonists. Congregations, communities, and some Protestant denominations split between the emotional "New Lights" revivalists and the rational "Old Lights" of established religion. Old Light clergymen resented the challenge to their authority and the new style of worship promoted by the New Light preachers. These revivalists encouraged the colonists to form their own church if they weren't satisfied with their established one. Some did just that. The new Protestant denominations that arose led to a greater tolerance of religious diversity throughout the colonies.

The Great Awakening also affected education. Some New Light preachers established colleges to train ministers for the new congregations. These colleges included Princeton University and Rutgers University in New Jersey, Brown University in Rhode Island, and Dartmouth College in New Hampshire.

The Great Awakening lessened the influence of the Enlightenment among many colonists and changed their view of religion and morality. In certain ways, however, the two movements had a similar impact on the colonies. Like the Enlightenment, the Great Awakening encouraged people to challenge authority and think themselves equal to those in power. In addition, both movements would eventually lead the colonists to question their British rulers and pave the way for revolutionary fervor.

HISTORICAL THINKING

1. **READING CHECK** What led to the Great Awakening?

2. **MAKE INFERENCES** Why do you think Edwards compared members of his audience to a spider?

3. **SUMMARIZE** How did the Great Awakening affect the colonists' ideas about authority and equality?

ENGLISH AND COLONIAL RIGHTS

For hundreds of years, English monarchs ruled with absolute power. But, bit by bit, those under their thumb began to chip away at the monarchs' control. In time, the colonists would do the same.

THE RISE OF PARLIAMENT

The English began their quest for legal rights in 1215, when the **Magna Carta**, or "Great Charter," was created. The document served as a peace treaty between King John of England and his barons, or noblemen, who had objected to the heavy taxes the king had levied against them. Most of the 63 clauses in the Magna Carta dealt with the rights of the barons and other wealthy nobles. But two of the clauses protected all free English citizens from being stripped of their rights or possessions without "the lawful judgment of [their] peers or by the law of the land."

Britain's Parliament meets in London's Palace of Westminster, often called the Houses of Parliament. This 2017 photo shows a meeting of the House of Lords. Today, the legislative powers of this house are limited to ensure the government represents all its people. For example, an act passed in 1911 prevents the House of Lords from opposing laws strongly supported by the House of Commons.

The Magna Carta laid the groundwork for a more democratic government in England and became the first written constitution in European history.

The Magna Carta also fostered the rise of **Parliament**, England's legislative body. When it was first created, Parliament consisted of two houses: the House of Lords, made up of nobles and high church officials; and the House of Commons, whose members were elected by male landowners. In the late 1600s, Parliament's power significantly increased following the Glorious Revolution, the bloodless overthrow of King James II. As you may remember, this was the king who formed the Dominion of New England and took away some colonial rights in the region. Parliamentary leaders also thought James had overstepped his authority in England. When William and Mary ascended the throne in his place, Parliament permanently limited the monarch's control and balanced powers more equally between the ruler and the legislature. For example, Parliament would control taxation, pass laws, and be called on to give its consent for raising an army in peacetime and for sending an army to fight against foreign invasions. The **English Bill of Rights of 1689** formally protected the rights of English citizens and Parliament.

The American colonists modeled their governments on Parliament. Property owners in every colony elected representatives to serve in assemblies that were similar to the House of Commons. But unlike those in England's legislature, assembly officials lived in the area they represented so they would better understand local interests and needs. The colonists enjoyed making their own decisions and managing some of their affairs and resented the fact that they had no representation in Parliament, especially when it passed laws they didn't like. For the most part, though, the English government adopted a policy of **salutary neglect** toward the colonies, which means the government usually left them alone. The government generally avoided enforcing colonial policies—unless it suited them to do so.

THE ZENGER TRIAL

In 1733, the English government chose to enforce its laws in the colonies after a series of objectionable articles had appeared in the *New-York Weekly Journal*, a newspaper published by **John Peter Zenger**. The articles reported the corrupt activity of William Cosby, the British colonial governor of New York. Cosby had removed a judge who had ruled against him and had also tampered with the outcome of an election. The accusations were true, but at that time, it was illegal to criticize the government. Since the newspaper didn't print the name of the articles' author, Cosby turned on Zenger and accused him of **libel**, or the publishing of lies. Zenger was arrested in November 1734 and remained in jail until his trial began in August 1735.

Even though Governor Cosby felt confident about the trial's outcome, he packed the jury with his supporters just to make sure. But Zenger's wife Anna, who continued to publish the *New-York Weekly Journal* after her husband's arrest, found out what Cosby had done and reported the fact in the paper. The judge in the trial dismissed Cosby's jury and replaced it with a jury of colonists. However, the judge also dismissed Zenger's team of lawyers for questioning his authority. Andrew Hamilton, a well-known lawyer from Philadelphia, took over the case.

Hamilton knew that Zenger would be found guilty if he simply tried to defend his client against the libel charge. There was no question the paper had criticized the governor, and any such criticism, true or not, was considered libelous. So Hamilton decided to admit Zenger had printed the articles, but he also pointed out that the criticism was true. Why, he argued, should Zenger be punished for printing the truth? A free press, Hamilton insisted, needed to be protected. And wasn't it especially important that the colonists challenge colonial governors when the latter abused their authority? Echoing Enlightenment ideals, Hamilton reminded the jury to allow "that, to which Nature and the Laws of our country have given us a Right, . . . both of exposing and opposing arbitrary Power . . . by speaking and writing Truth."

After a brief deliberation, the jury returned a verdict of not guilty, stunning Cosby and the judge and delighting most of the colonists who thronged the courtroom. The verdict was a major victory for freedom of the press, and it helped ignite the colonists' determination to protect their rights. But the colonists still considered themselves British citizens. When British forces went to war, they would fight alongside them.

HISTORICAL THINKING

1. **READING CHECK** Why was the Magna Carta an important document?

2. **COMPARE AND CONTRAST** In what ways were Parliament and colonial assemblies alike and different?

3. **DRAW CONCLUSIONS** How might the Zenger trial have altered the colonists' attitude toward British authority?

CONFLICT IN THE COLONIES

Can't we all get along? Many of the Native Americans who lived in North America didn't. But in the 1600s, some tribes united and agreed to defend each other against their common enemies. These agreements would influence where they would stand in the war that was brewing on the continent.

THE IROQUOIS CONFEDERACY

Before Europeans came to North America and claimed land there, Native Americans began forming alliances with one another. One of these alliances was formed by a group of tribes who called themselves the Haudenosaunee (hah-duh-NAH-suh-nee), or "People of the Longhouse," for the style of the houses they built. The French, however, called the group the Iroquois. As you have read, the Iroquois spoke the Iroquoian language and lived in the area around lakes Ontario, Huron, and Erie in present-day New York State and Pennsylvania and in the southern regions of Ontario and Quebec in present-day Canada. Five Iroquoian tribes living primarily in New York—the Mohawk, Oneida, Onondaga, Cayuga, and Seneca—forged the alliance

between 1570 and 1600. They wanted to put an end to the fierce wars they had been fighting against each other for years. The alliance was called the **Iroquois Confederacy**. With the addition of the Tuscarora tribe in 1722, the confederacy's name would change to the Six Nations.

The Iroquois also joined together to create a united force against their common enemies, the Algonquian and Huron. The Algonquian consisted of a band of tribes, including the Pequot and the Lenape, who spoke similar languages and lived along the Atlantic coast. The Huron lived along the St. Lawrence River.

As Europeans began to arrive in the region, Native Americans also began to form alliances with the British and French. The Iroquois—in particular, the

The Seneca Bark Longhouse at Ganondagan State Historic Site in Victor, New York, is a full-scale replica of a traditional longhouse.

War would erupt between Britain and France in 1754. American artist Junius Brutus Stearns depicts the war's Battle of the Monongahela in his circa 1851 painting, *Washington as a Captain in the French and Indian War.* In this scene from the battle, the general leading the British and American troops falls wounded before George Washington, who sits astride his horse.

Mohawk—formed an alliance with the British and Dutch, with whom they often traded furs for firearms. After the English took control of New York, the alliance came to be known as the Covenant Chain. Iroquois leaders maintained that their covenant, or binding promise, with the English was linked by a "chain of silver" that would never rust or break. The Iroquois believed the chain was linked by peace and friendship. Meanwhile, the Lenape and Huron allied with the French.

In the 1600s, the French and Iroquois battled for control of the fur trade. The Iroquois dominated the headwaters of the major waterways in the East, which were the key trade arteries to the interior of the continent. However, the Iroquois moved west after the demand for beaver fur led to a scarcity of the animals. The Native Americans warred with competing tribes along the way.

They also fought in New France, hoping to put an end to French trading in the Ohio Valley and beyond. In 1689, the Iroquois attacked the French settlement of Lachine (luh-SHEEN), a small fur-trading settlement

near Montreal. The attack was in retaliation for a raid on Iroquois corn two years before. The Iroquois killed about 250 settlers at Lachine and destroyed the trading settlement.

Clashes between the French and Iroquois continued until both sides grew weary of fighting. In 1701, at the request of the governor of New France, roughly 1,300 representatives from as many as 40 Native American tribes arrived in Montreal. The participants signed a treaty, known as the **Great Peace of Montreal**, that ended hostilities between the Iroquois and the French. In accordance with the treaty, the battle-weakened Iroquois agreed to remain neutral, or not take sides, in future wars.

CONFLICT BETWEEN BRITAIN AND FRANCE

As you have read, when French fur traders first came to North America in the 1600s, they set up a few forts and trading posts in the St. Lawrence River Valley. After they had trapped and killed many of the animals in the area, they resettled in the Ohio Valley. The British also claimed this land, and, in the 1740s, began pushing the French traders out of the valley. Colonial settlers bought land shares in the fertile Ohio Valley from the Ohio Company of Virginia in 1749. Nevertheless, the French still tried to maintain their claim on the land.

To block the British, the French began building a chain of forts from Lake Ontario to the Ohio River. Then in 1752, the French destroyed Pickawillany, a colonial trading post. In an effort to settle the dispute over the Ohio Valley, the British governor of Virginia sent a young colonial army officer, **George Washington**, to Fort LeBoeuf (luh-BUHF) in October 1753. The French fort was located in northwest Pennsylvania near Lake Erie. Washington was charged with delivering a message from the governor, informing the French they were on British land and requesting that they leave the fort. However, the French politely refused.

In May 1754, the British sent the newly promoted Colonel Washington and a few troops under his command to capture Fort Duquesne (doo-KAYN) in present-day Pittsburgh. The French fort was strategically located on land where the Allegheny and Monongahela rivers meet to form the Ohio River. When he reached the fort, Washington realized he

was outnumbered. He retreated about 40 miles from Fort Duquesne, where he and his troops hastily built a wooden stockade they fittingly called Fort Necessity.

But their situation was hopeless. French troops and their Native American allies soon surrounded the encampment and attacked. Washington's troops suffered heavy losses. After only a few hours of fighting, about 30 of Washington's men had been killed and about 70 were wounded. Accepting defeat, Washington surrendered to the French and abandoned Fort Necessity. Many historians consider this battle the start of the **French and Indian War**.

For Britain and France, this war would become part of a larger conflict, called the Seven Years' War, which officially began in 1756. The larger war involved all the great powers of Europe in a struggle over land on the continent. The French and Indian War was fought between Britain and France in their struggle to control North America.

Meanwhile, the colonists were also concerned about holding on to land in North America. In 1754, seven colonies sent delegates to a congress in Albany, New York, to negotiate an alliance with the Iroquois

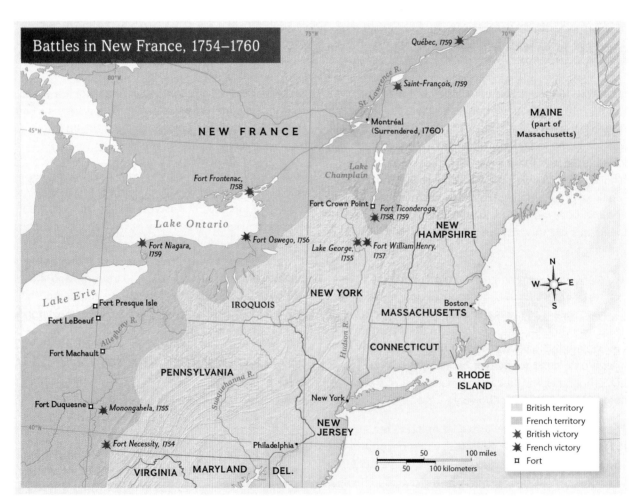

Battles in New France, 1754–1760

against the French. The Iroquois refused, however, because they were bound by the peace treaty they had signed with the French in 1701.

The delegates then discussed the defense measures the colonies might take against the French. They voted to adopt the **Albany Plan of Union** suggested by Benjamin Franklin. The plan proposed empowering a central government to tax, pass laws, and oversee military defense for the colonies. When the delegates returned home with the proposal, none of the colonies approved it. Nevertheless, the colonists were united in their determination to fight for the land they believed was theirs.

EARLY YEARS OF THE WAR

British general Edward Braddock landed in the colonies with two British regiments in 1755. In July of that year, he led his troops and about 700 colonial soldiers—including Washington, serving as an aide—through the Virginia backcountry on a mission to capture Fort Duquesne. Braddock's army was also accompanied by a group of Native Americans who served as scouts along the way.

The army's progress was slow, however. Braddock's wagons were too big for the narrow paths they encountered, and many of the scouts deserted, offended by the treatment they received at the hands of the British soldiers. The French and their Native American allies had plenty of time to track Braddock's progress and prepare for his arrival.

After Braddock and his troops crossed the Monongahela River about 10 miles east of Pittsburgh, the French forces ambushed them, shooting from behind trees. The **Battle of the Monongahela** lasted for several hours, as the French and their Native American allies continued to use the same tactic. Washington tried to convince Braddock to fight from behind trees as well, but the general refused. He and his troops were used to fighting on European battlefields, where the opposing armies formed neat rows.

The battle was a devastating defeat for Britain. About 1,000 of the 1,459 British soldiers who took part in the battle were killed or wounded, including Braddock himself. With his uniform pockmarked by bullet holes, Washington struggled to save what was left of Braddock's army and helped organize the retreat. British losses continued to pile up in the early years of the war. In New York, French forces seized Fort William Henry and Fort Oswego. Despite being outnumbered four to one, they captured 2,000 British soldiers at Lake George. In addition, between 1755 and 1757, France's Native American allies burned backcountry settlements in Virginia, Maryland, and Pennsylvania and killed or captured thousands of colonists. So far, the war was not going well for Britain and the colonies.

HISTORICAL THINKING

1. **READING CHECK** Why did some Iroquoian tribes form an alliance?

2. **MAKE INFERENCES** Why do you think none of the colonies approved the Albany Plan of Union?

3. **EVALUATE** What qualities did George Washington demonstrate during the Battle of the Monongahela?

4. **INTERPRET MAPS** Where were most of the battles of the French and Indian War fought?

BRITISH VICTORY

The colonists had fought valiantly alongside the British soldiers and rejoiced in Britain's victory. But soon after the war, the British government took steps that made the colonists wonder what they had fought for.

THE TIDE TURNS

The course of the conflict reversed after British statesman **Sir William Pitt** heavily financed the war and raised more troops to fight in it. In July 1758, the British captured Louisbourg in Nova Scotia, forcing the French in the Ohio Valley to pull out and rush to the defense of Quebec and Montreal. Soon after the removal of the French, supplies ran out for their Native American allies, and they, too, withdrew from the backcountry. As a result, the British took control of the western region.

Not even the French reinforcements from the Ohio Valley could save Quebec. In 1759, General James Wolfe laid siege to the city. Although both Wolfe and the commander of the French troops would die during the **Battle of Quebec**, the British captured the city. These victories persuaded many Iroquois to abandon their neutrality and join Britain and the colonies in the war effort. Then in 1760, General Jeffrey Amherst led his troops to Montreal. Only about 2,000 French soldiers remained to defend the city. Within three days, they surrendered to the British. The capture of Montreal ended French control of—and power in—Canada. It also marked the end of the French and Indian War.

In 1763, British diplomats traveled to Paris to negotiate a treaty with the French. Although many Native American tribes had been heavily involved in the conflict, no representatives from these groups were invited to take part in the negotiations. The **Treaty of Paris of 1763** officially ended the French and Indian War. According to its terms, Britain gained Canada from France. As Britain's ally, Spain acquired New Orleans and the Louisiana Territory west of the Mississippi River. Spain agreed to cede Florida to the British in exchange for Cuba and the Philippines, a group of islands in Southeast Asia. Britain now controlled all of the land in North America east of the Mississippi.

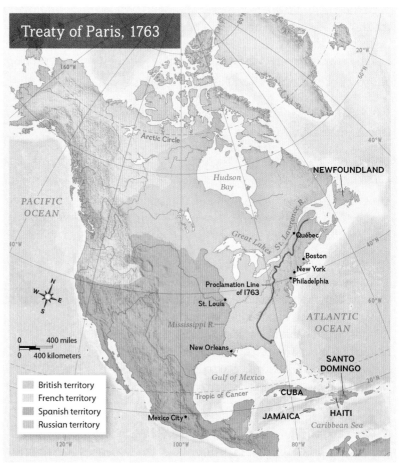

Treaty of Paris, 1763

British territory
French territory
Spanish territory
Russian territory

IMPACT OF THE WAR

With the end of the war, the colonists gained some advantages. The treaty gave them the right to fish the waters of the North Atlantic off the coast of Canada. And the colonists assumed they were now free to settle the Ohio Valley. For Native Americans, however, the war was a disaster. With the French removed from North America, they lost a powerful ally and trading partner. And trade with the British was much less favorable. The British didn't present the Native Americans with annual gifts as the French had. They also raised prices on trade goods and placed limits on what and how much Native Americans could trade. Perhaps worst of all, colonial settlers began streaming into Native American lands in the Ohio Valley, violating treaties that were still in effect.

The changes in trade policies and the land-grabbing by colonists drove large numbers of Delaware, Shawnee, Iroquois, and other Native Americans to rebel. Ottawa leader **Pontiac**, who had allied with the French during the war, urged Native Americans in the region to band together and fight against the British. In 1763, Pontiac began a series of coordinated attacks on British forts in what is known as **Pontiac's Rebellion**. His forces defeated 13 forts but were unable to seize the most important ones, including Fort Pitt (named in honor of William Pitt) in Pennsylvania. In addition, Pontiac had hoped to receive aid from the French, but that never came. During the siege at Fort Pitt, representatives from the Delaware tribe met with officers at the fort to ask them to give up. The British officers refused. Instead, some historians maintain that the officers gave the Native Americans smallpox-infested blankets to intentionally spread disease among them.

Fighting would continue for two more years. In the meantime, **King George III** of England grew frustrated with the ongoing war between the colonists and Native Americans. In an effort to keep the peace, King George issued the **Proclamation of 1763**, which required colonists to remain east of a line that, on a map, ran along the crest of the Appalachian Mountains from Maine to Georgia. The proclamation angered the colonists. The right to settle the lands west of the line had been the reason most of them had fought in the French and Indian War. Many colonists ignored the proclamation and continued to move westward. But the French and Indian War had been costly for the British government. It couldn't afford to send soldiers to enforce the proclamation. Soon Britain would demand that the colonists help pay down these expenses.

It is important for us, my brothers, that we exterminate from our lands this nation which seeks only to destroy us. You see as well as I do that we can no longer supply our needs, as we have done from our brothers, the French. The English sell us goods twice as dear [expensive] as the French do, and their goods do not last. Scarcely have we bought a blanket or something else to cover ourselves with before we must think of getting another; and when we wish to set out for our winter camps they do not want to give us any credit as our brothers the French do.

—from a speech to a council of Native Americans given by Chief Pontiac, near Detroit, May 1763

HISTORICAL THINKING

1. **READING CHECK** Why did the tide turn toward the British in the French and Indian War?

2. **SUMMARIZE** How did Britain's victory in the war affect Native Americans?

3. **ANALYZE CAUSE AND EFFECT** What led King George III to issue the Proclamation of 1763?

4. **INTERPRET MAPS** Why do you think Britain wanted to exchange Cuba and the Philippines for Florida?

VOCABULARY

Use each of the following vocabulary words in a sentence that shows an understanding of the term's meaning.

1. overseer
   The overseer didn't allow the enslaved laborers to stop working until well after sunset.

2. subsistence farming

3. backcountry

4. maritime

5. Parliament

6. salutary neglect

7. libel

8. salvation

READING STRATEGY
SUMMARIZE

When you summarize, you restate text in your own words and shorten it. A summary includes only the most important information and details. Use a diagram like this one to summarize the factors that led to the expansion of cities in the colonies.

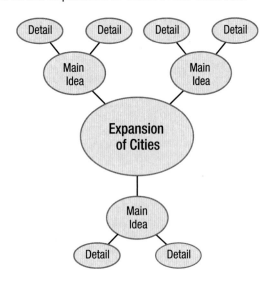

9. Why did most of the colonial cities arise in New England and the Middle Colonies?

MAIN IDEAS

Answer the following questions. Support your answers with evidence from the chapter.

10. Why did New England become the center of colonial trade in the early 1700s? **LESSON 1.1**

11. Why did the Middle Colonies come to be called the "breadbasket of the colonies"? **LESSON 1.2**

12. Where did most of the Germans who immigrated to the Middle Colonies settle? **LESSON 1.3**

13. Why did little industry develop in the Southern Colonies? **LESSON 2.1**

14. How did enslaved Africans in the Southern Colonies create resilient and rich cultures? **LESSON 2.2**

15. What was the Enlightenment? **LESSON 3.1**

16. In what way was the Great Awakening a reaction against the Enlightenment? **LESSON 3.2**

17. Why was John Peter Zenger arrested and jailed? **LESSON 3.3**

18. What sparked the French and Indian War? **LESSON 4.1**

19. How did the Proclamation of 1763 impact the colonists? **LESSON 4.2**

HISTORICAL THINKING

Answer the following questions. Support your answers with evidence from the chapter.

20. **MAKE INFERENCES** What was life probably like for subsistence farmers in the New England colonies?

21. **DRAW CONCLUSIONS** How did the Quakers live by the Bible's golden rule, which says to act toward others as you would want them to behave toward you?

22. **ANALYZE CAUSE AND EFFECT** What happened because enslaved people from West Africa taught southern plantation owners how to cultivate rice?

23. **FORM AND SUPPORT OPINIONS** Which movement do you think had the greater impact on the colonies—the Enlightenment or the Great Awakening? Remember to support your answer with evidence from the chapter.

24. **COMPARE AND CONTRAST** How did the relationship between the Native Americans and the British differ from that between the Native Americans and the French?

25. **MAKE PREDICTIONS** How do you think the colonists will react when Britain tries to make them help pay for the war?

INTERPRET GRAPHS

Study the graph below, which shows colonial population growth between 1670 and 1770. Then answer the questions.

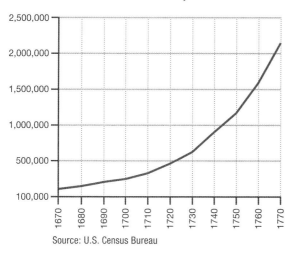

Population Growth in the Colonies, 1670–1770

Source: U.S. Census Bureau

26. In which decade did the American colonies experience the largest population growth?

27. What do you think accounts for the growth in population in that decade?

28. By how much did the population increase between 1670 and 1770?

ANALYZE SOURCES

In 1735, an essay supporting the education of women was reprinted in John Peter Zenger's *New-York Weekly Journal* after it had appeared in another newspaper. Read the excerpt from the essay and answer the question.

> I Have often wondered that Learning is not thought a proper Ingredient in the Education of a Woman . . . they have the same improvable Minds as the male Part of the Species, why should they not be cultivated by the same Method?
>
> Learning and Knowledge are Perfections in us, not as we are Men, but as we are reasonable Creatures, in which Order, of Beings the Female World is upon the same Level with the Male. We ought to consider in this Particular, not what is the Sex, but what is the Species to which they belong.

29. What Enlightenment ideals might have influenced the author of this essay?

CONNECT TO YOUR LIFE

30. **EXPLANATORY** Think about the challenges faced by those who moved to the American colonies. Then consider the difficulties immigrants to the United States encounter today. How are their challenges similar, and how do they differ? Write a paragraph in which you compare the two sets of experiences.

TIPS

- List the challenges the colonists faced in the cities, rural areas, and backcountry. Then list the challenges immigrants endure when they come to the United States today.

- Describe the factors that may have compelled the colonists and the modern immigrants to move.

- Use two or three vocabulary terms from the chapter in your paragraph.

- Conclude the paragraph with a sentence that ties the colonists' experiences to those of modern immigrants.

NATIONAL GEOGRAPHIC | CONNECTION

Colonial New York

by Andrea Stone

Adapted from "New Online Archive Shows Colonial New York Was Rowdy, Filthy, Smelly," by Andrea Stone, news.nationalgeographic.com, December 21, 2014

Decrees limiting the sale of alcohol and outlining penalties for fighting were some of the first ordinances issued in the Dutch colony, New Netherland. Peter Stuyvesant, the colony's director-general, issued these decrees in the mid-1600s.

Most of the inhabitants of the colony's capital, New Amsterdam, likely never read the official decrees. But today, anyone with an internet connection can read them—some of the earliest laws declared in North America. New York City's Municipal Archives has posted a digitized collection of ordinances from 1647 to 1661, when the island of Manhattan in New York City was run by the Dutch and known as New Amsterdam.

The nation's origin story is dominated by the prim, religious monocultures of the Pilgrim and Puritan colonies of New England. The mixture of religions, races, and ethnic groups found in unruly New Amsterdam are often overlooked. However, we know New Amsterdam was an exuberant center of commerce, open to settlers of diverse backgrounds. Pauline Toole, commissioner of New York City's Department of Records and Information Services, remarks, "These ordinances show how New Amsterdam officials tried to maintain order in a fractious and rowdy city, and shed a light on our city's early development."

SUNDAY DRINKING AND FIGHTING

When Stuyvesant replaced an inept and tyrannical director-general, he found a city where alcohol was made or sold in one of every four buildings. Alcoholism was rampant. Despite his immediate crackdown on Sunday drinking and fighting, less than a year later, a frustrated Stuyvesant acknowledged that few had paid attention to his new regulations.

Stuyvesant, however, never tried to enact total prohibition. When he and his council weren't trying to moderate drinking, they were trying to tax it, often unsuccessfully. Several decrees dealt with the government's inability to collect excise taxes on illegal homemade beer and wine.

HOGS RUNNING FREE IN THE STREET

To tamp down frequent fires, Stuyvesant appointed chimney inspectors; required buckets, ladders, and hooks on street corners; and banned roofs made of hay and reeds. He also issued standards for bakers to follow and tried mightily to clean up the streets. The city's health and building departments can trace their beginnings back to Stuyvesant's New Amsterdam decrees.

In 1650, just 25 years after the Dutch built Fort Amsterdam to protect New Amsterdam and the rest of the colony, an ordinance was passed forbidding animals to run free. It noted the "decayed fortress, formerly in fair condition, has mostly been trodden down by hogs, goats and sheep." The loose animals also created an awful smell. To curb the stink lingering in the city, the council also banned the common practice of throwing "any rubbish, filth, ashes, oyster-shells, dead animals or anything like it" in the street.

The online portrait of New Amsterdam "sounds like kindergarten gone wild and the leaders trying to impose order desperately," says Russell Shorto, author of *The Island at the Center of the World*. But he added that the ordinances alone skew the picture of life in the colonial city. As thousands of court documents and other pieces of correspondence are posted to the archive, a more well-rounded portrait should emerge of New Amsterdam and North America's first Dutch colony.

"There's something about the actual written documents and something beyond the words—the paper, the texture, the change in handwriting, the stains on the document," Shorto says. "It's a physical document, and to get some sense [of it] in digital form is a wonder."

For more from National Geographic, check out "The First Americans" online.

UNIT INQUIRY: Conceive a Utopia

In this unit, you learned about the various groups of Europeans who came to North America seeking better lives for themselves and their families. Some groups, such as the Pilgrims and the Puritans, came to form communities based on shared religious beliefs and values. Others focused on building wealth by utiliizing the continent's abundant natural resources. What did these groups consider to be an ideal community? How did they conceive and form their new communities? What conflicts arose as they established their communities?

ASSIGNMENT

The colonies in North America were begun by people who imagined and sought a better way of life in a new place. Envision an ideal community, or a utopia, that you would like to live in. Think about such factors as the goals and values of your community and how it would function. Be prepared to present your utopia to the class.

Plan As you conceive your utopia, review the unit to gather evidence about the ways in which newcomers to North America devised or structured particular components of their communities and how they handled conflicts that arose. Use a graphic organizer like this one to take notes on the variety of ways you find.

Goals	Values
Religion	
Economy	
Government	
Education	
Gender roles	
Conflict	

Produce Review your notes and think about what you consider to be features of an ideal community. Produce a detailed conception of your utopia by writing a short paragraph on each feature.

Present Choose a creative way to present your community and its goals and values to the class. Consider one of these options:

- Create a commercial to persuade people to move to your new community. Include details telling where it is, what it's like, and what kind of people would prosper there.

- Lead a class discussion on the features of an ideal community. To begin the discussion, describe the features of your community.

- Develop a survey asking questions about what makes an ideal community. Encourage classmates to complete the survey, and then use their feedback to present ways your utopia matches their needs.

NATIONAL GEOGRAPHIC | LEARNING FRAMEWORK ACTIVITIES

Map Migrations

SKILLS Observation, Collaboration

KNOWLEDGE Our Human Story

Working with a partner, create a world map showing the migration routes of groups of people who settled in North America up to the mid-1700s. Skim the unit and make a list of immigrant groups and the dates of their migrations. Then create an outline map of the world. You might draw arrows of different colors to represent migration routes of various groups. Include a key that identifies the groups and provides dates of key movements. After you have finished your map, share it with your classmates and compare it with the maps of other partners. What patterns of migration do you notice? Why do you think these patterns occurred?

Establish a Trade Network

ATTITUDE Empowerment

SKILL Collaboration

Trade expanded the colonial economies and created important industries during the 17th century. Working with a small group, establish a trade network among your classmates. Decide what products or resources your group will trade with other groups and what products or resources you want to acquire. Negotiate prices and set quantities of products and resources to be traded. Then determine how the network will exchange goods. List the trading partners and details on the board. Discuss how the trade network might establish new industries or the need for additional infrastructure to support the exchange of goods.

CRITICAL VIEWING Reenactors fire muskets as they portray an American Revolution battle scene in Mount Vernon, Virginia. What details in the photograph convey what it may have been like to fight in the American Revolution?

REVOLUTION AND A NEW NATION

THE UNITED STATES

1783
The United States defeats Britain, and the American Revolution ends when representatives from both sides sign the Treaty of Paris.

1776
The Declaration of Independence is adopted on July 4.

1773
Colonists board British ships and throw 342 boxes of tea into the waters of Boston Harbor in an act known as the Boston Tea Party. *(This bottle contains tea that washed up on shore following the Boston Tea Party.)*

1775
The American Revolution begins with the battles at Lexington and Concord in Massachusetts after a shot is fired in Lexington. *(statue of Captain John Parker, who commanded the colonial militia at the Battle of Lexington)*

1765
The British impose the Stamp Act, which taxes American colonists for every piece of paper they use.

1760

1780

THE WORLD

1770

1779 AFRICA
Luanda, a city on Africa's Atlantic coast, becomes the leading port in the African slave trade.

1765 ASIA
Chinese forces invade Burma. *(a seal of Chinese emperor Qianlong, who launched the invasion)*

1776 EUROPE
Scottish economist Adam Smith publishes *The Wealth of Nations*, in which he argues against government control of the economy.

1783 AMERICAS
Future revolutionary leader Simón Bolívar is born in present-day Venezuela in South America.

1789
George Washington becomes the first president of the United States. *(commemorative button from Washington's first inauguration with his initials and the words "Long Live the President")*

HISTORICAL THINKING

DETERMINE CHRONOLOGY What earlier events might have inspired Haiti's fight for independence?

1804
Thomas Jefferson sends Meriwether Lewis and William Clark on an expedition to explore the western territory included in the Louisiana Purchase. *(Clark's compass and Lewis's watch used during the expedition)*

1787
Delegates at the Constitutional Convention draft and sign the U.S. Constitution.

1812
The War of 1812 erupts between Britain and the United States over British violations of American rights at sea.

1820

1791
The Bill of Rights, guaranteeing individual rights, is added to the U.S. Constitution.

1800

1814 EUROPE
British forces defeat French emperor Napoleon at the Battle of Toulouse in France.

1804 AMERICAS
Haiti gains its independence from France. *(Haitian banknote featuring Toussaint L'Ouverture, who led the revolution)*

1789 EUROPE
The French Revolution begins.

1787 AFRICA
Freed American slaves settle in Freetown, Sierra Leone, in West Africa.

CHAPTER 4

THE AMERICAN REVOLUTION

1764–1783

HISTORICAL THINKING How did the colonists' emerging American identity lead to revolution?

The Old North Bridge, located in Concord, Massachusetts, is the site of a skirmish between the Continental and British armies in 1775.

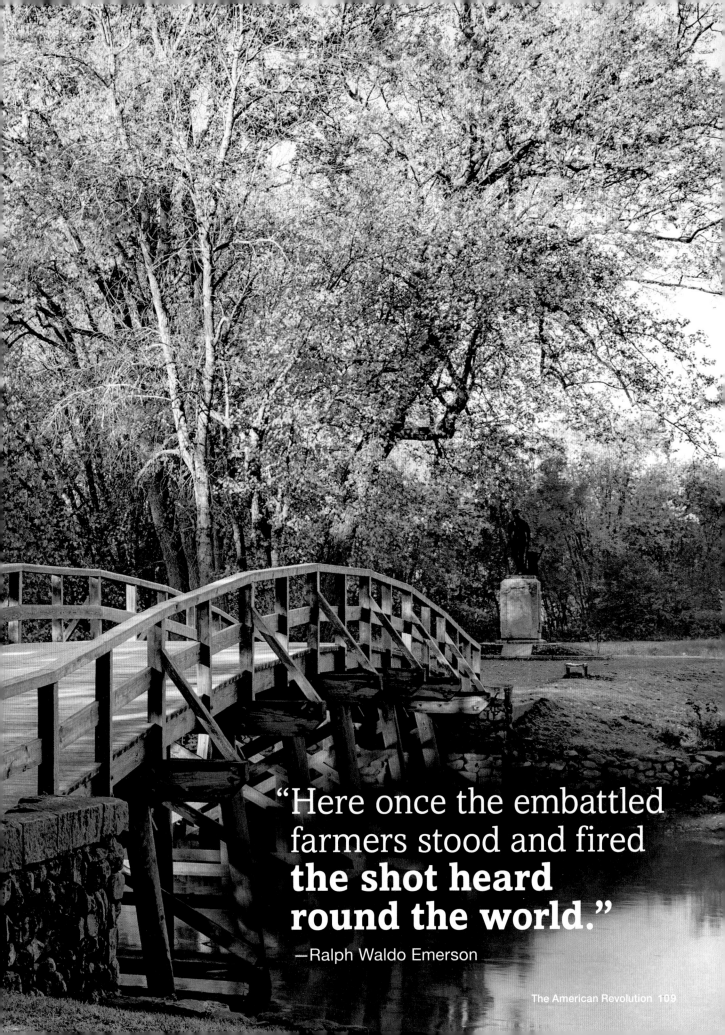

"Here once the embattled farmers stood and fired **the shot heard round the world.**"

—Ralph Waldo Emerson

MAIN IDEA Britain's attempt to raise revenue by taxing the colonies led the colonists to resist.

BRITISH ACTIONS AND AMERICAN REACTIONS

If you have an after-school job, you know about taxes. Even today, Americans complain about paying taxes. But we pay taxes that have been set by our elected representatives. The colonists had no such representatives in Parliament to promote their ideas about taxation.

TAXATION WITHOUT REPRESENTATION

American colonists were British subjects, but they had grown used to self-government and the concept of individual rights. When the British Parliament imposed new taxes on the colonists, it threatened more than just their pocketbooks. By the mid-1700s, the colonists had begun to shake off British influence and develop an American identity. Parliament's attempt to enforce new taxes drove another wedge between Britain and the North American colonies.

After the French and Indian War, the British government faced massive debt. British authorities argued that the colonists should pay a large share of that debt. **George Grenville**, the prime minister appointed by King George, agreed and issued laws to tax the colonies directly, rather than allowing colonial assemblies to impose taxes. Grenville, who believed that Britain should strictly control the colonies, saw these taxes as a way of raising revenue and reinforcing British power over the colonies.

Among the first of the new taxes was the **Sugar Act** of 1764, which established **duties**, or taxes, on imports of refined sugar, molasses, and other goods. Parliament also passed the **Currency Act**, which prohibited colonies from issuing their own paper money. This created a shortage of currency and further curbed colonial merchants and trade.

Many British subjects justified the Sugar Act by claiming that American colonists should start pulling their economic weight because they paid only a fraction of the annual taxes that people in Britain paid. Grenville believed that colonists should pay because the British army had reduced the threat of French colonial expansion by winning the French and Indian War. But some colonists openly accused the British of tyranny, coining the slogan "no taxation without representation." The colonists believed that because they had no representation in Parliament, Parliament had no right to impose direct taxes on them. As one Philadelphia merchant said, "The point in dispute is a very Important one, if the Americans are to be taxed by a Parliament where they are not nor can be Represented, they are no longer Englishmen but Slaves."

Colonial potters began making teapots with slogans to celebrate the repeal of the Stamp Act in 1766.

THE SONS OF LIBERTY

The original Sons of Liberty were a group of small merchants and craftsmen in Boston who called themselves the Loyal Nine and organized in protest of the Stamp Act. One of their first acts was hanging an effigy, or dummy, of a local man, Andrew Oliver, from a tree on Washington Street. The same night, an angry mob destroyed his home and carriage house. Ironically, the Act had appointed Oliver as distributor of the stamps without his knowledge and he had yet to accept the position. The Loyal Nine soon changed their name to the Sons of Liberty as the organization and its protest movement began to spread. By the end of 1765, there were Sons of Liberty operating in every colony.

In response to Britain's direct taxation, colonists began to organize protests, which included a series of **boycotts** against British goods. By refusing to import or purchase these goods, the colonists hoped to avoid taxes and send a clear message to Britain.

THE STAMP ACT

In 1765, Parliament passed the **Quartering Act**, which required colonists to provide housing for British soldiers in stables, inns, ale houses, and abandoned buildings. That same year, Parliament also passed the **Stamp Act**, a law that sent an even greater storm of protest sweeping through the colonies. Only documents marked with an official stamp were considered legal, and the only way to acquire the stamp was by paying a tax. Printed materials subject to this law included deeds, business licenses, court documents, newspapers, and even playing cards. The law also demanded the tax be paid with gold or silver coins, which colonists had difficulty doing because they generally used paper money and credit. British courts in the colonies enforced the act by confiscating any land, property, or goods involved in transactions conducted without the special government stamps.

Colonial assemblies formally protested the Stamp Act. **Patrick Henry**, newly elected to Virginia's House of Burgesses, led the protest. Henry was a strong supporter of colonial rights and would later become a leader in the fight for independence. He persuaded the House of Burgesses to pass a series of resolutions defending the colonists' right to tax themselves rather than to be taxed by Parliament. Massachusetts, Connecticut, New York, New Jersey, Pennsylvania, Maryland, and South Carolina passed resolutions similar to Virginia's. Rhode Island simply instructed its officials to ignore the stamp tax.

In October 1765, representatives from nine colonies traveled to New York City to attend the **Stamp Act Congress**. The congress upheld the power of representative colonial assemblies, not Parliament, to tax the colonists. It also defended the right to trial by jury, which the colonists believed was threatened by the expanded authority of the British colonial courts.

Protests broke out across the colonies, and by the end of 1765, they had forced official stamp distributors in every colony except Georgia to resign. The protest leaders called themselves **Sons of Liberty** and established networks throughout the colonies to organize boycotts and other protest actions. Merchants in New York City, Philadelphia, and Boston signed pacts to stop accepting British imports until Parliament repealed the act. Colonial resistance aimed to cancel the stamp tax, not end British authority. The efforts succeeded in 1766, when Parliament repealed the Stamp Act.

The controversies surrounding British actions led to a sharp division among colonists, and the erosion of individual rights and tax legislation created further animosity. **Loyalists** supported the authority of Parliament and wanted to continue living as British subjects. **Patriots** supported colonial self-government and increasingly began to call for independence from Britain.

HISTORICAL THINKING

1. **READING CHECK** How did British actions lead to resistance in the colonies?

2. **MAKE CONNECTIONS** Why did many colonists claim Parliament's decision to tax them was unfair?

3. **ANALYZE CAUSE AND EFFECT** How did the Sons of Liberty help bring about the repeal of the Stamp Act?

CRISIS IN BOSTON

Everyone has a boiling point. The colonists had successfully forced the repeal of the Stamp Act, only to find Parliament saddling them with more taxes and regulations. Protests and boycotts led to a partial repeal, but rising tensions would eventually inspire revolt.

THE TOWNSHEND ACTS

Although Parliament repealed the Stamp Act, the threat of new taxes did not disappear. After all, Parliament had the authority to tax citizens living in Great Britain "in all cases whatsoever." It claimed that its authority also extended to subjects living in Britain's North American colonies.

Charles Townshend became Britain's finance minister shortly after the Stamp Act was repealed. He had strongly supported the Sugar Act. In fact, he was partially responsible for coming up with the legislation. He agreed with the British government that the colonists reaped economic and political benefits from their connection to Britain, and they should pay their fair share to that nation.

In 1767, Parliament passed four acts designed to generate colonial revenue for the British treasury as well as to force the colonists to comply with Parliament's authority. These acts were collectively called the **Townshend Acts**. Britain planned to use some of the revenue collected to pay colonial governors and judges, who previously had been paid by colonial legislatures. British leaders believed Parliament would have greater control over colonial officials if it held its own purse strings.

The acts established a Board of Customs Commissioners to collect customs duties, or taxes on imported goods, from colonial traders. These duties included taxes on lead, glass, paper, paint, and tea, all goods that the colonies were required to purchase from Britain. To stop smugglers, the British Parliament gave the board extensive powers to overtake ships and seize cargoes it believed to be contraband, or smuggled goods. The acts also expanded the authority of courts to issue **writs of assistance**, or search warrants, which permitted customs officials to enter any building to search for and seize property from any trader who had not paid customs duties.

At first, there was little colonial reaction to the Townshend Acts. However, beginning in December 1767, John Dickinson, a Philadelphia lawyer who owned a Delaware plantation, published a series of 12 letters signed "A Farmer." Newspapers throughout the colonies reprinted these protest letters, and opposition to the acts soon grew. Colonists resisted paying the duties, and cries of "Tyranny!" rang through the streets.

John Singleton Copley painted this portrait of Mercy Otis Warren in 1763.

Paul Revere's engraved print of the Boston Massacre, *The Bloody Massacre in King Street*, is not quite accurate. The print does not show the colonists fighting back, and it does not include Crispus Attucks, the African-American man killed in the clash.

Contributing to rising tensions was the response from Great Britain to a letter sent by the Massachusetts assembly to the 12 other colonial assemblies. The letter was written by **Samuel Adams**, a prominent member of the Sons of Liberty, and lawyer James Otis. In the letter, they called once again for a boycott of British goods. The British monarchy saw this as a direct threat to its authority in the colonies. Parliament demanded that the Massachusetts assembly rescind, or withdraw, its call to action. It ordered colonial governors to dissolve their assemblies if they refused to ignore the call. Furthermore, Parliament sent British regiments into Boston to guard against further unrest. When the Massachusetts assembly refused to take back the letter, Parliament disbanded it, prompting a boycott in Boston that spread throughout the colonies.

Mercy Otis Warren, a writer and historian from Massachusetts, was close to many leading Patriots. After British troops were called to occupy Boston, she concluded that Britain was an enemy that could not be reasoned with. In her book *A History of the Rise, Progress, and Termination of the American Revolution*, she wrote, "the standing army is the most ready engine in the hand of despotism." For her, the stationing of troops in Boston represented the point of no return in relations between the colonists and Britain. While the Townshend Acts were being passed, she opened her home to other Patriots, such as John Adams and Samuel Adams, and it became a center of political resistance to Britain.

THE BOSTON MASSACRE

The movement of British troops into Boston kept tensions charged for the next two years. Some troops set up camps on Boston Common, a wide field in the middle of the city meant for all citizens to use. The soldiers were not paid well, so many of them sought local work when they were not on duty. The people of Boston resented this, claiming the soldiers were taking jobs from colonists. Children taunted the soldiers in the streets, mocking their red uniforms by calling them "redcoats" and "lobsterbacks." All of this prompted plenty of fistfights between colonists and British soldiers. Within a few years, that violence turned deadly.

Early in the morning of March 5, 1770, authorities posted a handbill stating British troops would defend themselves against any colonial harassment. Later that night, an angry band of colonists roamed the streets of Boston, itching for a fight. They came upon a lone British sentry guarding the Customs House, and they began hurling insults at him. According to some accounts, the sentry responded by hitting a boy in the crowd with his gun. This attracted a larger crowd, and a British officer, Captain Thomas Preston, led seven more armed soldiers to the scene to try to calm things down. Instead, the situation got worse.

The crowd threw snowballs, ice, rocks, and other objects at the soldiers and attacked them with sticks and clubs. Then one of the soldiers fired his weapon, and the rest followed suit. Three colonists were killed immediately, including **Crispus Attucks**, an African-American sailor. Two other victims were wounded and died later, bringing the death toll to five, and six colonists were injured in what would go down in history as the **Boston Massacre**.

Governor Thomas Hutchinson promised that justice would be served. He arrested the soldiers involved and accused them of murder. To many colonists' dismay, John Adams, Patriot and lawyer, agreed to defend the soldiers in court, stating that everyone deserved the right to a fair trial, even the loathed British soldiers. Adams mounted an eloquent case, arguing that the soldiers had fired in self-defense, fearing their lives were in danger. His argument convinced the jury, which acquitted Captain Preston and all but two of the soldiers. Adams feared this trial would end his legal career, but over time he earned the respect of his fellow Patriots and played a vital role in the founding of the nation.

On the same day as the Boston Massacre, Lord North, Townshend's successor, asked Parliament to repeal the Townshend Acts, except for the tax on tea. He maintained Britain's right to tax the colonists and wanted to avoid the perception that he was giving in to colonial protesters. However, he also realized the American boycotts resulting from the Townshend Acts were harming Britain's economy. Parliament agreed to his request on April 12, 1770.

For the next two years, the conflict between Great Britain and the colonists eased, but the calm did not last. In 1772, after Patriots in Rhode Island burned a British ship that had been hunting for smugglers, Parliament once again started passing laws intended to control unrest in the colonies. Samuel Adams organized a **committee of correspondence** in Massachusetts to collect a list of British offenses against the colonies, publish them in public spaces, and communicate them as much as possible. Virginia soon had its own committee, and within a year most colonies had coordinated such opposition to Britain's actions.

The part I took in Defence of Captain Preston and the Soldiers, procured me Anxiety. . . . It was, however, one of the most gallant, generous, manly and disinterested Actions of my whole Life, and one of the best Pieces of Service I ever rendered my Country. Judgement of Death against those Soldiers would have been as foul a Stain upon this Country as the Executions of the Quakers or Witches, anciently. As the Evidence was, the Verdict of the Jury was exactly right. This however is no Reason why the Town should not call the Action of that Night a Massacre, nor is it any Argument in favor of the Governor or Minister, who caused them to be sent here. But it is the strongest Proofs of the Danger of Standing Armies.

—from John Adams's diary, concerning his defense of British soldiers during the Boston Massacre trial, 1773

THE BOSTON TEA PARTY

It wasn't long before the committees of correspondence had a new target for protest. In 1773, Parliament passed the **Tea Act**, which was enacted to bail out the failing British **East India Company** and gave the company the sole right to import and sell tea in North America. Without competition from colonial tea merchants, the company was able to lower the price of its tea. While the act was not intended to raise revenue, it stirred up old debates about the Townshend duties on tea, which were still in effect. Soon more protests were underway.

At first, the protesters simply made it difficult for the East India Company to deliver its tea to the colonies. Dockworkers in New York and Philadelphia refused to unload the company's ships and sent them back to England with their original cargoes. Then, in Boston, the Sons of Liberty staged a grand act of rebellion.

On December 16, 1773, the band of Patriots disguised themselves as members of the Mohawk nation and, under cover of night, headed to Boston Harbor. The choice of disguise was not simply to keep their identities secret. The act of dressing as Native Americans signaled that they no longer considered themselves to be subjects of the British crown, but true Americans. They boarded three ships and dumped 342 chests of East India Company tea overboard in what came to be known as the **Boston Tea Party**.

Reenactors dump crates of tea into Boston Harbor on December 16, 2017, the 244th anniversary of the famous protest. The men stand on a replica of one of the three ships the Sons of Liberty boarded that night.

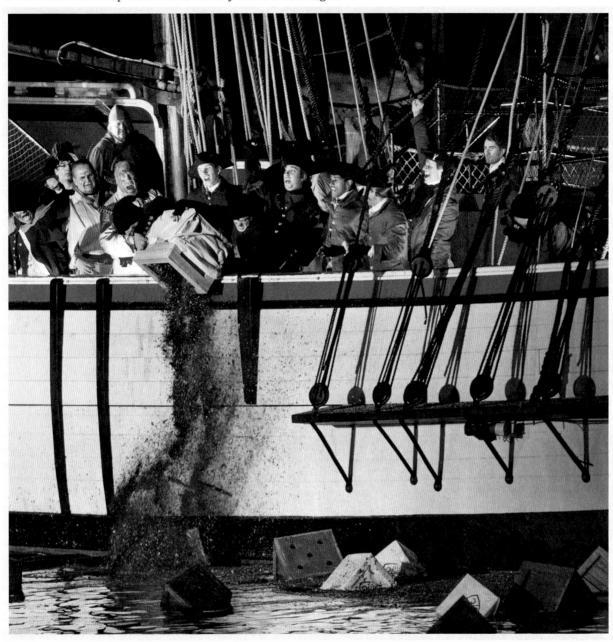

The Sons of Liberty took great care in planning and executing the Boston Tea Party. No one was hurt that night, and only one person, Francis Akeley, was imprisoned for the crime. Crates of tea leaves reportedly washed ashore in Boston and nearby towns during the weeks following the protest.

The incident sparked more bold protests, including a second Boston Tea Party in March 1774 and a similar event that took place in New York in April. But these acts of defiance only hardened Britain's resolve against the protests. New and more punishing laws would soon be inflicted on the colonies.

HISTORICAL THINKING

1. **READING CHECK** Why was Boston considered a center of resistance against the British?

2. **IDENTIFY MAIN IDEAS AND DETAILS** What were Parliament's two main purposes in passing the Townshend Acts?

3. **ANALYZE VISUALS** What kinds of different information can an engraving and a photograph convey to a reader?

4. **FORM AND SUPPORT OPINIONS** Were the Sons of Liberty justified in destroying the British cargo? Support your opinion with evidence from the text.

MAIN IDEA The British response to protests inspired an increasing number of colonists to consider breaking away from Britain, especially after shots were fired.

THE SHOT HEARD ROUND THE WORLD

No one likes to be insulted. For King George III, the colonists' organized protests, such as dumping tea into Boston Harbor, were too great an insult to bear. Britain struck back at the colonists with all its might.

THE INTOLERABLE ACTS

In 1774, after the Boston Tea Party, Parliament and King George III decided to punish the colonies in the form of the Coercive Acts. Colonists quickly renamed these four acts the **Intolerable Acts**, because they were intended to prevent Massachusetts from governing itself. The acts closed the port of Boston until the colony repaid the East India Company for the tea it lost. They replaced the colonial assembly with a ruling council of the king's appointees. The acts increased British control on Massachusetts's courts, protecting British officials, who, if charged with a crime, could go to England or another colony to be tried. Finally,

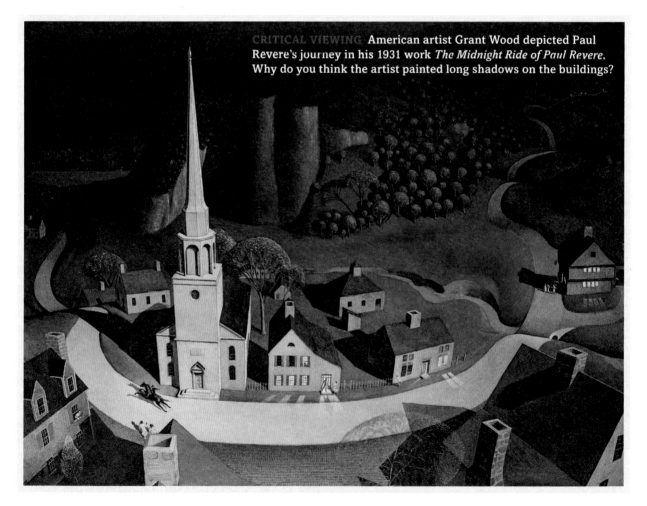

CRITICAL VIEWING American artist Grant Wood depicted Paul Revere's journey in his 1931 work *The Midnight Ride of Paul Revere.* Why do you think the artist painted long shadows on the buildings?

Britain expanded the Quartering Act, which gave the colonial governors more authority to house British troops in buildings or in private citizens' homes, if necessary. Basically, the Intolerable Acts put Boston under **martial law**, or military control.

Colonists were furious. Protests and organized resistance increased in Massachusetts and the other colonies. When Boston suffered severe unemployment and food shortages due to the port closure, neighboring towns sent supplies.

On September 5, 1774, representatives from every colony but Georgia—56 delegates in all—met in Philadelphia at the **First Continental Congress** to determine how to respond to Britain's actions and to air their grievances. The meeting lasted more than a month. Although most of the delegates wanted to remain loyal to Britain, they agreed to petition the Parliament and the crown to repeal the Intolerable Acts and other restrictions. They passed resolutions to end all trade with Britain and suspend exports to the West Indies. They also established local committees, elected by citizens, to enforce the ban on trade. These committees eventually took on other functions of local government, including collecting taxes and raising militias.

Parliament refused the Congress's request, and King George concluded that the New England colonists were openly rebelling. He predicted that "blows must decide whether [colonists] are to be subject to this country or independent." Less than a month before the Congress was set to meet for a second time, King George's words came true.

LEXINGTON AND CONCORD

Believing that armed conflict with the British was inevitable, Patriots formed militias made up of **minutemen**, citizen-soldiers who would respond to a call to action at a moment's notice. In the spring of 1775, **General Thomas Gage**, commander of British troops in Boston, ordered his army to seize and secure all weapons and gunpowder and keep them out of the militias' hands. The order also required Gage to arrest Patriots Samuel Adams and **John Hancock** in nearby **Lexington**, in hopes of subduing protests. On April 18, British troops began marching toward **Concord**, about 20 miles west of Boston, to seize the **arsenals**, or stores of weapons and ammunition, believed to be held there. Things did not go according to plan.

A spy inside the British high command had informed the Patriots of Gage's plan, allowing **Paul Revere**, a local silversmith active in the Sons of Liberty, to make plans of his own. He arranged for the caretaker of the Old North Church to convey information to Patriots in Charlestown about British troop movements by signaling: one lantern in the steeple meant the British were advancing by land; two meant they were coming by sea. Legend has it that the caretaker hung two lanterns that night.

Upon learning the British were on the move, Paul Revere rowed from Boston to Charlestown. From there, he raced on horseback toward Lexington. Another Patriot, **William Dawes**, rode from Boston. Together, they sounded the alarm for the militia to gather at Lexington. A third Patriot, **Samuel Prescott**, rode on to Concord. The British troops, 700 men strong, reached Lexington at dawn on April 19. About 70 minutemen were waiting for them on Lexington Green. British major John Pitcairn planned to disarm the small militia and move on, but an unexpected shot rang out, and the fight was on. When the firing ended, eight minutemen lay dead, and ten were wounded. Only one British soldier was wounded, and none were killed.

After the confrontation at Lexington, the British set out for Concord. They knew the Patriots had already hidden most of their weapons and gunpowder. When the British arrived, they burned what few arms they found. Nearby minutemen thought the British were going to burn the entire town. They rushed to the North Bridge, exchanging gunfire with a group of British soldiers who were defending it. Meanwhile, hundreds of minutemen from the surrounding countryside arrived. The British troops began marching back to Boston, but the minutemen pursued them, using **guerrilla tactics**. They ambushed the British, launching small surprise attacks from behind trees and buildings. By day's end, British casualties included over 60 dead and 200 wounded or missing. At least 39 minutemen were missing or wounded, and 49 had died in what most historians recognize as the first battle of the American Revolution.

HISTORICAL THINKING

1. **READING CHECK** How did the Intolerable Acts lead to a more organized colonial resistance?

2. **DRAW CONCLUSIONS** Why did the Battle of Lexington increase the likelihood of full-scale war breaking out between Britain and the American colonies?

3. **MAKE PREDICTIONS** How might the Continental Congress respond to the Battles of Lexington and Concord?

1.4 ◆

BOSTON COMMON
BOSTON, MASSACHUSETTS

Once used as an encampment for British soldiers during the American Revolution, Boston Common was the place where Americans, including George Washington and John Adams, gathered to celebrate their new independence from England. It was a place for antislavery speeches, Vietnam War protests, and rallies for civil rights—its grounds dedicated to free speech and public assembly.

Established in 1634, Boston Common is America's oldest public park. In the 1800s, residents leveled 50 acres of land where cows once grazed and added trees, fountains, and statues to transform the park into the popular public space we know today. Like Central Park in New York City, Boston Common embodies the trend in American cities to preserve nature within crowded areas of urban development.

CRITICAL VIEWING The sprawling Boston Common features landscaped paths, ballfields, a children's play area, and a pond for skating in the winter and splashing in the summer. Based on details in this photograph, how would you describe the urban setting that surrounds the park and the role the park likely plays in the city of Boston?

MOVING TOWARD INDEPENDENCE

The element of surprise is a powerful tool in war. An unexpected advance can send entire armies into disarray. One morning in 1775, British troops awoke to find the Continental Army right on top of them. They had to act quickly if they were going to survive.

THE SECOND CONTINENTAL CONGRESS

As many delegates at the First Continental Congress had expected, Parliament and King George ignored their list of grievances, so a **Second Continental Congress** convened on May 10, 1775. Many of those present had attended the First Continental Congress. The Second Continental Congress elected John Hancock from Massachusetts as its first president. A New York delegate named **John Jay** replaced Hancock as president in 1778. Other prominent delegates included Charles Carroll from Maryland, who was a radical member of the Board of War. John Witherspoon from New Jersey was an educator who had taught several other members of the Congress. A delegate from Pennsylvania, Benjamin Rush, published revolutionary newspaper articles promoting independence from Britain.

Early on, the Congress established the Continental Army. They named George Washington, the colonial army leader from Virginia, as its commander. Washington's job was to train recruits and maintain control over the armed forces in case war broke out. Washington proved to be an excellent choice.

Not all 65 delegates to the Second Continental Congress agreed on declaring independence or raising an army. A delegate from Pennsylvania proposed that the Congress refuse to discuss the possibility of independence during the meetings. In fact, the divide between Patriots and Loyalists within the Congress was wide. Patriots spoke of defending colonists' natural rights and liberties as a just cause. In contrast, Loyalists believed Patriot committees sometimes acted as mobs that gave individuals too much power and threatened the **rule of law**, or the idea that people and institutions are required to follow the regulations set forth by the government. Loyalists also argued that talk of a revolution threatened the stability they enjoyed as part of the British empire.

Soon after the Second Continental Congress convened, word came that a Patriot militia had won an important victory against the British at **Fort Ticonderoga**, a stronghold in northeastern New York. This significant event shifted the debate between Patriots and Loyalists to how effective military action would be in forcing Great Britain to accept their demands for change.

VICTORY AT FORT TICONDEROGA

In the early morning hours of May 10, 1775—the very day the Second Continental Congress first convened—**Ethan Allen**, a Patriot and military leader from Vermont, and **Benedict Arnold**, a captain from Connecticut, stood on the shore of Lake Champlain in northeastern New York. With them were about 300 members of a militia known as the Green Mountain Boys. They planned to use boats to cross the lake to Fort Ticonderoga and overtake the 40 people there.

Transporting the soldiers to the fort took longer than Allen and Arnold expected. Dawn quickly approached. Afraid they might lose the element of surprise, the commanders gave the order for the soldiers who had made the crossing to attack the southern gate of the fort. Without firing a shot, the men took the fort, gaining the first victory for the Patriot cause.

The colonial forces gained many advantages from their victory at Fort Ticonderoga. First, the fort's location was a key access point to towns in nearby British-held Canada and the Hudson River Valley.

A map from 1758 details Fort Ticonderoga's location on the shore of a long, narrow lake in northern New York State. The lake had become a key travel route for transporting soldiers between New France and the American colonies.

Redoubt finish'd by the orders of Monsr de Pontleroy

Place of Arms

Sarre

Redoubt which covers the Lower Town

LOWER TOWN

Stockaded

2nd Bat.ⁿ of Berry during the Action

Folses a Loup

Wooden Warehouse

HOSPITAL

The Place where Battoes & Canoes are Laid up

CRITICAL VIEWING Built in 1755 by the French, the fort has a star shape that allowed cannons to be positioned along the perimeter to reach every part of the battlefield. This architectural style is called a bastion fort. What other features do you observe in the photograph and on the map that might aid soldiers in battle?

With the capture of the fort, the Patriots blocked an important British military transit route between Canada and New York City. Without a direct way to transport troops, the British Army splintered. Also, capturing the artillery at Fort Ticonderoga provided the Continental Army with cannons and other pieces of heavy artillery at a time when munitions were in short supply. Less than a year later, the Patriots used these weapons to mount a successful attack on British forces in Boston, Massachusetts.

BATTLE OF BUNKER HILL

By April 1775, the British Army in Boston numbered about 5,000 troops, who positioned themselves throughout the city and the surrounding villages and towns. The British knew that by seizing control of Charlestown, they could prevent the Patriots from mounting an attempt to capture Boston. The British also saw an advantage in Charlestown's harbor. They sent long-distance communications by boat, so the harbor offered the British a base from which to stay in touch with their other forces. They planned to capture Charlestown's two hills, Bunker Hill and Breed's Hill, which provided clear views for observing Boston. But the Patriots had no intention of allowing the British to succeed.

George Washington ordered General Israel Putnam to lead a force of about 1,000 soldiers to block the British. On the night of June 16, 1775, Putnam's men marched to the hills above Charlestown and built **earthworks**, or human-made land modifications, to fortify their position on Breed's Hill. They also built small fortifications on Bunker Hill that would serve as a fallback point in case they needed to retreat.

The British awoke the next morning to find the Patriots overlooking their positions in Charlestown. General Thomas Gage instructed his soldiers to fire cannons at the Patriots. He ordered more than 2,000 troops to cross the Charles River and capture Breed's Hill. The British formed a line at the bottom of the hill and began their first charge. Through a stroke of luck, they had received the wrong size cannonballs from their armory, which meant their cannons were useless. Patriot General Putnam, keenly aware that his troops were also running out of ammunition, ordered his men to wait to open fire.

Well protected behind their earthworks, the Patriots forced the British to retreat, but the British soon regrouped and mounted a second charge. This charge was also unsuccessful, and soon hundreds

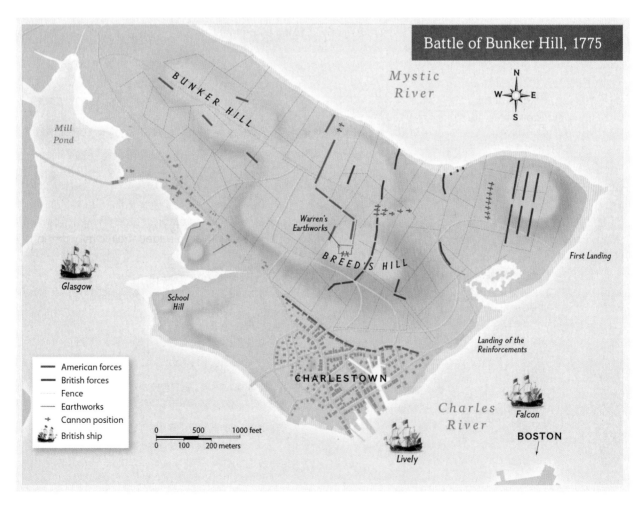

Battle of Bunker Hill, 1775

of British soldiers and officers lay dead or wounded. Forced to retreat for a second time, the British generals recognized that traditional fighting tactics would be unsuccessful. They ordered their troops to take off their knapsacks and coats so they would be more mobile. Colonel William Prescott, the commander, is said to have told his men, "Don't fire until you can see the whites of their eyes."

By the time the British advanced on Breed's Hill for the third time, the Patriots were resorting to throwing stones at them. General Putnam commanded his troops to retreat to Bunker Hill, but after a few unsuccessful attempts to defend it, he ordered a full retreat. In the end, more than 200 British soldiers and 100 Patriots lost their lives, and more than 750 British and 300 Patriots were wounded at the **Battle of Bunker Hill**. The British won the battle, but they suffered a great number of casualties, and fighting for control of the city of Boston continued. They realized that defeating the American colonists would be neither quick nor easy.

This Hessian brass drum was recovered from the Battle of Bennington in 1777. The sling in front was worn over the shoulder, leaving the drummer's hands free to hold drumsticks.

PEACE REJECTED

After the Battle of Bunker Hill, delegates from every colony except Georgia drafted a letter to King George, known as the **Olive Branch Petition**. The letter expressed hope for reconciliation while repeating the colonists' grievances against the Intolerable Acts. The colonists claimed that British "hostilities . . . have compelled us to arm in our own defense," but they made it clear that they were protesting Parliament's actions and were still loyal to Great Britain. King George did not believe them, though, and in August 1775, he declared without reading the petition that the colonists were in "open and avowed rebellion." In October, he stated that the colonists' actions were "carried on for the purpose of establishing an independent empire."

The king's statement dashed many Loyalists' hopes for reconciliation. They believed that the king had not realized how the Parliament's crippling

legislation would affect the colonists. The king's dismissal of the petition proved that he knew the consequences of the laws. Additionally, Parliament passed the Prohibitory Act on December 22, 1775, which authorized a blockade of all American ports to prevent any trade. Then the king made a deal with Germany allowing Britain to hire fierce German soldiers called **Hessians** and send them to North America. The Hessians were **mercenaries**, or soldiers for hire, who fought for whomever paid them. These acts increased tension between the Patriots and the British. John Adams noted that the blockade "throws the thirteen colonies out of the royal protections . . . and makes us independent in spite of our supplications and entreaties." However, many Loyalists continued to support efforts for reconciliation.

Attempting to divide the colonists even further, British authorities encouraged enslaved people in North America to revolt, claiming that their freedom rested on British military success. But the British only promised such freedom to those who fought on their side. Meanwhile, the colonists told enslaved people that the British were attempting to lure them away only to resell them in the West Indies, a much harsher place to be enslaved than the American colonies. With these conflicting narratives, enslaved people faced a tough decision. Predictably, some chose to join the British while others pledged their loyalty to the Patriot cause.

HISTORICAL THINKING

1. **READING CHECK** What was the significance of the Olive Branch Petition?

2. **ANALYZE CAUSE AND EFFECT** How did the capture of Fort Ticonderoga impact the Patriots' ability to wage war against Britain?

3. **DISTINGUISH FACT FROM OPINION** Was King George's claim that the colonies were taking actions "for the purpose of establishing an independent empire" fact or opinion? Explain your answer.

DECLARING INDEPENDENCE

Sometimes working as a team means putting differences aside for the greater good. In the years leading up to the American Revolution, people who held wildly differing views worked together to establish a government for all citizens. It was a tremendous undertaking.

HOSTILITIES AND *COMMON SENSE*

Two weeks after the Battle of Bunker Hill, George Washington arrived in Cambridge, Massachusetts, near Boston, to take charge of the Continental Army. Upset by the disorder he discovered there, Washington set out to instill strict discipline among the existing troops. He also began training new recruits whom he hoped would defeat the organized British troops.

In September 1775, the Second Continental Congress sent General Richard Montgomery and 1,200 members of the militia on a mission to attack Quebec City, a British military stronghold in Canada. Along the way, Montgomery's men battled British troops in Canada. But when they joined General Benedict Arnold's troops at their destination on December 31, the attack ended in a disastrous defeat. Montgomery died in the Battle of Quebec, and 400 Patriots were killed, captured, or wounded. Despite this loss, Benedict Arnold continued fighting against the British forces there.

Meanwhile, the fight for control of Boston raged on. In late January 1776, cannons, other artillery, and gunpowder from Fort Ticonderoga arrived. On the night of March 4, Washington had the cannons hauled to the top of a hill south of the city, which had clear views of the British troops below. Yet again, British soldiers awoke in the morning to find enemy guns aimed at them. General **William Howe** recognized he had been outmaneuvered. "These fellows have done more work in one night than I could make my army do in three months," he remarked. Washington agreed to allow the 10,000 British soldiers to evacuate safely in exchange for Britain's pledge not to burn the city as they went. The last of the British troops exited Boston on March 17, 1776. Howe sent his men to Nova Scotia, Canada, to regroup and resupply.

PRIMARY SOURCE

The cause of America is in a great measure the cause of all mankind. Many circumstances hath, and will arise, which are not local, but universal, and through which the principles of all Lovers of Mankind are affected, and in the Event of which, their Affections are interested. The laying a Country desolate with Fire and Sword, declaring War against the natural rights of all Mankind, and extirpating [destroying] *the Defenders thereof from the Face of the Earth, is the Concern of every Man.*

—from *Common Sense*, by Thomas Paine, February 14, 1776

Some members of the Second Continental Congress still wanted to reconcile with Britain even though battles had already taken place. The protection and stable economy that the British empire offered to colonists remained powerful reasons for their loyalty. But on January 9, 1776, as Arnold's campaign in Canada was failing and Patriots **mobilized** to protect the South from the British, **Thomas Paine** published a small pamphlet titled *Common Sense*.

Common Sense explained the struggle between the colonists and Britain from a new perspective. Rather than attacking King George directly, Paine defined the colonists' struggles as a question of how they wanted to be governed. Did they wish to have a representative democracy, or did they wish to continue to be ruled by a king or queen? Paine clearly chose the former. He called on colonists to declare independence, and he urged colonial merchants to break their ties to London businesses and expand their trade with other European countries for the sake of the colonial economy. "We have it in our power to begin the world over again," he wrote.

DRAFTING THE DECLARATION

The popularity of *Common Sense* spread rapidly among the growing number of Patriots both in the Congress and in the general public. In April 1776, the North Carolina delegates to the Congress pledged to vote in favor of independence. In May, New Jersey Patriots removed the last royal governor in the colonies from office. *Common Sense* won the endorsement of George Washington and many other leading Patriots, including Jonathan Trumbull, Sr., of Connecticut—the only colonial governor to favor independence. Loyalists, on the other hand, believed Paine's ideas were unrealistic and dangerous.

By the summer of 1776, 150,000 copies of *Common Sense* were in circulation. Colonists began destroying royal images and removing royal symbols from public buildings in their communities. A statue of King George in New York City was melted down for bullets by female volunteers

and used against British troops. The setting was now ripe for the Congress to draft a statement declaring the colonies' independence.

On June 11, 1776, the Congress chose five delegates—**Thomas Jefferson**, John Adams, Benjamin Franklin, Roger Sherman, and Robert Livingston—to draft a declaration of independence. The delegates became known as the **Committee of Five**. Among them, they selected Jefferson, a young politician and lawyer from Virginia, to write the official draft of the document. Jefferson had become famous for his writing skills through his publication of "A Summary View of the Rights of British America" in 1774, in which he argued that Parliament did not have authority over the colonies.

Jefferson incorporated many Enlightenment ideas into the **Declaration of Independence**, particularly John Locke's notions of natural rights and the existence of the social contract formed between people and their governments. Each section of the Declaration had a unique purpose. It began with a **preamble**, or introductory statement, which laid out the reasons colonists were declaring independence. A list of violations committed by King George followed, including the king's failure to approve certain laws created by colonial governments, his interruption of colonial trade,

The Committee of Five discuss the future of the country in this painting by Alonzo Chappel. He finished this piece in the 1850s as part of a series titled *The Drafting of the Declaration of Independence*.

U.S. Capitol Rotunda
Washington, D.C.

The painting is the first of four Revolutionary-era scenes that the U.S. Congress commissioned from painter John Trumbull. The artist had created a smaller version of this painting to document the events of the American Revolution, and he enlarged it for the Rotunda between August 1817 and September 1818. It was installed in 1826, along with three other Trumbull paintings.

and his levying of taxes without permission. The next section suggested that British citizens had ignored several appeals for justice from the colonists. The document concluded by declaring the newly independent nation as the United States of America, casting off all ties to Britain and pledging an oath that all states (all former colonies) supported the declaration.

The Committee presented the first draft of the Declaration to the Congress on June 28, 1776. However, delegates withdrew the draft because it included statements that morally objected to the institution of slavery and the slave trade. Those sentences were later deleted to gain the support from southern, as well as some northern, colonies.

APPROVING THE DECLARATION

By July 2, 1776, all of the colonial delegations except that of New York had a majority vote to approve the Declaration of Independence. The New York delegation approved it on July 9. However, there were individual holdouts. Some members of the Congress refused to sign it unless Jefferson withdrew statements that condemned the British people since many colonists wanted to avoid a direct attack on a culture to which they still felt connected. Jefferson made these revisions.

On July 19, the Congress titled the document "The Unanimous Declaration of the Thirteen United States of America," officially recognizing the new nation by this name. By August 2, most delegates had signed it. Newspapers printed copies, and colonists posted it on the doors of public buildings throughout the country. General George Washington instructed his officers to read it to the troops. Celebrations erupted throughout the nation, encouraging many Loyalists to support the Patriot cause. Suddenly, the Declaration had shifted the colonists' cause to a fight

for a united American republic instead of a struggle against Parliament in the king's name. You can read the Declaration of Independence in its entirety in the Citizenship Handbook.

CREATING A GOVERNMENT

On July 12, 1776, members of the Congress submitted their first draft of the **Articles of Confederation**, a list of resolutions loosely uniting the 13 states under a central government. The authors had worked hard to write resolutions that balanced the power of a central government with the power of state governments. The Articles created a central government with limited authority. For example, the government did not have the power to tax the states. The Articles also gave each state delegation one vote. This equalized the power of

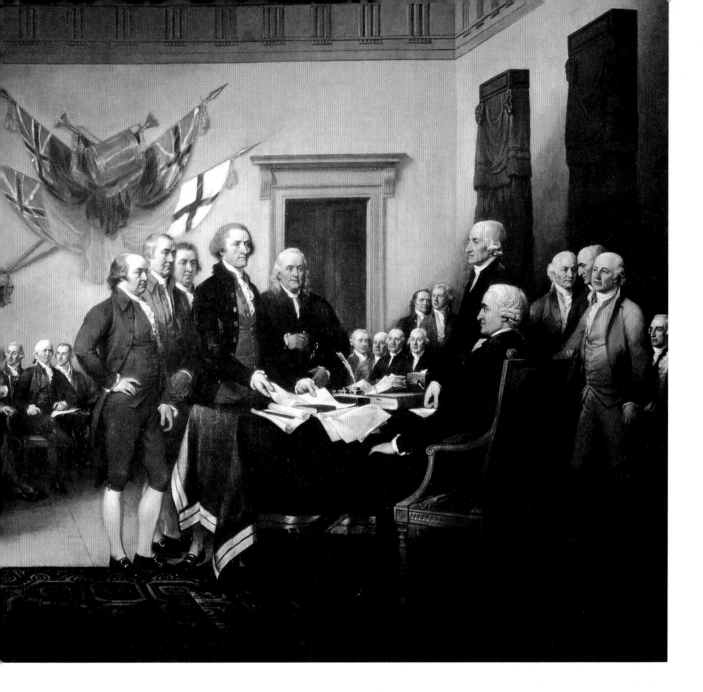

states with large and small populations. For the Congress to approve any act, nine states had to vote in favor of the proposal. And to avoid the creation of an elite political class, delegates to the Congress could only serve for three years.

While delegates agreed on the structure of government created by the Articles, the Congress did not **ratify**, or formally approve, the document until 1781. This delay was due to some states' unresolved disputes over claims of lands outside the 13 colonies. States that held claims, such as Virginia, resisted giving up the land. States without claims wanted the central government to take control. In the end, the states without claims won, and the Congress ratified the Articles soon after. The Articles served as the foundation for the national government until 1789.

A FOUNDATION FOR THE COUNTRY

Although the Declaration of Independence is not a legally binding document in the same way the U.S. Constitution and the Bill of Rights are, it is the basis on which the United States was founded. As such, it holds pride of place with the other two founding documents in the Rotunda for the Charters of Freedom in the National Archives Museum in Washington, D.C.

In addition to the founding documents, the archives house the population censuses taken every ten years since 1790, significant treaties, and military and naturalization records for all soldiers and immigrants in the United States. But the archives do not keep every government document. Only those files that are deemed valuable are kept, which works out to be between 2 and 5 percent of the federal records generated annually.

CRITICAL VIEWING Why is it important for a country to showcase historical documents, such as the Declaration of Independence?

DOCUMENT ONE

**Primary Source: Legal Document
from the Declaration of Independence, 1776**

The goal of the Declaration was to unite the colonies as one nation. To accomplish this goal, the colonists informed King George that he no longer held power over them, and why.

CONSTRUCTED RESPONSE What does this excerpt suggest about the colonists' reasons for declaring independence?

When in the Course of human events, it becomes necessary for one people to dissolve the political bands which have connected them with another, and to assume among the powers of the earth, the separate and equal station to which the Laws of Nature and of Nature's God entitle them, a decent respect to the opinions of mankind requires that they should declare the causes which impel them to the separation.

DOCUMENT TWO

**Primary Source: Legal Document
from the Declaration of Independence, 1776**

The colonists listed a set of principles for how they believed a government should treat its citizens. The Declaration was written in accordance with these principles.

CONSTRUCTED RESPONSE What beliefs about the origin and purpose of government did the colonists hold?

We hold these truths to be self-evident, that all men are created equal; that they are endowed by their Creator with certain unalienable rights; that among these are Life, Liberty, and the pursuit of Happiness; that, to secure these rights, governments are instituted among Men, deriving their just powers from the consent of the governed; that whenever any form of government becomes destructive of these ends, it is the right of the people to alter or to abolish it, and to institute new government, laying its foundation on such principles, and organizing its powers in such form, as to them shall seem most likely to effect their safety and happiness.

DOCUMENT THREE

**Primary Source: Legal Document
from the Declaration of Independence, 1776**

The Declaration ends with a list of human rights violations the colonists felt Great Britain had committed against them. They state that these violations justify their act of separating from the British empire.

CONSTRUCTED RESPONSE Why did the colonists feel it was their duty to establish independence?

When a long train of abuses and usurpations [illegal seizures of power], pursuing invariably the same object, evinces a design to reduce them under absolute despotism, it is their right, it is their duty, to throw off such government, and to provide new guards for their future security. Such has been the patient sufferance of these colonies; and such is now the necessity which constrains them to alter their former systems of government. The history of the present King of Great Britain is a history of repeated injuries and usurpations, all having in direct object the establishment of an absolute tyranny over these states.

Read the full Declaration of Independence in the Citizenship Handbook.

SYNTHESIZE AND WRITE

1. **REVIEW** Review what you have learned about the writing and adoption of the Declaration of Independence.

2. **RECALL** On your own paper, write the main idea expressed in each excerpt of the document. Remember that main ideas should be supported by details from the excerpt.

3. **CONSTRUCT** Construct a topic sentence that answers this question: In what ways did the colonists feel Great Britain had violated their civil rights?

4. **WRITE** Write a paragraph that supports the statement in Step 3 using evidence from the excerpts.

3.1

MAIN IDEA From late 1776 to late 1777, the Continental Army suffered major defeats that threatened to end the colonists' efforts to achieve independence.

MILITARY STRATEGY IN THE EARLY STAGES

Success in a competition often comes from knowing your own and your opponent's weaknesses and strengths. For a year, the well-trained and well-armed British Army dealt devastating losses to the Continental Army. But a weakness in the British plan let the Continental Army win an important victory that kept the colonists' hope for independence alive.

TWO ARMIES

As you might expect, the British military had distinct advantages over the Continental Army—it had the world's most powerful army and navy and had defeated its fiercest rivals, France and Spain, in several conflicts over the previous century. It was also well equipped and well supplied by Great Britain's strong central government. The British had the support of Loyalists throughout the colonies, including the Mohawk and a number of other Native American tribes and nations. Nearly 25,000 colonists would directly support British military actions during the war.

On the other hand, the Continental Army had its own strengths, which the British underestimated. First, most Americans had a strong belief in the cause of independence and self-government. Furthermore, Americans had a much more detailed knowledge of the local terrain, which gave them an

🏛 Museum of the American Revolution
Philadelphia, Pennsylvania

William Waller, a soldier from Virginia, stored gun powder in the horn shown below. The horn was from a cow, an ox, or a buffalo. Ornate drawings, slogans, and personal information were necessary to identify the horn's owner if it went missing. British and Hessian soldiers captured Waller at a battle near New York City in 1776. A British officer most likely wore the silver gorget at right to protect himself from enemy fire. A gorget is a piece of armor military officers wore to show their rank. The ornamentation on this piece indicates that its owner held a high position.

British gorget

Revolutionary powder horn

advantage in battles. These factors contributed to the rise of resourceful American military leaders who were determined to use every strategy and resource necessary to win the nation's freedom.

Both forces had weaknesses, too. For the British, keeping troops supplied was a logistic and financial challenge. Ships carrying men, weapons, and food from Britain took months to reach North America. Distribution of those resources took time because the British Army was stationed up and down the eastern coast of the continent. British citizens quickly voiced concern about the cost of the war. In addition, the British soldiers found themselves far from home in a vast, unfamiliar country as they tried to control the widespread, rebellious colonists, move supplies over rough land and dangerous waters, and engage in combat. And some British generals hastily misjudged their enemy, which kept them from coordinating their own strategies effectively.

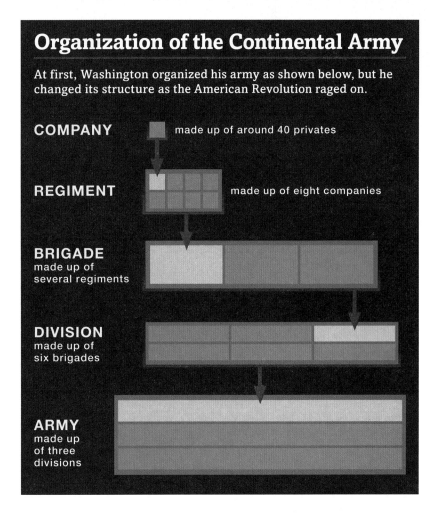

Organization of the Continental Army

At first, Washington organized his army as shown below, but he changed its structure as the American Revolution raged on.

COMPANY — made up of around 40 privates

REGIMENT — made up of eight companies

BRIGADE made up of several regiments

DIVISION made up of six brigades

ARMY made up of three divisions

For its part, the Continental Army suffered from a woeful lack of training and discipline. It was constantly confronted by a shortage of supplies and ammunition and was so poorly funded that troops often received no payment for their service. Called to action by the Congress, soldiers followed their leaders into battles while worrying about the families and livelihoods they left behind. Meanwhile, the Articles of Confederation had stripped the Congress of the authority to collect taxes to pay the military or even to provide blankets and food.

General Washington quickly devised a plan to unite citizen-soldiers and state militias into a disciplined Continental Army. His first step was to create a structure similar to that used by the British Army, which was divided into smaller and smaller groups. Washington structured the Continental Army with even more levels of command, from brigades of thousands of soldiers to companies of about 40 privates. By organizing the troops into manageable groups, Washington's generals and officers could train and instill discipline more easily. In addition, troops could be more readily **deployed**, or put to use, in battle as large brigades or small companies, depending on what strategy was needed.

To increase the odds of winning the war, Washington tried to unite the army in two ways. First, he brought together state militias and regular forces under commanders from their own regions, so they could remain connected to the homes they were fighting for. But Washington also knew that his army had to represent the diversity of the new nation. To that end, he persuaded the Congress to recruit soldiers for long terms of service and organized them into regiments with soldiers from different regions.

AMERICAN LOSSES IN NEW YORK

Knowing the weaknesses of the Continental Army, British generals expected a rapid, victorious end to the conflict. They launched a plan to crush the rebellion by taking control of the Hudson River Valley and New York City, dividing the northern colonies from the middle and southern colonies. Because the British believed New England to be the stronghold of the Revolution, they hoped to cut off that region's supply lines. Colonists would certainly reconsider supporting the war if shipments of food and supplies stopped. The British also believed that large numbers of Loyalists in the middle and southern colonies would then welcome back British rule.

They decided to capture the city first. On August 22, 1776, Howe landed 20,000 troops on Long Island and overpowered General Washington and the 10,000 Continental soldiers stationed there, forcing them to retreat. On September 15, Howe's forces landed at Kip's Bay on the eastern side of Manhattan, where, once again, they soundly defeated the Continental Army. The Americans retreated a second time to the northern tip of Manhattan. They defended the stronghold at Harlem Heights for another month.

The defeat in New York City was a disaster for Washington and the Continental Army. About 2,000 men were killed, wounded, or captured, and about half of the remaining enlisted soldiers' terms of service were scheduled to expire by the end of the year. Reinforcements came from other regiments, swelling the army to about 5,000 soldiers, but Washington knew that he needed a win to gain the numbers required to defeat the British.

Through October and November 1776, Howe's forces continued to advance west, capturing 3,000 Continental soldiers at Fort Washington north of Harlem and forcing the rest into full retreat across the Hudson River and into New Jersey. Howe dispatched General **Charles Cornwallis** and his soldiers to pursue them. By December, Washington's force—which now consisted of 2,400 men—retreated to Pennsylvania.

VICTORY AT TRENTON

Meanwhile, Howe called off Cornwallis's pursuit of General Washington and ordered Cornwallis's troops to set up winter quarters at various locations across New Jersey, including Princeton and Trenton. Among those fighting for Britain were Hessian mercenaries, about 30,000 of whom served the British Army throughout the course of the American Revolution.

On the night of December 25, Washington and his men stealthily crossed the icy Delaware River and launched an attack on Hessian **garrisons**, or station posts, at Trenton. Early the following morning, they converged on the town. In only an hour and a half, the Continental Army took the city, killing 22 Hessians and capturing another 918 at the **Battle of**

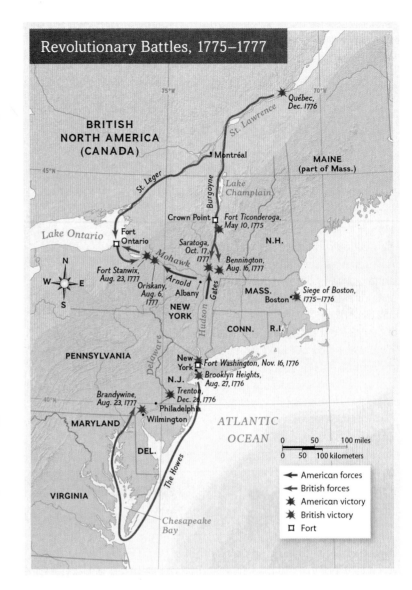

Revolutionary Battles, 1775–1777

Legend:
← American forces
← British forces
✴ American victory
✴ British victory
☐ Fort

Trenton. The Americans only suffered two dead and five wounded. Encouraged by this victory, more men stayed on and continued fighting the British.

A few days after their defeat at Trenton, Cornwallis and his troops returned to the city, hoping to win it back. On the night of January 2, 1777, Washington instructed his men to light campfires before telling them to evacuate their camps. His deception fooled the British into believing that the Continental Army had not moved during the night. The next morning, Washington launched a surprise attack, inflicting heavy losses on three British regiments at Princeton, a town about 13 miles from Trenton. Howe called most of his remaining troops to New Brunswick, Canada, and British hopes for a speedy end to the war disappeared.

DEFEAT AT PHILADELPHIA

In the spring of 1777, British generals William Howe and **John Burgoyne**, in addition to Lieutenant Colonel **Barry St. Leger**, coordinated a new plan involving three armies. Burgoyne would march from Canada, St. Leger from western New York, and Howe from New York City to take control of the Hudson River Valley. They would join forces at Albany.

Burgoyne and St. Leger and their armies made their way from Canada and waited for Howe's arrival to attack Saratoga. However, Howe had changed his plan. He had decided it would be a good time to attack Philadelphia, the capital city of the new, rebellious nation. He thought the attack would send a strong message to the Americans about the futility of continuing the war. Capturing Philadelphia would also give Britain the advantage of controlling both major shipping and overland supply routes in North America. Because the three men were communicating by letter through their superiors in Britain, the men did not know each other's whereabouts.

In August, General Howe and his brother, Admiral Richard Howe, sailed with 13,000 troops from New York to the Chesapeake Bay. From there, they marched toward Philadelphia. As Washington tried and failed to block the British advance, the Continental Congress fled the capital. Although Washington's soldiers mounted an attack on British-held Germantown on October 4, the British defeated them. Howe's army soon took control of Philadelphia and Germantown. Over the next month and a half, British forces captured key forts along the Delaware River, allowing Howe to establish supply lines and enabling him to control the entire region. Washington retreated, settling his troops into winter quarters, 20 miles northwest of Germantown.

HISTORICAL THINKING

1. **READING CHECK** What steps did Washington take to form and strengthen the Continental Army?

2. **INTERPRET VISUALS** About how many brigades were in the Continental Army?

3. **COMPARE AND CONTRAST** How were the advantages and disadvantages of the Continental Army different from those of the British military?

4. **INTERPRET MAPS** How many battles did the Americans win between 1775 and 1777?

General Washington (center left, standing) surveys the opposite shore in Emanuel Leutze's 1851 oil painting *Washington Crossing the Delaware*. On December 25, 1776, Washington and his army crossed the river on their way to attack Hessian troops in Trenton, New Jersey.

SARATOGA AND VALLEY FORGE

Keeping an opponent guessing about your next move can be a winning strategy. Both the British and the Americans used this tactic, but the Americans had to learn quickly how best to employ the element of surprise as they fought a much larger and better-equipped enemy.

AMERICAN VICTORY AT SARATOGA

As you have read, while the Howe brothers were on their way to attack Philadelphia, British general John Burgoyne was in Canada, preparing his march southward to gain control of the Hudson River Valley and overtake Albany, New York. He began his march with about 8,500 British, Hessian, and Canadian soldiers and almost 1,000 Native American warriors. Burgoyne might not have known that when General William Howe set sail to capture Philadelphia, he took most of his men with him, leaving a much smaller unit behind in New York City. Howe had no intention of leaving Philadelphia for Albany, so his decision left Burgoyne without the reinforcements he expected. And Burgoyne made some mistakes of his own.

At first, the plan to converge on Albany seemed to be working. Sailing southward on Lake Champlain, Burgoyne's forces easily recaptured Fort Ticonderoga in early July 1777. Greatly outnumbered by the British, the Continental soldiers abandoned the fort under cover of darkness and retreated south to the Hudson River.

After that victory, however, Burgoyne's progress slowed considerably. First, he had overloaded his troops with a mix of necessities and luxuries— along with heavy supplies and artillery. Soldiers also dragged cartloads of Burgoyne's personal possessions. Second, the rough terrain stalled the British as they marched on wilderness trails through marshes, ravines, and creeks swollen from rain. And finally, the Continental forces used guerrilla tactics to impede Burgoyne. They destroyed bridges, cut down trees and used them to block the path, and dug trenches to flood trails. British progress was reduced to one mile a day.

As Burgoyne was struggling to move south, St. Leger and his troops were advancing on Albany from the west. But St. Leger and a large group of Mohawk became involved in a 21-day siege at Fort Stanwix in the Mohawk Valley on their way to meet Burgoyne. When St. Leger learned that a substantial number of Continental reinforcements were marching toward the fort, he pulled his men out and headed north to Canada. Now, both St. Leger and Howe had abandoned the plan to capture the Hudson River Valley. Unaware that he was the only one still headed there, Burgoyne marched to Albany.

Meanwhile, forces of the Continental Army under the command of General **Horatio Gates** gathered along the Hudson River near Saratoga. With the help of Polish military engineer Tadeusz Kościuszko (tah-DAY-oosh kos-CHOOS-koh), the Continental troops had built fortified walls along Bemis Heights, overlooking the Hudson River and the nearby road, so they could see the British coming and fire on them. On September 19, 1777, the Americans and the British clashed at what is now called the First Battle of Saratoga, or the Battle of Freeman's Farm. Burgoyne's soldiers failed to cross Gates's lines. On October 7, Burgoyne attempted another attack, but General Benedict Arnold's unit drove the British back to their camp. This was the Second Battle of Saratoga.

By October 17, with the arrival of yet more Continental soldiers, Gates's forces numbered 20,000 or more. That was almost four times the strength of Burgoyne's army. Burgoyne sent out a desperate but futile call for reinforcements. The Americans surrounded him and cut his supply lines, forcing him to surrender. Upon learning about

CRITICAL VIEWING General John Burgoyne (center left, in red) surrenders to General Horatio Gates (center, in blue) after the Battle of Saratoga. Painter John Trumbull used elements of composition in his 1821 painting *Surrender of General Burgoyne* to portray the transaction as peaceful. What details do you notice in the painting that indicate this?

Burgoyne's defeat at Saratoga, both General Howe and Admiral Howe resigned. In 1778, General Henry Clinton took command of the British forces in North America.

The victory at Saratoga was a vital turning point in the American Revolution. In showing that they could defeat a large, professional army, the Americans impressed the French government. Despite having secretly sent money and military supplies to the Americans since 1776, France had yet to declare an official alliance. Finally convinced that the Americans could win the war, the French government negotiated in Paris with Benjamin Franklin. They signed a treaty in 1778 making the alliance official. Now the Americans had the backing of a wealthy nation with a large navy.

VALLEY FORGE

Meanwhile, after his defeat in Philadelphia, George Washington set up winter camp at **Valley Forge**. Valley Forge sat on a plateau above a series of hills in a forested area, which formed a natural protective barrier around the camp. About 11,000 men and 500 women and children lived there in wooden huts built by the men, but the winter of 1777–1778 was brutally harsh. Everyone suffered without enough clothing, blankets, or food. Washington remained at Valley Forge to share his troops' hardships, although he lived in a stone house and enjoyed somewhat better living conditions.

Despite the weather, the soldiers spent the winter training. In February 1778, **Friedrich von Steuben** (FREE-drihk von STOO-buhn), a former Prussian Army officer and expert in military tactics, arrived at Valley Forge. He instructed the Continental Army on how to care for their weapons, use the bayonet, march in drill formations, and plan their movements in the field, emphasizing the importance of taking care of their fellow soldiers. Von Steuben's training prepared the Continental Army to fight the British on equal terms. Unfortunately, the bitterly cold winter cost the lives of approximately 2,500 men in Washington's troop.

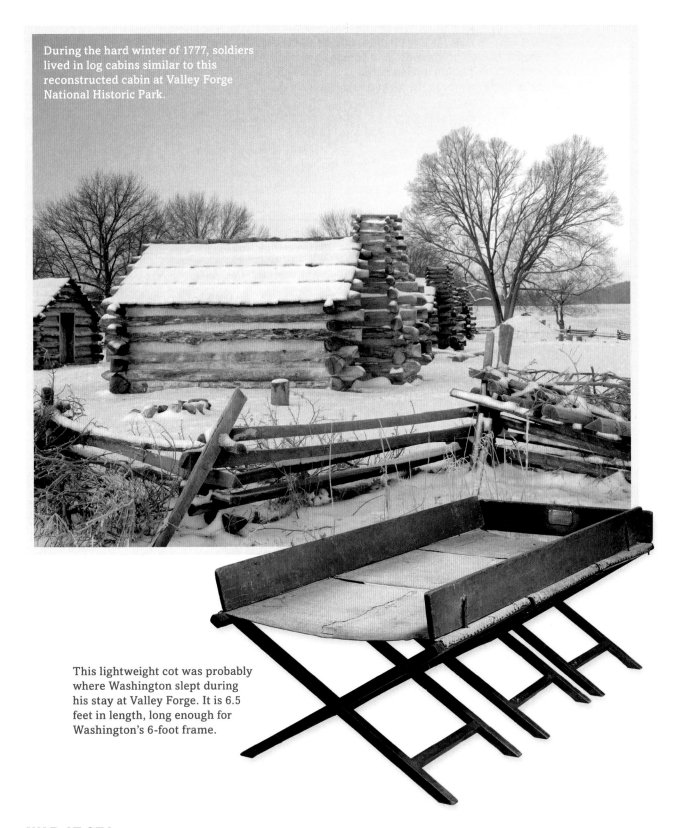

During the hard winter of 1777, soldiers lived in log cabins similar to this reconstructed cabin at Valley Forge National Historic Park.

This lightweight cot was probably where Washington slept during his stay at Valley Forge. It is 6.5 feet in length, long enough for Washington's 6-foot frame.

WAR AT SEA

The soldiers in the Continental Army were discovering that they could defend themselves and defeat their enemy by using the terrain and the element of surprise to their advantage. But the new Continental Navy, officially established by the Congress in 1775, had fewer advantages. It lacked both funding and time to build more ships. The lack of money made hiring and adequately training sailors to fight Britain's vastly superior Royal Navy difficult. From the earliest days of the war, the need for American sailors to defend themselves against the British Navy had been great. The British seized or harassed American merchant ships and routinely blockaded harbors up and down the coast.

By 1777, the Continental Navy had about 18 ships. The Royal Navy boasted almost 260. Looking for a strategy to overcome their naval disadvantage, the Americans relied on a common maritime practice known as *guerre de course*, or "war of the chase," which allowed private ships to attack the merchant ships of an enemy power. The American government hired these **privateers**, or privately owned ships authorized to participate in war. The Continental Navy deployed privateers, often in pairs or with naval ships, to capture British equipment and supplies if possible, and to disrupt and delay British shipping in the Atlantic and around the Caribbean.

When Benjamin Franklin secured the help of France and Spain, two powerful navies joined the Continental Navy in battles. The United States' formal alliance with France also gave the Americans access to French ports. Now American ships could sail farther from home waters, even into the North Sea near Great Britain.

American captain **John Paul Jones**, commander of the merchant ship *Bonhomme Richard*, pursued British merchant vessels being escorted by the Royal Navy. In 1779, Jones intercepted the larger British ship H.M.S. *Serapis*. Early in the fighting, two of the *Bonhomme Richard's* cannons exploded. The ship caught fire, but the battle continued with the ships literally locked side by side in combat. According to legend, when the British captain demanded the Americans surrender, Jones replied, "I have not yet begun to fight." The British finally surrendered. By this time, the *Bonhomme Richard* was almost destroyed and sinking, so Jones and his crew boarded the *Serapis*. This was one of the most notable naval victories of the American Revolution. It boosted the morale of soldiers and civilians as the conflict moved into its final stage.

PAYING FOR WAR

You might be wondering why the Second Continental Congress didn't fund the Continental Navy. The short answer is because it couldn't. The Congress had very little money and no authority to raise it. Remember, the Articles of Confederation prohibited the Congress from taxing individual states. The country was too new to have a treasury or to borrow money on credit. So, to help pay for the navy, the army, and the war in general, the Congress began printing a new paper currency called "Continental" dollars, even though the government had no real wealth, such as stores of gold or silver, to back it up. At the beginning of June 1775, about $2 million Continental dollars were printed, but as the war dragged on, the Congress printed more money to cover its expenses. This led to rapid **inflation**, a rise in the price of goods and services that causes a decrease in the value of money.

By 1781, it took $146 to buy an item that had cost a dollar before the war. Washington even commented that "a wagon load of money will scarcely purchase a wagon load of provision." Merchants began to reject the currency. People came to view Continental currency as worthless.

Making matters worse, goods were hard to come by. For most of the war, the British controlled major ports, such as New York City and Philadelphia, negatively affecting American trade. Some merchants who supplied goods to the Continental Army participated in **profiteering**, or charging high prices for items in high demand and short supply to make a quick fortune.

Although the French, Dutch, and Spanish had granted the Americans several large loans, these funds were not enough to cover all the costs of war. To help stabilize the financial situation, the Congress turned to **Robert Morris** of Pennsylvania. As a former finance superintendent, Morris had helped the state reform its currency. The Congress hoped he could do the same for the nation. Morris chartered the First Bank of North America, which had the sole right to issue paper currency. Together with **Haym Salomon**, an American Jewish **financier**, or money broker, Morris funded the new bank with his own money, Salomon's, and some of the funds borrowed from the French. Among many Americans who loaned money to help pay the costs of the Revolution, Salomon was noted for extending large interest-free loans to the government. Never repaid for his generosity, Salomon died penniless in 1785. His and Morris's efforts helped to slow the rate of inflation and allowed Washington to continue the fight.

HISTORICAL THINKING

1. **READING CHECK** How did both an informal and formal alliance with France affect the Congress's ability to pay for the war?

2. **ANALYZE LANGUAGE USE** What did Washington mean when he stated that "a wagon load of money will scarcely purchase a wagon load of provision"?

3. **DETERMINE CHRONOLOGY** While Burgoyne's troops marched south toward the Hudson River Valley, what were the other participants in the plan to capture Albany doing?

4. **MAKE PREDICTIONS** As France enters the Revolutionary War, how might the strategies of the Continental Army and British forces change?

WOMEN'S ROLES IN THE REVOLUTION

Colonial women did not have the same rights as men, but they shared the responsibilities, hopes, and dangers of Revolutionary times. And most of the women resolved to make a difference in the fight for the nation's independence.

BEFORE THE REVOLUTION

As the possibility of war grew and debates raged, many women worked to build support for independence. You have read how the Sons of Liberty organized boycotts against the British, but it was the **Daughters of Liberty** who assured the success of the boycotts. They knew that women generally purchased the household goods, and they urged their friends and neighbors to participate. One of these women was **Sarah Morris Mifflin**. Born in Philadelphia to a prominent Quaker family, she was moved to action after the violent clashes at Lexington and Concord. Although she was wealthy, she joined others in refusing to purchase luxury items and textiles from Britain. To avoid buying British thread, Mifflin and many other women began spinning their own sewing thread and weaving their own cloth.

Other Daughters of Liberty, such as Mercy Otis Warren and **Abigail Adams**, wrote letters and articles supporting the cause of independence. Warren also wrote a series of satirical political plays that emphasized how the colonists' liberties were under attack not only by Parliament but also by corrupt royal officials within the colonies. She criticized Massachusetts governor Hutchinson for carrying out British policies and praised those who participated in the Boston Tea Party. Warren also published political pamphlets and articles in local newspapers in support of boycotts and other protests. She even urged women to be ready to take up arms. Her efforts prompted John Adams to call her the "most accomplished woman in America."

John Adams's wife, Abigail Adams, was a brilliant thinker in her own right. She influenced many Revolutionary leaders with her skillful writing about

PRIMARY SOURCES

I have retrenched every superfluous expense in my table and family. Tea I have not drank since last Christmas, nor bought a new cap or gown . . . and what I never did before, have learned to knit, and am now making stockings of wool for my servants; and this way do I throw in my might for the public good. I know this, that as free I can die but once; but as a slave I shall not be worthy of life. I have the pleasure to assure you that these are the sentiments of my sister Americans. They have sacrificed assemblies, parties of pleasure, tea-drinkings and finery, to that great spirit of patriotism which actuates all degrees of people throughout this extensive country.

—from a letter written by Sarah Morris Mifflin to a friend, 1776

I long to hear that you have declared an independency—and by the way in the new Code of Laws which I suppose it will be necessary for you to make I desire you would Remember the Ladies, and be more generous and [favorable] to them than your ancestors. Do not put such unlimited power into the hands of the Husbands. Remember all Men would be tyrants if they could. If [particular] care and attention is not paid to the Ladies we are determined to foment a [Rebellion], and will not hold ourselves bound by any Laws in which we have no voice, or Representation.

—from a letter written by Abigail Adams to her husband, 1776 liberty, independence, and fair government. In letters to her husband, she also advocated for women's rights.

DURING THE REVOLUTION

Once the war began, women's roles increased in intensity and in range of activity. To provide for themselves, their children, and other relatives while the men were at war, women stepped in to run their husbands' businesses, which ranged from blacksmithing to publishing. On the farm, women took over the entire agricultural operation.

To aid the Continental Army, women formed public fundraising organizations. In Philadelphia, **Esther Reed**, the wife of Joseph Reed, a member of Philadelphia's Committee of Correspondence, published a **broadside**, or a single sheet of printed information, called "The Sentiments of an American Woman." It called on other women to show their patriotism by supporting activities that assisted the troops. As the wife of a high-ranking member of the Continental Army, she was well aware of equipment and clothing shortages, as well as the fact that many soldiers had not received the pay promised them. Canvassing the city, Reed's group gathered donations totaling more than $300,000 in paper currency. Similar women's organizations arose throughout the middle states.

The care of sick and wounded soldiers fell to women, both on and off the battlefield. In the summer of 1775, the Congress authorized the Continental Army to hire one nurse, at a monthly salary of $2, for every 10 soldiers needing care in a military hospital. Other women, such as Catherine Greene of Rhode Island, freely opened their homes as makeshift hospitals. In army camps and near battlefields, women often cooked meals and washed clothes.

Some women engaged in **espionage**, or spying, while others fought on the battlefield. As a member of a spy ring, **Anna Smith Strong** collected intelligence on British troop and ship movements along the coast of New York. Strong notified other spies of the information she had gathered through a code based on how she hung out her laundry. For example, a black petticoat on her clothesline meant a messenger was coming. Some female camp aides, known as Molly Pitchers because they brought water to the battlefield for the soldiers and to cool the cannons, are the subjects of Revolutionary legends. Famous Molly Pitchers **Margaret Corbin** and **Mary Ludwig Hays McCauly** are both said to have taken over firing artillery in the place of their wounded husbands.

Portrait of Abigail Adams, 1785

Sixteen-year-old **Sybil Ludington** rode 40 miles on horseback to warn her father's militia and villagers along her route that British troops were approaching. **Deborah Sampson** disguised herself as a man and joined the Fourth Massachusetts Regiment. She participated in multiple battles before she became ill and was relieved of service. She managed to keep her gender a secret until her illness required medical care. Even so, Sampson received an honorable discharge and became the only woman to receive a service pension from the Continental Army.

On a daily basis, colonial women helped the fight for independence and were a major influence in building the new nation. And, while their contributions to the war effort did not bring equal rights to women immediately, they expanded women's roles in society, laying the groundwork for women's rights campaigns a century later.

HISTORICAL THINKING

1. **READING CHECK** How did women build support for war efforts before the Revolution?

2. **DRAW CONCLUSIONS** How does Abigail Adams's letter to her husband signify that the war had sparked a movement among women?

3. **FORM AND SUPPORT OPINIONS** Which women's role discussed in this lesson do you think was most significant to the war effort? Cite evidence from the text to support your opinion.

THE WAR MOVES SOUTH

As a commander in the Continental Army, news of the French entering the war might give you high hopes of a quick victory. But subsequent defeats and a shift in British strategy put the end of the war temporarily out of sight.

ASSISTANCE ARRIVES

As you've read, France had been helping the Continental Army informally by sending supplies, but the French monarchy decided to adopt a wait-and-see strategy before it formally committed to aid the new nation. However, this earlier lack of a formal alliance didn't stop individual French volunteers from joining the fight. One such volunteer was the **Marquis de Lafayette**, a young aristocrat who had served in the French royal court. He arrived in Philadelphia in July 1777. Lafayette initially served on Washington's staff before taking command of his own division. But he soon found himself back in France, assisting Benjamin Franklin and John Adams on a diplomatic mission to secure French supplies and troops for the Patriot cause. He would eventually return to lead troops in Virginia as the war moved south.

Since the French and Spanish were already allied against the British, both nations pitched in to help the American war effort, drawing Britain's military and naval attention in different directions. The French navy pulled British resources away from the mainland by luring the Royal Navy into sea battles in the West Indies. On the mainland itself, Spaniard **Bernardo de Gálvez** led Spanish troops to the Mississippi Valley to re-occupy forts formerly held by Spain. This forced Britain to divert soldiers to the region, pulling them away from the Continental Army. Then Gálvez turned his attention to Florida, where he helped defeat the British, claiming the territory for Spain.

The Marquis de Lafayette (below) was also known as the "Hero of Two Worlds" because of his leadership in both the Continental and French armies. Born into a distinguished military family, Lafayette joined the French army when he was only 14 years old.

AFRICAN-AMERICAN RECRUITS

Meanwhile, many northern states recruited free African Americans to fight in the war. Even though African Americans had fought on the Patriot side during the battles of Lexington, Concord, and Bunker Hill, George Washington initially denied men of color the right to enlist in the Continental Army. The British, on the other hand, welcomed African Americans and lured enslaved African Americans into their ranks by promising them freedom. But when the need for fresh Patriot troops became dire, Washington lifted the ban, allowing all free men to enlist.

The British strategy of offering freedom to enslaved African Americans in exchange for their military service sometimes backfired on them. **James Armistead**, an enslaved man living in Virginia, sought and received his owner's permission to enlist in the Continental Army. He came to serve under Lafayette as a spy. Posing as a runaway slave, he joined a nearby British regiment and gained its leaders' trust. The information he gathered and shared with Lafayette and Washington helped the Americans win individual battles as well as the war itself.

By 1778, a significant number of free African Americans were recruited for service, with slaves and servants occasionally being accepted as substitutes for white landowners. That year, the First Rhode Island Regiment reformed, allowing recently freed African Americans to join because the state was unable to fill its quota of troops. Eventually, recruiters accepted any African American who chose to serve, whether free or enslaved. In all, an estimated 5,000 African Americans served in the Continental Army, in state militias, or at sea.

In this commendation letter dated November 1784, the Marquis de Lafayette writes of James Armistead, "His intelligences from the enemy's camp were industriously collected and faithfully delivered. He . . . appears to me entitled to every reward his situation can admit of." The illustration of Armistead at the top is by John Blennerhasset Martin.

THE FRONTIER WAR

From the beginning of the war, many Native American tribes formed alliances with the British because they had more weapons and supplies than the Patriots. The British also held more outposts in the frontier, so Native Americans often depended on them for trade. In addition, as many Americans began to settle west of the Appalachians, Native Americans saw them as a threat to their way of life. Soon, Native Americans launched devastating attacks on frontier settlements from the Great Lakes south to Georgia.

In early 1779, Virginia dispatched troops led by Lieutenant Colonel **George Rogers Clark** to deal with Native American attacks in the western backcountry. Clark's goal was to gain control of Fort Vincennes (also known as Fort Sackville), in present-day Indiana, from the British. By capturing the fort, he hoped to reduce British support for Native American raids on American settlements. Clark's surprise attack succeeded, and with the American victory at Vincennes, British domination in the frontier began to crumble. Once Native American tribes realized the

British could no longer protect their interests, they began declaring neutrality. But although their frontier raids became less frequent, they did not end entirely.

Not all Native Americans on the frontier supported the British. The Catawba of South Carolina were a great help to the Patriots. They searched for Loyalists and escaped slaves who might aid the British and supplied food to the Patriots. After the war, the South Carolina assembly compensated them for their loyalty, refusing to support the governor's plan to claim and lease out their lands.

THE SOUTHERN CAMPAIGN

Despite the entry of the French forces into the Patriot cause, neither the Americans nor the British could claim a clear advantage in the war in the North. The two armies had reached a **stalemate**, or a tie, as they fought in New York in late 1778, so the British decided to take the war south. They knew that larger Loyalist populations existed in the South than in the North, and their strategy was to build strongholds of

This mural depicts General Francis Marion, the "Swamp Fox," and his men escaping British capture in a swamp in South Carolina in 1780. After seven hours of pursuit, the British gave up hope of finding them.

British Movements, 1778–1781

support throughout the region. In December 1778, British general Henry Clinton sent troops to Georgia and captured Savannah and Augusta.

In response, the Congress sent General Benjamin Lincoln, commander of the Southern Continental Army, to Charleston, South Carolina, to defend the city and organize a counteroffensive. The attempt, which took nearly a year to plan, resulted in a disastrous defeat for the Americans. By May 1780, the British had captured Charleston as well.

By July, desperate for a change in command, the Continental Army sent General Horatio Gates to build a new southern army. Less than a month later, the British soundly defeated Gates and his poorly prepared troops at Camden, South Carolina. By the end of August, Britain had gained control over much of South Carolina, and Clinton took part of his force back to New York. He left General Cornwallis in charge of about 8,000 soldiers. It seemed as if this strategy might just win the war for Britain, but once again, the British miscalculated. This time, they made the mistake of counting on a significant number of Loyalists to flock to their aid.

SOUTHERN PATRIOTS TURN THE TIDE

George Washington sent **Nathanael Greene**, one of his best generals, to take charge of American troops in the South. During 1780 and 1781, Greene rebuilt the army using both traditional soldiers and guerrilla forces called **irregulars**, or soldiers who joined the regular army for various periods of time. These smaller brigades of irregulars were led by Brigadier General **Thomas Sumter**, Colonel **Andrew Pickens**, and General **Francis Marion**. Marion had become famous as the "Swamp Fox" because of his ability to evade capture as he chased down the British through the swamps of Georgia and the Carolinas.

Together these officers and their troops cut British lines of communication and sabotaged local bands of Loyalists. A backcountry "civil war" erupted between Loyalists and Patriots that helped the Patriots regain control over parts of the Carolinas. This conflict also involved many African Americans who fought on both sides. On October 7, 1780, a Patriot militia defeated a large group of Loyalists at King's Mountain. This rare American victory sent the British retreating south and bolstered morale, but Britain still had the upper hand.

Two months later, General Greene arrived in North Carolina with a small force of only 1,500 men who lacked sufficient equipment and clothing. He decided their best chance was to force the British to split up and chase them through the Carolinas instead of engaging them in direct warfare. Greene split his small army into two groups. He led one, and General **Daniel Morgan** led the other. Cornwallis sent part of his force after Morgan's unit, confronting them at the **Battle of Cowpens**, in South Carolina, in January 1781. Morgan and his Continental troops decisively defeated Cornwallis. Meanwhile, in March 1781, a small force of British regulars caught up with Greene's unit at the **Guilford Courthouse** in North Carolina. Although historians give the victory to the British, it was hard-won. Cornwallis's troops suffered heavy casualties and retreated to the North Carolina coast seeking naval support.

Greene, now reunited with Daniel Morgan's troops, moved the Continental forces south to re-establish control of South Carolina and Georgia. Starting in April 1781, Greene's troops and the guerrilla brigades of Sumter, Pickens, and Marion fought two major battles in South Carolina. Although, like Guilford Courthouse, these were not American victories, they continued forcing the British to abandon their posts. One by one, Greene's soldiers picked off the remaining British garrisons, so that by September 1781, the British had retreated to a narrow strip of land near Charleston. Putting their hope in the southern Loyalists had failed. Now the British had to reconsider their strategy in the South.

HISTORICAL THINKING

1. **READING CHECK** Why did the British change their strategy at the end of 1778?

2. **DRAW CONCLUSIONS** Why was the battle at Guilford Courthouse a significant turning point in the war in the South?

3. **INTERPRET MAPS** How does the map demonstrate the strategy that General Greene and General Morgan used against British forces?

YORKTOWN AND THE LEGACY OF THE REVOLUTION

Have you noticed how some people achieve success by knowing when to act? Sometimes in war, an opportunity presents itself while your opponent hesitates. As the British commanders disagreed on strategy, George Washington and the French seized the chance to defeat the British and end the war.

BRITISH SURRENDER AT YORKTOWN

As Greene and Morgan were winning the Carolinas and Georgia back for the Americans, Cornwallis returned to Virginia to take over the command of British general Benedict Arnold—the same Benedict Arnold who had been a Patriot hero at Fort Ticonderoga at the beginning of the war. Cornwallis decided to establish a stronghold in the area and requested additional troops from New York. But his superior, General Clinton, disapproved of this plan and refused the request. Cornwallis withdrew to the peninsula at Yorktown, Virginia, where he set up camp with an army of about 8,000 men. He fortified his position with the goal of keeping the harbor open for the British.

However, Cornwallis and Clinton continued squabbling, and the delay gave the Americans and the French a golden opportunity to organize an attack. Washington had been planning to combine forces with the French to launch a land-and-sea assault on New York City, but when he learned that a large French fleet under Admiral Comte de Grasse would arrive in the Chesapeake Bay in August, he changed his mind. Washington realized that a combined

CRITICAL VIEWING In John Trumbull's painting *Surrender of Lord Cornwallis*, British soldiers walk between French (left) and American (right) troops on horseback. What details suggest the historical significance of the scene?

French-American force could attack from both land and sea to destroy Cornwallis's army before British reinforcements arrived. Washington marched south with his troops and the French soldiers commanded by Comte de Rochambeau (ROH-sham-BOH).

By the time Washington arrived in late September, the French fleet had already blockaded Chesapeake Bay, cutting off Cornwallis's escape route. The combined French and American forces now numbered around 16,000. Within weeks, the bombardments of artillery from Washington's troops forced Cornwallis to admit that he was trapped, and Yorktown was lost. General Clinton dispatched reinforcements from New York, but it was too late. Cornwallis surrendered on October 19, 1781.

Claiming illness, Cornwallis did not formally surrender by presenting his sword to Washington that day, however. His second-in-command performed the symbolic act. The British military band played a song called "The World Turned Upside Down," a fitting comment on the victory. The **Battle of Yorktown** was the last major battle of the Revolution. The British Parliament voted to end the war in 1782.

THE TREATY OF PARIS OF 1783

In negotiating peace terms, the United States had to reckon with its **adversary**, or enemy, Great Britain, as well as its allies, France and Spain. American peace commissioners Benjamin Franklin, John Jay, and John Adams shrewdly worked with each party to obtain a desirable settlement. The result was the **Treaty of Paris of 1783**. Signed on September 3, 1783, the treaty included two **provisions**, or legal conditions, that gave immediate authority to the new country. First, Great Britain recognized the United States of America as a sovereign nation. Second, the treaty established the United States' official boundaries: the Mississippi River on the west, the southern border of Canada on the north, and the border of Florida on the south. In separate agreements, Florida, which Britain had divided into **East Florida** and **West Florida**, was returned to Spain, and parts of the West Indies and Canada were ceded to France.

Besides forcing the British to remove troops from North America immediately, the treaty also secured American fishing rights off the Atlantic coasts of Newfoundland and the St. Lawrence River. In return, the Congress would prompt state governments to return property seized from Loyalists during the war and honor all prewar debts owed by citizens of each country to citizens of the other.

Not everyone was happy with the treaty. Native Americans felt that the British, ignoring the many treaties they had made over the years, had signed away their lands without the authority to do so. And despite the promises of freedom given by the British, thousands of African Americans were re-enslaved in the British West Indies in the years following the treaty. Some free African Americans, Loyalists, and Native Americans moved to Canada, where they felt welcome and less threatened. And in spite of the treaty, the British continued to contest territory between the Appalachian Mountains and the Mississippi River for decades.

The coming years would present a series of challenges to the new nation. Besides the creation of an independent United States, the Revolution had also established a new American identity. Based on the ideals of self-government, this identity embraced equality before the law, freedom of religion, and the values of education and **nationalism**, or a sense of loyalty and devotion toward one's nation. Citizens of the United States would have to decide exactly how to apply these ideals and values moving forward. They would also have to decide how to establish a stable government.

BENEDICT ARNOLD, AMERICAN TRAITOR

Why did Benedict Arnold, who fought so valiantly for American independence at the beginning of the war, end up fighting for the British? According to most historians, his loyalties shifted after Saratoga, where he was wounded. Angered that General Gates did not give him the credit he thought he deserved when reporting the victory, Arnold switched his allegiance to Britain. In 1779, he plotted to surrender the American fort at West Point, New York, to the British. Before the plan could unfold, Washington's forces uncovered the plot and exposed Arnold as a traitor. Arnold escaped, and the British welcomed him as a commander of their forces in Virginia.

HISTORICAL THINKING

1. **READING CHECK** What was the significance of the Battle of Yorktown?

2. **FORM AND SUPPORT OPINIONS** Why was it important for Great Britain to recognize and accept the United States of America in the Treaty of Paris of 1783? Use text evidence to support your answer.

3. **INTERPRET VISUALS** Why do you think the artist chose to paint a dramatic background behind Cornwallis and his men?

MOUNT VERNON MUSEUM AND EDUCATION CENTER MOUNT VERNON, VIRGINIA

At its peak in the late 1700s, Mount Vernon was an 8,000-acre plantation estate with gardens and farms, lovingly managed by George and Martha Washington and painstakingly cared for by more than 300 slaves and workers. Today, about 500 acres of the original estate are preserved as a national historic site, which attracts around 1 million visitors each year.

The centerpiece of Mount Vernon is the Washingtons' home, the Mansion, which lies along the banks of the Potomac River and is surrounded by gardens and manicured grounds. The historic site also features reconstructed slave cabins and barns, as well as other original structures. A museum and education center tell the story of George Washington's life.

Martha Washington's Silk Gown

Martha Washington's granddaughter carefully preserved this brown silk gown with a pinned note that described it as "a favorite gown of my dear Grandmother Mrs. Washington." This gown is the only intact item of Martha Washington's clothing at Mount Vernon. Her descendants took apart her garments and distributed the fragments as heirlooms, or family possessions handed down from one generation to another.

What favorite personal artifact might you choose to leave behind as an heirloom?

Huntsmen blew curved horns like this one to direct the hounds during hunts.

Hunting Horn

George Washington often hosted fox hunts at Mount Vernon during the fall and winter. Enslaved brothers William and Frank Lee served as Washington's huntsmen, managing the 40 to 60 hounds that pursued the fox.

Samuel Vaughan's Journal

This journal belonged to a wealthy English merchant named Samuel Vaughan, who visited Mount Vernon in 1787. In his journal, Vaughan described the estate and made this sketch showing the Mansion and nearby buildings and gardens. Vaughan's sketch is the earliest known drawing of the central plan of Mount Vernon. His journal has served as a valuable reference source in the restoration of the plantation.

How might Vaughan's journal assist with present-day restoration projects at Mount Vernon?

George Washington's Telescope

Through this telescope, Washington could view the stars and planets in the night sky or identify ships cruising the Potomac River. Besides this large telescope, Washington owned 12 small, handheld ones called spyglasses. As a general during the American Revolution, he often used telescopes to observe the movements of British and American troops. Washington kept this brass Gregorian telescope, which was made in London, in his study at Mount Vernon.

This telescope is named after its designer, the Scottish astronomer James Gregory.

What do details on this weathervane reveal about its craftsmanship?

Dove of Peace Weathervane

Custom-built in Philadelphia while Washington ran the Constitutional Convention, this dove of peace weathervane tops the cupola, a structure on the roof of the Mansion, at Mount Vernon. Washington commissioned this piece himself, determining its design and even choosing the color black for the bird's bill and the color green for the olive branch. The weathervane was meant to symbolize that peace would prevail in the nation no matter how hard the winds might blow over the years.

THE AMERICAN REVOLUTION
REVIEW

Use each of the following pairs of key vocabulary terms in a sentence that shows an understanding of their meanings.

1. **boycott, committee of correspondence**
   Samuel Adams set up a committee of correspondence to organize a widespread boycott of British goods.

2. **guerrilla tactic, privateer**

3. **mercenary, deploy**

4. **rule of law, ratify**

5. **financier, profiteering**

READING STRATEGY
FORM AND SUPPORT OPINIONS

Forming opinions as you read history is important to help clarify your understanding and sharpen your perceptions of the words and actions of the people involved. Use the graphic organizer to state and support your opinion about an important event of the American Revolution. Then answer the question.

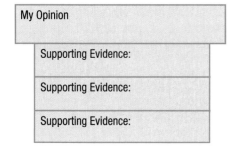

My Opinion

Supporting Evidence:

Supporting Evidence:

Supporting Evidence:

6. In your opinion, what was the most significant event of the American Revolution, and why?

MAIN IDEAS

Answer the following questions. Support your answers with evidence from the chapter.

7. How were the Sons of Liberty effective in leading resistance against British policies? **LESSON 1.1**

8. How was the Boston Massacre a result of both the Quartering Act of 1765 and the Townshend Acts? **LESSON 1.2**

9. Why did the colonies unite after the passage of the Intolerable Acts? **LESSON 1.3**

10. Why did King George III reject the Olive Branch Petition? **LESSON 2.1**

11. How were the ideas expressed in *Common Sense* put to use in the structure of the new national government established by the Articles of Confederation? **LESSON 2.2**

12. Why did the Continental Army's victories at Trenton and Princeton help keep the American effort for independence alive? **LESSON 3.1**

13. How did the Congress eventually find a way to help pay for the war? **LESSON 3.2**

14. How did women provide vital assistance to the Continental Army? **LESSON 3.3**

15. How did General Nathanael Greene help prevent the British from achieving success in their southern strategy? **LESSON 4.1**

16. What gave the Continental Army an advantage over the British at the Battle of Yorktown? **LESSON 4.2**

HISTORICAL THINKING

Answer the following questions. Support your answers with evidence from the chapter.

17. **ANALYZE CAUSE AND EFFECT** How did the Daughters of Liberty set the groundwork for changes in the social status of women during and after the war?

18. **MAKE CONNECTIONS** How did the United States' alliance with France contribute to the British defeat in the southern states?

19. **DRAW CONCLUSIONS** Why do you think that widespread public support for declaring independence was slow to form even after the events at Lexington and Concord?

20. **IDENTIFY PROBLEMS AND SOLUTIONS** What problem did the entry of the French into the war present for the British, and how did they attempt to solve it?

21. **DESCRIBE** How did women writers help to push colonial attitudes in favor of independence?

22. **IDENTIFY MAIN IDEAS AND DETAILS** How did disagreements among the British play a pivotal role in allowing George Washington to force the surrender at Yorktown?

23. **FORM AND SUPPORT OPINIONS** How would you rate Washington's handling of the Continental Army from late 1775 through late 1776? Support your opinion with evidence from the text.

INTERPRET MAPS

Look closely at the map that shows the boundaries of the original United States of America, established by the Treaty of Paris of 1783. Then answer the questions that follow.

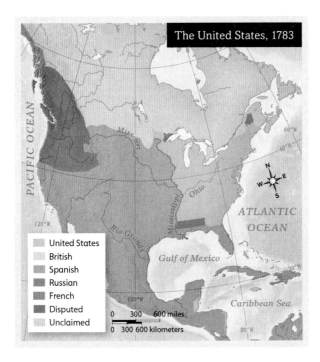

The United States, 1783

Legend:
- United States
- British
- Spanish
- Russian
- French
- Disputed
- Unclaimed

0   300   600 miles
0 300 600 kilometers

24. What nations claim land bordering on the United States, and where, geographically, do those borders lie?

25. Assuming that North America includes the Caribbean Islands, which European nations hold the most and the least land in North America, according to this map?

ANALYZE SOURCES

During the run-up to the American Revolution, Native Americans faced the difficult question of whether to remain neutral or to side with the Americans or the British. Read the excerpt below, which explains the concerns of the Oneida about choosing sides. Then answer the question that follows.

> We cannot intermeddle in this dispute between two brothers. The quarrel seems to be unnatural. You are two brothers of one blood. We are unwilling to join on either side in such a contest, for we bear an equal affection to both you Old and New England. . . . We Indians cannot find, nor recollect in the traditions of our ancestors . . . a similar instance.

26. Based on the excerpt, why did the Oneida wish to remain neutral in the conflict between the Americans and the British?

CONNECT TO YOUR LIFE

27. **EXPOSITORY** The American Revolution was fueled by a desire to protect people's rights to life, liberty, and the pursuit of happiness. Yet this desire was not applied equally to African Americans, women, and Native Americans during and after the war. Think of a social conflict the United States is experiencing today. Using the war as one example, write a short essay explaining the importance of having fair solutions to social conflicts.

TIPS

- Use textual evidence and two or three key vocabulary terms from the chapter in your explanation.

- Describe the problems of equality during and after the American Revolution and the problem you are addressing today.

- Connect the two ideas, and explain how better understanding can help prevent social conflicts.

- Explain how Americans can improve their understanding of modern social conflicts.

CHAPTER 5

FORGING A NEW GOVERNMENT
1780–1790

HISTORICAL THINKING How did American ideals and culture shape the new government?

Independence Hall in Philadelphia, Pennsylvania, is the birthplace of the United States. The public can now tour this Georgian-style, red brick building where the Declaration of Independence and the Constitution were debated and signed.

"The way to secure liberty is to **place it in the people's hands.**"

—John Adams

1.1

MAIN IDEA The Articles of Confederation created a weak federal government, which caused serious problems for the new republic.

PROBLEMS IN THE NEW REPUBLIC

Have you ever tried to organize a new club or team? Imagine trying to create an entirely new kind of government. The nation's leaders grappled with this challenge and, like all of us, had to learn from their mistakes.

GOVERNING PROBLEMS

When the Patriots declared independence from Great Britain, they said that the American people had the power to create their own government. This new and radical idea was sparked in part by Enlightenment ideals of **egalitarianism**, the belief that all people should be treated equally, and **republicanism**, the belief that a government's power comes from its citizens and the representatives they choose to make their laws. According to John Jay, one of the American negotiators of the Treaty of Paris of 1783, Americans were "the first people whom heaven has favored with an opportunity of deliberating upon, and choosing the forms of government under which they should live."

In practice, however, the ideals of egalitarianism and republicanism did not apply to all people in the new republic. Women, Native Americans, most free men of color, and, of course, none of the enslaved had much of a political voice, if any. The individual states determined who qualified for **suffrage**, or the right to vote. In most states, only white males who owned property were allowed to vote.

As you have read, the United States' first plan of government— the Articles of Confederation— featured a weak central government. **Sovereignty**, or the power to govern, remained with each of the 13 new states. The Articles loosely bound these

self-governing states together under a national legislature called the Confederation Congress, which acted as their agent. Each state had an equal vote in Congress. The national government did not include executive and judicial branches, which meant there was no president or federal court system. Congress itself had few powers. It could conduct foreign affairs, negotiate treaties, declare war, create a postal service, and issue money. But it could not impose taxes; that right belonged to the states. If Congress needed money, it had to request funds from the states.

This 1777 copy of the Articles of Confederation includes its full title. The reference to "Perpetual Union" reflects the representatives' hope that the union would continue forever.

FINANCIAL PROBLEMS

The emphasis on state sovereignty failed to promote a sense of national identity. This lack of unity made it difficult for the new nation to take effective action on important issues, such as paying off the huge debt amassed during the Revolution. Individual states refused to contribute enough money to help pay the debt. In 1785, Congress stopped making interest payments to France. By 1787, it was defaulting on loan payments to France, Spain, and private Dutch investors who had helped finance the war.

Meanwhile, the states faced their own financial difficulties. A postwar **depression**, or severe economic downturn, created hardship for farmers throughout the United States. State governments made the situation

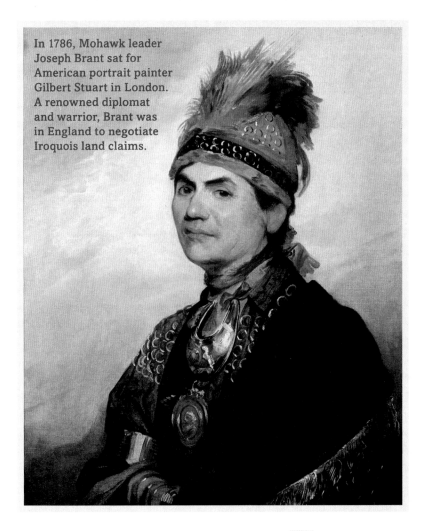

In 1786, Mohawk leader Joseph Brant sat for American portrait painter Gilbert Stuart in London. A renowned diplomat and warrior, Brant was in England to negotiate Iroquois land claims.

worse by imposing heavy taxes in order to repay **war bonds** issued to fund the Revolution. During the war, people had bought the bonds for less than their face value with the assurance they could sell them back for their full value when the bonds matured. As the war debt rose, many bond holders believed they would never be paid back, and they sold their bonds to wealthy lenders for cash, but at discounted prices.

When states levied high taxes, farmers had an especially hard time paying. Most farmers were used to paying debts with crops or livestock and rarely did business in cash. In many states, all or a portion of taxes had to be paid in gold and silver coins. If farmers failed to pay taxes, local courts seized their land and livestock and sold them, often at a fraction of their value. The courts imprisoned anyone whose assets failed to cover debts and back taxes until someone paid the sum owed.

CONFLICTS WITH OTHER NATIONS

Under the Articles of Confederation, conflicts with other countries also proved difficult to resolve. Without the ability to raise money and assemble a strong army, the American government could

not enforce its policies. In the Treaty of 1783, for example, the British pledged to remove their troops from forts in the Great Lakes region. Through the 1780s, however, they refused to withdraw, hoping to regain the territory. They barred American ships from the Great Lakes and allied with Native Americans who wanted to halt white settlement. British diplomats claimed the actions were justified because Americans had failed to pay prewar debts to British creditors and to return property they had confiscated from Loyalists during the Revolution.

Native Americans allied with both Britain and Spain to slow the influx of American settlers. In return for an alliance and weapons, the Creek offered to block the Americans from settling in Spanish territory. The Cherokee and Shawnee also battled Americans through the 1780s, mostly in Tennessee, Kentucky, and Alabama, thus slowing settlement in what was then the southwestern frontier. In the Ohio Territory and surrounding northwest areas, Mohawk leader Thayendanegea (thahy-ehn-DAHY-naw-gah), also known as **Joseph Brant**, rallied Native Americans against white settlement.

During the 1780s, as settlers rapidly filled the region between the Appalachian Mountains and the Mississippi River, Spain feared it might lose control of Louisiana and Florida. In 1784, to protect its interests, the Spanish government closed the port of New Orleans to American ships and trade. The lower Mississippi River remained closed to U.S. navigation until 1788, when the Spanish permitted Americans to bring goods through New Orleans as long as they paid duties, or taxes, to Spain.

HISTORICAL THINKING

1. **READING CHECK** What problems did the nation experience under the Articles of Confederation?

2. **DRAW CONCLUSIONS** Why was the Confederation Congress unable to pay off the large national debt?

3. **COMPARE AND CONTRAST** How was the government of the new republic similar to and different from British rule of the colonies?

THE NORTHWEST ORDINANCES

How do 13 separate governments resolve a shared problem? The 13 states all had overlapping claims to western frontier lands, and the new Congress faced one of its first challenges in crafting a fair solution.

LAND ORDINANCE OF 1785

As you have read, the Treaty of Paris of 1783 granted the United States most of the land between the Atlantic Ocean and the Mississippi River. Besides the original 13 states, this area consisted of the lands west of Pennsylvania, north of the Ohio River, and east of the Mississippi River. These "western lands" collectively became known as the Northwest Territory and included present-day Ohio, Indiana, Illinois, Michigan, Wisconsin, and part of Minnesota.

By ceding this territory to the United States, the Treaty of Paris also invalidated the many treaties between the British and the Native American nations who lived there. The question of who really controlled the area became a pressing issue. Some states claimed parts of the territory. Virginia, for example, claimed all the land between its western border and the Mississippi River. Other states argued that the

Northwest Territory, 1787

Boundaries indefinite

BRITISH NORTH AMERICA (CANADA)

L. Superior

L. Michigan
L. Huron
L. Ontario
L. Erie

Mississippi

SPANISH LOUISIANA

N.Y.

PENN.

Ohio

VIRGINIA

KENTUCKY
Cumberland Gap

TENNESSEE

NORTH CAROLINA

0   100   200 miles
0   100   200 kilometers

Northwest Territory
Present-day state boundary

Confederation Congress should control the area. Clearly, the nation needed a system to guide the settlement of the Northwest Territory.

Operating under the Articles of Confederation, Congress passed three **ordinances**, or laws, designed to provide order and regulate settlement in the Northwest Territory. These ordinances established a system for transferring federally owned land into private holdings and forming townships and states.

The first ordinance, passed in 1784, divided the Northwest Territory into seven districts. The law allowed the settlers of each district to govern themselves by choosing a constitution and laws from any of the existing states. When a district's population reached that of Rhode Island, the smallest of the original 13 states, the district would become a state. Congress retained responsibility for selling public lands in the seven districts.

The second law, the **Land Ordinance of 1785**, set the procedures for surveying, dividing, and distributing land in the Northwest Territory. The ordinance called for dividing districts into townships 6 miles square, which would be further subdivided into 640-acre lots. Each lot would be sold at a minimum of $1 per acre, or $640 per lot.

The ordinance of 1785 reserved land in each township for a public school. By setting aside land for schools, Congress established the **precedent**, or example, of supporting public education, forwarding the ideals of egalitarianism, democracy, and republicanism. Thomas Jefferson pointed out that a republic could only work if voters were educated enough to make informed choices. About the importance of public education, Jefferson wrote, "Above all things I hope the education of the common

The painting *Daniel Boone—The Home Seeker: Cumberland Valley* (c. 1940) by American artist N.C. Wyeth depicts the legendary frontiersman and his family moving westward. Boone's trailblazing helped later settlers reach the Northwest Territory. What do details in the painting imply about journeys through the wilderness?

people will be attended to; convinced that on their good sense we may rely with the most security for the preservation of a due degree of liberty."

Because of the relatively high cost of the township lots, Congress had difficulty selling them to individuals. In fact, many settlers set up farms on lots without government approval. Frustrated by the lack of sales and in need of funds to pay off war debts, Congress agreed to sell 1.5 million acres for less than 10 cents an acre to the Ohio Company. The Ohio Company was a group of New England **speculators**. A speculator is a person who invests in property or stocks, hoping to sell at a profit.

NORTHWEST ORDINANCE OF 1787

The third ordinance, the **Northwest Ordinance of 1787**, created a process for organizing territorial governments and states. The ordinance called for Congress to appoint a governor, secretary, and three judges to administer a newly established territory. Once 5,000 adult males resided in a territory, they could elect an assembly. The right to vote was limited to free men who owned at least 50 acres of land. A territory qualified to enter the Union as a state when its population reached 60,000. Congress anticipated that three to five states would be created from the Northwest Territory.

The 1787 ordinance included provisions for such individual rights as religious liberty and trial by jury. It also banned slavery. After the Revolution, the issue of slavery grew in importance as some citizens noted that it conflicted with the principles of the Revolution. By the mid-1780s, several state governments had passed legislation against slavery. Vermont banned slavery in its constitution in 1777. In 1780, Pennsylvania passed a law providing for a gradual end to slavery in the state. In 1783, the Massachusetts Supreme Court declared that slavery violated the state constitution, which effectively ended slavery in the state. New Hampshire began abolishing slavery in the same year. In 1784, legislatures in Connecticut and Rhode Island followed Pennsylvania's example by passing laws gradually ending slavery.

HISTORICAL THINKING

1. **READING CHECK** What was the purpose of the three ordinances governing the Northwest Territory?

2. **INTERPRET MAPS** Besides land, what natural resources visible on the map of the Northwest Territory would benefit settlers?

3. **MAKE INFERENCES** How did the Northwest Ordinance of 1787 reflect democratic values?

THE CONSTITUTIONAL CONVENTION

If you had lived through more than six years of war, what would you most want? A peaceful life? That's probably what Americans wanted after the end of the Revolution. So what pushed a group of American farmers to take up rifles and fight again?

SHAYS'S REBELLION

As you have read, an economic depression after the Revolution caused great hardship for farmers. Before the war, British companies had encouraged Americans to buy goods on **credit**, which meant they could obtain the goods immediately and pay for them over time. Many farmers had paid their debts with such goods as crops or livestock or with **currency**, or paper money, issued by the states. Now that the war was over, the British manufacturers demanded Americans pay their debts in **specie**, or money in the form of gold and silver coins. Both specie and currency backed by specie were in short supply. At the same time, state governments imposed high taxes on their citizens, in part to repay war debts, and many demanded that a portion of these taxes be paid in specie.

The requirement to pay most debts and taxes in specie forced many Americans, particularly farmers, to run up enormous personal debts. As you have read, if people couldn't pay their debts or their taxes, they could be imprisoned. In addition, their property would be seized for nonpayment of taxes.

In this lithograph of Shays's Rebellion (1786–1787), a mob of rebels watch as one protester fights with a government official. The rebels gathered in September 1786 to prevent the court in Springfield, Massachusetts, from meeting.

Debtors around the country protested, but none more forcefully than the farmers of western Massachusetts. Beginning in August 1786, a farmer and veteran of the American Revolution named Daniel Shays staged an uprising that became known as **Shays's Rebellion**. Shays led armed farmers into Massachusetts courthouses to stop debt hearings and **foreclosures**, or the taking possession of property to cover outstanding debts.

In response to the attacks, Massachusetts called up 1,200 members of the state militia and implored Congress to help the state put down the armed rebellion. Congress, proving to be ineffectual in a crisis, responded by asking the states to send money and recruits to form a federal army. The Massachusetts government—and every state except Virginia—refused to raise the money. In late January 1787, Shays and the rebels attacked the federal armory at Springfield, intent on seizing its large store of weapons. Outnumbered but well-armed, the militia defeated them, and the rebellion was over by February. But the debt problem and the mounting discontent did not go away. The rebellion highlighted those issues, and voters turned to the ballot box to elect candidates who were sympathetic to debtors. Shays and many of his followers later received pardons.

The angry militancy of indebted farmers drew attention to the disastrous state of the nation's finances. The revolt highlighted the inability of Congress under the Articles of Confederation to resolve the nation's financial problems and maintain law and order. The rebellion concerned George Washington enough that he returned to public life.

A CONSTITUTIONAL CONVENTION

For years, Patriot leaders such as **Alexander Hamilton** of New York and Robert Morris of Pennsylvania had argued in favor of a more powerful central government. Shays's Rebellion brought more people around to their way of thinking.

In September 1786, as Shays's Rebellion grew stronger, state delegates assembled in Annapolis, Maryland, to discuss amending the Articles of Confederation in order to give Congress the power to regulate trade. But only five state delegations arrived on time, so the convention was canceled. Several delegates called for another convention to meet in May 1787 in Philadelphia to work on a broader revision of the Articles.

The Philadelphia meeting, called the **Constitutional Convention,** started on May 25, 1787. Every state except Rhode Island sent delegates. The delegates who gathered to create the Constitution—all wealthy and well educated—would become known as the **Framers**. Many of them, such as Benjamin Franklin of Pennsylvania, had been leaders during the Revolution and the first years of the republic. The Framers elected George Washington of Virginia as the leader of the convention.

To preserve the papers he acquired during the Constitutional Convention, George Washington stored them in this leather and brass-tack document box.

At the time of the convention, the weather in Philadelphia was punishingly hot and humid. Even so, the delegates insisted on keeping all the windows and doors shut in order to keep their discussions private. Men's fashions of the period added to the delegates' discomfort. Men wore coats and vests at all times, and the New England delegates were even wearing wool. Today, some historians believe that the delegates' desire to escape the stifling heat of Philadelphia made them more efficient and willing to compromise.

One of the most influential and prominent delegates was **James Madison** of Virginia, a 36-year-old planter, slaveholder, and intellectual who had served in the Virginia assembly and in Congress. In response to what he saw as major problems in Congress and in state governments, Madison felt compelled to push for a stronger central government. Ordinarily a shy man who avoided public speaking, he took such a dominant role in the proceedings that he was later called the "Father of the Constitution." Even though the purpose of the convention was to amend the Articles of Confederation, Madison arrived with a prepared document in which he proposed a powerful federal government to link all the states together. This document shifted the debate from how to revise the Articles to how to create an entirely new plan of government.

HISTORICAL THINKING

1. **READING CHECK** What was the historical significance of Shays's Rebellion?

2. **DRAW CONCLUSIONS** Why do you think the states wanted farmers to pay their debts in specie?

3. **IDENTIFY PROBLEMS AND SOLUTIONS** What financial problems did farmers and the states face after the Revolution, and why were they difficult to solve?

MAIN IDEA Delegates to the Constitutional Convention compromised to create a plan for a constitutional republic with three branches of government: legislative, executive, and judicial.

A CONSTITUTIONAL REPUBLIC

Meet each other halfway. Make a deal. Find a happy medium. These expressions all mean the same thing: compromise. That's what the delegates to the Constitutional Convention did to create our American form of government.

THE GREAT COMPROMISE

In 1787, when the delegates in Philadelphia began to debate what form the new government of the United States should take, they had a variety of competing interests to consider and issues to resolve. But they could agree on a few things. For example, they wanted the federal and state governments to share power, a system called **federalism**. They also wanted the state governments to have certain powers that the federal government could not overrule, an idea called **dual sovereignty**. But how should power be divided? How would the rights of small states and large states be balanced? Should the federal government include a head of state, and how much power should that office hold? Should there be federal courts, and how much power should they have?

Convention delegates created a **constitutional republic,** a government in which the representatives gain their authority from the consent of the governed— that is, from the voters who elect them. The delegates agreed that the new government needed the same three branches as the British government: a **legislative branch** to make the laws, an **executive branch** to enforce the laws and lead the nation, and a **judicial branch** to interpret the laws. But the delegates expanded on the concept. Influenced by the writings of French political philosopher **Montesquieu** (MON-tuh-SKYOO), the Framers decided the three branches should have separate responsibilities and powers, so that no branch could become too powerful. This principle of **separation of powers** proved to be essential in the creation of the U.S. Constitution. As John Adams explained, "It is by balancing each of these Powers against the other two, that the Effort in human Nature towards Tyranny can alone be checked and restrained, and any degree of Freedom preserved in the Constitution."

During the first seven weeks of the Constitutional Convention, one issue overshadowed all others—the power of large states versus small states. James Madison's **Virginia Plan**, presented by fellow Virginian Edmund Randolph, proposed a powerful central government anchored by a **bicameral legislature**—one made up of two houses. Qualified voters would elect members to the lower house. For the upper house, members of each state's legislature would nominate candidates, and members of the lower house would choose from among them. The federal legislature would appoint members of the executive and judicial branches of the central government and could veto state laws. This plan gave more power to the larger states, because the number of representatives from each state depended on the state's population.

Several smaller states opposed the Virginia Plan. Delaware, Maryland, New Jersey, and Connecticut feared the power of Virginia, Pennsylvania, and Massachusetts, which together were home to almost half of the American population. If the Virginia Plan were adopted, just four states could dominate the legislature. In mid-June, William Paterson of New Jersey introduced the **New Jersey Plan**, which proposed a one-house, or unicameral, Congress in which all states had equal representation. In this plan, Congress would appoint an executive council, which would choose a supreme court. As in the Virginia Plan, Congress had greater authority than under the Articles of Confederation, with powers to tax, regulate commerce, and compel states to obey its laws. But the large states objected to the New Jersey Plan, arguing that Delaware, with a population of just 59,000, should not have as much power as Virginia, which had a population of 748,000.

TOTAL POPULATION OF THE UNITED STATES, 1790: 3,929,214

Population of Virginia
19%, 747,610

Population of New Jersey
4.7%, 184,139

NH
ME
VT
GA
KY
RI
DE

SC
PA
NC
NY
MA
CT
MD

= one representative from New Jersey

= one representative from Virginia

Edmund Randolph's
Virginia Plan
TWO HOUSES

UPPER HOUSE

LOWER HOUSE

The number of representatives from each state is proportionate to the state's population.

William Paterson's
New Jersey Plan
ONE HOUSE

Each state has an equal number of representatives, regardless of population.

ROGER SHERMAN'S
GREAT COMPROMISE

HOUSE OF REPRESENTATIVES

The number of representatives from each state is proportionate to the state's population.

SENATE

Each state has an equal number of representatives, regardless of population.

Source: United States Census Bureau

Roger Sherman of Connecticut finally broke the stalemate by proposing a plan known as the **Great Compromise.** This plan included a bicameral Congress. Representation in the lower house, the House of Representatives, would be based on population. The members of this house would be elected directly by the voters every two years. Only this house would have the power to initiate revenue bills, which meant that voters would elect the representatives who taxed them.

In the upper house, called the Senate, each state legislature would choose two senators to serve six-year terms. The idea of a bicameral Congress resolved the debate between small and large states. It also satisfied leaders who wanted to limit the influence of ordinary voters. These leaders expected that senators would come from the wealthier, upper classes of society. The senators' long terms and the fact that they were appointed by state legislators rather than elected by citizens would shield them from public opinion and provide a stabilizing influence. The plan required both houses of Congress to approve legislation.

Under the Great Compromise, the United States would become a single nation rather than a confederacy of states. At the same time, the states retained some rights, including equal representation in the Senate.

THE EXECUTIVE AND JUDICIAL BRANCHES

Remembering the colonies' problems with the British monarchy, delegates to the Constitutional Convention did not want to assign too much power to one person. But they also wanted the executive branch to serve as a check on the legislature. Ultimately, they decided that the executive branch would feature a single president who would serve a four-year term.

But how should the president be chosen? Some delegates thought the president should be directly elected by the voters. Others wanted Congress or the state legislatures to make the choice. The delegates finally arrived at a solution: an **electoral college** made up of electors from each state would cast official votes for the president and vice president. The number of electors from each state would be the same as the state's number of representatives in Congress, and each state could decide how to choose its electors.

Of the three branches of government, the judicial branch is least clearly defined in the Constitution. While the Framers created a judiciary with a Supreme Court to interpret the laws, they left many of the details to Congress. However, Section 2 of Article 3 prescribes one of the basic rights enjoyed by American citizens: the right to a trial by jury. The Framers felt this right was essential to protect citizens from tyranny.

To reinforce the separation of powers, the Framers included **checks and balances** in the Constitution. This system allows each branch of government to amend or veto acts of another branch so that the power of the three branches remains balanced. The president was given the power to veto laws passed by Congress, but legislators could override the veto if two-thirds of both houses approved. Congress had the authority to remove the president by **impeachment** and trial for treason, bribery, and "other high Crimes and Misdemeanors." Impeachment is the process of bringing formal charges against

a public official. Congress also had the power to declare war and raise an army and navy, but the president served as commander-in-chief of the military. Only with the "advice and consent" of the Senate could the president negotiate treaties and appoint ambassadors, Supreme Court justices, and other officials. The courts had the power to strike down laws judged to be unconstitutional.

SLAVERY AND COMMERCE

In addition to determining the structure of the government itself, the Framers had to address two other major issues: slavery and commerce. The words *slave*, *slavery*, and *slave trade* do not appear anywhere in the 1787 Constitution, and yet the issue influenced debates on representation in Congress, the election of the president, and the regulation of commerce. The southern states wanted to count slaves in a state's population when calculating the

TO BE SOLD. on board the Ship *Bance-Yland*, on tuesday the 6th of *May* next, at *Afhley-Ferry*; a choice cargo of about 250 fine healthy NEGROES, just arrived from the Windward & Rice Coast. —The utmost care has already been taken, and shall be continued, to keep them free from the least danger of being infected with the SMALL-POX, no boat having been on board, and all other communication with people from *Charles-Town* prevented.

Auftin, Laurens, & Appleby.

N. B. Full one Half of the above Negroes have had the SMALL-POX in their own Country.

The 1787 Constitution allowed for the importation of slaves for at least 20 years. This advertisement from a Charleston, South Carolina, newspaper in the late 1700s announces the importation and sale of Africans on the ship *Bance Island*. To appeal to plantation owners seeking rice-farming expertise, the ad mentions that the captives are from the Windward and Rice Coast, the rice-growing area of Sierra Leone. The ad also notes that the Africans are likely free from or immune to smallpox.

number of delegates to the House of Representatives and votes in the electoral college. Because enslaved persons made up a significant portion of the population in southern states, northerners protested that white southerners would gain an unfair advantage by such a plan. They argued that slaves should not be counted because they could not vote. The convention settled on the **Three-fifths Compromise**, which stated that five enslaved African Americans would count as three free persons for determining representation and direct taxes, which were to be levied on income or profits rather than on goods or services.

The Framers approved other measures that upheld slavery, which was not surprising since George Washington himself owned more than 300 slaves. While few northern delegates supported slavery, they did almost nothing to promote its end. Instead, the Framers supported southern interests by approving a **fugitive slave clause**, which prevented people who had escaped slavery in the South from living as free people in the North. The delegates also included a slave importation clause, which stated that Congress could not prohibit the importation of slaves for 20 years. North and South Carolina and Georgia demanded this option because they expected settlement to expand into western Georgia and what are now the states of Alabama, Mississippi, and Tennessee.

Besides the issue of slavery, the Framers had to address the issue of **interstate commerce**, or trade between the states. Under the Articles of Confederation, Congress had no power to regulate trade, except with Native American nations, or to make trade agreements with foreign governments. Each state made its own trade regulations and agreements, which often conflicted with those of nearby states. In the commerce clause of the Constitution, the Framers gave the federal government the right to "regulate commerce with foreign nations, and among the several states, and with the Indian tribes."

Finally, the Framers understood that they needed to devise a method for adding amendments, or changes, to the Constitution when necessary. They

The Three-fifths Compromise

In some regions, the Three-fifths Compromise could make a big difference in the number of allotted representatives. As you can see from the table, enslaved people made up a small proportion of the population of New England in 1790. In contrast, enslaved people made up more than one-third of the South's population.

Under the Three-fifths Compromise, about 2,300 people would be added to the population of New England for the purpose of determining representation, which was not enough to add one representative. But more than 387,000 people would be added to the population of the South, thus giving a major boost to the power of southern white voters by increasing the number of their representatives in Congress by more than 12.

Percentage of Enslaved Population by Region, 1790

Region	Total Population	Enslaved Population	Percentage Enslaved
New England	1,009,522	3,886	0.38%
Middle Atlantic	1,017,726	45,371	4.46%
South	1,866,387	645,023	34.56%
TOTAL	**3,893,635**	**694,280**	**17.83%**

Source: United States Census Bureau

decided, however, that the process should not be too easy because frequent changes would make the Constitution less stable and enduring. To make changes possible—but not easy—they decided that two-thirds of both houses of Congress or two-thirds of the state legislatures must propose an amendment. Then three-fourths of the state legislatures must ratify the amendment for it to be added to the Constitution. In more than 225 years, only 27 amendments have been added.

HISTORICAL THINKING

1. **READING CHECK** How did the Framers create a strong central government with checks on its power?

2. **COMPARE AND CONTRAST** How is the form of government outlined in the Constitution different from that prescribed in the Articles of Confederation?

3. **SUMMARIZE** How did the Great Compromise address the concerns of both large and small states?

4. **INTERPRET CHARTS** How did the southern states benefit from the Three-fifths Compromise? Support your answer with evidence from the population chart and the text.

3.1

MAIN IDEA Politicians and everyday citizens alike intensely debated the pros and cons of adopting the Constitution.

FEDERALISTS AND ANTIFEDERALISTS

Imagine a conversation among a group of small farmers in rural Pennsylvania in late 1787. They say the proposed Constitution will create a central government that is too large and powerful—and out of touch with the needs of everyday people. Sound familiar? Some of the original criticisms of the form of government outlined in the Constitution still surface in political arguments today.

THE BATTLE OVER RATIFICATION

In Philadelphia on September 17, 1787, the Framers signed the Constitution. They quickly sent it to the Confederation Congress, which forwarded it to the states without much debate. According to Article 7 of the Constitution, at least nine state conventions had to ratify, or approve, it for the Constitution to become the basis for a new government. Leaders who supported ratification knew the process had to move quickly, before an effective opposition could arise.

Disagreements flared over the key issue of power—specifically, who held most of it. How much power should the central government have, and how strong should the executive branch be? How much power should the states have? A significant argument against the Constitution was that it did not guarantee certain basic rights, which had factored so prominently in the Declaration of Independence.

The pro-ratification group included such powerful leaders as James Madison, Alexander Hamilton, and John Jay. This group came to be called **federalists** because they argued in favor of the Constitution's federalist provisions—those that kept certain powers for the states—in addition to supporting the elements calling for a strong central government. The anti-ratification group acquired the name **antifederalists**

American artist Joseph Wright painted this portrait of federalist John Jay in 1786.

American artist Thomas Sully painted this portrait of antifederalist Patrick Henry in 1815.

because they disagreed with the federalist position. Concerned about the potential abuse of power by the federal government, they opposed a strong central government and favored giving more power to state governments. The antifederalists also included a number of prominent political leaders, such as George Mason and Patrick Henry, both of Virginia.

THE TWO SIDES

Citizens in both cities and rural areas joined the ratification debate. People with federalist and antifederalist viewpoints could be found in every state and among every economic group, debating the Constitution's pros and cons intensely.

Merchants, professionals, artisans, and commercial farmers tended to be federalists. They favored ratifying the Constitution because it gave the federal government, not state governments, the authority to issue money. The Constitution would put an end to state-issued currencies and result in one national currency, which would facilitate trade. They believed a strong central government would encourage the growth of a market economy, make it easier to trade with other states and countries, provide greater stability and strength, and raise the stature of the United States in the eyes of European nations.

The federalists thought the purpose of government was to help balance the opposing interests of different groups. They believed that society benefited when people pursued their own individual goals. Madison claimed that the Constitution would establish a large republic with so many different factions that no single interest group could monopolize power.

Antifederalists disagreed with this viewpoint. They favored small, homogeneous republics or states in which people shared similar needs. Many antifederalists were small family farmers who were in debt to wealthy merchants. They believed that a central government would be too large and too remote and that the interests of the citizens of the 13 states were too diverse for one body to govern them all effectively. They argued that a member of Congress could not possibly know the will of 30,000 voters. With so few people elected to Congress and such large electoral districts, wealthy, well-known candidates would have a strong advantage over ordinary people who ran for office. To the antifederalists, the Constitution lacked important safeguards against corruption and abuse of power. They argued for term limits and more frequent elections. Antifederalists also objected to the lack of a list of citizens' rights in the Constitution.

PRESENTING THEIR CASES

The federalists had some advantages over the antifederalists. The federalists were organized nationally, and many lived in the coastal cities and towns, where it was easier to influence public opinion than it was in rural areas. To promote their position, three of the most prominent federalists—Hamilton, Jay, and Madison—began publishing anonymous essays in New York newspapers explaining in detail why the Constitution should be ratified. In 1788, these 85 essays were gathered together into a book called *The Federalist*, which gained attention beyond New York. It is still considered a major work in American political theory.

The antifederalists also wrote anonymous newspaper columns that explained their position on the Constitution. Two of the most prominent antifederalist essayists called themselves Brutus and Cato, after famous ancient Roman politicians, and wrote in response to an anonymous pro-ratification essayist called Caesar. However, the antifederalist columns were never published in a single volume.

WHY WERE THEY ANONYMOUS?

The war of words between the federalists and the antifederalists in American newspapers was waged anonymously. Why? Historians cannot be certain, but many have speculated that it was the name recognition of the writers themselves that forced them to adopt pseudonyms. They believed their arguments needed to be judged on their own merits, not on the notoriety or political power of the author. The antifederalists in particular adopted a number of pseudonyms, such as Cato, Brutus, a Columbian Patriot, and so on. It's been speculated that "Cato" was George Clinton, governor of New York; that "Brutus" was Judge Robert Yates; and "a Columbian Patriot" was Revolutionary playwright and essayist Mercy Otis Warren.

HISTORICAL THINKING

1. **READING CHECK** What was the process for adopting the Constitution?

2. **COMPARE AND CONTRAST** What were the positions of the federalists and the antifederalists?

3. **MAKE GENERALIZATIONS** What groups tended to support the federalist view and why?

4. **MAKE INFERENCES** Why might small farmers in a largely rural state prefer that most power remain with their state government?

RATIFICATION AND THE BILL OF RIGHTS

Most Americans think of the Bill of Rights as an essential part of the U.S. Constitution. Probably few remember that it wasn't part of the original Constitution. A new Congress added it as a group of amendments, which persuaded two holdout states to agree to ratification.

THE ROAD TO RATIFICATION

As you have read, the Constitution required approval by the conventions of nine states to become law. Ratification proceeded smoothly at first. Delaware approved the Constitution unanimously on December 7, 1787, becoming the first state to ratify. In Pennsylvania, where supporters worried about resistance developing in the backcountry, federalists moved quickly and secured approval by a two-to-one margin. New Jersey and Georgia followed by ratifying unanimously. Connecticut ratified in January 1788. Except for Pennsylvania, these states were relatively small and recognized the advantages of joining a union in which they had equal representation in the Senate.

Soon the smooth road to ratification became bumpy. Maryland and South Carolina ratified easily, but the vote in Massachusetts was very close: 187 for and 168 against. The lack of a list of citizens' rights was a major obstacle to agreement, and Massachusetts recommended a series of amendments to protect individual rights and limit the powers of Congress. In June 1788, New Hampshire became the ninth state to ratify, satisfying the number of states required. Nevertheless, two crucial states had yet to accept the Constitution: Virginia and New York. While their ratification was technically not needed, their size and economic importance made their approval necessary to the success of the Constitution and the new government.

Virginia was home to some of the most vocal and respected antifederalists. Among their chief concerns was the Constitution's lack of a bill of rights that named and protected such fundamental liberties as freedom of speech and freedom of religion. The federalists argued that a bill of rights was superfluous, or unnecessary, because state constitutions already offered those protections. In reality, the protected rights varied from state to state. Federalists also argued that, while a bill of rights was necessary to protect citizens from a powerful king, the people themselves were sovereign under the Constitution and so there was no need to protect their rights.

Virginia won the battle over the bill of rights. It ratified the Constitution in late June after recommending a series of amendments that included a bill of rights, which Congress agreed to add. New York finally approved the Constitution in late July 1788. With ratification by 11 states, the United States began a new experiment in republican government. North Carolina and Rhode Island were the last two states to ratify.

THE BILL OF RIGHTS

In February 1789, members of the electoral college met in their state capitals to cast votes and elect the nation's first president. The unanimous election of George Washington came as no surprise. Washington's leadership during the war, his dignity and character, and his support for republican government made him the obvious choice. John Adams was elected vice president. On April 23, 1789, Washington arrived in New York City, which had been named the temporary federal capital, on a decorated barge. Thousands of cheering New Yorkers turned out to welcome him. He took the oath of office a week later.

CRITICAL VIEWING Artist Howard Chandler Christy's oil painting *Scene at the Signing of the Constitution of the United States* (1940) includes authentic period details and the likenesses of 40 men who attended the signing at Independence Hall in 1787, including George Washington, standing on the dais, and Benjamin Franklin, seated in the center. How would you characterize Chandler's portrayal of this historic event?

Meeting for the first time on March 4, 1789, the newly elected Congress addressed the question of amending the Constitution. Several states had criticized the document for failing to protect the rights of citizens, and those objections still kept North Carolina and Rhode Island from joining the Union. James Madison became the chief advocate in Congress of the group of amendments that became known as the **Bill of Rights**, in spite of his earlier opinion that such amendments were not necessary. But some antifederalist leaders still wanted to scrap the Constitution entirely. They refused to support the Bill of Rights because they knew it would add to the Constitution's popular support.

After much negotiation between the Senate and the House, on September 25, 1789, Congress sent a total of 12 amendments to the states for ratification. The addition of the Bill of Rights was enough to secure the ratification of the two remaining states. North Carolina ratified the Constitution in November 1789, and Rhode Island followed suit in May 1790. By December 15, 1791, three-quarters of the states had approved 10 of the amendments, which formed the final and official Bill of Rights.

Of the 10 amendments that became the Bill of Rights, the First through Eighth Amendments enumerate basic individual rights. The Ninth Amendment protects any personal freedoms that are not specified in previous amendments. The Tenth Amendment states that "powers not delegated to the United States by the Constitution, nor prohibited by it to the States, are reserved to the States respectively, or to the people." It addressed concerns that the federal government might assume powers that were not mentioned in the Constitution.

HISTORICAL THINKING

1. **READING CHECK** Before voting for ratification, what did Virginia insist that Congress add to the Constitution?

2. **DRAW CONCLUSIONS** Why was it important for Virginia and New York to ratify the Constitution?

3. **SUMMARIZE** What were the federalists' arguments against adding a bill of rights to the Constitution?

4. **FORM AND SUPPORT OPINIONS** Do you think it was important to include the Bill of Rights in the Constitution? Support your opinion with evidence from the text.

SETTING A BALANCE

The Framers of the Constitution wanted to establish an effective government, protect citizens' liberty, and guard against corruption and power-grabbing. To accomplish these goals, they crafted a government with three branches, assigned the branches different responsibilities, and provided ways for each branch to check the power of the others.

Gilbert Stuart painted portraits of five U.S. presidents, including James Madison. Dolley Madison wrote of Stuart, "He is a man of genius, and therefore does everything differently from other people." Her words could describe her husband's work to form a new nation.

CRITICAL VIEWING In this portrait of James Madison (c. 1805–1807), Gilbert Stuart placed drapery and other items typical in portraits of royalty in the background. In contrast, how do Madison's pose and the foreground reflect democratic ideals?

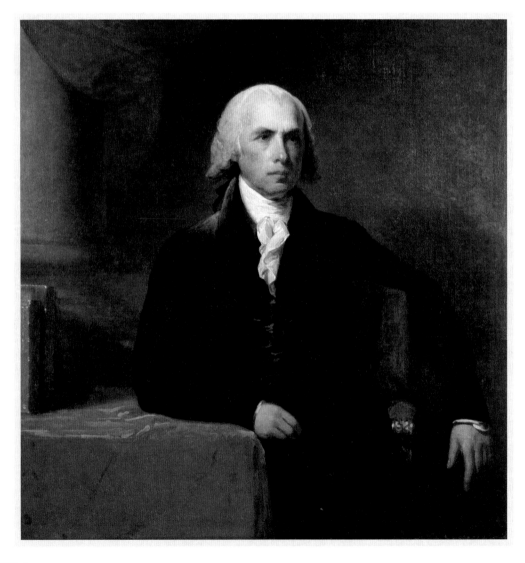

DOCUMENT ONE

Primary Source: Book
from *The Spirit of the Laws,* Book XI, Chapters 4 and 6, by Montesquieu, 1748

The Spirit of the Laws by French philosopher Montesquieu was one of the most influential books of 18th-century political thought. The book was widely read in the colonies and even excerpted in many newspapers. In the book, Montesquieu introduced and described the concept of separation of political powers. His ideas influenced the Framers as they debated the details of the Constitution.

CONSTRUCTED RESPONSE What kind of check on power does Montesquieu describe in this excerpt?

To prevent this abuse [of power], it is necessary from the very nature of things that power should be a check to power. A government may be so constituted, as no man shall be compelled to do things to which the law does not oblige him, nor forced to abstain from things which the law permits. . . . When the legislative and executive powers are united in the same person, or in the same body of magistrates, there can be no liberty. . . . Again there is no liberty if the judiciary power be not separated.

DOCUMENT TWO

Primary Source: Essay
from *Federalist* No. 51 by James Madison, 1788

In 1788, a group of American federalists published a collection of 85 essays entitled *The Federalist,* in which they argued in favor of the ratification of the U.S. Constitution. Essay No. 51, which James Madison originally published anonymously, dealt with the importance of autonomy, or independence, for the various departments of government.

CONSTRUCTED RESPONSE What does Madison prescribe as a way for each department of government to maintain its autonomy?

In order to lay a due foundation for that separate and distinct exercise of the different powers of government, which to a certain extent is admitted on all hands to be essential to the preservation of liberty, it is evident that each department should have a will of its own; and consequently should be so constituted that the members of each should have as little agency as possible in the appointment of the members of the others.

DOCUMENT THREE

Primary Source: Document
from The Constitution, Article 1, Section 7, Clause 3

The Framers took the ideas of Montesquieu and those of the federalists into account as they crafted their own version of a government. Each branch of this government would have the means to limit the power of the others. By extension, this form of government would help establish balance among the interests, classes, and factions of a diverse nation.

CONSTRUCTED RESPONSE How does Clause 3 set up a relationship of checks and balances?

Every Order, Resolution, or Vote to which the Concurrence [agreement] of the Senate and House of Representatives may be necessary (except on a question of Adjournment) shall be presented to the President of the United States; and before the Same shall take Effect, shall be approved by him, or being disapproved by him, shall be re-passed by two thirds of the Senate and House of Representatives, according to the Rules and Limitations prescribed in the Case of a Bill.

Read the full United States Constitution in the Citizenship Handbook.

SYNTHESIZE AND WRITE

1. **REVIEW** Review what you have learned about the idea of separation of powers and how it came to be part of the U.S. Constitution.

2. **RECALL** On your own paper, write notes about the responsibilities of each branch of government and the ways each branch checks the power of the others.

3. **CONSTRUCT** Construct a topic sentence that describes why the separation of powers is an important concept in a constitutional republic.

4. **WRITE** Using evidence from this chapter and the documents, write a paragraph explaining how the principle of separation of powers is applied in the United States government.

VOCABULARY

Use each of the following vocabulary words in a sentence that shows an understanding of the word's meaning.

1. sovereignty

   Each state was guaranteed sovereignty and so had the authority to rule itself.

2. egalitarianism

3. ordinance

4. suffrage

5. federalism

6. bicameral legislature

7. constitutional republic

8. antifederalist

READING STRATEGY
COMPARE AND CONTRAST

To understand how a government evolves, it helps to compare and contrast its plans for governance. Use a Venn diagram to compare and contrast the main features of the Articles of Confederation and the U.S. Constitution, placing each feature in the proper circle. If the plans share any features, list them in the space where the circles intersect. Then answer the question.

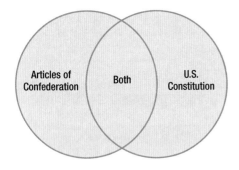

Articles of Confederation | Both | U.S. Constitution

9. How did the U.S. government evolve from its founding to the ratification of the U.S. Constitution?

MAIN IDEAS

Answer the following questions. Support your answers with evidence from the chapter.

10. What was the main problem with the government formed under the Articles of Confederation? **LESSON 1.1**

11. What was the political status of the states under the Articles of Confederation? **LESSON 1.1**

12. What was a major problem with the Land Ordinance of 1785, and how was it solved? **LESSON 1.2**

13. Why did taxation lead to a revolt among farmers in 1786? **LESSON 2.1**

14. In what way did James Madison influence the direction of the 1787 convention in Philadelphia? **LESSON 2.1**

15. How did the Great Compromise combine elements of the Virginia Plan and the New Jersey Plan? **LESSON 2.2**

16. What are the main responsibilities of the three branches of the U.S. government? **LESSON 2.2**

17. How did the group that favored ratification of the Constitution get its name? **LESSON 3.1**

18. Why were some Americans opposed to ratification of the Constitution? **LESSON 3.1**

19. What issue slowed down the ratification of the Constitution? **LESSON 3.2**

HISTORICAL THINKING

Answer the following questions. Support your answers with evidence from the chapter.

20. **IDENTIFY PROBLEMS AND SOLUTIONS** How did the Articles of Confederation make it difficult for Congress to resolve conflicts with other countries?

21. **ANALYZE CAUSE AND EFFECT** What effect did the high price of lots have on land distribution in the Northwest Territory?

22. **MAKE CONNECTIONS** What political groups today oppose a strong central government, and what are their reasons?

23. **DRAW CONCLUSIONS** How might the Three-fifths Compromise have influenced the continuation of slavery in the United States?

INTERPRET VISUALS

American artist Ralph Earl and the subject of his portrait, Elijah Boardman (1760–1823), chose an unusual setting for this painting: Boardman's dry goods store. Boardman was a Revolutionary War veteran and a successful merchant in Connecticut. He eventually entered politics and became a U.S. senator. In this painting, he stands in front of his counting desk, where he managed bills and inventory. The open door reveals shelves of costly fabrics, including imports from Europe and Asia.

24. What do Boardman's clothing and manner imply about his status in the new republic?

25. How does Boardman typify the kind of leaders many Framers envisioned for the new republic?

ANALYZE SOURCES

As state legislators debated ratification of the U.S. Constitution, other citizens had fiery debates on its merits in the public press, most often signing their essays and letters to the editor with pseudonyms. In this excerpt from the October 18, 1787, edition of the *New York Journal*, antifederalist "Brutus" warns against establishing one large republic. Read the excerpt and answer the question.

> History furnishes no example of a free republic, any thing like the extent of the United States. The Grecian republics were of small extent; so also was that of the Romans. Both of these, it is true, in process of time, extended their conquests over large territories of country; and the consequence was, that their governments were changed from that of free governments to those of the most tyrannical that ever existed in the world.

26. What danger is "Brutus" warning readers about in this quotation?

CONNECT TO YOUR LIFE

27. **ARGUMENT** The U.S. Constitution is one of the oldest constitutions in use in the world. Its longevity is largely due to the amendment process, which allows the document to adapt to changing conditions. If you could propose a constitutional amendment, what would it be? Why is it important, and how might it affect Americans? Write a proposal describing your amendment and the problems it would alleviate. Include supporting reasons, details, and evidence.

TIPS

- Read the amendments to the Constitution to become familiar with the kinds of changes that have been made.

- Address opposition to your amendment.

- If appropriate, include two or three key terms from the chapter in your proposal.

- Conclude your argument by summarizing the benefits of your amendment.

HISTORICAL THINKING How did government, expansion, and war unify the nation?

CRITICAL VIEWING George Washington inherited this northern Virginia estate, called Mount Vernon, sometime after 1752. Before moving there in 1759, he started expanding the house. His renovations continued until 1787. Some of the design ideas, such as the covered walkways connecting the buildings, were uniquely his own. What does this photo of Mount Vernon suggest about Washington's design preferences and choices?

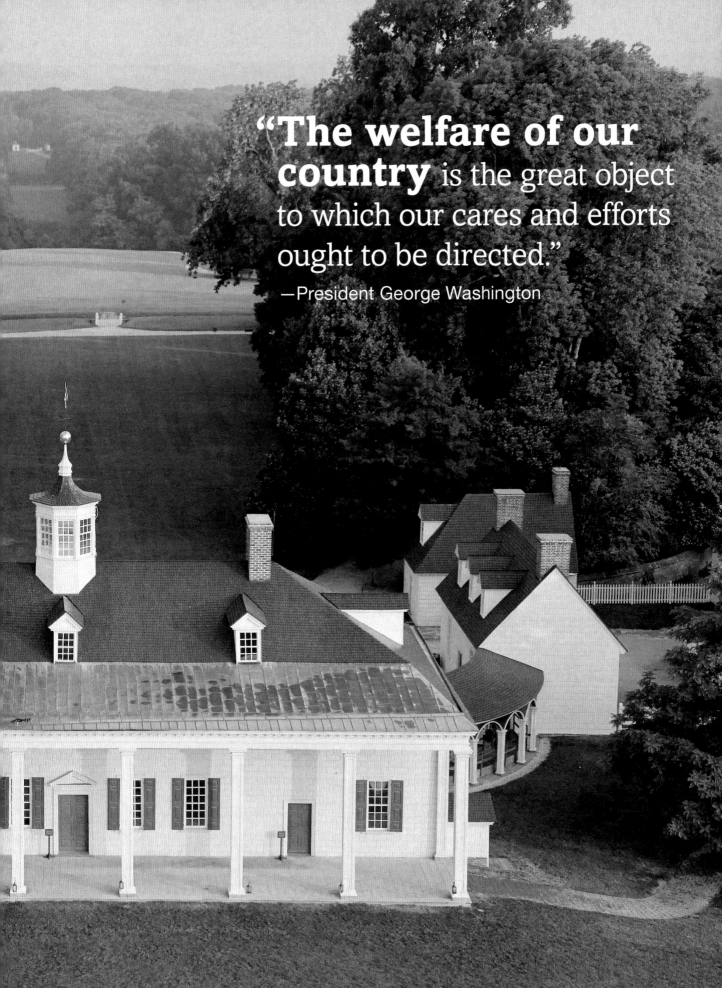

"**The welfare of our country** is the great object to which our cares and efforts ought to be directed."

—President George Washington

CRITICAL VIEWING American artist Gilbert
Stuart painted this portrait of George Washington
around 1800. How do you think the artist wanted
to portray Washington, and what details in the
painting might help represent him that way?

THE FOUNDING FATHERS

Why do we use the term "Founding Fathers" to describe George Washington, Thomas Jefferson, Benjamin Franklin, and their contemporaries at the Constitutional Convention of 1787? The obvious answer is that these individuals helped establish the United States as an independent country and created its stable, lasting government structures. In a deeper sense, the Founding Fathers earned that title not just through their actions but by the qualities of character they embody. Each man personified traits such as patriotism, forward-thinking, and innovation that Americans admire and strive to incorporate into our national identity.

GEORGE WASHINGTON: THE PATRIOT

To most people, being elected president of the United States would most likely be cause for jubilation. George Washington, however, wrote to a friend that he was sacrificing "all expectations of private happiness in this world" by accepting the office. His personal aspirations lay elsewhere, on a plantation in Virginia called Mount Vernon.

When Washington inherited Mount Vernon sometime after 1752, he was already managing the plantation. He was dedicated to it, and his chief ambition was to remain there running the plantation in the company of his wife and stepchildren. Between 1775 and 1781, as Washington campaigned with the Continental Army, Mount Vernon remained on his mind. He gratefully returned there when the American Revolution ended.

Within a few years, however, Washington went back to public life and eventually became a key figure in the Constitutional Convention of 1787. Shortly afterward, the electoral college unanimously elected him president, and he felt obligated to serve his country.

> "Every post is honorable in which a man can serve his country."
> —George Washington, 1775

Washington knew his actions would set the tone for all future presidencies. In a letter to fellow Founding Father James Madison, he wrote "As the first of everything in our situation will serve to establish a precedent, it is devoutly wished on my part that these precedents may be fixed on true principles." He strove to fulfill his office with integrity and respect for the principles of democracy, and he retired after two terms.

Washington would have less than three years to enjoy his well-deserved and long-delayed retirement at Mount Vernon. On December 14, 1799, he died of a throat infection surrounded by his family members, trusted friends, and close members of his staff.

THOMAS JEFFERSON: THE FORWARD THINKER

On April 29, 1962, President John F. Kennedy hosted a banquet at the White House for 49 Nobel Prize winners. In his speech to some of the most brilliant people in the world, Kennedy said, "I think this is the most extraordinary collection of talent and of human knowledge that has ever been gathered together at the White House—with the possible exception of when Thomas Jefferson dined alone."

Kennedy had a point: Jefferson's intelligence, coupled with his curiosity and his relentless quest for knowledge, made him one of the

> "The tree of liberty must be refreshed from time to time with the blood of patriots and tyrants."
>
> —Thomas Jefferson, 1787

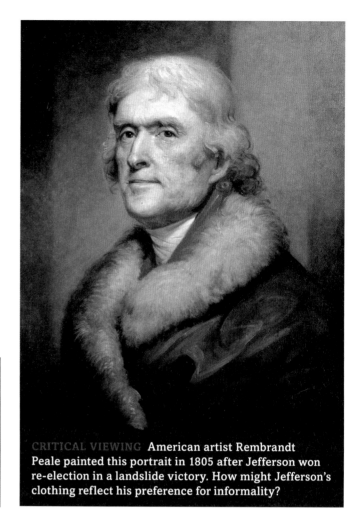

CRITICAL VIEWING American artist Rembrandt Peale painted this portrait in 1805 after Jefferson won re-election in a landslide victory. How might Jefferson's clothing reflect his preference for informality?

FOUNDING MOTHERS?

In 2016, when *The Atlantic* magazine asked, "Who is the greatest supporting player of all time?" historian Richard Norton Smith nominated Martha Washington, George's wife. According to Smith, "She ran Mount Vernon during his long absences; acted as his wartime secretary, sounding board, and surrogate; and charmed members of Congress who agreed on little else." Many historians acknowledge that Martha Washington was a patriot in her own right and played a pivotal role in supporting George in both the private and public spheres.

CRITICAL VIEWING This 1878 oil painting of Martha Washington is part of the White House art collection. What does artist Eliphalet Frazer Andrews convey about Mrs. Washington through the portrait's details?

leading intellectuals of his time. These qualities also allowed him to form a vision for the future of the North American colonies as an independent country, which he boldly articulated as the principal writer of the Declaration of Independence. Later, as president, he purchased the Louisiana Territory to ensure an expansive future for the United States.

Jefferson's restless intellect drove him to study topics as diverse as architecture, wine making, natural history, and many others. Wherever he found himself, he would take time each day to make notes about the weather, what plants were blooming, and the patterns of migratory birds. When he dispatched Lewis and Clark to explore the land west of the Mississippi, he was eager not just to stake the United States' claim to the territory, but to learn of the new animals, plants, people, and geographic features they would discover.

After his second term in office as president, Jefferson was succeeded in 1809 by his friend James Madison and retired to Monticello, his home in Virginia. At the age of 76, once again looking to the future, he founded the University of Virginia. Jefferson died on July 4, 1826.

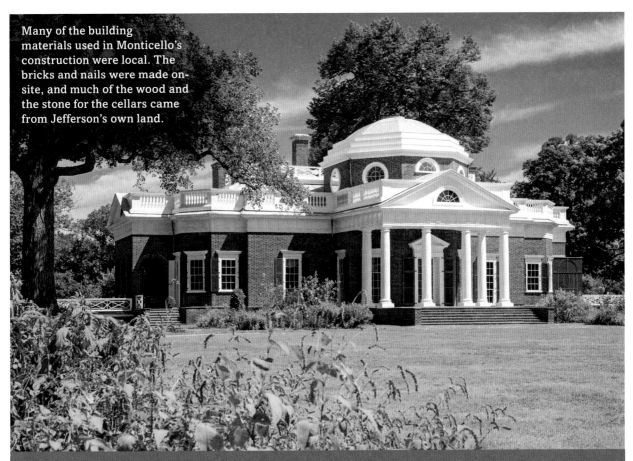

Many of the building materials used in Monticello's construction were local. The bricks and nails were made on-site, and much of the wood and the stone for the cellars came from Jefferson's own land.

AT HOME IN MONTICELLO

For Jefferson, Monticello was both a dream house and a lifelong project. He began designing and building the home near Charlottesville, Virginia, in 1768, and devoted more than 40 years to altering it. The current structure was finished in 1809.

Many elements of Monticello bear witness to Jefferson's genius. The dome that tops the house, for example, had to be meticulously designed and built in order to fit safely on top of the load-bearing walls. From the inside, the "dome room" features large circular windows and a skylight.

Jefferson also installed a pair of doors that both opened when only one of them was pushed. It was not until Monticello was renovated in 1950 that experts discovered the ingenious mechanism he had devised to connect the doors. A sundial in the garden that Jefferson built himself demonstrates his solid understanding of astronomy.

Today, the home and historic gardens of Monticello, are maintained by the Thomas Jefferson Foundation and open to visitors. The estate is also listed as a UNESCO World Heritage Site.

> *"To succeed, jump as quickly at opportunities as you do at conclusions."*
> —Benjamin Franklin

BENJAMIN FRANKLIN: THE SELF-MADE MAN

By the time Benjamin Franklin died in 1790, he had been a printer, author, newspaper publisher, scientist, inventor, diplomat, and statesman. He is the only Founding Father to have signed the Declaration of Independence, the Treaty of Alliance with France, the Treaty of Paris, and the Constitution. He is also arguably the best-known entrepreneur among the Founding Fathers.

Such greatness probably seemed unimaginable when Franklin was born in 1706, the tenth son of a Boston soap maker. Franklin's family could not afford to educate him, and at 12 years old, he was apprenticed to his older brother, a printer. At 17, he ran away to Philadelphia, where he continued in the printing business. There he wrote and published the wildly popular annual *Poor Richard's Almanack* from 1732 to 1757. In addition to weather predictions and household advice, the almanac contained pearls of wisdom and wit, such as "Early to bed and early to rise, makes a man healthy, wealthy and wise" and "Three may keep a secret, if two of them are dead."

Like Jefferson, Franklin had a broad range of scientific interests and pursued them whenever the opportunity presented itself. When crossing the Atlantic Ocean to Europe, for example, he took accurate measurements of ocean temperatures that enabled him to make the first chart of the Gulf Stream, a powerful ocean current that flows from North America to Europe. This information helped reduce the sailing time from Europe to North America by two weeks. He also greatly advanced the understanding of electricity by conducting a variety of experiments, including the famous incident in which he flew a kite tied to a key during a lightning storm.

But it is as a statesman that Franklin is best known—and revered. When the Stamp Act was passed in 1765, he was in England, serving as a colonial representative of Pennsylvania. The colonists' negative response to the passage of the act took him completely by surprise. Stirred to action, he spoke eloquently to Parliament, condemning the act and explaining the colonists'

Ben Franklin, shown above in a portrait by Joseph Siffred Duplessis, shared many important ideas with the world. But his proposal to eliminate the letters C, J, Q, W, X, and Y from the alphabet was not well received.

position. His speech was instrumental in its repeal. The experience made Franklin feel what he called his "Americanness" as never before. He also began to question his loyalty to Britain and its treatment of the colonies. As colonial protests mounted against Britain and the king, Franklin became a strong voice for independence and democracy. He would help draft the Declaration of Independence and was among the first to sign it.

Through his accomplishments, wit, energy, and personal charm, Franklin lived his final days wealthy and admired on both sides of the Atlantic.

THINK ABOUT IT

What American ideals do the Founding Fathers represent for you?

WE ARE INDEBTED TO YOU, BEN FRANKLIN

Some of Franklin's inventions, incorporating later improvements, are still in use, while others have been overtaken by more modern technologies. Here is a partial list of his creations, discoveries, and new ideas:

Bifocal glasses

- bifocal glasses

- the lightning rod

- *Poor Richard's Almanack*

- the Franklin stove, which allowed for more efficient home heating

- swim fins (for the hands)

- the glass armonica (a musical instrument)

- extension arm (a device for reaching books on high shelves)

- the first successful lending library in the United States

- a map of the course of the Gulf Stream

- the terms "charge," "condenser," and "conductor" to describe concepts in electricity

Poor Richard's
Almanack, **1739**

Romanticized painting of Franklin harnessing lightning

THE GLASS ARMONICA

Glass armonica

One of Franklin's odd-looking inventions to modern-day eyes is the glass armonica, a musical instrument consisting of glass bowls of various sizes mounted on a spindle. The armonica relied on an effect similar to creating musical notes by rubbing a wet finger around the rim of a partially filled glass. To coax music from a glass armonica, the player would turn the spindle and touch the edges of the rotating bowls with a moistened finger to produce different notes. Glass armonicas are rare today, but they were popular in the late 18th century. Both Mozart and Beethoven wrote pieces for the instrument.

WASHINGTON'S LEADERSHIP

Voted unanimously into office, George Washington reluctantly took on the role of president. As he himself described it, the nation faced "an ocean of difficulties." So what did he do? He gathered an A-list of team members to help him.

FORMING A GOVERNMENT

As you have read, the founders faced the unique challenge of forming a republican government from the ground up. The Articles of Confederation, which had given almost all the power to the states and practically none to the central government, hadn't worked well. Now the nation had a new Constitution that split power between a strong central government and the individual states. The challenge was to make that balancing act work.

As the newly written Constitution directed, the electoral college—not the people—determined who would be president in this first election. When the members of the electoral college met in their state capitals in February 1789 to cast their votes for president, they were instructed to vote for two candidates each. Every one of the 69 electors who participated cast one vote for Washington. Washington won the presidency hands down. John Adams, who was runner-up with 34 votes, became the vice president.

Washington's leadership during the revolution, his dignity and character, his support for republican government, and his commitment to the success of the new Constitution made him the obvious choice to unite the nation. He took great pains to make it clear that he would be the nation's president, not its king, and that he answered to the American citizens. At

his first presidential **inauguration**, or swearing-in ceremony, he did as he had when asked to lead the Continental Army: he renounced any formal salary for his position. Instead, in his inaugural address, he declared that any money paid to him as executive "be limited to such actual expenditures as the public good may be thought to require."

One of the first tasks the new president and Congress faced was to organize the government. In the summer of 1789, Congress created the Departments of State, Treasury, and War as part of the executive branch. Washington appointed the heads of these departments, called secretaries, and they formed his **Cabinet**.

CRITICAL VIEWING On April 30, 1789, Washington was sworn in as president on the balcony of a hall in New York City, the newly declared U.S. capital. What details in Ramon de Elorriaga's painting *The Inauguration of George Washington* show the importance of the event?

Washington chose a group of highly talented men from a variety of geographical areas and with a mix of political views to make up his Cabinet. He strongly advocated political moderation and tried to keep himself, as president, above the bickering that went on between political factions. He encouraged his Cabinet to do the same.

To oversee relations with foreign nations, Washington chose Thomas Jefferson as Secretary of State. Alexander Hamilton, well known as a good money manager, was chosen to be Secretary of the Treasury. And former general Henry Knox was selected to supervise the nation's military as Secretary of War. Congress created another Cabinet position, the office of **attorney general**, charged with the primary role of representing the United States before the Supreme Court. Unlike the other Cabinet members, the attorney general would not lead an executive department. Washington named lawyer and politician Edmund Randolph as the nation's first attorney general.

THE JUDICIARY AND THE CENSUS

President Washington and Congress also needed to establish a system of courts. With the **Judiciary Act of 1789**, Congress fleshed out the line of text in Article III of the Constitution, which states: "The judicial power of the United States shall be vested in one Supreme Court, and in such inferior courts as the Congress may from time to time ordain and establish." The act established a Supreme Court of six justices—one Chief Justice and five associate justices. (Today, eight associate justices sit on the court.) The Chief Justice was to preside over the judicial branch of the U.S. government as well as over the Supreme Court itself. John Jay, who had helped negotiate the Treaty of Paris in 1783, became the nation's first Chief Justice.

The act also created a dual-court system, with responsibilities split between state and federal courts. A few "inferior" federal courts, that is federal courts other than the Supreme Court, existed to deal with federal crimes. State courts presided over most civil and criminal cases. A **civil case** is a legal dispute between two or more individuals or organizations, often involving contract issues or other business problems. In a **criminal case** the defendant is

THE CENSUS, THEN AND NOW

In 1790, the U.S. Census was little more than a head count. It measured race, age, gender, and whether someone was free or enslaved. Today, the census involves more than 200 different surveys that track information about people living in the United States, whether they are citizens or not. Why does the government need so much data? Information such as income, home ownership, and relationships among people sharing a residence help the government anticipate what its population will need. The number of people that live in a state continues to serve as the basis for determining how many representatives a state should have in the House. More specific information about each person helps government agencies decide how to allot government funds meant for maintaining education, healthcare, and other social systems nationwide.

accused of breaking the law and endangering society, and the government initiates the case in coordination with law enforcement. The U.S. Supreme Court might agree to hear appeals for civil and criminal cases decided by the highest state courts.

Representing each state's population fairly with the right number of delegates in the House of Representatives and electoral college was a vital concern for the country. It meant the nation had to keep track of how many people were living in each state. The Constitution had stipulated that within three years of Congress's first meeting, a **census**, or population count, would be taken. It was to be repeated every ten years after that. Congress set August 1790 as the date of the first census, which took 18 months to complete.

Although sketchy and incomplete, the **U.S. Census of 1790** helped measure the dynamic population growth of an expanding nation. The first census results showed that the United States had nearly 3.9 million people, not including Native Americans. "Free white males" numbered about 1.6 million. "Free white females" numbered around 1.54 million. The category "All other free persons," mainly free African Americans, numbered nearly 60,000. Almost 700,000 of those counted in the census were enslaved.

HISTORICAL THINKING

1. **READING CHECK** What steps did Washington and Congress take to establish the new government?

2. **SUMMARIZE** Choose one political decision described in this lesson. How did it help organize the new nation's government?

3. **COMPARE AND CONTRAST** How were the nation's new federal and state courts different from one another?

WOMEN'S ROLES IN THE NEW REPUBLIC

Two steps forward, one step back. During the war, women ventured outside of the home to battle, farm, and do business. Afterward, a new spotlight shone on the importance of women's household roles. Was this progress?

REPUBLICAN MOTHERHOOD

When George Washington traveled to his inauguration in New York, Americans along the route showed their patriotic spirit with celebrations, banners, and speeches. Americans also felt bound together by a new spirit of nationalism. They had a sense they were participating in **civic republicanism** —or the tradition of political thought that stresses individual freedom, active citizenship, and support for the common good.

Civic republicanism dates back to the ancient Greeks and Romans. In the United States, it represented a government and constitution that promised justice for all. In order to guarantee freedom and justice, a nation needed to promote principles such as civic virtue, patriotism, and individual freedom, and it needed to oppose excessive government power. In connection with these ideals, many Americans believed that raising children and educating them was important to the republic, as these activities passed the qualities of effective republican citizenship on to the next generation.

Women were crucial to civic republicanism in the role that historians now refer to as republican motherhood. The concept of **republican motherhood** was a powerful force in the late 18th and early 19th centuries. The goal was to raise children—especially sons—to participate actively and wisely in civic life by voting, becoming property owners, taking part in local government, and behaving morally. Though voting

Best known for his art depicting colonial America, John Singleton Copley painted this portrait of himself (top left) with his family in 1776–1777. Historians believe that through lighting, gesture, gaze, and color, Copley's work expresses some popular ideals of his time—including the concept of republican motherhood.

rights at the time varied from state to state, they were generally limited to property-owning white males. So the notion of republican motherhood mostly applied to upper- and middle-class white women.

The ideal was for a republican mother to pass on her wisdom in a tranquil home, a refuge protected from conflicts in the outside world of politics and business. By avoiding such outside influences, the republican mother was expected to live out her once-revolutionary principles by raising and teaching children. While this ideal elevated the traditional status of mother and wife, it also solidified gender roles in which men ruled the public sphere.

WOMEN, RESPONSIBILITIES, AND RIGHTS

During the war, women stepped in to manage farms and businesses while men served as soldiers. Some women even served on the battlefield. Many American women hoped that their lives would change after the Revolution, and they would be able to continue taking on more active roles as citizens.

After the war, women's rights did not improve. Women still could not vote or hold office. They still had very limited access to educational opportunities and had virtually no right to purchase property. Though they were allowed to inherit more property after the American Revolution, women usually came into their inheritance after marriage, so their husbands ended up being the legal owners of property they inherited. Ironically, as limited as the role of republican motherhood was, it was one of the only paths many women could follow to gain control over parts of their own lives.

A woman's stature as a republican mother opened up possibilities to serve the new nation in ways beyond just raising good citizens. Often seen as more "moral" than men who battled in politics, courtrooms, and businesses, the republican mother—tasked with shaping the moral and intellectual character of future generations—found opportunities to become active in church and community groups.

Women provided much of the support for establishing public schools and mental asylums. They opposed activities that they deemed immoral, such as alcohol abuse, and many worked to abolish slavery. They also formed "Maternal Associations" to teach new ideas about raising children and to provide childcare for working mothers who often took on domestic work for other families to support their own. And, since women were expected to teach their children to become responsible citizens, they argued for more educational opportunities for themselves.

SUPPORT FOR EDUCATION

Female essayist and playwright **Judith Sargent Murray** was a strong supporter of education for women. She argued against the common belief of the day that women were intellectually inferior to men, claiming that the nation's daughters could not reach their full capabilities if the only roles they were trained for in society were those of wife, mother, and housekeeper. She pointed out that if mothers were expected to teach their children the basics in all subjects, they should be educated in the sciences and higher mathematics, which were traditionally reserved for male students.

Through the first decades of the new republic, women would take an ever-increasing role in the education of children, both within the home and in public schools. They also became involved in establishing schools for other women. The more active women became in this enterprise and in promoting the public good, the more they began to work toward securing rights for themselves and their daughters. They formed organizations to help orphans, the physically handicapped, and war widows. These organizations would lead to larger social movements in the future.

PRIMARY SOURCE

I expect to see our young women forming a new era in female history. . . . The partial distribution of advantages, which has too long obtained, is, in this enlightened age, rapidly giving place to a more uniform system of [education] . . . and the revolution of events is advancing in that half of the human species, which [has until now] been involved in the night of darkness, toward the irradiating sun of science.

—from Judith Sargent Murray, 1798, as quoted in *No Small Courage: A History of Women in the United States*

HISTORICAL THINKING

1. **READING CHECK** What was "civic republicanism," and why did Americans feel they were participating in it?

2. **FORM AND SUPPORT OPINIONS** Did the concept of republican motherhood give women greater or less independence and autonomy? Support your opinion with details from the lesson.

3. **MAKE CONNECTIONS** What ideas that rose from the concept of republican motherhood might have led to later events in history, such as the fight for women's right to vote?

OPPOSING VISIONS OF AMERICA

Which came first, the United States or its national debt? If you said "its debt," you're right. Patriots had borrowed $54 million to fund the American Revolution. And now the already struggling nation was in conflict about how to pay it back.

OPPOSING VISIONS OF AMERICA

The arguments that had plagued the constitutional debates continued into the new government. During Washington's first term, these political divisions widened, and two political parties developed. Alexander Hamilton, Washington's secretary of the treasury, saw the nation's future greatness in commerce and manufacturing. His followers, who joined to form the **Federalist Party**, favored commercial development, a strong central government, and a **loose constructionist** interpretation of the Constitution, which gave expansive powers to Congress and the president.

On the other side of the political coin, the **Democratic-Republican Party** favored a **strict constructionist** interpretation of the Constitution, one that followed the document to the letter, honoring the rights of states over federal power. Thomas Jefferson and James Madison founded the party, and Jefferson became the Democratic-Republicans' chief spokesman. He believed that the United States should be an **agrarian**, or agricultural, society made up of small farmers. The role of commerce should be to allow these farmers to sell their surplus crops in Europe and purchase manufactured goods in return.

DISPUTES OVER DEBTS

The nation owed more than $10 million in war debts to foreigners, mostly the French, and more than $40 million to Americans in payment of bonds. The bonds were issued to civilians in exchange for wartime supplies and to soldiers in exchange for wages. After the war, many ordinary Americans, unable to wait for repayment, sold their bonds to wealthy speculators, often at only 10 or 15 percent of their value. In addition to the national debt, individual states owed about $25 million collectively.

In his *Report on the Public Credit* in January 1790, Alexander Hamilton presented a plan in which the national government took on the responsibility for all of these debts, including those owed by the states. He proposed repaying the foreign debt immediately but repaying the domestic debt more slowly, using import duties, income from the post office, and an **excise tax**, or a tax levied on one particular product, in this case on the purchase of whiskey.

The Democratic-Republicans opposed Hamilton's proposal. They argued the plan would allow speculators to profit from the hardships of citizens— many of them farmers—who had sold their bonds at a fraction of their value. And many of the southern states had already paid off their war debts. They did not want to be taxed again to pay debts of other states. Debate continued for months. The matter was finally settled after Hamilton, Jefferson, and Madison struck a bargain.

Jefferson and Madison wanted to move the nation's capital from New York to a place farther south, specifically, on the banks of the Potomac River, which separated Virginia from Maryland. If Hamilton agreed, Jefferson and Madison would persuade southern delegates to approve his financial proposal. He did, and Congress passed Hamilton's plan and authorized a new capital, carved out of Virginia and Maryland, but belonging to neither. The capital city would be called Washington, and it would lie on land renamed the District of Columbia. **Pierre L'Enfant**, a French architect who had served with Washington at Valley Forge, was hired to plan the new capital.

Finally, to stabilize the nation's finances, Hamilton proposed a national bank and a common currency. The **Bank of the United States** and its branches would hold federal funds and regulate state banks.

Based on the life of the Founding Father, Tony Award-winning *Hamilton* mixes hip-hop music with traditional elements of Broadway musicals. The result is a unique biography that has propelled writer and actor Lin-Manuel Miranda (right) and his main character, Alexander Hamilton, into the national spotlight.

In addition to commemorating Hamilton's contributions to establishing the Federalist Party and advocating for the National Bank, the musical considers how Hamilton's childhood shaped his life and explores his roles as a soldier, a lawyer, and an economist throughout his political career.

Its chief purposes would be to expand the money supply and encourage commerce and economic growth. As it prospered, stockholders would receive **dividends**, or interest for depositing their money. The government would also receive dividends, which would help to lower the national debt.

Madison and Jefferson took a strict constructionist stance on the national bank, arguing that the federal government lacked constitutional authority to create such an institution. Hamilton countered with the loose constructionist interpretation that some federal powers are implied rather than stated outright. He argued that the Constitution gave Congress and the president the power to collect taxes, pay debts, coin and regulate money—and to "make all laws which shall be necessary and proper for carrying into execution the foregoing powers." Congress chartered the bank in 1791 for 20 years. After studying the matter carefully, President Washington approved Congress's charter.

THE WHISKEY REBELLION

The excise tax on whiskey led to unrest in the states, particularly in western Pennsylvania. Farmers there had resisted the tax from the start, because whiskey was their main source of cash. It was much cheaper to transport and sell whiskey than the heavy grain it was made from. The excise tax harmed farmers'

finances and made them furious. In what became known as the **Whiskey Rebellion**, they tarred and feathered tax collectors, burned barns, and even destroyed the whiskey stills of fellow farmers who paid the tax. They believed their battle was a struggle for "the virtuous principles of republican liberty." The farmers had other complaints, too, about the federal government's failure to open lands in the Ohio Territory for settlement and to end trade restrictions with the Spanish on the Mississippi River.

In July 1794, about 500 farmers surrounded and burned a tax inspector's home, exchanging gunfire that killed several people. The violence soon spread to neighboring states. Washington sent 13,000 militia, but the revolt had ended before the troops arrived. The threat of military force had stopped the rebellion.

HISTORICAL THINKING

1. **READING CHECK** How did a loose constructionist and a strict constructionist interpret the Constitution differently?

2. **ANALYZE CAUSE AND EFFECT** What was the primary cause of the Whiskey Rebellion?

3. **DISTINGUISH FACT FROM OPINION** What was one fact and one opinion used in the debate over Hamilton's plan to repay the nation's war debt?

POLITICAL ENTANGLEMENTS

Washington's presidency wasn't getting any easier. As the young nation grew, so did its internal conflicts between political parties and external conflicts with other nations. Agreeing on which conflict to resolve first was a problem, too.

EXPANSION TO THE WEST

During the 1780s, the lands west of the Appalachian Mountains and south of the Ohio River developed quickly, as American settlers moved to Kentucky and Tennessee in search of available farmland. State governments, speculators, and frontiersmen took the land from the Cherokee who had inhabited the territory for thousands of years.

In the 1780s and 1790s, the Cherokee joined the Creek and Shawnee, who also lived in the region, in attacking the American settlers. To stop the attacks, the U.S. government issued the 1791 Treaty of Holston, which promised that if the Cherokee ceded settled territory, they could keep their remaining lands. However, Governor William Blount of the Tennessee Territory, known by Native Americans as "dirt king" for his greed for land, ignored the promise to the Cherokee. The treaty collapsed and the battles continued until 1794, when U.S. forces fought and defeated the Native Americans.

Farther north, settlement in Ohio country was slower. This was partly because the federal government kept a tighter control in the territory than in the West— but more so because Native Americans strongly resisted giving up their land there. Throughout the 1780s, the United States obtained land in the area from some Native American groups, while the Delaware, Shawnee, Iroquois, Miami, and other Native American nations rejected the agreements. Native American tribes in Ohio formed a confederacy against U.S. settlement and attacked any settlers that trespassed on their land. The confederacy extended its influence, forming alliances with Native Americans to the south. The Spanish and the British, who still had their eyes on these lands, provided aid to the Native American confederacy.

In the early 1790s, Washington sent two military expeditions against the confederacy. Both were unsuccessful. Then in 1794, U.S. forces defeated the Shawnee and the Miami at the **Battle of Fallen Timbers** near present-day Toledo, Ohio. The British, who had helped the confederacy in the past, refused to enter this battle because they were already fighting a war with France. The Native American confederacy eventually signed the **Treaty of Greenville** in 1795, giving up their lands in present-day Ohio and parts of Indiana, Illinois, and Michigan.

THE SPANISH FRONTIER

By the 1790s the young nation faced difficult relations with European rivals, both in North America and abroad. A major challenge came from Spain. At that time, Spain's lands in what is now the United States extended from Florida to Louisiana, Texas, New Mexico, Arizona, and California. Even though Spanish officials were wary of U.S. population growth, they opened their lands to U.S. settlers to bolster their own population and economy. Spain offered free land in Florida and Louisiana to American planters and relaxed restrictions to promote more trade. Such policies eventually led to the U.S. acquisition of Florida and Louisiana. As Jefferson had predicted, Spain provided "the means of delivering to us peaceably, what may otherwise cost us a war."

Meanwhile, **Thomas Pinckney**, an American statesman, traveled to Spain and negotiated the Treaty of San Lorenzo in 1795 to maintain friendly relations between the United States and Spain. Also known as "Pinckney's Treaty," it opened the Mississippi River to free navigation, allowing Americans free use of the Spanish port of New Orleans. The treaty also settled a conflict regarding the Spanish colony of West Florida.

DIFFICULTIES WITH FRANCE AND GREAT BRITAIN

In 1789, Americans were intrigued by the events unfolding in another country across the Atlantic. The people of France sought to put an end to upper-class privilege and demanded equality for the lower classes. This caused the country to change from a strict monarchy to a constitutional monarchy and started the **French Revolution**. Many in the United States, particularly the Democratic-Republicans, supported this revolution. However, in 1792, as the French Revolution continued, **radicals**, or people who support complete social or political change, took control and established the First French Republic. Within a year, the radicals had executed King Louis XVI. The French Republic then declared war on Britain, Spain, and other neighboring nations. In this international conflict, the Federalists sided with Britain, thereby increasing the division between the two American parties. So even though France had supported the American Revolution, Washington declared in 1793 that the United States would remain neutral, not taking sides with anyone.

The 1778 Franco-American Alliance, forged during the American Revolution, did not require the United States to enter France's conflicts in Europe, but France expected favorable trade policies and informal American military help. Though Secretary of State Jefferson favored France, he agreed that neutrality, or official impartiality, was essential. Jefferson knew American commerce was tied to Britain, which could also sweep U.S. ships from the seas with its powerful navy.

Washington issued a Proclamation of Neutrality in April 1793, warning citizens to avoid hostile acts, including selling weapons and privateering, or licensing of private ships by a warring nation to attack enemy vessels. Still, France enlisted American privateers against British vessels.

On July 14, 1789, an angry crowd in Paris attacked and captured the Bastille, the fortress prison that had become a symbol of the tyranny of King Louis XVI. The event, as represented in this painting by Jean Pierre Houel, signaled the beginning of the French Revolution, a decade when long-oppressed French commoners seized power from the upper classes.

Meanwhile Washington also faced increasing aggression from the British. In the early 1790s, the British began **impressment**, or recruitment by force, of U.S. merchant sailors. They captured American sailors and forced them to serve the British navy. Then, in 1793, the British blockaded the French West Indies, seizing more than 250 American ships.

Problems eased when the British weakened their French West Indies blockade, allowing Americans to trade food and consumer goods, but not weapons. Washington sent John Jay, chief justice of the Supreme Court, to persuade the British to leave their Western forts, pay for the slaves who had left with Britain's army, end impressment, open the British West Indies to American trade, and compensate

the United States for their Caribbean shipping losses. **Jay's Treaty** succeeded only in obtaining British withdrawal from Western forts, payment for confiscated ships in the Caribbean, and began to open trade in the British West Indies to most ships.

Washington kept the treaty secret from the Senate until it was debated in June 1795. With heavy Federalist support, the Senate approved Jay's Treaty and Washington signed it. Jay's failure to achieve all of the treaty's goals enraged many politicians. Democratic-Republicans gained support from former Federalists, especially Southerners, as Americans throughout the nation protested what they viewed as a failed treaty. But the treaty had eased tensions with the British enough to avoid open war.

A GLOBAL PERSPECTIVE Chinese artist Ai Weiwei created 176 portraits of "prisoners of conscience"—people imprisoned for holding views their governments do not allow—out of colorful LEGO® blocks. In 2014, his exhibit of the portraits, called *Trace*, was installed on the floor of Alcatraz Prison in San Francisco. From a distance, the images look cheerful. But details in them, such as handcuffs, surveillance cameras and Twitter bird logos (symbolizing tweets challenging authority), allude to a story of repression.

Ironically, Weiwei could not view the installation of his work. Due to his public criticisms of the Chinese government, he was not allowed to leave his country. There are many prisoners of conscience across the world today. Similar to the Sedition Act of 1798, which targeted anyone who criticized the U.S. government, laws exist in other countries that enable governments to violate citizens' basic freedoms. Governments that protect their citizens' civil and human rights have policies in place to limit and balance government power.

THE ADAMS PRESIDENCY

Once conflicts had subsided, American settlement and trade in the West increased. The economy flourished, and the success of the American republic seemed ensured. As the 1796 election approached, President Washington announced his retirement. His health had started to decline, and the angry Senate debate over Jay's Treaty had left him exhausted. He also wanted to establish the precedent, or example, of limiting the presidency to two terms. Before leaving office, Washington delivered a farewell address, in which he warned against the dangers of rivaling parties.

In spite of this warning, the Federalists and Democratic-Republicans waged a bitter campaign in 1796. John Adams ran on the Federalist side, and Thomas Jefferson represented the Democratic-Republicans. Other candidates ran too. As you have read, every elector of the electoral college cast two votes, but no more than one for any candidate. The 1796 election results were close: Adams won the presidency with 71 votes, and Jefferson won the vice presidency with 68. It was not a happy arrangement.

Adams's background was certainly presidential. A Patriot leader from the earliest rumblings of the Revolution, Adams had strongly supported Jefferson's writing of the Declaration of Independence and had served as a delegate to the Continental Congress. He had helped negotiate the Treaty of Paris of 1783 and had been minister, or ambassador, to Great Britain. Adams possessed an excellent understanding of government and diplomacy and had a reputation for honesty and fairness; but he lacked Washington's charisma, military bearing, and flair for leadership.

TROUBLE WITH FRANCE

Relations with France had worsened by the time John Adams took office. France began seizing American ships in an effort to prevent the United States from trading with Great Britain. War with France appeared inevitable. In 1797, the United States responded to the ship seizures by fortifying its harbors with warships and militia. Adams sent three **envoys**, or ambassadors, to France to settle the problem. The envoys communicated with the French foreign minister through **intermediaries**, or go-betweens, later known to the American public simply as X, Y, and Z. When the French agents made unreasonable demands and even insisted on being paid a bribe to begin negotiations, the shocked envoys turned them down and returned home.

The **XYZ Affair**, as the negotiations came to be called, further soured American relations with France. It also hurt the reputation of the Democratic-Republicans, who had supported the French Revolution. When Adams made reports of the affair public, most Americans felt their honor had been attacked, and war fever swept the country. Congress expanded the army, established the navy, and authorized naval vessels to attack French ships that threatened American merchant ships. Without officially declaring war, the United States battled France in the Caribbean from 1798 to 1800. After consistent French defeats at sea, the United States was reassured that France was not a threat.

THE ALIEN AND SEDITION ACTS

In 1798, as feelings of American patriotism rose against the French, the Federalists passed the **Alien and Sedition Acts**. The Alien Act allowed the president to expel, for any reason, new immigrants, or aliens, living in the United States—most of whom were Democratic-Republicans. The Sedition Act targeted U.S. citizens, including journalists, who criticized the government. **Sedition** is the act of provoking rebellion.

Democratic-Republican Thomas Jefferson condemned the Alien and Sedition Acts, claiming they violated citizens' freedom of speech and freedom of the press. His writings spurred a theory called **nullification**—the idea that a state could veto a federal law it considered unconstitutional. The theory represented a strict interpretation of the Constitution, denying implied powers of the federal government. By 1802, most of the acts had expired or been repealed, but they had undermined Adams's popularity. In the presidential election of 1800, Jefferson defeated him. The election marked the first peaceful transfer of power from one party to another.

HISTORICAL THINKING

1. **READING CHECK** What conflict did the United States have with Great Britain in the 1790s, and how was it resolved?

2. **SUMMARIZE** How did the United States deal with Native American groups who opposed U.S. settlement of the West in the 1780s and 1790s?

3. **FORM AND SUPPORT OPINIONS** Was John Adams successful as president? Support your opinion with evidence from the text.

4. **DRAW CONCLUSIONS** In what ways did the Proclamation of Neutrality that Washington issued in 1793 protect the United States?

MAIN IDEA Thomas Jefferson narrowly won the 1800 presidential election on his promise to limit government and lower taxes.

JEFFERSON'S "REVOLUTION"

What happens when a presidential election is tied? Back in 1800, the House spent seven days casting votes to try to break it. The 36th time was the charm. Jefferson won.

THE ELECTION OF 1800

As the 1800 presidential election approached, the Federalists faced a growing backlash based on concerns over the Alien and Sedition Acts. At the same time, the United States was still hostile toward France. The Federalists hoped to take advantage of the continued conflict during the election. They planned to paint Jefferson and the Democratic-Republicans as pro-French and anti-American, since they had strongly supported the French Revolution when it began. However, President Adams did not halt negotiations with France for election strategies. The result was the Convention of 1800, an agreement with France that normalized relations and called for "a firm, inviolable, and universal peace."

Peace with France destroyed the Federalists' main campaign strategy and put the Democratic-Republicans in a good position going into the election. The party chose Jefferson as its presidential nominee and supported **Aaron Burr**, an accomplished attorney and statesman, for vice president. President Adams once again received the Federalist nomination for president. Charles Pinckney was the Federalists' choice for vice president. When the electoral vote came in, the two Democratic-Republicans were tied at 73 votes, Adams had 65 votes, and Pinckney had 64.

No one had expected such a result. The Jefferson-Burr tie sent the election to the House of Representatives, with each state delegation receiving one vote. The House cast 36 ballots over seven days before awarding the presidency to Thomas Jefferson. Burr became vice president. To keep the arduous process from happening again, Congress approved the **12th Amendment** to the U.S. Constitution in 1803. The amendment requires each elector to cast

AMERICAN PLACES
Jefferson Memorial
Washington, D.C.

The Jefferson Memorial, which faces the White House from across the Potomac River, was completed in 1943. It follows an architectural style, called neoclassical, that is prevalent on Capitol Hill. Like the earlier Greek and Roman styles that inspired it, the neoclassical style is characterized by symmetrical shapes, tall columns, and domes. Inside the memorial building, a bronze statue of Jefferson stands 19 feet tall.

a ballot for both a president and a vice president. The states ratified this amendment in 1804, just in time for the next general election.

Jefferson's inauguration took place in March 1801, the first to be held in the new capital city of Washington, D.C. The Democratic-Republicans dominated Congress. Many Federalists feared what they considered Jefferson's radical views. They saw what had happened in France, when revolutionaries took control and executed thousands of people. In his inaugural address, Jefferson tried to soothe such fears by saying, "We are all Republicans; we are all Federalists." His speech expressed his beliefs in power for state governments, freedom of religion and the press, majority rule with protection for political minorities, and the reduction of federal debt.

Jefferson aspired to create an agrarian republic in which the federal government minimized its role. In contrast to the Federalists' attempts at European grandeur, Jefferson adopted informality and frugality, or thriftiness, in his administration. He met Congressional delegates and foreign diplomats in small groups. He wrote Congress messages instead of making speeches. With Congressional support, he cut the defense budget and repealed all excise taxes, including the whiskey tax that had sparked a rebellion during Washington's administration. Almost two decades later, Jefferson described his election as "the revolution of 1800" because it was the first time that power passed from one party to another in the United States.

MARBURY v. MADISON

Although the Democratic-Republicans had won the presidency and Congress in 1800, the judiciary remained in Federalist control. Just before the Democratic-Republicans took over, Adams and his outgoing Federalist Congress passed the Judiciary Act of 1801, which amended the Judiciary Act of 1789. The act reduced the number of justices on the Supreme Court from six to five, thereby denying Jefferson the chance to appoint a new justice when the next justice died or resigned the lifetime position. The act also allowed Adams to appoint many new, Federalist lower-court judges before he stepped down. Adams worked late into the night of his last day signing commissions for these judges, who became known as the "**midnight judges**."

THE DUEL BETWEEN HAMILTON AND BURR

The rivalry between Aaron Burr and Alexander Hamilton had been building for a decade. In 1791, ill will began when Burr defeated Hamilton's father-in-law in an election. In 1800, Burr published a private essay Hamilton had written that criticized President John Adams. The essay publicly shamed Hamilton.

When Burr ran for governor of New York in 1804, Hamilton actively campaigned against him, and Burr lost the election. Irate, Burr challenged Hamilton to a duel with pistols, a common though illegal practice. Hamilton did not believe in dueling, but he accepted the challenge. The two men met at Weehawken, New Jersey, on July 11, 1804. Burr shot Hamilton in the stomach, and Hamilton died the next day. The murder ended Burr's political career. Despite being charged for Hamilton's death, Burr was never tried for it and received no punishment for the crime.

Adams also appointed a new Chief Justice of the United States, **John Marshall**—a Federalist. One of Marshall's earliest and most important cases was **Marbury v. Madison**. The case arose because the commission for one of the midnight judges, William Marbury, had not been delivered on time. Adams believed his signature alone made the commission valid. Jefferson disagreed and ordered his secretary of state, James Madison, to block the commission. Marbury sued to secure his commission.

The case seemed straightforward. Observers expected Chief Justice Marshall and his Federalist court to direct Secretary of State Madison to comply. Instead, Marshall explained that he could not remedy Marbury's problem because Congress had erred in giving the court such authority. In an unprecedented decision, Marshall declared that the existing 1789 Judiciary Act was unconstitutional.

With this ruling, Marshall established **judicial review**, the authority to invalidate any law the Court deems unconstitutional. By establishing judicial review, Marshall strengthened the balance among the three branches of government, promoting the principle of checks and balances.

HISTORICAL THINKING

1. **READING CHECK** How did judicial review strengthen the balance among the three branches of government?

2. **ANALYZE CAUSE AND EFFECT** Why did the election of 1800 lead to the adoption of the 12th Amendment?

3. **DRAW CONCLUSIONS** How did reduced tensions between the United States and France affect Jefferson's chances of winning the presidency?

THE LOUISIANA PURCHASE

All purchases, even the greatest deals with the most benefits, have drawbacks. The Louisiana Territory was a great purchase for the United States that came with some big challenges.

NEGOTIATIONS FOR LOUISIANA

A chain of unlikely events led to the United States' purchase of the **Louisiana Territory.** It began in 1800, when France signed a treaty with Spain to recover the North American lands it had ceded to Spain in 1762. When Jefferson and Madison heard about the agreement, they instructed the U.S. minister to France, **Robert Livingston**, to prevent the territory from changing hands, or at least to obtain the important port of New Orleans.

Louisiana Purchase, 1803

Above all, the United States wanted to keep France from controlling the Mississippi River. As American settlers moved west, their economy increasingly depended on access to the Mississippi River and New Orleans. In October 1802, before the land transfer from Spain to France had gone through, Spain suspended the right of Americans to store goods in New Orleans, endangering the entire economy of what was then known as the American West. Americans believed that **Napoleon Bonaparte,** the leader of France, was behind the ban. Americans were anxious about what might happen when France took over the region. Many Americans—including frontiersmen and lawmakers—wanted to take New Orleans by force. Jefferson pushed for negotiations instead.

While U.S. minister Livingston negotiated in France, Napoleon made a surprising offer. Instead of selling only New Orleans to the United States, he suggested selling the entire Louisiana Territory—all 828,000 square miles of it. After years of rebellion, France's hold on its West Indian colony of Saint-Domingue on the island of Hispaniola (present-day Haiti) was

unstable. **Toussaint L'Ouverture** (TOO-sahnt LOH-ver-toor), a formerly enslaved man, led a successful rebellion to free slaves in the colony in 1791. He governed until 1802, when Napoleon staged an unsuccessful attempt to take it back. Without land in the Caribbean, Napoleon felt that Louisiana had little value. He had lost troops both to the revolt and to tropical diseases. The monetary costs of the conflict had also been high, and France was on the brink of war with Britain, another expensive enterprise.

In documents dated April 30, 1803, the United States agreed to pay France $15 million, or about three cents an acre, for the Louisiana Territory. The contract for the **Louisiana Purchase** did not specify the region's boundaries, however. The United States would have to negotiate those boundaries with Spain and Britain.

DOUBLING THE SIZE OF THE UNITED STATES

With the Louisiana Purchase, the United States nearly doubled in size, including land from the Gulf of Mexico north to Canada and from the Mississippi River west to the Rocky Mountains. Native Americans lived throughout the region. At the time of its purchase, the territory had a sparse white population of about 50,000 people, which included a mix of French, Spanish, Dutch, British, and Americans. Afterward, 3,000 free Africans moved into the region from Cuba. By 1810 approximately 7,600 free African Americans and 35,000 African-American slaves had entered the territory.

Some Federalists disapproved of the purchase, but most Americans celebrated it. The Mississippi River was once again open to commerce, while eastern merchants profited from the trade. As a strict constructionist, Jefferson worried that the federal government had no constitutional power to acquire territory. He put aside his concerns, however, confident that the Louisiana Purchase would provide spacious lands for generations of independent American farmers. Of those lands, Jefferson said, "The fertility of the country, its climate and extent, promise in due season important aids to our freedom, an ample provision for our posterity, and a widespread field for the blessings of freedom."

The United States took possession of Louisiana in December 1803, raising boundary issues and displeasing the Spanish, who had only recently transferred control to the French. Jefferson pushed for a generous interpretation for the United States, demanding that West Florida, Texas, and part of New Mexico be included. Spain, however, only agreed to give up a narrow strip along the west bank of the Mississippi River from northern Missouri to the Gulf of Mexico. More than a decade later, in 1819, the United States purchased Florida from Spain and came to an agreement on the Louisiana Territory's southwestern border.

THE TRIAL OF AARON BURR

As you have read, Aaron Burr killed Alexander Hamilton in a duel in 1804. Afterward, he fled arrest and alienated himself from Jefferson. He also hatched a plot or two, which included an invasion of New Spain and the **secession**, or political separation, of the American West. The plot fell through when an accomplice warned Jefferson of the plan. Burr was arrested and faced trial for treason in 1807. U.S. law defines treason as the act of anyone

In 1904, a centennial celebration of the Louisiana Purchase was held in St. Louis, Missouri. To honor the event, the march "A Deed of the Pen" was composed by Neil Morét. The title is a reference to the signing of the contract with France, and its sheet music had this specially designed cover.

"owing allegiance to the United States" who wages war against the United States or gives aid and comfort to its enemies.

Chief Justice John Marshall presided over Burr's trial. A jury acquitted Burr after Marshall argued that, according to the Constitution, treason required an overt act of war. Jefferson considered impeaching Marshall for favoring Burr during the trial, but found little support in Congress. Meanwhile, the president had other things to think about. He had been busy supervising an ambitious exploration of the new lands the nation had recently acquired.

HISTORICAL THINKING

1. **READING CHECK** What are some geographical borders that surround the area of land acquired in the Louisiana Purchase?

2. **INTERPRET MAPS** What rivers did the United States acquire the rights to in the Louisiana Purchase?

3. **FORM AND SUPPORT OPINIONS** Do you think Aaron Burr should have been found guilty of treason? Support your opinion with evidence from the text.

THE LEWIS AND CLARK EXPEDITION

Imagine the president asked you to explore unchartered territory. How would you prepare for your trip? When packing for the unexpected, Lewis and Clark made sure to bring their journals.

THE CORPS OF DISCOVERY

Even before the Louisiana Purchase was finalized, Thomas Jefferson had planned to explore the lands west of the Mississippi River. Several times since 1783, Jefferson had tried to organize expeditions for scientific knowledge and to promote American interests in the region. As president, he now had the authority and the country had the financial resources to support the enterprise. The Louisiana Purchase gave the plan a concrete purpose.

In 1803, Jefferson commissioned the exploration of those lands all the way to the Pacific Northwest. Jefferson named his private secretary, **Meriwether Lewis**, as captain of his **Corps of Discovery**, the group of men who undertook the expedition. Lewis chose as his co-leader his former military commander **William Clark**. In Lewis, Jefferson had the kind of leader he wanted: "a person who to courage, prudence, habits [and] health adapted to the woods, [and] some familiarity with the Indian character, joins a perfect knowledge of botany, natural history, mineralogy [and] astronomy." Lewis and Clark had battled Native Americans together in the Northwest Territory while serving in the army during the early 1790s. Both had experienced rugged frontier conditions. Clark also proved to be an expert mapmaker.

Jefferson had a list of goals for the Corps of Discovery. The explorers were to travel to the source of the Missouri River and from there try to find the elusive Northwest Passage, a transcontinental water route long sought by European mariners. However,

Born in 1774, Captain Meriwether Lewis (left) was four years younger than Second Lieutenant William Clark (right). Both men were born in Virginia and had successful military careers. Lewis helped quell the Whiskey Rebellion in 1794. That same year, Clark helped defeat the Shawnee and the Miami at the Battle of Fallen Timbers in the Ohio region.

repeated attempts to find the passage had all failed. The explorers would also be recording information about the plants and animals that lived throughout the new territory. The president hoped Lewis and Clark also would be able to make peaceful contact with Native Americans and expand the fur trade. Ultimately, the expedition would fill huge gaps in geographic, scientific, and cultural knowledge of the region.

Jefferson thought Lewis and Clark's expedition could solidify U.S. claims to the region. As you have read, the United States and Spain were still negotiating the boundaries of the Louisiana Territory. The United States could use exploration of the West and alliances with Native Americans to help support its claims to the broad boundaries of the territory.

In January 1806, Lieutenant William Clark and some Corps of Discovery members walked along the Oregon coast in search of a beached whale. On the way, they traveled past these sea stacks on what is now called Cannon Beach. The view inspired Clark to write, "from this point I beheld the grandest and most pleasing prospects which my eyes ever surveyed."

Lewis and Clark were commissioned as U.S. army officers to lead the Corps of Discovery. In May 1804, the expedition departed St. Louis with about 40 men, traveling north along the Missouri River, sometimes navigating, sometimes pushing their 55-foot keelboat and towing two canoes. Clark charted their course and drew maps. Lewis frequently went ashore to investigate minerals, soil, plants, and animals.

Along the way, the expedition experienced threatening encounters with the Teton branch of the Lakota nation. In one tense meeting, Clark pulled his sword and Lewis brandished the boat's swivel gun. Thanks in part to the diplomacy of Teton Chief Black Buffalo, both sides calmed down before fighting broke out. At that point, the goal of friendly relations with Native Americans seemed distant.

The expedition navigated up the Missouri through autumn until, soon after the first snowfall, it arrived at the Mandan and Hidatsa villages in what is today North Dakota. The Corps of Discovery members constructed Fort Mandan nearby as a place to spend the winter, safe from the bitter, below-zero cold. Through the winter, they hunted buffalo, repaired their gear, traded with the Mandan and Hidatsa, and learned about the surrounding lands from those Native Americans.

SEARCH FOR A WATER ROUTE WEST

In April 1805, some members of the Corps of Discovery returned to St. Louis with scientific notes, maps, artifacts, minerals, plants, and animals. The remaining 33 headed west in dugout canoes. By then the expedition had acquired two interpreters—French Canadian fur trapper Toussaint Charbonneau (TOO-sahnt shar-buh-NOH) and his Shoshone wife **Sacagawea** (SAK-uh-juh-WEE-uh), who had been captured by the Hidatsa at age 12. The interpreters brought along their baby, Jean-Baptiste, also known as Pomp.

Throughout the summer, the Corps made progress toward the Rocky Mountains, watching as the snow-capped peaks seemed to grow taller and taller. They had hoped to travel on the Missouri River all the way there. But then they reached the part of the river known as the Great Falls, where five waterfalls ranged over 21 miles of river, making navigation impossible. The expedition had to **portage**, or carry their canoes and supplies overland for 18.5 miles in order to get around the falls. Extreme summer heat, dangerous storms, prickly pear cacti, and brush made the portage more challenging and time-consuming than anticipated, and the journey took about three weeks.

Meriwether Lewis drew this life-size illustration of a smelt (also called a eulachon or candlefish) when he first encountered it at Fort Clatsop. Below is part of Lewis's description of the fish.

The chief [Clatsop] and his party had brought for sail a Sea Otter skin some hats, stergeon and a [s]pecies of small fish which . . . are taken in great quantities in the Columbia R. about 40 miles above us by means of skiming or scooping nets . . . the first bone of the gills . . . is of a bluis cast . . . the puple of the eye is blak and the iris of a silver white. the underjaw exceeds the uper; and the mouth opens to great extent, . . . it has no teeth.

—from the journal of Meriwether Lewis, February 24, 1806

In August, the Corps reached a Shoshone village just east of the mountains, where they had hoped to buy horses to help them cross the mountains. To everyone's shock and delight, the villagers recognized Sacagawea. The chief of this group was her long-lost brother.

At the end of August, the party set out to cross the rugged mountains with 29 horses they had purchased. The expedition trekked the Lolo Trail through the Bitterroot Mountains for 11 days, passing over more than 200 miles of mountain crags and through dense forests. Clark wrote in his journal: "I have been wet and as cold... as I ever was in my life, indeed, I was at one time fearful my feet would freeze." After climbing over the Bitterroots, the explorers were overjoyed to finally see flat land. Lewis wrote, "The pleasure I now felt in having triumphed over the [Rocky] Mountains and descending to a level and fertile country where there was every rational hope of finding a comfortable subsistence [food supply] for myself and party can be more readily conceived than expressed, nor was the flattering prospect of the final success of the expedition less pleasing."

The explorers followed the Clearwater River to the Columbia River and then beyond to the Pacific Ocean. Paddling their canoes, they arrived at the Columbia in mid-October. They rested there before heading down the river to its estuary, 20 miles from the coast. An **estuary** is a wide body of mixed salty and fresh water where a river meets the ocean. There, torrential storms forced the explorers to remain for three weeks.

LEWIS AND CLARK'S RETURN

In mid-November 1805, the expedition finally reached the Pacific Ocean. There they built **Fort Clatsop**, which they named after the local Native Americans. They spent a rainy, uneventful winter there, making clothes and moccasins, drawing maps, writing in journals, and preserving food. The explorers hoped to meet one of the British or American ships that were reported to trade at the mouth of the Columbia River, but they never saw one. Finally, in late March 1806, the expedition began the long trip back home, first battling the strong current of the Columbia, then heading overland, including another difficult climb through the Bitterroots, sometimes through ten feet of snow.

Once across the Bitterroots, the expedition separated, taking two different routes to investigate more territory. Lewis led one group north along the Marias River, while Clark led the other south, heading toward the Yellowstone River. The plan was to meet back up where the Yellowstone flowed into the Missouri. Along their route, Lewis's group had a violent encounter with eight Blackfeet. At first the Native Americans seemed friendly, and the two groups even camped together. But fighting broke out the next morning, and the explorers killed two of the Blackfeet. Fearful that the Blackfeet were pursuing them, Lewis and his group fled. On August 11, Lewis was shot below his left hip while hunting elk. Some of the expedition suspected Native Americans, but it's more likely Lewis was shot accidentally by one of his own men. Lewis's wound was painful but not life-threatening, and he continued the trek.

Meanwhile, Clark's party followed the Yellowstone River, taking notes and looking for good timber to construct carriages for their canoes. In his journal, Clark described finding the huge bones of a "fish" jutting out of a rock. Based on his account, scientists believe he discovered part of a dinosaur fossil. The day after Lewis was injured, the two groups reunited and began canoeing homeward along the swift current of the Missouri River.

After leaving Sacagawea and some other members of the expedition at the Mandan and Hidatsa villages, the Corps rode the river south. When they finally reached St. Louis at noon on September 23, 1806, they had traveled about 8,000 miles. Because the explorers had been gone for so long—two years, four months, and ten days—many Americans assumed that the Spanish or Native Americans had killed them. In fact, Spanish officials had tried unsuccessfully to intercept the expedition, which they correctly suspected would make Native American allies for the United States. When the Corps returned safely, they were met by a cheering crowd of about a thousand people.

A grateful president and Congress gave the explorers double the pay they had been promised as well as grants of land. Jefferson named Meriwether Lewis governor of Upper Louisiana Territory and promoted William Clark to brigadier general and made him an Indian agent. In 1809, Lewis was just 35 when he died of gunshot wounds at an inn in Tennessee while traveling to Washington, D.C. In 1813, Clark became the governor of the Missouri Territory.

🏛 National Museum of American History Washington, D.C.

The Corps of Discovery relied on compasses to navigate to the Pacific Ocean and back. Before the expedition, Lewis purchased 3 pocket compasses for $2.50 each, and this silver-plated compass in a mahogany box for $5.00. It was one of the few instruments to survive the journey.

A WEALTH OF NEW KNOWLEDGE

Although Lewis and Clark never found the Northwest Passage, the expedition was a great success. The explorers made contact with numerous Native American groups, including the Blackfeet, Lakota, and Nez Percé. They brought back information about Native American societies, noting that their interactions had been mostly friendly.

The expedition also gathered much scientific and geographical knowledge, such as identifying 178 new varieties of plants, including bitterroot, prairie sagebrush, Douglas fir, and ponderosa pine. They recorded 122 new species of animals, including the grizzly bear, the prairie dog, and the pronghorn antelope. The Corps collected valuable information about the geography and geology of the territory and brought back numerous mineral samples. Lewis, Clark, and at least five other Corps of Discovery members kept journals, providing notes on soil, climate, latitude, and longitude, as well as drawings of landforms and living things. Clark, a skilled cartographer, drew a series of detailed maps, published in 1810 and 1814, which became the most accurate maps of the West for decades. The expedition strengthened U.S. claims to the West, inspiring future exploration and waves of settlement.

HISTORICAL THINKING

1. **READING CHECK** What were Jefferson's political and scientific goals for authorizing the expedition?

2. **MAKE GENERALIZATIONS** How did the Corps of Discovery's interactions with Native American groups help the United States?

3. **INTERPRET VISUALS** What does the sketch on the journal page suggest about Lewis and Clark's priorities during the expedition?

4. **DETERMINE WORD MEANINGS** How would you explain the meaning of the word *expedition* as it is used in the context of this lesson?

SACAGAWEA C. 1788–1812

"[Sacagawea] deserved a greater reward for her attention and services on that route than we had in our power to give her." —William Clark

William Clark is referring to Sacagawea's contribution to the success of the expedition into the Louisiana Territory carried out by Clark, Meriwether Lewis, and other members of the Corps of Discovery between 1804 and 1806. The only woman on the expedition, she acted as a translator and shared her knowledge of the wilderness with the explorers as they moved westward—all while carrying her infant son. And, actually, for these services and others, Sacagawea received no reward at all.

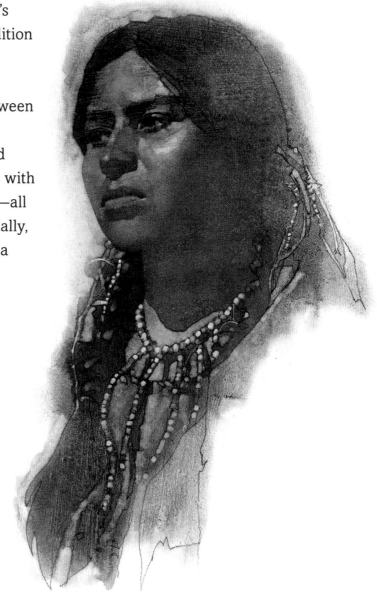

VALUABLE TEAM MEMBER

Sacagawea is a legendary figure, but little is known about her life. Most historians agree that she was born in 1788 or 1789 and was a member of a Native American tribe called the Shoshone. However, they disagree about the spelling of her name and what it means. Spelled *Sacajawea*, the name may be a Shoshone word meaning "boat launcher." But spelled *Sacagawea* (or *Sakakawea*), the name is a word in the Native American language of Hidatsa and translates as "bird woman." Around 1800, when Sacagawea was 11 or 12 years old, the Hidatsa kidnapped her. She lived for a few years among the Hidatsa people until she was sold to French-Canadian fur trapper Toussaint Charbonneau and became one of his wives.

Lewis and Clark hired Charbonneau to be an interpreter on their expedition. Sacagawea set out with her husband and the explorers in 1805, even though she had given birth just two months before. During their travels, Lewis and Clark hoped to buy horses from the Native

Artists can only speculate about what Sacagawea looked like, but surviving records of her actions provide insight into her character. When a boat capsized during the expedition, she alone kept her head and fished out articles from the water that, according to Clark, were necessary to "insure the success of the enterprize."

Americans they encountered. Since Sacagawea could speak both Hidatsa and Shoshone, they thought she could serve as a translator during the transactions. By an amazing coincidence, when Lewis and Clark did cross paths with a group of Shoshone, its leader turned out to be Sacagawea's brother. After the siblings' emotional reunion, Sacagawea helped secure the horses the explorers needed.

She made herself useful in other ways as well. After Sacagawea joined the expedition, she sometimes recognized landmarks and provided important information on the terrain—even though she had not set foot on it since she was a little girl. She also knew the medicinal qualities of some of the roots and plants found along the way and used them to treat sick members of the expedition. On the return trip, she helped the explorers navigate a mountain pass—today known as the Bozeman Pass—to the Yellowstone River. The Corps probably benefited from her presence alone. A group of men traveling through the wilderness could appear threatening to others. As Clark wrote in his journal, "A woman with a party of men is a token of peace."

IN THE WORDS OF LEWIS AND CLARK

Most of what we know about Sacagawea comes from the journals of Lewis and Clark. In an early entry, Lewis seems to regard Sacagawea with contempt. He wrote, "If she has enough to eat and a few trinkets to wear, I believe she would be perfectly content anywhere." However, in at least one instance, she showed more spirit than Lewis initially gave her credit for. When the Corps reached the Pacific Ocean and saw a beached whale, Sacagawea asked the explorers to let her accompany them to witness these wonders. Eventually, they gave in. Lewis later commented in his journal, "She observed that she had traveled a long way with us to see the waters, and that now that monstrous fish was also to be seen, she thought it very hard she could not be permitted to see either."

Clark, on the other hand, was kind to Sacagawea, whom he nicknamed "Janey" and referred to as "pilot" in his journal. And he was quite fond of her child, Jean Baptiste. Clark called him "his little

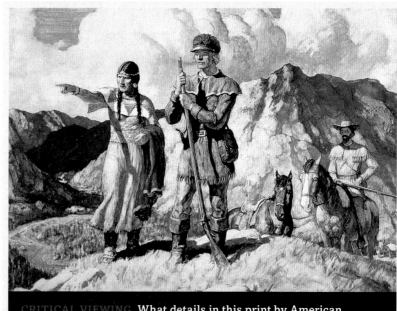

CRITICAL VIEWING What details in this print by American illustrator N.C. Wyeth suggest that Sacagawea was a valuable member of the Corps of Discovery?

dancing boy, Pomp" and named a sandstone formation near the Yellowstone River "Pompey's Pillar" after the boy. When Jean Baptiste's neck was swollen, Clark himself applied an ointment, made of items such as beeswax and onions, to help reduce the swelling.

In August 1806, Sacagawea and her family returned to their village by the Missouri River. Then in 1812, Clark received word that she had died shortly after giving birth to a second child. However, just as debate surrounds Sacagawea's birth, controversy swirls around her death. Some historians maintain that another one of Charbonneau's wives died in childbirth, not Sacagawea. These researchers claim that Sacagawea rejoined the Shoshone and died on the Wind River Reservation in Wyoming Territory in 1884. Although much of her life remains a mystery, Sacagawea captured the American imagination. She has been honored with monuments, statues, a gold coin, and the title of honorary sergeant for her role on the Lewis and Clark expedition.

HISTORICAL THINKING

1. **READING CHECK** What are some of the mysteries that surround Sacagawea's life?

2. **EVALUATE** What do Sacagawea's actions and the journals of Lewis and Clark convey about her character?

3. **MAKE INFERENCES** Why do you think Sacagawea has captured the American imagination?

MORE CONFLICT WITH BRITAIN

Two sides are fighting. You say you don't want to get involved. Then you start trading supplies with both sides as they fight. Business is good for you. But there's a problem—now you *are* involved.

IMPRESSMENT AND INTERFERENCE

As you have read, Napoleon sold the Louisiana Territory to focus French efforts on a looming war with Britain. French expansion across Europe had sparked hostility between the two nations. Soon after France sold the Louisiana Territory to the United States in 1803, Great Britain declared war on France.

The United States took an official stance of neutrality in the war, and American merchants were more than willing to sell goods and weapons to both countries. But Britain and France were determined to keep their enemy from receiving supplies. By 1806, each country blockaded the other's harbor to keep American ships from delivering provisions. In addition, Britain authorized its navy to impress American sailors by capturing American ships and forcing the sailors to serve the British Navy.

Many Americans began calling for war. But Jefferson hoped to avoid hostilities and remain neutral during foreign disputes. He approved the Non-Importation Act of 1806, which banned specific British imports, and he attempted, unsuccessfully, to negotiate with Britain to end impressment and assure trading rights.

In June 1807, men on the British ship *Leopard* fired on and boarded the American ship *Chesapeake*, capturing four sailors. As more Americans clamored for war, Jefferson closed U.S. ports and waters to British vessels. But the British continued impressment and challenged Jefferson's port closures. They fired on coastal towns in Maine and sailed into Chesapeake Bay.

At Jefferson's urging, Congress passed the **Embargo Act of 1807**, which prohibited American exports to any country and most British imports. An **embargo** is a government order to ban trade with a particular nation or to halt the trading of a specified product. The embargo had devastating effects on American businesses, and merchants were soon staging protests. Congress replaced the Embargo Act with the Non-Intercourse Act in 1809. The new legislation banned trade only with Britain and France. Days later, Jefferson's second term as president ended without a resolution to the nation's problems with Britain.

HEADING FOR WAR

Despite the impact of the embargo, Jefferson remained popular. His endorsement of fellow Democratic-Republican James Madison in the 1808 presidential election resulted in a landslide victory against the Federalists. The election proved that Americans still supported the policies of Jefferson's Democratic-Republicans.

Madison moved into the still-unfinished president's mansion with his wife, **Dolley Madison**, who would play an important role in his presidency. According to one observer, "There was a frankness and ease in her deportment [behavior], that won golden opinions from all, and she possessed an influence so decided with [Madison]." The first lady transformed the presidential residence into a true executive mansion, frequently hosting gatherings and inviting Federalists and Democratic-Republicans to socialize together.

Meanwhile, the problems with Britain continued. In 1811, Madison appointed **James Monroe** of Virginia to be Secretary of State. Monroe hoped to ease tensions over British trade with diplomacy, but Britain continued to insist that American exports be licensed in England before shipping them to France. When Napoleon partially lifted France's blockade in 1811, the United States resumed trading with France. The British responded by attacking U.S. ships, and tensions between the two countries continued.

CRITICAL VIEWING Having started before dawn, much of the Battle of Tippecanoe took place in the dark. What details in this 1880s lithograph by Kurz and Allison reveal the difficulties that each side faced?

At the same time, conflict with Native Americans was brewing in the West—and Americans suspected the British were behind it. American settlement of the West was increasing, and many Native Americans feared they would be pushed out. Shawnee chief **Tecumseh** (tuh-KUM-suh) attempted to build an alliance among the Native Americans to protect their lands against the United States.

The last straw for the Native Americans had been the Treaty of Fort Wayne of 1809, in which several tribes were persuaded to sell the United States 2.5 million acres of their lands for about two cents an acre. Tecumseh met with **William Henry Harrison**, governor of the Indiana Territory, who refused to overturn the treaty. Next Tecumseh went south, seeking allies among the Creek and Seminole. But Tecumseh's plan for a broad Native American alliance failed. By 1811, American settlements in Tennessee, Kentucky, and Ohio had grown large enough to form a barrier between the Native Americans living to the north and south.

In November 1811, Harrison led about 1,000 troops toward Prophetstown, a village that Tecumseh and his brother, the Shawnee prophet Tenskwatawa (tens-qwah-TAH-wah), had founded on the Tippecanoe River in Indiana Territory. Tecumseh was still in the south. In the early morning on November 7, Tenskwatawa's forces attacked Harrison's camp.

The Native Americans were repelled and withdrew. At dawn, Harrison's forces struck back, destroying Prophetstown and claiming victory in what became known as the **Battle of Tippecanoe**.

When news of the battle reached Washington, D.C., many misinterpreted it as evidence of a threatening alliance between the British and Native Americans. **War Hawks** in Congress, led by Speaker of the House Henry Clay of Kentucky and John C. Calhoun of South Carolina, called for another war with Britain. In Calhoun's words, the United States had to show "the World, that we have not only inherited that liberty which our Fathers gave us, but also the will and power to maintain it." But many Americans wondered if the United States was prepared for such a conflict.

HISTORICAL THINKING

1. **READING CHECK** How did the United States become involved in the war between France and Great Britain?

2. **MAKE INFERENCES** What argument might Britain have made for its many acts against American commerce on the seas? Use evidence from the text to support your response.

3. **MAKE CONNECTIONS** Why do you think so many Americans thought that Britain was instigating the Native American unrest in the Northwest Territory?

THE WAR OF 1812

Twenty-nine years after winning their war for independence, Americans were fighting the British again. The young United States was not the economic or military powerhouse it is today, and waging war against an empire was a risky prospect. But the war had consequences for Great Britain as well.

THE WAR BEGINS

Spurred on by Britain's interference with maritime commerce, cries from War Hawks, and rumors of a British-Native American alliance, Madison issued a war message on June 1, 1812. He signed Congress's declaration of war against Great Britain on June 18, and the **War of 1812** began.

The United States was ill-prepared for the war. The Democratic-Republicans in power supported a limited federal government that carried little debt and collected few taxes. They believed that financial responsibility, even for defense, lay with the states. The Bank of the United States charter had been allowed to expire in 1811, so state banks were the only source for war loans. The United States had declared war, but it did not have the financial resources to fight effectively. To make matters worse, the New England states refused to provide their share of funding for the war, and neither Massachusetts nor Connecticut sent militias.

Madison dispatched U.S. forces to Canada, hoping to win some victories while Britain focused on fighting France in Europe. U.S. General William Hull attacked Fort Malden, in Canada, which was commanded by British General Isaac Brock with support from Tecumseh's forces. Hull failed, though, and he even surrendered Detroit. The British went on to take control of much of the region. By this time, Britain really had joined forces with several Native American nations. Britain and its new allies captured Fort Dearborn, at the site of modern-day Chicago. American forces suffered another defeat in October near Fort Niagara.

Madison ran for reelection during the unsuccessful Canada campaign. His opponent, DeWitt Clinton of New York, criticized the war effort. However, the American navy won some surprising victories during the presidential campaign, including the U.S.S. *Constitution's* sinking of Britain's *Guerrière* near Nova Scotia. This boosted Madison's support, and he not only won the electoral vote 129 to 89, but his Democratic-Republican party secured a majority in Congress.

THE STAR-SPANGLED BANNER
This was the American flag that flew amid flaming rockets and exploding bombs at the battle of Fort McHenry. It inspired **Francis Scott Key** to memorialize the scene in his poem "Defense of Fort McHenry," which eventually became a song called "The Star-Spangled Banner." Congress made it the official U.S. national anthem in 1931.

Then 1813 began with another disaster. British and Native American forces staged a new offensive in the West, killing or capturing nearly 900 American troops near Detroit. The U.S. Army managed to hold Fort Meigs and Fort Stephenson in northern Ohio, but it needed naval support to end British control of Lake Erie. On September 10, U.S. ships commanded by **Oliver Hazard Perry** defeated the British at Put-in-Bay and seized control of Lake Erie.

Perry's victory allowed General William Henry Harrison to attack Fort Malden again, sending the British and Native Americans into retreat and reestablishing control of Detroit. Harrison's forces caught up with the British at Moraviantown in Upper Canada on October 5, winning the Battle of the Thames (tehmz) and killing Tecumseh. U.S. forces also burned York (Toronto), the capital of Upper Canada, but they met defeat in Montreal and lost Fort Niagara.

This painting by Tom Freeman, called *Burning of the White House, 1814*, shows the executive mansion in flames after British soldiers torched it during the War of 1812. Before their arrival, Madison's wife, Dolley, had a full-length portrait of George Washington carried from the building for safekeeping.

A WELCOME PEACE

After defeating Napoleon in April 1814, Britain turned greater attention to the American war. Britain sent forces into Chesapeake Bay and attacked Washington, D.C., in August. British troops burned the Capitol Building and the executive mansion. The president's family fled in the nick of time. Thanks to Dolley Madison's quick thinking, official documents and a famous portrait of George Washington were saved. In September, Americans won an important naval victory on Lake Champlain that saved New York City from invasion. That same month the British turned to Baltimore, but despite heavily bombarding Fort McHenry, they failed to take the city.

British forces sailed south to blockade the Mississippi River. However, as U.S. General **Andrew Jackson** prepared to defend New Orleans, Great Britain and the United States both realized a clear victory in the war was hopeless. As the British considered peace negotiations, they learned of American successes at Lake Champlain and Baltimore. Many in Britain now wanted to resume normal trade relations with the United States.

In August 1814, James Madison sent a delegation to Ghent, a city in what is now Belgium, and on Christmas Eve negotiators agreed to end the war. Due to the reliance on ships for communication, news of the **Treaty of Ghent** did not reach the United States until February 1815. Meanwhile, British forces continued to move against U.S. forces in New Orleans.

On January 8, 1815, the British unleashed a bold attack on the city, but they found Jackson ready and waiting. Jackson's troops, behind earthworks, fired into the charging British lines. In less than an hour, the British commander, two generals, and almost 300 British soldiers lay dead; more than 1,200 were wounded and 484 captured. Only 13 Americans were killed, with 39 wounded and 19 captured. News of the victory at the **Battle of New Orleans** reached Washington, D.C., just before notification of the Treaty of Ghent—signed two weeks before the Battle of New Orleans.

HISTORICAL THINKING

1. **READING CHECK** Why was the United States ill-prepared to fight the War of 1812?

2. **DESCRIBE** What major defeats and victories occurred for the United States at the beginning of the War of 1812?

3. **ANALYZE CAUSE AND EFFECT** What developments persuaded the British to agree to sign the Treaty of Ghent?

VOCABULARY

Write a sentence using each of the following vocabulary terms.

1. civil case
   My family had a legal dispute with our insurance company, so we filed a civil case against them.

2. criminal case

3. civic republicanism

4. loose constructionist

5. strict constructionist

6. sedition

7. nullification

8. judicial review

9. secession

10. War Hawks

READING STRATEGY
SUMMARIZE

Summarizing can help a reader understand a text and see its important ideas. One way to summarize is to answer these questions: Who? What? Where? When? Why? and How? Use a graphic organizer like the one below to summarize a lesson in the chapter. Then answer the question.

Who?	
What?	
Where?	
When?	
Why?	
How?	
Summary	

11. How did the events described in this lesson help unify the nation?

MAIN IDEAS

Answer the following questions. Support your answers with evidence from the chapter.

12. During the first presidential election, why did Americans see George Washington as the obvious choice to unite the nation? **LESSON 1.1**

13. In what ways did "republican motherhood" give women new freedom and autonomy, and in what ways did it maintain the status quo? **LESSON 1.2**

14. Describe the political divisions that arose in the early years of Washington's presidency. **LESSON 1.3**

15. What problems did the United States face in its relationships with foreign nations during the 1780s and 1790s? **LESSON 1.4**

16. What changes did Jefferson bring in his first term as president? **LESSON 2.1**

17. In what way did the Louisiana Purchase contradict Jefferson's political beliefs, and how did he rationalize the purchase? **LESSON 2.2**

18. In what ways was the Lewis and Clark Expedition successful in fulfilling Jefferson's goals for their exploration? **LESSON 2.3**

19. What pressures brought the United States closer to war with Britain in the years leading up to the War of 1812? **LESSON 3.1**

20. What developments helped bring an end to the War of 1812? **LESSON 3.2**

HISTORICAL THINKING

Answer the following questions. Support your answers with evidence from the chapter.

21. **COMPARE AND CONTRAST** In what ways was Jefferson's Democratic-Republican political philosophy different from that of the Federalists? Support your response with details from the text.

22. **MAKE INFERENCES** How did the Lewis and Clark Expedition help to secure U.S. claims to the Louisiana Territory and the Pacific Northwest, and open the entire West to American settlement?

23. **SYNTHESIZE** What effects do you think the Louisiana Purchase had on the American identity at that time?

24. **DRAW CONCLUSIONS** How do you think Britain's leaders viewed the outbreak of war with the United States in 1812?

25. **DISTINGUISH FACT FROM OPINION** As relations with France deteriorated, Federalists questioned the patriotism of Democratic-Republicans, journalists, immigrants, and all critics of the battles with France. Were their charges based on facts or opinions? Explain your response with evidence from the text.

INTERPRET VISUALS

In 1912, the Smithsonian Institution hired Amelia Fowler to repair the original Star-Spangled Banner. Fowler and her team of 10 workers replaced the deteriorating canvas backing that supported the flag, allowing it to be displayed for more than 80 years before its next, more extensive restoration, which began in 1998. The symbolic flag is now displayed in the National Museum of American History in Washington, D.C.

26. What tools were probably needed to restore the backing of the flag?

27. Why did Fowler require such a large team to finish the project?

ANALYZE SOURCES

George Washington announced his retirement as president in a letter published in Philadelphia's *American Daily Advertiser* on September 19, 1796. The letter, which came to be known as his "Farewell Address," advised building national unity by avoiding regionalism, factionalism (political parties), and foreign entanglements. Read the passage and answer the question.

> The common and continual mischiefs of the spirit of party are sufficient to make it the interest and duty of a wise people to discourage and restrain it.
>
> . . . It agitates the community with ill-founded jealousies and false alarms, kindles the animosity of one part against another, foments [provokes] occasionally riot and insurrection. It opens the door to foreign influence and corruption.

28. How does Washington believe the establishment of political parties can lead to corruption?

CONNECT TO YOUR LIFE

29. **EXPLANATORY** George Washington was adamantly opposed to political parties for the reasons he set forth in the excerpt quoted above. Today, there are wide divisions between the two major American political parties—the Republican Party and the Democratic Party. Choose one of Washington's arguments for avoiding the establishment of political parties, state whether or not you think it applies to American politics today, and write a paragraph explaining your thoughts on the matter.

TIPS

- List Washington's reasons for opposing political parties in your own words.

- Choose the one you think best applies to today's political situation.

- Support your response with evidence and examples from current events.

- Restate your main idea to help you write a strong conclusion to your paragraph.

Map Drawing

by Betsy Mason

Adapted from "19th-Century Schoolgirls Were Incredibly Good at Drawing Maps,"
by Betsy Mason, news.nationalgeographic.com, July 27, 2016

The beautifully detailed early 19th-century map of the United States pictured above would be snapped up quickly by a collector if it were to hit the market today. It could go for several hundred or a couple thousand dollars. But not because it was made by a well-known cartographer or a prestigious map publisher. This map was hand-drawn by a 15-year-old girl as part of her schoolwork.

For a brief period at the beginning of the 19th century, many schoolgirls in the United States were expected to draw elaborate maps as a central part of their education. "It was hugely popular for about 30 years," says historian Susan Schulten of the University of Denver. "Chances are if you come across one [of these maps], it's from 1800 to 1835."

This practice likely originated in Europe and then spread to female academies, which were becoming popular in the states at the time. Though there are some nice examples of maps drawn by boys, boys were more often taught surveying and navigation instead of map drawing, Schulten says. For the girls, drawing maps wasn't to prepare them to be cartographers or even geographers. Instead, the activity was supposed to help them gain, retain, and demonstrate general knowledge, become good citizens, and show off their artistic skill.

"I think it very nicely fits in [with] what were the central goals of female education after the revolution," says Schulten, who first became interested in the schoolgirl maps while researching her book *Mapping the Nation*. Back then, geography was seen as an appropriate avenue for girls to become culturally literate, "to prepare them for a life of usefulness and social exchange," according to Schulten.

Another primary goal of drawing maps was mastery of the art of penmanship. The lettering on most of the schoolgirls' maps is very careful and neat, with multiple fonts, sizes, and weights for various kinds of features, like states, cities, and rivers, just like the professionally made maps these drawings were based on. "The lettering was sort of what drew me to them," Schulten says. "Sometimes I notice that [the girls] paid so much attention to penmanship and lettering that they chronically misspell words."

The maps were clearly labor-intensive assignments that would have taken weeks, if not months, to finish. So how did the schoolgirls create them? Information on how the maps were made is scarce, but a couple of techniques seem likely. Students who copied the maps by sight may have laid a grid over the original map as a guide. They would then put a similar grid on a blank sheet and copy the contents of each small box, one at a time—far easier than eyeballing an entire map at once.

Many of the maps were almost certainly traced, but some are on paper too thick to trace through. In this case, the girls could have used a common trick of the time to make a sort of carbon copy. They would use a pencil to cover an entire piece of paper with graphite, lay that facedown on a blank sheet of paper, and put the original map on top. Tracing the map with some sort of pointer would transfer the graphite outline to the blank sheet.

The various techniques, base maps, and personalities of the schoolgirls led to a wide range of map styles. Some girls just replicated versions of existing maps. Others displayed real artistry or added their own personal touches. Stephanie Cyr, co-curator of the "Women in Cartography" exhibit at Boston Public Library, comments, "[The girls] were able to express themselves artistically at a time when their whole world was dominated by men."

For more from National Geographic, check out "Searching for Sacagawea" online.

UNIT INQUIRY: Explore a Contradiction

In this unit, you learned about the American colonists' path to independence—from breaking ties with Great Britain and staging a revolution to establishing a new form of government for a new nation. The concept of liberty, or individual freedom, was a core ideal in the American Revolution and central to the emerging American identity. How did the Founding Fathers embrace liberty for all and yet allow the practice of slavery? Many of them owned slaves. Didn't they recognize the contradiction?

ASSIGNMENT

Research the Founding Fathers' positions on slavery and how they reconciled the practice of slavery with their ideal of liberty for all. Find out which of the Founding Fathers were slaveholders. Investigate the discussions of slavery that occurred during the drafting of the Articles of Confederation and the Constitution. Present your findings to the class.

Plan As you explore the contradiction between the Founders' ideal of liberty and the practice of slavery, gather evidence from this unit and the internet about the Founders' attitudes toward slavery. Research individuals such as John Adams, Samuel Adams, Samuel Chase, Benjamin Franklin, Alexander Hamilton, John Hancock, Patrick Henry, John Jay, Thomas Jefferson, James Madison, Thomas Paine, and George Washington. Think about motivations they may have had for accepting slavery. Use a graphic organizer like this to organize your notes.

Founding Father	State	Slaveholder, yes or no	Position on slavery
J. Adams			
S. Adams			
S. Chase			

Produce Review your notes and think about the reasons these prominent Founders failed to oppose slavery during the drafting of the Constitution. Write a summary that answers this question: How did the Founding Fathers reconcile their core value of liberty with their acceptance of the practice of slavery?

Present Choose a creative way to present your summary of the Founding Fathers' positions on liberty and slavery to the class. Consider one of these options:

- Taking on the role of one of the Founders, prepare and deliver a speech or monologue in which you present your views to the class.

- Write a journal entry or letter as one of the Founders in which you present your thoughts and feelings. Share your journal entry or letter with classmates.

- Design a poster or digital presentation that addresses the conflict between Americans' promotion of liberty for all and the practice of slavery.

NATIONAL GEOGRAPHIC | LEARNING FRAMEWORK ACTIVITIES

Stage a Debate

ATTITUDE Curiosity

SKILLS Communication, Collaboration

Review the unit and conduct further research to determine why some colonists did not support separating from Great Britain at the time of the American Revolution. Team up with a partner and prepare arguments for and against independence from Great Britain from the perspectives of both a Patriot and a Loyalist. Then create two props, such as different hats, to transform yourselves into a Patriot and a Loyalist. Begin by giving short speeches summarizing your positions and then debate the issue with your class.

Create a Storyboard

SKILLS Communication, Collaboration

KNOWLEDGE Our Human Story

Working in a small group, create a storyboard that tells the "story" of the formation of the United States. You might use a software program or simply pencil and paper to draft your storyboard. First review the chapters in this unit to determine which significant events to portray. Pick events that will show the story from the British taxation of the colonists to the election of President Washington. Make a list of the main events and their dates, and then work together to sketch the events and write a script. Display your storyboard in the classroom.

New industries and inventions transformed the United States in the early 19th century. In this painting titled *Emigrants Crossing the Plains*, by American artist Albert Bierstadt, what details suggest how expanding transportation networks may have affected the growing country?

THE UNITED STATES

1836
Texans declare independence from Mexico. *(bronze plaque depicting a scene from the Texas War for Independence)*

1838–1839
The journey of about 17,000 Cherokee forced to leave their homeland becomes known as the Trail of Tears.

1813
The Boston Manufacturing Company opens in Waltham, Massachusetts, marking the beginning of the Industrial Revolution in the United States. *(glass jug made in a Boston factory in the early 1800s)*

1831
Enslaved African-American Nat Turner organizes a slave rebellion in Southampton County, Virginia. Rebels kill about 55 white people before Turner is caught.

1825
The Erie Canal opens, linking Lake Erie with the Hudson River.

1810

1830

THE WORLD

1821 AMERICAS
Venezuela and Mexico gain independence from Spain.

1838 AFRICA
Zulus clash with Boers in what is known today as South Africa.

1815 EUROPE
French emperor Napoleon gives up his throne after his defeat at the Battle of Waterloo in Belgium. *(two-cornered hat worn by Napoleon during a battle in Europe)*

1839 ASIA
The Opium Wars begin in China as the Qing dynasty fights Britain and France in an effort to end the opium trade in China.

1846
The Mexican-American War begins in a dispute over Texas. *(medal awarded to an American soldier who fought in the war)*

HISTORICAL THINKING

DETERMINE CHRONOLOGY Which prior event may have been a factor in the outbreak of the Mexican-American War?

1849
After gold is found in California's Sacramento Valley, thousands of people rush to the site. *(a metal case containing a gold scale and weights used by California miners)*

1848
A convention calling for women's rights is held in Seneca Falls, New York.

1850
Congress passes the Compromise of 1850, which seeks to settle slavery issues in newly admitted states and keep the Union united.

1854
Congress passes the Kansas-Nebraska Act, which allows the people of the two states to decide for themselves whether to allow slavery.

1840

1860

1847 AFRICA
Freed U.S. slaves and free African Americans found the republic of Liberia in West Africa.

1848 EUROPE
Revolutions and unrest erupt across Europe.

1850 ASIA
Chinese Christian rebels rise up against China's Qing dynasty, starting the Taiping Rebellion.

1845 EUROPE
The Irish Potato Famine kills more than 1 million people and forces many others to immigrate to the United States. *(This sculpture is part of Philadelphia's Irish Memorial and honors the Irish people who journeyed to America.)*

REGIONAL AND NATIONAL GROWTH

1814–1831

HISTORICAL THINKING How did rapid change create new opportunities and new tensions for the growing nation?

"If we look to the history of other nations, ancient or modern, **we find no example of a growth so rapid, so gigantic, of a people so prosperous and happy.**"

—James Madison

In the mountains of West Virginia, this steam locomotive takes passengers on a scenic ride to the heights of Bald Knob, at the summit of Back Allegheny Mountain. The train, now part of Cass Scenic Railroad State Park, once hauled lumber from mountain logging camps to the sawmill in the town of Cass.

AMERICAN INVENTIONS

CRITICAL VIEWING A farmer uses a plow to work the stubble of an earlier grain crop into the soil before planting a soybean crop. How do you think American inventions like the steel plow affected society and the economy?

The first half of the 19th century was a time of vigorous economic growth in the United States, fired in part by industrial innovations imported from Britain, but also by American inventions that revolutionized the fields of manufacturing, communication, and agriculture. This American Story highlights a few of the American inventions that helped spur the country's growth in the 19th century and laid the groundwork for the economy and technologies of the 21st century.

AGRICULTURE: THE COTTON GIN AND THE STEEL PLOW

The agriculture and economy of two American regions, the Midwest and the South, were each largely shaped by a single invention. In the South, that invention was the cotton gin, patented by Eli Whitney in 1794. The cotton gin consisted mainly of a rotating drum with protruding hooks that could separate the seeds from cotton plants 50 times more quickly than a person doing the job by hand. Whitney's invention had an enormous effect on the economy of the southern states, vastly improving the productivity of cotton plantations. By the middle of the 19th century, cotton was the United States' leading export. Cotton's increased profitability due to the cotton gin had unintended social consequences. Both the plantation system and slavery became more deeply entrenched in the South as the demand for labor to harvest the ever larger cotton crops increased.

In the region we now call the Midwest, the crucial invention was the steel plow. The fields of grain that stretch from horizon to horizon in Iowa, Nebraska, Kansas, and other states may be said to have originated from this innovation. In the first decades of the 19th century, settlers were pouring into the western territories seeking to establish farms. The cast iron plows they brought with them from the East, however, did a poor job of breaking through the rich but sticky prairie soil. Farmers were forced to stop frequently and remove the clumps of soil that accumulated on their plow blades.

In 1837, a young blacksmith from Illinois named John Deere forged a plow using steel instead of cast iron while also giving the plow a slightly different shape. Combined, these two innovations allowed Deere's plow to cut cleanly through the dense soil. Farmers eagerly adopted the invention, which they nicknamed the "singing plow" because they claimed it made a musical sound as it dug furrows in the prairie soil. John Deere continued innovating and improving his designs, and by 1846, he was producing 1,000 plows a year. In the 21st century, the John Deere Company is one of the world's largest manufacturers of agricultural equipment.

MANUFACTURING: THE SEWING MACHINE

Elias Howe, an American machinist, was not the first person to imagine or even to build a sewing machine. However, he was the first to create and patent a device that incorporated key features of modern home and industrial sewing machines. One of these was a new form of needle that allowed for a type of stitching called a lockstitch. To see an example of lockstitch sewing, you can examine the hem of almost any machine-sewn garment in your wardrobe.

With Howe's sewing machine, garments could be made much more quickly and cheaply. The New York clothing maker Brooks Brothers, for example, was able to make its overcoats in six days, rather than three weeks, and sell the coats at a lower price. As companies adopted sewing machines, garment factories expanded, and employment opportunities opened up for workers, especially women. A *New York Times* article from January 7, 1860, paints an optimistic picture of "sewing girls," claiming that "it is no uncommon thing for those who, toiling night and day, could earn only one or two dollars per week, to now receive from three to ten dollars per week for operating a sewing machine." By the early 20th century, the Chicago clothing maker Hart, Schaffner & Marx alone employed 8,000 workers. Today, garment factories using sewing machines based on Howe's novel ideas employ millions of people worldwide.

ELIAS HOWE

la meilleure

CRITICAL VIEWING The French phrase *la meilleure* in this 1900 advertisement for an Elias Howe sewing machine means "the best." How do you think the ad is supposed to make people feel about purchasing a Howe sewing machine? What details in the image support your response?

INVENTIONS BY AMERICAN WOMEN

There is no way of knowing how many American inventions were created, at least in part, by women because women were not allowed to apply for patents in the country's early years. Some historians believe, for example, that plantation owner Catherine Greene was the principal designer of the cotton gin, but she could not patent the invention under her name. This time line traces notable inventions by American women between 1813 and 1975.

1871 machine for making paper bags (Margaret Knight)

1813 circular saw (Tabitha Babbitt)

1825

TYPING IT UP

The first commercially successful writing machine—or typewriter—was the result of intensive research by inventors Christopher Latham Sholes, Carlos Glidden, and Samuel Soulé in Milwaukee, Wisconsin. Others had tried to invent similar machines, but most of them were difficult to use and very large—as big as a piano in some cases.

In June 1868, Sholes filed a patent for a small, more efficient typewriter that could put words onto paper far faster than a pen. The machine featured the QWERTY keyboard still used on computer keyboards today, a cylinder that placed equal spaces between each typed line, and key levers that struck an ink ribbon to print each letter on the inserted sheet of paper.

In 1873, Sholes contracted with the New York gun manufacturer E. Remington and Sons, to mass-produce the typewriters. The machines were soon renamed "Remingtons." Author Mark Twain owned a Remington and was the first writer to submit a typed book manuscript to a publisher.

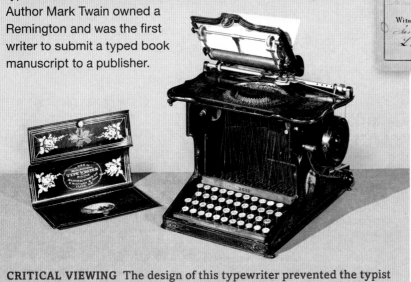

Sholes's 1868 typewriter patent (above) featured a machine that could type only in capital letters. A shift key introduced in 1878 allowed capitals and lowercase letters.

CRITICAL VIEWING The design of this typewriter prevented the typist from seeing the words while he or she typed. What differences do you observe between early typewriters and computer keyboards?

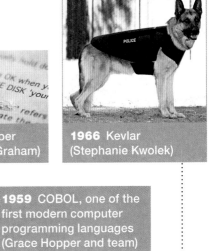

1886 dishwasher (Josephine Cochrane)

1903 windshield wipers (Mary Anderson)

1948 the first solar-powered house (Maria Telkes)

1958 Liquid Paper (Bette Nesmith Graham)

1959 COBOL, one of the first modern computer programming languages (Grace Hopper and team)

1966 Kevlar (Stephanie Kwolek)

1900

1975

The telegraph system below is a replica of one of the units used on Samuel Morse's line between Baltimore and Washington, D.C., in 1844. The replica includes the key that the operator would tap, a paper tape reel, and a register, which received the transmitted signals.

COMMUNICATION: THE TELEGRAPH

At the start of the 19th century, long-distance communication was carried out via trains, horseback riders, mail carriages, and ships. As a consequence, it was both slow and unreliable. In the 1830s and 1840s, the American inventor and painter Samuel Morse built on the work of other thinkers to solve this problem by designing an easy-to-operate telegraph.

Morse's telegraph was a simple device. An operator tapped a key that completed an electrical circuit, sending a signal along a wire to another telegraph. The operator could transmit patterns of long and short signals (called "dots" and "dashes") that would be recorded on a piece of paper moving through the receiving telegraph. Each pattern represented a letter of the alphabet in a code developed by Morse, which is still known as Morse Code.

The telegraph quickly found a multitude of civilian and military uses. Journalists on assignment could rapidly transmit stories to newspapers back home. During the Civil War, army units would string telegraph wires as they advanced so that they could receive orders and relay intelligence without delays.

An article in *Harper's Weekly* magazine from 1862 reported on the Union Army's use of the telegraph: "The army signal-telegraph has been so far perfected that in a few hours quite a large force can be in constant connection with head-quarters. This, while a battle is progressing, is a great convenience."

Perhaps as important as the telegraph device itself was the network of wires that were strung across the continent, and then the world, to connect all the individual telegraphs. This network would evolve into the system that carries 21st-century instant communication through telephones and the Internet.

THINK ABOUT IT

Which invention do you think had the greatest influence on the American economy or society in the 21st century?

EVERYDAY TREASURES

Not every invention must be large or momentous to have a noteworthy effect on our everyday lives. Each of these American innovations dating from the 19th century or earlier has made its particular contribution to our comfort, convenience, or pleasure.

1774 mail order catalog

1796 cupcake

1806 coffee percolator

1775

1800

THE U.S. PATENT OFFICE

The framers of the U.S. Constitution were anxious to encourage new ideas by ensuring that inventors could reap the benefits of their work. Article 1, Section 8, Clause 8 of the Constitution states that the legislative branch should "promote the progress of science and useful arts, by securing for limited times to authors and inventors the exclusive right to their respective writings and discoveries."

The United States Patent and Trademark Office is the agency that oversees the fulfillment of this constitutional mandate. An inventor can file an application with the patent office, describing the invention in detail. If the agency recognizes that the invention is original and does not duplicate an existing invention, it issues a document called a patent. Receiving a patent provides certain rights and protections to an inventor, including the right to exclude all others from exploiting the invention to make money for up to 20 years. At the same time, the patent document is available to the public, so that others may study the invention and improve on it.

The United States is not the only country with a government patent office. An international treaty exists to allow inventors to seek patents internationally.

This specification for improvements to the rotary engine was filed by Margaret Knight with the U.S. Patent Office in 1902.

1815 dental floss

1829 Graham cracker

1843 ice cream maker for home use

1847 doughnut

1849 safety pin

1859 pencil eraser

1867 paper clip

1874 spork

1825   1850   1875

THE INDUSTRIAL REVOLUTION

By definition, a revolution involves dramatic change. The American Revolution gave birth to the United States. Just a few decades later, a different type of revolution transformed the way most Americans lived.

THE EFFECTS OF THE WAR OF 1812

Even though the War of 1812 ended in a stalemate, many Americans felt a sense of triumph. The United States had held its own against Great Britain, the most powerful military force in the world. The war inspired nationalism among Americans as it reinforced the nation's independence and sovereignty. Soon after peace returned, the newly confident United States entered a period of economic growth driven by industry.

Riding the wave of optimism that swept across the country, James Monroe, Madison's secretary of state, easily won the 1816 presidential election, becoming the third straight Democratic-Republican from Virginia to hold that office. During his distinguished career, Monroe had served as a delegate to the Continental Congress, senator from Virginia, and governor of Virginia before Jefferson sent him to France to help negotiate the terms of the Louisiana Purchase. He had earned a reputation for honesty and dependability.

Monroe and his wife Elizabeth set a new tone for the presidency, with greater emphasis on style, entertaining, and celebrating the new national stature of the United States. The Monroes had the executive mansion painted a brilliant white to cover the smoke stains that remained from the fire set by the British forces during the war. The mansion has ever since been known as the "White House."

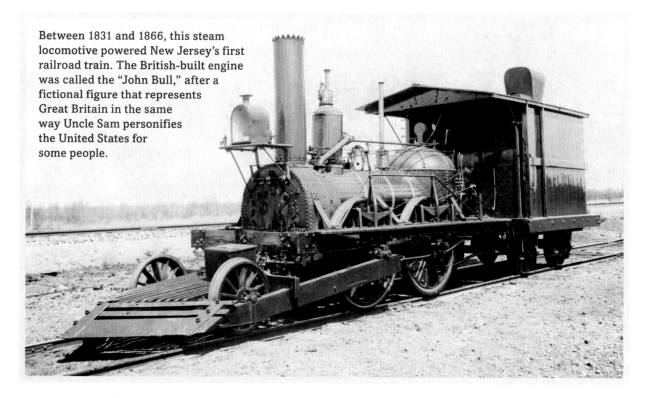

Between 1831 and 1866, this steam locomotive powered New Jersey's first railroad train. The British-built engine was called the "John Bull," after a fictional figure that represents Great Britain in the same way Uncle Sam personifies the United States for some people.

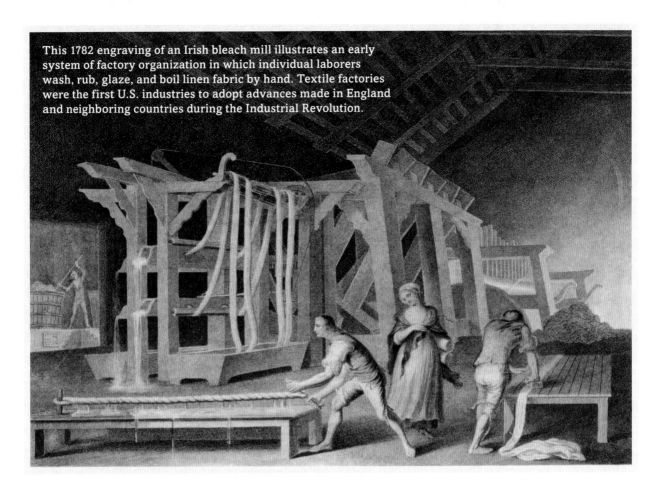

This 1782 engraving of an Irish bleach mill illustrates an early system of factory organization in which individual laborers wash, rub, glaze, and boil linen fabric by hand. Textile factories were the first U.S. industries to adopt advances made in England and neighboring countries during the Industrial Revolution.

The country that Monroe presided over was united in name, but its various regions had developed different economic strengths and distinct cultures. Sometimes the states had sharply conflicting policies, and their economies did not connect with one another very effectively. Certain similarities persisted across all regions, however. For example, most Americans in the early 1800s supported themselves through farming. They had few possessions and little money, and they made many of the things they needed by hand, including clothing and basic tools. For other items, they relied on skilled artisans, or craftspeople, in their communities. But a change was coming.

THE INDUSTRIAL REVOLUTION IN BRITAIN

Roughly a half-century earlier, in the mid-1700s, a sweeping transformation had begun in Great Britain that historians would later call the **Industrial Revolution**. The name implies rapid change, but this revolution unfolded over the course of many decades. It was characterized by a number of technological developments, each influencing the next advancement. One of the most significant of these developments was the invention of the steam engine to power factories and, when used in a vehicle such as a train locomotive, to transport goods. New machines greatly increased production

while decreasing the amount of human effort needed to perform specific tasks. These machines included the spinning jenny, which spun thread, and the power loom, which wove thread into cloth. The two inventions played a major role in completely transforming the way textiles were produced.

Another key development was the introduction of **interchangeable parts**, or precisely manufactured parts that are identical to one another. Using such parts, unskilled workers could quickly assemble products such as firearms. Interchangeable parts made possible **mass production**, or the production of manufactured goods in great quantities. Previously, such goods were made in small workshops by skilled artisans who crafted each part individually.

The Industrial Revolution began in Britain for many reasons. Britain enjoyed an abundance of flowing rivers and coal, natural resources that could provide energy to power the newly invented machines. Further, Britain's expanding network of roads, canals, and, eventually, railroads made it relatively easy and inexpensive to transport raw materials and finished goods over long distances. British investors were willing to provide large amounts of **capital**, or money needed to fund a business. They invested heavily in machines and factories, hoping to make a healthy profit when the enterprises succeeded. They eventually extended their investments throughout the United Kingdom, which, by 1801, included the countries of England, Scotland, Wales, and Ireland.

The Industrial Revolution brought profound changes to Britain. The old economy based on agriculture and handicrafts gave way to a new economy focused on manufacturing and industry. Society shifted from an agrarian economy and became far more urbanized as large numbers of people left farms to work in factories, which were usually located in cities.

THE AMERICAN INDUSTRIAL REVOLUTION

The advances of the early Industrial Revolution gave Great Britain's textile industry a tremendous advantage over its rivals in other countries. To keep this advantage, the government prohibited skilled workers from emigrating and forbade the export of textile machinery and drawings of that machinery.

In late 1789, a young cotton-mill worker named Samuel Slater left Britain illegally and sailed to the United States. In 1793, with the support of a wealthy American businessman, he built the first water-powered textile mill in Pawtucket, Rhode Island. Amazingly, he built it from memory. Slater constructed a spinning frame, a machine that produced stronger threads than regular spinning wheels. Since no satisfactory power loom yet existed, Slater's mill performed only the first two steps of cloth production: carding, or preparing the cotton fibers for spinning, and spinning the thread. Slater distributed the thread to local farm families, who wove cloth on looms in their homes. The textile industry became the first American industry to use methods of mass production. Slater has been called the "father of the American factory system" for the way he divided factory work into simple steps.

Even so, the United States continued to rely heavily on Great Britain for imports of textiles and other manufactured goods into the early 1800s. But then Britain imposed trade restrictions on the United States for continuing to do business with France while the two European powers were at war with each other. As you have read, Congress responded by passing the Embargo Act of 1807, which prohibited all foreign trade. This act and the subsequent War of 1812 nearly cut off all British imports. The U.S. economy suffered, leading to hardship among farmers, who could no longer sell their produce for export, and New England merchants, who had relied on international trade. The American textile industry, however, eventually benefited from the trade disruption. U.S. manufacturers developed their own power looms and other technologies to increase production and sell to people who had formerly bought imported textiles.

As in Great Britain, a wealth of natural resources played an important role in the early stages of the American Industrial Revolution. The United States

This illustration, copied from an oil painting by an unknown artist, shows Samuel Slater's first U.S. mechanical cotton mill rising up above nearby buildings and Rhode Island's Pawtucket Falls.

had an abundance of waterpower, the energy derived from flowing rivers and waterfalls, that could be harnessed to drive machinery. It also had plenty of iron ore and coal. The coal could be burned to power steam engines and to fuel the furnaces used in the production of iron and steel.

NEW ENGLAND'S TEXTILE MILLS

In 1810, almost 20 years after Samuel Slater's textile mill began operating, a Boston businessman named Francis Cabot Lowell traveled to Great Britain for a two-year visit. Through his business connections, he toured textile mills in Scotland and in the English county of Lancashire and became fascinated by the water-powered looms that wove thread into cloth at great speed, generating wealth for the mill owners. He carefully studied the looms, memorizing details of their construction and workings.

Upon returning home, Lowell worked with an engineer to recreate a power loom from memory. He and two business partners raised $400,000 in capital—a spectacular sum at the time—from a group of investors called the Boston Associates. In 1813, ten miles west of Boston, they opened the Boston Manufacturing Company, the first factory that combined all the steps of making cloth under a single roof. The company started as a four-story textile mill built along the Charles River in Waltham, Massachusetts, where a waterfall with a ten-foot drop offered free waterpower. Bales of cotton entered the mill, and bolts of cloth left it. This represented the real beginning of the Industrial Revolution in the United States.

Unlike earlier textile mills, Lowell's Waltham factory used unskilled labor and machines for weaving, which had been the most expensive part of the cloth-making process. Lowell and his partners were concerned that the introduction of factories into the United States might create the same problems with child labor and poverty-stricken workers they had seen during their visits to England. With this in mind, they recruited young New England farm women and girls as "operatives," or factory workers. The operatives, unlike British laborers, considered millwork a three- or four-year commitment before they left the factory, often to marry and raise a family. They worked 14 hours a day, 6 days a week, and earned $2.00 a week or more, depending on the type of job they performed.

By today's standards, the long hours and the often unpleasant and dangerous working conditions that the "mill girls" endured seem **exploitative**, or unfair and abusive. At the time, however, their employment

represented a significant step forward for society. It was rare in the early 1800s for women to have the freedom to leave their homes, live on their own, and earn their own money. The Boston Manufacturing Company provided housing and offered greater educational and cultural opportunities than the girls and women would have encountered at home.

The Waltham mill was tremendously profitable, and in 1822 its investors broke ground for a larger mill located 30 miles northwest of Boston. The mill was the centerpiece of the country's first planned industrial town, which was given the name "Lowell" in honor of the man who had transformed the U.S. textile industry. In the following decades, the Boston Associates continued to expand their textile empire into Lawrence, Massachusetts, and other parts of New England.

HISTORICAL THINKING

1. **READING CHECK** How were most goods produced in the United States before the Industrial Revolution?

2. **DRAW CONCLUSIONS** What role did capital play in the Industrial Revolution?

3. **ANALYZE CAUSE AND EFFECT** How did trade with Britain affect the American Industrial Revolution?

4. **FORM AND SUPPORT OPINIONS** Do you think the "operatives" who worked at the Lowell mill were exploited as workers? Support your opinion with evidence from the text.

COTTON AND SLAVERY IN THE SOUTH

Comfortable, versatile, and attractive, cotton cloth was the high-performance fabric of the 1800s, and everyone wanted it. As factories spun and wove, planters in the South picked up speed to meet the demand for cotton fiber.

KING COTTON

As Britain's textile mills continued to produce cotton cloth more cheaply and in larger quantities, the market for affordable cotton garments expanded. After the War of 1812, demand soared for raw cotton that British factories could spin and weave into the popular fabric. And no region of the world was as well prepared to meet this demand as the American South.

Cotton is categorized by staple length—that is, the length of the fibers. **Long-staple cotton** is prized because its long, silky fibers can be used to produce fine cloth and lace. But it is difficult to grow. In the United States, it flourished only in the coastal lowlands of Georgia and the Carolinas. **Short-staple cotton**, on the other hand, could be grown successfully across nearly the entire South. Cotton fibers are found in the plant's bolls, or pods, which contain small, sticky seeds. Separating the seeds from the raw fiber was an extremely slow and laborious process.

In 1793, while visiting a cotton plantation in Georgia, a New Englander named **Eli Whitney** came up with the idea for a machine that could quickly separate the cotton fibers from the seeds. His invention was called the cotton engine, or **cotton gin**, and it greatly increased the efficiency of cotton production. A single gin could produce as many as 50 pounds of cleaned cotton fiber each day. In contrast, a person removing the seeds by hand could produce only about one pound of fiber in a day. Since seeds accounted for more than half the weight of harvested cotton, removing the seeds before the cotton was shipped dramatically lowered transportation costs from plantation to cotton mill. Textile factories in the North began to purchase more cotton from the South. As profits increased, cotton growers expanded their production, causing the demand for enslaved workers to grow.

Seeking fertile land to meet the demand for cotton, small farmers and planters moved westward to the new states of Alabama, Mississippi, and Louisiana. Cotton soon surpassed tobacco as the most important southern crop, accounting for more than half of all U.S. exports. **King Cotton**, as the industry came to be called, would have a long reign and would profoundly affect the South and the country.

CRITICAL VIEWING Artist William Henry Brown used pen, watercolor, and cut-out figures to create *Hauling the Whole Weeks Picking* (c. 1842), a four-panel artwork depicting life on a South Carolina plantation. What does the title of this illustration mean, and what are the enslaved people doing?

EXPANDING SLAVERY

By the late 1700s, more and more voices were being raised against slavery, mostly in the northern states. In 1807, at the urging of **abolitionists**, or activists who work to end (or abolish) slavery, Congress passed an act that prohibited "the importation of slaves into any port or place within the jurisdiction of the United States . . . from any foreign kingdom, place, or country." The United States would no longer be part of the trans-Atlantic slave trade, which had begun 300 years earlier. The 1807 act did not, however, prohibit owning slaves or selling them within the borders of the United States.

The enslaved population continued to grow even after it became illegal to import slaves. As you have read, under chattel slavery, children born to enslaved parents were themselves enslaved. Also, traders persisted in smuggling slaves into the United States. In 1810, nearly 1.2 million enslaved people lived in the United States. By 1820, that number increased by roughly 29 percent to nearly 1.54 million. Although the enslaved population was much higher in the South than in the North, both sections of the country participated in and benefited from slavery and the slave trade.

The quick expansion of cotton plantations from southeastern coastal states into Alabama, Mississippi, and Louisiana created a tremendous demand for labor. Large numbers of field workers were needed to do the backbreaking work of clearing and cultivating the land and harvesting the cotton. Enslavers in the states along the Atlantic seaboard, faced with a surplus of labor, eagerly sold enslaved people to planters moving west. As a result, around

🏛 The Henry Ford Museum Dearborn, Michigan

The cotton gin designed by Eli Whitney pulled the cotton through a set of narrow wire teeth mounted on a spinning cylinder, leaving behind the larger seeds. Capable of being operated by people, animals, or water power, the machine was both simple and efficient. In the 1790s, the first saw-tooth gin was developed by several inventors, including Eli Whitney and Hodgen Holmes. The saw-tooth cotton machine in the photograph below was made around 1830.

HAULING THE WHOLEWEEKS PICKING

1815, the price of enslaved people began to rise, and the practice of separating families in order to sell individuals to the highest bidders also increased.

Hundreds of thousands of enslaved people were forced to migrate to the new states in the 1810s and 1820s. Some moved along with their enslavers to the new plantations, but many individuals were sold to slave traders in the East and North. The traders then brought them to slave markets in New Orleans, Mobile, and other cities in the new states. This domestic slave trade, a complex network of traders, suppliers, and insurers, contributed to the northern economy and made up as much as 13.5 percent of the total southern economy. The combined population of Alabama, Mississippi, and Louisiana more than tripled between 1810 and 1820, and by 1860, nearly half of those people were enslaved.

But not all African Americans were enslaved, even in the South. In 1810, the South was home to around 97,000 free African Americans, and roughly 77,000 lived in the North. Some had purchased their freedom, some had been freed by their former enslavers, and some had managed to escape slavery, take new identities, and start new lives.

Free African Americans were a small minority, however. Slavery was expanding, partly in response to developments in the North, particularly in the growing textile industry. In northern mills, demand increased for the South's cheap cotton, which was made possible by enslaved labor. But even as slavery became more deeply ingrained in the South and in the country's economy, opposition to it was growing in the North. Slavery was becoming a fault line that would threaten to split the nation.

EFFECTS OF KING COTTON

The Industrial Revolution began making itself felt in the United States by the 1810s, but its immediate effects were largely confined to northern states. While an industrial society began to develop in the North, the South remained primarily agricultural, in large part because of the cotton boom.

The expansion of King Cotton's realm did not occur in a direct east-to-west sweep across the South. Instead it followed the geographic and political outlines of lands once controlled by Native Americans. As you have read, during the War of 1812 many Native Americans had fought on the side of the British. They did so in a desperate effort to stop the United States

Now a museum of African-American history, arts, and crafts, the Old Slave Mart in Charleston, South Carolina, is the former site of many slave auctions. In locations such as this one, slaves were displayed and inspected by buyers prior to purchase.

CRITICAL VIEWING Enslaved African Americans place baskets of cotton into a cotton-press machine, which flattens it to be packed into square bales, or bundles. From the details in this illustration, what role do you think the young man on the horse plays in the process?

from intruding farther into their territories. The end of the war dealt a strong blow to this hope as the United States took quick steps to establish firm control over the entire eastern half of the continent.

Andrew Jackson, the general who had won the Battle of New Orleans, negotiated with the Creek, Cherokee, Chickasaw, and Choctaw nations of Alabama, Florida, and Mississippi. Using heavy-handed tactics, he forced Native Americans to sign treaties giving away their lands. Many resisted the enforcement of these treaties, objecting that the leaders who signed them had no authority to do so. Their resistance and arguments were in vain, and they were driven off the land.

After Jackson secured the lands from the Native Americans, white settlers rushed into the newly acquired territories, eager for the fertile land and the fortunes they planned to earn from it. Meanwhile, the Native Americans of the region, all of whom lived in agrarian societies, were pushed into hilly and mountainous areas poorly suited to farming.

Another effect of the cotton boom was to tie the South more closely to the economy of Britain. To meet the demand of its booming textile industry, Britain imported raw cotton from the West Indies, the East Indies, Brazil, and the Mediterranean region as well as from the southern United States. In 1790, cotton from the South represented less than one percent of total British cotton imports. By 1800, the figure had risen to 24 percent, and by the late 1820s, Britain imported nearly 75 percent of its cotton from the southern United States.

HISTORICAL THINKING

1. **READING CHECK** Why was cotton referred to as "King Cotton"?

2. **ANALYZE CAUSE AND EFFECT** Why did the auction prices of enslaved people rise, even after the international slave trade was outlawed on American soil?

3. **DRAW CONCLUSIONS** How did the Industrial Revolution affect the lives of the people who were enslaved in the South?

4. **DETERMINE WORD MEANINGS** What context clues help you understand what "heavy-handed" means in describing Andrew Jackson's tactics in negotiating with Native Americans in the South?

THE ECONOMY EXPANDS

Today, goods travel all over the world on container ships, airplanes, trucks, and high-speed trains. Two hundred years ago, the pace of life was slower, but merchants were beginning to call for speedier modes of transportation.

FULTON'S STEAMBOAT

From the earliest days of European settlement, the fastest and cheapest way to travel and transport goods long distances in North America was by boat on natural waterways. However, rivers could be dangerously fast in some seasons and so slow and shallow as to be impassable in others. They often froze for months in the winter. Floating downstream was easy, but traveling upstream against the current could be almost impossible. Flatboats that carried goods down the Ohio and Mississippi rivers to New Orleans did not make the return trip. Instead, they were broken up and their crews journeyed home on foot. Keelboats, longer and slimmer than flatboats, could be poled, paddled, sailed, or pulled upstream, but the work was backbreaking and the progress slow. Not surprisingly, soon after the power of steam was harnessed in the mid-1700s, people began to dream of riverboats propelled by steam engines.

The first practical steamboat in the United States was built by an inventor named John Fitch. He successfully tested the boat on the Delaware River in 1787, and four years later he received a U.S. **patent**, or a license that gave him the sole right to manufacture and sell his steamboats. He built several more steamboats, but because they were very costly to make and operate, he failed to start a profitable business. Another person excited by the possibility of steam propulsion was Robert Livingston, the statesman who, as the American minister to France, had negotiated the Louisiana Purchase. Livingston secured a 20-year monopoly on all steam navigation in the state of New York. A **monopoly** is the complete control of an industry or business venture by one person or company. Once Livingston had his monopoly, he partnered with an inventor named **Robert Fulton** to build a steamboat.

By the fall of 1807, a Fulton-designed steamboat was making regular trips on the Hudson River between New York City and Albany, the state capital. By 1811, Fulton managed to build a steamboat that was powerful and sturdy enough to take on the powerful currents of the Mississippi River. Soon, dozens of steamboats designed by other engineers were traveling up and down the river in competition with Fulton's model. Within a decade, the upstream journey on the Mississippi and Ohio rivers from New Orleans to Louisville, Kentucky, had been reduced from several months to just 14 days. "If anyone had said this was possible thirty years ago," a journalist marveled, "we should have been ready to send him to a mad-house."

Steamboats, along with the invention of the cotton gin and demand from textile mills, contributed to the rapid growth of the cotton industry in the South by providing efficient transportation between the plantations of the lower Mississippi Valley and the port of New Orleans. The increasing speed and frequency of the steamboats also encouraged the growth of villages and towns along the rivers. Louisville, Kentucky; Pittsburgh, Pennsylvania; Cincinnati, Ohio; and St. Louis, Missouri, were among many cities that grew into major business centers thanks to the arrival of the steamboat.

CLAY'S AMERICAN SYSTEM

The United States was experiencing a transition from a pre-industrial economy to a market-oriented, capitalist economy—the **market revolution**. While each region in the United States developed differently, the country's leaders saw the need to improve transportation between the regions in order to build the national economy. The Democratic-Republicans had long been known for

CRITICAL VIEWING This 1803 wooden scale-model reveals the technology of Robert Fulton's first steamboat. The black metal engine, a steam boiler, powered the two paddle wheels placed on either side of the hull. Why do you think inventors build scale-models like this one?

their opposition to federal power, but the surge of nationalism after the War of 1812 inspired leading members of the party to view the central government more favorably. Younger party members, such as **Henry Clay** of Kentucky and **John C. Calhoun** of South Carolina, urged Congress and the president to take strong steps to promote economic stability and encourage the growth of businesses.

Clay and Calhoun believed the future of the country lay in commerce and industry, and this led them to propose a three-part economic plan that Clay dubbed the **American System**. First, the plan called for internal improvements, such as clearing rivers and constructing roads and canals, which would make it easier to transport agricultural produce and manufactured goods from one part of the country to another. To provide the funds for these improvements, Clay and Calhoun supported the use of government subsidies. A **subsidy** is an amount of money or land granted to an individual or business by the government to promote commerce or fund improvements.

Second, the plan called for the re-establishment of a national bank to stabilize currency and encourage trade. Finally, the American System advocated a tariff to protect the United States' growing industries. A **tariff** is a tax on goods imported from other countries. By making imported goods more expensive, tariffs encourage people to buy goods produced in their own countries. Tariffs are also a way for governments to collect money.

THE NATIONAL ROAD

Relying on the support of the American System, the United States experienced a frenzy of roadbuilding after 1815. Investors, states, and even the federal government built thousands of miles of private roads, called **turnpikes**, that charged tolls to cover the roads' notoriously high maintenance costs. In 1818,

the U.S. government opened the **National Road**, also called the Cumberland Road, which wound through the rugged Allegheny Mountains and connected Cumberland, Maryland, on the Potomac River, with Wheeling, Virginia (now West Virginia), on the Ohio River. Both George Washington and Thomas Jefferson had pushed for the construction of such a road as a means of unifying the country and opening western lands for expansion.

The National Road was the best that technology could provide at the time, and it proved to be wildly popular. It featured excellent bridges and a relatively smooth stone surface. To ensure that rainwater drained quickly, the center of the roadway was raised higher than the sides. The road was soon crowded with travelers—on foot, on horseback, in carriages, in stagecoaches—and livestock. Traffic jams often slowed movement to a crawl. As a result of heavy usage, the road's condition quickly deteriorated due to wear and tear.

THE ERIE CANAL

In addition to building roads, state governments and private **corporations**, businesses that have most of the legal rights of an individual, began planning the construction of dependable canals. These canals would have **locks**, or gated enclosures used to raise or lower boats as they pass from one level to another. Locks solved the problem of building canals through hilly or uneven terrain.

In New York, ground was broken in 1817 on an extremely ambitious project: a canal that would connect the Hudson River with Lake Erie. It would allow water transportation between the Atlantic Ocean and the entire Great Lakes system, which extends deep into North America's interior. When completed, the **Erie Canal** would be roughly 365 miles long—more than 10 times longer than any existing canal at the time.

Mockingly called "Clinton's Big Ditch" after the governor of New York State who promoted its construction, the Erie Canal soon won over its critics. Several engineers who helped build the canal traveled to Britain to study canal construction, and local U.S. workers often invented tools to solve specific problems. Over the life of the canal, laborers, like those in this photograph taken around 1907, have maintained and rerouted the canal and locks.

Year by year, the canal advanced steadily toward Lake Erie, transforming the countryside along the way. As soon as workers completed a segment, canal boats crowded its waters, paying tolls that financed the portions yet unfinished. The Erie Canal was completed in October 1825, seven years after work had begun and two years ahead of schedule. It was considered one of the engineering marvels of its time. It boasted 83 stone locks and 18 stone **aqueducts**, or water bridges, that carried it over streams and ravines. Cutting through swamps, forests, and solid rock, it climbed more than 500 feet in elevation from east to west. Near its western end, a staircase-like series of locks transported it up a steep 75-foot-high slope called the Niagara Escarpment.

From the start, the canal was a spectacular success. The cost of transporting goods between Lake Erie and New York City, at the mouth of the Hudson River, plummeted. Canal traffic became so heavy that boats sometimes had to wait a day or two to pass through the locks. Buffalo, Rochester, Syracuse, and other canal-side cities flourished, and New York City became more firmly established as the country's most important seaport and commercial center. Like the National Road, the Erie Canal played a large role in westward expansion. By providing a safe and reliable route as well as easier, cheaper access to more markets, it drew large numbers of settlers to western New York and, from there, to the country's western territories.

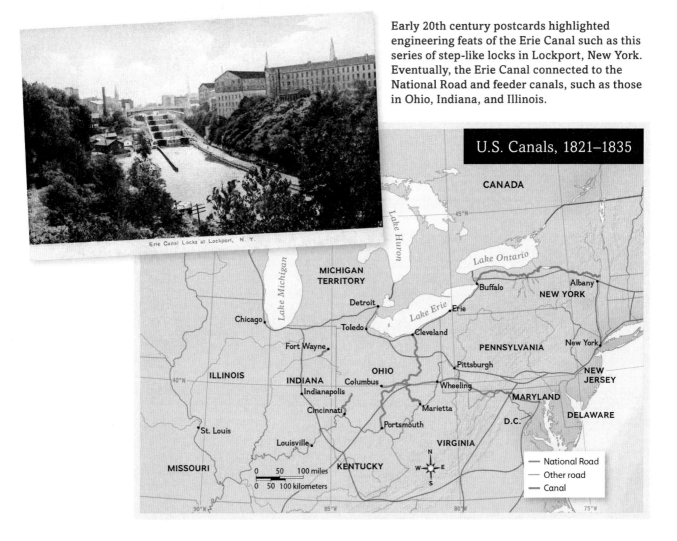

Early 20th century postcards highlighted engineering feats of the Erie Canal such as this series of step-like locks in Lockport, New York. Eventually, the Erie Canal connected to the National Road and feeder canals, such as those in Ohio, Indiana, and Illinois.

Erie Canal Locks at Lockport, N. Y.

U.S. Canals, 1821–1835

— National Road
--- Other road
— Canal

TARIFFS

As you have read, the War of 1812 disrupted trade between the United States and Britain. By the end of the war in 1815, the British had large stockpiles of iron products, glassware, and textiles. At the same time, production of these goods had been growing in the United States. In an effort to reduce their inventories and to restrain American manufacturing, the British began sending their goods to the American market at very low prices. Most Americans bought the cheaper British goods, leaving American goods unsold. **Bankruptcies**, or business failures, among American manufacturers grew sharply.

In their proposed American System, Henry Clay and John C. Calhoun promoted a tariff as the best way to protect and promote U.S. industry. Congress agreed and passed the **Tariff Act of 1816**, which imposed a tax on British imports, leveling the playing field between Britain's strong manufacturing sector and the United States' emerging one. Revenue from the tariff was intended to help fund the internal improvements that were also part of Clay and Calhoun's grand plan.

Tariffs became one of the country's most divisive issues. Manufacturers in the Northeast welcomed them because they protected the region's growing industries. On the other hand, farmers in the South, West, and Midwest opposed tariffs because they raised the price of imported goods. Southerners also worried that the British would retaliate and impose a tariff on cotton and other agricultural imports, which would hurt the South's cotton-centered economy. The issue of tariffs would continue to raise problems throughout the first half of the 19th century.

HISTORICAL THINKING

1. **READING CHECK** What was the American System?

2. **DRAW CONCLUSIONS** How would a British tariff on cotton imports from the United States hurt the South's economy?

3. **ANALYZE CAUSE AND EFFECT** How did the American System drive the building of roads and canals in the United States in the early 1800s?

4. **INTERPRET MAPS** How could someone send goods from coastal Maryland to Detroit in 1835?

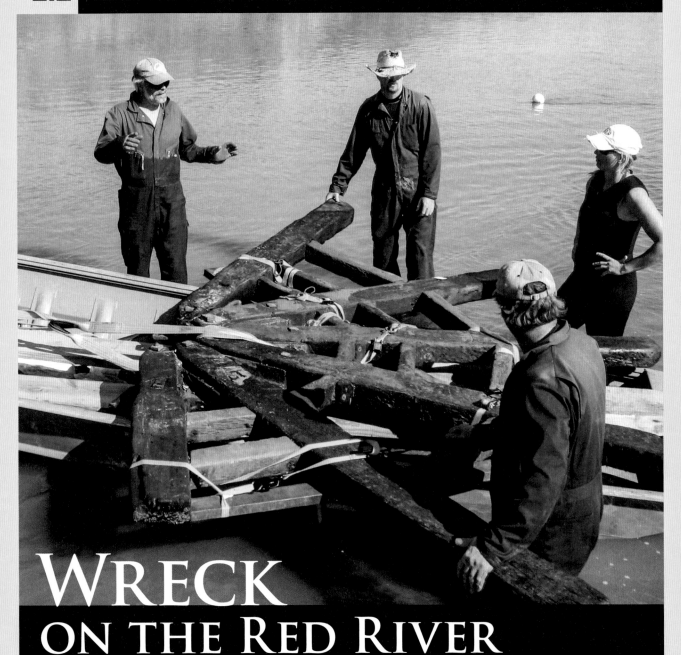

WRECK
ON THE RED RIVER

"There are a million stories to be told through this boat." —Kevin Crisman

For about six years, Kevin Crisman drove through a cattle ranch, donned diving gear, and jumped into Oklahoma's Red River. Day after day, he dove down and explored the wreck of a steamboat, bringing up artifacts to be studied and cataloged. Just a typical day at the office for this underwater archaeologist. But this was no typical find. The steamboat, called the *Heroine*, had sunk in 1838 and remained hidden in its watery grave for more than 150 years. It became the earliest example of a North American western river steamboat to be studied archaeologically.

^
National Geographic Explorer Kevin Crisman (far left) and his team carefully pull a paddle wheel assembly belonging to a steamboat called the *Heroine* from the Red River in 2006. Flooding during the mid-1800s buried the wreck in sand, where it remained for more than a century.

MAIN IDEA Underwater archaeologist Kevin Crisman's study of the *Heroine* has provided new information about early steamboats and river culture.

Passengers on steamboats such as the *Heroine* had to be patient. Low water levels sometimes made it impossible for the boats to move until rainstorms raised the river's water level again.

LOST AND FOUND

The 140-foot-long *Heroine* was bringing supplies to soldiers at Oklahoma's Fort Towson when a snag, or submerged log, in the river tore through its hull and brought the boat down. Stories about the *Heroine* circulated for years, but no one really tried to find it. After all, many steamboats from the 1800s had sunk, but very few had been found. Some sank when the steam boilers that powered their engines exploded—a common occurrence. Other hazards lurked beneath the river's surface, with sandbars, shifting logs, and snags lying in wait for unwary ship captains. It's no wonder the average lifespan of a steamboat in the early to mid-1800s was less than six years. The *Heroine* itself was about that age when it sank into the sands of the Red River. It remained there until the 1990s, when flooding led to its discovery on the riverbank.

In 2002, enter National Geographic Explorer Kevin Crisman. Working with the Oklahoma Historical Society and Texas A&M University's Institute of Nautical Archaeology, Crisman led the exploration of the steamboat—while it remained in the water. Crisman and his team couldn't remove the *Heroine* from the river because doing so would have caused its wooden frame to shrink, crack, and fall apart. Besides, the boat was well preserved in the sand.

So Crisman extracted everything he could from the wreck, but the process was challenging. After the team carefully dug a hole in the sediment, rain sometimes washed sand back in, filling up the hole. And much of the work was carried out in dark, murky water. As Crisman says, he and his team often "saw with our fingertips." Still, they managed to bring many artifacts to the surface: tools, machinery, cargo, and personal items. Based on data and pieces of the steamboat gathered at the site, researchers have also been able to create models of the *Heroine*.

TRANSPORTATION REVOLUTION

Among the cargo found on the *Heroine* were two intact pork barrels, the first ever recovered. The finding gave researchers insight into the meatpacking practices of the early 1800s. "That's the thing about shipwrecks," claims Crisman. "You find all of these things that you would have never thought to ask questions about." In their haste to abandon ship, passengers left some items behind. The spoons, buttons, and shoes help archaeologists imagine the lives of the passengers.

The items also help identify the social standing of the passengers. According to Crisman, the boats were "cultural blenders." For a couple of weeks, people from all walks of life were thrown together as they sailed on a steamboat: the wealthy and the poor, businessmen and laborers, mountain men and settlers. The boats sometimes even carried African Americans to slave auctions.

People sailed on steamboats in the early 1800s because they provided a quick—an astounding five to eight miles per hour!—and inexpensive form of transportation. Also, unlike earlier craft, steamboats could run upstream; they didn't have to be hauled manually. The boats brought about a transportation revolution that transformed the West. Steamboats carried immigrants and their cultures all over the region, and goods such as oranges made their way west for the first time as well. As Crisman says, "The floodgates opened, and the world rushed in."

HISTORICAL THINKING

1. **READING CHECK** Why didn't Crisman haul the *Heroine* out of the river to explore it?

2. **MAKE INFERENCES** What does Crisman mean when he says, "The floodgates opened, and the world rushed in"?

AMERICAN PLACES
THE GREAT LAKES

The largest surface freshwater system on Earth, the Great Lakes have played a major role in the colonization and development of North America. The movement of massive glaciers gave the Great Lakes basin its shape through a geological process that began about one million years ago.

In the early days of European exploration and expansion, the lakes served as a convenient transportation route into the middle of the continent. Explorers soon realized the value of the fertile land, thick forests, and mineral-rich vast shorelines. These resources, plus the endless supply of fresh water, drew people and industries to the region, where cities grew and flourished. Today, over 30 million people live in the Great Lakes basin. Lakes Michigan, Ontario, Superior, Erie, and Huron continue to attract people and businesses. But the lakes themselves have not benefited from this development. They have been seriously affected by such issues as pollution, overfishing, and invasive species—issues environmentalists are scrambling to address today.

STRENGTHENING THE NATIONAL GOVERNMENT

Since the nation's founding, Americans have argued over how much power they should grant the federal government. That question drove decisions of voters, lawmakers, and the Supreme Court in the first half of the 19th century.

THE SUPREME COURT AND NATIONAL POWER

Between 1814 and 1828, a series of Supreme Court decisions further expanded federal power and encouraged economic development. One case, **Gibbons v. Ogden**, focused on the steamboat monopoly New York State had granted to Robert Livingston. The case required the court to interpret the Constitution's vaguely worded commerce clause, which grants Congress the power "to regulate Commerce with foreign Nations, and among the several States, and with the Indian Tribes."

Aaron Ogden, who owned a fleet of steamboats, had an agreement with monopoly holder Robert Livingston to operate his boats in waters between New Jersey and New York. Thomas Gibbons joined him in this enterprise, but the partnership fell apart when Gibbons ran his own steamboat from Elizabethtown, New Jersey, to New York City. Ogden sued him. Gibbons argued that Congress alone had the power to regulate interstate commerce, or business affairs between states, and that New York had been wrong to grant the monopoly in the first place. The Court decided in favor of Gibbons, ruling that federal laws regulating interstate commerce take precedence over state laws.

This ruling greatly expanded Congress's power to regulate commerce between states. By making it illegal for states to grant monopolies and enact laws restricting interstate commerce, the decision also encouraged competition. It triggered a boom in steamboat traffic on the Mississippi and other major rivers, accelerating the country's westward expansion and economic development.

New Hampshire's Dartmouth College was at the center of another key Supreme Court ruling. In 1769, King George III of England had granted the college a charter, giving authority for managing the school to a board of trustees. In 1815, after a religious controversy led the board to remove the college's president, the New Hampshire legislature passed laws that amended the charter. Its actions made the once-private school a public college, changed the duties of the trustees, and altered the trustee selection process.

The trustees sued, and the case, called **Dartmouth College v. Woodward**, eventually reached the Supreme Court. The court ruled in favor of the trustees, holding that the charter was a contract, and the Constitution prohibits states from passing laws that alter the obligations of a contract. The ruling had a powerful effect on the U.S. economy. Shielded from one form of state interference, businesses were more secure and likelier to attract investors and expand.

THE SECOND BANK OF THE UNITED STATES

The Bank of the United States played an invaluable role in helping the young country handle its huge Revolutionary War debt and establish an effective financial system. But, as you have read, the bank faced strong political opposition based on questions of its constitutionality. After a bill to renew its charter failed in Congress, the Bank of the United States was forced to close its doors in 1811. It didn't take long for economic problems to arise again.

The United States at this time relied heavily on credit, or the ability to borrow money or obtain goods or services before paying for them. Credit is given based on trust that payment will be made in the

Surprisingly, the Supreme Court was not provided with its own building until 1935. Chief Justice William Howard Taft, who had also served as president, persuaded Congress to construct a permanent home for the Court. The architect built it in the style of an ancient Roman temple. The result was as Taft wished: "a building of dignity and importance suitable for its use as the permanent home of the Supreme Court of the United States."

future. Because far too little cash was available in the country's growing territory, business dealings were often based solely on trust. But when a chain of transactions is based on credit, the failure of one borrower can bring down many lenders. By 1815, states had chartered more than 200 private banks in an effort to solve their cash-shortage problems. These banks issued notes that served as currency in cash-starved areas.

Many influential leaders, including Henry Clay, John Calhoun, and President Monroe, wanted to create a new national bank to stabilize the economy and distribute scarce cash more uniformly. They argued that the state bank notes varied too much in value. Some were at risk of losing value entirely, destabilizing the whole economic system. The expanding nation needed a central financial institution to coordinate the flow of money.

In 1816, Congress chartered the **Second Bank of the United States**. Based in Philadelphia, the bank was a blend of public institution and private enterprise. The federal government deposited funds in the bank, controlled a fifth of its shares of stock, and appointed a fifth of the directors, but otherwise the bank operated as a private business. It pumped large amounts of paper currency into the system in an attempt to fuel the postwar economy and make it

easier to pay debts. This was especially helpful in the new states of the West, where buyers were making numerous land purchases on credit.

The Second Bank provoked as much hostility as the first had. Its opponents still argued that the Constitution did not grant Congress the power to establish corporations of any type, including a national bank. In the case of **McCulloch v. Maryland**, 1819, the Supreme Court ruled the bank was constitutional and protected it from state taxation. In his decision, Chief Justice John Marshall declared that the laws of the federal government "form the supreme law of the land." Business flourished in the new legal environment created by the Supreme Court's **landmark decisions**, or legal cases that settle important questions about new or existing laws.

HISTORICAL THINKING

1. **READING CHECK** How did a Supreme Court ruling affect traffic on the Mississippi River?

2. **DRAW CONCLUSIONS** How did the Supreme Court decision in *Dartmouth College* v. *Woodward* affect the relationship between state governments and businesses?

3. **IDENTIFY PROBLEMS AND SOLUTIONS** What problems led to the call for a second national bank?

NATIONALISM AND FOREIGN POLICY

Picture a jigsaw-puzzle map of the United States with its present-day borders. After the War of 1812, the puzzle was far from complete, but the fast-growing nation would soon add several key pieces.

SETTLING THE COUNTRY'S BOUNDARIES

When the War of 1812 ended, a wave of nationalism swept over the United States. As you have read, nationalism is a strong feeling of loyalty and devotion to one's country, often emphasizing the idea that the nation is superior to all others. The optimistic national mood influenced—and was influenced by—developments in foreign affairs as the United States began to increase its interactions with other countries.

After taking office in early 1817, President James Monroe worked to establish clearer borders for the United States. **John Quincy Adams**—a skilled diplomat, a member of the U.S. delegation that had negotiated the Treaty of Ghent that ended the War of 1812, and the son of second president John Adams—helped negotiate the Rush-Bagot Agreement of 1817 with Britain. The goal of this treaty was to calm diplomatic tensions on the Great Lakes and Lake Champlain, near the Canadian border, by limiting naval fleets that patrolled the waters. Under its terms, each side was allowed one military vessel each on Lake Champlain and Lake Ontario and two on each of the other Great Lakes. As Monroe's Secretary of State, Adams also helped negotiate the Convention of 1818, an agreement with Britain that fixed the border between the United States and Canada at the **49th parallel**—that is, the line of latitude established at 49 degrees north latitude.

Monroe and Adams also negotiated with the Spanish minister to settle the U.S. borders with Spain's territories. In the resulting **Adams-Onís Treaty** of 1819, Spain ceded both East and West Florida to the United States and dropped its claim to the Oregon Territory. The United States, in return, recognized Spanish sovereignty over the vast territory stretching

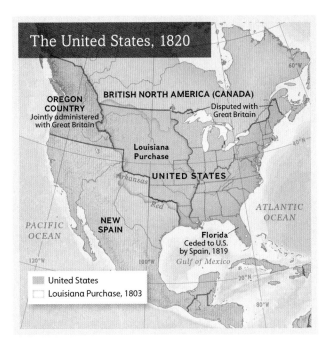

The United States, 1820

from Texas to present-day California. Adams referred to the accord as the Transcontinental Treaty because it extended the borders of the United States from the Atlantic to the Pacific.

THE PANIC OF 1819

As world demand for cotton cloth increased each year, prices skyrocketed for land on which to grow cotton in the southern United States. This led to a dramatic spike in Southern cotton prices. British manufacturers turned to other cotton suppliers, such as India. This sent American cotton prices tumbling, and the value of land that produced cotton fell with them. Meanwhile, something similar was happening in the country's new western lands, where easy credit and high European demand for American agricultural products helped to create a speculative "bubble" in land prices. The cost of land kept increasing, and many people thought it would continue to rise indefinitely. But the bubble burst, in part for the same reasons as the drop in Southern cotton values. Prices for American crops had risen along with the cost of the land on which they grew, which in turn caused European demand to decrease.

As land prices fell, many who had borrowed money based on future profits were unable to repay their loans. Banks and businesses began to fail, and they fell like dominoes. The **Panic of 1819** had begun, an economic crisis that sent the nation into the worst financial downturn it had yet experienced. The economy took three years to recover.

Farmers were hit hard, but many managed to get by through subsistence farming. In the cities, business ground to a halt due to bank failures and a lack of sources of credit. About half a million workers lost their jobs. Americans shuddered to see "children freezing in the winter's storm—and the fathers without coats and shoes." Charitable groups opened soup kitchens, while many families who had moved to towns and cities for work returned to the countryside to live with relatives.

As the fifth president of the United States, James Monroe was the last of the Founding Fathers to remain active in national politics. Like Thomas Jefferson and John Adams, two presidents who preceded him, Monroe died on the Fourth of July.

THE MONROE DOCTRINE

Despite the economic downturn, President Monroe remained popular, and he easily won re-election in 1820. The years of his presidency became known as the **Era of Good Feelings** because of the near absence of party politics and conflict, both within the United States and in its direct dealings with European nations. Elsewhere in the Western Hemisphere, however, conflict abounded.

Throughout the first two decades of the 19th century, South and Central America faced one struggle after another. Once-powerful Spain had been weakened by war and domestic upheaval, and colonial leaders such as Simón Bolívar in Venezuela and José de San Martín in Argentina pushed ahead with their long-simmering plans for independence. By 1822, the former Spanish colonies of Chile, Mexico, and Venezuela had won their independence, as had the former Portuguese colony of Brazil.

Fearing that France or Russia might attempt to fill the vacuum left by Spain in the Americas, President Monroe urged Congress to recognize the new Latin American republics. In December 1823, the president formalized a new foreign policy that eventually became known as the **Monroe Doctrine**: "The American continents, by the free and independent conditions which they have assumed and maintained, are henceforth not to be considered as subjects for future colonization by any European power." Monroe made it clear that, while the United States would not involve itself in any European wars, it would defend the Americas against any interference from Europe. Through this bold statement, the United States claimed the role of protector and leader of the Western Hemisphere.

HISTORICAL THINKING

1. **READING CHECK** What was the Monroe Doctrine?

2. **DRAW CONCLUSIONS** Why do you think Americans did not blame President Monroe for the Panic of 1819?

3. **INTERPRET MAPS** What areas of North America did the United States gain under the Adams-Onís Treaty?

4. **MAKE CONNECTIONS** What connections existed between Spain's domestic situation and the terms of the Adams-Onís Treaty?

WESTWARD EXPANSION AND TENSIONS OVER SLAVERY

Think about a time you had to make a compromise. What did you give up in order to get what you originally wanted? Were you satisfied? Compromises are important ways to manage conflict, but they don't always solve the underlying problem.

SETTLING THE NORTHWEST TERRITORY

The growing nationalism in the United States was mirrored by a dramatic expansion to new territories in the West. In the first two decades of the 19th century, the number of Americans living west of the Appalachian Mountains grew from about 300,000 to more than 2 million. "Old America seems to be breaking up, and moving westward," one man wrote in 1817, as he watched people move their possessions down the Ohio River on flatboats.

The region called the Old Southwest—the area that included Alabama and Mississippi—was growing fast due to the cotton boom, but the Northwest Territory, or Old Northwest, was growing even faster. Bounded by the Appalachian Mountains in the east, the Ohio River in the south, and the Mississippi River in the west, much of the region's land was ideally suited for farming, thanks in large part to its glacial past. For millions of years, ending about twenty thousand years ago, vast sheets of ice had plowed across this part of North America, smoothing and flattening the land and leaving behind thick deposits of silt, sand, clay, and rock called **glacial till**. Over the centuries, it became exceptionally fertile soil.

As you have read, when the Northwest Territory was formally opened for settlement, the Northwest Ordinances of 1784, 1785, and 1787 established laws calling for the territory to be divided into a number of self-governing districts. The plan was for these to become states once they met certain requirements. The laws also specified such things as lot sizes and prices. Importantly, the Northwest Ordinance of 1787 prohibited slavery from the region forever.

Most white settlers were dissatisfied with the first land they claimed; about two-thirds of them moved again within a few years. There was always talk of

In this illustration from a series called "Life of Lincoln," the very young future president Abraham Lincoln maneuvers a flatboat full of cargo down a river in the early 1800s. The flatboat was a practical mode of transportation at the time.

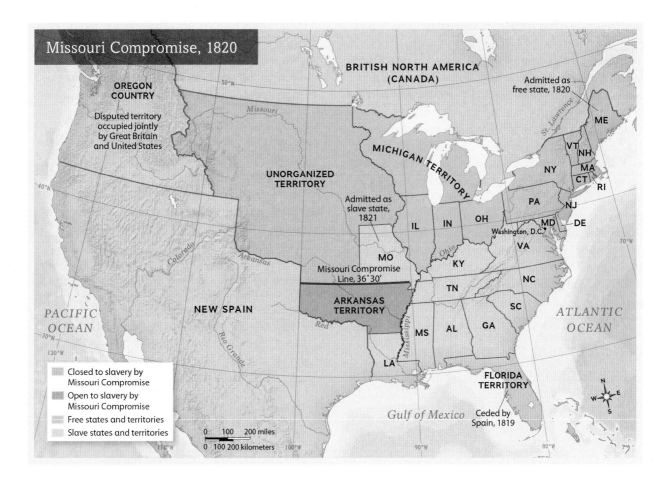

Missouri Compromise, 1820

OREGON COUNTRY
Disputed territory occupied jointly by Great Britain and United States

BRITISH NORTH AMERICA (CANADA)

Admitted as free state, 1820

UNORGANIZED TERRITORY

Admitted as slave state, 1821

MO

Missouri Compromise Line, 36°30'

ARKANSAS TERRITORY

NEW SPAIN

PACIFIC OCEAN

ATLANTIC OCEAN

Gulf of Mexico   Ceded by Spain, 1819

FLORIDA TERRITORY

Legend:
- Closed to slavery by Missouri Compromise
- Open to slavery by Missouri Compromise
- Free states and territories
- Slave states and territories

0 100 200 miles
0 100 200 kilometers

richer land a bit farther west, or a new town that was certain to mushroom into a major city, or greater opportunity just over the horizon. Settlers who remained in a community often became its leading citizens, consolidating land into larger farms, setting up gristmills and sawmills, holding political offices, and establishing the small towns that served as county seats and trading centers. In many cases, the storekeepers who were among the first to arrive often made small fortunes through trade.

THE MISSOURI COMPROMISE

As the United States expanded, each region began to establish a separate identity. People came to feel strong loyalty toward the part of the country in which they lived, a concept known as **sectionalism**. Several factors drove the development of sectionalism in the United States, including economic differences among regions—dependence on industry in the northeast, for example, as opposed to the agriculture that drove the southeast and west—and a variety of cultural differences. But slavery was one of the major causes of sectionalism, and westward expansion was making that more evident.

In 1815, the United States was evenly divided between slave states and free states; there were nine of each. The balance held over the next four

years as Mississippi and Alabama were admitted to the Union as slave states and Indiana and Illinois were admitted as free states. Politically, this balance was extremely important. Although the free states held a large and growing numerical advantage in the House of Representatives, the two sides were equally represented in the Senate. That meant neither could force through legislation opposed by the other. Southerners feared that if the free states gained control of the Senate, they would outlaw the practice of slavery nationwide.

The upcoming statehood of the Missouri Territory threatened to upset that balance in 1819. About 10,000 enslaved people lived in the territory. If Missouri were admitted as a slave state, as its territorial legislature had decreed, then the slave states would have a majority in the Senate. Slavery in Missouri, an area at roughly the same latitudes as much of Illinois, Indiana, and Ohio, seemed to violate the assumption, long held by many in the free states, that if slavery expanded at all, it would do so only in the South. The Constitution's Three-fifths Compromise, which allowed states to count enslaved people as a fraction of free persons in the census, had already given the slave states 20 more members of Congress and 20 more electors for the presidency. The South seemed to be getting extra and unfair representation.

Debate in the Senate raged for weeks in early 1820. Finally, a group led by Henry Clay succeeded in negotiating the **Missouri Compromise**. Under its terms, Missouri would be admitted to the Union as a slave state and Maine would be admitted as a free state, preserving the balance between slave and free states. Going forward, slavery would be prohibited in all the lands acquired in the Louisiana Purchase north of the southern border of Missouri, which was 36° 30' north latitude. Under this provision, slavery would be allowed to continue in the Arkansas territory, but it would be prohibited in **unorganized territory**, the vast expanses of the Louisiana Territory that lay farther north. This included the future states of Iowa, Minnesota, Wisconsin, the Dakotas, Nebraska, and Kansas. Another provision stipulated that any slaves who escaped to the free states would be returned to their owners upon capture.

DISAGREEMENTS OVER SLAVERY

The dispute over Missouri made it clear that slavery was becoming an increasingly divisive issue, but no one seemed to have a solid plan for what might happen should slavery end. Slavery had entrenched in Americans' minds the idea that whites and African Americans were somehow fundamentally different. Many white citizens, both in the North and the South, believed it would be impossible for the two races to live together in the United States. That was the message of the **American Colonization Society**, founded in 1816 and based in Washington, D.C. The society bought land in western Africa where it established a colony called **Liberia**, which means "land of freedom." Over the next 50 years, the society sent about 12,000 free African Americans to the colony, many of whom died of tropical diseases. As time went by, fewer African Americans migrated—and most were never interested in emigrating in the first place.

Meanwhile, unrest brewed among African Americans, both free and enslaved. In Charleston, South Carolina, a free and literate African American named **Denmark Vesey** had followed the Missouri controversy in the newspapers, which reinforced his belief that slavery was immoral. Taking inspiration from a successful slave revolt in Haiti decades earlier, Vesey organized a large-scale rebellion scheduled for June 16, 1822.

The rebels planned to seize Charleston's arsenals, guardhouses, and roads, and then to kill slaveholders before fleeing to Haiti, where slavery had been abolished. Before the rebellion could take place, insiders leaked the plans, and Vesey called

off the attack. Over the next two months, authorities captured and hanged 35 alleged conspirators, including Vesey. White southerners blamed Vesey's rebellion on the agitation against slavery in the Missouri debate.

Nine years later, **Nat Turner**, an enslaved but literate field hand and traveling preacher, led a deadly revolt in Virginia. Turner claimed God sent him visions urging him to lead a slave rebellion. During the night of August 22, 1831, Turner and his followers moved from farm to farm, slaughtering white families, including children and infants. By dawn, Turner's band of about 75 men had killed more than 50 people. A militia of 3,000 soon arrived to put down the rebellion, and Turner and his men were either killed or captured, later to be hanged.

Fearing more uprisings, the Virginia legislature met to discuss the issue. Some argued for a crackdown on the free black community's activities. Others

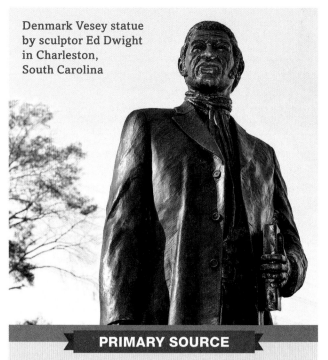

Denmark Vesey statue by sculptor Ed Dwight in Charleston, South Carolina

PRIMARY SOURCE

At his trial, Denmark Vesey kept his head held high, facing his prosecutors with the heroism of someone who believed he was doing the right thing even though he was resigned to bear the most severe punishment for it. His behavior rattled the sentencing judge, who addressed him directly at trial.

It is difficult to imagine, what infatuation could have prompted you to attempt an enterprise so wild and visionary. You were a free man, comely, wealthy, and enjoyed every comfort compatible with your situation. You had, therefore, much to risk and little to gain.

—from Judge to Denmark Vesey at his trial, 1822

called for an end to slavery, either immediately or gradually. Finally, Virginia and other southern states passed laws further limiting the freedom of both enslaved and free African Americans.

THE REINVENTION OF POLITICS

Slavery and the power of the federal government were central issues in the presidential election of 1824. James Monroe had run unopposed in 1820, but the 1824 election featured five strong candidates, including Secretary of State John Quincy Adams, Secretary of War John C. Calhoun, Secretary of the Treasury William Crawford, House speaker Henry Clay, and war hero Andrew Jackson. The election ended with Adams, Crawford, Clay, and Jackson vying for the presidency. Jackson won the popular vote and more electoral votes than the other candidates, but he needed more than half of the electoral votes to win the election.

Per the Constitution, it fell to the House of Representatives to decide the election. Adams narrowly prevailed with Clay's help. Although he had been a brilliant secretary of state, Adams struggled as president and could not rally public or political support for a stronger national government, internal improvements, or a tariff to protect American industry. This was due in part to fierce opposition from Jackson's supporters who remembered what they called Adams's "corrupt bargain" with Clay to win the election.

As the Era of Good Feelings faded, a very different era was coming into view. In New York, politicians developed a political strategy based on party organization and the **spoils system**, also known as the patronage system. Candidates who won an election were expected to remove people who had been appointed to city and state jobs by their predecessors and replace them with their own campaign workers and supporters. They were also expected to distribute political favors to loyal supporters. **Martin Van Buren**, a young lawyer and politician from New York, took advantage of the spoils system to create a powerful statewide organization. His goal was to combine party unity with personal advancement for party members, creating a self-reinforcing network of political power.

In the 1824 election, Van Buren had thrown his support behind Andrew Jackson, who shared his political ideas. Traveling throughout the United States, Van Buren forged a **coalition**, or group united to achieve a common goal, of ambitious state politicians willing to back Jackson. The coalition eventually split from the Democratic-Republicans to

CRITICAL VIEWING Cartoonist Thomas Nast illustrates the spoils system as a statue of Andrew Jackson surrounded by money bags while riding a pig. On the pedestal is the motto "To the Victors Belong the Spoils." How does the image of the pig add to the cartoon's ironic message?

form a new party called the Democratic Party, or the Democrats. Their candidates did extremely well in the congressional elections of 1827, exploiting public disapproval of Adams and his party, the National Republicans. After the election, the Democrats controlled both the House and the Senate. The stage was set for a showdown in the 1828 elections.

HISTORICAL THINKING

1. **READING CHECK** Why was the balance between slave states and free states politically important?

2. **FORM AND SUPPORT OPINIONS** Were white southerners correct in believing Denmark Vesey's rebellion was caused by debates about the Missouri Compromise? Support your opinion with evidence from the text.

3. **INTERPRET MAPS** Which areas did the Missouri Compromise close to slavery, and which did it open?

4. **DRAW CONCLUSIONS** Why did politicians establish the spoils system?

VOCABULARY

Use each of the terms below in a sentence that demonstrates an understanding of a concept or development discussed in the chapter.

1. capital

   The Industrial Revolution was dependent on investors willing to provide capital to fund the purchase of factories and machinery.

2. cotton gin

3. mass production

4. short-staple cotton

5. abolitionist

6. tariff

7. landmark decision

8. 49th parallel

9. sectionalism

10. spoils system

READING STRATEGY

DRAW CONCLUSIONS

Drawing conclusions about how events and ideas connect is important to building understanding. Complete a graphic organizer like the one below to draw a conclusion about the importance of technology during the early 19th century. Then answer the question.

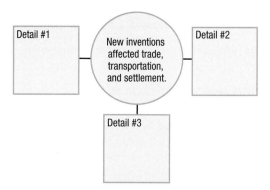

11. How did technology help transform the United States' economy?

MAIN IDEAS

Answer the following questions. Support your answers with evidence from the chapter.

12. Why were waterfalls important in the early decades of the Industrial Revolution? **LESSON 1.1**

13. How did the Embargo Act of 1807 and the War of 1812 affect industry in the United States? **LESSON 1.1**

14. How did Eli Whitney contribute to the expansion of cotton production? **LESSON 1.2**

15. What effect did the cotton boom have on slavery? **LESSON 1.2**

16. What three things did Henry Clay propose in the economic plan he called the American System? **LESSON 2.1**

17. How did the Tariff Act of 1816 help American industry? **LESSON 2.1**

18. In what area did the Supreme Court's decision in *Gibbons* v. *Ogden* expand the federal government's power? **LESSON 2.4**

19. What was the purpose of the Convention of 1818? **LESSON 3.1**

20. Why was Maine important to the Missouri Compromise? **LESSON 3.2**

HISTORICAL THINKING

Answer the following questions. Support your answers with evidence from the chapter.

21. **IDENTIFY** Identify five major changes or developments that took place in the United States in the period after the War of 1812.

22. **DRAW CONCLUSIONS** What economic reasons might the British have had for wanting to repair diplomatic relations with the United States after the War of 1812?

23. **COMPARE AND CONTRAST** In the early decades of the 1800s, were the North and the South becoming more or less alike? Explain.

24. **SUMMARIZE** What were the overall negative and positive effects of the Tariff Act of 1816 on the American people?

25. **FORM AND SUPPORT OPINIONS** Do you think Denmark Vesey should be viewed as a hero? Support your opinion with evidence from the chapter.

26. **ANALYZE CAUSE AND EFFECT** Why did President Monroe initiate the foreign policy that became known as the Monroe Doctrine?

INTERPRET GRAPHS

Between 1810 and 1830 the percentage of people enslaved in the North went from about 0.7 to 0.3 percent; in the South, it went from about 33 percent to 34 percent. Study the graph below, which shows the sizes of the enslaved populations of southern states in 1810 and 1820. Then answer the questions that follow.

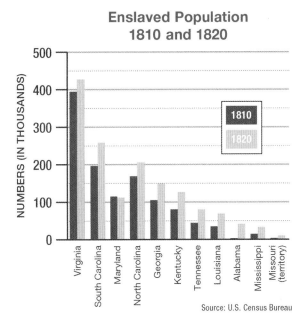

Enslaved Population 1810 and 1820

Source: U.S. Census Bureau

27. Identify which state on the graph had the greatest growth in slave population between 1810 and 1820. How many more people were enslaved in that state in 1820 than in 1810?

28. What conclusion can you draw about where slavery increased the most during the decade between 1810 and 1820?

ANALYZE SOURCES

In August 1807, Robert Fulton conducted the first trial of his newly built steamboat, traveling from New York City up the Hudson River to Albany and back. Afterward, he described the successful trip in a letter to his friend, Mr. Barlow.

> My steamboat voyage to Albany and back has turned out rather more favorable than I had calculated. The distance from New York to Albany is one hundred and fifty miles; I ran it up in thirty-two hours, and down in thirty. I had a light breeze against me the whole way, both going and coming, and the voyage has been performed wholly by the power of the steam engine. I overtook many sloops and schooners [sailboats] . . . and parted with them as if they had been at anchor. The power of propelling boats by steam is now fully proved.

29. Why do you think Fulton included the sentence about sloops and schooners?

CONNECT TO YOUR LIFE

30. **ARGUMENT** In this chapter you learned about the rise in nationalism after the War of 1812. Now think about the role nationalism plays in American life today. Do you think nationalism is a good thing or a bad thing? Write a short argumentative essay in which you explain why you feel this way.

TIPS

- Find evidence in the text that shows how nationalism affected the United States after the War of 1812.

- List examples of nationalism you see in the United States today.

- Weigh positive and negative aspects of nationalism against each other.

- Begin your essay by stating your claim.

- Include details and evidence that support your argument.

- End your essay with a concluding statement.

THE
JACKSON ERA
1828–1840

HISTORICAL THINKING How did Andrew Jackson change politics and the presidency?

CRITICAL VIEWING This statue of Andrew Jackson, erected in 1856, stands at the center of Jackson Square in New Orleans, Louisiana. It is one of four identical statues by sculptor Clark Mills. The equestrian monuments celebrate Major General Jackson's 1815 victory against the British at the Battle of New Orleans during the War of 1812. At the dedication of this statue, Mills said that he tried to capture Jackson reviewing his troops just before leading them into battle. How would you describe Jackson's attitude as portrayed here by Mills?

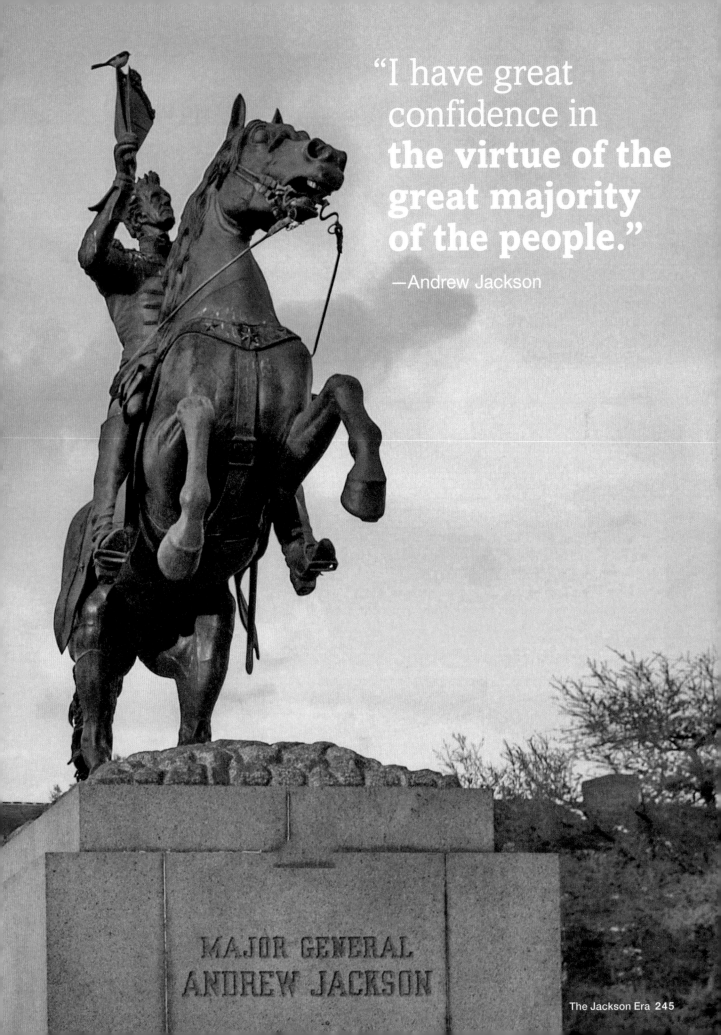

"I have great confidence in **the virtue of the great majority of the people.**"

—Andrew Jackson

MAJOR GENERAL
ANDREW JACKSON

THE CHEROKEE

Stereotypes about Native Americans persist in the United States. Many people believe that Native American cultures are simple and unsophisticated and have remained unchanged over time. The reality is that when the first European explorers arrived in North America, the Native American societies on the continent varied greatly, each with its own well-developed culture. In the centuries that followed, tribes followed different paths in their quests to resist or adapt to white settlement, and their cultures evolved in response to the realities of U.S. expansion.

The Cherokee tribe is one example of a Native American society that wrestled for many years with the issues of adapting to white American culture while still maintaining its own distinct identity. Like other Native Americans, the Cherokee endured forced relocation and other assaults on their way of life. Nevertheless, today the Cherokee Nation stands as a resilient, modern Native American society.

EARLY HISTORY

The Cherokee and their cultural ancestors have lived in the mountainous parts of North Carolina for thousands of years—since the end of the last ice age—but the Cherokee culture as it is recognized today began to develop about 1,000 years ago. This group called itself the *Ani'-Yun'wiya'*, which means the "Real People" or the "Principal People." Later, Europeans would use the word "Cherokee," a corruption of *Tsála̐gi̐* or *Tsa̐ra̐gi̐*, the name another tribe called them that meant "people of a different speech."

According to estimates, in 1650 roughly 22,500 Cherokee controlled an area of around 40,000 square miles in the Appalachian Mountain regions of present-day Georgia, Tennessee, North Carolina, and South Carolina.

Cherokee society was organized along matriarchal lines, meaning that property and certain aspects of family identity were passed down through the women of the tribe, not the men. Cherokee groups lived in villages that centered on a council house used for meetings and religious ceremonies. They practiced extensive agriculture and

CRITICAL VIEWING A young Cherokee takes part in a powwow festival, a celebration of Cherokee heritage. Unlike Native Americans of the Great Plains, who wore long feathered headdresses, the Cherokee wore a few feathers tied at the crown of the head. Why do you think the Cherokee might choose to wear traditional clothing at their festivals today?

farmed large plots of land. Crops included corn, beans, and squash, which were known as the "three sisters" because they benefited from being planted close together. Spirituality was an important part of Cherokee life, with beliefs and ceremonies focused on maintaining a sense of balance among humans, nature, and the spiritual world.

The Cherokee first encountered Europeans in 1540, when the Spanish explorer Hernando de Soto led his expedition across the tribe's land in search of gold and other riches. This first meeting was devastating for the Native Americans. De Soto and his followers demanded food and tribute from the Cherokee, and they enslaved people from the villages. Worst of all were the diseases the Europeans introduced, such as smallpox and measles. The Cherokee, like other Native American groups, lacked immunity to these illnesses, and their population suffered great losses. According to some estimates, European diseases wiped out up to 95 percent of the Native American population within 150 years of Columbus's arrival.

FRIENDS AND FOES

By 1650, the Cherokee had established regular trade relationships with English settlers. Contact with the new immigrants brought about some changes in farming patterns as the Cherokee began to cultivate species brought from Europe, such as

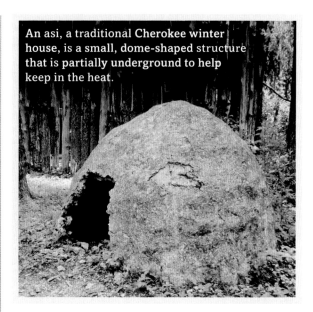

An asi, a traditional Cherokee winter house, is a small, dome-shaped structure that is partially underground to help keep in the heat.

peaches and watermelons. Alliances between the Cherokee and settlers were marked by outbreaks of hostility. For example, in 1693, the tribe sent a delegation to the British authorities in Charleston, South Carolina, to formally protest after colonists purchased some Cherokee people taken as slaves by enemy groups.

Trade and conflict continued in the 18th century as white settlers encroached on Cherokee land in rapidly increasing numbers. When the American Revolution erupted, most Cherokee allied with

This illustration depicts a 1566 meeting between the Spanish conquistador Juan Pardo and members of the Creek and Cherokee nations.

the British and fought for the return of their land. Receiving little support from Britain, however, the Cherokee were defeated in 1777 by the Continental Army and forced to sign away even more territory in western North Carolina, South Carolina, and portions of present-day Tennessee and Kentucky.

During the 1780s, a steady stream of settlers flowed from Virginia and North Carolina into the region west of the Appalachians and south of the Ohio River in search of fertile land. State governments, speculators, and frontiersmen quickly proceeded to push out the Cherokee. Colonial governments did sometimes declare in favor of Cherokee land rights, but the progress of white settlement was unstoppable.

The Cherokee began to explore the strategy of assimilation and adopted elements of white culture. They established a new government and constitution that they modeled on that of the United States. They also abandoned their traditional log dwellings to build homes in the American style and used American agricultural methods. Many Cherokee children even attended schools run by Christian missionaries, who persuaded a considerable number of tribe members to convert to Christianity. White authorities praised the Cherokee for adapting so well to European culture and adopting what the authorities considered to be "civilized" behavior.

Despite their many adaptations, the Cherokee and other tribes of the Southeast had no desire to leave their home regions. In their view, they had already given up more land than they should have and were determined to hold on to what they had left. The pressure to force the Indians out, however, was intense. Most whites, especially those who coveted the rich lands under the Native Americans' control, bristled at the continuing presence of the native inhabitants. The discovery of gold in Georgia only served to intensify their hunger for land.

In 1830, President Andrew Jackson required tribes in the Southeast to move west of the Mississippi to a dry prairie region called the Great American Desert. The Cherokee contested their removal in the Supreme Court and through other peaceful means, but to no avail. After years of negotiations and resistance, the Cherokee were among the last of the southeastern tribes to go. Their journey was brutal and became known as the "Trail of Tears." Thousands of Cherokee died of hunger, disease, exposure, or sheer exhaustion during the journey.

THE CHEROKEE TODAY

As tragic as it was, the Trail of Tears did not put an end to the Cherokee. Resilient in the face of hardship, they promptly began rebuilding their institutions and businesses after their removal. The new Cherokee capital was the town of Tahlequah, in present-day Oklahoma. There, the Cherokee reinstated their democratic form of government, and in 1839, they adopted a new constitution. In 1828, the Cherokee began printing periodicals in their own language. The tribe also established an extensive school system with 144 elementary schools and 2 institutes of higher learning—the Cherokee Male and Female Seminaries. These schools were so well regarded that white settlers living nearby paid to have their children attend. Some historians have termed this time of relative calm and prosperity the "Cherokee Golden Age."

THE CHEROKEE WRITING SYSTEM

Around 1809, a Cherokee named Sequoya began creating a system to write words in the tribe's language using symbols to represent syllables. After the Cherokee people adopted the writing system—known as a syllabary—literacy rates within the tribe soared. In 1824, the General Council of the Cherokee Nation awarded Sequoya a silver medal to honor his achievement. In 1828, the U.S. Congress granted him an honorary award of $500, although he only received $300. Texas leader Sam Houston once told Sequoya, "Your invention of the alphabet is worth more to your people than two bags full of gold in the hands of every Cherokee."

SEQUOYAH'S CHEROKEE ALPHABET.

The symbols in the Cherokee syllabary, shown here, are similar to English letters and usually written from left to right.

CRITICAL VIEWING
The Cherokee Female Seminary opened in Park Hill, Oklahoma, in 1851. It was the first school of higher learning for women west of the Mississippi. After the school burned down in 1887, a new one—shown in this photo—opened in 1890 in Tahlequah. Why might education have been important to the Cherokee people?

In the 1860s, the Civil War put an end to the golden age. Tribal members, some of whom were slave owners, were divided over which side to take in the bloody conflict. Over the course of the war, Cherokee territory was overrun by both the Union and Confederate armies at different times, leaving the tribe's economy in tatters.

Still, the Cherokee maintained a partly independent state until 1906. At that point, in the lead-up to Oklahoma's statehood, the land was divided into lots, some of which were given to individual Cherokee who had been listed in a special census. Other lots were given to freed slaves or homesteaders or retained by the federal government. Many of the Cherokee who held the lots became U.S. citizens, and the tribal government was essentially dissolved.

In the later 20th century, the Cherokee government saw a revival as the tribe regained a large measure of independence. In 1990, the Cherokee Nation negotiated and signed an agreement with the U.S. Congress on self-governance. The Cherokee Nation today numbers around 300,000 members throughout the United States and governs a jurisdictional service area—not a reservation—in northeastern Oklahoma, where around 126,000 members live. The tribal government is founded on democratic principles and is composed of executive, judicial, and legislative branches. It also owns several successful businesses, including Cherokee Nation Entertainment, which operates

entertainment venues, and Cherokee Nation Industries, which supplies defense contractors. According to the Cherokee Nation's website, its businesses have "a positive financial impact of over one billion dollars annually" for the state of Oklahoma.

In North Carolina, the descendants of those few who succeeded in avoiding the enforced removal formed the Eastern Band of the Cherokee. Like the Cherokee Nation, they operate under a tribal government with three branches. The Eastern Band has more than 14,000 enrolled members, the majority of whom live in the 57,000-acre area the group purchased, called the Qualla Boundary.

Like all groups of people, the Cherokee are diverse in their thoughts, opinions, and ways of navigating the modern world. Some adhere closely to tribal traditions, while others have largely abandoned them. The Cherokee Nation hosts numerous celebrations and ceremonies, and members are free to choose whether or not to attend. What all Cherokee have in common is belonging to a living, evolving culture that defies flat stereotypes of Native American life and occupies a unique place in today's United States.

THINK ABOUT IT

What aspects of Cherokee society do you think helped the tribe survive and move toward success in the 21st century?

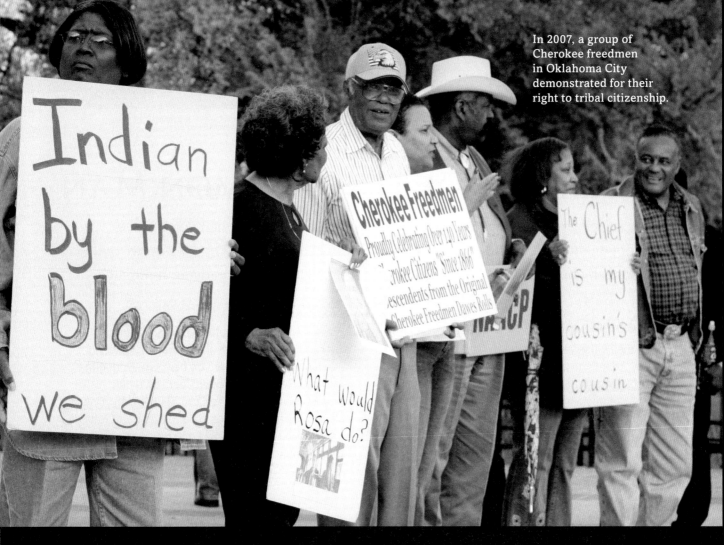

In 2007, a group of Cherokee freedmen in Oklahoma City demonstrated for their right to tribal citizenship.

THE CHEROKEE FREEDMEN CONTROVERSY

When the Cherokee assimilated into white American society in the early 1800s, some established plantations and acquired African-American slaves to work on them. The enslaved people were forcibly moved along with their masters to the Great American Desert, where they continued in servitude.

After the Civil War, the Cherokee signed a treaty with their former slaves, or freedmen, granting them "all the rights of Native Cherokees." However, in 2007, the Cherokee amended their constitution and made having "Indian blood" a requirement for being considered a citizen of the tribe. As a result, about 2,800 descendants of the freedmen lost their Cherokee citizenship. The freedmen responded with protests, demonstrations, and, eventually, lawsuits.

Finally, in 2017, 10 years after the amendment's passage, U.S. District Court judge Thomas Hogan ruled that Cherokee freedmen had tribal citizenship rights. In his decision, Judge Hogan wrote, "The Cherokee Nation can continue to define itself as it sees fit but must do so equally and evenhandedly with respect to native Cherokees and the descendants of Cherokee Freedmen." The attorney general for the Cherokee Nation stated that the decision would not be appealed.

RIGHTS RESTORED

Marilyn Vann was a leader of the descendants and a plaintiff in the lawsuit against the Cherokee.

PRIMARY SOURCE

Following the ruling, Vann told a reporter what it meant to her.

There can be racial justice—but it doesn't always come easy. What this means for me is the freedmen people will be able to continue our citizenship . . . and also that we're able to preserve our history. All we ever wanted was the rights promised us to continue to be enforced.

—from an interview with National Public Radio, 2017

CHAMPION OF THE COMMON MAN

A loss in any contest can be hard to take, but it is especially so when you believe your opponent used underhanded methods to win. That's exactly how Andrew Jackson felt about his loss in the 1824 election. By 1828, he was ready for a rematch.

THE COMMON MAN

When the House of Representatives chose John Quincy Adams as president in 1824, Andrew Jackson viewed the win as another triumph for the rich. Jackson claimed to represent the rights of hardworking people, whom he called the "common man," and he considered himself one of them. Born into poverty in 1767, Jackson grew up on the border between North and South Carolina. His father died before his birth, so his mother struggled to raise him and his brothers on her own. During the American Revolution, young Jackson risked his life carrying messages to the Continental Army. British soldiers captured him during a mission and took him prisoner. While held captive, the boy was ordered to shine a soldier's shoes. When Jackson refused, the

Soldiers cheer for Jackson astride his white horse as he surveys the battle scene in this 1856 painting by Dennis Malone Carter, *The Battle of New Orleans*. In the background, British soldiers fall before the Americans' fire.

soldier slashed him with his sword. By the age of 14, Jackson had lost his mother and brothers to various illnesses. Jackson himself contracted smallpox but survived the disease.

Jackson was determined to overcome his hard childhood and make a success of his life. As a young man, he studied law and became a lawyer. Then he moved to Tennessee, where he met the woman he would marry, Rachel Donelson Robards. Jackson also served in the House of Representatives and Senate. In 1804, he purchased a 425-acre farm, later called the Hermitage, near Nashville. As you've read, Jackson rose to national prominence when he defeated the British at the Battle of New Orleans in the War of 1812.

After he lost the presidential election in 1824, Jackson and the Democratic Party that eventually formed sought to limit Adams to a single term and lay the groundwork for the next election. Jackson's allies in Congress weakened Adams's presidency by blocking many of his programs. The Democrats also benefited from the expansion of voting rights in many states, which granted suffrage to white men who did not own property, including farmers, craftsmen, laborers, and middle-class businessmen. (Women, African Americans, and Native Americans still could not vote, however.) To appeal to these new voters, the Democrats tried to make political participation attractive. They organized barbecues and picnics at political rallies and wrote entertaining campaign songs. Political gatherings became events that united people with common interests.

The movement that supported the rights of the common man became known as **Jacksonian democracy**. Due in part to broadened voting rights, over 800,000 more men voted in the 1828 presidential election than in the 1824 election. As the 1828 election approached, there was a general restlessness and desire for change. Many voters were ready for a president who had risen from a humble background through hard work rather than one who had inherited his wealth and power. Andrew Jackson would be their man.

THE ELECTION OF 1828

The election once again pitted Jackson against Adams. During the campaign, both sides did everything in their power to get their candidate elected. They organized speeches, held parades, and came up with slogans and songs to build enthusiasm for their man. These tactics changed the way all future American politicians would run their campaigns.

PRIMARY SOURCE

You are supported by the great body of the people . . . because they have entire confidence in your wisdom, and integrity; and it is believed that the men now in power have obtained, and are endeavoring to retain their places by "bargain management and intrigue," and in direct violation of the will of the people.

—from a letter written by Robert Y. Hayne to Andrew Jackson, 1828

The 1828 campaign was also marked by mudslinging, or nasty personal attacks. Previous campaigns had used insults to criticize an opponent, but communication had been more limited then. In 1828, newspapers across the country carried the candidates' attacks. Jackson's supporters portrayed Adams as a man who only represented the interests of the wealthy and who had gained the presidency through a "corrupt bargain" with key members of the House. The Adams campaign, in turn, charged that Jackson was a slave trader and murderer. In fact, Jackson used slaves at the Hermitage and had engaged in many duels, one of which resulted in the death of his challenger. But the most vicious attacks directed against Jackson involved his wife, who had divorced her first husband. Rachel's divorce had not been properly finalized when she and Andrew married in September 1793. Once the divorce went through, however, the couple legally remarried in January 1794. Still, the Adams campaign characterized Rachel as a bigamist, or someone who is married to two people at the same time.

In spite of the mudslinging, Jackson won in a landslide, with 178 electoral votes to Adams's 83. Sadly, Jackson would enter the White House without Rachel by his side. She died of a heart attack a few weeks after the election. Jackson believed his political enemies and their personal attacks had caused his wife's death. In December, he buried Rachel on the grounds of the Hermitage in the dress she had planned to wear to her husband's inauguration.

HISTORICAL THINKING

1. **READING CHECK** How did the expansion of suffrage benefit Jackson in the election of 1828?

2. **DISTINGUISH FACT FROM OPINION** How did both Adams and Jackson use facts and opinions to try to sway voters?

3. **DRAW CONCLUSIONS** Why were so many people excited over the prospect of Jacksonian democracy?

THE PEOPLE'S PRESIDENT?

Seeing a new president installed in the White House is always a cause for celebration—at least among his or her supporters. But Andrew Jackson's backers may have been a bit too enthusiastic.

A NEW POLITICAL CLASS

About 20,000 people arrived in Washington, D.C., to witness Andrew Jackson's inauguration on March 4, 1829. Some traveled 500 miles to attend the event. In a tradition established by Thomas Jefferson, Jackson opened the White House to the public so that he could greet the people. However, the White House staff was not prepared for the thousands who showed up. As the crowd grew and became more unmanageable, the new president fled the White House and was taken to a hotel.

Rumors circulated that the guests had destroyed items in the White House and stood on the furniture in their muddy shoes. But Jackson supporters claimed these accounts were exaggerated. And actually, most newspapers reported little or no damage. At least one writer, Margaret Bayard Smith, was dismayed by the simply dressed men and women who came to the White House. Nevertheless, she recognized that their presence—and Jackson's—represented a fundamental change in American democracy. Smith wrote, "What a pity what a pity! No arrangements had been made, no police officers placed on duty and the whole house had been inundated [invaded] by the rabble mob." However, as she also pointed out, "Ladies and gentlemen only had been expected at this Levee [reception], not the people en masse [as a whole]. But it was the People's day, and the People's President and the People would rule."

To the established political class, the scene at the White House represented the dangers of Jacksonian democracy. Members of the establishment thought they were better able to govern the country than the common man. But Jackson's election had broadened democracy, and he symbolized the age. He was the first president who did not come from a wealthy family in Virginia or Massachusetts. To many supporters, he also represented the shift of power to the West. Many people believed they finally had a president who represented them and their interests.

A ROCKY START

When Jackson took office, he began to carry out the reforms he'd promised during his campaign. He started by replacing a number of government officials from the previous administration with people who had supported him during the campaign, including newspaper editors. Jackson replaced only about 10 percent of the officials he had authority over, but this was far more than other presidents had replaced. The new president referred to his actions as "the principle of rotation in office." He claimed this rotation prevented government officials from permanently holding on to their jobs and becoming too powerful. Jackson's opponents, however, claimed he was simply rewarding his friends.

Critics charged Jackson with instituting the spoils system, which comes from the saying "to the victors belong the spoils of the enemy." They claimed that what he had done was corrupt and that he was using his appointments to gain greater control of the federal government. You may remember that Martin Van Buren had used the spoils system to create a powerful statewide network when he served as a New York senator. Jackson was the first to use the spoils system in the federal government.

Like the presidents before him, Jackson also selected his Cabinet members. He made Van Buren, who had directed the 1828 campaign, his Secretary of State. His close friend, John Eaton, became Secretary of War. Jackson's vice president, John C. Calhoun, recommended men for some of the other Cabinet positions.

CRITICAL VIEWING President Jackson—in the black jacket—is pinned against a wall by his supporters during the White House reception following his inauguration in this 1970 painting by Louis S. Glanzman, *The Rowdy Party*. What details in the painting convey a negative impression of the people at the reception?

Meanwhile, gossip was swirling about Eaton's new wife, Peggy, who was said to have a scandalous past. As a result, many of the Cabinet members' wives and Calhoun's wife refused to socialize with Peggy. Calhoun supported his wife, which angered Jackson. The rumors recalled those that had upset Jackson's wife during the 1828 campaign. The Eaton affair, as it came to be called, caused a rift between Jackson and Calhoun. Van Buren, on the other hand, behaved courteously to Peggy Eaton and would become Jackson's most trusted advisor. Policy issues would also divide the Cabinet. To ease the tension, Van Buren and Eaton withdrew from their positions. Jackson fired most of the other members in 1831.

Instead, he turned to a group of unofficial advisors—all trusted friends. Jackson's opponents dubbed this group the **kitchen cabinet**, suggesting that the members had "back door" access to the president.

For a time, Van Buren was a member of the kitchen cabinet. Calhoun, who wanted to succeed Jackson as president, became increasingly resentful of Van Buren. His resentment turned out to be well founded. When Jackson ran for re-election in 1832, Van Buren replaced Calhoun as his running mate.

HISTORICAL THINKING

1. **READING CHECK** What did Jackson symbolize to his supporters?

2. **MAKE INFERENCES** Why might some people have wanted to characterize those who came to the White House after Jackson's inauguration as a "rabble mob"?

3. **FORM AND SUPPORT OPINIONS** Do you think a president should only appoint friends and supporters to positions of power? Why or why not?

TENSION OVER TAXES

Sometimes you take a stand, and it doesn't work out. In 1828, Adams supported a bill he hoped would help him get re-elected, but the move backfired. Andrew Jackson won the election but had to deal with southern opposition to the bill.

DIFFERENCES BETWEEN THE NORTH AND THE SOUTH

The Eaton affair and Cabinet infighting weren't the only problems Andrew Jackson faced early in his presidency. Tensions between the North and the South were rising over tariffs, the taxes a government charges on imported goods. By the 1820s, the two regions had developed strong, but very different, economies. You've learned that the economy of the North had become increasingly industrialized by the 1820s. The trend had brought great population growth and wealth to the region. Some of this population growth was due to the influx of immigrants drawn by the hope of obtaining work in northern factories. By contrast, the agrarian South depended largely on agricultural production, particularly cotton. And, as you know, large plantation owners used enslaved labor to work their fields.

Industries in the North benefited from tariffs because the taxes increased the price of foreign manufactured goods. The tariffs made the lower-priced goods produced in the North more attractive, which boosted local sales. On the other hand, tariffs hurt the South. Southern farmers bought manufactured goods from Europe. Tariffs on these goods made them more expensive. In 1828, Congress would pass a bill that underscored the economic differences between the North and the South.

THE TARIFF OF 1828

The bill, which would be called the Tariff of 1828, was passed in the final months of John Quincy Adams's presidency. It greatly raised tariffs and, therefore, the prices of foreign goods sold in the United States. The bill was intended to protect northern industries from foreign competition. As you know, Adams represented the interests of the Northeast, where many factories were located. With the next presidential election approaching, Adams promoted the bill, in part to appeal to northeastern voters. The bill, he believed, would also benefit the federal government. At that time, tariffs represented the government's main source of revenue. Defenders of the tariff pointed out that its passage would be in the interest of the entire country. Southerners didn't buy it. They hated the tariff so much they called it the **Tariff of Abominations**.

The Tariff of 1828 made the foreign goods the South needed more expensive. However, it also contained a clause that raised taxes on some of the imported raw materials that were necessary to both the North and the South, including wool. Democrats in Congress had proposed the clause because they believed its inclusion would persuade northeastern representatives to vote against the tariff. After all, many textile manufacturers in the Northeast depended on imports of wool, and the clause made the fiber more expensive. Nevertheless, the bill passed with the support of representatives from the middle and western states as well as a few key congressmen from New England.

Adams signed the bill into law even though he knew it would probably hurt him in his bid for re-election. People in many regions of the country disliked the bill, but southerners especially loathed it. The South voted against Adams partly in reaction to the tariff. One of its greatest opponents was John C. Calhoun, who was John Quincy Adams's vice president. As you know, Calhoun was also elected vice president under Andrew Jackson. Once in office, Jackson supported the tariff, but Calhoun continued to voice his opposition to it. As a result, the split between the two would deepen even further.

TARIFFS TODAY

Americans continue to disagree over tariffs. In 2017, the U.S. government threatened to impose tariffs on steel imported from China and other countries. Ships carrying containers of imported steel continually arrived in American ports, including this one in South Carolina.

The president at that time, Donald Trump, claimed the countries were using the United States as a "dumping ground" for their cheap steel. He also insisted that the imported steel was harming national security by preventing the United States from manufacturing steel for its own defense purposes. Critics said the tariffs would raise the price of domestic steel and, as a result, the price of U.S. goods made of steel. Opponents also pointed out that European countries might retaliate by levying tariffs on some U.S. imports. In spite of these objections, President Trump ordered tariffs on most imported steel and aluminum in 2018.

HISTORICAL THINKING

1. **READING CHECK** How did the economies of the North and the South differ in the 1820s?

2. **IDENTIFY MAIN IDEAS AND DETAILS** Why did southerners call the Tariff of 1828 the Tariff of Abominations?

3. **MAKE INFERENCES** Why might those in the middle and western states have supported the tariff?

4. **DRAW CONCLUSIONS** In what ways was the passage of the Tariff of 1828 a no-win situation for Adams?

THE NULLIFICATION CRISIS

Where do you stand on states' rights? Do you believe a state should be able to decide which federal laws it will obey? The people in many southern states thought they should have that right after Congress passed the Tariff of 1828.

THE DOCTRINE OF NULLIFICATION

Vice President John C. Calhoun represented South Carolina, his home state, in the fight against the Tariff of 1828. He invoked the **doctrine of nullification**, also known as the states' rights doctrine, to make his case. As you may recall, nullification refers to an idea first proposed around 1798 by Thomas Jefferson and James Madison. According to this idea, states have the right to determine when the federal government has exceeded its power. In these instances, states can reject federal laws and declare them "void [invalid] and of no force." The doctrine of nullification became a key issue in the debate over states' rights versus federal power.

Calhoun further developed this doctrine in a document called the *South Carolina Exposition and Protest*, which was published in 1829 without his name on it. In the document, Calhoun insisted that a state should only be compelled to obey a federal

Daniel Webster debates the doctrine of nullification in the Senate while his opponent, Robert Y. Hayne, sitting cross-legged in the foreground, listens. This bronze relief is set in the pedestal of a statue of Webster in Washington, D.C.

The Webster-Hayne debate took place over several days in January 1830 and established Webster's reputation as a gifted orator. In the following excerpts from their speeches, first Hayne and then Webster state their views on nullification.

If the Federal Government, in all or any of its departments, is to prescribe [impose] the limits of its own authority, and the States are bound to submit to the decision, and are not to be allowed to examine and decide for themselves when the barriers of the Constitution shall be overleaped, this is practically "a Government without limitation of powers." The states are at once reduced to mere petty corporations [insignificant organizations] and the people are entirely at your mercy.

—Robert Y. Hayne, 1830

I . . . have kept steadily in view the prosperity and honor of the whole country, and the preservation of our federal Union. It is to that Union we owe our safety at home, and our consideration and dignity abroad. It is to that Union that we are chiefly indebted for whatever makes us most proud of our country. . . . And although our territory has stretched out wider and wider, and our population spread farther and farther, they have not outrun its protection or its benefits.

—Daniel Webster, 1830

law with which it disagreed if the law were amended to the Constitution. This process would protect states' rights—especially those of the less populated South—from being violated by a northern majority. Otherwise, Calhoun believed, federal enforcement of the law should be considered unconstitutional.

Andrew Jackson was angered by the position his vice president had taken on nullification. Jackson didn't like the tariffs, but he didn't repeal the Tariff of 1828. His inaction disappointed many of the southerners who had voted for him. They'd expected he would at least modify the law once he became president. Jackson supported states' rights, but he opposed Calhoun's notion that states should have the power to prevent the federal government from enacting national laws. Only the Supreme Court, Jackson asserted, had the power to declare a law unconstitutional. He also feared the doctrine of nullification threatened the preservation of the Union.

THE WEBSTER-HAYNE DEBATE

Daniel Webster, a senator from Massachusetts, disagreed with Jackson on many issues, but he also perceived nullification as a threat to the Union. Other politicians joined in the debate over nullification, but the **Webster-Hayne debate** held in 1830 became the most famous. Over the course of the debate, Webster argued against nullification, calling for "Liberty and Union, now and forever, one and inseparable." Senator Robert Y. Hayne of South Carolina presented Calhoun's ideas and made the case in favor of nullification. Hayne criticized those whom he said "are constantly stealing power from the States and adding strength to the Federal Government."

The nullification crisis escalated in 1832. In an effort to make some concessions to the South, Congress passed the Tariff of 1832, which reduced tariffs. However, most southerners viewed the new law as little better than the old one, and South Carolina decided to put Calhoun's nullification theory to a test. The South Carolina legislature declared the tariffs of 1828 and 1832 "null and void." Furthermore, if the federal government used force to collect the tariffs, the representatives claimed South Carolina would secede, or withdraw, from the Union. South Carolina tried to persuade other states to join their protest, but none did.

Jackson responded by issuing a statement reaffirming the authority of the federal government and warning that any attempt to leave the Union would be considered treason. In addition, Congress authorized the president to use force against any state that refused to pay the tariffs. Finally, Senator Henry Clay of Kentucky proposed the Compromise Tariff of 1833, which would gradually reduce tariffs over the next 10 years. South Carolina agreed to the compromise, and the nullification crisis ended. Jackson had succeeded in preventing secession. However, tensions over states' rights would continue to grow and divide the country throughout much of the 1800s.

HISTORICAL THINKING

1. **READING CHECK** What is the doctrine of nullification?

2. **DISTINGUISH FACT FROM OPINION** How did Hayne and Webster use facts and opinions to make convincing arguments in their debate?

3. **DRAW CONCLUSIONS** Why did Jackson believe the nullification crisis could lead to secession?

SEIZING NATIVE AMERICAN LAND

Almost from the moment Europeans arrived in North America, Native Americans had struggled to hold on to their homes. They would encounter one of the greatest threats to their traditional lands in Andrew Jackson.

PROMISES MADE AND BROKEN

You may remember that Andrew Jackson had dealings with Native Americans before he became president. After the War of 1812, the federal government authorized then-General Jackson to negotiate treaties with Native Americans in the Southeast, including the Creek, Cherokee, Choctaw, and Chickasaw. The Creek signed their treaty after losing a war against U.S. Army troops led by Jackson, and the treaty's terms were highly unfavorable to the Native Americans. They were required to hand over about 22 million acres of land—an area roughly the size of South Carolina—to the federal government. After more battles and treaties with other Native Americans, white settlers moved into the fertile lands the tribes had occupied for generations. The Native Americans were edged onto lands less suitable for farming.

As president, Jackson wanted to get hold of more Native American territory for white settlers. He offered Native Americans two options. They could either **assimilate**, or adopt, European culture and submit to the laws of their state government, or they could move west of the Mississippi River. Some Native American tribes chose assimilation. The Cherokee, Chickasaw, Creek, Choctaw, and Seminole adapted so well to European culture that some people referred to them as the "Five Civilized Tribes." Among these tribes, none assimilated as fully as the Cherokee. They dressed in western-style clothing and owned businesses and farms. Some built plantations and ranches and even used enslaved people to work their land.

One Cherokee named **Sequoya** (sih-KWOY-uh), who had fought for the United States during the War of 1812, developed a **syllabary**, written symbols or characters used to represent a word's syllables,

for the Cherokee language. The syllabary was used to translate many books, including the Bible, and literacy spread rapidly among the Cherokee. The Cherokee also printed a newspaper called the *Cherokee Phoenix*, the first newspaper published by Native Americans as well as the first in a Native American language. They even wrote a constitution based on the U.S. Constitution and, having established a sovereign government, founded the **Cherokee Nation**.

However, assimilation did not protect the Cherokee or any of the southeastern tribes from being pressured to leave their homes. The pressure mounted when gold was discovered on Cherokee land in Georgia in 1828. As a result, southern states passed laws that ignored previous treaties and allowed farmers, miners, and other settlers to claim Native American lands for themselves.

THE INDIAN REMOVAL ACT

Jackson supported the laws enacted in the southern states and went even further. In 1830, he pushed Congress to pass a law called the **Indian Removal Act**, which reversed the federal government's policy of respecting Native American claims to their lands. The law granted the president power to negotiate removal treaties with Native American groups living east of the Mississippi. The treaties required Native Americans to give up any claim to their homes and move to an area of land that came to be known as **Indian Territory**, which included present-day Oklahoma and parts of Kansas and Nebraska. Native Americans who wished to remain in the eastern states would become citizens of their home state.

The Indian Removal Act called for peaceful negotiations and specified that Native Americans would not be forced off their land. But Jackson did

Native Americans continue to fight for their homes today. In 2016, Native Americans protested the installation of an oil pipeline that crossed the Missouri River near North Dakota's Standing Rock Sioux Reservation, claiming that it could contaminate the reservation's drinking water. In this photo, U.S. Army veteran Catcher Cuts the Rope leads a protest march. Despite protesters' efforts, the pipeline opened in June 2017.

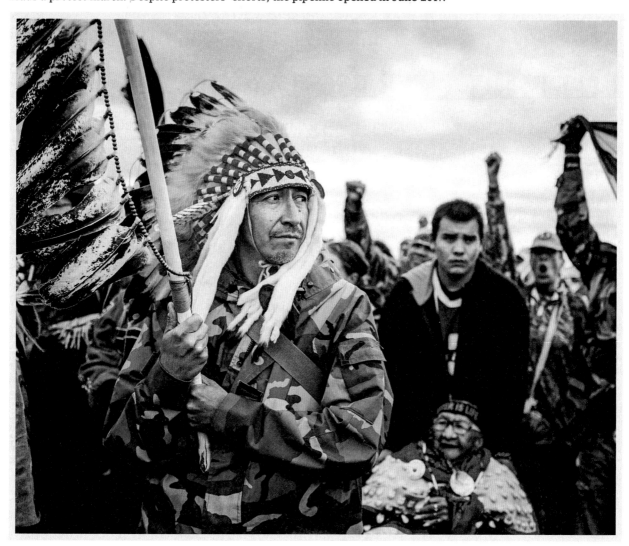

not always abide by this ruling. He regarded Native Americans as children who needed to be guided. Jackson believed removal was in their best interests. Not all Americans agreed with the removal act, however. Some protested the cruelty of sending Native Americans to unknown lands. Others, like the Quakers, objected on moral grounds, claiming the Indian Removal Act was neither just nor right. But their protests had little impact. The removal of Native Americans soon got underway.

The act affected not only Native Americans in the Southeast but also tribes farther north. Many Native Americans left their homes peacefully. The Choctaw became the first southeastern tribe to sign a treaty. While some Choctaw chose to remain in Mississippi under the terms of the act, thousands elected to move westward beginning in 1831. On foot and carrying insufficient supplies, the first group to relocate encountered the worst winter yet recorded. About 2,500 Choctaw died of exposure, starvation, and disease during the move. The Chickasaw faced similar hardships when they headed west in the winter of 1837. But not all Native Americans gave up their homes. Some would not go without a fight.

HISTORICAL THINKING

1. **READING CHECK** What options did Jackson offer Native Americans in his effort to acquire land for white settlers?

2. **DISTINGUISH FACT FROM OPINION** Was Jackson's attitude toward Native Americans based on fact or opinion or both? Explain your answer.

3. **MAKE INFERENCES** Why do you think many Native Americans chose to leave their homes peacefully and relocate to Indian Territory?

3.2

MAIN IDEA Some Native Americans resisted relocation, but most were forced to leave their homeland and endured great suffering.

PUTTING UP RESISTANCE

Sometimes people stand up to injustice, even when they're outnumbered and overpowered. Despite the size and strength of the United States, some Native Americans tried to defy Andrew Jackson and the U.S. government.

THE SECOND SEMINOLE WAR

The Seminole, who had first settled in the northern area of Florida, were among the Native Americans who fought against relocation. Most of the Seminole refused to sign a removal treaty, and President Jackson and the U.S. government declared war on them in 1835.

This wasn't the first time Jackson had gone to war against the Seminole. The First Seminole War was waged between 1817 and 1818, when General Jackson led his troops on frequent raids into Florida, which belonged to Spain at that time. The Seminole had provided a refuge for slaves who had escaped from their owners. Jackson and his soldiers invaded the Spanish territory to combat the Native Americans, burn their villages, and recapture the slaves. The Americans also seized Spanish-held territory. As a result, Spain ceded Florida to the United States in 1819, and the Seminole were confined to an area of land in the central and southern parts of the territory.

The Second Seminole War posed a tougher challenge for the U.S. Army. Under their leader **Osceola** (ahs-ee-OH-luh), the Seminole used guerrilla tactics to fight the American soldiers. The warriors hid within the swamplands of the Everglades, a wetlands region in southern Florida,

CRITICAL VIEWING Little is known about Osceola's early life, but many historians believe he was born in Alabama in 1804 to a Creek mother and a Scottish father. He was known as Billy Powell until he went to live among the Seminole in the Everglades. There, he embraced his Native American heritage and became known as Osceola. What does this 1838 portrait of Osceola, painted by American artist George Catlin, convey about the leader?

and took the Americans by surprise during battles. Armed with tomahawks and muskets, the Seminole ambushed and attacked the soldiers. The Seminole also tried to drive out white settlers already living in the region by setting fire to their homes and farmland.

In 1837, the U.S. government and the Seminole called a truce, or an agreement to stop fighting, and the Americans arranged to meet Osceola at a peace conference. But the conference turned out to be a trap. Osceola was taken prisoner and died in captivity three months later.

Occasional skirmishes in Florida continued for five more years before the Seminole finally surrendered. Nearly 2,000 American soldiers died during the war, which cost the government more than $40 million. Some Seminole eventually migrated to Indian Territory and became one of the Five Civilized Tribes. However, many remained in the Everglades. The Seminole still live there today.

THE BLACK HAWK WAR

As you've learned, Native Americans in other parts of the country faced removal. Some of them resisted relocation as well. Tribes in Illinois, including the Shawnee, Ottawa, Potawatomi, Sauk, and Fox, signed a treaty and moved west of the Mississippi River. However, once they settled in their new home, they struggled to grow enough food on the land. Rather than starve, they rebelled. In April 1832, Sauk warrior **Black Hawk** led about 1,000 Sauk, Fox, and other Native American people to take back their lands in Illinois.

Their return angered and frightened the white settlers who had moved onto the lands the tribes had surrendered. A force of about 7,000 volunteers, consisting of settlers, U.S. soldiers, and even members of other Native American tribes, joined together to fight Black Hawk and his followers. The brief but bloody Black Hawk War ended in August and resulted in the deaths of as many as 600 Native Americans and 70 soldiers and settlers. A number of those who participated in the war on the American side would become prominent figures in U.S. history. For instance, a young **Abraham Lincoln** served as a captain in the Black Hawk War. Another future president, **Zachary Taylor**, also took part.

Black Hawk surrendered and was held prisoner by the U.S. Army for several months. While imprisoned, he told his captors that he was not sorry for trying to take back Native American land. Black Hawk believed he was defending the land and his people from those he said aimed to "cheat them." When the American public learned what Black Hawk had said, many people sympathized with him.

Following his imprisonment, Black Hawk was brought to Washington, D.C., to face Andrew Jackson. The president had Black Hawk take a tour of four major eastern cities to show the Sauk leader that he was no match for such a large, powerful nation. Many Americans turned out to see the famous Sauk warrior. While in Baltimore, Black Hawk was quoted as saying, "I ought not to have taken up the tomahawk, but my people have suffered a great deal." He died in 1838.

🏛 National Museum of the American Indian Washington, D.C.

Seminole men wore pouches called bandolier bags strapped over their shoulders. Made of wool and decorated with beads, the bags were used to carry flint, steel, and tobacco. The bag shown at right is believed to have been taken from a Seminole chief during the Second Seminole War.

Removal of the Native Americans, 1830s

SOUTHEASTERN GROUPS RELOCATED

Group	Number Relocated
Cherokee	12,000
Chickasaw	4,750
Choctaw	13,000
Creek	14,500
Seminole	3,000

CANADA

Lake Superior

MAINE

VT.
N.H.

WISCONSIN
TERRITORY

OTTAWA

MICHIGAN

Lake Michigan

Lake Huron

L. Ontario

NEW YORK

MASS.

RHODE
ISLAND

IOWA
TERRITORY

SAUK
AND
FOX

POTAWATOMI

SHAWNEE

OHIO

PENNSYLVANIA

CONNECTICUT

NEW JERSEY

L. Erie

Mississippi

Missouri

UNORGANIZED
TERRITORY

ILLINOIS

INDIANA

D.C.

DELAWARE

MARYLAND

Arkansas

Indian
Territory

MISSOURI

Trail of Tears

Ohio

VIRGINIA

KENTUCKY

disputed
between
Texas and
Mexico

ARKANSAS

CHICKASAW

TENNESSEE

NORTH
CAROLINA

CHEROKEE

SOUTH
CAROLINA

ATLANTIC
OCEAN

Red

CHOCTAW

CREEK

GEORGIA

REPUBLIC
OF TEXAS

ALABAMA

Rio Grande

MISSISSIPPI

LOUISIANA

MEXICO

Gulf of Mexico

FLORIDA
TERRITORY

SEMINOLE

N
W E
S

0   100   200 miles
0   100   200 kilometers

Removal routes
- Cherokee
- Chickasaw
- Choctaw
- Creek
- Seminole
- Other tribes

In 1988, thousands of reenactors embarked on the journey taken by the Cherokee to commemorate the 150th anniversary of the Trail of Tears.

THE TRAIL OF TEARS

As a sovereign nation, the Cherokee took legal action to resist their removal from Georgia. In the 1823 case *Johnson* v. *M'Intosh*, the Supreme Court declared that only the U.S. government could buy land from Native Americans, not private citizens. The Cherokee brought two cases before the Court in their fight: *Cherokee Nation* v. *Georgia* in 1831 and *Worcester* v. *Georgia* in 1832. In the second case, the Supreme Court ruled that the Cherokee Nation could not be regulated by the state and determined the Indian Removal Act violated previous treaties with the Cherokee. However, the decision did not help the Cherokee. Both the state of Georgia and Jackson ignored the Supreme Court ruling. The president reportedly declared, "[Supreme Court Chief Justice] John Marshall has made his decision, now let him enforce it!"

A few Cherokee leaders negotiated a removal treaty with the U.S. government and headed to Indian Territory in the mid-1830s. But most of the Cherokee—about 17,000—opposed the treaty and remained on their land. **John Ross**, the principal chief of the Cherokee, tried to work out a more favorable treaty with the United States, but Jackson refused to engage in further negotiations. In 1838, General **Winfield Scott** and 7,000 troops were sent into Cherokee lands in Georgia and Alabama. The soldiers took the Cherokee from their homes and placed them in camps. White settlers then destroyed the Cherokee villages and stole the people's belongings, leaving the Native Americans with only the few items they'd taken to the camps.

After months of confinement, the Cherokee were forced to begin the long march to Indian Territory. They were ill-equipped for the long journey, which took place over the fall and winter of 1838 and continued through the spring of 1839. And the soldiers didn't provide the Cherokee with adequate food, shelter, or clothing. Some soldiers even stole what few supplies the Native Americans possessed. As a result, about 4,000 Cherokee died.

One of the soldiers accompanying the Cherokee later described the march: "On the morning of November the 17th [1838] we encountered a terrific sleet and snow storm with freezing temperatures and from that day until we reached the end of the fateful journey on March the 26th 1839, the sufferings of the Cherokee were awful. The trail of the exiles was a trail of death. They had to sleep in the wagons and on the ground without fire. And I have known as many as twenty-two of them to die in one night of pneumonia." Survivors described the journey as "the place where they cried." Today it is known as the **Trail of Tears**.

PRIMARY SOURCE

Before the Cherokee were taken from their homes and forced on the march to Indian Territory, John Ross still hoped to appeal to the U.S. government for justice. In this excerpt from a letter Ross wrote to members of the House of Representatives, he describes what his people had already suffered.

We are stripped of every attribute of freedom and eligibility for legal self-defense. Our property may be plundered before our eyes; violence may be committed on our persons; even our lives may be taken away, and there is none to regard our complaints. We are denationalized; we are disfranchised [denied legal rights]. *We are deprived of membership in the human family! We have neither land nor home, nor resting place that can be called our own.*

—from Cherokee chief John Ross's letter to the U.S. House of Representatives, 1836

The Cherokee who survived the march faced more challenges when they reached Indian Territory. During the journey, the American soldiers had made the Cherokee pay settlers for the right to cross their land and boatmen for passage across rivers. By the time the Cherokee arrived in their new home, they had little money left. And the Native Americans who had already settled in the territory weren't pleased to see the newcomers. The Cherokee fought with the Osage over land. They also sought revenge against their people who had signed the removal treaty.

More than 47,000 people from the five southeastern tribes were moved to Indian Territory. As one historian has said, "All went through their own versions of the Trail of Tears."

HISTORICAL THINKING

1. **READING CHECK** How did the Seminole use the geography of the Everglades to fight the U.S. Army in the Second Seminole War?

2. **DRAW CONCLUSIONS** Why were the numbers of U.S. soldiers and Native Americans killed in the Black Hawk War so unequal?

3. **EVALUATE** What did Jackson reveal about his presidency when he challenged the Supreme Court to enforce its ruling in the Cherokee cases?

4. **INTERPRET MAPS** Why was Indian Territory probably established where it is shown on the map?

GILCREASE MUSEUM TULSA, OKLAHOMA

A Scotch-Irish, French, and Native American heritage and a love for American history and artwork inspired Tulsa oilman Thomas Gilcrease to found Gilcrease Museum in 1949. He had admired artwork by the masters in Europe but chose to curate a collection that reflected Native American history and culture—a nod to his Creek ancestry.

With a focus on the preservation and study of American art and history, Gilcrease Museum and its research center house the world's largest collection of art, artifacts, and historical documents relating to the American West. Its collection includes more than 12,000 pieces of western fine art and more than 100,000 rare books and manuscripts.

Silver Thunderbird Necklace

In some Native American folklore, the thunderbird is a symbol of power, but it may also represent a trickster—the interpretations abound. Regardless, the thunderbird appears on Native American artifacts from many different groups and regions.

This 1900s necklace from the Zuni group in the American Southwest features seven thunderbird pendants adorned with turquoise, jet, coral, and mother-of-pearl.

To many Native American groups of the Southwest and Mexico, turquoise symbolized life: the blue of water and the green of growing plants.

The Night Rider by Frederic Remington

Remington was one of the premier artists of the American West, and his oil paintings are an important part of the Gilcrease collection. This 1905 painting and others still serve as source material for modern filmmakers and historians of this region.

Ceramic Vessel by Annie Healing Nampeyo

While some modern southwestern potters now experiment with different colors and effects in their work, many adhere to techniques dating back to 300 B.C. A Hopi Tewa potter from Arizona, Annie Healing Nampeyo (1884–1968) followed in her mother's footsteps, using traditional Puebloan designs and patterns in her work. This piece dates to around 1900.

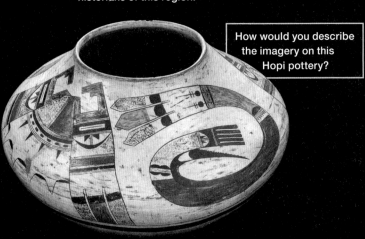

How would you describe the imagery on this Hopi pottery?

Antelope Head with Pedernal by Georgia O'Keeffe

A modern artist who trained in New York City and Chicago, O'Keeffe (1887–1986) spent many summers in New Mexico developing a love for the Southwest. This 1954 oil painting embodies what O'Keeffe is best known for—abstract close-ups of animal bones, flowers, clouds, and landscapes. She is considered the mother of American modernism.

Wooden Kachina Doll

Within the traditional beliefs of the Hopi and Zuni groups, a kachina is considered one of many spirit-beings that interact with humans. These spirit-beings can be represented through masks and hand-carved wooden dolls, such as this one. The dolls teach children about ceremony, legends, and history. Many kachina are elaborately decorated and presented as gifts on special occasions.

What types of materials were used to decorate this kachina?

The Cheyenne

Frederic Remington wasn't just a painter. This 1913 bronze sculpture is part of a collection of riders and horses he sculpted after traveling through the Southwest in the 1880s with "a desire to record the vanishing wilderness." The details in the sculpture capture the strength and grace of both the horse and its Native American rider.

Remington was also a writer, authoring short stories and eight books about the West.

What can you infer about Native American warriors from this sculpture?

THE END OF THE SECOND BANK

What do you do when you perceive something as a threat? Do you run from it, or do you confront it head-on? Never one for running away from anything, President Andrew Jackson went on the attack against the Second Bank of the United States.

JACKSON'S BANK WAR

You've read that Congress approved the creation of the Second Bank of the United States in 1816. This bank was established after the charter, or permit to do business, of the First National Bank, proposed by Alexander Hamilton, expired. During Andrew Jackson's presidency, the Second Bank had helped regulate the economy and stimulate its growth. Because the huge federal bank controlled the country's money supply, inflation had been kept down. Inflation is a decrease in the value of money that causes an increase in the price of goods and services. The bank had also provided loans to finance the purchase of property and businesses.

Much of the success of the Second Bank was due to its president, **Nicholas Biddle**, who had assumed the post in 1823.

In spite of the prosperity fostered by the Second Bank, Jackson hated the bank. Under Biddle's leadership, the number of bank notes, or paper money, issued by the Second Bank had increased, and Jackson distrusted paper money. In 1795, he had sold some land, and the buyer had paid Jackson in bank notes. When the buyer went bankrupt, the bank notes were worthless. Jackson believed the nation's money supply should only consist of specie, or silver or gold coins. He also thought the Second Bank favored wealthy industrialists over working people

After Jackson's presidency ended, money began to lose its value. The 50-cent bank note below is actually a political cartoon showing Jackson, on the far right, grabbing for gold. The token, which features Jackson and the words "I take the responsibility," mocks his economic policies.

and limited its support of farmers and westward settlers. In addition, the president felt the bank and those who directed it were too powerful. Because the Second Bank could grant loans to members of Congress, Jackson feared that Biddle could use his power to influence these legislators.

The Second Bank became the central issue during Jackson's run for re-election in 1832. The charter for the bank was due to expire in 1836. But Jackson's opponent in the presidential race, National Republican Henry Clay, supported the bank and sponsored a bill to renew its charter early. Congress passed the bill, but Jackson vetoed it. In his veto message to Congress, Jackson wrote, "[It is my] belief that some of the powers and privileges possessed by the existing bank are unauthorized by the Constitution, subversive of the rights of the States, and dangerous to the liberties of the people."

When Jackson beat Clay in the 1832 election, he interpreted the win as support for his position on the Second Bank and as a **mandate**, or authorization, to destroy it. So during the four years that remained of its charter, Jackson directed funds from the Second Bank to be deposited in various state banks. Critics called these state banks Jackson's "pet banks." Biddle fought back by withholding bank loans from customers, but his actions backfired and turned more people against the Second Bank. By the time the bank's charter expired, Jackson had already stripped it of its power. Although Biddle tried to keep the Second Bank in operation with a state charter from Pennsylvania, the bank went out of business in 1841.

A NEW PARTY

In 1834, Henry Clay, who lost the presidential race but remained senator of Kentucky, persuaded Congress to censure Jackson over his handling of the Second Bank and refusal to hand over classified documents relative to the veto. Jackson was the first president to receive this "formal disapproval" from Congress. That same year, Clay and fellow senator Daniel Webster formed a new political party. They called it the **Whig Party** after a political party in Britain that had criticized the monarchy's abuse of power. The Whigs believed Jackson had exceeded his authority as president. In fact, members of the new party often referred to Jackson as "King Andrew." The Whigs promoted a national program to improve infrastructure, such as roads and buildings, much like the one Clay had laid out in his American System. They also supported business and industry interests.

CRITICAL VIEWING This political cartoon, "King Andrew the First," was issued around 1833. What details in it convey the idea that Jackson abused his power when he vetoed the Second Bank bill?

After the Second Bank lost its power, Jackson's pet banks made it easier to take out loans, and people flocked to them. At first, the federal government benefited from these loans because many citizens used them to purchase government land in the West. The revenue from these land sales was so great that, in 1835, Jackson paid off the national debt. However, the flow of easy credit led to inflation. To help curb this trend, Jackson required purchasers of government land to pay in gold or silver instead of paper money issued by banks. But this policy prompted banks to reduce available credit. An unstable currency and banking system would lead to a severe economic downturn shortly after Jackson's second term in office ended.

HISTORICAL THINKING

1. **READING CHECK** Why did Jackson hate the Second Bank of the United States?

2. **SYNTHESIZE** How did Jackson's attitude toward the Second Bank reflect his role as the representative of the common man?

3. **MAKE INFERENCES** Why did the Whigs call Jackson "King Andrew"?

AN ECONOMIC CRISIS

In good economic times, people tend to be content with the government in office. But when the economy plunges, people often cast blame on those officials. Martin Van Buren was about to find that out.

THE PANIC OF 1837

As the 1836 presidential election approached, the U.S. economy still seemed to be in good shape. With his second term coming to an end, Andrew Jackson backed his vice president, Martin Van Buren, as the Democratic candidate, and Van Buren won easily. The young Whig Party had nominated three candidates to try to gain support from three different regions of the country. Senator Daniel Webster of Massachusetts was chosen to attract voters in the East. Senator Hugh White from Jackson's own state of Tennessee was the Whigs' hope for support in the South. And William Henry Harrison, a congressman from Ohio, represented the West. You may recall that Harrison became well known after he fought the Shawnee at the 1811 Battle of Tippecanoe in Indiana. He'd also been a hero during the War of 1812. Harrison was the most popular Whig candidate and secured more electoral votes than Webster or White. Nevertheless, Van Buren won more electoral votes than the three Whig candidates combined.

Van Buren had had his eyes on the presidency for years. As Jackson's trusted friend and advisor, Van Buren was the most likely candidate to succeed the president. Van Buren was a skilled politician, but he lacked Jackson's charisma, or charm. Still, his supporters were confident that he would continue Jackson's policies and defend the rights of working people. However, just weeks after Van Buren's inauguration, the state banks began to struggle. Americans soon realized an economic crisis was brewing. Jackson's impact on the banking system and insistence on the use of specie were among the factors that led to the crisis. The fear over the state of the economy that swept the country became known as the **Panic of 1837**.

Many people rushed to the banks to exchange their paper money for gold and silver. But the banks didn't have enough of the precious metals to meet the demand. As a result, about 800 banks closed in 1837. The closures led businesses to collapse, which in turn caused many thousands of Americans to lose their jobs and land. Some of the unemployed went hungry and were forced to live on the streets. Before long, the country had spiraled into a deep economic depression that would last for seven years. Van Buren, who believed the federal government should not interfere with the economy, did little to address the problem. Because the depression didn't improve throughout his presidency, many voters blamed him for the nation's economic woes.

Public Land Sales, 1836–1854

Data: United States Census Bureau

THE 1840 ELECTION

Van Buren's opponents were quick to criticize the new president's reaction to the crisis. Henry Clay and Daniel Webster insisted that the federal government should help dig the country out of the depression. They called for higher tariffs on imports to raise the price of imported goods and encourage Americans to buy products made in the United States. But Van Buren didn't take their advice. As the depression dragged on and more and more people turned against Van Buren, the Whigs believed they had a good chance of winning the presidential election in 1840.

This time, the Whigs nominated William Henry Harrison as their sole candidate. They chose **John Tyler** of Virginia to be Harrison's running mate. During the campaign, the Whig Party focused on Harrison's war experience, particularly at the Battle of Tippecanoe. Banners and flags carried the slogan "Tippecanoe and Tyler too." Harrison was also portrayed as a frontier man of the people and the "log cabin" candidate. The Whigs painted Van Buren as rich and out of touch with the common man. Actually, although Harrison lived on a farm, he was born into a wealthy family. It was Van Buren who came from a humble background. Whig Party organizers held parades for their candidate and came up with catchy songs. Harrison himself went out on the campaign trail to meet with people. He was the first presidential candidate to do so.

Harrison won the election with 234 electoral college votes to Van Buren's 60. It was a huge victory for Harrison and for the Whigs, who took control of both houses of Congress. At age 67, Harrison was the oldest man ever elected president up to that time, but his term was brief. On a chilly day in March 1841, Harrison delivered an inaugural address that lasted almost two hours. He caught a cold that developed into pneumonia and died 31 days later. Harrison became the first president to die in office.

Consequently, Tyler became the first vice president to assume the presidency after his predecessor's death. Even though he was a Whig working with a Whig Congress, Tyler received little support from his party. Many of his views aligned with those of the Democrats. The Whigs had only chosen him for vice president to appeal to southern voters. Dubbed "His Accidency" by his enemies, Tyler used the veto 10 times during his presidency and was kicked out of the Whig Party. Even though the country began to emerge from the depression in the early 1840s, Tyler would be limited to one term in office.

HISTORICAL THINKING

1. **READING CHECK** Why did voters blame Van Buren for the economic depression?

2. **ANALYZE CAUSE AND EFFECT** What happened as a result of the depression?

3. **DISTINGUISH FACT FROM OPINION** How did the Whig Party use facts and opinions to promote Harrison during the 1840 presidential campaign?

The Democrats gave the Whigs the idea for running a "log cabin campaign" after one of their newspapers ridiculed Harrison as a dull backwoodsman who, with a small pension, would be content "to sit the remainder of his days in his log cabin." This pin from the 1840 campaign shows Harrison standing in front of a log cabin shaking Uncle Sam's hand.

VOCABULARY

Use each of the following vocabulary words in a sentence that shows an understanding of the term's meaning.

1. **Tariff of Abominations**
   Southerners called the Tariff of 1828 the Tariff of Abominations because it made the imported goods the South needed more expensive.

2. kitchen cabinet

3. Whig Party

4. syllabary

5. assimilate

6. Trail of Tears

7. Jacksonian democracy

8. Panic of 1837

READING STRATEGY
DISTINGUISH FACT FROM OPINION

When you separate someone's personal beliefs and feelings on a topic from information that can be proved to be true, you distinguish fact from opinion. Use a chart like this one to record statements from the chapter and identify them as fact or opinion. Then answer the question.

Facts	Opinions

9. What facts and opinions were voiced during Andrew Jackson's war on the Second Bank of the United States?

MAIN IDEAS

Answer the following questions. Support your answers with evidence from the chapter.

10. What groups of people did Andrew Jackson promise to represent as president? **LESSON 1.1**

11. Why did the Eaton affair cause a rift between Jackson and his vice president, John C. Calhoun? **LESSON 1.2**

12. Why did President John Quincy Adams promote the Tariff of 1828? **LESSON 2.1**

13. How did Jackson respond to the nullification crisis? **LESSON 2.2**

14. Why did Jackson strongly support passage of the Indian Removal Act? **LESSON 3.1**

15. What measures did the Cherokee take to resist relocation? **LESSON 3.2**

16. Why did Henry Clay and Daniel Webster call their new party the Whig Party? **LESSON 4.1**

17. How did the Panic of 1837 affect Martin Van Buren's presidency? **LESSON 4.2**

HISTORICAL THINKING

Answer the following questions. Support your answers with evidence from the chapter.

18. **EVALUATE** How would you describe Jackson's character?

19. **MAKE INFERENCES** Why do you think some Native Americans were willing to adopt European culture?

20. **DRAW CONCLUSIONS** How did Calhoun's call for states' rights during the debate over the Tariff of 1828 underscore the divide between the North and the South?

21. **COMPARE AND CONTRAST** In what ways were the presidencies of Van Buren and John Tyler similar and different?

22. **MAKE CONNECTIONS** How has Jacksonian democracy influenced politics today?

23. **FORM AND SUPPORT OPINIONS** In your opinion, is Jackson's legacy primarily good or bad? Explain your answer.

This 1831 political cartoon, "The Rats Leaving a Falling House," was published after members of Jackson's Cabinet resigned. Jackson is seated in the chair. The rats represent, from left to right, Secretary of War John Eaton, Secretary of the Navy John Branch, Secretary of State Martin Van Buren, and Secretary of the Treasury Samuel Ingham. Study the cartoon and then answer the questions that follow.

24. Why is Jackson's foot pressing down on the tail of the rat represented by Van Buren?

25. What details in the cartoon tell you that its creator was not a Jackson supporter?

26. Why do you think these department secretaries are shown trying to flee Jackson's Cabinet?

ANALYZE SOURCES

In his inaugural speech in 1829, President Jackson discussed his policies on the economy and Native Americans. Read the following excerpt from his speech and then answer the questions.

> Under every aspect in which it can be considered, it would appear that advantage must result from the observance of a strict and faithful economy. This I shall aim at the more anxiously both because it will facilitate the extinguishment [elimination] of the national debt . . . and because it will counteract that tendency to public and private profligacy [wastefulness] which a profuse expenditure [extravagant spending] of money by the Government is but too apt to engender [cause]. . . . It will [also] be my sincere and constant desire to observe toward the Indian tribes within our limits a just and liberal policy, and to give that humane and considerate attention to their rights and their wants which is consistent with the habits of our Government and the feelings of our people.

27. What were Jackson's goals with regard to the nation's economy?

28. How well did Jackson carry out the position he states here on Native Americans?

CONNECT TO YOUR LIFE

29. ARGUMENT In the 1828 presidential campaign, mudslinging on both sides was used to sway voters. Think about the campaign ads, speeches, remarks, and tweets made by recent candidates for government offices. Did they use mudslinging against their opponents? Do you think such personal attacks persuade voters or disgust them? Write a paragraph in which you make the case for or against mudslinging in political campaigns.

TIPS

• Review the mudslinging tactics used in the 1828 presidential campaign.

• Recall or research the campaign ads and speeches made by a recent candidate for government office and note the mudslinging used.

• Determine whether the mudslinging helped or hurt the candidate.

• State your position on mudslinging in political campaigns and support it with evidence from the text or your own experience and observations.

• Conclude your paragraph with a sentence summarizing your position.

AN AGE OF REFORM

1820–1850

HISTORICAL THINKING How did cultural and social reform influence American society?

CRITICAL VIEWING The Hudson River begins high in the Adirondack Mountains of New York and runs south to the Atlantic Ocean. North of New York City, the river winds through the Hudson River Valley, where this photograph captures the region's unspoiled fall beauty. In the early 19th century, writers and landscape painters flocked to the valley. Why do you think the terrain of the Hudson River Valley inspired 19th-century Americans?

"Nothing can bring you peace but **the triumph of principles.**"
—Ralph Waldo Emerson

RELIGION AND REFORM

If you've been part of a large crowd at a sports event or concert, you know how exhilarating that experience can be. In the early 19th century, enthusiastic crowds flocked to religious events known as revivals.

THE SECOND GREAT AWAKENING

The 1820s and 1830s marked a period of reform in the United States motivated by new ideas about religion and a changing society. Many adults were leaving home at a younger age to take advantage of newly available land in the West. Emerging industrial work drew young men to growing cities, leaving their family farms or businesses. Young women and girls, too, left their communities to work in mills and factories. As people sought to cope with these changes, revival meetings brought many people together for a common purpose.

Revivalism was not a new idea. As you've read, Jonathan Edwards and George Whitefield hosted revival meetings in frontier towns during the First Great Awakening in the late 1700s. During the first few decades of the 19th century, similar gatherings attracted thousands of people who listened to stirring sermons, prayed, studied the Bible, and sang hymns. The movement became known as the **Second Great Awakening**, which emphasized a new idea: having a direct and emotional relationship with God encouraged personal responsibility and would lead to spiritual salvation.

This print, titled *Methodist Camp Meeting*, captures the typical activities of a 19th-century revivalist meeting held in the wilderness. After building the preachers' shelter, participants set up tents, listened, prayed, and socialized.

CRITICAL VIEWING In *The Progress of Intemperance*, four panels of a 19th-century print concisely illustrate the path to alcoholism, which the temperance movement blamed for much family hardship. What does each step describe, and what is the overall purpose of this illustration?

TEMPTED.   PERSUADED.   HARDENED.   WRECKED.

The influential ministers of this movement shifted the religious viewpoint of American society in an important way. Like the leaders of the First Great Awakening, these **evangelists**, or preachers of the Gospel—the part of the Bible that describes the life and teachings of Jesus—enthusiastically urged believers to experience a spiritual rebirth and accept Jesus as their personal savior. However, later revivalist preachers broke with their predecessors on the crucial point of salvation. Edwards and Whitefield believed that only the grace of God could save people, while preachers of the Second Great Awakening taught that people could achieve salvation for themselves through their own actions. They believed that by turning away from sin, helping others to do so, and improving the overall morality of society, individuals could work to establish the kingdom of God on Earth and, by doing so, save their own souls.

One minister in particular, **Charles Grandison Finney**, embodied the movement's zealous spirit. As a young attorney living in Adams, New York, Finney began attending church at his fiancée's request. There, he unexpectedly found himself struck by what he identified as the power of God's love, saying that "an overwhelming sense" of his wickedness brought him to his knees. Speaking in the plain, direct language of everyday life, Finney set himself apart from other ministers. His masterful sermons delivered his hopeful message to believers and nonbelievers alike: he believed that all people had it within themselves to embrace God and turn away from sin.

Those converted by Finney brought his optimistic message to their own churches and communities. Women's prayer groups met daily, traveling from home to home to spread their religious message. Employers encouraged their workers to attend revivals. All the Protestant denominations worked together, setting aside differences in their beliefs to recruit hundreds of new and former Christians, spread the message of salvation, and work to improve the moral character of their families and communities. These efforts led to reforms throughout 19th-century society.

MIDDLE-CLASS REFORMS

People looked to churches for moral direction, and church ministers responded by encouraging their congregations to build a solid, religious home life for their children. The church pointed specifically to middle-class women to serve as the moral center of the American family. As you may remember, the idea of Republican Motherhood was much admired in the years following the American Revolution. In the early 1800s, with more children attending school and husbands' incomes rising in a growing economy, housewives and mothers had more time and resources to teach their children and encourage their husbands to live devout, or faithful, lives. They could also spend their free time improving the lives of people in the community.

The **temperance movement** became a center of social reform for many of these women. The word *temperance* means "self-restraint" or "moderation."

Most women in this movement saw drinking as a sin, and they believed that those who drank alcohol lacked self-control. And members of the temperance movement had evidence to back up their beliefs.

At that time, alcohol consumption was a real problem. By 1830, the average American drank about seven gallons of pure alcohol a year—triple the amount that Americans drink today. Drunkenness resulted in impoverished families, immoral behavior, damaged health, and poor job performance. By 1833, around 6,000 temperance societies had sprung up around the nation. These were generally religious groups, and the majority of their members were women. Temperance societies spread their anti-alcohol message through marches, meetings, and published literature, often urging people to make public pledges to refrain from drinking.

Reformers also took up the cause of universal public education. They campaigned for a public investment in education for every American child as the path to good citizenship and a more moral society. But when education depended on a family's ability to pay for private schools, many lower-income, working-class, and immigrant children, who had to work to help support their families, could not attend. Men, who were typically the main wage earners, were more likely to receive formal educations than women, whose main duties were to home and family. Enslaved African Americans were prohibited from obtaining any education at all, while free African Americans could only attend certain schools.

To address some of these issues, **Prudence Crandall** opened the Canterbury School for girls in 1831, and soon repurposed it as a school for African-American girls only, stirring controversy in her small Connecticut town. The local authorities arrested Crandall more than once for "unlicensed instruction," and the school was threatened and attacked. Meanwhile, reformers began to push for all American children to have free public education managed by local governments, an education reform known as the **common school movement**.

In Massachusetts, **Horace Mann** put the ideas of this movement into action. He championed the need to set basic standards for the training of professional teachers, especially women. He also wanted public schools to prepare students of all social classes, genders, races, ethnicities, and faiths for society and the workforce. Mann put another common school movement idea into action: funding free public schools through local property taxes. Soon other states began to follow Massachusetts's lead.

Reformers also looked to change institutions housing prisoners, the poor, and the mentally ill. Instead of concentrating only on punishment, reformers sought to establish a different kind of prison called a **penitentiary**, whose goal was to rehabilitate criminals. In a penitentiary, inmates were confined in individual jail cells, alone with their thoughts and the Bible. Reformers hoped that the inmates might become penitent, or remorseful, as a result and later return to society as better people. Reformers also sought to establish compassionate asylums, or hospitals, for the deaf and blind, the mentally ill, orphans, and the poor. At the time, many of these people were locked away in prisons or confined to poorhouses because there was no other place for them to go.

A social reformer named **Dorothea Dix** became famous throughout the country for her crusade on behalf of the mentally ill and people otherwise forgotten. Dix lobbied tirelessly for cleaner, healthier, and safer institutions for people in need. She persuaded at least nine state legislatures to establish publicly funded asylums to help care for those patients. Dix also worked on improving conditions in jails and poorhouses.

In addition to pursuing prison and asylum reforms, Dorothea Lynde Dix was an innovative educator. She wrote numerous books, including the popular *Conversations on Common Things*, a guidebook to help schools and parents answer a variety of children's questions.

The lead story in the December 1840 edition of the *Lowell Offering* was a spirited response to an editorial from the *Boston Quarterly Review* that painted an unflattering picture of the lives and morals of "factory girls."

"'She has worked in a factory' is sufficient to damn to infamy the most worthy and virtuous girl." So says Mr. Orestes A. Brownson [writer of the original editorial]; and either this horrible assertion is true, or Mr. Brownson is a slanderer. . . . And whom has Mr. Brownson slandered? A class of girls who in this city alone are numbered by thousands, . . . girls who generally come from quiet country homes, where their minds and manners have been formed under the eyes of the worthy sons of the Pilgrims, and their virtuous partners, and who return again to become the wives of the free intelligent yeomanry [farmers and small business owners] of New England, and the mothers of quite a portion of our future republicans.

—from *Lowell Offering*, December 1840

WORKERS BEGIN TO ORGANIZE

By the 1820s, widespread factory work was changing how people lived and worked. Industry provided many new jobs, but working conditions in most factories were far from ideal. The employees often worked 14 hours per day, 6 days a week, regardless of age. Children as young as 10 commonly worked in some factories, such as textile mills. Worker safety was a low priority, and serious on-the-job injuries and even deaths occurred too frequently. An injured employee was either fired for being unable to work or received no pay until he or she could return to work.

Naturally, workers wanted better treatment, including safer working conditions, shorter hours, and job protection following accidents. They also wanted better pay because the country's growing economy meant that the cost of living, reflected in prices for food, clothing, and rent, kept rising. Workers realized they stood little chance of changing conditions individually, so in the 1820s, they began to organize **labor unions**, or groups that advocate for workers' rights and protections. Because they bargain and act collectively, labor unions can promote reform and advancement efforts more effectively. Craftspeople and artisans who practiced a specialized skill, such as carpenters and shoemakers, also formed their own organizations known as craft unions. While most members of craft unions did not work in factories, their goals for better wages and working conditions were the same.

Despite heavy resistance from factory owners, unions made progress in improving workplace conditions until an economic depression hit the nation, prompting the Panic of 1837. Within a year, many factory workers and artisans were unemployed. As the economy struggled, the power of labor and craft unions decreased. Improved work conditions became less important than having work to begin with, as jobs became scarce. When the economy improved again in the early 1840s, unions began to regain some of their power.

Women in the Massachusetts textile mill town of Lowell joined together in 1844 to establish the Lowell Female Labor Reform Association (LFLRA), the first union of working women. Female millworkers built public support for their goals by writing and publishing the *Lowell Offering*, a monthly magazine of articles, poetry, and songs about their lives. By courting public opinion and pressuring the Massachusetts legislature to support their cause, the LFLRA was able to shorten millworkers' average workday from 14 to 10 hours.

HISTORICAL THINKING

1. **READING CHECK** Who was Charles Grandison Finney?

2. **MAKE INFERENCES** Why do you think universal public education was considered an important part of the 19th-century reform movement?

3. **DRAW CONCLUSIONS** Why did changes in society lead to religious revivalism in the early 19th century?

4. **FORM AND SUPPORT OPINIONS** Why do you think business owners fought against workers' demands during this era? Support your opinion.

A Young Nation's Literature and Arts

Writers and artists help create and define a nation's culture and identity. Which writers and artists do you think best capture the American spirit? In the 19th century, as the United States grew and changed, so did its art and literature.

AN AMERICAN LITERATURE

Culture in the United States during the 19th century had its roots in the colonial era. But in the country's early days, literature and art took a backseat to war, economic panic, and political conflict. As the American people grew more prosperous, they started to create a new identity separate from their European past. Artists and writers played a significant role in that effort.

In 1773, **Phillis Wheatley** became the first African-American woman to achieve fame as a poet. About seven years before she wrote or published her poems, Wheatley was a child kidnapped from Africa and taken to Boston on a slave ship. Purchased by a couple who recognized her talents, she soon learned to read and write in English, Greek, and Latin. Some of Wheatley's poetry addresses the colonial struggle for independence, as well as racial freedom. The couple freed her shortly after her book *Poems on Various Subjects, Religious and Moral* was published in London.

By the early 1800s, a uniquely American literature was taking hold and gaining recognition. **Washington Irving** became an internationally recognized writer, best known for his short stories "Rip Van Winkle" and "The Legend of Sleepy Hollow," both published between 1819 and 1820. In 1823, **James Fenimore Cooper** began publishing his five-book series of novels known as the "Leather-Stocking Tales" that include *The Last of the Mohicans*, an American classic. These popular books recount the life and exploits of the idealized frontiersman Natty Bumppo, or Hawkeye. Poet **Henry Wadsworth Longfellow**

In the legend of Rip Van Winkle, who sleeps through the Revolutionary War, author Washington Irving cleverly contrasts America's sleepy colonial society to that of the bustling United States. Artist N.C. Wyeth is one of many American artists who portrayed the aged Rip Van Winkle after his 20-year nap.

immortalized the earliest days of the American Revolution in his famous poem, "Paul Revere's Ride," bringing the event into the realm of national myth. His poems made many American legends famous, including the legend of Hiawatha, the Iroquois leader who helped establish the Iroquois Confederacy.

Some authors of the time wrote about both historic and contemporary conflicts and individualism. Although he wrote and published in the mid-1800s, **Nathaniel Hawthorne** set his major novels in Massachusetts during its early years when Puritanism ruled. *The House of the Seven Gables* was inspired by a home one of Hawthorne's relatives owned and a curse supposedly placed on his relatives by a woman accused of being a witch during the Salem witch trials. His best-known novel, *The Scarlet Letter*, focuses on love, guilt, revenge, and judgment in the Massachusetts Bay Colony of the 1640s. In his more contemporary novel, *Moby Dick*, **Herman Melville** describes life on a whaling ship as he recounts the tale of Captain Ahab, who relentlessly pursues the great white whale of the book's title. The novel is Melville's allegory for Americans' obsession with wealth and westward expansion.

In their writing, poets **Walt Whitman** and **Emily Dickinson** turned away from the flowery, sentimental poetry popular in the 1800s. Instead, they both wrote honestly and directly about their beliefs and experiences. In his most important work, *Leaves of Grass*, Whitman wrote in free verse, or poetry that does not rhyme or depend on a strict meter. The collection includes the poem "Song of Myself," in which he celebrates his life as a journey toward individual growth and a more democratic self. While Dickinson's poetry is leaner and more abstract, she also played with rhythm and theme in unexpected ways. During her life, she wrote over 1,700 poems.

THE TRANSCENDENTALISTS

Many American writers embraced a philosophical movement called **transcendentalism** in the 1830s and 1840s. Transcendentalism was based on the goal of transcending, or rising above, the

Walt Whitman was in his 30s and about to publish his first book of poetry, *Leaves of Grass,* when this photograph was taken. Many of his poems praise America as an experiment in democracy.

expectations society typically placed on people. The movement started in New England with a group of people who attended the Unitarian Church—a liberal, Christian church that urged members to embrace their feelings rather than texts and sermons. Like the revivalists of the Second Great Awakening, the Unitarians believed in the need to work toward social reform. Rather than a quick conversion experience at a revival meeting, however, Unitarians believed individual spiritual changes took time, as people relied on reason and their own consciences to lead them on the correct path.

Transcendentalists took this a step further. They believed that the path to spirituality lay in following one's heart and taking inspiration from nature, art, and literature. They emphasized the importance of practicing self-reliance as opposed to conformity. As a group, transcendentalists supported women's rights, abolition, and other social reforms, and they believed that organized religion, restrictive laws and social institutions, and industrialization kept individuals from fully expressing themselves and their spirituality.

Transcendentalist leader **Ralph Waldo Emerson** incorporated **Romanticism**, another philosophy that rejected the logic and rationality of the Enlightenment and emphasized imagination, emotion, and action, into his movement. Emerson's book *Nature* (1836) reflects his belief that experiencing nature leads one to grasp the divine, spiritual, or mystical aspects of life. In a speech at Harvard University, Emerson famously argued that action, risk, and endeavor should be the hallmarks of a true American scholar.

The New England writer, editor, and educator **Margaret Fuller** was closely associated with Emerson and his philosophy. She edited the transcendentalist magazine *The Dial* in the early 1840s and also wrote *Woman in the Nineteenth Century* (1845). The book states her feminist beliefs, which included her conviction that women deserved to have political equality and the right to seek emotional fulfillment.

In July 1846, Thoreau was briefly jailed for refusing to pay taxes he believed supported slavery and the Mexican-American War. He framed his refusal to pay as an act of protest and civil disobedience, which he outlined in his essay "Civil Disobedience."

I ask for, not at once no government, but at once a better government. . . . Must the citizen ever for a moment, or in the least degree, resign his conscience to the legislation? Why has every man a conscience then? I think that we should be men first, and subjects afterward. It is not desirable to cultivate a respect for the law, so much as for the right. The only obligation which I have a right to assume is to do at any time what I think right. . . . How does it become a man to behave toward the American government today? I answer, that he cannot without disgrace be associated with it. I cannot for an instant recognize that political organization as my government which is the slave's government also.

—from "Civil Disobedience,"
    by Henry David Thoreau, 1849

One of Emerson's students, **Henry David Thoreau**, however, was probably America's best-known transcendentalist. In his book *Walden: Life in the Woods* (1854), Thoreau describes the two years he lived alone in harmony with nature in a simple cabin beside Walden Pond, a small lake in Concord, Massachusetts. He also wrote a famous essay, "Civil Disobedience," which explains why he supported **civil disobedience**, or the purposeful breaking of a law that contradicts one's conscience. Fuller and Emerson shared Thoreau's beliefs. All three believed the United States was waging a war in Mexico to expand slavery in the Southwest, and they denounced it. Emerson and Thoreau were ardent abolitionists who opposed the institution of slavery.

Louisa May Alcott, famous for her novels about family relationships and what it was like to grow up female in 19th-century society, was the daughter of transcendentalist leader Bronson Alcott. She grew up in the company of Thoreau, Fuller, and Emerson, and her father's dedication to transcendentalist philosophy and the importance of education informed her life and work. She is best known for her novel *Little Women*.

Some transcendentalists, including Bronson Alcott, organized **utopian communities**. The word *utopian* means "ideal or perfect," and the aim of these small towns was to

CRITICAL VIEWING Inspired by his trips westward, Albert Bierstadt's painting *Sunset in the Rockies* is a romantic landscape with the luminism, or clear, radiant light, characteristic of the Hudson River School. How might this painting have influenced Americans to participate in the country's westward expansion?

gather believers together to live in a way that was as close to ideal as possible. These communities attempted to be self-sustaining, but few, if any, could thrive on their own. Most of them disbanded after only a few years.

PAINTERS OF NATURE

Romanticism and transcendentalism also influenced American visual artists as they sought inspiration in the natural world. **Thomas Cole**, a key figure in American fine arts in the 1830s and beyond, lived on the Ohio frontier. After visiting New York's Hudson River Valley in 1825, Cole began to paint its dramatic landscapes. Soon younger painters, such as **Asher B. Durand** and **Frederic Edwin Church**, joined Cole in their fascination with the stirring American landscape, both along the Hudson River and throughout the region. The style created by these painters and their followers became an American art movement known as the **Hudson River School**. **Albert Bierstadt**, a German immigrant and accomplished artist, traveled far to the West. He gained international fame for using the style of the Hudson River School in his panoramic paintings of the Rocky Mountains, the Grand Canyon, the high Sierra, and the hanging valleys of Yosemite. In their paintings, all of these artists celebrated the diverse beauty of the American landscape and often emphasized the human relationship with nature.

Several noted artists of the time began painting in the style of the Hudson River School, but went on to embrace other less precise and realistic styles of painting. For example, **George Inness** began his career painting finely rendered American landscapes, but over the years and under the influence of French painters of the era, his focus changed to vivid colors and depictions of shimmering light. Like the transcendentalists and their belief that the divine and spiritual could be found in nature, Inness's later paintings transcend realism and reveal a mystical world where light and color work in harmony to suggest, rather than strictly depict, a landscape.

Little Blue Heron exemplifies the scientifically precise images John James Audubon created in his paintings. But Audubon also reveals the bird's intangible qualities, explaining, "You may see this graceful Heron, quietly and in silence walking along the margins of the water, with an elegance and grace."

Other important artists followed their own paths through the American landscape. Beginning in the 1830s, **George Catlin** lived among the Native Americans of the Great Plains and made hundreds of drawings and paintings. As a young man, Catlin was moved by the sight of a Native American delegation visiting Philadelphia. He vowed that "nothing short of the loss of my life shall prevent me from visiting their country and becoming their historian." Art and nature enthusiasts could also view the country's wildlife in the remarkable watercolors of **John James Audubon**, who set out on daunting journeys to record the birds of the young nation in their natural environments. It took ten years for Audubon to produce four immense volumes. He completed the project in 1838.

HISTORICAL THINKING

1. **READING CHECK** How does James Fenimore Cooper's work mark him as a writer of truly American literature?

2. **MAKE CONNECTIONS** What philosophical belief do the transcendentalists and the members of the Hudson River School have in common?

3. **MAKE INFERENCES** Why might members of the Hudson River School of painting be considered followers of Romanticism?

4. **ANALYZE VISUALS** How does the Bierstadt painting reflect the views of transcendentalists?

ROCKY MOUNTAIN NATIONAL PARK, ESTES PARK, COLORADO

Artifacts prove humans began exploring the Rocky Mountain region 11,000 years ago. Recently, archaeologists have discovered evidence of migration patterns of these early native peoples within the area. We do know the Ute tribe dominated the area until the 1700s, reaping the benefits of the lush valleys, meadows, and clear, cold lakes. With the 1803 Louisiana Purchase, the United States acquired the land that includes what we now call Rocky Mountain National Park, and it was only a matter of time before the stunning landscape attracted more and more visitors.

Like the Grand Canyon, the valleys of Yosemite, and the Hudson River, the landscape of Rocky Mountain National Park inspired many Romantic artists—and continues to inspire artists today. The geography and diversity of life in this unique region allow artists to capture the human relationship with nature, something painters like Albert Bierstadt and Charles Partridge Adams aspired to do. And surely the elk, mule deer, and moose, along with hundreds of species of birds and plants, make it easy to feel inspired.

CRITICAL VIEWING Beginning millions of years ago, massive glaciers scraped across the earth, shaping the meadows and peaks of Rocky Mountain National Park. Compare this photograph to the Bierstadt painting, *Sunset in the Rockies*, you saw earlier in this chapter. What elements from this natural environment likely influenced and inspired Bierstadt and other Romantic artists?

LIFE UNDER SLAVERY

The fact that fewer than 200 years ago, our country allowed people to hold others captive, buy and sell them, force them to work, and freely abuse them is unjustifiable to us today. It was unjustifiable to many people then, too.

AFRICAN AMERICANS AND THE SOUTH

As you have read, in the early 1800s the domestic slave trade expanded beyond the southern coast as planters in Alabama, Mississippi, and Louisiana cleared more land to plant cotton. Enslaved people also helped grow and harvest many other agricultural commodities, such as hemp, wheat, corn, rice, sugar, and tobacco. They worked with livestock, practiced trades such as carpentry and blacksmithing, and even labored in southern factories, in shipyards, and on docks. Wherever there was work to be done in the South, enslaved African Americans were likely being forced to do it.

Despite their bondage, African Americans created a strong, uplifting culture that influenced the larger American culture. Families were at the center of this culture, but they were often split apart by the slave trade. You may remember reading that slave owners could sell a child away from his or her mother, or a husband away from his wife. Enslaved African Americans had to rely on extended families for support, and grandparents, aunts, and uncles often played significant roles in child rearing. When even extended family was unavailable, enslaved people created "fictive kin," or friends and neighbors given honorary titles of "brother" or "aunt" and treated as relatives. These kinship bonds helped enslaved families stay resilient.

THE SLAVE DWELLING PROJECT

In 2010, Joseph McGill, Jr., was an office worker who had a unique hobby: Civil War reenactment. In "battle," he wore the uniform of the 54th Massachusetts Volunteer Infantry Regiment, the first Union military unit of African-American soldiers during the Civil War. For McGill, it was a thrilling way to experience history, so when an opportunity to sleep in a former slave cabin arose, he said yes. It led him to found the Slave Dwelling Project, a journey to locate and stay overnight in former slave dwellings.

The project's mission is to encourage people to preserve the places where enslaved people lived. McGill believes that when people—black and white—know the history, they are more able to have frank discussions about slavery's legacy. In this photograph, Johnnie Leach looks over a slave cabin slated for restoration in South Carolina. Leach once lived with his family in a slave cabin like this one while working nearby.

Slave owners placed these heavy iron shackles on young children's ankles to punish them or keep them from running away.

PLANTATIONS AND FARMS

Plantation owners commonly placed responsibility for day-to-day operations in the hands of professional overseers, or supervisors. These overseers were often young white men hoping to gain experience and money to buy their own land one day. Slave owners and overseers held the ultimate threat of force against slaves, but they much preferred to keep the work moving smoothly. Conflicts and discipline problems meant the loss of productive work. On larger plantations, enslaved people often worked in groups called gangs, which were managed by trusted male slaves who served as "drivers." These men tended to be especially intelligent, strong, and skilled. Some drivers were respectful to and, in turn, were respected by the people they managed. Others took advantage of their authority, and they were neither liked nor respected by the people who worked under them.

Slavery was an institution of power, designed to create profit for the slaveholder and break the will of the enslaved. In addition to working as many as 15 hours a day in the fields or as domestic servants, enslaved African Americans had very little privacy and were subject to severe discipline by their owners. Slaves who were accused of being disobedient or disrespectful were often whipped, branded, shackled, or even locked up in sweltering enclosures. Female slaves often suffered sexual abuse. Partly because most expectant mothers were forced to continue working in the fields until giving birth, about a third of all enslaved babies died before they reached their first birthday. Enslaved people generally ate poorly, were provided only meager shelter, and had little or no access to effective health care. Many constantly feared violence from the drivers and overseers.

Slave owners often justified their behavior by claiming they provided "their people" a better life than they would have had in Africa. Indeed, southern plantation owners tried to justify slavery to themselves and to the North by stressing their Christian **stewardship**, or careful and responsible management, of the slaves. As one clergyman wrote to his fellow slaveholders in the early 1840s, slaves "were placed under our control . . . not exclusively for our benefit but theirs also."

POLITICS OF THE SOUTH

In southern cities, white plantation owners and cotton merchants enjoyed among the highest per capita incomes in the nation. They had the finest homes and access to public entertainment that rivaled any city in the country. They owed their position to slavery. Without it, the southern economy would collapse. So it is not surprising that southern landowners were determined to protect the institution of slavery.

Both of the major U.S. political parties in the South—the Whigs and the Democrats—clamored for the southern landowners' votes. The Whigs, who portrayed themselves as the party of progress and prosperity, appealed to lawyers, editors, merchants, and wealthy planters. They believed the best way to protect slavery was for the South to develop its region's economy and build strong economic and political ties with the North and Europe.

The Democrats, on the other hand, found their strongest supporters among the small farm owners of the South who resented paying taxes on their property, including any slaves they owned. They saw the Democrats' platform of limiting the power of the federal government as the best way to protect slavery. They also liked the party's approach to western expansion and its policy of removing American Indians from locations that had fertile, rich soil or mineral resources.

HISTORICAL THINKING

1. **READING CHECK** Why did some enslaved people create a network of "fictive kin"?

2. **DRAW CONCLUSIONS** Why do you think both Whigs and Democrats in the South positioned themselves as friends of slavery?

3. **DISTINGUISH FACT FROM OPINION** What facts from the lesson prove false the claim of the southern preacher that African Americans were enslaved "not exclusively for our benefit but theirs also"?

ABOLITIONISTS SPEAK OUT

If you speak up about a cause or injustice from personal experience, people usually listen with more interest and empathy. In the 19th century, when former slaves spoke out with powerful stories about their horrifying experiences, more people listened and joined the abolitionist cause.

THE ABOLITION MOVEMENT

The first efforts to end slavery in North America arose even before the United States was founded, but in the late 1820s, the push to abolish slavery began to gain momentum. The Second Great Awakening had sparked interest in social reform, and some northern church members argued that it was their Christian duty to work for immediate **emancipation**, or freedom, of the enslaved. These abolitionists called for slaveholders to free their slaves as soon as possible; hire them as free, paid workers; and reimburse them for their years of unpaid labor.

A crusading newspaper writer and editor, **William Lloyd Garrison** was also one of the leaders of the abolition movement. He became involved by working with the colonization movement, which, as you've read, aimed to relocate freed slaves to West Africa. After attending antislavery meetings organized by African Americans, he realized that the colonization movement was not good-hearted, but racist. In 1831, Garrison began to publish *The Liberator*, a newspaper that promoted the antislavery cause.

This cotton and silk banner was designed to spread the abolitionist message and honor journalist William Lloyd Garrison (above). It was displayed at antislavery gatherings.

Despite being respected for his speaking and writing, Frederick Douglass often faced racism, exclusion, and isolation. In a subtle response to bigotry, Douglass engaged in a 19th-century version of "photo ops." Photographed frequently, he purposefully chose to dress formally and to convey the image of a stern, dignified, and educated African American.

In it he condemned the colonization plan and pushed the idea of emancipation. "I *will* be as harsh as truth," Garrison announced, "and as uncompromising as justice. On this subject, I do not wish to think, speak, or write, with moderation. . . . AND I WILL BE HEARD." And he was heard. Although his message was no different from those running in newspapers published by African Americans, through *The Liberator* these ideas reached a larger white audience.

In 1833, Garrison joined with other abolitionists to found the American Anti-Slavery Society. By the late 1830s, the organization had more than 2,000 chapters and as many as 250,000 members, primarily in the Northeast and Midwest. The organization held that slavery violated not only natural law but also the will of God and that the U.S. Constitution gave people the right to end slavery. It spread this message through its publication, the *National Anti-Slavery Standard* and through meetings, petitions, and lectures. Other abolition groups also published and distributed antislavery articles in their publications, which were powerful weapons for their cause.

Both whites and African Americans banded together to support the abolitionist cause. **Frederick Douglass** was among the most prominent African-American abolitionists. He wrote the *Narrative of the Life of Frederick Douglass, an American Slave* (1845) to detail his years of enslavement in Maryland. While there, he broke the law by learning to read. Sent to Baltimore by his owner, Douglass worked in the shipyards, read widely, and plotted his escape to freedom. After several attempts, he finally succeeded in 1838. He borrowed the papers of a free African-American sailor and rode a train to freedom in New York City. There, he met a man who introduced him to the New York Anti-Slavery Society.

Douglass was a compelling speaker who lectured throughout the North with William Lloyd Garrison. He also cofounded and edited an influential abolitionist newspaper called the *North Star*. The newspaper's name referred to the fact that escaping slaves used the North Star to guide them to freedom. Douglass eventually became a consultant to President Abraham Lincoln and, in later years, a U.S. official and diplomat.

SPREADING THE WORD

Between 1834 and 1835, abolitionists sent out a million pieces of mail, much of it to the South where they hoped to appeal directly to ministers and others open to the idea of emancipation. Angry white southerners protested, declaring that the literature would provoke more rebellions such as those led by Nat Turner and Denmark Vesey. In Charleston, South Carolina, mobs of southern slavery sympathizers burned sacks of mail that came from northern cities. A group of plantation owners from Georgia offered a $12,000 reward for the capture of a wealthy abolitionist merchant who funded much of the antislavery postal campaign.

Among the abolitionists who went on the lecture circuit, **Angelina** and **Sarah Grimké** were popular speakers for the cause because they were the daughters of a prominent South Carolina slave-owning planter. The Grimkés' personal experiences with slavery gave them a credibility that white northern abolitionists could not match. "All moral beings have essentially the same rights and the same duties, whether they be male or female," Angelina Grimké said. The women of the South, who "now wear the iron yoke of slavery in this land of boasted liberty and law . . . are our countrywomen—they are our sisters."

African Americans were more effective at spreading the word than any other abolitionists. They electrified audiences and readers with descriptions of their captivity and their daring escapes to the North.

Sojourner Truth, born into slavery in New York around 1797, attracted a wide readership with her book, *The Narrative of Sojourner Truth.* So, too, did **Solomon Northup**, a free man of color from New York who was kidnapped and sold into slavery in the deep South, with his account *Twelve Years a Slave.* **Harriet Tubman**, who escaped bondage in 1849, helped hundreds of enslaved people escape the South. She was a riveting speaker who pulled no punches in her description of slavery and the dangers of trying to escape it. Despite the respect they gained from telling their stories, African-American abolitionists continued to face restrictions from fellow reformers and enemies alike. They responded by demanding greater rights for African Americans in the North, as well as those in the South.

David Walker was another powerful, resourceful abolitionist voice. Born in the South to a free mother and an enslaved father, Walker moved to Boston, where he opened a secondhand clothing store in the 1820s. Walker printed antislavery pamphlets and sewed them into the clothes he sold to sailors. He hoped his pamphlets would travel to many ports, reaching as many people as possible, especially in the South. In 1829, Walker printed his pamphlet *Appeal to the Colored Citizens of the World*, which became one of the most radical antislavery documents of the abolitionist movement. In the pamphlet, he denied that slaves felt or owed any loyalty to their masters and called for African Americans to be full American citizens in both the government and the economy, even if that required violent revolt.

PRIMARY SOURCE

In this excerpt from his pamphlet known by many simply as *Appeal*, David Walker emphasizes his themes of justice and freedom by challenging Americans to judge their colonization plan as well as the institution of slavery.

Americans! . . . you have and do continue to treat us more cruel than any heathen nation ever did a people it had subjected to the same condition that you have us . . . we must and shall be free. . . . You may do your best to keep us in wretchedness and misery, to enrich you and your children, but God will deliver us from under you. And wo[e], wo[e], will be to you if we have to obtain our freedom by fighting. Throw away your fears and prejudices then, and enlighten us and treat us like men . . . and tell us now no more about colonization, for America is as much our country, as it is yours.

—from *Appeal to the Colored Citizens of the World,*
by David Walker, 1829

DIFFERENCES AMONG ABOLITIONISTS

Just as Americans could not agree on the subject of slavery, abolitionists themselves differed on how to react to the opposition they faced. William Lloyd Garrison told his followers not to respond to any acts of violence. He renounced all ties to either major political party because both were tolerant of slavery. But other abolitionists courted political parties and politicians, seeing them as the most effective way to achieve abolition.

The differences among the abolitionists became clear at the annual meeting of the American Anti-Slavery Society in 1839. The various factions differed in their attitudes toward the role of women in the movement. Women made up perhaps half of all antislavery organizations, but some male abolitionists believed it best to keep them in a subordinate role, preventing women members from voting, speaking publicly, and serving on committees with males. Unable to resolve their differences, the society split. The more conservative members, who advocated for the gradual emancipation of enslaved peoples, created the Liberty Party. They put their hope in politics, attempting to run a candidate for president in the 1840 election. Garrison founded the Friends of Universal Reform, which continued to work for the immediate emancipation of slaves and welcomed women as full and equal members.

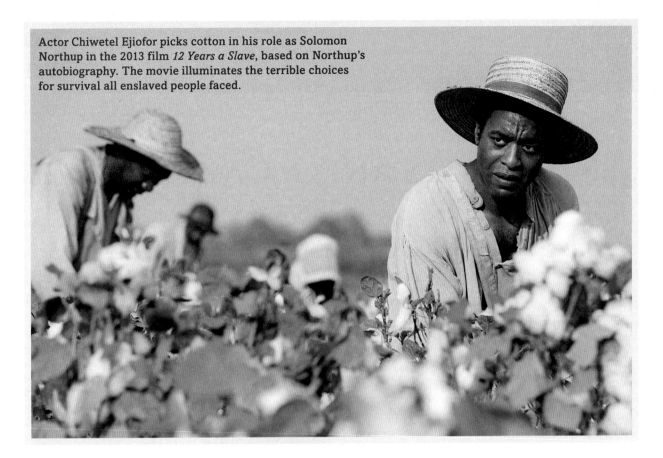

Actor Chiwetel Ejiofor picks cotton in his role as Solomon Northup in the 2013 film *12 Years a Slave*, based on Northup's autobiography. The movie illuminates the terrible choices for survival all enslaved people faced.

Both sides overwhelmed Congress with more than 300 petitions signed by 40,000 people demanding the abolition of slavery in the District of Columbia. Once again, southerners argued that the petitions threatened to incite slaves to rebellion and called for Congress to reject them. Seeking to avoid conflict, Congress set the petitions aside without consideration. This congressional practice of disregarding petitions is called the **gag rule**. During the next decade, many northern abolitionists spoke out against the gag rule, which they believed violated a basic American freedom and supported slavery.

Former president John Quincy Adams, now a Massachusetts congressman, thought the gag rule unconstitutional and fought for Congress to recognize the antislavery petitions. Finally, the gag rule was overthrown in December 1844. Adams also successfully defended Africans who had taken control of the slave ship *Amistad* on its way to Cuba and sailed it to Long Island, New York. The Africans were arrested and charged with murdering the ship's captain. Supported by a large network of abolitionists, Adams tried the case before the U.S. Supreme Court. In 1841, he won the case, securing the acquittal and freedom of the defendants.

As the antislavery movement grew stronger, it met with more determined opposition in the North as well as in the South. In 1835, mobs in Boston destroyed

the homes of African Americans, pelted antislavery speakers, and dragged William Lloyd Garrison through the streets of town at the end of a rope. After denouncing a local judge who prevented the trial of a crowd that had burned a black man alive in Missouri, abolitionist editor **Elijah P. Lovejoy** moved across the Mississippi River to the free state of Illinois to escape the wrath of offended readers. He didn't move far enough. In November 1837, a pro-slavery mob shot and killed him as he and his assistants tried to protect his printing equipment from them. Local law officers arrested Lovejoy's assistants for inciting the violence. Clearly, there was no agreement, in the North or South, on the question of abolishing slavery.

HISTORICAL THINKING

1. **READING CHECK** What methods did abolitionists use to spread their message?

2. **MAKE INFERENCES** Why do you think William Lloyd Garrison came to believe the colonization plan was racist?

3. **ANALYZE CAUSE AND EFFECT** What effect did publications such as *The Liberator* have on the public, and why was this effect important?

4. **DRAW CONCLUSIONS** How did learning to read affect Frederick Douglass's life?

An Age of Reform **291**

SENECA FALLS AND A CALL FOR RIGHTS

Today women vote, protest, and are active in social and political causes. But before the 1830s, the idea of women demanding to vote was considered laughable, and the thought of a woman governor, member of Congress, or president was unimaginable. Then women began to find and use their collective voice.

THE CULT OF DOMESTICITY

As the rapid advances of the Industrial Revolution changed the U.S. economy in the first half of the 19th century, a substantial middle class began to form in the United States. In middle-class homes of that era, men left home each day to go to work, and women took care of the children and the household. Middle-class women were expected to be the moral center of the household and provide strong models of clean living for their children and husbands. This social ideal became known as a **cult of domesticity**.

Catharine Beecher, the sister of Harriet Beecher Stowe, renowned abolitionist and author of *Uncle Tom's Cabin*, was a teacher, author, and advocate for women's education. While Beecher felt that women's duties were as important as men's, she also believed that each partner had a distinct sphere to which he or she was suited. And for Beecher, a woman's sphere was the home and family. She opposed women's suffrage for this reason, claiming that politics were corrupting and far removed from women's place in the home. Her 1841 book, *A Treatise on Domestic Economy*, was a comprehensive guide for domestic duties. It contained practical lessons in how to keep a home, feed a family, raise children, and provide simple medical care. For the middle-class women who could afford luxuries such as domestic servants and store-bought foods, following such advice for efficient household management allowed them more free time.

The cult of domesticity empowered some women to consider restrictions they faced in society. Individual state laws, for instance, governed women's rights

Catharine Beecher, 1848

and freedoms according to their marital status. Often, unmarried women shared many legal rights with men, including the ability to own property and make contracts. In contrast, married women deferred these rights to their husbands the moment they married. A married woman could not give away or sell any property. She could not bring a lawsuit, nor could she be sued. She could not enter into a contract or make a will. And every American woman was barred from voting in national elections and serving on juries. Chafing under these restrictions, women began to demand reforms.

SENECA FALLS CONVENTION

Of course, some women had been speaking out about their lack of rights since before the American Revolution. You'll recall that Abigail Adams admonished her husband John, who was then serving as a delegate to the Continental Congress, to "remember the ladies" because they will not "hold [themselves] bound by any laws in which [they] have no voice or representation." But for more than 50 years, American women had allowed themselves to be bound by those very laws. That was about to change.

In 1840, abolitionist **Elizabeth Cady Stanton** attended the World's Anti-Slavery Convention in London, England. As a female delegate, she found herself seated in a separate, roped-off area away from the important discussions, and she felt "humiliated and chagrined" by the experience. While there, Stanton met another attendee, **Lucretia Mott**, a devout Quaker and feminist, who shared her feelings. In fact, the Quakers had recognized the spiritual equality of women from the faith's earliest days, allowing them the same rights to speak in meetings as men and expecting them to take on social causes with the same vigor. Just as Quakers were staunch abolitionists, they enthusiastically embraced the fight for equal rights for women.

Stanton and Mott vowed to begin a movement for women's rights in the United States. Their plan was temporarily set aside when both women returned to the United States. Mott, meanwhile, joined a group of Quaker women who traveled around the nation, spreading the word about both abolition and women's rights. They hoped to bring the idea of equality for women into the national consciousness. Then in 1847, Stanton moved from Boston to Seneca Falls, a small town in upstate New York.

Living in Seneca Falls, Stanton grew frustrated with the limitations the small town placed on her and other women. She reached out to Mott and, in 1848, the two women joined together with three of Mott's Quaker friends to plan a convention for women's rights activists in Seneca Falls. Their plan included the drafting of a list of rights all women should strive for. They called their plan the **Declaration of Sentiments and Resolutions**. Using the Declaration of Independence as a model, Stanton and Mott demanded women's suffrage, or the right to vote, and insisted on equal treatment concerning property rights, education, employment, divorce, and legal matters.

A historical roadside marker designates the Wesleyan Chapel in Seneca Falls, New York, as the site of the first national women's rights convention in 1848.

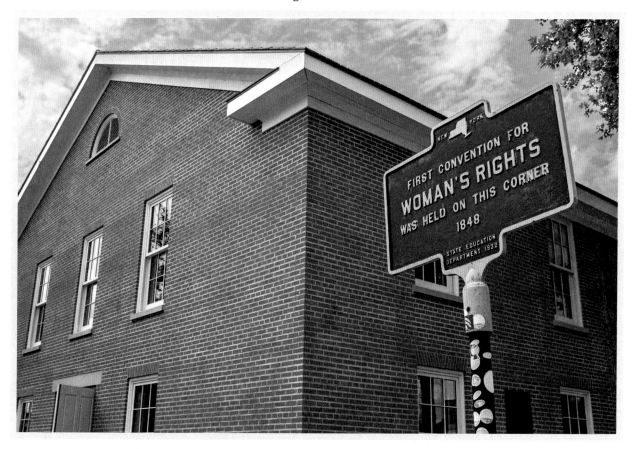

They held the **Seneca Falls Convention** in July 1848. Stanton read the 12 resolutions of the declaration. Afterwards, those attending voted to pass each resolution individually. The only resolution that failed to pass was the call for women's suffrage. Many attendants felt that resolution asked for too much and might hurt their efforts to achieve their other goals. The convention ended with 68 women and 32 men signing Stanton and Mott's document.

IMPACT OF THE CONVENTION

The Seneca Falls Convention—and the declaration, when it was published—was met with considerable hostility, even from those who believed in improved rights for women. But the organizers of the convention succeeded in their major goal: calling attention to the need for women's rights in the United States.

The Seneca Falls Convention is viewed as the beginning of the women's rights movement and the organized attempt to gain women's suffrage. News of the convention spread to women's rights and reform groups across the country. Beginning with the 1850 women's rights convention in Worcester, Massachusetts, national meetings convened regularly and their goals became national talking points for the growing women's rights movement.

The work of abolitionists and women's rights activists often overlapped in the 1800s. Frederick Douglass was one of the men who attended the Seneca Falls Convention and signed the Declaration of Sentiments. He returned to Rochester, New York, where he was living, and gave the convention a positive review in his newspaper, the *North Star*. At a women's rights meeting in Akron, Ohio, in 1851, African-American abolitionist and women's rights activist Sojourner Truth addressed the audience. She told her story of escaping slavery in New York in 1826, leaving all but one of her children behind. When New York freed all enslaved people in 1827, she was reunited with most of her children. She learned that her son Peter had been sold illegally to a plantation owner in Alabama. Truth sued both Peter's former owner and the Alabama planter and won. In 1844, she joined a reform group run by abolitionists that advocated for women's rights. She soon began speaking for both causes.

In her speech, later named "Ain't I a Woman?," Truth criticized the abolitionists who failed to seek the same freedoms for both African-American men and women. She worried that when slavery ended, African-American men would receive rights and become citizens, leaving behind the cause

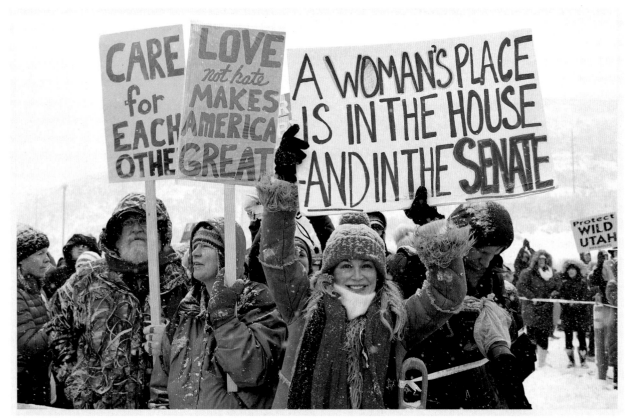

CRITICAL VIEWING People gather at a Respect Rally in Park City, Utah, in 2018 on the anniversary of the first Women's March, which was held on January 20, 2017. Thousands of demonstrations took place around the world on the same day in 2018. Why do you think people choose to participate in public demonstrations? Support your answer with details from the photograph.

PRIMARY SOURCE

There are several accounts and transcriptions of Sojourner Truth's "Ain't I a Woman?" speech available. The most famous, excerpted below, was recounted and published 12 years after she first delivered it. It presents her words in a thick Southern dialect that most historians dispute. After all, Truth was born in New York, and her first owners were Dutch planters in the Hudson River Valley. She grew up speaking Dutch; English was not her first language. Read the excerpt and consider how views of African Americans at the time may have influenced the person who transcribed this version of the speech.

I think that 'twixt the negroes of the South and the women at the North, all talking about rights, the white men will be in a fix pretty soon. That man over there says that women need to be helped into carriages, and lifted over ditches, and to have the best place everywhere. Nobody ever helps me into carriages, or over mud-puddles, or gives me any best place! And ain't I a woman? Look at me! Look at my arm! I have ploughed and planted, and gathered into barns, and no man could head me! And ain't I a woman? I could work as much and eat as much as a man—when I could get it—and bear the lash as well! And ain't I a woman? I have borne thirteen children, and seen most all sold off to slavery, and when I cried out with my mother's grief, none but Jesus heard me! And ain't I a woman?

—from "Ain't I a Woman?," by Sojourner Truth, 1851

for women's rights, black or white. Her speech highlighted the complex relationship among white abolitionists, white **suffragists**, or people who supported granting voting rights to women, and African Americans. White women's rights advocates generally phrased their demands for equal rights in terms of education and a broad range of freedoms, and this appeared to neglect African-American women and their needs.

Several years after the 1848 Seneca Falls Convention, Elizabeth Cady Stanton and **Susan B. Anthony** met. Like Lucretia Mott, Anthony was a Quaker, and she also began her activism with the abolition movement, working with William Lloyd Garrison. Later, she crusaded for temperance and founded the Woman's New York State Temperance Society after she was barred from speaking at a New York state Sons of Temperance meeting in 1852.

Stanton and Anthony quickly became friends and joined forces. Stanton's and Anthony's backgrounds, personalities, and strengths were different, but these differences worked together to make them a formidable team. They complemented each other, with Stanton providing the intellectual and theoretical foundations of the movement, and Anthony acting as its chief organizer, activist, and agitator. For the next 50 years, the two drove and dominated the crusade for women's rights and suffrage.

HISTORICAL THINKING

1. **READING CHECK** What rights did married women lack in the mid-1800s?

2. **DETERMINE CHRONOLOGY** What events led to Elizabeth Cady Stanton becoming a leader in the women's rights movement?

3. **MAKE INFERENCES** Why might Sojourner Truth worry that some activists would stop supporting the women's suffrage movement once African-American men won the right to vote?

4. **MAKE CONNECTIONS** Describe the connection between the abolition and women's rights movements.

ELIZABETH CADY STANTON 1815–1902

"The history of the past is but one long struggle upward to equality."
—Elizabeth Cady Stanton

Elizabeth Cady Stanton certainly joined the historical struggle for equality. She fought the uphill battle for women's rights and suffrage for most of her life. Many of Stanton's views, including those on marriage and divorce, were considered radical in her time. Brave and outspoken, she often alienated others—sometimes even those on her own side—but Stanton never backed down. As she said, "The best protector any woman can have . . . is courage."

A YOUNG REBEL

At an early age, Elizabeth Cady recognized the unequal treatment accorded women. She grew up in a wealthy home in Johnstown, New York, where her father, Daniel Cady, was a prominent lawyer and statesman. Tragedy repeatedly struck the family, however, and only 4 of the 11 Cady children survived into adulthood—all daughters. After his last remaining son died, Elizabeth's father said to her, "Oh, my daughter, I wish you were a boy!" Elizabeth tried to make his wish come true. She later wrote: "I thought that the chief thing to be done in order to equal boys was to be learned and courageous. So I decided to study Greek and learn to manage a horse."

Daniel Cady probably didn't believe that women were inferior, but he was realistic about their status in society. He knew his daughter would never have the rights and

Elizabeth Cady Stanton put her views on equal rights into practice in her own marriage. At her insistence, the promise to obey her husband, which was typically included in a woman's wedding vows at that time, was removed. Stanton fought for women's political rights and their social and cultural rights.

opportunities that men enjoyed. Still, he made sure Elizabeth received the best education available to girls at that time. She attended the Johnstown Academy and graduated from Emma Willard's Troy Female Seminary in 1832. Elizabeth also gained an education by helping out in her father's law office, where she learned firsthand about the legal restrictions imposed on women. Visits to the home of her abolitionist cousin, Gerrit Smith, also opened Elizabeth's eyes. Through Smith, Elizabeth met some of the leading social and political reformers of the day.

One of these reformers was Henry Stanton. An abolitionist and ten years older than Elizabeth, Henry had donated most of his money to the fight against slavery. In spite of her father's objections, Elizabeth and Henry married in 1840. The couple decided to spend their honeymoon in London where they attended the World's Anti-Slavery Convention. It was there, as you have read, that Elizabeth Stanton met Lucretia Mott. They would soon join forces and organize their own convention at Seneca Falls.

A CONTROVERSIAL LEADER

Stanton worked with Mott at Seneca Falls, but it was with Susan B. Anthony that she forged an enduring partnership beginning in 1851. The two were an impressive political team. Stanton was the better writer and orator. While she stayed at home to care for her seven young children, she wrote pamphlets, essays, letters, and speeches for herself and for her partner. Anthony, on the other hand, had greater organizational skills. She planned meetings, distributed Stanton's pamphlets, and pressured the New York legislature to pass laws that supported women's rights.

Many of their efforts focused on marriage and divorce. Stanton called for the government to grant married women property rights. At that time, all property in a marriage belonged to the husband by law. Stanton also wanted to relax divorce laws and allow women the right to leave an unhappy marriage, which scandalized other crusading women.

As you know, Stanton was an abolitionist, and she intensified her work in the abolition movement during the Civil War. After the war, however, she criticized the 14th and 15th amendments, which granted voting rights to African-American men. Stanton believed the government should pass

CRITICAL VIEWING This cartoon ridicules the women who chose to join Stanton and Anthony's National Woman Suffrage Association. How does the cartoonist portray women who demanded the right to vote?

legislation that granted universal suffrage and so refused to support the amendments. Her stand created a rift with other abolitionists. As a result, Stanton and Anthony established the exclusively female National Woman Suffrage Association in 1869. Less radical feminists formed the American Woman Suffrage Association.

Stanton cut back on her speaking tours as she got older and focused on her writing. Together with Anthony and suffragist Matilda Joselyn Cage, Stanton wrote the *History of Woman Suffrage*, which would become a six-volume publication on the struggle for women's rights. The work helped heal the split between the two rival suffrage organizations, and they merged to form the National American Woman Suffrage Association in 1890. However, Stanton stirred controversy once again by claiming that organized religion and the teachings in the Bible discriminated against women. She enraged many people in the suffrage movement in the mid-1890s when she published her critique of biblical texts in *The Woman's Bible*. Stanton anticipated her critics by stating in that work: "Come, come, my conservative friend, wipe the dew off your spectacles, and see that the world is moving."

HISTORICAL THINKING

1. **READING CHECK** What elements of Stanton's upbringing led her to support women's rights?

2. **FORM AND SUPPORT OPINIONS** Do you think Stanton was justified in her opposition to the 14th and 15th amendments? Why or why not?

3. **EVALUATE** What did Stanton mean when she urged her critics to "see that the world is moving"?

THE SENECA FALLS CONVENTION

As the 19th century progressed, women played huge roles in reform movements that took hold in the United States. They held meetings, gave talks, protested, and generally helped raise awareness about abolition, temperance, the needs of the poor and mentally ill, and many other issues in society. But by mid-century, the women who played leading roles in attempting to help others faced another problem within U.S. society—the subordinate, or lesser, role of women. Their work in previous reform movements armed them with tools to take action.

On July 19, 1948, the United States issued a three-cent stamp commemorating the first women's rights convention at Seneca Falls, New York, and celebrating the 100 years of progress toward equality made by women following the convention. Featured on the stamp were three 19th-century activists and reformers, Elizabeth Stanton, Carrie Chapman Catt, and Lucretia Mott. Besides serving a practical purpose, postage stamps are sometimes valuable to historians for the cultural and historical insights they contain.

CRITICAL VIEWING If you were a historian, what would this stamp tell you about how people in 1948 thought about the Seneca Falls convention of 1848? Include information about the three women portrayed on the stamp in your answer.

DOCUMENT ONE

Primary Source: Historic Document
from the Declaration of Sentiments,
by Lucretia Mott and Elizabeth Cady Stanton, July 20, 1848

Mott and Stanton issued the Declaration of Sentiments and Resolutions at the Seneca Falls Convention in New York. It begins by echoing the Declaration of Independence to establish that women should have the same rights as men. This excerpt is from the Declaration of Sentiments, a pointed list of women's grievances against men.

CONSTRUCTED RESPONSE Why do you think the right to vote is listed as the first grievance? Explain.

Declaration of Sentiments

He has never permitted her to exercise her inalienable right to the elective franchise [right to vote].

He has compelled her to submit to laws, in the formation of which she had no voice.

He has made her, if married, in the eye of the law, civilly dead.

He has taken from her all right in property, even to the wages she earns.

He has denied her the facilities for obtaining a thorough education— . . .

He has endeavored, in every way that he could to destroy her confidence in her own powers . . .

DOCUMENT TWO

Primary Source: Newspaper Article
from "Women Out of Their Latitude," the *Mechanic's Advocate*, August 12, 1848

The reaction to the Seneca Falls Convention and the Declaration of Sentiments and Resolutions was mostly negative and often dismissive or condescending. This newspaper article is a typical example of these reactions, making reference to both the concept of proper "womanliness" and the Bible.

CONSTRUCTED RESPONSE What part of this writer's critique of the convention might the organizers actually agree with? Explain.

The women who attend these meetings, no doubt at the expense of their more appropriate duties. . . . affirm, as among their rights, that of unrestricted franchise [right to vote], and assert that it is wrong to deprive them of the privilege to become legislators, lawyers, doctors, divines [members of the clergy].

Now, it requires no argument to prove that this is all wrong. Every true hearted female will instantly feel that this is unwomanly. Society would have to be radically remodeled . . . and the order of things established at the creation of mankind . . . would be completely broken up.

DOCUMENT THREE

Primary Source: Speech
from "Solitude of Self," by Elizabeth Cady Stanton, January 18, 1892

After the 1848 Women's Rights Convention at Seneca Falls, Elizabeth Cady Stanton continued her work for women's suffrage. For more than 20 years, she led suffrage organizations, including the National American Woman Suffrage Association. This excerpt is from her resignation speech from that group, 28 years before the 19th Amendment guaranteed women the right to vote in 1920.

CONSTRUCTED RESPONSE What overall effect does Stanton believe the contemporary state of women's rights in 1892 was having on American women?

To throw obstacle in the way of a complete education is like putting out the eyes; to deny the rights of property, like cutting off the hands. To deny political equality is to rob the ostracized of all self-respect; of credit in the market place; of recompense in the world of work; of a voice among those who make and administer the law; a choice in the jury before whom they are tried, and in the judge who decides their punishment.

SYNTHESIZE & WRITE

1. **REVIEW** Review what you have learned about the reasons and theories behind the movement for improved women's rights in the mid-1800s.

2. **RECALL** List the main ideas about the women's rights movement expressed in the three documents.

3. **CONSTRUCT** Construct a topic sentence that answers this question: Why did American women campaign for increased rights?

4. **WRITE** Using evidence from the chapter and the documents, write an informative paragraph that supports your topic sentence in Step 3.

AN AGE OF REFORM
REVIEW

VOCABULARY

Use each of the following terms in a sentence that shows an understanding of the term's meaning.

1. Romanticism
   Followers of Romanticism rejected logic in favor of emotion.

2. penitentiary
3. suffragist
4. labor union
5. stewardship
6. temperance movement
7. gag rule
8. transcendentalism
9. emancipation

READING STRATEGY
MAKE INFERENCES

When you make inferences, you use what you already know to understand the meaning of a text. Use a chart like the one below to make inferences about how the era's social and cultural reforms influenced America. Then answer the question.

I Read	I Know	And So
"Americans seemed to fear that their society was becoming less unified."	People can react strongly to change and disunity.	An upsurge in religious zeal, the Second Great Awakening, took hold.

10. What changes did the era's social and cultural reforms make to American society?

MAIN IDEAS

Answer the following questions. Support your answers with evidence from the chapter.

11. Where did the Second Great Awakening have its geographical roots? **LESSON 1.1**

12. What overall outcome did Dorothea Dix hope for in her movement to help the mentally ill and those who were imprisoned? **LESSON 1.1**

13. What set John James Audubon apart from the painters of the Hudson River School? **LESSON 1.2**

14. Why might it be to a slave owner's advantage to use one of his slaves as a driver? **LESSON 2.1**

15. What role did violence play in the running of a plantation? **LESSON 2.1**

16. Why did the speeches of Frederick Douglass and the sisters Angelina and Sarah Grimké carry more significance for some northerners than those of other white abolitionists? **LESSON 2.2**

17. Explain the ways in which former president John Quincy Adams contributed to the abolitionist movement. **LESSON 2.2**

18. How was the legal status of men and women both similar and different in the mid-1800s? **LESSON 3.1**

19. How did the cult of domesticity influence the women's rights movement? **LESSON 3.1**

HISTORICAL THINKING

Answer the following questions. Support your answers with evidence from the chapter.

20. **FORM AND SUPPORT OPINIONS** In what ways do you think Charles Grandison Finney epitomized the spirit of not only the Second Great Awakening but also of the reform era?

21. **ANALYZE CAUSE AND EFFECT** What methods did members of the temperance movement use to try to persuade people to refuse or drink less alcohol?

22. **MAKE CONNECTIONS** Explain how Romanticism and transcendentalism are related to each other.

23. **DRAW CONCLUSIONS** Which of the middle-class reform movements do you think had the most concrete, long-lasting effect on U.S. society? Explain.

George Catlin is famous for his paintings of Native Americans and their lives and cultures in the early 1800s. Look closely at his painting *Buffalo Chase, a Single Death*. Use your observation of the painting and information from the chapter to answer the questions that follow.

24. How does this painting illustrate the contribution George Catlin made to the development of uniquely American art forms?

25. In what ways does Catlin's painting reflect the ideas of Romanticism and transcendentalism?

Elizabeth Cady Stanton was in many ways well ahead of her time. In this quotation from her book, *The Woman's Bible*, published in 1895 and 1898, she expresses a desire for equality between men and women that many would argue has still not been achieved to this day.

> We should give to our rulers, our sires and sons no rest until all our rights—social, civil and political—are fully accorded. How are men to know what we want unless we tell them? They have no idea that our wants, material and spiritual, are the same as theirs; that we love justice, liberty and equality as well as they do; that we believe in the principles of self-government, in individual rights, individual conscience and judgment, the fundamental ideas of the Protestant religion and republican government.

26. In what ways does this quotation from Elizabeth Cady Stanton echo the motives and tactics of the Second Great Awakening and the middle-class reforms that followed?

27. EXPOSITORY Think about the movement for women's rights that had its beginnings in the era of reform and the fact that this movement is ongoing today. Write a paragraph that discusses the progress of the movement over time and its status today.

TIPS

- Introduce the topic with a clear main idea statement concerning your assessment of the progress of women's rights over time.

- Use textual evidence from the chapter to highlight the ways in which U.S. society and government limited women's rights at the time the movement began.

- Summarize which of these limitations have been done away with.

- Include at least two areas in which U.S. society still falls short of giving equal rights to women.

- Provide a concluding statement that follows from and supports the ideas and information you have presented.

CHAPTER 10 WESTWARD EXPANSION

1830–1854

HISTORICAL THINKING How did the idea of manifest destiny shape the future of the United States?

As the United States expanded westward, it gained such natural treasures as these huge sandstone pillars in Utah's Valley of the Gods. Adjacent to Bears Ears National Monument, Valley of the Gods is protected public land managed by the Bureau of Land Management. In 2017, the U.S. government reduced the size of Bears Ears by 85 percent to allow natural resources to be extracted from the land.

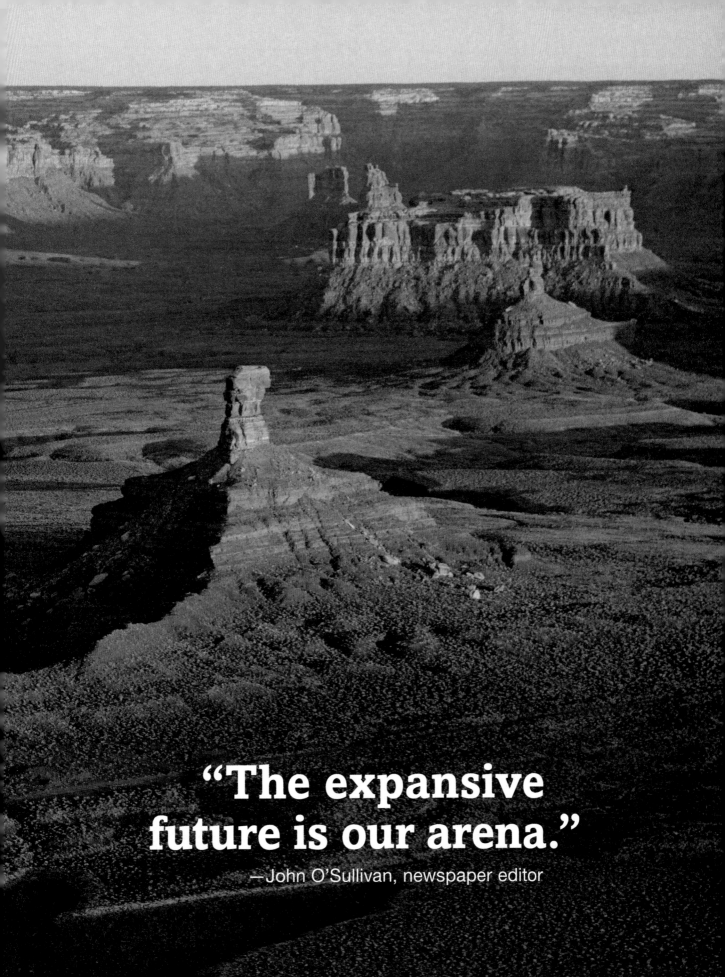

"The expansive future is our arena."

—John O'Sullivan, newspaper editor

CHICANO
HISTORY AND CULTURE

Vehicles draped in Mexican flags
and banners are a familiar sight at the annual Cinco de
Mayo parade in Modesto, California. What impressions
of Chicano culture do you gain from the photo?

In 1821, Mexico was the largest country in North America, reaching well into what is now the northern United States. Newly independent from Spain, Mexico was nearly twice the size it is today. It encompassed territories that include parts or all of the present-day states of California, Utah, Nevada, Colorado, Wyoming, New Mexico, Oklahoma, and Arizona.

Away from the Pacific Coast, the land north of the Rio Grande was sparsely inhabited. To spark economic development, the Mexican government enticed settlers from the United States and Europe by granting them colonies in Texas. Americans flocked into the region, but they soon rebelled against the laws imposed by the distant central government in Mexico City. In 1836, Texas gained its independence from Mexico, unleashing debates within the United States over whether to annex, or add, the new republic as a state—which would guarantee war with Mexico. In 1845, the annexation was approved, and war followed.

The Mexican-American War was hard-fought and bloody. In 1847, Mexico was defeated and forced to cede all of its land north of the Rio Grande to the United States. After the war, many Mexicans who had made their homes north of the Rio Grande found themselves living in the United States. Over time, these Mexican Americans and their descendants helped form the unique cultures of the states they lived in.

In the nearly 200 years since the end of the Mexican-American War, later waves of immigrants from Mexico have continued to enrich the cultures of the border states, creating unique art forms, music, and cuisines. Today, a number of states have large Mexican American populations, especially those that once formed part of Mexico, including New Mexico, Colorado, Nevada, Arizona, California, and Texas. This American Story highlights the Mexican American, or Chicano, history and culture of those states.

EARLY CALIFORNIA

Before the Mexican-American War, the state we know as California was called Alta California, or Upper California, to distinguish it from Baja California, or Lower California. Baja California extends as a long peninsula south of the present-day border of California. The Spanish settlement of Alta California began in 1769 with the establishment of the first Catholic missions and the military forts called presidios.

Alongside the missions and presidios, a civilian society of Spanish-speaking landowners arose. The Californios, as they were known, received generous land grants from the Spanish government to encourage settlement in Alta California. The Californios established large farms and cattle ranches, relying on the labor of Native Americans and Mexicans from lower social classes. Some Californio families controlled enormous estates. Legally, a land grant could not exceed about 50,000 acres, but some families received multiple grants.

The Californios had comfortable lifestyles, supported through trade with U.S. merchants who arrived by sea to buy hides and tallow produced at the ranches. The elite families were known for their lavish entertainments and parties. A Californio wedding celebration could last a week or more.

After the Mexican-American War ended in 1847, all Mexicans living in the lands ceded to the United States became American citizens by default, unless they officially declared themselves to be Mexican citizens. On paper, the Californios retained title to their land. But the reality was that their vast holdings and control of society were quickly threatened. The California gold rush caused large numbers of people to pour into California from the United States. Additionally, westward-expanding railroads demanded land grants from the government. Soon the Californios were facing legal challenges to their land ownership. Many families were forced to sell their property piece by piece to pay legal fees. By the end of the 19th century, most elite Californios had lost much or all of their property.

A NEW CENTURY OF SETTLEMENT

The 20th century saw new waves of immigration from Mexico into California and other southwestern states. The Mexican migrants were not seeking land but better-paying jobs. At times, the new arrivals faced prejudice and open hostility, even when they were filling existing labor gaps.

In the early 1900s, the spread of irrigation, agriculture, railroads, and mining in California created a demand for inexpensive labor. Many migrants worked for a few months and then returned to Mexico, but between 35,000 and 75,000 stayed every year. Some cities in California developed lively centers of Mexican American culture, but prejudice against Chicanos remained strong.

In 1942, a new wave of Mexican workers arrived at the invitation of the U.S. government in response to a shortage of farm and transportation workers caused by World War II. Under the Bracero Program, Mexican laborers replaced American workers who were serving in the armed forces. Over a span of 22 years, the Bracero Program brought more than 4 million Latino workers into the country.

ENGLISH FROM SPANISH

Hundreds of English words have Spanish origins, and many of these words made their way into the United States via the former Mexican territories that now form the American Southwest. This chart features words that are related to the experiences of early Mexican cowboys working on ranches in the region.

ENGLISH	SPANISH	SPANISH MEANING
buckaroo	vaquero	cowboy
lasso	lazo	tie
lariat	la reata	rope
mustang	mustango or mesteño	wild horse
patio	patio	courtyard
ranch	rancho	ranch
rodeo	rodear	to encircle

The Bracero Program had a strong influence on California's economy and resulted in an increase in long-term Mexican American residents. Like earlier waves of immigration, this one caused flare-ups of prejudice and hostility. In 1943 in Los Angeles, for example, white soldiers, sailors, and civilians went on a weeklong spree of violence against Mexican American youths. The outbreak came to be called the Zoot Suit Riots because of a style of dress that was fashionable among young Mexican American men: extravagant-looking outfits called zoot suits and a distinctive duck-tail haircut. The aggressors forcefully removed the Mexican American young men's suits, cut their hair, and beat them brutally. At the time, rumors were spread that Mexican Americans were hindering the war effort by evading the draft. In fact, the reverse was true: Mexican Americans served in the armed forces in World War II in numbers far greater than their percentage of the general population. Seventeen were awarded the Congressional Medal of Honor.

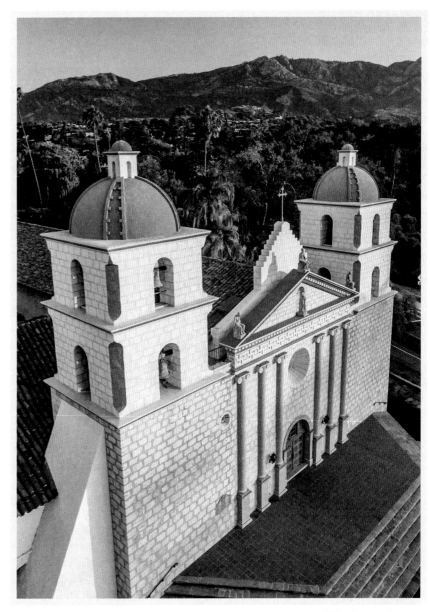

A Catholic religious order called the Franciscans founded Old Mission Santa Barbara in Santa Barbara, California, in 1786. Still home to a community of Franciscan friars, the mission is considered a cultural and historic landmark.

In the 1950s and 1960s, Mexican Americans in California joined with other groups to counter the effects of prejudice and to empower communities. A union called the United Farm Workers, organized by labor activist Cesar Chávez, took up the cause of migrant farmworkers, demanding better pay and improved working conditions. In 1968, a group of Mexican American high school students and their supporters organized what became known as the Los Angeles Blowouts. About 15,000 students walked out of 5 East Los Angeles high schools to protest their substandard education. Both the union and the students were part of a larger civil rights movement called the Chicano Civil Rights Movement. The term Chicano had long existed as a negative nickname for Mexican Americans, but the movement adopted it as a symbol of cultural pride.

Today, California's Mexican roots are visible throughout the state. The names of cities such as Los Angeles, San Francisco, San Diego, and Sacramento all originated with the Spanish colonizers. California streets and towns bear the names of old Californio families, such as Yorba, Pico, Vallejo, and Peralta. Many cities proudly celebrate their Mexican heritage and the state's unique Mexican American cultures. Olvera Street in Los Angeles, for example, has been called the heart of that city's Chicano community and hosts an annual celebration of the Mexican Revolution and such religious festivals as *Día de los Muertos* (Day of the Dead) and the feast of the Virgin of Guadalupe.

ON BEING MEXICAN AMERICAN

Mexican American novelist and poet Sandra Cisneros (left) was born in Chicago, but in her youth, she frequently traveled with her family to Mexico to visit relatives. In interviews, she commented on the experience of growing up in multiple cultures.

PRIMARY SOURCE

If you know two cultures and two languages, that intermediate place, where the two don't perfectly meet, is really interesting.

I think that Mexican American kids live in a global world. It's not even bi-, it's multi-. You know, for those of us who grew up with different countries on our block, different nationalities, you know, we moved into multiple worlds.

San Francisco's Mission District, with its historic buildings and bright murals, is home to local Chicano organizations. A carnival is held every May in the district to celebrate the food, music, and dance of the Chicano culture. In 1999, the city of San Jose opened Mexican Heritage Plaza, a community and cultural arts center with a theater, art gallery, and classrooms. Visitors from all ethnic backgrounds come to California every year to enjoy the riches of the state's Mexican American heritage.

THE CHICANOS OF TEXAS

It's a popular question for trivia contests: How many flags have flown over Texas? In fact, beginning in the 1500s, Texas has been under six flags: those of France, Spain, Mexico, the Republic of Texas, the Confederacy, and the United States. Over the centuries, the governments have changed, but the Tejanos have remained.

The word *Tejano* refers to Texans of Mexican or Spanish descent. Unlike the Californios, the Tejanos did not form an upper-class landowning society, though the majority earned a living by farming or ranching. Throughout the 1700s, the Spanish government tried to persuade people to settle in Texas, but the isolation, poor living conditions, and danger from Native American attacks held most prospective settlers back. By the end of the 18th century, Texas had only about 5,000 residents of Mexican heritage.

In the 1800s, the trickle of Mexican settlers increased to a larger flow, and in 1850, a federal census counted 14,000 residents of Mexican descent. Like California, Texas also had an influx of Mexican immigrants at the start of the 20th century. By one estimate, the number of Tejanos had reached about 700,000.

The immigration tide turned during the Great Depression, which began in 1929. Faced with growing unemployment in the Southwest—and throughout the United States—President Herbert Hoover created a program to deport Mexicans and other Hispanics so that Americans could take their jobs. Mexican Americans remaining in the country struggled to find jobs or federal assistance.

All southwestern states were affected but Texas was impacted the most. In all, between 400,000 and 500,000 Mexicans and their American-born children returned to Mexico, more than half of them from Texas. Not all the returnees were officially deported. Some left on their own in fear that they would be forced out of the country.

Immigration to the United States from Mexico increased once again in the 1940s due to labor shortages in the United States, the Bracero Program, and a high rate of poverty in Mexico. In 1990, the census counted about 3.9 million people of Mexican descent in Texas, and more than 80 percent were born in the United States.

As in California, Chicanos in Texas have encountered prejudice, segregation, and sometimes violent treatment. Before World War II, most Tejanos lived in rural areas, farming, working as ranch hands, or building railroads. In towns, some managed to start small businesses that catered to Tejano communities. During World War II and after, many Tejanos moved to larger cities for better-paying, more highly skilled jobs. In the 1960s, many organizations worked as part of the Chicano Movement to fight for equal rights and greater political involvement for Mexican Americans in Texas.

Tejanos have developed their own unique culture based on Mexican traditions but incorporating outside elements. One example is the music genre called *conjunto*. Combining musical elements from two continents, conjunto mixes themes from northern Mexican traditions with accordion sounds and polka music borrowed from 19th-century German settlers in the region. A typical conjunto band features an accordion, guitars, and drums. The Tejano Conjunto Festival draws appreciative audiences to San Antonio, Texas, every year, and the Conjunto Hall of Fame has inducted more than 70 musicians.

Another prominent aspect of Tejano culture is Tex-Mex food, which blends elements of Mexican and American cooking. Cheese, beans, beef, and the spices cumin and chili powder are common ingredients in Tex-Mex cooking. Fajitas and nachos are popular Tex-Mex creations.

CHICANOS TODAY

Southwestern states, especially California and Texas, continue to attract the majority of Mexican immigrants today. After California and Texas, the state that receives the largest number of Mexican immigrants is Illinois. Chicago, the city with the third highest population in the United States, has a large and vibrant Mexican American community that has attracted new immigrants for decades.

CRITICAL VIEWING Artist Domingo Ulloa was committed to promoting social justice through his artwork. He painted *Braceros* in 1960 after visiting a migrant workers' camp in Holtville, California. What does this painting suggest about the experiences of migrant workers under the Bracero Program?

Between 1965 and 2000, 4.3 million Mexicans moved to the United States. In 2014, more than 11.7 million Mexicans came to the United States, making up 28 percent of the foreign-born population. Since the end of the Great Recession of 2007–2009, however, more Mexican migrants have returned to Mexico than have arrived in the United States.

While the Mexican American community is well established in the United States, some people have concerns about illegal immigration from Mexico. The number of unauthorized immigrants coming into the country has dropped in recent years. But millions of illegal immigrants remain in the United States, some of whom were brought here as children. Under President Trump, who was elected in 2016, the U.S. government has increased its efforts to stop illegal immigration and to deport unauthorized immigrants.

Americans have differing opinions on the subject of deporting unauthorized immigrants. Some oppose deportation, arguing that unauthorized immigrants help the American economy by performing jobs that few citizens want. Others favor deportation, claiming that unauthorized immigrants take jobs that would otherwise go to American citizens. The treatment of illegal immigrants who came to the United States as children is a particularly divisive issue.

In the meantime, Mexican Americans continue to enrich the culture of the United States with their contributions in literature, art, architecture, government, agriculture, science, and other fields. Cities and small towns across the country boast restaurants serving Mexican and Tex-Mex food. Vibrant Chicano neighborhoods invite visitors to join in appreciating Mexican American art, music, and celebrations. Two major Spanish-language television networks, Univision and Telemundo, are headquartered in the United States, providing news and entertainment to a diverse audience. Mexican American culture will always be an integral part of the American scene.

THINK ABOUT IT

What elements of Chicano culture do you experience in your everyday life?

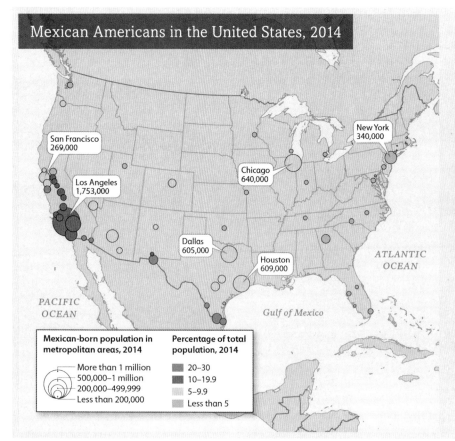

Mexican Americans in the United States, 2014

San Francisco
269,000

Los Angeles
1,753,000

Chicago
640,000

New York
340,000

Dallas
605,000

Houston
609,000

ATLANTIC OCEAN

PACIFIC OCEAN

Gulf of Mexico

Mexican-born population in metropolitan areas, 2014	Percentage of total population, 2014
More than 1 million	20–30
500,000–1 million	10–19.9
200,000–499,999	5–9.9
Less than 200,000	Less than 5

In the period between 2010 and 2014, most immigrants from Mexico settled in California (37 percent), Texas (21 percent), and Illinois (6 percent). The U.S. cities with the largest number of Mexican immigrants were greater Los Angeles, Chicago, Houston, and Dallas. These four metropolitan areas were home to about 39 percent of the Mexican immigrants in the United States.

What conclusions can you draw about the distribution of the Mexican American population in the United States?

NATIONAL GEOGRAPHIC

JASON DE LEÓN

A spiky cactus bristles in the scorching Sonoran Desert sun. Caught on its thorns—a baby diaper. Miles away, a tattered backpack contains one roll of toilet paper, a love letter, and a prayer card. Beside it, a tiny child's shoe. Until Jason De León, a National Geographic Explorer and the founder of the Undocumented Migration Project, arrived on the scene, such items were all considered garbage, or never discovered at all.

People view undocumented migration into the United States from Mexico from a wide variety of perspectives, often focusing on the effects the immigrants have on the politics, culture, or economy of the United States. De León may be the first to study the topic from the perspective of an archaeologist. He applies scientific techniques to gain a deeper understanding of the migrants' experiences. In addition to collecting the objects they leave behind, he conducts interviews to help illuminate the meaning of the items. De León explains, "We use archaeological surveys, linguistics, forensics, and ethnography to document how people prepare to cross the border, who profits from helping them, how they deal with physical and emotional trauma during their journey, and what happens to those who don't make it." His goal is to learn more about the effects of immigration on all who are involved in it on both sides of the border, including migrants, law enforcement officers, smugglers, and everyday citizens. "It's an emotional subject, but my focus has to be science first," explains De León.

De León is a Mexican American who grew up in South Texas and Southern California. "Being raised on the border in a bicultural household with a long immigration history makes me very attuned to issues of cultural identity and discrimination," he explains.

What might the study of undocumented migrants reveal about U.S. history?

De León collaborated with American artist Amanda Krugliak and photographer Richard Barnes on a traveling exhibit called *State of Exception*, a wall of discarded backpacks left by migrants trying to cross into the United States through the Sonoran Desert.

THE CALL OF THE WEST

What is "the West" to you? Americans' notions of "the West" have changed over time. Almost every section of the United States beyond the eastern coastal region has been considered "the West" at some time in American history. As Americans migrated, the designation of the West changed.

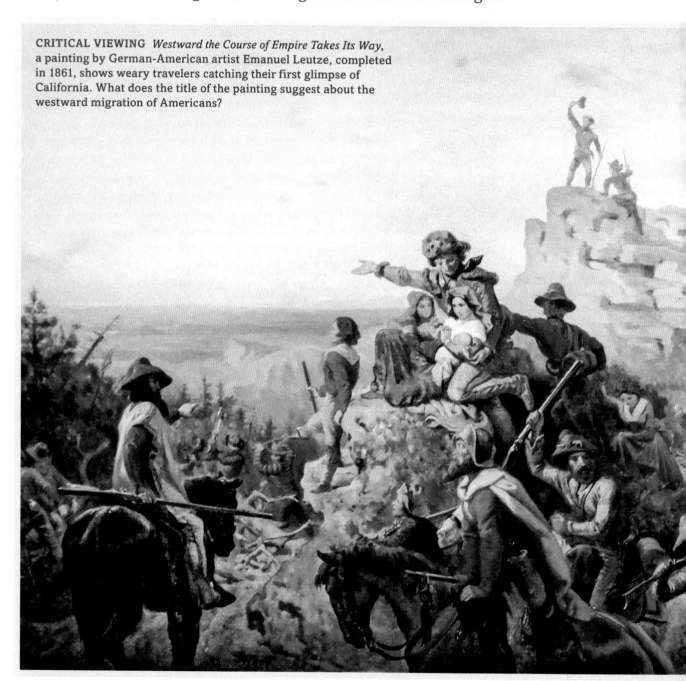

CRITICAL VIEWING *Westward the Course of Empire Takes Its Way*, a painting by German-American artist Emanuel Leutze, completed in 1861, shows weary travelers catching their first glimpse of California. What does the title of the painting suggest about the westward migration of Americans?

REASONS FOR MIGRATING

Europeans began pushing westward shortly after they established their first settlements along the eastern seaboard of North America. Many people migrated west along the same latitudes as they lived, moving to places with familiar weather and soil. For example, in the early 1800s, people from New York migrated to Michigan, while people from Virginia, Tennessee, and Kentucky headed to Missouri.

In the 1840s, the number of people moving west of the Mississippi River increased dramatically, forming one of the largest migrations in U.S. history. Between 1841 and 1866, up to a half million Americans migrated west of the Mississippi. Most of these migrants were young men in their teens and early adulthood. About 30 percent were women and children. While people from all over the United States moved west in the 1840s and 1850s, the largest number came from the South and the Midwest.

People packed up and headed west for a variety of reasons. One of the main reasons was population growth. The population of the United States grew from 5.3 million in 1800 to a whopping 23 million by 1850.

During this period, most people in the United States needed land because they made their living by farming. Younger children in farm families often inherited little or no property. In some places, overuse had made existing farmland less fertile and productive, so it took more acreage to produce the same yields. Tobacco and cotton, the cash crops of the South, were particularly tough on the soil, depleting it of nutrients and decreasing its fertility. Many southern farmers were looking for fertile land to grow these crops. Recent immigrants wanted land as well.

Changes in government policy in the 1830s made moving to the West much more attractive, contributing to the boom in migration and settlement. In 1801, a settler had to pay $2.00 per acre and buy a minimum of 320 acres to secure public land from the government. In the 1830s, the price was about $1.25 per acre and a settler only had to buy 80 acres.

Iron bands were added to wooden wagon wheels to withstand the long journeys of pioneers through the rugged terrain of the West.

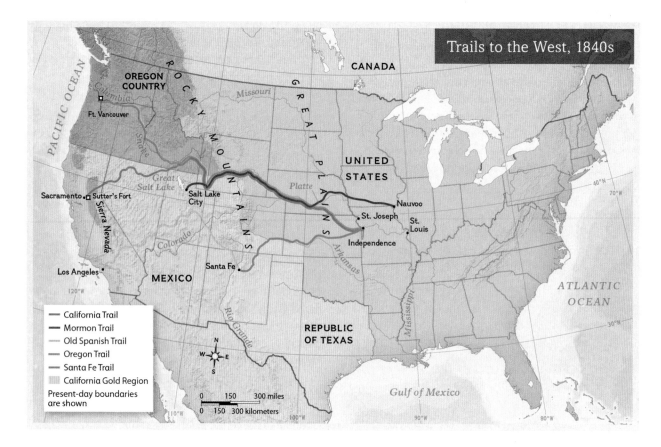

Besides needing farmland to make a living, Americans tended to link open land and land ownership with the ideals of liberty and independence. Many moved several times in their lives, looking for better land and more freedom.

As Americans pushed west, they gained access to natural resources that either had been depleted in the East or did not exist there. For example, while farmers gained fertile land, trappers and fur traders, called **mountain men**, made fortunes selling beaver pelts and other furs. The Great Plains provided ranchers with grazing land for livestock. The discovery of valuable deposits of coal, copper, silver, gold, and other minerals drew miners to the West. The area's forests prompted the development of the timber industry in the Pacific Northwest.

THE CONCEPT OF "MANIFEST DESTINY"

The West was not simply an area of vast, unoccupied land, however. Hundreds of Native American groups lived there, while Spain and later Mexico claimed much of the territory. Americans needed a justification for taking the land from the people who already lived there or considered it theirs. In 1845, newspaper editor John O'Sullivan provided that justification. He wrote that it was the **manifest destiny**, or inevitable fate, of the United States "to overspread the continent allotted by Providence for the free development of our yearly multiplying

millions." In other words, O'Sullivan proposed that God intended for the people of the United States to take over the North American continent.

Not surprisingly, the idea of manifest destiny and the westward expansion of the United States led to disputes with Native Americans who already lived in the West and with Mexicans who claimed much of the region. Not only was land at stake, but also the culture and way of life of many groups of people.

TRAILS WEST

While some migrants sailed to California and the Pacific Northwest, most traveled overland by wagon. The overland migrants followed trails marked by earlier trappers and fur traders who, to some degree, probably used even earlier trails made by Native Americans as well as by migrating herds of animals.

Some of the trappers and traders became legends to the people of the eastern United States. One of the most famous was **Jim Beckwourth**, a free African American who worked on western expeditions and lived with various Native American tribes. Beckwourth established a trail west through the Sierra Nevada, the high mountain range along part of the eastern border of California.

Other explorers also blazed trails and drew maps to guide westward migrants. **John C. Frémont** and **Kit Carson** were two of the most important

Jim Beckwourth, an American mountain man and explorer, established a trail through the Sierra Nevada for migrants traveling to California.

trailblazers. Frémont was a soldier with the U.S. Army, and Carson was a famous mountain man who served as his guide. They explored the Rocky Mountains region in 1842, making use of a gap through the mountains in what today is southern Wyoming. This crossing point, called the South Pass, became essential to overland travel to the West Coast. In the following years, the pair traveled through the Oregon Territory, California, and the Southwest. Their journeys led to Frémont's famed map of the West, the first map of the area that was scientifically based.

Migrants and traders typically followed two main trails west. The **Santa Fe Trail** started at Independence, Missouri, and led to Santa Fe in present-day New Mexico. From Santa Fe, the trail extended into Mexico. Access to the city of Santa Fe gave traders the chance to exchange U.S. products for Mexican silver, furs, and mules. The **Oregon Trail** stretched for about 2,000 miles from Independence, Missouri, to Oregon City, near present-day Portland, Oregon. A southern spur, the California Trail, led to Sacramento, California.

Hundreds of thousands of people traveled the Oregon Trail from the 1840s through the 1860s. Those who traveled the spur trail to California sent back reports of crowded campsites and dust-filled air from the large number of oxen and wagons.

Ruts made by the wheels of the many wagons that rolled over the land can still be seen in parts of the Great Plains today.

MIGRATION OF THE MORMONS

One of the groups migrating west was the **Mormons**, who believed in a religion founded by Joseph Smith in New York in 1830. Members of the religion, called the Church of Jesus Christ of Latter-day Saints, believe in the Christian Bible but consider it incomplete. They also follow additional scriptures found by Smith, who claimed they had been revealed to him by divine beings.

Smith and his followers moved from New York and established settlements in Ohio and Missouri. However, their non-Mormon neighbors viewed them with suspicion and hostility. Forced to leave Ohio and Missouri, they gathered in Illinois in 1839 and founded the town of Nauvoo.

By the mid-1840s, Nauvoo had become one of the largest cities in Illinois, with a population exceeding 15,000 people. However, the Mormons again faced harassment, which erupted into violence. After a mob killed Smith in 1844, the Mormons chose a new leader, **Brigham Young**. He decided to lead the Mormons west to find a remote and protected place where they could practice their religion.

Young and his followers chose the region around the southern shore of the Great Salt Lake in what is now the state of Utah. Surrounded by mountains in the east and deserts in the west and south, the site was effectively cut off from the rest of the country. Two years after the death of Joseph Smith, 15,000 Mormons followed what came to be called the **Mormon Trail** and began arriving at their new home. About 55,000 Mormons traveled the Mormon Trail to Salt Lake City over the next 20 years.

HISTORICAL THINKING

1. **READING CHECK** What was the concept of manifest destiny, and how was it connected to westward migration?

2. **ANALYZE CAUSE AND EFFECT** Why did so many Americans move west of the Mississippi River in the 1840s and 1850s?

3. **IDENTIFY MAIN IDEAS AND DETAILS** What role did geography play in the Mormons' choice of a site to settle in the West?

4. **INTERPRET MAPS** What physical features did all the trails shown on the map pass over or through?

CRITICAL VIEWING The giant sequoias of California inspired awe in the first pioneers who encountered them in the 1850s. This tree in Sequoia National Park is the second largest in the world, measured not by height but by volume. It contains at least 54,000 cubic feet of wood and bark and, at 3,200 years old, is still growing. How does the perspective from which Nichols captured this shot help convey the tree's size?

MICHAEL NICHOLS

National Geographic photographer Michael Nichols worked more than two weeks with a crew of climbers and assistants to get this shot of a giant sequoia named "the President." Then he climbed the tree himself to "say goodbye." Born in Alabama, Nichols has devoted his career to capturing the wonders of the natural world, striving to inspire people to conserve Earth's amazing living things, from African elephants to giant sequoias.

MAIN IDEA The pioneers endured many hardships on their migrations west, while Native Americans faced the loss of homeland and culture.

PIONEERS AND NATIVE AMERICANS

Can you imagine traveling in a covered wagon for six months across vast grasslands and over mountains to make a new life in an unknown land? Or watching your homeland being overtaken by people who do not respect your rights? Pioneers and Native Americans faced these separate challenges in the mid-1800s.

THE PIONEER EXPERIENCE

Traveling west on the Oregon Trail was nothing like the relatively safe and easy cross-country trips of today. An estimated 4 to 10 percent of travelers died on the trail, mostly from diseases or accidental shootings. People often contracted such diseases as cholera, dysentery, and typhoid fever from drinking unsanitary water or eating contaminated food. In the mountains, migrants faced the threat of early snowstorms. Some mountain passes were so dangerous and steep that wagons had to be dragged up one side and then carefully eased down the other using ropes, chains, and pulleys. Before reaching the end of the trail, some travelers ran out of food and suffered from malnutrition. But contrary to popular myth, conflicts with Native Americans were rare along the trails west.

Most pioneers traveled overland in a smaller version of a Conestoga wagon, which, as you have read, is a type of covered wagon. The vehicles' white canvas covers reminded people of the sails on

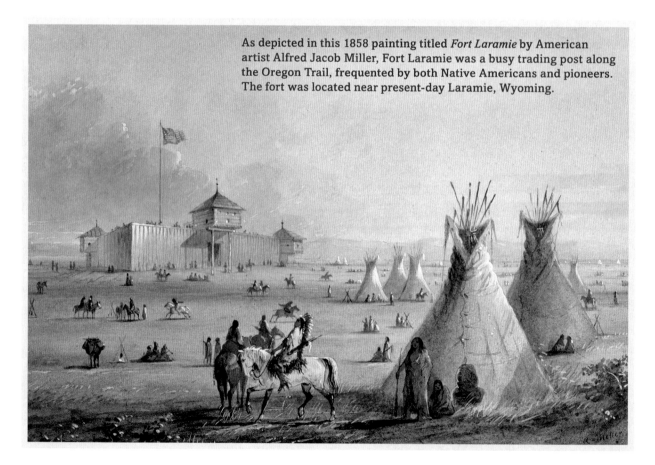

As depicted in this 1858 painting titled *Fort Laramie* by American artist Alfred Jacob Miller, Fort Laramie was a busy trading post along the Oregon Trail, frequented by both Native Americans and pioneers. The fort was located near present-day Laramie, Wyoming.

ships called schooners, which led people to call the wagons **prairie schooners** . During the day, the pioneers rode in or walked next to their wagons, herding their livestock along the way. When they stopped, they had to set up camp, find fuel and make a fire, cook meals, and make any necessary repairs on wagons and other equipment.

On the journeys west, women typically did not follow strict gender roles. They still cared for the children, gathered fuel, and cooked meals, but they also took on such traditionally male roles as driving wagons, repairing equipment, herding cattle, putting up tents, and pulling oxen out of the mud.

CONFLICTS OVER LAND AND CULTURE

As you have read, millions of Native Americans lived in North America when Columbus first set foot in the Western Hemisphere. However, European diseases soon began to decimate their population. Despite these losses, hundreds of established tribes still lived west of the Mississippi when explorers and settlers began moving there. According to some historians, more than 325,000 Native Americans lived in the Southwest, the Great Plains, California, and the Pacific Northwest in 1840.

Westward migration from the United States threatened these Native Americans with the loss of their homeland, access to vital resources, and ways of life. The United States forced many tribes into treaties that took away their land and limited their freedom. When they resisted the changes pressed upon them, the U.S. government's reaction was usually swift and brutal.

These changes particularly threatened the nomadic way of life of the Plains tribes, who moved from place to place following the herds of bison, or buffalo. These tribes depended on the buffalo for most of their needs, including food, clothing, shelter, weapons, and tools. The wild buffalo herds migrated seasonally across enormous areas of open grazing land. The nomadic culture of the Plains tribes clashed with that of settlers who sought their own plots of land for farming, ranching, and mining.

The settlers even encroached upon land that had been specifically set aside for Native Americans. Under the Indian Removal Act of 1830, several southeastern tribes were forced to move to Indian Territory in present-day Oklahoma and parts of Kansas and Nebraska. Eventually, the pioneers began to claim that land as well.

While traveling west, pioneers used Dutch ovens like this one to cook food on hot coals.

PRIMARY SOURCE

Amelia Stewart Knight set out on the Oregon Trail in 1853 with her husband and seven children. She recorded their experiences in her diary.

Cold; breakfast the first thing; very disagreeable weather; wind east, cold and rainy, no fire. We are on a very large prairie, no timber can be seen as far as the eye can reach. Evening—Have crossed several bad streams today, and more than once have been stuck in the mud. We . . . have just crossed Grand river, and will camp in a little bottom, plenty of wood, and we will have a warm supper, I guess. Came 22 miles today. My head aches, but the fire is kindled and I must make some tea, that will help it, if not cure it.

—from the diary of Amelia Stewart Knight, April 18, 1853

HISTORICAL THINKING

1. **READING CHECK** How did the westward migration of people from the United States affect Native Americans?

2. **MAKE INFERENCES** Why do you think pioneer women did not follow strict gender roles on their journeys west?

3. **EVALUATE** In your opinion, what were the greatest hardships that pioneers faced on their journeys west?

4. **ANALYZE LANGUAGE USE** What inspired the pioneers to call their covered wagons "prairie schooners"? Cite evidence from the lesson in your response.

SETTLING THE SOUTHWEST

It's impossible to look at a map of the Southwest without recognizing the Spanish influence on the region's place names: San Antonio, Los Angeles, Rio Grande. Can you identify the Native American influence as well? Of course, the names you read reflect the region's history.

SPANISH COLONIES IN THE SOUTHWEST

As people from the United States moved westward, they encountered not only Native Americans but also Spanish citizens. As you have read, beginning in the 1500s, Spanish conquistadors explored and claimed the parts of western and southwestern North America that became Arizona, New Mexico, Nevada, Texas, Utah, and California.

Spain had a different colonial system than that of Great Britain. Spain was more interested in converting local Native Americans to Christianity and exploiting their labor than in replacing them with Spanish settlers. As a result, Roman Catholic clergy traveled with the conquistadors and set up missions throughout Spanish America. The goal was to gather the Native Americans into a community ruled by soldiers and priests, teach them European agricultural techniques, and make them Christians. Some Spanish treated the Native Americans well, but many punished and enslaved those who refused to convert or openly rebelled.

Some Native American tribes sought to build alliances with the Spanish against their enemies, but many resisted Spanish colonization. You have read about the Pueblo rebellion against the Spanish conquistador Juan de Oñate in New Mexico in the late 1500s. It was followed by more uprisings, including a revolt at Acoma Pueblo, during which the community was destroyed. The largest and most successful rebellion in New Mexico was the 1680 **Pueblo Revolt**, also called Popé's—or Po'pay's— Rebellion. During the rebellion, the Pueblo killed a number of priests, destroyed missions and Christian artifacts, and drove all 2,400 Spanish settlers out

of New Mexico. After 4 attempts over 12 years, the Spanish recaptured the territory and subdued the Pueblo people once again.

The Spanish had a significant impact on North American culture, including agriculture, language, music, art, law, and food. The Spanish introduced goats, sheep, horses, and cattle to the Western Hemisphere. Many ranching techniques come from the Spanish, including the use of **vaqueros**, or cowboys, to manage large herds of cattle. The words *lariat* and *lasso* are Spanish in origin. So are many western and southwestern place names, including Colorado, California, Los Angeles, and Tucson. In Spanish America, new cultures emerged that combined elements of Spanish culture and a number of Native American cultures of the Southwest.

The Spanish government left North America in 1821 after Mexico won its 11-year revolution against Spain. The new nation of Mexico included lands that make up parts or all of present-day Texas, New Mexico, Arizona, California, Nevada, Utah, Colorado, and Wyoming.

The newly independent nation had difficulty establishing a stable government and a healthy economy. Its northernmost states and territories, which included Tejas (TAY-hahs), or present-day Texas, were distant from the center of government in Mexico City, and few Mexicans were interested in settling there.

GONE TO TEXAS

Hoping that a larger population would help stabilize Tejas and prevent the territory from becoming part of the quickly expanding United States, the Mexican government offered land grants to encourage American immigration. Agents called **empresarios** contracted with the Mexican government to settle a certain number of families in Tejas in exchange for large land grants. An empresario controlled how property on a land grant was allotted and even how the law was enforced. The Mexican government gave out 41 empresario grants over 14 years after the country gained its independence.

Many Americans found the idea of migrating to Tejas enticing. Tejas had fertile soil for farming, vast forests for providing lumber, and expansive grasslands for raising cattle. In 1827, the Mexican government agreed it would not ban slavery entirely in Tejas. As a result, a number of plantation owners immigrated there, bringing along enslaved people.

The first and most famous empresario was **Stephen F. Austin**, an American who agreed to settle 300 families on land between the Brazos and Colorado rivers in Tejas. These first settlers are still called the Old Three Hundred. Most of them were farm families from west of the Appalachian Mountains rather than the East Coast. The majority were from Louisiana, and others hailed mostly from Alabama, Arkansas, Missouri, and Tennessee. They had been part of an earlier westward migration and were now seeking to move even farther west.

American empresario Stephen F. Austin, known as the "Father of Texas," established settlements of English-speaking people in Tejas in the 1820s.

Mexico's immigration plan was a far bigger success than Mexico expected or ultimately wanted. By 1830, about 21,000 Americans were living in Tejas, significantly more than the number of **Tejanos**, or settlers of Hispanic descent. Only 5 years later, the number of American settlers in Tejas had grown to about 38,000, which included about 3,000 enslaved African Americans.

HISTORICAL THINKING

1. **READING CHECK** What parts of North America did Spain control in the early 1800s?

2. **COMPARE AND CONTRAST** How was the Spanish colonial system different from the British system?

3. **ANALYZE CAUSE AND EFFECT** Why did the Americans in Tejas outnumber the Tejanos by the 1830s?

4. **INTERPRET MAPS** Based on the map, why do you think Tejas was so attractive to settlers from the United States?

TEXAS FIGHTS FOR INDEPENDENCE

Perhaps you've heard this saying by Mark Twain: "It's not the size of the dog in the fight, it's the size of the fight in the dog." Texans would likely apply this saying to those who fought to free their state from Mexico.

REBELLION IN TEXAS

As you have read, Americans in Tejas, or Texas as they called it, vastly outnumbered Mexicans by 1830. Concerned about the imbalance, the Mexican government outlawed further immigration from the United States and also prohibited Americans from bringing any more enslaved people into Texas. The ban did not actually stop immigration—of free or enslaved Americans—but it angered many Texans.

Both Americans and Tejanos, all proud residents of the Texas territory, began to call for greater representation in the central government and statehood within Mexico for Texas. Texans staged two revolts in 1832 and 1833. Then in 1834, General **Antonio López de Santa Anna** suspended the Mexican constitution and named himself dictator of Mexico. Both Americans and Tejanos were outraged at the disregard for their rights. Stephen Austin

and other Texans formally petitioned the Mexican government to allow Texas to become a separate Mexican state under its own administration. When their request was denied, they decided to fight.

As with the American Revolution, the **Texas War for Independence**, also called the Texas Revolution, started with a skirmish. In early October 1835, Mexican commander Francisco de Castañeda (kah-stah-NYAY-duh) led a small troop of soldiers to Gonzales, Texas, to retrieve a cannon that the Mexican government had provided the town. Castañeda had orders to avoid conflict, but the town's local militia attacked him and his men, forcing them to retreat. This incident became known as the Battle of Gonzales. More battles followed, and soon Santa Anna was on the march, leading an army north to put down the rebellion.

TEXAS WAR FOR INDEPENDENCE
1835–1836

October 10, 1835
Texans win the
Battle of Goliad.

December 9, 1835
Texan troops seize the
Alamo. (Alamo building
located in San Antonio, Texas)

| OCT | NOV | DEC | JAN | FEB |

October 2, 1835
Texans win the
Battle of Gonzales.

December 1835
Antonio López de Santa Anna
arrives in San Luis Potosí to raise
troops against Texans. (portrait
of Santa Anna by Carlos París)

In February 1836, Santa Anna and his army attacked and occupied San Antonio, Texas, where about 180 Texan rebels refused to surrender an old mission called the **Alamo**. About 1,800 Mexican soldiers held the rebels under siege for 13 days, during which time no food, ammunition, or reinforcements could enter the mission. Among those who occupied the Alamo were **Davy Crockett**, a famous frontiersman and congressman from Tennessee, and **James Bowie**, a Texan slave trader. Bowie commanded the volunteer troops at the Alamo. He shared power with **William Barrett Travis**, who commanded the regular troops. On March 2, 1836, Texas declared its independence from Mexico and named itself the **Republic of Texas**.

The Alamo's defenders held out for nearly two weeks. On March 6, the Mexicans stormed the mission and killed almost everyone inside. On orders from Santa Anna, the Mexican Army stripped the bodies of the rebels and burned them. After the battle, "Remember the Alamo!" became a rallying cry, and all those who died were considered heroes of Texas independence.

Another major skirmish began on March 23, 1836. The Mexican Army captured about 400 men from the United States who had joined the Texan army at Goliad, Texas. Many of these men surrendered with the understanding that they would be allowed to return to the United States. They did not know that the agreement depended on Santa Anna's approval. Santa Anna instead ordered the execution of all the captives. "Remember Goliad!" now became a rallying cry alongside "Remember the Alamo!" Santa Anna's cruelty at the Alamo and Goliad not only roused people in Texas but also many in the United States and other countries who decided to support the Texan cause.

THE LONE STAR REPUBLIC

In the spring of 1836, Santa Anna was on the verge of ending the Texas Revolution. But on April 21, the Texan army, led by **Sam Houston**, surprised a larger Mexican force at the San Jacinto (yuh-SIHN-toh) River. A force of 910 Texans attacked Santa Anna's 1,200 soldiers during their afternoon nap, taking only 18 minutes to win the **Battle of San Jacinto**. Santa Anna was wounded but escaped, only to be captured a day later. Houston forced Santa Anna to sign treaties withdrawing Mexican troops from Texas, granting Texas its independence, and recognizing the Rio Grande as the boundary between Mexico and the Republic of Texas.

Mexico's Congress renounced the treaties on the grounds that Santa Anna had signed them under penalty of death. But the fight was over, and Texas became an independent nation. Its flag featured a single large star, which earned Texas the nickname **Lone Star Republic**. The new nation legalized slavery and banned free African Americans from entering or living in the country. Texans elected Sam Houston, the hero of San Jacinto, as president. The people of Texas also voted to seek immediate **annexation**, or takeover, by the United States. However, Texas remained independent longer than anyone expected.

HISTORICAL THINKING

1. **READING CHECK** What events led to the Texas War for Independence?

2. **DETERMINE CHRONOLOGY** When did the tide turn in favor of the Texans during their fight for independence?

3. **MAKE INFERENCES** Why did Tejanos fight for independence from Mexico?

February 23, 1836
Santa Anna and his troops begin the siege of the Alamo.

March 6 ,1836
Santa Anna storms the Alamo.

March 23, 1836
Santa Anna orders the Goliad Massacre.

April 21, 1836
Texans win the Battle of San Jacinto and capture Santa Anna a day later. (Surrender of Santa Anna by William Huddle)

| MAR | APR | MAY | JUN |

March 2, 1836
Texas declares its independence from Mexico. (flag of the Republic of Texas)

May 14, 1836
Santa Anna signs the Treaties of Velasco.

MEXIC-ARTE MUSEUM
AUSTIN, TEXAS

The Mexic-Arte Museum presents traditional and contemporary Mexican, Latino, and Latin American art with the goal of reaching visitors of all ages. Its permanent collection and special exhibitions showcase the work of established and emerging artists in such media as prints, sculptures, photographs, masks, murals, and installations.

The museum's mission of youth outreach is evident in its educational programs. For example, artist educators teach courses for underserved students at local schools. The museum also provides formal gallery space for local teens to display their artwork and teams up with other museums to present teacher workshops during the summer.

Illustrated Encyclopedia

Among the Mexic-Arte Museum's collection of rare books is this encyclopedia volume titled *México a través de los siglos (Mexico Through the Centuries)*. When the encyclopedia was published in 1884, it was advertised as the complete social, political, religious, military, artistic, scientific, and literary history of Mexico from ancient times to the late 1800s. This rare book is among the more than 5,000 books and periodicals housed in the museum's library, which has a collection that dates from the 19th century to the present day.

Calaveras Print

This 19th-century print by Mexican artist Manuel Alfonso Manilla (1830–1895) features imagery of skeletons, or *calaveras*, which is common in indigenous Aztec art. Manilla often used calaveras to depict religious themes and create caricatures. A caricature is an illustration that exaggerates prominent characteristics of a subject, usually in order to ridicule the subject.

From 1882 to 1892, Manilla worked as an illustrator and engraver with a Mexico City publishing house. He created artwork to accompany songs, or *corridos*, and drew story characters and scenes of street life, bullfighting, and circuses.

Tree of Life

A Tree of Life is a form of Mexican folk art inspired by the metal candelabras, or candleholders, and incense burners that Spanish friars brought to Mexico. Originally sculpted from clay, early Trees of Life depicted the biblical story of creation. Today's sculptures display a wide variety of themes. This ceramic Tree of Life by renowned Mexican potter Alfonso Castillo Orta (1944–2009) focuses on the theme of spring. The goddess of spring appears in the center of the tree near the bottom.

How does Alfonso Castillo Orta represent spring in this Tree of Life?

Queen of the Huipil

In this 1988 photograph, Mexican-born photographer Jesse Herrera (1945–) captures the coronation of the Queen of the Huipil during an annual festival held in the community of Cuetzalan in Mexico. Elders from the community select a festival queen based partly on the quality of her *huipil*, a traditional woven garment. The queen is crowned with a white cloth and paraded on an ornate chair, as shown here.

Tecuani Mask and Costume

Tecuani means "jaguar" or "tiger" in Nahuatl, a language spoken by indigenous people in central and southern Mexico. This mask and costume come from the state of Guerrero in southwestern Mexico. Dancers wear this kind of costume in performances of a traditional Mexican dance called *Danza de los Tecuanes*, or Dance of the Jaguars.

Originally, the dance represented an event in which two tribes joined together to fight a jaguar that had been attacking their livestock. Today, the dance is performed at religious celebrations and cultural events in Mexico and in the United States, including Day of the Dead celebrations. Day of the Dead is a Mexican holiday in November that focuses on remembering family members and friends who have died.

This mask is made of hand-carved glass with boar bristles and a leather tongue.

TENSIONS WITH MEXICO

What would you consider a legitimate reason to wage war? Like people around the world, Americans have different answers to this question. In the 1840s, many Americans—both prominent leaders and everyday citizens—doubted the reasons for waging war with Mexico.

THE ELECTION OF 1844

Debate about adding Texas as a state in the Union began almost as soon as the Republic of Texas won its independence in 1836 and continued for years. The presidential campaign of 1844 brought the issue to the forefront of American politics. The Democrats nominated **James K. Polk**, a former governor of Tennessee and a staunch supporter of manifest destiny, as their candidate. Polk had supported Martin Van Buren as the party's presidential nominee and had only wanted to be vice president. But Van Buren did not support the annexation of Texas, which cost him the support of southerners—and the nomination.

Polk was the first **dark horse** to run for the nation's highest office. A dark horse is a little-known candidate whose nomination is unexpected and usually the result of a compromise between factions. Polk and the Democrats appealed to both northerners and southerners with a platform promoting U.S. expansion. They addressed the issue of slavery by proposing to balance the admission of Texas as a slave state with the admission of Oregon as a free territory.

The Whigs nominated prominent Kentucky statesman Henry Clay for president on a platform opposing further U.S. expansion. However, Clay soon came to believe that such a stance would cost him the presidency. He changed his position and supported the annexation of Texas on the condition that it be achieved peacefully. But his strategy backfired, and he won only a few expansionist votes while losing those of abolitionists and other opponents of annexation. Clay's campaign was damaged even more by the presence of a third party, the abolitionist Liberty Party, in the election. Though the Liberty Party only won 62,000 votes, its strong showing in New York drew enough votes away from Clay to give the state's electoral votes to Polk, which made the difference in the national election. Although Polk won only 49.5 percent of the popular vote, he received 170 votes from the electoral college against Clay's 105 votes. That was enough to secure him the election. He entered office with the clear goal of annexing Texas and Oregon.

This presidential campaign ribbon from 1844 features portraits of Democratic candidate James Polk and his running mate, George Dallas.

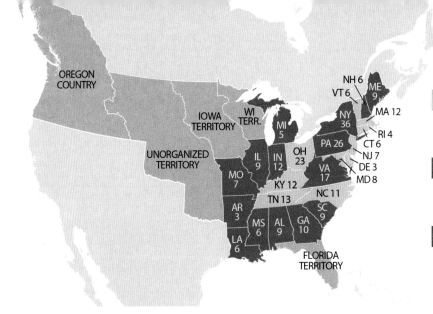

The 1844 Election

POLK'S FOUR GOALS

Polk had promised to serve only one term as president, but he planned to accomplish a great deal in those four years. He had campaigned on four goals. One was to add two new states to the Union by annexing the Republic of Texas and acquiring full control of the Oregon Territory from Great Britain. His second goal was to reduce tariffs on imports, which he believed would lower the cost of products for American consumers. His third goal was to re-establish an independent U.S. Treasury, which would manage all government funds, thus limiting the influence of unregulated state banks. The lending practices of the state banks had contributed to a depression in the late 1830s. Polk's fourth goal was to acquire the territories of California and New Mexico. Polk eventually would achieve all four goals.

Even before Polk took office, Congress voted to annex Texas as a new slave state in 1845. But the admission of Texas to the Union meant that slave states outnumbered free states in the U.S. Senate. The admission of Oregon as a free state would be needed to restore the balance.

For years, expansionists had sounded the rallying cry "Fifty-Four Forty or Fight." They wanted the United States to gain control of all the Oregon Territory up to its boundary with Russian territory at the latitude of 54° 40'. During the presidential campaign, Polk had agreed. But after winning the election, he instructed his secretary of state, James Buchanan, to negotiate secretly with Great Britain to relinquish, or give up, its claims to the Oregon Territory below the 49th parallel, which formed the northern boundary of the United States to the east. This deal angered northern Democrats, who had supported Polk on Texas, because it would decrease the size and eventual electoral power of Oregon. In 1846, the United States and Great Britain signed the Oregon Treaty, setting the border between Oregon and Canada at the 49th parallel.

POLK PROVOKES WAR

The Mexican government had never recognized the independence of Texas, so the United States' annexation of Texas increased tensions between the two countries. In addition, the two countries did not agree on the boundary between them. Polk insisted that the **Rio Grande** was the border between Texas and Mexico, but Mexico considered the **Nueces River**, which was much farther north, to be the border.

Polk wanted to fight Mexico but did not want to be blamed for starting a war. Instead, he provoked one. In July 1845, Polk ordered American troops under the command of General Zachary Taylor to cross the Nueces River into disputed territory. The Mexican government claimed that the United States had invaded Mexico, committing an act of war. Even though the Mexican Army lacked funds, effective weapons, and training, Mexican president José Joaquín de Herrera ordered troops to assemble at the Rio Grande.

There, on April 25, 1846, American and Mexican forces fought a battle that left 11 Americans dead and 5 wounded. The Mexicans captured the remainder of the American troops. More skirmishes followed, and on May 11, President Polk announced to Congress that Mexico had "invaded our territory and shed the blood of our fellow citizens on our own soil." In response, Congress declared war, and the **Mexican-American War** began on May 13, 1846.

While the United States was negotiating a peace treaty with Mexico, Senator John Calhoun of South Carolina delivered a speech to his peers in which he opposed a proposal to annex all of Mexico because he did not want Mexicans or Native Americans to become American citizens. In this excerpt from his speech, he explains why he argued against the Mexican-American War from the beginning.

I opposed the war then, not only because I considered it unnecessary, and that it might have been easily avoided; not only because I thought the President had no authority to order a portion of the territory in dispute and in possession of the Mexicans, to be occupied by our troops; not only because I believed the allegations upon which it was sanctioned by Congress, were unfounded in truth; but from high considerations of reason and policy, because I believed it would lead to great and serious evils to the country, and greatly endanger its free institutions.

—from a speech to the Senate by John C. Calhoun, January 4, 1848

DIFFERENT ATTITUDES TOWARD WAR

The Mexican-American War had widespread support in the South and West, where people hoped a victory would open new lands for American settlement and the expansion of slavery. Although many northerners denounced the war and American motives, Polk had no difficulty getting congressional approval because he linked the war to support for U.S. troops.

Debate over the war continued, however. Some Americans, particularly those who opposed slavery, viewed the conflict as an immoral land grab that violated the nation's democratic principles. Former president John Quincy Adams opposed the war, as did such northern abolitionists as William Lloyd Garrison and Charles Sumner, who believed that it was being fought so that southerners could expand slavery and increase cotton production. Author Henry David Thoreau spent a night in jail for refusing to pay taxes that would fund the war. In response to the opposition, Polk accused his critics of treason and insisted that the war was just and necessary.

As the war dragged on for more than a year, opposition grew. In December 1847, Illinois congressman Abraham Lincoln, then a young newcomer to the U.S. House of Representatives, introduced the "Spot Resolutions." This legislation called on President Polk to identify the "spot" where American blood had first been spilled in order to determine if the bloodshed had actually occurred on U.S. soil. Congress never acted on the resolutions. But in January 1847, the House of Representatives passed a law censuring Polk for "unnecessarily and unconstitutionally" beginning the Mexican-American War.

AMERICAN PLACES

The Rio Grande, Texas

The Rio Grande forms the southern boundary of Big Bend National Park, a protected area of canyons and waterfalls at the southernmost bend of the river in southwest Texas. The huge bend in the river curves around the largest protected portion of the Chihuahuan Desert. The Rio Grande serves as the border between Mexico (top) and the United States for about 1,000 miles. Early in the Mexican-American War, this border, and therefore access to this important river, was disputed.

HISTORICAL THINKING

1. **READING CHECK** What were the four goals of James Polk's 1844 presidential campaign?

2. **ANALYZE CAUSE AND EFFECT** How did James Birney and the Liberty Party affect the election of 1844?

3. **COMPARE AND CONTRAST** How did attitudes about the Mexican-American War differ among Americans?

4. **INTERPRET MAPS** How would you describe the voting pattern in the 1844 election?

WAGING WAR IN THE SOUTHWEST

The Southwest is known for its breathtaking landscape. The Grand Canyon, Bryce Canyon, and Yosemite Valley are just a few of the region's stunning features. Once belonging to Mexico, these natural treasures are part of the bounty the United States gained with its victory in the Mexican-American War.

WAR WITH MEXICO

The United States began the Mexican-American War on strong footing. In June 1846, General **Stephen Kearny** led about 1,700 American soldiers from Fort Leavenworth, Kansas, to Santa Fe, the capital of the New Mexico Territory. Kearny's troops traveled for two months before reaching their destination, but they took control of the city without firing a shot. With this one victory, the United States claimed all of the New Mexico Territory.

Kearny's next goal was to gain control of California. By the time Kearny arrived in San Diego in December 1846, U.S. Navy Commodore Robert Stockton had captured and blockaded the three major ports of California: San Francisco, Los Angeles, and San Diego. A power struggle emerged between the two men, each believing that President Polk had put him in charge. When Lieutenant Colonel John C. Frémont, also under orders from Polk, joined the two officers, he sided with Stockton. In return, Stockton named Frémont governor of California.

Frémont had been serving in California clandestinely, or secretly, with possible orders to encourage Americans living in California to rebel against the Mexican government. On June 14, 1846, about 30 American settlers in Sonoma, California, took control of the town and raised their own flag, which featured a grizzly bear. The design later became the inspiration for California's state flag. The flag also inspired the name of the **insurrection**, or rebellion, which became known as the **Bear Flag Revolt**. The rebels declared California an independent republic—the **Bear Flag Republic**. A few weeks later, Frémont

took command of the American rebels and seized the **presidio**, or Spanish military settlement, of San Francisco, which was empty at the time.

The independent Bear Flag Republic ended three weeks after it began, however. American forces soon claimed San Francisco and the surrounding region for the United States. By January 1847, all of California was under American control. Kearny took over and became territorial governor of California. He arrested Frémont and sent him east to Washington, D.C., where he was court-martialed for disobedience and other offenses. But President Polk stepped in and reversed Frémont's sentence. Frémont retained public support and eventually returned to California, where he became the first senator to represent the state in the U.S. Congress.

Westward Expansion, 1783–1853

An 1851 print by German artist Carl Nebel captures the moment General Winfield Scott discovered that the Mexican Army had retreated from Mexico City overnight, forcing local politicians to surrender the capital to the Americans.

AMERICANS INVADE MEXICO

Meanwhile, in Texas, General Zachary Taylor had been moving south. He crossed the Rio Grande on May 18, a few days after war was officially declared. In September 1846, he conquered the city of Monterrey after a five-day siege. In early 1847, at the Battle of Buena Vista (BWAY-nuh VEES-tuh), Taylor fought against Mexican troops led by General Santa Anna. While no clear winner emerged, the Mexican Army suffered far greater casualties than the Americans did, and Taylor became a hero in the United States.

Taylor's troops next joined those commanded by General Winfield Scott on the east coast of Mexico, near Veracruz. The Mexican fort at Veracruz was considered to be nearly impossible to capture. Scott employed the largest **amphibious force** ever used by the United States up to that time. An amphibious force consists of troops attacking from both land and sea. After a three-week siege, Scott succeeded in taking Veracruz without losing many of his soldiers. Then he headed inland toward Mexico City, where Americans fought for days before they finally captured the last fort protecting the city in September 1847. With its capital city under American control, Mexico surrendered.

Mexico and the United States signed the treaty that officially ended the war, the **Treaty of Guadalupe Hidalgo**, on February 2, 1848. Under the terms of the treaty, the Rio Grande became the boundary between Texas and Mexico. In exchange for $15 million, Mexico relinquished all of its northernmost territories, including all or part of the present-day states of California, New Mexico, Arizona, Utah, Nevada, Colorado, and Wyoming. The U.S.-acquired territory constituted more than half of Mexico's total territory and increased the area of the United States by one-third. Polk had achieved his fourth goal of acquiring the territories of California and New Mexico.

In 1853, the United States completed its last land deal with Mexico. In the **Gadsden Purchase**, the United States paid $10 million for an area of land located along the southern borders of present-day Arizona and New Mexico. The United States wanted this land to complete a southern transcontinental railroad. The transaction completed the borders of the **contiguous**, or connected, United States.

HISTORICAL THINKING

1. **READING CHECK** How did the Mexican-American War end?

2. **SUMMARIZE** What were the consequences of the Mexican-American War for the United States and for Mexico?

3. **INTERPRET MAPS** Through what single land purchase or treaty did the United States gain the largest area of land between 1845 and 1855?

SETTLING CALIFORNIA

Today, California is the leading economic powerhouse of the United States. But both the Spanish and the Mexicans largely ignored the territory when they owned it. Even so, their influence on California is readily apparent.

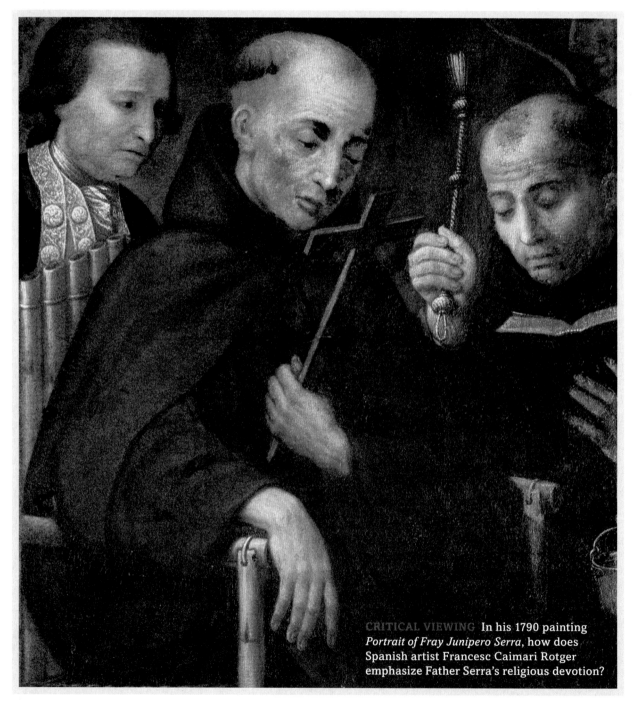

CRITICAL VIEWING In his 1790 painting *Portrait of Fray Junipero Serra*, how does Spanish artist Francesc Caimari Rotger emphasize Father Serra's religious devotion?

MISSIONS AND RANCHOS

As you have read, Spain first explored and claimed California in the 1500s but was slow to establish settlements there. In the mid-1700s, Russian and British fur trappers in the Pacific Northwest began to expand their hunting and trading activities farther south. To reinforce their land claims, the Spanish then sent priests and soldiers to establish settlements.

In 1769, **Father Junípero Serra** (hoo-NEE-peh-roh SEH-rah), a Catholic priest from Spain, built the first mission in California at San Diego. The Spanish went on to establish 21 missions throughout California, each a day's ride apart. Protected by soldiers housed in nearby presidios, these church-centered missions grew into villages and agricultural centers. They formed the foundations for many California cities, including San Diego, Los Angeles, and San Francisco.

Like other mission priests, Father Serra sought to convert the local Native Americans to Christianity. As you have read, the mission system was devastating to many Native Americans, who were often mistreated and exploited for their labor. Father Serra's relationship with the Native Americans under his authority is the subject of controversy. While a number of historians believe he was a generous, caring, and courageous man who did his best to improve the lives of Native Americans, others claim he participated in the abuse and oppression of Native Americans at the Spanish missions.

Mexico won its independence from Spain in 1821 and ended the mission system in California in 1833. The Mexican government granted most of the mission land to **Californios**, or settlers of Spanish or Mexican descent. These land grants formed large estates called **ranchos**. Each rancho covered thousands of acres. The rancheros, or owners, raised large herds of cattle for their hides and tallow, or processed fat. They traded the hides and tallow for manufactured goods, which were shipped along the Pacific Coast. Most of the hides went to New England boot- and shoemakers, while the tallow was processed into candles and soap in South America. Many Native Americans ended up working on the ranchos, often receiving only basic housing and food for their labor.

California was too far away for the authorities in Mexico City to govern it effectively. Feeling neglected and yet also increasingly independent, Californios staged numerous revolts against the Mexican government. By 1845, residents had effectively achieved home rule and had a locally born governor, Pío Pico, a ranchero of mixed Mexican and African descent. But California remained sparsely populated, with a Native American population numbering less than 150,000 and about 7,000 non-native people living there. By the end of 1849, the non-native population would reach nearly 100,000.

A GROWING AMERICAN PRESENCE

In the 1830s, Americans began migrating to California as part of the overall westward movement. A majority of the American immigrants were male traders, who typically blended into the local culture, married local women, learned Spanish, and became Mexican citizens. Most of these traders lived in the coastal cities, such as Los Angeles, San Diego, and San Francisco.

Fur trappers and farming families also moved to California, following the California spur of the Oregon Trail. These groups settled more often in northern California and usually remained separate from the Californios, due to differences in culture and religious beliefs. While most Californios were Roman Catholics, the majority of immigrants were Protestants. The immigrants tended to form their own settlements. Some received land grants from the Mexican government to establish ranchos.

One of the largest of these immigrant settlements was Nueva Helvetia, or New Switzerland, which later became the city of Sacramento. Swiss immigrant **John Sutter**, who received several land grants from the Mexican government to start a colony, founded the settlement. By the late 1840s, Sutter's settlement had become a thriving farm community. Besides raising herds of cattle like other California rancheros, residents also grew grapes and wheat, thus helping to diversify the region's agriculture.

Despite the influx of immigrants from the United States and other countries, Californios still formed the majority of the population when the United States acquired California in 1848 through the Treaty of Guadalupe Hidalgo. But that situation would soon change.

HISTORICAL THINKING

1. **READING CHECK** What was a rancho?

2. **SUMMARIZE** How did Native Americans in California fare under Spanish rule?

3. **MAKE INFERENCES** Why was it difficult for the government in Mexico City to effectively govern California?

4. **COMPARE AND CONTRAST** How is the history of Mexican California similar to the history of Mexican Texas?

THE GOLD RUSH

Eureka is an ancient Greek word meaning "I have found it." Supposedly, shouts of "Eureka!" rang through the Sierra Nevada foothills in the first few months of the California gold rush. But the supply of easy gold had dwindled by the time most of the gold seekers showed up.

GOLD DIGGERS

The Native Americans of California had always known about the gold in the rocks and creeks of their homeland, but they did not value it the way Europeans did. On January 24, 1848, when a worker building a sawmill for John Sutter spied glittering flecks of gold in the stream that powered the mill, everything changed. Sutter swore the worker to secrecy, but it didn't take long for word to spread. By the end of the year, **prospectors**, or people in search of valuable natural resources, swarmed the western foothills of the Sierra Nevada, collecting nuggets and gold dust worth about $6 million. Local Native Americans were among the first to participate in the mining. Territorial governor Richard Mason estimated that in 1848, more than half the gold miners were Native Americans. By the end of 1849, more than 700 ships carrying in excess of 45,000 prospective gold miners—most of them from the eastern United States—had sailed to California. About 55,000 new settlers followed, arriving from the overland trails that cut across the continent. The newcomers formed a **gold rush**, a large-scale, rapid movement of people to a place where gold has been discovered.

CRITICAL VIEWING American and Chinese miners work on a site outside Sacramento, California, in 1852. Based on what the men hold and wear, what equipment was essential to search for gold?

Whether they came by sea or land, the fortune-seekers were a mixed group. The majority of **forty-niners** —gold miners named for the year they began arriving in California—were Americans, but people came from all over the world. Stories of *Gam Saan*, or "Gold Mountain," sparked gold fever in China. In 1852 alone, over 20,000 Chinese gold seekers arrived in California. Prospectors from Peru, Chile, and especially from Sonora, Mexico, which had experienced a gold rush of its own in the early 1800s, also streamed into California. In fact, many Latino gold-seekers were skilled miners. Some African Americans came too. Most were from the cities of New England or were enslaved people bound to southern forty-niners. Women were less likely to be victims of gold fever. By 1850, only 8 percent of California's entire population was female. But a few women made a good living as **entrepreneurs**, or organizers of new businesses. And some women did try their luck at mining and struck gold.

Whatever their ethnicity or gender, few miners made a fortune, aside from the lucky handful present at the beginning of the gold rush. However, California flourished. Many who first came to find gold decided to stay and became farmers, teachers, builders, and traders. In fact, the largest fortunes in California were made not in the gold fields, but from supplying miners with clothing, food, and equipment. One of the most famous California gold rush entrepreneurs was Levi Strauss, a dry goods salesman who had emigrated from Germany. He moved to San Francisco, where he produced and sold the tough denim blue jeans still popular today.

THE MINING FRONTIER

Although movies and books romanticized it, mining was a dangerous, unpleasant business. Disease, violence, and miserable living conditions were part of daily life in mining camps. The death rate from illness, accident, murder, and suicide was extremely high. One out of every five forty-niners died within six months of arriving in the gold fields.

Mining life was especially hard for certain ethnic groups. Some Native Americans were worked to death, while others were driven away or murdered. The government sanctioned this violence. In 1851, California's first governor, Peter Hardeman Burnett, declared that "a war of extermination will continue to be waged between the two races until the Indian race becomes extinct." Latino and Chinese miners also were frequently exploited as laborers, sifting gold from the sand and gravel of streambeds. The Foreign Miners License Tax, passed in 1852, was imposed

almost solely on the Chinese. Until it was declared unconstitutional in 1870, it provided nearly a quarter of California's yearly revenue.

Most miners did not intend to settle in California permanently; they planned to make their fortunes and go back home. Mining camps that had turned into **boomtowns**, or towns that grow suddenly, were abandoned on an almost daily basis. Maintaining law and order amid such chaos was extremely difficult. The territorial, and later the state, government passed mining codes and established mining districts. But many mining areas were too remote to govern effectively, and the stream of new prospectors was constant. Miners ended up forming their own self-governing districts. Each district elected an official who recorded all the claims and settled disputes. Miners administered justice themselves, often by banishing or hanging offenders.

The lawlessness in the mining camps created a demand for stronger government, which statehood would bring. California easily met the population requirements for statehood, but residents wanted it to be admitted as a free state. California's constitution explicitly stated: "neither slavery nor involuntary servitude . . . shall ever be tolerated in this state." Even though its admission would upset the balance between slave and free states, California became the nation's 31st state in September 1850.

HISTORICAL THINKING

1. **READING CHECK** How were the largest fortunes in California made during the gold rush?

2. **ANALYZE CAUSE AND EFFECT** How did the discovery of gold in 1848 affect California?

3. **IDENTIFY MAIN IDEAS AND DETAILS** What was life like in the mining camps of California during the gold rush?

4.3 **GEOLOGY IN HISTORY**

MAIN IDEA In the 1850s and 1860s, geology largely determined the railroad route that would connect California with the rest of the country.

How Geology Built the Transcontinental Railroad

By Andrés Ruzo, National Geographic Explorer

People often say that the shortest distance between two points is a straight line. But a railroad route between two places is rarely straight. The area's geology has to be dealt with.

CONNECTING THE EAST WITH THE WEST

After California achieved statehood, many people believed the United States needed a **transcontinental railroad**—a railroad that would cross the continent to the West. Trains already linked the East, South, and Midwest. But settlers heading to the Pacific Coast had to travel by wagon or stagecoach on a journey that took months. A railroad connecting the regions would not only provide more efficient transportation but also unite all parts of the growing country.

Many of those who supported the creation of a transcontinental railroad were nonetheless divided over what route it should take. In general, northerners called for a route passing through northern states and territories. Southerners, on the other hand, advocated for a route that would run through the territory acquired in the Gadsden Purchase: present-day southern Arizona and southern New Mexico. Both sides knew that a transcontinental railroad would bring new businesses and industries and increased trade to the stops along the route.

In the 1850s, Congress sponsored several groups of surveyors to explore possible routes for the railroad. The surveyors mapped the **topography** of the land west of the Mississippi, studying its physical features, including mountains, valleys, and bodies of water, as well as its human-made features. They also documented the Native American tribes living in the West and the region's plants and animals. The surveyors looked for areas with fertile soil, forests, and navigable rivers. Having these resources accessible along the chosen route would not only make construction cheaper and easier but also promote settlements along the way. Above all, the surveyors tried to plot routes that would run mostly along flat or gently sloping terrain.

OVERCOMING GEOLOGIC FEATURES

A man named Theodore Judah, however, had his own ideas about the route. Judah was a construction engineer who had helped build the first railroad in California. For the transcontinental railroad, he proposed a northern route through Nebraska, Wyoming, Utah, Nevada, and California. Those who objected to Judah's plan pointed out the many

Trains used the Summit Tunnel at Donner Pass, shown here, for 130 years. Today, this line of the railroad is bypassed, and the tunnel has been abandoned.

Andesite Peak
8,215 ft *(2,504 m)*

DONNER RIDGE

Donner Pass
7,093 ft *(2,162 m)*

Donner Lake

Mount Judah
8,245 ft *(2,513 m)*

Mount Lincoln
8,369 ft *(2,551 m)*

Transcontinental Railroad

Elevation above sea level	
7,550–9,200 ft	2,301–2,804 m
6,700–7,549 ft	2,042–2,301 m
6,200–6,699 ft	1,890–2,042 m
1,800–6,199 ft	549–1,889 m

scale varies with perspective

physical obstacles, including the Sierra Nevada, the mountain range running along the eastern edge of California. To build level tracks, engineers would use explosives to blast tunnels through the range's granite peaks.

Daniel Strong, a drugstore owner in California, liked Judah's proposed route and offered his help. Strong showed Judah a path through the Donner Pass, a mountain pass in the northern Sierra Nevada. A **mountain pass** is a passageway through a mountain range that is lower than the surrounding peaks. As geologic forces, such as glaciers and earthquakes, eroded and shaped mountain ranges over millions of years, they created these passes. The Donner Pass would require the railroad route to cross one of the Sierra Nevada's summits rather than two. Judah's route would also follow already established trails, including the Oregon and Mormon trails.

Together, Judah and Strong found investors to fund their plan, and Judah presented it to Congress in 1861. The legislators expressed doubts about the proposal, but President Abraham Lincoln, who was a great supporter of a transcontinental railroad, endorsed it. And by that time, the country was engaged in the Civil War between the North and the South. That meant that the southern route was no longer under consideration. Congress passed the **Pacific Railways Acts** in 1862 and 1864, which authorized two companies to build the railroad: the **Central Pacific Company** and the **Union Pacific Company**. It was decided that the Central Pacific Company would begin laying tracks in Sacramento, California, while the Union Pacific Company would start in Omaha, Nebraska. The two lines would meet in the middle.

After laborers worked 12 to 16 hours a day, 7 days a week for about 6 years building bridges, blasting tunnels, and laying tracks, locomotives from each company met nose to nose at Promontory Point, Utah, on May 10, 1869. The president of the Central Pacific Company drove a golden spike into the tracks to commemorate the route—an achievement dictated by geology.

THINK LIKE A GEOLOGIST

1. **READING CHECK** Why did many Americans want to build a transcontinental railroad in the 1850s?

2. **MAKE INFERENCES** What physical features besides mountains might have posed a challenge to those building the transcontinental railroad?

3. **DRAW CONCLUSIONS** In what ways did geology dictate the railroad's route?

Use each of the following vocabulary words in a sentence that shows an understanding of the term's meaning.

1. mountain man

   The mountain man lived alone and trapped beaver in the Rocky Mountains.

2. manifest destiny   7. rancho

3. vaquero   8. gold rush

4. empresario   9. forty-niner

5. dark horse   10. boomtown

6. presidio

READING STRATEGY
ANALYZE CAUSE AND EFFECT

Analyzing causes and effects can help a reader understand the reasons that an event occurred. Complete the following graphic organizer with reasons for the westward migration of the 1840s and 1850s and answer the question.

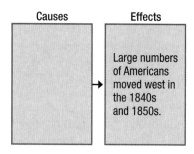

Causes   Effects

Large numbers of Americans moved west in the 1840s and 1850s.

11. What push and pull factors contributed to the westward migration of Americans in the 1840s and 1850s?

MAIN IDEAS

Answer the following questions. Support your answers with evidence from the chapter.

12. What role did the concept of manifest destiny play in the westward migration of Americans? **LESSON 1.1**

13. Why did the westward migration of the pioneers particularly threaten the way of life of the Plains tribes? **LESSON 1.3**

14. Why did the Mexican government encourage American immigration to Tejas? **LESSON 2.1**

15. Why did both Tejanos and Americans in Tejas want to separate from Mexico? **LESSON 2.2**

16. Why did the Mexican-American War have widespread support in the South? **LESSON 3.1**

17. How did the outcome of the Mexican-American War benefit the United States? **LESSON 3.2**

18. How did the change from Spanish to Mexican rule affect California? **LESSON 4.1**

19. How did the gold rush of 1848 affect the drive for statehood in California? **LESSON 4.2**

HISTORICAL THINKING

Answer the following questions. Support your answers with evidence from the chapter.

20. **IDENTIFY PROBLEMS AND SOLUTIONS** What problems did the annexation of Texas create for the United States?

21. **SEQUENCE EVENTS** In what order did the United States acquire the lands west of the Louisiana Purchase?

22. **ANALYZE CAUSE AND EFFECT** What effect did the gold rush of 1848 have on Native Americans in California?

23. **DRAW CONCLUSIONS** What was the ultimate goal of the Texan fight for independence from Mexico?

24. **FORM AND SUPPORT OPINIONS** What is your opinion of the concept of manifest destiny?

25. **DESCRIBE** Who were the forty-niners? Describe their characteristics and backgrounds.

The political cartoon by Nathaniel Currier at right is titled "The Independent Gold Hunter on His Way to California" and was first published in 1849. This cartoon contrasted with other popular depictions of the forty-niners. Newspapers sensationalized stories of miners getting rich after a short time in California. Many artists portrayed the forty-niners as brave and ambitious heroes. Study this illustration closely. Then answer the questions that follow.

26. What equipment is the man carrying?

27. What is unusual about the way the man is dressed?

28. Based on details in the cartoon, what is the artist's attitude toward the gold hunter?

ANALYZE SOURCES

The United States Constitution states that only Congress can declare war. On May 11, 1846, after American forces had clashed with Mexican troops in eastern Texas, President Polk addressed Congress and requested a declaration of war on Mexico. Read this excerpt from his address. Then answer the question.

> Mexico has passed the boundary of the United States, has invaded our territory and shed American blood upon American soil. She has proclaimed that hostilities have commenced and that the two nations are now at war.
>
> As war exists, and, notwithstanding all our efforts to avoid it, exists by the act of Mexico herself, we are called upon by every consideration of duty and patriotism to vindicate with decision the honor, the rights, and the interests of our country.

29. How does Polk characterize Mexico's actions and the position of the United States?

30. How does Polk justify declaring war on Mexico?

CONNECT TO YOUR LIFE

31. **ARGUMENT** Think about the migrants who headed west in the 1840s. Many were Americans who were moving to Mexican territories in search of land and better opportunities. Today, emigrants from Mexico and many other nations come to the United States in search of a better life. Should the United States welcome such immigration or severely limit it? Write a short essay stating your opinion and supporting it with reasons and evidence.

TIPS

• State your opinion on whether immigration to the United States should be encouraged or severely restricted.

• Provide at least two reasons that support your opinion.

• Use information from the chapter, if possible, as well as your own observations and facts obtained by research to provide evidence for your argument.

• Address any counterarguments.

• Conclude your essay by summarizing your position.

Nat Turner's Complex Legacy

by Justin Fornal

Adapted from "Nat Turner's Slave Uprising Left Complex Legacy,"
by Justin Fornal, news.nationalgeographic.com, October 5, 2016

Nat Turner was an African-American slave preacher in Virginia who led the bloodiest slave rebellion in American history.

In the 185 years that followed, Turner's place in history has been reinterpreted and revised. His legacy is debated, and even more so today, with Turner's Bible now on display in the National Museum of African American History and Culture and the release of the 2016 film *The Birth of a Nation*, chronicling Turner's life and revolt.

After the revolt, Turner was captured, tried, and executed. Much of our knowledge of Turner comes from the town where he was jailed, which is today Courtland, Virginia. There, he was interviewed by lawyer Thomas Ruffin Gray. The interviews were compiled in a pamphlet titled "The Confessions of Nat Turner: The Leader of the Late Insurrection in Southampton, Virginia." This serves as the main historical record of who Nat Turner was. But it's an imperfect record. Some historians think Gray took personal liberties with how he presented Turner.

Nat Turner was born into slavery on October 2, 1800, on the Benjamin Turner family plantation in Virginia. Having learned to read at an early age, Turner was considered an intellectual at the time, as teaching slaves to read was highly frowned upon.

Throughout his life, Turner would look to the Bible to better understand the reasons behind slavery. His wisdom and natural oratorial skills led him to become a respected preacher among the surrounding slave community. Early on, he interpreted that the Bible said that slaves should remain subservient to their earthly masters, but a series of prophetic visions and a solar eclipse changed his views. These events convinced Turner that it was his destiny to unite black men and women, both enslaved and free, to fight against slavery.

On August 21, 1831, Turner met with a group of fellow conspirators and took a vow to kill all slave owners they encountered, including women and children. The group traveled from farm to farm, slaughtering whites and freeing blacks. Many of the enslaved chose not to join the revolt, and some even fought to protect their masters. At most stops the rebel force grew, at one point reaching around 40 recruits. Over the next two days the rebels killed at least 55 whites. Soon the local militia caught the group. However, Turner delayed capture by hiding in the woods for two months. Once found, Turner was sentenced to death for "conspiring to rebel and make insurrection." On November 11, he was hanged.

Desperate to regain control in the wake of the rebellion, white militias unleashed a wave of violence and intimidation against both enslaved and free blacks throughout the region. Many innocent people who had nothing to do with the incident were killed.

It is rumored that after Nat Turner was hanged, he was decapitated, quartered, and skinned. Allegedly, pieces of his skin were given out as souvenirs. This would have been done in an attempt to crush Turner's legacy and prevent him from being a martyr.

But Turner's story is now undergoing a resurgence. The 2016 film presents Turner as a patriot. And his descendants and the descendants of survivors of the revolt are in the news debating his legacy.

Today in Courtland, monuments stand in honor of the Confederate military. There's a plaque noting the rebellion, but those who see Nat Turner as a hero believe that just as the Confederate memorials stand to benefit descendants of southern soldiers, it is only fair that descendants of the enslaved should have a place to pay homage to figures such as Nat Turner, who gave his life to fight for their freedom.

For more from National Geographic, check out "The Way West" online.

UNIT INQUIRY: Document a Migration

In this unit, you learned about the physical expansion and growth in population of the United States during the first half of the 19th century. As the nation enlarged its boundaries, hundreds of thousands of Americans migrated westward, undertaking long and challenging journeys. What drove Americans to pull up roots and move their families west? What were their journeys like? What did they find when they arrived at their final destinations?

ASSIGNMENT

Assume the role of a 19th-century American who is moving west. Create a journal in which you describe:

- who you are and where you live now
- the reasons you want to move (push-pull factors)
- why you chose a particular destination
- the route you take
- what you pack
- challenges and encounters on the journey
- how many miles and days you travel
- what you find and do at your destination

Be prepared to share your journal with the class.

Plan As you plan your journal entries, review the unit to gather evidence about the experiences of those who journeyed west in the early 1800s. Conduct additional research as necessary. Use a graphic organizer like this one to take notes.

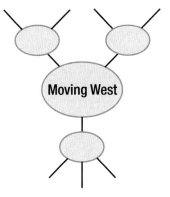

Moving West

Produce Begin your journal entries with actual dates. Include a map of your route and sketches or photographs of the landscapes you travel through. Focus on creating a realistic account of the experiences of migrants of the time. Be sure to cover these topics: *decision* (push-pull factors); *planning* (route and destination, what to pack); *journey* (landscapes, challenges, hardships, encounters); *destination* (miles covered, number of days, result).

Present Choose a creative way to present your journal to the class. Consider one of these options:

- Introduce yourself and select a few journal entries to read aloud to the class. Then allow class members to pose questions for you to answer.

- Post your journal online and invite the class to access it. Encourage readers to share their reactions and comments and to ask questions. Answer classmates' questions after they are posted.

- Hold a discussion in which classmates share what they learned from the journal writing assignment. Take a poll of the class, asking how many would actually be willing to risk such a trip.

NATIONAL GEOGRAPHIC | LEARNING FRAMEWORK ACTIVITIES

Depict Nature

SKILL Observation

KNOWLEDGE Our Living Planet

During the 19th century, many artists and writers celebrated the beauty and wonder of the American landscape in their work. Select and explore a natural site near you. It could be a park, beach, nature trail, or some other natural site. While you are there, take notes or photographs of what you observe, including physical features, animals, or plant life. Choose a way to depict your observations to share with your class. Either present the photos you took or use your notes to write a poem or create a drawing.

Create Slogans to Promote Reforms

ATTITUDE Responsibility

KNOWLEDGE Our Human Story

While many Americans moved west in the early 1800s, others worked to address social problems in settled parts of the country. Working in a small group, review the unit to make a list of the various problems and injustices that reformers focused on. Write a short summary of each problem or injustice, including who was affected and how they were affected, and then create a slogan that identifies the kind of change that reformers sought. Share your slogans with the class in a creative way.

ARCHAEOLOGY AND U.S. HISTORY

Fredrik Hiebert

Archaeologist-in-Residence,
National Geographic Society

Dr. Hiebert directs archaeology
projects around the world and
recently curated an exhibition of
more than 500 Greek artifacts in
the National Geographic Museum.

Making sense of past events can be a complicated process. If history is the study of the past through written documents, such as firsthand accounts, letters, news reports, and inscriptions, then archaeology is the study of the human past through the **material record**—the buildings and objects that survive from a previous era. Archaeologists and historians are partners in preserving the human record.

Archaeology is the study of human-made objects, or **artifacts**, and the artifacts' context. An artifact tells a story by its style of manufacture, decoration, or inscription (words written on it). **Context** is the location of artifacts in the place of their last use or disposal. Context refers to where the artifacts were found, whether in the remains of buildings, in burial sites, on battlefields, or even in garbage pits.

This archaeological information sheds light on written histories that might tell only one side of the story. In fact, archaeology is one of the most important contributors to the interpretation of history here in the United States, from the original peopling of the continent right up to contemporary events.

For a look at American archaeology, start with the features on the opposite page. Then check out the map of U.S. archaeological sites that follows—archaeology may be just around the corner.

How does archaeology add to our understanding of U.S. history?

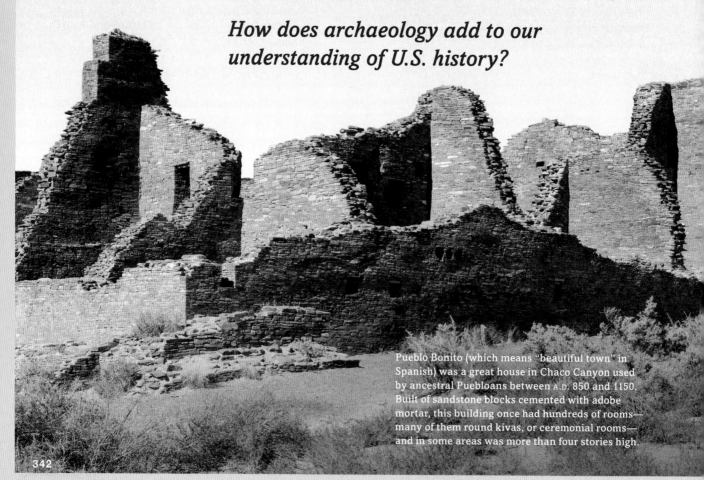

Pueblo Bonito (which means "beautiful town" in Spanish) was a great house in Chaco Canyon used by ancestral Puebloans between A.D. 850 and 1150. Built of sandstone blocks cemented with adobe mortar, this building once had hundreds of rooms—many of them round kivas, or ceremonial rooms—and in some areas was more than four stories high.

ARCHAEOLOGY AT A GLANCE

Archaeologists as First Responders

When disaster strikes, archaeologists are often among the first emergency personnel on the scene. Their expertise in proper excavation techniques is vital to the careful recovery of human remains and material evidence. The work of archaeologists, for example, sheds light on the real impact of the 9/11 devastation in New York City and the extent of the damage from Hurricane Katrina in New Orleans.

When the World Trade Center towers were destroyed, first responders included archaeologists. Instead of collecting artifacts such as ancient pottery, they collected wallets, briefcases, office supplies, and personal memorabilia of terrified workers forced to leave their belongings behind.

NatGeo Archaeology

National Geographic Society has a long history of archaeological exploration, including Hiram Bingham's work at the Inca site of Machu Picchu in the Andes in 1911. Today, Dr. Fredrik Hiebert is archaeologist-in-residence at National Geographic's headquarters in Washington, D.C. The Society has also been instrumental in conducting repatriations, the return of illegally excavated artifacts to their countries of origin.

National Geographic helps support ongoing excavation at Jamestown in Virginia, the site of the first permanent European settlement in North America.

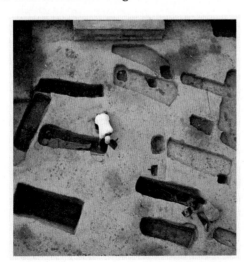

State Archaeologist

Did you know that every state in the union has an official archaeologist? These experts help direct archaeological research and discovery on nonfederal land and bring that information to the public through stewardship and education.

Native American Graves Protection and Repatriation Act (NAGPRA)

This 1990 act provides protection for Native American burial sites and better control over the removal of Native American human remains and artifacts. The act requires federal agencies to return excavated cultural items, including human remains, funerary objects, sacred objects, and objects of cultural heritage, to descendants and culturally affiliated Indian tribes.

ARCHAEOLOGY SITES
ACROSS THE COUNTRY

The *Indiana Jones* movies put the academic study of archaeology on the map—the *world* map, that is. You might be surprised to learn about the range of archaeological projects right in your own backyard. Use the map on this page to get familiar with some of the exciting and important work underway in the United States, and go to *America Through The Lens* online to find archaeological sites in your state.

Ozette, Washington
A Makah village, excavated after a mudslide in 1970, yielded more than 55,000 artifacts, thousands of them wooden.

Little Bighorn River, Montana
Archaeology has changed historical accounts of the Battle of the Little Bighorn in 1876. There, Native Americans of the Great Plains engaged with U.S. Army troops under General George Custer. Analysis of artifacts and bones found there revealed this to be a major Native American victory, despite reports—and legend—to the contrary.

Pueblo Bonito, New Mexico
Archaeologists have found nearly 300,000 artifacts here, including wooden flutes, human effigy vessels, and cylindrical pottery jars. This site continues to draw archaeologists and other scientists hoping to uncover new information on the culture that thrived here.

PACIFIC OCEAN

Santa Rosa Island, California
This is the home of Arlington Man, possibly the oldest human remains found in North America, dating to 13,000 years ago. Additional sites suggest Paleo-Indian occupation dating to 8,000–11,000 years ago.

U.S.S. *Arizona*, Pearl Harbor, Hawaii
In 2016, National Park Service archaeologists and National Geographic photographers used an ROV (remotely operated vehicle) to explore this U.S. battleship, sunk on December 7, 1941. The team collected artifacts for analysis and took sediment and water samples for further study.

MT

ND

SD

NE

KS

CA

AZ

NM

OK

TX

AK

HI

PACIFIC OCEAN

PACIFIC OCEAN

Jeffers Petroglyphs, Minnesota
These rock carvings, some dating possibly to 9,000 years ago, include humans, elk, buffalo, turtles, and dragonflies. Archaeologists had to carefully remove lichen that covered the rocks in order to examine the carvings underneath. They speculate that the carvings were used for sacred ceremonies or to record events.

World Trade Center site, New York
A visit to the 9/11 Memorial Museum in New York City has been called an "archaeological walking tour." Archaeologists worked to recover human remains and artifacts from the tons of debris left after the towers collapsed.

Cahokia Mounds, Illinois
This 2,200-acre site of a pre-Columbian Native American city is the largest archaeological site in the United States. The roughly 80 mounds that remain today suggest a sophisticated urban Mississippian culture. Artifacts uncovered at Cahokia include pottery, tools, stones, shells, knives, arrowheads, and tattoo kits.

Mount Vernon, Virginia
The home of George and Martha Washington, Mount Vernon continues to yield a great deal of data that document life on an 18th-century plantation. One effort has focused on an archaeological survey of slave burials on the grounds.

Underwater Archaeological Preserves, Pensacola, Florida
The battleship U.S.S. *Massachusetts* from the Spanish-American War was towed to Pensacola in 1921 and eventually scuttled at the entrance to the harbor. Today, the ship is an artificial reef and home to an array of marine life in the Gulf of Mexico.

The Alamo, San Antonio, Texas
Once a fortress and mission, the Alamo is a moving reminder of the Texan forces who faced Santa Anna's Mexican troops there in 1836 as part of the Texas Revolution. Archaeologists are still excavating to identify the original structure's adobe walls and inventory thousands of artifacts.

MN · WI · IA · IL · MO · AR · MS · LA · TN · AL · GA · FL · NC · VA · DC · MD · DE · NJ · PA · NY · CT · RI · MA · NH · VT · ME

ATLANTIC OCEAN

CRITICAL VIEWING The first major conflict to be extensively photographed was the American Civil War. This photo, taken by G.H. Houghton in the early 1860s, shows Union troops stationed at Camp Griffin in Langley, Virginia—a Confederate state. Based on the details in this photograph, what do you predict may have taken place shortly after it was taken?

THE UNITED STATES

January 1, 1863
Abraham Lincoln signs the Emancipation Proclamation, which frees slaves in states that had seceded from the Union. *(print of the proclamation featuring a portrait of Lincoln)*

1850
Congress passes the Compromise of 1850 to address the issue of slavery in newly acquired territories and keep the Union from splitting apart.

1861
The Civil War begins after the South attacks Fort Sumter, a garrison in South Carolina under federal control. *(This flag was torn by bullets as it flew over Fort Sumter during the attack.)*

1855
A period known as "Bleeding Kansas" begins, as the territory becomes a battleground between proslavery and antislavery forces.

1860
Abraham Lincoln is elected president. Soon after, South Carolina secedes from the union.

1850

1860

THE WORLD

1857 ASIA
Indian soldiers revolt against British rule in India.

1861 EUROPE
The serfs in Russia are freed.

1855 AFRICA
Scottish explorer David Livingstone is the first European to see a spectacular waterfall along the Zambezi River and names it Victoria Falls in honor of Britain's Queen Victoria.
(photo of Victoria Falls)

1858 ASIA
France begins colonizing Vietnam and eventually expands its control to include Cambodia and Laos.

July 1–4, 1863
Union forces defeat the Confederates at the battles of Gettysburg, in Pennsylvania, and Vicksburg, in Mississippi, with great losses on both sides. *(insignia from the cap of a Union commander who led his regiment at Gettysburg)*

1867
Congress passes the Reconstruction Acts of 1867, requiring southern states to satisfy several conditions, including granting African-American men suffrage. *(a slot-topped wooden ballot box used during Reconstruction)*

1864
Union general William T. Sherman leads his soldiers on a march through Georgia, burning the homes of those who try to fight back.

1865
On April 9, the Civil War ends when southern general Robert E. Lee surrenders to northern general Ulysses S. Grant. On April 14, Lincoln is assassinated.

1877
Through the Compromise of 1877, Rutherford B. Hayes becomes president in exchange for the withdrawal of federal troops from the South, thereby ending Reconstruction.

1865

1875

1871 EUROPE
Otto von Bismarck unites the German states to form the German Empire and becomes its first chancellor.

1869 AFRICA
The Suez Canal opens, connecting the Mediterranean and Red seas.

1864 AMERICAS
Napoleon III crowns Archduke Ferdinand Maximilian Joseph of Austria emperor of Mexico. *(the jewel-encrusted seal of Maximilian I of Mexico)*

1867 ASIA
The Tokugawa shogunate is overthrown, and Meiji rule brings a period of modernization to Japan.

349

TENSIONS BETWEEN NORTH AND SOUTH

1846–1861

HISTORICAL THINKING How did tensions over slavery divide the North and the South?

CRITICAL VIEWING This monumental statue of Abraham Lincoln overlooks the National Mall from within the Lincoln Memorial in Washington, D.C. The memorial was dedicated in 1922. A team of sculptors had spent 4 years carving the 19-foot-tall and 19-foot-wide marble statue. Its designer, Daniel Chester French, wanted to depict Lincoln at the height of the Civil War. What do Lincoln's posture, clothing, and expression say about him as a leader?

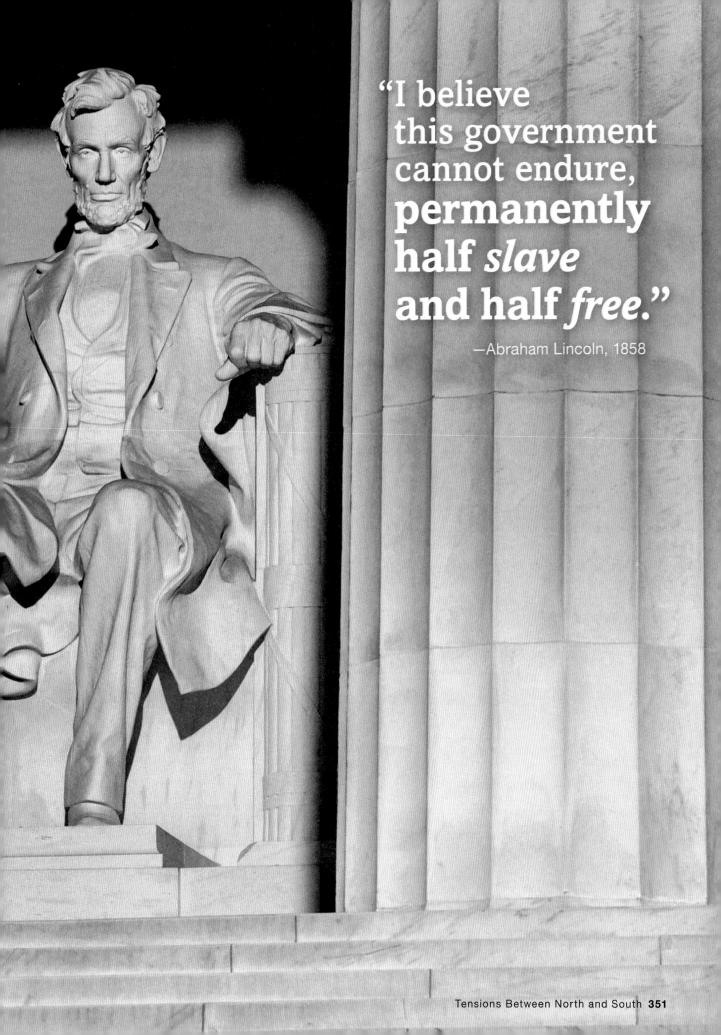

"I believe this government cannot endure, permanently half *slave* and half *free*."

—Abraham Lincoln, 1858

CRITICAL VIEWING
Alexander Hesler's 1860
photograph of Abraham
Lincoln captures the man
before his presidency.
How does this photo
compare to others you
have seen of Lincoln
later in his life? Explain.

ABRAHAM LINCOLN

THE GREAT EMANCIPATOR

Over the course of his life, Lincoln was called many names. Barbarian. Unshapely man. Even the original gorilla. But those who admired him called him Honest Abe, the Ancient One, and with the highest level of respect—the Great Emancipator.

In 1864, Lincoln wrote, "I am naturally anti-slavery. If slavery is not wrong, nothing is wrong." His actions and writings indicate not just lifelong opposition but also personal disgust with slavery. In an undated note, he reflected sarcastically that "although volume upon volume is written to prove slavery a very good thing, we never hear of the man who wishes to take the good of it, by being a slave himself." Lincoln abhorred the institution of slavery, but his attitudes toward African Americans could not be described as "modern." Although he never publicly embraced the idea of full equality, his ideas about the capabilities of African Americans and their roles in society did evolve with time and experience.

Lincoln's negative view of slavery may date back to his early childhood and to his parents' position on the matter. When he was born in Kentucky in 1809, slavery was legal in the state, and some of his family members were slaveholders. Lincoln's parents, however, appear to have been against it. In fact, when their church divided over the question of whether slavery was justified, they joined the antislavery group. In 1816, Lincoln's father moved the family across the Ohio River into Indiana, a free state. In his autobiography, Lincoln wrote that his father made this change "partly on account of slavery."

Lincoln witnessed slavery on many occasions during his youth in Kentucky and while traveling on the Mississippi and Ohio rivers. The experiences disturbed him, as is indicated in a letter he wrote to his friend Joshua Speed. "In 1841 you and I had together a tedious low-water trip, on a Steam Boat

TIME LINE OF LINCOLN'S LIFE

February 12, 1809
Abraham Lincoln is born in a one-room log cabin in Kentucky to parents Thomas Lincoln and Nancy Hanks Lincoln.

1824
At 15, Lincoln is an avid reader and hard worker. He attends school in the fall and winter and plows, plants, and does odd jobs for neighbors.

1827
Lincoln gets a job ferrying passengers to steamboats on the Ohio River.

1830
The Lincolns move to Illinois. Lincoln makes his first political speech.

| 1800 | 1810 | 1820 | 1830 |

from Louisville to St. Louis. You may remember, as I well do, that from Louisville to the mouth of the Ohio there were, on board, ten or a dozen slaves, shackled together with irons. That sight was a continual torment to me; and I see something like it every time I touch the Ohio, or any other slave-border."

Lincoln supporters wore pins like this one during his second presidential campaign.

Lincoln began his career as a public servant in 1834, when he was elected to the Illinois General Assembly for the first of four terms. Despite his personal beliefs, he did not advocate for the immediate abolition of slavery. He believed it was permitted under the Constitution in the states where it existed and that the federal government did not have the power to abolish it in those states. In 1837, at the age of 28, Lincoln made one of his first public statements about slavery before the Illinois General Assembly, and it neatly summarized his views:

> [We] believe that the institution of slavery is founded on both injustice and bad policy; but that the promulgation of abolition doctrines tends rather to increase than to abate its evils.
>
> [We] believe that the Congress of the United States has no power, under the constitution, to interfere with the institution of slavery in the different States.

In 1846, Lincoln was elected to the U.S. House of Representatives. During his single term in office, he became known for his antislavery views, and he proposed legislation to begin abolishing slavery in the District of Columbia. Because this zone was directly under federal government control, Lincoln believed Congress did have the authority to make

rules regarding slavery there. After completing his term in 1849, Lincoln returned to Illinois and retired from politics to practice law, but he was unable to embrace life as a private citizen for long. In 1854, the topic of slavery drew Lincoln back to the public stage after Senator Stephen A. Douglas persuaded Congress to pass the Kansas-Nebraska Act, which opened up the possibility of slavery's expansion into a large part of the Midwest. Incensed, Lincoln delivered three speeches from Illinois in which he eloquently outlined the case against slavery. "I hate it because of the monstrous injustice of slavery itself," he said. "I hate it because it deprives our republican example of its just influence in the world—enables the enemies of free institutions, with plausibility, to taunt us as hypocrites."

At the same time, however, he didn't insist on the abolition of slavery in the South, and he admitted he didn't know what steps should be taken if all the slaves were to be liberated at once. "My first impulse would be to free all the slaves, and send them to Liberia—to their own native land," he remarked.

Mary Todd had a life of privilege before she married Lincoln.

TIME LINE CONTINUED

April 1832
The Black Hawk War breaks out. Lincoln joins the Illinois militia but sees no action.

August 4, 1834
Lincoln is elected to the Illinois General Assembly as a member of the Whig Party. He begins to study law, using books borrowed from a friend.

November 4, 1842
Lincoln and Mary Todd marry and live in Springfield.

August 3, 1846
Lincoln is elected to the U.S. Congress as a member of the Whig party.

1830

1840

Liberia, on Africa's Atlantic coast, had been settled by freed American and Caribbean slaves since 1822 and had become a republic in 1847. Lincoln went on to admit he viewed African Americans as somewhat less than equal. If it were not practical to send all the former slaves to Liberia, he asked, "What next? Free them, and make them politically and socially, our equals? My own feelings will not admit of this; and if mine would, we well know that those of the great mass of white people will not."

During a debate against Senator Douglas in 1858, Lincoln made himself even clearer. "I will say then that I am not, nor ever have been, in favor of bringing about in any way the social and political equality of the white and black races," he declared, going on to assert his opposition to African Americans serving on juries, voting, or holding office. He did insist, however, that African Americans had the right to be free, receive pay for their labor, and improve their conditions through their own hard work.

In the years that followed, Lincoln continued to support the concepts of gradually ending slavery and sending former slaves out of the country— an idea called colonization that was popular among some leaders. In 1862, while drafting the Emancipation Proclamation, which would outlaw slavery in the South, President Lincoln met with a group of formerly enslaved people at the White House and presented a plan to send emancipated slaves to colonize a region of Central America. Abolitionists and African-American leaders alike angrily disagreed with this plan, insisting African Americans had the same right to live in the United States as whites.

As the tensions over slavery mounted and the country moved inexorably into the Civil War, Lincoln continued to speak out, although his message seemed contradictory at times. In a famous speech in Springfield, Illinois, in 1858,

Frederick Douglass Appeals to President Lincoln
by William Edouard Scott, 1943

LINCOLN AND DOUGLASS

When Lincoln happily spotted his friend Frederick Douglass at the reception following the president's second inauguration, he immediately asked what Douglass thought of the inaugural speech. "There is no man in these United States whose opinion I value more than yours," Lincoln explained.

The friendship between Lincoln and Douglass seems both unlikely and perfectly logical. They were self-made men who were born into poverty and educated themselves before rising to positions of prominence. But Douglass had experienced the cruelties of being enslaved. He was also an abolitionist who demanded immediately ending slavery, while Lincoln favored gradually phasing it out. With the brutal honesty of a friend, Douglass criticized Lincoln's colonization plans, writing that the president "seems to have an ever increasing passion for making himself appear silly and ridiculous."

March 31, 1849
Lincoln returns to Springfield, leaving politics to practice law.

1854
Lincoln re-enters politics to oppose the Kansas-Nebraska Act. He chooses to run for the U.S. Senate, but loses the Senate election in 1855.

June 16, 1858
Lincoln gives his "House Divided" speech in Springfield and engages in seven debates with Stephen Douglas, his Democratic opponent in the Senate race. In 1859, Lincoln loses the Senate election to Douglas.

November 6, 1860
Lincoln is elected as the first Republican president of the United States.

1850

1860

he declared, "A house divided against itself cannot stand. I believe this government cannot endure permanently half slave and half free. I do not expect the Union to be dissolved . . . but I do expect it will cease to be divided. It will become all one thing or all the other." Lincoln gave his first inaugural address as president in 1861 a little more than a month before fighting broke out between the Union and the Confederacy. However, he insisted, "I have no purpose, directly or indirectly, to interfere with the institution of slavery in the States where it exists. I believe I have no lawful right to do so, and I have no inclination to do so."

CRITICAL VIEWING In this 1862 photograph, Lincoln confers with General George McClellan in Antietam, two weeks after that bloody battle. What does this photograph reveal about Lincoln's relationship with McClellan?

On December 20, 1860, South Carolina became the first state to secede from the Union. On April 12, 1861, the Civil War began with the Confederate Army attack on Fort Sumter, South Carolina. By August 1862, the Confederacy had won several important victories, and Lincoln had written a preliminary draft of the Emancipation Proclamation. Lincoln's change in attitude toward abolition was more a matter of strategy than a serious change of heart.

By the summer of 1862, thousands of African Americans had fled their places of enslavement and sought shelter behind Union lines. Neither the federal government nor the Union Army had a policy for dealing with these individuals. Lincoln realized that proclaiming freedom for those enslaved in the South could serve two purposes: First, giving the former slaves an official status in the Union would allow them to support Union army units. Second, more slaves might be encouraged to free themselves, deserting the plantations in the South and thus helping to starve the Confederacy.

In an August 22, 1862, letter to Horace Greeley, Lincoln explained his priorities: "My paramount object in this struggle is to save the Union, and is not either to save or to destroy slavery. If I could save the Union without freeing any slave I would do it; and if I could save it by freeing all the slaves I would do it; and if I could save it by freeing some and leaving others alone I would also do that."

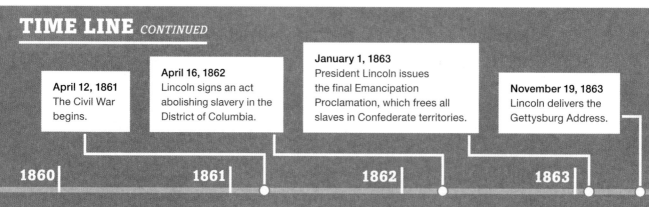

TIME LINE CONTINUED

April 12, 1861 The Civil War begins.

April 16, 1862 Lincoln signs an act abolishing slavery in the District of Columbia.

January 1, 1863 President Lincoln issues the final Emancipation Proclamation, which frees all slaves in Confederate territories.

November 19, 1863 Lincoln delivers the Gettysburg Address.

1860 1861 1862 1863

⛪ The Abraham Lincoln Presidential Library and Museum Springfield, Illinois

From 1837 until he moved into the White House in 1861, Lincoln made his home in Springfield, Illinois. Today, Springfield's Abraham Lincoln Presidential Library and Museum shares his legacy with thousands of visitors every year. The library houses a unique collection of Lincoln-related papers and artifacts, and the museum immerses visitors in Lincoln's life and career through interactive exhibits.

Lincoln's letter sealer

In reality, when the final version of the Emancipation Proclamation was issued on January 1, 1863, it did not actually free any slaves, because it applied only to the Confederate states that were fighting against the Union—states that did not recognize Union laws. Border slave states and parts of the Confederacy that had been taken by the Union were exempted. Still, it was a powerful statement and a meaningful step toward the true abolition of slavery that would come with the 13th Amendment in 1865. The proclamation also marked an evolution in Lincoln's own thinking, as it did not mention colonization at all, and Lincoln never alluded to it again.

In the turbulent years following the Emancipation Proclamation, Lincoln's attitude toward African Americans continued to evolve and was likely influenced by the actions of the formerly enslaved. As historian T.J. Stiles observed, "The enslaved moved *themselves* off farms and plantations and into federal lines, asserting their autonomy in a positive act of resistance. Many carried it further by enlisting as soldiers, with profound implications for the status of African Americans." The escaping slaves were the Great Emancipators in their own lives, and their service in the Union Army cast them in an entirely new light. By the end of the war, 200,000 African Americans had served in the U.S. Army and Navy,

many of them with great bravery and distinction. Some historians connect the former slaves' self-assertion and courage in defense of the Union with Lincoln's willingness to envision a greater role for them in society.

In his last speech, Lincoln took one step farther away from his earlier prejudices, promoting partial suffrage for African Americans, an idea that seems timid by today's standards but was radical for its time. He declared, "It is also unsatisfactory to some that the elective franchise [voting] is not given to the colored man. I would myself prefer that it were now conferred on the very intelligent, and on those who serve our cause as soldiers." Three days later, Abraham Lincoln was assassinated. It's impossible to know whether and how his views on African Americans would have continued to evolve had he been given the chance to live to a ripe old age.

THINK ABOUT IT

How did Lincoln's views toward slavery and racial equality evolve throughout his lifetime?

November 8, 1864
Lincoln is re-elected, defeating Democrat George B. McClellan.

April 9, 1865
General Lee surrenders his Confederate Army to General Grant following the Battle of Appomattox Court House in Virginia.

April 14, 1865
John Wilkes Booth shoots Lincoln, who dies at 7:22 the following morning.

December 6, 1865
The 13th Amendment, which was passed by Congress on January 31, 1865, is ratified. Slavery is abolished in the United States.

1864   1865   1866

MAIN IDEA As a sharp distinction developed between the economies of the North and the South, the two regions also formed different ideas about what they expected from the federal government.

INDUSTRIAL NORTH AND AGRICULTURAL SOUTH

If you've spent your entire life living on a farm, it might be difficult to envision life in a huge city. Likewise, if you've lived in towns or cities your whole life, you may have trouble understanding life in the country. How might rural and urban communities have different expectations of their federal government?

NORTHERN INDUSTRY AND COMMERCE

During the 1830s and 1840s, economic differences between the North and the South started to form. The northern economy, though still primarily agricultural like the South, began to be driven more and more by industry.

As you have read, textile mills represented one of the earliest major industries in the North. Samuel Slater brought the British secrets of textile machinery to New England in the 1790s, where he established a number of plants. In the early 1800s, Francis Cabot Lowell helped develop the first power loom and revolutionized the conversion of raw cotton into finished cloth so the entire process could be done under one roof. He created company towns around his factories, providing housing, stores, and other businesses to support the needs of his wage workers. Lowell's factories also changed the makeup of the worker population by recruiting young, female immigrants, who would work for lower wages than other laborers.

The geography of New England, with its many swift rivers, provided the water power to run the mills' mechanical looms. Other industries soon emerged throughout the North, using that same water power to manufacture machinery, guns, paint, paper, and other products. Manufacturing, in turn, boosted secondary industries that supported the factory-based economy. Banking expanded to provide loans and capital, or money for investment, to businesses. And business owners needed better transportation systems, such as canals and railroads, to transport supplies and goods. Many wealthy northern

industrial families, such as the Lowells, invested in railroads, financial institutions, and other businesses that helped their manufacturing endeavors.

Factory workers toiled long hours in often unsafe conditions for wages that barely covered their basic needs. Still, for many, such work offered greater security and a better life than they might have had otherwise. The growth of American factories and the need for more workers in the North coincided with natural and political crises in Europe. Millions of Europeans fled their homelands for a better life in the United States, providing a ready and willing workforce for northern industries.

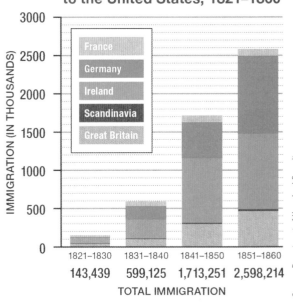

European Immigration to the United States, 1821–1860

Legend:
- France
- Germany
- Ireland
- Scandinavia
- Great Britain

IMMIGRATION (IN THOUSANDS)

1821–1830	1831–1840	1841–1850	1851–1860
143,439	599,125	1,713,251	2,598,214

TOTAL IMMIGRATION

Source: Department of Homeland Security

From 1845 to 1849, a blight, or disease, struck potato crops in Ireland. Potatoes had become a staple Irish food following their introduction to Ireland in the late 1500s, and the extended crop failure caused a devastating famine, or time of mass starvation. More than 2 million people fled the **Irish potato famine**, hoping to find work in the northern United States. Once they landed, Irish immigrants faced hard times and discrimination because of their Roman Catholic faith and their willingness to take almost any job for any pay. Some workers born in the United States complained that Irish immigrants drove down wages for everyone.

As the Irish potato famine came to an end, a political upheaval in Germany caused another wave of immigrants to move to the North. Many German immigrants came with money to invest in businesses and land. Most of them settled in cities or headed to the Midwest and beyond. Some German immigrants maintained their culture and language by settling in large groups. As industries and transportation expanded and Americans continued to move west, German immigrants settled and established businesses in growing midwestern cities, such as Chicago and Detroit.

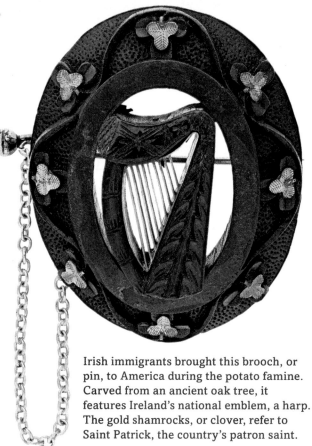

Irish immigrants brought this brooch, or pin, to America during the potato famine. Carved from an ancient oak tree, it features Ireland's national emblem, a harp. The gold shamrocks, or clover, refer to Saint Patrick, the country's patron saint.

SOUTHERN AGRICULTURAL ECONOMY

As the North became more industrial and urban, the southern economy and culture continued to focus on agriculture, especially growing cotton. Large-scale plantations were so profitable that few wealthy southerners saw value in investing in factories, although the availability of cotton drove the development of textile mills in the South. Still, few other types of manufacturing took hold. Great Britain purchased so much southern cotton for its textile factories that a healthy trade system grew between Great Britain and the South. Rather than make goods themselves, southerners relied on British manufactured goods. And some southern states traded more cotton with Britain and other foreign countries than they did with the northern states.

Most wealthy southerners invested in property, especially land and enslaved people. Some historians have argued that the region's reliance on plantation agriculture delayed economic diversity. Southern leaders defended their agricultural system against criticisms about its dependence on slavery by declaring it was more stable than northern industries and less prone to the ups and downs of economic **recessions**, periods of decline in economic activity. They argued that northern factory owners used and abused their workers, discarding

them if they got hurt or became ill and could not work. In contrast, they reasoned, enslavers had an interest in looking out for the welfare of their enslaved workers, even in illness and old age.

Some newer southerners, however, questioned this system and its reliance on slavery. Few mid-century German immigrants who settled in Texas supported slavery. Some spoke out loudly against it. But since most immigrants did not want to cause disputes with their new neighbors, the majority of German immigrants opposed to slavery kept their thoughts to themselves.

HISTORICAL THINKING

1. **READING CHECK** Other than geography, what circumstances helped the textile industry to flourish in the North?

2. **ANALYZE CAUSE AND EFFECT** How did northern industries benefit from overseas crises like the Irish potato famine?

3. **COMPARE AND CONTRAST** How did the southern economy develop differently from that of the North?

4. **INTERPRET GRAPHS** According to the graph, what happened to Irish and German immigration in the period between 1851–1860?

TENSIONS OVER EXPANDING SLAVERY

The call of the West continued to inspire Americans. There was no stopping the rush of settlers toward new land. But what about the spread of slavery across the country? Was that inevitable, too?

THE WILMOT PROVISO

Before the Mexican-American War ended in 1848, debates about the expansion of slavery were heating up. Would slavery be allowed in any of the new territory acquired by the United States? Should it be? Not surprisingly, northerners and southerners had opposing views.

At issue was the balance of political power between slave and free states. So far, Congress had kept a balance under the Missouri Compromise of 1820, which simultaneously admitted Missouri as a slave state and Maine as a free state—keeping the total number of free and slave states equal. At this point, the more densely populated free states held a majority of seats in the House of Representatives. In the Senate, each state received equal representation, preserving a balance. But this balance was challenged as the United States acquired more land.

In 1846, a bill before Congress addressed the acquisition of more land. It proposed that the United States spend $2 million to end the Mexican-American War and purchase California and Mexican territory north of the Rio Grande. Representative **David Wilmot**, a Pennsylvania Democrat, seized the opportunity to address slavery. Like most northerners, Wilmot was concerned that the expansion of slavery to new territory would strengthen the institution and increase southern political power. He proposed adding a **proviso**, or condition, to the bill that would prohibit the establishment of slavery in any territory the United States might acquire from Mexico. His plan is known as the **Wilmot Proviso**.

The House passed the proviso, with most votes in favor of it coming from the North. But the proviso was defeated in the Senate in 1847, with 15 slave states and 14 free states in the Union at that time. This spurred a desire among the representatives of free states to weaken the influence of the slave states in Congress. From 1846 onward, divisions between the North and the South would threaten party unity.

THE PONY EXPRESS

After California's statehood in 1850, better communication was needed between the East and the West. In 1860, a service to deliver mail by horseback riders—called the Pony Express—was introduced as a solution. Riders traveled in relays at full speed on a nearly 2,000-mile route between Missouri and California. Along the way, fresh riders and horses were exchanged at stations, such as the one shown in this painting by Frederic Remington titled *The Coming and Going of the Pony Express.*

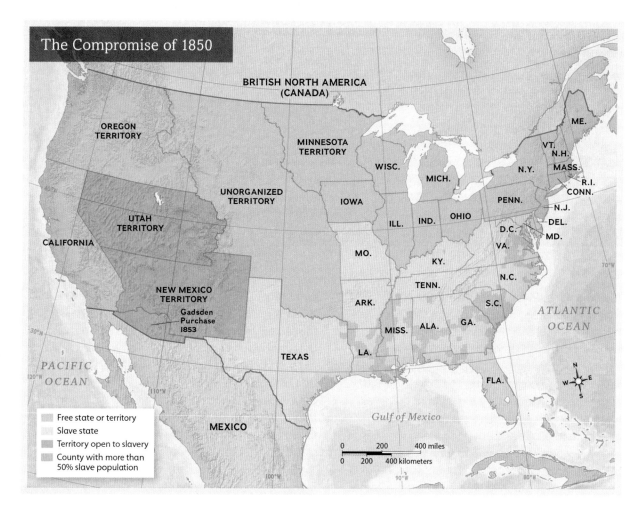

The Compromise of 1850

BRITISH NORTH AMERICA
(CANADA)

OREGON TERRITORY

MINNESOTA TERRITORY

WISC.

MICH.

UNORGANIZED TERRITORY

IOWA

N.Y.

PENN.

UTAH TERRITORY

ILL.   IND.   OHIO

CALIFORNIA

MO.

KY.

VA.

NEW MEXICO TERRITORY

Gadsden Purchase 1853

ARK.

TENN.

N.C.

S.C.

ATLANTIC OCEAN

MISS.   ALA.   GA.

TEXAS

LA.

PACIFIC OCEAN

FLA.

ME.
VT.
N.H.
MASS.
R.I.
CONN.
N.J.
DEL.
MD.
D.C.

Free state or territory
Slave state
Territory open to slavery
County with more than 50% slave population

MEXICO

Gulf of Mexico

0   200   400 miles
0   200   400 kilometers

To further complicate matters, part of the agreement that had been established by the Missouri Compromise was now in question. It had to do with its allowance of slavery into new territories south of Missouri's southern border. Many residents in the Southwest opposed the idea of slave states in their region. Though some settlers in isolated areas of the Southwest had slaves, most communities in the newly acquired territories did not accept slavery. This was especially true in California, where the discovery of gold, among other factors, contributed to its status as one of the fastest-growing areas of the far West.

A good portion of California fell below the Missouri Compromise line, so it did not clearly fit the geographic boundaries established for being a free state or slave state. But as a former territory of Mexico, California had been "free" since 1829. And many Americans who had migrated there did so to establish small farms or to work on large ones. Introducing slave labor into California's agricultural economy would cost them their livelihoods. In 1849, a year before California became a state, the California constitution banned slavery. Californians petitioned for California to enter the Union as a single free state in violation of the Missouri Compromise.

Southerners drew a hard line at allowing California to break the Missouri Compromise and join the Union as a free state. If they gave in to California, they feared a balance of representation and power in government could not be maintained. Outraged southern politicians even argued that to deny slave states equal representation in the Senate was to risk war between the North and the South.

COMPROMISE OF 1850

As debates heated up over California's petition to join the Union as a free state, tensions rose between the North and the South over yet another slavery issue: runaways. Under the Fugitive Slave Act of 1793, authorities of one state could order the return of runaway slaves to their owners in another state. Northern states increasingly ignored this law, however, often turning a blind eye to abolitionists who helped many enslaved people flee to freedom. Southern enslavers argued that by refusing to enforce the Fugitive Slave Act, authorities in the North encouraged enslaved people to flee and unfairly deprived enslavers of their property. They wanted a tougher federal law to ensure that runaways would be returned to bondage or owners would be compensated for their loss of slave labor.

In Charleston, South Carolina, enslaved laborers hired out by their owners were required by law to be licensed and to wear copper identification badges like these while they were leased out. Stamped on each badge is the city name, the job, such as porter or carpenter, an identification number, and the year. Although badge laws existed in several cities, Charleston was the only city known to have followed a formal regulatory system for the leasing of enslaved people, and only metal badges from that city have been found. Leased slaves were sometimes allowed to keep a percentage of what they earned.

Slave tax badges

In the meantime, these various debates were reshaping political alliances. In August 1848, supporters of the Wilmot Proviso, upset by the actions of northern Democrats and Whigs whom they felt were too moderate on slavery, held a convention to launch a new political party. The **Free-Soil Party** brought together antislavery forces from the Whig, Democratic, and Liberty parties to oppose any further spread of slavery. Adopting the motto "free soil, free speech, free labor, and free men," the Free-Soil Party attracted a wide coalition of voters. Small farmers and wage laborers who opposed the spread of slavery on the basis of economic competition rather than moral grounds supported the new party. Former president Martin Van Buren ran as the Free-Soil Party's presidential candidate in 1848. Although he did not win, the party picked up numerous seats in state and local legislatures, proving that its stance was growing in appeal.

The rise of the new party contributed to split loyalties among voters. As a result, war hero and Whig Party candidate **Zachary Taylor** was elected U.S. president in 1848. Taylor angered those on both sides of the slavery issue by supporting California statehood without any reference to its slave or free status. He proposed that the courts should decide the fate of slavery in the region. When California applied for statehood as a free state in December 1849, some southern states threatened to secede, or separate politically, from the Union. Kentucky Representative Henry Clay hoped to broker a compromise but received little support from Taylor.

Clay proposed what would become known as the **Compromise of 1850**. It attempted to balance the political interests of free states and slave states, while also taking into consideration **popular sovereignty**, or the right of local citizens to determine their own laws. Clay's proposal was an **omnibus bill**, or

comprehensive legislation, which addressed almost all divisive slavery concerns. He hoped to balance the territory issue with other matters that drove debates about slavery. He suggested keeping slavery legal in the District of Columbia, but abolishing the domestic trading of slaves there. On the one hand, the bill called for a stronger fugitive slave law in the North. On the other hand, it announced that Congress had no power to regulate the interstate slave trade. The legislation sought to admit California

PRIMARY SOURCES

When the Compromise of 1850 was proposed, it set off a great debate in the Senate between northerners and southerners. The arguments below illustrate how the slavery issue was starting to threaten the Union.

Unless something decisive is done, I again ask, What is to stop this agitation before the great and final object at which it aims—the abolition of slavery in the States—is consummated? Is it, then, not certain that if something is not done to arrest it, the South will be forced to choose between abolition and secession? If the agitation goes on, . . . nothing will be left to hold the States together except force.

—from speech by John C. Calhoun, March 4, 1850

I wish to speak to-day, not as a Massachusetts man, nor as a Northern man, but as an American, . . . I speak to-day for the preservation of the Union. . . . I speak to-day, out of a[n] . . . anxious heart for the restoration to the country of that quiet and that harmony which make the blessings of this Union so rich, and so dear to us all.

—from speech by Daniel Webster, March 7, 1850

as a free state, but broke from the Wilmot Proviso by leaving the status of other territories won from Mexico undetermined. Hard-liners on both sides of the issues opposed the compromise. Fierce debate raged among members of Congress.

DEBATING THE COMPROMISE

In January 1850, John C. Calhoun, Henry Clay, and Daniel Webster—among the most influential American legislators of the time—took the lead in the national debate over California. Calhoun, from South Carolina, was the most vocal and extreme spokesman for the South. He warned that if slave states did not unite, they would be overtaken by free states in the North and West. Clay of Kentucky reassumed the role of the Great Compromiser that he had played during the Missouri Compromise 30 years earlier. Massachusetts's Webster tried to convince angry northerners that accepting the South's demand for respect was in the best interests of the Union because it would keep the nation together. Arguments went on for months. Meanwhile, President Taylor offered no support for the legislation. The Compromise of 1850 seemed doomed.

Then a series of unexpected events brought new interest to the legislation. In the summer of 1850, Zachary Taylor died from a sudden illness. The new U.S. president, **Millard Fillmore**, openly supported the compromise. John Calhoun, who had been ill throughout most of the debates, passed away. Daniel Webster left the Senate to become Secretary of State. And the elderly and exhausted Henry Clay left Washington, D.C., to recover. Younger, less prominent members of Congress began to build coalitions in support of the compromise. **Stephen A. Douglas**, a promising young Democrat from Illinois, steered the various components of the compromise through committees and votes.

By September, the five major components of the Compromise of 1850 had become law. California was admitted as a free state, and the boundary of Texas was established. Congress formed the territories of Utah and New Mexico, where popular sovereignty would decide the slavery issue. And to balance ending the slave trade in Washington, D.C., Congress passed a much more restrictive and controversial fugitive slave law.

The **Fugitive Slave Act of 1850** raised much dissent in free states because it allowed for the punishment of anyone who aided runaway slaves in their escape. Marshals and sheriffs had the authority to force any bystanders, including abolitionists, to help capture fugitives. Once arrested, an alleged runaway could

CAUTION!!

COLORED PEOPLE
OF BOSTON, ONE & ALL,
You are hereby respectfully CAUTIONED and advised, to avoid conversing with the
Watchmen and Police Officers of Boston,
For since the recent ORDER OF THE MAYOR & ALDERMEN, they are empowered to act as
KIDNAPPERS
AND
Slave Catchers,
And they have already been actually employed in KIDNAPPING, CATCHING, AND KEEPING SLAVES. Therefore, if you value your LIBERTY, and the *Welfare of the Fugitives* among you, *Shun* them in every possible manner, as so many *HOUNDS* on the track of the most unfortunate of your race.

Keep a Sharp Look Out for KIDNAPPERS, and have TOP EYE open.
APRIL 24, 1851.

Printed by abolitionists as a warning to runaway slaves, this poster reflects the impact of the Fugitive Slave Act of 1850 in Boston.

not testify in his or her own defense or call witnesses. And no matter how long it had been since a person had escaped, no matter how settled or accepted the runaway had become in a new place, an enslaver could capture and return the fugitive to bondage. Abolitionists adamantly opposed the Fugitive Slave Act. While parts of the Compromise of 1850 quieted conflict between the North and the South, the law provoked it.

HISTORICAL THINKING

1. **READING CHECK** What connection did the Wilmot Proviso have to California statehood?

2. **IDENTIFY MAIN IDEAS AND DETAILS** What political factions made up the Free-Soil Party?

3. **SUMMARIZE** How did the Fugitive Slave Act of 1850 acknowledge and enforce slave states' practice of slavery?

4. **INTERPRET MAPS** Based on the map, how did the Compromise of 1850 balance the issue of free versus slave states?

THE UNDERGROUND RAILROAD

It's the mid-1800s and your family is part of a secret operation to help slaves escape through the North to Canada. From all outward appearances, it's just a regular day of chores. But family members are on edge. Then a soft, coded knock signals that your guests have arrived.

GROWTH OF THE ABOLITION MOVEMENT

As you have read, the abolition movement grew out of religious groups who opposed slavery on moral grounds. White abolitionists, free African Americans, and enslaved people who had successfully escaped bondage in the South pooled their efforts to work to end American slavery.

As the movement grew, the role of African Americans, especially former slaves, also expanded within the movement. Sharing their personal experiences helped put human faces to the political issue. Abolitionist publishing houses and newspapers produced numerous narratives recounting life under slavery, horrifying incidents of abuse, and harrowing experiences of escape. As you have read, abolitionist groups sponsored inspiring speakers such as Frederick Douglass and Sojourner Truth. But the most dangerous and daring abolitionist effort, especially in the face of the Fugitive Slave Act, was the **Underground Railroad**, a network of secret routes and safe houses run mainly by free African Americans and devoted white abolitionists in the North.

A ROAD TO FREEDOM

Escaping from slavery was very difficult. Runaways were hunted like animals, and if they were captured, they were returned to bondage where they faced whippings and other terrible, sometimes deadly, punishments. With the passage of the Fugitive Slave

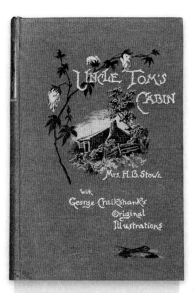

Today people read *Uncle Tom's Cabin* very differently than they did in 1852. They often discuss how Stowe's use of literary elements moved the nation.

Act of 1850, the best way for escaping slaves to avoid being caught was to make it all the way into Canada, where U.S. authorities and slave hunters had no jurisdiction, or legal power. This effort required months of slow, careful travel to avoid detection.

The Underground Railroad was not a physical railroad with trains and tracks, but rather a network of escape routes extending throughout all the free northern states. By the 1830s, those involved with the effort had adopted language from the rail system as part of their code. Homes and businesses of allies who helped shelter runaways were "stations" or "depots." Guides who led runaways to stations were "conductors." Runaways and conductors usually traveled at night, covering only 10 to 20 miles until they reached the next station, which would have been alerted to expect them. Sometimes abolitionist groups working with the Underground Railroad provided new clothes to help disguise the runaways' appearance or paid their passage on boats for quicker movement north. Wealthy abolitionists who secretly donated money to keep the Underground Railroad running were code-named "stockholders."

One of the most famous conductors on the Underground Railroad was Harriet Tubman, who, as you have read, escaped slavery and then helped hundreds of runaway slaves reach freedom in the North. After her escape in 1849, she worked and

CRITICAL VIEWING African-American artist Jacob Lawrence depicts an escape from slavery in his 1997 silkscreen *Forward Together (Harriet Tubman and the Underground Railroad)*. What shapes, colors, and other details in the work help convey what it was like for runaways on the Underground Railroad?

saved her money so she could return to the South to smuggle more slaves to freedom. Over the next 10 years she made approximately 13 trips back and forth, leading about 70 people to freedom. Tubman perfected a variety of techniques to avoid capture. Her bravery and skill earned her the admiration of other abolitionists and the hatred of southern slaveholders. In 1849, southern authorities had offered a reward for her arrest. Tubman once bragged to Frederick Douglass that as a conductor on the Underground Railroad she "never lost a single passenger."

UNCLE TOM'S CABIN

While some abolitionists actively helped enslaved people escape, others used the power of the pen to spread their message. In 1852, author **Harriet Beecher Stowe** published a popular antislavery novel that some historians believe persuaded many readers to oppose slavery. Stowe was one of minister and reform activist Lyman Beecher's 13 children. Raised to believe that they had a duty to address injustices in the world, almost all of the Beecher children grew up to be involved in reform causes, including abolition and women's rights.

Objecting to the Fugitive Slave Act and its effects, Stowe wrote **Uncle Tom's Cabin** in the style of popular melodramas, appealing to readers who might otherwise not read abolitionist literature. The main character, Uncle Tom, is a kindly older slave who lives under a wicked, abusive master named Simon Legree.

The plot involves tragedy, redemption, and heart-pounding escapes north for some of the characters. Although a work of fiction, the book reflects real-life experiences of African Americans who told their stories of escape to northern audiences.

Uncle Tom's Cabin sold an unheard-of 300,000 copies within a year of publication. It was the bestselling novel of the 19th century, as readers throughout the world empathized, or felt a connection, with the enslaved people in the story and were mortified by their treatment. Abolitionist groups held theatrical performances of the story to further spread its message. Southerners, however, harshly criticized the book, arguing that the reprehensible Simon Legree did not reflect the actions of most slaveholders. Some historians who claim the book was partly responsible for the Civil War cite the story of Abraham Lincoln meeting Stowe and declaring, "So this is the little lady who made this big war."

HISTORICAL THINKING

1. **READING CHECK** How did the Underground Railroad get its name?

2. **DRAW CONCLUSIONS** How did the Fugitive Slave Act of 1850 affect abolitionists who wanted to help people who had escaped slavery?

3. **IDENTIFY MAIN IDEAS AND DETAILS** What major contributions did African Americans make to the abolitionist movement?

HARRIET TUBMAN c. 1820–1913

"There are two things I've got a right to, and these are, Death or Liberty— one or the other I mean to have."—Harriet Tubman

Born into slavery, Harriet Tubman fought for her right to liberty— and, as she says, would have chosen death if she couldn't be free. When she was a teenager, she even defended the rights of another enslaved person by refusing to help capture him. The man's overseer threw a two-pound weight at Tubman and hit her in the head. As a result of the blow, she suffered headaches and seizures for the rest of her life. But none of the abuse she endured as a slave kept her from seeking freedom.

UNDERGROUND CONDUCTOR

Tubman seized her chance to escape in 1849 when her master died. She fled the Maryland plantation and the fields she'd worked for years and set off on foot for Pennsylvania. With the help of a sympathetic white woman along the way and guided by the North Star, Tubman made her way to Philadelphia. Recalling her feelings upon her arrival, she said, "I looked at my hands to see if I was the same person. . . . I felt like I was in Heaven."

She found work in the city and used the money she earned to return to Maryland and bring members of her family to freedom along the Underground Railroad. In time, as you know, Tubman rescued many other enslaved people and claimed, "I never ran my train off the track."

Much of her success on the Underground Railroad was due to the strategies she perfected. Tubman carried drugs to keep fretful babies quiet, and she typically set

Unlike many photographs that captured Harriet Tubman later in her life, this one shows her as a young woman in her 40s. It was taken by Benjamin Powelson after the Civil War for use as Tubman's calling card. As was the custom of the time, Tubman would have left this card when she paid someone a visit.

off with her passengers on a Saturday night, knowing that the escape wouldn't be reported in the newspapers until Monday. Tubman could also improvise. Once, after a bounty had been placed on her head, she overheard some men reading her wanted poster. When they read aloud the part that stated she was illiterate—she was—she picked up a book and pretended to read it.

SPY AND MILITARY LEADER

In recognition of her achievements on the Underground Railroad, Tubman earned the nickname "Moses." The name referred to the Jewish prophet who, according to the Hebrew Bible, led his people out of Egyptian slavery. She was also known to some as "General Tubman." This would prove prophetic.

During the Civil War, Tubman decided she could free more slaves by working with the Union Army. She served as a spy and even led a military expedition— the first woman to do so. On one occasion, she and other former enslaved people gathered information about Confederate positions and maneuvers along a river in South Carolina. Tubman helped plan a raid on the southern troops that resulted in the destruction of buildings, bridges, and plantations and freed about 750 slaves. In this and all the challenges she faced, Tubman's religious faith sustained her. As she once said, "I prayed to God to make me strong and able to fight."

After the war, Tubman retired to New York, where she lived until her death in 1913. Tubman will always be remembered as the most famous conductor on the Underground Railroad, but a more tangible memorial of her legacy may be in the works. In 2016, President Barack Obama's treasury secretary announced his plan to replace Andrew Jackson with Harriet Tubman on the $20 bill in 2020. However, after a new administration entered the White House in 2017, President Donald Trump's treasury secretary suggested he might block that plan or place Tubman on a $2 bill. Still, the honor of being on the $20 bill would be fitting. After all, Tubman, once enslaved herself, would take the place of a man who had been a slave owner.

Tubman keeps watch over a group of fugitive slaves as they sleep in a barn in this illustration from *Harriet and the Promised Land*, a book about the Underground Railroad by Jacob Lawrence.

HISTORICAL THINKING

1. **READING CHECK** What did Tubman decide to do after she gained her freedom?

2. **MAKE INFERENCES** Based on Tubman's accomplishments, what inferences can you make about her character?

3. **FORM AND SUPPORT OPINIONS** Do you think Tubman should appear on U.S. currency? Explain.

KANSAS AND NEBRASKA

Just four years after the Compromise of 1850 was finally passed, the balance between free and slave states was upset again. And this time the controversy erupted into violence. What was it going to take to resolve this recurring, seemingly unending problem?

THE KANSAS-NEBRASKA ACT

As you have read, the Missouri Compromise of 1820 prohibited slavery in any territory north of the 36° 30' line of latitude. When California, located partly below this boundary, petitioned to join the Union as a free state, Congress eventually passed more extensive legislation known as the Compromise of 1850, which appeased both sides of the issue yet again.

Illinois Senator Stephen A. Douglas, who worked to pass the Compromise of 1850, soon turned his attention to the future of the unorganized territory west of Iowa and Missouri. Douglas supported the vision of a railroad system that would cross the entire continent, passing through his home state of Illinois. However, the railroad could not be built through unorganized territory. Douglas believed the next step toward realizing the railroad system was to organize the lands into two new territories named Kansas and Nebraska, which could later become states. These new territories lay north of the 36° 30' latitude line. Once again, the balance of power between free and slave states was a hotly debated issue.

Douglas was not a supporter of slavery, but he was an advocate of popular sovereignty. He submitted a bill to the Senate that would repeal the Missouri Compromise and let the residents of each new territory and state decide on the matter of slavery for themselves—regardless of whether they resided on land north of the 36° 30' latitudinal line. Douglas hoped his legislation, which became the Kansas-Nebraska bill, would help him gain southern support for organizing the two territories. He also believed

The Kansas-Nebraska Act, 1854

Free states
Territories closed to slavery
Slave states
Territories open to slavery

that, even if the territories opted to allow slavery, the practice would not survive in any northern territories or states. The proposal unleashed a wide range of objections that had supposedly been resolved by earlier compromises. Free-Soil Party members and abolitionists protested loudly and angrily against a bill that might allow slavery to spread beyond its current borders.

The opposing factions could not coordinate their efforts to fight the bill, though, and the **Kansas-Nebraska Act** passed in 1854. It repealed the Missouri Compromise and created two new territories—Kansas and Nebraska—that would decide the legality of slavery through popular sovereignty. Both sides on the slavery issue knew there was still a chance to influence the voting. Plans for how to do so were already underway.

FORMATION OF THE REPUBLICAN PARTY

The issue of slavery was having an impact on political parties. As you have read, slavery was a major reason for the formation of the Free-Soil Party. As old alliances began to fracture, new ones formed. The fight over slavery in the new territories sped up these changes. But slavery wasn't the only matter driving the political shifts that were taking place.

For many political leaders in the early 1850s, halting the flood of immigrants to the United States was a higher priority than stopping the spread of slavery. **Nativists**, or those who opposed foreign immigration, organized the American Party around this issue. People began to call this political faction the **Know-Nothing Party** because it was initially organized much like a secret society, and when asked about party platforms or business, members were instructed to respond, "I know nothing." At first, the Know-Nothings shook up conventional party politics by winning a number of elections, many by write-in vote, in 1854. Eventually, however, the party

was unable to keep its promise to citizens to stem the tide of immigrants. The American Party's members split along proslavery and antislavery lines. By 1856, it had lost almost all its influence.

New parties such as the Know-Nothings had benefited from the declining power and unity of the Whigs, who were also being torn apart over slavery. The Kansas-Nebraska Act brought about the end of the Whig Party. By 1854, most northern antislavery Whigs had split from the party, while most of the proslavery members had joined the Democrats.

Some former Whigs, Free-Soilers, Know-Nothings, and Democrats were fed up with their party's support for southern causes and met at Ripon, Wisconsin, in May 1854 to form a new party more firmly devoted to stopping the spread of slavery. Its platform stated it would not permit slavery in the territories or in new states. This new political faction, called the **Republican Party**, was relatively successful as a new party. Its members quickly won election to

CRITICAL VIEWING A Know-Nothing political cartoon published in 1854 portrays an Irish and a German immigrant running from a voting site with the ballot box, which they have stolen in the midst of a brawl. What details in the cartoon reflect nativist attitudes toward immigrants?

local offices throughout the country. In 1856, the Republican presidential candidate, John C. Frémont, won 11 northern states and two-fifths of the electoral vote overall. The presidential winner, Democrat **James Buchanan**, held no strong position on the slavery issue and was considered by most to be noncontroversial. Buchanan seemed happy to let the courts decide the future of slavery.

"BLEEDING KANSAS"

In spite of the disputes surrounding the Kansas-Nebraska Act, the future of slavery in the Nebraska Territory was not controversial. The territory's climate was not conducive to plantation agriculture, and only a few slaves resided in the area. The 1860 census identified a total of 15 enslaved African Americans in the entire territory.

Kansas was a different story. Activists on both sides of the slavery issue believed they had the opportunity to turn the Kansas Territory in their favor. Antislavery forces quickly organized emigrant aid societies to provide assistance to those who would move to Kansas and vote against allowing slavery in the territory. Expecting trouble from proslavery forces, some of these societies encouraged the settlers to arrive well armed. Abolitionist minister Henry Ward Beecher, of the famous Beecher family, personally outfitted some migrants with new rifles. These gifts came to be known as "Beecher's Bibles."

In response to these efforts, proslavery forces from neighboring Missouri organized to cross the border and influence the territorial vote. In November 1854, when Kansas residents went to the polls to choose between a proslavery or antislavery congressional representative, proslavery Missourians flowed into Kansas Territory to stuff the ballot boxes with illegal votes. The proslavery delegate won the election.

Election tampering was even worse in March 1855, when Kansas voters had to choose between a proslavery and antislavery territorial government. Illegal voting increased as so-called "border ruffians" crossed over from Missouri to threaten anyone opposed to slavery. Their efforts were unnecessary, however, because many Kansas residents had migrated from the South and were proslavery in the first place. Once again, the proslavery delegates won. They took over the territorial legislature and passed laws prohibiting "free-soilers" and other antislavery men from serving on juries and holding public office. The proslavery delegates made assisting a fugitive slave a capital offense, punishable by death.

But this time antislavery forces in Kansas refused to recognize the proslavery legislature's authority. As the newly elected Kansas government passed laws protecting slavery in the territory, antislavery forces established their own government with its own elected legislature and governor, and a separate constitution. Most antislavery supporters in Kansas were not

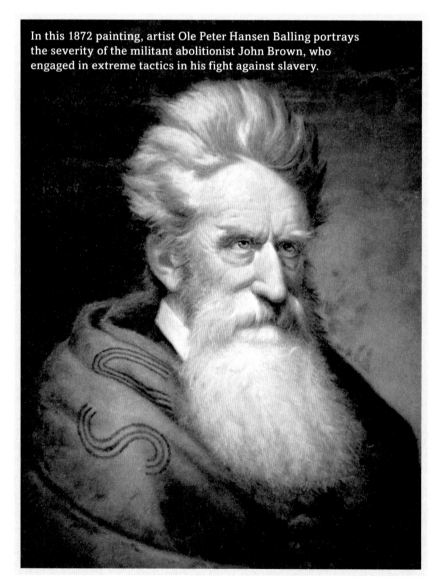

In this 1872 painting, artist Ole Peter Hansen Balling portrays the severity of the militant abolitionist John Brown, who engaged in extreme tactics in his fight against slavery.

A number of antislavery emigrant parties came to Kansas Territory armed with cannons to fight any proslavery forces that tried to keep them out. A photographer captured this group of northerners and their cannon in Topeka, Kansas Territory, in 1856.

full-fledged abolitionists. They were simply opposed to competing with plantation agriculture and its institution of slavery. While federal authorities tried to find a way to fix the election mess in Kansas, the territory was split between the two opposing state governments. In 1856, the proslavery government moved its capital to Lecompton, not far from Lawrence, which was a center of antislavery activism in the territory. The conflict in Kansas dragged on and became increasingly violent.

Violence escalated in May 1856 when a group of proslavery advocates ransacked Lawrence, set a hotel on fire and destroyed a newspaper office. They burned down the newspaper office and the Free State Hotel. The "**sack of Lawrence**," as this attack came to be known, shocked people throughout the country. Even more shocking, three days later the zealous abolitionist **John Brown** led his sons and several other followers in a violent revenge attack on a group of proslavery supporters. Brown's men dragged five men from their homes and hacked them to death on the banks of Pottawatomie Creek. Each of the victims had been connected in some way with the territorial court, but Brown's motives for choosing whom to attack have never been clearly established. Neither Brown nor his sons were ever punished for the murders.

Newspapers began to refer to the region as "**Bleeding Kansas**." The brutality even extended to the halls of Congress. During the height of the Kansas violence, Massachusetts senator and abolitionist Charles Sumner gave a speech calling out fellow senators, whom he blamed for causing the chaos in Kansas. He targeted Stephen Douglas, the popular sovereignty advocate from Illinois and author of the Kansas-Nebraska Act, and Andrew Butler, a proslavery leader from South Carolina. Sumner's verbal attacks on the elderly Butler were particularly harsh and personal. Congressman Preston Brooks, Butler's nephew, decided to avenge his family's honor by taking action against Sumner. On May 22, 1856, Brooks attacked Sumner as he was sitting at his desk in the Senate chamber, beating him over the head with a metal-tipped cane. The attack left Sumner severely injured and permanently scarred. Though the storm of violence in Kansas finally subsided after a new territorial governor took charge in September 1856, its rippling effect in Congress indicated a greater disturbance in the nation was to follow.

HISTORICAL THINKING

1. **READING CHECK** Why were abolitionists opposed to the Kansas-Nebraska bill?

2. **IDENTIFY MAIN IDEAS AND DETAILS** What was the main platform of the newly formed Republican Party?

3. **SUMMARIZE** What incidents led to the use of the term "Bleeding Kansas"?

4. **INTERPRET MAPS** How did the Kansas-Nebraska Act affect the balance of power between slave states and free states?

Dred Scott and the Debate over Slavery

Boundaries between slave states and free states were negotiated to maintain a balance of power in Congress. But what happens when a slave owner moves with his slave from a slave state to a free state? What do these boundaries mean *then*?

DRED SCOTT DECISION

In 1857, the U.S. Supreme Court made a ruling that would increase discord about slavery. The case involved an African American named **Dred Scott**. John Emerson, a doctor in the U.S. Army, had purchased Scott as a slave in 1833. Emerson then relocated to the Wisconsin Territory, where slavery was illegal under the provisions of the Missouri Compromise. Scott continued to work for Emerson without wages while in the territory. However, because Emerson's work required him to be away for long periods, Scott was hired out to others for pay. While living in Wisconsin Territory, Scott also met and married Harriet Robinson, who was enslaved by a federal Indian agent. Emerson purchased Harriet, and the Scotts eventually had two daughters, who were also Dr. Emerson's property.

Emerson married in 1838 and moved back South, bringing the Scotts with him. Three years later, Emerson died in Missouri. In his will, he instructed that the Scott family and his other slaves be left to his wife's family. Dred Scott wanted to use the money he had been saving to purchase freedom for himself, his wife, and their daughters, but the family's new owners refused. Dred Scott sued, arguing that his time living in the free Wisconsin Territory made him a free man. The case worked its way up through the court system, with various outcomes for and against Scott until it finally wound up before the Supreme Court in 1846.

At this time, southerners, led by Chief Justice **Roger B. Taney**, dominated the Supreme Court. Its 1857 decision in **Dred Scott v. Sandford**, written by Taney, not only went against Scott's request, but went further than anyone expected. In the **Dred Scott decision**, the Court declared that it could not rule on the merits of Scott's request because as property, enslaved African Americans "had no rights which the white man was bound to

🏛 **Missouri History Museum St. Louis, Missouri**

During the 1880s, the artist Louis Schultze painted this life-size portrait of Dred Scott for the Missouri Historical Society as part of a series depicting notable residents of St. Louis. Although painted after Scott's death, the image was based on the only known photograph taken of Scott, who wore a similar suit jacket, white shirt, and bow tie.

respect." In other words, Scott had no standing to sue in federal court as African Americans could not be considered U.S. citizens, even those who had been born free. Furthermore, the decision declared that the ownership of slaves was a property right, and Congress had no authority to limit slavery in territories such as Wisconsin, so the Missouri Compromise had been illegal. This essentially meant that slavery could extend anywhere in the United States, regardless of local opinion or established law.

Reaction to the decision was swift. Many southerners were relieved, although even they were surprised by how far the Court went. Rather than resolving the issue, however, the decision only enraged abolitionists and Free-Soil supporters. If the Dred Scott decision were followed to its logical conclusion, they warned, the United States would reopen the slave trade with Africa and even extend slavery into northern states, where it had been banned. Most authorities quietly ignored the ruling rather than enforce it. The case unintentionally boosted support for the rising Republican Party.

You are probably wondering what happened to Dred Scott and his family. During the trial and its many appeals, Dred Scott received assistance from a surprising source: the original family who had sold him to John Emerson. The adult sons of Scott's first owner paid his legal fees as the case worked its way through the courts. After the Supreme Court decision, the family purchased Scott and his family and granted them their freedom. Dred Scott died just 16 months after finally becoming free.

LINCOLN-DOUGLAS DEBATES

The Dred Scott case played an important role in the 1858 race for U.S. senator from Illinois, which would set the stage for the next presidential election. Incumbent Democratic Senator Stephen A. Douglas was running for re-election against Republican lawyer Abraham Lincoln. Although state legislatures, rather than individual voters, elected U.S. senators at this time, the candidates held seven public debates that newspapers covered nationally.

The Lincoln-Douglas debates highlighted the candidates' differing views on expanding slavery into new territories. Douglas reaffirmed his commitment to popular sovereignty. Lincoln expressed his personal belief that slavery was immoral and should be placed on a path toward "ultimate extinction." In terms of policy for the meantime, however, Lincoln reaffirmed the Free-Soil position that slavery needed to be confined rather than rashly abolished. Douglas

PRIMARY SOURCES

Lincoln and Douglas gained the attention of the nation during their race for the Illinois U.S. Senate seat. Because they mainly debated the issue of slavery, the outcome of their contest had repercussions for the entire country.

Judge Douglas declares that if any community want[s] slavery, they have a right to have it. He can say that, logically, if he says that there is no wrong in slavery; but if you admit that there is a wrong in it, he cannot logically say that anybody has a right to do wrong.

—from a speech by Abraham Lincoln during one of the Lincoln-Douglas debates, 1858

I hold that the people of the slaveholding States are civilized men as well as ourselves; . . . It is for them to decide, therefore, the moral and religious right of the slavery question for themselves within their own limits.

—from a speech by Stephen Douglas during one of the Lincoln-Douglas debates, 1858

seized on Lincoln's statements to portray him as a dangerous radical whose views could further tear the country apart.

During one of the debates held in Freeport, Illinois, Lincoln challenged Douglas to discuss how popular sovereignty could exist after the Dred Scott decision. Douglas argued that local communities could undermine the ruling by refusing to enact slave codes (similar to local police regulations), which were used to control enslaved people and prevent them from running away. And because few slaveholders would choose to live in communities without laws protecting their right to hold humans as property, slavery would be kept at a minimum in the areas where communities refused to enact slave codes. This concept became known as Douglas's **Freeport Doctrine**.

But Douglas's doctrine only widened a growing sectional division within the Democratic Party. Some northern Democrats were satisfied with Douglas's position. Many southern Democrats adamantly opposed it. To them, Douglas was not an ally they could count on to protect their interests. Although Douglas won the election and retained his seat in the U.S. Senate, he lost national standing within his own party. Lincoln, on the other hand, lost the election but won a national following within the Republican Party.

THE RAID ON HARPERS FERRY

With tensions already rising over slavery in the territories, a familiar face reemerged to fan the flames of conflict. Radical abolitionist John Brown, who had worked with the Underground Railroad and led the murderous attack on slavery supporters at Pottawatomie Creek during the "Bleeding Kansas" crisis, launched his boldest effort yet. After his action in Kansas, Brown and his followers led a group of newly freed slaves to assured freedom in Canada.

Brown had fled capture in Kansas, and for the next few years he spent most of his time in the North, speaking about slavery and abolition to audiences. Hatching a plan to lead a larger-scale slave revolt in Maryland and Virginia, Brown solicited money from wealthy and willing contributors to fund this insurrection. With this money, he purchased weapons for his planned initial attack.

On October 16, 1859, Brown led 21 men—only 5 of them African American—in an attack on the federal arsenal at **Harpers Ferry, Virginia**. The group took several slave owners hostage, believing their slaves would take arms from the arsenal and join the revolt. They hoped an army of liberators would rise up across the South and overthrow slavery in a bloody rebellion.

Instead, U.S. Army forces overtook the arsenal, killing several of Brown's followers and wounding Brown himself, whom they captured alive. The federal government quickly tried Brown and sentenced him to hang for treason. A defiant Brown went to the gallows, still claiming that his actions were necessary and called for by God.

Once again, reactions to John Brown's deeds and execution varied by region. Some northern abolitionists hailed him as a righteous victim who had sacrificed himself to the antislavery cause. Southerners were horrified by the violence carried out by Brown and his followers. To them, he was an example of growing extremism within the abolition movement.

HISTORICAL THINKING

1. **READING CHECK** What legal argument did Dred Scott rely on when he sued for his freedom?

2. **IDENTIFY MAIN IDEAS AND DETAILS** What reasons did the Supreme Court give to support its decision in the Dred Scott case?

3. **SUMMARIZE** Why did national newspapers cover the debates in Illinois between Lincoln and Douglas?

4. **FORM AND SUPPORT OPINIONS** Was John Brown justified in attempting to raid the Harpers Ferry arsenal? Support your opinion.

Harpers Ferry National Historic Park, West Virginia

Harpers Ferry lies where the Potomac and Shenandoah rivers converge, as shown in this aerial image taken by National Geographic photographer Ken Garrett. The scene of John Brown's 1859 raid on the armory, the town later became the site of one of the nation's first integrated schools—attended by both African Americans who had been enslaved and whites. Today it is part of Harpers Ferry National Historical Park at a point in the Blue Ridge Mountains where West Virginia, Virginia, and Maryland meet.

THE ELECTION OF 1860

It was clear that "a house divided" couldn't stand, and a presidential election wasn't going to fix the problem. It was becoming obvious that whoever won the election of 1860 would have the unlucky task of keeping the nation from falling.

NOMINATING LINCOLN

Going into the national Republican convention of 1860, the front-runner, or leading candidate, for the presidential nomination was U.S. Senator **William Seward**, a former governor of New York. Seward was a fierce abolitionist who had left the Whigs to join the Republican fight against the expansion of slavery into new territories. However, a relative newcomer to the national spotlight overshadowed Seward. As you have read, just two years before the convention, Abraham Lincoln had lost his bid for the U.S. Senate seat from Illinois to Stephen A. Douglas. But Lincoln's riveting performances during the much-publicized Lincoln-Douglas debates had won him nationwide attention.

Lincoln was firm in his stance on slavery: he did not expect it to be abolished anytime soon, but it should not be allowed to spread. Seward was much more outspoken in his opposition to slavery. Slavery was such a divisive issue in the country that many Republican party members viewed Lincoln as the more moderate, practical choice. And it didn't hurt Lincoln's chances for nomination that the 1860 Republican National Convention was being held in Lincoln's home state of Illinois. Thousands of Lincoln's supporters descended upon the convention site in Chicago—a makeshift structure called the Wigwam—to promote "Honest Abe." The majority of Republicans at the convention soon saw Lincoln as the future of the party. After three ballots, Lincoln had secured the party's nomination.

A political banner from 1860 advertises presidential candidate Lincoln and his running mate Hannibal Hamlin.

A BROKEN PARTY

Meanwhile, as the Republican Party rallied behind Lincoln, sectional differences were splitting the Democratic Party in two. The Democrats had long depended on attracting voters and support from both the South and the North, but that ability was nowhere to be found in Charleston, South Carolina, at the first Democratic National Convention of 1860. Disagreements over slavery led southern Democrats to walk out of the convention.

As Stephen A. Douglas, Lincoln's former senatorial opponent, was securing his candidacy at the convention, the southern delegates who had walked out were holding their own separate convention. They nominated **John C. Breckinridge** of Kentucky as their candidate. Northern democrats staged yet another convention in Baltimore, Maryland, to try to bring the southern delegates back into the fold, but it became clear the split could not be mended. The race now had a northern Democrat, Douglas, and a southern Democrat, Breckinridge, running against one another—as well as against Republican candidate Lincoln—for the presidency.

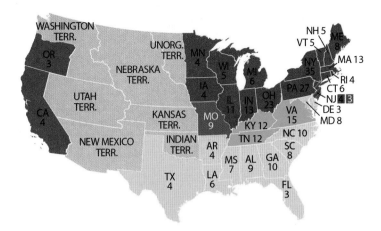

The 1860 Election

Abraham Lincoln, Republican	
Electoral Vote: 180 votes, 59.4%	
Popular Vote: 1,866,452 votes, 39.8%	

Stephen A. Douglas, Northern Democrat	
Electoral Vote: 12 votes, 3.9%	
Popular Vote: 1,380,202 votes, 29.5%	

John C. Breckinridge, Southern Democrat	
Electoral Vote: 72 votes, 23.8%	
Popular Vote: 847,953 votes, 18.1%	

John Bell, Constitutional Unionist	
Electoral Vote: 39 votes, 12.9%	
Popular Vote: 590,901 votes, 12.6%	

Then a fourth candidate entered the race. Hoping to unite the country beyond sectional differences, some former members of the Whig Party and what few remnants were left of the Know-Nothings joined forces to create the **Constitutional Union Party**. The party appealed to people who believed that preserving the Union and protecting the Constitution outweighed concerns about slavery. It nominated **John Bell**, a highly regarded former U.S. senator from Tennessee and a slaveholder. With so many candidates for the presidency, the Unionists—as members of the Constitutional Union Party were called—counted on there being a deadlock that the House of Representatives would have to settle. Unionists hoped that legislators in the House would end up voting for Bell.

A FIERCE ELECTION

With four candidates running in an increasingly divided nation, the individual campaigns operated as if there were two separate elections taking place: one in the North and one in the South. Northern voters focused on choosing between Lincoln and Douglas, while southern voters considered Bell and Breckinridge as options. Some southern states did not even include Lincoln or Douglas on their ballots.

Lincoln did not campaign in the South, or in the North for that matter. Following the practice of the time, he remained at home in Springfield, Illinois, where he received Republican delegations and discussed important issues of the day. Constitutional Union Party candidate Bell did not go out on the campaign trail either, and southern Democrat Breckenridge gave only one speech, in Lexington, Kentucky. Stephen A. Douglas, on the other hand, traveled all over the North and as far South as Alabama warning voters not to let sectionalism drive their votes. However, Douglas's efforts went unrewarded, especially in the South, where he endured insults and had rotten fruit thrown at him.

On election day, Lincoln won 40 percent of the overall popular vote and a commanding 60 percent majority of electoral votes. He swept the North—with the exception of New Jersey, which he split with Douglas—and the western states of Oregon and California. Lincoln did not win electoral votes in a single southern state. Douglas won almost 30 percent of the popular vote but received a mere 12 electoral votes: 9 from Missouri and 3 from New Jersey. Breckinridge won the entire South except for the three states that straddled the North and the South—Tennessee, Kentucky, and Virginia—which voted for Bell. Southerners were shocked that Lincoln had won the presidential election without a single electoral vote from the South.

HISTORICAL THINKING

1. **READING CHECK** What factors helped Lincoln defeat Seward in the Republican Party nomination of 1860?

2. **IDENTIFY MAIN IDEAS AND DETAILS** What did the Constitutional Union Party hope to achieve?

3. **DRAW CONCLUSIONS** Why were there two Democratic candidates in the 1860 presidential election?

4. **INTERPRET MAPS** Would the winner of the 1860 presidential election have been different if the states that voted for Bell had voted for another candidate? Explain your answer.

THE CONFEDERACY FORMS

In hindsight, it's hard to believe that some people wanted to leave their country after finding out that Abraham Lincoln was their president. Yet Lincoln's election was the straw that broke the camel's back— or broke the nation in two, in this case.

SECESSION

"THE DEED'S DONE" shouted a Mississippi headline announcing that Abraham Lincoln had won the presidential election. Lincoln's victory outraged many southerners. To them, it signaled the eventual destruction of slavery, and sooner rather than later. Despite Lincoln's assurances that he did not intend to threaten slavery where it already existed, many southern leaders believed it was only a matter of time before abolitionists achieved their goal. Few southerners believed that popular sovereignty or appeals to states' rights would protect the institution of slavery within the United States. Instead, they began seriously discussing the matter of secession.

Different perspectives of secession existed in both the South and the North. Some white southerners argued that secession was treason, while others felt it was the best way to present a united front against the North. Northerners were also split, with some northern Democrats calling for conciliation with the South. In December 1860, Kentucky Senator John J. Crittenden tried to play the role of peacemaker, proposing a compromise plan in Congress that he hoped would stop talk of secession. His **Crittenden Plan**, which was also called the Crittenden Compromise, would remove any federal power to abolish slavery in states where it already existed. It would also restore the north-south division of the Missouri Compromise and extend it to the Pacific Ocean. This would nullify the Compromise of 1850 and disregard popular sovereignty, except in states south of the Missouri Compromise line.

The plan found support in both the North and the South, and President James Buchanan pushed for its speedy approval in Congress. However, many

Republicans—including President-elect Abraham Lincoln—strongly objected to extending slavery into any new territories. By the middle of January 1861, the Senate had killed the plan.

Many southerners saw their options dwindling, with secession as the only remaining solution. Although southern leaders had repeatedly threatened to secede from the Union over the first half of the 19th century, no state had formally attempted it. Lincoln did not even believe secession was legal under the U.S. Constitution. Others argued that since the United States was originally formed as an agreement between states, any state had the right to leave the Union if it so desired.

Lincoln was due to take office in March 1861, and some southern states wanted to secede before his inauguration. In South Carolina, delegates held a convention in December 1860 to declare they were leaving the Union. Among their reasons were that northern states had "denounced as sinful the institution of slavery" and elected a president "whose opinions and purposes [were] hostile to slavery." Southerners serving in President Buchanan's outgoing cabinet began to resign. In January and February 1861, six states from the Deep South followed South Carolina's lead and seceded: Mississippi, Florida, Alabama, Georgia, Louisiana, and Texas. Delegates from these states met in Alabama to create a provisional constitution, which was similar to that of the United States except in its explicit guarantee of slavery and states' rights.

Although he publicly declared that states did not have the right to secede, President James Buchanan did little else in response. In fact, he refused to take any action to stop the secession.

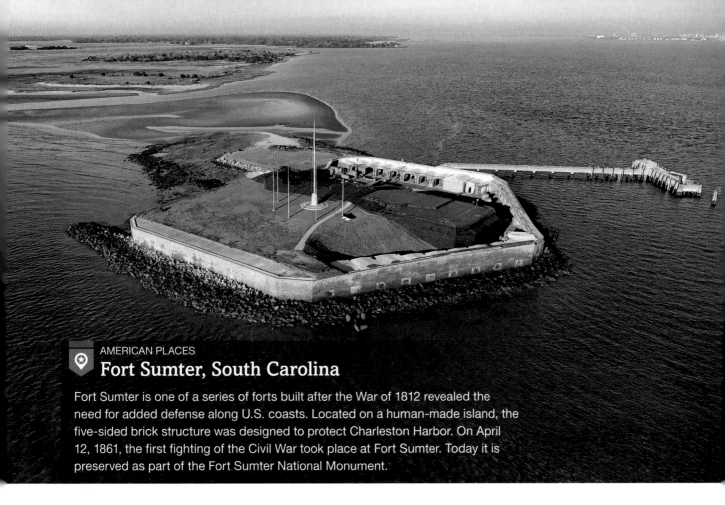

AMERICAN PLACES
Fort Sumter, South Carolina

Fort Sumter is one of a series of forts built after the War of 1812 revealed the need for added defense along U.S. coasts. Located on a human-made island, the five-sided brick structure was designed to protect Charleston Harbor. On April 12, 1861, the first fighting of the Civil War took place at Fort Sumter. Today it is preserved as part of the Fort Sumter National Monument.

THE CONFEDERATE STATES OF AMERICA

At their February 1861 meeting, delegates from the seceding states formally established a new country, called the **Confederate States of America**, also referred to as the **Confederacy**. They launched a temporary government headquartered in Montgomery, Alabama, where they inaugurated **Jefferson Davis** as provisional president with Alexander H. Stephens as vice president. The Confederacy eventually adopted a constitution that limited its president to one six-year term.

In the meantime, with President Buchanan refusing to use force against the seceding states, local militias in the Confederacy began seizing U.S. government property. In most cases, U.S. officials and military forces gave up the property peacefully and retreated from the seceded state back into Union territory. However, in some places stalemates occurred. That's what happened at **Fort Sumter**, a U.S. fort located on an island in Charleston Harbor, South Carolina.

Two days after South Carolina seceded, U.S. Army Major Robert Anderson and his troops secured control of the fort, which was still under construction, and they refused to surrender. Rather than attack Fort Sumter and drive out the troops, the South Carolinians held siege, preventing supply ships from reaching the island. Anderson alerted authorities in Washington, D.C., that his troops had about four months' worth of supplies. By that time, Abraham Lincoln would be president. James Buchanan decided to let Lincoln deal with the crisis.

As Lincoln prepared for his inauguration, he faced challenges on numerous fronts. Seven slave states had seceded from the Union, and eight slave states remained. The use of force or threats would likely cause the remaining slave states to secede. People throughout the country waited to see what would happen next.

HISTORICAL THINKING

1. **READING CHECK** Why did Lincoln's election prompt the secession of some states?

2. **SUMMARIZE** What process did the first seven states to secede follow to separate themselves from the United States?

3. **DRAW CONCLUSIONS** Why do you think most U.S. officials in the South gave up federal property without a fight?

4. **MAKE CONNECTIONS** How did the Crittenden Plan build on past legislation in its effort to resolve the secession crisis?

VOCABULARY

Use each of the following vocabulary terms in a sentence that shows an understanding of the term's meaning.

1. recession
   During the recession, many factories closed because people could no longer afford to buy their products.

2. proviso

3. popular sovereignty

4. omnibus bill

5. nativist

6. Dred Scott decision

7. Underground Railroad

8. Confederacy

READING STRATEGY
IDENTIFY MAIN IDEAS AND DETAILS

Identifying the main ideas and details of a text helps a reader understand the content and follow all the parts of a narrative. Use a graphic organizer like the one shown here to identify the details contributing to the growing problem of sectionalism in the United States. Then answer the question.

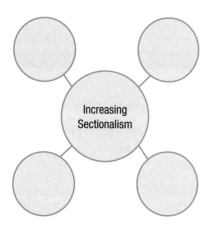

Increasing Sectionalism

9. In what ways did slavery divide the North and the South in the mid-19th-century United States?

MAIN IDEAS

Answer the following questions. Support your answers with evidence from the chapter.

10. During the 1840s and 1850s, why did large groups of Irish and Germans immigrate to the United States? **LESSON 1.1**

11. What were the main provisions of the Compromise of 1850? **LESSON 1.2**

12. Why was Harriet Beecher Stowe famous? **LESSON 2.1**

13. Why was the Kansas-Nebraska Act so controversial? **LESSON 2.3**

14. Explain the Freeport Doctrine. **LESSON 2.4**

15. When and why was the Constitutional Union Party formed? **LESSON 3.1**

16. How were Abraham Lincoln's and Stephen Douglas's ideas about the issue of slavery alike and how were they different? **LESSON 3.1**

17. What was the Crittenden Plan? **LESSON 3.2**

HISTORICAL THINKING

Answer the following questions. Support your answers with evidence from the chapter.

18. **SUMMARIZE** What role did cotton play in both the northern textile industry and southern plantation agriculture?

19. **IDENTIFY MAIN IDEAS AND DETAILS** What was the most controversial part of the Compromise of 1850 for northerners, and why?

20. **ANALYZE CAUSE AND EFFECT** What political developments led to the creation of the Republican Party?

21. **EVALUATE** How did the Dred Scott decision by the U.S. Supreme Court worsen the conflict over slavery?

22. MAKE INFERENCES What trends and events in the United States gave rise to the American Party, also called the Know-Nothing Party?

23. FORM AND SUPPORT OPINIONS Based on the evidence provided in this chapter, do you think it was inevitable that the South would split from the North? Explain your response.

INTERPRET VISUALS

This lithograph by T. H. Maguire titled *Outward Bound, The Quay of Dublin*, depicts a man in Dublin, Ireland, studying a poster advertisement about ocean voyages to New York City. It was engraved sometime before 1860. Examine the cartoon and answer the questions that follow.

24. Why do you think the artist chose to show this particular view from within the city of Dublin?

25. What details in the lithograph help you understand why the man might be interested in leaving Ireland?

ANALYZE SOURCES

On July 5, 1852, Frederick Douglass delivered a scathing speech against slavery in Rochester, New York. The city's leaders had asked him to speak at the local Independence Day festivities, and speak he did. Read the excerpt from the speech and answer the question that follows.

> It is not light that is needed, but fire; it is not the gentle shower, but thunder. We need the storm, the whirlwind, and the earthquake. The feeling of the nation must be quickened [made to live]; the conscience of the nation must be roused; the propriety of the nation must be startled; the hypocrisy of the nation must be exposed; and its crimes against God and man must be proclaimed and denounced.

26. How does this excerpt explain Douglass's reasons for giving a fiery speech against slavery rather than delivering a standard flag-waving Fourth of July address?

CONNECT TO YOUR LIFE

27. EXPLANATORY Think about how the issue of states' rights surrounding slavery divided the nation to the point of its breaking apart. Now consider the issues that divide American citizens today. Choose one of these issues and write an essay summarizing its impact on the United States.

TIPS

- Brainstorm a list of divisive issues the people of the United States are facing today and choose the one you find most compelling.

- Research to learn more about both sides of the issue.

- Form a topic sentence naming the issue and explaining why you believe it to be important.

- Develop the topic with relevant facts and concrete details. Be sure to address both sides of the issue.

- Conclude your essay by restating and briefly supporting your topic sentence.

THE CIVIL WAR

1861–1865

HISTORICAL THINKING How did the Civil War change the way different groups of Americans viewed themselves and the nation?

"Whatever happens, there will be no turning back."

—Ulysses S. Grant

CRITICAL VIEWING Ball's Bluff National Cemetery near Leesburg, Virginia, is one of the nation's smallest Civil War-era cemeteries. Established in 1865, this quiet spot is the final resting place for 54 Union soldiers killed in a battle fought nearby. What does the perspective of this photograph reveal about the site?

AMERICAN STORIES

NATIONAL GEOGRAPHIC

NAVAL BATTLES
OF THE
CIVIL WAR

The Battle of Hampton Roads in 1862 pitted a Confederate ship once described as "a floating barn roof" against a Union ship called a "tin can on a shingle." The vessels may have not have been graceful, but they heralded the beginning of modern naval warfare.

The confrontation between these two ships, the Confederacy's C.S.S. *Virginia* and the Union's U.S.S. *Monitor* is the most famous naval battle of the Civil War. It marked a turning point in military technology and secured the Union's dominance when it came to sea power. Hampton Roads was, however, just one of several key naval battles of the Civil War. This American Story spotlights three of these engagements.

HAMPTON ROADS

Both the *Virginia* and the *Monitor* were ironclads, a new breed of steam-powered warship. As the name implies, an ironclad was sheathed in iron plates. The Confederates salvaged a Union ship called the U.S.S. *Merrimack* and renamed it the *Virginia*. They then replaced its upper hull with a structure made of iron. In all, the ship was 263 feet long. The *Monitor*, the Union ship, was an entirely new design. Its 172-foot hull rose just above the waterline, making it hard to hit. It also had a revolving gun turret so that its cannons could fire in any direction.

Hampton Roads is a harbor at the mouth of the James River in Virginia. On March 8, 1862, it was under blockade by powerful wooden Union warships, including the *Congress* and the *Cumberland*, when the *Virginia* steamed into the harbor. The *Congress* unleashed its 20 cannons in a thunderous bombardment, but the *Virginia* shrugged off the assault. It pushed forward, one sailor recalled, "like the horrid creature of a nightmare," and pounded the *Congress* with multiple rounds of cannon shot. The *Virginia* next attacked the *Cumberland*. As the Union ship fired volley after volley, the *Virginia* rammed the *Cumberland* and sank it. Finally, the *Virginia* turned back to the *Congress* and finished it off, too.

Three other Union warships had hurried into the harbor to pursue the *Virginia*, but all three had run aground. Two had managed to escape, leaving the *Minnesota*,

CRITICAL VIEWING The crew of the U.S.S. *Monitor* pose for a photo on deck while the cook (left) tends the stove. The ship's revolving gun turret rises in the background. What do you think life was like for the sailors aboard the ironclad?

still stuck, to exchange fire with the *Virginia*. When evening fell and it became too dark to shoot, the *Virginia* returned to its moorings. Later that night, the *Monitor* quietly slid into Hampton Roads and tied up to the *Minnesota*. The next day would see a change in fortunes for both the Union and Confederacy.

When the *Virginia* approached the *Minnesota* on the morning of March 9, it was confronted by the Union ironclad. However, neither the *Virginia* nor the *Monitor* could gain the advantage. Eventually, the *Virginia* scored a hit on the *Monitor*'s pilothouse that partially blinded the ship's commander, Lieutenant John Worden. Worden immediately turned over command to his executive officer, and the *Monitor* retreated to shallow water where the *Virginia* could not follow. The *Virginia* prepared to renew its attack on the *Minnesota*, but it had a leak in its bow and was running short of ammunition. The Confederate ship was forced to withdraw for repairs.

Today, historians still debate who won the Battle of Hampton Roads. The fight between the *Monitor* and the *Virginia* was inconclusive. Craig Symonds, professor emeritus of history at the U.S. Naval Academy, believes the results of the fight favored the Union. "The battle was certainly a draw in the tactical sense," he says, "but in the strategic sense it was a clear Union victory. The *Monitor* neutralized the offensive potential of the *Virginia*, which allowed the Union Navy to remain in Hampton Roads." In terms of naval history, the battle was a landmark. March 8, 1862, came to be seen as the day the wooden warship died.

VICKSBURG

It is almost impossible to overestimate the importance of the Mississippi River to both sides in the Civil War. The Father of Waters, as the river was often called, was a major route for transporting goods to markets. When Mississippi and Louisiana seceded from the Union, free passage down the great river was blocked. Once the war began, the blockade threatened the northern economy and prevented the Union from transporting troops to southern battlefields.

The Union had gained control over much of the Mississippi by 1862, but the Confederacy still held a 200-mile stretch along Vicksburg, Mississippi. Sitting on a high bluff above a bend in the river,

INSIDE THE *MONITOR*

The *Monitor* was a radical departure from previous warship designs. Among the most revolutionary features was the gun turret that could pivot in any direction using steam power. Other innovations included a steam engine specially designed to fit into a tight space, a forced-air ventilation system, and flush toilets. Modern warships may not look much like the "tin can on a shingle," but the *Monitor* is the ancestor of today's battleships. The cutaway diagram below of the *Monitor* reveals its interior and compartments and provides information on the ship's size, speed, and engine.

Engineer and inventor John Ericsson designed the Union's first ironclad and even gave it its name: the *Monitor*.

- 360-degree rotating turret
- Two 11-inch shell guns
- Turret armor: 8-inch iron plating
- Engine exhaust vents
- Hatch
- Officer quarters
- Pilothouse
- Engine room
- Rudder
- Galley
- Berth deck/ Crew quarters
- Wardroom
- Captain's quarters

- Crew: 58 men
- Speed: 7 knots
- Length: 173 feet

Cutaway of the U.S.S. *Monitor*, created by Matt McIntosh, courtesy of NOAA's Monitor National Marine Sanctuary

CRITICAL VIEWING
Vicksburg's Battery Sherman, shown here in a photograph taken between 1863 and 1865, was built by the Union after it won the Battle of Vicksburg in 1863. The battery was named for Union general William Tecumseh Sherman, who played an important role in the battle. What geographic advantages did the battery give the Union over the Confederate Army?

Vicksburg commanded the perfect position to block passage on the Mississippi. Heavily fortified batteries, or artillery units, in and around the city could target any ship that attempted the stretch with a punishing barrage. To Abraham Lincoln, Vicksburg was the key to all the productive land in the southern states. As long as Vicksburg commanded the river, southern troops could be supplied with food by ships plying the Mississippi.

The difficult job of taking Vicksburg fell to General Ulysses S. Grant. Grant's troops were on the east side of the river, across from the city. His plan of attack required him to find a way to land the soldiers on the west side of the river south of Vicksburg. To make it happen, Grant called on Union admiral David Porter. Grant later recalled in his memoirs, "The cooperation of the navy was absolutely essential to the success (even to the contemplation) of such an enterprise."

At first, Grant requested only that Porter supply a few gunboats, but Porter proposed a bolder scheme. He would take nearly half of his squadron down the Mississippi, including ironclad gunboats and transports, in two separate sorties, or defensive attacks. At 10 p.m. on April 16, 1863, the first fleet, consisting of 7 ironclads, 1 warship equipped with rams, and 3 army transports, set out to make its way past the Vicksburg batteries under cover of night. Each ship had barges tied to it carrying baggage and supplies. Porter had also ordered bales of cotton and hay and sacks of grain to be stacked around the ships' boilers to protect them from Confederate shots and to conceal the boiler fires. The Union Army could use these supplies, too, once they were unloaded downstream.

In the end, the effort at secrecy was in vain. As Grant recalled, "The enemy were evidently expecting our fleet, for they were ready to light up the river by means of bonfires on the east side and by firing houses on the point of land opposite the city on the Louisiana side. The sight was magnificent, but terrible."

The night was turned to thunderous daylight by the bonfires and the nonstop firing of the Vicksburg batteries. Grant observed that the fleet was under attack for more than two hours, while other accounts claimed that the barrage lasted for four. Witnesses claimed the sound of the guns could be heard from 30 miles away.

Despite the furious shelling, Porter's small first fleet suffered very little damage. One transport was destroyed, but its crew abandoned ship and was rescued. Other ships suffered some damage but remained largely intact. Even better, no men were killed during the passage, although a dozen were wounded. The second fleet also emerged relatively unharmed. Grant's men, meanwhile, marched south to meet the boats and gain transport across the river to the Vicksburg side. Once the troops landed, the Union Navy continued to provide support by bombarding key sites from the river.

The Battle of Vicksburg was far from over with the landing of the troops. The city finally surrendered to Grant on July 4, 1863, after hard fighting and high casualties on both sides. However, without the participation of Porter and his fleets, the battle to completely open the Mississippi might have been even more costly in lives lost.

CRITICAL VIEWING The *Monitor* (in the foreground) and the *Virginia* exchange fire in this 19th-century print. Note that shots from the *Monitor* issue from its round, rotating turret. Why do you think the battle between the two ironclads ended in a stalemate?

MOBILE BAY

Have you ever heard the expression "Damn the torpedoes, full steam ahead!"? People use the phrase to express a determination to go forward with an action, no matter the obstacles. Few know that it originated with Union admiral David Farragut, the victor at the Battle of Mobile Bay.

In August 1864, Mobile Bay, Alabama, was a heavily fortified Confederate naval base. The bay's entrance was defended by two forts and by a field of floating mines, which were called torpedoes at that time. The Confederates had left a narrow channel free of torpedoes so that their blockade runners could slip into the harbor. Inside Mobile Bay lurked the *Tennessee*, a powerful ironclad under the direction of Confederate admiral Franklin Buchanan, who had also commanded the *Virginia*. His fleet included two lesser ironclads.

Admiral Farragut was in command of a fleet of four ironclads and several wooden steamships. He formed a plan to enter Mobile Bay through the narrow torpedo-free channel with his ironclads arranged in one column and the wooden vessels in another. The plan quickly went wrong, however, when some of the ships veered from their columns, and the ironclad *Tecumseh* hit a torpedo that sank it within 25 seconds. In an attempt to avoid total defeat, Farragut directed his own ship, the wooden-hulled *Hartford*, into the field of floating mines, shouting, "Damn the torpedoes!"

Incredibly, the *Hartford* proceeded through the minefield without setting off any torpedoes, possibly because many of them had faulty trigger mechanisms. The rest of the Union ships followed carefully in the *Hartford*'s path. As the ships entered the bay, Buchanan tried to ram them with the *Tennessee*, but the ironclad couldn't keep up with the faster wooden warships.

Then, Buchanan and Farragut engaged in a duel between the *Tennessee* and the *Hartford*. The ships slowly sailed toward each other—it took 15 minutes to cover the 4 miles that separated them. When they finally faced off, a sailor on the *Hartford* threw a spittoon at the other ship, and a sailor on the *Tennessee* succeeded in stabbing a *Hartford* crewman with his bayonet. Neither ship, however, scored a fatal hit against the other.

After the odd confrontation concluded, the *Tennessee* found itself surrounded by Union ships, all firing as rapidly as possible. The *Tennessee*, meanwhile, was experiencing problems with its ammunition. The fight was all but over when Buchanan was struck by flying debris and fell with a broken leg. He passed command to his captain, who surrendered shortly thereafter.

THINK ABOUT IT

What do battle narratives like these help you understand about events in history?

The two cannons shown in this photograph were removed from the *Monitor*'s revolving gun turret in 2004.

SAVING THE *MONITOR*

Both the *Monitor* and the *Virginia* ended their careers as wrecks on the sea bottom. Because the *Virginia* was scuttled intentionally in 1862, its location was known, and several salvage operations after the war brought up parts of the ship. Finding the *Monitor*, which sank in a storm off North Carolina in 1862, was more of a challenge.

In 1973, an expedition partially funded by the National Geographic Society located the shipwreck at last, using sonar, photography, and remotely operated vehicles. In 1975, the site of the *Monitor* shipwreck became the nation's first national marine sanctuary. In more recent years, the Mariners' Museum and Park in Virginia, the National Oceanic and Atmospheric Administration, the U.S. Navy, and other agencies have joined forces to raise and conserve parts of the *Monitor*. The ship's propeller was raised in 1998, and its innovative steam engine was returned to daylight in 2001. The *Monitor*'s most famous feature, its unique turret, was brought to the surface in 2002, after lying under the warship's overturned hull on the sandy sea bottom for 140 years.

The next step in the conservation process was to plunge the massive artifacts back into water, this time in special tanks at the Mariners' Museum and Park. These tanks contained a solution designed to remove the salt that had accumulated on all the artifacts' surfaces after sitting on the ocean floor for more than a century. Today, the propeller has been fully preserved and is on display in the museum's extensive *Monitor* exhibit. Other artifacts are still undergoing the preservation process in the museum's lab complex, where visitors can watch conservators at work revealing the secrets of the gun turret and other items.

In addition to many artifacts large and small, researchers made a gruesome discovery when they found the remains of two crewmen among the wreckage. These unknown sailors were among the 16 who perished when the *Monitor* went down.

DURING THE BATTLE OF HAMPTON ROADS

William F. Keeler, paymaster on board the *Monitor* during the Battle of Hampton Roads, described the harrowing experience in a letter to his wife.

PRIMARY SOURCE

In this excerpt from his letter, Keeler describes a moment during the battle when the *Monitor* and *Virginia* are firing at each other, and the grounded Union ship, the *Minnesota*, also joins the fight against the *Virginia*.

The sounds of the conflict at this time were terrible. The rapid firing of our own guns amid the clouds of smoke, the howling of the Minnesota's *shells, which was firing whole broadsides [a barrage of fire from one side of a ship] . . . just over our heads (two of her shots struck us), mingled with the crash of solid shot against our sides & the bursting of shells all around us. Two men had been sent down from the turret, who were knocked senseless by balls striking the outside of the turret while they happened to be in contact with the inside.*

—from William F. Keeler's letter, 1862

BEGINNINGS OF WAR

It was January 9, 1861. The *Star of the West* was headed to secessionist South Carolina to resupply army forces holed up at Fort Sumter. Suddenly the ship was overtaken by rebel gunfire and retreated. What would become of the soldiers at Fort Sumter now?

DECISION AT FORT SUMTER

In February 1861, president-elect Abraham Lincoln began a long railway trip from Illinois to Washington, D.C., pausing to speak to the people who came out to meet him along the way. At first, he downplayed the talk of secession coming from the South. But as the train rolled on, threats of war and even threats against the president himself increased. For his own safety, Lincoln sneaked into the nation's capital in the dark of night.

Abraham Lincoln took the oath of office on March 4, 1861. In his inaugural speech, he addressed concerns from the southern states, assuring that he had no intention of interfering with slavery where it already existed, that he would not use force against the South, and that he would not attempt to fill offices with men not supported by local communities. But he also warned that secession was illegal and that it was his duty to maintain the integrity of the federal government. Lincoln pleaded with his countrymen to move slowly and let heated feelings cool.

Lincoln believed the country was best served by having the most talented people in the Cabinet, even if they disagreed with him, so he appointed several Cabinet members who had previously been his political rivals. Three in particular—Secretary of State William H. Seward, Treasury Secretary Salmon P. Chase, and Attorney General Edward Bates—had run against him for the

Republican presidential nomination. This "team of rivals" grew to respect and become extremely loyal to Lincoln. He hoped that bringing together these men, some of whom held opposing ideas, would help him find ways to avoid war. However, events soon took over, elevating the simmering conflict into violence.

As you have read, by the time Lincoln took his oath of office, Fort Sumter, a Union fort on an island in Charleston Harbor, was surrounded by Confederate

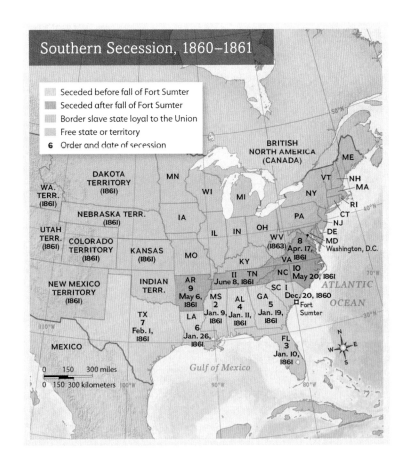

Southern Secession, 1860–1861

- Seceded before fall of Fort Sumter
- Seceded after fall of Fort Sumter
- Border slave state loyal to the Union
- Free state or territory
- **6** Order and date of secession

forces in South Carolina. Union soldiers held the fort, refusing to surrender. After Lincoln's inauguration, the commander at Fort Sumter reported that his troops would soon be out of food. Lincoln decided to send noncombat supplies to the fort.

Meanwhile, Jefferson Davis and his Confederate government had already decided that they would consider any attempt to supply the fort to be an act of war, and they determined that the Confederate commander in Charleston, P. G. T. Beauregard, should attack Fort Sumter before the Union relief ships had a chance to arrive. In the early hours of the morning on April 12, 1861, Beauregard's troops opened fire on Fort Sumter. The shelling continued for more than 30 hours before the Union forces finally surrendered. Luckily, no lives were lost in the attack, and the southern forces allowed the northern troops to evacuate the fort peacefully.

To Lincoln and other leaders of the federal government, the shelling of Fort Sumter was an act of war. As the president prepared to defend the Union by force, it became clear that the time for a peaceful resolution to political disagreements between the North and the South had run out.

ADVANTAGES AND DISADVANTAGES

The day after the Confederates raised their flag over Fort Sumter, President Lincoln called out 75,000 soldiers to help put the rebellion down. As a result, Virginia seceded. Confederate leaders then voted to move their capital to Richmond, Virginia, the largest and most industrialized city in the South.

Arkansas, Tennessee, and North Carolina soon followed Virginia's example and joined the Confederacy. Lincoln knew that if Maryland seceded, the District of Columbia would be completely surrounded by Confederate territory. Accordingly, he acted quickly to keep Maryland in the Union, jailing secessionist advocates and suspending the **writ of *habeas corpus***, a law that allowed prisoners to petition to a judge if they believed they had been arrested unlawfully. The suspension only applied to areas near rail lines between Philadelphia and Washington, and its goal was to protect the movement of troops, supplies, and weapons to the capital. With *habeas corpus* suspended, any secessionist arrested as a threat to the Union was effectively blocked from being released. Despite being a slave state, Maryland chose to remain in the Union. The other slave states on the border of the South—Kentucky, Missouri, and Delaware—also remained in the Union under pressure from the federal government.

Even in strongly pro-Confederate states, some people remained loyal to the federal government. In the mountains of western Virginia, delegates met to declare their allegiance to the Union. These 50 counties formed the new state of **West Virginia**, which joined the Union in 1863 as a slave state. The strategic need to keep the slave-holding **border states** from seceding was one of the reasons Lincoln did not focus on the future of slavery in the initial days of the war, but instead emphasized the illegality of secession and the need to preserve the Union. Many people in the North and the South found his tactics, such as suspension of the writ of *habeas corpus*, to be an abuse of federal power.

At the outset of the war, the North held an advantage in terms of overall resources. The Union states had greater industrial capacity; a more extensive system of railroads and canals; more food, draft animals, and ships; and four times as many free citizens eligible for military service as the South. However, the North faced fighting an **offensive war**, meaning that victory depended on invading the Confederates' home territory. Lincoln's government also had to convince skeptical northerners that it would be worth the cost in lives and resources to keep the southern states in the Union by force.

The Confederacy possessed considerable military advantages. It could wage a **defensive war**, protecting its homeland and fighting on ground that was familiar to local forces. The Confederates also had an initial advantage in military leadership. Some of the most experienced U.S. military generals resigned to fight for the South. For example,

SCOTT'S GREAT SNAKE.

The Anaconda Plan was meant to strangle the South by cutting off trade between slave states in the East and the West and between the Confederacy and Europe. General Winfield Scott believed his plan would put an early end to the war and limit the number of casualties.

Scott proposed sending a large naval force down the Mississippi River that would capture forts and towns along its banks.

Union ships patrolled the coastal border to prevent deliveries of weapons and supplies to southern states.

Scott's plan was never fully implemented, but a naval blockade was maintained throughout the war, largely cutting off the South's access to money, food, and war supplies from abroad. Scott himself believed the war would last for two years.

coal

corn

cotton

peaches

oranges

cattle

hay

banking

tobacco

sheep

apples

sugar cane

horses

A Confederate hundred-dollar bill (left) features enslaved African Americans working fields, the Greek goddess Minerva, and former Vice President John C. Calhoun. An eagle, Liberty, and Abraham Lincoln are featured on the U.S. ten-dollar bill (below).

Robert E. Lee, who had served the United States as an officer in the Mexican-American War and as superintendent of the United States Military Academy at West Point, refused to fight against his home state of Virginia. Although he did not strongly support secession, Lee eventually became commander of the Army of Northern Virginia. Meanwhile, Lincoln struggled to find a leader for the Union Army who could win decisive victories on the battlefield.

STRATEGIES ON BOTH SIDES

When fighting first broke out, neither side expected the conflict to last long. Lincoln's initial call for troops was supposed to be for only 90 days of service. The Confederates believed northerners lacked the desire to fight an offensive war and would quickly negotiate a settlement. But by summer, both North and South began to recognize that the war might last beyond a few months. The Confederate Congress authorized 400,000 volunteers in May 1861, and in July 1861, the U.S. Congress authorized 500,000 troops. New soldiers enlisted for three years.

In terms of military strategy, the South saw itself as purely on the defensive, but if the opportunity arose, it hoped to carry out a decisive strike against Washington, D.C. The North, for its part, counted on General Winfield Scott's **Anaconda Plan**, named after the large snake that squeezes its prey to death. That plan depended on sending an overpowering force down the Mississippi, dividing the South in two. At the same time, the Union Navy would blockade southern seaports on the Atlantic coast and Gulf of Mexico to seal the South off from its global trading partners.

On the civilian side, Confederate leaders decided to print paper money to help fund the expensive war effort. Since the Confederacy had little gold or silver to back the value of this money, Confederate currency was really more like a **promissory note**, or an agreement to pay, that could be redeemed once the South won the war. As the war dragged on, the Confederates printed millions of dollars of currency even as the value of their money tumbled, leading to massive inflation and dire economic circumstances for the South. The Union relied more on taxes and bonds—loans to be repaid later—to fund the costs of the war. Eventually, however, it also had to issue paper money. More than $450 million in U.S. paper currency, called **greenbacks** because the backs of the bills were printed in green ink, circulated during the war.

HISTORICAL THINKING

1. **READING CHECK** Why did the Confederates fire on Fort Sumter?

2. **COMPARE AND CONTRAST** What advantages and disadvantages did each side have in the conflict?

3. **FORM AND SUPPORT OPINIONS** How do you think the Anaconda Plan could have shortened the war?

4. **INTERPRET MAPS** Of the four states that seceded after the attack on Fort Sumter, which one shared a border with only Confederate states?

1.2

MAIN IDEA Early battles proved that the Civil War was not going to be easy for either side to win.

EARLY COURSE OF THE WAR

Can you imagine packing a lunch and spending the afternoon watching a battle? In July 1861, civilians from Washington, D.C., heard that Confederate and Union troops were about to clash just outside town. Expecting a quick and exciting Union victory, many lined the battlefield carrying picnic baskets and champagne. The realities of war soon dimmed their spirits.

BATTLE OF BULL RUN

In the summer of 1861, both the North and the South were strategizing for a quick victory. With the opposing capitals of Richmond, Virginia, and Washington, D.C., so close to one another, a decisive attack by either side on the other's capital could mean a swift end to hostilities, which is why many of the early battles occurred in Virginia. Some Union leaders thought they should attack before the Confederates had time to

mobilize, or organize and train, their forces. But both Union and Confederate armies already had troops in position in northern Virginia.

Lincoln made the first move, sending out Union troops under the command of General Irvin McDowell with the goal of capturing Richmond. The soldiers marched south from Washington to Manassas, Virginia, where, on July 21, 1861, they

National Geographic photographer Ken Garrett captured a smoke-filled reenactment of the Battle of Bull Run in Manassas, Virginia.

faced off against Confederates commanded by General P.G.T. Beauregard in the first major battle of the war. Because it took place near a stream called Bull Run, the action is known in the North as the **First Battle of Bull Run**. In the South, it's called the First Battle of Manassas. Civilian spectators came out from Washington to watch, expecting a quick Union victory.

The fighting was harder than anyone expected, but Confederate troops took heart when one of their leaders pointed out General Thomas J. Jackson and his men holding their line and shouted, "There is Jackson standing like a stone wall!" From that time on, the general was known as **Stonewall Jackson**. The Confederates rallied and took the advantage when **J.E.B. Stuart**, the leader of the Confederate **cavalry**, or soldiers on horseback, sent his men to charge through the Union lines of **infantry**, or foot soldiers, forcing the Union troops to retreat. The Confederates won their first victory, but at a cost. The casualties were high on both sides.

Lincoln soon replaced McDowell with **George B. McClellan**, a hero of the Mexican-American War who had studied military tactics in Europe. McClellan had already frustrated Confederate forces under Robert E. Lee in western Virginia. Lincoln had high hopes for McClellan, but soon grew impatient as his general hesitated to launch a major offensive. Meanwhile, weakened by heavy casualties, Confederate forces failed to pursue further attacks against the North to follow their Bull Run victory.

WOMEN AND WAR

As both sides recruited men to fight in the war, women were also called upon to serve in a variety of ways. Within two weeks of the war's beginning, Union and Confederate women organized thousands of local aid societies to help supply uniforms and other necessities to their respective armies.

Many of these supplies were destined for hospitals. The sheer number of troops involved, along with the new and ever more destructive weapons used in the war, led to high numbers of casualties that overwhelmed understaffed hospitals. Women began filling nursing positions, even though only men had served as military nurses prior to the Civil War. Secretary of War Simon Cameron appointed Dorothea Dix, long known as a champion of the poor and mentally ill in the years before the war, to be superintendent of nurses for the Union Army. In spite of her title and responsibilities, neither she nor any of the female nurses who served in the Civil War received official military appointments.

PRIMARY SOURCE

If I were to speak of war, it would not be to show you the glories of conquering armies but the mischief and misery they strew in their tracks; and how, while they march on with [the] tread of iron and plumes proudly tossing in the breeze, some one must follow closely in their steps, crouching to the earth, toiling in the rain and darkness, shelterless like themselves, with no thought of pride or glory, fame or praise, or reward; hearts breaking with pity, faces bathed in tears and hands in blood. This is the side which history never shows.

—from remarks written by Clara Barton, date unknown

Female nurses worked long hours and tended to gruesome injuries previously believed to be too horrific for women to handle. Many distinguished themselves, earning the respect of career military men. **Kate Cumming**, from Alabama, was among the most honored Confederate nurses in the Mississippi region. She later wrote one of the most accurate memoirs about life in Confederate field hospitals. **Phoebe Pember**, the daughter of a prominent Jewish family in the South, wrote another famous southern hospital memoir. Pember served as a nurse and administrator at what was at the time the world's largest military hospital, in Virginia.

For some women, serving as Civil War nurses inspired future careers. Union nurse **Clara Barton**, nicknamed the "Angel of the Battlefield" for her service, went on to found the American Red Cross. Another Union nurse, Louisa May Alcott, became a famous author. Her wartime experiences shaped her fiction books, including *Little Women*.

On the home front, women took on the work of men serving in the war. In the North, women ran farms and worked in factories in addition to raising families all by themselves. In the South, women managed plantations, farmed, and fed their families in the face of high inflation and increasing food shortages. The burden of war was heavy for women on both sides.

HISTORICAL THINKING

1. **READING CHECK** How did the Battle of Bull Run end?

2. **IDENTIFY MAIN IDEAS AND DETAILS** Why did many early battles take place in Virginia?

3. **MAKE INFERENCES** In what ways did the Civil War affect the northern workforce?

4. **MAKE CONNECTIONS** How has the role of women in the medical profession changed since the Civil War?

MANASSAS, VIRGINIA

Near the town of Manassas, Virginia, flows a small stream called Bull Run. This was the site of the two major Civil War battles named after both the town and the stream. The First Battle of Bull Run, also known as the First Battle of Manassas, was fought on July 21, 1861, near the residence in the photograph, called the Stone House. During the battle, wounded Union soldiers sought refuge in the home's basement. Soon they could hear the cries of other wounded soldiers seeking shelter on the floor above.

The Second Battle of Bull Run, or the Second Battle of Manassas, took place more than a year later. Once again, the Stone House served as a Union aid station where medical officers treated wounded soldiers. Both battles resulted in Confederate victories and a staggering number of casualties. Today, the Stone House is part of Manassas National Battlefield Park, which covers about eight square miles and preserves the sites of the two historic battles.

CRITICAL VIEWING The landscape of Manassas National Battlefield Park features gently rolling hills covered by a patchwork of open meadows and mostly deciduous forests. The park spans nearly 5,100 acres with more than 40 miles of hiking trails, including paths that loop through the sites of the two battles. How would you characterize the mood of this photograph by National Geographic photographer Ken Garrett?

EARLY BATTLES ON LAND AND SEA

Maryland brothers Andrew and William Shriver not only grew up together, but lived next to one another as adults. When war broke out, however, Andrew sided with the Union while William aided the Confederacy. Their situation was a real-life example of the divisions that pitted brother against brother and neighbor against neighbor.

THE WAR IN THE WEST BEGINS

While Union and Confederate leaders eyed each other's capitals in the East, fighting expanded in the western border states, especially Missouri. Southern forces hoped to rally slaveholders in divided communities to their side, believing that victories over Union troops might lead those states to secede and join the Confederacy.

A few days after the Battle of Bull Run, Lincoln installed former Republican presidential candidate John C. Frémont as commander of the forces in Missouri. On August 10, 1861, two regiments of Confederate troops attempted to surround Union forces near Springfield, Missouri. Although the Union soldiers were outnumbered, they attacked the poorly equipped Confederates. Both sides suffered heavy casualties during the fighting, and both sides retreated, but the Union troops withdrew the farthest. For the time being, southwestern Missouri remained under Confederate control.

Confederate forces also staged guerrilla attacks throughout the state. With Missourians divided over the war, Frémont placed the entire state under martial law, or military authority. He ordered the death penalty for captured guerrillas and seized the slaves and other property of Confederate sympathizers. Slaveholders in the border states of Kentucky and Maryland threatened to join the Confederacy if Lincoln did not make Frémont back off. When Frémont resisted, Lincoln removed him from his post. Missouri remained in a state of turmoil throughout the war.

A descendant of Massachusetts Bay colonists, Ulysses S. Grant was born in Ohio in 1822. After graduating from West Point, he served with Winfield Scott in the Mexican-American War, participating in the sieges of Veracruz and Mexico City.

By 1862, Union generals in the West began to advance aggressively. Troops under the command of General **Ulysses S. Grant** pushed Confederates from southern Kentucky down the Tennessee and Cumberland rivers and across the Kentucky border into Tennessee. Important Confederate forts guarded both rivers, but Grant hoped to overwhelm them with combined attacks from water and land. He successfully assaulted Fort Henry on the Tennessee River in early February. He then marched his men overland to Fort Donelson on the Cumberland River. There, the Confederates fought desperately, destroying several Union gunboats, but Grant ultimately won control of the fort and the region it served. When the Confederate general in command of Fort Donelson attempted to negotiate with Grant for its surrender, Grant responded: "No terms except an unconditional and immediate surrender can be accepted." Within days, Union troops took nearby Nashville, the capital of Tennessee, the first capture of a southern state's capital during the war.

Artist J. G. Wells illustrated the close-range battle between the *Monitor* (front left) and the *Virginia* (front right) in this 1891 oil painting.

BATTLE OF THE IRONCLADS

From the beginning of the war, the Confederacy had hoped to win support from European trade partners that relied on southern cotton, especially France and England, both of which had already abolished slavery. But citizens of other nations were also divided by the Civil War in the United States. Many Europeans sympathized with the Confederates' desire for self-determination. European abolitionists, however, opposed any efforts to protect slavery. The South also overestimated its importance to European markets. British factories had stockpiled cotton in anticipation of the war, and Britain and other nations also began investing heavily in Egyptian cotton. European countries planned to remain neutral until they were more certain of which side would win the conflict. Meanwhile, the Union Navy continued to tighten its blockade under the North's Anaconda Plan, limiting the ability of southern smugglers to sneak cotton overseas.

As the naval war heated up, both sides began to experiment with new and improved maritime weapon technologies. The Confederacy was the first to build an **ironclad**, or ship covered in iron plates. After southern shipbuilders redesigned and cladded a captured Union ship, the U.S.S. **Merrimack**, the Confederacy changed the ship's name to the C.S.S. **Virginia**. The Union countered by designing its own ironclad, the U.S.S. **Monitor**. On March 8, 1862, the *Virginia* attacked several Union ships in the harbor at Hampton Roads, Virginia. Luckily for the Union Navy, the *Monitor* was nearby. The next day, the two ironclads engaged in a battle that lasted for hours

and technically ended in a draw. Many consider the battle a victory for the Union, which remained in possession of Hampton Roads.

Naval experiments eventually led to the first combat submarines—and the first combat submarine attack. The Confederates built a vessel they hoped could strike the enemy while remaining entirely underwater. The work was very dangerous. Several men lost their lives in test runs of the tiny, hand-cranked submarine called the *H. L. Hunley*. Despite this poor track record, by the latter part of the war Confederate leaders were so desperate to break the Union blockade that they called the experimental submarine into action. On February 17, 1864, the *Hunley* torpedoed the U.S.S. *Housatonic* in Charleston Harbor. Although most of the *Housatonic* crew escaped, the ship became the first ever sunk by a submarine. But the *Hunley* crew never lived to celebrate the victory. The submarine failed to resurface.

HISTORICAL THINKING

1. **READING CHECK** Why did Lincoln remove John C. Frémont as commander of the Union forces in Missouri?

2. **ANALYZE CAUSE AND EFFECT** What effect did the Battle of Hampton Roads have on the Union blockade of the South?

3. **MAKE CONNECTIONS** How did the war influence later naval technology?

THE BATTLES OF 1862

The pictures were startling. Using recently developed technology, Civil War photographers started capturing graphic images of bodies that lay strewn about battlefields after the fighting. The gruesome photos undermined any remaining optimism about a quick end to the war.

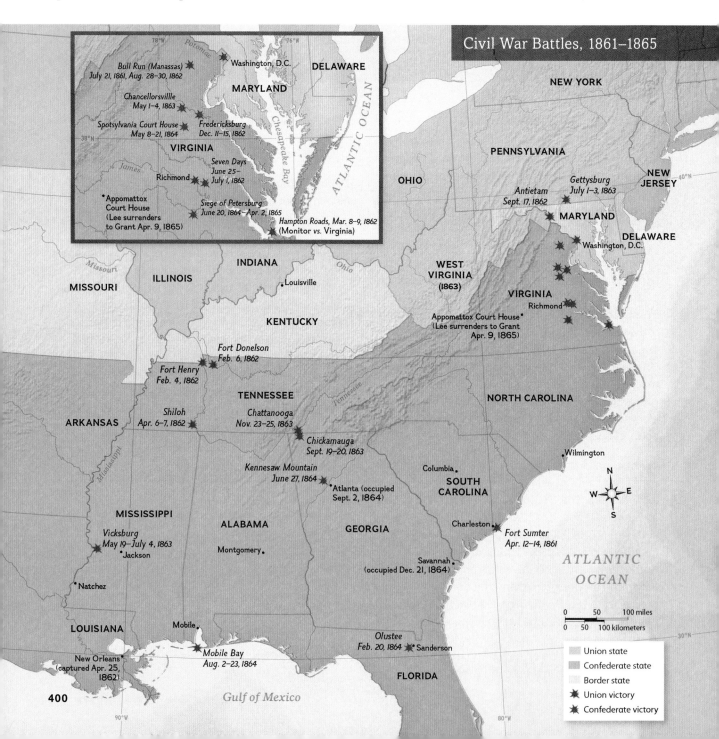

Civil War Battles, 1861–1865

Bull Run (Manassas)
July 21, 1861, Aug. 28–30, 1862

Washington, D.C.

DELAWARE

MARYLAND

Chancellorsville
May 1–4, 1863

Spotsylvania Court House
May 8–21, 1864

Fredericksburg
Dec. 11–15, 1862

VIRGINIA

Seven Days
June 25–
July 1, 1862

Richmond

Appomattox
Court House
(Lee surrenders
to Grant Apr. 9, 1865)

Siege of Petersburg
June 20, 1864–Apr. 2, 1865

Hampton Roads, Mar. 8–9, 1862
(Monitor vs. Virginia)

Chesapeake Bay

ATLANTIC OCEAN

NEW YORK

PENNSYLVANIA

OHIO

Antietam
Sept. 17, 1862

Gettysburg
July 1–3, 1863

NEW
JERSEY

MARYLAND

DELAWARE
Washington, D.C.

INDIANA

ILLINOIS

Louisville

MISSOURI

WEST
VIRGINIA
(1863)

VIRGINIA
Richmond

Appomattox Court House
(Lee surrenders to Grant
Apr. 9, 1865)

KENTUCKY

Fort Donelson
Feb. 6, 1862

Fort Henry
Feb. 4, 1862

TENNESSEE

NORTH CAROLINA

Shiloh
Apr. 6–7, 1862

Chattanooga
Nov. 23–25, 1863

ARKANSAS

Chickamauga
Sept. 19–20, 1863

Wilmington

Kennesaw Mountain
June 27, 1864

Columbia

Atlanta (occupied
Sept. 2, 1864)

SOUTH
CAROLINA

MISSISSIPPI

ALABAMA

GEORGIA

Charleston

Fort Sumter
Apr. 12–14, 1861

Vicksburg
May 19–July 4, 1863

Jackson

Montgomery

Savannah
(occupied Dec. 21, 1864)

ATLANTIC
OCEAN

Natchez

LOUISIANA

Mobile

Mobile Bay
Aug. 2–23, 1864

Olustee
Feb. 20, 1864   Sanderson

New Orleans
(captured Apr. 25,
1862)

FLORIDA

Gulf of Mexico

N
W   E
S

0   50   100 miles
0   50   100 kilometers

Union state
Confederate state
Border state
Union victory
Confederate victory

BATTLES IN THE EAST AND WEST

Combat on all **fronts**, or battle lines between armies, heated up by the spring of 1862. It seemed as if Union general George McClellan was finally ready to launch his long-delayed offensive in the East. McClellan planned to attack Richmond from the south to shift fighting farther away from Washington, D.C. But even after getting the go-ahead from President Lincoln, McClellan took several more weeks to prepare his men for what he expected to be the war's conclusive, or final, battle.

Meanwhile, in the West, generals Ulysses S. Grant and **William Tecumseh Sherman** pushed their troops deeper into Tennessee after their victories at Fort Henry and Fort Donelson. Their objective was Corinth, Mississippi, a major southern rail center, where 45,000 Confederate soldiers waited for them. If the Union could capture the railroads at Corinth, it would control most of the western Confederacy. However, Confederate general Albert Sidney Johnston learned about the plan and ambushed Grant's troops near a church in Shiloh, Tennessee, on April 6, 1862. The **Battle of Shiloh** began as a series of brutal fights among scattered groups of desperate men with little coordinated leadership. When General Johnston was killed leading an attack, he was replaced by P.G.T. Beauregard, who then succeeded in pushing the Union troops back two miles.

The Confederate advantage proved short lived, however, as 20,000 Union reinforcements arrived overnight. The next day Grant and his army regained the ground they had lost, and the Confederates retreated to Corinth. Although the southern forces had been badly beaten, Grant's troops were too exhausted to pursue them. The loss of life at what the press called "Bloody Shiloh" exceeded anything anyone had ever seen. With more than 23,000 casualties overall, Shiloh was the deadliest battle of the war so far. Horrified at the loss of life, some people urged Lincoln to remove Grant from his command, but the president refused. He is said to have responded, "I can't spare this man [Grant]; he fights!"

As Grant's forces were working to secure the upper Mississippi, Union naval forces under Commander **David Farragut** were trying to seize control of New Orleans. The city was protected by two well-armed

Confederate Memorial Hall New Orleans, Louisiana

Confederate and Union soldiers launched these three- to five-pound hand grenades like darts into enemy territory during the battles at Vicksburg and Petersburg, among others. New Yorker William Ketchum designed and patented this particular grenade. On impact, metal parts inside the grenade would grind against each other, causing a spark that would ignite gunpowder.

forts as well as a river blocked with thick cables. On April 24, Farragut and his fleet of 43 ships attacked the city, breaching the cables and sailing right up to the New Orleans docks. On April 25, Confederate leaders ordered more than 3,000 southern soldiers to evacuate New Orleans. Union ground troops soon arrived to occupy the city while Farragut's fleet continued up the Mississippi River, capturing Baton Rouge, Natchez, and Memphis. However, they were unable to dislodge the Confederate forces holding Vicksburg, Mississippi.

FIGHTING TO A STALEMATE

Throughout the war so far, Washington, D.C., remained a target for the Confederates. Lincoln and McClellan feared the capital faced a direct threat from Confederate troops stationed in the Shenandoah Valley under the command of Stonewall Jackson. For three months in the spring of 1862, Jackson led his men up and down the valley, creating the impression that his forces were larger than they were. As a result, the Union divided its troops, and McClellan cancelled his plans for an overland assault on Richmond, which would have required his army to march through the Shenandoah Valley. Instead, McClellan set sail from Washington, D.C., with around 100,000 soldiers, landing on the Virginia Peninsula and battling to within a few miles of Richmond. There, rather than pushing forward, McClellan decided to pull his men back because he feared they might be outnumbered when they reached the Confederate capital.

Meanwhile, in early June, Robert E. Lee replaced the wounded Joseph Johnston as commander of the Army of Northern Virginia, the largest field army of the Confederacy. Lee then ordered an attack against McClellan's larger force. He sent out cavalry leader

J.E.B. Stuart, whose soldiers rode all the way around McClellan's troops, scoping out their position and stealing their supplies. Lee soon brought in Jackson and his men to join the effort. The series of clashes that followed are called the **Seven Days' Battles** because they took place over seven days, between June 25 and July 1. The Confederates managed to protect Richmond and drive the Union troops back down the Virginia Peninsula, but they sustained heavy losses.

By July 1862, the war seemed to have reached a stalemate, with neither side gaining the upper hand. McClellan's hesitant performance in the Seven Days' Battles weakened Lincoln's already waning confidence in his leadership. Lincoln placed Major General Henry Halleck, who advocated a more aggressive stance, in charge of all the Union forces. McClellan remained a commander working under Halleck's command.

ANTIETAM

To better protect Washington, Lincoln and Halleck decided to remove McClellan from the Virginia Peninsula and consolidate his troops with others from the Shenandoah Valley. This unit would be under the joint command of McClellan and General John Pope. As McClellan's forces began to retreat from the peninsula in August, the Confederates saw a window of opportunity for an offensive attack. Lee decided to strike Pope's troops near Bull Run, before McClellan's group could join them. After defeating the Union at the Second Battle of Bull Run, Lee decided to continue his offensive and push into Maryland. But as McClellan's men were on the move, one soldier made a fortuitous discovery. He stumbled upon a packet of cigars in a field, dropped by a careless Confederate officer. Wrapped around the cigars were Lee's detailed plans for his attack on Maryland. The plans revealed that Lee had split his forces into two groups marching several miles apart. If McClellan moved quickly, he could ambush Lee's army before the two groups could meet up again. But once again, McClellan took action too late.

On September 17, Lee and McClellan met in battle once more, this time at Antietam (an-TEE-tuhm) Creek, near Sharpsburg, Maryland. The Confederates had only 35,000 men to McClellan's 72,000, but Lee's forces held their ground. The terrible **Battle of Antietam** ended in confusion and stalemate. More men were killed, wounded, or declared missing on this day than on any other single day during the war. Lee lost nearly a quarter of his army. Despite the massive Confederate casualties and the weakened state of Lee's troops, McClellan held back, allowing them to retreat.

Charles Carleton Coffin, a journalist who was present at Antietam, reported a chilling description of the battle in the magazine *The Century Illustrated*: "It was no longer alone the boom of the batteries, but a rattle of musketry—at first like pattering drops upon a roof; then a roll, crash, roar, and rush, like a mighty ocean billow upon the shore, chafing the pebbles, wave on wave, with deep and heavy explosions of the batteries, like the crashing of the thunderbolts."

Neither side was satisfied with the battle's outcome. The Confederate offensive had failed, but McClellan, despite his numerical advantage, had been unable to win a decisive victory. Many historians have argued that if McClellan had continued to attack Lee's

CRITICAL VIEWING In December 1862, army engineers built floating bridges for Union troops to cross a river near Fredericksburg, Virginia. What materials were needed to construct them?

After the Battle of Antietam in 1862, photographer Alexander Gardner documented a few of the thousands of soldiers who lost their lives.

forces, the war might have been over at this point. Lincoln complained, "If General McClellan does not want to use the army, I would like to borrow it for a time." The president named Ambrose E. Burnside as the new commander of Union forces working under Major General Halleck.

Despite Lincoln's dissatisfaction with the outcome at Antietam, the Union won an important political and economic advantage. Seeing the South thwarted in such an important battle, the European powers decided to withhold their support from the Confederacy for the time being.

FREDERICKSBURG

In November, Burnside planned another assault on Richmond. Hoping to fool Lee by taking an unusual route, he decided to cross the Rappahannock River at Falmouth, near Fredericksburg, Virginia, then follow the railroad lines to Richmond. Burnside's engineers needed hollow metal cylinders called **pontoons**, to build floating bridges over the river, but these did not arrive until two weeks after Burnside reached the Rappahannock. Two Confederate units arrived at Fredericksburg and took potshots at Burnside's men as they worked on the bridges.

Meanwhile, Lee positioned his troops and artillery high in the hills above Fredericksburg. When the Union soldiers finally crossed the Rappahannock, they had to march through a valley where the Confederate troops perched above could easily

pick them off. "A chicken could not live on that field when we open on it," declared one Confederate at Fredericksburg. With southerners able to fire down on them at will from protected positions, more than 12,000 Union soldiers were killed, wounded, or declared missing during the three-day **Battle of Fredericksburg**. Burnside was eventually forced to retreat across the river. Watching the attack, Lee noted, "It is well that war is so terrible. We should grow too fond of it."

At battle's end, both armies found themselves where they had been at the battle's beginning. The North fell into mourning, humiliation, and anger at this sacrifice. By the winter of 1862–1863, many men had died for little apparent purpose and with no end in sight to the increasingly bloody war.

HISTORICAL THINKING

1. **READING CHECK** Why was Corinth, Mississippi, an important objective for the Union Army?

2. **FORM AND SUPPORT OPINIONS** Was the battle of Antietam a greater loss for the Union or the Confederacy? Explain your answer.

3. **MAKE INFERENCES** Why were the Confederates successful in fighting the Union Army to a stalemate in the East?

4. **IDENTIFY MAIN IDEAS AND DETAILS** Why did McClellan attack Richmond from the Virginia Peninsula?

SHIFTING THE FOCUS TO SLAVERY

It was dusk on the evening of July 18, 1862. The men of an African-American regiment in the Union Army readied themselves to lead a dangerous charge against a heavily protected fort in South Carolina. Many in the North and the South doubted the fighting ability of African-American soldiers. Their commander told the men, "The eyes of thousands will look upon what you do tonight."

SLAVERY UNDER ATTACK

Although neither side was satisfied with the bloody outcome at Antietam, President Lincoln decided that it represented enough of a Union victory to justify tying the outcome of the war to the end of slavery. This would stir greater support for the war among northern abolitionists, and it might also discourage European powers that had banned slavery on their own soil from supporting the Confederacy. Even northerners who did not support abolition could see that slavery offered the South an economic advantage. Slaves provided a huge labor force at home while white males went off to fight for the Confederacy. Anything that undermined that system was good for the Union.

Up to this point, slavery in captured territories had presented a dilemma for advancing Union forces. Military leaders had to decide whether enslaved people should be treated as **contraband**—captured enemy property—or as free. When Union soldiers overran South Carolina's Sea Islands during the Battle of Port Royal in November 1861, most of the white residents fled, leaving behind 10,000 slaves and a wealth of cotton fields. Rather than treat the enslaved people as contraband, Union leaders put the **Port Royal Experiment** in place, treating the former slaves as free. Most of these **freedmen** continued to work in the islands' cotton fields, but now they received wages. In January 1862, a Union general put in a request for teachers to help educate the freedmen. Soon after, the federal government expanded this call into a formal effort to not only educate the freedmen, but also to build hospitals for them and help them gain ownership of lands from the plantations they had once worked as slaves.

Some northerners saw the Port Royal Experiment as a model for what could be done throughout the South. In the spring of 1862, abolitionist and Union general David Hunter declared slavery abolished in South Carolina, Georgia, and Florida. President Lincoln immediately revoked Hunter's proclamation. In the months before Antietam, he was not yet prepared to end slavery where it existed.

Some legislators sided with General Hunter. **Radical Republicans**, or abolitionist members of Congress who supported African-American rights, wanted to make abolition a condition for ending the war. Many northern Democrats who were sympathetic to the South, called **Copperheads**, opposed this position, believing it would spur the Confederates to fight harder. They wanted slavery to remain in place so that the South would return to the Union, and they were hostile to ideas of racial equality. In the first year of the war, Lincoln tried to steer a course between the Radical Republicans and the Copperheads.

PRIMARY SOURCE

That on the first day of January . . . all persons held as slaves within any State or designated part of a State, the people whereof shall then be in rebellion against the United States, shall be then, thenceforward, and forever free; and the Executive Government of the United States, including the military and naval authority thereof, will recognize and maintain the freedom of such persons, and will do no act or acts to repress such persons, or any of them, in any efforts they may make for their actual freedom.

—from Abraham Lincoln's Emancipation Proclamation, 1863

The 54th Massachusetts Infantry Regiment, led by Colonel Shaw, stormed the walls of Fort Wagner on July 18, 1863. For their bravery, soldiers wounded in the battle were each given a badge like the one above. The 1890 print shown here was made by Kurz and Allison, a printing company based in Chicago.

THE EMANCIPATION PROCLAMATION

By the end of 1862, Lincoln was shifting course. The loss of life had made many northerners question whether keeping the Union together was worth the cost. Lincoln needed a moral cause to rally the Union.

In the wake of Antietam, Lincoln issued the **Emancipation Proclamation**, which decreed all slaves in states that were still in rebellion against the United States were "thenceforward, and forever free." The official document took effect on January 1, 1863, and it was denounced throughout the South and in much of the North as well. The proclamation did not free any of the enslaved people in the border states, for fear that those states would shift their loyalty to the Confederacy. And, of course, slaveholders in the Confederacy did not consider themselves bound by U.S. law, so the proclamation did not affect them. However, the decree ruled out any compromise that would bring the Confederate states back into the Union with slavery intact. Slavery had been the central cause of the war, and now Lincoln proclaimed that a Union victory would end it.

AFRICAN-AMERICAN SOLDIERS

Although northern civilian and military leaders remained deeply divided over abolition, many began to realize that African Americans could be of great value to the Union. Very quickly after Lincoln announced the Emancipation Proclamation, Union leaders began to enlist African-American troops. In May 1863, two African-American regiments stormed a fortified Confederate installation at Port Hudson, Louisiana. That same month, the War Department founded the **Bureau of Colored Troops** and began a wide-scale effort to recruit African-American soldiers.

In February 1863, the governor of Massachusetts issued the first formal call for African Americans to enlist in the **54th Massachusetts Infantry Regiment**, led by white colonel **Robert Gould Shaw**. In two weeks, more than 1,000 African Americans had enlisted, including Charles and Lewis Douglass, two of Frederick Douglass's sons. In July 1863, the unit lost Shaw and nearly half of its 600-man attack force when the regiment stormed **Fort Wagner**, which guarded the port of Charleston, South Carolina. Greatly outnumbered and forced into hand-to-hand combat, the regiment lost the battle, but the valor of the 54th inspired many more African Americans to enlist and fight for the Union.

HISTORICAL THINKING

1. **READING CHECK** Who were the Radical Republicans?

2. **DISTINGUISH FACT FROM OPINION** Does the statement "The Emancipation Proclamation ended slavery in the United States" represent a fact or an opinion? Explain your response, based on evidence from the text.

3. **MAKE INFERENCES** Why do you think so many African Americans enlisted to fight for the Union after the Emancipation Proclamation was issued?

DISCONTENT IN THE NORTH AND THE SOUTH

Few places reflected the human cost of war more than military hospitals. As one witness recalled, "The surgeon snatched his knife . . . wiped it rapidly once or twice across his bloodstained apron, and the cutting began. The operation accomplished, the surgeon would look around with a deep sigh, and then—'Next!'"

SOLDIERS AND THE MEANING OF WAR

As the war dragged on, both sides used new technologies to gain an edge over the enemy. In addition to advances in maritime technology, such as the ironclad, each side made improvements in land transportation and communication. The Union, which already held an advantage in terms of the railroad and telegraph lines it controlled at the beginning of the conflict, greatly expanded these networks. Telegraph lines could be rapidly extended in the wake of troops on the march, permitting nearly instant communication even from the battlefield. Both the North and the South also experimented with using hot-air balloons to spy on enemy lines from above.

Some of the most significant technological advances involved the weapons and equipment carried by everyday soldiers. The development of the Minié ball, a cone-shaped bullet, made rifles more accurate and easier to load. By 1863, Union soldiers were using repeating rifles, which allowed them to shoot more than one bullet without reloading. The fastest of these could fire off 7 rounds in less than 30 seconds. Due to its industrial advantage, the Union was better able to equip its troops with

Dr. Child likely would have used a medical kit such as this one. Saws, knives, and scalpels were a military doctor's most useful tools during the Civil War.

PRIMARY SOURCE

Surgeons and nurses who staffed the hospitals of the Civil War wrote letters describing the horror of combat and the hardships their patients suffered.

The days after the battle are a thousand times worse than the day of the battle—and the physical pain is not the greatest pain suffered. How awful it is. . . . The dead appear sickening but they suffer no pain. But the poor wounded mutilated soldiers that yet have life and sensation make a most horrid picture. I pray God may stop such infernal work—though perhaps he has sent it upon us for our sins. Great indeed must have been our sins if such is our punishment.

—from a letter written by Dr. William Child, Union Army surgeon, 1862

A soldier stands in the trenches of fortifications at Yorktown, Virginia, in May 1862. Based on the photograph, what do you believe were the advantages of living and fighting in the trenches?

these newer rifles, while the South lagged behind. Both sides were using rifles with grooved barrels, an invention that became commonplace in the 1850s. The grooves caused bullets to spin, making them much more accurate at longer ranges than the bullets fired from the smooth-barreled muskets used in the American Revolution.

To counter the increasingly efficient rifles and larger cannons, Civil War soldiers resorted to **trench warfare**. Opposing armies dug ditches, or trenches, roughly parallel to each other. The trenches provided each army with both a vantage point from which to fire at the enemy and a place to shelter from incoming fire.

Improved weaponry added to higher casualty rates on the battlefield. In addition, poor hygiene in military camps and hospitals led to high rates of infection and disease. Doctors did not understand the role germs play in spreading infections, so they did not employ practices that are considered basic today, such as hand-washing. A Civil War soldier was actually more likely to die from illness than from battle wounds. In some ways, those killed quickly in battle faced an easier end than the majority of those who died slowly from infected wounds. Often the only way to treat infection in an arm, leg, or foot was to amputate. Thousands of wounded who survived the war returned home missing parts of their bodies.

Despite the miserable conditions in the camps, which also included poor food and long, lonely hours, soldiers found ways to keep their spirits up. They sang songs, played games, and gambled. Many spent long hours writing letters home and savored any letters from loved ones that reached them at the front.

CHALLENGES IN THE CONFEDERACY

Although many of the battles of the spring of 1862 had been close, with high casualties on both sides, the outcomes generally favored northern goals. As the war dragged on and the body count grew, Confederate leaders had a hard time keeping experienced troops in the field. Many of those who had enthusiastically volunteered for service had expected the fighting would be over quickly. They were not prepared to spend years in fear and misery far away from their homes and families. When the first year-long enlistments in the Confederate Army ran out in April 1862, many soldiers opted to return home rather than re-enlist.

The Confederate Congress, fearful that its army would be short of men as the Union stepped up its attacks, decided that it had no choice but to enact **conscription**, issuing an order that forced men into military service. Conscription is also known as the **draft**. All white men between the ages of 18 and 35 were required to serve in the Confederate military for three years. However, the order exempted one white man on plantations with 20 or more slaves, a provision known as the "twenty negro law." This loophole divided southerners by class, since those with few or no slaves could not escape the draft. Many resented this **exemption**, or release from the obligation to serve. They claimed the Confederacy was simply using poor white southerners to benefit the interests of wealthy planters. Some derided it as "a rich's man's war and a poor man's fight."

Class conflict also broke out in the streets of the Confederate capital in the spring of 1863. Convinced that greedy merchants were holding supplies of flour until shortages and inflation drove prices even higher, a crowd of poor women in Richmond broke open merchants' stores and took what they needed. The **Richmond Bread Riot** subsided after authorities threatened violence and arrests, in addition to promising free supplies, but similar events occurred in several other southern cities.

The rioters were not the only ones who took what they needed. That same spring, the Confederate government passed several laws, including the Impressment Act, that allowed it to **confiscate**, or seize and hold, crops and other supplies from citizens. Volunteer efforts were not producing enough food, clothing, and other necessities to supply the Confederate Army. Some desperate soldiers had

already taken to stealing crops. Under the new laws, farmers were supposed to receive a fair price in exchange for their goods. Instead, many felt used, further fueling tensions within the South.

THE NORTHERN HOME FRONT

The war also made life difficult in the North. Prior to the Emancipation Proclamation, many northerners objected to the war and Lincoln's approach to it. Wealthy business owners were eager to re-establish trade with their former southern partners. Northerners whose families had come from the South wanted to renew connections that the war had broken. As a result of these feelings, Copperheads won significant victories in congressional elections in 1862.

Opponents of the war feared, for good reason, that the Union would establish a draft that would force men to fight for a cause they did not support. The Union was facing the same problem as the South—volunteer recruitment efforts could not keep up with the needs of the battlefield. Congress passed the Conscription Act in March 1863, instituting its first draft. Like the Confederate draft, the law allowed wealthy men to avoid service. If drafted, a man with enough money could hire a substitute to fight in his place, or he could pay a fee of $300 directly to the government.

After a battle at Savage Station, Virginia, in 1862, wounded Union soldiers wait for medical care. Confederates captured the hospital the day after this photograph was taken.

In the 2016 film *Free State of Jones*, Newton Knight, center, and fellow soldiers defend themselves against Confederate troops trying to put down their rebellion.

Poor and working-class northerners, especially those who lived in cities, opposed the draft. Emotions were particularly strong in areas with large communities of Irish immigrants. They had fled famine in Ireland only to face discrimination and difficulty finding jobs upon arriving in the United States. Few wanted to risk their lives to free slaves who might compete with them for jobs after the war ended.

Protest demonstrations broke out in several northern cities. The worst occurred in New York City. On July 13, 1863, a group of protesters destroyed a draft office, sparking the **New York City draft riots**. Violence escalated into four days of attacks on newspaper offices, businesses that supported the war effort, and African Americans. In fact, African Americans became scapegoats, or innocent people blamed for the mistakes or faults of others. In this case, some of the rioters blamed African Americans for the war and taking jobs away from white workers. During the uprising in New York, rioters destroyed homes owned by African Americans and lynched, or hanged, 11 African Americans. Many African-American families abandoned the city.

Local police were unable to calm the rioting. By July 16, some 4,000 Union troops, fresh off the battlefield of Gettysburg, were called to assist. When the smoke cleared, more than 100 people were dead and millions of dollars in property had been destroyed. Nearly 20 percent of the African-American

THE FREE STATE OF JONES

Southern class conflict manifested itself in unusual places and ways. Angered by what he believed to be unfair conscription laws, a white farmer in Mississippi named Newton Knight initiated a local guerrilla war against the Confederacy in October 1863. His "Jones County Scouts" eventually declared Jones County, Mississippi, to be the Free State of Jones, aligned with the Union. They even raised the American flag over the county courthouse. Knight and his supporters managed to elude Confederate capture for the remainder of the Civil War.

population left the city. Those that stayed either moved to neighborhoods with police stations close by or to the outskirts of the city where the danger of race rioting was lower.

The draft continued to be enforced, but with one important difference: Some New York men with families who had no other means of financial support were now eligible to receive exemptions.

HISTORICAL THINKING

1. **READING CHECK** How did both the Union and Confederacy respond to the lack of military volunteers?

2. **ANALYZE CAUSE AND EFFECT** How did new battlefield technology contribute to higher casualties?

3. **COMPARE AND CONTRAST** How were the uprisings in Richmond and New York City similar and different?

4. **MAKE PREDICTIONS** What simple advancement in medical science do you think was needed before army surgeons and nurses would be able to save a greater number of wounded soldiers?

VICKSBURG AND CHANCELLORSVILLE

A good leader knows just what actions are necessary to get the desired results. General Grant knew that if his troops could capture Vicksburg, it would work in the Union's favor. In Virginia, Union forces were thinking the same thoughts about Richmond. But first they had to fight their way through Chancellorsville.

THE SIEGE OF VICKSBURG

As you have read, the Union gained control over much of the Mississippi River in the spring of 1862 when its forces captured New Orleans, Baton Rouge, Natchez, and Memphis. The Confederacy, however, still held a nearly 200-mile-long stretch of the river between **Vicksburg**, Mississippi, and Port Hudson, Louisiana. Vicksburg was the only remaining location in Mississippi where the Confederacy controlled railroad heads on both sides of the river.

Vicksburg's geography made it a formidable stronghold. The city sat atop high bluffs overlooking a hairpin bend in the river. Union ships attempting to sail around the bend had to make it past a multitude of Confederate cannons positioned along the cliffs' edges. From the start of the war, President Lincoln had considered Vicksburg one of the keys to a Union victory.

In May and June 1862, Union gunships shelled the city's defenses, but with little effect. Meanwhile, Union troops started digging a three-mile-long canal across the DeSoto Peninsula, a long finger of land surrounded by the river bend, hoping to change the course of the river to bypass Vicksburg entirely, rendering the city irrelevant. However, disease, heat exhaustion, and sunstroke claimed the lives of many of these soldiers, and the Union gave up working on the canal in July.

In December, General Ulysses S. Grant moved on Vicksburg once again. He ordered General William Tecumseh Sherman to lead an attack on the city in late December. Sherman's troops advanced on Vicksburg from the northeast, struggling across muddy bayous. At Chickasaw Bayou, Sherman's men encountered Confederate forces waiting for them in strong defensive positions. Sherman was soon sounding the retreat.

Following this defeat, Grant decided to try again to build the canal and reroute the river. Day after day from January through March, soldiers as well as slaves from nearby plantations dug in the cold mud. Disease once again plagued the project, and so did clouds of mosquitoes, continuous rain, floodwater from the rising river, and shelling from Confederate **batteries**, or groups of artillery pieces.

In spring 1863, Grant finally gave up on the canal in favor of a bold new plan. He marched his 40,000 soldiers down the west side of the Mississippi to a point roughly 30 miles south of Vicksburg. From there, they crossed the river on barges and gunboats that Union admiral **David Porter** had managed to run south past Vicksburg under cover of night. The army marched northeast, capturing Jackson, Mississippi, the state's capital, and several other towns along the way. Then Grant's troops turned and battled their way westward to the eastern edge of Vicksburg. After two unsuccessful assaults on the well-entrenched Confederates, Grant blocked every road leading into the city, beginning the Siege of Vicksburg.

Over time, the situation became increasingly grim for the city's residents and its 31,000 defenders. To escape Union shelling, many people began living in caves dug into the hills. Supplies of ammunition, food, and water began to run perilously low. After 47 days, Confederate general John C. Pemberton surrendered the city to Grant on July 4, 1863. The Union soon controlled the entire Mississippi River, and the Confederacy was split in two. "The Father of the Waters again goes unvexed to the sea," said President Lincoln.

CRITICAL VIEWING During the siege of Vicksburg, the Shirley family, who owned the house shown in this 1863 photograph, was forced to live in an artificial cave, like the ones dug into the hillside. What sacrifices might be required of the people living in these caves?

THE BATTLE OF CHANCELLORSVILLE

Meanwhile, back in Virginia, Lincoln replaced General Burnside after the Union's disastrous defeat at Fredericksburg. General **Joseph Hooker** took command of the Army of the Potomac, the official name of the Union forces battling in Virginia. But no one was certain how "Fighting Joe" Hooker would fare against Robert E. Lee, who had yet to be decisively defeated despite the men, resources, and determination the Union had thrown against him.

As Grant's soldiers were landing south of Vicksburg, Hooker staged an attack on Lee's Army of Northern Virginia, which remained entrenched in the hills south of Fredericksburg. Hooker commanded 130,000 troops, but rather than trying to overwhelm Lee with numbers, Hooker intended to outsmart him. He planned to send a large Union force to sweep around Lee in a **flanking maneuver**, or a troop movement around the side of an enemy line in the hope of gaining an advantage. Some of the soldiers would attack the Confederates from behind as others attacked from the front, forcing Lee out of his strong defensive position. But Lee wasn't so easily fooled. He divided his troops and sent General Stonewall Jackson to circle around Hooker's men and attack, outflanking Hooker's own flanking maneuver.

On May 2, Jackson surprised and defeated Hooker's troops near a crossroad called **Chancellorsville**. Southern jubilation over the victory ended that very night, though, when nervous Confederate soldiers accidentally shot Stonewall Jackson as he returned from surveying the front lines.

The next day, Lee managed to contain another Union assault on Fredericksburg, forcing Hooker's troops to retreat. Lee had overcome Hooker's superior numbers, but his losses were staggering: 13,000 casualties, or roughly 22 percent of his men. The most significant loss was General Jackson, who died of his wound after the fighting ended.

HISTORICAL THINKING

1. **READING CHECK** Why was the Battle of Chancellorsville both a victory and a loss for General Lee?

2. **ANALYZE CAUSE AND EFFECT** What was the effect of Hooker's flanking maneuver around Lee's troops?

3. **MAKE INFERENCES** Why do you think Grant decided to put Vicksburg under siege?

4. **ANALYZE LANGUAGE USE** What do you think President Lincoln meant when he said "The Father of the Waters again goes unvexed to the sea"?

COMPOSE AND WAIT

"Photography is an act of appreciation. If it can become an act of affection, you are at one with your subject."
—Sam Abell

When a young Sam Abell became a photography intern at *National Geographic* magazine in 1967, he thought to himself, "This is the right place for me; this is my life." He was also convinced he was the least qualified person ever hired for the role, having graduated from a college that did not have an actual photography program. Fifty years and thousands of memorable photos later, Abell has amply proved himself wrong about his qualifications—but he was correct in his realization that National Geographic was the perfect place for him.

⌃ In 2001, Abell captured this photograph of the swollen Mississippi River overtaking its banks and spilling floodwater onto Water Street near Muscatine, Iowa.

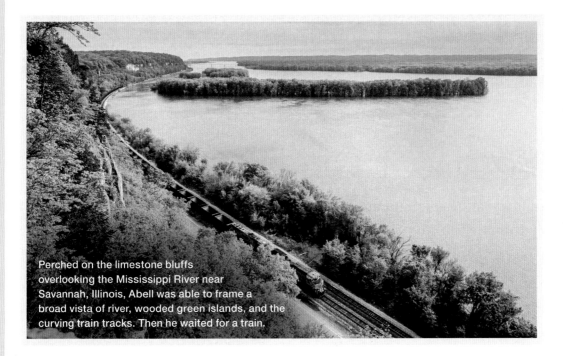

Perched on the limestone bluffs overlooking the Mississippi River near Savannah, Illinois, Abell was able to frame a broad vista of river, wooded green islands, and the curving train tracks. Then he waited for a train.

MAIN IDEA National Geographic photographer Sam Abell captures American culture and geography with his camera.

NOT THE TYPICAL PHOTOGRAPHER

Born in Sylvania, Ohio, in 1945, Sam Abell had a camera in his hand at an early age. His first photography teacher was his father, an enthusiastic amateur photographer. In a darkroom they built in their home, Abell and his father spent hours learning to develop photos and forging a loving bond over their shared fascination with the photographic image.

The University of Kentucky, where Abell went to college, didn't have an official photography program, but he received an abundance of real-world practice taking pictures for the university's School of Journalism. After graduating in 1967, he was hired by National Geographic as a photography intern and became a staff photographer for *National Geographic* magazine in 1970. In a decades-long career, he photographed subjects as diverse as maritime culture in Newfoundland, the tiny town of Hagi, Japan, and the expansive American West.

Abell is not the typical journalistic photographer, and his images have often been described as "quiet," not a quality generally associated with the lively, action-oriented scenes that magazines often seek. He considers himself a charter member of the "compose and wait" school of photographic thought. He will choose a location and frame his shot, then wait—for weeks, if necessary—for the perfect moment, gesture, or even shadow that brings what he calls a "breath of life" to the image. A photo editor once noted that Abell "records everyday physical existence but simultaneously suggests other possibilities. It is this steady looking for another life behind things that characterizes his work." Abell elaborates, "I have been drawn to that which in life is enduring."

CONNECTING TO THE MISSISSIPPI

One subject that Abell has returned to more than once is the Mississippi River, which he has explored extensively, recording both its pristine wildernesses and its bustling industrial areas—geographic America and economic America.

Reflecting on why the river is such an iconic symbol of the American story, Abell observes that if you spread out a map of North America, it looks like the entire continent drains into the Mississippi. That's not quite true, of course, but for Abell, visualizing the continent in this way illustrates "the power of the Mississippi's physical location." He also acknowledges the sophisticated Native American civilizations that grew along its banks, the role of its tributaries in carrying Lewis and Clark westward, and the river's importance during the Civil War as the North and South fought for control of its waters. "It's the great confluence of water and exploration and the history of North America," he says.

HISTORICAL THINKING

1. **READING CHECK** What does Sam Abell mean by the expression "compose and wait"?

2. **ANALYZE VISUALS** Look at the photos on these pages. How do they reflect Abell's ideas about photography?

THE BATTLE OF GETTYSBURG

As you walk among statues and monuments, a group of children exit the Gettysburg Museum and Visitor Center, running and laughing across the grass. It's a peaceful place now, but you can't help but be reminded of how many fought and died on this very spot, and how it changed the course of the war.

LEE INVADES THE NORTH

General Lee's stunning victory at Chancellorsville was one bright spot in an otherwise gloomy picture for the Confederacy in early May 1863. In Mississippi, Union forces under General Grant were winning battle after battle as they marched toward the key city of Vicksburg. The Union's Army of the Cumberland, commanded by General William Rosecrans, was threatening to break through Tennessee into Georgia. And the Union's blockade was drawing an ever-tighter net around the southern coast.

Some of Lee's generals urged him to pull Grant away from Vicksburg by rushing his troops to Tennessee to defend the center of the Confederacy. But Lee decided that his most effective move would be to invade the North again, taking the pressure off Virginia, where much of the fighting had taken place up to that point. A successful invasion of the North would dishearten the Union, and it might persuade Britain and France to recognize the Confederacy. It might also strengthen the position of Peace Democrats, northerners who wanted to abandon the war effort and negotiate a settlement with the South. These were the same people the Union called "Copperheads."

In early June 1863, Lee began to move his army of 75,000 men north through the Shenandoah and Cumberland valleys into southern Pennsylvania. There, they occupied several towns and advanced within striking distance of Harrisburg, the state capital. Meanwhile, General Hooker had also been moving northward, keeping the 95,000-strong Army of the Potomac between Lee's forces and Washington, D.C.

Hooker's relationship with his superiors and President Lincoln had grown increasingly strained, and in late June, Hooker threatened to resign his command. Lincoln abruptly replaced him, putting General **George Meade** in charge. Now it was up to Meade to figure out how best to stop the greatest threat the

Born into a celebrated Virginia family, Robert E. Lee enrolled in the U.S. Military Academy at West Point in New York and was one of only six soldiers in his class who graduated with a clean record of behavior.

Union had yet faced from Confederate forces. Washington and Baltimore were vulnerable, along with the cities, towns, and farms of Pennsylvania. Confederate troops not only helped themselves to the abundant food and livestock the rich land offered as they marched through, but they also seized free African Americans and fugitive slaves and forced them to the South and into slavery.

Still, Lee and his men found themselves in a dangerous situation. Lee had sent a cavalry corps commanded by his "eyes and ears," J.E.B. Stuart, to gather information about Meade's forces, but Stuart ranged too widely from the main army. As a result, Lee had little idea of the Union Army's plans. For their part, Meade and his fellow officers decided to pursue Lee, but not too aggressively; they wanted to choose the right time and place for a decisive battle.

On June 30, fate intervened. That day, a Confederate brigade in search of supplies happened upon a large Union cavalry force in a place that neither side knew or cared much about: Gettysburg, Pennsylvania. Gettysburg was a crossroad town of about 2,400 people located some 35 miles south of Harrisburg.

Lee's army was scattered across a large area of south-central Pennsylvania, and Meade's army was strung out along a 25-mile-long front moving northward from Maryland into Pennsylvania. Messengers quickly spread the news of the Gettysburg encounter, and reinforcements from both armies hurried to the town.

FIGHTING FOR THE HIGH GROUND

The **Battle of Gettysburg** began the morning of the following day, July 1, when a large **contingent**, or group, of Confederates advancing from the west clashed with Union cavalry that had taken up positions on a set of ridges along the town's western border. Union infantry soon arrived to support the cavalry, but the Union forces were still outnumbered. The fighting intensified and spread as the two sides battled for the high ground. By afternoon, the Union forces were in retreat through Gettysburg.

At first, the Confederates thought they had gotten the better of the first day's fighting, but as the smoke cleared late in the day, they discovered that the Union forces had consolidated themselves on the most advantageous ground. Meade's men occupied

Gettysburg Battlefield, Pennsylvania

In 1863, most roads in south-central Pennsylvania led to Gettysburg, so it was not surprising that enemy armies would encounter one another here. This statue of Union general Gouverneur K. Warren stands on Little Round Top, a hill overlooking the battlefield that he and his troops defended from a Confederate assault. Warren, who was nicknamed the "Hero of Little Round Top," survived the furious fighting. The statue of Warren shown in this photograph was raised after his death in 1882.

Artist Paul Philippoteaux painted this scene of Pickett's Charge in the early 1880s. It is part of a larger mural that measures 42 feet high and 377 feet long. How would you describe the nature of the fighting at the Battle of Gettysburg?

a four-mile-long, fishhook-shaped line of hills and ridges—including Cemetery Hill, Cemetery Ridge, Culp's Hill, Little Round Top, and Big Round Top— that permitted them to protect their flanks. When Meade arrived during the night, he strengthened the Union positions with artillery and additional troops.

During the second day of the battle, the Confederates slowly mobilized their forces to attack the Union positions late in the afternoon. Fierce attacks and counterattacks raged on the slopes of Little Round Top and the boulder-strewn hill known as the Devil's Den, as well as in a nearby wheat field and peach orchard. The fighting produced horrific casualties—35,000 men were killed or wounded—but the Union managed to keep control of the high ground.

PICKETT'S CHARGE

Despite the Union's superior position, and against the advice of General James Longstreet, one of his top officers, Lee decided to mount a frontal attack the next day. Early in the afternoon, his artillery forces began a massive, deafening bombardment of Union positions. For nearly 2 hours, some 150 Confederate cannons blazed, focusing much of their shelling on the middle of the Union lines along

Cemetery Ridge. Union artillery forces shot back, but because of limited space they had fewer than half as many big guns. To fool the Confederates and to save ammunition for later battles, the Union commander ordered his men to slow their fire.

Mistakenly believing that the artillery **barrage**, or bombardment, had substantially weakened the Union forces, Lee ordered General **George E. Pickett** and two other generals to lead roughly 13,000 men in an assault on the middle of the Union line. As Confederate attackers marched and then raced in waves toward Cemetery Hill across nearly a mile of open ground, many were mowed down by deadly artillery crossfire or by rifle fire from the Union soldiers. Nevertheless, in what would later be called "the high-water mark of the Confederacy," several hundred of the attackers managed to pierce Union lines. Within an hour, however, they were repulsed and forced to retreat. **Pickett's Charge** had been a catastrophic failure.

Lee's troops spent the next day, July 4, on Seminary Ridge, a short distance west of Cemetery Ridge, waiting in a drenching rain for a Union counterattack that never came. That night, as the rain continued to fall, the Confederates began their long retreat back to Virginia. Meanwhile, a thousand miles away, General Pemberton had just surrendered Vicksburg to General Grant.

AFTER THE BATTLE

The three days of fighting at Gettysburg had been a disaster for the Army of Northern Virginia. About one-third of the entire force—around 28,000 of Lee's men—had been killed or wounded. The Confederates, short of supplies and soldiers, had gambled on an aggressive assault and lost. Although the North's casualty count was similar, its total number of troops was still far greater than the South's. Elation swept the North. The Union's victories at Gettysburg and Vicksburg would prove to be major turning points in the Civil War.

Hoping to end the war as soon as possible, President Lincoln used persuasion as well as fighting to try to entice the Confederacy back into the Union. In early December 1863, five months after Gettysburg, he issued a proclamation of amnesty and reconstruction. To southerners who would take an oath of loyalty to the Union, Lincoln promised a full pardon and the return of all property with the exception of slaves. Although he excluded Confederate leaders and high officers from this offer, Lincoln tried to include as many white southern men as possible. He decreed that once 10 percent of the number of voters in a state had sworn their loyalty to the Union, they could begin forming a new state government. He also promised education and apprenticeship programs that would aid formerly enslaved people in the transition to full freedom. He made no allowances for African-American participation in the new state governments of the South, however.

Implementing this plan turned out to be problematic. Lincoln, northern Republicans, and much of the public had underestimated the intensity of southern bitterness over years of war and occupation. Even in Tennessee and Kentucky—areas that were under Union control—guerrilla bands and raiders terrorized the local population and disrupted elections. Civilians in border states often found themselves in an impossible situation. Washington Elliott, a brigadier general in the Union Army, called citizens of the border states who failed to aid Union forces "enemies of mankind" with "the rights due to pirates and robbers." Those who actively aided the Union, on the other hand, were liable to find their crops trampled, their barns burned, and other acts of vandalism carried out by secessionist neighbors.

One of the civilian witnesses of the Battle of Gettysburg was a 15-year-old girl named Tillie Pierce, whose family lived in the center of the town. On July 5, 1863, two days after the fighting had ended, she and some friends climbed the hill known as Little Round Top and looked out over the battlefield. In a book she wrote 25 years later, she described the scene:

As we stood upon those mighty boulders, and looked down into the chasms between, we beheld the dead lying there just as they had fallen during the struggle. From the summit of Little Round Top, surrounded by the wrecks of battle, we gazed upon the valley of death beneath. The view there spread out before us was terrible to contemplate! It was an awful spectacle! Dead soldiers, bloated horses, shattered cannon and caissons [horse-drawn carts to transport the cannons], thousands of small arms. In fact everything belonging to army equipments, was there in one confused and indescribable mass.

—from *At Gettysburg, or, What a Girl Saw and Heard of the Battle* by Matilda "Tillie" Pierce Alleman, 1889

Abolitionists and their allies attacked Lincoln's plan as far too lenient to Confederates and not helpful enough for former slaves. In February 1864, Republican members of Congress introduced the **Wade-Davis Bill**, which attempted to enforce a standard set of laws to be enacted and administered across the South after the war ended. These laws would require 50 percent, rather than 10 percent, of a state's population to swear an oath of past as well as future loyalty before the state could form a new government. Lincoln hoped to entice Arkansas and Louisiana to rejoin the Union, and he was looking ahead to the upcoming election. He decided he had no choice but to refuse to sign the bill.

HISTORICAL THINKING

1. **READING CHECK** What are two things that General Lee believed might be accomplished by a Confederate invasion of the North?

2. **IDENTIFY MAIN IDEAS AND DETAILS** Why were the casualties at Gettysburg a greater blow to the Confederacy than to the Union?

3. **MAKE CONNECTIONS** What connection can you make between Lee's victory at Chancellorsville and his strategy at Gettysburg?

4. **DRAW CONCLUSIONS** Why do you think General Meade did not order a Union counterattack the day after Pickett's Charge?

NATIONAL CIVIL WAR MUSEUM HARRISBURG, PENNSYLVANIA

The National Civil War Museum in Harrisburg, Pennsylvania, describes itself as the only museum in the United States to tell the entire story of the Civil War "without bias to Union or Confederate causes." The museum immerses visitors in the Civil War period through living history demonstrations, videos, dioramas, and interactive exhibits that represent the experiences of common soldiers, civilians on the home front, enslaved African Americans, and prominent leaders. Artifacts on display include drums and bugles carried by young boys in the armies, a wide variety of weapons, and a brass slave collar. The great suffering caused by the war becomes evident through the museum's collection of war photography.

Lincoln's Note to McClellan

On August 27, 1862, President Abraham Lincoln sent this brief note to Major General George McClellan in Alexandria, Virginia, inquiring: "What news from the front?"

At the time, McClellan had been ordered to move Union troops toward Manassas to aid General Pope's soldiers in an upcoming battle with Confederate forces. McClellan failed to follow orders and never sent troops to Manassas, which led to a disastrous defeat for the Union at the Second Battle of Bull Run.

A lead musket ball like the one lodged in this Bible would create a large wound.

Bible with Musket Ball

Private Adam Troutman of the Confederate Army of Northern Virginia carried this Bible in his pocket during the Battle of Antietam in 1862. The Bible stopped a musket ball and probably saved his life. Troutman gave the Bible to his brother and was later killed in another battle.

Union Navy Flare Gun

Guns that launch flares—bursts of bright, colored light—were used by the Union Navy for signaling during the Civil War. The guns shot cartridges high up into the night sky, where they exploded as flares. Ships could send coded messages by launching flares of different colors in various combinations. The flares might convey orders, distress, the location of troops, or other messages.

How does this flare gun appear to differ from a pistol?

Union Signal Corps Decoding Device

Both the Union and the Confederate armies had signal corps—squads of soldiers who were responsible for communicating information across a battlefield.

A signal corps member typically waved flags or torches to send messages from one commander to another. These flag or torch movements represented different numbers, which were then translated into letters using a decoding device like this one. The codes themselves could be changed by rotating the disk to alter the alignment of numbers and letters.

Do research to identify modern veterans' groups similar to the G.A.R.

Grave Marker

The Grand Army of the Republic (G.A.R.) was an organization made up of veterans who had fought for the Union in the Civil War. The Ladies of the G.A.R. is a still-active organization of female descendants of those veterans. The members place markers like this one on the graves of their deceased family members.

TOTAL WAR

Sometimes duty calls us to do things we'd rather not. According to some historians, William Tecumseh Sherman wept when he learned that South Carolina had voted to secede and civil war had become inevitable. Four years later, Sherman led a brutal campaign through the South that all but assured a Union victory.

BATTLES IN SPRING 1864

In late November 1863, four and a half months after his successful siege of Vicksburg, General Ulysses S. Grant helped lead Union forces to victory in two battles near another key city, Chattanooga, Tennessee. The victories ended a Confederate siege of the city and opened a path for the Union to enter Georgia, as Chattanooga lay just north of the Georgia-Tennessee state line. This development ultimately spelled disaster for the Confederacy.

Grant had earned President Lincoln's confidence with his battlefield successes and the strategic initiative he displayed. In March 1864, Lincoln awarded him command of the Union Army. Grant and Lincoln agreed that the Union should use its superior numbers, naval strength, military equipment, and supplies to attack the Confederacy on every front at once and force it to sacrifice at least some of its territory. Grant would head to Virginia to meet General Robert E. Lee head on and fight toward the goal of capturing Richmond. Lincoln left General Sherman in charge of Union forces in Chattanooga. From there, Sherman would launch an invasion of Georgia and attack Atlanta, a vital industrial and railroad center. A Union capture

REMOVING CONFEDERATE STATUES

In the first half of the 20th century, organizations dedicated to remembering Confederate Civil War heroes erected statues of Confederate military officers in parks and other public spaces in more than 30 states. In the 2010s, many Americans began to question why Confederate officers should be so honored, viewing the statues as symbols of the white supremacist ideals that are the legacy of slavery.

A controversial movement began, urging city governments to remove these monuments. Two descendants of Stonewall Jackson even joined in, writing an open letter asking for his statue on Monument Avenue in Richmond, Virginia, to be taken down. Several cities responded. The statue of Jefferson Davis at left, for example, was removed from a New Orleans, Louisiana, monument in May 2017. The worker is wearing a bulletproof vest to protect him from the possibility of a violent protest.

of Atlanta would disrupt rail transportation throughout the South and cut the Confederacy into pieces too small to resist the Union forces.

More than 180,000 African Americans enlisted just when the Union needed them most. By spring 1864, the Union Army had established the means of recruitment, training, and pay for these soldiers. The Confederates, however, refused to recognize the same rules of warfare for African-American soldiers that they acknowledged for whites. In April 1864, at Fort Pillow in western Tennessee, Confederate cavalry under the command of **Nathan Bedford Forrest** shot down African-American Union soldiers who attempted to surrender. The **Fort Pillow Massacre** and other racist atrocities committed by the Confederates provoked outrage in the North and strengthened the determination of African-American soldiers, for whom "Remember Fort Pillow!" became a battle cry.

In May 1864, two months after assuming command of the entire Union Army, Grant marched into Virginia with his largest unit, the Army of the Potomac, to destroy Lee's forces and capture the Confederate capital of Richmond. The first engagement between Grant and Lee was the **Battle of the Wilderness**, which took place in thick woods near Chancellorsville. Two days of savage fighting ended in horrible losses on both sides. Shells exploding in dry brush caused fires that trapped wounded men, burning them alive. Grant lost more men than Hooker had at the Battle of Chancellorsville. Hooker had treated such losses as a decisive defeat and retreated, but Grant pushed forward.

Hoping to position a large Union force between Lee's army and Richmond, Grant hurried his soldiers southward to the crossroad of **Spotsylvania Court House**. Lee's troops got there first, however. For two weeks, both sides fought fiercely around Spotsylvania until the Confederates managed to halt the Union advance. After withdrawing, Grant tried repeatedly to swing his troops around Lee's right flank, but each time Lee anticipated his move and blocked him. Finally, in mid-June, Grant tried another strategy.

Grant aimed to capture Petersburg, a vital rail center located 25 miles south of Richmond, but the Confederates were able to repulse the North's

The National Museum of American History, Washington, D.C.

Abraham Lincoln used the latest technology to his full advantage during the 1860 and 1864 elections. His campaign team made pins featuring a portrait of the candidate that supporters could wear on their jackets. Though Lincoln's pins didn't become popular again until the 1890s, they are a precursor to the campaign buttons we are familiar with today.

initial attack. Grant then began a siege, pinning down Lee's main force around Richmond and Petersburg and forcing the Confederates to construct longer lines of earthworks to protect the capital. In an attempt to break through Lee's defenses, Union soldiers from Pennsylvania who had been coal miners before the war volunteered to tunnel under the South's fortifications and plant explosives. Throughout July, they dug; finally, at the end of the month, they detonated 320 kegs of gunpowder, blowing an enormous crater in the Confederate lines and killing several hundred Confederate soldiers. The attack that followed the explosion, however, failed. Union troops piled into the crater, where the rallying Confederates trapped them.

LINCOLN'S RE-ELECTION

In early May 1864, as Grant set off on his Virginia campaign, Sherman began his invasion of Georgia, moving southward from Chattanooga with an army of about 110,000 men. Throughout June and July, he pushed relentlessly through northern Georgia. By the end of July, the Confederates had fallen back to Atlanta, preparing to defend it from siege. It seemed only a matter of time before the Union triumphed, but how much time? This question loomed large for the Confederacy because 1864 was a presidential election year for the Union. If Lincoln were to lose the election, southern leaders might be able to negotiate an end to the war and recognition of Confederate independence.

Forced to fight off strong political challenges even within his own party, Lincoln himself believed that his chances of winning a second term were low. The Republicans tried to broaden their appeal by nominating Andrew Johnson, a former Democrat from Tennessee, for the vice presidency.

The Democrats, meanwhile, felt they were in a good position to win back the presidency. They knew that in the eyes of his critics, Lincoln had caused the war, trampled on constitutional rights, consolidated too much power, and refused to end the war when he had a chance. To take full advantage of such criticisms, they chose as their candidate General George McClellan, one of many generals Lincoln had removed from command. McClellan and the Democrats portrayed themselves as the party committed to restoring the United States to its prewar unity and grandeur. McClellan campaigned on a promise to end the war by re-admitting the southern states to the Union and allowing them to continue to practice slavery. It was a bargain that appealed to many in the North.

Just when it appeared certain that the Democrats would win the election, news from the battlefield began to alter the political landscape dramatically. Sherman had swung around Atlanta and begun destroying the railroads that made the small city an important transportation hub. Unable to defend Atlanta, the Confederates set much of it on fire and abandoned it. Sherman and his army marched into the city on September 2. About two weeks later, Union general **Philip Sheridan** soundly defeated Confederate forces in the Shenandoah Valley and then set about systematically destroying the valley's ability to support the South's war effort again.

Throughout most of the war, the Shenandoah Valley had been a rich agricultural resource, providing crops to feed the Confederate Army. The railroads that ran through the valley supplied southern soldiers with food, clothing, and ammunition, much of which was stored at Staunton, Virginia. Sheridan burned the valley's fields, farms, and mills; ripped up its railroad tracks; and destroyed the storehouses in Staunton. Then he took a regiment across the Blue Ridge Mountains to Charlottesville and destroyed the railroad hub there.

These successes lifted spirits in the North and gave a tremendous boost to Lincoln's campaign. On Election Day in November, Lincoln won with relative ease, capturing 55 percent of the popular vote and 212 of the available 233 electoral votes. Unexpectedly strong support from Union soldiers contributed significantly to his victory.

SHERMAN'S MARCH TO THE SEA

In the first few years of the war, the Union had generally refrained from targeting civilians and their property. By 1864, however, generals Grant and Sherman had come to believe, as had President Lincoln, that in order to bring the South to its knees, the Union must wage **total war**. In this harsh method of warfare, illustrated by Sheridan's destruction of the Shenandoah Valley, traditional rules and laws of war are ignored and all resources are poured into defeating the enemy no matter what. Little distinction

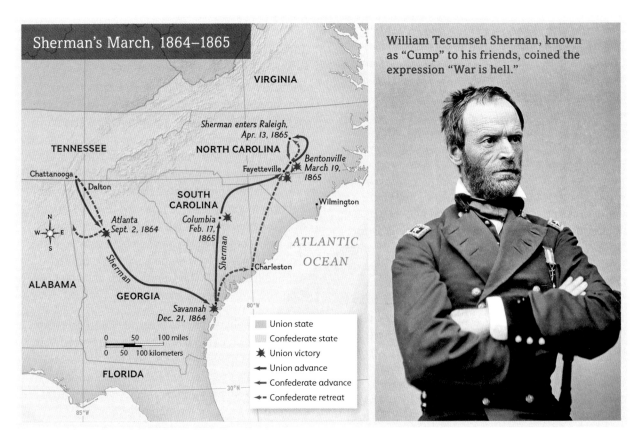

Sherman's March, 1864–1865

William Tecumseh Sherman, known as "Cump" to his friends, coined the expression "War is hell."

Union soldiers dismantle railroad tracks in Atlanta, Georgia, in 1864.

is made between combatants and noncombatants, private property is considered fair game, and every effort is made to destroy the enemy's economic and emotional capacity to continue fighting. "We are not only fighting hostile armies," explained Sherman, "but a hostile people, and must make old and young, rich and poor, feel the hard hand of war."

A week after Lincoln's re-election, Sherman and his troops set out from Atlanta toward Georgia's Atlantic coast, taking the war to the southern people themselves. The march was as much a demonstration of northern power as a military maneuver. "If we can march a well-appointed army right through [Confederate] territory," Sherman argued, "it is a demonstration to the world, foreign and domestic, that we have a power which [Confederate president] Davis cannot resist."

As Sherman's army of 62,000 men swept triumphantly across the state, living off food confiscated from farms along its route, it left a wide path of devastation. The troops tore up railroads, blew up bridges, cut telegraph lines, destroyed fences, and burned crops and supplies. Large numbers of deserters from both sides, fugitive slaves, and outlaws took advantage of the situation to prey on the towns and plantations in Sherman's wake, inflicting additional destruction and panic.

On December 10, Sherman's force reached the important coastal city of Savannah and took up positions around it. Sherman demanded that the city surrender, and on December 21 it did so. Savannah was spared the destruction Atlanta had endured. "I beg to present to you, as a Christmas gift, the city of Savannah," Sherman buoyantly telegraphed Lincoln. Contrasting sharply with the devastation of the South, the president's annual message to Congress presented a portrait of a North gaining strength with "more men now than we had when the war began."

HISTORICAL THINKING

1. **READING CHECK** What developments brought new life to Lincoln's 1864 presidential campaign?

2. **MAKE INFERENCES** Why do you think Lincoln assigned Grant to lead the Army of the Potomac rather than allowing him to continue waging war in the West?

3. **COMPARE AND CONTRAST** How did Lincoln and McClellan differ in their positions on the slavery issue? Support your answer with text evidence.

4. **INTERPRET MAPS** Where did Sherman and his troops go after they captured Savannah?

LINCOLN'S VISION

Abraham Lincoln's speeches are remembered today as among the finest in the history of the United States. Lincoln was not known as a speaker gifted with a captivating voice or dramatic delivery. The force of his speeches—and of his most significant written documents—came from the words themselves.

The beginning of 1862 was not a happy time for Abraham Lincoln. His son Willie died of typhoid fever, the Union Army was in a deadlock with the Confederates, and the American people were restless. In the summer, Lincoln moved his family to a cottage north of Washington, D.C. There, he wrote one of the most important laws in U.S. history.

On July 22, 1862, Abraham Lincoln read a first draft of the Emancipation Proclamation to his Cabinet. Although he was not delivering a formal speech, he knew his words must win over his chief advisors if his plan to change the focus of the war was to succeed.

The painting below shows Lincoln alone in a messy study. His left hand is resting on a Bible and the U.S. Constitution. A bust of former president James Buchanan, who was seen as a weak leader against secession, hangs from a noose in the corner. Pro-Union Andrew Jackson stares at Lincoln from the mantle of the fireplace. With these details, the artist is hinting at the great weight of history Lincoln must have felt as he wrote the Emancipation Proclamation.

CONSTRUCTED RESPONSE Study the painting carefully. What other examples of symbolism do you notice in the painting?

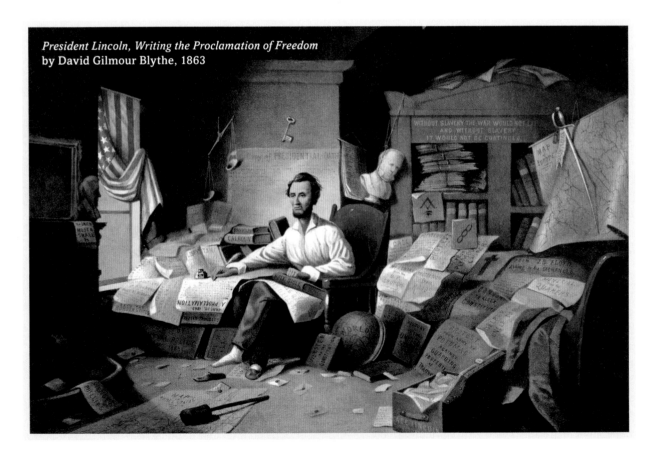

President Lincoln, Writing the Proclamation of Freedom
by David Gilmour Blythe, 1863

DOCUMENT ONE

**Primary Source: Speech
The Gettysburg Address, by Abraham Lincoln, November 19, 1863**

In November 1863, Abraham Lincoln was invited to speak at the dedication of a cemetery at Gettysburg for the Union soldiers who had perished in the battle. Despite its extreme brevity, or shortness, Lincoln's address to the gathered crowd soon came to be seen as one of the greatest speeches in American history. In it, Lincoln attempted to frame the war as not simply a struggle to keep the Union together but as a fight for the principles of freedom and democracy upon which the country was founded.

CONSTRUCTED RESPONSE To what is Lincoln referring when he speaks of "unfinished work" and "the great task"?

Four score and seven years ago our fathers brought forth on this continent a new nation, conceived in Liberty, and dedicated to the proposition that all men are created equal. Now we are engaged in a great civil war, testing whether that nation or any nation so conceived and so dedicated, can long endure. We are met on a great battlefield of that war. We have come to dedicate a portion of that field, as a final resting place for those who here gave their lives that that nation might live. It is altogether fitting and proper that we should do this. But, in a larger sense, we cannot dedicate—we cannot consecrate—we cannot hallow—this ground. The brave men, living and dead, who struggled here, have consecrated it, far above our poor power to add or detract. The world will little note, nor long remember what we say here, but it can never forget what they did here. It is for us the living, rather, to be dedicated here to the unfinished work which they who fought here have thus far so nobly advanced. It is rather for us to be here dedicated to the great task remaining before us—that from these honored dead we take increased devotion to that cause for which they gave the last full measure of devotion—that we here highly resolve that these dead shall not have died in vain—that this nation, under God, shall have a new birth of freedom—and that government of the people, by the people, for the people, shall not perish from the earth.

DOCUMENT TWO

**Primary Source: Speech
from Abraham Lincoln's Second Inaugural Address, March 4, 1865**

The war that had begun a month after Lincoln first took office as president was still dragging on when he began his second term in 1865. In his brief second inaugural address, Lincoln suggested that the war was God's punishment for slavery—a sin for which the South and the North shared guilt. And although the end of the war was in sight, he spoke not of triumph but of reconciliation and healing.

CONSTRUCTED RESPONSE What do you think a *bondsman* is, and to what is Lincoln referring with the phrase "two hundred and fifty years of unrequited toil"?

Fondly do we hope, fervently do we pray, that this mighty scourge of war may speedily pass away. Yet, if God wills that it continue until all the wealth piled by the bondsman's two hundred and fifty years of unrequited toil shall be sunk, and until every drop of blood drawn with the lash shall be paid by another drawn with the sword, as was said three thousand years ago, so still it must be said "the judgments of the Lord are true and righteous altogether." With malice toward none, with charity for all, with firmness in the right as God gives us to see the right, let us strive on to finish the work we are in, to bind up the nation's wounds, to care for him who shall have borne the battle and for his widow and his orphan, to do all which may achieve and cherish a just and lasting peace among ourselves and with all nations.

SYNTHESIZE AND WRITE

1. **REVIEW** Review what you have learned about Lincoln's Gettysburg Address and Second Inaugural Address.

2. **RECALL** On your own paper, write the main ideas expressed in each document.

3. **CONSTRUCT** Select one to three key words from either the Gettysburg Address or the Second Inaugural Address and then construct a topic sentence to answer this question: What is the significance of these words to the speech?

4. **WRITE** Using evidence from this chapter and the documents, write a one-paragraph argument that supports your topic sentence in Step 3.

SURRENDER AND TRAGEDY

Have you ever wondered how two opposing forces can work together after waging war on one another? When it became clear that the Union was the victor in the Civil War, the next challenge for the North and the South was to reunite as one nation. Would both sides win that victory?

SURRENDER AT APPOMATTOX

In mid-January 1865, several weeks after achieving his triumphant March to the Sea, General Sherman issued Special Field Order No. 15. This order reserved confiscated land along the coasts of South Carolina, Georgia, and Florida for former slaves, granting 40-acre plots to those who settled there. Two weeks later, the Republicans in Congress passed the **13th Amendment**, which abolished slavery in the United States forever. One congressman wrote to his wife that "we can now look other nations in the face without shame."

Sherman's 60,000-man army had begun moving northward from Georgia into the Carolinas. As they had during the March to the Sea, the troops lived off the countryside and destroyed much of the local infrastructure. Meanwhile, growing numbers of Confederate soldiers were deserting their armies.

President Lincoln met with Confederate officials in early February at Hampton Roads, Virginia, to try to negotiate an end to the war. He offered slave owners compensation for their freed slaves if the Confederacy would immediately cease fighting, but Confederate president Jefferson Davis refused to submit to the "disgrace of surrender." A month later, Lincoln was sworn in for his second term as president. In his inaugural address, he offered a message of forgiveness and reconciliation, calling for his fellow citizens to "bind up the nation's wounds."

Meanwhile, Grant was finally poised to capture Richmond, which the Union had besieged for months. As Grant's troops worked to surround Petersburg and cut Confederate supply lines, Lee's force was stretched thinner and thinner. Finally, on the night of April 2, Lee evacuated both Richmond and Petersburg, hurrying the Army of Northern Virginia westward along the Appomattox River. Union forces entered Richmond, only to find the Confederates had burned it to the ground rather than allow it to fall intact into enemy hands.

Grant's army set off in hot pursuit of Lee. Seven days later, they confronted each other near the village of **Appomattox Court House** in central Virginia. Lee was moving his troops south to reinforce Confederate forces battling Sherman in North Carolina, but now he was surrounded. With all avenues of escape blocked, Lee had no choice but to surrender.

On April 9, 1865, Lee and Grant met in the living room of a civilian's home in Appomattox Court House, Lee in his full dress uniform and Grant in his muddy field outfit. Lee accepted Grant's terms and surrendered. All Confederate soldiers were pardoned and allowed to keep their private property—including their horses, which they would need for farm work when they returned home. Confederate officers were allowed to keep their sidearms. "The war is over," Grant said. "The Rebels are our countrymen again." But the Confederate soldiers were in bad shape. Many were starving. Grant made sure that all of Lee's men received Union rations.

Though a number of Confederate troops had yet to surrender, and Jefferson Davis remained at large, it was clear that the war had ended. All of the passion and courage the Confederates displayed throughout the war was not enough to defeat the resources and manpower of the industrial North. Celebrations erupted among relieved citizens in cities and towns throughout the North.

CRITICAL VIEWING The National Geographic Society commissioned Tom Lovell to paint *Surrender at Appomattox* in 1965. Why do you think the artist chose to show the Union officers gazing toward Lee, who is dressed in gray and seated apart from them?

In the South, Confederate soldiers and displaced persons began to straggle home. On April 11, 1865, Lincoln addressed a crowd outside the White House on **Reconstruction**, or the process of reorganizing and rebuilding the former Confederate states. He admitted that northerners differed "as to the mode, manner, and means of Reconstruction" and that the white South was "disorganized and discordant."

LINCOLN'S ASSASSINATION

Among the crowd that had gathered to hear Lincoln's address on Reconstruction was a failed actor and southern sympathizer named **John Wilkes Booth**. The previous summer, Booth and several co-conspirators had begun plotting to kidnap the president, but their plans eventually changed from kidnapping to **assassination**, or murder committed for political reasons.

On the evening of April 14, Lincoln and his wife went to Ford's Theater in Washington to see a play. There, Booth approached Lincoln from behind and shot him in the back of the head before leaping to the stage and fleeing. Lincoln died early the next morning. The news stunned Americans and sparked an explosion

of anti-southern sentiment in the North. One newspaper mourned that Booth and his conspirators "have stricken down the MAN who stood forth their best intercessor [negotiator] before the nation . . . their truest, most forgiving friend, he who pleaded with his people to temper justice with mercy." In death, Lincoln was transformed from a careworn president into a hero who had given his life to hold the nation together.

Lincoln's funeral train left Washington, D.C., on April 21. Its final destination was Springfield, Illinois, where Lincoln had lived before becoming president. Along the train route, thousands of Americans lined up to mourn and pay respects to the president, who was finally buried on May 4.

THE EFFECTS OF THE WAR

The costs and consequences of the Civil War were profound. The Union expended about $3 billion on for the conflict, while the cost to the Confederacy was about $1 billion. But the monetary cost was dwarfed by the price paid in suffering and loss of life. Total casualties on both sides—including soldiers who were wounded, killed in action, died in prisoner

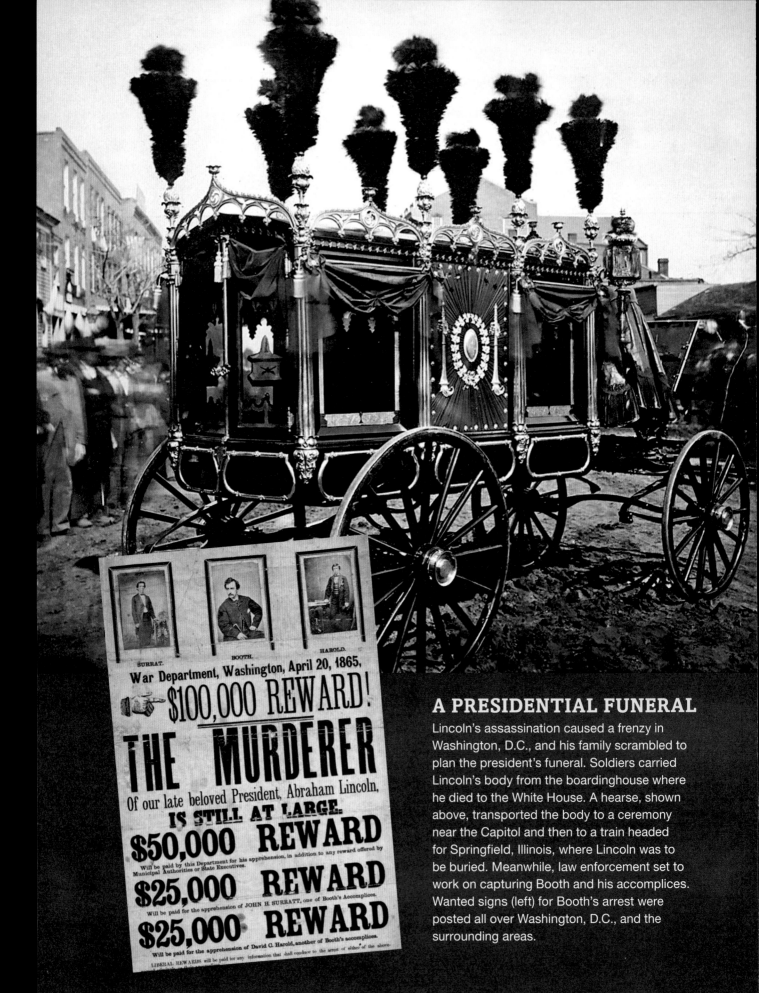

SURRAT.   BOOTH.   HAROLD.

War Department, Washington, April 20, 1865,

☞ **$100,000 REWARD!**

THE MURDERER

Of our late beloved President, Abraham Lincoln,

IS STILL AT LARGE.

$50,000 REWARD

Will be paid by this Department for his apprehension, in addition to any reward offered by Municipal Authorities or State Executives.

$25,000 REWARD

Will be paid for the apprehension of JOHN H. SURRATT, one of Booth's accomplices.

$25,000 REWARD

Will be paid for the apprehension of David C. Harold, another of Booth's accomplices.

LIBERAL REWARDS will be paid for any information that shall conduce to the arrest of either of the above-

A PRESIDENTIAL FUNERAL

Lincoln's assassination caused a frenzy in Washington, D.C., and his family scrambled to plan the president's funeral. Soldiers carried Lincoln's body from the boardinghouse where he died to the White House. A hearse, shown above, transported the body to a ceremony near the Capitol and then to a train headed for Springfield, Illinois, where Lincoln was to be buried. Meanwhile, law enforcement set to work on capturing Booth and his accomplices. Wanted signs (left) for Booth's arrest were posted all over Washington, D.C., and the surrounding areas.

of war camps, and succumbed to disease—topped 1 million: about 640,000 from the Union and more than 480,000 from the Confederacy.

Two out of three deaths occurred not on the battlefields, but in the field hospitals, as diseases and infections took their toll. Army surgeons prescribed millions of doses of **morphine**, a highly addictive medication, to ease their patients' pain, and many Civil War **veterans**, or people who served in the military, became addicted to it.

The war affected the financial situations of families in both the North and the South. Many wounded veterans were permanently disabled and could no longer work, and thousands of fathers, sons, and brothers never returned home at all, resulting in the loss of the family breadwinner. Some families fell into poverty, and many homes, farms, and businesses had to be rebuilt. This was especially true in the former Confederacy.

Major southern cities had been reduced to ruins and ash. Much of the South's infrastructure had been destroyed; weeds and brush had taken over fields, and farm values fell by half. However, abolition of slavery and the resulting loss of "free" slave labor was the largest blow to the southern economy. Paying wages for the masses of workers needed to keep a large plantation going hit the owners hard.

Things were not as dire in the North. While the war did not fundamentally change the North's economy, it did speed up processes already well underway. Northern manufacturers saw their businesses and profits expand during the war due to the demand for their products. Northern farmers began using machinery to plant, harvest, and process their crops, reducing the amount of farm labor required.

The war also resulted in a major change in the United States government. The balance of power shifted from individual states and regions to Washington, D.C., and the Union victory boosted Republican power in both the legislative and executive branches. The success of the Republican party—which would continue for decades—and the creation of a national currency and banking system aided the flow of money, spurred the growth of business, and triggered an expansion of the federal government.

NEW LAWS LOOK FORWARD

Before the war even ended, the federal government began asserting its new power. In 1862, the Republicans succeeded in passing three important pieces of legislation. The **Morrill College Land Grant Act** provided each state with 30,000 acres

of federal land grants for each member of its congressional delegation. The states then sold the land and used the proceeds to fund 69 public colleges, most of which focused on agriculture and the mechanical arts. These "land grant colleges" include Cornell University, the Massachusetts Institute of Technology, and the University of Wisconsin at Madison.

The **Homestead Act** also involved land grants, but the recipients were individuals. Any adult citizen who headed a family could qualify for a grant of 160 acres of public land by paying a registration fee and living on the land continuously for 5 years. The act also permitted a farmer to purchase the land from the government at a reduced rate after only six months of residency. By the end of the 19th century, the U.S. government had distributed more than 80 million acres to Americans through the provisions of the Homestead Act.

Finally, the Pacific Railway Acts provided funds and land grants for the creation of a nationwide railroad network, specifically one that would connect the Atlantic and the Pacific coasts by train—a transcontinental railroad. The acts authorized both the Union Pacific and the Central Pacific companies to construct rail lines from the Missouri River to the continent's west coast. The war slowed this effort, but interest in a transcontinental railroad picked back up once the conflict was over.

The United States emerged from the Civil War a changed nation. The demands of wartime had led to the draft and government involvement in transportation and business. The war had also profoundly shifted the balance of power among the regions of the country: After Lee's surrender at Appomattox, the South's political dominance over the national agenda was broken. Now it was time to bring the South back into the Union.

HISTORICAL THINKING

1. **READING CHECK** What happened at Appomattox Court House?

2. **DETERMINE WORD MEANING** Reread the last sentence of "Surrender at Appomattox." What do you think *discordant* means in this context?

3. **IDENTIFY PROBLEMS AND SOLUTIONS** What problem was Sherman addressing when he issued Special Field Order No. 15?

4. **FORM AND SUPPORT OPINIONS** What do you think was the biggest problem facing the United States after the Civil War? Explain your answer.

VOCABULARY

Write a sentence using each of the following key terms.

1. writ of *habeas corpus*

   Thanks to the writ of habeas corpus, he was able to appear before a judge and claim that his arrest was illegal.

2. border state
3. defensive war
4. cavalry
5. ironclad
6. contraband
7. Copperhead
8. draft
9. total war

READING STRATEGY
MAKE INFERENCES

When you make inferences, you use what you already know to understand the meaning of a text. Complete the following chart to make inferences about the major challenges the nation faced immediately following the Civil War. Then answer the question.

Before the War	During the War	After the War

10. What major challenges did the nation face as it began to reunite after the war?

MAIN IDEAS

Answer the following questions. Support your answers with evidence from the chapter.

11. Why was fighting a defensive war an advantage for the South? **LESSON 1.1**

12. Why did civilian spectators come out from Washington to watch the First Battle of Bull Run? **LESSON 1.2**

13. What was the outcome of the battle between the *Monitor* and the *Virginia*, the first two ironclads that faced each other in the war? **LESSON 2.1**

14. Why was the Battle of Antietam considered a stalemate? **LESSON 2.2**

15. What did the Emancipation Proclamation declare about slaves in rebelling states? **LESSON 3.1**

16. Why was General Grant's capture of Vicksburg a turning point in the war? **LESSON 4.1**

17. What was the outcome of the Battle of Gettysburg? **LESSON 4.3**

18. Why was the Union's presidential election of 1864 important to the Confederacy? **LESSON 5.1**

19. What was the outcome of the siege of Richmond and Petersburg? **LESSON 5.3**

HISTORICAL THINKING

Answer the following questions. Support your answers with evidence from the chapter.

20. **IDENTIFY** How did views about the "proper" role of women in the medical field change during the war?

21. **DRAW CONCLUSIONS** Why did Missouri become the site of heated conflict during the war?

22. **MAKE INFERENCES** Why might some people have thought General McClellan was an indecisive leader?

23. **DISTINGUISH FACT AND OPINION** Some Copperheads said the Radical Republicans' insistence on making the end of slavery a condition of peace would only lead to more bloodshed. Is this statement a fact or an opinion? Explain.

24. COMPARE AND CONTRAST How were the siege of Vicksburg and the siege of Richmond and Petersburg alike and different?

25. FORM AND SUPPORT OPINIONS Should Robert E. Lee and other Confederate officials be remembered as heroes or as villains? Explain your answer.

Examine the graph at right, which illustrates how inflation affected the North and the South by showing how much buying power Americans had in each region throughout the war. Then answer the questions.

26. If a northerner paid $1.46 for three pounds of tea in 1865, how much would a southerner pay for the same item?

27. How many times higher was the cost of that tea in the South in 1865 compared with 1862?

Inflation: North and South

Source: Todd, Richard Cecil. 1954. *Confederate Finance.* Athens: The University of Georgia Press, p. 198.

ANALYZE SOURCES

In the early years of the Civil War, Confederate forces often took advantage of the rich agricultural resources of Virginia's Shenandoah Valley. In September 1864, Union general Philip Sheridan embarked on a strategic campaign of destruction throughout the valley. In November, a Confederate soldier named Richard Habersham described the devastation he saw as his army marched through the area.

> It is a sad sight to see this beautiful valley desolated as it is. All along the route from Staunton to this place houses are leveled to the ground and tack wantonly destroyed and horses by the hundreds lying scattered over the fields or stretched off on the roadside either killed in [Confederate general Jubal] Early's last fight or died and left unburied. . . . Our infantry is now in line of battle[,] the bugle is sounding for the horses to be taken up and we are—I think about to have a little excitement of some kind, probably a battle, as the sharpshooters are all in the front ready for action.

28. What emotions does Habersham express in this excerpt?

CONNECT TO YOUR LIFE

29. ARGUMENT Think about the principles that people were willing to fight for during the Civil War. Consider how people battled to abolish slavery or uphold it, to preserve the Union or secede from it. Now think about the principles you believe are worth fighting to protect. Would you be willing to go to war to uphold them? Write a paragraph defending your principles and explaining why it is important to stand up for them.

TIPS

• Make a list of what you consider to be the most important principles a person should follow. Note where you see a potential conflict between two of your listed principles.

• Note events in your life when you needed to stand up for your beliefs and how you dealt with these challenges.

• Connect one of the events in your personal life with the struggle over principles that took place during the Civil War.

HISTORICAL THINKING How did the United States change because of Reconstruction?

Founders Library is located in the center of Howard University in Washington, D.C. Howard was chartered in 1867 during post-Civil War Reconstruction to educate newly freed African Americans. A historically black university, the present-day Howard consists of 13 schools and colleges noted for their rigorous learning environments and cultural diversity.

"I have confidence . . . in the endurance, capacity, and destiny of my people."

—Blanche K. Bruce, African-American senator during Reconstruction

RECONSTRUCTION UNDER ANDREW JOHNSON

Even the best of friends can break up after a bitter argument. But how do you become friends again? The Civil War had divided the United States between the North and the South. After the war, would it be possible to repair this division and reunite the nation?

THE NATION'S CHALLENGES

The nation was still deeply divided after the surrender of the Confederacy. Plans for a postwar Reconstruction had first been discussed in December 1863, when President Lincoln proposed an **amnesty**, or pardon, plan. This plan would allow Confederate states to organize new governments once 10 percent of the male population took an oath of loyalty to the United States. Lincoln's approach echoed his call from the Second Inaugural Address to act "with malice toward none, with charity for all."

But Lincoln was dead, assassinated in April 1865, and the nation was left to steer the course of rebuilding without his thoughtful guidance and strong leadership. Vice President **Andrew Johnson**, a former Democrat from Tennessee who was chosen for the 1864 Republican ticket to attract more voters, assumed the presidency. Johnson was a southerner and a former slaveholder who had remained loyal to the Union. He had served in Congress and retained his seat in the Senate even after his home state of Tennessee seceded. Before being elected vice president, Johnson had also served as the military governor of Tennessee. Now he faced the difficult challenge of rebuilding the United States politically, socially, and economically.

Although loyal to the Union, Johnson did not support equal rights for African Americans. This position, along with his southern background, did little to win him the trust of northern Republicans. But southerners did not trust him either, due to his support of the Union. As Lincoln had, Johnson believed that moderate measures would be most effective in reuniting southern states with the Union.

Andrew Johnson, the 17th president of the United States, was born in 1808. After the death of his father, his family struggled financially. Johnson never went to school and was apprenticed to a tailor at age 14, but he taught himself to read and write. His eloquent speaking style helped propel his advance in politics.

AMERICAN PLACES
Arlington National Cemetery
Arlington, Virginia

Arlington National Cemetery is the resting site for more than 400,000 veterans of every American war, from the Revolutionary War to conflicts of the 21st century. It was officially designated a military burial ground in 1864 when land available to bury Civil War fatalities became scarce in nearby Washington, D.C. Now a 612-acre cemetery, Arlington was once part of an estate owned by descendants of First Lady Martha Washington and the Confederate leader Robert E. Lee.

Incorporating the South back into the political life of the United States in a fair and just manner was one of the largest challenges looming for Johnson. While the new president supported more lenient treatment of former Confederates, northern Republicans in Congress argued for harsher punishment for the South. They thought the South should pay a heavy political price for the war, which would include banning Confederate leaders from participating in the nation's politics in the future. Northern politicians also realized that if African Americans were granted the right to vote, southern representation in the House of Representatives would increase—a possible threat to northern Republicans' control in the House.

The nation also had to grapple with the South's continued resistance to granting any rights to African Americans or taking steps to **integrate**, or bring them into society as equals. Many African Americans worried that their former owners and other white southerners would keep them from owning property

and taking advantage of employment opportunities. President Johnson had made no secret of the fact that he did not support equal rights for the newly freed African Americans. This, along with his support of states' rights, led many Republicans and other northerners to fear that the president's actions would only encourage white southerners to resist African-American equality.

Perhaps the most overwhelming and immediate problem facing the nation was rebuilding the South and its economic system. By the war's end, large portions of the South lay in ruins, and its economy had crumbled. Land values had decreased dramatically, crop fields had been destroyed, and herds of livestock had been reduced significantly. Confederate money and bonds were worthless. Before emancipation, planters had used their slaves as collateral for loans, since the enslaved were, legally, property. **Collateral** is property or money a borrower puts up as security when he or she takes out a loan. If the borrower does not repay the loan, the lender can take the collateral as payment. With the destruction of that "collateral," the fortunes of many formerly wealthy southerners collapsed, and few banks outside the South were willing to loan money to them to rebuild or revive the economy. The emancipation of African Americans destroyed the South's slave-based agricultural system and left nothing in its place.

PRESIDENTIAL RECONSTRUCTION

Congress was in recess when Lincoln was assassinated, and it was not scheduled to reconvene until December 1865. Johnson used the opportunity to implement his plan to reunite the North and the South. Through his **Presidential Reconstruction** plan, Johnson offered amnesty to former Confederates who agreed to take an oath of loyalty to the Union, restoring their political and civil rights and assuring that the government would not seize their property or prosecute them for treason. High-ranking Confederate leaders and wealthy planters were not offered amnesty at this time, although Johnson eventually pardoned many of them

individually. In fact, by 1866, Johnson had granted more than 7,000 pardons to wealthy southerners and Confederate senior officers.

In addition to loyalty oaths, Johnson also mandated that states convene constitutional conventions to reject secession and ratify the 13th Amendment, which abolished slavery nationwide. Johnson's Reconstruction plans, however, left out any provision for allowing African Americans the right to vote or participate in politics.

For the most part, the southern states met Johnson's conditions and began electing new members to Congress. Little had changed politically, however. Many of the thousands of former Confederates whom Johnson had pardoned were elected to seats in Congress, including Alexander H. Stevens, the former vice president of the Confederacy, who represented Georgia. With the entire African-American population now counted as single individuals when apportioning representatives—not merely as three-fifths of a person as before the war—the South stood to gain even greater legislative power than it had held before the war.

This wood engraving by Alfred R. Waud depicts the May 1866 riot in which white men shot at unarmed African-American citizens in Memphis, Tennessee. Although the violence began after a minor disturbance between former Civil War African-American soldiers and local police, it quickly escalated.

RESISTANCE IN THE SOUTH

The South welcomed the lenient terms established by Johnson's Presidential Reconstruction. Many southerners and their state legislatures, including members of the state conventions elected in 1865, proudly displayed their contempt for the North. Some refused to fly the American flag, some refused to ratify the 13th Amendment, and some even refused to admit that secession had been illegal. Even Johnson recognized that "there seems, in many of the elections something like defiance."

Beginning with Mississippi in 1865, southern states began passing post–Civil War black codes, which were special laws to control and limit the rights of African Americans. These laws were not all that different from those enacted in the colonial era when slavery first took hold. By keeping African Americans poor and dependent on white society for work, these black codes, although varying from state to state, were all intended to maintain the constant supply of available cheap labor that the 13th Amendment had removed. Although the southern state legislatures granted African Americans some rights, such as the right to marry, to own personal possessions, and to sue and be sued, most black codes defined what African Americans could not do: move from one job to another, own or rent land, testify in court, or practice certain occupations.

As African Americans adjusted to the new black codes in southern states, they also faced a wave of violence in many areas of the postwar South. In Texas alone, roughly 1,000 African Americans were murdered by whites between 1865 and 1868, some for merely refusing to remove a hat or for not obeying a command issued by a white person.

Sometimes the violence turned into rioting. For three days in May 1866, white mobs in Memphis, Tennessee, angered when a group of African Americans attempted to stop a white policeman from arresting an African-American man, attacked the camps and neighborhoods of African Americans. Even white police officers and firefighters joined in the violence. A Congressional investigation concluded that competition over jobs fueled the rioting and reported that 46 African Americans and 2 whites were murdered in the uprising. Many more of both races were injured, and homes, churches, and schools were robbed, burned, or destroyed. The violence and jailing of hundreds of blacks forced most of Memphis's African-American community to flee the city until order was restored.

PRIMARY SOURCE

Section 2. All freedmen, free negroes and mulattoes [biracial people] *in this State, over the age of eighteen years, found on the second Monday in January, 1866, or thereafter, with no lawful employment or business, or found unlawfully assembling themselves together, either in the day or night time, and all white persons so assembling themselves with freedmen, Free negroes or mulattoes, or usually associating with freedmen, free negroes or mulattoes, on terms of equality . . . shall be deemed vagrants, and on conviction thereof shall be fined in a sum not exceeding, in the case of a freedman, free negro or mulatto, fifty dollars, and a white man two hundred dollars, and imprisoned at the discretion of the court, the free negro not exceeding ten days, and the white man not exceeding six months.*

—from "Black Codes" of Mississippi: An Act to Amend the Vagrant Laws of the State, 1865

Riots also broke out in July 1866 in New Orleans, when white citizens murdered 35 black citizens and wounded more than 100. As with the Memphis riots, the New Orleans attacks were carried out with the tacit, or unspoken, approval of local government officials and the city's police force. This violence showed the failings of Reconstruction: No one group seemed to have the political will necessary to punish the perpetrators and protect African Americans.

Northerners and congressional Republicans were enraged by the enacting of black codes and the recurring violence against African Americans in the South. In response, they took action against Johnson's Reconstruction efforts.

HISTORICAL THINKING

1. **READING CHECK** Why did most congressional Republicans resist President Johnson's Reconstruction plans?

2. **SUMMARIZE** What challenges did President Johnson face in trying to rebuild the nation?

3. **IDENTIFY** What requirements did the former Confederate states have to meet before being readmitted to the Union under Presidential Reconstruction initiated by Johnson?

4. **MAKE INFERENCES** Why might Lincoln, a northerner, have advocated for a plan that was lenient in its treatment of the former Confederate states and its leaders?

RADICAL RECONSTRUCTION

You may have heard the saying, "To the victor belong the spoils." And, after the Civil War, that's why many northern congressional Republicans believed they should win control of the South's reconstruction. But many southerners and the president himself had different plans, inciting a power struggle for the South.

CONGRESS TAKES CONTROL

The South might have been generally pleased with Johnson's Presidential Reconstruction plan, but northerners—and especially Republicans in Congress—were not. In the North, public opinion called for severe punishment of the South. As you have read, the Radical Republicans, who had supported abolition during the war, agreed with this plan. They were led by Representative **Thaddeus Stevens** of Pennsylvania and Senator Charles Sumner of Massachusetts. You may recall that Sumner was the senator who was beaten with a cane on the Senate floor during debates surrounding the Kansas-Nebraska Act in 1856. Stevens was a

fierce abolitionist who fought for the rights of African Americans before, during, and after the Civil War. He had practiced law in Pennsylvania and served in Congress from 1859 to 1868, where he became an early leader of the Republican Party.

The Radical Republicans were furious over the South's institution of black codes and Johnson's lenient Reconstruction plans. They argued for harsher treatment of former Confederate leaders and wealthy plantation owners, such as seizing their land and giving it to those who had been enslaved on it. They supported immediate and universal voting rights for African Americans. As violence against African Americans increased in the

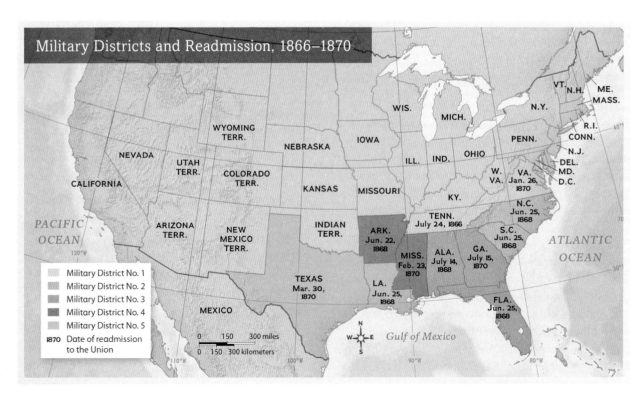

Military Districts and Readmission, 1866–1870

Military District No. 1
Military District No. 2
Military District No. 3
Military District No. 4
Military District No. 5
1870 Date of readmission to the Union

South, many moderate Republicans allied with the Radical Republicans. In December 1865, House and Senate Republicans created a Joint Committee on Reconstruction, tasked with investigating the political and social conditions in the former Confederate states before considering their readmission to the Union.

Attempting to eliminate the black codes through federal legislation, the House passed the **Civil Rights Act of 1866**. The act granted full equality and citizenship to "every race and color," with the exception of Native Americans. Johnson vetoed the bill, but Congress overrode the veto.

As you know, upon the ratification of the 13th Amendment in December 1865, all enslaved people were released from bondage. To prevent any future erosion of African-American rights, Radical Republicans proposed the **14th Amendment**, which guaranteed citizenship and equal protection under the law to all American-born people. The amendment decreed that any state that abridged, or reduced, the voting rights of any male citizen who was older than 21 would suffer a proportionate reduction in its congressional representation. On Johnson's advice, the southern states refused to ratify the amendment.

For much of the summer and fall of 1866, northerners watched in disbelief as southerners ignored the reforms Congress had crafted. Delegates at southern state conventions refused to ratify the 14th Amendment and resisted further attempts to rebuild the South. Then Republicans won control of Congress in the 1866 elections, and they decided it was time to take Reconstruction out of the president's hands.

RECONSTRUCTION ACTS OF 1867

The results of the 1866 elections overwhelmingly reflected northern disapproval of Johnson's plans for Reconstruction. Even though Johnson undertook a speaking tour to regain support for his policies, his Republican opponents won control of two-thirds of the seats in both the House and Senate as well as the governorships and legislative majorities of every northern state.

The Republicans felt they had a mandate, or command from the people, to institute a harsher Reconstruction plan, but they couldn't agree among themselves about the vote, land distribution, the courts, and education. Some wanted to put the South under military control and keep it there for an undetermined time, while others thought it was better to return southern states to civilian control as

---

PRIMARY SOURCE

Only months after Andrew Johnson took office, Thaddeus Stevens—the leader of the Radical Republicans in Congress—wrote him a letter arguing against his plan for Presidential Reconstruction.

His Excellency Andrew Johnson,

Sir

I am sure you will pardon me for speaking to you with a candor [frankness] to which men in high places are seldom accustomed. Among all the leading Union men of the North with whom I have had [communication] I do not find one who approves of your policy. They believe that "restoration" as announced by you will destroy our party (which is of but little consequence) and will greatly injure the country. Can you not hold your hand and wait the action of Congress and in the meantime govern them by military rulers? Profuse pardoning also will greatly embarrass Congress if they should wish to make the enemy pay the expenses of the war or a part of it.

With great respect Your obt Servt [obedient Servant]
Thaddeus Stevens

—from Representative Thaddeus Stevens's letter to President Andrew Johnson, July 6, 1865

---

soon as possible. Finally, in March 1867, they passed the **Reconstruction Acts of 1867**, which undid all of Johnson's policies and began the period of **Congressional Reconstruction**, which lasted until the end of 1877.

The Reconstruction Acts, which collectively came to be called **Radical Reconstruction**, placed the South under military rule. All southern states except Tennessee, which had been readmitted to the Union in July 1866 after ratifying the 14th Amendment, were divided into five military districts. A Union general was placed in charge of each district. Southern states were required to convene conventions to write new constitutions, which had to grant the right to vote to all adult male citizens, regardless of race. After ratifying its new constitution, each state had to ratify the 14th Amendment before it was allowed to elect members to Congress. Once these conditions were met and both the U.S. Senate and House of Representatives had approved its new constitution, the state could be readmitted to the Union.

With Radical Reconstruction underway, some northerners began to move to the South looking for business opportunities created by the rebuilding efforts. Southern Democrats and others called these northern immigrants **"carpetbaggers"** because they often arrived carrying cheap suitcases made of carpet fabric. Most southerners viewed these people as intruders, looking to take advantage of others and exploit the South. Some of them were buying up the property of southerners who, due to the region's dire economic situation, could not afford to pay taxes. If a property owner failed to pay taxes, his or her land could be sold for pennies on the dollar. The northerners who came South included Republicans who wanted to engage in politics, and many of them became delegates to the constitutional conventions in the former Confederate states. But most of the northerners who traveled South were former Union soldiers, preachers, teachers, and social workers who hoped to help African Americans adjust to society as free individuals.

White southerners who supported Radical Reconstruction also earned the disdain of many in the South, who considered them traitors and called them "scalawags."

CRITICAL VIEWING Republican Carl Schurz moved from Wisconsin to Missouri, where he was elected U.S. senator in 1868. In this 1872 political cartoon by Thomas Nast, Schurz appears as a carpetbagger. What qualities does Nash link to Schurz, and whose opinion would that caricature most likely represent?

The term **scalawag** is an insult used to describe a worthless, dishonorable person. Southern supporters of Radical Reconstruction came from a variety of backgrounds. Many were small plantation owners or backcountry farmers who wanted to prevent the wealthy planters from regaining power. Others were southern business owners who supported the North's efforts to rebuild the South's economy. Enough "scalawags" were scattered throughout the South to help build the Republican Party into a political force in the mountains of eastern Tennessee, western North Carolina, eastern Kentucky, northern Alabama, and northern Georgia.

THE IMPEACHMENT OF JOHNSON

As Republicans in southern state governments carried on with their rebuilding efforts, congressional Republicans sought to curb Andrew Johnson's presidential power. In a special session of Congress, Republicans voted to limit Johnson's authority as commander in chief of the army and passed the Tenure of Office Act, which prevented the president from removing officials who had been confirmed by the Senate. The passage of this act clearly violated the U.S. Constitution, which granted the president the right to hire or fire Cabinet members.

In August 1867, Johnson defied the new law by replacing his Secretary of War, Edwin Stanton, with war hero Ulysses S. Grant. Stanton, a strong supporter of the Republicans in Congress, had been the only member of Johnson's Cabinet to support Radical Reconstruction. Stanton, with the support of his Radical Republican allies, locked himself in his office and refused to leave.

On February 24, 1868, the House of Representatives voted to impeach Johnson, charging him with 11 articles of impeachment, most centered on the violation of the Tenure of Office Act. The Senate trial began in March 1868 and lasted for 11 weeks. Finally, in May, Johnson was acquitted in the Senate by one vote. Even his political foes realized that using impeachment to address anything less than criminal offenses was unwise. However, the constitutional and political significance of Johnson's impeachment endured.

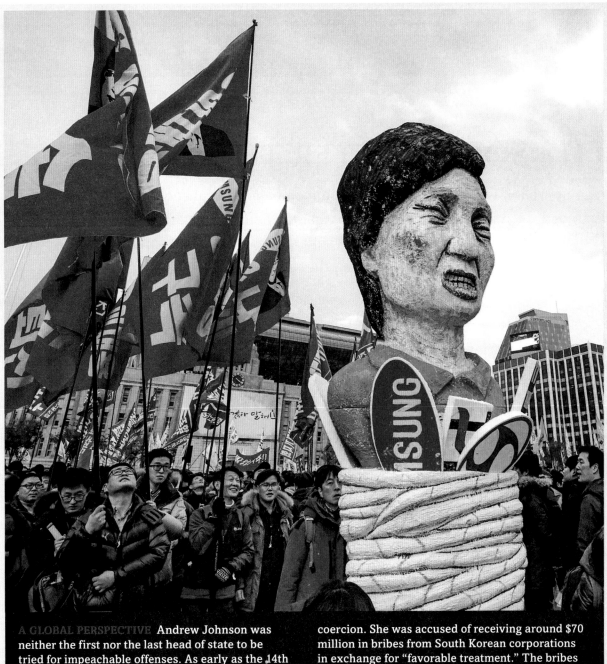

A GLOBAL PERSPECTIVE Andrew Johnson was neither the first nor the last head of state to be tried for impeachable offenses. As early as the 14th century in England, a member of Parliament faced impeachment, and the process eventually became a law in many nations. In the 21st century, several world leaders have been impeached, including President Park Geun-hye of the Republic of Korea. Removed from office in 2016, Park was arrested and put on trial for bribery, abuse of power, and coercion. She was accused of receiving around $70 million in bribes from South Korean corporations in exchange for "favorable treatment." The bribes were revealed when files kept by Park's friend, Choi Soon-sil, were leaked to the press. In 2018, Choi and Park were convicted in separate trials. Choi was sentenced to 20 years in jail, and Park to 24 years. In this photograph, South Koreans protest the corruption by displaying an effigy of Park tied to the logos of companies accused of the bribery.

HISTORICAL THINKING

1. **READING CHECK** What issues concerning Reconstruction plans divided President Johnson and the congressional Republicans?

2. **MAKE INFERENCES** What political purpose did the Radical Republicans have for supporting equal rights for African Americans?

3. **DETERMINE WORD MEANINGS** Why might some people call the Reconstruction Act of 1867 "radical"?

4. **INTERPRET MAPS** Based on the map, which Military District was first to return to the Union in its entirety, and which states were part of this district?

MAIN IDEA The postwar South was forced to develop a new system of labor and increase its industry, but the region continued to rely mainly on labor-intensive agriculture to drive its economy.

THE SOUTH AFTER THE WAR

Imagine what it would be like if the foundation of your local economy were destroyed, seemingly overnight. That's what the South faced after the war. Along with the end of slavery came a massive shift in the labor force, especially on the huge plantations that had supported the region's once-thriving agricultural economy. Change would not be easy.

ECONOMIC DEVASTATION

As profound social and political problems plagued the South after the Civil War, Republican leaders in the early years of Reconstruction keenly focused on economic development. These politicians believed that with appropriate aid, the South could be transformed. It could become a modern society dominated by large, prosperous cities, productive factories, and an agricultural industry not based on the plantation system and enslaved labor.

The Civil War left large parts of the South in ruins and devastated its economy. Most of the fighting had taken place in the South, and its major cities, such as Atlanta, Charleston, and Richmond, were severely damaged. Little infrastructure remained standing. Energy supplies were depleted, and nearly two-thirds of the South's railroad system was in a shambles. Steamboats no longer traveled the rivers, and roads had been mangled by wartime use. Protective levees near rivers had been demolished, ruining large strips

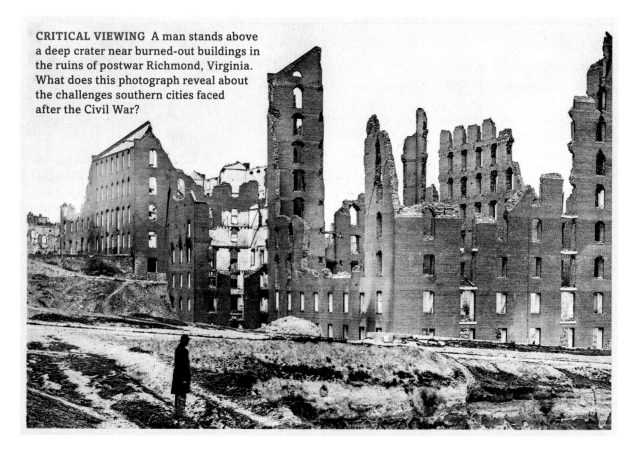

CRITICAL VIEWING A man stands above a deep crater near burned-out buildings in the ruins of postwar Richmond, Virginia. What does this photograph reveal about the challenges southern cities faced after the Civil War?

of Mississippi delta cotton lands. Cotton that had not been destroyed in the war had been seized by Union troops.

Throughout the South, land values had decreased dramatically, wiping out hundreds of millions of dollars in insurance investments and bank assets based on the value of now nearly worthless property. Confederate money and bonds were also worthless. Consequently, little capital was available to pay for rebuilding. Perhaps the greatest impact on the South's economy was the emancipation of African Americans. Enslaved workers accounted for the largest share of capital investment in the South, roughly $4 billion, which was more than the land itself was worth. Emancipation completely upended the South's agricultural system, which relied on enslaved labor. Consequently, the disappearance of both enslaved labor and capital meant that the South's agricultural economy required a complete overhaul.

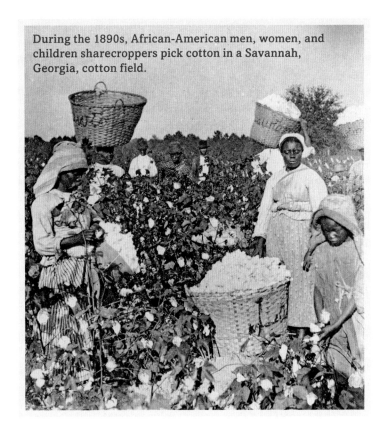

During the 1890s, African-American men, women, and children sharecroppers pick cotton in a Savannah, Georgia, cotton field.

Naturally, these factors had a negative effect on southern crop production. The cotton crop would not rise to prewar levels until 1879. Likewise, tobacco and sugar production didn't rebound until the 1880s and 1890s. Other traditional southern crops fared worse. Some, such as the rice industry along the East Coast and the hemp industry of Kentucky, never returned to their prewar levels.

A CHANGED SOCIETY

The southern economy clung to life as both whites and African Americans struggled to find an alternative to slavery and the plantation system. People responded in a variety of ways. Some former slaveholders simply gave up and left the country to settle in Latin America, while others continued to treat the freed African Americans as though they were still enslaved to keep them from leaving. Other planters provided living accommodations to former slaves and paid them wages for the work they performed on the plantations.

Immediately after the war, in the spring of 1865, many planters insisted that their formerly enslaved workers continue to work in "gangs," as they had before emancipation. In exchange for their labor, they received a portion of the crop, shared among all the workers. Few African Americans agreed to this method. They preferred to work as individuals or in family groups. Landowners soon found they had little choice but to permit African Americans and their families to take primary responsibility for farming a portion of land under an agricultural system called **sharecropping**.

Under this system, sharecroppers—who were also known as **tenant farmers** because they did not own the land they worked—provided all the labor on a portion of land and turned over the majority of the crop to the landowner. The profit on the crop served as payment of rent on land and shelter, and the sharecroppers also were allowed to keep a very small portion of the profit for themselves. Some poor white families, devastated by the war, also became sharecroppers.

But sharecropping could also leave sharecroppers in debt to landowners. Most sharecroppers lacked necessary supplies, including seeds and tools for farming their allotted land. Landowners and local supply shops would often step in to rent or sell the supplies to the sharecroppers on credit at a high rate of interest. To assure that they would be paid back, the landowners and merchants would place **liens**, or legal claims on a borrower's crops and any property owned. By the time the crops were harvested, the sharecropper had usually run up a considerable amount of debt, and as a result, would receive only a tiny part of the profits, or none at all. If sharecroppers could not pay back their loans, the planter and anyone else they owed could claim even more of the profits on the crops they grew.

The cycle would continue for many sharecroppers, leading to a financial condition called **debt peonage**. In this situation, sharecroppers were financially bound to continue under the unfair sharecropping system because they could not make enough money to pay off their debts or move off the land. Sharecroppers who failed to pay off debts could be sent to prison or placed into forced labor. So many African Americans fell into debt peonage that some people called the condition "black peonage."

Despite the challenges facing the South, the region was making economic progress. Wealthy, powerful northern and southern politicians and business owners provided money to rebuild infrastructure and to develop new industries. These efforts to transform the South from a mostly agrarian society into an industrial one reflected the desire for a "New South." For example, the land around Birmingham, Alabama, contained large deposits of coal, iron ore, and limestone necessary for producing steel. By the late 1880s, Birmingham had become one of the largest producers of iron and steel in the nation. But despite the industrial progress, most southerners remained closely linked to traditional agriculture, which remained the driving economic force in the South.

THE KU KLUX KLAN

As Radical Reconstruction gained traction in the South, southern whites looked for ways to fight racial integration that they believed the North was forcing on them. Because they were politically powerless to battle the Republicans running their state governments, many organized secret societies to undermine efforts to promote African-American equality. The largest and most powerful of these societies was the **Ku Klux Klan**, founded in 1866 by Confederate veterans in Pulaski, Tennessee. The Ku Klux Klan, also known as the KKK or simply, the Klan, dedicated itself to maintaining white supremacy. It saw itself as a military wing of the Democratic Party, intimidating and killing both whites and African Americans who dared to associate with Republicans or support African-American rights. Under the leadership of its "grand wizard" Nathan Bedford Forrest, the KKK rallied resistance against Radical Reconstruction. Forrest was a former Confederate

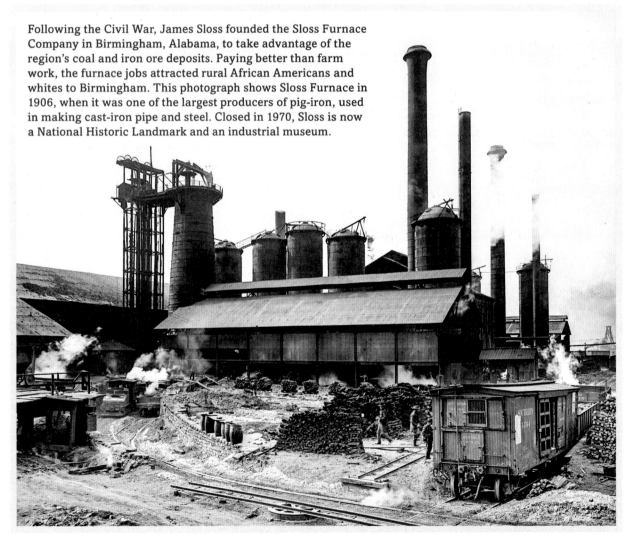

Following the Civil War, James Sloss founded the Sloss Furnace Company in Birmingham, Alabama, to take advantage of the region's coal and iron ore deposits. Paying better than farm work, the furnace jobs attracted rural African Americans and whites to Birmingham. This photograph shows Sloss Furnace in 1906, when it was one of the largest producers of pig-iron, used in making cast-iron pipe and steel. Closed in 1970, Sloss is now a National Historic Landmark and an industrial museum.

general who had won a handful of victories over Union forces in the war. His reputation attracted many members to the organization.

Klan violence spread across the South and continued into the 1870s. Local Klan members, along with other white supremacist groups such as the Knights of the White Camelia, White Leagues, and the White Brotherhood, terrorized communities in many parts of the South. Hooded and robed to disguise their identities, the KKK attacked at night, breaking up Republican meetings; burning African-American homes, churches, and schools; and running their political opponents out of their communities. They even lynched, or tortured and hanged, their victims.

The Klan threatened both African Americans and white Republicans, pledging to harm or kill them and their families if they tried to cast a ballot, and these **voter intimidation** tactics proved very effective. By keeping opponents away from the polls, the Democratic Party began to regain its political foothold in the South. Driven by white racism, the KKK framed each election as a battle between African Americans and whites. With these tactics, the Klan helped the Democratic Party eventually win back the support of many southern whites who had been voting for Republicans. By the mid-1870s, the Democrats regained power in all but three southern states.

ANTI-KLAN EFFORTS

Republicans realized that racist violence and brutality were undermining the party's ability to survive and grow in southern states, but they were split on how to address the issue. Many came to the conclusion that using military forces to influence politics was not working in the South. Others, influenced by the persistent violence, questioned if staying in the South was worth the party's cost and effort.

Unable to ignore the Klan's violent activities, Congress passed three Enforcement Acts between 1870 and 1871 to address the problems in the South. The first, in 1870, made it illegal for groups of people to "go in disguise upon the public highways, or upon the premises of another" in order to violate any citizen's rights. The two Enforcement Acts passed in 1871, also known as the **Ku Klux Klan Acts of 1871**, gave the federal government control of national elections (including the supervision of polling places), outlawed organized attempts to deprive voters of their civil rights, and banned efforts to bar any citizen from holding public office.

CRITICAL VIEWING In 1874, this political cartoon by Thomas Nast appeared in *Harper's Weekly*. From the symbols and elements incorporated in the cartoon, what overall statement is Nast making about the condition of the United States in the years following the Civil War?

The Enforcement Acts also gave the federal government broader powers to fight the Klan, including the right to override state laws. The acts gave the president the authority to use military force to detain and aid the prosecution of Klan members, resulting in the arrests of more than 5,000 Klan leaders and the eventual conviction of 1,250 of them. Although the Enforcement Acts were used to force southern states to comply with the rule of law, sentiment in the North for such stern measures was fading, and the United States Supreme Court declared the Ku Klux Klan Acts unconstitutional in 1882.

HISTORICAL THINKING

1. **READING CHECK** What is sharecropping?

2. **ANALYZE CAUSE AND EFFECT** Why were many African Americans trapped by the sharecropping system in the postwar South?

3. **DRAW CONCLUSIONS** What impact did the actions of the Ku Klux Klan have on Republican Reconstruction?

4. **IDENTIFY** What were the chief aims of the Ku Klux Klan Acts of 1871?

PROMISES AND REFORMS

Like many Americans, you probably take your education and political rights for granted. But to African Americans during Reconstruction, opportunities to learn and participate in politics were significant signs of their new freedoms.

SOUTHERN LAND REFORM

Reconstruction aimed not just to rebuild the South but also to reunite the nation without slavery. Those efforts began even before the war was over. As Union forces took over Confederate territories near the end of the Civil War, they freed enslaved people they encountered. Some African Americans seized their freedom at the first opportunity; others moved to Union camps or even joined the army. For most, simple survival remained the highest priority. This meant being able to find shelter and food.

Most newly freed African Americans stayed in the South, and many based this decision on rumors that the government would award them land. As you have read, after General Sherman completed his "March to the Sea" and confiscated roughly 400,000 acres of coastline stretching from South Carolina to

Florida, he issued Special Field Order No. 15. The order set the land aside exclusively for the settlement of freedmen, with each family receiving no more than 40 acres. By June 1865, more than 40,000 African Americans had established a self-governing community on the confiscated "Sherman Land." Sherman also instructed his army to lend mules to the community to help in development. This was the source of the promise of "40 acres and a mule." But after the war, in the fall of 1865, President Johnson overturned Sherman's order and returned most of "Sherman Land" to its former owners.

In early 1865, in anticipation of the war's end, Congress created the Bureau of Refugees, Freedmen, and Abandoned Lands, more commonly called the **Freedmen's Bureau**. The bureau's main purpose was to oversee the South's transition from a

African-American women and children practice reading in this photograph, taken at the Freedman's Village in Virginia. The federal government established the village to aid enslaved people who were escaping from the South during the Civil War.

In this 1877 oil painting, *Sunday Morning in Virginia*, Winslow Homer captures young African Americans as they practice a new freedom—learning to read.

slave economy to a **wage economy**, or an economy in which people are paid for their work. Army officers, who acted as bureau agents, dispensed medicine, food, and clothing to formerly enslaved African Americans and poor white southerners. The Freedmen's Bureau created courts to draw up labor contracts between landowners and laborers and resolve conflicts. It also established schools and coordinated female volunteers who came from the North to teach in them. In fact, the bureau's commissioner, former Union general Oliver Otis Howard, believed education was the key to improving the lives and opportunities of former slaves. By 1869, the Freedmen's Bureau had built thousands of schools for African Americans.

THE IMPORTANCE OF EDUCATION

Having been denied educational opportunities during slavery, many southern African Americans were eager to attend school. They viewed education as a path to better jobs as they adjusted to a wage economy. Learning to read and write and gaining a basic understanding of mathematics would help them deal with contracts, budgets, and other labor issues. A solid education would also allow them to become active, informed citizens, aware of their civil rights and knowledgeable about the political process.

The Freedmen's Bureau worked with African-American churches, individuals, and aid groups to help fund, build, and staff hundreds of schools for African-American children and adults. The schools were often built on land owned by African Americans. Although the schools were free, sending children to school often cut into total household income. As you have read, many recently freed African Americans, including children, continued to work at the same jobs they had performed when they were enslaved, whether on farms or in towns, only now they were being paid for their labor. Most families relied on their children's wages to help cover living costs.

African-American schools grappled with many challenges, including shortages of teachers and classroom space. Students often had to rotate in and out of a classroom in shifts. Typically, teachers taught children all day and then held classes for adults at night. Teachers included soldiers who had a basic education and were stationed in the area to oversee Reconstruction. In some schools, children and adults learned side by side in the same classroom.

Along with establishing schools to teach basic skills, the Freedmen's Bureau also created institutions of higher learning for African-American students during Reconstruction. As you have read, General Oliver Otis Howard, the commissioner of the Freedmen's Bureau, supported education within African-American communities. Howard University in Washington, D.C., founded in 1867 and named in Howard's honor, established the first law school for African Americans. Howard served as the university's third president. Other African-American colleges and universities were founded throughout the South, creating a vital education network for formerly enslaved people and their families. Many of these colleges and universities are still thriving today.

THE FIGHT FOR SOCIAL JUSTICE

Following the Civil War, African Americans quickly established their own churches. Many African Americans were drawn to the Baptist denomination because of its flexible organization, which allowed congregations the freedom to determine how they wanted to worship. More than a million southern African Americans were members of a Baptist church by 1890, significantly more than those who joined any other denomination.

Churches were central to the lives of African-American families and helped to strengthen their growing communities. Importantly, churches led the battle for **social justice**, or the fair distribution of opportunities and privileges, including racial

African-American men, dressed according to their profession, cast their ballots during Virginia's 1867 election in *The First Vote*, an illustration by Alfred Waud. That year, African Americans in Virginia were given the right to vote.

equality and rights, for all. In addition to conducting religious services, churches hosted political, social, and educational events. In places where African Americans did not have strong political representation, African-American ministers stepped in to become community leaders and advocates for social justice. African Americans also formed a range of fraternal and benevolent societies, clubs, and lodges, and even trade associations to provide aid and support within their communities.

Like religion, family was a foundation of African-American life. Slavery had torn apart unimaginable numbers of families, and during Reconstruction, many African Americans tried to reunite with lost family members. Many turned to the Freedmen's Bureau to locate missing relatives. The Freedmen's Bureau also helped strengthen African-American families by legitimizing marriages that had usually been prohibited during slavery.

GAINING A VOICE

Radical Reconstruction gave southern African Americans the right to vote, allowing them to gain a political voice and become active participants in the nation's electoral process. Ambitious African-American southerners, many of whom had been free and relatively prosperous before the Civil War, put themselves forward as natural leaders. African Americans from the North came to the South, also hoping to secure appointed and elective offices. During their service in the Union military, African-American veterans had gained useful leadership skills. Such men became the backbone of the Republican Party in districts that had a predominantly African-American population.

Many African Americans looked to the **National Equal Rights League** for political support. This organization advocated the expansion of civil rights and established state leagues throughout the nation. With the help of the Equal Rights leagues, many local African-American leaders mobilized enormous numbers of African-American voters in the fall of 1867. African Americans were the majority of delegates in South Carolina's and Louisiana's conventions, although they accounted for smaller proportions of convention delegates in the other southern states. Even so, African-American delegates throughout the South played an instrumental role in drafting democratic constitutions for their states.

Republican support and voter turnout among African Americans propelled many formerly enslaved men into community and political leadership positions. More than 1,400 African Americans were elected to

This 1872 print depicts the first seven African Americans to serve in the U.S. Congress. Representing five southern states, the men are (from left to right), Senator Hiram Rhodes Revels of Mississippi (who filled the Senate seat that Jefferson Davis had once held) and Representatives Benjamin S. Turner of Alabama, Robert C. De Large of South Carolina, Josiah T. Walls of Florida, Jefferson F. Long of Georgia, Joseph Rainey of South Carolina, and Robert B. Elliot of South Carolina.

political office in the South during Reconstruction, including a total of 16 African Americans elected to Congress. Of those, **Blanche K. Bruce** and **Hiram Revels** represented Mississippi in the U.S. Senate.

Although Bruce had been born into slavery, the son of an enslaved woman and a white planter, he was a well-educated man. The Republican-led Mississippi legislature elected Bruce to a seat in the U.S. Senate in 1874, where he served until 1881, fighting for equal rights for African Americans and Native Americans, as well as for Chinese immigrants.

Born to free African Americans in the South, Hiram Revels was a minister who was educated in the North. After winning a seat in the Mississippi State Senate in 1869, Revels was elected to assume a vacant Mississippi U.S. Senate seat in 1870, where he worked to integrate public schools and passenger rail service. He left the Senate to become president of Alcorn Agricultural and Mechanical College, which today is Alcorn State University, in Claiborne County, Mississippi.

African-American politicians, including Revels and Bruce, worked with other Republicans to repeal black codes, increase the number of elective political offices open to African Americans, and establish state hospitals and other institutions for people with disabilities. They passed legislation to rebuild roads, railways, and other infrastructure, and they achieved a major goal when Reconstruction governments established public school systems in the South.

Despite their many political achievements during Reconstruction, no African American was elected governor of a state in that era. However, after a

corruption scandal toppled the elected governor of Louisiana, **Pinckney Pinchback** stepped in to serve as acting governor from late 1872 to early 1873. Pinchback had been born free in Macon, Georgia, the son of an African-American mother and a white planter who raised him together. After his father's death, Pinchback and his mother fled the South for Ohio in fear of being enslaved. During the war, Pinchback returned South to recruit soldiers for the Union in New Orleans and remained in the region.

Oscar Dunn was the nation's first elected African-American lieutenant governor, serving in Louisiana from 1868 to 1871. Born into slavery in New Orleans, Dunn was self-educated and learned public speaking from actors who rented rooms in his mother's boarding house. After escaping slavery, he purchased his freedom. During Reconstruction, he served in the Louisiana State Senate and helped organize the 1870 Republican convention. Before his death in 1871, Dunn was a vocal supporter of African-American suffrage, equal rights, and land ownership. He was a fierce opponent of leniency for former Confederate officials.

HISTORICAL THINKING

1. **READING CHECK** What does the term "social justice" mean?

2. **SUMMARIZE** How did the Freedmen's Bureau help African Americans in the South?

3. **ANALYZE CAUSE AND EFFECT** How did education empower African Americans?

4. **DESCRIBE** How did the social and political lives of African Americans change during Reconstruction?

GRANT'S PRESIDENCY

Elections have consequences. The Republicans knew that they needed to win the presidential election to keep their Reconstruction policies going. Few, if any, realized that electing a popular but inexperienced executive might cause a host of other problems.

THE ELECTION OF 1868

Politically wounded and weak, Andrew Johnson finished his term in office but decided against running in the 1868 election. Republicans nominated Union war hero Ulysses S. Grant, whom they trusted to support their Reconstruction policies. Although Grant had no political experience, Republicans thought his independence and reputation would lead to less partisanship throughout the country. Accepting the nomination, Grant said, "Let us have peace," a phrase that became the theme of the Republican campaign.

The Democrats nominated the former governor of New York, **Horatio Seymour**. Seymour was a Copperhead, a former Confederate sympathizer, who relied on racial bigotry and white supremacy to attract voters. Seymour's message resonated with midwestern farmers and urban whites who felt misunderstood by Eastern politicians or threatened by freedmen, whom they thought would take their jobs.

This 1868 campaign badge promotes Ulysses S. Grant's presidential candidacy with patriotic symbols.

Grant prevailed over Seymour, thanks in part to African-American support in the South. Even in the face of violence and voter intimidation, enough federal troops were stationed in southern states to protect and enable the large numbers of African-American voters—nearly 500,000 of them—who turned out to cast their ballots. Grant carried six states in the South and most states in the North to win the election with 53 percent of the vote, and the Republicans retained their large majorities in both houses of Congress.

In his inaugural address, Grant declared, "I shall on all subjects have a policy to recommend, but none to enforce against the will of the people." He promised to uphold the laws Congress passed, and he was true to his word. With Andrew Johnson and his veto pen a memory, Congress was finally able to put one final Reconstruction amendment into place.

THE 15th AMENDMENT

You have read about the 13th Amendment, which abolished slavery in the United States. The 14th Amendment, which guaranteed citizenship to all American-born people and equal protection under the law for all citizens, was finally ratified in July 1868. In the years that followed, the 14th Amendment opened the door to other landmark legislation, including laws that expanded rights for women, mandated school integration, and guaranteed voting rights and equal employment opportunities for women and minorities.

After Grant's election, Congress passed the **15th Amendment**, which prohibited federal and state governments from restricting the right to vote because of race, color, or previous condition of servitude, or slavery. The amendment was intended to limit the legal right of the southern states to exclude African Americans from the political process, and it completed the political reforms sought by Reconstruction.

Congress approved the amendment quickly in February 1869. Democrats viewed it as a step toward equality for African Americans and heavily opposed it. In fact, the amendment did not ensure African

CRITICAL VIEWING Called *The 15th Amendment*, this 1870s print features a parade celebrating the amendment. Portraits of those who helped pass the amendment, as well as one of Abraham Lincoln, surround the central image. How do the scenes depicting African-American life relate to the 15th Amendment?

Americans the right to hold office, and it left in place certain restrictions that both southern and northern states imposed on voting rights. These restrictions included **poll taxes**, or fees charged when people register to vote, and **literacy tests**, which require voters to prove they can read and write before registering. Such measures were enacted mainly to keep African Americans from voting. Even so, state legislatures ratified the 15th Amendment promptly, and it became part of the Constitution in 1870.

WEAK LEADERSHIP

By 1870, many Americans were thinking less of the war and more of the future. Northern voters were losing interest in the South's issues and becoming more concerned about those closer to home. But Grant's inexperience impeded his ability to help the nation face challenges. Because of his "hands-off" approach to governing and attempts to avoid partisan battles, he seemed weak. Congress stepped in to make decisions about controversial issues.

The Republicans were losing support in the South to the Democratic Party as Reconstruction-era policies faded. And within the party itself, rifts arose over protective tariffs, currency issues, and competing Reconstruction plans. Among the most powerful party factions were a group of disgruntled, unhappy members who called themselves the **Liberal Republicans**. In the 1870s, the word *liberal* described someone who favored smaller government, lower tariffs, civil-service reform, and, most important, an end to Reconstruction. But Grant's administration had other problems, too. Rumors of scandal were beginning to surface.

HISTORICAL THINKING

1. **READING CHECK** What effect did the 15th Amendment have on voting rights for African Americans in the North?

2. **ANALYZE CAUSE AND EFFECT** How did African Americans help pass the 15th Amendment?

3. **COMPARE AND CONTRAST** How closely did Grant's inaugural promises align with his actions as president? Support your response with evidence.

THE END OF AN ERA

Think about how complicated and difficult it is to keep track of U.S. economic and political issues today. In the 1870s, Americans were also faced with a host of political scandals and a financial panic that nearly took their minds off the problems of Reconstruction. Nearly.

SCANDAL AND PANIC

The first accusations of scandal arose in the summer of 1869. Two speculators, Jay Gould and Jim Fisk, were caught manipulating the gold market to make huge profits for themselves. The scheme involved members of Grant's own family, leading many Americans to question the ethical standards of Grant and his administration.

But despite Grant's weak leadership and connection to scandal, Republicans chose him again as their 1872 presidential candidate. The Liberal Republicans allied with Democrats to throw their support behind newspaper publisher Horace Greeley, whose platform was based on ending Reconstruction. Grant, who supported Reconstruction, remained popular enough with the public to win re-election easily, even though more government scandals were already brewing.

Corruption in the railroad industry surfaced in September 1872. The **Crédit Mobilier** (KREH-diht moh-BEEL-yay) was a construction company created by directors and stockholders of the Union Pacific Railroad. The stockholders signed contracts with the company to work on the railroad, and then they overcharged for work completed,

American illustrator Howard Pyle captures the fear and chaos sparked by the Panic of 1873 in this painting, *The Rush from the New York Stock Exchange on September 18, 1873*.

passing the huge profits on to themselves. To avoid a congressional investigation, Crédit Mobilier's managers bribed some congressional Republicans and, allegedly, Vice President Schuyler Colfax, allowing them to buy company shares at prices well below market value. When the lawmakers sold their shares, they pocketed the difference. A newspaper, the *New York Sun*, broke the story in late 1872, sparking an investigation that further damaged the Grant administration's credibility. Another scandal arose when Congress forced Secretary of War William Belknap to resign after accusing him of accepting cash gifts from army suppliers.

Then, in September 1873, the influential banking firm of Jay Cooke and Company declared bankruptcy due to a European stock market crash and bad investments made in the Northern Pacific Railroad. More bank and railroad business failures followed, sending a wave of fear known as the **Panic of 1873** through the financial industry and the country. Thousands of businesses closed, many people lost their savings, and unemployment increased. To make matters worse, there was no system of unemployment insurance or social security to cushion workers against the economic shocks. The nation slid into a depression that lasted until 1879.

Scandals and economic panic harmed Grant and the Republicans politically, and in the 1874 midterm elections, Democrats won control of the House of Representatives and secured more seats in the Senate. Grant's administration retreated from southern politics, and southern Democrats gained more power. Racial intimidation and racist propaganda increased, and in 1876, two important Supreme Court cases diminished African Americans' hopes of securing equal rights.

RECONSTRUCTION ENDS

In *U.S.* v. *Cruikshank*, the Court ruled that, while the 14th Amendment allowed the federal government to prohibit states from abusing African Americans' civil rights, only the states could prosecute and punish violations of the amendment. In *U.S.* v. *Reese*, decided the same day, the Court ruled that the 15th Amendment only made it illegal to deny a citizen's voting rights based on race. States were free to use other criteria to determine a voter's fitness, such as poll taxes and literacy tests. These decisions paved the way for nearly a century of racial discrimination.

Democrats felt optimistic as the 1876 presidential election approached. They nominated the governor of New York, Sam Tilden, a vocal opponent of

corruption. Republicans nominated Rutherford B. Hayes, a respected Union officer, former member of the House of Representatives, and governor of Ohio. Both candidates were known for their honesty.

Tilden captured 184 electoral votes against Hayes's 165, but Tilden needed one more electoral vote to secure a victory. Of the 20 votes still in doubt, 19 were from the southern states of Louisiana, South Carolina, and Florida, and one was from Oregon. Both sides declared victory. The Constitution did not provide guidance on contested presidential elections, but the two houses of Congress had specific roles. The House of Representatives was responsible for electing the president if no one won an electoral majority, and the Senate was responsible for verifying the electoral vote. Neither the Republican Senate nor the Democratic House could proceed without the support of the other.

Congress created a 15-member electoral commission with five members each from the House, Senate, and Supreme Court. The commission's eight Republicans and seven Democrats voted along party lines, recommending the disputed electoral votes go to Hayes, but the Democratic House would still have to accept Hayes as the winner. To prevent a crisis, Republicans and Democrats struck a deal that became known as the **Compromise of 1877**: Democrats agreed to award Hayes the presidency in exchange for ending Reconstruction. Within a month of taking office, Hayes pulled federal troops out of the South.

Reconstruction had begun the long struggle to overcome the racism borne of centuries of chattel slavery, but to complete the effort would have required an expansion of federal power few Americans, even those in the North, were willing to accept. Instead, racial discrimination became entrenched throughout the nation. Reconstruction may have fallen short of its goals, but the 13th, 14th, and 15th amendments eventually paved the way for the civil rights movement of the 1960s.

HISTORICAL THINKING

1. **READING CHECK** What was the outcome of the Compromise of 1877?

2. **DRAW CONCLUSIONS** Why was the Crédit Mobilier scandal particularly disturbing to many Americans?

3. **ANALYZE CAUSE AND EFFECT** What set off the Panic of 1873 and how did it affect the nation?

4. **COMPARE AND CONTRAST** How were the two Supreme Court cases involving the 14th and 15th amendments similar and different?

VOCABULARY

Use each of the terms below in a sentence that expresses an understanding about an event or topic from the chapter.

1. **amnesty**
   President Johnson's support of amnesty for former Confederates suggested he would willingly grant them official pardons.

2. carpetbagger

3. scalawag

4. sharecropping

5. voter intimidation

6. social justice

7. integrate

8. collateral

9. poll tax

READING STRATEGY
COMPARE AND CONTRAST

Use a Venn diagram like the one shown below to compare and contrast the principles of Presidential and Congressional (Radical) Reconstruction. Then answer the question.

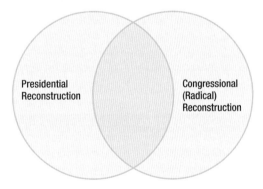

Presidential Reconstruction

Congressional (Radical) Reconstruction

10. On which issues were Presidential Reconstruction and Congressional Reconstruction alike and on which issues were they different?

MAIN IDEAS

Answer the following questions. Support your answers with evidence from the chapter.

11. Why were many congressional Republicans not surprised that Andrew Johnson supported leniency toward former Confederate states? **LESSON 1.1**

12. Why did the Radical Republicans think it necessary to implement their own Reconstruction plans? **LESSON 1.1**

13. What pushed congressional Republicans to consider impeaching Johnson? **LESSON 1.2**

14. What proposals were made to help rebuild the South and reform its economy? **LESSON 2.1**

15. In what area of African-American life did the Freedmen's Bureau have the most impact? **LESSON 2.2**

16. Why was education considered crucial as well as a symbol of freedom to African Americans in the South? **LESSON 2.2**

17. Why did Congress wait until Grant was elected to pass the 15th Amendment? **LESSON 3.1**

18. How was the 1876 election dispute settled? **LESSON 3.2**

HISTORICAL THINKING

Answer the following questions. Support your answers with evidence from the chapter.

19. **SEQUENCE** How did ratification of the 13th, 14th, and 15th amendments advance the rights of African Americans?

20. **DRAW CONCLUSIONS** What impact did the emergence of sharecropping in the South have on the region after the Civil War?

21. **SUMMARIZE** What were the political ramifications of the Panic of 1873?

22. MAKE INFERENCES Why were the elections and political successes of Hiram Revels and Blanche K. Bruce important to African Americans in the South?

23. FORM AND SUPPORT OPINIONS Given what you have read about Presidential and Congressional (Radical) Reconstruction, which plan do you think offered the best way to reunite the nation? Explain your opinion.

INTERPRET VISUALS

Look closely at the two-panel political cartoon, which compares the South during Reconstruction with the South after Reconstruction. Use information from the chapter and the cartoon to answer the questions that follow.

24. What does the woman in the first panel symbolize, and why?

25. How does the artist depict the South in the second panel?

ANALYZE SOURCES

In this excerpt from President Grant's Second Inaugural Address delivered on March 4, 1873, Grant discussed his approach to civil rights in the South as Reconstruction continued. Read the excerpt and answer the question.

> The effects of the late civil strife have been to free the slave and make him a citizen. Yet he is not possessed of the civil rights which citizenship should carry with it. This is wrong, and should be corrected. To this correction I stand committed, so far as Executive influence can avail.
>
> Social equality is not a subject to be legislated upon, nor shall I ask that anything be done to advance the social status of the colored man, except to give him a fair chance to develop what there is good in him, give him access to the schools, and when he travels let him feel assured that his conduct will regulate the treatment and fare he will receive.

26. What distinction does Grant make between the meaning of "civil rights" and "social equality"?

CONNECT TO YOUR LIFE

27. EXPLANATORY Ratification of the 15th Amendment in 1870 prohibited the government from denying a person's right to vote on the basis of race. Recall what you learned about the issues during Reconstruction that drove many African-American men to feel empowered and to take an active role in the political process by voting. Think about the first time you were or will be eligible to vote as an active citizen in your local, state, and national elections. Write a paragraph identifying an issue about which you have strong opinions and why you think your vote and your voice should be heard.

TIPS

- Use textual evidence from the chapter in your explanation.

- Address the issues that arose when some southern states tried to limit the legal rights of African Americans to vote.

- Explain under what circumstances voters can have their voices suppressed either legally or illegally.

A Sketch in Time

by Harry Katz

Adapted from "A Sketch in Time,: Bringing the Civil War to Life,"
by Harry Katz, *National Geographic*, May 2012

At the time of the Civil War, camera shutters were too slow to record movement sharply. Photographers, burdened by large glass negatives and bulky horse-drawn processing wagons, could neither maneuver the rough terrain nor record images in the midst of battle. So newspaper publishers hired illustrators to sketch the action for readers at home and abroad. Embedded with troops on both sides of the conflict, these "special artists," or "specials," were America's first pictorial war correspondents or reporters. They were young men—none were women—from diverse backgrounds, including soldiers, engineers, fine artists, and a few veteran illustrators, all seeking income, experience, and adventure.

The English-born Alfred Waud and Theodore Davis were the only specials who covered the war from the opening gun battle in April 1861 through the fall of the Confederacy four years later. Davis later described what it took to be a war artist: "Total disregard for personal safety and comfort; an owl-like propensity [ability] to sit up all night and a hawky style of vigilance during the day; capacity for going on short food; willingness to ride any number of miles horseback for just one sketch, which might have to be finished at night by no better light than that of a fire."

In spite of the remarkable courage these men displayed and the events they witnessed, their harrowing stories have gone unnoticed. W.T. Crane heroically covered the events taking place in Charleston, South Carolina, from within the rebel city. D.H. Strother, a Union supporter, was arrested as a spy for sketching the Confederate Army encampments outside Washington, D.C. Frank Vizetelly witnessed Jefferson Davis's final flight into exile.

Special artists worked fast, identifying a war scene's focal point, blocking out the composition in minutes, and fleshing it out later in camp. They took great pride in making their renderings as faithful as possible. The artists dispatched their sketches from the battlefield by horse, train, or ship to the publisher's office, where the image was copied onto blocks of wood and engraved for printing. Usually it took two to three weeks for the drawing to be published, although important events or battles could be rushed into print in a matter of days.

Two journals led the national scene in 1861, *Harper's Weekly* and *Frank Leslie's Illustrated Newspaper*. *Leslie's* claimed to be strictly neutral in its coverage of the growing divide in the country and then of the war. In contrast, *Harper's* stood firmly with the Republican Party, President Lincoln, the abolitionists, and the Union. Both publishers, however, censored images considered too negative or graphic and altered drawings to make them more stirring or upbeat. *Harper's* editors, for instance, made Alfred Waud's drawing of a leg amputation at an Antietam field hospital look less gory to accommodate squeamish readers. Engravers freshened another Waud sketch of exhausted horses dragging artillery carts, giving them lifted heads and spirited tails and making them kick up clods of mud. The enhanced sketch provided an animated portrait of the drivers of the team of horses racing ammunition to the front.

Nonetheless, by depicting scenes as realistically as they could, specials undermined the popular myth of the war as a romantic adventure. As citizens grew accustomed to the violent imagery, censorship eased.

Within a generation, photographers using Kodak cameras surpassed sketch artists. But artists are still going to battlefronts. For instance, both the military and the media send artists to Afghanistan to interpret warfare in ways cameras cannot, capturing for the record the inner lives of the soldiers caught up in a larger drama.

For more from National Geographic, check out "Lincoln" online.

UNIT INQUIRY: Analyze the Legacy of Slavery

In this unit, you learned about one of the most divisive periods in American history— the years before, during, and after the Civil War—when the issue of slavery ripped the country apart. Did the practice of slavery, and the racism that accompanied it, cause problems that continue to affect the lives of Americans today? Do the effects of slavery and racism still cast a shadow over the country, more than 150 years after the end of the Civil War?

ASSIGNMENT

Compare the social, political, and economic status of African Americans during the Civil War era and today. Identify areas of progress as well as lingering problems that are part of the legacy of slavery and racism. Be prepared to present your analysis to the class.

Plan As you consider the legacy of slavery and racism, review the unit to gather evidence about the treatment of both free and enslaved African Americans during the Civil War era. Make a list of the areas in which African Americans experienced discrimination and describe the treatment. Then consider the situation today. Do additional research if necessary. Use a graphic organizer like this one to help organize your findings and observations.

	Civil War Era	Today
Segregation		
Employment		
Education		
Property ownership		
Voting rights		
Family units		
Hate group activity		

Produce Use your notes to write an essay in which you analyze the legacy of slavery and racism in the United States. Describe what life was like for free and enslaved African Americans during the Civil War era. Then identify the strides that have been made as well as the connection between slavery and problems of racism, prejudice, and privilege that remain.

Present Choose an engaging way to present your analysis to the class. Consider one of these options:

- Team up with a partner to present an imaginary dialogue between two people, one from the Civil War era and one from the present time, discussing educational and employment opportunities for African Americans in the United States.

- Create your own graphic that clearly compares the situation in the two time periods.

- Prepare talking points for both sides of a debate on this question: Have the issues of race, prejudice, and privilege improved in the United States since the Civil War era? Work with a partner to stage the debate for the rest of the class.

NATIONAL GEOGRAPHIC | LEARNING FRAMEWORK ACTIVITIES

Create a Compromise Guide

SKILLS Collaboration, Problem-Solving

ATTITUDE Responsibility

The Missouri Compromise, the Compromise of 1850, and the Kansas-Nebraska Act helped keep the United States together, postponing the Civil War. Review information about the three acts. Then think about a time you, or a group you are part of, compromised. Consider this question: What makes compromise successful? Then work with a partner to create a guide for successful compromise. Include conditions necessary for agreement. Present your guide to the class and discuss the conditions that existed during the creation of the acts in the 1800s.

Investigate Medical Care

ATTITUDE Curiosity

KNOWLEDGE Our Human Story

About 620,000 soldiers died in the Civil War, and about two-thirds of those deaths were caused by disease rather than injury. Research the medical care that soldiers received in camps and field hospitals. Find out the factors that contributed to the high rate of disease and the large number of deaths. Investigate treatments for diseases and surgical techniques used. Then give an oral report to the class in which you identify medical advances that would have reduced the disease and death rate.

Similar to today, New York City around 1900 was a
bustling, congested place where cultures and social classes
intermingled, influenced one another, and sometimes
clashed. Rapid urban growth and the influx of immigrants
contributed to some of the social challenges cities like
Chicago, San Francisco, and New York faced. In this photo,
children eagerly wait in line with empty tubs to collect free
ice that could be used to keep food from spoiling.

THE UNITED STATES

1882
The Chinese Exclusion Act severely limits the immigration of Chinese laborers to the United States.

1894
Railway workers for the Pullman Palace Car Company go on a strike that disrupts rail traffic throughout the country.

1892
Farmers form the Populist, or People's, Party to focus on issues such as better pay and working conditions.

1877
Thomas Edison invents the phonograph.

1890
Federal troops kill more than 150 Lakota Sioux at Wounded Knee Creek in South Dakota.

1896
In *Plessy* v. *Ferguson*, the Supreme Court rules that facilities for African Americans can be "separate but equal."

1890

1870

1889 EUROPE
The Eiffel Tower is built in Paris, France, and becomes the world's tallest structure.

1884 AFRICA
European powers meet at the Berlin Conference to divide up Africa, triggering a race for territory on the continent.

THE WORLD

DETERMINE CHRONOLOGY What two consecutive events indicated that the United States was expanding its influence?

1906
President Theodore Roosevelt pushes Congress to pass the Meat Inspection Act and the Pure Food and Drug Act. *(uninspected medicine sold before the acts were passed)*

1911
More than 140 workers—mostly young immigrant women—die in New York City's Triangle factory fire.

1920
The 19th Amendment is ratified, granting women the right to vote.

1909
W.E.B. Du Bois helps found the National Association for the Advancement of Colored People (NAACP). *(pin used during the anti-lynching movement)*

1913
Henry Ford uses the assembly line system to mass-produce his automobiles.

1920

1898
The Spanish-American War erupts after U.S. intervention in Cuba's war of independence against Spain.

1917 EUROPE
The Russian Revolution begins.

1900

1910 AMERICAS
The Mexican Revolution begins.

1914 EUROPE
World War I begins in Europe. *(helmet worn by German officers in the war)*

1899 ASIA
The United States proposes the Open Door Policy in China.

1900 ASIA
A secret society in China rebels against the spread of Western and Japanese influence during the Boxer Rebellion.

EXPANSION & CONFLICT IN THE WEST

1877–1900

HISTORICAL THINKING How did expansion alter the West and its native populations?

National Geographic photographer Jim Brandenburg captured these wild American bison crossing the prairie near the Missouri River in South Dakota. In the first half of the 19th century, millions of bison roamed freely over North America. During the second half of the century, however, their numbers fell sharply, in part because settlers pushed westward, and farmers and ranchers killed off many of the animals. By the early 20th century, only a few hundred wild bison remained in North America.

"These soldiers cut down my timber; they kill my buffalo; and when I see that, **my heart feels like bursting.**"

—Chief Satanta of the Kiowa

THE WILD WEST

CRITICAL VIEWING The 2016 Columbia Pictures movie *The Magnificent Seven* was a remake of the 1960 Western by the same name. What does this photo reveal about the cast of characters?

In the 1950s and 1960s, you couldn't flip through the television channels during prime time without seeing at least one Western—a fictional series about the American West set in the late 1800s. Movie screens were also filled with images of scheming outlaws pursued by handsome, heroic lawmen, and cool, confident cowboys protecting herds from cattle thieves. In other words, the Wild West lived and breathed through the entertainment industry, and the American public loved it.

THE REAL WEST

The legend of the Wild West did not start with TV or the movies. First came the dime novels (pictured below): short, inexpensive paperback books that told thrilling tales of adventure, hardship, and daring rescues. Even as the real cowboys, outlaws, lawmen, and pioneers went about their business in the real West, dime novel writers were spinning the stories of these individuals into tall tales and wild adventures. At the same time, Buffalo Bill's Wild West show was touring the eastern states. This outdoor extravaganza featured mock shootouts, cowboys demonstrating their skills, buffalo, and other Wild West icons.

And so was born the larger-than-life image of the West as a place of theatrical violence, with masked bandits stalking every bank and frequent shootouts between the good guys and the bad guys. Life in the real West was by no means boring, and the West did have its colorful characters. But the day-to-day reality was not nearly as exciting as the stories on the pages and screens.

Two of the most popular "set" pieces from Westerns—the shootout between the sheriff and the villain in the town streets and the daring bank robbery—were extremely uncommon in real life. Historians have studied crime statistics for several western towns in the late 1800s. Using the information, these researchers estimated that the Wild West was no more violent than cities and towns today. Historian Larry Schweikart concluded

> *There are more bank robberies in modern-day Dayton, Ohio, in a year than there were in the entire Old West in a decade, perhaps in the entire frontier period!*
>
> — Historian Larry Schweikart

that fewer than a dozen bank robberies likely took place in the final decades of the 19th century. He remarked, "There are more bank robberies in modern-day Dayton, Ohio, in a year than there were in the entire Old West in a decade, perhaps in the entire frontier period!"

As for dramatic shootouts on Main Street, most of the life-altering disagreements in the West were over land, and people fought them out in court. In a book about the frontier, historian Patricia Nelson Limerick commented, "The showdowns would occur in the land office or the courtroom; weapons would be deeds and lawsuits, not six-guns."

DIME NOVELS

"Purple prose" is an expression used to describe writing that is elaborate, flowery, and over the top. It's also a good description of the style in which many dime novels were written. This 1910 novel features a dramatic image of Buffalo Bill in action. But the novel's title is relatively tame compared to more "purple" ones like *Adventures of Buffalo Bill from Boyhood to Manhood: Deeds of Daring, Scenes of Thrilling Peril*; and *Romantic Incidents in the Early Life of W. F. Cody, the Monarch of Bordermen*.

CALAMITY JANE

Men weren't the only real-life characters who found their way into the myth of the Wild West. Martha Jane Cannary was orphaned in 1867, soon after her family moved to Salt Lake City, Utah. The 12-year-old girl was uneducated and desperately poor, but she was tall, strong, and able to do the jobs that were mainly available to men. Dressing and working like a man, taking whatever jobs she could, the teenager acquired the nickname Calamity Jane.

We know for certain that Calamity Jane moved to Deadwood, South Dakota, in 1876 and met American frontiersman, army scout, and officer of the law, Wild Bill Hickok. At that point, the stories take over. Jane, an enthusiastic participant in the creation of her own tall tale, claimed that she had single-handedly caught the man who killed Hickok—a fact disproved by newspaper accounts of the time. She also claimed to have rescued a runaway stagecoach with its six passengers and driver.

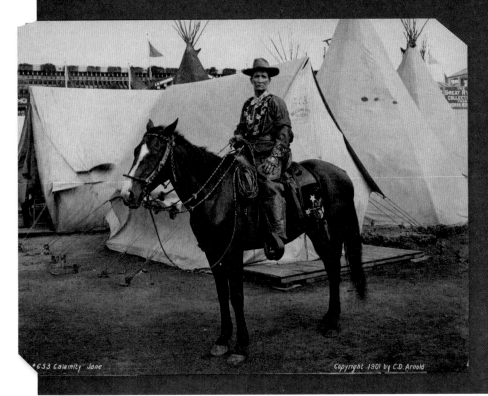

In 1895, Jane joined Buffalo Bill Cody's Wild West show as a horseback rider and sharpshooter, further expanding both her legend and her fan base. Dime novels about Calamity Jane spun ever more fanciful tales of her adventures, including a marriage to Hickok. Though reports of a relationship between Calamity Jane and Hickok are highly suspect, she was buried next to him at Mount Moriah Cemetery in South Dakota.

An accomplished rider, Jane was often photographed on horseback. Here she poses in front of tepees and tents at the Pan-American Exposition in Buffalo, New York.

The life of the cowboy, too, was not exactly as portrayed in the Westerns. On-screen cowboys were almost exclusively white, and they seemed to spend their days with pistols drawn. In reality, of the approximately 40,000 cowboys on the Great Plains, 30 percent or more were African-American or Mexican. Several hundred were Native Americans. And the actual work of a cowboy? It was unromantic, poorly paid, and often revolved around the boredom of 14-hour days in the saddle herding cattle.

WILD BILL HICKOK: A CASE STUDY

The story of Wild Bill Hickok is a useful case study for examining how a real-life event was turned almost instantly into a Wild West legend. The tale begins with one of the few true instances of a quick-draw gun duel in the street. In 1865, James Butler Hickok,

known as "Wild Bill," was a gambler and a drifter who made his temporary home in Springfield, Missouri. He got into a disagreement over a gambling debt with a man named Davis Tutt. It culminated on the evening of July 20, when both men drew their pistols and fired at each other in the town square. Tutt fell dead, with a bullet through the heart; Hickok was unharmed.

Within a few months, Hickok was on his way to Wild West stardom. Colonel George Ward Nichols started the process with an article about the showdown for *Harper's New Monthly Magazine.* Nichols's account of the shootout was mostly factual, but he went on to tell his readers that Hickok had once fought off 10 attackers on his own and that he had killed 100 men, among other fictions. The article was hugely popular and was soon followed by dime novels with titles such as *Wild Bill, the Indian Slayer.*

CRITICAL VIEWING American film stars Montgomery Clift (left), John Wayne (center), and Noah Beery, Jr., (right) endured long days of filming on the set of the 1948 Western *Red River*. What do you observe about the sets and process used to produce this film?

Hickok himself contributed to his legend by appearing in Buffalo Bill's Wild West show. It was as a gambler, however, that Hickok would meet an abrupt and unglamorous end, when a man named Jack McCall crept up and shot him while he was playing poker in a saloon in Deadwood, South Dakota, in 1876. Even after his death, the dime novels continued to embellish the Wild Bill Hickok lore with titles such as *Wild Bill, the Pistol Prince; Buffalo Bill, the King of the Border Men;* and *Wild Bill's Last Trail.*

WHY THE LEGEND?

Why have the tall tales of the Wild West persisted for more than a century after the real American frontier began to fade from memory? Perhaps it is because the Old West embodies a spirit of toughness and independence that Americans admire. Perhaps, too, the legends recall a time when much of the country was untamed and new—to American settlers, at least. For the Native Americans of the West, many of the events of the frontier period are distinctly lacking in romance or nostalgia. For those who still enjoy the legends of the Wild West, and those who seek out the truth behind them, perhaps the greatest draw is the universal human love of a good story.

THINK ABOUT IT

How do films or TV shows you have seen that feature the Old West or the American frontier compare to the legends and realities you have learned about? What evidence of bias or historical inaccuracies have you observed?

THE LONE RANGER

"Hi-Yo Silver! Away!" was a call recognized by millions of Americans in the 1930s through the 1950s and beyond. It was the signature call of the Lone Ranger to his valiant horse, Silver, as he set off on another weekly adventure to bring order to the lawless West. Accompanied by his Native American sidekick, Tonto, the Lone Ranger protected the innocent and brought evildoers to justice. Unlike some heroes of Wild West tales, the Lone Ranger was entirely fictional and not based on a real-life individual.

The Lone Ranger began as a radio show in 1933, featuring the adventures of a mysterious masked man who fought for justice in the Wild West. In 1949, it debuted as a TV show and became wildly popular in its own right, running in syndication well after the series was canceled in 1957. The appeal of *The Lone Ranger* has continued into the 21st century. A TV movie with that title was made in 2003, and a new version was released in 2013.

PRIMARY SOURCE

Across the country in the 1930s, families would tune in their radios to hear the thrilling introduction to *The Lone Ranger* radio show, which many could recite by heart:

A fiery horse with the speed of light, a cloud of dust and a hearty Hi-Yo Silver! The Lone Ranger! With his faithful Indian companion Tonto, the daring and resourceful masked rider of the plains led the fight for law and order in the early western United States! Nowhere in the pages of history can one find a greater champion of justice! Return with us now to those thrilling days of yesteryear! From out of the past come the thundering hoofbeats of the great horse Silver! The Lone Ranger rides again!

—from *The Lone Ranger*, by Fran Striker, 1933

Actor Clayton Moore took his job as a role model very seriously and made frequent public appearances as the Lone Ranger when he wasn't filming episodes.

Collectors love television memorabilia, and items from *The Lone Ranger* television series are no exception. This 1954 metal lunch box is a prized piece of pop culture.

MAIN IDEA Western settlement was spurred by economic opportunities in farming, ranching, and mining and by the federal government's goal of expanding the nation's boundaries.

FARMING, RANCHING, AND MINING

When there's a lot of open space, people tend to spread out. After the Civil War ended, Americans once again hitched their wagons and headed west of the Mississippi River, eager to settle the untamed land and begin their new lives.

MANIFEST DESTINY

As you have read, many of those who migrated west were inspired by the concept of manifest destiny, the belief that Americans were intended to settle all the land between the Atlantic and Pacific coasts. While American communities were thriving in the East, many eastern farmers, hungry for greater stretches of land, moved westward. In 1860, the unsettled West included the grassland prairie region in the middle of North America, called the Great Plains, an area that was wide open for new settlement.

During the Civil War, the U.S. government had tried to make it easier for farmers to migrate to the Great Plains by passing the Homestead Act in 1862. As you know, the act offered plots of land in the region to American citizens or to those intending to become citizens. For a small filing fee, each person was eligible for 160 free acres as long as he or she lived on the land and cultivated it for five years. That may sound like a lot of land, but a settler had to purchase two or three times that acreage to grow enough crops for a reasonable profit. And the Homestead Act did not provide the money to go west, file a claim on the land, or purchase farming equipment.

Still, many pioneers left their homes and settled on the Great Plains. They were rewarded for their efforts when the transcontinental railroad opened in 1869. The railroad provided transportation for the settlers and brought new immigrants across the frontier. The lines also carried household goods, tools, and other merchandise to the homesteaders—items sometimes purchased through catalog companies such as Montgomery Ward.

After the Civil War, many African Americans also migrated west with the goal of seeking a life free from discrimination and establishing communities of their own. The settlers were called **Exodusters** because they made their exodus, or exit, from the South after Reconstruction had failed to end the racial oppression of African Americans. On the Great Plains, many became farmers, and some even established towns of their own. Many African-American men also worked as miners and cowboys. By 1890, about 520,000 African Americans lived west of the Mississippi River.

LIFE ON THE GREAT PLAINS

The settlers' lives weren't easy. The first order of business upon arrival on the Great Plains was building a house. Because there were no forests on the plains, and therefore no lumber, homesteaders cut thick blocks of earth, called "sod bricks," out of the prairie soil. It took about 3,000 sod bricks to construct a single sod house. The thick sod walls kept out the cold in the winter and the heat in the summer. Some homes were built right into a hill or ridge with only a single opening for a door and grass growing on the "roof." Lacking firewood, farmers burned buffalo chips—dry dung—or sunflower plants for fuel to cook their meals and provide warmth.

The arid climate and tough prairie soil proved challenging for farmers, but new technology in farming machines helped increase productivity. In 1837, an Illinois blacksmith named John Deere invented a plow tough enough to break through the prairie's dense soil. Cyrus McCormick's reaper, a machine that helped harvest grain, was widely used by 1850. During the 1880s, inventors created steam-powered threshers to process wheat and machines that husked corn, or removed the ears' outer leaves. In 1873, Joseph Glidden devised a practical form of barbed wire for fencing. Soon a machine could produce this wire on a large scale, and it was used widely to keep livestock in and predators out.

Technology alone could not help the farmers cultivate crops. The region received little rain, and few rivers crossed the plains. Farmers who lived near the Rocky Mountains could build irrigation systems to bring water from mountain streams, but farther east, farmers came to rely on **dry farming** techniques to make the most use of what little rain did fall. They plowed widely spaced rows and planted their seeds between deep furrows so that rainwater would drain into the trench formed between the rows. They kept fields free of weeds to ensure that only food-producing plants received moisture.

One of the challenges of living on the Great Plains was dealing with its sheer size. On the vast prairie, tall grass stretched as far as the eye could see, and farms were far apart. The nearest neighbor was often miles away. Although families set up networks to meet socially and support each other during difficult times, homesteads were isolated. Loneliness was a fact of life.

THE LIFE OF A COWBOY

While lonely, the grasslands of the western plains were perfect for grazing cattle, and a number of wealthier settlers established ranches from Texas to Montana. At the same time, the once numerous herds of bison that had roamed the region were dwindling, victims

PRIMARY SOURCE

In 1880, former slave Benjamin "Pap" Singleton testified at congressional hearings regarding the migration of African Americans to the Great Plains. In this excerpt from the hearings, he states his reasons for promoting the exodus.

Well, my people, for the want of land—we needed land for our children—and their disadvantages—that caused my heart to grieve and sorrow; pity for my race, sir, that was coming down, instead of going up—that caused me to go to work for them. I sent out there perhaps in '66— perhaps so; or in '65, any way—my memory don't recollect which; and they brought back tolerable favorable reports; then I . . . went into Southern Kansas, and found it was a good country, and I thought Southern Kansas was congenial [agreeable] to our nature, sir; and I formed a colony there, and bought about a thousand acres of ground.

—from Benjamin "Pap" Singleton at congressional hearings, 1880

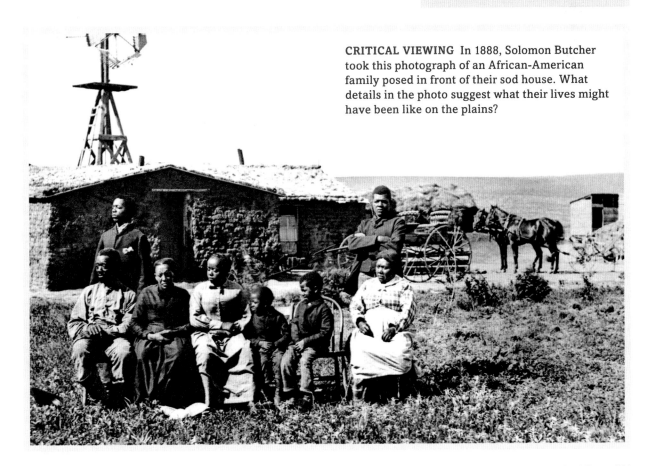

CRITICAL VIEWING In 1888, Solomon Butcher took this photograph of an African-American family posed in front of their sod house. What details in the photo suggest what their lives might have been like on the plains?

of overhunting and conflicts between the U.S. government and Native Americans. Their loss left even more land for cattle to roam.

Ranchers employed cowboys to round up their cattle and drive them to "cow towns" in Kansas, Nebraska, and Wyoming. From there the animals were loaded into boxcars and shipped by rail to the stockyards and meatpacking plants of Chicago. Improved slaughtering and packaging techniques as well as ice-cooled boxcars made beef more widely available throughout the nation. Americans developed a taste for beef, and its consumption soared.

Cattle drives took three to five months, depending on how far the ranch was from a cow town. More than 2,000 head of cattle were rounded up for a big cattle drive. Before the drive could begin, cowboys had to check each animal's brand—an identifying mark burned into its hide—to make sure that all the cattle belonged to the ranch they were working for. Cowboys also tamed horses, branded calves, herded the cattle safely across rivers, and prevented stampedes, or animals racing out of control.

Men of many different ethnicities worked as cowboys, but they all used the techniques and traditions developed by Mexican vaqueros, or cattle drivers. These cowboys also adopted Mexican tools and apparel, such as spurs, chaps, and lariats. One of every seven cowboys was an African American. Although they were paid the same wages, African-American cowboys were not as likely to manage herds or hold other positions of authority on the cattle trail. Even so, some African-American cowboys became successful ranchers themselves when they retired from driving cattle.

When the use of barbed wire spread across the plains, and fences enclosed the once open range, the role of the cowboy faded. Today, as you know, many Western movies and novels portray cowboys as rugged heroes who led exciting lives, but wrangling cattle was hard work. Cowboys could easily work 14 hours or more every day. During cattle drives, cowboys worked in shifts to watch the herds through the night, rode throughout the day, and pocketed only about $30 or $40 per month for their labors.

IN SEARCH OF TREASURE

Farmers, ranchers, and cowboys worked hard for their money, but some people hoped to gain instant wealth. After the California gold rush of 1849, prospectors found gold and silver deposits in Colorado, Montana, and the Dakotas, as well as rich deposits of copper in New Mexico and Arizona.

The story was almost always the same. With the discovery of a **lode**, or vein of ore, a horde of hopeful miners rushed to the area, staked claims, and set up camp. Then the merchants arrived, bringing goods to sell to the miners at exorbitant, or very steep, prices. As in California during the gold rush, if the mineral lode was substantial, a wild and lawless mining camp might grow quickly into a boomtown. Some boomtowns, such as Denver, Colorado, grew into large, prosperous cities. But most of the boomtowns went bust once the lode had been mined out. Abandoned as quickly as they sprang up, these boomtowns became ghost towns.

Initially, miners used **placer mining** techniques to search for gold, panning for gold nuggets and dust in riverbeds and streams with lightweight tools. They set up wooden runs called **sluices** to strain the water. But these techniques were not enough to eke, or obtain, every bit of precious metal from a rich lode. Soon mining companies stepped in and funded a much more intensive, aggressive process.

The companies used dynamite for **shaft mining**, blasting vertical channels into mountains. Once these dark passageways were carved out, men were lowered down shafts to mine for 10 to 12 hours a day using picks and shovels. Lack of oxygen, pockets of toxic gases, and cave-ins made these mines dangerous places to work. Other companies shot pressurized water onto the mountainsides to remove topsoil and gravel and expose the precious minerals beneath, a process known as **hydraulic mining**, or hydropower mining. Debris and the toxic chemicals used in the process—including mercury—flowed downstream, contaminating farmers' water sources. Farmers sued the mining companies and put an end to hydraulic mining, but it took decades for the land and water to recover.

Mining spawned many stories of fortune and failure. It also helped to spread the Union from coast to coast. People demanded law enforcement and government in the hastily organized, unruly mining camps. This eventually led to the creation of new territories and several new states, including Colorado in 1876. The Dakotas, Montana, and Washington were admitted to the Union in 1889.

Western expansion and advances in technology enriched the nation and made work more efficient, but this progress often came at a price—especially for farmers. Even as their farms became productive, many farmers found themselves falling into a cycle of debt. In time, they decided to get together and do something about it.

Art Institute of Chicago

On a trip to Mexico in 1889, American artist Frederic Remington made sketches of the horsemen he saw there. He used this material to create many illustrations and paintings, including this one in 1890 called *A Mexican Vaquero*. The portrait of the *vaquero*, shown here sitting on his horse and looking directly at the viewer, was also made into a wood engraving for *Harper's New Monthly Magazine* in 1891.

HISTORICAL THINKING

1. **READING CHECK** What attracted settlers to the Great Plains after the Civil War?

2. **ANALYZE ENVIRONMENTAL CONCEPTS** In what ways were the byproducts of shaft mining and hydraulic mining detrimental to several natural systems?

3. **DRAW CONCLUSIONS** How was the establishment of new states and territories in the West connected to unruly behavior in mining camps?

4. **MAKE INFERENCES** What qualities did settlers need to survive on the Great Plains?

1.2 GEOLOGY IN HISTORY

MAIN IDEA A huge underground reservoir of water allows the farmers of the Great Plains to water their crops.

HOW GEOLOGY WATERS THE GREAT PLAINS
By Andrés Ruzo, National Geographic Explorer

Fresh water is one of our most rare and precious resources. We can't survive without it. Thanks to modern plumbing and water purification techniques, about 99 percent of Americans can get water right from the tap, but this ease of access is misleading. Only about 3 percent of Earth's water is fresh, and most of this water is locked away in ice caps and glaciers. Of all the water on Earth, less than 1 percent is available to humans as usable fresh water.

FROM THE GREAT AMERICAN DESERT

Most Americans get their fresh water from either surface or groundwater **reservoirs**, contained bodies of water that can be tapped. As rain flows over the land's surface, some of it collects in rivers and lakes, and some seeps into the earth. The water that soaks into the surface fills the space between soil particles and fractures in rock to become groundwater. Certain geologic formations have the right conditions below the surface to hold large groundwater reservoirs. These formations are called **aquifers**.

The water in some aquifers flows to the surface naturally. To get water from other aquifers, however, engineers must drill down and raise the water to the surface. Depending on the type of rock, an aquifer will produce different amounts and types of water. Fault zones, areas of easily dissolved rock, and expanses of gravel often result in productive aquifers. The groundwater can effectively flow through the fractures and spaces in the rock. Areas of rock that are solid and not porous or fractured usually do not form aquifers because water cannot penetrate.

In 1820, U.S. Army major Stephen H. Long dubbed the Great Plains, "the Great American Desert." He considered this dry, flat land, "almost wholly unfit for cultivation, and of course uninhabitable by a people depending upon agriculture for their subsistence." Despite this warning, settlers moved to the Great Plains in droves beginning in the 1860s and 1870s. While many did manage to make a living,

it was tough. The thick sod of the plains had to be broken up before crops could be planted. And though farmers were able to use pumps powered by windmills to bring some underground water to the surface, this technique had its drawbacks. Farmers were not usually able to dig deep enough wells, and the pumping mechanisms did not work when the wind was not blowing. By the 1930s, drought and poor farming practices had so eroded parts of the Great Plains, they became known as the Dust Bowl because of the terrible dust storms that blew through the region.

Before pump technology improved in the 1950s, farmers struggled to create irrigation systems to water their fields, as shown in this photo of an Oklahoma farmer in the 1930s.

TO AMERICA'S BREADBASKET

Those settlers would never have believed that this same region would become part of America's breadbasket by the 1950s—all thanks to the **Ogallala Aquifer** (also called the High Plains Aquifer). For the past 15,000 years, water has been slowly collecting in the space between underground sand and gravel grains to form the Ogallala Aquifer. Spanning eight states, it's one of the world's largest aquifers.

Unfortunately, farmers didn't have access to this aquifer during westward expansion. In fact, full access to this reservoir wasn't available until the 1950s, when new technology made it economically viable to drill deep into the aquifer and access its water using powerful pumps. Today, Ogallala waters help grow nearly one-fifth of the wheat, corn, and beef cattle produced in the United States.

However, overuse has been drying up the Ogallala Aquifer. By the 1960s, geologists realized its water was limited, and natural processes refill it very slowly. Without rules for responsible groundwater extraction, some estimates indicate the aquifer will run dry as early as 2028. Once drained, it will take more than 6,000 years for it to naturally replenish.

Ogallala Aquifer

Though groundwater is often accessible at less than 100 feet below the surface, much of the Great Plains lacked sufficient groundwater to support agricultural development.

50–100 feet below surface

Groundwater

300 feet below surface

Ogallala Aquifer

In some places, the water of the Ogallala Aquifer is as much as 300 feet below the surface; it wasn't accessible until drilling and pump technology advanced in the 1950s.

THINK LIKE A GEOLOGIST

1. **IDENTIFY MAIN IDEAS AND DETAILS** Why are aquifers important to humans?

2. **DRAW CONCLUSIONS** Why is the fact that early settlers were unable to fully tap into the Ogallala Aquifer beneficial to farmers today?

3. **ANALYZE ENVIRONMENTAL CONCEPTS** What human practices in the 1950s altered the natural processes within the Ogallala Aquifer?

CRITICAL VIEWING Center-pivot irrigation systems, widely used to distribute water from the Ogallala Aquifer, operate equipment and sprinklers that rotate around a central point, or pivot, giving farm fields this circular pattern. How might this current form of irrigation be more efficient than others in this region?

FARMERS AND THE POPULIST MOVEMENT

Staying afloat in any business is tough. You've probably seen restaurants and stores close after they failed to thrive. In the late 19th century, small farmers struggled against the odds to make a profit. Some just didn't make it.

FARMERS ORGANIZE

Around 1870, farmers in the South, Midwest, and West all faced economic hardship. Technology had increased farm productivity, but the surplus of agricultural products resulted in falling prices. For example, a bushel of wheat cost $1.50 in 1865. By 1894, the price had fallen to $0.49. The loss of income and the rising costs of farm equipment and shipping charges put farmers in a cycle of debt.

To make matters even worse, a boll weevil infestation struck the South in 1892. The boll weevil is a beetle that eats the buds and flowers of the cotton plant, preventing the boll, or the rounded, fluffy seed capsule of the cotton, from forming. The boll is what is harvested, processed, and spun into thread. Without the boll, there is no crop. The failed crops affected the livelihoods of southern landowners, sharecroppers, and merchants. Many people were ruined financially and fled the South. Those who remained diversified their crops and eventually brought new agricultural industry to the region.

Dependent on merchants, railroads, and banks, which also charged high interest rates, farmers started to organize and unite in protest. In the 1870s, a group of farmers in Texas formed the first **Farmers' Alliance**. By the 1880s, other alliances arose with millions of members in the South and the Midwest. These alliances served not only a social, cultural, and political purpose but also an economic one.

To help resolve their economic grievances, farmers in local Granges, or lodges within an alliance, formed

A GLOBAL PERSPECTIVE
Today, farmers' cooperatives, like those that arose in the late 1800s in the United States, have been established in countries all over the world. In this photo, African farmers belonging to the Orinde Farmers' Cooperative Society in Kenya sort coffee beans on a drying bed. About 700,000 small-scale farmers belong to more than 500 cooperatives in Kenya. These agricultural cooperatives help create jobs and provide training and financial help for members.

cooperatives. **Cooperatives** are organizations run and funded by their members, who contribute funds into a pool of money. The farm cooperatives used the money to buy seeds and equipment. The larger the order for goods or services, the easier it was to negotiate good prices, lower shipping and storage rates, and lower-interest bank loans.

One of the most significant problems farmers faced was overproduction, which kept farm prices low. To address this problem, Charles Macune proposed the **subtreasury system**. The government would set up storage silos, or subtreasuries, in urban centers. When a farmer deposited a crop in the silo, the government would give the farmer a low-interest loan for a percentage of the crop's value to buy seeds for the next season. In 1889, Macune presented his system at a conference in St. Louis, but politicians refused to support it. The plan was never tried.

African-American farmers, who were banned from joining the mostly white Farmers' Alliances, formed the **Colored Farmers' National Alliance** in 1886. At its peak, about 250,000 African-American farmers belonged to the alliance. In 1891, the Colored Alliance went on strike, refusing to pick cotton unless landowners raised their wages. The strike, organized by Ben Patterson of Arkansas, ended when 15 strikers were lynched, including Patterson himself. The Colored Alliance soon dissolved.

THE POPULIST PARTY

In 1892, Farmers' Alliance leaders formed a third political party, known as the **People's Party** or the **Populist Party**, declaring that the Republican and Democratic parties did not support their interests. **Populism** is the belief that ordinary people should control government rather than elite politicians. The populists' political platform promoted subtreasuries and called for regulations to control rates for storage and shipping. It also supported workers' rights, specifically an eight-hour workday.

The Populist Party's most well-known concern was the issue of silver coinage. At the time, American currency was backed by gold. The **gold standard** required the U.S. government to print only an amount of money equal to the total value of its gold reserves. Strictly following the gold standard kept a limited amount of currency in circulation, which, in turn, kept the economy from growing, even though the nation's population was rapidly expanding. The only way the United States could distribute more money was to obtain more gold. The limited number of dollars in circulation affected the value of each one. Farmers found they had to work harder to maintain the same

At the Democratic Convention in 1896, William Jennings Bryan gave a fiery speech in support of free silver. He compared the gold standard to the crown of thorns Christians believe was placed on Jesus' head before he was crucified.

If they dare to come out in the open field and defend the gold standard as a good thing, we shall fight them to the uttermost, having behind us the producing masses of the nation and the world. Having behind us the commercial interests and the laboring interests and all the toiling masses, we shall answer their demands for a gold standard by saying to them, you shall not press down upon the brow of labor this crown of thorns. You shall not crucify mankind upon a cross of gold.

—from William Jennings Bryan's "Cross of Gold" speech, 1896

level of income. As a result, they looked for ways to inflate the currency—that is, put more dollars into circulation—and help lift themselves out of debt.

With western mines providing an abundant supply of silver, the Populist Party supported the **free silver movement**. According to the plan proposed, anyone holding silver could have it minted into U.S. coins for a small fee, and the coins could then be placed into circulation. Introducing free silver would increase the money supply and inflate prices substantially. In 1896, the Democratic nominee for president, **William Jennings Bryan**, supported free silver. The Republican nominee, **William McKinley**, was for the gold standard. As a result, farmers threw their support behind the Democrats. When the Populist Party as a whole supported Bryan, its members joined the Democratic Party. The Populist Party came to an end. However, Bryan's support of free silver lost him the 1896 election. The Republicans fanned voters' fears that free silver would lead to inflation, and McKinley won the presidential election. The gold standard remained in place until 1933.

HISTORICAL THINKING

1. **READING CHECK** How were farmers affected by industrialization?

2. **DRAW CONCLUSIONS** Why do you think Bryan used a biblical metaphor to argue his case in favor of free silver?

3. **ANALYZE CAUSE AND EFFECT** How did the free silver movement affect the Populist Party and the 1896 presidential election?

AMERICA'S BREADBASKET: THE GREAT PLAINS

For a long time, the term "breadbasket" referred literally to the basket that held your family's bread or rolls during meals. Today, it's a common name for a country's food-producing region, and in the United States, that's the Great Plains. Parts or all of 10 different states fall within the Great Plains, and most of them—Nebraska, Kansas, Iowa, Illinois, Indiana, and North Dakota, to name a few—are considered the breadbasket of North America because of the abundance of grains they produce.

The notion that an agricultural region could provide grain to cities that can't produce their own food isn't a new one. It dates back to the classical Greeks and Romans. In the United States, the farmers, fertile soils, and inexpensive available land of the Midwest have been growing reliable staple crops since the 1700s, and feeding not only Americans, but people across the world. Chances are great that the wheat, barley, corn, rice, or soybeans you eat each day are the product of your country's breadbasket.

Like other breadbasket states, Iowa is known for its cornfields. In 2015, the state's farmers grew 2.5 billion bushels of corn on 13 million sprawling acres of farmland. To preserve soil quality, corn is rotated with soybeans, growing here in front of the corn in the distance.

GROWING PRESSURES ON NATIVE AMERICANS

When settlers pushed westward, the Native Americans in the region were forced to leave their homelands. Some went quietly, but many Native Americans chose to resist and fight back.

BATTLES AND RESERVATIONS

Approximately 325,000 Native Americans inhabited the lands west of the Mississippi River prior to white settlement. Each tribe or nation had its own culture and customs, and sometimes groups fought one another for land and access to resources. As migrants began to head west along the Oregon and Santa Fe trails and miners pursued gold in California in 1848, Native Americans in the region sometimes launched attacks on the settlers and miners who were pushing westward.

In an attempt to stop the violence, U.S. officials and Native Americans met in Wyoming in 1851 and signed the **Treaty of Fort Laramie**. The treaty guaranteed the Native Americans in the territory an annual cash payment. In exchange, the Native Americans agreed to remain within specified boundaries, end their attacks on settlers, and allow the U.S. military to build forts in the area. The treaty worked. Wagon trains filled with settlers passed safely through tribal lands, and the U.S. Army encountered no resistance as it built its forts.

However, conflicts arose once again when even greater numbers of American pioneers and homesteaders began to migrate to the West in the 1860s. The constant flow of white settlers and the expansion of the transcontinental railroad threatened to push the Native Americans off the lands they'd been guaranteed. In addition, the settlers' cattle, sheep, and horses competed for grazing land with the vast herds of bison that roamed the region, and commercial hunters slaughtered many of the huge animals. Native Americans living in the West relied on bison for food and supplies, using every part of the animal. Throughout the 1860s and 1870s, growing tensions over land and the bison erupted into frequent battles between Native Americans and U.S. forces.

The U.S. government tried to put an end to the conflicts by establishing reservations to confine Native Americans. A **reservation** is an area of land designated for and managed by a particular Native American tribe. However, most Native Americans found it hard to survive on reservations, which were typically located on undesirable land that was not good for farming. Most Native American cultures were based on a lifestyle of hunting and **foraging**, or searching for plants. The animals and plants Native Americans traditionally sought for food, medicines, and rituals were often scarce on reservations.

Native Americans were supposed to be safe on their reservations, but that was not always the case. In 1864, the governor of the Colorado Territory told the Cheyenne living there to gather near Fort Lyon on Sand Creek. He promised them protection from the battles raging in the region. Chief Black Kettle, leader of the Cheyenne, had his people set up camp along the creek. To show that the Cheyenne were friendly, he flew an American flag. Others in the village raised white flags, indicating their desire to communicate.

Ignoring these signs of peace, Colonel John Chivington, commander of a group of volunteer militiamen, swept into the camp after the able-bodied men had left to hunt. The militiamen slaughtered at least 150 unarmed women, children, and elderly men in the **Sand Creek Massacre**. In retaliation, the Cheyenne, Lakota, and Arapaho living in the territory conducted raids on unsuspecting settlers.

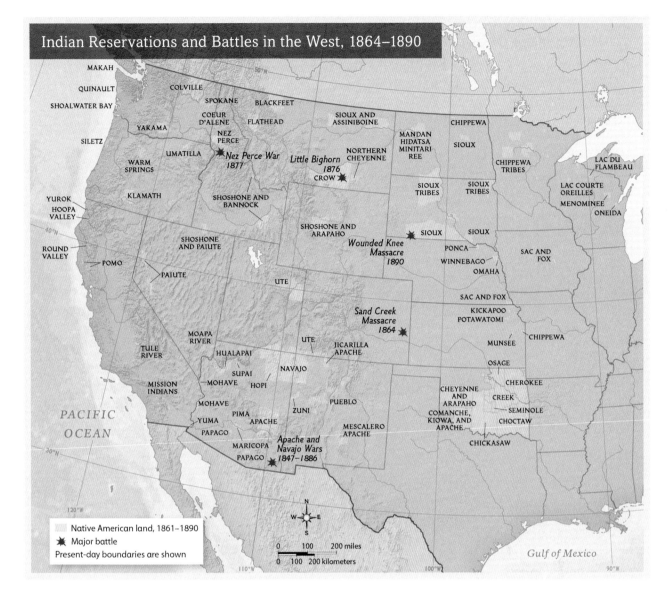

Indian Reservations and Battles in the West, 1864–1890

MAKAH
QUINAULT
SHOALWATER BAY
COLVILLE
SPOKANE
BLACKFEET
COEUR D'ALENE
FLATHEAD
SIOUX AND ASSINIBOINE
CHIPPEWA
YAKAMA
SILETZ
NEZ PERCE
Nez Perce War 1877
Little Bighorn 1876
NORTHERN CHEYENNE
MANDAN HIDATSA MINITARI REE
SIOUX
CHIPPEWA TRIBES
LAC DU FLAMBEAU
UMATILLA
WARM SPRINGS
CROW
SIOUX TRIBES
SIOUX TRIBES
LAC COURTE OREILLES
MENOMINEE
ONEIDA
YUROK
HOOPA VALLEY
KLAMATH
SHOSHONE AND BANNOCK
SHOSHONE AND ARAPAHO
SIOUX
SIOUX
ROUND VALLEY
SHOSHONE AND PAIUTE
Wounded Knee Massacre 1890
PONCA
WINNEBAGO
OMAHA
SAC AND FOX
POMO
PAIUTE
UTE
MOAPA RIVER
UTE
SAC AND FOX
KICKAPOO POTAWATOMI
TULE RIVER
HUALAPAI
JICARILLA APACHE
Sand Creek Massacre 1864
MUNSEE
CHIPPEWA
SUPAI
NAVAJO
OSAGE
MISSION INDIANS
MOHAVE
HOPI
CHEROKEE
PACIFIC OCEAN
MOHAVE
YUMA
PIMA
APACHE
ZUNI
PUEBLO
CHEYENNE AND ARAPAHO
CREEK
SEMINOLE
PAPAGO
MESCALERO APACHE
COMANCHE, KIOWA, AND APACHE
CHOCTAW
MARICOPA
PAPAGO
Apache and Navajo Wars 1847–1886
CHICKASAW

Native American land, 1861–1890
★ Major battle
Present-day boundaries are shown

0 100 200 miles
0 100 200 kilometers

Gulf of Mexico

THE LITTLE BIGHORN

Few Native Americans liked being confined to a specific territory. But after the U.S. government promised the Lakota that miners and settlers would not encroach on their territory, they reluctantly agreed to settle on a reservation in the Black Hills in present-day South Dakota. When gold was discovered in the Black Hills, however, Colonel **George A. Custer** allowed miners to cross into Lakota hunting territory, in violation of a new Fort Laramie Treaty drawn up in 1868.

In 1874, the treaty was officially voided, and the commissioner of Indian affairs demanded that all Lakota leave the Black Hills by the end of January 1876. Sitting Bull, leader of the Lakota, refused to move, and troops arrived to force the relocation. Eventually Sitting Bull moved his band to a camp in the valley of the Little Bighorn River in Montana.

There the Cheyenne, Lakota, and other Native Americans who had abandoned their reservations joined Sitting Bull in his fight.

On June 25, 1876, Colonel Custer and his 7th Cavalry entered Sitting Bull's encampment on the Little Bighorn River. The roughly 2,000 Native American warriors were in an advantageous position. Custer had only about 200 men, but the U.S. troops attacked anyway. The warriors killed nearly all of them, including Colonel Custer, in the **Battle of the Little Bighorn**. It marked the worst defeat for the U.S. Army in the Native American wars.

After their victory, the Lakota did not go on the offensive, but the U.S. government did. Fighting continued for another five years, and the U.S. Army ultimately forced the Lakota to relinquish their hunting grounds and relocate to reservations. The United States seized the Black Hills.

National Geographic photographer Anand Varma captured this scene overlooking a canyon in the Black Hills, a small mountain range that rises in South Dakota and extends into Wyoming. The Lakota—often called the Sioux—have refused offers of payment as compensation for the land from the U.S. government. The Lakota only want the Black Hills, which they consider their spiritual home.

CHIEF JOSEPH AND GERONIMO

A similar pattern of resistance played out in other regions as well. The Nez Perce (NEHZ PURSE), who had traditionally lived in the Pacific Northwest, refused to give up their territory and relocate to a small reservation in Idaho. Despite being outgunned and outnumbered, **Chief Joseph** fought U.S. troops while leading his band of about 700 Nez Perce in a retreat toward the Canadian border. The Nez Perce journeyed about 1,600 miles, climbing steep mountains and trudging across hot plains, but the U.S. Army apprehended them just 30 miles from the border.

PRIMARY SOURCE

Chief Joseph made his surrender speech at Bear Paw, Montana, in 1877. In this excerpt from the speech, Chief Joseph reflects the despair of all Native Americans whose efforts to resist the U.S. government had failed.

It is cold, and we have no blankets; the little children are freezing to death. My people, some of them, have run away to the hills, and have no blankets, no food. No one knows where they are— perhaps freezing to death. I want to have time to look for my children, to see how many I can find. Maybe I shall find them among the dead. Hear me, my chiefs! I am tired; my heart is sick and sad. From where the sun now stands, I will fight no more forever.

—from Chief Joseph's surrender speech, 1877

When Chief Joseph's band finally surrendered at Bear Paw Mountain in Montana, they were guaranteed settlement in Idaho, but the government broke that promise. Instead, the Nez Perce were sent to the Oklahoma Territory, where disease caused mass casualties. In 1884, after the public became aware of the tribe's plight, advocates pressured the government to allow the Nez Perce to return to their native lands. Today, they belong to a confederation of tribes in eastern Washington State.

In the Southwest, Apache chief **Geronimo** also resisted forced government confinement. In the 1870s, the Apache had been confined to a reservation in Arizona. Geronimo frequently left the reservation with a small band of followers to raid towns and settlements. In September 1886, Geronimo and 400 other Apaches were captured, exiled to Florida, and imprisoned there. Many of the prisoners died in Florida because the unfamiliar tropical environment made them susceptible to diseases. The U.S. government denied Geronimo's request to return his people to Arizona. Instead, in 1894, his band was transferred to Fort Sill in Oklahoma, where Geronimo died at the age of 80 in 1909.

Some people call the treatment of Native Americans **genocide**, or the deliberate killing of a large group of people and its culture. Many historians consider the Native American wars to have ended with Geronimo's capture. While in captivity, the Apache chief became a celebrity and sometimes appeared in public. When his autobiography was published in 1906, he dedicated the book to President Theodore Roosevelt. Geronimo believed Roosevelt was "fair-minded" and would treat the Apache people with justice in the future. However, on his deathbed, the chief told his nephew, "I should never have surrendered; I should have fought until I was the last man alive."

HISTORICAL THINKING

1. **READING CHECK** Why did the U.S. government break the Treaty of Fort Laramie?

2. **INTERPRET MAPS** Locate areas on the map with several reservations clustered together. What inferences can you make about the type of land in these areas and why tribes were placed there?

3. **MAKE PREDICTIONS** How might history have unfolded differently if the United States had not forced Native Americans to relocate to reservations?

4. **DRAW CONCLUSIONS** What did Chief Joseph mean when he said, "From where the sun now stands, I will fight no more forever"?

BROKEN PROMISES

Relations between the U.S. government and Native Americans were characterized by a trail of broken promises. No matter how many treaties Native Americans signed, their situation grew ever more desperate.

DAMAGE TO NATIVE CULTURES

The American public began to recognize the wrongs committed against Native Americans. In 1877, President Rutherford Hayes spoke out about how the nation had repeatedly broken its promises to them. Writer **Helen Hunt Jackson** also drew attention to the Native American plight in her 1881 book *A Century of Dishonor*. She submitted her work to Congress, hoping to stir its members to pass legislation that would improve Native American lives.

To that end, Congress passed the **Dawes Severalty Act** in 1887, which divided reservations into land **allotments**, or sections, of 160 acres. Native Americans who received an allotment were expected to establish farms. After 25 years, those who had successfully established a farm could become U.S. citizens. Sponsors intended the law as a positive alternative to the reservation system. However, the law also allowed the public to purchase any unoccupied allotments. Since most Native Americans of the Great Plains had lived as nomadic hunters and gatherers, few wanted to settle on the farms. So white settlers rushed to purchase the best reservation land. In the end, the allotments only weakened Native American communities.

THE TRAGEDY AT WOUNDED KNEE

By the 1880s, many Native Americans lived in poverty on reservations. They also suffered from illness, malnutrition, and despair. This was the case at the Pine Ridge Reservation on Wounded Knee Creek, to which Lakota leader Sitting Bull and his band had been sent. The United States considered Sitting Bull an agitator, or someone who seeks to rouse anger and stir rebellion as a means of forcing change. Sitting Bull refused to sign government treaties and boldly voiced his doubts over government promises.

U.S. officials also believed Sitting Bull was the driving force behind the **Ghost Dance** movement.

Actually, the movement got underway in 1889 after a Northern Paiute named Wovoka had a vision of a rescuer destroying white men and restoring the world to Native Americans. Wovoka taught followers the ceremonial Ghost Dance, which would usher in this deliverer. Once every six weeks, the participants danced for five nights; on the final night, they danced until morning. The practice spread to many reservations in the West—including the Pine Ridge Reservation—giving demoralized Native Americans hope. Fearing the Ghost Dance would result in uprisings, the U.S. government tried unsuccessfully to ban it.

In autumn 1890, when government officials came to the Pine Ridge Reservation to distribute land allotments to the Lakota, Sitting Bull declared he and his followers would refuse them. This rebuff, as well as the fact that the officials believed Sitting Bull had instigated the Ghost Dance, led the government to issue a warrant for his arrest. On December 15, 1890, authorities tried to seize Sitting Bull. He resisted arrest and was fatally shot during the scuffle.

But his death did not end the Ghost Dance. Two weeks later, the U.S. Army confronted Lakota Ghost Dancers gathered at Wounded Knee Creek and demanded they hand over their weapons. During the tense transaction, a shot was fired—no one knows by whom—but U.S. troops immediately opened fire in return, killing about 300 Lakota. The **Massacre at Wounded Knee** failed to put an end to the Ghost Dance, but from then on, the ceremony was conducted in secret. However, the massacre did halt any further Native American resistance.

CRITICAL VIEWING In 1890, the U.S. government attempted to assimilate Native American children, or change their language, habits, and dress, by sending them to boarding schools to learn white values and culture. The Apache children shown in these two photos taken by John Choate were among those captured with Geronimo in Arizona in 1886. The children were sent to the Carlisle Indian Industrial School, a boarding school in Pennsylvania.

Choate took the top photo shortly after the children's arrival at the school. The bottom photo, showing the same children, was taken after four months at the school. What does the children's physical appearance reveal about the ways they were changed by the school?

HISTORICAL THINKING

1. **READING CHECK** What were the aim and results of the Dawes Severalty Act?

2. **MAKE INFERENCES** Why might U.S. officials have believed that Sitting Bull started the Ghost Dance movement?

3. **SYNTHESIZE** What series of misunderstandings led to the Massacre at Wounded Knee?

4. **DRAW CONCLUSIONS** What effect did assimilation have on the Native American community?

THE FIELD MUSEUM CHICAGO, ILLINOIS

The Field Museum of Natural History arose as a result of the World's Columbian Exposition, an international fair held in 1893 in Chicago. The fair celebrated the 400th anniversary of Christopher Columbus's landing in the so-called "New World" in 1492. Its exhibits showcased the development of civilization, with a focus on American culture.

Leading citizens of Chicago established the Field Museum in 1893 to commemorate the exposition and house its exhibits, which included an extensive collection of Native American artifacts. Over time, the Field Museum developed into a renowned natural history museum, covering such fields as anthropology, botany, zoology, and geology.

> "The wonderful thing about museums is that you can **interact directly with other cultures—** ancient and modern—through their artifacts."
>
> —Bill Parkinson, Associate Curator

The White City

This postcard from the Columbian Exposition shows the "White City," which showcased the fair's main exhibition buildings. Painted white, these buildings housed exhibits of industrial technology, agricultural production, and fine art. Running at a right angle to the White City was the Midway Plaisance, a mile-long avenue with live exhibits of indigenous people of many cultures. The Midway was intended to display humanity's progress toward the "ideal" civilization of the White City.

Columbian Exposition tickets cost 50 cents for adults and 25 cents for children under 12.

Sioux Beaded Vest

This Sioux beaded vest was worn by a child in a "live display" at the Columbian Exposition. At the fair, Native American performers lived in reconstructed villages to demonstrate their traditional life for fairgoers. The Sioux were one of the Plains Indian groups who lived in tepees and hunted bison. As this vest demonstrates, they were also highly skilled at beadwork.

How might a "live display" have been perceived differently by performers and spectators?

This mask was made before 1893 by a Kwakiutl artist named Xániyus.

Kwakiutl Transformation Mask

Known for their painted carvings, the Kwakiutl originally lived in what is now British Columbia, Canada. This Kwakiutl carving is a transformation mask, which can be opened by strings to reveal another image. Shown in the open position, this mask represents a shaman, a priest believed to have magic powers. The Kwakiutl thought a transformation mask represented the inner change believed to occur when it was worn, such as a transformation from a human to a particular animal.

Formed from thin, flat copper, this fish model has characteristics of two different species native to the Mississippi River system.

Hopewell Copper Fish

The Field Museum has one of the world's largest collections of artifacts from the Hopewell culture, which flourished more than 2,000 years ago in what is now southern Ohio. Most of the museum's collection comes from an excavation that was undertaken specifically to obtain Native American artifacts for the Columbian Exposition. The Hopewell culture produced especially fine metalwork, as represented by this copper fish.

CLOSING THE FRONTIER

Westerns, with their strong, quiet heroes and dastardly bad guys, have been a staple of films for more than 100 years. That tradition was born after the frontier vanished and stories of the rugged people who settled it took hold in people's imaginations.

TRANSFORMED BY THE FRONTIER

As the U.S. government forced Native Americans onto reservations, white settlers flooded deeper into western states and territories. By 1890, census data showed there was no longer a western region in which the population numbered fewer than two people per square mile. The frontier, once marked by open, unpopulated land, had ceased to exist.

In response to the census data, historian **Frederick Jackson Turner** developed a theory about the importance of the frontier. He presented his frontier theory in the paper "The Significance of the Frontier in American History," which he delivered to the American Historical Association in 1893. His views influenced generations of historians. Turner maintained that

PRIMARY SOURCE

In this excerpt from one of William Cody's autobiographical writings, he explains why the Wild West show was important to him and popular with his audience.

It was because of my great interest in the West, and my belief that its development would be assisted by the interest I could awaken in others, that I decided to bring the West to the East through the medium of the Wild West show. I am sure the people enjoyed this spectacle, for they flocked in crowds to see it. There was never a day when, looking back over the red and white men in my cavalcade, I did not know the thrill of the trail, and feel a little sorry that my Western adventures would thereafter have to be lived in spectacles.

—from *Buffalo Bill's Own Story: An Autobiography of Buffalo Bill,* by Colonel W.F. Cody, 1920

western settlement had shaped America's national identity. He portrayed the frontier as a place that encouraged individualism and the belief that a person's independence and self-reliance were more important than the rules and concerns of society as a whole. As each generation pushed farther west, it became more democratic and egalitarian, or equal. The people relied on themselves and their neighbors instead of institutions or government officials. For example, if a horse was stolen, the sheriff often gathered together a **posse**, or group of armed men formed to capture an outlaw.

Turner's characterization of the frontier and the people who conquered it became widely accepted. Like most Americans of the late 19th century, he ignored the stories of many groups of people who were an important part of western history: Native Americans, Latinos, African Americans, Asians, and women of all ethnicities. Turner's frontier was solely one of white settlement and expansion.

THE WILD, WILD WEST

Incomplete though it may have been, Turner's characterization of the West began to be reflected in popular culture. Easterners and those living in urban areas developed a particular fascination with stories of the West, no matter how embellished, or exaggerated, they were. Novels, songs, plays—and, in time, films—portrayed bold characters and their adventures on the now vanished frontier.

One figure in particular captured the imagination of Americans from all walks of life: **Buffalo Bill Cody**. William Cody was born on the prairie in 1846, and he worked as a messenger, livestock wrangler, gold prospector, and Pony Express rider delivering mail throughout the West. In 1867, he began hunting bison—which many people at the time referred to as *buffalo*—to feed railroad construction crews. He hunted and killed more than 4,000 buffalo in 17 months, but he actually earned his nickname by taking part in an 8-hour buffalo shooting match with another hunter named William. Cody also fought in numerous battles during the Native American wars.

Cody became the larger-than-life protagonist, or main character, of a series of novels penned by E.Z.C. Judson. Judson wrote **dime novels**, popular fiction that sold for 10 cents a book, that were made widely available through improved printing methods and shipping. Dime novels were the forerunners of modern paperback books. Judson, who published his books under the pen name Ned Buntline, created a Buffalo Bill character that became as iconic as American folk hero and frontiersman Davy Crockett had been to earlier generations.

In 1872, Judson encouraged Cody to portray his fictional character on stage. Cody discovered he was a natural showman, and his first performances were so well received that he launched Buffalo Bill's Wild West show, a traveling act that was part circus and part theater. In his Wild West show, Cody featured Native Americans and bison in different scenes, telling mostly true—but often sensationalized— stories. Besides Buffalo Bill himself, the indisputable star of the show was **Annie Oakley**, an excellent markswoman. She performed for crowds at the Wild West show for 16 years and is widely considered America's first female superstar. Lakota leader Sitting Bull also joined the show for a short time. The show toured for three decades throughout the United States and Europe.

Dime novels laid the foundation for Western films, which appeared at the dawn of the movie industry. The first Western, *The Great Train Robbery,* was a black-and-white film released in 1903. It was so successful that producers quickly made more films in the same genre. Initially, Westerns were filmed in eastern cities, but as plots grew more complicated, they required more authentic-looking scenery. Thus, producers moved to California-based studios, where Westerns became a significant percentage of the movies produced—and Hollywood was born. The public viewed cowboy characters as heroes. In the 1950s and early 1960s, Westerns were the most popular genre of television programming. Though tastes in entertainment have changed somewhat since then, Western stories continue to find eager audiences in movies, television, and novels.

Annie Oakley was born Phoebe Ann Moses in 1860. Her family had a small farm, and as a child, Annie helped support it by shooting small wild game to sell to grocery stores. At age 15, she won a shooting contest against a traveling marksman named Frank Butler, who was charmed by Annie. The two married and soon began performing together, with Annie using the name "Oakley." Sitting Bull saw their show and gave Annie the Lakota name *Watanya Cicilla*—"Little Sure Shot." In 1885, she joined the Wild West show. Oakley continued performing into her sixties.

HISTORICAL THINKING

1. **READING CHECK** According to Frederick Jackson Turner, how did western settlement shape America's national identity?

2. **MAKE INFERENCES** Why do you think city dwellers became especially entranced with tales of the West?

3. **FORM AND SUPPORT OPINIONS** Do you agree with Turner's theory about the impact of western settlement on American identity? Explain why or why not.

LITERATURE OF THE WEST

As a writer, how would you describe a place that is unfamiliar to most people so that they could imagine being there? In the late 1800s, authors captivated readers with strange and elaborate depictions of the West and new American experiences.

SETTLERS' VOICES

The dime novels that mythologized the Wild West grew out of a much larger literary movement of the late 1800s, marked by a writing style known as regional realism, or **local color**. Through this writing style, the unique and sometimes very peculiar traits of a region came to life through vivid descriptions of its people, customs, dialects, folklore, and landscape. Local color grew in popularity after the Civil War, as Americans became intrigued with areas of the country they had once found too distant or strange to consider settling in.

Humorist **Mark Twain**, whose real name was Samuel Langhorne Clemens, was one of the most notable local colorists of the era. Before he began writing travel narratives and fiction, Twain piloted steamboats up and down the Mississippi River, mined for silver, and worked as a newspaper reporter in Nevada and California. His accounts of traveling down the Mississippi and throughout the West paint

a detailed picture of life in those regions, and his most famous novels, *The Adventures of Tom Sawyer* and *Adventures of Huckleberry Finn*, rely on his rich memories of growing up in Missouri.

The mining camps and boomtowns of the American West also inspired local colorists. **Bret Harte**, famous for his exaggerated characters in short stories, such as "The Luck of Roaring Camp" and "The Outcasts of Poker Flat," spent time in the gold camps of California before becoming a journalist,

Mark Twain's first famous story was "The Celebrated Jumping Frog of Calaveras County," the source of this fanciful illustration of the author.

PRIMARY SOURCE

Roughing It is an account of author Mark Twain's experiences in the West.

And now, at last, we . . . were perched upon the extreme summit of the great range of the Rocky Mountains. . . . We were in such an airy elevation above the creeping populations of the earth, that now and then when the obstructing crags stood out of the way it seemed that we could look around and abroad and contemplate the whole great globe, with its dissolving views of mountains, seas and continents stretching away through the mystery of the summer haze.

—from *Roughing It* by Mark Twain, 1872

In Zitkala-Sa's "The Soft-Hearted Sioux," a young man returns to his Lakota village after attending a Christian mission school.

I did not grow up the warrior, huntsman, and husband I was to have been. At the mission school I learned it was wrong to kill. . . . In the autumn of the tenth year I was sent back to my tribe to preach Christianity to them. With the white man's Bible in my hand, and the white man's tender heart in my breast, I returned to my own people.

Wearing a foreigner's dress, I walked, a stranger, into my father's village.

—from "The Soft-Hearted Sioux" by Zitkala-Sa, 1901

fiction writer, and poet. Author **Mary Hunter Austin** wrote about life on the eastern slopes of the Sierra Nevada and in the Great Basin. Her most famous work, *The Land of Little Rain*, describes the animals, plants, and people of that region in the late 1800s.

NATIVE AMERICAN VOICES

Native Americans were among the emerging Western literary voices after the Civil War. The nations and tribes of the Great Plains had long passed down oral histories of their lives and beliefs. But as more Native Americans were sent to boarding schools in the late 1800s, a number of them began to write extensively about their experiences. Activist **Sarah Winnemucca Hopkins**, the daughter of a Paiute chief, was one of the first Native Americans of the plains to have such accounts published. Her autobiography and only book, *Life among the Piutes [Paiutes]: Their Wrongs and Claims*, describes the lives of the Northern Paiute and how they were affected by U.S. settlement.

Two Lakota writers of the late 1800s struggled to reconcile the cultures in which they were raised with their assimilation into white society. **Zitkala-Sa** (ziht-KAH-lah SAH), or "Red Bird," was born and raised on the Pine Ridge Reservation in South Dakota. After attending a Quaker missionary school in Wabash, Indiana, where Lakota ways were discouraged, Zitkala-Sa found herself caught between two cultures. She drew on her personal experience to write essays and short stories, a number of which were published in literary magazines of the time.

Charles Alexander Eastman was raised in the Lakota tradition until his father, who had converted to Christianity, encouraged him to convert as well. Eastman became a doctor and eventually returned to the Lakota as a government physician on the Pine Ridge Reservation, where he witnessed the aftermath of the massacre at Wounded Knee. He

later described the event in *From the Deep Woods to Civilization*, but his most notable work is an account of his Lakota upbringing, called *Indian Boyhood*.

BORDER BALLADS

American settlement of the Southwest changed the lives of the Spanish-speaking people in this region. Newly introduced cultural and language differences sparked conflicts, especially near the Mexican border. Mexican ballads called ***corridos*** (koh-REE-dohs), told dramatic stories of heroes' defiant encounters with the new U.S. authorities, based on real events.

The earliest known corrido is about Mexican folk hero Juan Nepomuceno Cortina, who shot a U.S. marshal for mistreating his mother's servant in the late 1850s. The incident escalated into a series of border conflicts that inspired a ballad and established the typical plot for most corridos that followed: an outnumbered Mexican hero north of the border outwits and outruns American forces. The most famous corrido, "El Corrido de Gregorio Cortez," tells the story of a ranch hand who was falsely accused of stealing a horse in 1901. He led his pursuers for hundreds of miles before he was captured.

The exciting literature that came out of the American West helped define the region and the nation as a whole. Some critics even credit the literary trend with helping the nation mend after the Civil War and establish a new American identity for the future.

HISTORICAL THINKING

1. **READING CHECK** What topic was common among the Native American writers discussed in this lesson?

2. **DETERMINE WORD MEANING** Why do you think the terms "local color" and "regional realism" are used to describe the literature of the West?

3. **MAKE INFERENCES** Why do you think the border corridos became so popular in the Southwest?

VOCABULARY

Use each of the following vocabulary terms in a sentence that shows an understanding of the term's meaning.

1. **shaft mining**
   Some companies used shaft mining to blast the passageways needed to reach the veins of gold deep within the mountain.

2. Exoduster

3. lode

4. populism

5. forage

6. allotment

7. cooperative

8. dime novel

9. local color

READING STRATEGY
DRAW CONCLUSIONS

When you draw conclusions, you make a judgment based on what you have read. You analyze the facts, make inferences, and use your own experiences to form your judgment. Use a diagram like this one to draw conclusions about the impact of expansion and conflict in the West.

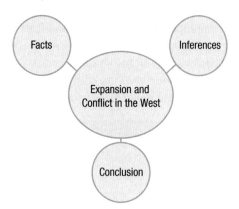

10. What impact did westward expansion and conflict with Native Americans have on American identity in the late 1800s?

MAIN IDEAS

Answer the following questions. Support your answers with evidence from the chapter.

11. Why did Exodusters migrate west? **LESSON 1.1**

12. How did farmers respond to industrialization? **LESSON 1.1**

13. Why did farmers in the South and the Midwest form alliances? **LESSON 1.3**

14. What happened when William Jennings Bryan basically co-opted much of the Populist Party platform and ideology? **LESSON 1.3**

15. What contributed to the decline of the great bison herds? **LESSON 2.1**

16. What was the result of the Lakota victory at the Battle of the Little Bighorn? **LESSON 2.1**

17. Why did the U.S. government try to ban the Ghost Dance? **LESSON 2.2**

18. What piece of data clearly indicated that there was no longer a western frontier? **LESSON 2.4**

19. How did local colorists bring the West to life for Americans in other regions? **LESSON 2.5**

HISTORICAL THINKING

Answer the following questions. Support your answers with evidence from the chapter.

20. **SYNTHESIZE** How did the federal government affect the country's growth in the years following the Civil War?

21. **ANALYZE CAUSE AND EFFECT** How did the boll weevil infestation affect cotton production in the South?

22. **EVALUATE** What impact—both good and bad—did settlement have on the Great Plains?

23. **MAKE INFERENCES** How did Buffalo Bill Cody's life serve as inspiration for a character in a dime novel?

24. **DRAW CONCLUSIONS** In the context of westward expansion, why did the U.S. government believe Native Americans would benefit from being assimilated into white culture?

25. **COMPARE AND CONTRAST** In what ways were the lives of Chief Joseph and Geronimo both similar and different?

This poster advertises land a railroad company sold on the Great Plains in 1872. Look at the poster and then answer the questions that follow.

26. Based on what you've learned about the Great Plains, do you think the image in this poster of land in Iowa and Nebraska is an accurate depiction? Why or why not?

27. Why might those trying to sell this land use both valid and fallacious, or flawed, arguments in a poster like this one?

Helen Hunt Jackson was best known as a poet, but in 1881, she published *A Century of Dishonor*, a nonfiction book that exposed the injustice of U.S. government policies toward Native Americans. Read the excerpt from the book below and answer the question.

> There is not among these three hundred bands of Indians one which has not suffered cruelly at the hands either of the Government or of white settlers. The story of one tribe is the story of all, varied only by differences of time and place. Colorado is as greedy and unjust in 1880 as was Georgia in 1830, and Ohio in 1795, and the United States government breaks promises now as deftly [effortlessly] as then, and with the added ingenuity [inventiveness] from long practice.

28. What does the passage tell us about Jackson's historical interpretation of the U.S. government?

29. **ARGUMENT** You've read that westward expansion helped shape a new American identity. What do you think our identity is today, and what factors have shaped it? Write a paragraph in which you defend your ideas about what American identity means today.

TIPS

• Think about how westward expansion shaped American identity in the late 1800s.

• Consider present-day events that have had a similar impact on our identity, including immigration and technology.

• Determine how these events have affected and changed our national identity.

• Write an opinion statement in which you state what you believe our American identity is today.

• Support your opinion with facts and reasons.

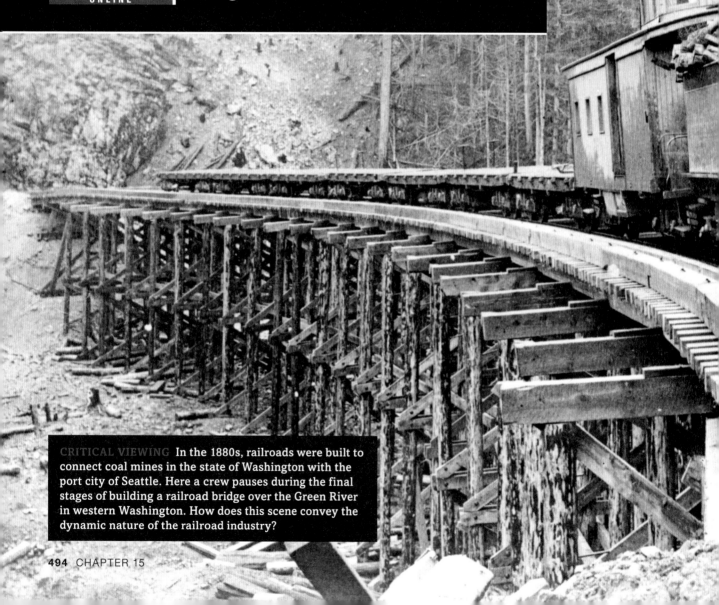

CHAPTER 15
INDUSTRIAL AMERICA 1877–1920

HISTORICAL THINKING What were the overall positive and negative effects of industrialization on America?

CRITICAL VIEWING In the 1880s, railroads were built to connect coal mines in the state of Washington with the port city of Seattle. Here a crew pauses during the final stages of building a railroad bridge over the Green River in western Washington. How does this scene convey the dynamic nature of the railroad industry?

"**Make money—**
honestly if you can—but make it."

—Jay Gould, financier
and railroad executive

WORKING IN
AMERICA

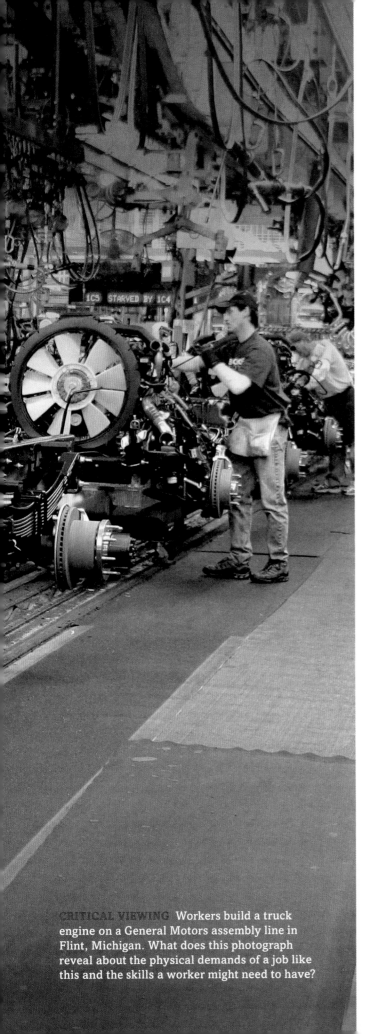

During the late 19th century, the nature of labor in the United States changed profoundly. In 1877, the country had 15 million non-domestic workers, with more than half in agriculture and another 4 million in manufacturing. In the decades that followed, the balance would shift as increasing numbers of Americans and new immigrants were attracted to factory work because it paid well. Manufacturing earnings went up about 50 percent between 1860 and 1890, prices of everyday goods fell, and wages increased. Earnings jumped again by 37 percent between 1890 and 1914.

Despite these improvements, working conditions weren't even close to what would be considered safe or even reasonable today. In 1890, the average pay rate for factory work was less than 16 cents per hour. The average workweek was 53 hours, and 2-day weekends were unheard of. In many industries, workers put in 12-hour workdays. At the same time, factory conditions were unsafe and largely unregulated by state or federal governments. At even greater risk than the adult workers—and earning lower wages—were the 1.75 million child laborers who were at work then.

The frustrations of the growing working class provided fertile soil for the seeds of the modern labor movement. Several large unions took up the cause of workers in industries such as steel, the railroads, and mining. Some of those unions no longer exist, but others, such as the American Federation of Labor, are still major forces today. In many ways, labor unions molded the 21st-century workplace. It is to their efforts that we owe reforms such as a 40-hour workweek and the end of child labor in factories and mines.

The story of American labor was shaped by a diverse group of charismatic activists, and it has influenced the lives of millions. This American Story focuses on a few of the many individuals who exemplify the diversity of labor in the United States.

CRITICAL VIEWING Workers build a truck engine on a General Motors assembly line in Flint, Michigan. What does this photograph reveal about the physical demands of a job like this and the skills a worker might need to have?

MOTHER JONES

Round-faced, with a kindly expression and white hair in a messy bun atop her head, Mary Harris Jones looked like somebody's sweet elderly grandmother, and not the firebrand that she was in reality.

Born in Ireland around 1837, Harris and her family crossed the Atlantic to flee the devastation of the Great Irish Famine. In 1861, she married an American ironworker who was also a union supporter, but he and their children died in a

The first thing is to raise hell. That's always the first thing to do when you're faced with an injustice and you feel powerless. That's what I do in my fight for the working class. —Mother Jones

Mother Jones (center-right) and her army of striking textile workers are shown here descending upon New York City to protest unfair working conditions.

yellow fever outbreak. Jones moved to Chicago and worked as a seamstress until she lost her home in the Great Chicago Fire of 1871. She then became a labor activist, campaigning for unions and workers' rights. In the 1870s, she traveled extensively, giving speeches to striking coal miners, railroad workers, and other laborers. The workers nicknamed her "Mother," a nod to her care for them. In 1905, Mother Jones helped found the Industrial Workers of the World union.

Mother Jones's efforts continued well into retirement age. While in her eighties, she actively supported a mine strike in West Virginia and traveled through Pennsylvania to encourage steel workers to vote in favor of a nationwide strike. She was arrested more than once for her activities but

was never deterred. When one judge asked her who had given her a permit to speak on public property, she answered tartly, "Patrick Henry; Thomas Jefferson; John Adams!"

Unsurprisingly, Mother Jones elicited strong and varying reactions from workers, union organizers, factory owners, and government officials. Labor leader Eugene Debs called her the "heroine of a thousand battles." On the other side, one U.S. congressman condemned Mother Jones as a "notorious and troublesome woman" in a speech to the House of Representatives. One attorney for the government is said to have called her "the most dangerous woman in America," a label that is frequently used in biographies and other writings about the colorful activist.

THE JAPANESE-MEXICAN LABOR ASSOCIATION

Some early labor unions were exclusive, refusing to admit African Americans, women, or workers from certain ethnic groups. But others created bonds across ethnic groups as workers united to improve their conditions.

One such mixed union was the Japanese-Mexican Labor Association (JMLA), which was the first labor union formed by members of different racial backgrounds. The JMLA represented workers who had been hired by the Western Agricultural

Contracting Company (WACC), a labor contractor, to work for a beet farming company in Oxnard, California. In February 1903, the JMLA presented a list of grievances to the WACC claiming workers were being paid less than they had been promised, and demanding that workers be allowed to shop in places other than the overpriced company store. When the JMLA went on strike, 90 percent of the laborers in the American beet industry stopped work to support them. Eventually, the WACC agreed to most of the JMLA's demands.

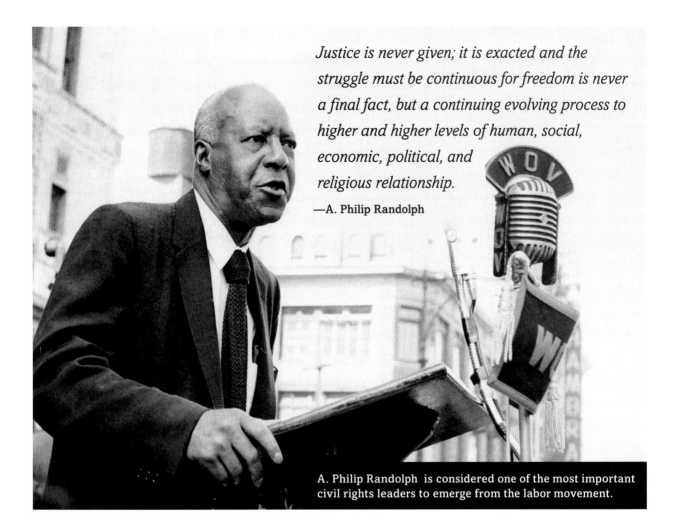

Justice is never given; it is exacted and the struggle must be continuous for freedom is never a final fact, but a continuing evolving process to higher and higher levels of human, social, economic, political, and religious relationship.
—A. Philip Randolph

A. Philip Randolph is considered one of the most important civil rights leaders to emerge from the labor movement.

A. PHILIP RANDOLPH

Asa Philip Randolph was born in Florida in 1889. In 1911, he moved to New York City, where he attended college at night and ran an employment agency. He attempted to organize black workers through his employment agency and later, during World War I, he advocated for more jobs for African Americans in the armed forces.

In 1925, Randolph became the founding president of the Brotherhood of Sleeping Car Porters, the first successful black trade union. At the time, long-distance travel within the United States often meant riding on a passenger train and, perhaps, spending the night in a sleeping car—a specialized railroad car with small bedroom compartments. Nearly all the porters who assisted sleeping-car passengers were African-American men. In 1937, the Brotherhood contracted with the Pullman Company, which manufactured and operated sleeping cars. Randolph's vision, however, extended well beyond any single union—he was determined to improve African Americans' job prospects overall.

In 1941, the American defense industry was rapidly expanding to provide arms and supplies to the country's European allies in World War II. Randolph observed that few African Americans were being hired to fill the new job openings, and the federal government was not taking action. Randolph began to plan a massive protest march on Washington, D.C., warning President Franklin D. Roosevelt that thousands of African-American workers would converge on the city. In response, Roosevelt issued an executive order forbidding defense contractors and the federal government from discriminating against African Americans. After the war, Randolph was instrumental in prompting President Harry S. Truman to eliminate segregation in the armed forces.

In 1955, Randolph became vice president of the American Federation of Labor and Congress of Industrial Organizations (AFL-CIO), where he continued to fight discrimination within the member unions. In 1963, he revived his plan for a giant protest in the country's capital, helping to organize the March on Washington for Jobs and Freedom. On August 28 of that year, around 200,000 people joined to support equal opportunities for African Americans—a goal that motivated A. Philip Randolph for decades.

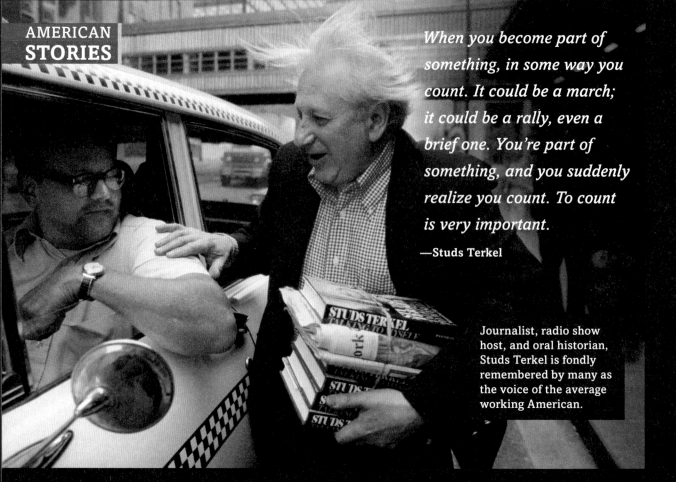

When you become part of something, in some way you count. It could be a march; it could be a rally, even a brief one. You're part of something, and you suddenly realize you count. To count is very important.

—Studs Terkel

Journalist, radio show host, and oral historian, Studs Terkel is fondly remembered by many as the voice of the average working American.

STUDS TERKEL

Louis Terkel was born in 1912, but later adopted the name "Studs" after the title character in a trio of books about a fictional youth growing into troubled manhood during the Great Depression.

Unlike the character in the book, Terkel was well educated, earning a law degree from the University of Chicago in 1934. After a varied career that included stints as a radio actor and writer and a period in the Air Force, he began hosting his own radio show in 1944. He found his voice in radio with a program that mixed music and interviews with Americans from all walks of life, both celebrities and everyday workers. Terkel's guests regularly opened up to him, revealing fascinating insights into their experiences, thoughts, and feelings. Of his gentle questioning style, he remarked, "The thing I'm able to do, I guess, is break down walls. If they think you're listening, they'll talk."

Terkel wrote books on many topics, including firsthand accounts of life during the Great Depression and World War II. In 1974, he published *Working*, a collection of interviews with dozens of people about their working lives. In the book, Terkel allowed individuals to tell their own stories. He took a broad view of the definition of labor, speaking with factory workers, farmers, office workers, stay-at-home mothers, business executives, musicians, and athletes, among many others.

One theme that runs through the book is workers' desire to find meaning in their work by taking pride in their jobs and asserting some control over their working conditions. According to Terkel, when that sense of purpose eludes them, they despair. Some of the people Terkel interviewed found meaning and satisfaction even in jobs that were poorly paid and sometimes perceived as menial. For example, waitress Dolores Dante described the highs and lows of her work to Terkel, explaining how she provided a special level of service. "I don't want to change the job," she told him during her interview.

Terkel once interviewed a union organizer who found his purpose in helping auto factory workers. These laborers often struggle to find meaning in their own jobs when they feel they have little or no say in their working conditions. The union organizer explained that workers "don't want to tell the company what to do, but simply have something to say about what *they're* going to do. They just want to be treated with dignity."

THE STATE OF THE UNIONS

The nature and power of labor unions have changed somewhat since the days of Mother Jones and A. Philip Randolph. Union density—the proportion of union members in the workforce—peaked in 1955, when it reached nearly 35 percent. Since then, union membership has declined steadily, especially in the private, or nongovernment, sector. Between 1970 and 1984, the number of private-sector union members dropped from 17 million to 11.6 million. By 2016, it dropped to 7.4 million. Public-sector unions representing teachers, police officers, and firefighters have had more success in keeping up their numbers, maintaining a density of around 35 percent between 1980 and 2016.

Various reasons may account for the decline in union membership. Many companies vigorously resisted attempts to unionize their workforces. Some moved the manufacturing of their products to factories in countries with lower labor costs. In the 1980s, the federal government enacted legislation that weakened unions' power. More recently, several state governments have also passed laws that make it harder for unions to organize workers and to bargain collectively for pay and benefits.

With the decline in private-sector unions, the face of union membership has changed. While the term "labor movement" often brings to mind gritty black-and-white images of 1930s factory strikes, a large proportion of 21st-century union members are white-collar workers. In fact, today, there are millions more unionized teachers than unionized truckers.

Nobody can predict with any certainty the future of labor unions in the United States. Some commentators believe the unions' influence will continue to be eroded by powerful corporations, government policies, and market forces such as globalization and the automation of workplaces. Others see hope in new ways of organizing and the increasing diversity of union membership. While the future is uncertain, unions will continue to search for ways to evolve as American workers confront the challenges of the 21st-century workplace.

THINK ABOUT IT

How do forces beyond workers' control affect union membership?

MEET LENNY RYBCZYK

In the present day, millions of workers still belong to unions. Lenny Rybczyk, who retired in 2016 after a 43-year career as a carpet installer, credits his union with his successful and satisfying work life.

Rybczyk has a family history of union membership. His mother belonged to the upholsterer's union in the 1950s and 1960s. His older brother apprenticed with the Chicago Carpenters Local Union 1185 in 1962, working four days a week and attending trade school (with pay) one day a week. When Rybczyk graduated from high school in 1973, he followed in his brother's footsteps, signing up as an apprentice to learn his trade. Recalling his early years, he says, "The work gave me structure as a young man, confidence, loyalty, equality, camaraderie, and also the ability to work independently with no supervisor."

Looking back on his career, Rybczyk takes pride in his work, which took him to such locations as Chicago's Sears Tower, the tallest building in the world at the time, and Argon National Laboratories, a high-level scientific research facility—in addition to banks, hospitals, and everyday office buildings. Without Local 1185, he believes, the story of his life would have been very different. "I have what I have only because of the union," he explains.

CRITICAL VIEWING Rybczyk takes tremendous pride in his union button collection. Based on what you have read about American laborers, what do you think fuels the intense pride many take in their unions?

MAIN IDEA During the 1870s and 1880s, the United States experienced a second Industrial Revolution distinguished by rapid industrialization and the development of the railroad, steel, and oil industries.

RAILROADS, STEEL, AND OIL

Being able to transport goods and people from coast to coast became a reality in the 1860s with the opening of the transcontinental railroad. This monumental achievement led to an explosion of business and technological innovations.

AN EXPANDING NATION

The invention of the steam engine and the cotton gin in the late 18th century sparked the first Industrial Revolution in the United States. Technological advances and the growth of railroad transportation brought about a second Industrial Revolution in the second half of the 19th century.

With the passage of the Pacific Railway Acts in 1862, two railroad companies began work on the nation's first transcontinental railroad, intent on making it easier to travel and move goods from the East Coast to the West Coast. The work crews of the Central Pacific, including thousands of Chinese immigrants, built eastward from California, and Union Pacific crews built westward from Nebraska. They blasted tunnels through mountains, constructed bridges over rivers, and laid 1,776 miles of track before connecting the railroad lines in Utah in 1869. The transcontinental railroad enabled overland commerce from coast to coast, accelerating industrialization and affecting every aspect of American society.

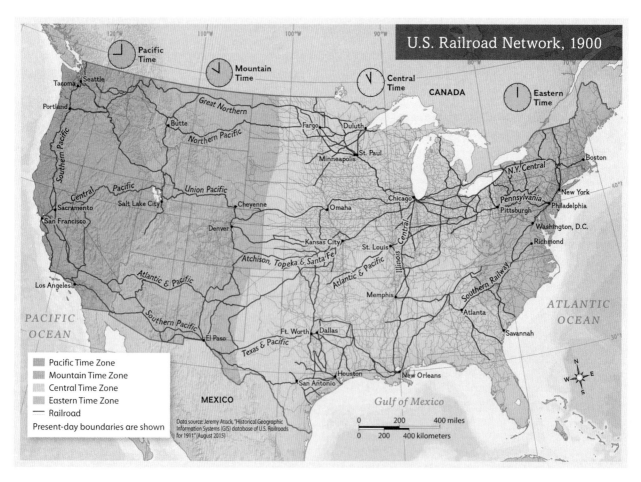

U.S. Railroad Network, 1900

Pacific Time Zone
Mountain Time Zone
Central Time Zone
Eastern Time Zone
— Railroad
Present-day boundaries are shown

Data source: Jeremy Atack, "Historical Geographic Information Systems (GIS) database of U.S. Railroads for 1911." (August 2015)

Over the next 25 years, the country added four more transcontinental rail lines, and railroad companies employed tens of thousands of employees. Goods such as coal and industrial machinery moved from one part of the country to another on a nationwide network of railroads. Special railroad cars transported food and livestock. Railroads became the nation's first big business.

CONSOLIDATING POWER

Entrepreneurs, or people who accept risk in starting a business, found that they could pool capital with partners to create security. As workers built the railroads, businessmen built corporations, companies or groups of people that invest in a business and then share its profits. The many investors that make up a corporation provide access to large amounts of capital. Such access is useful, and even necessary, for large industries. Large corporations were able to accumulate cash reserves, enabling them to weather a depression that began in the 1870s, as well as several recessions in the 1880s. As you have read, a depression is a severe and long-term economic decline in which many businesses fail, industrial output is reduced, and unemployment is high. A recession, often part of a normal business cycle, is a shorter-lasting downturn.

While some business owners were largely immune to economic fluctuations, downturns affected workers substantially. As corporations hired more and more people, when the economy faltered, more workers lost their jobs. The perceived economic progress of the late 19th century was repeatedly disrupted by prolonged periods of decline as the country suffered a number of economic recessions during the intense boom-and-bust cycles.

Entrepreneurs generated levels of wealth not imagined before, even in spite of economic ups and downs. People began to question the practices of industry executives and owners. For example, railroad owners **Cornelius Vanderbilt** and **Jay Gould** had reputations for treating competitors ruthlessly. Their behavior earned them the negative description of "**robber barons**," or businessmen who sought to buy out their competitors and who conspired to set prices, enriching themselves, but often violating state laws. Such practices eventually enabled larger railroad companies to consolidate and control even more of the railroad business, forming the nation's first industrial giant.

In response, states set up commissions, or agencies composed of experts, to investigate the railroads' practices and settle issues of rates, finance, and service. Railroads rejected such oversight, and in the mid-1870s, the Illinois commission was challenged in the Supreme Court case *Munn* v. *Illinois* by a grain warehouse. The firm argued that it could set its own storage and railroad rates. Regulations that varied from state to state violated its 14th Amendment right to equal protection. But the court upheld the right of a state to regulate private industries that affect public interest and all railroads. In 1887, Congress passed the **Interstate Commerce Act**, establishing a commission to investigate complaints and sue companies that violated its regulations.

CARNEGIE'S EMPIRE

As the railroad industry grew, it created a demand for more steel for railroad tracks and train parts. As a result, the steel industry vastly increased its production between 1877 and 1880 alone. The main technology for steel production was the **Bessemer process**. In this process, workers forced air through molten pig iron to remove impurities. Doing this first made the process of adding carbon to transform the iron into steel cheaper and more efficient.

Andrew Carnegie became the dominant figure in the steel industry. To build his empire, Carnegie adopted the strategy used by Gustavus Swift in the meatpacking industry: **vertical integration**, or the control of all phases of production from start to finish. Carnegie purchased the mines to gather raw materials, bought boats and railroads to transport materials, built and controlled the steel mills, and developed a sales force to sell his products. By employing vertical integration, Carnegie maximized profits by not having to pay outside companies.

In dealing with his competition, Carnegie employed **horizontal integration**, which means he purchased other companies to reduce the number of competitors. Carnegie's use of horizontal integration allowed him to come close to achieving a monopoly on, or exclusive control over, the steel industry.

Carnegie believed the ability to create wealth came naturally for some people because the natural order of society determined that some people would be wealthy while others would be resigned to poverty. His assumption derived from a misapplication of Charles Darwin's theory of evolution, which states, in part, that the fittest animals and plants survive to reproduce and pass on their genes, while the less fit die off. British writer Herbert Spencer applied Darwin's theory to human society in a new philosophy. According to the ideas of **Social Darwinism**, wealthy individuals, who represented the fittest of humans, were destined to survive and succeed.

In an 1889 article "The Gospel of Wealth," Carnegie refined his ideas about wealth and Social Darwinism. He acknowledged his belief in a natural division between the wealthy and the poor, but Carnegie also believed that the wealthy were duty-bound to share that wealth with society. His philanthropy, or desire to promote the welfare of others through financial support, set an example for business leaders. Throughout his life, Carnegie donated millions of dollars to many causes, including educational institutions, libraries, and theaters. Between 1883 and 1929 he funded 2,509 libraries worldwide, 1,689 of them in the United States.

OIL TYCOON

In 1859, oil prospectors struck the first American oil near Titusville, Pennsylvania. The rise of the railroad and steel industries made oil more readily available nationwide. Railroads transported oil long distances, and the steel industry provided a strong material for constructing pipelines, drilling equipment, and tanks. Initially, oil's main purpose was to fuel lamps, but soon oil became necessary to lubricate the machinery that ran American industries. In the early 1900s, oil was an essential part of the new automobile industry and would later provide heat and electric power to the country as well.

AMERICAN PLACES
Carnegie Hall, New York City

Andrew Carnegie donated 90 percent of his wealth to worthy organizations and causes. He also supported educational institutions and promoted American arts and culture. One of his most long-lasting contributions is Carnegie Hall, which opened in New York City in 1891 as the "Music Hall." The first performances in the hall featured Peter Tchaikovsky, the Russian composer, conducting his own works.

Another successful and powerful business leader who shaped American industry was the oil tycoon, **John D. Rockefeller**. Rockefeller built his first oil refinery in Ohio in 1863 to convert crude, or raw, unprocessed oil into specialized oil products. Just a few years later, in 1870, he founded the **Standard Oil Company**. Rockefeller used tactics such as price-cutting to lure customers to his company. Like Carnegie, he also employed horizontal integration, taking over most of his competitors to ensure his company's dominance in the market.

Within a decade, Rockefeller controlled about 90 percent of the country's oil-refining capacity. But he had done so by engaging in secret deals to get railroad companies to charge him less than other producers for transportation costs. Regulators put a stop to that, so in 1881, he reestablished his corporation as a **trust**, or a company managed by members of a board rather than by owners or stockholders. These board members are called trustees. Unlike those who oversee the management of a company, trustees are not investors with a stake in profits. The switch allowed Rockefeller, through his trustees, to buy controlling amounts of stock in other oil companies, and to do so across various states.

Rockefeller's questionable business tactics did not go unnoticed by state and federal government or by the general public. Beginning in 1902, journalist **Ida Tarbell** wrote a series of articles called "The History of the Standard Oil Company" for *McClure's Magazine*. Tarbell's father had worked in the oil industry in Pennsylvania, and she learned firsthand the effects of Rockefeller's strategies. For example, the secret rebates Rockefeller had arranged with the railroad companies made the costs of transporting oil prohibitively high for independent producers like Tarbell's father, but generously low for Standard Oil. As a result, Tarbell's well-to-do family was soon living in poverty. Tarbell spent nearly two years researching Standard Oil before writing her articles exposing Rockefeller's unethical practices. Her reporting had a profound influence on the public's opinion of corporations and trusts in general. In fact, Tarbell and other investigative reporters became known as **muckrakers**, or journalists who expose misconduct by an organization or a person.

Still, despite Rockefeller's suspicious business strategies, he, like Carnegie, contributed enormous sums of money to philanthropic organizations, such as educational institutions and medical facilities. Additionally, in 1913 he established the Rockefeller Foundation, which for more than 100 years has supported research and initiatives to improve the well-being of people and the planet.

PRIMARY SOURCE

In the excerpt below, journalist Ida Tarbell evaluates John D. Rockefeller's takeover of oil producers in and around Cleveland, Ohio, by fixing transportation costs.

Mr. Rockefeller's capture of the Cleveland refineries in 1872 was as dazzling an achievement as it was a hateful one. The campaign . . . viewed simply as a piece of brigandage [piracy], was admirable. The man saw what was necessary to his purpose and he never hesitated before it. His courage was steady—and his faith in his ideas unwavering. He simply knew what was the thing to do, and he went ahead with the serenity of the man who knows.

—from "The History of the Standard Oil Company," by Ida Tarbell, in *McClure's Magazine*, 1903

The second Industrial Revolution profoundly changed Americans' relationships with work, transportation, and communication. As in the first Industrial Revolution, the development of new materials and new processes upended the roles of labor and attracted more people to jobs in cities. However, the second Industrial Revolution was characterized by government's increased role in social and business affairs. Ownership in company stocks became more common, unlike during the first Industrial Revolution. The trend toward groundbreaking inventions and the growth of big business continued throughout the late 19th century, ushering in the modern United States and a new American identity.

HISTORICAL THINKING

1. **READING CHECK** What strategies did leaders of different industries use to maximize profits and reduce competition?

2. **IDENTIFY PROBLEMS AND SOLUTIONS** What solution did the states and Congress create to investigate concerns about the railroad industry's practices?

3. **COMPARE AND CONTRAST** In what ways are vertical integration and horizontal integration similar and different?

4. **FORM AND SUPPORT OPINIONS** Do you think Ida Tarbell is biased in her assessment of John D. Rockefeller's practices in her articles? Use evidence from the text to support your opinion.

California State Railroad Museum, Sacramento

Home to 225,000 square feet of exhibits, restored railroad cars, and iconic engines, this museum brings railroad history in California and the West to life. One exhibit features early communication methods—the bells, whistles, flags, lanterns, and lights used by railroads before modern electronic communication methods existed. Another tells the story of Abraham Lincoln and his steadfast support of the railroad, highlighting the construction of the world's first transcontinental railroad, the Union Pacific Railroad, which has carried America through natural disasters, wars, and a changing transportation industry. There's even a train simulator for museum visitors who want to "pilot" a high-speed train.

2717 – Southern Pacific Motor Car, Sacramento Valley Lines, California.

Southern Pacific Motor Car

Completed in 1908 and retired in 1920, the Southern Pacific Railroad's McKeen Motor Car Number 9 operated along the railway's Sacramento Valley Lines. McKeen Motor Cars were the first steel self-propelled train cars in the world, and the first example of aerodynamic design in North America. This postcard, dated 1915, demonstrates the comfort of traveling via motor car.

Steam Locomotive

Built in New Jersey in 1863, this small steam-powered locomotive traveled on a ship called the *Mary Robinson*, which departed from New York, sailed around Cape Horn, and arrived in San Francisco in March 1864. The Central Pacific Railroad would have preferred to purchase a larger engine, but because of the Civil War, only smaller engines were available.

Why would the Civil War have impacted the availability of train engines? Do research to find the answer.

Railroad Time Schedule

Railroad companies proposed dividing North America into four time zones as a way to make rail transportation more efficient. Before the implementation of time zones in 1883, most towns in the United States kept their own local time based on the movement of the sun. As railroads made it easier and faster to move between cities, the fact that each city had its own local time made it impossible to track and set arrival and departure times. Major railroad companies collaborated on a plan to divide the country into four time zones, which greatly helped regulate their train schedules.

Station Clock

Train stations and their buildings, or depots, range in size tremendously, from the one-room country station to the grand union station serving more than one railroad line. But historically, most depots had some common features: benches, a clerk's office complete with a desk and safe, windows for selling tickets, and, of course, a traditional station clock hanging from the wall.

How might this 1873 schedule for the Central Pacific Railroad, which was based on local times, have contributed to confusion?

Moving Fresh Foods

By combining images, photographers and artists around the turn of the century created humorous scenes boasting of a region's agricultural capabilities. In this exaggeration or tall-tale postcard, a Southern Pacific flat car is loaded with six enormous California peaches. Since the late 1890s, real peaches have been shipped worldwide in refrigerated railcars and containers.

A Car Load of California Peaches.

INVENTIONS AND NEW TECHNOLOGIES

Without even realizing it, you have been experimenting with and inventing things since you were young. During the late 19th century, men and women of varied backgrounds also experimented—and they created transformative technologies.

BELL'S TELEPHONE

The growth of the railroad, steel, and oil industries changed American life, but their rise was not the only economic development to transform the United States. At the same time, inventors were developing technologies and creating devices that would have profound impacts on daily life.

During the 19th century, people relied on the **telegraph**, a machine that transmitted messages along connected wires, to communicate over long distances. An operator tapped out the electric signals for a word with the telegraph key. The key completed an electric circuit and sent the message to a receiver at the other end, where the message could be transcribed or printed. In the 1870s, **Alexander Graham Bell**, a Scottish scientist, began to experiment with sending multiple messages at the same time. While trying out ways to subdivide a telegraph wire into many channels, Bell began transmitting musical tones over the telegraph. Ultimately, he hoped to transmit people's voices.

Bell devised a simple machine from which sounds were carried over wires—the first telephone. In February 1876, Bell filed a request for a patent, or a license that would give him the sole right to make and sell his new invention. He was just in time. Bell had submitted his patent request just two hours before another inventor

Surrounded by curious onlookers, Alexander Graham Bell speaks into his new invention. By the time the first telephone connection opened between Chicago and New York City in 1892, 950 miles of copper wire had been strung between the two cities to make telephone communication possible. Bell became president of the National Geographic Society in 1898. Under his leadership, photography became a central feature of the Society's magazine, *National Geographic*.

presented his own plans for a similar device. A few weeks later, the U.S. Patent and Trademark Office awarded Bell his patent. Within a week, Bell spoke the first words ever heard on a telephone, saying to his assistant: "Mr. Watson—come here—I want to see you."

Later that year, Bell demonstrated his invention at the Centennial Exposition in Philadelphia, and in 1877, he and two partners formed the Bell Telephone Company. In 1885, Bell created the American Telephone and Telegraph Company as a wholly owned **subsidiary**, or secondary business, of American Bell. The original purpose of American Telephone and Telegraph was to build and operate long-distance telephone lines, but its role expanded, and it eventually became the **parent company**, or controlling company, of the Bell System. The company, also known as AT&T, still exists today.

THE WIZARD OF ELECTRICITY

Not long after the debut of the telephone, another inventor unveiled one of the most important advancements of the 19th century. In 1880, **Thomas Edison** patented his most famous work: a practical electric light bulb. Just three years later, Edison put this invention to work by establishing the first electrical system in New York City. Within a year, 500 customers in the city had electric lights.

Although Edison's first career was as a telegraph operator, by the time he was in his 20s, he was an active inventor who had already patented some of his almost 1,100 inventions. His range of patents included both entirely new devices and improvements to existing ones, such as an efficient electrical generator, a motion picture projector, and an electric pen.

In 1876, Edison established an industrial research laboratory—the first of its kind—to work on his inventions. The lab, located in Menlo Park, New Jersey, became the site of many future discoveries. While there, Edison invented the **phonograph**, or record player, in 1877. The Menlo Park lab was also the site of Edison's experiments with electric lighting.

Edison's light bulbs relied on a direct electric current, which initially caused some problems. When the current traveled long distances, the amount of usable electric power decreased. A former colleague of Edison's, an immigrant named **Nikola Tesla**, developed a system for delivering electric power using an alternating current. Alternating current, or AC, electric power could travel longer distances

than the direct current, or DC, power Edison and his team developed. Tesla sold his patent to industrialist **George Westinghouse**, who quickly embraced and marketed Tesla's new and improved method.

In 1886, Edison built a second research lab in West Orange, New Jersey, known as the Edison Laboratory. At this lab, Edison and his workers invented a motion picture camera and built the first motion-picture stage, launching the silent-film industry. They also improved his phonograph and developed an alkaline storage battery. For the wealth of contributions he made to technology, Edison became known as the "Wizard of Menlo Park."

A WAVE OF INVENTIONS

Although Bell and Edison undoubtedly produced some of the most important inventions of the late 19th century, many other inventors also introduced life-changing technologies. Products such as the cash register, the typewriter, and the linotype, which the newspaper industry used to set type, helped improve efficiency in the workplace. The Kodak Company's portable camera allowed anyone to become a photographer.

George Washington Carver was among the many African-American innovators who emerged during the late 19th century. Carver served as the head of the agriculture department at the Tuskegee Institute in Alabama, where he encouraged crop diversification in the South to address a major problem: soil quality. Because of decades of **monoculture**, or the practice of growing only one crop, the quality of soil in the South had diminished. Carver experimented with solutions by asking southern farmers to grow a variety of crops, such as peanuts and sweet potatoes. The problem was, however, that these crops didn't generate enough market demand. So Carver began developing new products derived from these crops, such as oils, flour, soap, and cosmetics. Peanuts eventually became one of the South's biggest cash crops.

Another African-American innovator was **Lewis Latimer**, who drew the blueprints for Alexander Graham Bell's telephone patent and also worked in the field of electric lighting. Latimer was a mechanical draftsman for the U.S. Electric Lighting Company, and in 1882, he invented an improved process for manufacturing the carbon filaments inside lamps. Latimer then went to work for Edison, first as an engineer and then as an inventor—the only African-American member of Edison's team.

Lewis Latimer was the youngest child of George Latimer, who had escaped from slavery. At Edison's urging, Latimer wrote a book about how electric lighting worked, but he also wrote about issues African Americans faced in the workplace. In the following excerpt, Latimer writes to a colleague planning a civil rights meeting in Detroit.

[O]ur history conclusively proves that the attempt to degrade any portion, class or race of common people, has always been fraught with more danger to the oppressor than to the oppressed.

If our cause be made the common cause, and all our claims and demands be founded on justice and humanity, recognizing that we must wrong no man in winning our rights, I have faith to believe that the Nation will respond to our plea for equality before the law, security under the law, and an opportunity by and through the maintenance of the law to enjoy with our fellow citizens of all races and complexions the blessings guaranteed us under the [Declaration of Independence], of "life, liberty and the pursuit of happiness."

—from a letter written by Lewis Latimer to be read at the National Conference of Colored Men, December 12–13, 1895

African-American inventor and electrical engineer **Granville T. Woods** left elementary school at the age of 10, yet went on to develop many important patents related to the field of transportation. One of his inventions was a telegraph system that enabled the transmission of messages between moving trains and train depots. Another was a safety feature that helped people avoid injury from accidental contact with electrical wires by running them above streetcars. Woods and his brother Lyates also received patents for emergency braking systems. In total, Woods patented more than 45 inventions during his lifetime, and he sold the rights to many of them to large companies.

Elijah McCoy was born in Canada to a family who had escaped slavery in Kentucky on the Underground Railroad. After studying mechanical engineering in Scotland, he returned to the United States and worked for the Michigan Central Railroad. Like Woods, McCoy also invented an important product related to transportation. Over the course of two years, McCoy experimented with a device to lubricate railroad engines automatically. In 1872, he patented the "lubricating cup," which continuously oiled a steam engine's gears.

During the late 1800s, enterprising women were also carving out a place as inventors, developing new labor-saving devices and safety-inspired products. **Margaret Knight** received patents for a variety of machines and products relating to both industry and the home. Some of Knight's patents were for shoe-manufacturing devices and rotary engines, while others related to sewing machines and clothing. By the time she died in 1914, Knight held a total of at least 27 patents for her inventions.

In 1886, **Josephine Garis Cochrane** patented the first commercially successful dishwasher. The daughter of a civil engineer and granddaughter of an inventor, Cochrane was also someone who entertained often. She set out to find a way to wash dishes quickly and safely. In 1886, Cochrane patented her dishwasher design and began building them for friends. She displayed her invention at the 1893 World's Columbian Exposition and later formed a company to sell the product, although the dishwasher did not become popular in American homes until the 1950s.

The number and variety of inventions developed during the late 19th century helped create factory and office jobs, and the country's workforce grew as a result. These innovations also enabled greater efficiency and constructive improvements in work, which led to greater economic gains and better working conditions for some, although not for all. The country's desire for inventions may have been motivated by practical considerations, but it also provided opportunities for resourceful and creative women and African Americans.

HISTORICAL THINKING

1. **READING CHECK** What contributions did Alexander Graham Bell and Thomas Edison make to American innovation in the late 19th century?

2. **MAKE INFERENCES** Why do you think the inventions of the women mentioned were oriented toward safety and efficiency?

3. **IDENTIFY PROBLEMS AND SOLUTIONS** What problem was George Washington Carver hoping to solve by diversifying crops in the South?

4. **ANALYZE CAUSE AND EFFECT** What factors contributed to the invention and innovation that occurred during the 19th century?

TWO PATHBREAKING INNOVATORS

Innovators and inventors throughout history share a common skill: problem-solving. George Washington Carver lived in the South and witnessed the effects of monoculture on southern farmers, so he innovated ways to improve soil nutrition. Margaret Knight was frustrated by slow and inefficient production in the factory where she worked, so she improved the process by inventing a machine.

GEORGE WASHINGTON CARVER

As an agricultural chemist, George Washington Carver spent a lot of time experimenting in his lab, as he is doing in the photo above. Carver's ideas about replenishing soil nutrients and growing more varied crops helped southern farmers, both in their harvests and their nutrition. His reputation earned him many invitations to work in other labs, but he declined, preferring to stay at Tuskegee.

MARGARET KNIGHT

In 1870, Margaret Knight invented a machine that produced flat-bottomed paper bags by cutting, folding, and gluing paper together. In 1871, she submitted the drawing at the left with her patent application. Knight built her first paper-bag machine from wood and brass, and it produced more than 1,000 bags. It also served as the prototype, or example, for a stronger machine made with iron, which was used in mass production.

THE STATE OF WORKERS

Rapid societal changes can have both positive and negative consequences. During the late 19th and early 20th centuries, many changes took place in the workforce—some for the better and some for the worse.

NEW INVENTIONS, NEW JOBS

Amid the explosion of technology in the late 1800s, the labor force expanded rapidly. In the 1870s alone, it increased by a whopping 29 percent. As new machines and office equipment made their way onto the market, factories and offices became common places of employment. This new work environment signaled a switch from work involving independent, skilled craftspeople to machine-driven jobs in large organizations—jobs that required little or no skill. Suddenly, many workers found themselves at the mercy of managers whose only concerns were maintaining order in the workplace and meeting profit expectations. Many workers had little chance of improving their circumstances.

When photographer Lewis Hine asked this cotton mill worker her age, she replied that she didn't remember, but that she knew she was too young to work. Hine took this 1908 photo in his role as an investigative photographer for the National Child Labor Committee.

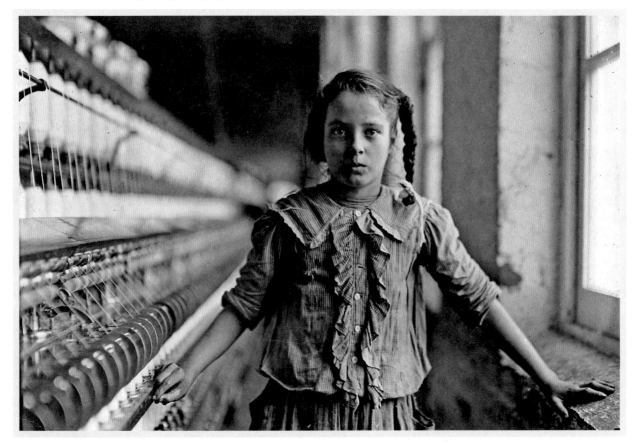

People moving to urban areas as part of this workforce expansion included immigrants as well as native-born Americans. Workers experienced some benefits from the growth of factory and office work. Increased productivity made possible by technology created a surplus of goods, resulting in **deflation**, or a decrease in the prices of goods and services. Workers' buying power increased, and in many cases, employees could work fewer hours. Women's participation in the workforce also expanded, as they took positions as teachers, office workers, sales assistants, domestic workers, and factory workers. However, women earned less than men, and fewer opportunities were available to them.

DANGEROUS WORK

Though wages and work hours improved during the late 19th and early 20th centuries, safety conditions did not. Workers in the railroad, coal mining, steel, and meatpacking industries faced constant danger of mishaps and even death on the job. A 1906 novel by **Upton Sinclair**, *The Jungle,* described the deplorable working conditions in the meatpacking industry. In his novel Sinclair wrote that men "fell into the vats . . . sometimes they would be overlooked for days, till all but the bones of them had gone out to the world." In the coal mining industry, an estimated 3,242 miners died in job-related accidents in 1907. More than 350 of those deaths resulted from just one mine explosion in West Virginia. That same year, a journalist investigating a U.S. Steel plant in Chicago found that as many as 12 percent of its employees died or suffered injuries every year.

Factory managers often blamed the workers themselves for the accidents that caused their injuries. But many observers realized that the hazards workers faced in many industrial jobs were real. In response, states began providing **workers' compensation**, which meant that a worker who had been injured could receive assistance for medical care and loss of income. Wisconsin passed the first comprehensive workers' compensation law in 1911. By 1920, 43 states had passed some type of workers' compensation.

As the workforce expanded in the late 19th and early 20th centuries, child labor also peaked. Factory managers hired children because they were easier to control than adults, and they could be paid lower wages. Often, children worked to help support their families. In 1880, nearly 182,000 children younger than age 16 worked in such places as textile mills, glass factories, and even coal mines. Like adults, children endured long hours under dangerous

conditions with few safety or health protections. Many children could not attend school because they had to spend their entire day at work.

The nonregulatory approach to business that allowed practices such as child labor is called **laissez-faire economics**, in which the government rarely interferes in the free market and businesses choose how they will operate, with little or no oversight. An American sociologist named **William Graham Sumner** offered the ideas of Social Darwinism as justification for this approach, arguing that social reforms imposed a financial burden on the "forgotten men" of the middle class. However, despite the popularity of Social Darwinism—or indeed perhaps because of it—workers of the late 19th and early 20th centuries began to assert their rights and demand improvements and protections in their workplaces.

HISTORICAL THINKING

1. **READING CHECK** What changes took place in the workforce during the late 19th and early 20th centuries?

2. **ANALYZE CAUSE AND EFFECT** What larger social and economic issues did the large-scale use of child labor in 1880 impact?

3. **DRAW CONCLUSIONS** How common were injuries in the coal and steel industries in 1907?

4. **IDENTIFY MAIN IDEAS AND DETAILS** What protections did workers have during the late 19th and early 20th centuries? Support your answer with details from the text.

ORGANIZING INTO UNIONS

Fighting for your rights takes a lot of perseverance, courage, and conviction. You could be putting your job or maybe even your life on the line. In the late 1800s, dangerous and unfair working conditions led many workers to fight for their rights—but not without a cost.

ORGANIZING FOR CHANGE

You have read that American workers began to organize labor unions, or groups of workers who band together to achieve better pay, safer working conditions, and other benefits, in the 1820s. After the Civil War, this effort gathered new energy. Unions formed in the cigar manufacturing, shoe-making, and coal mining industries, but their popularity grew in other industries as well—most notably, the railroads. Strikes, or work stoppages, became a strategic tactic employed by unions when companies or bosses refused to negotiate with them. In industries with highly trained employees who performed specific jobs, such as a railroad brakeman, management struggled to replace workers when all of them walked off the job at once. Unionized workers knew they had a lot of leverage in this situation, and they used it.

PRIMARY SOURCE

The demand for an 8-hour workday dates from the early 1800s, but nearly 100 years later, it was not yet a reality. In this excerpt, Terence Powderly provides arguments in its favor.

Men who work short hours are better educated than those who do not; they have more time in which to study. A thinking, studious man will learn that overexertion shortens life, and he will guard against it. Thousands go to early graves through overwork every year, and until the struggle for existence is shortened by cutting down the hours of toil, this condition of affairs will continue.

—from "The Plea for Eight Hours," by Terence V. Powderly, 1890

What does Powderly imply will happen if workers' hours aren't reduced?

In July 1877, railroad workers launched a strike in Martinsburg, West Virginia, when the Baltimore and Ohio (B&O) Railroad Company announced it would immediately cut pay by 10 percent. Workers had already experienced one pay cut that year, and they balked at the company's decision. Soon the strike had spread to larger cities such as Baltimore, Pittsburgh, and Chicago. In total, about 100,000 workers across the country participated in what came to be known as the Great Railroad Strike. When management's attempt to break the strike resulted in rioting, federal troops arrived. Though the riots led to the deaths of about 100 people, the strike succeeded in sharpening the focus on workers' rights.

One of the first major unions was the **Knights of Labor**, founded in 1869. Like other unions at the time, the Knights of Labor sought an 8-hour workday to replace the more typical 10- to 12-hour workday. But the union also pressed for social reforms and equality. It offered membership to women and African Americans. Its inclusivity set the Knights of Labor apart from other 19th-century labor and trade unions.

In 1879, **Terence V. Powderly** assumed control of the Knights of Labor. After the Great Railroad Strike of 1877, the union's membership climbed from approximately 9,000 members in 1879 to more than 100,000 in 1885. Though Powderly himself did not generally support the practice of striking, the Knights of Labor mobilized a strike in 1885 against Jay Gould, an executive for the Union Pacific railroad known for his ruthless dealings with both employees and competitors. In 1886, the Knights of Labor called another strike against Gould's company—this one much more widespread than the first. Prompted by

Chicago History Museum

After witnessing the Haymarket Riot, Paul Hull, a reporter for the *Chicago Daily News,* wrote *The Chicago Riot: a Record of the Terrible Scenes of May 4, 1886.* In July and August of 1886, Hull and four other *Daily News* reporters also served as witnesses at the trial of those accused in the bombing. In addition to an account of the riot, Hull's book includes details of the bombing investigation that began on the day following the riot. This book is housed in the library of the Chicago History Museum.

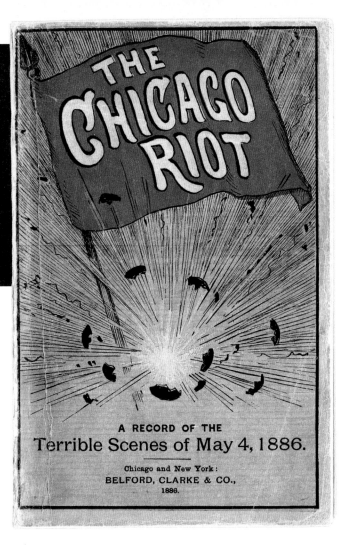

THE CHICAGO RIOT

**A RECORD OF THE
Terrible Scenes of May 4, 1886.**

Chicago and New York:
BELFORD, CLARKE & CO.,
1886.

the firing of a union member in Texas, the Great Southwest Strike spread to several states and halted railroads in the region, but Gould held fast, and the strike ended after a month and a half.

DESCENT INTO CHAOS

Meanwhile, Chicago experienced its own labor uprising in 1886. On May 3, striking union members at McCormick Works, a McCormick harvesting machine factory, were harassing **scabs**, or nonunion workers willing to cross strike lines in order to work, who were going into and out of the factory. The situation turned violent, and police killed one person and injured several others. In response, labor leaders called for a public protest rally in Haymarket Square the following day.

The May 4 rally began peacefully. In fact, Chicago's mayor, who lived only a mile away, even visited the event. Unconcerned that trouble might start, he returned home. However, the situation became chaotic when someone threw a bomb and police responded with gunfire. The blast was so powerful, the mayor heard it from his home. In the end, several police officers and protesters died, and dozens of people suffered injuries. Police blamed labor leaders for the bombing, giving rise to the argument that the labor movement supported terrorism and **anarchism**, or anti-government beliefs.

The event, later known as the **Haymarket Riot**, resulted in the arrests of eight people. Despite the fact that their guilt was questionable and the evidence flimsy, seven of those arrested were sentenced to death, and the eighth defendant was sentenced to life in prison. Though the Knights of Labor had no direct association with the events in Haymarket Square, many people nonetheless blamed the organization for what took place, and the union's membership declined.

In contrast, the **American Federation of Labor (AFL)**, which formed the same year that the Haymarket Riot occurred, suddenly drew many members to its ranks. Leader **Samuel Gompers,** a critic of the Knights of Labor, wanted to focus on labor's economic gains and less on social reform. He emphasized issues such as better wages, benefits, and working conditions rather than changing the structure of society. As labor unions gained strength in numbers, the steel and railroad industries faced increasing numbers of labor strikes.

HISTORICAL THINKING

1. **READING CHECK** In what way was the Knights of Labor a unique labor union in the late 1800s?

2. **IDENTIFY PROBLEMS AND SOLUTIONS** What problem did workers hope to solve by calling a strike? Explain by using information from the text.

3. **DETERMINE CHRONOLOGY** What was the order of the main events around the Haymarket Riot? Explain what happened before, during, and after the riot.

LABOR CONFLICTS

Worker protests and union strikes might not seem newsworthy today, but in the late 1800s, they made headlines. When labor unions took on the giants of industry, they encountered the combined forces of police, the National Guard, and the U.S. government.

STRIKING AGAINST STEEL

Though union membership grew in the late 1800s, the public reactions to two major strikes—the **Homestead Strike** and the **Pullman Strike**—set the labor movement back in the 1890s. As you have read, Andrew Carnegie controlled much of the steel industry. Workers at his steel plant in Homestead, Pennsylvania, belonged to the Amalgamated Association of Iron and Steel Workers union, and their contract with Carnegie Steel was scheduled to expire on July 1, 1892. Carnegie, away in Scotland, gave permission to his operations manager, **Henry Clay Frick,** to break the union, or destroy its power, in advance of this date.

Frick strongly opposed the union—more so than Carnegie—and wasted no time. First, he tried cutting the workers' wages, a move the union rejected. Next, Frick locked the workers out of the mill, literally, by surrounding the mill with barbed wire so that workers could not get in. Then on July 2, he fired all of the union workers at the mill—a total of 3,800 employees.

Union workers knew that Frick would try to replace them with scabs, so the strikers charged the mill. Meanwhile, Frick had hired 300 security guards from the **Pinkerton Detective Agency**, whom industrialists often enlisted to break strikes, to guard the mill. In the battle that ensued, at least seven workers and three Pinkerton guards died. The workers took control of the mill for several days, but the National Guard advanced on July 12 and removed them. A few days later, scabs replaced union workers at the mill.

Neither labor nor Carnegie Steel fared well in the wake of the Homestead Strike. Union workers lost their jobs, and some also faced criminal charges for their roles in the violence. Public opinion of Carnegie Steel suffered because of the way the company had treated its workers.

THE PULLMAN STRIKE

In 1894, another major strike made headlines, this time in the railroad industry. Workers struck against the Pullman Palace Car Company near Chicago, Illinois. The company, owned by George Pullman, manufactured railway sleeper cars known as Pullman cars.

In 1881, Pullman had established a company town—Pullman, Illinois—near his factory to accommodate its workers. The town featured housing, shops, a library, parks, and other amenities for the workers. It might sound ideal, but it allowed Pullman great control over his workers. He did not allow free discussion, independent newspapers, or the observance of any religion other than Protestant Christianity. Pullman also charged a higher rent than landlords in nearby areas, enabling him to profit from his ownershp of the company town.

When an economic recession hit in 1893, Pullman cut his workers' wages and extended their work hours, but he still expected Pullman residents to pay the same amount in rent and other expenses. In response, angry workers joined the American Railway Union, a new union led by **Eugene V. Debs**.

The American Railway Union was the country's first union to consolidate workers across an entire industry. Before Debs succeeded in combining the many different railway unions, workers had organized themselves according to their individual crafts.

The solidarity, or united purpose, of the American Railway Union turned a local strike into a national labor conflict.

When the Pullman union workers tried to discuss their grievances with their employer, he fired them. In response, the workers called for a strike. Debs coordinated a union boycott of Pullman cars on all rail lines. With members of the American Railway Union refusing to handle any Pullman cars, rail traffic in the Midwest screeched to a halt. Debs hoped the work stoppage would cause the railroads to discontinue their relationship with Pullman.

Instead, President Grover Cleveland sent federal troops to Illinois to facilitate train movement. Violence erupted, and members of the National Guard shot and killed several strikers. As a result of the bloodshed, Debs tried to end the strike, but his involvement with the boycott and strike led to his arrest. While in prison, Debs became interested in **socialism**, the political theory that advocates that the community as a whole should control the production, distribution, and exchange of goods and services. Debs later formed and became the leader of the Socialist Party of America.

Labor was not the only segment of society to experience change during the late 1800s. Greater transformations lay ahead for the United States as more immigrants began to arrive.

HISTORICAL THINKING

1. **READING CHECK** What actions led to the Homestead Strike and the Pullman Strike?

2. **IDENTIFY PROBLEMS AND SOLUTIONS** Describe solutions that indicate different directions events could have taken in the cases of the Homestead and the Pullman strikes.

3. **EVALUATE** What does the structure of the company town of Pullman say about George Pullman's attitude toward its residents? Use examples from the text to support your answer.

ELLIS ISLAND AND ANGEL ISLAND

Athlete. Artist. Gamer. Musician. Environmentalist. Your identity is a combination of traits and experiences, and it is likely to change as you grow. Likewise, the American identity was reshaped by the arrival of millions of new immigrants in the late 1800s.

THE NEW IMMIGRANTS

Until the early 1870s, most immigrants to the United States were from northern and western Europe. But between 1890 and 1920, immigrants began to arrive from southern and eastern European countries such as Italy, Greece, Hungary, Poland, Russia, and Czechoslovakia. Unlike many of their predecessors, few of these new immigrants were Protestant Christians, but instead were largely Catholic, Jewish, and Orthodox. They also typically did not speak English. Although seeking a better life, just as those who arrived before them, they were often treated with prejudice.

Like earlier groups of immigrants to the United States, southern and eastern European and Asian immigrants were motivated by several **push-pull factors**, or pressures that forced them from their home countries and drew them to a new one. The factors that pushed immigrants away from their home countries included a lack of economic opportunities, a shortage of farmland, too few educational opportunities, religious discrimination, and the threat of being drafted to fight in wars. For the Irish, the massive emigration that began with the Great Potato Famine of 1845–1849 stretched into the latter half of the century, as hunger and poverty continued to plague Ireland.

The pull factors that drew immigrants to the United States included the hope for greater economic opportunity, plentiful farmland available for purchase at affordable prices, political and religious freedom, and the absence of war. Following the Civil War, rapid industrial growth created an unprecedented demand for labor. Industries across the country needed both skilled and unskilled workers. Communities established by previous groups of immigrants in cities such as Chicago and New York welcomed the newcomers.

As the influx of non-English-speaking immigrants continued into the early 20th century, an **Americanization** movement emerged. Proponents of Americanization wanted to immerse immigrants in what they defined as American culture and transform them into "true" Americans. During the 1910s, schools, community organizations, and businesses offered immigrants English classes and lessons in American history and government. Some immigrants embraced Americanization efforts, but others rejected them, preferring instead to maintain their own languages and cultures.

Support for Americanization peaked during World War I and waned in the 1920s. In its place came a new appreciation by some for the coexistence of different groups, known today as pluralism. This new appreciation also applied to religious beliefs, as growing numbers of Catholics and Jews continued arriving from Europe.

WELCOME TO ELLIS ISLAND

Beginning in 1892, most of the European immigrants who arrived on the East Coast were processed through the immigration station at **Ellis Island** in New York Harbor. Before it opened, immigrants had arrived at a facility called Castle Garden in Lower Manhattan. Between 1855 and 1890, officials processed 8 million immigrants at the Castle Garden location, but the facility was no longer large enough to manage the large numbers of new immigrants. Ellis Island became the site of a new and more comprehensive immigration processing facility.

THE FACES OF ELLIS ISLAND

Augustus Francis Sherman was the chief registry clerk at Ellis Island in the early 1900s. He took photographs of incoming immigrants, and in 1907, *National Geographic* magazine published some of them. In 2016, artist Jordan Lloyd digitally colorized many of these photos, including the four that appear below. The colorization specialists took care to reproduce historically accurate colors in order to bring to life the intricacies and beauty of the traditional clothing worn by immigrants who walked through the doors of Ellis Island.

Woman from Ruthenia, a region of present-day Ukraine and Belarus, wearing an embroidered linen blouse and sheepskin jacket

Bavarian man, wearing a trachtenjanker, or wool jacket, with horn buttons

East Indian boy, wearing a topi (cap), homespun cotton cloth called khadi, and prayer shawl

Italian woman, wearing a traditional dress with blue shawl and veil

Once they arrived at Ellis Island, immigrants faced a series of examinations that generally took anywhere from three to seven hours. They answered questions about how they were going to support themselves in the United States and received medical exams to ensure they were free of contagious diseases. Aid workers and social workers also provided immigrants with other needs, such as clothing, counseling, or even money. Immigrants who were found to have a contagious disease or deemed unable to support themselves could be barred entry and sent back to their home countries. About 2 percent of immigrants met this fate. By the time Ellis Island stopped functioning as an immigration center in 1924, more than 12 million immigrants had passed through its doors.

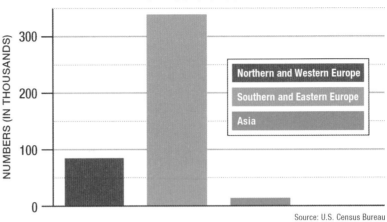

Immigrants Arriving in the United States in 1900

Legend:
- Northern and Western Europe
- Southern and Eastern Europe
- Asia

NUMBERS (IN THOUSANDS)

Source: U.S. Census Bureau

One experience shared by immigrants entering the United States through Ellis Island was seeing the **Statue of Liberty** as they arrived in New York Harbor. Unveiled on a wet and foggy day on October 28, 1886, with President Grover Cleveland in attendance, the statue was greeted with great celebration. The copper figure was designed and constructed as a gift from France, and the pedestal was built by the United States. Holding the torch of freedom in her upraised hand, "Lady Liberty" came to symbolize the welcoming spirit of the United States. **Emma Lazarus**'s poem "The New Colossus" was etched into a plaque at the base of the statue in 1903, reinforcing a message of inclusion: "From her beacon-hand / Glows world-wide welcome."

CONTROLLING IMMIGRATION

On the West Coast, immigrants arrived at **Angel Island,** a facility in San Francisco Bay that processed immigrants during the early 20th century. Unlike the mainly European immigrants who arrived at Ellis Island, those who arrived at Angel Island came from Asia, primarily China and Japan. Other Asian immigrants included Filipinos, Hindus, and Sikhs.

The Angel Island facility opened in 1910 not only to process immigrants but also to control the number of Chinese immigrants allowed into the country. Many native-born Americans harbored prejudices toward Chinese immigrants and believed Chinese laborers, who often worked for low wages, took jobs away

from American workers. Anti-Chinese sentiment had intensified in the 1870s when unemployment ran especially high. In 1882, Congress passed the **Chinese Exclusion Act** to prevent Chinese immigrants from working in the United States. Although states had already passed their own versions of immigration laws, the Chinese Exclusion Act became the nation's first federal immigration law.

Immigration from Asia continued despite laws created to suppress it. Those who came for purposes other than work could still seek admission to the United States. However, they had to prove they were not laborers by providing certification from the Chinese government. Because the act included such a wide definition of who qualified as a laborer, proving their occupation was difficult for immigrants.

As a result, the act severely limited Chinese immigration for 10 years. Officials turned away more than 5 percent of Chinese immigrants who tried to enter the country—far more than the 2 percent of European immigrants turned away from Ellis Island. Even the Chinese people already living in the United States had to obtain certification to reenter the country if they traveled outside the United States and wanted to return. When the Chinese Exclusion Act expired in 1892, Congress enacted the **Geary Act**, which extended the restrictions on Chinese labor for an additional 10 years. When that act expired in 1902, Congress made the extension permanent. In fact, Congress did not finally repeal these exclusionary acts until the 1940s.

Chinese immigrants denied admission and detained at Angel Island could appeal, but they often had to endure difficult conditions while waiting to hear the results. The wait could last weeks, months, or

Japanese women aboard an incoming ship await processing at Angel Island in 1925. Between 1900 and 1925, more than 250,000 Japanese immigrated to the United States.

in some cases more than a year, and prospective immigrants had to submit to lengthy interrogations about their families and villages in China. To pass the time and express their feelings while waiting, some detainees carved poems in the walls. Facilities on Angel Island were often crowded, and some featured barbed wire and armed guards to prevent people from escaping. The island seemed more like a prison than an immigration center.

Also contributing to the diversity of the United States in the early 20th century was the openness of its southwestern borders. People crossed freely between the United States and Mexico. But the migration process could be difficult for new arrivals to the United States, and the struggle did not end there. Once admitted to the country, immigrants frequently faced prejudice and poverty as they settled into their new homes.

HISTORICAL THINKING

1. **READING CHECK** What were some of the push-pull factors that led immigrants to come to the United States during the late 19th and early 20th centuries?

2. **INTERPRET GRAPHS** From what region did the most immigrants to the United States come in 1900?

3. **IDENTIFY PROBLEMS AND SOLUTIONS** How could a Chinese person immigrate legally under the terms of the Chinese Exclusion Act?

4. **MAKE GENERALIZATIONS** Explain connections between the experiences of immigrants arriving in the late 19th and early 20th centuries with the larger issue of worldwide migration in the 21st century.

Sikh immigrants from India, Angel Island, c. 1925

Japanese immigrant, Angel Island, c. 1925

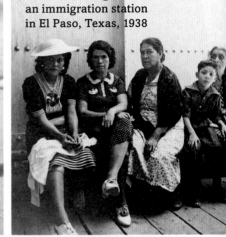

Mexican immigrants at an immigration station in El Paso, Texas, 1938

3.2

THROUGH THE LENS

IMMIGRATION

As President John F. Kennedy famously acknowledged in the title of a book he published as senator in 1959, the United States is "a nation of immigrants." Except for those of us with Native American ancestry, we all can trace our heritage back to somewhere else. From English colonists seeking religious freedom on the shores of a distant land, to Asian, Latin American, and European immigrants eager for work opportunities and a chance to make a better life, the rich tapestry of this country is interwoven with the stories of many immigrants. How is immigration a piece of your American story?

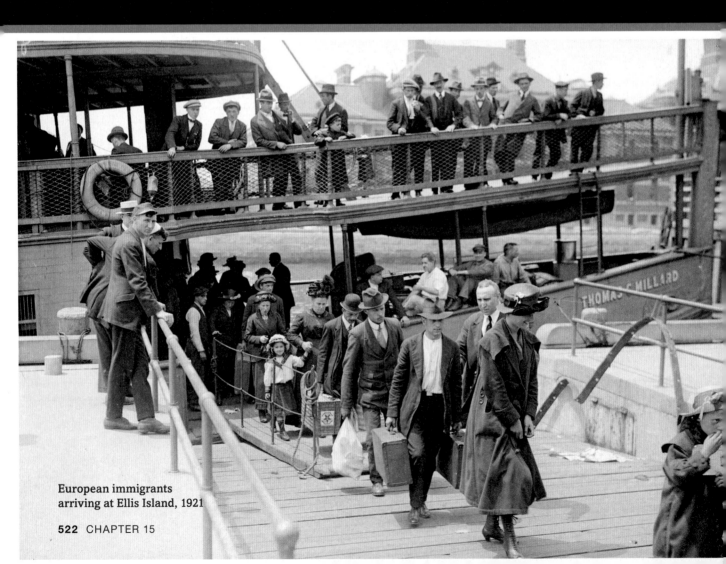

European immigrants arriving at Ellis Island, 1921

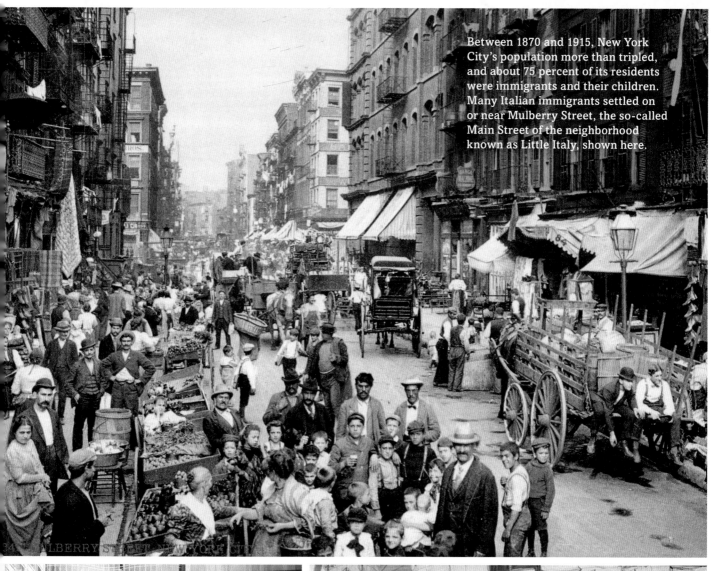

Between 1870 and 1915, New York City's population more than tripled, and about 75 percent of its residents were immigrants and their children. Many Italian immigrants settled on or near Mulberry Street, the so-called Main Street of the neighborhood known as Little Italy, shown here.

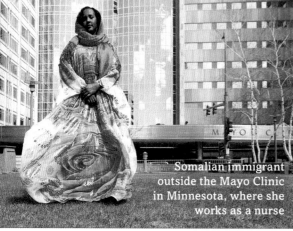

Somalian immigrant outside the Mayo Clinic in Minnesota, where she works as a nurse

Little Havana, Miami, Florida

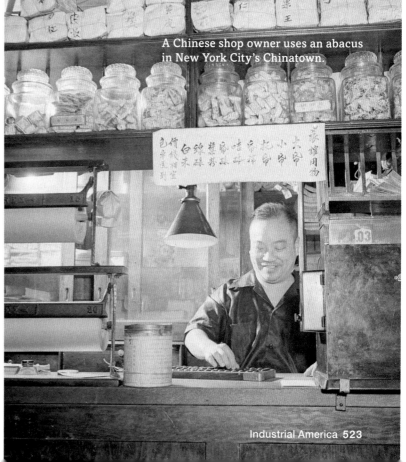

A Chinese shop owner uses an abacus in New York City's Chinatown.

MAIN IDEA Immigrants in the early 20th century often faced discrimination and poverty, but social welfare groups were ready to assist them in their new country.

DIFFICULT LIVES IN A NEW LAND

Adapting to a new country was especially difficult for newly arrived immigrants, whose languages, religions, food, and traditions often set them apart as they searched for shelter and work.

A PLACE TO LIVE AND WORK

Immigrants brought with them a hopeful optimism about a new future in a new country. At the same time, navigating daily life in an unfamiliar place sometimes brought a series of complex and frustrating encounters. For some, the language barrier was significant. In 1910, almost one-quarter of all immigrants spoke languages other than English. They were further isolated by their traditional dress, ethnic foods, and religious practices that were sometimes unfamiliar to the largely Protestant American population. Catholics and Jews, in particular, often faced religious prejudice, such as anti-Catholicism and **anti-Semitism**, or prejudice against Jewish people. For instance, throughout the late 19th century, American Jews were often barred from attending particular universities and conducting certain businesses.

Once settled, immigrants gained employment in a variety of jobs. Many immigrant men worked in construction. They dug tunnels and laid rails for the new subway system in New York, and they built steel mills in Pittsburgh. In Chicago, immigrants helped construct some of the world's first skyscrapers, or very tall buildings.

Some immigrant groups migrated toward specific types of work. For example, Italian women often sewed for the garment industry, Greek immigrants took jobs with the railroads, and Filipinos, Japanese, and Hindus and Sikhs from India, moved to California and other western states to work in the agriculture and service industries. Many immigrants started businesses.

The influx of new immigrants added to the population growth of cities across the country. In cities such as Chicago and New York, housing could not keep up with increased demand. Wealthier residents lived in spacious apartment buildings and townhomes, but working-class residents—including newly arriving immigrants—often found housing in structures called **tenements**. Most tenements were six- or seven-story, multi-resident buildings, constructed on narrow lots. They were typically poorly ventilated, crowded, and ill-maintained.

In New York City, tenements were designed to house as many people as possible. Individual residences featured small, narrow rooms and few windows. The space between the tenement buildings was often so narrow that people could reach out a window and touch someone living in the next building. Only the top floors actually received much light. Because of poor ventilation and substandard or nonexistent sanitation, diseases spread quickly in the tenements. The structures were also prone to fires because of overcrowding and poor construction.

STRENGTH IN NUMBERS

Many immigrants settled in neighborhoods that reflected their own ethnic backgrounds so their native languages and customs surrounded them. They built churches and synagogues and formed mutual aid, or self-help, societies to provide services and support for residents and incoming immigrants.

One of these societies was the Polish National Alliance, formed in Philadelphia and Chicago in 1880. Its purpose was to bring Polish immigrants together in support of Poland's independence and to help one another assimilate, or blend in with and adopt American ways of life in the United States. One year after forming, the alliance established a Polish-language newspaper. Later, it set up an insurance program for members and provided loans and scholarships to those seeking an education.

CRITICAL VIEWING Children play in the streets of New York City, amid traffic and trash. Lewis Hine captured this photograph in 1910. Based on details you notice in the photo, how would you describe this street and its tenements?

The Hebrew Immigrant Aid Society, founded in 1881 on Manhattan's Lower East Side, originally formed to aid eastern European immigrants fleeing to the United States to escape religious persecution. The organization provided food, clothing, transportation, and employment to Jewish refugees. In 1904, it established a bureau on Ellis Island to assist newly arrived immigrants with translation and other services, such as loans for the $25 landing fee.

In addition to forming self-help societies, immigrants also contributed to their neighborhoods by constructing schools, theaters, and concert halls. These investments demonstrated the immigrants' commitment to their new country—an idea the Americanization movement promoted. The Polish National Alliance and the Hebrew Immigrant Aid Society still operate today, helping immigrants and others in need.

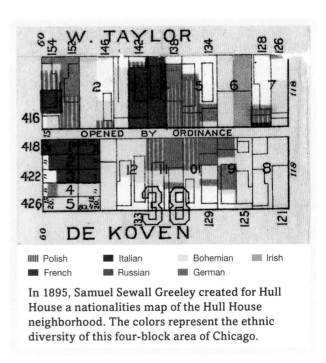

IIIII Polish   ■ Italian   Bohemian   ■ Irish
■ French   ■ Russian   ■ German

In 1895, Samuel Sewall Greeley created for Hull House a nationalities map of the Hull House neighborhood. The colors represent the ethnic diversity of this four-block area of Chicago.

ENCOUNTERING PREJUDICE

Despite many immigrants' attempts to assimilate into their new home, some Americans still harbored prejudices against them. These nativists felt threatened by what they saw as changing cultural values and competition for employment. They vehemently opposed immigration and wanted to restrict it by using literacy tests and quotas based on national origin. Many nativist groups worked actively against immigrants, taking particular aim at certain religious groups, such as Catholics and Jews.

For example, in 1887, the American Protective Association formed in Iowa. In essence, this organization was a secret society of white, native-born Protestants that exploited Americans' fears about an unstable economy and what they perceived as a negative influence of immigrants in the country. The organization specifically targeted Catholic immigrants, spreading rumors and **propaganda**, or purposely misleading and usually negative information, to try to bar Catholics both from entering the United States and from serving in public office. In fact, the oath that members took included a pledge that they would not "vote for, or counsel others to vote for, any Roman Catholic." The organization boasted more than 2 million members in the 1890s, though by 1900, its membership had dwindled significantly, and it had little or no influence.

Of course, prejudice extended beyond anti-Catholic and anti-Semitic boundaries. Just as the

CRITICAL VIEWING Anti-immigrant sentiment, though prevalent, was not unchallenged. This 1896 cartoon drawn by Frank Beard appeared in *The Ram's Horn*, a Social Gospel magazine. How does Beard portray both the United States and the immigrant trying to enter the country?

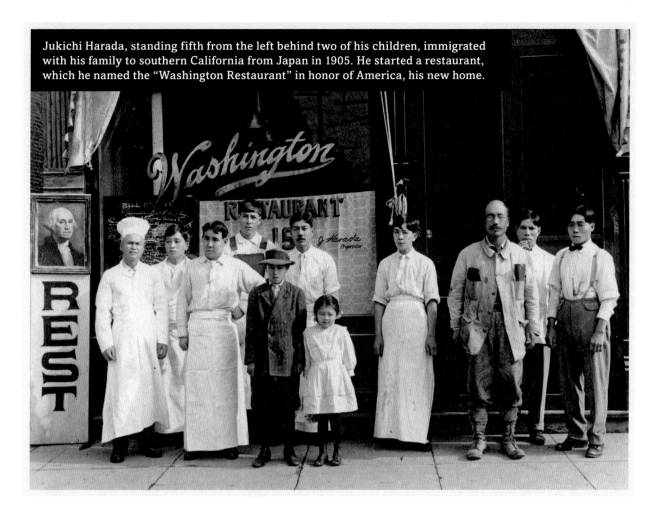

Jukichi Harada, standing fifth from the left behind two of his children, immigrated with his family to southern California from Japan in 1905. He started a restaurant, which he named the "Washington Restaurant" in honor of America, his new home.

Chinese Exclusion Act of 1882 had barred many Chinese immigrants from entering the country, the **Gentlemen's Agreement of 1907** between the United States and Japan had a similar effect, though not quite as severe.

This understanding between President Theodore Roosevelt and the Japanese government affirmed that the Japanese would grant passports for Japanese emigration to the United States only to educated businessmen and other professionals and their direct family members—not to peasants (farmers) or laborers. In exchange, Roosevelt agreed that the San Francisco School Board would stop separating Japanese schoolchildren from white students. Californian nativists had drummed up the need for the Gentlemen's Agreement out of a fear that Japanese immigrants would ultimately control all the best farmland in the state. At the time, 1,000 Japanese immigrants were arriving in the state every month, and most of them were farmers.

Like the Chinese, most Japanese arrived at Angel Island in San Francisco Bay. But thanks to the Gentlemen's Agreement, Japanese immigrants rarely had to stay on the island beyond a couple of days. In the end, both Roosevelt and the Japanese government stuck to their promises, but the agreement did nothing to end discrimination against the Japanese in the United States.

Urban centers continued to expand as native-born Americans and newly arrived immigrants moved to the growing, crowded cities. At the same time, the gap between the wealthy and the poor continued to increase.

HISTORICAL THINKING

1. **READING CHECK** Who immigrated to the United States between 1877 and 1911, and why?

2. **DESCRIBE** Why did immigrants form self-help societies?

3. **EVALUATE** In what ways did the treatment of immigrants to the United States show both the strengths and weaknesses of American democracy at the turn of the 20th century?

4. **IDENTIFY PROBLEMS AND SOLUTIONS** Explain the problem that the Gentlemen's Agreement set out to address.

JANE ADDAMS 1860–1935

"She is the truest American I have ever known, and there has been none braver."—Harold Ickes, United States Secretary of the Interior

In the late 1800s, Chicago was a tough place to live for the thousands of immigrants who came to work in the city's booming factories and stockyards. The journalist Lincoln Steffens described Chicago as "first in violence, deepest in dirt, loud, lawless, unlovely, ill-smelling. Criminally, it was wide-open; socially it was thoughtless and raw." Onto this grim and seemingly hopeless stage stepped an unlikely hero: Jane Addams.

THE FOUNDING OF HULL HOUSE

Jane Addams was born into a financially comfortable family in the small town of Cedarville, Illinois—far from the poverty and bustle of Chicago. A bright and intellectually curious young woman, she attended college and went on to study medicine, although she did not complete her medical degree. Instead, she spent several years traveling in Europe and considering her choices for leading a meaningful life. During a visit to London, Addams and her friend Ellen Starr toured a settlement house—an urban community center that provided needed services to people in the neighborhood. There, Jane Addams discovered her purpose.

In 1889, Addams and Starr leased a house, called Hull House after the man who had built it, in a poor, immigrant neighborhood of Chicago. Hull House would be Addams's home for the rest of her life. Addams and her partner, Starr, moved into the house and immediately began renovating the space, creating programs to help the people in the neighborhood, and fundraising among wealthy Chicagoans to support their work.

In this photo taken in 1930, Jane Addams holds a little girl during the celebration of Hull House's 40th anniversary. The settlement house was located in a neighborhood that, at the time, had one of the city's highest infant mortality rates. In response, Hull House residents researched this problem as well as others that affected people in their neighborhoods. Their findings, often published in sociology journals, provided evidence for activists lobbying for reforms.

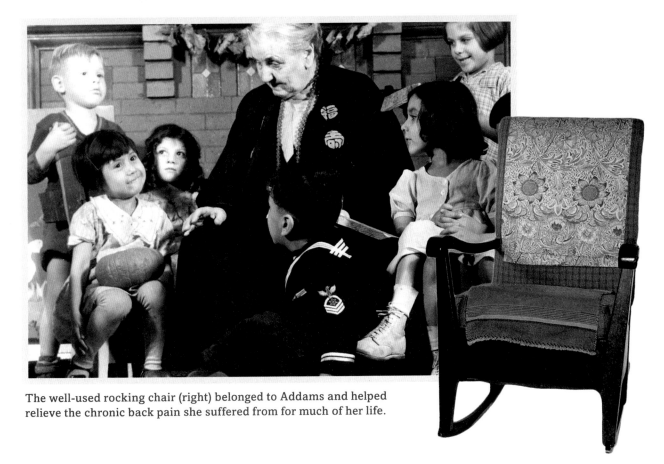

The well-used rocking chair (right) belonged to Addams and helped relieve the chronic back pain she suffered from for much of her life.

Hull House provided a generous range of desperately needed services, including a kindergarten, day care, afternoon clubs for older children, classes and activities for adults, a playground, a library, and a boarding house for girls. Addams crusaded for improvements throughout the city as well as in her own neighborhood. She served on the city's board of education and, at one point, worked as the garbage inspector in the ward where Hull House was located.

BEYOND HULL HOUSE

Addams's work at Hull House gained her respect and admiration from people throughout the country. However, when she took her activism onto the national scene, she was not afraid to take public stances she knew would make her deeply unpopular. She was opposed to war under any circumstance and spoke out against fighting in World War I, even after the United States had joined the war and most Americans strongly supported it. After the war, she continued to be critical of the military. She also supported labor unions and openly criticized elements of the American capitalist system. By the 1920s, J. Edgar Hoover, the director of the Federal Bureau of Investigation (FBI), was calling Jane Addams "the most dangerous woman in America"— the same description that had been applied to Mother Jones several years earlier by a U.S. attorney.

Then came the stock market crash of 1929 and the beginning of the Great Depression, a time of poverty and struggle for many Americans. Once again, Addams's efforts on behalf of the poor came to the forefront. She rose in the national esteem at the same time she received international recognition. In 1931, she was awarded the Nobel Peace Prize.

Jane Addams died only a few years later. Her legacy of support for all people continues today in the organizations she helped found, including the National Association for the Advancement of Colored People (NAACP), the American Civil Liberties Union (ACLU), and the Women's International League for Peace and Freedom. After 122 years of service, Hull House closed in 2012. However, the site now houses a museum dedicated to continuing Addams's vision through research, education, and social engagement.

HISTORICAL THINKING

1. **READING CHECK** Why was Jane Addams unpopular during World War I?

2. **IDENTIFY PROBLEMS AND SOLUTIONS** What are some of the problems that Jane Addams worked to solve during her lifetime?

3. **MAKE CONNECTIONS** Think of an issue of local, national, or international concern today. What do you think Jane Addams would say about it?

GROWING URBANIZATION

Some people prefer the wide-open spaces of a rural environment, but others crave the energy of city life. In the late 19th and early 20th centuries, Americans moved to cities for a host of reasons, and the cities grew to accommodate them.

FROM COUNTRY TO CITY

Between 1860 and 1920, American cities grew immensely, especially in the Northeast and Midwest. For example, Chicago's population swelled from about 109,000 in 1860 to about 1.1 million by 1890. However, rapid urbanization was not confined to the Northeast and Midwest. In the 1890s, a new railroad connected south Florida, including Miami, with northeastern cities. By the following decade, the swampy land of southern Florida was drained to attract new residents with its affordable property and warm climate. Miami's expansion was so rapid that it acquired the nickname "Magic City."

Many factors contributed to American urbanization. The ever growing number of immigrants—more than 8 million between 1870 and 1890 alone—generally settled in the cities where they arrived. Increased industrialization and trade played a role as well. As a result of extensive railroad systems, cities such as Chicago could receive large shipments of food and other goods, which brokers then sold and transported to markets throughout the nation. Declining crop prices also drove people from rural areas into the cities when farming no longer provided them with a livable income.

Cities offered exciting opportunities for people to meet others, enjoy cultural events, and live independent lives. Many single men and women took advantage of these opportunities. A great many of them rented rooms in boardinghouses, a living arrangement where a landlord or lady leased rooms in his or her home for a reasonable amount of money per week. The proprietor of the boardinghouse provided three meals a day, served in a common dining room, and kept the boarders' rooms clean. Boarders also had access to the parlor, where they could socialize with each other. It was an economical way for newcomers to make friends and learn about the city in a safe home environment.

Cities also offered a wide variety of entertainments. Young and old Americans alike enjoyed amusement parks, dance halls, and **vaudeville** theaters. Vaudeville, a type of show featuring a variety of specialty acts such as singing and instrumental music, dancing, comedy, drama, and acrobatics, was popular with urban audiences.

Colorful posters like this one from 1894 advertised vaudeville productions and promised thrilling and exotic entertainment—including strongmen lifting humans high overhead.

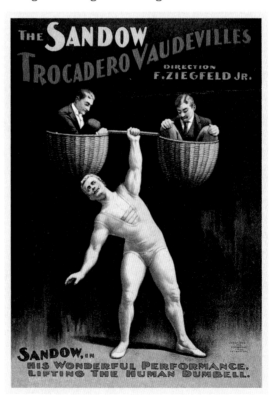

CITY STRUCTURES

Busy, crowded, and growing cities need efficient forms of public transportation. In the 1880s, **streetcars** became the main form of transportation in urban centers, and cities that had streetcar systems, such as Boston, San Francisco, Chicago, and New York, became known as "streetcar cities." Streetcars helped foster the development of a city's central district because they gave people a means for traveling to and from the city to shop and work. At the same time, streetcars allowed people to travel easily to the outskirts of the city, so those who wanted to escape city living could move to emerging communities on the city's edge, called **suburbs**.

A city's central district featured businesses such as banks, railroad terminals, and the growth of new places to shop: **department stores**. First introduced in the United States in the mid-1800s, department stores offered a unique shopping experience by providing a wide variety of merchandise all under one roof. They drew shoppers from the suburbs. Chicago's Marshall Field & Company and New York's R.H. Macy & Company brought many customers into the big city.

As city populations grew, finding enough space to house all the residents quickly became a problem.

When cities could not spread out, they found another solution: they built up. The revolutionary use of steel frameworks in construction allowed builders in Chicago to erect the first skyscraper—an incredible 10-story building—in the 1880s. Skyscrapers were soon standing 30 stories high or more in American cities, making efficient use of limited available urban space. Moreover, the development of the commercial electric passenger elevator just a few years after the first skyscraper's construction added to the practicality and usefulness of these tall buildings. But not everyone could afford to live in a roomy apartment in a skyscraper or move to the suburbs. Many city dwellers rented space in tightly packed, poorly ventilated tenements. The intense overcrowding in poor urban neighborhoods led to many public health problems that required solutions, and reformers ultimately took up the cause.

HISTORICAL THINKING

1. **READING CHECK** What factors contributed to urbanization between 1860 and 1920?

2. **ANALYZE CAUSE AND EFFECT** What effect did the use of steel have on building construction and the growth of cities?

3. **EXPLAIN** How and why did suburbs emerge in the late 19th century?

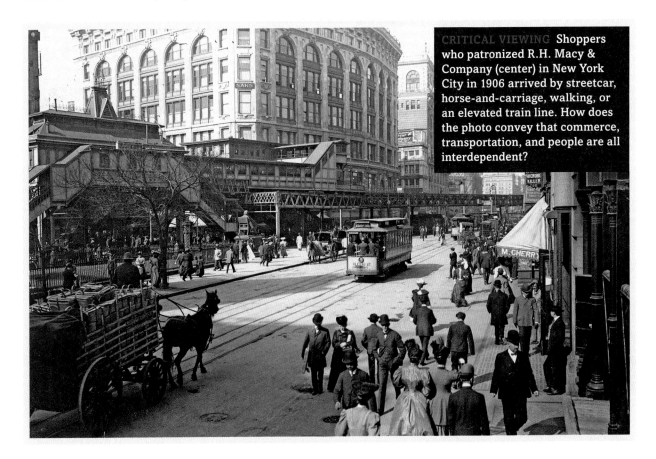

CRITICAL VIEWING Shoppers who patronized R.H. Macy & Company (center) in New York City in 1906 arrived by streetcar, horse-and-carriage, walking, or an elevated train line. How does the photo convey that commerce, transportation, and people are all interdependent?

TACKLING URBAN PROBLEMS

When big problems are not solved by those in charge, sometimes ordinary citizens step up and become the agents of change. In the late 1800s, reformers took on social and political problems that had been brewing for several decades.

CITY PROBLEMS, CITY POLITICS

The growing density of urban populations during the late 19th century caused great concern among both public health officials and social reformers. Before 1895, effective departments of **sanitation**, or proper waste disposal and a system for providing clean water, did not exist in cities. Horse manure and garbage accumulated in the streets, while noxious factory smoke filled the air. Such unsanitary conditions made poor sections of cities particularly susceptible to outbreaks of illnesses such as

cholera, a deadly disease that people sometimes contract after drinking contaminated water. Crowded conditions increased the amount of damage caused by fires and the likelihood of violent and criminal acts.

Corruption in big city governments was an accepted practice, and political machines were in charge. **Political machines**, or agreed upon, exclusive power structures, involved city officials bribing politicians, contractors, and constituents with all manner of favors to keep the city running. Bribes,

Butchers pause for a photo in Chicago's meatpacking district in 1904. Upton Sinclair exposed the ill treatment of workers and unsanitary and dangerous conditions in slaughterhouses. Through one of his characters in *The Jungle,* he asserts that "one of the consequences of civic administration by ignorant and vicious politicians, is that preventable diseases kill off half our population."

promises, and favors were the oil that greased the political machine. In cities such as Chicago and New York, political machines were efficient but corrupt methods of city management.

New York's William Magear Tweed, or "Boss Tweed," ran one of the most notorious political machines. In the 1860s, Tweed led a Democratic Party committee called **Tammany Hall**, and, similar to the spoils system that arose during the Jackson presidency, he used his position to award city contracts to associates and supporters. Newspapers accused Tweed of corruption, but the inner-city residents, whom the machine depended on for votes, saw value in the system. The contracts that Tweed awarded improved the residents' neighborhoods by paving roads, installing sewers and gas lines, and building parks and elevated train lines. Corruption charges eventually brought Tweed down in the early 1870s but did not disable political machines as a whole.

Because of the political corruption and gaudy excesses of the wealthy, the years between 1870 and 1900 became known as the **Gilded Age**. To gild something means to coat it with a thin layer of gold that can disguise what lies underneath. The phrase "Gilded Age" originated with the novel *The Gilded Age* by Mark Twain and Charles Dudley Warner. The authors used the term to highlight the way spectacular wealth masked the greed and corruption of industrialists and politicians.

REFORMING SOCIAL ILLS

Many Americans knew what was underneath the gilded layer, and they believed that governments did not do enough to solve the problems that stemmed from urbanization. In the 1890s, individuals organized a number of different reform movements to address social problems. These reformers were mostly native-born, middle class, white, and Protestant. They believed that society was responsible for the common good of all its citizens and that social ills resulting from industrial growth and political corruption had to be addressed.

Because one of the root values of these reformers was a belief in progress, the various reform movements became known as **progressivism**. Progressive reformers worked in many different capacities to achieve reforms. Some focused on improving urban living conditions. Some addressed the injustices of child labor, and others challenged big-city bosses and government corruption. While they may have focused on different issues, progressive reformers shared similar goals: addressing social problems such as poverty and exploitation, exposing corruption, reforming government, and expanding democracy.

Thanks to the writings of several novelists and journalists, even Americans who did not live in places like New York City or Chicago learned about the horrendous living conditions in these cities. As you have read, Upton Sinclair's 1906 novel *The Jungle* exposed the dangerous and filthy working conditions of Chicago's stockyards and the abusive treatment immigrant workers endured in the city. Like Ida Tarbell and other muckrakers, Sinclair shined a light on suffering and injustice and the need for reform.

The authors **Theodore Dreiser** and **Frank Norris** also highlighted social problems in their novels. Dreiser had grown up in poverty, and he used his experiences to inform his writing. He described urban poverty in *Sister Carrie* and targeted the legal system in *An American Tragedy*. Likewise, Frank Norris, in his novels *McTeague* and *The Octopus,* explored social issues such as the wheat industry's conflicts with railway monopolies.

Besides addressing social problems, progressive reformers aimed to clean up government by passing new laws that gave citizens the right to initiate **referendums**, or public votes on individual issues, and the right to recall, or remove, an elected official from office. These measures were one way to keep political figures and political machines from gaining too much power. Other progressive reforms included enforcing state regulation of industry and giving voters, instead of party officers, the chance to choose nominees for important political offices.

The late 1800s saw the beginning of many reforms in society and government. Even so, some deeply held prejudices still lurked in American society.

HISTORICAL THINKING

1. **READING CHECK** What steps did reformers take to try to improve citizens' lives and government practices?

2. **IDENTIFY PROBLEMS AND SOLUTIONS** In what ways did change in the late 19th and early 20th centuries affect politics, values, and beliefs?

3. **DESCRIBE** Why did poor city residents have positive feelings about political machines such as Tammany Hall?

JIM CROW AND SEGREGATION

Sometimes the struggle against injustice runs into obstacles, as personal and institutional prejudices get in the way of making laws that are fair for everybody. Although progressive reformers had made headway with social and political reforms, many African Americans still faced massive challenges.

SUPPRESSING THE VOTE

As you have read, during Reconstruction, laws were enacted in the South to protect the rights of African Americans and bring them into the larger society as full-fledged citizens. The 13th, 14th, and 15th amendments, respectively, abolished slavery, granted equal protection under the law to all Americans, and extended the right to vote to African-American males. But after Reconstruction ended, southern states and communities passed laws meant to undermine these reforms. African Americans experienced what historians refer to as the "black nadir," or the lowest point since the end of the

Civil War. Racial violence and legalized discrimination inhibited African Americans' economic opportunities and political participation.

Southern state, county, and local legislatures set their sights on the 15th Amendment in particular. Tactics targeting African-American voting rights, such as the implementation of poll taxes and literacy tests, were complicated and difficult to get around. For example, poll taxes were typically between one and two dollars, but the equivalent of a dollar in 1877 equaled more than $22.00 by 2017 standards. That was unaffordable for many poor people of any

Poll taxes were common throughout the nation in the latter 19th century, and faded away in the 20th century, except in the South. This receipt from San Francisco, California, shows that James Leonard paid a poll tax of $2.00 in 1890. California abolished the tax in 1914. Fifty years later, the 24th Amendment abolished the poll tax nationwide.

ethnicity. In addition, counties, cities, and towns sometimes each levied their own separate poll taxes, which put an even greater burden on those hoping to register.

Poll taxes were an impediment to poor white citizens as well as African Americans, but several southern states found a way around that problem through the use of a legal provision called a **grandfather clause**. The clause stated that those who had the right to vote prior to 1866 or 1867—or their direct descendants—were not subject to some or all voting requirements, such as poll taxes or literacy tests. This allowed poor and illiterate white men to register to vote, but denied that right to many African Americans.

The first literacy tests required for voter registration didn't arise in the South, but in New England. In 1855, Connecticut instituted a law requiring a year's residency in the state and successful completion of a literacy test before a citizen could register to vote. The state's intent was to discourage Irish immigrants from voting. After Reconstruction, southern states adopted this practice. Literacy tests took many forms, from requiring a citizen to read and answer questions to interpreting a portion of a state's constitution. But the registrar of voters had the final say over who passed. A white applicant might answer all questions incorrectly and pass, while an African-American applicant might provide accurate answers and fail.

Perhaps the worst hurdle for African Americans wishing to register to vote was intimidation. Most voter registration applications had to be made at the courthouse where, in some places, white police officers waited to arrest applicants on petty or made-up charges. In many southern locales, white business owners organized White Citizens Councils that retaliated against minorities who attempted to vote. Registrars released applicants' personal information to the councils, which then punished prospective voters by encouraging their employers to fire them or persuading their landlords to evict them.

Many council members were also part of the Ku Klux Klan. Due to the federal anti-Klan legislation of the early 1870s, Klan membership had dwindled by 1880, but the racism that fueled the organization never died out. Despite the low profile of the Klan during the 1890s, the practice of lynching continued, and its members murdered on average 187 African Americans every year throughout the decade. The Klan began to build its membership again in 1915.

People wear badges to identify as members of a group. In the 1920s, some Americans wore these badges to be identified as Klan members. The badge on the left is in the shape of a Klan hood.

SEPARATION BASED ON RACE

Discrimination against African Americans was common practice throughout the United States, but it occurred most rampantly in the South. After the end of Reconstruction, southern politicians remained intent on enforcing **segregation**, or the separation of different groups of people, usually based on race. They passed a series of laws to ensure that African-American and white citizens attended separate schools and used separate public facilities, such as restrooms, theaters, restaurants, and public transportation. In states such as Florida, Louisiana, and Mississippi, whites enforced these laws, known as **Jim Crow laws**, to establish and maintain power in society. Jim Crow was an African-American character in minstrel shows of the day—a dim-witted, comic fellow, portrayed by a white actor in blackface, who was the target of ridicule and the butt of jokes. That the name of this character became associated with segregation laws is just one more affront to those to whom the laws applied.

One Jim Crow law had a particularly significant effect. In 1890, Louisiana passed the Separate Car Act, which required "equal but separate accommodations" for white and African-American train passengers. In other words, the railroads had to offer the same accommodations to whites and African Americans, but in separate rail cars.

A New Orleans committee that supported African-American rights decided to test the act's constitutionality. Because the act did not define the meaning of *white* or *African-American*, the committee

CRITICAL VIEWING White bi-plane passengers tow a group of African-American passengers behind them in this 1913 cartoon from the New York humor magazine, *Puck*. What details in the cartoon demonstrate a northern critique of the "separate but equal" policies legalized by *Plessy* v. *Ferguson*?

claimed the railroads could not consistently apply the act. To prove its point, in 1892, the committee enlisted Homer Plessy to purchase a train ticket in Louisiana. Plessy was one-eighth African-American. When he purposely sat in the car reserved for whites, a conductor told Plessy to move to the African-American car. Plessy refused and was arrested.

Plessy challenged the railroad company in the 1896 Supreme Court case *Plessy* v. *Ferguson*. The court decided that the Separate Car Act did not violate the 14th Amendment's guarantee of "equal protection of the laws" because the railroad company offered equal accommodations, even if they were separate. In a strong dissent from the majority of the court, Justice John Marshall Harlan wrote, "I am of the opinion that the statute of Louisiana is inconsistent with the personal liberties of citizens, white and black, in that State, and hostile to both the spirit and the letter of the Constitution of the United States." By ruling against Plessy, the Supreme Court upheld the practice of segregation, thereby allowing other businesses and institutions to apply a "**separate but equal**" treatment to African Americans for decades.

Public schools enforced "separate but equal" segregation policies. African-American and white students attended different schools, but they were rarely equal. Whites had much better access to schools and the public funding needed to pay for them. African Americans, on the other hand, often had to pay to build schools themselves and resort to using second-hand supplies, such as outdated textbooks that white schools gave them.

SELF-RELIANCE VS. SOCIAL REFORM

African-American leaders responded to segregation laws, but in very different ways. Some supported the idea of working to make changes from within the system. Others championed open protest because they believed that was the only route to securing their denied rights.

Booker T. Washington was an educator who founded the Tuskegee Institute in Alabama in 1881 to train African Americans to be teachers. Eventually, though, Washington incorporated vocational classes at the institute, teaching manual trades and developing students' agricultural skills.

Our greatest danger is that in the great leap from slavery to freedom we may overlook the fact that the masses of us are to live by the productions of our hands, and fail to keep in mind that we shall prosper in proportion as we learn to dignify and glorify common labor and put brains and skill into the common occupations of life. No race can prosper till it learns that there is as much dignity in tilling a field as in writing a poem. It is at the bottom of life we must begin, and not at the top. Nor should we permit our grievances to overshadow our opportunities.

—from the "Atlanta Compromise" speech, by
  Booker T. Washington, 1895

How does Washington's speech reflect the
Tuskegee Institute's goals?

The supplementary truths must never be lost sight of: first, slavery and race-prejudice are potent . . . causes of the Negro's position; second, industrial and common-school training were necessarily slow in planting because they had to await the black teachers trained by higher institutions . . . and, third, while it is a great truth to say that the Negro must strive and strive mightily to help himself, it is equally true that unless his striving be not simply seconded, but rather aroused and encouraged, by the initiative of the richer and wiser environing group, he cannot hope for great success.

—from *The Souls of Black Folk,* by
  W.E.B. Du Bois, 1903

What is Du Bois's main critique of Washington's
theories?

Washington also promoted self-reliance among African Americans, believing they should focus on hard work and personal development rather than on trying to reform entrenched, systemic racism. He thought the best way for African Americans to win the respect of whites was for them to prove themselves worthy of that respect. In 1895, Washington presented his ideas in a speech at the Cotton States and International Exposition in Atlanta, Georgia. In his speech, known as the "Atlanta Compromise" speech, Washington encouraged African Americans to refrain from openly and actively promoting social equality.

Washington's emphasis on self-reliance helped him raise money for the institute, especially from white donors. Although Washington did not publicly promote social reform, he did privately fund court challenges to segregation.

In contrast, historian, sociologist, and reformer **W.E.B. Du Bois** (doo-BOYS) believed that protest was the best path toward gaining equality and ending segregation. Du Bois charged that Washington's acceptance of discrimination helped promote bigotry rather than deter it. He critiqued the ideas of self-reliance in his book *The Souls of Black Folk*, and, in the process, motivated others to oppose Washington's approach.

By 1903, the year *The Souls of Black Folk* was published, eight years had passed since Washington's "Atlanta Compromise" speech. Little had improved in the daily lives of African Americans,

however. Racial violence, discrimination, and segregation worked against African Americans' limited ability to participate in the political process, and the activism proposed by Du Bois gained favor.

In 1905, Du Bois founded a small organization called the Niagara Movement, which attacked Washington's ideas. The organization died out in 1909, but that same year Du Bois co-founded the **National Association for the Advancement of Colored People (NAACP)** with other African-American leaders and white supporters. DuBois served as the organization's director of research and edited its magazine, *The Crisis*. His hope was that the NAACP could be a force for change in ending segregation and discrimination against African Americans. In fact, reform did begin to attract greater attention as the nation entered a new period of rapid change.

HISTORICAL THINKING

1. **READING CHECK** What were Jim Crow laws, and why were they instituted?

2. **ANALYZE CAUSE AND EFFECT** How might poor white citizens in the South avoid voter suppression tactics such as poll taxes and literacy tests?

3. **EVALUATE** Regarding the events discussed in this lesson, evaluate what aspects of African Americans' lives changed and what aspects stayed the same.

4. **IDENTIFY PROBLEMS AND SOLUTIONS** What different solutions did Booker T. Washington and W.E.B. Du Bois propose as ways to fight discrimination against African Americans?

CONFRONTING RACIAL VIOLENCE

Beginning in the 1870s, African Americans realized the freedoms they had gained following the Civil War were under attack. Many white people sought to manipulate laws to return African Americans to what, in effect, would be slavery. When laws failed to work, some white people turned to violence, wrecking the property of African Americans and resorting to lynching. In retaliation, some African Americans fought violence with violence. Others fled their homes. But many turned to nonviolent protest.

CRITICAL VIEWING One way white southerners terrorized African Americans during the years after the Civil War—and well into the 20th century—was by burning down their houses and farms and destroying their crops and belongings. *Burned Out*, painted by William H. Johnson around 1943, depicts an African-American couple standing in front of their burning house with the few possessions they managed to rescue. How does the painting convey the vulnerability of African Americans in a hostile society?

🏛 **Smithsonian American Art Museum Washington, D.C.**

William H. Johnson grew up in South Carolina, left for New York at age 17, and studied art in Paris. He traveled throughout Europe and North Africa with his Danish wife before returning to New York, where he spent most of the rest of his life. There, he developed his distinctive style, using a limited number of colors applied to a flat surface such as plywood. Like many artists, Johnson brought his own life experiences into his art. From his studio in New York, Johnson recalled life in the South from his childhood, which he depicted in paintings and in works on paper. After his death in 1970, more than 1,000 of Johnson's paintings and drawings were discovered by friends. His work is now housed in the Smithsonian American Art Museum.

DOCUMENT ONE

Primary Source: Newspaper Editorial
from "Mrs. Ida Wells-Barnett Calls on President McKinley," by Ida B. Wells-Barnett, 1898

Ida B. Wells-Barnett, an African-American journalist, wrote extensively about lynching. She traveled to England to speak about the topic and formed anti-lynching societies. Wells-Barnett devoted particular attention to the topic after mobs lynched three of her friends.

CONSTRUCTED RESPONSE How does Wells-Barnett characterize lynching in the United States?

For nearly twenty years lynching crimes . . . have been committed and permitted by this Christian nation. Nowhere in the civilized world save the United States of America do men . . . go out in bands of 50 and 5,000 to hunt down, shoot, hang or burn to death a single individual. Statistics show that nearly 10,000 American citizens have been lynched in the past twenty years. To our appeals for justice the stereotyped reply has been that the governor could not interfere in a state matter. We refuse to believe this country, so powerful to defend its citizens abroad, is unable to protect its citizens at home.

DOCUMENT TWO

Primary Source: Document
from "Platform Adopted by the National Negro Committee," 1909

In response to racial violence, William English Walling and others, mostly whites, formed the National Negro Committee, which eventually became the NAACP. Written by the committee, the platform's signers include Ida B. Wells-Barnett and Jane Addams. This document emphasized that violence benefits no one.

CONSTRUCTED RESPONSE According to the statement, who is affected by violence against African Americans?

The systematic persecution of law-abiding citizens . . . on account of their race alone is a crime that will ultimately drag down to an infamous end any nation that allows it . . . and it bears most heavily on those poor white farmers and laborers whose economic position is most similar to that of the persecuted race. Indeed persecution of organized workers, peonage, [and] enslavement of prisoners . . . already threaten large bodies of whites in many southern States.

DOCUMENT THREE

Secondary Source: Newspaper Article
from *Fort Worth Star-Telegram*, by Tim Madigan, 2011

In July 1910, a white mob, emboldened by rumors, randomly attacked African-American residents of Slocum, Texas. Anywhere from 20 to 200 people were killed. Newspaper accounts of the massacre were conflicting, and most articles falsely reported that it was begun by armed African Americans. Not until 2011 did the town officially acknowledge the massacre. This newspaper article relates what is known of the killings 100 years after they happened.

CONSTRUCTED RESPONSE What important information does this source provide about the 1910 events in Slocum?

Some initial newspaper accounts erroneously reported that whites had also been killed, describing the Slocum incident as a race riot. But Slocum was no riot. "Men were going about killing Negroes as fast as they could find them, and, so far as I was able to ascertain, without any real cause," Anderson County Sheriff W.H. Black, a white from nearby Palestine, was quoted as saying. Seven white men were indicted on murder charges and had their cases transferred to Houston on a change of venue. But none ever came to trial.

SYNTHESIZE & WRITE

1. **REVIEW** Review what you have learned about racial violence from the passages and the painting.

2. **RECALL** On your own paper, write down some of the different reactions American citizens had to racial violence in the late 19th and early 20th centuries, as demonstrated in the passages.

3. **CONSTRUCT** Construct a topic sentence to answer this question: In what ways did African-American journalists and activists reveal the extent of racial violence?

4. **WRITE** Write an informative paragraph supporting your topic sentence in Step 3 by using evidence from the passages, the art, and the chapter.

15 REVIEW

VOCABULARY

Write a paragraph using each key vocabulary term from the chapter listed below in a way that conveys its importance. A sample beginning sentence is provided for the first term.

1. push-pull factors
    Lack of opportunity in their home countries and opportunities in the United States were push-pull factors for immigrants.

2. muckraker

3. tenement

4. sanitation

5. propaganda

6. progressivism

READING STRATEGY
IDENTIFY PROBLEMS AND SOLUTIONS

Identifying problems faced by individuals and nations and tracking their solutions can help readers understand the way history unfolds. Complete the Problem-and-Solution Chart to analyze several problems the United States faced as it continued to industrialize and solutions to those problems. Then answer the question.

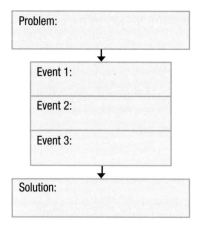

7. Describe one problem the United States faced as industrialization grew, beginning in the 1890s. Then list events that led to a solution.

MAIN IDEAS

Answer the following questions. Support your answers with evidence from the chapter.

8. How did expansion of the railroad industry help the steel industry grow? **LESSON 1.1**

9. Why are Alexander Graham Bell and Thomas Edison considered significant inventors of the late 19th century? **LESSON 1.3**

10. Why did states provide workers' compensation? **LESSON 2.1**

11. Why did workers resume forming labor unions in the late 1800s? **LESSON 2.2**

12. What was unique about the American Railway Union's structure? **LESSON 2.3**

13. What did the Americanization movement hope to accomplish? **LESSON 3.1**

14. Why did nativists oppose immigration? **LESSON 3.3**

15. Why were fires and diseases especially deadly in large cities such as Chicago and New York? **LESSON 4.2**

16. Why did many white southerners react the way they did to Reconstruction reforms after Reconstruction ended? **LESSON 4.3**

HISTORICAL THINKING

Answer the following questions. Support your answers with evidence from the chapter.

17. **ANALYZE CAUSE AND EFFECT** What part did greed play in the growth of industry?

18. **EVALUATE** In what ways did the late 19th and early 20th centuries represent both advancement and turmoil for African Americans?

19. **SYNTHESIZE** How did writers in the late 19th and early 20th centuries help expose injustices in society, and why was it important?

20. **IDENTIFY PROBLEMS AND SOLUTIONS** What problems did progressive reformers seek to solve?

21. **DRAW CONCLUSIONS** How did Jim Crow laws and "separate but equal" treatment impact economic mobility and opportunity for African Americans?

22. **FORM AND SUPPORT OPINIONS** What were positive effects of industrialization on living and working conditions? Support your opinion using evidence from the chapter.

INTERPRET GRAPHS

Look carefully at the graph showing causes of death on the job for workers at steel mills in one Pennsylvania county. Then answer the questions that follow.

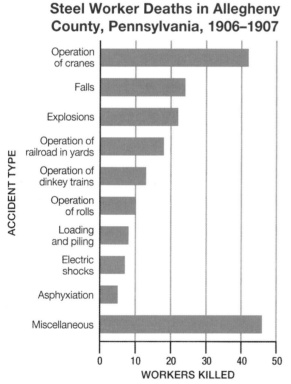

Steel Worker Deaths in Allegheny County, Pennsylvania, 1906–1907

Source: Crystal Eastman, *Work-Accidents and the Law: The Pittsburgh Survey*, 1916

23. How many workers were killed by various causes not specified in the graph?

24. How do the numbers of deaths from operating different types of equipment, such as cranes, the railroad in yards, dinkey trains, and rolls, compare?

25. What were the causes of the third and fourth highest numbers of deaths?

ANALYZE SOURCES

In 1900, writer and journalist Theodore Dreiser published *Sister Carrie*, a novel about a young woman who moves from rural Wisconsin to Chicago. In this scene, the narrator describes Carrie's visit to a department store, a new kind of consumer experience that arose in the late 1800s.

> Carrie passed along the busy aisles, much affected by the remarkable displays of trinkets, dress goods, stationery, and jewelry. Each separate counter was a show place of dazzling interest and attraction. She could not help feeling the claim of each trinket and valuable upon her personally, and yet she did not stop. There was nothing there which she could not have used—nothing which she did not long to own.

26. What was the effect of the department store on Carrie?

CONNECT TO YOUR LIFE

27. **ARGUMENT** This chapter discusses the rise of cities and some of the benefits and drawbacks of city life. Is solving the problems of cities worthwhile, or should people just move out of cities? Write an argument supporting your position.

TIPS

• Reread the chapter, listing the advantages and disadvantages of urban living.

• Look over your lists and add your own thoughts and experiences to them.

• Decide on a position to take. Then choose two or three of your strongest pros or cons to develop and support your argument.

• Include two or three vocabulary terms from the chapter in your argument.

• Address any opposing views you identify. Use your list to help in choosing an opposing view to challenge.

• Conclude with a summary that explains your arguments clearly and directly.

HISTORICAL THINKING What reforms and expansion took place during the Progressive Era?

AMERICAN STORIES | The Triangle Waist Company Factory Fire

SECTION 1 **Progressivism**

SECTION 2 **Progressive Administrations**

SECTION 3 **America in the Age of Empire**

AMERICAN GALLERY ONLINE | **New York City at the Turn of the Century**

At the same time Americans were working to solve social, economic, and political problems at home, the United States was expanding its overseas territories. The island chain of Hawaii, where American companies operated pineapple plantations like the one pictured here, became a U.S. territory in 1900.

"A great democracy has got to be progressive, or it will soon **cease to be either great or a democracy.**"

—President Theodore Roosevelt

THE TRIANGLE WAIST COMPANY

FACTORY FIRE

March 25, 1911, was a normal day for the 500 workers at the Triangle Waist Company, a factory located on the 8th, 9th, and 10th floors of the Asch Building in New York City. That is to say, the workers, most of them immigrant women between the ages of 16 and 23, had put in several grueling hours sewing shirtwaists—a type of women's blouse—for a pay rate that came to around $15 for a week of 12-hour days.

In 1909, the Ladies Garment Workers Union had led a strike against New York clothing manufacturers. Their demands had included higher pay, shorter hours, and safer working conditions. Most of the smaller factories quickly agreed to the union's demands, but Isaac Harris and Max Blanck, the owners of the Triangle factory, resisted. Instead, they joined a group of manufacturers who fought back with dirty tactics, including paying police officers to beat or intimidate the striking workers. Eventually, Harris and Blanck relented, offering their employees higher wages and shorter working hours but refusing to allow them to unionize. Despite these improvements, work at the Triangle Waist Company was still exhausting, unsafe, and poorly paid. The factory remained a sweatshop with working conditions just as harsh as that name implies.

Around 4:40 p.m. on March 25, 1911, Isidore Abramowitz was preparing to go home from his job cutting fabric on the eighth floor, when he spotted sparks in a bin used for discarded scraps of fabric. At once, he seized one of the buckets of water placed throughout the factory in case of fires and dumped it on the flames. Abramowitz's fellow cutters rushed to throw water from other buckets onto the fire, but the workers were in a gigantic room filled with long wooden tables and piles of fabric scraps. They were surrounded by extremely flammable materials.

Within moments, the fire was out of control, and panicked employees were struggling toward the exits. Sylvia Kimeldorf, an 18-year-old who was working on the eighth floor that day, recalled, "The place was filling up with heavy black smoke, and we were all choking."

Limited firefighting technology, including short ladders and poor water pressure, made battling the Triangle factory fire and rescuing factory workers a serious challenge for firefighters.

MAURR I BLUM

CLOTHING SPECIALTIES

23-29

HARRIS BROS MFRS OF MENS CLOTHING

BERNSTEIN & MEYERS CLOAKS AND SUITS

n 1909, a fire insurance inspector recommended that Triangle factory owners keep the building's doors unlocked during the day and conduct fire drills with factory workers. Harris and Blanck did not follow through on either request. As a result, when Ladder Company 20 arrived on the scene of the horrific fire here two years later, there was little they could do

Fabric scraps provided fuel for what one fire captain called "a mass of traveling fire." Staircases were too few in number, and the fire escape didn't reach the ground. Short ladders and poor water pressure made putting out the fire and rescuing workers nearly impossible. All firefighters could do was mist the outside of the building.

The Asch Building had stairways and elevators located on the northeast and southwest corners, but the northeast corner was almost instantly consumed by flames. On the eighth and ninth floors, workers rushed for the stairway doors on the southwest side of the building but found them locked. It was company policy to lock the doors during working hours to prevent workers from stealing supplies or taking unauthorized breaks. On the eighth floor, one employee had a key, and most of the workers on that floor were able to escape.

Workers on the 10th floor managed to take the stairs up to the building's roof, from which they were rescued by a group of students at the neighboring New York University School of Law building, who placed ladders between the rooftops. Factory owners Isaac Harris and Max Blanck were able to escape the fire in this way. But for workers on the ninth floor, there was no escape via the staircases. They were unable to unlock or force the doors open, so their only hopes for survival were the southwest elevators or the fire escape.

Elevator operators Joseph Zito and Gaspar Mortillalo saved as many people as they could, making several trips to the burning floors before conditions became unbearable. Later, bodies of workers who had tried to escape down the elevator shaft but had fallen to their deaths were found piled on top of the elevators. A few people did survive the breakneck trip down the elevator shaft by gripping the cables. One of them, Sam Levine, recalled, "I can remember getting to the sixth floor. While on my way down, as slow as I could let myself drop, the bodies of six girls went falling past me."

The metal fire escape ladder on the outside of the building was not sufficiently strong to support the weight of the fleeing crowd, and it was further weakened by the fierce heat of the fire. Some workers were able to descend the fire escape to the sixth floor before the fragile ladder crashed to the ground. Nellie Ventura was one of those survivors. "At first I was too frightened to try to run through the fire," she recalled. "Then I heard the screams of the girls inside. I knew I had to go down the ladder or die where I was."

THE TRIANGLE FACTORY FLOOR

This diagram shows how the ninth floor of the Asch Building was laid out. The fire blocked access to the stairs and freight elevators on the Greene Street side of the building. Look at the spacing of the long tables and the location of the passenger elevators on the Washington Place side. One survivor described the space between the rows as "narrow and blocked by chairs and baskets." Other sources indicate that the stairs in the stairwells were 33 inches wide and the stairs of the fire escape were 17½ inches wide. In addition to the locked stairway door, what difficulties did the workers face in trying to escape the fire?

WHAT IS A SHIRTWAIST?

It is ironic that the shirtwaist, produced in sweatshops by an underpaid, mainly female workforce, was a symbol of social progress and women's growing empowerment. Popular in the late 19th and early 20th centuries, the shirtwaist was a style of blouse for women, featuring buttons down the front and modeled after men's shirts.

Practical and relatively comfortable, shirtwaists came to symbolize the modern working woman who earned her own wages and thus was not fully dependent on a man to support her. Women wearing shirtwaists as they demonstrated in the streets were the backbone of the women's movement around the turn of the 20th century.

As it gained in popularity, the shirtwaist also had a democratizing effect on fashion. Because the blouses were available in a range of prices, from 25 cents to 7 dollars, they were worn by women from every economic level, from salesclerks to wealthy socialites. According to the *Gimbel Brothers Illustrated 1915 Catalog*, "the women of other lands occasionally wear a shirtwaist—the American woman occasionally wears something else. Her daily apparel is a smart tailored skirt and neat blouse."

CRITICAL VIEWING What can you infer about women's fashions during the early part of the 1900s based on this 1905 shirtwaist and 1901 advertisement?

CRITICAL VIEWING The Triangle factory fire caused extensive damage. What can you infer about the intensity of the fire from this photo?

CRITICAL VIEWING The bodies of the Triangle factory workers who did not survive the fire were taken to the New York City morgue to be identified by their loved ones. What does this photo reveal about the impact the fire had on New Yorkers?

Meanwhile, on the ground, the New York City fire department was trying desperately to quell the blaze, but the department's ladders reached only as high as the sixth floor of the Asch Building. Firefighters and onlookers watched helplessly as young women, trapped and in danger of burning to death, leapt from the factory windows.

Some firefighters tried to deploy safety nets to catch the falling workers, but all those who jumped died on impact. Sylvia Kimeldorf, who had managed to escape by the stairs, remembered reaching the ground floor of the building and being held back by firefighters: "The bodies were falling all around us and they were afraid to let us go out because we would be killed by the falling bodies." Within 40 minutes, all three floors of the Triangle factory had been destroyed by the blaze, and 146 workers were dead. Even seasoned police officers were appalled by the grim scene. "It's the worst thing I ever saw," one older officer told the *New York Times* that night.

Could the Triangle factory fire have been prevented, or could it at least have resulted in fewer fatalities? In the aftermath, angry New Yorkers and factory workers believed so. Outraged crowds took to the streets to protest dangerous factory working conditions. On April 5, 1911, a mourning parade of more than 100,000 factory workers marched along one of New York City's main streets as 300,000 spectators turned out to witness the event.

CRITICAL VIEWING This household sewing machine from around 1900 didn't run on electricity. The user "powered" it by turning the crank to make the needle move up and down. What do you notice about the craftsmanship of this machine?

SEWING MACHINES AT HOME AND AT WORK

The sewing machine is arguably one of the most influential American inventions in both the industrial and domestic domains. Before the sewing machine, garments were mostly stitched by women working at home. In New York City in 1850, around 5,000 women were employed hand-stitching shirts in their homes for very little pay. Beginning in the late 1800s, industrial sewing machines allowed entrepreneurs to hire women to work in factories, turning out clothing much more quickly and cheaply. Some sources touted the benefits of the new invention for "sewing girls," but as the Triangle story illustrates, the move from home to factory did not necessarily improve the situation for poor, immigrant working women.

In middle-class and wealthier homes, the sewing machine helped support the "cult of domesticity," the idea that a woman's home was her particular sphere of influence. In the words of an 1860 *New York Times* article, the sewing machine had "stitched its way onward as an agent of domestic economy." By acquiring a sewing machine—and perhaps a sewing room—a woman proved that she could master relatively complex machinery and produce and mend clothing for the family. Believers in the cult of domesticity conveniently overlooked the fact that the men in the home were usually in charge of the finances, and thus the decision to purchase a sewing machine.

Later that year, the New York state legislature formed a commission, which included union leader Samuel Gompers, to investigate ways to prevent disastrous workplace fires in the future. In 1912, the commission issued the first of a series of reports that resulted in numerous changes to health and safety laws in New York. Buildings were required to have fire alarms, fire extinguishers, well-built fire escapes, and sprinkler systems on higher floors. In addition, it became illegal to lock fire exits during working hours or to block stairways. Many of these laws were adopted in other states as well. Future

Secretary of Labor Frances Perkins had been in New York on March 25, 1911, and had watched the tragedy unfold with gruesome swiftness. "Something must be done," she said, encapsulating the country's mood. "We've got to turn this into some kind of victory, some kind of constructive action."

THINK ABOUT IT

Do you think a workplace disaster like the Triangle factory fire could happen in the United States today? Why or why not?

An unlikely trio, a young garment worker, mink brigade member and social activist Flora Dodge LaFollette, and social reformer and missionary Rose Livingston (from left to right), march together during a 1913 strike of New York City garment workers.

THE MINK BRIGADE

When female garment workers went on strike in 1909, prior to the Triangle factory fire, they garnered unlikely allies in wealthy, prominent women. Anne Morgan, daughter of the powerful financier J.P. Morgan, had never needed to earn a living—much less toil at a sewing machine for 12 hours a day. Still, she and her friends were moved by the plight of the young immigrant sweatshop workers. Morgan recruited other upper-class women, including social activist Flora Dodge LaFollette, to come to the workers' defense. The "mink brigade," as the women were

mockingly called because of their extravagant furs, walked the picket lines, feeling less likely to be attacked due to their social status. The mink brigade also defended striking workers who had been arrested and paid their fines.

Women like Anne Morgan and Flora Dodge LaFollette engaged in other philanthropic projects and worked to advance women's rights. In a statement in 1927, Morgan pictured a time when women "will take their places beside men as partners, unafraid, useful, successful, and free." To what extent do you think this vision has been realized in the 21st century?

MODERN-DAY TRIANGLES

In the 21st century, factory disasters in China, India, and Bangladesh have served as disturbing modern-day reminders of the Triangle factory fire. Bangladesh has become a world leader in garment manufacturing. The country's more than 5,000 factories, staffed with a largely female workforce, produce clothing for major international brands.

In November 2012, more than 100 people died in a fire at the Tazreen Fashions factory outside Dhaka, the capital of Bangladesh. The problems in the Tazreen factory—and other factories in Bangladesh—resembled those in the Triangle Waist Company factory: insufficient fire escapes, blocked exits, and poor safety measures. Then, in April 2013, the Rana Plaza building, in Savar, which is northwest of Dhaka, collapsed.

Rana Plaza had housed several garment factories. More than 1,100 workers were killed and 2,500 more injured in the catastrophe. The ensuing investigation revealed that the top four floors of the building had been built illegally, with no permits issued, and that the foundation was poorly constructed.

The disasters sparked a public outcry against the factory owners, the international brands that contracted the factories to make their garments, and the Bangladeshi government. Activists demanded improved safety measures and working conditions in the country's garment factories. The case of the Rana Plaza collapse resulted in criminal charges against the owners of the building and the factories housed inside. In addition to building code violations, charges in the case included murder.

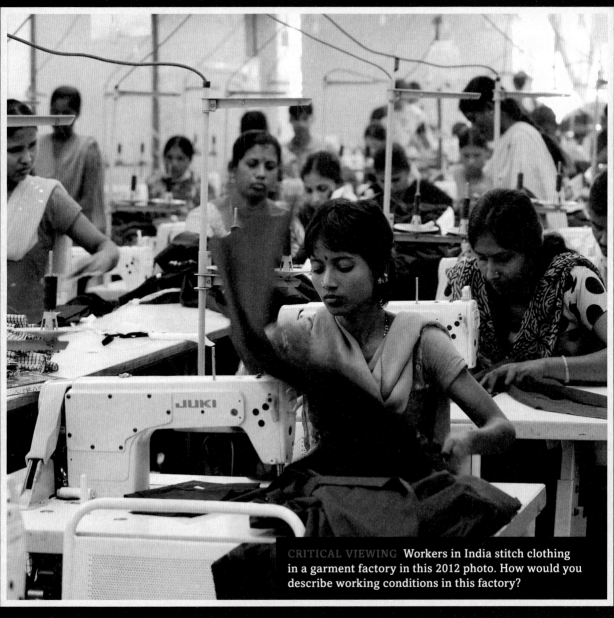

CRITICAL VIEWING Workers in India stitch clothing in a garment factory in this 2012 photo. How would you describe working conditions in this factory?

THE ROOTS OF PROGRESSIVISM

At the dawn of the 20th century, children as young as eight years of age helped support their families by working in dusty mines sorting coal. This situation was one of many that reformers at the time wanted to change.

GOALS OF PROGRESSIVISM

As you have read, the United States had quickly become more industrialized and urbanized after the Civil War, and its immigrant population had grown dramatically. These changes brought new social and economic problems that reformers pressured the government to address. The push for reform reached a peak during the **Progressive Era**, a period from about 1890 to 1920 in which reformers sought to correct many social, economic, and political inequalities and injustices in the United States. The era brought sweeping changes that had a lasting impact on American society. In fact, many laws, policies, and ideas that shape life in the United States today trace back to this period.

The Progressive Era featured numerous reform campaigns led by progressive-minded people who were primarily white, middle class, Protestant, and college educated. The various campaigns often shared the same general aims of helping the disadvantaged and making the United States a more equitable and democratic country. One of the progressives' major goals was to end the widespread corruption of political bosses and government officials. Progressives wanted government at all levels to be honest and more open, efficient, democratic, and responsive. The people, they felt, should have a stronger and more direct role in electing officials and creating laws.

Many progressives also sought reforms in business and labor. Rejecting the laissez-faire, or hands-off, approach to economic affairs that had prevailed previously, they called for the government to regulate business practices and to break up monopolies and trusts. They hoped to end child labor and bring about improved working conditions, higher pay, and better benefits for all workers, including immigrants.

Theodore Roosevelt was an avid horseback rider throughout much of his life. In this photo from 1902, Roosevelt jumps a horse over a fence on a friend's farm near Washington, D.C.

Women played a major role during the Progressive Era and fought for an equal voice in government. At the time, only a few states allowed women to vote in elections. Progressives sought an amendment to the U.S. Constitution guaranteeing women's suffrage.

SPREADING PROGRESSIVISM

Progressivism arose in response to a multitude of problems. These included poverty, the spread of urban slums, poor working conditions in factories and mines, corruption in government, and the power of large corporations over the economy and government. These problems gained the attention of most Americans through **exposés**, writings that publicize a scandal or injustice. You have read about Upton Sinclair and his book *The Jungle,* which exposed the horrors of working in the meatpacking industry. You have also read about Ida Tarbell and her exposé of Rockefeller's Standard Oil Company. Sinclair and Tarbell were just two of the many muckrakers who helped bring the nation's social ills to wide public attention.

Helen Hunt Jackson, who had achieved fame as a poet and novelist, became a fierce advocate for the rights of Native Americans. In her nonfiction book *A Century of Dishonor,* published in 1881, Jackson condemned the federal government and white settlers for their shameful and often brutal treatment of Native Americans. Her popular 1884 novel *Ramona* called attention to the struggles of Native Americans living on missions in the Southwest.

Journalist and photographer **Jacob Riis** drew public attention to the crime, disease, and squalor in New York City's slums, which he had experienced firsthand as a struggling immigrant and a police beat reporter. His influential book *How the Other Half Lives,* published in 1890, jolted readers with stark photographs, unsparing descriptions, and shocking statistics. The book helped bring about laws regulating tenements, and it strongly influenced then president-to-be Theodore Roosevelt.

Joseph Mayer Rice, a physician by training, became a leader in a movement to reform education. From 1891 to 1897, he authored a series of articles that appeared in a journal called *The Forum.* Rice's articles shocked Americans by revealing poor teaching methods, low achievement, and unhealthy conditions in the nation's public schools.

In his 1902 magazine article "Tweed Days in St. Louis," muckraker **Lincoln Steffens** revealed the destructive effect of corruption on the government of St. Louis, Missouri, then one of the country's largest cities. The popularity of that article led Steffens to report on the troublesome relationship between business and government in five other major cities. His articles were collected and published in 1904 in a book called *The Shame of the Cities.* They made a powerful impression on the American public.

The Lithuanian-born political activist and anarchist **Emma Goldman** spoke out in her writings and lectures for the rights of workers and the empowerment of women. When World War I erupted, she fought strongly against U.S. involvement in the

SOCIAL GOSPEL AND FUNDAMENTALISM

Two distinct religious movements, Social Gospel and fundamentalism, took root during the Progressive Era. Social Gospel was based on Christian liberal theology, fundamentalism on a literal interpretation of the Bible. Two leading fundamentalists of the time were **Dwight L. Moody** and **Billy Sunday**. A former shoe salesman, Moody began preaching in the mid-1800s and devoted his life to winning souls and educating impoverished children in Chicago. Sunday left professional baseball to travel the country preaching against alcoholic beverages, declaring, "Whiskey and beer are all right in their place, but their place is in hell." Fundamentalists and followers of Social Gospel alike opposed the teachings of such Social Darwinists as William Graham Sumner, who portrayed the results of dire poverty as a natural mechanism to weed out the "unfit" in society.

war and against military conscription, in which the government requires men to enlist and serve in the armed forces. As a result of her antiwar activism, she was arrested and convicted of conspiracy against the conscription law. She spent two years in prison. After her release, she was deported to her home country.

The progressive movement coincided with and was strongly influenced by a religious movement known as **Social Gospel**, which originated around 1870 among Protestant ministers who sought to apply Christian liberal theology to societal problems. This theology emphasized helping others by following the moral and ethical example of Jesus. Like Social Darwinism, Social Gospel addressed the poverty in urban, industrial society. However, followers of Social Gospel rejected the tenet of Social Darwinism that people are engaged in a struggle for existence in which only the strong survive. In contrast, they believed that by creating a kinder and more equitable society, they could help build the kingdom of God on Earth. They worked for such reforms as an end to child labor, a living wage for workers, a shorter workday, and safer working conditions.

HISTORICAL THINKING

1. **READING CHECK** What were the goals of progressivism?

2. **ANALYZE CAUSE AND EFFECT** How did journalists help spread progressivism?

3. **COMPARE AND CONTRAST** How do the teachings of Social Gospel conflict with the theory of Social Darwinism?

WOMEN FIGHT FOR RIGHTS

When the Progressive Era began, the campaign to allow women to vote was about a half century old. How much longer would women have to fight before they gained something as basic as the right to cast a ballot?

MIDWEST LEADERS

In the early 20th century, American society still strongly restricted the roles of women. Women could not vote or hold office in most states, and many companies barred women from working in certain professions. For decades, American women had been working in support of social reforms, even as they began to demand that their own rights be expanded to include all the rights and responsibilities of citizenship. Women were the foot soldiers of progressive reform.

One of the best known foot soldiers was Jane Addams. As you have read, she founded Hull House in Chicago, one of the most famous settlement houses in the nation. Hull House provided many resources and services to struggling immigrants. Addams also fought for such progressive causes as workers' rights, women's suffrage, or women's right to vote, and the regulation of tenements. She helped bring about the first juvenile law court, and she played a role in the founding of the **American Civil Liberties Union (ACLU)**, an organization that fights to this day for the constitutional rights of all citizens.

Hull House became a magnet for bright, ambitious women who were dedicated to social work and reform. One such women was **Florence Kelley**. While residing at the settlement house, she investigated sweatshops and tenement conditions and conducted a thorough survey of Chicago's 19th Ward, a political district in the city. Her reports on the appalling conditions she observed helped bring about an Illinois law that banned child labor, limited working hours for women, and established regulations for sweatshops. Kelley's reports earned her an appointment as the state's chief factory inspector.

In 1899, Kelley moved to New York City to become the general secretary of the newly created **National Consumers League**, an organization dedicated to defending the rights of consumers and workers. For the next 30 years, she led the league's fight for a minimum wage law for women, protection of in-home workers from exploitation, and restrictions on child labor.

Another social reformer drawn to Hull House was **Julia Lathrop**, who arrived in 1890. Lathrop worked to improve the lives of children, the disabled, and the mentally ill. In 1893, after becoming the first female member of the Illinois Board of Charities, Lathrop set out to inspect all of the state's poorhouses and "poor farms." These facilities housed, at state expense, people who could not support themselves, which included the mentally ill, physically ill, disabled, and aged—all mixed together. The inspections led her to push for separate facilities for the mentally ill. In 1912, President Taft appointed Lathrop as the first head of the **Children's Bureau**, the first federal agency dedicated to improving the lives of children and families. Lathrop worked to address the issues of child labor, infant and maternal mortality, juvenile delinquency, and the treatment of the mentally ill.

WEST COAST REFORMERS

On the West Coast, in San Francisco, women were working to solve other kinds of problems. The Chinese Exclusion Act of 1882 banned the immigration of Chinese laborers. As a result, Chinese men who had emigrated before the ban were cut off from their wives and families. Secret criminal societies called *tongs* arose in San Francisco's Chinatown, as well as in Chinese neighborhoods in other cities, to bring Chinese women to the United States. The tongs

🏛 Jane Addams Hull-House Museum, Chicago

Jane Addams appears with children at Hull House, the settlement house she established, in this photo from the collection of the Jane Addams Hull-House Museum. By 1907, Hull House consisted of 13 buildings occupying an entire block in Chicago. The museum is housed in one of the two original Hull House buildings.

kidnapped women and girls from China, smuggled them into California, and sold them as slaves to men or to brothels, or houses of prostitution. **Margaret Culbertson**, superintendent of the Occidental Mission Home for Girls, a Chinatown settlement house, was fearless in her efforts to rescue these women and girls. Once safe at the mission house, they received shelter, food, clothing, education, and security.

When Culbertson became too ill to continue her rescues, her assistant, **Donaldina Mackenzie Cameron**, took over. In the nearly 4 decades that she served as superintendent, Cameron rescued more than 3,000 women and girls from slavery, daring to run across rooftops and break down doors to carry out her work. The tongs hated and feared her, but those she rescued and sheltered called her *Lo Mo*, or "Beloved Mother."

COMBINING FORCES

In 1890, two competing women's rights organizations merged to form the **National American Woman Suffrage Association (NAWSA)**. Elizabeth Cady Stanton and Susan B. Anthony, pioneers in the women's suffrage movement, served as the new organization's first presidents. When Anthony retired in 1900, the presidency went to **Carrie Chapman Catt**, who stated that the enfranchisement of women would be the crowning glory of democracy. **Enfranchisement** is the act of granting full citizenship, including the right to vote. The right to vote is also referred to as the **franchise**.

For several decades, the strategy of suffragists, or people seeking the franchise for women, had been to push for a national constitutional amendment guaranteeing women the right to vote. By 1910, however, the movement had stalled. Southern Democrats in Congress opposed women's suffrage for fear it would include the enfranchisement of African-American women. In addition, companies that manufactured liquor worried that women's suffrage would strengthen the movement to prohibit the sale of alcohol. Faced with those roadblocks, suffragists began focusing their efforts at the state level. The result was a string of victories in western

CRITICAL VIEWING This print from 1874 depicts the actions of reformers who wanted to end the sale and consumption of alcohol. Why might the reformers' actions have been considered controversial?

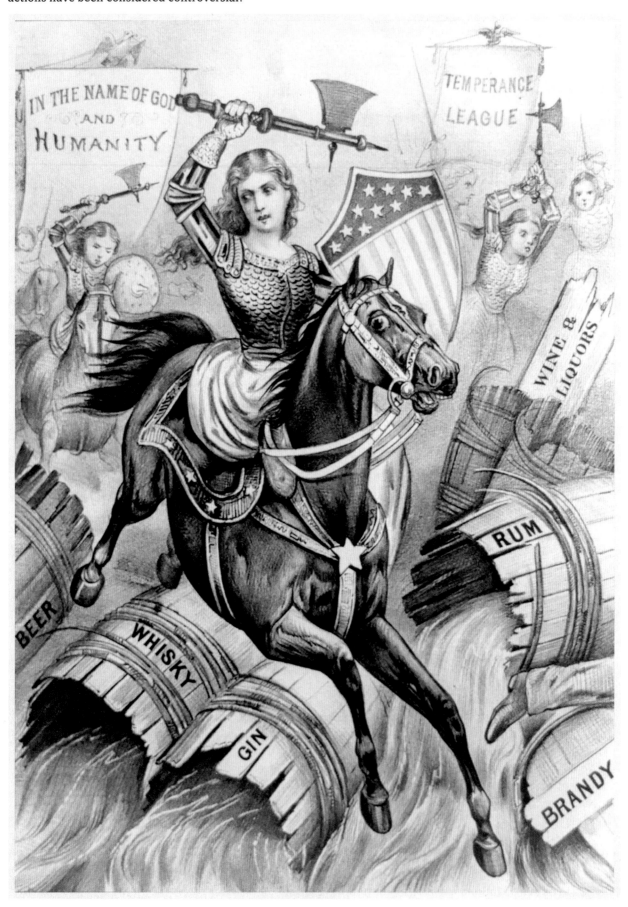

states as well as several eastern states. Some of the victories were only partial—that is, women were granted the right to vote only in certain elections—but others fully enfranchised women. In California, women gained full voting rights in 1911.

Another important figure in the suffrage movement was **Alice Paul**, who led its radical wing. She had fought for the vote in England and now wanted to apply aggressive tactics, such as marches and protests, in the United States. Other women joined her, including Harriot Stanton Blatch, who was the daughter of Elizabeth Cady Stanton.

For a few years, Paul and her allies worked on NAWSA's congressional committee. NAWSA stressed that female voting would result in purer and more honest politics. The organization also played down the argument that women should have equal political rights. Instead, it argued that suffrage would offset the votes of immigrants and racial minorities in large cities. Thus, suffragists would be protecting traditional values against "alien" assaults. Frustrated with NAWSA's cautious tactics, Paul left the organization in 1913. Along with **Lucy Burns**, the suffragist known for spending the most time in jail for the cause, she formed the Congressional Union for Woman Suffrage.

In 1916, the Congressional Union for Woman Suffrage reorganized itself as a single-issue political party and adopted a new name: the **National Woman's Party (NWP)**. Although the NAWSA and the NWP were fighting for the same cause, their strategies could not have been more different. While the NAWSA continued to rely on lobbying, petition gathering, and state-level campaigns, the NWP opted for direct action. Its members staged marches, picketed the White House, went on hunger strikes, and committed acts of civil disobedience. The effort to win the vote for women would take several more years and a war to bring about victory.

THE PROHIBITION MOVEMENT

Women also took the lead in reviving the temperance movement, which had first emerged in the early 1800s and encouraged people to temper, or moderate, their consumption of alcohol, or to abstain from alcohol altogether. Temperance reformers pointed out that although men did much of the drinking, alcohol-related problems often hit women and children hardest. Some men, they argued, spent money on alcohol that could be used to provide for the needs of their families. Excessive alcohol consumption, reformers believed, often caused men

to become abusive, abandon or neglect their families, turn to crime, or fall into poverty and homelessness.

The Anti-Saloon League, founded in 1893, became one of the leading national organizations in the crusade against alcohol. Through propaganda and educational materials that often focused on women, children, and families, the league developed a strong base, especially among devout Protestant Christians. Promoting the idea of **prohibition**, the league pressured local and state governments to create laws restricting or prohibiting the production, sale, and consumption of alcohol. Oklahoma was the first state to adopt prohibition in 1907, and by 1914, eight other states had done the same. Militant prohibitionists, however, were discouraged by the state-by-state approach. The Anti-Saloon League set its sights on a bigger goal: a constitutional amendment to ban the sale of alcohol in the United States.

HISTORICAL THINKING

1. **READING CHECK** What reforms did Florence Kelley help bring about?

2. **FORM AND SUPPORT OPINIONS** What is your opinion of the NAWSA's claim that granting women the right to vote would offset the votes of immigrants and racial minorities? Give reasons for your opinion.

3. **COMPARE AND CONTRAST** How did the strategies of the NAWSA and the NWP differ?

4. **IDENTIFY PROBLEMS AND SOLUTIONS** What social problems did leaders in the temperance movement work to solve?

FOR OR AGAINST WOMEN'S SUFFRAGE?

From its beginnings in the 1840s to the start of the Progressive Era in the 1890s, the women's suffrage movement grew dramatically. Nevertheless, many Americans remained firmly opposed to the idea of extending the franchise to women. For every argument offered by suffragists, the anti-suffragists had a counterargument.

On November 2, 1915, voters in Massachusetts and New York—meaning men—cast ballots on whether to amend their state constitutions to grant the vote to women. The pennant shown below was part of the New York publicity campaign. In both states, the outcome was *No*: by a narrow margin of 175,000 votes in New York, but by 2 to 1 in Massachusetts. In another referendum 2 years later, voters in New York finally granted the franchise to women, becoming the 16th state to do so. Massachusetts women did not obtain the right to vote until the 19th Amendment was ratified in 1920.

CRITICAL VIEWING In 1910, this cartoon showing a male protester being arrested by two female police officers appeared on a *Life* magazine cover. Do you think this cartoon is satirical, or making fun of the idea of men's rights, or is it presenting that idea as a legitimate issue? What message does the cartoon convey about women's right to vote?

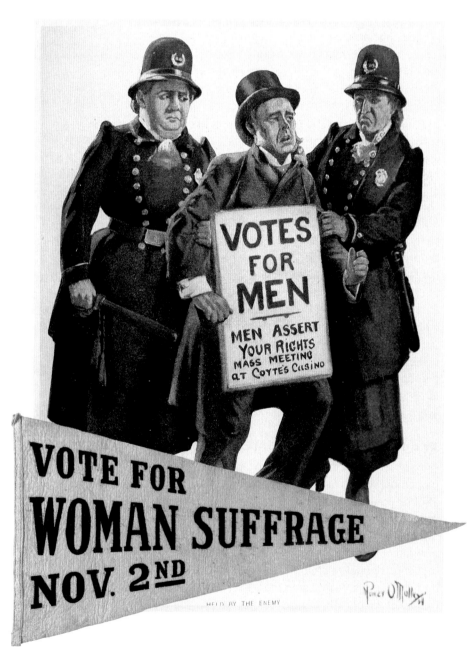

558 CHAPTER 16

Primary Source: Leaflet
from "Twelve Reasons Why Women Should Vote," by the
National American Woman Suffrage Association, 1918

NAWSA produced posters, booklets, leaflets, and
other printed materials that presented arguments in
favor of women's suffrage. Local suffrage groups often
purchased large quantities of the reading materials for
rallies and women's suffrage campaigns.

CONSTRUCTED RESPONSE
Which of the 12 reasons do you think would have had
the strongest impact on readers, and why?

Twelve Reasons
Why Women Should Vote

1. BECAUSE those who obey the laws should help
   to choose those who make the laws.
2. BECAUSE laws affect women as much as men.
3. BECAUSE laws which affect WOMEN are now
   passed without consulting them.
4. BECAUSE laws affecting CHILDREN should
   include the woman's point of view as well as
   the man's.
5. BECAUSE laws affecting the HOME are voted on
   in every session of the Legislature.
6. BECAUSE women have experience which would
   be helpful to legislation.
7. BECAUSE to deprive women of the vote is to
   lower their position in common estimation.
8. BECAUSE having the vote would increase the
   sense of responsibility among women toward
   questions of public importance.
9. BECAUSE public spirited mothers make public
   spirited sons.
10. BECAUSE millions of women in the United States
    have become wage workers and the conditions
    under which they work are controlled by law.
11. BECAUSE the objections against their having the
    vote are based on prejudice, not on reason.
12. BECAUSE to sum up all reasons in one—IT IS
    FOR THE COMMON GOOD OF ALL.

Primary Source: Pamphlet
from "Vote NO on Woman Suffrage," by the National
Association Opposed to Woman Suffrage, c. 1915

As the women's suffrage movement gained strength,
opposition groups, such as the NAOWS, sprang up.
They often directed their messages at women. The
anti-suffrage arguments below appeared on the back of
a pamphlet offering household tips for women.

CONSTRUCTED RESPONSE What do you think is
meant by "petticoat rule" in the fifth reason, and why
would women consider it undesirable?

Vote NO on
Woman Suffrage

BECAUSE 90% of the women either do not
    want it, or do not care.

BECAUSE it means competition of women with
    men instead of co-operation.

BECAUSE 80% of the women eligible to vote
    are married and can only double or annul
    their husbands' votes.

BECAUSE it can be of no benefit commensurate
    with the additional expense involved.

BECAUSE in some States more voting
    women than voting men will place the
    Government under petticoat rule.

BECAUSE it is unwise to risk the good we
    already have for the evil which may occur.

Vote "No" button,
c. 1910

SYNTHESIZE & WRITE

1. **REVIEW** Review what you have learned about the
   women's suffrage movement.

2. **RECALL** Summarize the main arguments for and
   against women's suffrage presented in the two
   documents.

3. **CONSTRUCT** Construct a topic sentence that
   answers this question: How do the arguments for
   and against women's suffrage reflect different
   views of women's role in society?

4. **WRITE** Using evidence from this chapter and the
   documents, write an explanatory paragraph that
   supports your topic sentence.

REFORMING GOVERNMENT

If you were running for political office, how would you convince people to vote for you? Offer them money? Promise them jobs? Across the United States, candidates were using such tactics to gain and keep political offices in the late 1800s and early 1900s.

REFORMING CITY GOVERNMENT

The earliest push for political reform during the Progressive Era occurred at the level of city government. The city mayors and councils struggled to deal with expanding populations divided by ethnicity, race, religion, and economic class. Council members often traded favors with one another and blocked legislation that hurt their districts, which made city government ineffective.

This situation gave rise to "boss politics." You have read about Boss Tweed and his political machine, Tammany Hall, but Tweed was not an isolated example. Throughout many big cities, powerful bosses commanded hierarchical political party organizations that operated at the district, the neighborhood, and even the block level. These corrupt political machines provided services, jobs, and favors in exchange for votes.

Reformers worked to take city government out of the hands of corrupt officials. After a hurricane devastated Galveston, Texas, in 1900, the Texas legislature suspended Galveston's city council and established a five-member commission to temporarily oversee the city. This new form of **commission government**, dubbed the "Galveston plan," worked so well that it was made permanent. It quickly spread to Dallas, Fort Worth, and other Texas cities.

CRITICAL VIEWING Two boys explore the wreckage of St. Patrick's Church in Galveston, Texas, after a devastating hurricane in 1900. The city council handled the disaster so poorly that a new form of government was instituted, and a commission of experts took charge of the various city departments. What details in the photograph indicate the scale of the hurricane damage?

In 1907, Des Moines, Iowa, became the first city outside Texas to adopt commission government, but it staged a vote so citizens could choose their own city commissioners. Des Moines became a model for cities around the United States that were seeking to overhaul their governments.

Staunton, Virginia, became another model. In 1908, Staunton's city council hired a professional manager to take charge of the city's struggling public services. The council-manager approach proved to be an effective way of taking politics out of city administration. Dayton, Ohio, adopted and popularized this form of government in 1913 following a devastating flood.

REFORMING STATE GOVERNMENT

The reform movement soon spread from the city level to the state level. Progressives, including future presidents Theodore Roosevelt and **Woodrow Wilson**, worked to make state government less corrupt, more efficient, and more democratic. Progressives instituted such structural changes as the **direct primary**, in which party candidates are nominated by a direct vote, and the direct election of U.S. senators.

At the time, party political bosses often controlled who was nominated to run for political offices. Direct primary elections gave this control to voters. In accordance with the U.S. Constitution, senators had always been elected by state legislatures, which often were strongly influenced by rich and powerful political supporters. In 1899, Nevada changed its law to allow voters to elect U.S. senators directly. Soon, other states did the same. Then, in 1913, progressive efforts helped pass and ratify the **17th Amendment**, which mandated that all U.S. senators be elected by popular vote.

Progressives also promoted such democratic reforms as the **initiative** and the referendum. An initiative enables citizens to bypass the legislature and propose new laws to be voted on. In a referendum, as you have learned, a proposal is submitted to voters directly for approval or rejection. During the Progressive Era, nearly 20 states adopted statewide processes for initiatives and referendums.

After he was elected New York's governor in 1898, Theodore Roosevelt worked with the state legislature to enact laws regulating tenements, corporations, and the civil service, and he fought against corruption and political machines. In 1906, New York gained another reform-minded governor with the election of Charles Evans Hughes. Hughes helped

In his first inaugural address as governor of California, Hiram Johnson warned against corrupt business leaders and politicians who had only their own power and prosperity in mind.

I prefer, as less dangerous to society, the political thug of the waterfront to the smugly respectable individual in broadcloth of pretended respectability who from ambush employs and uses that thug for his selfish political gain.

—from Governor Hiram Johnson's first inaugural address, 1911

How can a corrupt politician be more dangerous than someone who uses physical violence to accomplish goals?

regulate public utilities, such as gas and water, and expanded the state's involvement in policing. He also pushed through laws that made political campaigns more open, honest, and democratic.

During his two-year tenure as governor of New Jersey beginning in 1911, Woodrow Wilson established a commission to oversee the state's public utilities and helped pass a workers' compensation law to help employees who were injured on the job. On the other side of the country, California governor **Hiram Johnson** led the charge for constitutional state amendments on the initiative, referendum, and **recall**, or the right of citizens to remove an elected official by direct vote.

But the leading symbol of state reform was **Robert M. La Follette**, a Republican who was elected governor of Wisconsin in 1900. During his two terms, he established direct primary elections, regulated Wisconsin's railroads, and levied higher taxes on corporations. He forged a close relationship between the state government and the University of Wisconsin faculty, who advised him on policy. This reliance on academic experts as government advisors was called the "Wisconsin Idea."

HISTORICAL THINKING

1. **READING CHECK** How did progressives give voters a larger voice in state government?

2. **MAKE CONNECTIONS** How did reforms instituted in city governments help shape reforms adopted in state governments?

3. **DRAW CONCLUSIONS** Why do you think Governor La Follette sought the advice of the faculty at the University of Wisconsin?

REFORM UNDER ROOSEVELT

Theodore Roosevelt had a strong commitment to reform, which fit perfectly with the mood of Americans at the start of the 20th century. He led the way in expanding the power of the federal government in order to carry out the reforms he thought were necessary.

ROOSEVELT BECOMES PRESIDENT

In November 1900, voters elected President William McKinley to a second term. McKinley's presidency was cut short, however. On September 6, 1901, a young Michigan-born anarchist, a person who opposes all government, shot the president at a world's fair in Buffalo, New York. The president died eight days later. His vice president, Theodore Roosevelt, took over as president.

At 42, Roosevelt was the youngest person ever to hold the office of president. Roosevelt was brash and energetic. He loved the outdoors, and he led an active lifestyle that included horseback riding, swimming, boxing, and hunting.

Roosevelt came to office at a time when there was strong momentum for social, economic, and political change in the United States. He became the first progressive president and took the lead in bringing about many reforms.

Since entering politics around 1880, Roosevelt had been either elected or appointed to a variety of government positions, including member of the New York State Assembly, assistant secretary of the U.S. Navy, and governor of the state of New York. He had earned a reputation for political independence and for commitment to eradicating, or getting rid of, political corruption.

After the deaths of his wife and his mother on a single day in 1884, Roosevelt had retreated to a cattle ranch he owned in the Dakota Territory and spent much of the next two years there. He became increasingly dedicated to **conservation**, or the management and protection of natural resources, as he saw how human activities were damaging the land and reducing the populations of such wildlife as bison, bighorn sheep, and elk.

🏛 The National Museum of American History, Washington, D.C.

Rose Michtom, the wife of a candy store owner, created the first Teddy bear in Brooklyn, New York, in 1902, after she and her husband saw a political cartoon involving President Theodore "Teddy" Roosevelt on a bear hunt. The couple put the bear on display in their store window, and many passers-by wanted to buy it. Rose and her husband, Morris, wrote to Roosevelt asking permission to use the name *Teddy* for the bear. On receiving the president's approval, Morris formed a toy company and began manufacturing Teddy bears.

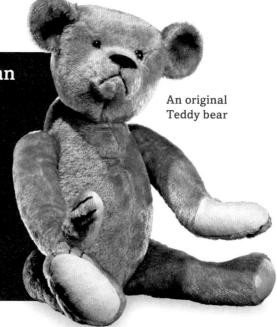

An original Teddy bear

THE SQUARE DEAL

Nine months after taking office, President Theodore Roosevelt faced one of the first major challenges of his presidency. On May 12, 1902, the 140,000 members of the United Mine Workers union, an organization formed to protect the interests of workers, walked off their jobs in the coal fields of eastern Pennsylvania after the mine operators refused to meet with union representatives. The miners were seeking higher pay, shorter hours, and recognition of their union. The mine operators, who had lost a strike two years earlier, wanted to break the strike—and the union.

The drop in production caused coal prices to soar. As the walkout stretched into autumn, the threat of winter coal shortages loomed. Republicans worried that if voters' homes were cold, people might vote against the Republican Party in the congressional elections in November. Roosevelt, in a letter to Massachusetts's governor Winthrop Murray Crane, expressed concern that the shortages could cause "untold misery . . . with the certainty of riots which might develop into social war."

After much agonizing, Roosevelt decided to act. But he did not call in troops to break up the strike, as

President Grover Cleveland had done in the Pullman Strike eight years earlier. Instead, he brought the two sides together and worked with them to negotiate a reasonable settlement. Roosevelt called his approach the **Square Deal** because he wanted to ensure fairness and balance to both sides. This approach in disputes between big business and labor would be a hallmark of Roosevelt's presidency.

Roosevelt believed that as president, he should take action to promote the general welfare of the people and to protect the country's natural resources. He saw the presidential office as a "bully pulpit," or a position of high authority and prestige from which he could promote his ideas and push his social and economic agenda more aggressively than presidents who came before him. For this reason, many historians consider Theodore Roosevelt the first modern president.

BUSTING THE TRUSTS

Corporations were a major source of concern for Roosevelt. Some of them were growing large and extremely powerful through **mergers**, in which two or more companies combine as one. One example was the 1901 merger of the Carnegie Steel Company with steel companies owned by J.P. Morgan, which created the mammoth United States Steel Corporation. Valued at more than $1.4 billion, it was the largest corporation in U.S. history. It had 168,000 employees, and it controlled 60 percent of the steel industry's production. By eliminating other employment opportunities, United States Steel used its size to drive down workers' wages, and so other steel companies were able to do the same.

In a cartoon entitled "The Lion Tamer," which appeared on the cover of *Harper's Weekly* in 1904, President Roosevelt is portrayed as taming the power of trusts in various industries.

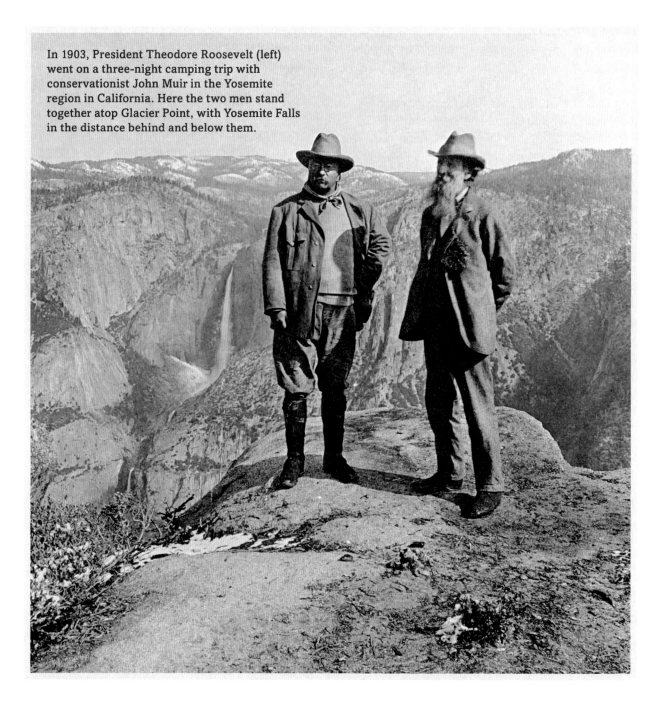

In 1903, President Theodore Roosevelt (left) went on a three-night camping trip with conservationist John Muir in the Yosemite region in California. Here the two men stand together atop Glacier Point, with Yosemite Falls in the distance behind and below them.

Roosevelt saw industrial mergers as unavoidable, but he thought that the federal government should play an active role in regulating business instead of sitting back and allowing corporations to do as they pleased. He believed in encouraging corporations to behave in a socially responsible way and in monitoring and controlling those that did not. Roosevelt's idea of a good company was one that paid a living wage to its employees, provided safe working conditions, did not overcharge its customers, and did not contribute to political corruption to gain an advantage.

In 1890, Congress had passed the **Sherman Antitrust Act**, which gave the federal government the power to prosecute and break up corporations and trusts that monopolized, or threatened to monopolize, specific markets and industries. Unlike previous presidents, Roosevelt used the act aggressively. His first target was the powerful Northern Securities Company, which controlled three railroads. In 1904, the Supreme Court ruled that the company had violated the Sherman Antitrust Act and ordered it to be dismantled. Americans saw Roosevelt as a **trustbuster**, someone who would fight to curb the power of big business by vigorously enforcing antitrust legislation.

REGULATING BUSINESS

Progressives had a strong belief in the power of government to do good and to promote a better society. They rejected laissez-faire economics, feeling the government's hands-off approach had allowed corporations to abuse their power at the expense of workers, consumers, and smaller businesses. Instead, progressives pushed the government to regulate business more closely. This work fell to agencies such as the **Federal Trade Commission (FTC)** and the **Interstate Commerce Commission (ICC)**, which employed experts on the industries they supervised.

The ICC was created in 1887 through the Interstate Commerce Act, which was intended to control corruption in the railroad industry. It required the railroad companies to offer reasonable and fair rates for transporting goods, and it prohibited them from offering preferred rates to certain customers. The act had not been strongly enforced, however, and the railroads and corporations still engaged in unfair practices. In 1903, Roosevelt took action. He signed the Elkins Act, which levied heavy fines on railroads that offered rebates, or partial returns on money paid, and on the companies that received them. Three years later, he signed the Hepburn Act, which gave the ICC the power to establish maximum transportation rates and review the accounts and records of the railroads.

Other industries also came under the watchful eyes of the Roosevelt administration. In late 1905, Congress began writing a bill intended to ensure the purity and safety of foods and drugs. Roosevelt strongly supported the bill, but it faced steep business opposition.

Then, in the winter of 1906, Upton Sinclair's muckraking novel *The Jungle* was published. As you have read, the book described the unsanitary practices of the meatpacking industry. Roosevelt was among the thousands of Americans who read the book and were shocked and disgusted by its revelations. He launched an investigation of the industry and supported legislation that established a federal program for meat inspection. Meanwhile, Sinclair's novel produced a public outcry that spurred the House to pass what would become the **Pure Food and Drug Act**, which Roosevelt signed into law in June of 1906.

RACE RELATIONS

While breaking up corporations and establishing food safety laws, Roosevelt also wanted to be seen as a friend to African Americans. In October 1901, he invited Booker T. Washington, who had built a political machine among black Republicans in the South, to dine with his family at the White House.

Southerners were infuriated, and a Tennessee newspaper editor called the occasion "the most damnable outrage that has ever been perpetrated by any citizen of the United States." Roosevelt felt the backlash of his decision and never again invited another African American to dine at the White House. However, he appointed African Americans to positions in post offices and customs houses. The appointments could only help him win votes from black delegates in the upcoming election of 1904.

Beyond symbolic actions, however, Roosevelt did not challenge the racism that existed throughout the nation. Discrimination, segregation, poverty, and violence continued to be a scourge on the lives of African Americans.

THE CONSERVATION PRESIDENT

As a boy, Theodore Roosevelt had been frail and sickly, but he grew into a strong man who loved outdoor activities. As you have read, the two years he spent on a cattle ranch in the Dakota Territory helped transform him into a committed conservationist. He saw how human activities were ruining the land and destroying wildlife, and he felt an urgent need to protect the country's natural resources.

Conservation became one of the defining aspects of Roosevelt's presidency. He used his power as president to create 4 national game preserves, or areas set aside to protect wild animals, 51 refuges for wild birds, and 150 national forests. He also helped establish Crater Lake and Mesa Verde national parks. Through the Antiquities Act, he protected the Grand Canyon and many other areas of scenic or historical interest from destruction and development. He worked closely with Gifford Pinchot (PIN-show), head of the newly created National Forest Service, to create a policy that balanced the protection of natural resources with their industrial use. Because of his efforts, Roosevelt is remembered as the Conservation President.

HISTORICAL THINKING

1. **READING CHECK** Why did many Americans think of Theodore Roosevelt as a trustbuster?

2. **MAKE INFERENCES** What political reason might Roosevelt have had for inviting Booker T. Washington to the White House?

3. **ANALYZE ENVIRONMENTAL CONCEPTS** What actions did Roosevelt take to improve the viability of natural systems?

THE GRAND CANYON NORTHWESTERN ARIZONA

One of the seven natural wonders of the world, the Grand Canyon is the most spectacular gorge on Earth. Over millions of years, the Colorado River carved the canyon, which displays through its layers of rock the most extensive record of geologic history on Earth. In fact, rocks at the bottom of the canyon date back 2.5 billion years. Still, the aesthetic and geologic value of the Grand Canyon have not been enough to ensure its protection. When mining and tourism interests posed a threat, President Theodore Roosevelt stepped in to safeguard the canyon by making it a national monument in 1908. Roosevelt expressed the hope that no human activity would "mar the wonderful grandeur, the sublimity, the great loneliness and beauty of the canyon." Congress established Grand Canyon National Park in 1919, but developers have not stopped devising plans to "mar" the canyon. Today, environmentalists affiliated with National Geographic and other organizations continue to battle against commercial groups who have proposed building a tram near the park's eastern edge to shuttle visitors to the canyon's bottom.

CRITICAL VIEWING Although mostly red, as revealed in this photo by National Geographic photographer Pete McBride, the Grand Canyon's rock layers also display hues of green, pink, gray, brown, and violet. What do you think motivates activists like McBride to protect the Grand Canyon from development?

PROGRESSIVISM UNDER TAFT AND WILSON

The description "a tough act to follow" could certainly be applied to Theodore Roosevelt. His popularity helped the Republicans retain the presidency in 1908, but his successor looked weak in comparison.

A MIXED COURSE

Theodore Roosevelt had stepped into the presidency early in McKinley's second term, so by 1908, he felt he had already served two terms in office. Citing George Washington's decision to limit his presidency to two terms, Roosevelt declined to run again. Instead he supported his secretary of war, **William Howard Taft**, as the next Republican candidate. Taft handily won the presidency against William Jennings Bryan, a Democrat who had run and been defeated twice before.

Roosevelt chose Taft as his successor because he believed Taft would carry on his progressive agenda. He did not realize that Taft disagreed with his expansive view of presidential power. Taft believed that the president should act within the strict constitutional boundaries of his office. Although he aggressively enforced antitrust legislation, Taft lacked the will to urge progressive policies on the more conservative members of the Republican Party. Roosevelt's progressive agenda continued under Taft, but it faced setbacks.

Taft started off on the wrong foot after he failed to name any progressives to his cabinet. Then he offended progressives again when he sided against Gifford Pinchot, the Forestry Service chief and Roosevelt's good friend, in a dispute over the commercial use of public lands in Alaska. Pinchot had barred the lands from development, but Richard A. Ballinger, Taft's secretary of the interior, opened the lands to coal-mining companies. Pinchot accused Ballinger of acting as a member of a **syndicate**, or group of criminals, trying to sell valuable coal lands for profit. Taft investigated the charges and publicly agreed with Ballinger. He fired Pinchot for insubordination, or defiance of authority. This incident led progressives to doubt Taft's commitment to conservation. Some even sent letters to Roosevelt, at the time on safari in Africa, saying as much.

As the president and the progressives argued, Americans struggled with major social issues. In 1910, some 200,000 youngsters below the age of 12 labored in mills and factories. Attempts to limit child labor in southern textile mills brought few results. In 1912, after a six-year struggle, progressive reformers succeeded in establishing the Children's Bureau. Its mission was to investigate and report on the conditions of children working in factories and living in orphanages. Unfortunately, Congress failed to pass any legislation that would have allowed reformers to take action against businesses that overworked child laborers. One such measure was a bill that would have prohibited interstate shipment of products made using child labor.

Another pressing social issue was immigration, which had nearly tripled from 1910 to 1914. Many of the immigrants were from southern and eastern Europe, and some Americans felt that their presence threatened traditional American values. The growing Americanization movement strongly encouraged immigrants to adopt American culture, including speaking and writing English instead of their native languages. While many immigrants quickly assimilated, others refused to give up their own languages and customs. By 1913, both houses of Congress had passed a bill to impose a literacy test on immigrants. President Taft, however, vetoed the bill as a largely anti-immigration measure.

LABOR AND THE WORKPLACE

The progressive movement had made huge strides during Roosevelt's presidency, but it fell short in brokering deals between labor unions and corporations. During Taft's presidency, unions made progress in organizing workers and improving working conditions for their members. That progress was partly driven by a public outcry over workplace tragedies.

On March 25, 1911, a fire broke out near closing time on the top floors of the Triangle Waist Company in New York City. The company employed about 500 people, mostly young immigrant women, to produce fashionable blouses. The workers ran to the stairway doors, but they were locked. Many trapped, terrified women chose to jump out of the 10-story building, hoping to survive the fall. Tragically, 146 people died in the **Triangle Waist Company factory fire**, and an outraged American public cried out for factory reform.

The intense heat of the factory fire at the Triangle Waist Company weakened the metal of the fire escape ladder. Some workers were able to descend to a lower floor before the ladder collapsed.

On March 4, 1913, Woodrow Wilson was inaugurated as the nation's 28th president. In this photograph taken at the White House just before the inauguration, Wilson appears on the left and his predecessor, President William H. Taft, is on the right.

Another outcry arose after soldiers moved in to clear a tent city in Ludlow, Colorado. For about seven months, mine workers had been striking against the Colorado Fuel and Iron Company for higher pay and better treatment in company camps. The company owner, John D. Rockefeller, had the governor call in the National Guard to end the strike, which resulted in clashes between soldiers and miners. On April 20, 1914, troops shot into the workers' camps and set fire to tents. As many as 20 people, including women and children, were shot or died in the fire.

Labor unions such as the American Federation of Labor (AFL) and the International Workers of the World (IWW) had existed prior to the turn of the 20th century, but their membership swelled between 1900 and 1914. The IWW grew, in part, because it aimed to unite workers of every industry, including unskilled and African-American workers. The IWW played a major role in a strike against textile mills in Massachusetts. Workers walked out of the mills in January 1912 after company owners announced pay reductions. Strikers sang of "bread and roses,"

symbolizing both a living wage and hope for the future. With production at a standstill, company owners were eager to negotiate. By March 1, 1912, with the IWW's help, the workers won a raise in pay.

As labor unions made important gains for workers, company owners looked at ways to make their businesses more efficient. A mechanical engineer named **Frederick Winslow Taylor** developed **scientific management**, a method of running factories and other workplaces efficiently. Taylor studied individual tasks and determined the best way to complete them in the shortest amount of time. Taylor's findings resulted in sweeping changes in many industries. Factory managers expected workers to perform one specific activity for hours at a time, which made many workers feel like little more than machines. As workers in other countries attained benefits such as **social security**, a program in which the government provides money to the elderly, disabled, and unemployed, Americans continued their fight for improved working conditions and higher pay.

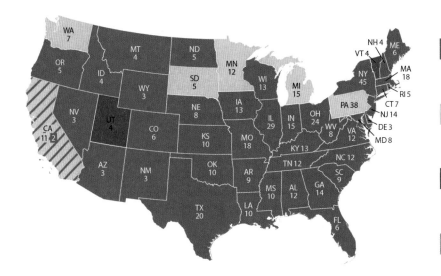

The 1912 Election

Woodrow Wilson, Democrat

Electoral Vote: 435 votes, 81.9%

Popular Vote: 6,294,327 votes, 41.8%

Theodore Roosevelt, Progressive

Electoral Vote: 88 votes, 16.6%

Popular Vote: 4,120,207 votes, 27.4%

William H. Taft, Republican

Electoral Vote: 8 votes, 1.5%

Popular Vote: 3,486,343 votes, 23.2%

Eugene Debs, Socialist

Popular Vote: 900,370 votes, 6.0%

A PROGRESSIVE DEMOCRAT

As Taft neared the end of his first term in office, many Americans viewed him as a weak president. Political divisions in the country became apparent during the 1912 election. Theodore Roosevelt, apparently forgetting his pledge not to seek another presidential term, started his own party, the Progressive Party, to run against Republican Taft. The Democrats nominated Woodrow Wilson, then the governor of New Jersey.

Another candidate, Eugene Debs, ran as the Socialist candidate. With the Republican vote split, Woodrow Wilson won the election by a landslide. Taft won only 8 electoral votes to Wilson's 435.

President Wilson set to work immediately on his pet project: lowering tariffs, or taxes imposed on imported goods. This issue was important to progressives because tariffs added to the price of imported household items. Cutting tariffs would cut prices for consumers. Wilson fought hard to persuade Congress to pass the Revenue Act of 1913 to reduce tariffs. However, there was a glaring problem: how to make up for the income lost by reducing tariffs.

To remedy this shortfall, Congress added another provision to the bill: an **income tax**, or money paid to the government based on how much a person earns. Earlier in the year, the states had ratified, or approved, the **16th Amendment**, which granted Congress the power to collect income taxes nationwide. Wilson's success with the Revenue Act helped build his image as an effective leader.

The Wilson administration then turned its attention to banking and trustbusting, or breaking up monopolies. The country needed a central bank to control the money supply and make sure it was adequate to meet the demands of the growing economy. Wilson's

solution was to form the **Federal Reserve System**, a system of 12 banks located around the country and overseen by board members appointed by the president. The Federal Reserve System functioned as the nation's central bank.

Wilson also urged Congress to strengthen the nation's antitrust laws. As you have read, the Sherman Antitrust Act, passed in 1890, gave the government the right to break up monopolies and illegal trusts. However, it did not forbid businesses from engaging in some questionable practices, such as allowing one person to direct two or more "competing" companies. The **Clayton Antitrust Act**, passed in 1914, closed many of the loopholes, or ways around the law, not specifically prohibited by the Sherman Antitrust Act.

While Wilson made significant contributions to the progressive movement, he opposed African-American causes. In addition, like Taft, he did not support women's suffrage, at least initially. Of the three progressive presidents, only Roosevelt supported women's right to vote.

HISTORICAL THINKING

1. **READING CHECK** How did Taft and Wilson further the progressive agenda?

2. **INTERPRET MAPS** If Roosevelt and Taft had not split the Republican vote, is it likely that the Republican candidate would have won the election? Use electoral and popular vote data from the map to explain your answer.

3. **ANALYZE CAUSE AND EFFECT** How did the Revenue Act of 1913 affect American consumers?

4. **MAKE INFERENCES** Why did many Americans view Taft as a weak president?

AMERICAN EXPANSIONISM

For more than a hundred years, the United States grew in size until it stretched from coast to coast. Then, in the late 1800s, the nation sought to gain a foothold in distant lands.

THE ROOTS OF IMPERIALISM

As Americans struggled with social issues at home, the United States began to take an interest in expanding its influence overseas. For most of its short history, the nation had kept a low profile in world affairs. While European powers pursued **imperialism**, a policy of exerting economic, political, or military control over weaker nations, Americans had followed the course of **isolationism**, avoiding entanglements in foreign countries. By the 1880s, however, the United States had begun to look beyond its borders.

Trade played a big role in this new outlook. American business was booming, and one of the results was a surplus of American-made goods. Business leaders wanted to increase opportunities to sell these goods overseas. Their desire to do so led many of them to endorse **expansionism**, a policy similar to imperialism. Expansionism focuses on increasing a country's territory. Such a policy would open up new markets for American products and provide access to more raw materials.

American leaders had watched closely as European powers carved up territories in Africa and Asia, adding colonies and **protectorates**, or countries that are partly controlled by a stronger country. Americans worried about being left behind. One expansionist leader, Captain **Alfred T. Mahan** of the U.S. Navy, proposed an international network of naval bases, a powerful battleship fleet, and an aggressive foreign policy that would make the United States a competitive world power.

More than a hint of racism ran through the aims of the imperialists and expansionists. They believed in the superiority of white, English-speaking people and thought the rest of the world should bend to their will.

EYES ON ALASKA AND HAWAII

Americans had already taken the first steps toward expansion years earlier. In 1867, the United States paid $7.2 million to purchase Russia's territory in Alaska. Most Americans believed the land was useless, but the discovery of gold there in the 1880s and 1890s lured prospectors to the territory, and the population began to grow. At the same time, the Alaskan salmon fishing industry began to thrive. When Alaskans discovered copper in 1898, Americans started to recognize the great deal they had made with the Russians.

The Hawaiian Islands, an **archipelago**, or island chain, in the midst of the Pacific Ocean, attracted American interest even earlier than Alaska did. American missionaries began preaching in the islands in the early 1800s, and by the 1850s,

PRIMARY SOURCE

After losing her throne in 1893, Queen Liliuokalani of Hawaii continued to demand that the United States give her country back to her. Here she presents her case to the U.S. government.

Therefore, supplementing my protest of June 17, 1897, I call upon the President and the National Legislature and the People of the United States to do justice in this matter and to restore to me this property, the enjoyment of which is being withheld from me by your government under what must be a misapprehension [misunderstanding] of my right and title.

—from Queen Liliuokalani's letter of protest addressed to the House of Representatives, 1898

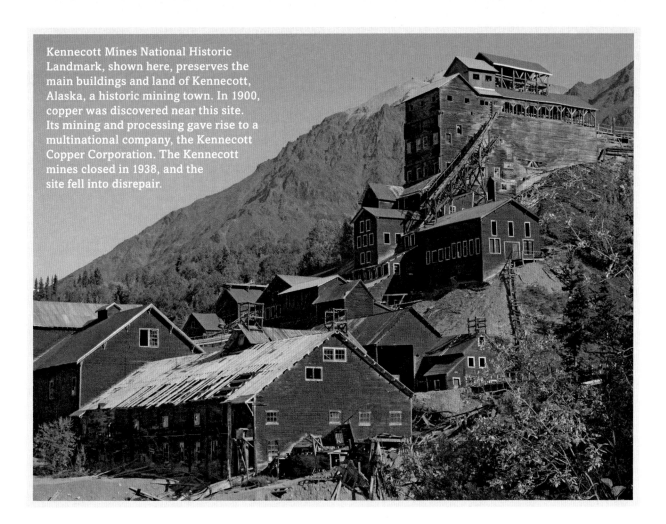

Kennecott Mines National Historic Landmark, shown here, preserves the main buildings and land of Kennecott, Alaska, a historic mining town. In 1900, copper was discovered near this site. Its mining and processing gave rise to a multinational company, the Kennecott Copper Corporation. The Kennecott mines closed in 1938, and the site fell into disrepair.

Americans were establishing businesses there, primarily growing and exporting sugarcane and pineapples. As early as the 1870s, the United States had recognized the strategic value of a naval base in Hawaii for protecting the Pacific Coast in wartime.

As more Americans came to the islands, their growing influence on the local economy and government soon sparked conflict with the Hawaiian monarchy. When **Queen Liliuokalani** came to power in 1891, she dismissed the legislature, which she felt was too sympathetic to Americans, and she presented a constitution that stripped white settlers of the powers they had secured for themselves. Most native Hawaiians agreed with the new constitution. But by this time, there were enough Americans and pro-American Hawaiians—including 150 U.S. Marines—living on the islands to stage a revolt against the queen. They overthrew the queen, established their own government, and requested that the United States annex, or take possession of, the islands.

President Benjamin Harrison agreed to sign a treaty with the pro-American, and mostly white, rebels to annex the islands, effective on February 14, 1893. But in the meantime, he lost the 1892 election to Grover Cleveland, who did not approve of the rebels' actions. Cleveland put the treaty on hold.

The fate of the islands remained unsettled until 1898, when the United States annexed Hawaii. By then, the islands were viewed as an essential naval asset in the Spanish-American War. In the "Organic Act" of 1900, Congress established a government for Hawaii, and the islands became an official U.S. territory. Meanwhile, the United States had set its sights on securing trading deals in Asia.

HISTORICAL THINKING

1. **READING CHECK** What were some reasons that the United States began an expansionist course in foreign policy in the late 1800s?

2. **EVALUATE** How did the acquisitions of Alaska and Hawaii benefit the United States?

3. **COMPARE AND CONTRAST** How are imperialism and expansionism alike and different?

EXTENDING INFLUENCE IN ASIA

Near the end of the 19th century, Japan and several of the most powerful European nations had secured exclusive trading deals in China. The United States wanted to trade in China as well. How did the Americans open the door to trade in China? They simply made a proposal.

OPENING THE DOOR TO CHINA

The United States successfully established a diplomatic and trading presence in Asia after Naval Commodore Matthew C. Perry negotiated the Treaty of Kanagawa with Japan in 1854. For centuries, Japan had a policy of isolation and limited trade with other countries. In 1853, Perry was sent to negotiate diplomatic relations and trade between Japan and the United States. As a result of the treaty the two countries signed, Japan opened its ports to American ships for the first time in more than 200 years. As the 19th century came to a close, the United States had begun to turn its attention to Japan's neighbor: China.

At that time, Great Britain had the strongest presence of any foreign power in China. But other countries, such as France, Germany, Italy, Russia, and Japan, had also carved out **spheres of influence**, or claims of exclusive economic and trading authority, in parts of the country. Within each sphere of influence, the controlling nation made deals with local banks and businesses that allowed it exclusive economic benefits within the community. The United States wanted a part of this economic action.

In 1900, U.S. Secretary of State **John Hay** proposed the **Open Door Policy** to all of the countries with spheres of influence in China. Hay suggested that all Chinese ports accept ships from every nation, not just those with which China had brokered deals. The plan honored the trading arrangements China had already made, but it extended those same provisions to other nations as well, giving the United States a foothold in China. The policy also calmed Chinese fears that the competition between the foreign powers would change the spheres of influence into

colonies and tear China apart. While the nations affected by this policy may not have agreed with the American proposal, they did not openly oppose it either.

Meanwhile, many Chinese were fed up with foreign interference in their country. Their discontent was about to erupt into open rebellion.

THE BOXER REBELLION

A secret society in China called the Righteous and Harmonious Fists had long opposed the presence of so many Westerners and Japanese in the country. Members of the society particularly resented the influence of Christian missionaries, who questioned the teachings of traditional religions. Bands of rebels started wandering the countryside outside Beijing, attacking foreigners, mostly Christian missionaries. The rebels were dubbed "the Boxers" because they exercised by sparring in a boxing ring. The Boxers also attacked Chinese leaders whom they believed were responsible for the preferential treatment that foreigners received. The attacks were called the **Boxer Rebellion**.

In 1898, forces within the Chinese government also began calling for an end to foreign meddling. The Boxers then changed the group's name to the Righteous and Harmonious Militia, and the government enlisted the militia and encouraged its violent actions.

The Boxers began burning Christian churches and buildings that housed foreign businesses. By the spring of 1900, the Boxers were staging attacks in the capital city of Beijing. An international relief force arrived in the city in June to stop the violence. China's empress dowager Cixi—the emperor's adoptive

CIXI, EMPRESS DOWAGER OF CHINA

Yehenara, a middle-class Chinese girl, started her political career by giving birth to a son in 1856. A mistress of the Chinese emperor, she became known as Cixi, meaning "kind and virtuous." Her son was the emperor's only male heir. When the emperor died, the six-year-old boy took the throne. Cixi became one of the regents, or officials who govern in place of a child monarch.

Cixi gave up the regency when her son became 17 years old. But he died two years later, and her three-year-old nephew, whom Cixi had adopted, ascended to the throne. Cixi again became a regent.

She ruled China until 1889, when she retired to a palace she had built near Beijing. However, Chinese officials returned her to power in 1898 after the country suffered a major defeat in a war with Russia and Japan. She fled Beijing during the Boxer Rebellion but returned in 1902 and continued to rule until her death in 1908.

A bright and ambitious woman, Cixi ruled China for almost half a century. She ranks as one of the most powerful women in Chinese history.

mother and the person who actually ruled China— sent troops to fight the relief force and declared war on the United States, the United Kingdom, France, Germany, Italy, Russia, Japan, and Austria-Hungary.

Another international force of 20,000 soldiers captured Beijing in August 1900. The empress dowager and her court escaped the city, and she had little to do with the negotiations that followed. In September 1901, China signed the treaty that officially ended the Boxer Rebellion. The treaty forced China to pay **reparations**, or forced compensation, to the foreign powers for damages and lost lives. Payment of these reparations had a disastrous effect on the Chinese economy, fueling a resentment that resurfaced later in the 20th century.

HISTORICAL THINKING

1. **READING CHECK** How did the United States gain a foothold in China in the late 1800s?

2. **ANALYZE CAUSE AND EFFECT** What were the causes of the Boxer Rebellion?

3. **DRAW CONCLUSIONS** Why do you think John Hay proposed the Open Door Policy instead of negotiating directly with China?

4. **COMPARE AND CONTRAST** How did the political system in China differ from that in the United States in the 1800s? Support your answer with evidence from the text.

Then a dramatic event changed the course of American involvement. The United States had sent a battleship, the U.S.S. *Maine*, to Havana, Cuba, to protect American citizens and property there. On February 15, 1898, the ship exploded in the Havana harbor, killing more than 250 men, or about two-thirds of the crew. Modern research suggests that naturally occurring chemical reactions in one of the ship's coal bunkers caused the explosion. At the time, however, a naval board of inquiry, along with the American public, blamed Spain.

Though they lacked any evidence, American newspapers claimed that Spain had blown up the battleship. The *New York Journal and Advertiser*, owned by newspaper publisher William Randolph Hearst, printed such unfounded headlines as "Destruction of the War Ship *Maine* Was the Work of an Enemy!" and "Spanish Treachery!" This type of sensationalized newswriting, using exaggeration, melodrama, and outright lies to attract readers, became known as **yellow journalism**.

While a Navy investigation never pinned blame on Spain, many Americans readily believed that the Spanish had caused the explosion. Proponents of U.S. military intervention in Cuba used the slogan "Remember the *Maine!*" to rally public support. As public opinion in the United States increasingly favored war, Spain tried to avert it by conceding to many U.S. demands. But then the U.S. Congress authorized the president to use force to gain the withdrawal of Spain's armed forces from Cuba.

Spain responded by declaring war on the United States on April 24, and the United States in turn declared war on Spain the next day, on April 25.

WAR IN THE PACIFIC

Although events in Cuba led the United States into war, the first battle of the Spanish-American War actually took place in the Philippines. The U.S. Navy believed their superior forces could easily disable the Spanish fleet in the Philippines, where Spain was also battling rebels. Because they wanted freedom from Spain, the Filipino rebels joined forces with the Americans.

On May 1, 1898, a U.S. naval squadron under the command of Commodore **George Dewey** attacked the Spanish navy at Manila Bay. Within hours, the Spanish fleet was destroyed in an uneven fight.

PRIMARY SOURCE

In an article entitled "Naval Officers Think the *Maine* Was Destroyed by a Spanish Mine," the *New York Journal and Advertiser* led Americans to believe that the U.S.S. *Maine* was deliberately blown up.

Assistant Secretary of the Navy Theodore Roosevelt says he is convinced that the destruction of the Maine in Havana Harbor was not an accident. The Journal offers a reward of $50,000 for exclusive evidence that will convict the person, persons or government criminally responsible for the [destruction] of the American battleship and the death of 258 of its crew. The suspicion that the Maine was deliberately blown up grows stronger every hour. Not a single fact to the contrary has been produced.

—from the *New York Journal and Advertiser*, February 17, 1898

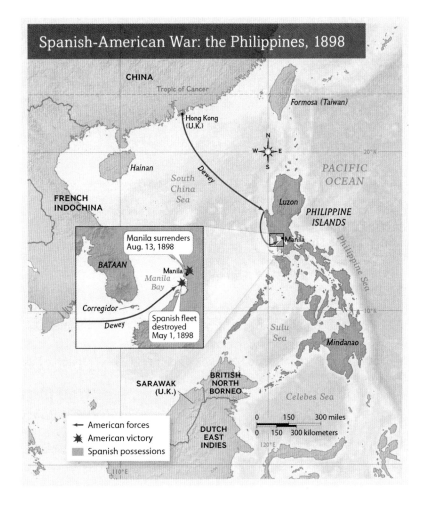

Spanish-American War: the Philippines, 1898

Theodore Roosevelt appears near the center in this 1898 photograph of the Rough Riders, a volunteer cavalry unit. The photograph was taken at the top of Kettle Hill, which the Rough Riders captured as part of the Battle of San Juan Hill. The battle became legendary, due largely to Roosevelt's fame. Although the Rough Riders trained as cavalry, they never fought on horseback because their horses did not arrive in Cuba in time.

Dewey had brought six steel ships to the battle, while the Spanish fleet consisted of seven unarmored wooden ships. The Spanish lost more than 350 men in the battle, while no Americans lost their lives. After the battle, Dewey reported to his superior officer: "There were . . . only seven men in the squadron very slightly wounded."

Dewey's victory was widely celebrated in the United States, even though it was incomplete. Though his squadron had control of Manila Bay, Dewey lacked enough troops to take Manila itself. He estimated that he would need 5,000 additional troops to seize the city. He soon received twice that number, and by August, U.S. troops occupied Manila. However, the United States still had to battle the Spanish in Cuba.

WAR IN THE CARIBBEAN

While Dewey's victory demonstrated the superiority of U.S. naval forces, the U.S. Army consisted of only about 25,000 troops, too small a force for the scale of fighting that was anticipated. The United

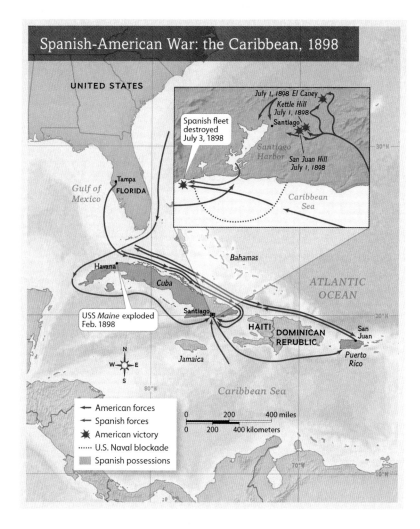

Spanish-American War: the Caribbean, 1898

UNITED STATES

July 1, 1898 El Caney
Kettle Hill
July 1, 1898
Santiago
Spanish fleet
destroyed
July 3, 1898
Santiago
Harbor
San Juan Hill
July 1, 1898
Caribbean
Sea

Gulf of
Mexico
Tampa
FLORIDA

Bahamas

Havana
Cuba
ATLANTIC
OCEAN

USS *Maine* exploded
Feb. 1898
Santiago
HAITI
DOMINICAN
REPUBLIC
San
Juan
Puerto
Rico

Jamaica

Caribbean Sea

American forces
Spanish forces
American victory
U.S. Naval blockade
Spanish possessions

0   200   400 miles
0   200   400 kilometers

northern plains. When they were ordered to Cuba and traveled through the southern United States, they encountered segregation and racial threats. Despite such unfair treatment, they fought fiercely in Cuba and earned numerous citations for bravery, including five Congressional Medals of Honor.

The war in the Caribbean came to an end after the U.S. Navy destroyed the Spanish fleet as it attempted to escape from the harbor at Santiago. The Spanish surrendered on July 16. American troops then invaded and took control of Puerto Rico on July 25, meeting with no opposition. On August 12, Spain and the United States signed a cease-fire agreement. From the first battle in the Pacific to the cease-fire agreement, the entire war had lasted just 16 weeks.

Representatives of the two countries met in Paris on December 10, 1898, to agree on a peace treaty. In the **Treaty of Paris**, Spain granted independence to Cuba, gave Puerto Rico and Guam to the United States, and allowed the United States to buy the Philippines for $20 million. The United States later convinced the new Cuban government to lease land for the Guantanamo Bay Naval Base. As the United States gained new territory, Spain's 400-year run as a colonial power in the Americas ended.

States had to turn to volunteers to fight the war. With enthusiasm for the war running high, about 1 million men volunteered, which was far more than the army could handle. About 280,000 men actually saw active duty in the war.

The war in the Caribbean began in late June 1898 with U.S. troops landing at Guantanamo Bay in Cuba and additional forces converging on the harbor city of Santiago. The most famous land battle in Cuba, the Battle of San Juan Hill, was fought near Santiago on July 1. A volunteer cavalry regiment called the Rough Riders and two African-American regiments, the Ninth and Tenth Cavalries, charged up Kettle Hill while other units attacked San Juan Hill. The Rough Riders were commanded by Leonard Wood and Theodore Roosevelt, who had resigned as assistant secretary of the Navy to lead the regiment. American newspapers portrayed Roosevelt as a hero in the battle, which contributed to his success in his future campaign for president.

At the time the war broke out, the U.S. Army included four regiments of African-American soldiers who had been headquartered in the West and on the

HISTORICAL THINKING

1. **READING CHECK** Why did the United States fight in the Spanish-American War, and what did the country gain from it?

2. **INTERPRET MAPS** Which American fleet had to travel farther, the one sailing from Hong Kong to Manila in the Philippines or the one departing from Tampa, Florida, to fight in Cuba? Use the scale of miles on the maps to determine your answer.

3. **ANALYZE CAUSE AND EFFECT** How did yellow journalism help drive the United States into war with Spain?

4. **MAKE CONNECTIONS** Describe a recent example of yellow journalism, and compare its effect with the effect of the reporting about the *Maine* explosion.

THE PHILIPPINE-AMERICAN WAR

After just 16 weeks of fighting, the United States defeated Spain in what the American secretary of state dubbed "a splendid little war." The United States gained Puerto Rico, Guam, and the Philippines, but not all of the countries involved felt "splendid" about it.

AN OPPORTUNITY TO EXPAND

Once Spain signed the Treaty of Paris in 1898, its empire dwindled to almost nothing. The United States, on the other hand, had become an imperialist nation at the stroke of a pen, claiming control over three island territories in two oceans. Americans were divided about McKinley's diplomatic success in acquiring those lands, however. The Americans who favored manifest destiny believed acquiring foreign territories was the next logical step for the nation. Many others, however, disapproved of such expansion, recalling how American colonists felt about British rule many years before.

As the Treaty of Paris was being negotiated, President McKinley headed to the Midwest in October 1898 to convince his fellow citizens that annexing the Philippines was in the nation's best interests. The president gave many speeches stating his case for a more expansive foreign policy. A territory in the South Pacific would bolster trade

A GLOBAL PERSPECTIVE In the Umbrella Revolution of 2014, tens of thousands of people took to the streets of Hong Kong to protest attempts by mainland China to control the island's elections. After police tried to break up the protests, the people used colorful umbrellas to protect themselves from pepper spray, as shown in this photo. Although Hong Kong became part of mainland China in 1997, the people were promised their autonomy for 50 years. How does the reaction of the people of Hong Kong compare to the reaction of many Filipinos when the United States claimed control of the Philippines?

with China, he argued, and the Philippines could supply certain goods that Americans needed, such as sugar. McKinley explained that the Germans and the Japanese had positioned ships around the Philippines, waiting for a chance to occupy the archipelago. He reasoned that it was better for the Filipinos to be taken under the wing of the United States than to be governed by any other nation. In Iowa, McKinley told his audience, "We do not want to shirk a single responsibility that has been put upon us by the results of the war."

Many Filipinos, however, did not agree with McKinley's reasoning. **Emilio Aguinaldo**, one of the leaders of the rebellion against Spain before and during the Spanish-American War, believed the United States had promised the Filipinos their independence. Now he felt that Filipinos had battled one colonial power only to be handed over to another. Aguinaldo and his men readied themselves to fight yet again.

A BRUTAL WAR

Only two days after ratifying the treaty ending the Spanish-American War, the United States became embroiled in the Philippine-American War. Aguinaldo and his troops took control of the largest island in the Philippines and proclaimed it a republic, prompting a swift U.S. reaction. President McKinley sent a fleet of ships to put down the rebellion.

During 1899, the U.S. Army defeated the Filipinos in conventional battles. However, when faced with the highly organized and fully supplied American army, Aguinaldo and his men switched strategies. They started a guerrilla war, a war fought by unconventional means, such as sabotage, ambushes, and unexpected raids. Aguinaldo's troops were a grassroots group—untrained and assembled from local residents—but they had some advantages. They knew the geography of their island, and they looked like the civilian population. They could hit selected targets and then escape by blending in with the crowd. Individual soldiers slipped into the American troops' camps at night and sabotaged or stole equipment. Faced with this new threat, the American military responded by killing and torturing Filipino prisoners to gain information about the rebels' plans. American troops also looted and burned down villages, moving the inhabitants into camps that they then failed to supply with food.

The American press reported the soldiers' brutality, and enthusiasm waned in the United States for pursuing further expansion. People who opposed

PRIMARY SOURCE

Why do the Imperialists wish to subjugate us? What do they intend to do with us? Do they expect us to surrender—to yield our inalienable rights . . . to the absolute control of the United States? What would you do with our nine millions of people? Would you permit us to take part in your elections? Or, would you tax us without representation?

—from a letter to the American people, by Galicano Apacible, Filipino political leader, 1899

imperialism began to organize. The **American Anti-Imperialist League** became a voice against McKinley's foreign policy decisions. By 1900, many Americans believed the existing empire should be retained and protected—but not increased.

Even some of the soldiers fighting in the Philippines struggled with their purpose in the war. One soldier wrote, "I am not afraid, and am always ready to do my duty, but I would like someone to tell me what we are fighting for." A Minnesota general lamented, "It seems to me that we are doing something that is contrary to our principles in the past."

American troops captured Aguinaldo in 1901, effectively ending the rebellion. Some minor uprisings occurred through the next summer, but without Aguinaldo, who took an oath of allegiance to the United States, the rebel forces slowly disbanded. On July 4, 1902, President Theodore Roosevelt forgave the Filipino nationalists and proclaimed the end of the war. The fighting had claimed the lives of 4,200 American soldiers and more than 20,000 Filipino rebels. In addition, some 200,000 Filipino civilians perished in the warfare or from starvation and disease. The Philippines would not become an independent nation until more than four decades later, in 1946.

HISTORICAL THINKING

1. **READING CHECK** What were the reasons for the Philippine-American War, and what were the results?

2. **ANALYZE CAUSE AND EFFECT** How did the Philippine-American War affect some Americans' views on expansionist foreign policy?

3. **ANALYZE LANGUAGE USE** The word *guerrilla* means "little war" in Spanish. How does this meaning help you understand the difference between conventional and guerrilla warfare?

4. **MAKE CONNECTIONS** How did the Spanish-American War lead to the Philippine-American War?

INVOLVEMENT IN LATIN AMERICA

Have you ever felt overshadowed by a stronger opponent in an athletic contest? In the early 1900s, the United States cast such a shadow over Latin America.

ACQUIRING PUERTO RICO

As you have read, the United States gained control of Puerto Rico at the end of the Spanish-American War in 1898. Before the war, many Puerto Ricans had long sought independence from Spanish rule. **Luis Muñoz Rivera,** a leader of the Puerto Rican independence movement, had worked with the Spanish government to negotiate for the island's independence. By 1897, Puerto Rico had won the right to self-governance, though it remained a Spanish colony. When the United States acquired Puerto Rico, Muñoz Rivera continued to advocate for independence. But the U.S. government had its own ideas.

After gaining control of Puerto Rico, the United States initially appointed military officers to govern the island. But on April 12, 1900, Congress ratified the Foraker Act, which established the island's first House of Representatives and Supreme Court. The act reserved for the U.S. president the authority to appoint a governor and an executive council, but it gave some political power to Puerto Ricans as well.

Control of high government positions in Puerto Rico was important to U.S. interests for a number of reasons. The tropical island could supply goods, such as sugar, to the United States, and it served as a new market for American goods, such as coal, a natural resource Puerto Rico lacked. The United States could enjoy exclusive rights to trade. In addition, Puerto Rico would become the site of an important U.S. naval base.

BIG STICK DIPLOMACY

In 1901, Theodore Roosevelt became president. By then, in addition to the territories discussed, the United States possessed the previously uninhabited Wake Island as well as part of the island chain of Samoa, which became American Samoa. Earlier, in 1867, the United States had annexed Midway Islands. Roosevelt began making plans to extend American influence worldwide, especially in Latin America. He relied on recommendations made by Alfred T. Mahan years before: build a strong navy, adopt an aggressive foreign policy, and connect the Atlantic and Pacific oceans by digging a canal through Central America.

In terms of foreign policy, Roosevelt said the United States should "speak softly and carry a big stick," meaning the nation should negotiate peacefully while

This cartoon from 1904 shows President Roosevelt pulling the Great White Fleet, a fleet of battleships that he ordered to sail around the world to demonstrate American naval strength.

U.S. Overseas Expansion, 1867–1903

Alaska 1867
RUSSIA
CANADA
Midway Islands 1867
CHINA
JAPAN
UNITED STATES
ATLANTIC OCEAN
Wake Island 1899
Hawaii 1898
Puerto Rico 1898
Philippines 1898
PACIFIC OCEAN
Guam 1898
Panama Canal Zone 1903
Equator
SOUTH AMERICA
AUSTRALIA
American Samoa 1899
U.S. territories and possessions
0   500   1,000 miles
0   500   1,000 kilometers

flexing its military strength. Roosevelt employed his **Big Stick Diplomacy** early in his presidency during an incident involving Venezuela. In 1902, German and British ships destroyed the Venezuelan economy by blockading its ports in order to collect debts owed to them. The event forced the president to act. Roosevelt "spoke softly" by negotiating a deal to end the crisis, and he "carried a big stick" by writing a declaration that, when necessary, the United States would intervene in the affairs of Latin American nations. The declaration, called the **Roosevelt Corollary**, amended the Monroe Doctrine, a much earlier U.S. declaration that opposed European interference in the Americas.

The Roosevelt Corollary came into play later as Roosevelt set out to build a canal in Central America. The canal would dramatically cut shipping times between the East and West coasts of the United States. Ships at the time had to sail around all of South America to complete this journey. In 1902, Congress pursued a treaty to lease a tract of land for the canal on an **isthmus**, or strip of land between two bodies of water, in Colombia. When the Colombian government refused, Roosevelt gently encouraged the people who lived on the isthmus to start an insurrection, or rebellion, against the Colombian government. The presence of American ships around the isthmus discouraged the Colombians from putting down the insurrection, which in turn allowed the newly formed nation of Panama to quickly claim its independence.

The Panamanians agreed to lease a 10-mile tract of land to the United States, giving it control over the area. On March 3, 1904, construction began on the **Panama Canal** and continued long after Roosevelt's presidency. The canal opened in 1914. With the Panama Canal Zone, the United States added another foreign territory to its collection. Technically, the acquisitions had all taken place by treaty and not by force, but that did not stop people around the world from calling the United States an empire.

Roosevelt passed the responsibilities of his administration to President Taft in 1909. Taft generally followed Roosevelt's diplomatic techniques, although when opportunities to invest in China arose, he replaced Roosevelt's "big stick" with money. For instance, when the Chinese asked for help to buy Japanese-owned railroads in their country in 1909, Taft and other world leaders loaned the money to them. In return, Taft requested that the Chinese be more accommodating to American trade. American journalists dubbed this approach "Dollar Diplomacy."

HISTORICAL THINKING

1. **READING CHECK** How did President Roosevelt apply Big Stick Diplomacy in gaining land for the Panama Canal?

2. **INTERPRET MAPS** Which territories did the United States acquire in 1898?

3. **FORM AND SUPPORT OPINIONS** What do you think were the pros and cons of Big Stick Diplomacy?

VOCABULARY

Use each of the following vocabulary words in a sentence that shows an understanding of the term's meaning.

1. **Progressive Era**
    As a result of Progressive Era initiatives, fewer children worked as laborers in factories.

2. enfranchisement

3. conservation

4. initiative

5. syndicate

6. isolationism

7. reparations

8. yellow journalism

9. trustbuster

10. protectorate

READING STRATEGY
ANALYZE LANGUAGE USE

Complete the Word Map to analyze the meaning of the quotation from Theodore Roosevelt that appears at the beginning of the chapter. Then answer the question.

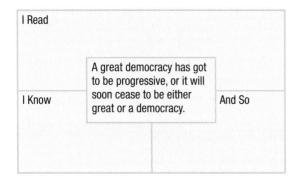

| I Read | A great democracy has got to be progressive, or it will soon cease to be either great or a democracy. | |
| I Know | | And So |

11. How did Roosevelt's progressivism impact the future of American democracy?

12. Where did women's suffrage fit within the progressive movement?

MAIN IDEAS

Answer the following questions. Support your answers with evidence from the chapter.

13. Why did the constitutional amendment guaranteeing women the right to vote become stalled? **LESSON 1.2**

14. Why were direct primaries considered a progressive idea? **LESSON 1.4**

15. Why is Theodore Roosevelt's presidency so strongly associated with the Progressive Era? **LESSON 2.1**

16. Why did progressives reject laissez-faire economics? **LESSON 2.1**

17. What problem did the Federal Reserve System solve? **LESSON 2.3**

18. What were some of the factors that changed Americans' minds about the purchase of Alaska from the Russians? **LESSON 3.**

19. Why did the United States seek to replace China's spheres of influence with the Open Door Policy? **LESSON 3.2**

20. What territories did the United States gain at the end of the Spanish-American War? **LESSON 3.3**

21. Why did some Americans oppose the United States' actions during the Philippine-American War? **LESSON 3.4**

22. How did President Roosevelt apply Big Stick Diplomacy in Latin America? **LESSON 3.5**

HISTORICAL THINKING

Answer the following questions. Support your answers with evidence from the chapter.

23. **MAKE GENERALIZATIONS** What methods did reformers use to achieve their goals during the Progressive Era?

24. **EVALUATE** In what way was President Roosevelt's Square Deal an innovative approach to labor disputes?

25. **MAKE INFERENCES** How did the United States' role in the world change after the Spanish-American War?

26. **SYNTHESIZE** What were the purpose and effects of the Open Door Policy?

27. **COMPARE AND CONTRAST** How did Roosevelt's Big Stick Diplomacy differ from Taft's Dollar Diplomacy?

28. **DRAW CONCLUSIONS** What was the impact of the Children's Bureau?

INTERPRET GRAPHS

Study the line graph below, which shows the results of censuses conducted on the Hawaiian Islands. Then answer the questions.

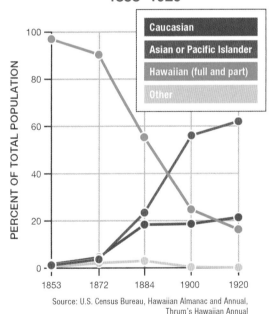

Hawaii's Changing Population, 1853–1920

Source: U.S. Census Bureau, Hawaiian Almanac and Annual, Thrum's Hawaiian Annual

29. Which population group declined the most and which increased the most during the time period covered on the graph?

30. What does the graph reveal about the non-native population of Hawaii during that time period?

ANALYZE SOURCES

In 1917, Carrie Chapman Catt delivered an address to Congress explaining why women's suffrage was inevitable and essential. Read the excerpt from the speech and answer the question that follows.

> Behold our Uncle Sam floating the banner with one hand, "Taxation without representation is tyranny," and with the other seizing the billions of dollars paid in taxes by women to whom he refuses "representation." Behold him again, welcoming the boys of twenty-one . . . to "a voice in their own government" while he denies that fundamental right of democracy to thousands of women public school teachers from whom many of these men learn all they know of citizenship and patriotism.

31. What point is Catt making about the United States government?

CONNECT TO YOUR LIFE

32. **ARGUMENT** Once the West was settled in the late 1800s, the United States turned its sights to the world outside its borders. American involvement in world affairs has increased ever since. Write an essay arguing whether or not the United States should have so much global influence, citing examples from the chapter and your own research.

TIPS

- Review American actions in the Pacific and the Caribbean discussed in the chapter.

- Research two or three current U.S. foreign involvements.

- Develop your topic by comparing U.S. actions described in the chapter with the present-day situations you researched.

- Use two or three vocabulary words from the chapter in your argument.

- End your essay with a recommendation on the role you believe the United States should have in world affairs.

NATIONAL GEOGRAPHIC | CONNECTION

Nature for Everyone

by Gary Strauss

Adapted from "Biologist Wants Nature for Everyone—Including Prisoners," by Gary Strauss, news.nationalgeographic.com, September 2016

National Geographic Explorer Nalini Nadkarni developed a reputation as "queen of the forest canopy," thanks to her extensive research among the towering branches of the forests of Costa Rica. On solid ground, she brings her knowledge of the natural world to unconventional settings. It's a long way from the Costa Rican rain forest to a U.S. prison, but Nadkarni navigates both environments with ease.

As a forest ecologist, Nadkarni spent her early career enmeshed in tree canopies. But after years of fieldwork and university life, she decided that her efforts needed a broader audience than scientists, academics, and natural history buffs. "I was preaching to the choir, so I began to ask myself how can I bring my message to others," says Nadkarni. "Rather than saying you need to read my articles or attend my lectures to understand my science, I took the approach of appealing to people in their own venues."

Nadkarni coordinated with rap artists to develop nature programs for at-risk youth, created a fieldwork outfit for a Barbie doll, and organized eco-fashion shows. She hoped that these entertaining yet educational initiatives would better connect people to trees and forests. Her work bringing science and nature programs to prisons could have that impact.

While teaching at Washington's Evergreen State College, she studied the movement of tree branches by attaching a paint brush to twigs. Measuring wind-aided changes and calculating them over 12 months, she found that a tree can sway back and forth up to 186,540 miles in a single year. "I began to think of other entities that are perceived to be static and stuck," she explains. "Prisoners are also stuck. But whether you're a CEO or an inmate stuck in solitary confinement, what we have in common is humanity and a connection to nature."

She put her observations into action by developing science and nature programs at Washington's Cedar Corrections Center. There, inmates working with biologists raised threatened Oregon spotted frogs. They also grew mosses in an effort to help replace what had been commercially harvested in old growth forests.

Those efforts evolved into the Sustainability in Prisons Project, funded in part by the National Science Foundation. The project spread to 10 Washington state prisons and facilities in Oregon, California, Ohio, and Maryland. The group's efforts include recycling programs, beekeeping, organic vegetable farms, tree planting, and flower nurseries. Inmates develop skills for future employment and gain a sense of purpose, responsibility, and teamwork. Nadkarni asserts that prisoners who participate are less likely to return to criminal activity after their release.

Now a biology professor and head of the University of Utah's Center for Science and Mathematics Education, Nadkarni has also brought nature to inmates housed in solitary confinement. She beamed images and videos of forests, oceans, mountains, and skies into their recreation rooms. While limited in scope, the impact has been dramatic. Some inmates housed for violent crimes or tendencies in the isolation unit at Oregon's Snake River Correctional Institution were shown nature videos. Those shown recordings of nature scenes committed 26 percent fewer violent infractions, according to a study presented in August 2016 to the American Psychological Association.

"We can't bring nature programs to maximum security," Nadkarni says. "But what we've found is that exposing violent offenders to images of nature for an hour a day brings down their stress and anxiety levels and reduces violent tendencies." She wants to bring her successes to other prisoners as well to further demonstrate her simple but profound approach.

For more from National Geographic check out "21st Century Cowboys" online.

UNIT INQUIRY: Produce a Documentary

In this unit, you learned about the changes that occurred in the United States in the late 1800s and early 1900s. From the displacement of Native Americans on the western frontier to the influx of immigrants into the growing industrial cities of the Northeast and Midwest, these changes produced a wide range of social, political, and economic problems. Writers and photographers documented the problems to call public attention to them.

ASSIGNMENT

Assume the role of a reporter and produce a short documentary that examines an important problem in American life between 1877 and 1920. Topics include poverty, child labor, substandard housing, unsafe working conditions, and political corruption in city governments. Explain the causes and effects of the problem and outline attempted solutions. Be prepared to present your documentary to the class.

Plan Review the social, economic, and political problems covered in this unit and choose one to investigate. Reread the text's description of the problem and make a list of questions you have about its causes, effects, and solutions. Use library and online resources to research multiple points of view on the issue. Evaluate each source's explanation of the cause of the problem. Determine which explanation best agrees with the text evidence provided to include in your documentary. Take notes using a graphic organizer like this one.

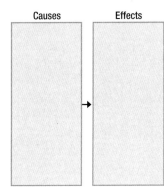

Causes → Effects

Produce Create an outline for your documentary. Then write a script in which you introduce the problem, identify its causes and effects, describe attempted solutions, and conclude by stating the outcome of the events. Revise the script as necessary. Consider your audience, and make sure to address the most significant points of the problem and solution. Choose photographs and other graphics from books and online sources to help convey your main points. Make a video of the narration and graphics.

Present Show your documentary to the class. You might consider one of these options:

- Post the documentary on a class website and invite your classmates and friends to view it. Invite viewers to share their feedback and questions with you. Respond to the feedback and questions you receive.

- Work with your teacher to schedule a class viewing of the documentary. After the viewing, ask classmates for their reactions and lead a class discussion of the issue.

NATIONAL GEOGRAPHIC | LEARNING FRAMEWORK ACTIVITIES

Write a Position Statement

`ATTITUDE` Responsibility

`SKILL` Communication

In the late 1800s and early 1900s, disadvantaged groups of Americans struggled to gain rights and improve their situations. These groups included farmers, Native Americans, laborers, immigrants, African Americans, and women. Choose one of these groups and research the group's struggles. Write a position statement addressed to a government official or agency of the time in which you detail your concerns and demands. Present your position statement to the class and discuss possible reactions of the government official or agency, taking into account historical context.

Plan a Protest

`ATTITUDE` Empowerment

`KNOWLEDGE` Critical Species

The settlement of the West and the expansion of farming had a negative impact on the natural environment in the late 1800s and early 1900s. A prime example of this negative impact was the fate of the American bison, which were hunted to the point of near extinction. Working with a partner or small group, research the bison's decline and plan a protest to persuade the government to take action to protect current and future herds. Create a slogan and protest signs. Outline where you will stage the protest and how you will draw participants. Present your plan to the class and solicit their reactions.

CRITICAL VIEWING Artist Franz Kline painted *Lower East Side Market Scene* (detail) around 1938, soon after moving to New York City. It shows an open-air market likely inspired by the artist's Greenwich Village neighborhood, with its older buildings and working-class residents. What does the painting reveal about American culture?

FROM THE GREAT WAR TO THE NEW DEAL

THE UNITED STATES

1920
Henry Ford produces more than 1 million cars, called Model Ts, and sells each one for $335.

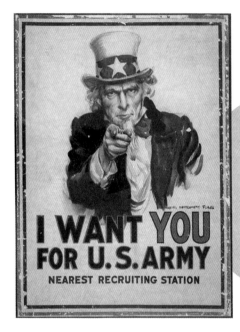

I WANT YOU FOR U.S. ARMY
NEAREST RECRUITING STATION

1917
The United States enters the war under President Woodrow Wilson. *(More than 4 million copies of this poster featuring "Uncle Sam" were printed between 1917 and 1918 to recruit soldiers.)*

1919
Congress passes the 19th Amendment, which, once ratified, grants women the right to vote.

1918
The Allies defeat Germany, bringing an end to the war.

1914
The assassination of Archduke Franz Ferdinand of Austria-Hungary triggers the start of World War I.

1910

1920

1919 EUROPE
The Treaty of Versailles is signed in France, which officially brings World War I to a close.

THE WORLD

1917 EUROPE
The Russian Revolution begins. *(Vladimir Lenin, who led the revolution)*

1916 AMERICAS
Mexican military leader Pancho Villa leads a raid in New Mexico, killing about 17 Americans.

HISTORICAL THINKING

DETERMINE CHRONOLOGY What other conflict
began the year the United States entered World War I?

1929
The stock market crashes, marking
the start of the Great Depression.
*(men wearing signs in downtown Chicago
advertising their qualifications, 1934)*

1933
To address the Great
Depression, Roosevelt
enacts a series of domestic
programs called the
New Deal. *(mural created
by Charles Wells under
the New Deal's Works
Progress Administration)*

1940
Roosevelt signs into
law an act creating
the first peacetime
draft in U.S. history.

1931
As a result of drought
and overplowed land,
terrible dust storms
sweep across the
Great Plains states, a
region some call the
Dust Bowl.

1932
Franklin Delano
Roosevelt is
elected to his
first term as
president.

1937 ASIA
Japan goes to war with China
and occupies Chinese cities
including Shanghai, Beijing,
and Nanjing.

1933 EUROPE
Adolf Hitler
becomes dictator
of Germany.
*(postage stamp of
Hitler made by the
Nazi regime)*

1922 AFRICA
Egypt gains
independence from
Great Britain.

THE GREAT WAR

1914–1920

HISTORICAL THINKING How did World War I affect the United States politically, economically, and socially?

CRITICAL VIEWING Trench warfare meant endless hours in muddy, wet conditions for soldiers during the Great War. In this 1916 photograph taken by John Warwick Brooke, British troops prepare to fight the Battle of the Somme in France, one of the bloodiest battles of the war. On the first day alone, the British suffered more than 57,000 casualties. What details in this photo convey the hardships of trench warfare?

"It is a fearful thing to lead this great peaceful people into war . . . **civilization itself seeming to be in the balance.**"

—President Woodrow Wilson

CRITICAL VIEWING The luxury ocean liner *Lusitania* departed for her last voyage from Pier 54 in New York City on May 1, 1915. Why do you think a crowd would have gathered to see the *Lusitania* off on its voyage?

THE SINKING
OF THE
LUSITANIA

Today you can board a plane anywhere in the continental United States and arrive in Europe in less than a day. In 1915, the only option for trans-Atlantic travel was by ship, and the fastest crossing you could expect to make was 4 days, 11 hours, and 42 minutes—a record set by the British passenger liner R.M.S. *Lusitania*, the swiftest and possibly the most luxurious ship afloat at that time.

A DISTANT WAR

On May 1, 1915, the *Lusitania* was set to depart New York for England with approximately 2,000 passengers and crew aboard, including nearly 200 Americans. The ship was also carrying war material, including ammunition, for the British war effort. Great Britain and its allies had been at war with Germany for nearly a year. Germany had taken the battle to the seas, deploying submarines to attack not only naval vessels but also civilian ships suspected of carrying ammunition or other war materials to Britain.

On the morning the *Lusitania* sailed, the German Embassy in the United States placed an advertisement in several newspapers stating, rather ominously, that Germany considered the seas around Great Britain to be a war zone, and that "vessels flying the flag of Great Britain . . . are liable to destruction in these waters."

This cork life ring covered in yellow fabric bears the name of the ill-fated passenger ship.

CROSSING THE ATLANTIC

The *Lusitania*'s passengers represented all walks of life, from the extremely wealthy who took up residence in the most glamorous cabins, to the third-class passengers who shared dormitory-type rooms. One of the most celebrated passengers aboard the *Lusitania* was the American millionaire Alfred Gwynne Vanderbilt, who had inherited a lavish fortune from his father, the railroad baron Cornelius Vanderbilt. Before the ship sailed, a reporter asked Alfred about the German newspaper threat. He replied, "I don't take much stock in it myself. What would they gain by sinking the *Lusitania*?"

Other notable American passengers included Theodate Pope, one of the first female architects in the United States, and Charles Lauriat, a well-known Boston book dealer. Pope spent the six-day Atlantic crossing reading and chatting with her traveling companion, Edwin Friend. Lauriat was transporting an extremely rare book by British writer Charles Dickens, and a priceless set of drawings.

Among the younger passengers was an American named Dorothy Conner, who found the uneventful trip across the Atlantic to be frustratingly dull. She remarked to a dinner companion, "I can't help hoping that we get some sort of thrill going up the [English] Channel." Later, when a friend remarked that she'd had her thrill, Conner replied, "I never want another."

A DISASTROUS COURSE

Captain William Turner appears to have sailed the *Lusitania* in a straight line through the dangerous waters of the Irish Sea. A zig-zag course would have made the ship a more difficult target for the U-boat torpedoes. Turner was later heavily criticized for his decision. How might a different course have changed history?

Embarked: May 1, 1915

WAR ZONE

German subs

United Kingdom

Germany

Sunk: May 7, 1915

New York

ATTACK NEAR IRELAND

At a little after 2 p.m. on May 7, the *Lusitania* was steaming into the Irish Sea, about 20 miles from the Irish Coast. Lurking in the same waters was the U-20, a German submarine with a mission to target British ships. The *Lusitania*'s captain ordered a turn to starboard, unknowingly placing the liner directly within the submarine's sights.

Passengers and crew alike watched, transfixed, as a German torpedo streaked toward the helpless ship. One passenger described himself as "spellbound" by the sight, adding, "I felt absolutely sick."

This moment of fearful anticipation ended when the torpedo slammed into the *Lusitania*'s side, blasting a hole in the hull. Immediately, seawater began to pour into the vessel at an estimated rate of 100 tons per second. The *Lusitania* began to list—or tilt—at an extreme angle, making it nearly impossible for passengers to

clamber into the lifeboats. Panicked passengers and crew members scrambled to find and put on their life vests, and parents desperately searched for their children in the crowds. Some people leaped into the sea while others clung to the sinking ship. Within 18 chaotic minutes, the *Lusitania* had disappeared beneath the surface of the sea.

Newspapers, including this May 8, 1915, edition of the *New York Times*, spread word of the event across the world.

ONE SHIPWRECK: TWO PERSPECTIVES

There are many survivor accounts of the sinking of the *Lusitania*, and it is valuable to compare these primary sources to better understand the event. The captain of the German U-boat that sank the ship offers a different perspective entirely from that of the survivors. Read and compare the two accounts below.

PRIMARY SOURCE

A SURVIVOR'S STORY

Dwight Harris, a young New Yorker, was carrying an engagement ring when he boarded the *Lusitania,* planning to propose to his beloved in England. He also brought with him a custom-made life preserver he had bought the day before. Pacing anxiously on deck on the day of the attack, he saw the torpedo: "a white and greenish streak in the water!" Harris hurried to his room to locate his life preserver, failed to get into a lifeboat, and jumped overboard.

Floating in the sea, he witnessed the *Lusitania's* plunge toward the bottom. He later described, "A terrible mass of iron, wood, steam, and water! And worst of all, human forms!—A great swirling greenish white bubble formed where the ship went down, which was a mass of struggling humanity and wreckage!" The ring Harris carried survived the catastrophe and he later offered it to Aileen Cavendish Foster, whom he married on July 2, 1915.

This illustration of survivors fleeing in lifeboats from the sinking of the *Lusitania* appeared in an Italian weekly newspaper.

PRIMARY SOURCE

THE SUBMARINE CAPTAIN'S STORY

The submarine that sank the *Lusitania* was the U-20, under the command of Captain Walther Schwieger. The U-20 left Germany on April 30 with a mission to destroy shipping vessels destined for Liverpool, England. It was a successful cruise: by May 7, the submarine had already sunk three vessels off the coast of Ireland. That morning, Captain Schwieger decided to turn for home, since the U-20 was running low on both fuel and torpedoes. Then, at 1:20 p.m., an officer at the periscope spotted the distinctive shape of the *Lusitania.*

In his ship's log, Schwieger provided one of the clearest eyewitness accounts of the torpedo's aftermath. He recorded, "There was a terrific panic on her deck. Overcrowded lifeboats, fairly torn from their positions, dropped into the water. Desperate people ran helplessly up and down the decks. Men and women jumped into the water and tried to swim to empty, overturned lifeboats. It was the most terrible sight I have ever seen."

The "terrible sight" did not dampen Schwieger's enthusiasm for his job. On a single cruise in September 1915, he sank 11 ships, including the passenger ship *Hesperian*, which was carrying home the body of a Canadian passenger who had been killed on the *Lusitania*. By the time the war in Europe was over, German submarines had sunk more than 4,000 ships, around one-fourth of the world's shipping vessels.

AFTERMATH

During the hours and days immediately following the disaster, the main concern for family and friends of the victims was the frantic search for survivors—or for the bodies of those who had perished. Alfred Vanderbilt had last been seen helping others escape the wreckage. His body was never found. Dorothy Conner survived the sinking and went on to serve in France, supporting the troops. Charles Lauriat also survived, but his irreplaceable book and drawings were lost in the icy Irish Sea. When rescuers pulled Theodate Pope aboard their boat, they believed she was dead and left her on deck with the other bodies. Fortunately, another rescued passenger realized she was alive and called for help to revive her. Her companion, Edwin Friend, was among those who disappeared.

It is believed that 1,191 people died in the sinking of the *Lusitania*. Of those, 129 were Americans. Exact totals have remained elusive because of the difficulty in identifying stowaways and last-minute changes to crew and passenger lists. Naturally, the news of the sinking sparked shock and horror in the United States. In private, President Wilson expressed his fury to his secretary. "In God's name, how could any nation calling itself civilized purpose [plan] so horrible a thing?" he asked. In public, however, he made speeches counseling a restrained response to the German aggression.

Despite their anger, most Americans agreed with Wilson; they opposed the idea of the United States entering the war in Europe. Still, the sinking of the *Lusitania* can be seen as the first in a series of events that did finally engage the United States in the conflict that would engulf the world. By the time Wilson declared war in 1917, American public opinion had turned firmly against Germany.

THINK ABOUT IT

1. What factors likely contributed to the sinking of the *Lusitania*?

2. If the ship hadn't been sunk, do you think the United States would have been drawn into the war? Why or why not?

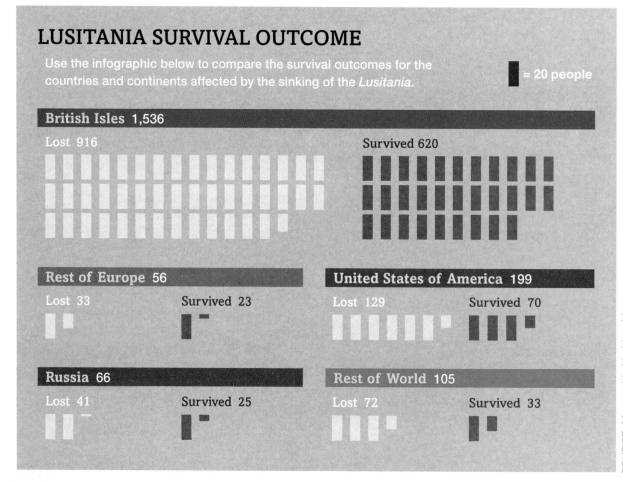

LUSITANIA SURVIVAL OUTCOME

Use the infographic below to compare the survival outcomes for the countries and continents affected by the sinking of the *Lusitania*.

█ = 20 people

British Isles 1,536

Lost 916   Survived 620

Rest of Europe 56

Lost 33   Survived 23

United States of America 199

Lost 129   Survived 70

Russia 66

Lost 41   Survived 25

Rest of World 105

Lost 72   Survived 33

SOURCE: Merseyside Maritime Museum

A SECOND EXPLOSION?

The *Lusitania* was a well-constructed ship, designed to survive the flooding of one or two of its internal compartments. Why, then, did it sink almost instantly after just one torpedo strike? Many witnesses claimed that a second explosion followed the torpedo strike, and several theories have been used to explain this blast, but none have been proven.

Some have claimed that the *Lusitania* was secretly carrying explosives for Britain's military and that these were ignited by the torpedo strike. As you have read, the ship was in fact carrying rifle ammunition and other war supplies, but none of these materials would have caused a massive explosion.

National Geographic Explorer-in-Residence Robert Ballard explored the *Lusitania's* wreck in 1993 and proposed the theory that the ship's coal bunkers exploded. The coal bunkers were enormous compartments that stored the 5,690 tons of coal needed to fuel the engines. By the end of the long voyage, only highly combustible coal dust remained in those spaces, but the dust may have been too damp to explode.

During hearings after the sinking, the *Lusitania's* captain proposed that the torpedo could have ruptured the line that carried steam from the boiler rooms to power the propellers. Tests conducted by a National Geographic team in 2012 seem to support this explanation, but definitive proof remains elusive. The wreck of the *Lusitania* guards its secrets.

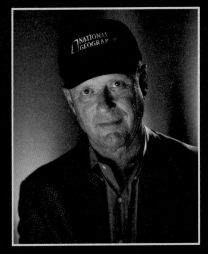

Says Robert Ballard of the *Lusitania* wreckage: "She is now a faint ghost of the ocean greyhound she once was, one of the saddest wrecks I've ever seen. But when I visualize her upturned bow, I can imagine the pride of those who once sailed on the swiftest ship in the world."

A small submersible called *Delta* took Ballard to the *Lusitania* for a firsthand look at the wreckage.

WAR BREAKS OUT IN EUROPE

Have you ever built a house of cards? Each card must be placed perfectly in order to support the delicate structure. Nudge just one card, and the whole building collapses. In 1914, Europe was a house of cards, just waiting for the nudge that would lead to fighting and chaos.

EUROPE AT THE EDGE OF WAR

In 1914, Europe was divided into hostile nations and poised for war. At the heart of the tension was lingering animosity between France and Germany in the wake of the Franco-Prussian War. In 1870, Germany had conquered France and then demanded $1 billion. Germany also seized the eastern French provinces of Alsace and Lorraine. For Germany, the acquisition of the provinces was the final step in unification. German leaders brought together several regions under the control of the kingdom of Prussia and declared a German Empire in 1871.

Frustrated by the military loss and determined to reclaim the lost provinces, the French worked to rebuild their economy and military. To further strengthen its position against Germany, France also formed alliances, or agreements of mutual support, with Russia and Great Britain. The German government had similar understandings with Austria-Hungary and the Ottoman Empire. Italy had been part of an earlier alliance with Germany and Austria-Hungary, but those ties had become frayed by 1914.

Because of these complex and delicate networks of treaties and alliances, an attack on one country could—and did—trigger retaliation by others and plunge all of Europe into a state of war. The conflict would come to be called "the Great War" because of the enormous number of casualties that resulted from it and the large number of nations involved in it. As war once again loomed in Europe in the 1930s, many historians began to refer to the conflict that began in 1914 as "World War I."

THE THREE –*ism*'s

Alongside the alliances, three cultural attitudes helped push Europe down the path to conflict. Nationalism is a strong belief in one's own country and its superiority to others. In Europe, nationalism often conflicted with individuals' ethnic ties to a certain region or group of people.

Imperialism is the drive to conquer or colonize other territories and form an empire. Great Britain, Germany, and France were imperial powers, competing for colonies in Africa and Asia and the raw materials and markets that the colonies provided.

Militarism is the belief that a government must create a strong military and be prepared to use it to achieve the country's goals. By 1914, Germany was a major military power, and France was working to catch up. Britain did not have a strong military presence on the ground, but it did have a large and powerful navy and felt threatened by Germany's push to expand its own seagoing forces.

AN ASSASSINATION SPARKS WAR

On June 28, 1914, **Archduke Franz Ferdinand** of Austria-Hungary and his wife were assassinated, or murdered for political reasons, during a parade in the capital city of Bosnia. Their killer was a Serbian nationalist. Serbia was allied with Russia and had a history of conflict with Austria-Hungary.

One after another, European alliances were activated. The Austrians, supported by the Germans, made harsh demands of the Serbs to punish them for the assassination. Russia came to Serbia's defense, and France declared its support for its ally Russia.

Alliances and Major Battles in World War I, 1914–1916

Legend:
- Allied Powers
- Central Powers
- Neutral nation
- German U-boat activity
- Naval blockade
- ✷ Battle

NORWAY
SWEDEN
Oslo
Stockholm
Helsinki
•Petrograd (St. Petersburg)
Tallinn
North Sea
Blockade 1914–1917
✷ *Jutland 1916*
DENMARK
Copenhagen
•Riga
•Moscow
Baltic Sea
Danzig
✷ *Masurian Lakes 1914*
Tannenberg 1914
•Vilnius
UNITED KINGDOM
NETHERLANDS
Amsterdam
see inset
•Berlin
•Warsaw
RUSSIA
London•
Brussels•
BELGIUM
LUX.
GERMANY
Frankfurt
•Prague
Kiev•
•Kharkov
Paris•
Strasbourg
•Vienna
•Budapest
FRANCE
SWITZ.
Geneva•
•Odessa
Milan•
Venice•
•Trieste
Fiume
AUSTRIA-HUNGARY
Don
Dnieper
Dniester
ATLANTIC OCEAN
Genoa•
Zara
Sarajevo•
Belgrade•
ROMANIA
Bucharest
•Sevastopol
ITALY
•Rome
MONTE-NEGRO
SERBIA
Danube
Black Sea
Adriatic Sea
ANDORRA
Corsica
Naples•
ALBANIA
BULGARIA
Sofia•
•Constantinople
PORTUGAL
SPAIN
Sardinia
GREECE
✷ *Gallipoli 1915*
OTTOMAN EMPIRE
Athens•
Izmir (Smyrna)•
Spanish Morocco (Sp.)
Sicily
Malta (U.K.)
Crete
Dodecanese (It.)
Cyprus (U.K.)
Euphrates
Tigris
MOROCCO (Fr.)
ALGERIA (Fr.)
TUNISIA (Fr.)
Mediterranean Sea
Ifni (Sp.)
LIBYA (It.)
•Cairo
NEJD
Rio de Oro (Sp.)
FRENCH WEST AFRICA (Fr.)
Tropic of Cancer
EGYPT (U.K.)
Nile
Red Sea

The Western Front, 1914–1916

Legend:
- ✷ Battle
- ← Allied troop movement
- → German troop movement

North Sea
52°N
NETHERLANDS
UNITED KINGDOM
Ostend•
•Antwerp
Calais•
✷ *Ypres, Second Battle 1915*
•Brussels
Aachen•
Strait of Dover
Ypres, First Battle 1914
•Lille
BELGIUM
Liège•
Namur•
English Channel
•Mons
Meuse
Coblenz•
Rhine
✷ *Somme 1916*
Somme
ARDENNES
Amiens•
Mézières•
Trier•
LUXEMBOURG
•Luxembourg
Moselle
WESTERN FRONT 1914
Oise
Aisne
FRANCE
Argonne Forest
Metz•
GERMANY
Reims•
✷ *Verdun 1916*
Seine
Marne
Nancy•
Strasbourg•
Paris•
✷ *Marne, First Battle 1914*
Épinal•
VOSGES
Rhine
Meuse
Moselle
Basel•
SWITZ.
48°N
9°E
N W E S
0 25 50 miles
0 25 50 kilometers
2°E 4°E 6°E 8°E

N W E S
0 200 400 miles
0 200 400 kilometers

LIBERIA
ANGLO-EGYPTIAN SUDAN (U.K.)
ERITREA (It.)
FRENCH SOMALILAND (Fr.)
ETHIOPIA
Niger

We entered the trenches about midnight, we found them very uncomfortable, as there was only one dug-out for our company. . . . I spent six hours making myself a shelter in a communication trench, a sort of sofa with a waterproof sheet above it, cut out of one side of a five-foot trench. I worked most of the night throwing earth up to shield my bed, as the Germans were sniping at our parapet all day long. Meals were wretched, as we had nowhere decent to eat them, and we also lost our principal ration bag, containing tinned fruits and other joys.

—from the personal account of British Lieutenant William Andrew Turnbull, regarding the trenches near Hooge, France, 1915

In early August, Germany declared war on both Russia and France, invading Belgium in a push to reach France's northern border.

Alarmed by the actions of belligerent, militaristic Germany, which lay just across the English Channel, Britain declared war on the country. Within months, Europe was consumed by a war between two alliances: the **Central Powers** (primarily Germany, Austria-Hungary, and Turkey) and the **Allies** (primarily Great Britain, France, and Russia). Italy remained neutral at first but eventually joined the Allies in 1915.

The sudden outbreak of fighting in Europe surprised Americans. Although the arms race among the great powers had seemed potentially dangerous, it had been a century since a war involving all of the major European countries had erupted. Additionally, American faith in progress and the betterment of humanity, a principal part of the Progressive Era's creed, made war unthinkable.

TRENCH WARFARE ON TWO FRONTS

For years before the events of 1914, Germany had been preparing to wage war on France and Russia. **The Schlieffen Plan**, devised by a German army officer and completed in 1906, called for a rapid conquest of France, so that German troops could then turn east and

IN THE TRENCHES

The Great War is known for its trench warfare. Troops fighting for the Allies and Central Powers dug trenches fairly close to each other to attack and defend from below ground level. Trench warfare is typically used when the troops defending themselves from an attack have superior firepower, forcing the opposition to give up their mobility by digging trenches for protection.

Great War trench systems usually included 2–4 parallel trenches connected by communication trenches.

Soil or stone parapets ran in front and behind each trench and contained places for soldiers to fire at the enemy.

Trenches were usually dug in a zig-zag pattern to prevent the enemy from firing straight down it from either end.

parapet

NO MAN'S LAND

communication trench

Barbed wire was used to defend the trenches and trap the enemy.

No Man's Land was the area between the trenches of the opposing armies.

CRITICAL VIEWING This colorful 1917 postcard features the flags of the Allies in the Great War. From left: Portugal, Serbia, Belgium, Italy, France, Great Britain, the United States, Romania, Russia, and Japan. What might have been the goal behind the creation of artwork like this during the Great War?

march on Russia. This strategy failed, however, when the British Army joined France in stalling the advance of the German Army before it reached Paris. By the end of 1914, Germany found itself fighting enemies on two fronts, or battle lines. On the Western Front in northern France, German troops battled French and British forces; on the Eastern Front, Germany faced off with Russia.

On both fronts, a type of fighting called trench warfare prevailed. To shelter from enemy artillery fire, troops would dig complex networks of trenches into the ground, often starting with simple foxholes that could hold one or two soldiers. The holes were then deepened and connected by shallow crawling trenches. From there, the trenches were excavated further underground to strengthen them, and lined with boards to ease movement along the passageways. The boards also helped troops avoid potential diseases caused by mud and dirty water.

Fighting between the trenches took a brutal toll on all sides. One army might take an enemy trench at the cost of thousands of lives, only to lose it again within a matter of weeks. In one battle along the Somme River in France, more than a million soldiers were killed or wounded in order for the Allies to advance

a meager six miles. The space between enemy trenches, called "No Man's Land," had an average width of 150 to 250 yards, but the distance could vary from just a few yards to miles across. Once productive farm fields or lush open meadows, No Man's Land quickly turned into a nightmarish dead landscape filled with rubble, bomb craters, and the bodies of soldiers killed by artillery or machine-gun fire. Sometimes wounded soldiers suffered for days there before they died.

HISTORICAL THINKING

1. **READING CHECK** Why was trench warfare so costly in human lives?

2. **ANALYZE CAUSE AND EFFECT** How did the conclusion of the Franco-Prussian war lead to hostilities between Germany, France, and Britain?

3. **MAKE GENERALIZATIONS** How do militarism and nationalism affect a country's attitude toward going to war?

4. **MAKE INFERENCES** Based on the diagram of trench warfare and what you have read in the chapter, what can you infer about the effectiveness of this type of fighting?

1.2   **MAIN IDEA** When war broke out in Europe, President Wilson declared
that the United States would not take sides, and most Americans
supported this decision.

WILSON'S NEUTRALITY

In 1914, Americans were eagerly following the baseball pennant race between
the New York Giants and the Boston Braves and flocking to the movies to
escape into the world of silent films. The guns of war in Europe seemed like
distant and muffled thunder.

WILSON'S MORAL DIPLOMACY

In 1914, when the war began in Europe, the United
States began to supply the Allies with weapons
and goods. However, President Woodrow Wilson
firmly declared the country would follow a policy
of neutrality, or refusal to support either side in the
war. He asked his fellow citizens to "be neutral in
fact as well as in name" and "impartial in thought as
well as in action." Elected president in 1912, Wilson
had wanted to concentrate on a domestic policy of
economic reform. In 1913, he remarked to a friend,

"it would be the irony of fate if my administration had
to deal chiefly with foreign affairs." When confronted
with the question of whether to support one of the
warring sides in Europe, Wilson left no doubt of
his opinion. "Our whole duty for the present . . . is
summed up in the motto America First," he said. "Let
us think of America before we think of Europe."

In fact, however, Wilson did actively pursue matters
of foreign policy even before being confronted with
the war in Europe. Wilson believed in a concept
called **moral diplomacy**, which required that the

Woodrow Wilson, shown here giving a speech after his 1912 nomination for
president of the United States, had been elected New Jersey's governor in 1910
and was elected U.S. president just two years later.

United States drastically reduce its intervention in the affairs of other countries. Wilson felt that the role of the United States should be to act as an example of democracy and to support the efforts of other peoples to elect their own governments. Wilson contrasted his philosophy to the "dollar diplomacy" practiced by his predecessor. Dollar diplomacy was a theory used to justify U.S. interference with the governments of countries in which American companies stood to make a profit. Pursuing the ideal of moral diplomacy, Wilson tried to lessen U.S. involvement in the Philippines and Latin America.

AMERICAN PUBLIC OPINION

Most Americans were solidly in agreement with Wilson's stance on the war in Europe. Still, many expressed sympathy for one or more of the countries embroiled in the fighting. The United States was home to more than five million German Americans, who tended to favor the Central Powers. The three million-plus Irish Americans strongly resented England and cheered for its enemies. Russia, with its authoritarian government, was generally regarded with suspicion. On the other hand, many Americans felt a kinship with Britain and France, which were both democracies and had a great deal of shared history with the United States.

Germany initiated an extensive propaganda campaign to sway American public opinion in its favor. The campaign was conducted principally through pamphlets and newspaper advertisements. At the same time, the German government used espionage, or spying, and sabotage to harm the Allied war effort by preventing American goods from being shipped to Britain. German agents would find ways to destroy the goods in the United States before they could be loaded onto ships, costing American businesses a great deal of money and sometimes injuring or killing civilians. When instances of sabotage were eventually discovered, they helped turn American public opinion against Germany.

American public opinion of the Central Powers was further soured by stories appearing in the *New York Times* in December 1915, reporting the killing or forced deportation of millions of Armenian civilians by the Turkish government. This campaign by the Turks became known as the **Armenian genocide**.

ECONOMIC TIES

While Americans were divided in their emotional loyalties to the European powers, the U.S. government had close economic ties to the Allies. In 1914, exports to Britain and France totaled $754

million. In contrast, that same year Germany received $190 million worth of imported products from the United States. As the war continued, the economic difference widened. In 1916, exports from the United States to Britain and France stood at $2.75 billion, while trade with Germany had dwindled to practically nothing because the British Navy was blockading German ports.

The United States had other growing financial ties to the Allies. In order to pay for American goods used in their war efforts, the Allies borrowed billions of dollars from the U.S. government, as well as from American banks and investors. Thus, a victory for the Allies would benefit many American investors.

This political cartoon draws attention to the U.S. government's conflicting attitude toward the war. It portrays Uncle Sam advertising peace on the front of his two-sided "sandwich board" and promoting the sale of ammunition to warring countries on the back.

HISTORICAL THINKING

1. **READING CHECK** Why did some Americans favor the Central Powers while others favored the Allies?

2. **COMPARE AND CONTRAST** What are the differences in the principles behind moral diplomacy and dollar diplomacy?

3. **MAKE INFERENCES** Why might a military defeat for the Allies cause a loss to American investors?

PRESSURES TO ENTER THE WAR

In 1914, the war in Europe seemed remote. Its violence was taking place on the far side of the ocean and was hardly relevant to life in the United States. By 1917, the war was on America's doorstep, and American blood had been shed.

GERMAN ATTACKS AT SEA

Since colonial times, the U.S. government had generally followed a policy of isolationism by declining to become involved in politics or wars in Europe. Even though certain groups within the United States sympathized with either the Allies or the Central Powers, the American public as a whole saw no reason to depart from the centuries-old policy. Even so, two strong forces were slowly pushing the United States toward engagement in the war: the economic ties with Britain and France that have already been discussed and the risk posed to American lives by the fighting.

American civilians were mainly at risk when they were at sea. Germany was confronted with a British naval blockade that prevented imported goods such as food and ammunition from reaching German ports. In 1914, the German Navy turned to a new

This 1916 campaign button reflected Wilson's isolationist platform.

weapon to combat the blockade: submarines, also called **U-boats** (short for *unterseeboot*, the German word for "submarine"). German submarines targeted not only enemy warships but also merchant ships that might be carrying war-related supplies from the United States to British or French ports. Even trans-Atlantic passenger ships, which often carried U.S. citizens, were not safe from the U-boats, since they were often suspected of also carrying cargo destined for the Allied war effort.

As you have read, on May 1, 1915, the passenger ship *Lusitania* left New York harbor for Liverpool, England. The *Lusitania* was huge, luxurious, and the fastest ship afloat. Its legendary speed offered no protection, however, when a German submarine encountered the ship in the Irish Sea on May 7 and sank it with a torpedo. Wilson and the nation were angered by the deaths of 129 Americans aboard the ship. The president demanded an apology from the German government, as well as a pledge to limit submarine warfare. Eventually, Germany agreed to stop attacking civilian ships without warning.

GERMAN U-BOAT

The German U-boat was less than 150 feet long and only 12 feet in diameter. The crew of 35 were packed into a tiny space no bigger than a double-decker bus.

Ship's Engines
Ship's battery engines generated explosive hydrogen gas.

GERMANY BREAKS ITS PROMISE

Despite the sinking of the *Lusitania* and the deaths of American citizens in other submarine attacks, Wilson refused to join the war. In the 1916 election, he ran on a platform of prosperity, progressivism, and peace. He won re-election after a campaign that featured the slogan "He kept us out of the war." Wilson then proposed ending the war through negotiation, but both Britain and Germany rejected his offer to broker a peace treaty. In response, Wilson addressed the Senate in January 1917 with a speech that called for a "Peace Without Victory" in which he argued that "only a peace among equals can last." The warring powers remained unwilling to cooperate, convinced that the only place to find a solution was the battlefield.

By 1917, the British naval blockade was successfully starving Germany of much-needed war supplies. On land, the Central Powers' armies were bogged down in the trenches and making no progress in either the east or the west. Becoming desperate, Germany decided to resume unrestricted submarine attacks to choke off the stream of supplies arriving in Great Britain by sea. The German military commanders knew this move would enrage Wilson and the American public, but they gambled that all-out submarine warfare would bring down the Allies before the United States could declare war and send troops to Europe.

THE ZIMMERMANN TELEGRAM

At the same time, another incident helped propel the country toward war. British intelligence had intercepted and decoded a secret telegram from the German foreign minister, Arthur Zimmermann, to Germany's ambassador in Mexico. The **Zimmermann Telegram** laid out a plan to ally with Mexico and offer financial aid to the country if it attacked the United States. The telegram promised that Arizona, Texas, and New Mexico would be returned to Mexico as part of this deal. Wilson released this diplomatic bombshell to the public on March 1, 1917.

PRIMARY SOURCE

The world must be made safe for democracy. Its peace must be planted upon the tested foundations of political liberty. We have no selfish ends to serve. We desire no conquest, no dominion [control over another country]. We seek no indemnities [promises to pay for any damages] for ourselves, no material compensation for the sacrifices we shall freely make. We are but one of the champions of the rights of mankind. We shall be satisfied when those rights have been made as secure as the faith and the freedom of nations can make them.

—from President Woodrow Wilson's Joint Address to Congress Leading to a Declaration of War Against Germany, April 2, 1917

From that point, events moved quickly to bring the United States to war. On March 18, the Germans sank three American ships. On April 2, Wilson called Congress to a special session and asked for a declaration of war against Germany. He pledged to fight for "the ultimate peace of the world and for the liberation of its peoples, the German peoples included." In many ways, Wilson's war declaration was also an effort to continue promoting America's vision for the world. Congress agreed and declared war on Germany on April 6, 1917.

HISTORICAL THINKING

1. **READING CHECK** What events led President Wilson to ask Congress to formally declare war on Germany?

2. **IDENTIFY PROBLEMS AND SOLUTIONS** Why did Germany choose to launch unrestricted submarine warfare in 1917?

3. **EVALUATE** For Germany, what were the advantages and disadvantages of submarine warfare?

Crew's Quarters
Up to 35 men slept in very cramped conditions.

Torpedoes
The U-boats were armed with six torpedoes.

MAIN IDEA As the United States prepared for war, the government acted to increase the production of war goods, recruit soldiers and sailors, and gain Americans' support, but efforts to raise morale also eroded important liberties.

AMERICA ENTERS THE WAR

On every public surface, colorful posters encouraged young men to join the armed forces. Factories converted their assembly lines to make uniforms instead of children's clothes. Americans were asked to have a "meatless" and a "wheatless" day each week so that more food could be sent to Europe. The United States was going to war, and life was changing for everyone.

BUILDING A MILITARY—AND FAST

By 1917, both Germany and the Allies were battle weary, and the number of casualties on both sides was staggering. On the Western Front, where the Allies and the Germans confronted each other in France, more than 1.4 million French soldiers had been killed or wounded in 1915 alone. In a single battle at the French town of Verdun in 1916, both sides lost more than 300,000 men. Gigantic battles also occurred on the Eastern Front between the Russians and the Germans and their Austrian allies.

Although American entry into the Great War came later than the Allies had hoped, they greatly welcomed the help. Unfortunately, in 1917, the United States was in a poor position to supply desperately needed soldiers to the Allies; together, the regular U.S. Army and National Guard numbered only 379,000 troops. The power of the federal government began to increase in response to the need to mobilize people for war. In fact, the war initiated a century-long growth of the federal government. Average citizens found they had to respond to government programs in strange and unfamiliar ways, including accepting new rules for their businesses and changing their eating habits.

The government grew first through the administration of the draft. In May 1917, Congress adopted the **Selective Service Act**, which required all men between the ages of 21 and 30 to register for the draft. By the end of World War I, 3.7 million American men would serve as soldiers or sailors. The corps of soldiers sent to fight in Europe was called the **American Expeditionary Forces (AEF)**. At the head of these troops was

General **John J. Pershing**, an experienced military leader who had commanded troops in Cuba, Mexico, and the American West.

THE WARTIME ECONOMY

As the United States entered into the most extensive conflict it had ever faced in terms of dollars, American businesses were also caught unprepared for war. The war effort would require the manufacturing of ships, airplanes, guns, and ammunition, but after a decades-long peacetime economy, American factories were accustomed to producing items like cars, bicycles, and kitchen stoves. They too would need to be readied for war.

To help solve this problem, the government undertook the organization of the war at home. Wilson began by establishing the **War Industries Board (WIB)**. The WIB oversaw manufacturing in the United States, finding ways to make factories more efficient as they converted to wartime production. Some labor unions threw their support behind the war effort and the WIB. In exchange for a voice in deciding economic policy, the American Federation of Labor promised that it would not strike or insist that factories hire only union members. Through the creation of the WIB and other agencies, the federal government increased its role in the U.S. economy.

Outside of the workplace, the government also promoted civilian support for the war. All Americans were asked to buy **Liberty Bonds**. As you have read, purchasing a war bond was, in essence, loaning money to the U.S. government. The government would repay the cost of the bond after 30 years, and in the meantime, the buyer received

CRITICAL VIEWING During the war, women were recruited into jobs vacated by men who had gone off to fight. New factory jobs, especially in munitions factories like the ones shown above, were also created as part of the war effort and became the largest employers of women in 1918. How might the work women did during the war have related to their quest for suffrage?

annual interest at a rate of 3.5 percent. Those who failed to buy war bonds were deemed unpatriotic and said to be helping the Germans. Ultimately, the total cost of the war to the United States exceeded $35 billion. The United States had loaned over $11.2 billion to the Allies, most of which was never repaid. Yet President Wilson counted on the Allies' financial dependence on the United States to leverage achieving the goals he had for postwar diplomacy.

WARTIME FOOD

In addition to financial support, the Allies needed food. To mobilize the agricultural resources of the United States, Congress passed the Lever Act, which established the Food Administration. Wilson named **Herbert Hoover** to head the agency. A mining engineer from California, Hoover had gained international fame through his work to feed the starving people of Belgium. He asked Americans to observe days without meat and wheat because "wheatless days in America make sleepless nights in Germany." Additionally, families planted "victory gardens" to grow fruits and vegetables. With the price of wheat rising higher, farmers were induced to expand their production, increasing the wheat crop from 637 million bushels in 1917 to 921 million bushels a year later.

DISSENT AND CIVIL LIBERTIES

Americans on the home front had mixed reactions to the war. Some were vocal in expressing their dissent, or disagreement, with the government's official opinion. Many men proclaimed themselves **conscientious objectors**—people who refuse to fight in a war for religious reasons—while others simply failed to register for the draft. Opposition to the war was especially prevalent among German Americans and Irish Americans.

To counter possible dissent and raise the country's enthusiasm for the war, the government established the **Committee on Public Information (CPI)**, which launched a massive campaign of advertising and propaganda. George Creel, the head of the committee, declared that its task was to create a spirit of "[brotherhood], devotion, courage, and deathless determination." The CPI used pamphlets, posters, billboards, movies, and dynamic public speakers to spread its message. This was no easy task for Creel, who called it "the world's greatest adventure in advertising."

The campaign stirred up strong feelings of patriotism but also hostility toward everything German. Hamburgers, named after the German town of Hamburg, came to be called "Salisbury steak" or "liberty steak." Sauerkraut was renamed "liberty cabbage," and the people in some cities gave up pretzels. German literature vanished from library shelves, and schools stopped teaching the German language. More alarming, German Americans experienced prejudice and extreme nativism, or a policy that favors the interests of native inhabitants over those of immigrants, and became the targets of suspicion, threats, and even violence.

The government had legitimate reasons to be concerned about German espionage, but the measures taken to combat it during the war were excessive. The government began a campaign against radicals and progressives, a position that Wilson had opposed during his run for re-election in 1916. This reversal of policy undermined public support for the president in domestic politics. In his eagerness to win the war, Wilson alienated part of his own political base.

ENSURING PATRIOTIC BEHAVIOR

The Wilson administration and Congress enacted a number of laws designed to place limits on the rights of Americans to criticize the government or the war effort. National Security concerns led to the passage and enforcement of the Espionage Act of

ARE YOU A SLACKER?

Nobody likes to be called a slacker, but nowadays acting like one will only get you in trouble with a teacher, parent, or boss. In 1917 and 1918, the term "slacker" referred to a man who failed to register for the draft or declare a conscientious objection. At first, the government tried using publicity to shame slackers into registering. Then, in 1918, the Justice Department took more serious steps. Agents began raiding restaurants and ballparks or just approaching groups on street corners. Any man who could not show draft registration papers was promptly arrested and taken to jail.

1917. The act was designed to prevent sabotage and spying, but simply speaking out against the war could be considered illegal. The Trading with the Enemy Act authorized the postmaster general to suspend the delivery of foreign-language publications or any material he believed might be offensive to the government.

The Sedition Act of 1918 prohibited "uttering, printing, writing, or publishing any disloyal, profane, scurrilous [slanderous], or abusive language" about either the government or the armed forces. Thus, nearly any public criticism could be deemed punishable by law in an attempt to prevent sedition, the criminal act of trying to persuade individuals to undermine the government. These acts severely encroached on Americans' **civil liberties**—the right to engage in legal activities such as free expression without being hindered by the government. People were even jailed for making negative comments about Woodrow Wilson or calling the conflict a "rich man's war."

HISTORICAL THINKING

1. **READING CHECK** What steps did the U.S. government take to prepare for war?

2. **ANALYZE CAUSE AND EFFECT** How did entering the war affect the organization of the economy of the United States?

3. **DRAW CONCLUSIONS** How did the government's actions both unite and divide Americans?

4. **INTERPRET VISUALS** Select one of the propaganda posters (right) and consider its purpose. Who was its intended audience and what techniques were used to make the poster effective?

National World War I Museum and Memorial
Kansas City, Missouri

The National World War I Museum in Kansas City, Missouri, is positioned beneath the Liberty Memorial, a 217-foot granite monument to the veterans of World War I. The museum opened in 2006 to national acclaim and was recognized by Congress in 2014 as the National World War I Museum and Memorial. More than one million people have visited the museum, including presidents and American veterans like Frank Buckles, the country's last surviving Great War veteran.

The museum houses a vast collection of World War I-era propaganda posters, including those pictured here. Their high-interest, colorful graphics and thought-provoking messages called Americans to action and attempted to inspire great patriotism.

Shortly after the start of the war, the poster was recognized as an effective way to distribute national propaganda to a wide audience cheaply, vividly, and quickly. In almost every country involved in the war, posters like these played a significant role in spreading patriotism.

This poster features Uncle Sam and Germany's ruler, Kaiser, or emperor, Wilhelm II.

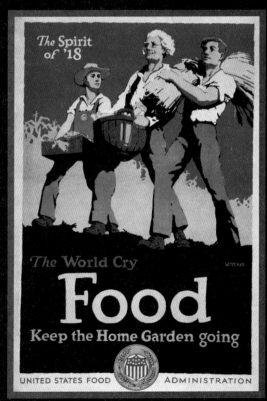

Posters encouraged people to plant victory gardens at home to provide food for soldiers.

Prominent studios produced short propaganda films to foster pro-war public sentiments.

A BRUTAL WAR

The trainee pilots were young and hopeful. They were eager to engage in daring aerial duels against the Germans, just like the glamorous Allied flying aces they idolized. Within weeks of their arrival in Europe, at least half of these young flyers died in action.

LETHAL TECHNOLOGY

When they arrived in France, American troops entered a war unlike any fought before. New technologies, as well as improvements to existing military machines, led to enormous numbers of casualties in every battle. **Machine guns**, for example, had existed since the late 1800s, but they were refined and improved over the course of World War I. Mounted atop trenches and able to fire hundreds of bullets per minute, machine guns could mow down attacking soldiers much more efficiently than single-shot rifles.

To counter the machine gun, the British invented the **tank**, an armored, heavily armed vehicle that used treads instead of wheels. Tanks could cross No Man's Land in the face of intense machine-gun fire and plow directly into enemy trenches. By the end of the war, both sides were using tanks to assault enemy lines.

This rotary engine came from the red Fokker Dr.1 Triplane of German ace pilot, the Red Baron.

For the first time ever, war also took to the skies. Only 11 years after the Wright brothers' first flight, airplanes were transformed into fighting machines and deployed over the battlefield. Pilots used cameras to take photos of enemy troop movements on the ground. German and Allied pilots engaged in one-on-one battles in the air, guiding their planes through acrobatic maneuvers high above the ground. At first, the pilots shot at each other with pistols, but eventually guns were installed on the planes themselves.

Being a pilot was extremely dangerous. On average, a new pilot survived three to six weeks in combat conditions. The most famous flyer on the Allied side was American ace fighter pilot, Eddie Rickenbacker, who was credited with shooting down 26 enemy planes. His impressive attack on 7 German aircraft in September 1918 earned him the U.S. Medal of Honor. On the opposing side, German Manfred von Richtofen, known as the Red Baron, was considered the ace of aces and credited with shooting down 80 Allied planes.

Nowhere near as nimble as airplanes, but also useful, were airships—also called dirigibles—whose cockpits were held aloft by gigantic rigid balloons filled with lighter-than-air gas. Airships could conduct aerial surveillance of enemy troop movements. Countering both planes and airships was the **antiaircraft gun**, a piece of heavy artillery modified so that it could be pointed skyward.

At sea, the Allies used a new strategy to end the threat of German submarines to Allied shipping. Convoys of destroyers and other warships—whose torpedoes, guns, and depth charges (bombs designed to explode under water) could easily sink a German submarine—surrounded and protected vulnerable merchant ships as they crossed the Atlantic. Escorted across the Atlantic by destroyers and other patrol vessels, these otherwise defenseless merchant vessels could move safely in groups.

WARBIRDS OF WORLD WAR I

The first aircraft used in World War I were extremely basic. Vulnerable pilots sat in open cockpits using unsophisticated and sometimes nonfunctional instruments. Navigation devices didn't exist, so they relied on paper maps and glimpses of the railway signs down below them. Sometimes lost pilots even landed in fields and asked directions! But air technology advanced throughout the war, and increasingly effective aircraft replaced the simple machines that took to the skies in 1914, transforming the airplane into a war machine.

BRITISH SOPWITH CAMEL BIPLANE
This plane's unusual name came from the slight hump in front of the cockpit. It shot down more German aircraft than any other Allied plane using twin machine guns that easily destroyed its flimsy opponents.

NIEUPORT 28
War hero Eddie Rickenbacker and many other American pilots flew these biplanes, which had a distinctive pair of machine guns mounted on their left sides.

SPAD XIII
Known as one of the most successful fighter planes of the Great War, this plane was widely used by French, American, and other Allied squadrons. Nearly 8,500 of them were produced.

FOKKER D VII
This popular German biplane was one of the best World War I fighters and was considered easy to fly, highly maneuverable, and safe. The Red Baron endorsed it wholeheartedly.

NORTH SEA 6 AIRSHIP
Along with the NS7, this airship became one of the more famous North Sea Class airships of the Great War. It could fly for 30 hours or more, escorting convoys and hunting for submarines.

AMERICANS ON THE WESTERN FRONT

In 1917, the situation for Britain and France took a dangerous turn when a revolution overturned the monarchy in Russia. The country's new government pulled out of the war, which freed the German troops from the Eastern Front to go fight in the west. At the same time, few American troops had arrived to reinforce the Western Front.

But in 1918, millions of American soldiers poured into France to turn the tide against Germany and eventually helped bring an end to the war. In contrast to the Allied troops, who were exhausted after years of brutal fighting, the Americans were fresh and well fed. In May 1918, one million American troops helped stop the German advance at the town of Cantigny.

Many members of minority groups who experienced discrimination at home served with distinction on the battlefields of Europe. A number of Asian Americans chose to serve in the armed forces and received U.S. citizenship as a result. Many Hispanic Americans from Texas and New Mexico also fought, although some refused to register for the draft to protest the discrimination they faced in everyday life. African-American leaders debated the merits of serving in the armed forces of a country that did not grant them equal rights. Still, thousands of black men did serve in segregated army units in Europe. With the exception of three exclusive fighting divisions, most African Americans were assigned behind-the-scenes duties instead of combat roles with white soldiers. But their wartime experience broadened the soldiers' views. Young men serving abroad found European ideas about race and sexuality very liberating.

HAZARDS FOR SOLDIERS

Charging into a barrage of machine-gun fire wasn't the only danger to soldiers fighting in the trenches. The Germans first used poison gas in 1915, but eventually both sides employed this fearsome weapon. Tossed into enemy trenches, the gas caused agonizing pain and killed soldiers by suffocation. After the Great War, most countries banned the use of poison gas. In addition, exposure to intense bombardment while in the trenches sent some soldiers home with physical injuries and others with a new syndrome known as "shell shock," a disorder brought on by the stress of war. Now known as PTSD, or post-traumatic stress disorder, symptoms included extreme nervousness, inability to sleep, and other severe emotional problems.

The trenches themselves posed other dangers to soldiers. Heavy rains filled the trenches with water

🏛 The National Portrait Gallery, Washington, D.C.

W.E.B. Du Bois, an African-American historian and author, is pictured here in Winold Reiss's 1925 drawing. In 1909, Du Bois helped found the National Association for the Advancement of Colored People (NAACP), which fought for equal rights for African Americans. He supported the war effort but believed the patriotism and heroism of African-American soldiers was not appropriately acknowledged or rewarded.

and mud, leading to diseases such as trench foot, which was caused by standing for hours in cold water with no possibility of changing into dry socks or boots. A severe case of trench foot could require amputation. Even the mud that filled the trenches could pose a drowning hazard for wounded soldiers waiting for medical assistance.

Many of the lesser-known heroes of World War I were women. Women and men drove ambulances, ferrying the sick and wounded from the front to hospitals behind the lines. The majority of the corps of nurses who treated the injured and comforted the dying were women. **Julia C. Stimson**, an American nurse, arrived at an army hospital in France just weeks after the United States joined the war. She was later appointed chief nurse of the Red Cross in France and then head of the nursing services of the American Expeditionary Forces. After the war, Stimson was awarded medals by the United States, Britain, and France for her bravery and life-saving service.

CRITICAL VIEWING The African-American soldiers of the 369th Infantry from New York City, nicknamed the "Harlem Hellfighters," fought with the French and were the first Americans to receive the French Croix de Guerre (War Cross) for Gallantry. What questions does this image—and what you've learned in this lesson—raise for you about the experiences African Americans had in the Great War?

PRIMARY SOURCE

The day has been tremendous, and the first in which I have not lost a life. We soldiers are hard pressed these days. The wounded pour in day and night by trains, by American autos too, but I can't take a minute to run out to salute my countrymen [American ambulance drivers]. We discharge our patients as fast as we can, and bury dozens a week. It is all like a weird dream, laughter (for they laugh well, the soldiers) and blood and death and funny episodes, and sublime also, all under the autumn stars.

—from *Mademoiselle Miss,* letters from an American nurse in France, entry dated October 27, 1915

HISTORICAL THINKING

1. **READING CHECK** How did women and minorities contribute to the war effort in Europe?

2. **DRAW CONCLUSIONS** Why did the Great War have more casualties than previous wars?

3. **ANALYZE CAUSE AND EFFECT** What effect does war have on the development of technology?

4. **EVALUATE** In 1918, W.E.B. Du Bois wrote in the NAACP's monthly journal that "while the war lasts [we should] forget our special grievances and close our ranks shoulder to shoulder with our white fellow citizens and allied nations that are fighting for democracy." This was viewed by some as puzzling, given his views on racial equality. What do you think about Du Bois's statement, based on what you know about the civil rights movement?

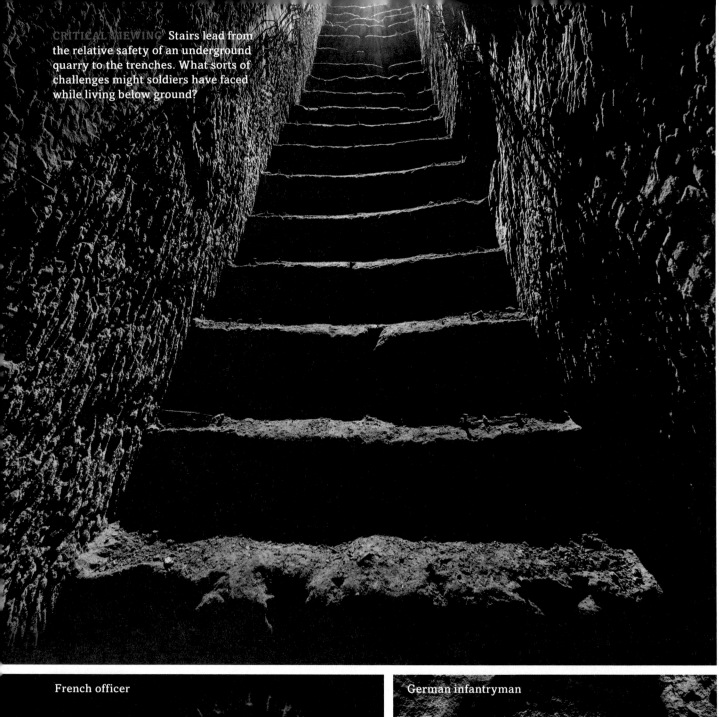

CRITICAL VIEWING Stairs lead from the relative safety of an underground quarry to the trenches. What sorts of challenges might soldiers have faced while living below ground?

French officer

German infantryman

Carving of "the disasters of the 20th century"

German military leader Field Marshal Paul von Hindenburg

THROUGH THE LENS

JEFFREY GUSKY

During World War I, some troops took refuge in centuries-old underground cities in northeastern France. They left their mark in the soft limestone in the form of signatures, sketches, carvings, and relief sculptures. National Geographic photographer Jeffrey Gusky captured the intimate stories of these soldiers, many of whom never made it out from the trenches.

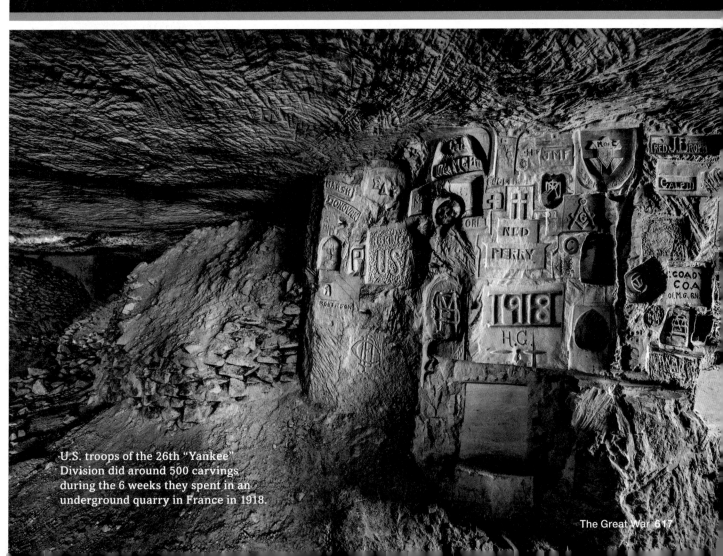
U.S. troops of the 26th "Yankee" Division did around 500 carvings during the 6 weeks they spent in an underground quarry in France in 1918.

MAIN IDEA The war abroad and reform movements at home combined to bring about changes in social and economic conditions for many Americans. At the same time, the world confronted a massive, deadly outbreak of a familiar disease.

THE HOME FRONT

Life didn't come to a halt in the United States while the young men fought overseas. The war accelerated far-reaching social changes that had already begun in America's cities, workplaces, and among the voting public. When the soldiers returned, they would find that home was not exactly the way they had left it.

🏛 The Phillips Collection, Washington, D.C.

Jacob Lawrence is considered one of the most influential visual artists of the 20th century. The painting above is Panel 1 of his 1941 series, *The Migration of the Negro*. This 60-painting collection pays tribute to southern African Americans, including his parents, who fled to cities in the American North and West during the Great Migration. To escape racial inequality, many migrants landed in cities like New York, St. Louis, and Chicago, transforming the culture, music, and politics of these locations.

THE WAR'S IMPACT AT HOME

Nearly every racial or ethnic group in the United States was affected by economic and cultural changes brought about by the war. As you've read, German Americans were viewed with suspicion by their fellow citizens. German Americans lost connections with their culture, as German-language newspapers were shut down, and speaking German in public was banned in half the states. Dissenters of any national background suffered a similar fate, being viewed with hostility by other Americans and persecuted by the government.

Some minority groups saw more positive changes. Jewish Americans had formerly been grouped according to their country of origin in Europe. Now they united to play a stronger international role by forming charities and donating millions to help victims of the war. Mexican American workers living in the southern and southwestern states moved north to follow job opportunities that opened up in factories when young men enlisted. Many women, too, left their traditional roles to take paying jobs in factories, offices, or loading docks.

For African Americans, the war years brought enormous changes. In the South, a variety of natural disasters crippled southern agriculture, which resulted in increasingly poor job prospects for black farm workers. African Americans had begun leaving the South for cities in the North around 1910, a mass movement known as the **Great Migration**. The outbreak of the war played a key role in this process. As immigration from Europe ended and white American factory workers enlisted, thousands of jobs opened up in industrial centers in northern cities. Between 1914 and 1920, more than 600,000 African Americans moved north.

African Americans who moved to these centers, however, were often met with hostility. And even after the war, the prospect of improved rights for African Americans remained bleak. The Wilson administration and the Democratic Party resisted efforts to reduce racism, and harsh policies toward black Americans persisted in many states.

PROHIBITION

At the start of the 20th century, saloons could be found in cities throughout the United States. They not only served beer and other alcoholic drinks, they offered places where working men could gather to socialize. Women were not permitted to enter a saloon—and many didn't want to. Reform organizations, such as the Anti-Saloon League and the Women's Christian Temperance Union, believed saloons encouraged drunkenness and overspending by men. Feeling that they were defending their families, many women supported **Prohibition**— making the sale of liquor illegal.

During the war, the Prohibition movement gained ground because the grain used to make beer was needed for food, and because most brewers (beer makers) were German. In December 1917, Congress approved the **18th Amendment** to the Constitution, prohibiting the sale of alcohol in the United States. The amendment was ratified after the war, in January 1919. Congress also passed the **Volstead Act**, which contained measures to enforce Prohibition.

In 1910, the National Woman's Christian Temperance Union (NWCTU) produced this "Vote No" Prohibition postcard. "Vote no" refers to localized "no license" campaigns that attempted to deny the license renewals of taverns in order to protect children and preserve family unity and values.

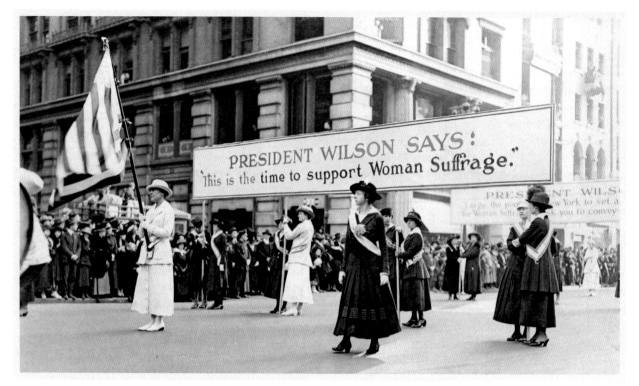

Suffragists align with Woodrow Wilson during his 1916 re-election campaign. While Wilson's political platform favored women's suffrage, the president didn't fully support it until 1918.

PRIMARY SOURCE

Do you realize that when you ask women to take their cause [suffrage] to state referendum . . . you drive women of education, refinement, achievement, to beg men who cannot read for their political freedom?

Do you realize that such anomalies as a college president asking her janitor to give her a vote are overstraining the patience and driving women to desperation? Do you realize that women in increasing numbers indignantly resent the long delay in their enfranchisement?

Your party platforms have pledged women suffrage. Then why not be honest, frank friends of our cause, adopt it in reality as your own, make it a party program, and "fight with us"? As a party measure —a measure of all parties—why not put the amendment through Congress and the legislatures? We shall all be better friends, we shall have a happier nation, we women will be free to support loyally the party of our choice, and we shall be far prouder of our history.

—from Carrie Chapman Catt's address to the U.S. Congress, November 4, 1917

WOMEN GAIN THE VOTE

Women had been demanding the right to vote since the 1840s, and by 1914, they could vote in several states. However, after Wilson's re-election, his support for a constitutional amendment giving women suffrage seemed lukewarm at best to those in the movement. In 1917, women picketed the White House, and many were imprisoned. Still, they continued to demonstrate, in spite of the threat of increasingly long jail terms.

World War I finally provided the context in which women's activism to secure the vote could finally succeed. Women saw the opportunity to strengthen their argument. Carrie Chapman Catt, a leader of the National American Woman Suffrage Association, claimed that women were patriotic voters. According to her argument, giving women the right to vote would counteract the potential influence of dissenters at the polls. At the same time, the pickets in front of the White House continued.

The combined impact of these tactics pushed the House of Representatives to pass the **19th Amendment**, granting suffrage to women in January 1918. The Senate took another year to approve the amendment, and the states ratified it in August 1920. Beyond the success of women's suffrage, however, the war did not produce lasting changes in the everyday lives of American women. As soon as the war ended, women were expected to relinquish their office and factory jobs to the returning soldiers and resume their traditional roles at home.

COLDS, INFLUENZA, PNEUMONIA, AND TUBERCULOSIS ARE SPREAD THIS WAY

Flu Epidemic 1918–1919

First cases reported at U.S. military bases
August 1918

September 1918 total U.S. deaths
12,000

October 1918 total U.S. deaths
195,000

Total U.S. deaths 1918–1919
600,000

Total deaths worldwide 1918–1919
50,000,000

Sources: PBS, U.S. National Library of Medicine

Despite attempts at public health education, like displaying this 1919 poster, the 1918 influenza pandemic was widespread and deadly. Scientists have since learned the virus was H1N1, which has resurfaced at various times throughout history.

THE FLU STRIKES

At the end of 1918, a particularly powerful strain of **influenza**, the contagious virus we now call "the flu," struck with dramatic suddenness and spread rapidly throughout the U.S. population. Scientists were not able to develop a vaccine quickly enough against the Spanish flu, as it was called. Antibiotics did not come into widespread use until around 1940, so they were not yet available to fight secondary infections, such as pneumonia, that could accompany the flu. More than 600,000 Americans died of the disease in 1918 and 1919, overwhelming the funeral facilities of many major cities. It was most deadly for people aged 20–40, which was unusual, since influenza is typically more likely to be fatal among the very young and the very old. As a result, soldiers and officers were in the most vulnerable age group.

The outbreak was a **pandemic**—a sudden spread of disease that covers a very large geographic area and affects a major portion of the population. By the time it receded in 1920, the flu had killed more than 50 million people worldwide. It is estimated that one-third of the world's population became infected. The pandemic sapped the strength of the Allied forces who had already lived through brutal trench warfare and had been tasked with enforcing the peace treaty at the end of the war. The outbreak also diverted attention from important social problems, and illustrated how vulnerable humanity was to infectious diseases.

PRIMARY SOURCE

1918 has gone: a year momentous as the termination of the most cruel war in the annals of the human race; a year which marked the end, at least for a time, of man's destruction of man; unfortunately a year in which developed a most fatal infectious disease causing the death of hundreds of thousands of human beings. Medical science for four and one-half years devoted itself to putting men on the firing line and keeping them there. Now it must turn with its whole might to combating the greatest enemy of all—infectious disease.

—from the *Journal of the American Medical Association*, 1918

HISTORICAL THINKING

1. **READING CHECK** What changes were reform movements able to bring about during and immediately after the war?

2. **MAKE GENERALIZATIONS** In what ways can a war help bring about social changes on the home front?

3. **EVALUATE** In Catt's appeal to Congress, what details suggest her frustration with having to beg for women's suffrage?

4. **FORM AND SUPPORT OPINIONS** Do you believe women and African Americans made large strides toward civil rights during the war years? Explain.

ROAD TO VICTORY

As you know, many people referred to the fighting as the Great War because it consumed so many countries in its fires. By the end, they were calling it "the war to end all wars" because the bloodshed and ruin were unlike anything that had gone before. But the participation of American troops in the war helped establish the United States as a global power.

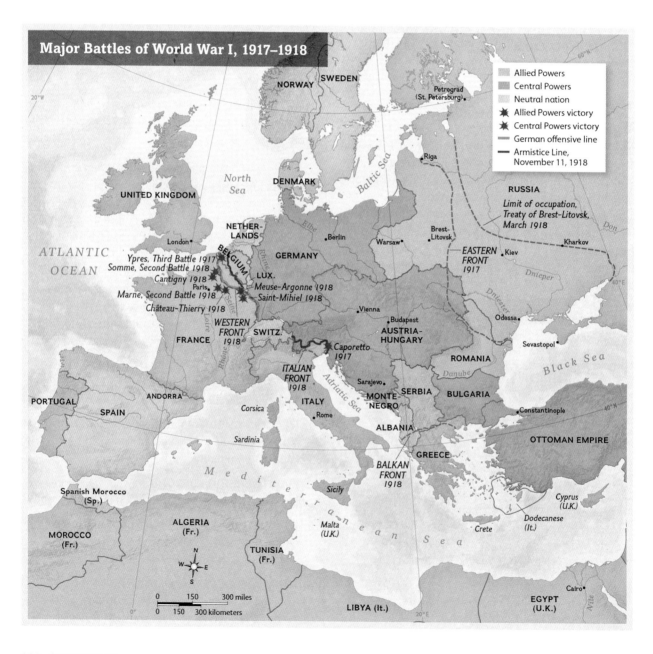

ATTACK AND COUNTERATTACK

During the late winter of 1918, the Allies faced a dangerous military crisis. As you may recall, by November 1917, revolution had erupted in Russia, and the second of two revolutions had taken that nation out of the Allied coalition. The revolutionaries placed the Bolsheviks, a party of communist extremists, in power and overthrew the Russian imperial government. This turmoil enabled the Germans to move troops to the Western Front. Berlin hoped to achieve victory before the Americans could reinforce the Allies.

On March 21, 1918, the German Army launched a renewed offensive to conquer France and end the war before large numbers of American forces landed in Europe. Over the next two months, the Germans gained ground in Belgium and France, only to be stopped in May by the American counterattack at Cantigny, France. With millions of U.S. soldiers now in France, the German drive for a quick victory had failed. The following month, the American Expeditionary Forces (AEF) stopped Germany from advancing in battles near Belleau Wood and Château-Thierry. In addition to their strategic value, these victories provided a tremendous morale boost to the flagging Allied armies.

The Germans made one more offensive push in July, but the British, French, and American troops repelled it. After that, the Allies went on the offensive, driving the German forces back, trench by trench. In September, the Allies began an operation called the **Meuse-Argonne offensive**, in which American divisions cut off the railroads that were bringing supplies to the German Army. As part of the offensive, General Pershing led AEF troops in the bloody and decisive **Battle of Argonne Forest** in October 1918. Looking back on the offensive years later, German general Erich Ludendorff wrote, "America thus became the most decisive power in the war." Still, American casualties in the Battle of Argonne were staggering, reaching 117,000, including 26,000 killed. French casualties totaled 70,000, and German casualties came to 100,000 soldiers.

WILSON'S PEACE PROGRAM

As the war ground toward its end, Wilson proposed a program for peace that he called the **Fourteen Points**. Among the key provisions of this plan were freedom of the seas, free trade among countries, and no more secret treaties. Wilson also advocated national self-determination, the idea that countries should reflect the national origins of the people who lived within their boundaries.

PRIMARY SOURCE

President Wilson's **Fourteen Points** were presented in a speech to Congress on January 8, 1918.

Points 1–5 dealt with diplomatic issues that Wilson believed were essential for preventing further war:

1. Open covenants [binding agreements] of peace, openly arrived at, after which there shall be no private international understandings of any kind but diplomacy shall proceed always frankly and in the public view.

2. Absolute freedom of navigation upon the seas, outside territorial waters, alike in peace and in war, except as the seas may be closed in whole or in part by international action for the enforcement of international covenants.

3. The removal, so far as possible, of all economic barriers and the establishment of an equality of trade conditions among all the nations consenting to the peace and associating themselves for its maintenance.

4. Adequate guarantees given and taken that national armaments [weaponry] will be reduced to the lowest point consistent with domestic safety.

5. A free, open-minded, and absolutely impartial adjustment of all colonial claims, based upon a strict observance of the principle that in determining all such questions of sovereignty, the interests of the populations concerned must have equal weight with the equitable [fair] claims of the government whose title is to be determined.

[Points 6–13 are not included here. These points dealt with boundary changes and called for ensuring the sovereignty of several nations. They also included a request for the break-up of the Ottoman Empire and the development of an independent Polish state.]

Point 14 called for the creation of an assembly of nations that would help safeguard the sovereignty of all countries:

14. A general association of nations must be formed under specific covenants for the purpose of affording mutual guarantees of political independence and territorial integrity to great and small states alike.

Which of the Fourteen Points do you think might have been controversial in the context of the war? Explain your answer.

CRITICAL VIEWING A wave of ceramic poppy flowers appears to tumble from the Tower of London in England as part of an evolving art installation called "Blood-Swept Lands and Seas of Red," created in 2014 by artists Paul Cummins and Tom Piper. Flowers were added daily from July 17 until November 11, 2014—the 100th anniversary of Britain's first full day of involvement in the Great War—until they reached the number of British fatalities in the war: 888,246. Beginning in the 1920s, the poppy, which grew in many of the war's battlefields, became a symbol of the sacrifice made by the soldiers. How does the name of this exhibition connect to the Great War?

The Fourteen Points would not be easy to achieve. Britain and France objected to the proposal because it did not include heavy sanctions on Germany. After four years of slaughter, these European nations wanted to punish Germany and cripple its ability to wage war in the future. They also disliked Wilson's interference with European policies. For the desperate Germans, however, the Fourteen Points seemed much more appealing than direct negotiations with Britain and France.

In early October, the German government asked Wilson to arrange an **armistice**, an end to the fighting, based on the provisions of the Fourteen Points. Britain and France objected to this proposal. However, by threatening to make a separate peace between the United States and Germany, Wilson convinced the two European nations to accept the Fourteen Points in general terms and attend a peace conference with Germany.

The fighting officially ended on November 11, 1918, at 11:00 a.m.—the 11th hour on the 11th day of the 11th month, or Armistice Day, as it would be called. Earlier that morning, Germany, lacking supplies and manpower and facing invasion at any moment, had signed an armistice, or peace agreement, with the Allies in a railroad car outside Compiégne, France. The details of the peace treaties among the formerly warring nations would be decided over the next year, but the relief that day was evident. British prime minister David Lloyd George stated, "This is no time for words. Our hearts are too full of gratitude to which no tongue can give adequate expression."

Nine million soldiers died in the Great War, and 21 million were wounded. France, Germany, Russia, Austria-Hungary, and Great Britain each lost nearly a million or more soldiers, and at least five million more civilians died from factors such as exposure, starvation, and disease. The Great War killed more people, involved more countries, and cost more money than any previous war in history. Its technology transformed the nature of modern warfare, introducing newer, deadlier, more effective weapons onto the battlefield.

The impact of the war was staggering, and many major global events that took place later in the 20th century can be tied to this first World War. The Russian Revolution, World War II, the Holocaust, and the creation of the atomic bomb, which you will read about later in this book, are all directly linked to the Great War. Even the Great Depression and the Cold War are connected to it in significant ways.

THE PARIS PEACE CONFERENCE

Breaking with the tradition that presidents did not travel outside the country, Wilson decided to attend the Paris Peace Conference. By the time he left for the conference, which began in January 1919, Wilson's political position at home had weakened considerably. He had alienated Republicans by keeping them out of the highest levels of his government and angered progressives with his harsh repression of dissent. In the October 1918 congressional elections, Americans voted Republican majorities into both the Senate and House of Representatives. This situation promised to make it difficult for a peace treaty negotiated by Wilson to be ratified.

In Europe, however, Wilson was heralded as a hero when he traveled to the Paris Peace Conference. The people greeted him with lavish applause and the nickname "Wilson the Just." Wilson, David Lloyd George, Georges Clemenceau, the president of France, and Italy's prime minister, Vittorio Orlando, made up the "Big Four" who directed the conference. The European leaders were hard-headed realists who did not share Wilson's idealism, and they were skeptical of the Fourteen Points. "God gave us the Ten Commandments and we broke them," said Clemenceau. "Wilson gives us the Fourteen Points. We shall see."

Notably absent from the Paris Peace Conference was one of the original Allies—Russia. As a result of the Russian Revolution, Russia's monarchy had given way to **communism**, a form of government in which all the means of production and transportation are owned by the state. The revolutionaries changed Russia's name to the Union of Soviet Socialist Republics (U.S.S.R.), or the **Soviet Union** for short. Its leader was Vladimir Ilyich Lenin. In March 1918, the Russian revolutionary party had made its own peace treaty with Germany.

HISTORICAL THINKING

1. **READING CHECK** What effect did the arrival of American troops have on the outcome of the war?

2. **MAKE INFERENCES** Why did Germany prefer to negotiate the terms of peace with Wilson rather than with France and Britain?

3. **EVALUATE** How did Wilson's Fourteen Points serve as a justification for America's entry into the war?

4. **MAKE PREDICTIONS** How might a later event in history, such as World War II or the Great Depression, be connected to the Great War?

VICTORY AND WILSON'S PEACE

Woodrow Wilson had a lofty dream of a world at peace and a great gathering of nations. It was a vision that blinded him to the necessities of everyday politics. In the end, the nations gathered, but the United States was not among them.

THE TREATY OF VERSAILLES

The **Treaty of Versailles**, which officially brought the war to a close, was signed in the Hall of Mirrors at the Palace of Versailles outside of Paris, France, on June 28, 1919. Although Wilson had a significant role in designing the Versailles Treaty, the negotiations over peace terms with Germany had produced both victories and defeats for the American president. Against his wishes, the final wording of the treaty included a clause assigning Germany the "guilt" for starting the war in 1914. The treaty also exacted severe financial penalties from Germany in the form of reparations, payments to make up for damages and casualties caused by the war, that eventually amounted to $33 billion. Both of these provisions fueled bitter resentment in Germany that would only deepen in the decades that followed.

With regard to self-determination for nations, Wilson was somewhat more successful. In the aftermath of the war, the Austro-Hungarian Empire was dissolved, and new boundaries were drawn. It was not possible to fully align national borders with the ethnic origins of the groups within each country. Still, borders in postwar Europe did more closely follow ethnic divisions than the prewar boundaries.

THE LEAGUE OF NATIONS

Wilson's main goal in the negotiations was to establish a **League of Nations**, a general assembly of countries that would stabilize relations among countries and help preserve peace. The final Treaty of Versailles included the league's charter. Each member country would have an equal voice in the general assembly, and the league would have an international court of justice. For Wilson, the "heart of the covenant" of the League of Nations was Article X, which required member nations to take unified action when any member country was attacked.

Because Democrats were in the minority in the Senate, Wilson would need some Republican votes to ratify the Treaty of Versailles. Many Republicans, however, objected to establishing the League of Nations, believing it infringed on U.S. sovereignty,

Three global powerhouses, British prime minister David Lloyd George (left), French prime minister Georges Clemenceau (center), and American president Woodrow Wilson (right), take a stroll during the Versailles Peace Conference in June 1919.

National Boundaries after World War I, 1920

Boundaries of German, Russian, and
Austro-Hungarian empires in 1914
Areas lost by Austro-Hungarian Empire
Areas lost by German Empire
Areas lost by Russian Empire
Areas lost by Bulgaria
Demilitarized Zones

or freedom from external control. Senator **Henry Cabot Lodge**, a Republican and chair of the Senate Foreign Relations Committee, was especially vocal in his opposition. Lodge and Wilson had been political enemies for a long time and disliked each other personally. Wilson did not help matters when he indicated that since the treaty's critics had offered no alternate plan, "it is a case of 'put up or shut up'".

In the political battle over the treaty, Lodge focused on Article X and the issue of whether Congress should be able to approve American participation in any actions taken by the league to defend its members from aggression. By September 1919, with the treaty in trouble, Wilson decided to take his case to the American people in a series of speeches in the Midwest and on the West Coast. The grueling schedule—32 major speeches in 22 days—exhausted him, and the heart and blood disorders that had

bothered him for years became aggravated. He was rushed back to Washington where he suffered a massive stroke that left his left side paralyzed.

The president's wife and his doctors did not reveal how sick Wilson was. As the first lady screened his few visitors and decided what documents he would see, Wilson became a shell of a president, and the government drifted. The Treaty of Versailles came up for a vote in the Senate in November 1919 and March 1920, and both times it was defeated. Wilson ultimately could not convince Congress to join the League of Nations. He died in 1924.

THE DECLINE OF PROGRESSIVISM

As you have read in this chapter, many goals of progressivism, including women's suffrage, a stronger labor movement, and Prohibition, had been attained by 1919. Enough states had ratified the 18th

Mounted Chicago police officers escort African Americans to a safety zone during the Chicago Race Riots of 1919. Thirty-eight people, most of them black, were killed, and another 500 were injured over the course of five violent days.

PRIMARY SOURCE

As revealed in this account of the Chicago Race Riots of 1919, racial tension and social unrest reached a boiling point that year across the United States.

The fury spread like wildfire. Workers in the stockyards, 10,000 or more of whom are [African American], were at first guarded as they entered and left, but few of them could get to their work when rioting made passage through the streets unsafe. Gangs of white and black hoodlums appeared and ran amuck [wild]. Armed men of either color dashed through the district in automobiles and beyond, firing as they flew. Two white men, wounded while shooting up the district, were found to carry official badges, one being thus identified as . . . a Chicago policeman.

—from *The Survey*, August 9, 1919

Amendment (the Prohibition amendment) by January 1919 to make it part of the Constitution. Additionally, thanks to the 19th Amendment, women could "take their appropriate place in political work," according to Carrie Chapman Catt. Americans began to turn their attention away from progressive ideas as they faced the switch from a wartime to a peacetime economy.

The end of the war created an uncertain situation for American businesses. Orders for guns, ammunition, and other wartime goods were canceled, leaving factories with a pressing need to retool themselves once again, this time to produce peacetime consumer items. When the war had broken out, the WIB had stepped in to help American industry remake itself, but now the government retreated from its earlier organizational role. At the same time, inflation raised prices considerably. By 1920, the government's cost of living index had gone up 105 percent over prewar levels, making goods more expensive. As returning

STRIKE CALLED
ALL UNIONS TO GO OUT

ANNOUNCEMENT OF STRIKE

Seattle Union Record

SIXTY THOUSAND TO RESPOND TO CALL

NO CONSTRUCTIVE LEGISLATION YET

35,000 SILK MILL WORKERS STRIKE

The photograph on the left shows a large crowd gathering at the entrance of the Skinner and Eddy Shipbuilding Corporation on Seattle's central waterfront during the nation's first citywide general strike. It began in the shipyards in January 1919, paralyzing the city for several days. On the right is the front page of the *Seattle Union Record* announcing the strike.

soldiers began to seek jobs, unemployment soared, reaching nearly 12 percent by 1921.

In the midst of economic hardship, social unrest also flared. In early 1919, labor unions staged major strikes demanding higher wages at shipyards in Seattle and steel mills across the country. The Industrial Workers of the World called for a general strike to support the shipyard and steel strikers. When 60,000 laborers took part in the strike, the mayor of Seattle, Ole Hanson, mobilized police and soldiers, earning himself the nickname "the Savior of Seattle." Inflammatory newspaper articles depicted the strike as a precursor to a communist revolution.

The largest industrial strike of the year was the Great Steel Strike of 1919. The American Federation of Labor tried to rally all steelworkers to end the grueling 7-day workweek and the 12-hour workday. In September 1919, 350,000 midwestern steelworkers left the mills. Steel manufacturers refused to recognize the union and replaced striking workers with unemployed minority workers and immigrants to keep their factories running during the strike. They waited for the strike to break due to police harassment and internal divisions within the unions themselves. Striking workers held their position for months, but could not withstand the financial and political pressure being exerted on them by management. The strike failed in early 1920.

Racial tensions also flared up in the turbulent postwar atmosphere. There were frequent lynchings in the American South. In the North, the flow of African-American migrants produced confrontations with angry whites. This tension erupted into race riots in Washington, D.C., Elaine, Arkansas, and Chicago, Illinois, during the summer of 1919, which one black

leader came to call "the red summer." Racism and antilabor sentiments fueled each other during these tense months.

With Wilson ill and the government leaderless, the Republicans expected Theodore Roosevelt to be their nominee in 1920, but he died in 1919. The party then turned to Senator **Warren G. Harding**, who promised frustrated voters a "return to normalcy." By *normalcy* he meant reducing government's role in business and stepping back into a more isolationist stance. Harding was elected by a large majority over the Democratic candidate, James M. Cox of Ohio. Voters wanted to turn the Democrats out of office because of their anger over big government, high taxes, and labor unrest. Americans were also prepared to let Europe grapple on its own with its new postwar realities. Although World War I transformed America into a world leader, the aftermath of the war ushered in a decade of isolationism. By the end of the 1920s, this policy would have serious consequences for the world economies.

HISTORICAL THINKING

1. **READING CHECK** How did the end of the war affect the U.S. economy?

2. **COMPARE AND CONTRAST** Compare the social climate of the United States at the beginning of the Great War to the social climate at the end of the war. How did they differ?

3. **FORM AND SUPPORT OPINIONS** Should the Senate have ratified the Treaty of Versailles? Support your opinion.

4. **MAKE INFERENCES** Why did some newspapers compare the steelworkers' strike to the beginning of a communist revolution?

VOCABULARY

For each pair of vocabulary words, write one sentence that explains the connection between the words.

1. **conscientious objector; civil liberties**
   A conscientious objector might have had to hide his negative feelings about the Great War to keep his civil liberties.

2. **militarism; moral diplomacy**

3. **influenza; pandemic**

4. **machine gun; tank**

5. **armistice; Fourteen Points**

6. **Treaty of Versailles; League of Nations**

READING STRATEGY
DRAW CONCLUSIONS

When you draw conclusions, you make a judgment based on what you have read. You analyze evidence, make inferences, and use your own experiences to form your judgment. Use a chart like this one to draw a conclusion about how the war changed the perception of the United States in the world. Then answer the question.

Conclusion

↑ ↑ ↑

Evidence   Evidence   Evidence

7. In what ways did World War I mark the beginning of a new role for the United States on the world stage?

MAIN IDEAS

Answer the following questions. Support your answers with evidence from the chapter.

8. How did the networks of alliances in Europe lead to the beginning of World War I? **LESSON 1.1**

9. Why did President Wilson declare a policy of neutrality toward the war in Europe? **LESSON 1.2**

10. What German actions eventually led the United States to declare war? **LESSON 2.1**

11. In what ways did the U.S. government support the war effort? **LESSON 2.2**

12. How were members of minority groups treated during the war ? **LESSON 3.1**

13. What effect did the flu pandemic of 1918–1919 have on the Allied forces? **LESSON 3.3**

14. In what ways did Wilson and the Allies disagree about a peace treaty for Europe? **LESSON 4.1**

15. Why did the United States refuse to ratify the Treaty of Versailles? **LESSON 4.2**

HISTORICAL THINKING

Answer the following questions. Support your answers with evidence from the chapter.

16. **MAKE GENERALIZATIONS** What general statement could you make about the power and usefulness of propaganda?

17. **DRAW CONCLUSIONS** How did Wilson's view of the United States' role in the world change during the war?

18. **IDENTIFY MAIN IDEAS AND DETAILS** What advantages made the United States instrumental in helping the Allied side win the war?

19. **SYNTHESIZE** How did the United States change its policies, both at home and abroad, because of World War I?

20. **MAKE CONNECTIONS** In what ways is the flu pandemic of 1918–1919 similar to modern disease outbreaks you have heard of? In what ways is it different?

21. **FORM AND SUPPORT OPINIONS** What do you think is the most important lasting effect of World War I on life in the United States? Explain your answer.

INTERPRET VISUALS

Study this propaganda poster created by the U.S. Food Administration during the war. Then answer the questions that follow.

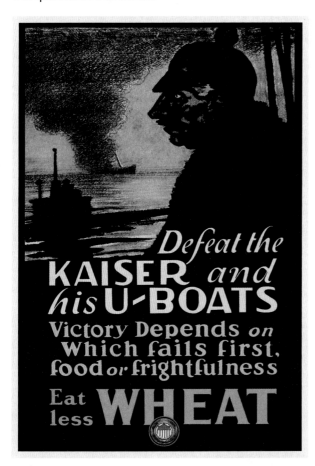

22. How do the poster's visuals and artistic details inspire fear?

23. What does the poster's slogan, "Victory depends on which fails first, food or frightfulness," mean?

ANALYZE SOURCES

Supporters of women's suffrage stood outside the White House day after day carrying signs and hoping to influence President Wilson. Often, the signs would elicit angry, or even violent, responses. Read the text of one such sign below. Then answer the question that follows.

> Kaiser Wilson
> Have you forgotten your sympathy with the poor Germans because they were not self-governed? 20,000,000 American women are not self-governed.
>
> —banner of the National Woman's Party, 1917

24. Why does the writer of this sign use the term "Kaiser Wilson"?

CONNECT TO YOUR LIFE

25. **EXPOSITORY** Imagine the year is 1919, and you spent the war working on the home front. The war has ended, and you are writing a letter to a friend explaining how events during and just after the war have changed your feelings about what it means to be an American.

TIPS

- Consider how the war affected all Americans, including the government's efforts to influence citizens' thoughts.

- Determine your identity as the letter writer. Are you male or female? Are you white, African American, a recent immigrant, or a member of a different group?

- Develop your topic by discussing ways in which your circumstances and your attitudes changed—and did not change.

- Use two or three vocabulary terms from the chapter in your letter.

- End the letter with a brief summary statement about how you feel at the current point in time.

THE JAZZ AGE AND MASS CULTURE

1921–1929

HISTORICAL THINKING How did the Roaring Twenties both divide and unite Americans?

The 2013 film version of F. Scott Fitzgerald's novel *The Great Gatsby* portrayed the Jazz Age as a swirl of activity. Director Baz Luhrmann interpreted the extravagant, self-indulgent world of the wealthy Jay Gatsby with vibrant party scenes like this one.

"Everybody's
youth is a dream."
—F. Scott Fitzgerald, author

ALL THAT
JAZZ

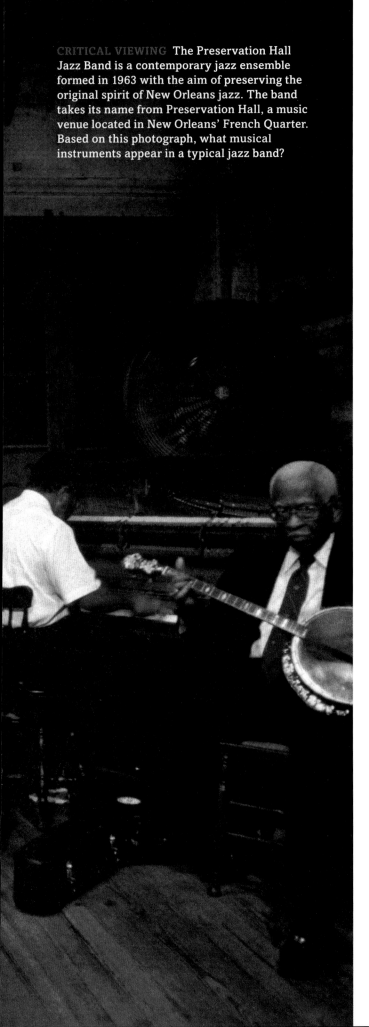

The Preservation Hall Jazz Band is a contemporary jazz ensemble formed in 1963 with the aim of preserving the original spirit of New Orleans jazz. The band takes its name from Preservation Hall, a music venue located in New Orleans' French Quarter. Based on this photograph, what musical instruments appear in a typical jazz band?

It seems that every generation chooses to rebel against previous ones, partly through the rhythms and melodies of new styles of music. In the 1950s and 1960s, the rebellious music of choice was rock and roll, described as "savage music" in an advertisement by the Citizens' Council of Greater New Orleans. In the 1980s and 1990s, rap and hip-hop came on the scene, once again rattling the sensibilities of older generations.

Though they are each unique, rock, rap, and hip-hop are cousins, bearing family resemblances because they are all descended from an earlier musical and social revolution—the birth of jazz and the blues.

THE ORIGINS OF JAZZ

New Orleans is generally considered to be the birthplace of jazz. A city like no other in the late 1800s, New Orleans was home to an extremely diverse population of whites, African Americans, and people of mixed races.

In this cultural whirlwind could be heard the sounds of music that had originated with enslaved people who worked in the cotton fields. The music was based on traditional African work songs and "field hollers." Work songs often had a call-and-response structure, with one person singing a line and other people singing a response. Field hollers were high-pitched calls used by individuals working alone to communicate with workers in other fields.

Late in the 19th century, New Orleans also hosted a lively European classical music scene, with several well-attended opera houses. At this time, new kinds of sounds emerged that blended various African and European influences. By the turn of the 20th century, the strains of jazz could be heard in the

CRITICAL VIEWING This 1943 oil painting by Chicago artist Archibald J. Motley, Jr., called *Nightlife*, depicts a crowded nightclub in a Chicago South Side neighborhood. What kind of mood does the painting convey?

streets of New Orleans. Two key features stood out as hallmarks of the jazz style: syncopation and improvisation. Syncopation is the temporary placement of stress on normally weak beats in a piece of music to create a complex rhythm. Improvisation is the act of composing and performing music on the spot. Modern-day jazz styles still feature catchy syncopated rhythms and dizzying original riffs improvised by performers.

NEXT STOP: CHICAGO

If New Orleans was the birthplace of jazz, Chicago was its nursery. In the 1910s and 1920s, many African Americans migrated north in search of better economic opportunities. Jazz musicians were part of this trend, and some of the most notable musicians landed in Chicago. Joe "King" Oliver was one of the best-known New Orleans transplants, playing with King Oliver's Creole Jazz Band on Chicago's South Side.

Today, Oliver is remembered not only for his own musical accomplishments but also for hiring one of jazz's legendary greats for his band. Trumpet player Louis Armstrong, also originally from New Orleans, brought the art of improvisation to new heights. Ron David, the author of *Jazz for Beginners*, describes Armstrong this way: "He built his improvisations like songs within a song, and his trumpet sound glowed." Also a singer, Armstrong had a distinctive vocal style and specialized in scatting, or singing improvised melodies in meaningless syllables.

The jazz craze spread like wildfire among diverse audiences in the 1920s, a decade now known as the Jazz Age. Young people flocked to nightclubs in Chicago, New York, Los Angeles, and other cities to hear jazz and to dance in ways their elders considered immodest. One of the most popular dances of the Jazz Age was the fast-paced, energetic Charleston, which featured quick kicking steps.

THE WOMEN OF JAZZ

Jazz singer Ella Fitzgerald performs with Duke Ellington's band in this 1964 photograph.

The female jazz musicians who have received the most acclaim are the great vocalists of the swing era and later, such as Ella Fitzgerald, Billie Holiday, and Lena Horne. Fitzgerald was a master of scatting, using her voice to weave complex improvised melodies around the beat of the band. Holiday, nicknamed "Lady Day," was known for her soulful and moving ballads. Horne, a dancer, singer, and actress, became one of the top African-American performers of her time, appearing in theater and movies and on television. She refused to accept any acting roles that stereotyped African-American women, and she became an activist in the civil rights movement.

A 1922 photograph shows Lil Hardin (center) performing with King Oliver's Creole Jazz Band in California.

Other lesser known but equally talented female jazz musicians include Lil Hardin and Mary Lou Williams. Born in 1898, Hardin was a pianist and composer. She started her career in New Orleans, where she played, wrote, and arranged music for several bands. After moving to Chicago, she played for King Oliver's Creole Jazz Band. She was married to Louis Armstrong from 1924 to 1938 and collaborated with him on a number of recordings. Williams was born in 1910 and was a composer, arranger, pianist, and bandleader whose work spanned several musical genres. During the swing era, she wrote and arranged pieces for Duke Ellington's band. Later, she worked in the style called bebop, which grew out of swing.

PRIMARY SOURCE

In a 1974 interview conducted by Canadian broadcast journalist Brian Linehan, Ella Fitzgerald was asked to explain her previous claim that she had "stolen from the horns" to create her singing style. In her reply, she spoke about the interaction between a singer and a musician, especially as she experienced it in jazz music.

You know, I think everybody steals from each other. I think that's the only way that we keep alive. As far as learning, it's just like going to school and learning history or learning anything. Actually when you're learning in school you're stealing something from another . . . from something from years back, but you add something to it, and that's the way people are.

We all learn something—the horns learn from another musician, and singers learn from another singer. And I like to try to sing like a horn sometimes in some of my songs, because to me, that's a great accomplishment, to try to feel like I'm playing what I hear a musician play.

—from Ella Fitzgerald, as interviewed by Brian Linehan on *City Lights*, a Canadian television show, 1974

SWINGING ON

A style of jazz called swing, which had a lively rhythm and was played by larger ensembles called big bands, became popular during the 1930s and 1940s. Some music scholars consider the swing era the golden age of jazz, and many would nominate Duke Ellington as the king of swing. Ellington was a bandleader, pianist, and composer. His songs, such as "It Don't Mean a Thing," are still recorded today.

During the swing era, most big bands were segregated. The white bandleader Benny Goodman was one of the few who hired both black and white musicians. Like many other successful bandleaders, Ellington was African-American. Even though his band toured nationally and played to both black and white audiences, Ellington and his musicians continually faced the possibility of being turned away from a gig because of the color of their skin.

THE COTTON CLUB

If you were trendy, fashionable, famous, or just hoping to hear some stellar jazz in 1920s New York City, the Cotton Club was the place to go. In this legendary nightclub, white audiences displayed a strange mix of admiration and disdain toward the conventionally African-American art form of jazz and those who performed it.

Located in Harlem, the Cotton Club had its heyday between 1922 and 1935. All workers and entertainers at the club were African Americans, but the clientele were exclusively white. The club's decor reflected a "stylish plantation environment," and the staff were dressed to reflect management's idea of enslaved people or plantation workers.

Despite the segregation and offensive depiction of African Americans, some of the greatest African-American jazz artists of the period played at the Cotton Club. Duke Ellington's orchestra performed as the house band between 1927 and 1931, after which the orchestra of another jazz great, Cab Calloway, took over. Cotton Club guest performers included Louis Armstrong, Ethel Waters, Lena Horne, and many other outstanding African-American musicians. Weekly radio broadcasts from the club brought their music to a national audience.

The Cotton Club moved to a new location after the Harlem riots of 1935, but it never regained its ranking as the premier New York nightclub. In 1940, it closed its doors for good.

How do you think the Cotton Club both helped and harmed the cause of African Americans?

This clapper, a percussion instrument, advertises the Cotton Club.

A Cotton Club poster from the 1930s publicizes the orchestra of Cab Calloway, a popular jazz singer and bandleader.

JAZZ AND THE FLAPPER

One popular image of the Jazz Age is the flapper, a young woman who bobbed her hair, sported a wide, lipstick-outlined smile, and wore a short, straight-waisted dress. Often, she was portrayed dancing.

Flappers were generally young white working women living in cities. As the economy improved in the 1920s, more jobs began opening up for women in offices, in department stores, and on telephone switchboards. At the same time, women had gained the right to vote. These changes helped produce a generation of newly independent-minded young women. Flappers abandoned the restrictive clothing of earlier times and adopted higher hemlines, bright colors, and cosmetics. In the evenings after work, they could be found dressed in daring new clothing styles and dancing to jazz music in nightclubs. They also engaged in smoking and drinking, activities formerly associated almost exclusively with men.

Not surprisingly, the flappers and their culture drew the condemnation of an outraged older generation. The president of the Christian Endeavor Society, for example, called jazz dancing "an offense against womanly purity." Nevertheless, even though the flappers' signature style faded away after the 1920s, their spirit of independence and youthful energy was passed on to the generations that followed.

Bobbed hair and shorter skirts were hallmarks of a flapper.

JAZZ TODAY

The popularity of jazz declined after the swing era, but the genre still has many dedicated fans and has evolved in a variety of directions. Some musicians have fused elements of jazz with the sounds of Latin and Caribbean music, while others have incorporated electronic instruments, such as synthesizers, and digital technology to move jazz into new realms. Still others continue to explore new ways to perform the classics of Duke Ellington, Louis Armstrong, Benny Goodman, and other jazz greats. Jazz in the 21st century is as diverse as those who perform it and those who listen to it.

THE EVOLUTION OF THE BLUES

Like jazz, the blues originated in the South, developing from such African roots as work songs and field hollers. The blues started out in rural areas rather than cities, sometime after the Civil War. Blues tunes principally expressed the singer's own feelings and struggles, and the instrument of choice was the guitar.

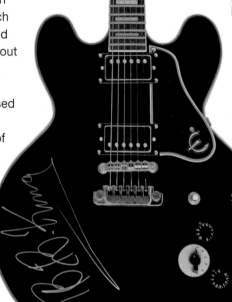

Even more than jazz, the blues featured improvisation, with singers making up both the words and melody as they played. Lyrics were often structured with one line being repeated two or three times, followed by a final line. Most of the early blues players were self-taught, and many could not read music. "The blues didn't come out of no book," the 1930s bluesman Big Bill Broonzy once remarked.

B.B. King named each of his trademark Gibson guitars Lucille. King also wrote a song called "Lucille," which is about his guitar and his music.

In the 1920s, blues musicians joined the northward migration to Chicago and other cities. Some of the most famous blues singers during this period were women, including Mamie Smith, who made the first blues record in 1920, and Bessie Smith, who became famous internationally. Born around 1898 to a poor family in Tennessee, Bessie Smith came to be known as the Empress of the Blues.

GREAT INFLUENCERS

Over the years, jazz and the blues would influence each other's sounds, but the two genres remained distinct. Unlike jazz, the blues never became a national craze. The blues remained popular mainly among African Americans. However, a few blues musicians, such as B.B. King, the King of the Blues, were able to cross over and appeal to a white audience.

In the 1940s, the blues branched out into rhythm and blues (R & B), and both genres influenced the development of rock and roll in the 1950s. Among the pioneers of rock and roll was the African-American singer, songwriter, and guitarist Chuck Berry, who influenced many later rock musicians. Elvis Presley recorded rock songs based on blues tunes, thrilling millions of avid young fans and scandalizing their parents with his energetic sound and his dance moves. As in the Jazz Age, parents and churches and other institutions sounded the alarm that the new music would surely warp young minds. Some of the criticisms were even racist in tone.

In later decades, rock and roll developed into rock music, which has gone in such diverse directions as heavy metal, alternative, and punk. In rap and hip-hop, listeners can trace the enduring blues elements of protest, personal expression, and irresistible rhythms. At the same time, jazz and the blues are still going strong in clubs, recording studios, and the hearts of fans.

THINK ABOUT IT

Why do you think young people turn to music to express their differences from their parents' generation?

JAZZ AND COMPANY

This chart shows the musical styles that blended to become jazz and blues, and many of the genres that evolved from jazz and blues. How many of the genres do you recognize? Which ones do you listen to?

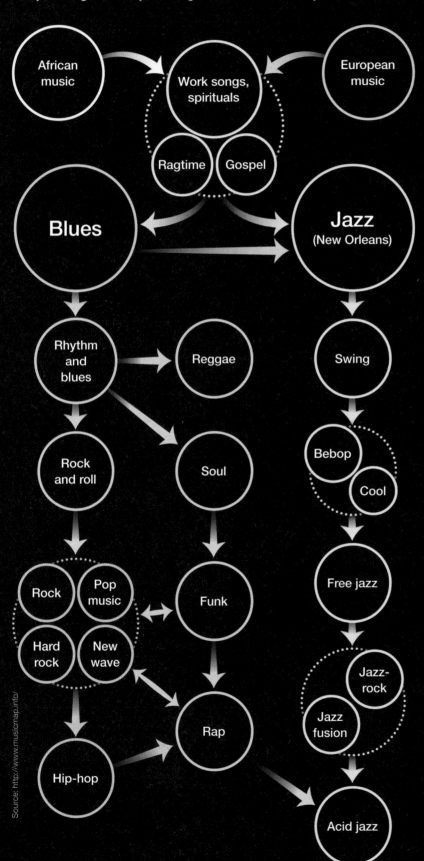

African music → Work songs, spirituals ← European music

Work songs, spirituals → Ragtime, Gospel

Ragtime, Gospel → Blues ↔ Jazz (New Orleans)

Blues → Rhythm and blues

Rhythm and blues → Reggae

Rhythm and blues → Rock and roll

Rhythm and blues → Soul

Jazz (New Orleans) → Swing

Swing → Bebop, Cool

Bebop, Cool → Free jazz

Rock and roll → Rock, Pop music, Hard rock, New wave

Soul → Funk

Rock, Pop music, Hard rock, New wave ↔ Funk

Free jazz → Jazz-rock, Jazz fusion

Hard rock, New wave → Rap

Funk → Rap

Hip-hop → Rap

Rock and roll → Hip-hop

Jazz fusion → Acid jazz

Rap → Acid jazz

Source: http://www.musicmap.info/

The influence of a great musician often spans generations and can spark the development of new genres. Blues giant B.B. King influenced the guitar playing of hard rock musician Jimi Hendrix, who in turn influenced funk musician Prince.

B.B. King

influenced

Jimi Hendrix

influenced

Prince

MAIN IDEA In the years following World War I, a fear of communism gripped the United States and led to tensions between individual rights and the power of government.

THE RED SCARE

Think about something that scares you. What makes it so frightening? Following World War I, the threat of communism spreading to the United States frightened many Americans and put the nation on edge.

CONCERNS ABOUT COMMUNISM

The 1920s would eventually become a decade of prosperity in the United States. But as you have read, the economy stumbled right after World War I as it shifted from wartime to peacetime. Production declined as the federal government canceled war contracts for the manufacturing of defense materials, such as rifles, bullets, and bombs. These slowdowns led to large-scale layoffs just as some 4 million soldiers were returning home in need of jobs, contributing to a two-year postwar recession.

The postwar economic slowdown spurred social unrest, from racial tensions to large strikes. During these anxious times, American leaders worried that the ideas of communism might spread to the United States. As you have learned, the Russian Revolution in 1917 resulted in the formation of the Soviet Union under communist-style rule, in which the government controls all business and the distribution of goods and food. As the United States struggled economically, some Americans viewed communism as fairer and more equitable than **capitalism**, an economic system in which private individuals or groups own the resources and produce goods for a profit.

FEAR GRIPS THE NATION

The emotions sparked by postwar unrest fueled the **Red Scare** of 1919 and 1920, a time when the federal government targeted suspected communists, anarchists, and

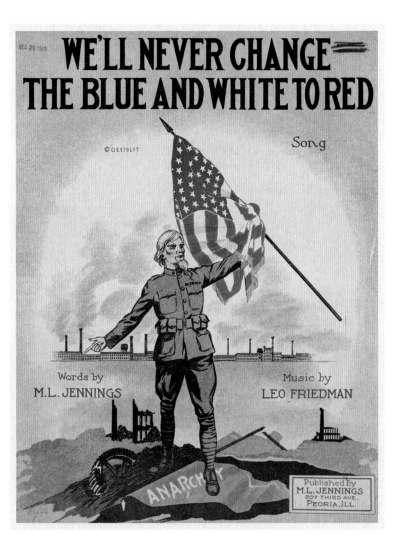

CRITICAL VIEWING Americans wrote songs such as "We'll Never Change the Blue and White to Red" after World War I amid growing fears of communism. What would "anarchy" lead to according to the cover of this sheet music?

radicals, or people who hold extreme political views. After these groups were blamed for a series of mail bombs, officials went on the offensive. Attorney General **A. Mitchell Palmer** obtained funding from Congress to establish a division in the Justice Department to hunt for radicals, naming **J. Edgar Hoover** as the head of the division. In November 1919, officials working under Palmer's direction conducted what were known as the **Palmer Raids**. Police broke into the homes and offices of suspected radicals, including labor union leaders and Russian immigrants. They made scores of arrests, often without obtaining search warrants. By January 1920, authorities had deported some 300 Russian immigrants to the Soviet Union under suspicion of communist activities.

Union leaders of the Industrial Workers of the World (IWW) "Big Bill" Haywood (seated, left) and George Speed (seated, right) appeared in court after their arrests during the Palmer Raids.

Throughout the country, Americans' civil liberties came under assault. Officials outlawed the Communist Party, and state legislatures imposed restrictions on groups and ideas they deemed radical. The Supreme Court upheld most of the laws restricting civil liberties during this time. In *Schenck* v. *United States* (1919), Charles Schenck faced espionage charges for handing out flyers encouraging citizens to resist the military draft. He claimed his arrest violated the First Amendment. However, Justice Oliver Wendell Holmes, Jr., argued that the flyers posed a "clear and present danger" to American society and were not protected by the amendment. Schenck served 10 years in prison for the flyers. In 1927, the Court reaffirmed the verdict in *Whitney* v. *California*. That case involved a Communist Party leader convicted for making a speech that some people interpreted as encouraging violence against the government.

Concern that the Red Scare was weakening freedoms protected by the Constitution led to the founding of the **American Civil Liberties Union (ACLU)** in 1920. The organization dedicated itself to defending the individual rights and freedoms of all Americans. The **Anti-Defamation League (ADL)** also worked to expose and counter the violence of extremist groups, including the Ku Klux Klan, which spread anti-Semitic and anticommunist propaganda. By late 1920, the Red Scare had lost momentum. Palmer had predicted ongoing violence, which never occurred, and his credibility was damaged.

The unrest and anxiety that immediately followed the war influenced the 1920 presidential election. Warren G. Harding easily won the election on his promise to "return to normalcy." He spoke of returning to an era of peace, wealth, and conservative values by reducing the power of government, lowering taxes, and reining in labor unions. Despite Harding's victory, the years ahead would be anything but normal. The 1920s would be a decade of extremes in the United States, combining broad cultural leaps toward modernity with deep anxiety about the country changing too fast and for the worse.

PRIMARY SOURCE

My best judgment of America's needs is to steady down, to get squarely on our feet, to make sure of the right path. Let's get out of the fevered delirium of war, with the hallucination that all the money in the world is to be made in the madness of war and . . . its aftermath. Let us stop to consider that tranquility at home is more precious than peace abroad, and that both our good fortune and our eminence [greatness] are dependent on the normal forward stride of all the American people.

—from Warren G. Harding's campaign speech, 1920

HISTORICAL THINKING

1. **READING CHECK** How did the end of World War I lead to a postwar recession?

2. **COMPARE AND CONTRAST** How was communism different from capitalism?

3. **EVALUATE** Why might the Palmer Raids be considered unconstitutional?

MAIN IDEA During the 1920s, Americans who embraced modern ideas about science and society clashed with those holding more traditional beliefs.

DIVISIONS IN SOCIETY

Sometimes it's hard to let go of old ideas, especially ideas that make you feel comfortable and secure. During the 1920s, changes in society challenged traditional ways and sparked anxiety and division.

POINTING FINGERS

After a few difficult years following World War I, the nation's economy began to recover. This triggered a wave of immigrants from around the world. More than 430,000 people sought entry to the United States in 1920, and another 805,000 immigrants came in 1921. Competition with immigrants for jobs—along with the Red Scare—contributed to a rise in nativism. This ideology favored people born in the United States over more recent immigrants. Nativists especially targeted immigrants from southern and eastern Europe, who were more willing to work for low wages. Adding to the anti-immigrant sentiment was a rise in the popularity of **eugenics**, the belief that some races are superior to others. Eugenicists thought that the more "desirable" race, which was usually western European and Protestant, should populate and grow.

The rise of nativists and eugenicists—who warned of the "degradation" of the population—prompted U.S. lawmakers to take action. Congress approved an emergency quota law in 1921 that limited immigration from Europe to 600,000 people per year. Three years later, lawmakers passed the **National Origins Act**, which reduced annual legal immigration from Europe to about 150,000 people. The act gave preference to people from western and northern European countries and blocked Asian immigrants entirely.

The courts often supported anti-immigrant legislation. One case that highlighted the courts' view involved an immigrant named Bhagat Singh Thind. Thind arrived in the United States from India in 1913 and began studying at the University of California at Berkeley. He volunteered for service in the U.S. Army during World War I. In 1920, he applied for U.S. citizenship, but he was denied under a 1917 law that barred all

PRIMARY SOURCES

Madison Grant was a nativist and a eugenics advocate. Franz Boas was an anthropologist and an opponent of such beliefs. The two held opposite views on immigration and diversity.

These immigrants adopt the language of the native[-born] American, they wear his clothes, they steal his name and they are beginning to take his women, but they seldom adopt his religion or understand his ideals and while he is being elbowed out of his own home the American looks calmly abroad and urges on others the suicidal ethics which are exterminating his own race.

—from *The Passing of the Great Race*, by Madison Grant, 1916

The fear of continued segregation of European national groups is not founded on facts, but on vague impressions obtained from the massing of immigrants in congested city quarters. It does not take into consideration the dispersion of the second and third generation, who become so thoroughly Americanized that in many cases it is quite impossible to obtain exact information in regard to the provenience [origin] of individuals.

—from "This Nordic Nonsense," by Franz Boas in *The Forum*, 1925

CRITICAL VIEWING Syracuse University is home to artist Ben Shahn's 1967 mosaic mural *The Passion of Sacco and Vanzetti* (above). The detail of the mural (right) shows the men who upheld the death sentence standing before Sacco's and Vanzetti's coffins. The trial judge is in the background. Shahn, like many people, thought the men hadn't received a fair trial. What does the artist suggest about the judge and these men by including them in this mural?

immigration from India. He took his case to the U.S. Supreme Court. In the 1923 case, *United States* v. *Bhagat Singh Thind*, the Court ruled that "Hindus" were "aliens ineligible to citizenship." In effect, the ruling established that the federal government could deny citizenship based merely on race or country of origin.

Concerns about immigration played into another prominent court case—a highly controversial murder trial that grabbed global headlines. In 1920, a robbery and murder took place in South Braintree, Massachusetts. Police arrested two Italian immigrants who were also known anarchists, Nicola Sacco and Bartolomeo Vanzetti. Despite claims that authorities had framed the two men, a jury found them guilty and sentenced them to death. People around the world protested against this trial, which came to be called the **Sacco-Vanzetti case**. Many believed that bias against immigrants and radical political beliefs had led to an unfair trial. During the next several years, the men's attorneys filed appeals to overturn the verdict. The American Civil Liberties Union even aided in their defense. However, by 1927, their appeals had run out, and the state of Massachusetts executed the men.

THE RISE OF THE KLAN

Nativist sentiments led to the re-emergence of the Ku Klux Klan. The Klan, as you have read, opposed Catholics, Jews, Asians, women, African Americans, and other minorities. The group, known for its white hoods, regained popularity in the 1920s and spread its beliefs of white supremacy into northern states. Its members often used violence and terrorist tactics to

intimidate those they opposed. Despite its reputation for brutality, including lynching and even torture, the Klan influenced many local and state leaders. Both Democrats and Republicans adopted some of the Klan's language to appeal to voters concerned about the rise of immigration.

The Klan claimed it had 3 million members by the early 1920s, but the organization's national influence began to decline around 1925 after scandals exposed widespread corruption. Meanwhile, groups such as the NAACP fought back against Klan violence through lawsuits and efforts to pass anti-lynching legislation. Despite ongoing racism, African Americans continued to make their voices heard during the 1920s, demanding more opportunities in all aspects of American society. In particular, African-American veterans of World War I expressed their beliefs that people who had risked their lives for their country should not be discriminated against.

To enforce prohibition, agents, often in disguise, identified places where alcohol was being served and confiscated it. In this photo from 1921, agents pour a barrel of beer down a sewer in New York City.

MOBSTERS AND BOOTLEGGERS

As you have read, the 18th Amendment and the Volstead Act had outlawed the sale of alcohol by 1920. Many progressives believed that these laws would decrease alcohol abuse in the United States. Overall, the laws achieved this goal. National consumption of alcohol declined significantly and rates of alcoholism dropped in the first few years of Prohibition.

However, Prohibition had unintended consequences. Across the United States, **bootleggers**, or people who made, transported, or supplied alcohol illegally, sold their products to saloons or **speakeasies**, illegal drinking clubs where people secretly gathered in the evenings. Most speakeasies were tucked away in the back room or basement of a legitimate business, such as a store or a restaurant. To assure security, patrons often had to give a password at the door to be allowed in. Eventually, millions of

middle-class Americans regularly broke the law by continuing to frequent speakeasies and purchase or make alcoholic beverages. Meanwhile, mobsters and their gangs became involved in the sale of illegal liquor, leading to a wave of violence and killing among rival crime organizations. Prohibition did not create organized crime. In fact, the 1920s was not a decade of rising crime rates overall. However, the nation became more aware of crime as a social problem due to the well-publicized activities of gangsters such as **Alphonse "Al" Capone**. In the later years of the decade, Capone ran a huge and notorious organization of illegal saloons, gambling houses, and other shady businesses in Chicago.

DISCOVERIES IN SCIENCE

The anxiety and unrest that emerged during the early 1920s was also fueled by new scientific theories that challenged traditional beliefs. Scientists like **Albert Einstein** argued that space, time, and mass

Albert Einstein won the Nobel Prize for Physics in 1921 for his work on relativity. Here, he was photographed while lecturing in Vienna, Austria, in 1921. That same year, Einstein, a German, visited the United States. He was impressed during his visit by what he called Americans' "joyous, positive attitude to life."

were all relative rather than absolute. This caused people to question traditional ideas about the nature of the universe. Psychologist **Sigmund Freud** suggested that the unconscious mind controlled much of an individual's behavior, an idea that opposed established notions about the causes of mental illness and emotional distress.

These new concepts spurred passionate debates among some American Christians over the proper position to take on scientific matters. Some Christians looked for ways to incorporate new scientific and social ideas into their traditional belief systems, but conservative church leaders preached about the dangers of moving away from the strict teachings of the Bible. This led to the rise of **fundamentalism**, a movement that promoted the idea that every word of the Bible was the literal truth.

Fundamentalists criticized many aspects of modern thinking. In particular, they targeted Charles Darwin's theory of evolution, which, as you will remember, stated that diverse species originated from common ancestors and only the strongest species have adapted and changed in order to survive. Fundamentalists argued that the theory undermined the Bible's teaching that God created all life, including human life, at one fixed point in time. Lawyer and politician William Jennings Bryan emerged as a leading opponent of evolution. "It is better to trust the Rock of Ages," he said, "than to know the age of rocks." In a dozen states, lawmakers introduced bills to ban the teaching of evolution in public schools. A group called the Anti-Evolution League formed to challenge Darwin's theory. Its members hoped to ban the teaching of evolution throughout the nation.

In 1925, Tennessee passed a law that prohibited spending public money "to teach any theory that denies the story of the Divine Creation of man as taught in the Bible." That same year, authorities arrested and tried teacher **John T. Scopes** for talking about evolution in his high school classroom in Dayton, Tennessee. The Scopes trial attracted national attention, with many viewing it as a clash between traditional and modern ideas.

Bryan agreed to help prosecute Scopes. The ACLU brought in noted trial lawyer **Clarence Darrow** to defend the teacher. The judge refused to let Darrow call in scientists to defend evolution, so Darrow called Bryan as an expert witness on the Bible. Bryan defended the literal interpretation of the Bible. However, under Darrow's cross-examination, Bryan came across as contradictory and uncertain. The jury found Scopes guilty and assessed him a small fine. Although Scopes lost the trial, many Americans believed that Bryan's fundamentalism had lost the battle to science and reason.

HISTORICAL THINKING

1. **READING CHECK** What prompted the wave of immigration to the United States in the early 1920s?

2. **MAKE INFERENCES** How did nativist and eugenic beliefs fuel opposition to immigrants?

3. **ANALYZE CAUSE AND EFFECT** What effect did Prohibition have on alcohol consumption in the United States?

4. **DRAW CONCLUSIONS** Why was the Scopes trial viewed as both a victory and a defeat for fundamentalism?

1.3 **GEOLOGY IN HISTORY**

MAIN IDEA Caves provided shelter for early humans and served another role thousands of years later: a place to locate speakeasies during Prohibition.

HOW GEOLOGY KEPT THE '20S ROARING
By Andrés Ruzo, National Geographic Explorer

A cave may not be where you choose to hang out with friends, but in the 1920s, caves had their attractions. For one thing, they made good hiding places. For another, in some of them, alcohol was served.

FINDING THE PERFECT SPEAKEASY

For many people during the 1920s, hiding out and drinking were both important considerations. As you have read, the 18th Amendment, popularly known as Prohibition, had passed, making the sale, production, importation, and transportation of alcoholic beverages illegal. Household consumption of the beverages was still legal, but unless people made their own, they had no way of getting a drink—except illegally, of course.

One of the best places to buy illegal alcoholic drinks was at a speakeasy. The word *speakeasy* suggests the need to whisper, and that's just what people often had to do to get into one of these establishments. Some required a password, others a secret knock or handshake. But these precautions didn't stop the determined. People flocked to speakeasies to drink, dance, enjoy music, and just have a good time.

Still, no one wanted to be arrested, so it was important to find the right speakeasy. Privacy, comfort, seclusion, safety, and getaway routes were all factors to consider. Speakeasies promising all these things popped up everywhere: in cities and in the country as well as in homes and businesses. Some were even in caves.

HUNKERING DOWN IN CAVES

In prehistoric times, early humans took refuge from their often hostile environment in caves. Geology was also on the side of Prohibition-era Americans who sought out caves because they provided shelter from the law. Caves form over hundreds or even millions of years in rocks as water drips through their cracks, eventually hollowing out underground channels. These make for perfect hideouts and even allow for secret passageways to be carved into the rock. And, with their thick walls, caves are insulated from the weather and so maintain near-constant temperatures all year round. As a result, speakeasies in caves were cool in the summer and relatively warm in the winter.

During Prohibition, these amenities attracted customers to the speakeasy at the Longhorn Cavern in Burnet, Texas, not far from the state capital of Austin. With its spacious dance room and dining area, the speakeasy provided a fairly respectable setting. In contrast, the speakeasy at the De Soto Cavern near Birmingham, Alabama, was known for its violence. Fights and shootings earned the speakeasy the nickname "the bloody bucket." Drunken patrons sometimes shot at the cave's **stalactites** and **stalagmites**—mineral deposits hanging from its ceiling or rising from its floor—and bullet holes can still be seen in the rock.

In 1933, Congress repealed the 18th Amendment—the only amendment to be entirely reversed—and liquor flowed freely once more. But Prohibition had forced people to think geologically and seek refuge in caves. The decade may have started on a dry note, but caves helped keep the '20s roaring.

THINK LIKE A GEOLOGIST

1. **READING CHECK** What factors did people look for in a speakeasy?

2. **ANALYZE ENVIRONMENTAL CONCEPTS** How did the formation of caves lead some people to benefit from this natural process during Prohibition?

3. **FORM AND SUPPORT OPINIONS** Would you like to explore a cave? Why or why not?

CRITICAL VIEWING The top photo shows the Longhorn Cavern in Burnet, Texas, which was converted into a speakeasy during Prohibition, complete with a wooden dance floor. The bottom photo shows the cavern today. What geologic elements shown in these pictures reveal why a cave would make an effective speakeasy?

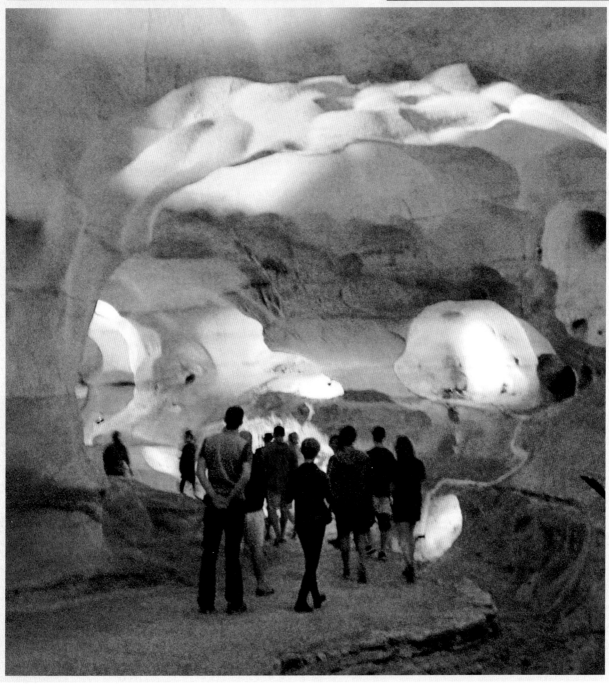

A New Consumer Society

The camera follows a gleaming red sports car as it races down a highway. Inside, we see its slick leather interior as the driver shifts gears. Americans today are accustomed to these irresistible images, but in the 1920s this form of advertising was just developing.

Tangee lipstick—which changed color for each individual wearer—combined new technology, modern advertising, and the flapper's look to become a symbol of the Jazz Age. Young women of the 1920s carried their makeup in small compacts, like the one below, designed in the elaborate art deco style.

Art deco makeup compact

A NEW WORLD OF ADVERTISING

Despite the social anxiety and turmoil of the postwar years, the U.S. economy began to recover during the 1920s. Factory output returned to its prewar levels, and the unemployment rate fell from 12 percent of the labor force in 1922 to only 4 percent in 1927. A good portion of the recovery was stimulated by a new consumer culture, built on an expanding middle class continually encouraged to buy new products.

Advertising boomed during the 1920s. Ad agencies developed effective ways to persuade Americans to buy the many goods produced in the nation's factories. New means of communication, such as the radio, helped advertisers spread their messages and contributed to the development of **mass markets**, or large numbers of consumers to whom manufacturers can sell goods. Before World War I, about $400 million was spent on advertising annually. That number soared to $2.6 billion by 1929. "Advertising," said one industry specialist, "literally creates demand for the things of life that raise the standard of living, elevate the taste, changing luxuries into necessities."

As advertising was coming into its own, so was a new mass audience: the youth market. The growing economy made households more secure, so fewer children were expected to work to help support the family. As a result, many young people had greater freedom and more leisure time. The teen years came to be seen as a distinct phase in the development of young Americans, and the youth culture became linked with seeking fun, excitement, and novelty. Appealing images of cars, cosmetics, motion pictures, fashions, and other attractions in advertisements gave young people ideas about how to have fun and where to spend their parents' money.

Advertisers also focused on the growing number and variety of home products, including electrical appliances. The electric power industry expanded rapidly during the 1920s. By 1928, two-thirds of American families had electricity in their homes. This boosted the market for a host of appliances, from refrigerators and vacuum cleaners to electric irons and washing machines. Advertisers promised these products would make housework easier than ever and give families more time for leisure and fun.

AN AUTOMOBILE CULTURE ARISES

Among the mass consumer goods that emerged during the 1920s, none had a bigger impact on American society than the automobile. Cars became affordable to more and more Americans, thanks in large part to people like carmaker **Henry Ford**.

Ford developed a simple and affordable vehicle, the **Model T**, and he devised an efficient way to mass-produce it. In his **assembly line** system, stationary workers each added a part to a vehicle as it moved along a conveyer belt. Ford's factories were soon turning out a car every 24 seconds, and millions of Americans were getting behind the wheel of the Model T. Ford shocked industry leaders by paying his workers five dollars a day—an unusually high rate for the time. But such wages ensured loyalty and limited turnover among his employees. Higher wages also pushed his factory workers into the middle class, and they, in turn, could afford to buy his cars.

The Model T was popular, affordable, and practical, but not particularly attractive. The Ford Motor Company's lack of varied car models was an opportunity for its competitor, General Motors (GM). Under the leadership of Alfred P. Sloan, Jr., GM introduced innovations that appealed to consumers, such as self-starters, fuel gauges, and reliable headlights. The constant flow of GM's new models and features led customers to want a fresh vehicle every few years. The General Motors Acceptance Corporation made it easy to acquire a car on credit, boosting profits for GM.

As car sales increased, so did the need for good roads throughout the nation. The Federal Highway Act of 1921 left road construction to the states, but it set national standards for concrete surfaces and access to roads. Gasoline taxes brought in revenues, enabling the state governments to build roads and highways. The national network of roads grew from 7,000 miles at the end of the World War I to 50,000 miles by 1927, and more than 20 million cars drove on them. A new category of businesses popped up along the roads to cater to travelers. Motels offered overnight accommodations, roadside restaurants provided food, and gas stations sold fuel and made car repairs. Even the advertising companies got in on the scene, erecting billboards along the roadways to promote local goods and services.

Other forms of transportation expanded as well during the decade. By 1927, there were more than 3 million trucks and buses on the roads. Glenn Curtiss, a champion bicycle racer, had made tremendous advances in motorcycle technology. After one of his early models tested at more than 136.3 miles per hour, he gained a reputation as the "fastest man on earth." Curtiss wasn't content to stick with motorbikes, however. He also helped advance the field of aviation, developing airplanes that set ever-increasing distance records.

Automakers like Henry Ford recognized that more efficient car manufacturing processes would allow them to make less expensive cars. In 1913, Ford pioneered the first large-scale moving manufacturing assembly line, and by the mid-1920s, the auto manufacturing process had achieved large-scale uniformity. In this 1914 photo, Model Ts move continuously along a Ford assembly line in Detroit, Michigan.

During the 1920s, the advertising industry grew rapidly as the proliferation of newspapers, magazines, and radios gave it greater access to consumers. But the public became wary of fraudulent product claims, so advertisers promoted the Truth-in-Advertising Movement, a self-regulating program that later became the Better Business Bureau.

Truth in advertising is not only an asset, but brings business. Untruth in advertising is not only a liability, but it does not bring business in any lasting form. It may thrive for a time on the poor prey . . . [but] How absurd to commit a crime for minnows when whales are to be had for the catching! Truth is the best form of advertising.

—from "Just Why Implicit Truth Is the Business Man's Greatest Asset" by Ed Wolff in *Associated Advertising*, March 1921

STRUGGLES AND SCANDALS

Even as prosperity returned, some Americans still struggled. The postwar recession continued to hit farmers hard. As European agriculture recovered from the war, many overseas markets closed for American farm products. American farmers' incomes generally leveled off after 1919, and the gap between farm earnings and urban wages widened. As a result, most farmers could not afford the modern appliances and conveniences that city dwellers enjoyed.

Not everyone in the cities flourished, either. Labor unions had lost some of their popularity during the Red Scare, and many factory workers struggled to get ahead. Increasingly, government officials and business owners, citing the cost of supporting labor, worked to weaken the power of unions.

On the positive side, some prosperous companies, such as General Electric, International Harvester, and Bethlehem Steel, offered their workers recreational facilities, benefit plans, and even profit-sharing opportunities, through which workers were paid a portion of profits when their company performed well. These extras, which would become known as **welfare capitalism**, were meant to satisfy workers' demands without relying on unions. But as the decade wore on, many of these programs stalled. The weakening of organized labor had removed the incentive for employers to make concessions to workers.

Away from the emerging mass consumerism, the nation's leadership struggled with corruption and scandal. An indecisive leader and a poor judge of people, President Warren Harding had allowed cronies and crooks to infest his administration. Attorney General Harry Daugherty was a political ally of the president, and his weak oversight of the Justice Department had allowed corruption to flourish.

The Harding administration's most serious scandal was called the **Teapot Dome scandal**. Secretary of the Interior Albert B. Fall leased federal oil reserves in Teapot Dome, Wyoming, to private oil companies. Soon after, Fall received $400,000 from his friends in the oil industry in what many taxpayers interpreted as payoffs for his leasing decisions. The Teapot Dome scandal exposed Harding's presidency as one of the more corrupt administrations in American history. The president himself did not make it to the end of his term. During a tour of the West Coast, Harding fell ill in San Francisco and died of heart disease on August 2, 1923.

Calvin Coolidge, Harding's vice president and the former governor of Massachusetts, became the nation's next president. Coolidge promised to continue growing the economy and to promote Harding's return to "normalcy." Coolidge was even more committed to conservative Republican principles than Harding had been. He proclaimed that "the chief business of the American people is business," and he endorsed policies designed to promote free enterprise. He extended tax-cutting policies and appointed pro-business individuals to head the regulatory agencies and departments that progressives had established a generation earlier.

President Coolidge used modern public relations techniques to bolster his image as the embodiment of old-time virtues of morality and frugality, or thrift. In addition, Coolidge succeeded in cleaning up much of the corruption that had plagued Harding's term in the White House.

HISTORICAL THINKING

1. **READING CHECK** How did advertising drive mass markets in the 1920s?

2. **IDENTIFY MAIN IDEAS AND DETAILS** How did Henry Ford's assembly line increase mass marketing of automobiles?

3. **ASK AND ANSWER QUESTIONS** What other questions do you have about the consequences of the new consumer economy in the 1920s, and where can you find the answers?

4. **MAKE GENERALIZATIONS** Why was the farming industry not as prosperous as other industries during the early 1920s?

MAIN IDEA In the 1920s, a distinct form of African-American music known as jazz emerged and gained popularity in the United States and parts of Europe.

THE BIRTH OF JAZZ

What do many of today's musicians have in common? They have been inspired by jazz artists. In fact, many rock and roll, hip-hop, and rhythm and blues musicians have been heavily influenced by jazz.

THE MUSIC OF NEW ORLEANS

After World War I, the music that came to be called **jazz** grew in popularity beyond its origins among African-American musicians in New Orleans. Jazz contains lively rhythms, sounds from a variety of instruments, and improvisation—the act of creating and playing music without prior rehearsal or reliance on a written score. Jazz is a uniquely American art form, and from its beginnings it brought together black and white musicians. The term *jazz* came into wide use after a New Orleans group, the Original Dixieland Jazz Band, produced a best-selling record album with mass appeal.

In the 1920s, radio stations broadcast live jazz concerts almost every night, making jazz singers and bandleaders famous. A leading jazz artist, **Joe "King" Oliver**, took his band on the road to cities such as Chicago and New York. Oliver trained many new artists in jazz techniques, and these

CRITICAL VIEWING Jazz and blues artists Ma Rainey (center) and her Georgia Jazz Band (from left), Gabriel Washington, Albert Wynn, Dave Nelson, Ed Pollack, and Thomas A. Dorsey, brought old country blues and new jazz to sold-out crowds in the 1920s. The innovative Ma Rainey was the first singer to record "See See Rider," a song still popular today. What image of jazz and the blues is projected by the musicians in this photo?

artists took what they learned and added their own variations and innovations. Jazz trumpeter **Louis (LOO-ee) Armstrong** was one of the musicians who worked with Oliver early in his career. Armstrong was nicknamed Satchmo, for "Satchel Mouth," because his cheeks puffed out like a bag when he played. Armstrong became one of the world's most successful musicians, and throughout his career, he helped spread American culture and goodwill through his talent.

JAZZ FROM COAST TO COAST

Modern forms of communication, such as record players and radio, helped spread the popularity of jazz from coast to coast and throughout the world. The music traveled from major American cities to smaller urban centers, such as Kansas City and Denver, and across the ocean to Britain, France, and even Russia. Part of the music's appeal lay in its fast-paced, unpredictable style. Many younger Americans looking for entertainment started attending nightclubs to dance to jazz music. The rhythms and sounds of jazz gave the 1920s its enduring title: the Jazz Age.

Trumpeter and singer Louis Armstrong is pictured on the cover of the sheet music for "Saint Louis Blues," an iconic jazz song written in 1914 by W.C. Handy. Armstrong first recorded the song in 1929.

Jazz also helped increase the crossover appeal of other African-American musical forms, especially the blues, the roots of which reach back to slave spirituals. Unlike upbeat jazz music, blues songs speak of sadness and heartache, sometimes covering adult themes such as alcoholism and drug abuse. Blues artists **Gertrude "Ma" Rainey** and **Bessie Smith** often drew upon their personal experiences in singing their sad, soulful tunes. Early in her career, a young Bessie Smith sang with Rainey and one of her bands. Both women performed and recorded songs with Armstrong. By the end of the 1920s, Smith was the highest paid performer in the world.

Some older, more conservative Americans considered jazz shocking. They associated the music with illegal drinking and other illicit activities. Jazz and the blues became one more point of generational conflict in the divide between traditional and modern cultural norms. Eventually, jazz gained widespread appeal and respect, particularly from Armstrong's global popularity and stars such as singer and bandleader **Cab Calloway**, dancer and singer **Josephine Baker**, and pianist and bandleader **Edward Kennedy "Duke" Ellington**.

The multitalented Calloway turned down a chance to play with the famous Harlem Globetrotters basketball team and left law school to sing with a band. He became a popular bandleader at the Cotton Club in Harlem, a composer, a scat singer (someone who sings jazz using only syllables instead of words), and a Broadway and film actor. Pianist, composer, and bandleader Duke Ellington is probably the most well-known American jazz musician. He is noted particularly for writing to showcase the talent of each member of his band. In describing his inspiration to write jazz, or what he liked to call "American music," Ellington said, "My men and my race are the inspiration of my work. I try to catch the character and mood and feeling of my people."

HISTORICAL THINKING

1. **READING CHECK** What were the origins of jazz?

2. **DESCRIBE** What are some characteristics of jazz music?

3. **FORM AND SUPPORT OPINIONS** Why do you think jazz was so popular in the 1920s?

4. **IDENTIFY** Through what methods was jazz music diffused across the United States and throughout the world?

POPULAR CULTURE AND ARTISTIC ACHIEVEMENT

Consider some of the things you like to do today, from watching videos on a computer or phone to going to movies, sporting events, or concerts. It all began in the 1920s, as mass forms of entertainment emerged and Americans began to enjoy the shared experience of popular culture.

MOVIES AND RADIO

With money to spend and more free time than ever, Americans found many ways to entertain themselves. One of the most popular activities was going to the movies. From uncertain beginnings at the turn of the century, motion picture studios had developed into large enterprises employing hundreds of people. Studio heads, including Adolph Zukor of Paramount Pictures and Louis B. Mayer of Metro-Goldwyn-Mayer (MGM), also controlled theater chains in order to show the films they had made on a tight schedule to maximize profits.

These posters, from the golden age of silent movies, advertise the films *It* (1927) with Clara Bow and *The Sheik* (1921) with Rudolph Valentino. In bright, bold colors, the posters feature the names and portraits of the stars, whose popularity drew the public into the movie "palaces," or theaters.

AN ORIGINAL AMERICAN ARCHITECTURE

During the 1920s, creative building designs flourished and became the basis of 20th century architecture. Among the most innovative architects of that time was **Frank Lloyd Wright**, who developed the Prairie style, a uniquely American design. Wright was influenced by the natural world, as represented here in his Fallingwater House, which was built in the mid-1930s in Bear Run, Pennsylvania. Today, skyscrapers and city centers throughout the world reflect aspects of Wright's distinctive Prairie style, which emphasizes geometric shapes and openness.

At the motion picture industry's peak during the 1920s, 20,000 theaters screened films attended by some 100 million people each week. Ticket prices were relatively affordable—admission was usually about 50 cents. Until the end of the decade, all the movies were silent. Live musicians in the theaters provided background music and sounds. Large urban movie palaces boasted entire orchestras to accompany silent films, but most smaller movie houses simply hired a pianist to put sound to the picture. Title cards in the films provided limited dialogue. The movie actors had to depend on their ability to convey emotions through facial expressions and actions, and actors who mastered the craft often became stars.

The movies provided a model for what young people wore, the slang they used, and even how they behaved. Women copied the fashions and bobbed haircuts of popular actresses, such as **Clara Bow**, nicknamed the "It Girl" for her on-screen appeal. Fans closely followed the personal lives of Hollywood celebrities, such as **Mary Pickford**, the biggest box office star of the decade and a leader in the film industry. Some historians consider Pickford and her husband, dashing action star **Douglas Fairbanks**, to have been the first Hollywood "supercouple." Comic actor **Charlie Chaplin** and mysterious, handsome

Rudolph Valentino also attracted a huge following of adoring fans.

In 1926, when Valentino died suddenly at the age of 31, many of his shocked fans became hysterical. Because they had seen him on-screen and read magazine articles about him, fans felt as if they had lost someone they knew. Thousands of people paid their respects at his funeral as hundreds of thousands stood on the street outside. It was the first time a celebrity was the object of such a public outpouring of grief. The reaction to Valentino's death reflected the growing influence movie stars had on American culture.

By the end of the decade, the film industry developed the technology to synchronize sounds with the actions of actors. Sound films, or "talkies," replaced silent pictures. The first major sound film, *The Jazz Singer* (1927), starred well-known entertainer **Al Jolson**. Fans loved the possibilities sound offered to enhance the film-going experience.

Radio technology, made possible by the expansion of electricity, added to entertainment options at home. The first radio station, KDKA in Pittsburgh, went on the air in 1920. In 1923, New York station WBAY began selling airtime to advertisers, who quickly saw the potential of radio to spread their messages. Radios soon became popular consumer items, and by 1923, they were in 400,000 households.

HEROES OF SPORT AND DARING FEATS

Another pastime that took off during the 1920s was following sports. During the decade, football grew into a national obsession. Large stadiums sprang up at colleges on the West Coast and in the Midwest. The most famous football player of the era was **Harold "Red" Grange** of the University of Illinois. When he scored 4 touchdowns in 12 minutes against the University of Michigan in 1924, his picture appeared on the cover of *Time*, a new magazine featuring news and popular culture. After he left college, Grange joined the newly formed National Professional Football League, a predecessor of today's National Football League, where he was paid $12,000 per game at the start. In contrast, the average worker in 1925 made 65 cents an hour.

Although football attracted millions of followers, baseball best captured the excitement and passion of the 1920s, especially after a phenomenal player named **George Herman "Babe" Ruth** emerged.

The National Museum of American History
Washington, D.C.

Popular for his dramatic home runs and generosity to fans, Babe Ruth (1895–1948) signed this baseball for a Pennsylvania fan. The Sultan of Swat played ball at St. Mary's Industrial School for Boys before joining the Red Sox and then the Yankees, the team he led to seven American League pennants and four World Series titles.

Babe Ruth was a pitcher for the Boston Red Sox when they traded him to the New York Yankees for $400,000 in 1918. Ruth was the first of the celebrity sluggers. He belted out 54 home runs during the 1920 season alone. His team constructed Yankee Stadium ("The House That Ruth Built") to hold the growing number of fans who flocked to New York City to watch him play. Baseball fans were captivated in 1927 when Babe Ruth hit 60 home runs, helping the New York Yankees capture the American League pennant and win the World Series in four games. Other sports heroes of the time included **Gertrude Ederle**, the first woman to swim the English Channel, and heavyweight boxing champion **Jack Dempsey**.

Athletes were not the only people who gained fans through their extraordinary feats. **Charles A. Lindbergh** secured his fame and fortune by making a historic, groundbreaking flight across the Atlantic Ocean. Lindbergh, an airmail pilot for the government, took up a challenge that offered a $25,000 prize to the pilot who could make the first solo nonstop flight between New York City and Paris, France, a distance of 3,610 miles. Lindbergh raised money to have a new plane built—the *Spirit of St. Louis*. On May 10, 1927, Lindbergh took off from Roosevelt Field in New York, headed across the Atlantic Ocean to Paris. When he landed in the French capital 33 hours and 30 minutes later, he was an international celebrity. Lucky Lindy, as he came to be known, was celebrated with a parade in New York City in his honor, medals from foreign nations, and a lifetime in the public eye. To the generation growing up in the 1920s, Lindbergh's laudable feat symbolized the ability of a single person to overcome any obstacle by sheer determination.

THE "LOST GENERATION" OF WRITERS

Not all artists and entertainers tried to appeal to popular tastes. Many leading authors of this time had come of age during World War I, and the horror of that war darkened their views of society. Their writing often struck a hard and realistic tone, a style that later became known as **modernism**.

The list of influential authors of the 1920s is long and distinguished. The most popular novelist of the early 1920s was **Sinclair Lewis**, whose books *Main Street* (1920) and *Babbitt* (1922) examined small-town life in the Midwest with brutal honesty. Novelists such as **Edith Wharton**, **Willa Cather**, and **William Faulkner** produced bodies of work that examined the lives of aristocratic women (Wharton), prairie pioneers (Cather), and life in the Deep South (Faulkner) with unflinching frankness rather than rosy nostalgia.

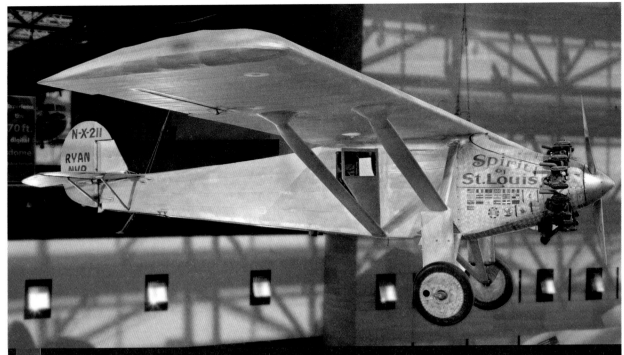

🏛 National Air and Space Museum, Washington, D.C.

The Ryan Airlines NYP *Spirit of St. Louis* plane hangs high above visitors in a flight hall at the National Air and Space Museum. In 1927, pilot Charles Lindbergh flew the monoplane across the United States and set a transcontinental record of 21 hours and 40 minutes for the flight. Eight days later, he made the 3,610-mile flight from New York to France. His risky venture brought immediate attention and financial support to the U.S. aeronautical industry. Upon his return, Lindbergh toured the United States, Mexico, and other countries in the Americas in the *Spirit of St. Louis* and had the flags of those countries painted around the plane's nose.

Two of the most popular fiction writers of the decade were **Ernest Hemingway** and **F. Scott Fitzgerald**. World War I and its aftermath greatly shaped the works of both authors. They were among a group of artists whom fellow writer **Gertrude Stein** nicknamed the "lost generation." The phrase refers to the uncertainty and despair many artists felt after the war. Influenced by writer **Ezra Pound**, Hemingway wrote in a sharp, understated style in best sellers such as *The Sun Also Rises* (1926) and *A Farewell to Arms* (1929), which spoke of the pain and doubt suffered by those who had fought in World War I. In *The Great Gatsby* (1925), Fitzgerald told the story of young Jay Gatsby, who tried to use his wealth to impress a lost love—with tragic consequences.

PRIMARY SOURCE

Toward the end of *The Great Gatsby*, the narrator, Nick Carraway, reflects on the life of a wealthy couple with whom he had once been friends but now concludes are partly responsible for Gatsby's untimely death.

They were careless people, Tom and Daisy— they smashed up things and creatures and then retreated back into their money or their vast carelessness, or whatever it was that kept them together, and let other people clean up the mess they had made.

—from *The Great Gatsby*, by F. Scott Fitzgerald, 1925

HISTORICAL THINKING

1. **READING CHECK** How did people spend their leisure time and money in the 1920s?

2. **ANALYZE VISUALS** Based on the 1920s movie posters, what ideas do you think motion picture studios were trying to sell to their audiences?

3. **COMPARE AND CONTRAST** What was different and similar about the heroes of sports and the heroes of daring feats?

4. **ANALYZE LANGUAGE USE** What does Fitzgerald's description of his characters imply about values of the Jazz Age?

CHANGING ROLES FOR WOMEN

Do you remember how you felt when you got your driver's license or your first job? That new sense of freedom and respect was similar to what a number of women felt in the 1920s as they gained greater independence in society.

EMBRACING NEW FREEDOMS

As it did for many people in America, World War I and its aftermath changed the lives of women. Having aided in the war effort and having won the right to vote, many younger women entered the postwar era with expectations very different from those of previous generations. Rather than moving straight from their parents' home to marriage and child-rearing, as was traditional before the war, more women sought to gain greater control over their lives by exercising personal choice in the timing of their education, career, marriage, and motherhood. After World War I, it became more common for a woman to postpone marriage or motherhood, in part because of access to new health care options, including family planning.

Standards for acceptable public behavior in the 1920s were changing for everyone, including young women. Dating young men without the presence of a chaperone and drinking in public—even though it was illegal—became commonplace. The most famous expression of these new social freedoms was conveyed through fashion. Many young women embraced a freer style of dress, and the media dubbed them "**flappers**." This name came from an illustration in a magazine showing a fashionable young woman whose rubber rain boots were open and flapping, but the real hallmarks of a flapper were her bobbed hair, her short dresses, and—perhaps most shocking of all—her use of cosmetics.

In 1925, a group of high school girls posed as flappers. The image of the flapper caught on as a symbol of a spontaneous approach to life.

AMELIA EARHART

Nicknamed Lady Lindy because she, too, was a record-breaking flier like celebrity pilot Lucky Lindy (Charles Lindbergh), aviator **Amelia Earhart** was a famous trendsetter of the 1920s. She was as skillful a flier and as knowledgeable about planes as any male pilot, and quickly established a huge fan following.

In 1928, Earhart became the first woman to fly across the Atlantic Ocean, and she was the first pilot of either gender to fly over both the Atlantic and Pacific oceans. Her dream was to become the first pilot to fly around the world. She set out on her journey in 1937, but she vanished with her navigator over the Pacific Ocean, more than 22,000 air miles into her trip. Her fate remains a mystery.

The flapper became associated with fun and fashion, and advertisers took notice. Magazines promoted this image to sell clothing and cosmetics to mass markets. As many young women looked to assert their independence, mass media pushed them to conform to the latest ideals of glamour and physical beauty. Many older suffragists scolded the younger generation for focusing on fun and glamour rather than on bringing about political and social changes. Most young women, however, were excited to break with traditional ideals, and to do it in their own ways.

ENTERING THE WORKFORCE

Women also wielded greater economic power, thanks to their increasing entry into the workforce. As the 1920s began, 8.3 million women worked outside the home, representing about 24 percent of the national workforce. Ten years later, the number of working women stood at 10.6 million, or 27 percent of the workforce. Despite this increase, the kinds of work available to women remained limited. A few occupations accounted for 85 percent of female jobs. One-third of employed women worked in clerical positions, one-fifth as domestic servants, and another third in factory jobs. And women were still paid less than men; on average, they made about half of what men earned for doing the same jobs.

In addition, not all women advanced equally. For the majority of working-class women, the barriers to opportunity remained high. Poor white women in the South often worked at dead-end jobs in textile mills or agricultural processing plants. Due to racial discrimination, African-American women found it difficult to secure nondomestic jobs in either the North or the South. Even upper- and middle-class white women faced formidable obstacles in the workplace. Many school districts forced newly married female schoolteachers to resign. The medical and legal professions employed more women than in the past, but men in power made it difficult for women to advance in these careers. In government, male employees regularly received favorable treatment. What's more, women were still expected to take care of all household duties—which made managing a full-time job all the more difficult.

HISTORICAL THINKING

1. **READING CHECK** In what ways did women's lives change in the 1920s?

2. **DESCRIBE** How did women exercise their new freedoms and increased independence after World War I?

3. **IDENTIFY MAIN IDEAS AND DETAILS** How did Amelia Earhart represent the changing roles of women in the 1920s?

4. **COMPARE AND CONTRAST** How were women's experiences in the workforce in the 1920s different from and similar to those of men and to those of women today?

WOMEN IN POLITICS

Hearing about women running for and being elected to prominent government positions is not uncommon today, but this is a relatively new development in the United States. It was only in the 1920s, after passage of the 19th Amendment, that women slowly began to enter politics.

WOMEN IN ELECTED OFFICE

As you have read, the 19th Amendment to the U.S. Constitution guaranteed women throughout the country the right to vote. Both supporters and opponents of women's suffrage had expected the amendment to change politics dramatically after it was ratified in 1920. It soon became apparent, however, that a majority of women tended to vote for the same candidates as the men in their lives. The notion of a unified bloc of female voters did not materialize.

Although women's suffrage did not usher in the sweeping political change some observers had predicted, increasing numbers of women served in political office in the 1920s. Two states, Wyoming and Texas, were the first to elect female governors. When Governor William Ross of Wyoming died shortly before votes were cast in his 1924 campaign for re-election, political leaders persuaded his widow, **Nellie Tayloe Ross**, to take his place on the ballot. Despite campaigning very little, Ross easily defeated her male opponent to become the United States' first female governor. She proved an excellent leader, remaining independent and refusing to bow to special interest groups. She narrowly lost her bid for re-election in 1926, after powerful business leaders backed her opponent. Ross went on to work for the federal government in Washington, D.C., as the first female director of the United States Mint, a position she held for more than 20 years.

The same year of Ross's election, **Miriam Amanda "Ma" Ferguson**, a housewife with no previous political experience, won the Texas governor's seat. The legislature had impeached and convicted her husband, the popular but corrupt James "Pa"

Ferguson, and barred him from holding state office. Ma Ferguson ran with the goal of carrying on her husband's work and clearing his name. Like Ross, she easily defeated her male opponent. Ferguson took office 15 days after Ross, making her the country's second female governor. Surrounded by the same cronies who had corrupted her husband's administration, Ferguson faced her own scandals, which kept her from winning re-election. Ferguson remained active in politics, however, and she made a comeback in 1932 when voters elected her as

Governor Nellie Tayloe Ross, c. 1925

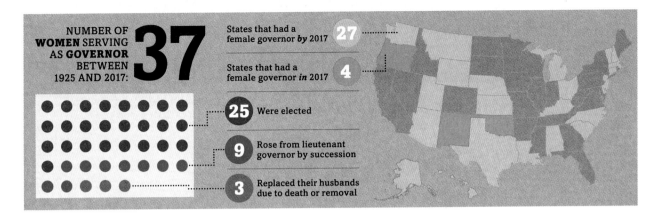

NUMBER OF **WOMEN** SERVING AS **GOVERNOR** BETWEEN 1925 AND 2017: **37**

States that had a female governor *by* 2017 — **27**

States that had a female governor *in* 2017 — **4**

25 Were elected

9 Rose from lieutenant governor by succession

3 Replaced their husbands due to death or removal

governor again. During her second term, a much more politically experienced Ferguson proved an effective leader to her **constituency**, or those who elected her, during tough economic times.

During the 1920s, voters elected 11 women to the House of Representatives, many of them as political heirs of their husbands. Many more women won seats in state legislatures and held local offices. Other women, such as **Eleanor Roosevelt**, the wife of a rising Democratic politician in New York, built up a network of support for women's causes and careers. In 1924, Roosevelt accepted a position as chair of the National Democratic Party's platform committee on women's issues. After male party leaders refused to allow the women of the committee to participate in the final party platform decisions, Roosevelt pressed for the inclusion of more female party delegates. In 1928, she organized one of New York's most successful campaigns ever to encourage women's political participation. "Women must learn to play the game as men do," she wrote.

EQUAL RIGHTS FOR WOMEN

Having achieved the vote, a more militant, or activist, wing of the suffragists campaigned to add an **Equal Rights Amendment (ERA)** to the U.S. Constitution. The purpose of the amendment was to end gender discrimination, which primarily affected women. Examples of discrimination, according to ERA proponents, ranged from women earning less than men for the same work to being excluded from various activities and jobs. Originally proposed by Alice Paul in 1923, the amendment states, "Equality of rights under the law shall not be denied or abridged by the United States or by any state on account of sex." Paul viewed the amendment as the next logical step in bringing "equal justice under law" to all U.S. citizens.

The amendment's language seemed simple and straightforward, but in reality it left much to interpretation. Some female reformers, such as Florence Kelley and Carrie Chapman Catt, opposed the ERA. They regarded it as a threat to hard-won laws that protected women in the workplace, such as maximum hours, minimum wage, and safe working conditions. Despite the lobbying efforts of Paul's National Woman's Party, the ERA did not gain wide support during the 1920s. Even so, the amendment was introduced in every session of Congress until it was approved in slightly modified form in the early 1970s.

A WOMAN RUNS FOR PRESIDENT

Nellie Ross and Ma Ferguson weren't the first women to run for office. At least one woman aspired to the highest position in the land decades before women were even allowed to vote. On April 2, 1870, the country's first female stockbroker, Victoria C. Woodhull, announced her candidacy for president. Her platform included an eight-hour workday, divorce laws that treated men and women equally, and support for social welfare—all issues that would come up in future decades. "I am quite well aware that in assuming this position I shall evoke more ridicule than enthusiasm at the outset," she wrote. Woodhull was disqualified for the candidacy due to her age. Presidents must be at least 35 years old; Woodhull was 34.

HISTORICAL THINKING

1. **READING CHECK** In what ways were Nellie Ross and Miriam Ferguson effective role models?

2. **MAKE INFERENCES** Why did some women see the need for an equal rights amendment?

3. **ANALYZE CAUSE AND EFFECT** Why didn't the ratification of the 19th Amendment bring about sweeping changes in American politics?

4. **INTERPRET CHARTS** Based on the chart, how many women became governor without initially running for the office?

MAIN IDEA The 1920s saw a major migration from the rural South to the urban North as African Americans sought new economic and political opportunities in large cities.

THE GREAT MIGRATION

As industry continued booming in the steel and car manufacturing cities of the North, thousands of African Americans arrived seeking better jobs and new lives. Most were not disappointed. One migrant to Chicago declared in a letter to his southern family, "Nothing here but money, and it is not hard to get."

DISCRIMINATION IN THE NORTH

During World War I, the need for northern factory workers led to the Great Migration, in which African Americans and other minority groups moved from the South to the North and West. The migration continued during the 1920s, as the economy boomed and industries expanded. In all, 1 million African Americans—about 13 percent of the South's entire black population—moved to cities such as Chicago, Detroit, New York, Los Angeles, and San Francisco.

Within their segregated neighborhoods, the migrants created vibrant communities. As African-American neighborhoods grew in the North, their residents gained greater local political influence. In addition, community magazines and newspapers, such as the *Chicago Defender*, focused on issues of local concern. Some publications gained national and international reputations, making it more difficult in some cases for political leaders to ignore the concerns of African-American citizens.

While African Americans found greater opportunity in the North and West, they still confronted racism. Whites who did not want the ethnic makeup of their cities to change or who feared economic competition, initiated conflicts with African-American migrants. In 1917, racial tensions boiled over in East

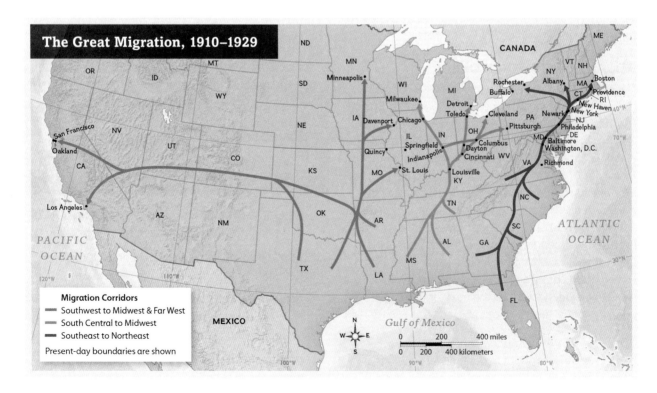

The Great Migration, 1910–1929

Migration Corridors
— Southwest to Midwest & Far West
— South Central to Midwest
— Southeast to Northeast
Present-day boundaries are shown

St. Louis, Illinois, across the Mississippi River from St. Louis, Missouri. Many migrants had moved to the area for work. Following rumors that a black man had killed a white man, roving bands of whites attacked African Americans, killing between 39 and 100 African Americans. They also destroyed $400,000 worth of property. The number of race riots increased during the postwar recession, as white workers saw African Americans as economic competitors.

In the face of growing violence and discrimination, many African Americans in the North looked to the NAACP for assistance. Since it began in 1909, the NAACP, which, as you have read, W.E.B. Du Bois helped found, had worked to build a network of local branches in cities across the country. Between 1917 and 1919 alone, the organization's membership jumped tenfold, from about 9,000 to 90,000 people.

Responding to the violence of the 1920s, civil rights leaders altered their strategies for overcoming segregation and discrimination. Focusing on the long view, the NAACP organized a team of lawyers to challenge segregationist laws in court and influence legislation. But change came slowly. It took more than 30 years for the organization to achieve one of its main goals: persuading Congress to pass a federal anti-lynching law.

A NEW HOMELAND

A number of African Americans believed the NAACP's methodical approach to combating racism and segregation was far too slow. As a result, they turned to more militant civil rights leaders who promised faster results. **Marcus Garvey**, who had immigrated to the United States from Jamaica in 1916, was among the most powerful of those leaders.

In part, Garvey followed Booker T. Washington's beliefs that African Americans should focus more on improving their personal economic conditions than on ending legal segregation. Garvey urged African Americans to support black-owned businesses and organizations to empower their communities. He also boosted the self-esteem of many followers by encouraging conversations about African pride.

The charismatic Garvey preached the doctrine of **Pan-Africanism**, a movement that sought to unify people of African descent. Many of Garvey's followers hoped to establish settlements in Africa so that African Americans could move there and live together. Garvey led this **back-to-Africa movement** and promised to "organize the 400,000,000 Negroes

At what he called the "First International Convention of the Negro Peoples of the World" in 1920, Marcus Garvey was elected the "Provisional President of Africa." This photo captured Garvey in his self-styled presidential uniform as he rode in a Harlem parade.

of the World into a vast organization to plant the banner of freedom on the great continent of Africa." He created a group called the Universal Negro Improvement Association (UNIA) to establish such settlements in areas of Africa that were not controlled by imperialist nations.

Pan-African rallies in New York and other cities often drew 25,000 people and raised funds for the UNIA. Ultimately, however, poor management caused Garvey's venture to fail. His health, finances, and political power gradually declined until his death in 1940. However, Garvey's ideas continued to influence generations of African Americans. Many civil rights groups throughout the 20th century adopted Garvey's message that urban blacks should band together to wield economic and political power.

HISTORICAL THINKING

1. **READING CHECK** Why did the Great Migration continue into the 1920s?

2. **SYNTHESIZE** What approach did the NAACP take to fight segregation and discrimination?

3. **INTERPRET MAPS** What generalization can you make about where African Americans migrated to and from?

THE HARLEM RENAISSANCE

It feels good to be part of a group where everyone gets along and shares similar interests. This is how many African Americans felt as they settled in the New York City neighborhood of Harlem and built a flourishing community.

In November 1934, Zora Neale Hurston went to Chicago to give a performance of African-American stories and songs she had collected in the South. Harlem Renaissance photographer Carl van Vechten captured this shot of Hurston.

AN ERA OF CREATIVE REBIRTH

One of the vibrant communities that emerged from the Great Migration is the neighborhood of Harlem in New York City. Located on the northern part of Manhattan Island, for decades the neighborhood attracted a variety of working-class immigrants from different ethnic groups. Starting around 1904, the Afro-American Realty Company began recruiting African-American families to move to the area.

Over time, Harlem became a majority African-American neighborhood. By the 1920s, it was the premier African-American community in the United States, a place where black culture thrived. African-American writers, artists, and musicians who lived there led a wave of creativity known as the **Harlem Renaissance**, which spread across the country.

Major figures in the Harlem Renaissance included poets **Countee Cullen** ("Yet Do I Marvel," a famous sonnet) and **Claude McKay** (*Harlem Shadows*, a collection of his celebrated poetry) as well as the memoirist and songwriter **James Weldon Johnson** (*God's Trombones*). Many artists crossed over into multiple genres, such as anthropologist and writer **Zora Neale Hurston** (*Their Eyes Were Watching God*) and poet, playwright, and novelist **Langston Hughes** (*The Weary Blues*). Then as now, their work provided readers with vivid descriptions of life during segregation. "For various reasons, the average, struggling . . . Negro is the best-kept secret in America," Hurston wrote. "His revelation to the public is the thing needed to do away with the feeling of difference which inspires fear, and which ever expresses itself in dislike."

Artists of the Harlem Renaissance often joined African traditions with their American experiences. **Aaron Douglas**, an illustrator, muralist, and celebrated painter, developed a modernist style based in African and Egyptian art. **Lois Mailou Jones** called upon African and Haitian traditions for her colorful abstract oil and watercolor paintings. Sculptor **Augusta Savage** gained fame for her sculpted busts of prominent African Americans such as W.E.B. Du Bois and Marcus Garvey. Some writers and artists, such as painter **Archibald J. Motley, Jr.**, who was born in New Orleans and spent most of his life in Chicago, found inspiration in the sights and sounds of the jazz and blues scenes. The music inspired young people and artists of all ages, and the venues were places for creative thinkers to socialize and share ideas.

In 1936, artist Jacob Lawrence painted *Ice Peddlers*, a vivid portrayal of the daily journey of ice sellers on a Harlem street. Lawrence was still a teen when he created this sophisticated streetscape of the peddlers at the forefront of the bustling city that surrounds them. As one of the first young men trained by other artists in the African-American community during the Harlem Renaissance, Lawrence drew on the life around him to chronicle African-American experiences and the effects of the Great Migration.

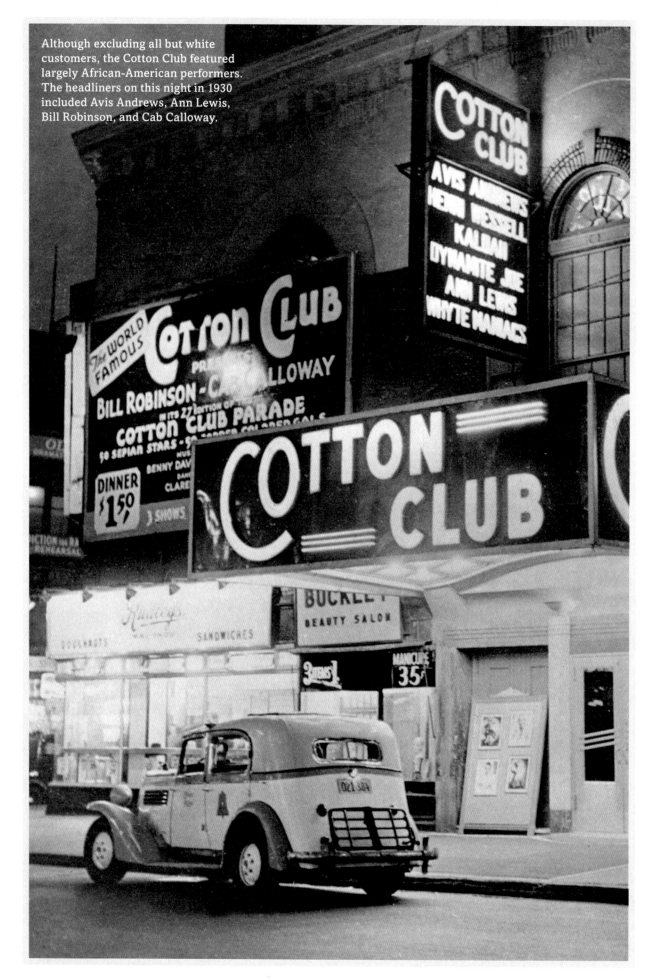

Although excluding all but white customers, the Cotton Club featured largely African-American performers. The headliners on this night in 1930 included Avis Andrews, Ann Lewis, Bill Robinson, and Cab Calloway.

The hottest nightclub in Harlem was the **Cotton Club**, originally opened as the Club Deluxe by African-American boxing champion Jack Johnson in 1920. The club featured the biggest names in jazz at the time, including Duke Ellington, Cab Calloway, and Louis Armstrong. In 1923, a white gangster named Owney Madden bought the club, expanded it, and remodeled it into a swanky, segregated venue he renamed as the Cotton Club. Although most of the Cotton Club's performers were African-American, only whites were allowed in the audience. The exclusive nature of the club enhanced its appeal among wealthy white club-goers while reinforcing racism and segregation. In many ways the Cotton Club served as a symbol of the limits of African-American success, even within black neighborhoods.

The Harlem Renaissance reached its peak in 1925. The neighborhood boasted an exciting nightlife filled with intellectuals, artists, and wealthy white patrons. A national magazine's special feature, titled "Harlem: Mecca of the New Negro," included an article describing the importance of the Harlem Renaissance for African Americans and the country:

> It has attracted the African, the West Indian, the Negro American. [Harlem] . . . has brought together the Negro of the North and the Negro of the South; the man from the city and the man from the town and village; the peasant, the student, the business man, the professional man, artist, poet, musician, adventurer and worker, preacher and criminal, exploiter and social outcast. Each group has come with its own separate motives and for its own special ends, but their greatest experience has been the finding of one another.

In the same year, Howard University professor **Alain Locke** published *The New Negro: An Interpretation*, a collection of works by Harlem Renaissance writers. The stories, essays, and poems in the book revealed a shift in how African Americans defined themselves. The work of many of the authors featured in the book has since been incorporated into American culture.

ON STAGE AND SCREEN

African Americans made advances in a variety of performing arts during the 1920s. As jazz and the blues wowed popular audiences, some African-American performers excelled in other musical forms. Opera singer **Roland Hayes** became an international star with his sensitive renditions of songs in multiple languages. He was the first African-American man to perform with a major American orchestra when he sang with the Boston Symphony.

PRIMARY SOURCE

In his introduction to *The New Negro*, Alain Locke states that his purpose was to "register the transformations of the inner and outer life of the Negro in America that have so significantly taken place in the last few years." This excerpt from an essay in the book describes life in Harlem.

[Harlem] has many unique characteristics. It has movement, color, gayety, singing, dancing, boisterous laughter and loud talk. One of its outstanding features is brass band parades. Hardly a Sunday passes but that there are several of these parades of which many are gorgeous with regalia and insignia.

—from "Harlem: The Culture Capital," an essay by James Weldon Johnson, in *The New Negro*, 1925

Actress **Ethel Waters** started her career singing the blues and jazz but soon branched out as a popular performer in Broadway and film musicals. Her signature song was the lively tune "Heat Wave." One of her occasional costars was **Paul Robeson**, the most popular African-American stage and film actor of his generation. Robeson's skills as a star student and football player in his youth led to the rare opportunity to earn college and law degrees. Discouraged by racism in the legal profession, the multitalented Robeson turned to acting. His physical stature, good looks, and booming bass voice cut an imposing figure in stage and film versions of the hit musical *Show Boat*, especially during the legendary scene in which he sang "Ol' Man River." He used his celebrity status to draw attention to human rights and civil rights concerns. In fact, the Harlem Renaissance, by fostering both self-determination and pride in African-American culture, helped set the stage for the civil rights movement to come.

HISTORICAL THINKING

1. **READING CHECK** What was the Harlem Renaissance?

2. **CATEGORIZE** Which arts did the Harlem Renaissance influence?

3. **COMPARE AND CONTRAST** How did the Cotton Club represent both opportunities and limitations for African Americans?

4. **DRAW CONCLUSIONS** Why do you think many African-American poets and other authors in the 1920s wrote about life under segregation?

LANGSTON HUGHES 1902–1967

"I, too, sing America. . . . I, too, am America." —Langston Hughes

Langston Hughes wasn't the first writer to "sing America" in his poetry. In fact, in the poem "I, Too," quoted above, he may have taken his cue from poet Walt Whitman, who celebrated the speech of ordinary Americans as a great symphony of song. For his part, Hughes sang about America to the strains of jazz and the blues. He infused his poetry with the rhythm and structure of these musical forms to speak to all African Americans. They, too, he affirms in his poems, are America.

YOUNG WRITER

Hughes was the first African American to make his living as a writer. But then, he came from a family of firsts. His grandmother was the first African-American woman to graduate from Oberlin College in Ohio. His great-uncle was the first African American elected to public office. Great things were expected of young Langston.

But what his father, at least, didn't expect was that his son would want to be a poet. When Hughes was a child, his parents divorced, and his father moved to Mexico. Hughes was raised first by his grandmother and then by his mother and stepfather. After Hughes graduated from high school, he spent a year with his father in Mexico. It was there that Hughes told his father he wanted to make his living as a writer.

The pair argued bitterly over Hughes's career choice. Then, a poem Hughes had written while traveling to Mexico, "The Negro Speaks of Rivers," was published in *The Crisis*, the official magazine of the NAACP. The poem connects the

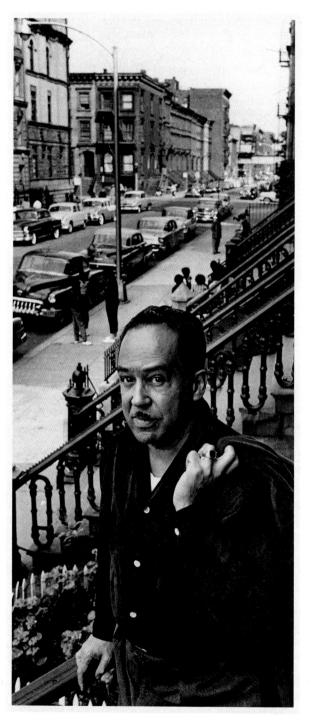

This 1958 photo shows Langston Hughes on the streets of New York, a setting he often explored in his poetry.

African-American experience with the dawn of civilization ("I bathed in the Euphrates when dawns were young") and the struggle for equality in America ("I heard the singing of the Mississippi when Abe Lincoln went down to New Orleans"). Impressed, Hughes's father agreed to pay for his son's education at Columbia University in New York City—as long as he studied engineering. As fortune would have it, though, when Hughes entered Columbia in 1921, the Harlem Renaissance was in full force.

He was hooked. The writers, artists, musicians, and thinkers of the movement fueled his passion for poetry and for creating a new African-American cultural identity. As a gay man, Hughes also felt a sense of belonging in 1920s Harlem, where the rules for acceptable gendered behavior seemed more flexible for black and white Americans than in other parts of society at that time. Hughes soon became a central figure in Harlem's literary community. After just two semesters at Columbia, he dropped out.

THE VOICE OF HARLEM

Hughes solidified his reputation in the Harlem Renaissance movement with the publication of his first volume of poetry, *The Weary Blues*. It was hailed a masterpiece—even by the white press. For many, Hughes became the poetic voice of Harlem. But some African Americans criticized his work. Fearing that his poems reinforced racial stereotypes, they claimed Hughes should represent African Americans in the best possible light. Angrily, they dubbed him the "poet low-rate" of Harlem. In response to the criticism, Hughes said, "I felt that the masses of our people had as much in their lives to put into books as did those more fortunate ones."

Throughout his career, Hughes wrote poetry and prose that often angered both his black and white critics. But he continued to write about ordinary African Americans and their suffering and common experiences. These black Americans became his most devoted audience because he reflected their culture back to them through their language and music. Arguably more than any other African-American poet or writer, Hughes diligently captured the small details and frustrations of black life during the early part of the 20th century.

Hughes sang of struggles and dreams deferred, but he tempered his themes with humor, affection, and optimism. In "I, Too," Hughes writes about being denied a place at the table with white America. At the end of the poem, however, he envisions a time when there will be a place there for him and all African Americans: "They'll see how beautiful I am / And be ashamed."

THE ART OF THE COVER
The books of Langston Hughes were works of art, both inside and out. For his book covers (shown from top to bottom), Hughes collaborated with the famous painters Miguel Covarrubias and Aaron Douglas and popular illustrator Cliff Roberts, all of whom conveyed the spirit of the time in stylized silhouettes.

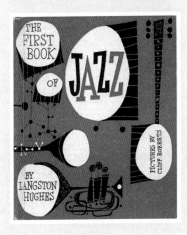

HISTORICAL THINKING

1. **READING CHECK** Who was the subject of and intended audience for Hughes's poetry?

2. **MAKE INFERENCES** Why do you think Hughes often used the rhythm and structure of jazz and the blues in his poetry?

3. **FORM AND SUPPORT OPINIONS** Do you think Hughes's critics were right when they said that he should portray African Americans in the best possible light? Explain why or why not.

VOCABULARY

For each pair of vocabulary words, write one sentence that explains the connection between the words.

1. **capitalism; Red Scare**
   During the Red Scare, many Americans were afraid of people who spoke out against capitalism.

2. **stalactite; stalagmite**

3. **assembly line; mass market**

4. **jazz; flapper**

5. **bootlegger; speakeasy**

6. **Pan-Africanism; back-to-Africa movement**

7. **American Civil Liberties Union; Anti-Defamation League**

READING STRATEGY
COMPARE AND CONTRAST

Comparing and contrasting concepts in a chart can help readers better understand the similarities and differences between people, events, and movements in history. In your chart, list traditional versus modern practices that emerged in major areas during the 1920s. Then answer the question.

Comparison Chart

	Traditional	Modern
Industry	Factories	Assembly line
Music		
Science		
Women's roles		

8. Which modern change had the most impact on a traditional practice, process, or idea? Explain your answer.

MAIN IDEAS

Answer the following questions. Support your answers with evidence from the chapter.

9. What factors led to the Palmer Raids? **LESSON 1.1**

10. What role did anti-immigration feelings play in the Sacco-Vanzetti case? **LESSON 1.2**

11. How did the Teapot Dome scandal affect Warren Harding's presidency? **LESSON 1.3**

12. How did new communications technology help popularize jazz? **LESSON 2.1**

13. What forms of entertainment grew popular during the 1920s? **LESSON 2.2**

14. How did the image of the flapper reflect the changing status of women? **LESSON 3.1**

15. Why did the passage of the 19th Amendment fail to have the immediate impact some people thought it might? **LESSON 3.2**

16. What factors made Marcus Garvey's back-to-Africa movement attractive to some African Americans? **LESSON 4.1**

17. Why did so many African Americans move to Harlem in the 1910s and 1920s? **LESSON 4.2**

HISTORICAL THINKING

Answer the following questions. Support your answers with evidence from the chapter.

18. **MAKE GENERALIZATIONS** How did culture change in the United States during the 1920s?

19. **ANALYZE CAUSE AND EFFECT** What were the main effects of the 18th Amendment and the Volstead Act?

20. **MAKE GENERALIZATIONS** What strides in politics did women make after passage of the 19th Amendment?

21. **DRAW CONCLUSIONS** Why do you think the NAACP worked to change laws even if it might take years to accomplish?

22. **FORM AND SUPPORT OPINIONS** Were the 1920s a "return to normalcy"? Support your opinion with evidence from the text.

INTERPRET VISUALS

The August 1927 cover of *McClure's* magazine features a vision of the Jazz Age by the artist John Held, Jr. Look at the cover (at right) and answer the questions that follow.

23. What do you think the portrait of the flapper symbolizes, and why?

24. In what ways does this illustration reflect the characteristics of the 1920s?

ANALYZE SOURCES

Colleen Moore was an actor during the 1920s and 1930s famous for playing flappers in numerous movies. Moore talked to author Joshua Zeitz about how she was influenced by the free-spirited young women of the 1920s during an interview for his 2006 book *Flapper: A Madcap Story of Sex, Style, Celebrity, and the Women Who Made America Modern*. Read the excerpt, which is a quotation from Moore. Then answer the question.

> They were smart and sophisticated, with an air of independence about them, and so casual about their looks and clothes and manners as to be almost slapdash. I don't know if I realized as soon as I began seeing them that they represented the wave of the future, but I do know I was drawn to them. I shared their restlessness, understood their determination to free themselves of the Victorian shackles of the pre–World War I era and find out for themselves what life was all about.

25. What were the attributes that Moore admired in flappers?

CONNECT TO YOUR LIFE

26. **ARGUMENT** Movies had a huge impact on fashion and other aspects of popular culture in the 1920s, and they still drive fashion and popular culture today. Then, as now, some people embraced this influence, and some people saw it as a threat to society and the status quo. Examine the influence of movies both now and in the 1920s, and write an argument that the art form exerts either a positive or a negative influence.

TIPS

- Use textual evidence from the chapter in your argument.

- Clearly state your point of view, briefly including the reasons for your stance.

- Acknowledge the opposite viewpoint by providing one or two valid alternative ideas.

- Provide examples from the text and your own understanding and experience to support each reason for your argument.

- Provide a conclusion that restates your argument, making your stand on the matter clear.

- Use two or three vocabulary terms from the chapter in your response.

HISTORICAL THINKING What impact did the Great Depression have on the American people, culture, economy, and spirit?

Walker Evans's photography during the Great Depression captured the essence of Americans' despair and worry. Here, the focus of his lens lands on the plates and bowls people are holding while they stand in line at a soup kitchen in Arkansas in 1937.

"**Brother,** can you spare a dime?"

—Yip Harburg, songwriter

THE DUST BOWL

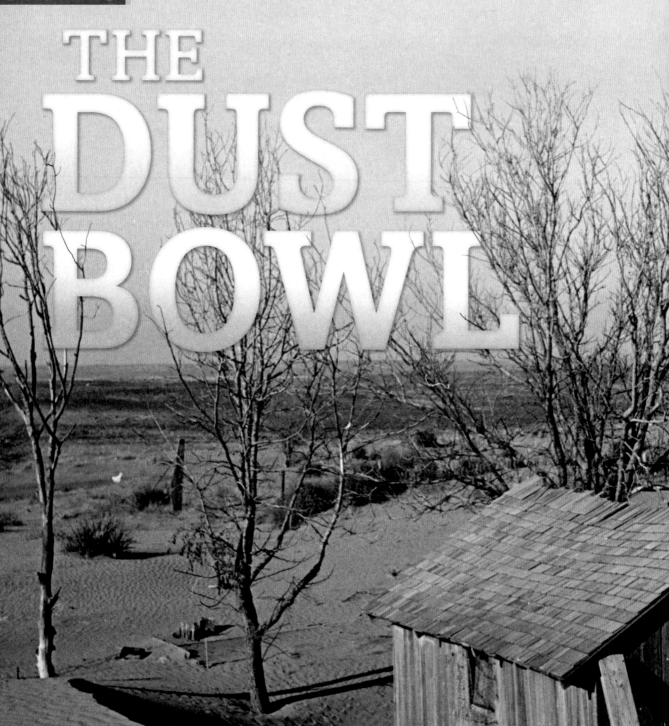

Piles of dust bury a farm near Liberal, Kansas, in this 1936 photograph by photojournalist Arthur Rothstein. Rothstein is known for his images of rural and small-town America.

Between 1931 and 1939, so-called "black blizzards"—dangerous dust storms—were frighteningly common across the Great Plains, especially in Texas, Oklahoma, Colorado, Kansas, and New Mexico. Journalist Robert Geiger coined the nickname "Dust Bowl" for this drought-stricken region in 1935. The name stuck because it was such an apt description for a bleak time and place, and possibly the worst environmental disaster ever to strike the United States.

When a black blizzard came howling into town, it looked and felt like the end of the world. One witness described one of these traumatizing storms after it assaulted a Texas town in 1935, writing, "The front of the cloud was a rolling, bumbling, boiling mass of dust and dirt about two hundred feet high, almost vertical, and as black as an Angus bull. . . . After the front passed, the darkness rivaled the darkness inside a whale resting on the bottom of the ocean at midnight." Lorena Hickok, a newspaper reporter, was in a car when a black blizzard hit. It was "[like] driving in a fog, only worse because of the wind that seemed as if it would blow the car right off the road," she recalled. "It was as though we were picked up in a vast, impenetrable black cloud which was hurling us right off the earth."

CAUSES AND REMEDIES

To a great extent, the Dust Bowl was a human-caused catastrophe. The Great Plains region has a semiarid climate, which means it receives light annual rainfall and is prone to occasional droughts. In the 1880s and 1890s, however, when millions of European settlers were arriving on the plains, the weather was exceptionally rainy, leading the new arrivals to the comfortable assumption that the bountiful rainfall would continue.

In the decades between 1880 and 1930, agricultural technology improved, allowing farmers to plow up increasingly wide swathes of native prairie grasses in order to plant their crops. These native plants had deep roots that anchored the soil when strong winds blew across the wide-open prairies, and they were perennials, which means they would survive from year to year. In contrast, wheat and other crops had shallow roots and were annuals, or plants that die after their growing season. Thus, in 1931, when heat and drought dried up the soil, there was nothing to hold it down when the turbulent winds blew. Wendell Berry, a writer and environmental activist, observed, "We plowed the prairie and never knew what we were doing, because we did not know what we were undoing." One perceptive Texas sheepherder put it more plainly when he asserted, "Grass is what holds the earth together."

A black blizzard could carry unimaginable quantities of dirt. In 1934, one storm traveled clear across the continent, deposited 12 million tons of former prairie soil on the city of Chicago, then carried dust so far east it darkened the sky in New York City and even reached ships 300 miles from shore in the Atlantic Ocean. On what became Black Sunday, April 14, 1935, another storm ripped up an estimated 300 million tons of topsoil from the Great Plains, trapping people who were caught outside in biting winds and absolute blackness.

The end of the Dust Bowl came about through both human solutions and nature's intervention. A federal agency called the Soil Conservation Service was established to introduce new farming techniques that would help retain the soil. The agency encouraged farmers to use contour plowing, a method of plowing furrows that follow the shape of the land, rather than plowing in a straight line regardless of hills or dips in the terrain. When occasional rains did fall, the contoured furrows would catch the water as it flowed downhill rather than channeling it through the parched land. The agency also suggested planting soybeans, sweet clover, and other crops that would help anchor the soil.

President Franklin Roosevelt also promoted his own plan, known as the Shelterbelt Project. According to the plan, the government would pay farmers to plant a broad line of trees from Texas to the Canadian border. This "shelterbelt" was intended to break the momentum of winds sweeping eastward across the plains and provide cooling to nearby areas. In the end, Roosevelt's shelterbelt was never completed, but it did help publicize the importance of taking action to reduce the negative effects of farming on the environment. By 1938, the drought continued unabated, but the tonnage of soil carried aloft by storms was reduced almost by half. In 1939, nature stepped in and rainfall resumed, putting an end to the lengthy drought.

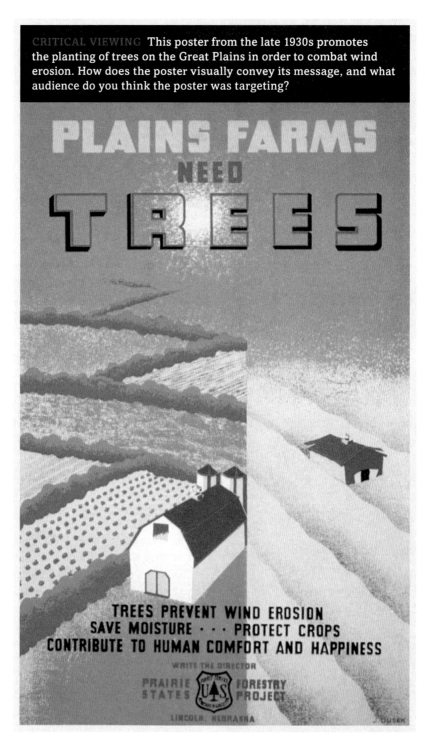

CRITICAL VIEWING This poster from the late 1930s promotes the planting of trees on the Great Plains in order to combat wind erosion. How does the poster visually convey its message, and what audience do you think the poster was targeting?

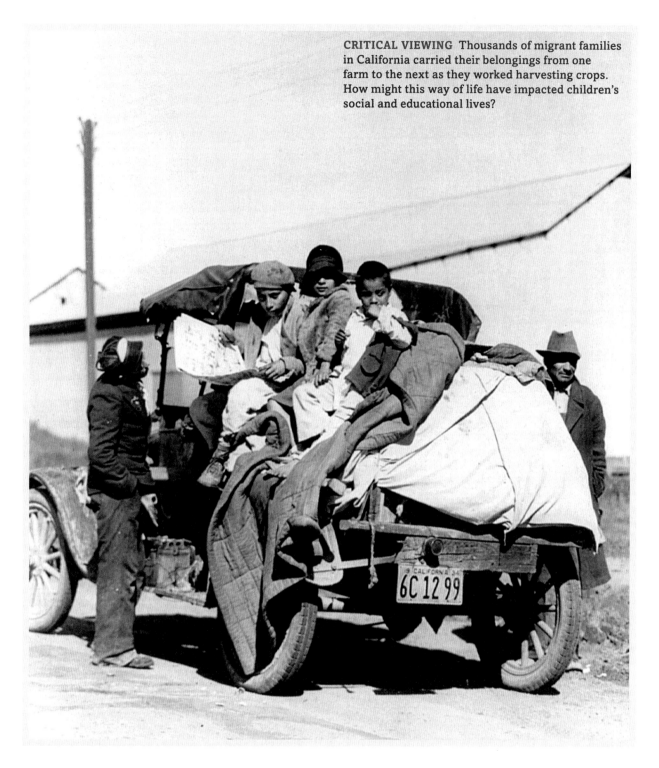

CRITICAL VIEWING Thousands of migrant families in California carried their belongings from one farm to the next as they worked harvesting crops. How might this way of life have impacted children's social and educational lives?

THOSE WHO LEFT

When the long drought began, the United States was already in the throes of the Great Depression. Farmers were struggling to make a living after a drastic fall in crop prices. For many, the arrival of the first severe dust storms in 1933 turned a difficult situation into a desperate one. Crops and livestock were already suffering from the lack of moisture, and now the black blizzards were carrying the soil away. Homes and buildings were half buried, while animals trapped outside in the storms sickened and died

from the dirt they inhaled. One grim joke of the time told of a farmer applying for a loan to support his farm, and then looking out the window of the bank to see that same farm blowing past in the wind.

Feeling they had no options, about one quarter of the people affected by the Dust Bowl decided to abandon their homes. Many of them packed their families and belongings into their cars and headed west for California, where they believed they would find work.

SEEMS LIKE ANOTHER COUNTRY

As the black blizzards raged and bread lines stretched along city streets, some Depression-era artists sought to imagine the country in more promising times. A group of American painters known as Regionalists aimed to create a purely American style, distinct from the styles of their contemporaries in Europe, and several used the American countryside as their subject. Instead of the ravaged scenery of the Dust Bowl, they painted idealized Midwestern farms that appeared green, fertile, and prosperous. Among the most prominent Regionalists were Grant Wood, Thomas Hart Benton, and John Steuart Curry. The painting below by Grant Wood is entitled *Young Corn*.

How does the image of rural life portrayed in this painting by Grant Wood differ from the image shown in the photographs in this article?

"THE NIGHTMARE IS BECOMING LIFE"

Many people who lived through the Dust Bowl wrote horrifying accounts of black blizzards. Avis D. Carlson, of Kansas, wrote the following description in 1935 for the magazine *The New Republic*. How does the line, "It is becoming Real," contribute to the excerpt?

PRIMARY SOURCE

The impact is like a shovelful of fine sand flung against the face. People caught in their own yards grope for the doorstep. Cars come to a standstill, for no light in the world can penetrate that swirling murk. . . . The nightmare is deepest during the storms. But on the occasional bright day and the usual gray day we cannot shake from it. We live with the dust, eat it, sleep with it, watch it strip us of possessions and the hope of possessions. It is becoming Real. The poetic uplift of spring fades into a phantom of the storied past. The nightmare is becoming life.

The rich California farm fields could not have looked more different to the exhausted migrants streaming into the state. The area of California known as the Inland Empire was home to large farms growing lemons, oranges, lettuce, grapes, and many other varieties of produce. Jobs, however, were not so plentiful, and the agricultural work was back-breaking. In addition, the farm owners used the influx of migrants to force down the already low wages for all workers, including native Californians and immigrants from Mexico.

As a result, local workers intensely resented the newcomers, whom they called "Okies." The term was short for Oklahoma, although most of the migrants were not from that state. Singer Woody Guthrie, who was well acquainted with the sufferings of Dust Bowl refugees, described the connotations of the name "Okie." According to him, the term "means you ain't got no home. Sort of meant, too, that you're out of a job. Or owe more than you can rake or scrape [up]."

Many Okies were met at the state line by police officers who informed them there was no work for them in California and told them to turn back. Californians weren't very friendly towards the migrants, either—in fact some were downright hostile, likely due to differences in regional culture. As a result, thousands of Okies found themselves living in roadside camps that were collections of ramshackle huts, and in the backs of cars and trucks. There was little or no sanitation or privacy. Eventually, the federal government stepped in to help provide better conditions for the migrants, but for many, life did not noticeably improve until the end of the Great Depression.

THOSE WHO STAYED

The people who remained in the Dust Bowl learned to endure nearly unbearable heat, extreme dryness, and inescapable dust. It was impossible to keep dirt out of the houses, no matter how tightly the doors and windows were sealed. One woman described sheltering in her home during a dust storm: "All we could do was just sit in our dusty chairs, gaze at each other through the fog that filled the room and watch the fog settle slowly and silently, covering everything—including ourselves—in a thick, brownish gray blanket." At night, people slept uncomfortably on gritty sheets. When setting the table, women placed plates and glasses upside-down until it was just time to serve the food, to avoid dirt settling onto the dishes.

It was impossible to avoid breathing in some dust, which could cause a variety of illnesses. Among the worst was silicosis, nicknamed "dust pneumonia," which was caused by sharp dust particles gradually scraping the lungs until the sufferer died.

People caught outside on foot or in cars during storms were at risk of becoming lost in the darkness and being suffocated by the violently blowing dirt. Some died just a few feet away from shelter that they could not glimpse through the black blizzard. One farmer recalled stretching a wire between his house and barn so that he could navigate his way home if a dust storm hit while he was in the barn.

Asked why people stayed on their farms, one woman from Kansas replied, "In part . . . we hope for the coming of moisture, which would change conditions so we can again have bountiful harvests. And in great part, because it is home. We have reared our family here and many have precious memories of the past. We have our memories. We have faith in the future, we are here to stay."

THINK ABOUT IT

What lessons about land use or management can be drawn from the Dust Bowl?

To get an overview of a field or a camp that she wanted to photograph, Dorothea Lange would often climb up on the roof of her car.

DUST BOWL PHOTOGRAPHER: DOROTHEA LANGE

Dorothea Lange was not planning to become an influential documentary photographer when she moved to San Francisco. Born into a wealthy family in 1895, she studied photography at Columbia University in New York City and then worked as an apprentice to several photographers before moving west to set up a successful portrait studio.

When the Great Depression hit San Francisco, it brought the same scenes of human misery as in other cities: homelessness, unemployment, and bread lines. Disturbed by the suffering she saw daily in the streets, Lange turned her camera to the people and events outside of her studio. Soon, she was working for the federal government, tasked with a mission to document the predicaments of people forced from their land by the Dust Bowl.

From 1935 to 1939, Lange traveled throughout the western United States photographing Dust Bowl refugees in settlement camps, in their cars, and at work. She used her skills as a portrait photographer to capture faces in unguarded moments of exhaustion, worry, and occasional relaxation. Paul Taylor, who accompanied Lange on her travels, explained her technique for putting her subjects at ease. "Her method of work," he recalled, "was often to just saunter up to the people and look around,

and then when she saw something that she wanted to photograph, to quietly take her camera, look at it, and if she saw that they objected, why, she would close it up and not take a photograph, or perhaps she would wait until . . . they were used to her."

The photo on the bottom of the next page is part of a series of images that became symbolic of the Great Depression, capturing the poverty, misery, and stress endured by migratory farmworkers in the 1930s. The main subject of the "Migrant Mother" photographs was 32-year-old Florence Owens Thompson, who was the sole supporter of her seven children. Lange claimed Thompson had sold her car's tires to buy food for her children and that the family had been surviving on vegetables that had frozen in a nearby field, but Thompson's children said Lange must have confused their mother with someone else.

Lange's images from the 1930s leave an indelible impression on viewers to this day. She and other Depression-era photographers helped ensure that all Americans would know about the struggles of those impoverished and left homeless by the upheavals of the time. After the Depression ended, Lange continued her work as a documentary photographer until her death in 1965.

In these photographs taken in California in the 1930s, Dorothea Lange captured rural people at work and at rest. The photo on the top left shows two workers loading cotton. The one on the right shows Dust Bowl refugees stopped along a highway. The bottom photograph from Lange's 1936 "Migrant Mother" series features mother Florence Owens Thompson sitting in a tent with two of her seven children.

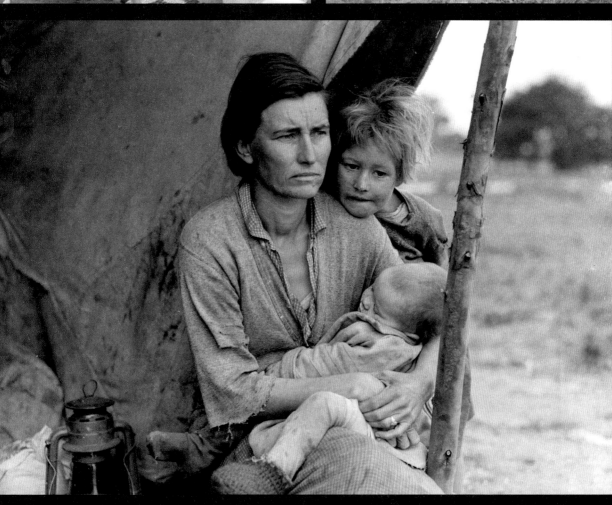

A DECEPTIVE PROSPERITY

The saying "All that glitters is not gold" is an apt description of the 1920s. When President Calvin Coolidge began his first full term in office, he believed the United States was prosperous and secure. But economic troubles lurked beneath the sparkling surface.

COOLIDGE IN THE WHITE HOUSE

In 1924, after serving out Harding's remaining term in office, Calvin Coolidge ran for and won the presidency. Strongly pro-business and against government intervention, his policy goals were modest. When Coolidge asked Congress for a cut in taxes, lawmakers responded with a measure that lowered taxes for people who made more than $100,000 a year. However, most married couples made less than $3,500 a year, so the tax cuts affected only the wealthiest Americans. The president also promoted laws to oversee the expansion of the new airline industry and to regulate the growing radio business. At the same time, Coolidge did little to help farmers and people living in rural areas. He twice vetoed a bill to aid farmers and did not support a federal government initiative to build dams on the Tennessee River that would provide affordable electric power to that region of the country.

In foreign policy, Coolidge opposed the use of military force, but he also believed the United States had an obligation to help countries in need. In 1924, the Coolidge administration had endorsed a plan to help a struggling Germany meet its huge war reparation debt. During the next four years, Germany borrowed almost $1.5 million from the United States. Similarly, when the Soviet Union faced a famine in the early 1920s, Americans sent large amounts of food and monetary aid. But when revolution and civil war took place in China, the U.S. government did not get

PRIMARY SOURCE

Coolidge focused on cutting taxes that were already low for most Americans and viewed taxation as funding "extravagance" in government.

We must have tax reform. We cannot finance the country, we cannot improve social conditions, through any system of injustice, even if we attempt to inflict it upon the rich. Those who suffer the most harm will be the poor. This country believes in prosperity. It is absurd to suppose that it is envious of those who are already prosperous. The wise and correct course to follow in taxation and all other economic legislation is not to destroy those who have already secured success but to create conditions under which everyone will have a better chance to be successful.

—from Calvin Coolidge's Inaugural Address, March 4, 1925

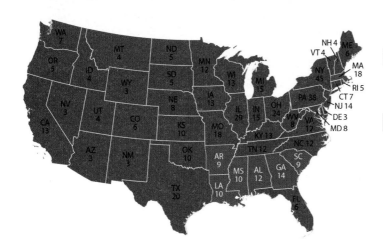

The Election of 1928

Herbert Hoover, Republican	
Electoral Vote: 444 votes, 83.6%	
Popular Vote: 21,391,381 votes, 58.8%	

Al Smith, Democrat	
Electoral Vote: 87 votes, 16.4%	
Popular Vote: 15,016,443 votes, 41.2%	

involved. In fact, the State Department preferred the idea of outlawing war altogether, an idea that peace groups supported. The resulting **Kellogg-Briand Pact** was a multinational agreement in which the signing countries agreed to renounce, or reject, war. Coolidge was among those who signed the pact in 1928, and it was ratified in 1929. However, there was no way to enforce the pact worldwide.

Believing that it would be difficult for anyone to be effective in the office for more than eight years, Coolidge declined to run for a second full term. Herbert Hoover, Coolidge's secretary of commerce, beat out his political rivals to win the Republican nomination for president. Hoover faced off against the Democratic candidate, Governor Alfred E. Smith of New York, who was Roman Catholic. In the general election, Hoover benefited from the religious intolerance many Protestants held against Smith's faith. Hoover won the electoral vote in a landslide.

A TROUBLED ECONOMY

When Hoover took office, the future looked bright, but the surface prosperity of the 1920s hid some serious economic problems. The most pervasive of these was the dramatically uneven distribution of income. Agricultural overproduction had driven down crop prices throughout the decade, so farmers did not benefit from the nation's general prosperity. Furthermore, by 1929, the economy was characterized by a lopsided distribution of income. At the top level, 5 percent of Americans received 33 percent of the total annual personal income, while half of all Americans received about 16 percent of the total. More than half of American families lived near or below the poverty line even though unemployment was low. More than 21 million families, or 80 percent of the national population, did not have any savings at all. But in order to expand, the economy relied on people purchasing consumer goods. If most ordinary

Americans lacked **disposable income**—or spending money—and purchasing power, it would have a big impact on the national economy.

Other warning signs signaled the economy was in trouble, including a recession in 1927. Wholesale prices fell nearly 4.5 percent, the production of goods slowed, and consumer spending dropped. The global economy was also fragile. Germany continued to struggle with its reparation payments, even after the United States reduced the burden of German war debts in 1924. In 1929, an international committee proposed another plan that further reduced Germany's total debt and established a longer period for repayment. These concessions eased economic pressures, but only temporarily. Weakness in the German economy continued to grow as banks closed and markets disintegrated.

Yet, despite multiple national and global warning signs, the U.S. banking system continued to expand credit. Americans increasingly speculated in the **stock market**, or the buying and selling of shares in companies. Earnings from stocks could be higher than interest paid by banks, but an investor could also lose money, especially over the short term. For the average American, though, it looked like the economy would grow forever.

HISTORICAL THINKING

1. **READING CHECK** What role did religion play in the presidential race between Hoover and Smith?

2. **ANALYZE LANGUAGE USE** How did President Coolidge's use of the phrase "any system of injustice" help his argument for tax reform?

3. **IDENTIFY MAIN IDEAS AND DETAILS** What warning signs suggested that the U.S. economy was not as prosperous as it appeared?

PANIC ON WALL STREET

We all know that what goes up must eventually come down. Investors in the 1920s didn't realize that old saying also applied to the stock market. On October 29, 1929, they learned just how wrong they were.

INVESTMENT FEVER

In the 1920s, Americans pointed to the growth of the stock market as an indication of the nation's growing prosperity. The market grew so quickly that many Americans saw it as the ideal place to make a fast buck. The U.S. Treasury's sale of Liberty Bonds during World War I had shown citizens that investments could lead to wealth.

More and more, corporations offered their stocks for sale to obtain cash to finance business growth. During the prosperous Harding and Coolidge years, generous government tax policies allowed the very wealthy to pay little or no income taxes, giving them extra money to invest in the stock market.

Smaller investors often bought stocks on **margin**. That is, they purchased stocks on credit, paying only 10 or 15 percent of the actual price up front. Buying on margin is a risky strategy because the investor is betting on being able to sell the stock at a higher price, pay off the stockbroker—the person who buys and sells stocks for his or her clients—and pocket a substantial profit. The lure of making easy money in the market was so great that people borrowed money to buy on margin. Banks happily loaned American investors that money, in spite of the Federal Reserve's warnings against the practice, which consequently gave rise to the establishment of weaknesses in the economy.

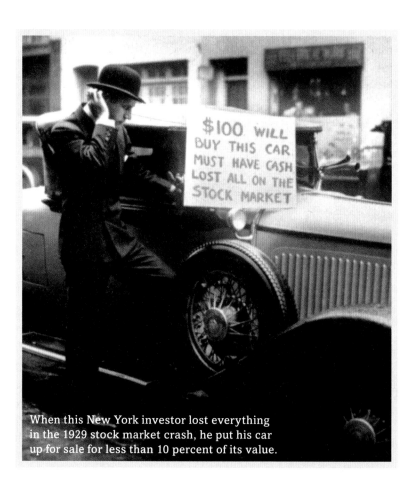

When this New York investor lost everything in the 1929 stock market crash, he put his car up for sale for less than 10 percent of its value.

Buying stocks on margin is a form of **speculation**. The buyer assumes, or speculates, that stock prices will always go up, even though there is no guarantee that they will. But in the 1920s, this looked like a sure bet. On September 3, 1929, the **Dow Jones Industrial Average (DJIA)**—a leading measure of general stock market trends—hit 381.17, a high for the decade, driven up in part by speculation and margin buying. Few suspected that the weakening market was headed for collapse.

OCTOBER 29, 1929

The problem began in September 1929. At the beginning of that month, the market hit its record high, but then stock prices declined. They regained some strength but began drifting downward again. Since there had been no abrupt collapse, many on Wall Street, their confidence unshaken, saw these events as one of the normal and temporary "corrections" that typically preceded another big increase in the stock market. A few people warned that problems lay ahead, but they were dismissed as chronic naysayers who had been wrong before.

But prices did not rise. On October 24, 1929, the day that became known as **Black Thursday**, stock trading began as usual, but few investors were willing to buy. Prices collapsed as investors, many of whom had bought on margin, tried to sell their stocks before prices fell even more. Nearly 13 million stocks were traded that day, which was then an all-time record. Stockholders absorbed, by some estimates, a $9 billion loss in the value of their stocks. During the afternoon, a large banking group led by bank executive J.P. Morgan, Jr., urged investors to be calm. Morgan even purchased some stocks himself. The market seemed to settle, leading to the hope that normal trading might recover.

Recovery was not in the cards. On the following Monday, the market fell sharply—around 13 percent—

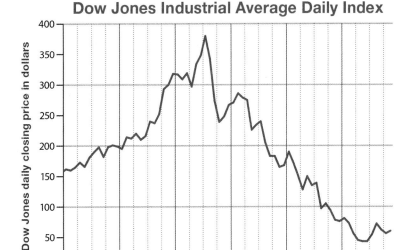

Dow Jones Industrial Average Daily Index

Source: The Dow Jones Averages (1885–1995)

and the DJIA plummeted to 260.64. Then the hammer fell on October 29, a day that is still known as **Black Tuesday**. When trading began, the sell-off continued, with more than 16 million shares changing hands in a single day. The DJIA fell to 230.07 and continued to drop for nearly three years.

The consequences of the crash were immediate and striking. The prices of individual stocks continued on their downward slide. The DJIA reached a low of 41.22 on July 8, 1932. Within a few months of the crash, General Electric's stock had dropped from $403 a share to $168, and Standard Oil shares fell from $83 to $48. During the next year, the **gross national product (GNP)** —the total goods and services produced by the nation plus the income earned by its citizens—shrank from nearly $88 billion to $76 billion. With the already existing difficulties in agriculture and the large debt crisis, the U.S. economy slumped into a long and severe decline, resulting in an economic catastrophe that became known as the **Great Depression**, the deepest and most prolonged economic downturn in American history with a substantial human toll.

PRIMARY SOURCE

Oral historian Studs Terkel interviewed people who lived through the Great Depression. In 1970, he published their stories in his book, *Hard Times*. In the following excerpt, composer Alec Wilder is speaking to Terkel of his losses in the stock market.

I knew something was terribly wrong because I heard bellboys, everybody, talking about the stock market. About six weeks before the Wall Street Crash, I persuaded my mother in Rochester to let me talk to our family adviser. I wanted to sell stock which had been left me by my father. He got very sentimental: "Oh your father wouldn't have liked you to do that." He was so persuasive, I said O.K. I could have sold it for $160,000. Four years later, I sold it for $4,000.

—from *Hard Times: An Oral History of the Great Depression,* by Studs Terkel, 1970

HISTORICAL THINKING

1. **READING CHECK** What effect did speculation and buying on margin have on stock prices?

2. **DRAW CONCLUSIONS** If trading reached record highs on October 24 and 29, why are these days called Black Thursday and Black Tuesday?

3. **INTERPRET GRAPHS** According to the graph, what were the highest and lowest averages in the DJIA in 1929, and how does the graph illustrate the cost and benefit of investing in the stock market?

THE DEPRESSION BEGINS

The reaction in a domino chain starts with the fall of the first domino, but it's the structure of the chain that causes the other dominos to fall. That principle applied to the economy during the Great Depression.

A WEAK FOUNDATION

The stock market crash of 1929 signaled the start of the Great Depression of the 1930s, the deepest and most prolonged economic downturn in American history. But the Depression was caused by broad underlying weaknesses more deeply rooted than falling stock values. The apparent prosperity of the 1920s hid the fact that the U.S. and world economies rested on an unsound foundation. Four main factors contributed to the problem: overproduction resulting in oversaturated markets, unequal income distribution, lack of proper banking regulations, and a weak worldwide financial system.

After World War I, American farmers continued to maintain high levels of wartime production, even though Europe was once again producing its own food or buying from U.S. competitors. Soon, the surplus of American crops and meat drove down prices on the global market. In the manufacturing sector—especially in one of the nation's leading industries, the automotive industry—new machinery and assembly lines led to increased productivity, and output jumped almost 32 percent between 1923 and 1929. Similarly, the other leading U.S. industry, construction, far outpaced demand for new houses. But by 1929, growth in the auto, housing, and consumer goods industries had begun to decline. Innovations that had enabled producing those items affordably meant that many people had already purchased what they needed. As demand decreased, workers were laid off.

Income inequality, or the unequal distribution of income and wealth between the few wealthiest Americans and the rest of the population, made the problem of overproduction worse, especially in the automobile and housing construction markets.

Similarly, the uneven distribution of wealth, or the value of what a household owns minus debts, factored into an unstable economy. The small percentage of wealthy Americans purchased only so many houses, cars, and luxury goods. To keep the consumer economy growing, the majority of the population needed to purchase newly built houses and to buy cars and consumer goods. Though unemployment was low, wages did not rise as fast as production, and soon more goods existed than people could afford to buy. As businesses accumulated profits rather than increasing workers' wages, demand weakened, prices and profits actually fell, and businesses laid off workers. By 1929, more than half of American families could not meet their basic needs with their income.

A lack of regulation in the banking and financial industries was another cause of the Depression. While the Federal Reserve regulated banking, district banks often had difficulty agreeing on regulation. For example, they could not decide on how best to rein in margin buying and overspeculation. Investors formed **trading pools**, groups formed to buy and sell large amounts of stocks. They made stocks appear active by buying and selling among themselves. This drove up the price of the stock artificially, and after they had sold off their stock at high prices, other investors' shares had little value. Lack of regulation also kept the Federal Reserve from acting quickly and decisively when, as the Depression deepened, American banks began to fail.

The fragile state of the global economy also contributed to the Depression. Internationally, the world stock market, international loans, economic policies, and World War I reparations formed a web of interconnected factors that helped lead to a

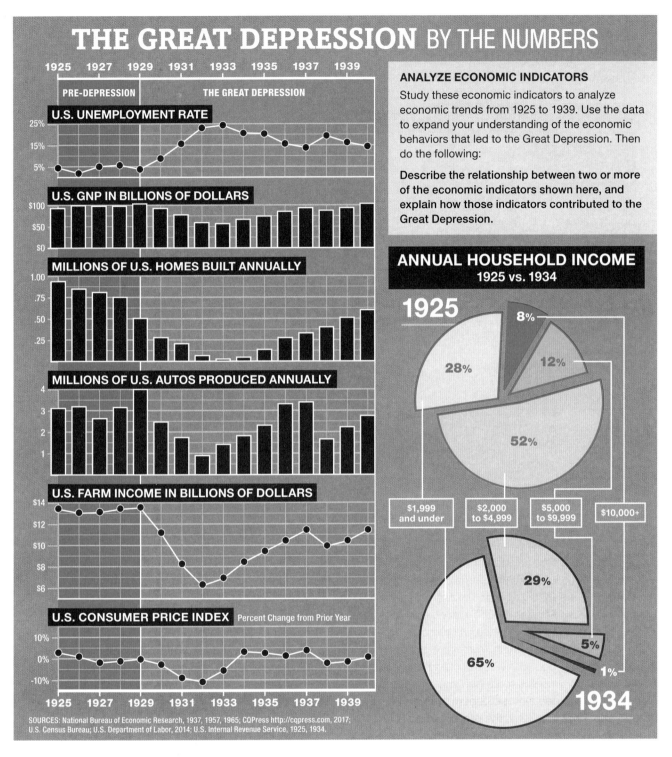

THE GREAT DEPRESSION BY THE NUMBERS

1925 1927 1929 1931 1933 1935 1937 1939

PRE-DEPRESSION   THE GREAT DEPRESSION

U.S. UNEMPLOYMENT RATE

25%
15%
5%

U.S. GNP IN BILLIONS OF DOLLARS

$100
$50
$0

MILLIONS OF U.S. HOMES BUILT ANNUALLY

1.00
.75
.50
.25

MILLIONS OF U.S. AUTOS PRODUCED ANNUALLY

4
3
2
1

U.S. FARM INCOME IN BILLIONS OF DOLLARS

$14
$12
$10
$8
$6

U.S. CONSUMER PRICE INDEX Percent Change from Prior Year

10%
0%
-10%

1925 1927 1929 1931 1933 1935 1937 1939

SOURCES: National Bureau of Economic Research, 1937, 1957, 1965; CQPress http://cqpress.com, 2017; U.S. Census Bureau; U.S. Department of Labor, 2014; U.S. Internal Revenue Service, 1925, 1934.

ANALYZE ECONOMIC INDICATORS

Study these economic indicators to analyze economic trends from 1925 to 1939. Use the data to expand your understanding of the economic behaviors that led to the Great Depression. Then do the following:

Describe the relationship between two or more of the economic indicators shown here, and explain how those indicators contributed to the Great Depression.

ANNUAL HOUSEHOLD INCOME
1925 vs. 1934

1925
8%
12%
28%
52%

$1,999 and under | $2,000 to $4,999 | $5,000 to $9,999 | $10,000+

29%
65%
5%
1%
1934

---

worldwide downturn. Europe was already weakened by Germany's inability to pay its war reparations. The United States had overtaken Britain after World War I as the world's financial leader and now passed protective tariffs it believed would enable American agriculture and industry to rebound. But the **Smoot-Hawley Tariff Act** of 1930, which raised customs duties to high levels, made it more difficult for European businesses to sell goods in the United States and obstructed the flow of capital, goods, and services in the world economy. Dozens of countries responded by passing retaliatory tariffs

that made it harder for the United States to export goods. International trade declined sharply, triggering international bank failures and adding to the suffering at home and abroad.

THE DEPRESSION DEEPENS

When the DJIA rose for a few months in early 1930, President Hoover told the nation, "I am convinced we have passed the worst and with continued effort shall rapidly recover." But as 1930 continued, it was clear the situation was only getting worse. Bank failures soared from 659 in 1929 to 1,350 a year later.

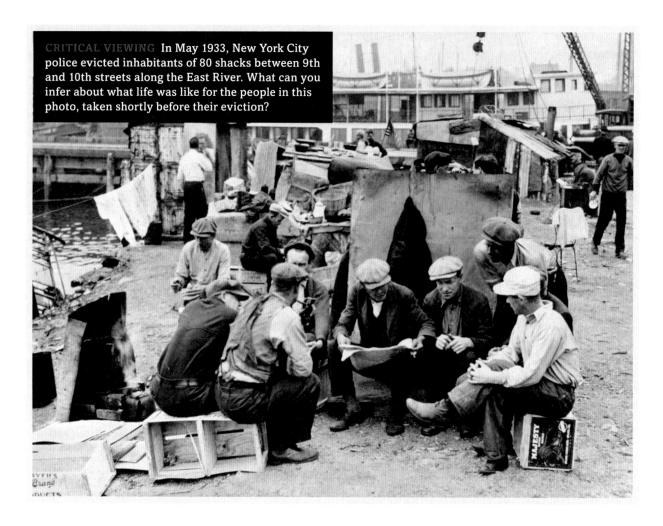

Businesses closed, investment declined, and profits fell. Industrial production was 26 percent lower at the end of 1930 than it had been 12 months earlier. Automobile manufacturing, a prime driver of the economy in the 1920s, operated at only 20 percent of capacity. By October 1930, 4 million people were jobless (almost 9 percent of the labor force), and the trend worsened each month. Within a year, nearly 16 percent of the labor force was out of work, and by 1932, unemployment had climbed to more than 23 percent. An additional 33 percent of Americans were underemployed: they were working but not earning enough to support themselves and their families.

The stock market crash left banks in a fragile position. Rural banks were particularly vulnerable, and many failed when farmers could not repay their loans. Small local banks also shut down, leaving their communities without functioning banks. Some of these banks had contributed to their own failure by providing loans for buying stocks on margin. When stock prices fell, investors and stockbrokers could not repay their loans. In addition, some banks had placed their own assets at risk by investing their deposits directly in the stock market.

When bank failures began, the Federal Reserve took a wait-and-see attitude. Some believed the failures would weed out weaker banks and strengthen the system, helping to combat the economic crisis. By the time larger banks began to fail, it was too late for action. Bank deposits were not insured by the government, so individual banks were vulnerable when customers requested to withdraw their money. Stronger banks called in loans they had made to smaller banks to save themselves, further damaging weaker banks. When a bank failed, its customers lost their savings with no hope of recovering the funds.

ECONOMIC REALITIES

For most Americans, there was no single moment after 1929 when they knew the economy was in trouble. But in the months following October 1929, families began making lifestyle changes as workers' hours were cut and the human toll became evident. People began postponing purchases and asking their children to contribute to the household's income. Job losses had a dramatic impact on families. Savings could help tide the family over for a while, but if a family had lost its savings in a bank failure or if its savings ran out, the family would have to put its home up for sale or wait for the bank to foreclose on, or take possession of, its mortgaged property.

Some responses to the economic crisis revealed underlying ideas about civil liberties and gender in the workforce. Many female workers were pressured to give up their jobs to men in an attempt to end the unemployment crisis. Men were considered to be the main "breadwinners," or the principal sources of income for the family, and working women were accused of taking their jobs away from men. Some corporations fired all married female employees, and southern school districts dismissed married female teachers. While the Depression did hinder women's participation in the workforce and slowed their economic progress, unemployment rates were lower for women than for men because women continued to work at their clerical and domestic jobs.

For already economically vulnerable Americans, the Depression presented still greater challenges. In the South, whites seeking work forced African Americans out of the low-paying service jobs they had traditionally filled. Sometimes this process was violent. Native Americans already trapped in a life of neglect and poverty fared even worse during the Depression. The infant mortality rate among Native Americans far exceeded the rate for the white population because of poverty, lack of healthcare facilities, and inadequate sanitation. The Bureau of Indian Affairs (BIA) did not address the many social problems that the people under its jurisdiction faced.

Like African Americans and Native Americans, immigrants faced serious challenges to their civil liberties during the Depression. Theirs were in the form of backlash. In an attempt to combat economic crisis, the Hoover administration instituted immigration quotas, or limits, to reduce the number of people looking for jobs and receiving government services. While potential restrictions applied to all immigrants, these efforts targeted Mexicans and Mexican Americans. Between 1930 and 1940, in a coordinated governmental effort known as the **Mexican Repatriation Program**, about 1 million people of Mexican descent were either **deported**, or forcibly removed from the country, or pressured to leave. An estimated 400,000 of those deported had been living in California. **Repatriation** means returning or being returned to the country of one's citizenship, but an astonishing 60 percent of those who returned to Mexico were actually U.S. citizens, and their deportation violated their civil rights.

PRIMARY SOURCE

In the 1980s, historian Vicki L. Ruiz interviewed Mexican women who had worked in California's canneries in the 1930s and 1940s. Carmen Escobar recounts an interaction with her foreman about how she was being paid.

When I caught the foreman cheating me, he said, "I love you like a daughter, Carmen, but who's the foreman, me or you?" "You are, but I came here to make money, not to stand around and not get my due." And then he would tell me, "Look, the poor bosses are losing money. One hour is nothing." "What do you mean one hour is nothing?" "Be quiet, Carmen."

—from *Cannery Women, Cannery Lives*,
  by Vicki Ruiz, 1987

Filipinos were also pressured to leave the United States. The Filipino Repatriation Act of 1935 provided transportation funds for Filipinos who agreed to move back to their home country permanently.

On the nation's farms, where many Mexican Americans worked, produce rotted in the fields because few people could afford to buy it. The Federal Farm Board was established in 1929 to stabilize farm prices. However, when farm surpluses around the world flooded grain markets in 1930, nothing could keep crop prices from plummeting. As banks foreclosed on farm mortgages, many former landowners became tenant farmers. All economic indicators, including GNP, consumer price index, and farm income, were in decline. And now an environmental disaster was about to deliver a crushing blow.

HISTORICAL THINKING

1. **READING CHECK** How did overproduction lead to weakness in key sectors of the economy?

2. **ANALYZE CAUSE AND EFFECT** What were the unintended consequences and complexities of the Smoot-Hawley Tariff Act of 1930?

3. **SYNTHESIZE** Why was there a Great Depression? State how individuals affected the U.S. economy.

4. **MAKE CONNECTIONS** How were African Americans, married women, Mexicans, and Mexican Americans hurt by the unemployment of white male workers?

CRITICAL VIEWING Safety liaison Jamison Walsh, photographed by Chin, climbs the spire of 1 World Trade Center after leading Chin's ascent. How are New York's skyscrapers symbols of the 1920s?

692

THROUGH THE LENS
JIMMY CHIN

National Geographic adventure photographer Jimmy Chin is used to extreme heights. He's skied down Mount Everest, photographed free climbers on Yosemite, and conquered the granite Shark Fin's wall of Meru Peak in the Himalayas. So 1,776 feet—the height of New York's 1 World Trade Center—is no big deal. In this shoot, Chin focused on capturing the great city of New York, a city of skyscrapers, many of which rose up around the Great Depression, from the spire of the building constructed where the World Trade Center once stood.

2.2

THE DUST BOWL

Sometimes nature and human actions mix in deadly and destructive ways. On the Great Plains, farmers had planted millions of acres of croplands with one main crop—wheat. When prolonged drought struck in the 1930s, the golden fields of wheat turned to dust, resulting in ecological disaster and human misery.

THE DIRTY THIRTIES

Farmers, already hit hard after World War I by falling crop and livestock prices, suffered a devastating blow in the early 1930s. Record high temperatures and drought, a prolonged period of low rainfall, gripped the Great Plains. In addition to the drought, strong winds whipped through the region, causing terrifying dust storms that swept through the plains and stripped nutrients from the dry soil.

Drought is a natural occurrence on the Great Plains, as are high winds and extreme temperatures. But the dust storms that plagued the region during the 1930s were unexpected and worsened by unwise agricultural methods and human modification of the landscape. Farmers had plowed millions of acres of grasslands on the Great Plains in order to plant wheat. After the crops were harvested, farmers used new machinery, such as disc plows pulled by small gas-powered tractors, to turn up the fields again. They then left them unplanted for months. Ranchers on the plains allowed their cattle and other livestock to overgraze what grassland remained. Without the deep roots of the prairie grasses, there was nothing to keep the soil in place. The wind picked up the dry soil and carried it for hundreds of miles.

CRITICAL VIEWING On April 14, 1935, a black blizzard hit the panhandles of Texas and Oklahoma. What details in this photo convey how threatening the cloud seems as it approaches a Texas town?

Some of the dust storms were caused by low-level winds that blew sand into huge drifts. Others were massive storms—black blizzards—with rolling dust clouds thousands of feet high that crackled with electricity, carried precious soil away to neighboring states, and turned daylight into dark. "This is the ultimate darkness," a Kansas woman wrote in her diary. "So must come the end of the world."

The blowing dust of a black blizzard destroyed crops and sickened and killed livestock and people. Dirt permeated everything, even the inside of houses, despite people's best efforts to seal every crack, window, and door. After the storm passed and light returned, farmers found their cattle and horses buried alive. The storms turned millions of acres of cultivated land in parts of Kansas, Colorado, Oklahoma, Texas, and New Mexico into a barren desert that became known as the **Dust Bowl**. The dust storms continued as the 1930s wore on—14 in 1932, then 38 in 1933—earning the decade the nickname the "Dirty Thirties."

HITTING THE ROAD

Many people living in the Dust Bowl region stuck it out because of pride, determination, or hope. Others stayed because they were simply too poor or too beaten down to leave. But a quarter of the population fled the region, some pushed off their land as they could not pay their mortgages. In one of the largest internal migrations in the nation's history, more than 3 million "Dust Bowl refugees" in Oklahoma, Kansas, the Dakotas, and other states abandoned their farms in the 1930s. Many set out for California seeking work and opportunity. The fortunate found low-wage work there, picking fruit, boxing vegetables, and baling

hay. Others went to cities to work as laborers. But few "Okies," as the Californians called them, found relief from the economic turmoil they had fled. Once in California, most lived in squatter camps along roads, often contracting diseases such as intestinal worms, typhoid, and dysentery as a result of the polluted water and lack of sanitation. The **Farm Security Administration (FSA)**, a federal agency charged with combating rural poverty, built camps to house families temporarily in somewhat improved conditions, but life was still difficult.

Okies were generally treated poorly, and they experienced discrimination at the hands of many native Californians. The Los Angeles police set up a task force called the "bum brigade" to turn Okies away at the border between California and Arizona. Residents complained about the tent communities, called "Okievilles," growing around the edges of Los Angeles, so sheriffs would ask the migrants to pack up and move on. In some towns, residents beat up the Okies and set fire to their camps.

Photographer **Dorothea Lange** documented the plight of the Okies as they traveled to California and tried to eke out a living there. Author **John Steinbeck** did the same in his 1939 novel, *The Grapes of Wrath*. His story chronicled the lives of the Joads, a fictional sharecropper family from Oklahoma, who migrated to California in search of work. Steinbeck and Lange, along with many other writers and photographers in the 1930s, captured the struggles of ordinary people weighed down by circumstances.

Once the depression lifted, some Okies returned to the plains, but many stayed in California. They infused their evangelical Protestantism, patriotic individualism, and downhome musical traditions into the culture of California's Central Valley.

HISTORICAL THINKING

1. **READING CHECK** Why did many people living in the Dust Bowl region stay during the 1930s?

2. **ANALYZE ENVIRONMENTAL CONCEPTS** How did the scale and duration of human actions, including modifying the landscape, affect the natural systems of the Great Plains during the Dust Bowl?

3. **MAKE INFERENCES** How might the social and economic impacts of the Dust Bowl refugees have influenced the reception the Okies received in California?

4. **ANALYZE LANGUAGE USE** How did Steinbeck characterize Route 66?

CULTURE DURING THE DEPRESSION

Maybe you take in a good movie or watch your favorite television show to cheer up when you're feeling down. Many people during the Great Depression tuned into their favorite radio shows, went to theaters to watch movies, and listened to music to escape reality—at least for a few minutes.

FORGETTING TROUBLES

Amid the challenges of the Depression, Americans found diversion in popular entertainment and **mass media**, or forms of communication such as radio, film, and musical recordings designed to reach large numbers of people. By the 1930s, radios had become more affordable, and they began to play a significant role in the worldwide diffusion of popular culture. Listening to a favorite radio show was a vital part of the daily lives of many families. Many listeners preferred daytime dramas such as *One Man's Family* or *Mary Noble, Backstage Wife*, which were quickly dubbed "soap operas" after the detergent companies that sponsored them.

Comic books also became popular during the Depression. The first comic books were collections of newspaper comic strips, and their heroes provided a sense that everything was going to be okay during a time of uncertainty. Among the most popular comic strip heroes were a police detective named Dick Tracy, a frontier lawman called the Lone Ranger, and Buck Rogers, a courageous space explorer living in the 25th century.

With ticket prices low and audiences hungry for a break from the stress of the Depression, movie theaters presented a wide choice of Hollywood films. Movies with sound had replaced the silent pictures of the 1920s, and people regularly went to the movies to forget their own troubles for a while.

Audiences enjoyed movie musicals and laughed at the Marx Brothers, W.C. Fields, and a new genre called screwball comedy, named for the unpredictable baseball pitch. Characterized by rapid-fire dialogue, social satire, and a blend of wacky situations and sophisticated settings, examples of screwball comedy include such hits as *It Happened One Night* (1934) and *My Man Godfrey* (1936). Not all films were pure escapism, however. Gangster films such as *The Public Enemy* and *Little Caesar* (both from 1931) were entertaining, but they also exposed viewers to the urban crime and corruption that existed in cities like Chicago and New York City.

Buck Rogers's Police Patrol Ship, a toy manufactured and sold in 1934 to accompany the Buck Rogers comic strip, is on display at the National Air and Space Museum in Washington, D.C.

The Depression was also a vibrant period for music. In Kansas City and other midwestern cities, African-American musicians developed a new jazz style known as "swing." Marked by complicated but compelling rhythms, swing was energetic and loud. As swing grew more popular, white musicians added elements of more sedate musical genres, such as classical music, to make swing more commercial. Many swing bands evolved into big bands with percussion, woodwind, and horn sections. **Benny Goodman**, from Chicago, led a big band that made swing popular with young people.

Not all music was flamboyant and brassy, however. Folk singers such as **Woody Guthrie**, Pete Seeger, and Huddie Ledbetter caught the public's attention by singing about the lives of the people hit hardest by the Dust Bowl and the Depression. Guthrie, an "Okie" who migrated to California, lived the life he sang about, riding the rails and sleeping in migrant camps. He sang on the streets for money and took whatever small jobs he could find to survive. Some of Guthrie's songs, such as "(If You Ain't Got That) Do Re Mi," describe the struggles of the Okies seeking a new beginning in California. But Guthrie also wrote the anthem "This Land Is Your Land," celebrating the beauty and diversity of the country while also commenting on the disparity between rich landowners and those who could not afford land.

Similarly, Huddie Ledbetter—nicknamed Lead Belly—chronicled the troubles of African Americans during the Depression through his songs. Lead Belly bridged a gap between folk music and the blues. He sang old folk standards of the rural South, gospel songs, the blues, and protest songs. He also composed his own music, including "Goodnight, Irene," which became a hit after his death in 1949.

CAPTURING THE DEPRESSION

Other artists joined musicians in telling Americans' stories during the Great Depression. As you have read, photographer Dorothea Lange captured images of Dust Bowl refugees. Photographer **Walker Evans** traveled throughout the South during the Depression, photographing rural life. Lange and Evans both worked for the Resettlement Administration, which later became the Farm Security Administration. Evans's photographs helped reveal the challenges faced by the rural poor. Evans also worked with

In 1943, *Life* magazine photographer Eric Schaal accompanied Woody Guthrie as he gave on-the-spot performances around New York City, where Guthrie lived from 1940 on.

writer **James Agee** to document the lives of three sharecropper families trying to farm on a dry hillside in the 1930s. In 1941, they published their text and photographs in *Let Us Now Praise Famous Men*.

Writer **John Dos Passos**, part of the "lost generation" you read about earlier, exposed the divisions in American society in his trilogy *U.S.A.*, which combined fiction, biographies of famous people, newsreels, and newspaper headlines to paint a picture of what he saw as the two halves of society: rich and poor. Novelist **Richard Wright** portrayed the discrimination and struggles faced by African Americans in his novel *Native Son*. The novel is about a young African-American man who lives in poverty on Chicago's South Side during the 1930s.

HISTORICAL THINKING

1. **READING CHECK** How did mass media trends help people cope with the Great Depression?

2. **MAKE CONNECTIONS** How did folk music, photography, and literature help recount the plight of the poor during the Great Depression?

3. **EVALUATE** Why is it important that artists document significant historical events through their art?

HOOVER'S INITIATIVES

President Hoover's assumption that private citizens and businesses could work together to solve the ills created by the Great Depression reflected a faith in human decency. But the problems were too big to solve without government intervention.

VOLUNTARY ACTION AND SELF-HELP

President Hoover's life experiences influenced how he handled the Great Depression. Raised as a Quaker, he believed in the power of individual effort and the obligation for all citizens to help one another. His success as a mining engineer and business leader reinforced his belief in the rewards of individual effort. His success in running relief programs during and after World War I convinced him of the effectiveness of voluntary action—private citizens and businesses working together to solve problems without government prompting or legal requirements. Hoover believed the traditional self-reliance and volunteer spirit of the American people provided the most dependable means of combating the economic crisis of the Great Depression.

Toward this end, Hoover set up presidential committees to coordinate volunteer relief efforts for the unemployed, such as the **President's Organization of Unemployment Relief (POUR)**. In an effort to keep the banking system afloat, he persuaded bankers to set up the National Credit Corporation, a private agency that would **underwrite**, or buy up the assets of, banks that had failed. That action was meant to safeguard the deposits of bank customers. Unfortunately, bank managers were reluctant to do this. Since that experiment was a failure, Hoover tried again with the Reconstruction Finance Corporation (RFC), a government agency to loan money to troubled banks that did not belong to the Federal Reserve System. During the year Hoover was to remain in office, the RFC was not particularly successful either.

Hoover's attempts to ease the misery that Americans were facing every day also failed. His programs were unable to deal with the scale of the unemployment situation. Eight million workers were jobless by 1931, a number that overwhelmed the resources of existing charitable agencies. The POUR program coordinated relief agencies and urged people to help their neighbors, but these efforts did little to alleviate the human toll of the Great Depression that gripped the country.

Millions of Americans were feeling desperate and hopeless. The homeless and unemployed took to the roads and rails, looking for work, better opportunities, or a simple meal along the way. Migrant workers moved through the farmlands of California, picking produce for whatever they could earn. Others traveled from city to city, doing their best to survive on the charity of relief stations and church groups. Homeless Americans lived in and around cities in shantytowns dubbed **Hoovervilles**. The name "Hooverville" mocked the president's failure to provide for the American people.

Yet when politicians begged the federal government to find a solution to the unemployment problem, Hoover refused to budge. His response to the drought that caused the Dust Bowl provided yet

PRIMARY SOURCE

Any lack of confidence in the economic future and the basic strength of business in the United States is simply foolish. Our national capacity for hard work and intelligent cooperation is ample [promise] of the future of the United States.

—from President Herbert Hoover's press conference, November 15, 1929

CRITICAL VIEWING One of the largest and longest-lasting Hoovervilles covered 9 acres outside of Seattle, Washington, and had a population of 1,200. Based on details you see in the photo, what were living conditions like in Hoovervilles?

another example of the administration's failures. Congress proposed to allocate $60 million to help disaster victims buy fuel and food. Hoover offered money to feed animals, but he rejected the idea of feeding farmers and their families. This concern for animals over starving citizens conveyed a lack of empathy on the president's part, and additional derogatory references to the president circulated. A pocket turned outward to show it was empty of money was called a "Hoover flag." A newspaper unfolded and used to cover oneself for warmth was a "Hoover blanket." In 1931, in Minneapolis and Oklahoma City, crowds stormed into grocery stores and took food for themselves, and more protests against Hoover's lack of help were to come.

TURMOIL ABROAD

As the U.S. economy deteriorated, so did the international economy, inspiring some Europeans to look to strong but authoritarian leaders for relief. Such a leader had already risen to power in Europe. Playing on the social unrest and economic turmoil of the postwar years, dictator **Benito Mussolini** had seized control of Italy in 1922. Mussolini was a proponent of **fascism**, a political movement that involves extreme nationalism, militarism, and racism. As the supreme leader, or *Duce*, Mussolini destroyed Italian labor unions, censored the press, abolished all

political parties but his own, and relied upon a secret police force to silence his critics. Global economic insecurity opened the door for fascism to grow in Europe. As people slid into poverty, many were willing to give up some of their rights on the basis of their authoritarian leader Mussolini's promises to bring back prosperity.

Asia was also affected. A 30 percent decrease in trade worldwide caused drops in income and productivity throughout the world. Japan, an island nation, needed raw materials for its industry and saw China as a likely source. Extreme nationalism provided a rationale for expanding its empire, and in 1931, Japan launched a war to occupy Manchuria, in China. Ultimately, Japan sought military, political, and economic control over the Pacific.

HISTORICAL THINKING

1. **READING CHECK** Why did President Hoover rely on voluntary action of citizens to try to address the economic crisis of the Great Depression?

2. **MAKE INFERENCES** Why was Hoover's response to drought victims in the Midwest unwise from a political standpoint?

3. **SYNTHESIZE** How did citizens and politicians try to deal with the effects of widespread unemployment?

THE BONUS ARMY

President Hoover was quickly reminded that sometimes things go from bad to worse. As unemployment rose, Hoover's popularity with Americans plummeted. As a result, the Democrats made progress in the 1930 elections and set their sights on victory in the 1932 presidential election.

HOOVER'S WANING POPULARITY

Hoover already had a low favorability rating with his constituents because of his policies to battle unemployment. Because Hoover was a Republican, many Americans assigned blame for the nation's struggles to his party. In the 1930 election, the Democrats picked up 8 seats in the Senate and 49 in the House. Neither gave the Democrats a majority, but by the time Congress next convened, Democrats had a majority in the House due to special elections held to replace representatives who had died.

To deal with a growing budget deficit, Congress passed the **Revenue Act of 1932**, the greatest peacetime increase in taxes in the nation's history.

At a time when the economy needed Americans to have more buying power to keep factories and businesses open, the tax measure drew money out of the hands of potential consumers. Raising taxes in an election year contributed to Hoover's decreasing popularity. On the other hand, Congress also passed the **Norris-LaGuardia Act of 1932**, which extended to workers "full freedom of association" in unions and labor representation. The law restricted the use of federal **injunctions**, or court orders, to stop labor strikes, boycotts, and picketing and barred actions that prevented workers from joining unions. This legislation strengthened the power of labor, and it was popular among many American workers.

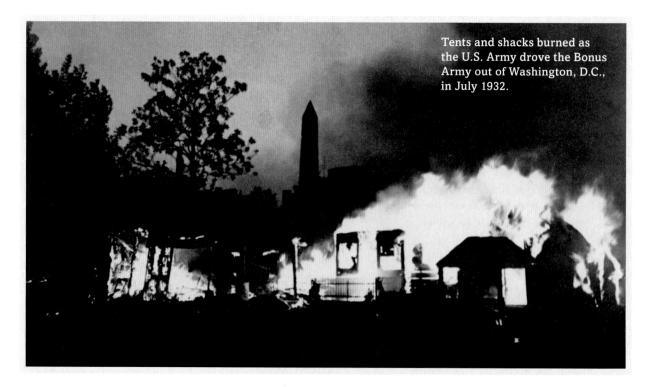

Tents and shacks burned as the U.S. Army drove the Bonus Army out of Washington, D.C., in July 1932.

To make matters worse, Congress introduced bills to provide direct assistance to the unemployed, but a coalition of Republicans and southern Democrats blocked their passage. Finally, as public pressure for action intensified, Congress passed the **Emergency Relief and Construction Act of 1932**. The act allocated federal funds to states for building public structures that could generate income, such as toll bridges, if the states proved they could not raise any money themselves. Although the law limited the kinds of construction projects that could be funded, it represented a symbolic step toward a greater federal role in combating the economic crisis and meeting the needs of desperate Americans.

THE BONUS MARCH

As the Depression worsened, economic distress triggered social protests, including one by war veterans. In 1931, a veterans organization passed a resolution demanding from Congress immediate payment of the cash bonus scheduled to be paid to World War I veterans in 1945. Veterans argued the early payment would not only help them but would also stimulate the economy. In December 1931, a bill authorizing this payment was introduced in the House. In May 1932, veterans began traveling to Washington, D.C., to show their support for the bill.

By June, more than 15,000 veterans calling themselves the Bonus Expeditionary Force, or the **Bonus Army**, had arrived in Washington to listen to Congress debate the bonus bill. While some slept in government buildings, most members of the Bonus Army camped out in makeshift tents and sheds on the banks of the Anacostia River. The Washington, D.C., police superintendent and the police captain in charge of Anacostia helped the veterans by providing food, medical care, and supplies for building their shacks. Hoover, on the other hand, ignored them. On June 17, the bill was rejected by the Senate. In July, the Hoover administration urged the Bonus Army to leave Washington and even allocated $100,000 to pay the men's transportation costs home. But many stayed on, hoping for a change in government policy.

On July 28, 1932, the secretary of war ordered the police to remove marchers from government buildings. Veterans resisted, and fighting broke out. When a police pistol went off, other officers began shooting, and soon two veterans lay dead. The president ordered the federal troops in Washington, commanded by Army Chief of Staff General **Douglas MacArthur**, to restore order. MacArthur took his

PRIMARY SOURCE

A 1932 editorial in the magazine *The New Republic* described the violence directed against the Bonus Army in Washington, D.C.

The orders which sent the soldiers to Anacostia, routing men, women and children out of bed, drenching them with tear gas, ruthlessly burning their poor shelters and whatever personal property they could not carry on their backs, then driving all of them, cripples, babies, pregnant women, up a steep hill at the point of a bayonet—these were the orders of a furious child who has been thwarted and is raging for revenge. It is profoundly humiliating to every decent American that he must see his government thus persecuting and stealing from these hungry and ragged men whom, fourteen years ago, it did not hesitate to send into the trenches at the risk of death.

—from "Bullets for the B.E.F.," *The New Republic*, August 10, 1932

men, armed with tanks and machine guns, across the Anacostia River into the Bonus Army's camp. His troops hurled tear gas canisters and burned tents and shacks as the veterans fled in terror. Documentary filmmakers captured the events, and moviegoers across the nation saw newsreels of MacArthur in full military dress directing the attack, cavalry soldiers charging veterans, and flames and smoke billowing from the camp. By the next day, the camp was a ruin and all the veterans had left. Many Americans were shocked. "If the Army must be called out to make war on unarmed citizens," wrote one newspaper editor, "this is no longer America." The public outrage spelled trouble for Hoover as the 1932 presidential election approached.

HISTORICAL THINKING

1. **READING CHECK** Why did veterans organize the Bonus Army?

2. **IDENTIFY PROBLEMS AND SOLUTIONS** What problem was the Emergency Relief and Construction Act of 1932 meant to solve?

3. **ANALYZE CAUSE AND EFFECT** How did public pressure and opinion affect the political actions of Hoover and his administration?

4. **DISTINGUISH FACT AND OPINION** Does the phrase "these were the orders of a furious child" convey a fact or an opinion? Explain your answer.

VOCABULARY

Write a paragraph about the topic using all the words in each group of words. A sentence is provided as a sample beginning.

1. Topic: the stock market crash
   Dow Jones Industrial Average
   margin   speculation
   trading pool   stock market
   Speculation was one factor impacting the Dow Jones Industrial Average.

2. Topic: effects of the Depression
   Dust Bowl   Bonus Army
   Hooverville   deportation

3. Topic: remedying the Depression
   underwrite   Smoot-Hawley   Tariff Act
   Revenue Act of 1932   injunction

READING STRATEGY
ANALYZE CAUSE AND EFFECT

Analyzing cause and effect can help you understand how situations develop throughout history. Complete the Cause-and-Effect Chain to identify the factors that led to the stock market crash in 1929 and the Great Depression that followed. Then answer the question.

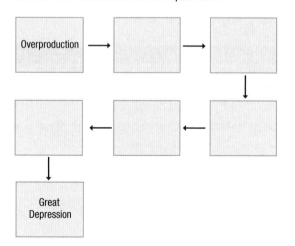

4. Describe the chain of causes and effects that resulted in the Great Depression.

MAIN IDEAS

Answer the following questions. Support your answers with evidence from the chapter.

5. What was the Kellogg-Briand Pact? LESSON 1.1

6. Why did intervention fail to stop the stock market slide between Black Thursday and Black Tuesday? LESSON 1.2

7. How did income inequality and overproduction in manufacturing work together to create problems during the 1920s? LESSON 2.1

8. In what ways did new farm machinery contribute to the conditions that caused the Dust Bowl? LESSON 2.3

9. Why was Woody Guthrie's music so important to people facing poverty during the Depression? LESSON 2.4

10. Why did Hoover's plan to help the banking system stay afloat fail? LESSON 3.1

11. How did worldwide economic problems influence the emergence of fascism? LESSON 3.1

12. How did the passage of the Revenue Act of 1932 hurt Hoover's popularity? LESSON 3.2

HISTORICAL THINKING

Answer the following questions. Support your answers with evidence from the chapter.

13. **ANALYZE CAUSE AND EFFECT** How did international loans and World War I reparations contribute to the Great Depression?

14. **MAKE CONNECTIONS** How did the Dust Bowl contribute to the depopulation of rural areas in the Great Plains?

15. **EVALUATE** In what ways did ordinary people respond to the Great Depression?

16. **ANALYZE CAUSE AND EFFECT** Did panic help cause the stock market crash, or was panic an effect of that crash? Explain your answer and describe how determining historical causes and effects can be complicated.

17. **FORM AND SUPPORT OPINIONS** How would you rate Hoover's handling of the Great Depression? Support your position with evidence from the text.

18. **ASK AND ANSWER QUESTIONS** Write a question you could ask about causes of the Great Depression, and describe how you could research the answer. Then explain the challenges of determining the causes and effects of a historical event like this.

ANALYZE VISUALS

Look closely at the political cartoon from 1929 depicting Herbert Hoover saying to a farmer, "It may not be perfect, but I'm sure it'll help quite a bit." Then answer the questions that follow.

19. What do each of the characters depicted in the cartoon represent?

20. What solution is Hoover offering the farmer, and what do the expressions of the scarecrow and crow convey about the solution?

ANALYZE SOURCES

California Industrial Scenes is a 1934 fresco by John Langley Howard depicting unemployed workers during the Great Depression.

21. How does the painting reflect the larger social and economic developments of the Depression era?

CONNECT TO YOUR LIFE

22. **EXPLANATORY** The Dust Bowl was an ecological disaster that may have been prevented if farmers had better understood the impact of their farming methods on the land. Find information about an ecological problem of today. Using the Dust Bowl as an example, write a short essay explaining why it is important that we understand problems before we can begin to solve them.

TIPS

• Think about the physical and human characteristics of the region.

• Use textual evidence from the chapter in your explanation.

• Make a connection between the Dust Bowl and the problem of today, and explain how being more informed can prevent ecological problems from turning into disasters.

• Use two or three vocabulary terms from the chapter in your response.

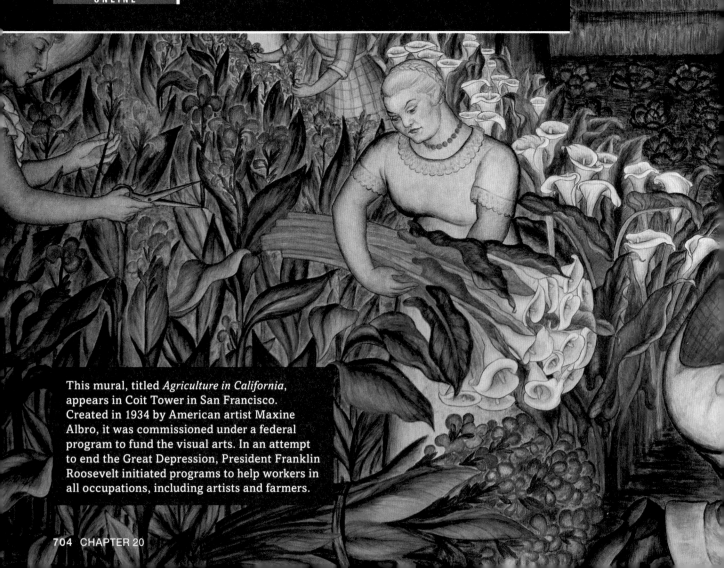

THE NEW DEAL
1933–1940

HISTORICAL THINKING In what ways were Franklin Roosevelt's policies during the Great Depression groundbreaking?

This mural, titled *Agriculture in California*, appears in Coit Tower in San Francisco. Created in 1934 by American artist Maxine Albro, it was commissioned under a federal program to fund the visual arts. In an attempt to end the Great Depression, President Franklin Roosevelt initiated programs to help workers in all occupations, including artists and farmers.

"We are helping, **and shall continue to help** the farmer."

—President Franklin D. Roosevelt

AMERICA'S
— FAVORITE —
PASTIME

CRITICAL VIEWING Sandlot baseball—baseball played by neighborhood kids on vacant lots, playgrounds, or open fields—filled many hours of a typical American childhood in the 1900s. What does this photo reveal about the changing landscape of New York City and the division of cities according to race, ethnicity, and class?

In our sundown perambulations of late, through the outer parts of Brooklyn, we have observed several parties of youngsters playing "base," a certain game of ball. . . . Let us go forth awhile and get better air in our lungs. Let us leave our close rooms. . . . The game of ball is glorious.

— American poet Walt Whitman, 1846

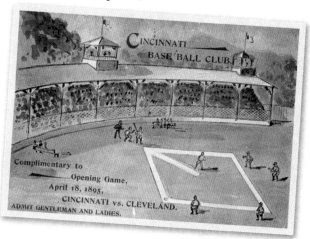

Opening day ticket for the Cincinnati Baseball Club, April 18, 1895

When you hear the expression "America's pastime," you know the topic is baseball. Although some other popular sports, such as basketball and football, also developed in the United States, there's something about baseball that uniquely symbolizes the American identity. Russell Lewis, Chief Historian of the Chicago History Museum, has this theory about the sport in the early 1900s: "Baseball was . . . extremely popular, and I think it really cut across the ethnic groups. I think a lot of minorities found baseball one of the ways they could participate in being an American."

IN THE STADIUM AND ON THE RADIO

During the 1930s, the United States was in the grip of the Great Depression, and its human toll was widespread, touching nearly every household. Struggling to make ends meet, many Americans could not afford the cost of a ticket to the ballpark, so attendance at major league fields suffered. Between 1930 and 1933, the number of spectators at games decreased by 40 percent. Still, many people made room in their budgets for an escape to the ballpark when they could. Writer Ray Robinson, who was a child in New York City during the Depression, remembered people would "go to the ballpark to get away from the economic horrors of empty wallets and ice boxes." Children like Robinson saw "guys selling apples on street corners for a nickel. Along the Hudson River," he explains, "you had some of these guys living in ramshackle huts in rags. So going to the ballpark was a big thing."

Those who couldn't get to the ballpark could follow the games on the radio. In the 1920s, commercial radio was still a concept unfamiliar to most. The airwaves were mainly used by the military and by a handful of amateur ham radio operators. But in 1921, the World Series was first broadcast "live" by a studio announcer who read the play-by-play descriptions relayed to him from a news feed printed on a strip of paper called ticker tape. In some early radio broadcasts, a special effects operator provided sounds of an imaginary ballpark. By the 1930s, announcers were broadcasting from actual stadiums—no special effects needed. Not all team owners permitted radio coverage of the games, fearing that fans would stay home to listen and ballpark attendance would drop.

Listening to baseball on the radio in the 1930s was more challenging than it is today. Radios, cumbersome and far from portable, resided in the family living room, and often produced scratchy or static-filled sound. Sportswriter Robert Creamer wrote about listening to the World Series during the 1930s: "As a nine-year-old boy, I heard those World Series games on our living-room radio, which my mother, who was not even a fan, turned on and tuned in before I came home from school. Those old radios took a long time to warm up, and tuning to the right station took patience and a deft hand." Still, the role of radio in terms of popularizing baseball within American culture was profound.

Toward the end of the 1930s, ballpark attendance began to rebound as the Depression lifted with the start of World War II. After the war ended and the soldiers returned, game attendance would return to—and even exceed—its pre-Depression levels. In the meantime, an intriguing new way to enjoy baseball made its debut during a game between the Brooklyn Dodgers and Cincinnati Reds on August 27, 1939. That day, station W2XBS in New York City broadcast live television coverage of the game to the fortunate TV owners who lived within 50 miles of the station. A *New York Times* sportswriter reported delightedly, "At times it was possible to catch a fleeting glimpse of the ball as it sped from the pitcher's hand toward home plate."

CRITICAL VIEWING Yankees hero Babe Ruth showed a group of attentive young boys in New York City how to grip a baseball bat. How might the relationship between professional athletes and their fans during the 1920s and 1930s compare to that of today?

BASEBALL LEGENDS

One name drew eager fans to the ballparks more than any other: that of legendary power hitter George Herman "Babe" Ruth of the New York Yankees. Ruth broke the single-season home run record in three consecutive seasons, hitting 29 in 1919, 54 in 1920 and 59 in 1921. In the early 1920s, he drew such a crowd that Yankees owner Jacob Ruppert built a new stadium to fit more spectators. Completed in 1923, Yankee Stadium was immediately given the nickname "The House that Ruth Built."

During the 1927 season, Ruth smashed 60 home runs, setting a record that remained unbroken until Roger Maris, who played in an era when the baseball season was 8 games longer, came along in 1961 and hit 61 home runs.

🏛 **National Baseball Hall of Fame and Museum Cooperstown, New York**

Baseball legend Babe Ruth hit three home runs with this 36-inch wooden bat—a bat worthy of a museum collection—in Game Four of the 1926 World Series.

During his stellar 1927 season, Ruth hit more home runs than most major league teams—only the St. Louis Cardinals, Chicago Cubs, New York Giants, and his own team, the Yankees, managed to out homer him. To the dismay of his opponents, he hit home runs in every stadium of the American League.

In the 1930s, even though his home run stats were in decline, Ruth remained a force to be reckoned with. In the 1932 World Series, he helped the Yankees to victory over the Cubs with a three-run homer and a single in the third game of the series. Ruth hit his last major league home run at Forbes Field in Pittsburgh, Pennsylvania, on May 25, 1935. Aging and out of shape, he nonetheless hit three homers in a single game. The last of these, described by the Pittsburgh pitcher as "the longest cockeyed ball I ever saw in my life," was the first ball ever hit completely out of that park. It was Babe Ruth's 714th and final home run.

While all eyes were on Babe Ruth, his teammate Lou Gehrig was quietly setting a major league record of his own. Between May 1925 and May 1939, he played in 2,130 consecutive games, earning the nickname "The Iron Horse." When asked why he wouldn't take a rest, Gehrig replied, "There's no point to it. I like to play baseball." Gehrig's record remained unbroken for 56 years, until Cal Ripken, Jr., of the Baltimore Orioles played his 2,131st consecutive game.

Gehrig was not far behind Ruth in slugging abilities, nearly equaling Ruth's record with 47 home runs of his own in 1927. In 1932, he surpassed one of Ruth's accomplishments by hitting four home runs in a single game. Perhaps because of Ruth's fame and flamboyant personality, Gehrig spent the first half of the 1930s in Ruth's shadow, even though he was scoring runs at a faster pace than the aging star.

The 1930s saw the birth of new baseball legends as well as the passing of an earlier golden age. Center fielder Joe DiMaggio made his debut with the New York Yankees in 1936, introducing himself to the major leagues by hitting 29 home runs and batting in 125 runs during his rookie year. DiMaggio helped lead the Yankees, without Ruth, to four consecutive World Series championships between 1936 and 1939.

Also in 1939, Ted Williams, playing for the Boston Red Sox, had possibly the best major league rookie year in all of baseball: 31 home runs, 145 runs batted in, and a batting average of .327. Both DiMaggio

Ted Williams was chosen three times (in 1954, 1957, and 1958) by baseball card manufacturer Topps as the "leadoff man," meaning his was the first card in the set.

TED Williams
BOSTON RED SOX OUTFIELD

and Williams would become dominant players in the major leagues in the 1940s. In 1941, DiMaggio went on a spectacular hitting streak, racking up hits in 56 consecutive games. That same year, Williams achieved an unheard-of batting average of .406. No player since then has ever approached either of these feats.

It seems appropriate that the Baseball Hall of Fame in Cooperstown, New York, was established in 1939. That year marked the end of a decade filled with legendary players, whose names are familiar to nearly all Americans. Babe Ruth was in the first group of inductees, along with greats from earlier eras, such as Ty Cobb and Honus Wagner. Lou Gehrig was elected to the Hall of Fame later that year, even though there is normally a waiting period between a player's retirement and his induction.

THINK ABOUT IT

What connections can you make between the popularity of baseball and the Great Depression?

THE NEGRO LEAGUES

Although such teams as the New York Yankees and St. Louis Cardinals dominated sports headlines throughout the 1930s, the all-white major leagues were not the only game in town. Prevented by prejudice and segregation from participating in the major leagues, African-American team owners and players formed their own leagues in the early 20th century. In 1920, Andrew "Rube" Foster, owner of the Chicago American Giants, organized the Negro National League, which consisted of eight teams in the Midwest. Other leagues soon followed, including the Negro Southern League later in 1920 and the Eastern Colored League in 1923.

Facing the same financial difficulties as the white major leagues during the Great Depression, Rube Foster's league disbanded after the 1931 season. It was soon replaced by a new Negro National League organized by Gus Greenlee, owner of the Pittsburgh Crawfords. From 1933 to 1949, Greenlee's league dominated the African-American baseball scene.

The best-known player in the Negro leagues was Leroy "Satchel" Paige, a tall, gangly pitcher with an unusual, high-legged windup and a spitfire delivery. Paige played for a number of teams, including the Pittsburgh Crawfords and the Kansas City Monarchs. There is little doubt that Satchel Paige would have been a star in the major leagues if teams had been integrated. Negro league teams did play

In a Negro league game in 1940, the Homestead Grays played the New York Black Yankees at Griffith Stadium in Washington, D.C.

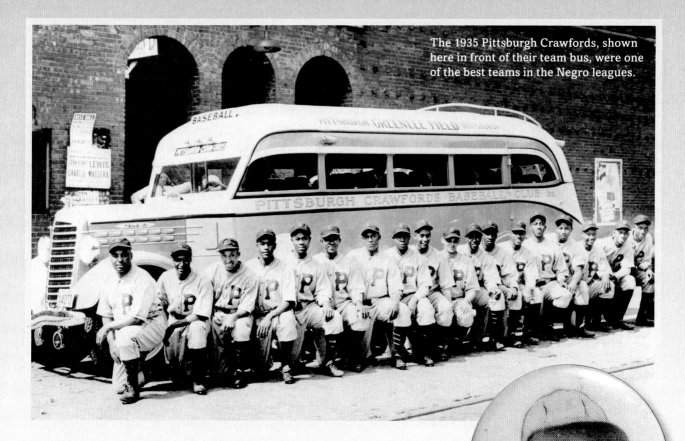

exhibition games against major league teams, and Paige struck out some of the toughest white hitters. Hack Wilson, a major leaguer, gave this description of Paige's fastball: "It starts out like a baseball, but when it gets to the plate it looks like a marble." Paige, known for his dazzling self-confidence and showmanship, gave this response: "You must be talking about my slowball. My fastball looks like a fish egg."

For all his brilliance, Paige may not have been the best pitcher in the Negro leagues. Some sportswriters and former players have suggested that Smokey Joe Williams or Bullet Joe Rogan may have been even better. Because the Negro leagues did not keep consistent records, it is difficult to compare players' statistics.

Despite their talent and popularity, even the top Negro league players were not allowed in most white-owned hotels and restaurants while they were on the road. However, by the end of the 1930s, some people were beginning to question the segregation of baseball. A group of African-American sportswriters was joined by the CIO labor union in calling for an end to the practice. Team owners in the major leagues ignored the calls, even though they were passing up the chance to sign extremely talented players. Over the course of the Negro leagues' existence, African-American teams played white teams in at least 438 exhibition games, and the Negro league teams won 309 times.

The racial barrier finally fell in 1947, when African-American player Jackie Robinson stepped up to the plate for the Brooklyn Dodgers. After that, the Negro leagues gradually dissolved as their best talent was hired by the now-integrated major leagues. In their later years, the Negro leagues were inclusive in a way that is not often recognized. Three women—Toni Stone, Connie Morgan, and Mamie "Peanut" Johnson—played on regular Negro league teams in the early 1950s.

This Negro leagues souvenir key chain from about 1940 features pitcher Satchel Paige.

WORTH THE WAIT

Much of baseball history focuses on traditionally dominant teams, such as the New York Yankees and the St. Louis Cardinals. Often overlooked are the teams that struggle a little—or a lot. One of those struggling teams—the Chicago Cubs—gained the limelight in 2016. When the opening pitch of the 2016 World Series was thrown, it had been 108 years since the Cubs had won baseball's most coveted prize. Teams like the Chicago White Sox and the Boston Red Sox hadn't fared much better.

The Cubs and the Red Sox had one other quirk in common: each team carried a famous curse. In the case of the Cubs, it was the so-called Curse of the Billy Goat. The tale goes that tavern owner William Sianis tried to bring his goat, named Murphy, to Game Four of the 1945 World Series at Wrigley Field, the Cubs' ballpark. When Murphy was turned away, Sianis supposedly proclaimed that the Cubs would lose that World Series and would never win another. The Cubs did in fact lose the 1945 World Series.

For all three long-suffering teams, the World Series drought ended in the 21st century. The Red Sox took the championship in 2004, and the White Sox in 2005. And in 2016, the Cubs won the World Series in a hotly contested, seven-game series against the Cleveland Indians. Lifelong fans across the country rooted for the team to break its epic losing streak, and after what may be the greatest World Series in history, it did. The score of the final game: Cubs 8, Indians 7.

Chicagoans welcomed their beloved Cubbies home after the win with a parade and rally that drew larger crowds than the city had ever seen. And longtime journalist Dan Rather posted his thoughts on the Cubs' historic win, reflecting at the same time on what baseball means to many Americans:

In a world of nanosecond news cycles, baseball is measured in what by comparison is geologic time. It ties us to those who came before us—the many generations. And it stretches to those yet unborn. Fans of the future will hear about a curse and the 2016 Cubbies without fully understanding the full import of the moment. A cosmic quirk in the law of averages has been reconciled.

But the sun will rise tomorrow. The calendar will turn to winter and then spring. And hope on the diamond always springs eternal.

First baseman Anthony Rizzo leapt into the air with Kris Bryant alongside Mike Montgomery, Javier Báez, and Addison Russell seconds after the Cubs made the winning out in the 2016 World Series.

FDR AND THE 1932 ELECTION

When a baseball team isn't doing well, sometimes the solution is to replace the manager. That's what happened in 1932 when the country was struggling through the Great Depression. Americans decided it was time for a new leader.

NOMINATING ROOSEVELT

In the years leading up to the 1932 presidential election, Republican Herbert Hoover, who was set to run for a second term, gradually lost public support. He had failed to ease the Great Depression, and many Americans had grown to resent him and wealthy people in general. The Democrats saw an opportunity to take back the presidency and began looking for an appealing and experienced candidate. **Franklin Delano Roosevelt**, popularly known as FDR, fit the bill. He was the distant cousin of a well-respected former president, Theodore Roosevelt, and he was married to Theodore's niece, Eleanor Roosevelt. Her political opinions and support of such causes as women's rights and labor had a great influence on her husband. Roosevelt was elected to

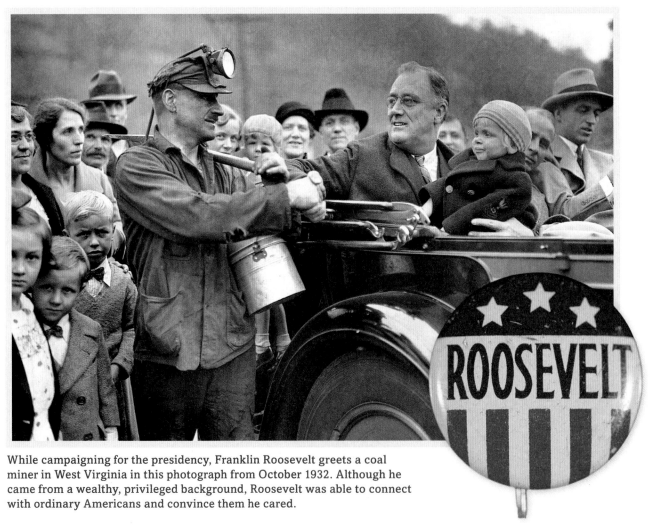

While campaigning for the presidency, Franklin Roosevelt greets a coal miner in West Virginia in this photograph from October 1932. Although he came from a wealthy, privileged background, Roosevelt was able to connect with ordinary Americans and convince them he cared.

the New York State Senate in 1910, and he served as assistant secretary of the Navy under President Wilson. In 1920, he ran as the Democratic candidate for vice president but did not win the election.

Unfortunately, in 1921, Roosevelt contracted an infectious disease called **polio** and lost the use of his legs. The public knew about his disability, though the press did not focus on his condition. Roosevelt assumed his bout of polio and the disability it caused meant the end of his political career, but Eleanor encouraged him to carry on. After taking time off to recover, Roosevelt worked hard to reenter politics. His determination paid off in 1928 when he narrowly won the governorship of the state of New York. As governor, he earned a reputation as a strong, reform-minded leader who actively worked to address such problems as unemployment and poverty.

FDR's forceful personality and "can-do" attitude impressed Democratic Party members. The Democrats felt Roosevelt's confidence and optimism would inspire hope in the many Americans who were struggling. They also believed his friendly, easy way of connecting with people would appeal to all Americans, rich and poor. At the party's national convention in Chicago, Roosevelt secured the presidential nomination, and John Nance Garner, a senator from Texas, was chosen as his running mate.

THE ELECTION OF 1932

The 1932 presidential race was not just a choice between Roosevelt and Hoover, however. The Socialist and Communist parties also nominated presidential candidates, hoping to appeal to Americans by proposing that their respective political systems offered the best solution to the Great Depression.

By October 1932, Hoover's public image was so unfavorable that Roosevelt's advisors assured the Democratic candidate that there was no need to campaign vigorously. FDR disagreed. Sensing that a passive campaign would not appeal to voters, he crisscrossed the country, giving speeches that convinced Americans their lives would improve if they elected him president.

On election day, November 8, 1932, Roosevelt won in a landslide, securing 57 percent of the popular vote and an overwhelming 89 percent of the electoral vote. Democratic candidates benefited from FDR's popularity, gaining 90 seats in the House and 13 in the Senate. The election proved a major

PRIMARY SOURCE

This is preeminently the time to speak the truth, the whole truth, frankly and boldly. Nor need we shrink from honestly facing conditions in our country today. This great Nation will endure as it has endured, will revive and will prosper. So, first of all, let me assert my firm belief that the only thing we have to fear is fear itself.

—from Franklin Delano Roosevelt's First Inaugural Address, March 4, 1933

disappointment to both the Socialist and Communist parties. The Socialist candidate received fewer than 1 million votes, and the Communist candidate collected only about 100,000. Herbert Hoover was now a **lame duck**, an outgoing elected official soon to be replaced by a successor. For many Americans, his exit could not come soon enough. In fact, Congress was in the process of ratifying the **20th Amendment**, which would move up the presidential inauguration from March to January.

Meanwhile, the Great Depression continued to deepen. By the morning of Roosevelt's inauguration on March 4, 1933, many banks in New York City, the nation's financial capital, were closing. Roosevelt took the presidential oath of office in a steady, chilling rain. "Only a foolish optimist can deny the dark realities of the moment," he told the huge crowd in attendance and the millions who listened on the radio. "This nation asks for action, and action now," he declared.

Roosevelt offered few specific solutions that day. His objective was to persuade a dispirited people to have faith in him and in themselves. Standing straight in his leg braces, he stressed four major themes: sacrifice, discipline, compassion, and hope.

HISTORICAL THINKING

1. **READING CHECK** Why did Democrats believe Franklin Roosevelt was a good candidate for president?

2. **DETERMINE CHRONOLOGY** Review Roosevelt's political career before the 1932 election. How did the positions he held and the order in which he held them prepare him for the presidency?

3. **MAKE INFERENCES** Why do you think the press did not focus on FDR's disability?

4. **DRAW CONCLUSIONS** What did FDR mean when he said "the only thing we have to fear is fear itself"?

MAIN IDEA As president, Franklin Roosevelt took immediate action to address the problems of the Great Depression and thus expanded the federal government's role in the nation's economy.

AN ACTIVIST GOVERNMENT

As the old saying goes, sometimes you have to spend money to make money. Roosevelt and his advisors believed that the best way to move the United States toward economic recovery was to spend government money, so they emptied the nation's wallet and invested in the thousands of desperate Americans in need of work.

THE FIRST HUNDRED DAYS

As soon as Roosevelt stepped into the White House, things began to change. Roosevelt asked several university professors, whom journalists called the "**brain trust**," to offer ideas on how to fix the still-floundering economy. With their help, he generated within his first few months in office 15 effective laws that fortified the nation's economy. This time of frenzied lawmaking was later dubbed the **First Hundred Days**.

The brain trust advised Roosevelt to proclaim a holiday for all the country's banks to prevent people from withdrawing their money in a panic. The **bank holiday**, which Roosevelt declared on March 6, 1933, stopped all banking operations nationwide. Roosevelt also called Congress back into a special session, so he could present laws designed to restore public confidence in the nation's banking industry. Americans were understandably anxious about the financial industry after many of them had lost their money when numerous banks closed throughout the nation. With both the House and the Senate now under firm Democratic control, Roosevelt had little trouble getting these bills passed.

The brain trust based their advice on theories developed by **John Maynard Keynes**, a leading British economist.

Years before, Keynes had proposed that the best way for a government to jump-start an economy was to invest all of its money back into the country, a strategy he called "priming the pump." The solution was risky because it created a **deficit**, or negative balance, in the national treasury. Basically, the idea was to print more money and give it to individual citizens, who would then stimulate the economy by spending it. The Federal Reserve Bank soon began printing more money. The brain trust also suggested a plan to regulate the banks. They called for the federal inspection of all banks, after which the banks with cash on hand would be allowed to reopen. The remaining banks would be reorganized, if possible, or closed for good.

Roosevelt then decided to address America's concerns about the banking industry directly. On March 12, 1933, he gave his first **fireside chat**, a radio broadcast that became a tradition throughout the rest of his presidency. More than 60 million Americans tuned in to listen. In the days that followed, as the stronger banks reopened, people began depositing money again. By the end of March, almost $1 billion had been returned to bank vaults. The banking crisis was over.

Roosevelt's strategy revealed his pragmatism, or practicality, and his belief in an activist government. Instead of taking a radical

🏛 The National Museum of American History Washington, D.C.

Instead of sitting before a fire for his chats, President Roosevelt sat before an array of microphones, including the first one used for the National Broadcasting Company (NBC). Carleton Smith, who set up the RCA type 50-A microphone for NBC and introduced the radio broadcasts, donated it to the museum.

In the 1930s, President Roosevelt was photographed as he delivered one of his 30 fireside chats. He began the practice 8 days after his inauguration in 1933 and continued it until 1944.

approach—giving the government control of all the nation's banks, for example—he demonstrated that his primary mission was to preserve capitalism. Roosevelt was willing to experiment with a wide array of ideas to save capitalism from its own excesses.

The special session of Congress continued meeting. In that time, the president established government agencies with the aim of creating jobs. One such agency was the **Civilian Conservation Corps (CCC)**, which combined the president's enthusiasm for conservation with his belief in national service. The corps provided outdoor jobs to young men ages 17 to 24. They worked on soil-erosion and flood-control projects and developed many state parks by paving roads, building cabins, and planting trees. Popular and successful, the CCC eased unemployment, lowered urban crime rates, and helped countless families.

Roosevelt chose a social worker and one of his closest advisors, **Harry Hopkins**, to help him manage the **New Deal**, a group of laws, agencies, and programs designed to combat the economic crisis. They coined the name of their plan from Theodore Roosevelt's Square Deal, and they hoped it would be as successful.

SUPPORT FOR RURAL AREAS

Roosevelt wanted to help all Americans through the Depression, including those who lived in rural areas. His New Deal featured programs designed to help poor farming families. Two major programs were in Tennessee and California.

The Tennessee River drained land in seven states. The 4 million people who lived there were some of the country's poorest farmers. Their communities were isolated and lacked doctors, proper schools, electricity, and paved roads. In May 1933, Roosevelt established a federal agency called the **Tennessee Valley Authority (TVA)** to construct dams and power plants along the river and its tributaries. Within a decade, 16 dams and hydroelectric plants operated along the river, providing thousands of jobs and bringing electrical power to residents.

In California, the New Deal funded the **Central Valley Project (CVP)**, a plan to irrigate the arid San Joaquin Valley, a portion of the state's vast Central Valley. Like the TVA, the CVP involved the construction of dams to create reservoirs for storing and delivering water.

Throughout the country, most farmers' incomes had been falling since the 1920s. In 1932, for instance,

The Southern Tenant Farmers' Union began during a meeting of 27 African-American and white sharecroppers held in a schoolhouse in eastern Arkansas in 1934. One man spoke up to convince the white farmers to join an integrated union.

We live under the same sun, eat the same food, wear the same kind of clothing, work on the same land, raise the same crop for the same landlord who oppresses and cheats us both. For a long time now [we] have been fighting each other and both of us has been getting whipped all the time. We don't have nothing against one another but we got plenty against the landlord.

—from a speech by African-American tenant farmer Isaac Shaw, given at an Arkansas schoolhouse, 1934

farmers were earning less than one-third of their 1929 incomes, even though the introduction of tractors and high-grade fertilizer allowed farms to produce more crops than ever.

The **Agricultural Adjustment Act (AAA)** was the New Deal's solution to declining farm incomes. Passed in 1933, the act limited the quantity of such staple crops as cotton, wheat, and corn that farmers could grow. It also paid farmers who voluntarily stopped growing crops on some of their land. The AAA was based on a theory called **planned scarcity**, in which the government lowers the supplies of certain products in order to create a high demand for them and raise their prices. The government also offered generous loans to farmers who stored their crop surpluses in government warehouses. Roosevelt funded the AAA by taxing businesses that processed farm goods, such as flour millers, cotton gin operators, and meatpackers. The plan worked. Within a year, more than 3 million farmers had signed individual contracts with the AAA. Farm incomes shot up almost 60 percent between 1932 and 1935.

In 1941, workers completed the construction of a turbine to generate hydroelectric power from water falling over the Cherokee Dam in Tennessee. The Cherokee Dam was one of 16 dams the TVA built between 1933 and 1943.

In the 1930s, members of the Civilian Conservation Corps could show their pride in the work they did for the CCC by purchasing and displaying items like this decorative pennant.

The AAA helped countless farm families, yet the system barely reached desperately poor tenant farmers, who did not own the land they farmed but rented it. Some tenant farmers were sharecroppers, who gave part of their harvest as rent. Tenant farmers made up almost one-half of the nation's white farm families and three-quarters of its African-American farm families. Under AAA regulations, tenants were supposed to get a fair share of the government payments, but this rarely occurred. Few landlords obeyed the rules, and some evicted their tenants in order to take even more land out of production.

In response, sharecroppers and other tenant farmers formed their own organization, the **Southern Tenant Farmers' Union**, to fight for their rights. But those who joined the union were evicted from their homes, ignored by potential employers, and denied credit at banks and stores. The union's organizers were beaten and jailed, and the union soon collapsed.

NATIONAL INDUSTRIAL RECOVERY ACT

The president's brain trust soon expanded to include such advisors as Eleanor Roosevelt and Harry Hopkins. The group experimented with centralized **economic planning**, or management of the economy by the federal government. The chief way Roosevelt centralized economic planning was through the **National Industrial Recovery Act (NIRA)**, enacted in June 1933. The act created two federal agencies: the **Public Works Administration (PWA)** and the **National Recovery Administration (NRA)**.

The Public Works Administration provided jobs for the unemployed and also generated new orders for factories in the steel, glass, rubber, and cement industries. It worked differently from most other New Deal agencies because it helped individual contractors hire and pay their own workers, instead of having the federal government pay the employees' wages. Roosevelt selected his Secretary of the Interior, **Harold Ickes**, to run the agency. Ickes managed hundreds of PWA projects, including the construction of the Hoover Dam in Nevada, the Golden Gate Bridge in San Francisco, the

Bonneville Dam between Washington and Oregon, and the Lincoln Tunnel in New York City.

The National Recovery Administration, led by General Hugh S. Johnson, established codes of fair business practices for individual industries. The idea was to set clear expectations for both business owners and workers in order to reduce labor strikes and allow the economy to stabilize. The NRA's main goals were to abolish child labor and give labor unions the right to organize and negotiate contracts. Johnson signed up major industries first—coal, steel, oil, automakers, and shipbuilders—and then moved on to smaller businesses. By the end of 1933, the NRA had 746 agreements in place.

But the NRA ran into trouble when small business owners complained that the codes encouraged monopolies and drowned them in paperwork. Labor leaders claimed that employers ignored the wage and hour expectations and continued to discourage union activity. To cover the cost of implementing the standards, manufacturers charged more for their products. Then consumers began to blame the NRA for rising prices.

During a court case in 1935, the Supreme Court declared the NRA unconstitutional on the grounds that Congress had delegated too much legislative authority to the president. Relieved, Roosevelt confided to an aide, "It has been an awful headache. I think perhaps NRA has done all it can do."

HISTORICAL THINKING

1. **READING CHECK** Describe the ways in which President Franklin Roosevelt used his increased presidential powers in response to the Great Depression.

2. **ANALYZE CAUSE AND EFFECT** In what ways did the expanded role of the federal government affect society and the economy in the 1930s?

3. **DRAW CONCLUSIONS** How does the Southern Tenant Farmers Union symbolize the advance and retreat of organized labor?

THE NEW DEAL

In the 1930s, the United States faced an enormous economic crisis. Many Americans, citizens and leaders alike, disagreed about how the federal government should respond to massive unemployment, business failures, labor strikes, and social unrest. It was a frightening time for the country.

Political cartoons during FDR's administration depicted Roosevelt in a variety of ways. Some painted him as strong, caring, and affable, while others characterized him as a sneaky politician, out for power. This cartoon from 1934 shows FDR surrounded by happy, dancing children who represent the various agencies established by the New Deal.

CRITICAL VIEWING Do you think this cartoon presents a positive, negative, or neutral characterization of FDR? Support your opinion with details from the cartoon.

DOCUMENT ONE

Primary Source: Speech
from Franklin D. Roosevelt's first fireside chat,
March 12, 1933

In his first fireside chat to the nation, President Roosevelt outlined his plans to restore confidence in banks. He faced a daunting challenge: how to rally a downtrodden citizenry from the depths of economic despair.

CONSTRUCTED RESPONSE What challenge does FDR present Americans in place of "rumors or guesses" about the failing financial system?

After all, there is an element in the readjustment of our financial system more important than currency, more important than gold, and that is the confidence of the people themselves. Confidence and courage are the essentials of success in carrying out our plan. You people must have faith; you must not be stampeded by rumors or guesses. Let us unite in banishing fear. We have provided the machinery to restore our financial system, and it is up to you to support and make it work. It is your problem, my friends, your problem no less than it is mine. Together we cannot fail.

DOCUMENT TWO

Primary Source: Letter
from an anonymous letter to Senator Robert F. Wagner,
March 7, 1934

Some Americans were wary of FDR's plans to get the country back on its feet. Many wrote letters to members of Congress and to the president himself, warning of the dire threats that the New Deal and other Roosevelt policies posed to the American social, political, and economic system.

CONSTRUCTED RESPONSE According to the author of this letter, what specific factors will lead to "disaster to all classes"?

My Dear Senator:

It seems very apparent to me that the Administration at Washington is accelerating its pace towards socialism and communism.

Everyone is sympathetic to the cause of creating more jobs and better wages for labor; but, a program continually promoting labor troubles, higher wages, shorter hours, and less profits for business, would seem to me to be leading us fast to a condition where the Government must more and more expand its relief activities, and will lead in the end to disaster to all classes.

DOCUMENT THREE

Primary Source: Newspaper article
from "The Roosevelt Record," *The Crisis*, November 1940

Roy Wilkins was one of the civil rights movement's most important figures. He was the editor of *The Crisis*, the official publication of the NAACP, from 1934 to 1949. From the 1940s through the 1960s, he helped organize legal efforts to overturn "separate but equal" segregation in public schools, participated in marches and protests, and served as the executive director of the NAACP.

CONSTRUCTED RESPONSE According to Wilkins, what problem could not be solved by the New Deal?

It is foolish to deny the imperfections and shortcomings of the New Deal. . . . The New Deal could not perform miracles. It could not overturn entrenched prejudices. The poor and the underprivileged, among whom are to be found most Negroes, need not look for comparison to the days of Herbert Hoover. They need only glance about them to see who is against the present administration. We are all Americans. We all seek security, justice, liberty, peace. But by what methods? And for whom?

SYNTHESIZE & WRITE

1. **REVIEW** Review what you have learned about the events surrounding the development and implementation of New Deal policies.

2. **RECALL** List the main ideas about the New Deal expressed in the three documents above.

3. **CONSTRUCT** Construct a topic sentence that answers this question: How did the federal government respond to the Great Depression, and what were the reactions to the New Deal?

4. **WRITE** Using evidence from this chapter and the documents, write an informative paragraph that supports your topic sentence in Step 3.

THE SECOND NEW DEAL

In 2007, the American economy almost collapsed, and more than 8 million people lost their jobs as a result. Double that number and you have some idea of the need that overwhelmed the country during the Great Depression.

JOBS, JOBS, JOBS

The progress made by Roosevelt's administration in its first hundred days was enough for Roosevelt to earn the American voters' loyalty. The economy was rebounding, and things were looking up. But the Roosevelt administration knew that too many citizens were still dealing with the persistence of poverty. When the Democrats gained even more seats in the House and Senate after the midterm elections of 1934, Roosevelt was confident Congress would pass more relief legislation. He presented Congress with a new set of reforms, the **Second New Deal**.

Despite the progress, millions of Americans remained unemployed. Roosevelt decided once again to rely on his pragmatic and activist government to address this problem. His administration launched the **Works Progress Administration (WPA)** in 1935, which provided jobs on small construction projects in communities around the country. WPA regional development projects ranged from building new schools, bridges, and landing fields for airplanes to improving more than 650,000 miles of roads. The WPA also funded projects that employed writers, teachers, musicians, and artists. Most of the WPA jobs were temporary and relatively low-paying, so as not to compete directly with private businesses. Nonetheless, the WPA, headed by Harry Hopkins, employed more than a quarter of the entire United States' workforce by 1936.

A separate division of the WPA, inspired by Eleanor Roosevelt, provided part-time jobs specifically for high school and college students. The agency, called the **National Youth Administration (NYA)**, employed several million young people.

SOCIAL SECURITY

In addition to promoting job opportunities, Secretary of Labor **Frances Perkins** urged the government to provide for those who could not work. The war years had led Americans to value independence, hard work, and sacrifice for the sake of their country. People were expected to be financially responsible for themselves. But the Depression changed that attitude. The crash proved that even the hardest workers could face financial setbacks created by economic forces over which they had no control.

In response to Perkins's request, Roosevelt proposed the **Social Security Act**, a law that would provide old-age insurance, unemployment insurance, and financial aid to the disabled and others in need. The program established a **pension fund**, or a pool of money used to pay people a small, established income after they retire. The Social Security Act was passed in 1935 and was funded by taxes paid by both employees and employers beginning in 1937.

Although the Social Security Act provided many benefits, it had some flaws and provoked controversies. It excluded millions of people, including the self-employed, farmers, and domestic workers. Benefits were not high—between $20 and $30 a month—but they were better than what those in need had been receiving: nothing. Some retired and disabled people were literally starving.

THE FASCIST CHALLENGE

While President Roosevelt labored to right the economic ship at home, some other countries were reacting to the Great Depression in very different, and in some cases, disturbing ways.

Artists working for the Works Progress Administration Federal Art Project designed posters that publicized WPA initiatives in such areas as education, recreation, safety, and health. WPA artists created the posters shown above between 1936 and 1941.

The changing face of European politics in the 1930s would challenge the United States' foreign policy as brutal authoritarian leaders emerged in several nations, particularly in Germany and Italy.

As you have read, Benito Mussolini had risen to power in the 1920s, instituting a fascist government in Italy that was based on extreme nationalism and militarism. A few years later, **Adolf Hitler** began his rise to power in Germany when he helped form the National Socialist German Workers Party. Also known as the **Nazi Party**, this organization was one of the many extremist groups that developed after World War I. Hitler modeled himself, to some degree, on Mussolini. Both were fascist dictators who established **totalitarian** regimes, in which the government relies on force to exert complete control over a country. Hitler's philosophy of **National Socialism** promoted the superiority of Germany and the German people, rejected communism, and carried anti-Semitism—hatred of Jewish people—to extreme levels. Both Hitler and Mussolini wanted to spread their power, which stirred fears of conflict in Europe and beyond.

Some leaders with fascist tendencies also gained popularity in the United States. **Huey P. Long**, the fiery governor of Louisiana, was a champion of the poor but acted ruthlessly in gaining power in his state. He abolished local government and took control of job appointments in education, police, and fire departments throughout the state. He also controlled the state militia, the judiciary, and the election system. In 1936, shortly after he announced that he would run for the presidency, he was assassinated in Baton Rouge, Louisiana.

Father Charles E. Coughlin, a Roman Catholic priest and an influential radio host from Michigan, also gained a loyal following by championing the poor. However, he began expressing anti-democratic and anti-Semitic views, which resulted in the Catholic Church ordering him to stop broadcasting in 1942. He went on to help form a new political group called the Union Party. Both Long and Coughlin were considered **populists**, or politicians who claim to represent the concerns of ordinary people.

PRIMARY SOURCE

Out of our first century of national life we evolved the ethical principle that it was not right or just that an honest and industrious man should live and die in misery. He was entitled to some degree of sympathy and security. Our conscience declared against the honest workman's becoming a pauper, but our eyes told us that he very often did.

—from *People at Work,* by Frances Perkins, 1934

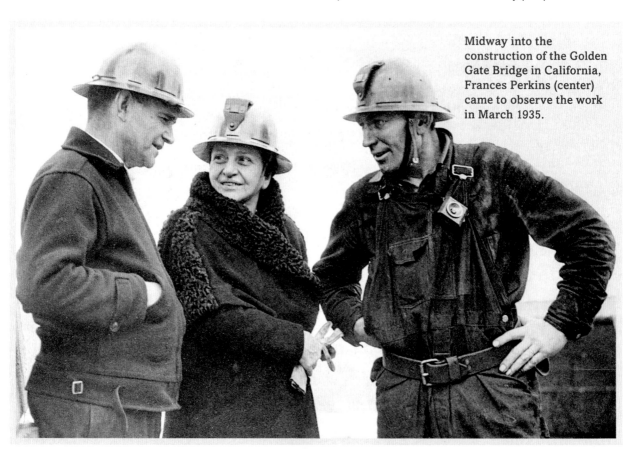

Midway into the construction of the Golden Gate Bridge in California, Frances Perkins (center) came to observe the work in March 1935.

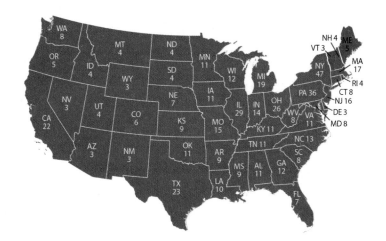

The 1936 Election

Franklin D. Roosevelt, Democrat		
Electoral Vote: 523 votes, 98.5%		
Popular Vote: 27,750,866 votes, 60.8%		

Alfred M. Landon, Republican		
Electoral Vote: 8 votes, 1.5%		
Popular Vote: 16,679,683 votes, 36.5%		

Union and Other Parties		
Popular Vote: 1,216,442 votes, 2.7%		

THE 1936 ELECTION

As the 1936 election approached, FDR had reason to be concerned about his political future. Although personal income and industrial production had risen dramatically, the country's unemployment rate was still very high. Some of his fellow Democrats argued that he needed to do more to ease Americans' suffering. In addition, more than 80 percent of the nation's newspapers and most of the business community remained loyal to the Republican Party, which meant that Roosevelt's major presidential opponent could count on strong editorial and financial support.

A coalition, or alliance, of Republican and Democratic opponents of the New Deal had formed an organization in 1934 called the **American Liberty League**. Members of the League claimed that some New Deal programs were unconstitutional because they gave increased power to the president to regulate the economy rather than to the judicial and legislative branches. League members were intent on defeating Roosevelt in the 1936 election.

But the Democrats had hope. Roosevelt's policies appealed to workers, farmers, African Americans, southern whites, and educated northerners. Many members of such religious groups as Catholics and Jews also backed the New Deal. This coalition had a good chance of keeping FDR in the White House.

The Republicans chose Kansas governor Alfred M. Landon to head their ticket, and Frank Knox, a Chicago publisher, as the vice presidential nominee. Landon, a political moderate, promised "fewer radio talks, fewer experiments, and a lot more common sense." However, Landon lacked the compassion and confidence that made Roosevelt so popular with many Americans.

Once again, Roosevelt faced presidential challenges from the Communist and Socialist parties. Both ran spirited campaigns in 1936, demanding more federal aid for the poor. Roosevelt was also opposed by the newly formed Union Party, which nominated William "Liberty Bill" Lemke, an obscure North Dakota congressman, as its presidential candidate.

Roosevelt's strategy in the 1936 election was to present himself as a champion of the common people, as opposed to the wealthy. In his final campaign speech in New York, he declared that the wealthy had "met their match" in the Roosevelt administration. If the rich and powerful hated him for that, he thundered, "I welcome their hatred."

On November 3, 1936, FDR crushed his opponents in the most one-sided election in over a century. The final totals showed Roosevelt with 27,750,866 popular votes, Landon with 16,679,683, and Lemke with about 890,000. The Socialist and Communist parties together won less than 270,000 votes. Roosevelt won every state except Maine and Vermont, securing 98.5 percent of the electoral vote. The Democratic Party added 9 seats each to its already huge majorities in the two houses of Congress.

HISTORICAL THINKING

1. **READING CHECK** In what ways did the Second New Deal improve people's lives?

2. **DRAW CONCLUSIONS** Why might people be drawn to fascist or ruthless leaders who promote extreme nationalism during difficult economic times?

3. **MAKE GENERALIZATIONS** What segments of American society did the Second New Deal target?

4. **COMPARE AND CONTRAST** How were Roosevelt's New Deal policies criticized by both Democrats and and Republicans?

MILWAUKEE PUBLIC MUSEUM MILWAUKEE, WISCONSIN

The Milwaukee Public Museum is the largest natural and human history museum in the state of Wisconsin, and one of the largest in the Midwest. Chartered in 1882, its collection contains more than 4 million objects, and its exhibits feature world cultures, life-size dioramas, walk-through villages, dinosaurs, a rain forest, and a live butterfly garden.

The museum's WPA Milwaukee Handicraft Project collection (MHP) contains artifacts and photographs that tell the story of one of the first national welfare programs. During the Great Depression, it employed more than 5,000 women and minorities in Milwaukee and broke gender and color barriers, while bringing fame to the city.

This giraffe pull-toy, which was cut from wood and painted by project workers, was sold to schools.

Integrated Workforce

Workers on the Milwaukee Handicraft Project were paid by the federal government to create handmade goods such as toys, dolls, furniture, coverlets, and books. The products were then sold to public institutions such as schools, for the cost of the materials alone. As shown in the photo above, the MHP was racially integrated while most WPA projects were segregated. The MHP also hired women, though most WPA projects were structured to provide work for the male head of a household.

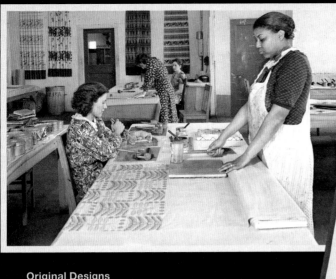

Original Designs

Although its focus was on providing work, the MHP produced beautiful, original, high-quality products that were sold throughout the United States. MHP products were designed by trained art educators and artists who taught basic crafting skills to the workers. The workers in the photograph above are printing designs onto fabric using linoleum blocks. This fabric would then be made into draperies or sold by the yard.

This coverlet is made of appliquéd cotton, with a design called "Horse." It was sold to nursery schools for children's napping cots.

> "The Milwaukee Public Museum's unique WPA collection **reflects the artistic focus** the WPA had in Milwaukee."

—Ellen Censky
Senior Vice President

This upholstered chair represents the variety of skills taught on the MHP: woodworking for the frame, weaving for the fabric, and upholstery for the chair seat and back.

Skills Training

Many of the female workers who came to the MHP had never worked outside of their homes. The impact of the Great Depression caused many women to seek jobs for the first time to help support their families. The MHP trained the women to produce handicrafts that gave them skills they could apply to work outside of the WPA, sewing as seamstresses, repairing books, and working in factories.

SUPPORTING LABOR

When you are used to having no car at all, you might be thrilled to finally own an old vehicle that still runs. But once you have that, you might wish for a nicer car. As Americans' lives got better under the New Deal, their acceptance of hardship and struggle gave way to a desire for more improvements in their lives.

GAINS BY LABOR

Despite his progressive leanings, Franklin Roosevelt never fully supported organized labor. He felt uneasy when the head of the United Mine Workers, **John L. Lewis**, tripled his labor union's membership by announcing to workers, "The president wants you to join a union!" When other major labor leaders began using the same tactic to increase membership numbers, Roosevelt became irritated.

Unions needed large memberships to maintain the authority to stand up to corporate managers. As you have read, one effective labor tactic was to organize strikes to persuade management to listen to workers' demands. The more people involved in a strike, the greater the impact.

Unions used strikes to fight for the right of **collective bargaining**, or negotiation between

New laws passed during FDR's first term guaranteed workers the right to organize and strike. The practice continues today. In this photo from April 2016, members of a janitors' union march peacefully in downtown Los Angeles to publicize their campaign for higher pay and benefits.

an employer and union leaders on behalf of all union members. Union members had become aware that pay rates and benefits were not uniform for workers doing the same job. Because workers negotiated their wages and benefits individually and secretly with factory managers, two workers hired for the same position could be offered different hourly wages. Before collective bargaining, employees might complain to management, but their complaints had little effect. Union organizers used collective bargaining to negotiate employment contracts that guaranteed standard pay ranges and equal benefits for all workers.

Unfortunately, labor disputes resulted in violence on numerous occasions as scabs—workers brought in to replace those on strike—and police fought with striking workers. In 1933, for example, 60 workers at the Spang-Chalfant Seamless Tube Company, which produced steel tubing and was located near Pittsburgh, went out on strike after management increased their work hours. As the strikers were protesting on a **picket line**, 200 armed police officers arrived. A picket line is a group of strikers who form a barrier to keep scabs, or strikebreakers, from entering a building to work in their place. When the strikers refused to leave the picket line, the police began firing tear gas. When that tactic failed, the police fired bullets, killing 1 bystander and injuring 15 strikers and onlookers. The strike finally ended after three weeks when the workers agreed that the company could make changes to the work schedule. In return, the company agreed to consult union leaders about shift changes and increases or decreases in work hours.

In response to this kind of violence, Senator Robert Wagner of New York wrote a bill to protect the rights of striking workers. His legislation, later called the **Wagner Act**, passed in 1935. A portion of the act—the **National Labor Relations Act**—required employers to allow unions to collectively bargain for wages and benefits. It also prohibited employers from engaging in a wide range of "unfair labor practices," such as discriminating against a worker because of union membership and punishing workers for filing complaints against an employer. In addition, it created the **National Labor Relations Board** to supervise union elections and assign union representatives to advocate for workers. This board still meets today.

The Wagner Act made forming unions easier, but its enforcement revealed deep racial divisions when workers in non-unionized factories attempted to organize. At the 1935 convention of the American Federation of Labor (AFL), an organization of labor

unions, John Lewis pleaded with fellow union leaders to begin serious membership drives in the steel mills, automobile plants, and rubber factories. These industries employed many African Americans and immigrants from eastern and southern Europe. But most AFL leaders, who represented such skilled trade workers as masons and carpenters, had little interest in organizing such unions.

Determined, Lewis joined with like-minded labor leaders who agreed with him to form the **Congress of Industrial Organizations (CIO)**. The goal of the CIO was to create powerful unions in mass-production industries, such as auto manufacturing and steel.

CONFLICT OVER THE SUPREME COURT

In his second inaugural address, which he delivered at the Capitol on January 20, 1937, Roosevelt emphasized the New Deal's unfinished business. "I see one-third of a nation ill-housed, ill-clad, ill-nourished," he declared. His landslide election had provided him with a strong popular mandate, or authority to act. In addition, he enjoyed huge Democratic majorities in the House and Senate, enabling him to continue his political agenda.

PRIMARY SOURCE

In 1937, President Franklin Roosevelt proposed changes to the Supreme Court, which had opposed some of his New Deal legislation. In a fireside chat, he explained to the American people his view of the conflict.

Last Thursday I described the American form of Government as a three-horse team provided by the Constitution to the American people so that their field might be plowed. The three horses are, of course, the three branches of government—the Congress, the Executive and the Courts. Two of the horses are pulling in unison today; the third is not. Those who have intimated that the President of the United States is trying to drive that team, overlook the simple fact that the President, as Chief Executive, is himself one of the three horses.

It is the American people themselves who are in the driver's seat.

It is the American people themselves who want the furrow plowed.

It is the American people themselves who expect the third horse to pull in unison with the other two.

—from a fireside chat given by President Franklin Roosevelt, March 9, 1937

The only branch of government not on FDR's side was the judicial branch—specifically, the Supreme Court.

The Supreme Court was dominated by elderly, conservative justices who strongly opposed the New Deal legislation. Roosevelt knew that in the coming months the justices would be reviewing two of the New Deal's most important accomplishments—the National Labor Relations Act and the Social Security Act. He took action to save his programs.

In February 1937, without consulting Congress, Roosevelt ordered a complete reorganization of the federal court system. Under his plan, the Supreme Court would gain six new members, raising the total number of justices to fifteen. Roosevelt would be able to fill these new positions with judges who shared his political views. This **court-packing plan** was legal; the Constitution set no limits on the size of the Supreme Court.

Roosevelt had miscalculated the power of his mandate, however. Some politicians worried that expanding the judicial branch would throw off the balance among the three branches of government. As opposition to the plan grew stronger, aides urged Roosevelt to withdraw it. The Senate later defeated it.

As it turned out, the president did not need to pack the court. In the spring of 1937, the Supreme Court changed course. By a vote of 5 to 4, the court upheld both the National Labor Relations Act and the Social Security Act. Then, one by one, the old conservative justices decided to retire, making FDR's plan unnecessary. Roosevelt—the only president in American history to make no Supreme Court appointments during his first four-year term—filled five vacancies over the next three years. The liberal justices he chose—especially Hugo Black, Felix Frankfurter, and William O. Douglas—would steer the court for decades to come.

Autoworkers at a General Motors plant in Flint, Michigan, staged a strike by sitting in the seats made to be installed in cars, as shown in this 1936 photograph.

Protected by state-of-the-art safety gear in 2016, a welder performs detailed work on aluminum for a lighting manufacturer. Welding has always been a hazardous occupation. Welders first began to wear modern safety gear in the 1930s, when factories invested in goggles and face shields at the urging of workers and unions.

CONFLICT OVER UNIONS

Away from Washington, new battles raged in the automobile plants of Michigan, the textile mills of North Carolina, and the coal mines of Kentucky. Workers in such major industries demanded union recognition under the banner of the CIO, but management ignored their demand.

On November 12, 1936, a small group of autoworkers at a General Motors (GM) plant in Flint, Michigan, staged a **sit-down strike**. Instead of leaving their jobs, the workers stayed in the plant, refusing to work. They thus prevented management from bringing in scabs to continue production and shut down the plant. Unlike the Spang-Chalfant strike, the Flint strike was effective and mostly peaceful.

In addition to seeking recognition for the CIO, the sit-down strikers wanted higher wages and safer working conditions. At the time, the average autoworker earned $900 a year, far below the $1,600 the government deemed necessary to support a family of four. In addition, hundreds of workers had died in auto plants in Michigan because of dangerous working conditions. Soon, the strike spread as workers at other General Motors plants began sitting down at their jobs. Journalists called this first major labor dispute between autoworkers and management "the strike heard 'round the world."

The 44-day Flint sit-down strike ended when GM recognized the CIO's United Automobile Workers (UAW) union as the bargaining agent for its employees and raised wages. The success of the strike motivated other autoworkers to protest as well. Within a few weeks after the strike, 87 more sit-down strikes occurred in the Detroit area alone. Chrysler came to terms with strikers a few months later. Other industry leaders followed suit after the UAW victory, including Firestone, General Electric, and RCA.

Some industry leaders were not so quick to give in to unions, however. Henry Ford hired an army of thugs to rough up union organizers and disrupt strikers on picket lines. The worst violence, however, occurred outside Republic Steel's South Chicago mill on Memorial Day 1937, when heavily armed police battled rock-throwing strikers on a picket line. Casualties included 10 workers killed by gunfire, and dozens more injured. Under pressure from the National Labor Relations Board, Ford and Republic Steel gradually accepted unions as a legitimate force in American manufacturing. With a membership approaching 3 million, the CIO had come a long way since its break with the conservative, trades-oriented American Federation of Labor a few years before.

The Supreme Court battle and the sit-down strikes slowed the political momentum that followed FDR's re-election landslide in 1936. In addition, a serious recession in 1937 eroded public confidence in the New Deal. Other problems loomed in Europe, where fascism continued to gain strength. For President Roosevelt, the road ahead appeared even steeper and rockier than before.

HISTORICAL THINKING

1. **READING CHECK** What gains did American labor make during the 1930s?

2. **EVALUATE** Why were unions important to American workers in the 1930s?

3. **FORM AND SUPPORT OPINIONS** Was the Wagner Act effective? Support your opinion with evidence from the text.

4. **DETERMINE CHRONOLOGY** What sequence of events made Roosevelt's court-packing plan unnecessary?

2.4 THROUGH THE LENS AMERICAN PLACES

GOLDEN GATE BRIDGE SAN FRANCISCO, CALIFORNIA

The iconic Golden Gate Bridge extends across the Golden Gate Strait and connects the city of San Francisco to Marin County, California. Opened in 1937, this steel suspension bridge is the product of thousands of hours of backbreaking, dangerous labor by hundreds of American workers. It was built during the Great Depression, a time when one out of four Americans were unemployed. Those who worked on it were grateful for their jobs. Bridge workers were hired through local unions, such as the Ironworkers Local Union 377, and included people from a wide range of backgrounds: farmers, lumberjacks, cowboys, and taxicab drivers. It took nerves of steel to work on the Golden Gate Bridge. Workers faced many physical challenges, including water, wind, and blinding fog. But creating this gateway to the "Golden City" during one of the lowest points in American economic history gave union workers financial stability and pride. "It was never just a job to me. I loved the work," said bridge worker Harold McClain.

CRITICAL VIEWING Measuring 1.7 miles long, the Golden Gate Bridge weighs nearly 900,000 tons. Two towers support two enormous carbon-steel cables, which are secured at each end by giant anchorages. Based on what you notice in the photograph, what challenges did workers probably face while building the bridge?

WOMEN DURING THE NEW DEAL

You probably take for granted that women hold important jobs and contribute to their families' financial security. But many jobs might still be closed to women if not for the efforts of pioneers like Eleanor Roosevelt.

OPPORTUNITIES FOR WOMEN

When the stock market crashed in 1929, men were not the only ones to lose their jobs. By 1933, about 2 million women were unemployed as well. In some families, the women were the main **breadwinners**, or contributors to a family's income. These women—in fact, all American women—had a powerful ally in Eleanor Roosevelt. The first lady was among the president's chief advisors, and her progressive beliefs strongly influenced him. An advocate for child welfare and equal rights for women and minorities, she traveled the country and reported to FDR on the social conditions she observed.

Eleanor worked to persuade those in charge of implementing the New Deal to include positions for women in their relief programs. She quoted girls and women who had written her letters telling how the Great Depression had affected them and their families. She pointed out that many women were earning their college degrees and entering the workforce with fresh ideas that the nation urgently needed. Influential leaders like Harry Hopkins listened.

Hopkins headed one of the first New Deal agencies designed to put people back to work, the Federal Emergency Relief Administration (FERA). He established a division in FERA called the Civil Works Administration (CWA), which was committed to finding jobs for women. Hopkins appointed his assistant and former Mississippi legislator, **Ellen Woodward**, to lead the CWA. Woodward required that each state hire a woman to direct the program.

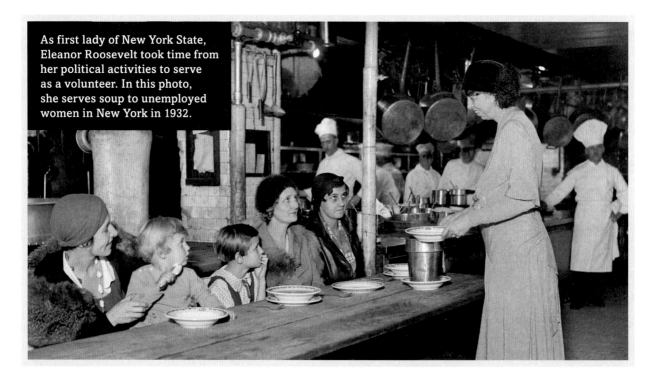

As first lady of New York State, Eleanor Roosevelt took time from her political activities to serve as a volunteer. In this photo, she serves soup to unemployed women in New York in 1932.

Eleanor Roosevelt received hundreds of letters from Americans asking for help during the Great Depression. After leaving the White House in 1945, she continued to fight for social change and to champion human rights.

I hope to complete my education, but I will have to quit school I guess if there is no clothes can be bought. Mrs. Roosevelt, don't think I am just begging, but that is all you can call it I guess. There is no harm in asking I guess [either]. Do you have any old clothes you have throwed back. The clothes may be too large but I can cut them down so I can wear them. Not only clothes but old shoes, hats, hose, and under wear would be appreciated so much.

—from a letter written to Eleanor Roosevelt by a 15-year-old girl from Alabama, 1936

Where, after all, do universal human rights begin? In small places close to home—so close and so small that they cannot be seen on any map of the world. Such are the places where every man, woman, and child seeks equal justice, equal opportunity, equal dignity without discrimination. Unless these rights have meaning there, they have little meaning anywhere.

—from a speech given to the United Nations by Eleanor Roosevelt, March 27, 1958

Women were also hired to renovate buildings, conduct public surveys, help develop museums, and carry out a variety of other projects. Job opportunities were far from equal, however. Women held only 7 percent of the jobs created by the CWA, and they were paid less than their male counterparts. The situation improved when FDR established the Works Progress Administration in 1935, replacing FERA. By 1938, more than 13 percent of the people working in the agency were women.

WOMEN LEAD THE WAY

Eleanor Roosevelt and Ellen Woodward were not the only influential women in the Roosevelt administration. Others included Frances Perkins, Josephine Roche, and Hilda Smith.

Frances Perkins, a labor rights activist from New York, was appointed secretary of Labor by FDR. She was the first woman in American history to hold a cabinet-level post. As secretary, she drew on her experiences inspecting working conditions in textile mills and advocating for working-class immigrants and African Americans. She outlined her goals for the president, including a 40-hour workweek, unemployment insurance, a minimum wage, and an end to child labor. FDR incorporated so many of Perkins's ideas that she was later called "the architect of the New Deal." As a member of the Special Board for Public Works, Perkins ensured that government funds were spent on roads, schools, and post offices. As chair of the Committee on Economic Security, she helped develop the Social Security Act, which provided aid for the elderly and workers who had been laid off and grants to states for maternal and child healthcare.

Roosevelt appointed **Josephine Roche**, Colorado's first policewoman and heir to a fuel company, as the assistant secretary of the Treasury in 1934. She had previously advocated for fair wages and health benefits for Colorado mine workers and had used her own money to establish unions in her family's mines.

Before joining the Roosevelt administration as the director of Workers' Education in FERA, **Hilda Smith** was a dean at Bryn Mawr College in Pennsylvania and had been active in social work and women's suffrage. As director, Smith ran FERA and WPA camps and schools for unemployed women. The camps provided food and clothing, and the schools taught such classes as literacy and typing. Unlike the men's camps, however, the women's camps failed to provide work. The women's camps were closed down after three years when New Deal opponents began complaining about the cost. "As so often the case," Smith wrote, "the boys get the breaks, the girls are neglected."

HISTORICAL THINKING

1. **READING CHECK** How did the New Deal affect the role of women in society?

2. **IDENTIFY MAIN IDEAS AND DETAILS** Why was Frances Perkins called the "architect of the New Deal"?

3. **DESCRIBE** How did Eleanor Roosevelt influence the appointment of women to important positions in New Deal agencies?

4. **ANALYZE CAUSE AND EFFECT** Why did the camps for unemployed women fail?

MIXED PROGRESS ON CIVIL RIGHTS

Perhaps the greatest challenge of American democracy has been making equal rights for all a reality. Every generation has faced this challenge.

AFRICAN AMERICANS AND THE NEW DEAL

President Roosevelt crafted his New Deal policies to apply to all Americans, no matter their ethnicity. African Americans appreciated this effort, and many of them supported him at the ballot box. As you have read, the Great Migration brought many African Americans to northern cities, where they often formed a **voting bloc**, or a large group of citizens who share a common concern and tend to vote the same in elections.

Historically, most African Americans had supported the Republican Party, an allegiance that dated back to Abraham Lincoln and the Civil War. With the New Deal, however, many African Americans shifted to the Democratic Party. This massive switch occurred because the Roosevelt administration provided jobs and relief benefits to all Americans, regardless of race.

Federal assistance was especially welcome in African-American communities, where the human toll of the Great Depression was especially evident. By 1933, unemployment among African Americans had reached 50 percent. Fortunately, the two New Deal administrators most responsible for creating jobs were sympathetic to minority needs. At the

AMERICAN PLACES
Lincoln Memorial, Washington, D.C.

On a chilly Easter Sunday in 1939, world-renowned opera singer Marian Anderson performed at the Lincoln Memorial in Washington, D.C., before a crowd of about 75,000 people. Previously, the Daughters of the American Revolution had refused to allow Anderson to perform at Constitution Hall because of her skin color. Anderson began her performance with a moving rendition of "My Country 'Tis of Thee."

Public Works Administration (PWA), Harold Ickes insisted that African Americans receive equal pay on all construction projects. Although local officials often ignored this rule, the PWA provided thousands of jobs for African Americans and built African-American schools and hospitals throughout the segregated South. At the Works Progress Administration, African Americans received a share of the work in northern cities. Many African Americans welcomed an administration that showed some interest in their well-being. They particularly admired the efforts of First Lady Eleanor Roosevelt, who took strong stands in favor of equal rights for minorities and women.

Eleanor Roosevelt's interest in civil rights had been fueled in large measure by her friendship with prominent African Americans, including

Mary McLeod Bethune, founder of Bethune-Cookman College in Florida. In 1936, Eleanor Roosevelt recommended Bethune to head the National Youth Administration's Office of Negro Affairs. As the New Deal's highest-ranking African-American appointee, Bethune presided over the administration's "black cabinet," an informal group of African-American leaders who advised the White House on minority issues. Bethune went on to play an important role many years later as one of the original U.S. representatives to the United Nations and its first black female delegate.

In 1939, Eleanor Roosevelt further demonstrated her commitment to African-American rights when she resigned from a historically all-white organization called the Daughters of the American Revolution. The group had refused to allow **Marian Anderson**, a gifted African-American opera singer, to perform at Washington's Constitution Hall. A few months later, Harold Ickes arranged for Anderson to sing at the Lincoln Memorial on Easter Sunday. An integrated audience of about 75,000 gathered to hear her stirring performance.

Yet the progressive work of Eleanor Roosevelt and others could not make up for larger New Deal failures in the field of civil rights. Throughout his presidency, for example, Franklin Roosevelt made no effort to dismantle segregation or to enable African Americans to vote. He remained on the sidelines as federal anti-lynching bills were narrowly defeated in Congress. Roosevelt argued that he could not support civil rights legislation without alienating southern Democrats, who controlled the most important committees in Congress. "They will block every bill I [need] to keep America from collapsing," Roosevelt said. "I just can't take that risk." The president's position did not prevent African Americans from supporting him in 1936, however. Roosevelt received 76 percent of their votes—the same percentage that Herbert Hoover, the Republican candidate, had won four years before.

MEXICAN AMERICANS AND THE NEW DEAL

As African Americans struggled with racism and discrimination, both Mexican immigrants and American citizens of Mexican descent, or Mexican Americans, faced their own challenges during the Depression.

THE SCOTTSBORO BOYS

In March 1931, nine young African-American men, ages 12 to 20, hopped aboard a freight train in northern Alabama to ride the rails as "hoboes," or homeless wanderers in search of work. A fight broke out between them and two white men. In the fray that followed, two white women, also riding the same train, accused the young black men of rape. Police arrested the nine African-American men and locked them up in the Scottsboro, Alabama, jail. From that point on, the nine were known as the Scottsboro Boys.

Over the course of the next seven years, the Scottsboro Boys would attend trials and retrials, which were marred by lies, bribes, and racial bias on the part of the accusers, the prosecuting attorney, and the judges. The victims gave vastly different accounts of the crime, and one even took back her accusation, admitting it was a lie. Even so, a series of all-white juries convicted and sentenced the young men to death several times. Each time, the defense appealed. The case went all the way to the U.S. Supreme Court, finally ending with five convictions and four dismissals. By 1950, all of the convicted Scottsboro Boys had been either pardoned or paroled.

Despite being recruited to work on American farms just 10 years before, Mexican immigrants met with deep resentment from white Americans who felt jobs were being taken away from them. In response to this resentment, in 1929, the federal government began the Mexican Repatriation Program, which, as you've read, deported hundreds of thousands of people of Mexican descent. In this context, repatriation is the act of sending an immigrant back to his or her home country to live. Some people left the United States voluntarily, accepting the government's free train fares. Others were coerced or tricked into leaving.

Many Mexican Americans were also deported to Mexico simply because authorities did not trust their claims of nationality or did not care. Of those who remained in the United States, many experienced unemployment because farm owners were hiring fewer migrant workers and giving jobs to white workers first. Farmers in various ethnic groups had begun working as migrant farm laborers after losing their farmland in bank foreclosures during the Great Depression. Many Mexican American farmers were among those who had lost their land and become migrant laborers.

Fortunately, the New Deal provided some relief. The Farm Security Administration (FSA), a New Deal agency, established camps to provide food and shelter for migrant workers and their families. Several camps were specifically for Mexican American workers. Farmworkers who lived in the camps were able to discuss labor issues among themselves. These discussions led to the formation of Mexican-American farm labor unions, which fought for higher wages and better working conditions.

In 2005, the California State Legislature passed the "Apology Act," a long-overdue response to the deportations that took place during and after the New Deal. California senator Joe Dunn wrote the act on behalf of his constituency to acknowledge the mistreatment Americans had suffered since the 1930s simply for being of Mexican descent.

However, Mexican Americans were not the only target of federal repatriation acts. In 1935, Congress passed a repatriation act targeting Filipinos. The act encouraged both Filipino immigrants and Americans of Filipino descent to return voluntarily to the Philippines, but the Filipino American community

CRITICAL VIEWING In 1930, a group of Filipino American farmworkers posed with tomatoes they harvested on California's Central Coast. The migrant workers followed the crops from the Mexican border to Alaska. Although migrant work was rough and the workers were often mistreated, why do you think these men mostly look happy in the photograph?

ENCOURAGING AN APPRECIATION OF NATIVE AMERICAN ART

As Commissioner of Indian Affairs from 1933 to 1945, John Collier worked to foster the economic independence of Native Americans, partly by promoting the work of Native American artists and craftspeople. This poster is one of a series designed by Native American artists to advertise a special exhibition held at the Museum of Modern Art in New York City from January to April of 1936. The goal of the exhibition was to expose white Americans to Native American cultures and encourage them to purchase works of art to decorate their homes.

resisted. One Filipino told an interviewer, "I would rather go hungry and die here than go home with an empty hand." At the end of the first year, only about 150 people had chosen to return to the islands, and by 1941 just 2,064 Filipinos had left the United States under the act.

NATIVE AMERICANS AND THE NEW DEAL

The New Deal brought major changes in federal policy toward Native Americans. As you have read, in 1871 the federal government had passed a law stripping Native Americans of their national sovereignty and making them wards of the state. The government had forced Native American children to attend "Indian schools," where all efforts focused on eliminating their languages and cultures. The goal was to assimilate Native Americans into mainstream American culture. The Dawes Act of 1887 attempted to turn Native Americans into farmers by dividing their reservation lands into plots intended for individual farms. However, most of the land was unsuitable for farming, and outsiders quickly bought up the best land.

When Roosevelt took office, he chose **John Collier**, a sociologist and author, as Commissioner of Indian Affairs. Collier was outraged by the effects of the Indian schools and the Dawes Act, and he set about making changes. He made sure that employers working on projects authorized by the CCC, NYA, WPA, and PWA hired Native American workers. He also encouraged Congress to authorize the **Indian Emergency Conservation Program (IECP)**. The IECP was similar to the CCC, but it employed Native Americans to work on physical improvements to reservations. Through the IECP, the government employed more than 85,000 Native Americans.

Collier worked to repeal the Dawes Act through Congressional passage of the 1934 **Indian Reorganization Act (IRA)**. The IRA provided tribes with federal funds to buy back some reservation lands. It also repealed laws that prohibited Native Americans from speaking their languages and practicing their customs. In addition, it provided for federal government recognition of tribal constitutions. Collier instituted a major shift in federal policy away from assimilation and toward autonomy.

HISTORICAL THINKING

1. **READING CHECK** How did the New Deal improve the lives of minorities in the United States?

2. **COMPARE AND CONTRAST** How did the Mexican Repatriation Program differ from the government program to repatriate Filipinos?

3. **SYNTHESIZE** What did the Scottsboro Boys case demonstrate about racism and discrimination in the United States at the time?

4. **DETERMINE CHRONOLOGY** Trace government treatment of Native Americans between 1871 and 1934. What changed and when?

4.1   **MAIN IDEA** The New Deal helped many people survive the
Great Depression, but as the decade and the depression
wore on, its effectiveness started to fade.

THE NEW DEAL WINDS DOWN

The New Deal featured many ambitious, expensive programs. It had its successes and its failures, its staunch advocates and its fierce critics. By 1937, President Roosevelt had to make some hard decisions about the New Deal.

THE ECONOMY STUMBLES AGAIN

As 1937 approached, the United States' national income and production rose nearly to the levels of 1929, before the stock market crash. However, the stock market itself had yet to reach its peak levels of 1929, even though stocks had enjoyed a minor boom over the preceding five years.

Roosevelt knew that government spending on programs such as the WPA had helped combat the economic crisis and fueled this recovery, and he knew that following John Maynard Keynes's economic guidance had been effective. Still, he was uncomfortable with the huge amount of government spending his programs had required. He worried that the ever-increasing national debt would cause inflation, or rising prices for goods and services,

and that federal welfare programs would diminish the recipients' initiative and self-respect. Indeed, Roosevelt had never intended for these programs to continue for the long term.

In 1937, the new Social Security payroll tax took effect, cutting into workers' take-home pay and removing billions of dollars of purchasing power from the economy. That same year, Roosevelt slashed funding for both the PWA and WPA, resulting in a loss of almost 2 million jobs. The new tax, combined with the program cuts, caused a recession. Unemployment began to rise, production plummeted, and people with no other choice began returning to breadlines and soup kitchens. The stock market fell yet again. Something had to be done, and quickly.

PRIMARY SOURCES

Elected to four terms, Franklin Roosevelt is still one of the most popular presidents in American history. But many people disagreed with his policies. For example, former president Herbert Hoover did not believe the New Deal had much chance for success.

The country is going sour on the New Deal, despite the heroic efforts of the Press. Unless there is a halt, the real question will be that, having cast off all moorings, will we swing to the "right" or to the "left." I fear first the "left," and then when the great middle class (80% of America) realizes its ruin, it will drive into some American interpretation of Hitler or Mussolini.

—from a letter written by Herbert Hoover, 1933

Four years after Hoover made his prediction, FDR was still promoting New Deal policies. In a speech to Congress, he introduced the Fair Labor Standards Act.

Our Nation so richly endowed with natural resources and with a capable and industrious population should be able to devise ways and means of insuring to all our able-bodied working men and women a fair day's pay for a fair day's work. All but the hopelessly reactionary will agree that to conserve our primary resources of man power, government must have some control over maximum hours, minimum wages, the evil of child labor and the exploitation of unorganized labor.

—from President Franklin Roosevelt's message to Congress, May 24, 1937

As the Fair Labor Standards Act took effect, it became the norm for teenagers to be in high school rather than in the workforce. In a 1941 photograph, energetic high school cheerleaders in Springfield, Pennsylvania, practice their routines.

TRIMMING THE NEW DEAL

Starting in October of 1937, Roosevelt and Congress took steps to approve $5 billion in federal funds for relief and public works programs. The economy in crisis responded positively, but Roosevelt's public image suffered because people felt he relied on government spending to solve economic problems.

By 1938, the New Deal had clearly lost momentum. Harry Hopkins, one of the architects of the New Deal, lamented that the public was "bored with the poor, the unemployed, the insecure." Congressional Republicans and conservative Democrats—in other words, Roosevelt's political opponents—gained control of the legislature in that year's midterm elections. Without a majority in Congress supporting him, Roosevelt could not enact any more progressive programs. On top of that, Roosevelt's court-packing scheme had taken a toll on his reputation. Many members of Congress had turned against him.

The passage of the Fair Labor Standards Act was among Roosevelt's few legislative achievements in 1938. The act stipulated a minimum hourly wage and a maximum 40-hour workweek. It immediately raised the wages of almost a million American workers and shortened the work hours of millions as well. The act also finally abolished child labor in most industries. As you have read, prior to the passage of the Fair Labor Standards Act, child labor was a common practice. In 1900, for example, 18 percent of American workers were under age 16. Now American children could concentrate on their education rather than on helping to support their families.

Without the support of Congress, most of the New Deal programs came to an end from a lack of funding in 1939. However, the nation's economic battle was not completely won. More than 8 million Americans were still unemployed. Roosevelt's critics pointed out that the New Deal strategy may have offered a measure of protection for unemployed and vulnerable workers, but it had not restored the nation to the prosperity of the 1920s. As it turned out, it would take another world war—and the full **mobilization**, or enlistment of soldiers, that followed—to bring back prosperity.

HISTORICAL THINKING

1. **READING CHECK** Why were most New Deal programs discontinued?

2. **MAKE CONNECTIONS** What types of economic indicators contributed to a recession in 1937?

3. **DRAW CONCLUSIONS** Why do you think a ban on child labor passed during the time of the New Deal?

4. **SUMMARIZE** What controversies and negative effects was Roosevelt concerned about in terms of the New Deal?

THE NEW DEAL'S IMPACT

Without realizing it, you've probably encountered the New Deal in your everyday life. If you have a part-time job, you may be paying Social Security tax. If you have a bank account, your money is safe because it's insured by an agency that was part of the New Deal.

AN EXPANDED GOVERNMENT ROLE

When the Great Depression began, some people believed restricting government spending was the best way to make the economy bounce back. But President Roosevelt did just the opposite. As you have read, he took an active role in combatting the economic crisis by enacting the New Deal and following a policy of **deficit spending**, or spending more money than the government receives from taxes.

The New Deal pumped millions of dollars into the economy by creating federal jobs. It regulated banking and investment activities and increased the government's participation in the settlement of labor disputes. The New Deal also set the precedent of providing federal aid to farmers.

As you have read, the Supreme Court nullified some New Deal legislation, claiming programs were unconstitutional because they gave the executive branch of the government too much authority. Because of the new powers assumed by the executive branch, some historians have labeled the New Deal as the beginning of the **Imperial Presidency**, a presidency that exercises more power than the Constitution allows.

Some New Deal programs, such as the National Industrial Recovery Act and the WPA, reflected the principle that government has a responsibility for its citizens' welfare. Such New Deal innovations as unions' right to collective bargaining, a minimum wage, a 40-hour workweek, and Social Security also reflected that principle. Thus, the New Deal contributed to the idea of the modern **welfare state**, a system in which the government provides for the health and well-being of its citizens.

CONSERVATIVE RESPONSES

Conservatives had criticized Roosevelt's New Deal policies from the start. They believed the New Deal expanded the size and power of the federal government too much, while curbing free enterprise. They also argued that the New Deal had not reached its goals. Pointing to continuing unemployment and poverty, they claimed the New Deal had been no kind of deal at all. Some liberals, who felt the New Deal could do more to remedy social and economic problems, joined the conservatives in this criticism.

Among the New Deal's most vocal critics was Ohio senator **Robert A. Taft**, the son of former president William Howard Taft. Although he supported some New Deal programs, such as unemployment insurance, he opposed big government and thought the New Deal exhibited some of its worst aspects, from wasteful spending to excessive interference in business. The New Deal's overregulation and high taxes hurt business, Taft asserted, accusing its supporters of attacking "individual opportunity, initiative, and freedom." He continued to be a thorn in progressives' sides throughout his career.

LASTING PROGRAMS

Today, supporters and critics agree on one aspect of the New Deal: its lasting impact on the United States. Many Americans still depend on government agencies and programs that began with the New Deal. For example, most Americans take advantage of Social Security at some time. Although never intended to provide a full pension, Social Security does grant senior citizens a measure of security and a hedge against poverty. It also aids workers who have become disabled or temporarily unemployed.

The Hoover Dam
Arizona and Nevada

Designed to control flooding of the Colorado River and to provide water to western states, the Hoover Dam was built during the Great Depression and employed more than 21,000 workers. Its construction was a huge and dangerous undertaking, claiming more than 90 lives.

The **Federal Deposit Insurance Corporation (FDIC)**, which insures the savings accounts of individual bank depositors, was part of the Glass-Steagall Banking Act of 1933. The FDIC continues to protect bank customers, insuring their deposits for up to $250,000 against loss in the event of a bank failure. After decades of urging from the big banks, Congress repealed most of the Glass-Steagall Banking Act in 1999, but it left the FDIC in place.

Another New Deal agency that still exists is the **Securities and Exchange Commission (SEC)**, created in 1934. As you have read, the economic crash in 1929 that caused the Great Depression was driven by the collapse of the stock market. Roosevelt created the SEC to protect investors in the stock market in ways similar to how the FDIC insures bank depositors. The SEC continues to oversee the stock market today, regulating stock-trading procedures and managing the nation's economic growth.

The National Labor Relations Board also continues to meet to this day. The board mediates labor disputes between unions and employers. Under the New Deal, workers gained protection of their right to organize and negotiate collectively with employers.

Thousands of bridges, dams, highways, schools, and other construction projects that remain today are another major legacy of the New Deal. Large public works projects, including the Hoover Dam, the Bonneville Dam, the California Central Valley Project, and the Tennessee Valley Authority, changed the lives of millions of Americans, providing them with flood control, irrigation, and electrical power.

HISTORICAL THINKING

1. **READING CHECK** How did the New Deal expand the role of the federal government in the nation's economy?

2. **DETERMINE CHRONOLOGY** What sequence of events led to the establishment of the Securities and Exchange Commission, and what is its function today?

3. **FORM AND SUPPORT OPINIONS** Do you agree or disagree with conservative critics of the New Deal? Give reasons for your opinion.

VOCABULARY

Use each of the following vocabulary words in a sentence that shows an understanding of the term's meaning.

1. **lame duck**
   Once Roosevelt won the 1932 presidential election, President Hoover was a lame duck.

2. **economic planning**

3. **First Hundred Days**

4. **New Deal**

5. **court-packing plan**

6. **voting bloc**

7. **collective bargaining**

8. **mobilization**

9. **deficit spending**

READING STRATEGY
DETERMINE CHRONOLOGY

Use a time line like the one below to organize the major events of the 1930s. Include dates and notes on the events. Then answer the question.

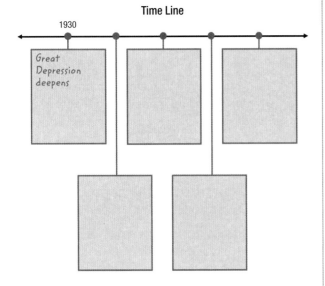

Time Line

1930

Great Depression deepens

10. How did New Deal policies change the lives of ordinary Americans?

MAIN IDEAS

Answer the following questions. Support your answers with evidence from the chapter.

11. In what way did Franklin Roosevelt's 1932 election indicate a change in direction for the country? **LESSON 1.1**

12. What did President Roosevelt accomplish in the First Hundred Days? **LESSON 1.2**

13. How did planned scarcity help the nation's economy recover? **LESSON 1.2**

14. What was the purpose of the Social Security Act? **LESSON 2.1**

15. What was the main goal of the Wagner Act? **LESSON 2.3**

16. How did Eleanor Roosevelt serve as the "conscience" of the Roosevelt administration? **LESSON 3.1**

17. Who was Mary McLeod Bethune? **LESSON 3.2**

18. Why did President Roosevelt view his New Deal programs as short-term solutions? **LESSON 4.1**

19. What New Deal programs still exist today? **LESSON 4.2**

HISTORICAL THINKING

Answer the following questions. Support your answers with evidence from the chapter.

20. **SYNTHESIZE** How did the New Deal attempt to remedy problems created by the Great Depression?

21. **MAKE INFERENCES** Why do you think President Roosevelt gathered the advisers known as the brain trust around him during the beginning of his presidency?

22. **COMPARE AND CONTRAST** How were the AFL and the CIO alike and different?

23. **MAKE PREDICTIONS** What direction might the country have taken during the Depression if FDR had not been elected president?

24. **DETERMINE CHRONOLOGY** What events led to increased labor union membership and activity in the 1930s?

25. **FORM AND SUPPORT OPINIONS** Was the development of an activist government during the 1930s positive or negative? Support your opinion with evidence from the chapter.

ANALYZE VISUALS

On February 11, 1937, the *Buffalo* [New York] *Evening News* ran a cartoon by Billy Warren portraying FDR walking up some steps with a cane. Study the cartoon and answer the questions that follow.

26. What actions do the steps on the stairs represent?

27. What does the cartoon reveal about the artist's bias toward FDR's actions?

ANALYZE SOURCES

In 1998, the National Parks Service interviewed men about their work for the CCC during the Depression. In the transcript that follows, Reed Engle (RE) interviews Arthur Emory (AE), a former CCC worker. Read the excerpt and answer the question.

RE: What do you think was the best thing about the CCC experience?

AE: The chance for learning. You see most of the people that went in there had dropped out of school. And they were just allowed to roam the street. Which was bad—that'd get you in a heap of trouble. It kind of gave them a chance to get their feet on the ground. So they could learn if they wanted to, which most of them did. It was actually the best thing that ever happened to kids our age at that time. Because you actually earned your way in it. They learned to do so many different things. Like, nobody wants to use a shovel, I don't believe. But they had to learn to use a shovel, and everybody learned something.

—from an interview with Arthur Emory, former CCC employee, 1998

28. How might this employee's experiences and personal biases have shaped his views toward the benefits of working for the CCC?

CONNECT TO YOUR LIFE

29. **INFORMATIVE** Research a New Deal artifact in your state, such as a WPA building or work of art. Write an essay describing the artifact and explaining how it reflects the New Deal.

TIPS

- Revisit the Curating History feature in this chapter. Then find more WPA artifacts at the Milwaukee Public Museum website.

- Organize your research in a two-column chart. In the first, write notes about the artifact. In the second, indicate how that information reflects the New Deal.

- Be sure to identify the New Deal agency that produced the artifact, the agency director, and who worked on the artifact, if possible. Cite information from the chapter describing the purpose of the agency.

- Conclude the essay with a paragraph that sums up what the artifact reveals about the New Deal's effects on American life.

NATIONAL GEOGRAPHIC | CONNECTION

The Hidden World of the Great War

BY EVAN HADINGHAM

Adapted from "The Hidden World of the Great War," by Evan Hadingham, in *National Geographic*, August 2014

The entrance is a small hole in the earth in northeastern France. I'm following Jeff Gusky, a photographer and physician from Texas who has explored dozens of underground spaces like this one. Here, shortly after the outbreak of the First World War, German military engineers would take turns listening for the slightest sound of enemy tunnelers. Muffled voices or the scraping of shovels meant that a hostile mining team might be only yards away. The danger grew if the digging stopped and you heard the sounds of the enemy laying high explosives at the end of the tunnel. Most nerve-racking of all was the silence that followed. At any moment the charges might detonate and blow you apart or bury you alive.

Nearby, on one of the tunnel walls, our headlamps illuminate graffiti left by the German engineers who manned this listening post. The pencil marks appear as if they were written yesterday. The soft chalk and limestone bedrock of France's Picardy region was ideal for World War I soldiers to record their presence in penciled signatures, sketches and caricatures, carvings, and even intricate relief sculptures.

The conflict began with confidence on all sides that the fighting would be over by Christmas. By the end of 1914, the German advance had stalled, the armies had dug in, and an extensive network of trenches stretched from the North Sea coast to the Swiss border. In the grip of this deadly stalemate, the Germans, French, and British resorted to siege-warfare techniques that had changed little over the centuries. The goal was to dig under key enemy strongpoints and blow them up.

But the underground war was not confined to narrow tunnels. Beneath Picardy's fields and forests are centuries-old abandoned quarries, some of which could shelter thousands of troops. One morning, we explore one such site, led there by the owner of the property. In one cavern, we peer at an array of finely engraved badges and memorials proclaiming the French regiments that had sheltered here. Then we encounter several chapels elaborately carved and painted with religious symbols, army insignia, and the names of notable French victories.

Life in the quarries was vastly preferable to the muddy hell of the trenches above. A journalist visiting one of the caverns in 1915 noted that "a dry shelter, straw, some furniture, a fire, are great luxuries for those returning from the trenches."

The quarries kept an even temperature year-round, but as one French soldier wrote home, "vermin devour us, and it's teeming with lice, fleas, rats and mice." To pass the time, the exhausted men would daydream. Images of women proliferate on the quarry walls, including many sentimental and idealized portraits.

Both sides converted the largest quarries into underground cities, many of them remarkably intact today. Not far from the landowner's property, we find ourselves in an astonishing quarry that stretches for more than seven miles, with twisting passageways and high ceilings. In 1915, the Germans connected this network to their frontline trenches. They installed electric lights and telephones, command posts, a bakery, a butcher's shop, a machine shop, a hospital, and a chapel.

The original diesel generator and barbed wire defenses are still in place. So are dozens of street signs neatly stenciled on every corner. On the cavern walls, German troops have inscribed their names and regiments, religious and military icons, elaborately sculpted portraits and caricatures, and sketches of dogs and other cartoons.

Safe underground from the inhuman chaos of the battlefield above, the men of the First World War left these personal expressions of identity and survival. Gusky's images bring to light the subterranean world soldiers inhabited and endured while sheltering from constant shellfire.

The traces they left behind reveal a forgotten world of World War I. They also connect us to individual soldiers, many of whom would not survive the nightmare of trench warfare.

For more from National Geographic check out "1918 Flu Pandemic" online.

UNIT INQUIRY: Create a Conflict Resolution Strategy

In this unit, you learned about conflicts the United States confronted on global, national, and local levels. From fighting in World War I to addressing political and labor unrest, embracing rights for women, and managing a massive economic downturn, American leaders and citizens alike had to navigate through new territories. Based on your understanding of the text, which conflict resolution strategies worked best? Which failed? How important were leaders' approaches in producing a positive or negative outcome?

ASSIGNMENT

Create a strategy you think could have been successful in resolving a conflict that took place in the United States between 1914 and 1940. Take into account factors that led to the conflict. Be prepared to present and defend your strategy to the class.

Plan As you create your conflict resolution strategy, think about the context in which the conflict unfolded, including the clash of old and new ideas of nationalism, government, and individual human rights. Also consider the impact of war, migration, and expanded citizenship. List the factors that sparked conflict, and address the most significant ones in your strategy. Use a graphic organizer to organize your thoughts.

Goals	Obstacles	Outcome
Summary		

Produce Use your notes to produce a detailed description of your conflict and design a solid conflict resolution strategy. Write your descriptions in outline or paragraph form.

Present Present your strategy to the class. You might consider one of these options:

- Host a debate on a conflict that you have learned about in this unit. Select volunteers to represent both sides of the conflict. Provide a short summary of the conflict to remind the audience of the main issues. Then have an appointed moderator pose prepared questions for the debaters. Allow time for the audience to pose questions as well. Conclude with a vote by the audience on which debaters proposed the best resolution to the conflict.

- Launch a campaign. Create election posters that summarize a conflict and its causes and that propose viable resolutions to the problem. Include a name for your campaign, slogans, and information that communicates the core issues.

- Write a speech that describes the origins of and proposes a resolution for the conflict through use of relevant factual evidence and sound reasoning.

NATIONAL GEOGRAPHIC | LEARNING FRAMEWORK ACTIVITIES

Write a Conflict Negotiator Profile

ATTITUDE Curiosity

KNOWLEDGE Our Human Story

Choose a historical figure you read about in this unit who demonstrated good conflict resolution skills. Research primary and secondary sources to gather evidence about his or her role in negotiating a resolution to a conflict. Note discrepancies among sources. Then write a profile for this individual or create something more visual, such as a poster or digital presentation. Your profile should include information such as birth and death dates, where the person lived, and the work she or he did. Your profile must also highlight a specific resolution to a conflict this person helped negotiate. Consider exploring what you think might have happened if she or he had not taken proactive action in negotiating a resolution.

Settle a Dispute

ATTITUDES Empowerment, Responsibility

SKILLS Collaboration, Problem Solving

Collaborate with a small group to research a dispute in your school or community. Assign roles to group members, such as researcher, interviewer, writer, and presenter. Scan the news and other diverse sources to gather evidence about the dispute, including people or groups on both (or all) sides of the conflict and important dates or events. Then, as a group, create a document or set up a poster or whiteboard on which you can chart the evidence you gather. Hold a meeting to discuss how your group might settle the dispute. Use the evidence you have gathered to put together a viable proposal. Once your group has settled on a solution, present both the dispute and your solution to the class.

As you will learn in this unit, World War II involved countries on almost every continent. After the major Allied powers, the United States and Great Britain, liberated North Africa from the Axis powers of Italy and Germany, they set out to defeat the Italian and German forces in Europe. The Allies' Italian campaign began with the invasion in July 1943 of the island of Sicily, where they successfully drove out German and Italian troops and prepared to assault the Italian mainland. Just outside the city of Palermo, Sicilian civilians (shown below) rejoice at the sight of American troops, cheering as the soldiers' jeeps and trucks navigate the rubble of the city's streets.

A NEW WORLD POWER

THE UNITED STATES

1945
The United States drops two atomic bombs on Japan; Japan and Germany surrender, ending World War II. *(an atomic bomb similar to those dropped on Japan)*

1942
Roosevelt issues Executive Order 9066, authorizing the internment of Japanese Americans in relocation centers.

1947
President Harry Truman signs a bill that would give rise to the Truman Doctrine, pledging support to democratic countries threatened by communist aggression.

1941
Japan attacks the naval base at Hawaii's Pearl Harbor, and the United States enters World War II. *(newspaper announcing the attack)*

1935
Roosevelt signs the first Neutrality Act in an effort to avoid involvement in future wars.

1940

1932
Franklin D. Roosevelt is elected to the first of his four terms as president.

1930

THE WORLD

1944 EUROPE
Allied forces invade Normandy, a region in France, and liberate western Europe from German control.

1933 EUROPE
Adolf Hitler is appointed chancellor of Germany.

1931 ASIA
Japan invades and conquers Manchuria, a northern province of China. *(Japanese naval flag)*

1949 ASIA
Communists defeat nationalist forces in China, and Mao Zedong becomes the leader of the new communist nation. *(poster featuring Mao Zedong)*

HISTORICAL THINKING

DETERMINE CHRONOLOGY What world events might have prompted the passage of the Neutrality Act in 1935?

1956
Congress passes the Interstate Highway Act, which calls for the construction of an extensive interstate highway system.
(car from the 1950s)

1960
John F. Kennedy becomes the youngest man ever elected president.
(profile of Kennedy on a half-dollar coin)

1953
Julius and Ethel Rosenberg are executed after being convicted of spying for the Soviet Union.

1954
Wisconsin senator Joseph McCarthy's campaign to expose communist subversion in government comes to an end when he accuses U.S. Army personnel.

1952
Dwight D. Eisenhower is elected president.

1960

1950

1959 AMERICAS
Fidel Castro leads a band of revolutionaries in Cuba and overthrows military dictator Fulgencio Batista.
(Castro and his fellow revolutionaries celebrate their victory.)

1957 EUROPE
The Soviets launch *Sputnik 1*, the first artificial satellite to orbit Earth, and trigger the space race between the United States and the U.S.S.R.

1952 AFRICA
The Mau Mau, a militant nationalist group in Kenya, revolts against British rule.

1950 ASIA
The Korean War begins.

HISTORICAL THINKING What ideas and events brought about
World War II?

"We shall never surrender."

—Winston Churchill

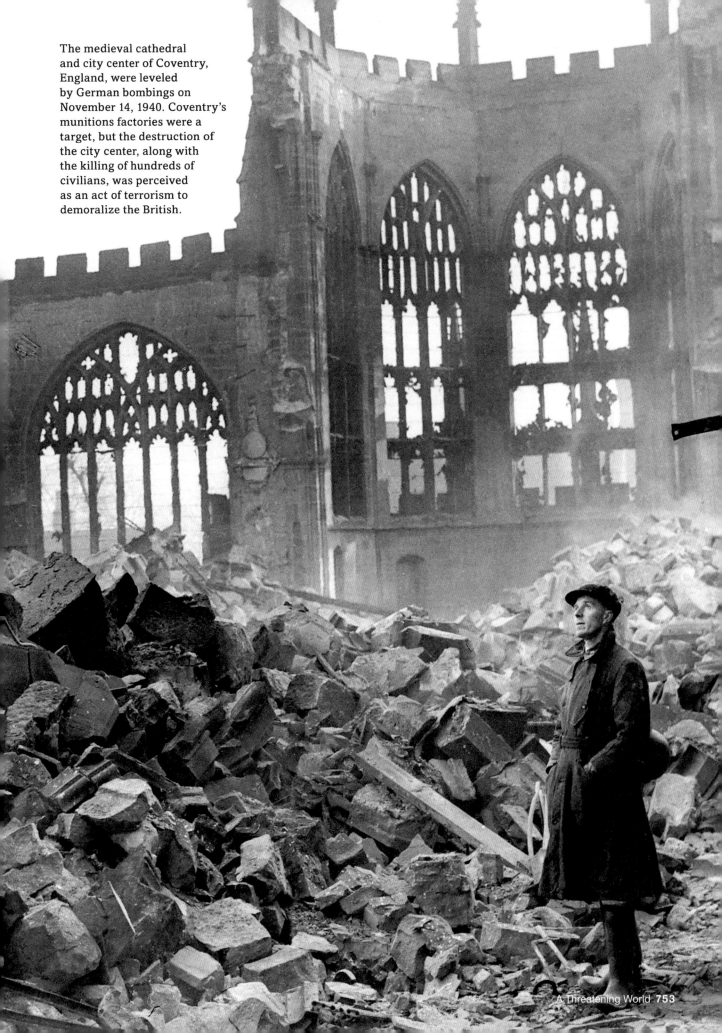

The medieval cathedral and city center of Coventry, England, were leveled by German bombings on November 14, 1940. Coventry's munitions factories were a target, but the destruction of the city center, along with the killing of hundreds of civilians, was perceived as an act of terrorism to demoralize the British.

FASCISM SPREADS IN EUROPE

Would you give up any of your personal freedoms to be more economically secure or more physically safe? Some people might say they would protect freedom at all costs, but history proves that security often comes first. That was certainly true in Europe in the 1930s.

TOTALITARIANISM TIGHTENS ITS GRIP

As the United States worked to pull itself out of the Great Depression, the nations of Europe were undergoing dramatic political change. With many European economies also suffering during the 1930s, great anxiety and unrest spread across the continent. Authoritarian leaders took advantage of the turmoil and uncertainty to seize power in several countries. They took control of government, built powerful armies, and looked to expand their territory.

As you have read, Adolf Hitler and his Nazi Party seized control in Germany. Hitler had risen to power as the German economy collapsed under the weight of the global depression. Millions listened as Hitler promised to create jobs, restore what he perceived as Germany's past glory, and avenge the "humiliation" of the Treaty of Versailles, which ended World War I. Nazi representation in the Reichstag, the German parliament, rose from 12 members in 1928 to 230 by 1932. A year later, Hitler became Germany's chancellor, or the head of its government.

Hitler's regime, which the Nazi Party dubbed the **Third Reich**, suspended constitutional rights and banned all competing political parties. *Reich* means "empire," and the term Third Reich acknowledged two powerful German states of the past while envisioning a strong, prosperous state that would endure into the future. The Nazis transformed German police departments into the **Gestapo**, a brutal secret police force that went after Hitler's political opponents and anyone else whom the Nazis deemed an enemy of the Reich.

Hitler began a massive **rearmament**, a rebuilding of Germany's stockpile of weapons. By 1934, German

THE CROOKED CROSS

Before it became associated with the Nazis, the swastika (pictured on the flags in the photo on the next page) was known as an ancient symbol of good fortune. In the ancient Asian language of Sanskrit, the word *swastika* means "well-being." At the beginning of the 20th century, many in the West saw it as a good luck symbol. The Boy Scouts adopted it, and the Girls' Club of America called their official magazine *Swastika*. The Nazis interpreted the cross as a symbol of racial superiority and adopted it as their party logo. After World War II, the swastika was banned in Germany and today is almost universally seen as a symbol of hate.

factories were churning out tanks and military aircraft at an ever-increasing rate. Hitler then began building an army by instituting a draft that forced men 20 or older to join the military. In 1936, in clear violation of the Treaty of Versailles, Nazi forces marched into the Rhineland, a region of Germany that had been occupied by the French after World War I. German soldiers conquered it without firing a shot.

Meanwhile, Benito Mussolini—the fascist dictator who had risen to power in Italy in the early 1920s— had dreams of recreating the Roman Empire by conquering territory in Africa. In October 1935, Mussolini invaded Ethiopia, a nation in east-central Africa. The League of Nations condemned the act, but that did little to stop Mussolini. Italian forces took the capital, Addis Ababa, in May 1936 and annexed Ethiopia to Italy. Several months later, in October, Mussolini signed a pact of friendship with Hitler,

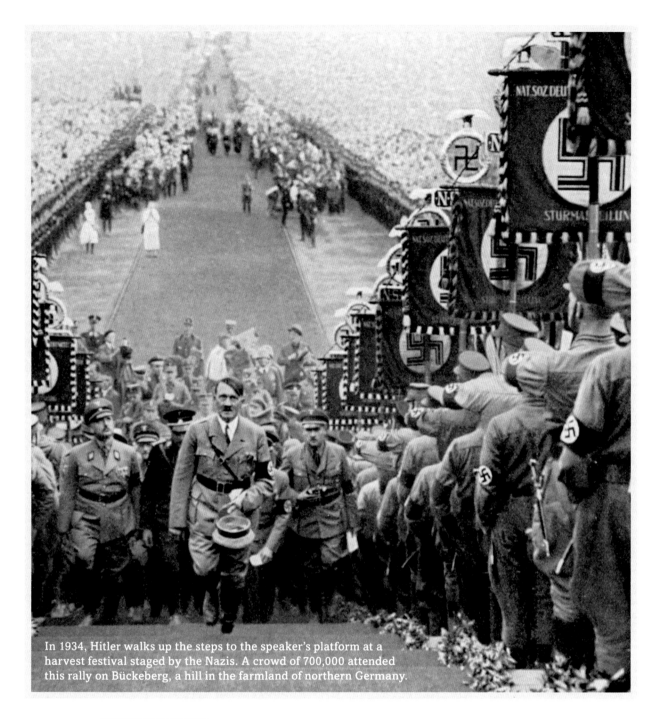

In 1934, Hitler walks up the steps to the speaker's platform at a harvest festival staged by the Nazis. A crowd of 700,000 attended this rally on Bückeberg, a hill in the farmland of northern Germany.

known as the **Rome-Berlin Axis**. Germany, Italy, and later Japan, would become known as the **Axis Powers**. The countries eventually opposing them would be referred to as the **Allied Powers**.

While Italy and Germany were hardening into dictatorships, **Joseph Stalin** was tightening his totalitarian grip on the Soviet Union. Stalin had come to power in 1924, and he steadily transformed his country from a peasant society into an industrial and military superpower. He ruled by terror during his brutal reign. Stalin expanded the powers of his secret police force, encouraged citizens to spy on one another, and had millions of people executed or sent to labor camps.

THE SPANISH CIVIL WAR

In 1936, civil war broke out in Spain, and Europe's dictators were eager to get involved. Spanish military officers led by **General Francisco Franco** attempted to overthrow the recently elected Spanish government, called the Republicans. Franco represented the Nationalists, a fascist group, and Hitler and Mussolini provided him with military aid, such as tanks, planes, and other weapons. Mussolini also sent 70,000 troops. Meanwhile, Stalin aided the Republicans, who represented a coalition of left wing groups, including communists, socialists, and liberal democrats, by sending weapons and money to help the government in its fight against Franco and the Nationalists.

CRITICAL VIEWING

Pablo Picasso (1881–1973), born in Spain, was one of the best-known artists of the 20th century. The large painting *Guernica*, completed in 1937—two years before Franco's victory—was the artist's reaction to the bombing of a northern Spanish coastal village by the German and Italian air forces in support of Franco's Nationalists. The title of the painting is the name of the village they destroyed, including its homes and shops, killing an estimated 1,650 people. Perhaps most disturbing, the attack was a terrorist bombing whose primary target was the civilians of the town. The first bomb fell on the center of the town on a market day.

Picasso used black, white, and gray shades of paint, depicting distorted human and animal forms and anguished facial expressions. Also shown are symbols of transition from a traditional to a modern world—a light bulb inside the sun and shapes filled with newsprint. According to Picasso's wishes, the painting was kept in New York's Museum of Modern Art until Spain restored its democracy. In 1981, the painting returned to Spain. At about 11 feet high by 25 feet wide, the painting occupies an entire wall in Madrid's Reina Sofia Museum. In applying the techniques he used, what do you think Picasso wanted visitors to feel as they viewed the painting?

Many international volunteers joined the war, including some from the United States. Some Americans praised Franco as an enemy of communism. However, many viewed him as a fascist thug trying to overthrow an elected government.

A group of several thousand Americans known as the **Abraham Lincoln Brigade** fought alongside the Spanish government. The famous American writer Ernest Hemingway, who covered the war as a reporter, summed up the anti-Franco view: "There is only one way to quell a bully and that is to thrash him." The fighting was widespread and brutal, with more than 500,000 killed. The war ended in 1939 with a complete victory for General Franco and his forces. Another dictator had taken power in Europe.

PERSECUTION OF JEWS

As Europe's dictators engaged in military actions outside their borders, they also tightened their grip on the home front. Their regimes silenced critics and oppressed people whom they deemed "undesirable." In Germany, the Nazis sought to reshape society according to their vision of a pure German "master race." The Nazis believed all other races and ethnicities to be inferior, and they targeted one group in particular: Jews.

In Europe, anti-Semitism, or hostility toward and discrimination against Jewish people, had deep historical roots. Many Europeans accused Jews of working to remain a separate social and religious group that refused to adopt the values of the countries in which they lived. After Germany's defeat in World War I, many Germans believed the German Army was betrayed by politicians, especially Jewish politicians. In addition, a number of Jews worked in the banking and money-lending industries, making them easy scapegoats for Germany's financial problems.

When the Nazis gained power, the persecution of Jews became government policy. Nazis began to exclude Jews from public life. At the annual Nazi rally in 1935, Hitler announced laws denying Jewish people citizenship and prohibiting marriage between Jews and people of "German or related blood." Three years later, under Hitler's personal orders, the Nazis destroyed the Great Synagogue in Munich.

On November 7, 1938, a 17-year-old Polish Jew, Hershel Grynszpan (GRIHNZ-pan), shot and killed

The riots of Kristallnacht, ordered indirectly by Goebbels and intended to appear as spontaneous expressions of rage, took place throughout Germany. This Jewish-owned shop in Berlin was one of more than 7,000 businesses destroyed during the two days.

Ernst vom Rath, a German diplomat in France. Joseph Goebbels (GEH-buhlz), the Nazi propaganda minister, immediately seized on the assassination to whip up rage against Jews. What followed became known as the **Kristallnacht**—the Night of Broken Glass. Between November 9 and November 10, 1938, Nazis destroyed Jewish homes, schools, and businesses, burned synagogues, and killed nearly 100 Jews. Officials arrested 30,000 Jewish men and sent them to concentration camps. Shortly after the attacks, U.S. president Franklin D. Roosevelt denounced the rising tide of anti-Semitism and violence in Germany. He also recalled Hugh Wilson, the U.S. ambassador to Germany. Nonetheless, the persecution of Jews in Germany continued.

HISTORICAL THINKING

1. **READING CHECK** What measures did Hitler take against Germany's Jews?

2. **ANALYZE CAUSE AND EFFECT** Why is it difficult to determine a single cause for four dictators all coming to power at about the same time in Europe?

3. **FORM AND SUPPORT OPINIONS** Do you think dictators and fascist regimes would have risen to power if Europe hadn't been so economically depressed after World War I? Explain your answer.

4. **MAKE CONNECTIONS** What similarities do you see among Hitler, Mussolini, and Stalin and one of today's world leaders?

MAIN IDEA Amid the growing possibility of another large-scale war, many Americans wanted the United States to remain neutral and to isolate itself from foreign conflict.

ISOLATIONISM AND NEUTRALITY

Maybe you have been in situations where you had your own conflicting opinions about an issue. In the 1930s, many Americans did not like what was happening in Europe, but they had concerns about the United States getting involved.

AVOIDING INVOLVEMENT IN EUROPE

As authoritarian leaders rose to power in Europe, U.S. president Franklin Roosevelt watched with increasing alarm. Roosevelt felt very early on that Hitler posed a threat to the world unlike any other. However, a majority of Americans did not feel the same way. Many had no wish to get involved in the turmoil they saw threatening Europe.

Americans voiced many reasons for wanting to stay out of the growing conflict. In the Great Plains and Upper Midwest, some were suspicious of international bankers and arms manufacturers, believing such businesspeople were responsible for pushing the United States into World War I for their own financial gain. Americans of German descent supported isolationism because they remembered how badly German Americans were treated during World War I. Americans of Irish descent opposed any kind of aid to Great Britain because of conflicts between Ireland and Great Britain, while many Americans of Italian descent admired Mussolini, due to a propaganda campaign by the dictator meant to win over Italian Americans. Furthermore, pacifism, the belief that war is morally wrong, appealed to clergy, peace groups, and many college students.

Following the will of the American public, the U.S. Congress passed a series of Neutrality Acts. The first act, passed in 1935, banned the export of "arms, ammunition, and implements of war" from the United States to any foreign nation at war. President Roosevelt opposed the act, but bowed to pressure from Congress and the public to maintain neutrality. Congress renewed the act in 1936 and 1937, and expanded it. U.S. citizens were now forbidden from traveling on ships owned by nations at war, and the United States could bar any warring ships from entering U.S. waters.

In a compromise with Roosevelt, the act did allow the United States to sell European nations materials and supplies—just not ammunition and arms. This enabled America to provide its allies with critical resources, such as oil. In an effort to limit the interaction, European nations had to arrange to pick up the materials and pay immediately in cash. The provision thus became known as "cash-and-carry."

ROOSEVELT CHALLENGES THE NATION

Standing in direct opposition to the American people and Congress, President Roosevelt continued to push for greater American involvement in Europe. He felt the United States could not remain strictly neutral, and the time would come when the democratic countries of Europe, especially Great

PRIMARY SOURCE

On October 5, 1937, President Roosevelt traveled to Chicago to speak at the dedication of a bridge completed under a New Deal program. Expected to praise the accomplishment of the bridge's construction, Roosevelt instead used the occasion to make his case for opposing tyranny in Europe. His speech at the bridge dedication became known as the **Quarantine Speech**.

The political situation in the world, which of late has been growing progressively worse, is such as to cause grave concern and anxiety to all the peoples and nations. Innocent peoples, innocent nations, are being cruelly sacrificed to a greed for power and supremacy which is devoid of all sense of justice and humane considerations. If those things come to pass in other parts of the world, let no one imagine that America will escape.

—from the Quarantine Speech, by Franklin D. Roosevelt, 1937

A GLOBAL PERSPECTIVE Refugees still flee dangerous situations and oppressive regimes to this day. In 2016, millions of men, women, and children fled a brutal civil war in the country of Syria. Hoping to find a better life in Europe, large numbers of these refugees packed into overcrowded boats and made a dangerous voyage across the Mediterranean Sea. Many died along the way. Those who made it struggled to fit in across Europe, as many nations opposed the influx of so many immigrants. For a single day in September 2016, at Parliament Square in London, international aid organizations displayed 2,500 life jackets worn by the refugees to help bring attention to their plight.

Britain, would need help from the United States. Roosevelt gave a speech in which he compared war with a disease, saying it was the responsibility of peace-loving nations to "quarantine" countries that threatened world peace.

In that speech, Roosevelt mentioned people and nations who were being "cruelly sacrificed," referring partly to the Jews suffering under the Nazi regime. But Roosevelt's speech did not go over well with the public, and the United States refused to ease the immigration restrictions that kept large numbers of German Jews from the safety of American shores. Each year between 1935 and 1941, the United States took in an average of 8,500 Jewish **refugees**, or people seeking shelter and protection from persecution. This was far below the annual quota of 30,000 for German immigrants set by the National Origins Act of 1924. Most Americans were still feeling the sting of the Depression and did not want foreigners competing with them for jobs and resources. A combination of economics, anti-

Semitism, and isolationism in the United States kept the "golden door" shut to most Jewish refugees.

Isolationists strongly criticized the president for trying to violate neutrality, while many average Americans remained opposed to deeper U.S. involvement in Europe's troubles. As Europe moved closer to war, the United States remained neutral.

HISTORICAL THINKING

1. **READING CHECK** Why did many Americans wish to remain neutral and not take sides in the growing conflicts in Europe?

2. **COMPARE AND CONTRAST** Compare the refugee crisis described in the lesson with what you know about the status of refugees today.

3. **MAKE INFERENCES** How do you think the American experience in World War I affected the country's attitude toward international events in the 1930s?

WAR ENGULFS EUROPE

Is it better to reason with a bully to achieve a compromise, or let the fight begin? The nations of Europe tried to compromise with Hitler as he rose to power and looked to conquer his neighbors. But in the end, they decided they had to fight.

THE MUNICH AGREEMENT

One of Adolf Hitler's main goals was to unite all German-speaking people into a "Greater Germany," or "Grossdeutschland." As you have read, Germany took its first steps toward this goal in 1936, when it reoccupied the Rhineland. In 1938, German troops marched into neighboring Austria. Hitler announced the "Anschluss" (AHN-shloos), or union, of Germany and Austria, adding six million German speakers to greater Germany.

With each aggressive step Hitler took, the nations of Western Europe made little attempt to confront him. Instead, Great Britain and France took an approach

Hitler's Advance, 1938–1940

Legend:
- Allied territory
- Axis powers
- Axis satellite
- Axis-controlled by 1940
- Soviet territory
- Neutral nation
- ← German troop movements

BLITZKRIEG

In invading Poland, the Germans demonstrated for the first time a new and seemingly unstoppable type of warfare—blitzkrieg (BLIHTS-kreeg), or "lightning war." Blitzkrieg was characterized first by bombing—to cripple the target's air capacity, railroads, and communication lines—followed by fast moving tanks, artillery, and waves of troops.

Using this new tactic of speed and overwhelming force, the Germans conquered Poland in a matter of weeks. In this photo, a German gunner fires from a plane attacking a Polish town.

known as **appeasement**—a policy of making political compromises in order to avoid conflict. Neither country had forgotten the horrors of World War I, and they sought to maintain peace at any price. In addition, many British politicians believed that Germany had genuine grievances, as the Treaty of Versailles had left hundreds of thousands of German-speaking people under the control of other countries in Europe. What's more, a number of Western leaders viewed communism, not fascism, as the greatest threat to Europe. Thus, they saw Hitler as a potential safeguard against Soviet expansion.

Facing little resistance, Hitler continued to invade and annex. After absorbing Austria, the German leader turned his attention to Czechoslovakia. He insisted that the Czechs surrender the Sudetenland (soo-DAY-tehn-land), a region of western Czechoslovakia where three million ethnic Germans lived. In September 1938, Hitler met with British Prime Minister Neville Chamberlain, French Premier Edouard Daladier, and Italian dictator Benito Mussolini in Munich. Under the **Munich Agreement**, the leaders agreed to Hitler's demand for the Sudetenland. In return, Hitler promised he would not occupy any more territory in Czechoslovakia. Daladier pressured the Czechs to accept the agreement and give the Sudetenland to Germany. Meanwhile, Chamberlain claimed the agreement had brought "peace in our time." Less than a year later, on March 15, 1939, Hitler violated the pact and sent German troops to seize the rest of Czechoslovakia.

GERMANY ATTACKS POLAND

In August 1939, the world was shocked to learn that two sworn enemies, fascist Nazi Germany and the communist Soviet Union, had signed a **nonaggression pact**. Under the pact, the two countries agreed to take no military action against each other for 10 years. The agreement also contained a secret section that detailed how the Soviets and Germans planned to divide up Eastern Europe. The first country targeted under their plan: Poland.

On September 1, 1939, Hitler sent the Wehrmacht—the German Army—across the German border into Poland. (The Soviets would invade weeks later and claim their share of Polish territory.) Hitler, it appeared, had finally gone too far. Two days after the German attack, Britain and France declared war on Germany. **World War II** had begun. What followed were months of quiet, known as the "phony war." During this time, the French and British hunkered down on one side of the French-German border, behind a series of fortifications known as the **Maginot** (MAJ-ih-noh) **Line**, and the Germans settled in on the other side.

GERMANY INVADES FRANCE

In April 1940, the calm came to an explosive end when German forces invaded Denmark and Norway, quickly conquering both nations and defeating British forces stationed in Norway. The defeat brought down Chamberlain's government, and he was replaced as prime minister by British statesman

Winston Churchill. Meanwhile, German forces rolled on, pushing into Belgium, Holland, and Luxembourg.

Next, Germany invaded France, and German forces seized Paris in June 1940. The French signed an armistice that divided France into two regions, one under German occupation and one under French authority, with the town of Vichy (VISH-ee) as its capital. Although French leaders oversaw Vichy, the Germans controlled the region—one of the most significant strategic outcomes of the war.

Despite the German victory, some of the French decided to fight on. The French general **Charles de Gaulle** set up headquarters in Britain to allow "Free French" forces to continue fighting as a resistance force. In the autumn of 1940, a number of French colonies in Africa declared their loyalty to de Gaulle, but they were a small force compared to the German enemy. The French resistance fighters did what they could to thwart the Nazis as the war progressed.

THE NAZIS TARGET GREAT BRITAIN

The Nazis had conquered most of Western Europe in less than two months. Now they targeted Britain. Winston Churchill rallied the British to fight on against Germany's overwhelming power, despite some calls for Britain to negotiate peace with Hitler. "We shall defend our island, whatever the cost may be," Churchill declared. "We shall fight on the landing grounds, we shall fight in the fields and in the streets, we shall fight in the hills; we shall never surrender."

From June through October 1940, British and German forces fought the **Battle of Britain**. It was primarily an air war, as Britain's Royal Air Force (RAF) and Germany's air force, the Luftwaffe (LOOFT-vahf-uh), clashed over the skies of Great Britain. Germany's attempts to bomb Britain into surrender met with stiff resistance. While German attacks inflicted heavy damage on British cities, the RAF continued fighting back and eventually forced Germany's air force to retreat. Unable to achieve victory, Hitler suspended further attacks on Britain and moved on. Referring to the RAF fighters who turned back the Germans, Churchill said, "Never in the field of human conflict was so much owed by so many to so few."

The British people suffered greatly during the Battle of Britain. Families were split up, as Londoners put their children on trains for the countryside, sending them as refugees to willing rural homes in hopes of keeping them safe from the nightly bombing. All too many children never saw their parents again, as the bombing campaign known as the London Blitz claimed the

PRIMARY SOURCE

Hitler knows that he will have to break us in this Island or lose the war. If we can stand up to him, all Europe may be free. But if we fail, then the whole world, including the United States . . . will sink into the abyss of a new Dark Age made more sinister, and perhaps more protracted, by the lights of perverted science. Let us therefore brace ourselves to our duties, and so bear ourselves that, if the British Empire and its Commonwealth last for a thousand years, men will still say, 'This was their finest hour.'

—from a speech before the House of Commons (British legislature), by Winston Churchill, 1940

lives of nearly 17,500 civilians in London. Thousands more were killed nationwide. Relentless German raids destroyed whole neighborhoods of London and other cities as the British took cover deep beneath ground in London's Tube—or subway system—or in designated bunkers and shelters. One of the more deadly attacks toward the end of the campaign killed nearly 1,500 civilians in a single night of bombing.

Across the Atlantic Ocean, Americans watched the onset of World War II with interest and alarm. Isolationists continued to argue that the country should stay out of the conflict. Interventionists insisted the United States must enter the fight to halt Hitler's march of conquest. President Roosevelt, in particular, felt that the United States should do more to help Britain. On September 21, 1939, soon after the war had begun, Roosevelt called Congress into special session. He pressed lawmakers to amend the Neutrality Act to lift the ban on arms sales and allow the United States to provide weapons to the nations threatened by Germany, specifically Great Britain. After much debate, Congress approved the amendment. The United States was slowly moving toward greater involvement in the war.

HISTORICAL THINKING

1. **READING CHECK** Explain the theory of appeasement. Why do you think it led to war in Europe?

2. **INTERPRET MAPS** From a geographical standpoint, why was it important that Germany capture France before battling with Britain?

3. **ANALYZE CAUSE AND EFFECT** How might events have taken a different turn if the world had not underestimated Hitler's intentions?

CRITICAL VIEWING British children of farmworkers take cover in a trench in southeastern England in 1940. In this photo, which appeared in *Life* magazine, the children watch an aerial fight between a British and a German fighter plane. What does the photo reveal about the children's reactions to what is happening in the sky above them?

JAPAN INVADES CHINA

By the time the nations of Europe went to war in the fall of 1939, another military power had risen on the other side of the globe. Japan was carving out an empire of its own, giving the world—and the United States—another serious threat to confront.

CHINA IN TURMOIL

China had been ruled as an empire for 2,000 years, and at the turn of the 20th century, it was poverty-stricken and underdeveloped. In 1911, a group of revolutionaries led by **Sun Yat-sen** overthrew the ruling Qing (CHING) Dynasty and established the Republic of China. Sun was elected China's first president, but he struggled to maintain control of the country—in reality ruled by a number of warlords, or local military leaders. After Sun's death in 1925,

power passed to **Chiang Kai-shek** (jee-AHNG ky-SHEHK). Chiang soon faced an armed resistance from the growing **Chinese Communist Party (CCP)**, led by **Mao Zedong** (MOW dzuh-DUNG).

In 1927, fearful of the CCP's increasing power, Chiang ordered a **purge**, or elimination, of CCP members in Shanghai and other Chinese cities. Chiang's troops, known as the Kuomintang, or KMT, killed tens of thousands of communists. By 1931, the KMT had

Mao Zedong arrives in Shaanxi Province in northern China in 1935, near the end of the Long March. Most officers rode horses, but all others walked on foot.

almost completely defeated Mao's forces. Some 700,000 KMT troops encircled communist positions in southeast China, preventing supplies from entering their territory. Hundreds of thousands of soldiers and peasants loyal to Mao were killed or died of starvation.

Facing almost certain defeat, the remaining Chinese communists decided to retreat to a more remote part of China. There, Mao hoped, the CCP could regroup and build its military power. In October 1934, at the beginning of what became known as the **Long March**, 86,000 communist troops and around 15,000 civilians marched out of southeast China, attempting to escape Chiang's KMT forces. They faced almost daily battles and skirmishes with KMT troops and local warlords, and they even were the targets of aerial bombardment. Many were killed in the fighting, and others died of starvation and exposure. Only 7,000 of the approximately 100,000 who had begun

the Long March the year before survived the journey. After the Long March, Chiang Kai-shek planned to wipe out the remaining communist forces, but by then a more serious threat had emerged from the neighboring nation of Japan.

JAPAN TAKES ACTION

By the early 20th century, Japan was a strong country with developed industries and a powerful military. In 1904, its forces had soundly defeated Russia in a war over several disputed territories in Asia. The easy victory had surprised observers and signaled that Japan was a rising world power. But as an island nation, it lacked the land and natural resources necessary for economic growth. Ambitious military leaders such as **Tojo Hideki** urged the young Japanese emperor **Hirohito** to seek out and conquer new land and build an empire. To achieve this goal, the Japanese turned their attention to China, their large neighbor to the west.

Japanese Territorial Occupation, 1931–1941

The Memorial Hall of the Victims in the Nanjing Massacre was built in 1985 in Nanjing, China. In 2015, students from the Nanjing University for the Arts painted huge Chinese violet cress flowers on the walkway before a Chinese holiday called "Tomb-Sweeping Day," when people honor their ancestors. How do the flowers contrast with other aspects of the Memorial?

China's land and resources—and its political instability—made it an attractive target to the Japanese. In 1931, as China was troubled with internal fighting, Japan invaded the Chinese province of Manchuria and made it an independent Japanese state, which it controlled completely. China turned to the League of Nations for help, and the League demanded that Japan withdraw its troops. Japan refused and withdrew from the League. By 1936, the Japanese military was in full control of Japan's government and intent on conquering new territory.

In 1937, Japan renewed its attack on China. Japanese Ambassador Hiroshi Saito defended the assault as an attempt to bring political and social order to the region. "If China's house were in order there would be no need for the presence of these foreign forces," he declared. "What our government and people want is peace and security in the Far East." Chiang reluctantly agreed to form a united front with Mao to fight the new threat, but just six months later, Japanese forces controlled all of northern China, including Beijing, Shanghai, and the Chinese capital of Nanjing. In Nanjing, Japanese forces committed horrific war crimes, actions that violate accepted international rules of war, when they killed as many as 300,000 Chinese civilians.

In November 1937, leaders of 18 nations met in the European city of Brussels to discuss ways of ending the conflict between Japan and China. The **Brussels Conference**, as it was known, ended with a call for Japan to cease all hostilities against its neighbor. The decree had little effect, however, as Japan had refused to attend the conference and claimed that western nations had no business meddling in its affairs.

TENSIONS RISE

At first, the United States did little to contest Japan's aggression. U.S. leaders were more concerned about the rise of Nazi Germany, and they hoped to avoid

PRIMARY SOURCE

Captain Frank Roberts was aboard the *Panay* during the attack. He recalled how he narrowly escaped death.

I had only taken a couple of steps when a shower of fragments [bomb pieces] hit me in the back and knocked me to my hands and knees. At the same time, I heard the sound of a machine gun and the splatter of bullets against the ship's side. Almost simultaneously, another bomb exploded to port, knocking down some of the bunks and breaking more glass. Being dazed and dizzy, I remained on the floor for some moments while two other bombs exploded somewhere near. Later I discovered that a bullet or a metal fragment had torn a three-inch rip in my left trouser leg at the top of the pocket. Still later, I found holes in my coat, the largest at the left shoulder, and there was a severe bruise, although the bullet or fragment did not penetrate.

—from *The Panay Incident,*
  by Hamilton Darby Perry, 1969

a crisis with Japan. In December 1937, Japanese warplanes sank the U.S. gunboat *Panay* on China's Yangtze (yang-tsee) River, killing 3 Americans and wounding nearly 30. President Roosevelt condemned the attack, but Japan apologized and the two nations settled the matter peacefully.

Japan, however, continued to expand its empire. In 1938, Japanese forces annexed European colonies in Southeast Asia and the Western Pacific. U.S. Secretary of State Cordell Hull warned that "Japan definitely contemplates securing domination over as many hundreds of millions of people as possible in eastern Asia." The United States responded to Japan's continued conquests by pulling back on trade. Japan purchased the bulk of its oil, steel, and machinery from America. In an effort to slow Japanese expansion, President Roosevelt declared an embargo, barring U.S. companies from selling a number of strategic industrial goods, such as oil and copper, to Japan. In May 1940, the president moved the headquarters of the U.S. Pacific Fleet from San Diego, California, to Pearl Harbor, Hawaii. The move was intended to enable the U.S. Navy to keep a closer watch on Japan. The United States had a base in the Philippines, but it was not prepared for war.

Relations grew more strained in September 1940, when Japan signed a war agreement with Germany and Italy, forming the Axis powers. They agreed to assist one another if any one of them were attacked by a nation not already involved in the war. Roosevelt retaliated by freezing all Japanese assets in the United States and blocking shipments of scrap iron and aviation fuel to Japan. Japanese Foreign Minister Teijiro Toyoda declared, "Commercial and economic relations between Japan and third countries, led by England and the United States, are gradually becoming so horribly strained that we cannot endure it much longer." The United States and Japan were now openly at odds, and tensions were mounting.

HISTORICAL THINKING

1. **READING CHECK** Who were the opposing sides in China's civil war?

2. **INTERPRET MAPS** Based on the information on the map, why was conquering China so appealing to Japan?

3. **EVALUATE** What led to the growing tensions between Japan and the United States?

MAIN IDEA At the onset of World War II, U.S. foreign policy reflected a struggle between Americans who wanted to maintain neutrality and those who favored greater involvement in the widening conflict.

SUPPORTING THE ALLIES

The question on every American's mind was, "Should the United States go to war, or should it stay neutral?" Even as Americans continued to debate this issue, the nation took greater steps to support the Allies.

A THIRD TERM FOR FDR

As the 1940 presidential election approached, the leading campaign issue was the war raging in Europe. France had fallen, and Great Britain was fighting alone against the Axis Powers. In this atmosphere of turmoil, President Roosevelt took the unprecedented step of running for a third term in the White House. No American president had ever served a third term. Roosevelt felt it was his duty to continue to lead the United States through the current world crisis, so he allowed himself to be drafted by the Democratic National Convention in 1940 as their candidate. Meanwhile, the Republicans nominated lawyer and businessman Wendell Willkie of Indiana as their presidential candidate.

The 1940 presidential campaign intensified the debate over U.S. neutrality. Roosevelt favored greater intervention, while Willkie took a more isolationist stance. "The President's attacks on foreign powers have been useless and dangerous," Willkie declared. "He has courted a war for which the country is hopelessly unprepared—and which it emphatically does not want."

As you have read, Roosevelt had persuaded Congress to amend the Neutrality Act in 1939 to lift the ban on arms sales to U.S. allies and continue cash-and-carry. American ships, however, were still barred from transporting goods to ports of **belligerents**, or the countries already fighting in the war. In September 1940, at Britain's request, and without informing Congress, Roosevelt took the step of supplying the British with 50 old but usable destroyers. In return, the United States obtained the rights to establish naval bases in various British territories. The agreement outraged isolationists, who viewed it as a clear violation of American neutrality.

Nonetheless, Roosevelt easily defeated Willkie in the November election, with about 27 million votes to 22 million votes (449 electoral votes to 82 electoral votes). Although many Americans were opposed to involvement in the war, most were rooting against Germany. A national poll in 1940 found that 83 percent of U.S. citizens favored a British victory. Many Americans believed that if Britain fell to the Nazis, the United States would be on its own and potentially Germany's next target.

AN "ARSENAL OF DEMOCRACY"

After his re-election, Roosevelt continued nudging the United States toward greater involvement in the war. In December 1940, the president declared the nation must devote its industrial might to helping Britain. "We must be the great arsenal of democracy," Roosevelt proclaimed. "For us this is an emergency as serious as war itself." An arsenal is a place where weapons are stored. In his declaration, Roosevelt indicated he envisioned the United States as the major supplier of arms for its allies. He went on to say, "No dictator . . . will weaken [our] determination."

Even before Roosevelt's declaration, the nation had begun ramping up its war effort. In August 1940, Congress passed the first peacetime draft in U.S. history. Like the original Selective Service Act from World War I, the **Selective Service and Training Act** again required able-bodied young men to register for potential military service. Congress also allocated $10.5 billion for defense spending. American factories began working around the clock to build weaponry, including tanks, warplanes, and warships. Unemployment virtually disappeared. The United States' urgent push to build up its arsenal had finally ended the Great Depression.

The "arsenal of democracy" included U.S.-made aircraft. In this 1940 photograph, a worker in a Los Angeles aircraft plant completes tail-fin assemblies for warplanes built for the Allies.

THE LEND-LEASE ACT

As the United States increased its military production, Winston Churchill sent a plea for help to Roosevelt. Churchill told the president that Great Britain was in deep financial trouble and unable to pay for arms from the United States. Roosevelt responded by crafting the **Lend-Lease Act**, which enabled countries to receive American military aid without immediately paying for it.

Proposed in late 1940 and passed on March 11, 1941, the Lend-Lease Act allowed the president to deliver arms and other defense materials to "the government of any country whose defense the President deems vital to the defense of the United States." The act enabled the United States to more directly aid nations at war against the Axis powers, while technically remaining neutral. Isolationists, such as Republican senator Robert Taft from Ohio, strongly opposed Lend-Lease as a violation of neutrality. FDR's isolationist opponents also included Henry Ford and Charles Lindbergh, who organized the America First Committee (AFC). The AFC opposed every effort by the president to move away from neutrality, and it strongly contested Lend-Lease.

Despite Taft's and the AFC's opposition, Lend-Lease proceeded, allowing the United States to supply weapons to the Allied powers.

Lindbergh argued that by supporting one side or another, the United States was being used to aid in that country's domination of the continent. He did not evaluate the countries of Europe in terms of their ideology or aggressiveness, but viewed them all as equally seeking advantage over the others. In his mind, there was no justification for sending Americans to further those causes. Some perceived Lindbergh's position as support for the Nazis.

HISTORICAL THINKING

1. **READING CHECK** Why did Franklin Roosevelt want to run for a third term as president?

2. **COMPARE AND CONTRAST** How did cash-and-carry and Lend-Lease differ, and which was more beneficial to the Allies?

3. **ANALYZE CAUSE AND EFFECT** How did Roosevelt's push to be an "arsenal of democracy" affect technology, the U.S. economy, and people's values and beliefs?

A NEW ALLIANCE

Sometimes no matter how much you try to stay out of a fight, circumstances force you to take action. When German warships began patrolling the Atlantic Ocean in order to stop supplies from reaching Great Britain, they targeted and tried to sink American ships. This brought the United States to the brink of battle.

THE ATLANTIC CHARTER

In the summer of 1941, the war in Europe took a dramatic turn. On June 22, Hitler pointed his army to the east and invaded the Soviet Union. The invasion was named Operation Barbarossa after the 12th-century Holy Roman Emperor, Frederick Barbarossa, and it ended the nonaggression pact between the two nations. Hitler had two objectives in mind: he wanted control of the oil supply in the Caucasus Mountains between the Black Sea and the Caspian Sea, and he wanted to conquer more territory for the expansion of Germany's population. More than 3 million German soldiers and 3,000 tanks plunged deep into Soviet territory. The German army defeated Soviet forces, captured more than 1 million prisoners, and moved toward Moscow and Leningrad.

Operation Barbarossa prompted many Americans to rethink their isolationist stance. The Nazis were becoming a true global threat. Following the German invasion, President Roosevelt offered Lend-Lease support to Soviet leader Joseph Stalin. While many Americans did not favor aiding a communist dictator, Roosevelt believed Hitler must be stopped at all costs. Over the next four years, Stalin received more than $11 billion in Lend-Lease aid from the United States to fight the Nazis.

In August 1941, two months after Germany marched on the Soviets, President Roosevelt and British prime minister Winston Churchill met aboard naval ships in Placentia Bay off the coast of Newfoundland in Canada. Even though the United States had not yet entered the war, the two leaders discussed their mutual aims and principles around fighting and winning the war. They drafted what became known as the **Atlantic Charter**. Under the eight-point charter, the two leaders agreed to such principles as freedom of the seas, greater trade among nations, and the right of people to choose the kind of government they

Operation Barbarossa, 1941

Operation Barbarossa launched June 22, 1941

Axis-controlled as of December 5, 1941
Soviet-controlled as of December 5, 1941
German-controlled Soviet territory as of December 5, 1941
Areas of fierce fighting
Neutral nation
Front line, December 5, 1941
German troop movements

desire. The charter stated the two countries would not wage war to gain territory, and they would oppose all changes in territory brought about by any war the people who lived there opposed. They would restore self-government to any nation that had lost it in the war, they would work together with other nations to improve living and working conditions throughout the world, and—perhaps most importantly—they stated that all countries should give up the use of force against one another.

By January 1942, 26 nations of North and South America, Europe, Asia, and Africa, along with Australia and New Zealand, had allied against the Axis Powers and pledged their support to the principles of the Atlantic Charter.

HOSTILITIES INCREASE

In the fall of 1941, tensions flared between the United States and Germany over activities in the Atlantic Ocean. German U-boats, or submarines, were targeting ships on the Atlantic sea-lanes. Roosevelt responded by authorizing U.S. destroyers—a type of warship—to hunt down the German subs. This policy was called **active defense**. On September 4, 1941, Germany fired on the U.S. destroyer *Greer*. The Germans claimed it was a case of mistaken identity, as they believed the ship to be a British vessel. President Roosevelt warned that any Axis ships that attacked American vessels in the North Atlantic would "do so at their own peril."

By October, U.S. Navy ships were providing escorts for civilian cargo vessels carrying war materials to Great Britain. This angered the Germans, who clearly saw the United States as aiding and supporting their enemy. In the early morning of October 31, a German U-boat sank the U.S.S. *Reuben James*, killing 115 crewmen. Americans were outraged. The United States appeared to be on the brink of entering the war. However, it would take a shocking attack from the other side of the world to ultimately push the United States into battle.

A FRIENDSHIP THAT CHANGED HISTORY

As the world plunged into war, the personal friendship between Winston Churchill and Franklin Roosevelt helped cement the historically strong bonds between the United States and Great Britain. The friendship helped lead to the Lend-Lease Act and the Atlantic Charter. In all, the two leaders met nine times. After one of these meetings, Roosevelt wrote to Churchill, saying, "It is fun to be in the same decade with you." After Roosevelt's death, Churchill wrote, "I felt I was in contact with a very great man, who was a warm-hearted friend, and the foremost champion of the high causes which we served."

HISTORICAL THINKING

1. **READING CHECK** How did Germany's attack on the Soviet Union affect Roosevelt's foreign policy and American public opinion about the war?

2. **INTERPRET MAPS** Along which German troop path were frictions and fighting the fiercest? Why do you think this was the case?

3. **EVALUATE** How did the Atlantic Charter seek to promote global peace?

4. **DETERMINE CHRONOLOGY** What events on the Atlantic Ocean heightened U.S.-German tensions to near-conflict?

VOCABULARY

For each pair of vocabulary words, write a sentence that explains the connection between the words.

1. **rearmament; Rome-Berlin Axis**
   After Hitler's rearmament began, he joined with Mussolini to form the Rome-Berlin Axis.

2. **Third Reich; Gestapo**

3. **Munich Agreement; appeasement**

4. **nonaggression pact; belligerent**

5. **Atlantic Charter; active defense**

6. **purge; Long March**

READING STRATEGY
COMPARE AND CONTRAST

Comparing and contrasting can help readers form a deeper understanding of concepts and events. Both Nazi Germany and Japan disrupted world peace in the 1930s and 1940s. Complete a Venn diagram to compare and contrast Nazi Germany and Japan. Include the following features:

single charismatic leader
desire for territorial conquest
disregard for established international laws
resentment over the outcome of World War I
lack of natural resources
policy of anti-Semitism
buildup of armed forces

Nazi Germany   Japan

7. In what way do you think Nazi Germany and Japan were most alike? Support your opinion with details.

MAIN IDEAS

Answer the following questions. Support your answers with evidence from the chapter.

8. What complex historical causes led to the rise of Adolf Hitler in Germany during the 1930s? **LESSON 1.1**

9. How did the views of President Roosevelt and a majority of Americans differ regarding involvement in the war? **LESSON 1.2**

10. How did the German-Soviet nonaggression pact contribute to the outbreak of World War II? **LESSON 2.1**

11. Why did Japan look upon China as a desirable target for invasion? **LESSON 2.2**

12. How did President Roosevelt intend to make America an "arsenal of democracy"? **LESSON 3.1**

13. How did the breaking of the German-Soviet nonaggression pact impact the debate between isolationists and interventionists in the United States? **LESSON 3.2**

HISTORICAL THINKING

Answer the following questions. Support your answers with evidence from the chapter.

14. **DETERMINE CHRONOLOGY** What 1940 military events preceded the Battle of Britain?

15. **EVALUATE** How did changes to the Neutrality Act over the years lead to greater U.S. involvement in the war effort?

16. **SYNTHESIZE** How did the onset of World War II help bring about the Atlantic Charter?

17. **DRAW CONCLUSIONS** Why do you think so many dictators were able to rise to power during the years before World War II?

18. **FORM AND SUPPORT OPINIONS** What events helped President Roosevelt build his case that Hitler posed a threat to the world unlike any other? Support your opinion.

INTERPRET VISUALS

During the Battle of Britain, many Londoners took shelter in the subway stations of the London Underground as Nazi bombs rained from the sky over their city. Study this photograph and then answer the questions.

19. A slogan during the bombing of London was "Your courage, your cheerfulness . . . will bring us victory." How does this photo reflect that philosophy?

20. What potential challenges do you see in living in these conditions for an extended period?

ANALYZE SOURCES

The Atlantic Charter, drafted in 1941 by Roosevelt and Churchill, consisted of eight general principles. Read the text of the eighth principle below. Then answer the questions that follow.

> Eighth, they [President Roosevelt and Prime Minister Churchill] believe that all of the nations of the world, for realistic as well as spiritual reasons must come to the abandonment of the use of force. Since no future peace can be maintained if land, sea or air armaments continue to be employed by nations which threaten, or may threaten, aggression outside of their frontiers, they believe, pending the establishment of a wider and permanent system of general security, that the disarmament of such nations is essential. They will likewise aid and encourage all other practicable measures which will lighten for peace-loving peoples the crushing burden of armaments.

21. What does the charter argue is "essential" to helping secure world peace?

22. Describe the complex cause and effect relationships between disarmament and peace. Support your answer with evidence from the text.

CONNECT TO YOUR LIFE

23. **NARRATIVE** Reread the summary of the Atlantic Charter from the chapter. Sum up the ideals Churchill and Roosevelt expressed to the world. To what extent have those ideals become reality since the charter was written? Think of what you know about the world today. Choose one or more of the principles of the Atlantic Charter, and describe the state of that principle in the world today.

TIPS

- Read the summary of the charter's principles, and state in your own words the principles and ideals expressed there.

- State the principle or principles you will compare with today's world—for example, the principle of not expanding territory, or of open trade among nations.

- Describe some aspect of the state of the world in terms of that principle.

- Use two or three vocabulary terms from the chapter in your narrative, if possible.

- Conclude your narrative with a summary of what exists now and how it could be changed to achieve the principle or principles you named.

AMERICA IN WORLD WAR II

1941–1945

HISTORICAL THINKING How did World War II and the Holocaust impact Americans and the world?

CRITICAL VIEWING During the Battle of Iwo Jima, an island near the Japanese coast, U.S. Marines took control of Mount Suribachi, the highest point of the island. In celebration, soldiers raised the U.S. flag at the top of the peak—twice. The second time, Joseph Rosenthal captured this image of the flag-raising, which won him a Pulitzer Prize and became one of the most iconic photos of World War II. What do you think the photo symbolized to Americans on the home front?

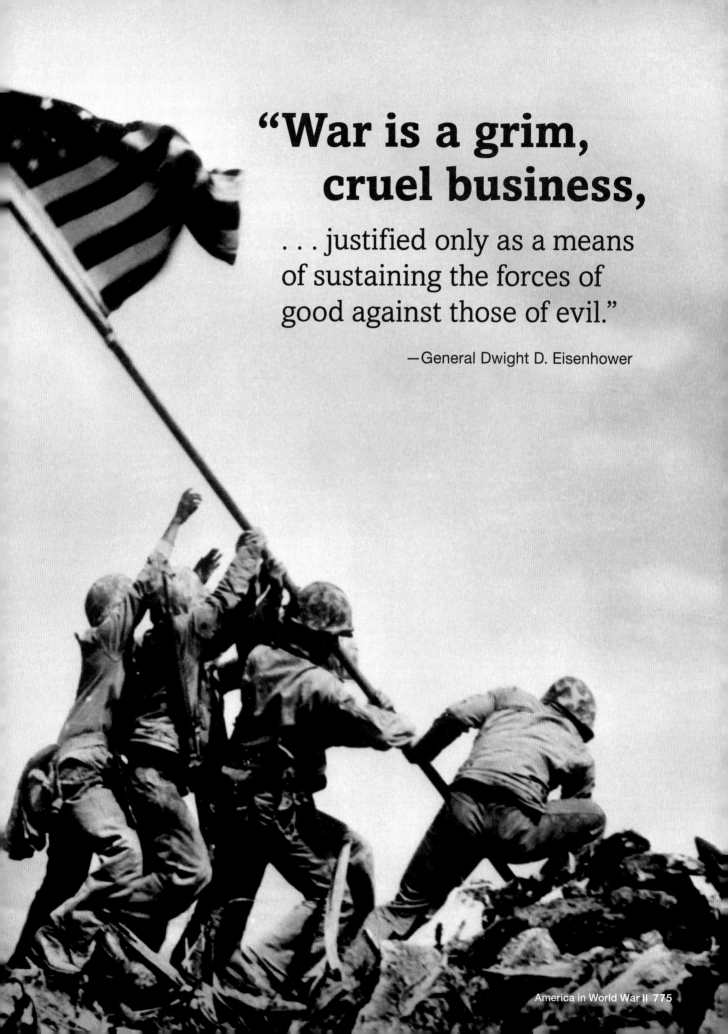

"**War is a grim, cruel business,** . . . justified only as a means of sustaining the forces of good against those of evil."

—General Dwight D. Eisenhower

CRITICAL VIEWING Navajo Code Talkers working with a U.S. Marine signal unit operate a portable radio in the jungles of Bougainville Island in the South Pacific. What does this photo reveal about the conditions of this military campaign?

The Code Talkers of
WORLD WAR II

When U.S. Marines disembarked onto Japanese-occupied beaches in the Pacific Islands during World War II, the battle scenes were unimaginable. Fighting their way inch by inch through firestorms of artillery, the "bullets fell like deadly sleet," reported one Marine of his landing on Guam. Bombs nicknamed "daisy cutters" rained down, spraying shrapnel outward in all directions to cause maximum damage to vulnerable human bodies.

DEVELOPING THE NAVAJO CODE

Amidst the chaos, it was essential for different military units to maintain communication. Messages had to be passed quickly, accurately, cryptically, in a way the Japanese could not interpret. To do this job, the Marines relied on an elite group of fighters—the Code Talkers.

The idea of using a Native American language as a wartime code originated during World War I. By transmitting messages in Choctaw, U.S. forces were able to orchestrate a successful surprise attack against the German army. In the years following World War I, scholars from Germany, Japan, and other countries visited the United States and studied various Native American languages including Cherokee, Choctaw, and Comanche. Few people in the United States or Europe spoke or understood the Navajo language. Navajo is complex in both its structure and its pronunciation. It is a tonal language, meaning that the tone used to pronounce a word can completely change its meaning. In addition, Navajo was almost never written down—both the language and its wealth of traditional stories were passed along orally.

NAVAJO CODE WORDS

The Navajo language did not have words for the technology of 20th-century warfare. When devising the code, the men first thought of an object that could symbolize the word they wanted to encode, then they chose the Navajo word for that object. These are some of the words for engines of war in the Navajo code.

ENGLISH	NAVAJO	MEANING
dive bomber	gini	chicken hawk
observation plane	ne-ahs-jah	owl
aircraft carrier	tsidi-ne-ye-hi	bird carrier
bombs	a-ye-shi	eggs
amphibious vehicle	chal	frog
submarine	besh-lo	iron fish

One non-native speaker who did have a basic understanding of Navajo was Philip Johnston, a civil engineer who had lived on a Navajo reservation as a child with his missionary parents. It was Johnston who suggested to the Marines that the Navajo language could form the basis of a wartime code.

In 1942, the Marines launched the Navajo code project with 29 Native American recruits. They gathered at a base in California, where they were charged with creating the code. The team devised a system of word substitutions in which a different Navajo word would stand for each letter of the English alphabet. To avoid spelling every word out, commonly used military terms were assigned their own Navajo words. For example, "fighter plane" became *da-he-tih-hi*, or "hummingbird" in Navajo. To make the code even more unbreakable, it was not written down.

The men, who came to be known as Code Talkers, memorized every single word of the code and practiced until they could quickly translate messages from English into Navajo code and back again. Chester Nez, one of the original 29, claimed that the Navajo tradition of oral storytelling helped the Code Talkers hone their memorization skills.

In an early test of the Navajo code, a message was sent over the radio from one post to another using the coding machines that were in common use. Simultaneously, one Code Talker relayed the same message orally to another. The Marine officers estimated the message would take four hours to transmit and decode using the machine method. The Code Talkers did it in under three minutes.

CODE TALKERS AT WAR

The Navajo were the largest group of Code Talkers, with around 420 members. They fought in the Pacific. Members of the Comanche, Cherokee, Chippewa, Kiowa, Pawnee, Lakota, and other tribes served as Code Talkers in Europe and other war zones. Code Talkers worked in pairs as battlefield radio officers. They carried a 30-pound radio that had to be cranked to generate electricity. As one man cranked the radio, the other transmitted coded messages to another pair of Code Talkers elsewhere on the battlefield or on a transport ship. Working under the deafening tumult of battle, the Code Talkers had to maintain enough focus to quickly translate and transmit messages, and be prepared to take part in the fighting.

The Code Talkers served with courage and distinction wherever they were assigned. In the Pacific, the Navajo Code Talkers were instrumental in several U.S. victories, including the famous battle for the island of Iwo Jima. According to one Marine officer, "The entire operation was directed by Navajo code. During the two days that followed the initial landings I had six Navajo radio nets working around the clock. They sent and received over 800 messages without an error. Were it not for the Navajo Code Talkers, the Marines never would have taken Iwo Jima."

COMING HOME

The return to civilian life after the war was difficult for many soldiers, including the Code Talkers. In their fighting units they had been respected by their fellow soldiers and treated as equals. Back in the United States, however, old prejudices were still in force. When Chester Nez returned to his home state of New Mexico after serving in the Marines, for example, he was not allowed to vote. Native Americans were not given the right to vote in that state until 1948.

Many of the returning Native American soldiers were also troubled by their experiences during the war, especially those that went against the traditions of their tribes. In his autobiography, Nez recalled being plagued with nightmares until he underwent a traditional ceremony called the Enemy Way that helped him return to the Right Way—a sense of balance between the physical and spiritual worlds.

The situation was made worse by the fact that the Code Talkers could not reveal the pivotal role they had played in so many hard-fought battles. The existence of Native American codes was kept secret until 1968, because the government did not want to reveal any possible keys to the only unbroken oral code from World War II.

After the work of the Code Talkers was declassified, or no longer declared an official secret, the soldiers were finally recognized for their true contributions to the war effort. In July 2001, the four surviving Code Talkers of the original 29 received the Congressional Gold Medal in a ceremony in Washington, D.C.

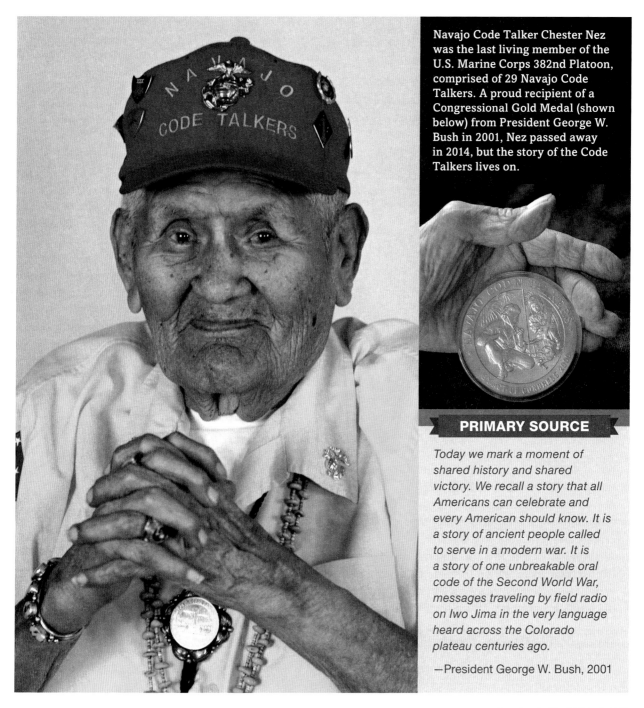

Navajo Code Talker Chester Nez was the last living member of the U.S. Marine Corps 382nd Platoon, comprised of 29 Navajo Code Talkers. A proud recipient of a Congressional Gold Medal (shown below) from President George W. Bush in 2001, Nez passed away in 2014, but the story of the Code Talkers lives on.

PRIMARY SOURCE

Today we mark a moment of shared history and shared victory. We recall a story that all Americans can celebrate and every American should know. It is a story of ancient people called to serve in a modern war. It is a story of one unbreakable oral code of the Second World War, messages traveling by field radio on Iwo Jima in the very language heard across the Colorado plateau centuries ago.

—President George W. Bush, 2001

OTHER CODES IN WORLD WAR II

While the Navajo worked to create a unique American code, others in the U.S. military were racing to break the German and Japanese codes. Like the non-Navajo codes used by the United States, the German and Japanese forms of encryption were machine-based.

The Germans used a machine known as the Enigma to create their coded messages. An operator would type a message in plain text on the Enigma's keyboard, and a series of notched wheels, or rotors, within the machine would turn, encoding the message into a seemingly random jumble of letters. The message would then be sent via radio to another operator who would use an Enigma machine to decode it. The second operator would have to know the exact sequence of rotor settings in order to correctly decrypt the message. The rotor settings for each day—called the daily key—were listed in codebooks that each Enigma operator possessed. Not surprisingly, these codebooks were some of the most closely guarded items of the war. The Enigma code was eventually penetrated by British code breakers building on earlier work by Polish intelligence.

American code breakers focused their efforts on the Japanese code known as Purple. The Japanese had purchased an Enigma machine from the Germans in the early 1930s, then added refinements to make it easier to use and harder to decrypt. Like the Enigma, the Purple machine required a daily key. Over the course of the war, U.S. code breakers were able to identify certain patterns in the way the Japanese daily keys were determined, and by the end of the war, Purple was broken.

World War II also saw the beginning of the digital age of encryption. The Allies quickly recognized the need for a way to communicate securely via telephone between the United States, London, and other locations. In cooperation with the U.S. Army Signal Corps, Bell Laboratories devised a digital method of encoding voice signals traveling over telephone wires. The code, called Sigsaly, was in use from 1943 to 1946, but it was not declassified until 1975. It was never broken.

THINK ABOUT IT

How did developments in communication during World War II affect its participants and outcome?

CRITICAL VIEWING Introduced on German U-boats sailing in the Atlantic Ocean in February 1942, the code produced by the MK 4 Enigma was not broken until December 1942. The cracking of German cypher codes by Allied intelligence was a major achievement in cryptanalysis, or code breaking, and played an important role in the outcome of the North Atlantic U-boat engagements during World War II. How might the course of the war have been different if the Enigma's code had not been broken?

Intelligent, rebellious, and quirky, Alan Turing, represented here by actor Benedict Cumberbatch in the 2014 movie *The Imitation Game*, was also gay. British law at the time made same-sex relationships illegal, which prevented Turing from being open about his personal life. But he found social acceptance at Kings College in Cambridge. In 1952, however, Turing was arrested and charged with "indecency" after a brief relationship with a man. He did not deny the charges.

According to Andrew Hodges, a mathematician and author of the Turing biography that inspired *The Imitation Game*, "When [Turing] was arrested, the first thing he said was he thought that this shouldn't be against the law." Defiantly mocking the absurdity of his arrest, Turing traveled to Norway and the Mediterranean, where the gay rights movement was beginning to gain momentum. However, 1950s British law considered homosexuality a security risk, and Turing's arrest and conviction cost him his job and the ability to travel. Hodges believes these consequences ultimately led Turing to suicide at the age of 41.

Homosexuality was not fully decriminalized for adults in Great Britain until the 1980s. In 2009, British Prime Minister Gordon Brown publicly apologized for Turing's "utterly unfair" treatment on behalf of the British government. Four years later, Queen Elizabeth II granted him a royal pardon.

FROM CODES TO COMPUTERS

The history of code breaking is entwined with the history of computers. Alan Turing, the mathematician in charge of Britain's cryptanalysis department during World War II, is viewed by many as the father of the modern computer. He played a key role in cracking the Enigma code by helping to develop an electromechanical machine called the bombe. An improvement on a pre-war Polish machine, the bombe greatly sped up the rate at which codes could be deciphered. In 1943, British code breakers designed another machine called the Colossus, which, like early computers, used vacuum tubes to control electric current. The Colossus could do basic mathematical calculations. It could also quickly perform the repetitive operations necessary to identify the patterns found in encrypted messages.

Interest in Britain's code-breaking operation, and in Alan Turing, has been awakened in recent years by historical accounts, novels, and the popular 2014 film *The Imitation Game*. It is less well known that by the end of the war, the U.S. Navy had developed electronic machines that were similar to the Colossus but had a greater number of vacuum tubes—and thus greater computing power. Also like the Colossus, these lacked the memory of a digital computer.

Further advancements in computer technology would come as researchers developed vacuum-tube computers that could work more quickly and run a greater variety of programs. Eventually, of course, digital technology would rapidly make computers much more powerful, versatile, and accessible to users outside the military and scientific communities.

A DEVASTATING ATTACK

Which of the freedoms you enjoy as an American citizen do you value the most? In 1941, President Franklin Roosevelt identified four freedoms he felt were the most essential—and worth fighting for. After an unprovoked attack, Americans would be doing just that.

FOUR FREEDOMS

In his annual address to Congress in January 1941, President Roosevelt named and discussed "four essential human freedoms" that were at stake in World War II. As a result, Roosevelt's address became known as the "Four Freedoms" speech.

> In the future days, which we seek to make secure, we look forward to a world founded upon four essential human freedoms.
>
> The first is freedom of speech and expression— everywhere in the world.
>
> The second is freedom of every person to worship God in his own way—everywhere in the world.
>
> The third is freedom from want—which, translated into world terms, means economic understandings which will secure to every nation a healthy peacetime life for its inhabitants—everywhere in the world.
>
> The fourth is freedom from fear—which, translated into world terms, means a world-wide reduction of armaments to such a point and in such a thorough fashion that no nation will be in a position to commit an act of physical aggression against any neighbor—anywhere in the world.
>
> —President Franklin D. Roosevelt, Annual Address to Congress, January 6, 1941

Roosevelt used his speech to frame the war as a conflict about fundamental values. After the United States entered the conflict, his words inspired artist Norman Rockwell to create four illustrations (at right) for the *Saturday Evening Post*, a popular weekly magazine, that translated the war aims into scenes of everyday American life.

A DAY OF INFAMY

Within a year of Roosevelt's speech, the United States would go to war against Japan to defend the freedoms he described. Relations between the two countries had long been strained. The United States had watched Japan's aggression and expansion into China with growing concern. This apprehension had increased when Japan signed the Tripartite Pact with Germany and Italy in September 1940. In an effort to put a halt to Japan's expansionism, Roosevelt froze Japanese business interests in the United States in 1941. He also established an embargo on essential goods such as oil to Japan. Many believed war between the United States and Japan was imminent. But most U.S. military analysts expected the Japanese would probably attack a European colony in the South Pacific, with an outside chance they would attack the United States in the Philippines. The U.S. military never imagined the Japanese would be bold enough to strike Hawaii.

The Japanese had planned their attack for months, and their goal was to destroy the U.S. Pacific fleet. So, in late November, a large convoy of Japanese battleships, destroyers, aircraft carriers, and cruisers headed toward the U.S. naval base at Pearl Harbor on the island of Oahu in Hawaii. On the morning of December 7, 1941, the fleet was within 200 miles of Pearl Harbor, and Japanese bomber planes took off from the aircraft carriers to launch the attack. Military personnel in Pearl Harbor had no idea they were in danger until the planes appeared on radar. And even then, they thought the planes were American fighters. In addition, the Japanese had deliberately attacked on a Sunday morning, when security at the base was likely to be more relaxed.

OURS...to fight for

Freedom of Speech

Freedom of Worship

Freedom from Want

Freedom from Fear

Norman Rockwell's paintings of the Four Freedoms appeared in the *Saturday Evening Post* in March and April 1943. The U.S. government printed and sold posters of the popular paintings in a campaign that raised more than $132 million for the war effort.

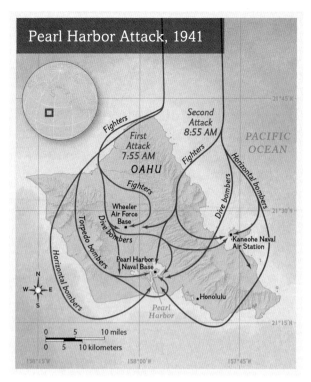

Pearl Harbor Attack, 1941

First Attack 7:55 AM
Second Attack 8:55 AM
OAHU
PACIFIC OCEAN
Fighters
Dive bombers
Horizontal bombers
Torpedo bombers
Wheeler Air Force Base
Kaneohe Naval Air Station
Pearl Harbor Naval Base
Honolulu
Pearl Harbor

0   5   10 miles
0   5   10 kilometers

Smoke billows from U.S. battleships anchored in Pearl Harbor following the Japanese attack on December 7, 1941. The map on the left shows the two waves of the attack carried out by 353 fighter, dive bomber, torpedo bomber, and horizontal bomber planes. The planes launched the assault from 6 aircraft carriers north of Pearl Harbor.

The assault came in two waves, with the first bombers arriving shortly before 8 a.m., and the second wave arriving an hour later. The planes rained their bombs and bullets down on U.S. battleships anchored in the harbor and American military aircraft sitting on the ground. Battleships, including the U.S.S. *Arizona*, were completely destroyed in the attack. In the end, the Japanese demolished or damaged nearly 20 American warships and about 200 planes. Far worse, more than 2,300 Americans were killed. The Japanese lost fewer than 100 men.

Roosevelt addressed Congress and the American people by radio the next day saying, "Yesterday, December 7, 1941—a date which will live in infamy—the United States of America was suddenly and deliberately attacked by naval and air forces of the Empire of Japan." **Infamy** refers to an extremely shameful or evil act. Roosevelt called for a declaration of war, and Congress—with only one dissenting vote—agreed. On December 8, Congress declared war on Japan. Three days later, Germany and Italy honored their allegiance to Japan and declared war on the United States. As you know, many Americans had been opposed to joining the war. But the bombing of Pearl Harbor had stunned the nation and instantly turned the tide of American opinion in favor of the war. Americans took their place among the Allied powers—including Great Britain, the Soviet Union, and China—in the fight against the Axis powers Germany, Italy, and Japan.

BATAAN DEATH MARCH

Within hours of the attack on Pearl Harbor, Japanese forces struck the Philippines, which was designated a commonwealth, or territory, of the United States in 1935. The United States Armed Forces in the Far East (USAFFE) had been mobilized earlier in case of attack and headquartered in the Philippines under the command of American general Douglas MacArthur. You may remember that President Hoover called on MacArthur to restore order when World War I veterans marched on Washington, D.C., in 1932.

The majority of the forces were Filipinos, but American troops also made up the ranks. However, the troops were unprepared for the full-scale attack the Japanese had planned. The Japanese air force bombed airfields, bases, harbors, and shipyards, and approximately 56,500 soldiers from the Japanese Army came ashore at Luzon, the largest island of the Philippines. By January 2, 1942, Japanese troops had taken Manila, the country's capital. Unable to defend the territory, the USAFFE strategically retreated to the jungles of the Bataan Peninsula.

Despite suffering from disease and starvation and fighting without any air support, the USAFFE troops defended Bataan for 99 days. Then, in March 1942, Roosevelt ordered MacArthur to leave the Philippines. The official story was that Roosevelt wanted MacArthur to go to Australia to coordinate the war effort. The truth was that MacArthur was too valuable an officer for the United States to lose, especially at the beginning of a war, so he was brought to safety. The general left the Philippines but vowed, "I shall return." Despite constant bombardment, the soldiers continued to fight under General Edward P. King, Jr., the Commanding General of the Luzon Force.

Finally, on April 9, King and his 75,000 Filipino and American troops surrendered to the Japanese. The troops were forced to march some 60 miles to their prison at Camp O'Donnell with no provisions for food, water, or shelter. Those who could no longer go on were beaten, bayoneted, shot, and in some cases, beheaded by their Japanese captors. Approximately 10,000 Filipinos and 750 Americans perished in what became known as the **Bataan Death March**.

Once imprisoned in Camp O'Donnell, another 20,000 Filipinos and 1,600 Americans died. A majority of the American prisoners were later transported in the hulls of unmarked vessels, known as "Hell Ships," to Japan, China, Formosa (present-day Taiwan), and Korea, where they worked as slave laborers. Thousands died on the ships and while in servitude. U.S. involvement in World War II had just begun, but Americans quickly realized it would take a lot of strength and resources to fight their formidable enemies.

HISTORICAL THINKING

1. **READING CHECK** What events brought on Japan's attack on Pearl Harbor?

2. **ANALYZE SOURCES** In Roosevelt's Four Freedoms speech, how did he frame American beliefs on both a personal and international level?

3. **DETERMINE CHRONOLOGY** What order of events took place within days of the attack on Pearl Harbor?

4. **INTERPRET MAPS** Based on the map, what conclusions can you draw about the attack?

GEARING UP FOR WAR

Once the United States entered the war, the country mobilized to prepare for it. World War II would require a massive buildup of resources to fight on both the Asian and European fronts.

THE WAR EFFORT

In order to gather the materials the country would need, President Roosevelt established the **War Production Board** in 1942. He called on automobile companies, such as Ford and General Motors, to build tanks and warplanes instead of passenger cars. Roosevelt knew these large corporations could fill the military's needs quickly and gave them the bulk of the work orders. He also offered the companies low-interest loans so they could convert their factories to war production and assured factory owners they would make a profit.

To help pay for the war supplies, Congress passed the **Revenue Act of 1942**, which increased taxes on individuals and corporations. However, this measure only provided about 45 percent of the funds needed to meet expenses. So the government issued war bonds. Citizens could purchase a bond for 75 percent of its face value and later cash it in with interest. To induce Americans to buy war bonds, the government appealed to people's emotions. Remember the illustrations Norman Rockwell created after Roosevelt's Four Freedoms speech? These illustrations became a centerpiece of the bond drive. By the war's end, about half of the nation's population had purchased bonds.

New developments in various fields also aided the war effort. In aviation, the powerful B-24 bomber helped the Allies defend against German submarines. **Napalm**, a thick, flammable substance used in bombs to cause and spread fires, first appeared in World War II. Strides in medical technology and, in particular, the development of penicillin, helped save soldiers' lives. **Penicillin** is an antibiotic, or bacteria killer, made from mold and used to treat infections and disease.

Industrial demands fueled by wartime needs helped end the Depression and set a model for an expanded governmental role in regulating the economy after the war. The defense-related industries became especially critical to California's economy, helping drive other developments in the manufacturing sector and in science and technology. The state played a huge role in America's successful war effort and built more military installations than any other state. The number of military bases in California increased from 16 to 41, more than those of the next 5 states combined.

MILITARY SUPPORT

New military bases were definitely needed. Six million Americans volunteered for service between 1942 and 1945, and the country drafted another 10 million men. The draft also conscripted conscientious objectors—those who opposed the war on religious grounds. However, COs, as they were sometimes called, were allowed to participate in public works projects or serve in other nonmilitary ways.

General **George Marshall**, the chief of staff of the U.S. Army in 1939, was largely responsible for training the troops and selecting commanders for the war. He put Lesley J. McNair in charge of the Army Ground Forces once the United States entered the war. McNair dedicated himself to ensuring the troops received the most realistic combat training possible. He staged huge mock battles and simulated real wartime situations.

Though the military training the troops received was similar, men from minority groups did not fight with white soldiers. Instead they were placed in segregated troops. Nevertheless, these troops made great sacrifices and demonstrated valor and

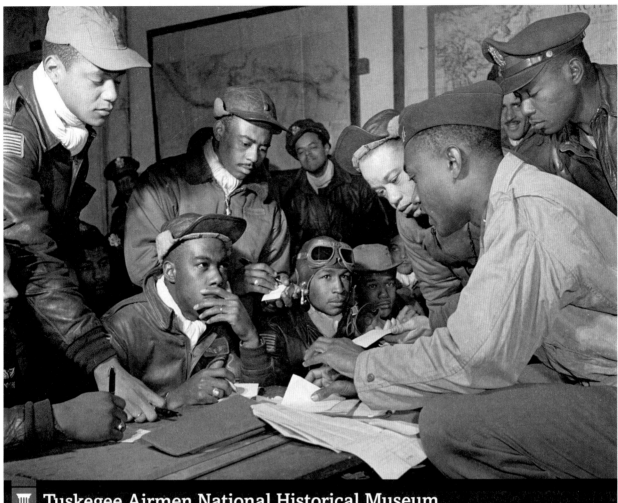

Tuskegee Airmen National Historical Museum
Detroit, Michigan

Toni Frissell photographed a group of Tuskegee Airmen receiving instructions for a mission at the Ramitelli airfield in Italy in 1945. Throughout the war, the Airmen played an important role, escorting allied bombers with one of the lowest loss records among escort fighter groups. They also flew about 15,500 combat missions. In recognition of their outstanding record and sacrifices, the Tuskegee Airmen received more than 150 Distinguished Flying Crosses.

distinction. The **Tuskegee Airmen** was a squadron of African-American pilots who trained in Tuskegee, Alabama, and shot down a dozen Nazi planes during an invasion in Italy in 1943. That same year saw the formation of the **442nd Infantry Regimental Combat Team**, a military unit that consisted entirely of Japanese Americans. The 442nd successfully fought in Europe in 1944 and rescued a regiment of Texas soldiers surrounded by German forces.

In April 1941, the U.S. government formed American Volunteer Groups to help the Nationalist government of China in its struggle against Japan. The "**Flying Tigers**" was the only American Volunteer Group to take part in combat. It sprang into action to help defend Burma and China against the Japanese after the attack on Pearl Harbor. Volunteer pilots from the American and Chinese air forces made up the Flying Tigers.

As you know, the Navajo provided an indispensable service to American forces during World War II. After it became clear the Japanese were intercepting and deciphering coded U.S. messages, the Marines enlisted Navajo men to transmit and translate messages using their native language. The men became known as the **Navajo Code Talkers**. The Navajo language was so difficult—and so few people spoke it—that the Japanese could not decode the messages. The Code Talkers were a major factor in the eventual Allied victory.

The military didn't welcome all Americans. Officials screened out and rejected homosexuals, though gay men and women still served in the armed forces in significant numbers. Some were tolerated because of the war effort, and their fellow soldiers often came to appreciate their service. However, many other gays were imprisoned or dishonorably discharged when their sexual orientation was discovered. That persecution set the stage for increased postwar oppression and organized resistance.

ON THE HOME FRONT

At home, World War II had many long-lasting effects. Increased production made employment skyrocket, resulting in 17 million new jobs—including jobs for women and minority groups. Income for the average American nearly doubled as well, largely as a result of the overtime factory workers logged in. The new jobs drew enormous numbers of migrants from all over the country to urban areas and eventually spurred the creation of expansive suburbs, highways, and shopping complexes.

The war also drew immigrants to the United States. In 1942, the government sponsored the **Bracero Program**, which continued until 1964 and was designed primarily to import Mexican laborers to replace native-born agricultural and transportation industry workers who were mobilizing for war. California particularly benefited from the braceros, which means "strong armed ones." Importing more than 40,000 workers in 1942 alone, the state came to depend on the agricultural laborers who came through the program. By the end of the war, California had the fastest population growth of any state—and an increasingly diversified society.

Meanwhile, Americans at home faced many everyday challenges. In 1942, Roosevelt enacted the **Office of Price Administration** to help limit inflation and **ration**, or control, the supply of goods made available to the public. The military desperately needed items such as gas, rubber, and certain foods, so civilians were urged to cut back on driving and consume less sugar, coffee, and meat. To supplement their food supplies, the government encouraged people to plant victory gardens, or plots of land on which they could grow their own food. Almost 20 million Americans planted victory gardens during the war. The gardens made people on the home front feel as if they were contributing to the war effort—much as the purchase of war bonds did.

Buying war bonds and planting victory gardens made people feel patriotic, but the stress of war was hard to avoid. Popular films and radio programs provided much needed distraction from the war. Diversions such as baseball games helped take people's minds off their worries as well. Some politicians had called for the suspension of major league baseball during the war, but Roosevelt disagreed. He explained that the game helped keep up people's morale. The **Office of War Information**, formed in 1942, also boosted Americans' spirits. The agency produced posters, photos, and films that celebrated the troops and encouraged Americans' support for the war.

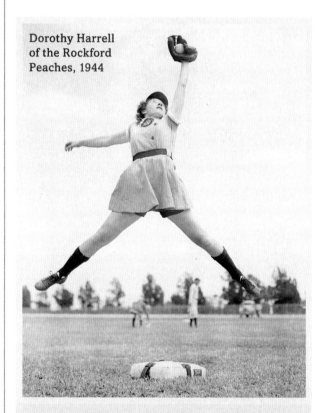

Dorothy Harrell of the Rockford Peaches, 1944

THE ALL-AMERICAN GIRLS PROFESSIONAL BASEBALL LEAGUE

As young men were drafted into the armed services during the war, minor league baseball lost most of its players. Philip Wrigley, owner of the Chicago Cubs, decided that a female ball league might bring fans to the parks and help keep the sport in the public eye. The result was the All-American Girls Professional Baseball League. After the athletes had been recruited and teams organized, the League first stepped up to the plate in 1943. The players were accomplished pitchers, batters, and hitters, but organizers insisted that they also be "lady-like." They attended charm school and wore make-up, even on the field. The League was an enormous success, and the women kept playing until 1954, nearly a decade after the war ended.

STRUGGLES AT HOME

As you've read, wartime factory work created new and higher-paying job opportunities for African Americans and other minorities. However, opening up the wage-labor market raised their expectations about what else they might be able to achieve. The contrast between the ideology of the war effort and the racial segregation of the armed forces sparked multiple efforts at minority equality and, in time, for civil rights activism after the war.

In 1941, a letter printed in the African-American newspaper, the *Pittsburgh Courier*, launched the "Double V" campaign. The campaign called on African Americans to fight for victory against fascism abroad and victory against racism at home. That same year, **A. Philip Randolph**, the head of the largely African-American **Brotherhood of Sleeping Car Porters** union, planned a march in Washington, D.C., to focus international attention on the hypocrisy of undemocratic practices at home while the country was poised to fight for democracy abroad. The march ultimately prompted Roosevelt to sign **Executive Order 8802** in 1941 to desegregate military-related industries.

But wartime racial discrimination went beyond the military and the workplace. In 1943, white shipyard workers attacked African-American workers in Mobile, Alabama, and a race riot between whites and blacks in Detroit resulted in more than 30 deaths and 700 injuries. That same year, Mexican Americans dressed in zoot suits also came under attack in Los Angeles, California. A zoot suit is a flamboyant man's suit that features wide-legged trousers and long jackets with wide lapels. The outfits were a fad among many African Americans and Mexican Americans. Many people considered those who wore zoot suits to be thugs.

The white American sailors who arrived in Los Angeles on leave in 1943 particularly objected to zoot suits—and the young Mexican Americans dressed in them. Tensions had long been growing between the two groups, who often fought and exchanged insults. Finally, the **Zoot Suit Riots** erupted in May when mobs of sailors attacked the zoot-suiters, beating the young men and tearing off their suits. Similar attacks continued for more than a week. During this time, the police sometimes stood by while the servicemen rampaged through the city. After the riots died down, a commission investigated the riots and identified racism as their central cause.

This photograph captured a couple of young African-American men, dressed in zoot suits, in 1943. During the war, the zoot suit became a part of the jazz world. Some people of color—including women—wore the suit to make a bold statement.

HISTORICAL THINKING

1. **READING CHECK** What measures did the U.S. government take to help pay for the war?

2. **SYNTHESIZE** What were some of the different ways in which civilians helped contribute to the war effort?

3. **MAKE INFERENCES** Why do you think African Americans, Japanese Americans, and Native Americans wanted to fight in the war?

4. **DRAW CONCLUSIONS** Why did Randolph call the treatment of African Americans at home hypocritical?

WOMEN AND THE WAR EFFORT

Throughout American history, women had stepped up in times of crisis but never in the numbers seen during World War II. Their reward was satisfaction in a job well done and pride in serving their country.

NEW OPPORTUNITIES

World War II provided women with an unprecedented opportunity to enter the workforce. Many men left their jobs to fight in the war, and women filled their places in factories and offices. The defense industries, particularly in aircraft and munitions, needed workers. These businesses employed 6 million women as welders, electricians, and assembly line workers during the war.

Some women also decided to join the military and served in the few branches the military allowed women to join. The establishment of the **Women's Auxiliary Army Corps (WAAC)** in 1942 offered women a chance to participate in noncombat roles as radio operators and air-traffic controllers, for example. Women who joined the WAAC earned a salary but were not given all the benefits men in the military received. However, within just a few months of the corps's establishment, more than 25,000 women had signed up. As a result, the army dropped the "auxiliary" designation in 1943, and members of the Women's Army Corps (WAC) received full U.S. Army benefits, comparable to those of male soldiers. A total of about 150,000 women served all over the world, including in war zones.

The navy equivalent of the WAC was the **Women Accepted for Volunteer Emergency Service (WAVES)**, which was also established in 1942. About 27,000 women joined in its first year. Unlike WACs, WAVES received full benefits from the beginning as well as the same salary as men. However, WAVES were not allowed to serve abroad. Members worked in fields such as aviation, medicine, intelligence, science, and technology. About one-third of WAVES were involved with naval aviation, while others performed duties such as calculating bomb trajectories or paths, and working as meteorologists. A total of about 100,000 women served as WAVES during the war.

By enabling women to fill noncombat roles, WACs and WAVES helped free up additional men for combat duties. These branches of the service also allowed women to take on vital and complicated responsibilities in the war effort. Though male officers at first anticipated that their female counterparts would only perform clerical duties, the women's dedication and capability soon changed the male officers' minds.

UNFAIR TREATMENT

Even as women sacrificed and worked hard for the war effort, they experienced unfair treatment in their new jobs. Some employers didn't even want to hire them. They didn't believe women had the strength or ability to do the jobs. Furthermore, many employers feared the women would distract male workers and prevent them from doing their work.

Another form of unfair treatment was **wage discrimination**, or receiving lower pay for the same job based on gender, race, or ethnicity. Though women who worked in defense industries generally made more money than they did working in other jobs, they still made far less than their male coworkers. In 1945, for example, a woman working in a factory earned an average of $32 a week, while a man made an average of $55—even though a law required equal pay for equal work. Some companies dodged the law by reclassifying higher-paying jobs into a lower pay scale or assigning women to lower-level positions.

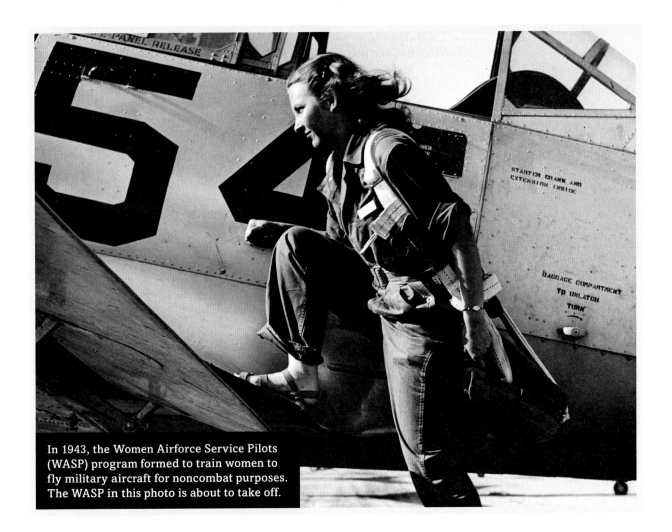

In 1943, the Women Airforce Service Pilots (WASP) program formed to train women to fly military aircraft for noncombat purposes. The WASP in this photo is about to take off.

After **demobilization**, or the release of soldiers from military duty, more women remained in the workforce than had done so following World War I. Still, most were forced to leave. Employers notified women they would have to give up their jobs to the returning soldiers. Employers—and society as a whole—still believed a woman's place was in the home. Advertisers also promoted a return to traditional women's roles.

As a result, even though the majority of women wanted to keep their jobs after the war, most either had to return to their roles as homemakers or take lower-paying jobs. By 1947, women's presence in blue-collar jobs had sunk to its prewar level. Nevertheless, women had briefly enjoyed a degree of liberation and financial security in their newfound workplace roles. Unfortunately, not all segments of American society would experience as much freedom as women had.

PRIMARY SOURCE

You have just made the change from peacetime pursuits to wartime tasks— from the individualism of civilian life to the anonymity of mass military life. You have given up comfortable homes, highly paid positions, leisure. You have taken off silk and put on khaki. And all for essentially the same reason. You have a debt and a date—a debt to democracy and a date with destiny.

—from Director Oveta Culp Hobby's remarks to the first WAAC officer training class, 1942

HISTORICAL THINKING

1. **READING CHECK** What new opportunities were available to women during World War II, and how do those opportunities compare to those woman have today?

2. **COMPARE AND CONTRAST** How were the jobs of WACs and WAVES alike and different?

3. **MAKE INFERENCES** Why do you think women wanted to keep their jobs in the defense industries after the war ended?

4. **EVALUATE** What tone did Hobby use in her remarks to the WAACs, and why did she use that tone?

ROSIE THE RIVETER 1942–1945

"She's making history, / working for victory / Rosie the Riveter."
— from "Rosie the Riveter," a song by Redd Evans and Jacob Loeb, 1943

Rosie the Riveter came to life in a song—some of its lyrics are quoted above. The song was a hit, and its title came to represent the millions of American women who took on the industrial jobs that were vacated as more and more men joined the war effort during World War II. Rosie became part of a U.S. government campaign to recruit women into the workforce. The campaign worked, and the women excelled in their new jobs. As the song says, "That little frail [woman] can do more than a male / will do."

A TALE OF TWO ROSIES

The face of Rosie the Riveter that most people were familiar with during the war was the one featured on the cover of the *Saturday Evening Post*. But this Rosie is no "little frail." In Norman Rockwell's painting, she's a muscular, monumental figure, based on the style Italian Renaissance artist Michelangelo used to depict biblical prophets in Rome's Sistine Chapel.

Apparently on her lunch break, Rosie holds a sandwich aloft and balances her riveting gun and lunchbox, etched with her name, on her lap. Her foot rests squarely on *Mein Kampf*, or *My Struggle*, Adolf Hitler's autobiography, in which he outlined his anti-Semitic views. Rosie's contempt for the German dictator and confidence that he will be defeated—with her help—are clear.

Mary Doyle Keefe, the model for Rockwell's illustration, was actually a petite young woman. Rockwell wanted to portray his Rosie as strong and powerful. Still, he apologized to Keefe for making her so brawny.

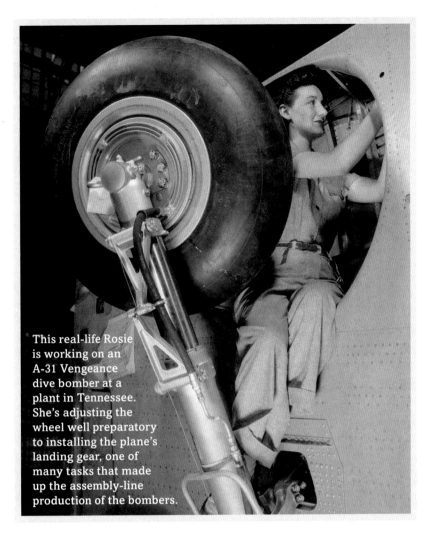

This real-life Rosie is working on an A-31 Vengeance dive bomber at a plant in Tennessee. She's adjusting the wheel well preparatory to installing the plane's landing gear, one of many tasks that made up the assembly-line production of the bombers.

men would get their jobs back. And the men, he said, weren't nearly as productive as they were.

Many of the women came to California to find jobs during the war. One named Bettye worked the graveyard shift—which began at midnight—building B-17 bomber planes. She entered the enormous plant through a tunnel covered in camouflage. Once there, Bettye and another woman worked as a team to install rivets into the part of the plane from which the turret gun, or multishot firearm, would be fired. Her teammate stood on the outside of the compartment and drove in the rivet, which is a permanent metal fastener that looks something like a thick screw. Bettye stood on the inside and bucked the end of the rivet, pounding and flattening it. But she insisted that the process "wasn't as easy as it looked." The "skin" of the plane was fairly thin. If the operator of the rivet gun didn't hold it steady, the gun would drill a bigger-than-desired hole in the plane, and a larger rivet would have to be installed. And that, Bettye said, would weaken the whole plane.

Rockwell fashioned his subject after a 19-year-old neighbor named Mary Doyle Keefe. The model for another iconic image of Rosie is unknown or, at least, contested. This image was one of a series of posters created for the Westinghouse Electric Corporation in 1942 and designed to boost workers' morale. The poster of a young woman in a red-and-white bandana, flexing her arm, and exclaiming, "We can do it!" only appeared in the Westinghouse factory and only for a couple of weeks. Now fast-forward to 1982, when the poster was rediscovered and became a symbol of the movement to expand women's rights. Although the woman in the poster wasn't given a name in the 1940s, for many people today, she is Rosie the Riveter.

REAL-LIFE ROSIES

Of course, behind the song, painting, and poster were millions of women eager to do their part for the war effort. As you've read, many of these real-life Rosies worked in the aircraft and munitions industries. In some cases, they apparently did their jobs too well. A foreman in one plant told the women not to work so fast because when the war ended, the

For many of the real-life Rosies, the work provided an experience of the world they may never have had otherwise. They met and worked alongside women from many different backgrounds and ethnicities. And the work gave them independence, an income—which was certainly welcome after the deprivations of the Depression—and a sense of pride and patriotism. As one Rosie named Bonnie remarked, "I wouldn't have missed the experience for anything. And we did do good. We won the war."

HISTORICAL THINKING

1. **READING CHECK** What purpose did Rosie the Riveter serve during World War II?

2. **MAKE INFERENCES** Why do you think the women's rights movement adopted the Westinghouse Rosie poster as a symbol?

3. **DRAW CONCLUSIONS** What did Bonnie suggest when she said, "We won the war"?

JAPANESE AMERICAN INTERNMENT

Have you ever been unfairly accused of something? During World War II, the U.S. government viewed Japanese Americans as a threat and removed them from their homes.

EXECUTIVE ORDER 9066

Entry into the war drew most Americans together in their support for the Allied cause, but others quickly discovered their heritage marked them as objects of fear. On December 8, 1941—the day after the Pearl Harbor attack—President Roosevelt issued a series of executive orders that established the **Enemy Alien Control Program**. An **enemy alien** is someone whose loyalty to the nation is suspect. Many persons of Italian and German origin who were in the United States when World War II began were classified as enemy aliens and had their rights restricted. Thousands were **interned**, or confined in prisons or camps for military or political reasons, while many others were sent back to Germany or Italy.

Photographer Ansel Adams took this image of Japanese Americans waiting for lunch at California's Manzanar Camp in 1943.

Japanese Americans were also classified as enemy aliens and interned. Public opinion had turned sharply against Japanese Americans after the attack on Pearl Harbor. Unlike the Italians and Germans who were interned, more than 60 percent of those with Japanese ancestry who were relocated to camps were **Nisei** (nee-SAY). Nisei are people born in the United States whose parents emigrated from Japan. The general population and the military believed Japanese Americans were a threat, even though the FBI did not consider them a danger. Military leaders feared the close proximity of Japanese American communities to American military bases and aircraft plants on the West Coast, and the public associated Japanese Americans with the actions of Japan's armed forces.

In response to the perceived threat, President Roosevelt signed **Executive Order 9066** in 1942, which authorized the relocation and internment of 110,000 Japanese Americans and "resident aliens" living within 60 miles of the West Coast and in parts of Arizona on grounds of national security. An **executive order** is a directive issued by a president that has the force of law.

Nearly all Japanese Americans lived on the West Coast, in California, Washington, and Oregon. The order violated their constitutional and human rights. However, the Supreme Court, in a decision heavily criticized today, upheld its implementation in *Korematsu* v. *United States*, arguing that, "When under conditions of modern warfare our shores are threatened by hostile forces, the power to protect must be commensurate with [in proportion to] the threatened danger." The government removed Japanese Americans to **internment camps** in military zones, where they lived in prison-like surroundings until the war's end.

INTERNMENT

Ten internment camps were set up in California, Arizona, Wyoming, Utah, Arkansas, and Colorado. Japanese American families were forced to sell whatever belongings they could not carry and relocate to the camps. Japanese American merchants had to sell their businesses in a matter of just days or weeks. By June 1942, the government had moved 120,000 Japanese Americans into the camps. The first camp to open, in March of that year, was Manzanar in California's Owens Valley. The largest of the camps was Tule Lake, also in California, which housed more than 18,000 internees by 1944.

This military dog tag, or ID, belonged to Jack Wakamatsu. While his family lived behind barbed wire at Manzanar, Wakamatsu fought in the 442nd Infantry Regimental Combat Team, the all Japanese American military unit.

Families at the camps were housed in army barracks surrounded by barbed wire and towers where armed guards kept watch. The barracks themselves were not insulated, and residents had to rely on coal-burning stoves for heat. Families slept on cots and shared bathrooms with other internees. Guards were authorized to shoot residents who tried to escape. Nonetheless, Japanese Americans tried to make the camps as much like communities as possible. They established schools, churches, newspapers, and farms, and children stayed active by playing sports. And even though their government had imprisoned them, many young Japanese American men volunteered to fight for their country. They were released from the camps to do so.

After the war ended, Japanese Americans were at last allowed to return to their homes. They lost personal property, businesses, farms, and homes as a result of their forced removal. After many years of campaigning for redress, or compensation, Japanese Americans finally obtained justice. Congress formally apologized for their internment and allocated funds to compensate the survivors in 1988.

HISTORICAL THINKING

1. **READING CHECK** Why were Japanese Americans relocated to internment camps?

2. **DESCRIBE** What constitutional issues were involved in *Korematsu* v. *United States*, and how did the case impact events on the U.S. home front?

3. **FORM AND SUPPORT OPINIONS** Given the circumstances of the war, do you think the U.S. government was justified in interning Japanese Americans? Explain your opinion.

JAPANESE AMERICAN NATIONAL MUSEUM, LOS ANGELES

The Japanese American National Museum in Los Angeles, California, presents over 150 years of Japanese American history and culture. It aims to inspire appreciation for America's ethnic and cultural diversity by sharing the struggles and triumphs of Americans of Japanese ancestry. The museum houses a permanent collection of over 60,000 items, including movies, photographs, artwork, letters, oral histories, textiles, and other artifacts that tell the stories of this group of Americans.

Many of those stories focus on the experiences of Japanese Americans whose lives were abruptly uprooted during World War II when they were relocated to internment camps. For example, the museum's collection of letters written by children in the camps to a sympathetic librarian in San Diego describe their living conditions and experiences. The museum also exhibits artwork by adults, including the pieces shown here, that document the fears and monotony of everyday life at the camps.

Hisako Hibi, Painter

In this oil painting titled *Morning*, female artist Hisako Hibi (1907–1991) depicts a scene at an internment camp in Topaz, Utah, in 1942. The painting shows U.S. soldiers marching into the camp at dawn to construct more barracks for internees. Two Japanese Americans watch the soldiers from behind a water tower.

Hibi was imprisoned at the Topaz camp along with her husband—who was also an artist—and their two young children. The Japanese Americans set up schools at the camps, and the Hibis both taught in an art school at the camp in Topaz. What does Hibi's painting suggest about the relationship between the internees and soldiers?

George Hoshida, Sketch Artist

A self-educated artist, George Hoshida (1907–1985) created a visual record of internment camp life in a series of notebooks in which he sketched portraits of inmates and painted scenes of everyday activities. In the watercolor at top right, Hoshida depicts two men playing a board game while others watch. The men in the ink drawing at bottom right are making pipes. The two ink portraits below are of internees Sawaichi Fujita (left), a tinsmith, and store owner Keizo Takata (right). Initially separated from his wife and daughters, Hoshida shared his drawing skills with other internees to pass the time and preserve history.

Jack Iwata, Photographer

Born in Seattle, Washington, professional photographer Jack Iwata (1912–1992) was forcibly relocated to an internment camp at Manzanar, California, along with his wife. Iwata and a fellow photographer established a photo lab at the camp and began documenting life there. In the photo at right, Iwata captured a group of internees arriving with their luggage at Manzanar.

In December 1944, the U.S. government announced the internment camps would be closed. Japanese Americans began leaving the camps in early 1945, and the last camp shut down in 1946. Upon release, former inmates had to rebuild their lives. In 1948, a law was passed to reimburse some of the property losses sustained by internees. And then in 1988, Congress passed the Civil Liberties Act, which awarded $20,000 to each camp survivor.

CAMPAIGNS IN EUROPE AND AFRICA

The Soviet Union received economic aid and supplies from the United States, but
Stalin did not like how the war was being fought in Europe. While some of the Allies
invaded Africa, Stalin's army battled the bulk of the German forces in Russia alone.

INVADING NORTH AFRICA

As the United States mobilized for war in the Pacific
and in Europe, President Roosevelt and British prime
minister Winston Churchill planned a course of
action against Hitler in Europe and North Africa. But
Soviet premier Joseph Stalin did not agree with the
other two leaders on the best strategy to use against
the Germans. Stalin wanted Allied help in battling the
Germans and defending the Soviet Union. As you
have read, Hitler's troops launched an invasion of the
Soviet Union in 1941, and Stalin wanted the Allies to
establish a second front, or line of battle, in western
Europe to help the Soviets combat the Germans.
Britain and the United States, however, preferred
invading French North Africa and reclaiming Nazi-
controlled areas there. The North African attack

The War in Europe and Africa, 1942–1943

Legend:
- Axis and Axis-controlled
- Allies
- Soviet-controlled
- Neutral countries
- ← Axis forces
- ← Allied forces
- ← Soviet forces
- ✳ Major battles

would be on a smaller, more manageable scale for the Americans, who were just entering the fight.

However, the first step toward victory in this campaign was for the United States to seize control of the Atlantic Ocean and ensure the safe mobilization of Allied troops in Africa. During the first few months of 1942, German submarines had been prowling the Atlantic, regularly sinking Allied ships. Eventually, new antisubmarine technologies and weapons such as radar and **depth charges**, underwater bombs that are programmed to explode at certain depths, enabled the Allies to strike back. By mid-1943, the German submarine threat in the Atlantic had been neutralized.

In November 1942, U.S. Army general **Dwight D. Eisenhower** led the Allied forces in an invasion of North Africa called **Operation Torch**. Eisenhower had been supreme commander of the Allied forces in Europe before taking charge of Operation Torch. By May 1943, the British and American forces had successfully recaptured Morocco and Algeria and defeated the army under German general **Edwin Rommel**, capturing more than 250,000

Nazi prisoners in Tunisia. Once they were firmly established in North Africa, the Allied forces planned to use it as a base of operations against Italy.

Germany's success in the first years of the war had been due in part to its superior fleet of tanks, known as **panzers**, which the Germans arranged in massed formations. Manufactured in Germany from the mid-1930s to the mid-1940s, the panzers were thickly armored and boasted impressive firepower, but their size and weight kept them from being speedy or easy to maneuver. The German panzers had a distinct advantage over the relatively older British tanks, but U.S. troops arrived in Europe and North Africa with American-built Sherman tanks, which could often outmaneuver the panzers. Sherman tanks had less substantial armor and firepower, but they were more agile. As a result, the British forces traded in their tanks for the Sherman tanks in 1943 and 1944.

GERMANY VERSUS THE SOVIET UNION

When Hitler's forces undertook their invasion of the Soviet Union in June 1941, they believed they could defeat the Soviet army in a matter of months. The Germans had caught the Soviets off guard, sending

ANTISUBMARINE TECHNOLOGY

The barrel-shaped depth charge was filled with explosives and contained a fuse set to detonate at a specific depth, based on water pressure. Depth charges were deployed in three major ways.

1 Rolled off a ship's drop rack

2 Launched from the K-gun, or depth charge projector, on a ship's deck into the water

3 Dropped from an escort plane or helicopter

escort plane

K-gun

drop rack

Shock Waves
A depth charge didn't usually explode close enough to a submarine to destroy it. But the shock waves from the explosion were powerful enough to damage the boat's structure, causing the submarine to rise to the water's surface. Once it did, naval gunners were ready to torpedo it.

shock waves

In October 1942, the Soviets sometimes sought defensive positions inside industrial buildings, including the Red October factory, while battling the Germans at Stalingrad. The factory protected the soldiers but was destroyed in the Battle of Stalingrad. In this photo taken by *Life* magazine photographer Thomas D. McAvoy, Soviet soldiers march German prisoners of war past the ruins of Red October.

200 divisions with 10,000 to 20,000 soldiers each to attack along a front stretching nearly 2,000 miles from the Baltic to the Black seas. Nonetheless, the Soviet army, or Red Army, put up strong resistance. Soviet forces employed a "scorched-earth" policy, destroying crops, bridges, and railroad cars as they retreated deeper into their homeland. This strategy left the German soldiers without food or shelter as they advanced east. Still, the Germans took hundreds of thousands of prisoners along the way. By mid-July, Hitler's troops were within a couple hundred miles of Moscow.

The next few months brought unexpected hardship to the German Army. An early and severe winter settled across the Soviet Union and impeded German advances. Some Nazi generals wanted to suspend fighting until spring, but they were overruled, and the army pressed on to Moscow. Both the German troops and their machinery suffered in the cold. Because the Germans had not expected the Soviet resistance to last so long, they had not brought enough supplies to last through the winter. By November 1941, 700,000 Germans had died. The following month, the Soviets launched an organized attack on the Germans, but Hitler would not allow

his army to retreat. As a result, the Germans held on to most of the ground they had captured earlier in the year.

By the summer of 1942, Soviet casualties stood at about 4 million. German numbers were high but not nearly as staggering. In July, Hitler decided to split his forces between the Caucasus Mountains near the Turkish border and the city of Stalingrad, located about 500 miles north on the Volga River. In August, Germany began bombing the city, and the **Battle of Stalingrad** began. With residents still living in Stalingrad, the two armies fought in the streets, causing high numbers of civilian casualties.

In November 1942, the Soviets launched a counteroffensive attack against the now freezing, starving, and poorly supplied German troops. Once again, Hitler refused to allow his army to retreat from the Volga River, ordering them to fight to the death. As the Nazis weakened, the Soviets surrounded them. The German troops surrendered at the end of January 1943. But battle resumed between the two armies about six months later in Kursk, a city to the west of Stalingrad. In the largest tank battle ever fought, the German Army was dealt a crushing defeat

A landing craft with General George Patton (wearing a helmet) aboard leaves the North African country of Tunisia for Sicily, in the combined British and American invasion of the island in 1943.

and suffered about 500,000 casualties. The Battle of Kursk was the last major offensive launched by the Nazis in the Soviet Union.

THE ITALIAN CAMPAIGN

In the summer of 1943, not long after the Allied victory in North Africa and the Soviet triumph in Stalingrad, the Allies turned their attention to Italy. The Soviets, still calling for a second front in Western Europe, were not happy with this turn of events, especially after the extreme losses they had suffered battling the Germans without the support of other Allied troops. Roosevelt tried to appease Stalin by promising him a second front the following year, but Stalin remained displeased.

In July 1943, Allied forces, led by American lieutenant general **George S. Patton** and British general Bernard Montgomery, began the Italian campaign by storming the island of Sicily. The invasion represented the biggest **amphibious assault** that had ever taken place. An amphibious assault uses naval support to protect military forces invading by land and air. The assault also demonstrated the cohesion of the American and British forces led by Patton and Montgomery, who successfully

worked together to secure the island. The Allies conquered Sicily in about a month, and their invasion indirectly forced a regime change in Italy. The Italian government removed, arrested, and eventually executed its leader, Benito Mussolini. Meanwhile, approximately 100,000 Axis troops retreated from Sicily and headed for Italy's mainland, having suffered many more casualties than the Allies in the battle over the island.

The Allies followed closely behind, landing on the southern coast of Italy in early September. Not long after their arrival, the new Italian government secretly agreed to sign an armistice with the Allies and help them fight against Germany. Additional Allied landings followed at Salerno and Naples along Italy's western coast, and by mid-October, Italy had officially changed sides and declared war against Germany. But Germany still occupied much of Italy. In November 1943, German troops began establishing defensive lines about halfway up the Italian peninsula to prevent the Allies from reaching Rome. Exhausting battles, the treacherous mountain terrain, and a lack of supplies slowed the Allied advance. It took four months for the Allies to move forward just 70 miles, and they were still 80 miles from Rome, Italy's capital.

For months, the Allies continued advancing up the peninsula. Then, in May 1944, they broke through one of the Germans' defensive lines and reached Rome about a month later. Fighting continued during the summer and into the fall and winter, leaving the Germans short of supplies—especially fuel. They were forced to use oxen to tow their tanks. In contrast, the Allies had received new reinforcements and weapons. German forces finally surrendered in May 1945, but the campaign had been costly on both sides. Allied casualties numbered around 300,000, while German casualties were about 434,000.

HISTORICAL THINKING

1. **READING CHECK** What strategy did Stalin want the Allies to follow against Germany?

2. **DETERMINE CHRONOLOGY** What events led to the German surrender at the Battle of Stalingrad in 1943?

3. **INTERPRET MAPS** Why did it make sense, geographically, for the Allied forces to invade Sicily and Italy's mainland after fighting in North Africa?

4. **DRAW CONCLUSIONS** Why did the Italian government switch to the Allied side during the Italian campaign?

WAR IN THE PACIFIC

If you've ever played a game of war strategy, you know that different types of battles require different plans of action. The Allies knew this as they fought Japan in the war in the Pacific.

BATTLING BY SEA AND AIR

The Americans were the primary fighting force in the Pacific and were supported by Allied troops from Australia, New Zealand, Canada, and Britain. The troops were led by General Douglas MacArthur, who, as you may recall, was ordered to leave his troops in the Philippines early in the war, and Admiral **Chester Nimitz** of the U.S. Navy. Their mission had four goals: maintain communication between the United States and Australia, where the Americans had established bases; defend North America against the Japanese; prevent the Japanese from venturing outside of the Pacific; and plan amphibious counteroffensives against them.

In spring 1942, the Japanese sought to take control of the sea north of Australia by establishing air bases in New Guinea and the Solomon Islands. From these bases, the Japanese planned to destroy U.S. naval bases along the eastern coast of Australia. However, Allied code breakers had uncovered their plan and alerted U.S. officials, who launched a preemptive attack. Over the course of several days in May, the two enemies battled by air and sea off the coast of New Guinea in what is known as the **Battle of the Coral Sea**. It was the first air-sea battle in history. Japanese forces sank one U.S. aircraft carrier and damaged another, and the Allies destroyed many Japanese planes and badly damaged a Japanese carrier.

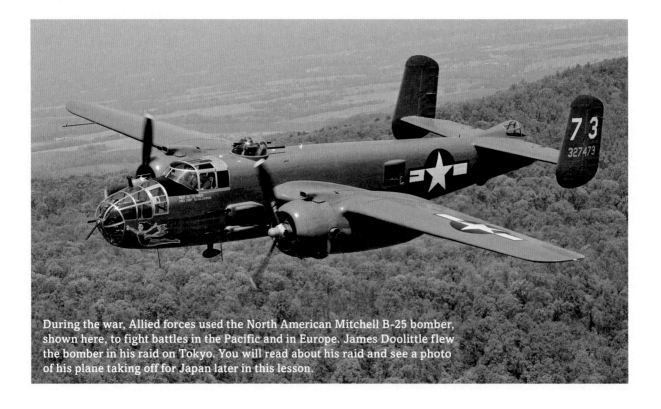

During the war, Allied forces used the North American Mitchell B-25 bomber, shown here, to fight battles in the Pacific and in Europe. James Doolittle flew the bomber in his raid on Tokyo. You will read about his raid and see a photo of his plane taking off for Japan later in this lesson.

But the Japanese remained determined. In June 1942, they tried to seize Midway Island, located 1,400 miles west of Hawaii, in an attempt to destroy a U.S. carrier fleet. Once again, the Allies had intercepted Japan's battle plans. Though the Japanese fleet far outnumbered the U.S. fleet during the three-day-long **Battle of Midway**, the Americans used the intelligence they'd received to stay one step ahead of their enemy.

On June 3, U.S. bombers attacked the Japanese fleet when it was still 500 miles from its destination. Undeterred, Japan attacked Midway the following morning, a decision it came to regret. The battle greatly reduced Japan's naval forces, including the destruction of four carriers and the loss of hundreds of planes and pilots. After its defeat at Midway, Japan canceled plans for several subsequent invasions.

ISLAND HOPPING

Having established control of the Pacific, the Allies' next move involved a two-pronged approach. Admiral Nimitz would travel west from Hawaii, and General MacArthur would travel north from Australia, carrying out a campaign of island hopping. This strategy was designed to capture and control islands in the Pacific one by one. The Allies planned to establish bases on the islands along a path to the Japanese homeland in preparation for an Allied attack on Japan.

The offensive began on the island of **Guadalcanal**, northeast of Australia in the Solomon Islands chain. In July 1942, the Japanese had begun constructing an air base there. A month later, the U.S. Marines were sent in to fight the Japanese and force them off Guadalcanal. As the battle dragged on, additional troops arrived to replenish both sides. By mid-October, the Japanese and the Americans each had more than 20,000 troops engaged in battle on the island. By January 1943, however, the Americans had managed to block the stream of Japanese reinforcements, while allowing the American troop strength to nearly double. The Japanese suffered many more casualties and, with their fewer numbers, soon evacuated the island. After six grueling months of battle, the Americans finally held Guadalcanal.

James Doolittle's B-25 taking off from the aircraft carrier, the U.S.S. *Hornet*

TOKYO RAIDERS

Since Japan's attack on Pearl Harbor in December 1941, the United States had wanted revenge. So in April 1942, Lieutenant Colonel James Doolittle led a squadron of B-25 bomber pilots on a surprise attack on the Japanese mainland.

As the planes flew over Tokyo, some citizens below waved to the pilots, believing the aircraft were Japanese. They were shocked when Doolittle and his raiders dropped their bombs, striking industrial and military facilities as well as civilian areas before retreating to free China, where most of them crash-landed.

Japanese casualties were relatively light, but the attack devastated Japanese morale and proved the nation was vulnerable. On the other hand, the raid gave the Americans new confidence and helped set the stage for the war in the Pacific.

More Pacific victories soon followed for the Allies. In November 1943, Nimitz led his forces west of Guadalcanal to the Gilbert Islands, where they also defeated the Japanese. Nimitz and MacArthur continued island hopping throughout 1944. MacArthur overpowered the Japanese in parts of New Guinea and the Philippines. Nimitz took control of the Marshall and Marianas islands in February and August, respectively. From there, the two commanders set their sights on the islands of Japan, only about 1,200 miles away. Meanwhile, the Allied forces in Europe were planning an invasion they hoped would turn the tide of war against Germany.

HISTORICAL THINKING

1. **READING CHECK** What was the Allied mission in the Pacific war?

2. **MAKE INFERENCES** What might have happened if the American military hadn't learned about Japan's plans for the battles of the Coral Sea and Midway?

3. **IDENTIFY PROBLEMS AND SOLUTIONS** Why was island hopping a good strategy for an Allied attack on Japan?

VICTORY IN EUROPE

When faced with a daunting task, you are never sure whether you have prepared well enough, and you don't know how it will turn out. As the Allied forces advanced on Europe, they met many challenges—both expected and unexpected.

OPERATION OVERLORD

With the war in the Pacific going well, the Allies began to make plans to drive the Nazis back to Germany. In November 1943, Roosevelt, Churchill, and Stalin gathered at the **Tehran Conference** in Iran in southwest Asia. It would be the first time Roosevelt had met Stalin. At the conference, the three leaders discussed their plans to invade western Europe—the second front in the west that Stalin had been pressing for—the following spring.

The plan was for General Eisenhower to lead an Allied invasion, code-named **Operation Overlord**, from Britain. Eisenhower organized 3 million soldiers for the invasion and stockpiled plenty of supplies, including food, planes, and smaller ships. To prevent the Nazis from learning their plans, the Allies deliberately planted false information indicating they intended to invade near Calais, France, directly across the English Channel from Dover, England. In addition, in the weeks leading up to the invasion, the Allied air forces kept the Nazis distracted by dropping bombs on German airfields, military bases, and bridges over the main rivers in France. The deception ultimately helped isolate and draw the Nazis away from the invasion's actual target: the French coastal province of Normandy.

Operation Overlord was originally planned to take place in May 1944, but naval vessels called **amphibious landing craft** were not assembled until June. A departure planned for June 5 was delayed by bad weather. At last, on June 6, 1944, thousands of amphibious landing craft, airplanes, and an armada, or fleet of warships, departed from several British ports. Eisenhower's huge force headed toward five different Normandy beaches, code-named Utah, Omaha, Gold, Juno, and Sword. By sundown that day, on what came to be known as **D-Day**, 150,000 American, British, and Canadian troops stormed the beaches.

American troops under the command of Major General **Omar Bradley** at Omaha, the largest assault area, endured some of the worst conditions. Many Americans drowned as they tried to reach the beach. The troops also faced heavy resistance from German soldiers who turned their machine-gun fire on the Americans as soon as they set foot on the beach. By the next morning, more than 2,000 American soldiers lay dead in the sand. Despite such difficult battles, the Normandy invasion was successful, and Allied forces soon began to move inland. Within two months of the initial landing, more than 1 million Allied troops were fighting to take back France.

BATTLE OF THE BULGE

It took Allied troops only about two months to reach Paris, France's capital, which was controlled by the Nazis. On August 19, 1944, Parisians—aware that the Allies would soon reach them—rose up against the occupying Germans. By the time the Allied forces arrived on August 25, the Nazis were ready to surrender. The liberation of Paris was complete. But the war was still far from over.

In early September, Allied troops advanced from northern France and captured Antwerp, Belgium, an important supply port. From there, they set out toward the German border. At this point, most people believed the end of the war was close. But as the Allies marched farther east, Nazi defenses strengthened. In mid-October, Hitler required all males between the ages of 16 and 60 to fight on behalf of the Third Reich. In mid-December,

Allied Invasion of Normandy, June 6, 1944

ENGLAND

London

Exeter

Plymouth

Falmouth

Southampton

Dartmouth

Weymouth

Poole

Portsmouth

Newhaven

Calais

Follow-up Force

U.S. Forces
British/Canadian Forces
Airborne Forces

E N G L I S H   C H A N N E L

Follow-up Force

U.S. 82nd Airborne

British 6th Airborne

Cherbourg

Utah

U.S. 101st Airborne

Carenten

Omaha

Le Havre

Gold

Juno

Brest

Caen

Sword

0   25   50 miles
0   25   50 kilometers

2°W

FRANCE

N
W   E
S

2°E

U.S. soldiers jump off their amphibious landing craft into the water and prepare for battle on the beach at Normandy on D-Day.

reinforced with fresh soldiers, the Germans launched an unexpected attack on the Allies in southern Belgium's Ardennes region. Their goal was to split up the Allied troops and retake Antwerp.

More than 200,000 German soldiers advanced into southern Belgium, greatly outnumbering the Allied troops there, and broke through the Allied front line. This break in the front line created a "bulge," giving the battle its name: the **Battle of the Bulge**. In just one day, approximately 4,000 American soldiers surrendered. General Eisenhower called in reinforcements, eventually enlisting a half million soldiers to fight the battle and, as he hoped, move the Allies closer to victory.

Many of the soldiers Eisenhower called came directly from basic training, however, with little or no experience in combat. Also among the reinforcements called to action were about 2,500 African-American soldiers, who fought shoulder-to-shoulder with white soldiers at Ardennes. An all-black tank unit also rolled in to fight in the battle. It was the first time desegregated troops had fought in a U.S. war.

Troops fought not only the enemy but also the weather. Snow and freezing temperatures tormented the soldiers, who lacked appropriate winter clothing. Many soldiers suffered from frostbite, and some of the wounded froze to death in their foxholes, the holes they dug in the ground to shield themselves as they fired on the enemy. Thick fog also made warfare more difficult for both the troops on the ground and the pilots above—and yet, the Allies kept fighting.

The Battle of the Bulge began in mid-December, and by Christmas, the Germans were calling for the Allies to surrender. But on December 26, General Patton and his army broke through German lines to capture the strategic Belgian town of Bastogne. Then in January 1945, thousands of Allied aircraft bombed the German troops and their supply lines, forcing the Nazis to withdraw in a matter of a few weeks. About 20,000 Americans died in the Battle of the Bulge, and the Germans wounded or captured another 60,000. But that paled in comparison with the 100,000 casualties sustained by the German troops. The battle was the biggest and bloodiest the U.S. Army had fought in World War II.

General Dwight D. Eisenhower (center) and Pierre Koenig (left), leader of the French resistance, take a symbolic walk under the Arc de Triomphe in Paris on August 27, 1944, two days after the Germans surrendered the city to the Allies.

END OF THE THIRD REICH

Meanwhile, the Soviet army was advancing toward the western front. Throughout January 1945, the Soviets had moved west across Poland toward Germany. By the end of the month, they were within 40 miles of Berlin. At the same time, more Allied forces pressed east from France and Belgium, while those involved in the Italian campaign continued to push German troops north along the Italian peninsula. To prepare the way for the ground-force invasion of Germany, the Allies intensified their aerial assault on the country in February 1945. Much of this strategic bombing targeted both industrial and civilian areas.

In 1945, Churchill, Roosevelt, and Stalin (from left to right) attend the Yalta Conference.

By late March, Allied ground troops began crossing the Rhine River into western Germany. Hitler ordered his retreating troops to destroy the country's industrial plants and power and water facilities, along with any food or clothing stores. He wanted to use the scorched-earth policy, much as the Soviets had done against the Germans. But Hitler's minister of war production refused, knowing it would lead to the suffering and deaths of many German citizens—a prospect that did not concern Hitler.

On April 11, Allied troops arrived at the Elbe River, within 60 miles of Berlin. Within two weeks, the Soviet troops joined them, and together they encircled the German capital. On April 30, with the Soviets closing in on his bunker, Hitler committed suicide. With their leader gone and their cause lost, the Nazis surrendered. The war in Europe officially ended on May 8, 1945. The Third Reich had fallen.

THE YALTA CONFERENCE

Before Germany surrendered, Roosevelt, Churchill, and Stalin met at Yalta, a Russian town in the Crimea, in February 1945. With the war turning in the Allies' favor, the leaders spent a week drawing up postwar plans for Europe. The decisions they made came to be called the **Yalta Accords**. The three leaders decided to divide Germany into different occupation zones controlled by the United States, the Soviet Union, Britain, and France. They also agreed to take control of or destroy German arms industries, try German war criminals in a court of law, and establish a commission in Moscow to decide on the reparations Germany would need to make. Stalin particularly pressed for reparations. German soldiers had killed or injured about 20 million Soviet citizens during the war and destroyed many Soviet towns and businesses. Stalin wanted to ensure the Soviet Union received appropriate compensation.

In addition, the leaders discussed Poland's geographic boundaries and political future as well as the establishment of a new international body called the United Nations. At the conference, Stalin agreed to respect free elections in Poland and elsewhere in the eastern European region of the Soviet Union. However, just weeks later, he ordered the arrest of Polish anti-communist leaders and the murder of political dissidents in Romania and Bulgaria.

The war in Europe was over, but the war in the Pacific dragged on. Japan refused to quit, even after crushing defeats. Nevertheless, the Allies hoped to bring a quick end to the war in the Pacific.

HISTORICAL THINKING

1. **READING CHECK** What was Operation Overlord?

2. **INTERPRET MAPS** Why might it have made sense to the Germans that the Allied forces would stage their invasion in Calais rather than in Normandy?

3. **MAKE INFERENCES** Why do you think defeat at the Battle of the Bulge made Hitler realize he might lose the war?

4. **EVALUATE** What did Stalin's actions after the Yalta Conference reveal about the Soviet leader?

VICTORY IN ASIA

The Allies found themselves up against a determined and relentless enemy in the Japanese. A strong sense of honor prevented Japanese soldiers from surrendering, even when the odds were heavily stacked against them. Faced with defeat, some even chose suicide.

LIBERATING THE PHILIPPINES

As the Allies gained ground and fought to secure victory in Europe, war continued to rage in the Pacific. In mid-September 1944, President Roosevelt and General MacArthur decided that the Philippines—which Japan had seized early in 1942—should be the next target of an Allied invasion, with American naval forces taking the lead. In preparation for the liberation, Filipino and American troops had formed guerrilla groups on the ground.

On October 20, 1944, General MacArthur led an amphibious landing on the island of Leyte, southeast of Luzon, where the Philippine capital, Manila, is located. The Allies had judged correctly that the Japanese did not have a strong defense on Leyte. In fact, the Japanese used a decoy ship to draw some of the U.S. naval fleet away from the island. They also sent forces to attack the American fleet at the landing. But the U.S. Navy had anticipated Japan's strategy and, on October 23, used submarines to sink two Japanese cruisers as they approached Leyte. The next day, American aerial attacks sank a Japanese battleship, and the fighting began in earnest.

The **Battles of Leyte Gulf** took place between October 23 and October 26, 1944, during which time the Japanese suffered heavy losses—far more than the Americans. Japanese losses were due, in part, to Japan's decision to deploy suicide bomber pilots called **kamikaze**, meaning "divine wind." These Japanese pilots volunteered to crash their planes, loaded with explosives, into American ships. Over the course of the rest of the war, the kamikaze destroyed 34 U.S. ships, but about 2,800 Japanese pilots sacrificed their lives in the process.

Though the United States did not achieve total control over Leyte until the end of December, the battles destroyed the Imperial Japanese Navy. The United States finally liberated the Philippines in March 1945. Filipino soldiers played an important role in the war effort, but the conflict had taken a terrible toll on their island nation. Manila became the second most devastated city in the world after Warsaw, Poland. By the end of the war, as many as 1 million civilians in the Philippines had died.

CLOSING IN ON JAPAN

Once the Philippines was under American control, the Allies turned their attention to Japan itself. The Allied forces wanted to establish a base for their B-29 bombers close to the Japanese mainland to conduct aerial attacks. They chose the Japanese island of Iwo Jima, located 760 miles southeast of Tokyo.

On February 19, 1945, the Allies, made up mostly of U.S. Marines, landed on Iwo Jima to confront the roughly 20,000 Japanese troops they believed were stationed there. Before the landing, however, the Allies had bombarded the island with napalm bombs and rockets. When the Marines set foot on the devastated island, they saw no sign of life and thought, for a moment at least, that they were going to take the island without a fight. Then suddenly, machine-gun fire erupted, seemingly out of nowhere. The Japanese were firing from a network of hidden natural caves and tunnels they had carved out all over Iwo Jima. And once again, they used kamikaze air raids, crashing their planes into American vessels, sinking one U.S. carrier and damaging many other ships. Fighting was intense, but eventually the Allies prevailed. About 6,000 Americans died while fighting

The War in Asia, 1942–1945

**Map labels:**
ALASKA (U.S.), Bering Sea, Kamchatka Peninsula, Aleutian Islands, Attu Island, Kiska Island May 1943, TANNU TUVA, SOVIET UNION, MONGOLIA, MANCHUKUO (MANCHURIA), Aug. 1945, Sakhalin, Kuril Islands, Beijing, KOREA, JAPAN, Tokyo, CHINA, Nanjing, Chongqing, Hiroshima Aug. 6, 1945, Nagasaki Aug. 9, 1945, TIBET, BHUTAN, NEPAL, Midway Islands (U.S.), Midway June 3–6, 1942, PACIFIC OCEAN, Hawaiian Islands (U.S.), INDIA (U.K.), BURMA (U.K.), Hong Kong, Formosa (Taiwan), Okinawa Apr. 1–June 21, 1945, Iwo Jima Feb. 19–Mar. 16, 1945, Wake Island (U.S.), Nov. 1943, Pearl Harbor Dec. 7, 1941, Apr. 1945, THAILAND, FRENCH INDOCHINA (Fr.), Philippine Islands (U.S.), Mariana Islands, Guam July 21–Aug. 10, 1944, Eniwetok Feb. 17–23, 1944, Marshall Islands, Nov. 1943, Leyte Gulf Oct. 23–26, 1944, BRITISH MALAYA, BRITISH BORNEO, Singapore, Borneo, Sumatra, Celebes, Caroline Islands, Japanese Mandate, Gilbert Islands (U.K.), Tarawa Nov. 20–23, 1943, Equator, DUTCH EAST INDIES (Neth.), Java, May 1944, Rabaul, Solomon Islands, Ellice Islands (U.K.), INDIAN OCEAN, New Guinea, Lae, Aug. 1942, Guadalcanal Aug. 7, 1942–Feb. 9, 1943, New Hebrides (U.K./Fr.), Coral Sea May 7–8, 1942, AUSTRALIA, New Caledonia (Fr.), Fiji Islands (U.K.)

Legend:
Japanese-controlled by Aug. 1942
Allied powers
Soviet Union and its allies
Allied advances
Major battle
Atomic bomb

Scale: 0 500 1,000 miles / 0 500 1,000 kilometers

the **Battle of Iwo Jima**, and nearly all the Japanese soldiers and civilians on the island perished. The Marines took Iwo Jima on March 16, and the United States staged about 2,000 B-29 bombers there.

That same month, just before the Marines secured Iwo Jima, the Allies used a new bombing technique on Tokyo, Japan: nighttime napalm firebombs. The first drop destroyed 25 percent of Tokyo's buildings and killed tens of thousands of people—most of them civilians. The Allies then used a similar technique on several other Japanese cities, hoping that the bombing campaigns would avoid the necessity of sending ground troops into Japan and force the Japanese to surrender.

On April 1, Allied troops landed on the island of Okinawa, located about 400 miles south of Honshu, Japan's main island, where Tokyo is located. Admiral Nimitz and 180,000 troops, most of his carriers, and 18 battleships faced off against 110,000 Japanese soldiers in the **Battle of Okinawa**. Nimitz's troops captured Okinawa's airfields, but the Japanese refused to back down. A few days later, Japan launched a counterattack that involved hundreds of kamikaze raids against the Allied fleet and a successful attack on a U.S. destroyer.

As a result of the kamikaze strategy, American casualty rates skyrocketed. And as on Iwo Jima, a maze of natural caves lay beneath the surface of Okinawa. Japanese soldiers hunkered down in the caves and in pillboxes, small concrete fortifications used to house weapons. American troops were forced to go from one hiding place to another and destroy them with dynamite. Fighting did not officially end on Okinawa until July 2. By then, 7,000 U.S. troops had died on land, and 5,000 more had died at sea. In addition, 40,000 American troops had sustained injuries. More than 100,000 Japanese died in the battle. The overwhelming losses on both sides would play a big role in the U.S. government's decision to use a new strategy to end the war.

A NEW PRESIDENT

Meanwhile, back on the home front, Roosevelt won an unprecedented fourth term in office. During his campaign, Roosevelt chose a new running mate for vice president, Senator **Harry S. Truman** of Missouri. When Roosevelt suddenly died of a massive stroke on April 12, 1945, just a few weeks after his inauguration, Truman became president. Truman was born in Missouri and had fought in World War I. He was an experienced politician, having served

The atomic bomb explodes over Hiroshima on August 6, 1945. In addition to the deaths caused by the explosion, tens of thousands of Japanese in both Hiroshima and Nagasaki died from radiation sickness.

first as a county judge and later as U.S. senator. But as the new president, he struggled to manage operations during the war.

President Truman was receiving conflicting advice about how to end the war and how to deal with Stalin, who was going back on promises he made at the Yalta Conference. Roosevelt's former vice president, Henry Wallace, encouraged Truman to negotiate with Stalin. The U.S. ambassador to the Soviet Union, however, urged the president to demand Stalin's compliance with the Yalta Accords. Truman took the ambassador's advice and pressed the Soviet foreign minister to convince Stalin to comply with the agreements, threatening that the United States would otherwise withdraw economic aid.

In mid-July 1945, Truman met with Churchill and Stalin in Potsdam, Germany, near Berlin. At the **Potsdam Conference**, the leaders agreed to the terms of peace for Germany and the procedure for bringing Nazi war criminals to trial, among other issues. The defeat of Churchill's Conservative Party interrupted the conference, as Churchill had to return to Britain to pass on his role as prime minister to a new leader. When the Potsdam Conference resumed, the friction between Truman and Stalin was apparent. Stalin brushed aside Truman's concerns about Poland and Eastern Europe, while Truman opposed Stalin's demand for reparations from Germany.

THE ATOMIC BOMB

Another talking point the leaders discussed at the Potsdam Conference was the possibility of using an **atomic bomb**, a type of nuclear bomb whose violent explosion is triggered by splitting atoms, which releases intense heat and radioactivity. Armed with this powerful weapon, Truman warned Japan about the disaster that would befall if the nation refused to surrender without conditions. But for the Japanese, any surrender would be a great dishonor to their country and to their emperor, Hirohito.

Truman had only learned of the atomic bomb's existence after he took office in April 1945. Roosevelt had decided to build the bomb after he was advised the Nazis were taking steps to build one themselves. The U.S. effort, known as the **Manhattan Project**, included top-secret facilities in Washington state, New Mexico, and Tennessee, where scientists designed, built, and tested the new weapon.

Truman formed committees to advise him on how best to deploy the atomic bomb. One of the committees recommended that the United States drop the bomb on four Japanese cities: Kokura, Niigata, **Hiroshima**, and **Nagasaki**. The president decided that although using atomic weapons would cause horrendous loss of life, it would also end the war more quickly, saving more lives in the long run.

In the end, Truman had two Japanese cities bombed. On August 6, 1945, a B-29 bomber called the *Enola Gay* dropped an atomic bomb on Hiroshima. At least 100,000 civilians died in the explosion and the firestorm that followed. A second atomic bomb was dropped on Nagasaki on August 9. Between 35,000 and 40,000 people died, and a similar number of Japanese were injured.

On August 15, Japan accepted the terms of surrender. World War II officially ended on September 2, 1945, when the Japanese signed the formal document of surrender aboard the battleship U.S.S. *Missouri* in Tokyo Bay. After the Japanese surrendered, the Allies occupied Japan, but they allowed the emperor to remain in power to restore order to the country. The Allies also conducted trials against Japanese military and government officials accused of war crimes.

Although American war casualties were small in comparison with those suffered by other nations, more than 400,000 Americans lost their lives. But in Europe as well as Japan, not only soldiers died in the war. The Allies would soon confront murder of civilians on a scale never seen before.

Photographer Alfred Eisenstaedt captured this moment of celebration in Times Square, New York, on August 14, 1945, the day the Japanese surrendered.

HISTORICAL THINKING

1. **READING CHECK** What strategies did the Americans and the Japanese use in the Battles of Leyte Gulf?

2. **COMPARE AND CONTRAST** In what ways were the Battles of Iwo Jima and Okinawa similar, and how did they differ?

3. **DETERMINE CHRONOLOGY** How soon after the Potsdam Conference were atomic bombs deployed over Japan?

4. **FORM AND SUPPORT OPINIONS** Do you think Truman was justified in dropping the atomic bomb on Hiroshima and Nagasaki? Explain your answer.

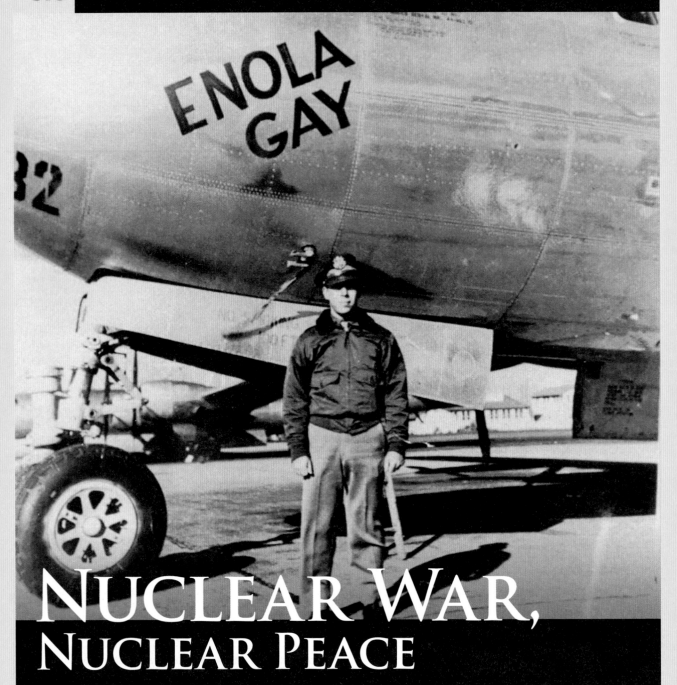

NUCLEAR WAR, NUCLEAR PEACE

"There is no one truth when it comes to World War II."
—Ari Beser

Ari Beser should know. His paternal grandfather was the only person to have flown in both of the planes that dropped atomic bombs on the Japanese cities of Hiroshima and Nagasaki. His maternal grandfather had employed a young Japanese woman who survived the bombing of Hiroshima. Spurred by this dual connection to these 1945 events, Beser set out to document his paternal grandfather's story, along with those of the survivors. "This is not just an American story or a Japanese story. It's a human story," he says.

^
Ari Beser's grandfather, Lieutenant Jacob Beser, poses in front of the B-29 bomber *Enola Gay*. This photo was taken before the plane dropped the first atomic weapon ever used in combat on the city of Hiroshima, Japan, on August 6, 1945.

Ari Beser (left) poses with Clifton Truman Daniel (right), grandson of President Harry Truman, who ordered the use of atomic weapons against Japan in 1945. They are joined by survivors of the bombs and their family members in Hiroshima.

ATOMIC HERITAGE

Growing up, Ari Beser had long heard tales of his grandfather's crucial role in the most historic of events. An engineer, Lieutenant (Lt.) Jacob Beser modified radar systems to suit the unique needs of the bombing mission. He was unapologetic about his part. He viewed the bombings as a necessary step in ending the war with Japan. Nonetheless, he expressed the wish that no such tragedy should ever happen again and made a point of ensuring that his grandchildren were aware of his story.

Lt. Beser left behind a technical memoir about his time on the Manhattan Project, the research and development initiative during World War II that produced the first atomic weapons. From the memoir, Ari Beser gained a wealth of firsthand information about his grandfather and his perspective on World War II. To better understand the perspective of the Japanese impacted by the bombing, Beser set out to talk to some of the remaining *hibakusha*—survivors of the bombs.

TRUTH AND RECONCILIATION

Through projects that aimed to raise awareness of the events at Hiroshima and Nagasaki, Beser did just that. A Fulbright–National Geographic Digital Storytelling Fellowship allowed him to travel to Japan in 2015 for the 70th anniversary of the bombings. The bombs together had killed some 200,000 people. Thousands more suffered radiation sickness. Beser has interviewed more than 50 *hibakusha* about their experiences during and in the wake of the bombings.

Despite the horrors they experienced, many *hibakusha* were eager to talk to Lt. Beser's grandson. The survivors bore no ill will toward the family of the man who had participated in the bombing missions. Ari Beser's frank but respectful approach gained him the trust of his interviewees. "How do you always get me to say things I've never said before?" asked a relative of Sadako Sasaki, who gained international renown for folding over 1,000 paper cranes as she battled leukemia caused by radiation exposure.

Gaining that trust was a necessary step. The accounts of the *hibakusha* are universally awful. They recount vividly the bright flash, the heat, and the wind generated by the bomb. And they all have tales of the carnage they witnessed in the aftermath. The rivers were choked with human remains, and horribly injured survivors wandered in search of help. Many were burned and stripped of skin. Even those who recovered endured years of chronic pain and wounds that wouldn't heal. As painful as reliving these memories is, the *hibakusha* insist that recording them is essential. Remarkably, many suspend judgment of the actions taken by the United States. Beser concurs. "We are each other's history," he says. "We all have a relative somewhere that fought in some war. This just happens to be my family's story."

It is his hope—and the hope of the *hibakusha*—that the exchange of these stories will put an end to nuclear warfare once and for all.

HISTORICAL THINKING

1. **READING CHECK** What does Beser hope to accomplish by talking to bomb survivors?

2. **EVALUATE** Compare the 1945 bombing of Japan to a similar recent event. What were the consequences of both events? What lessons were learned from them?

3. **MAKE GENERALIZATIONS** How do most survivors view the bombings?

THE HOLOCAUST

In the haze of war, Americans knew about Hitler's hatred of the Jews, but few allowed themselves to imagine the full extent of his anti-Semitic fervor. After the war in Europe was over, the world learned what the Nazis were capable of.

NAZI PERSECUTION OF JEWS

When the Allies invaded Germany and Poland in the spring of 1945, they encountered scenes of horror: **concentration camps** full of starving and dying prisoners. Most were Jews, but there were also non-Jewish Poles; Roma, or Gypsies; homosexuals; and political dissidents.

The nightmare began when Hitler became Germany's chancellor in January 1933. You've learned that Hitler considered Jews an inferior race, and he began almost immediately to devise a plan for their extermination. On Hitler's command, the Nazis began to systematically restrict the civil and political rights of Jews. They removed Jews from German schools and universities and banned them from many public areas. Businesses were taken away from their Jewish owners, and Jewish doctors and lawyers were not allowed to practice. In time, the Jewish people lost their right to vote.

Persecution of the Jews escalated with Kristallnacht on November 9, 1938, when, as you have read, rioters attacked and killed about 100 Jews and destroyed Jewish shops and synagogues. Many German Jews sought refuge in other countries, but the Nazis made travel outside of Germany difficult. Soon, Jews were forbidden to leave the country at all.

Germany invaded Poland in 1939, and the Nazis subjected both Jewish and non-Jewish Poles to brutal treatment. They made Poles perform hard labor and seized their property. They also created about 400 confined areas in Polish cities, called ghettos, forcing huge numbers of Jews to live in them. Barbed wire, thick walls, and armed guards surrounded the ghettos to prevent residents from escaping. Jews older than the age of six in Poland and in all German-occupied territories eventually were forced to wear a yellow Star of David with *Jew* written in the region's

Jews in the Netherlands were forced to wear a Star of David, like this one, with the Dutch word *Jood*, meaning "Jew." Any Jew in a German-occupied territory who refused to wear a star faced severe punishment or even death.

After putting up a fight in 1943, the Jews in Poland's Warsaw ghetto who survived were captured and deported to concentration camps. The Nazis systematically destroyed the city and blew up Warsaw's Great Synagogue. This photo is one of many taken by a Nazi photographer to document the Jews' removal.

language on it. With so many people living in such tight quarters, food was scarce, and disease spread quickly. In 1941, the Nazis rounded up others they had imprisoned as "undesirables" and sent them to the Polish ghettos. But the ghettos were just holding places until the Nazis came up with a plan to solve what they called "the Jewish question."

"THE FINAL SOLUTION"

When Germany invaded the Soviet Union, special military units accompanied the German Army. Their sole responsibility was to kill Jews, Gypsies, and Soviet heads of government departments. By 1943, these mobile killing units had executed an estimated 1 million Jews. This was the first step in what the Nazis called the "final solution." "Final solution" was code for the plan to murder all the Jews in Europe—approximately 11 million in all. Hitler had made

it known that this was his goal. In January 1942, **Reinhard Heydrich**, head of the Gestapo, called a meeting of high-ranking Nazis in Wannsee, a suburb of Berlin. Heydrich had gathered the men together at the **Wannsee Conference** to explain how the rest of the plan would be carried out.

Heydrich told the men that concentration camps would be constructed in eastern Europe. Jews would be sent to the camps, where the able-bodied among them would build roads and do other work. The work would be so hard that many Jews would die due to "natural reduction." Those who put up any resistance would be executed. But Jewish genocide, or the systematic destruction of a racial, cultural, or ethnic group and its culture, was the real purpose of the camps. The Nazis equipped most of the camps with facilities for carrying out the killings. The camps became known as extermination or death camps.

CRITICAL VIEWING These survivors of Buchenwald, one of the largest concentration camps inside Germany, were photographed as U.S. forces arrived at the camp in April 1945. Among them is Elie Wiesel, whose face appears farthest to the right in the second bunk from the bottom. Wiesel would describe his experiences in concentration camps in his memoir *Night*. What does the survivors' appearance suggest about their treatment in the camp?

Anne Frank, 1942

The most famous Jew who went into hiding from the Nazis is Anne Frank, a young girl who hid with her family in a secret attic apartment in Amsterdam, the Netherlands. Not long before the Nazis found the Franks and deported Anne to Auschwitz, she wrote the following in her famous diary. She died in Bergen-Belsen in 1945.

In spite of everything I still believe that people are really good at heart. I simply can't build up my hopes on a foundation consisting of confusion, misery, and death. I see the world gradually being turned into a wilderness, I hear the ever approaching thunder, which will destroy us too, I can feel the sufferings of millions and yet, if I look up into the heavens, I think that it will all come right, that this cruelty too will end, and that peace and tranquility will return again.

—from *The Diary of a Young Girl*, by Anne Frank, published in 1947

From 1942 until early 1945, the Nazis rounded up millions of Jews all across Europe. Jews were often ordered to gather in a town square, where Nazi officers terrorized them and then packed them into trains for "deportation," or transport, to the death camps. The overcrowded train cars were hot in the summer and freezing in the winter, and passengers did not receive food or water during the journey. Some died before they reached their destinations.

A number of Jews went into hiding or resisted rather than board the trains. The most famous example of resistance took place in 1943, when Jews in the Polish ghetto of Warsaw fought back against the Nazis. Armed with weapons they had managed to smuggle into the ghetto, the group held off the Nazis for a time. But in the end, the far better-equipped German troops overpowered the Jews. About 7,000 of those in the Warsaw ghetto were shot immediately. The rest—about 50,000—were sent to the camps.

DEATH CAMPS

The most notorious death camps were located in Poland and included Chelmno, Treblinka, and **Auschwitz** (OWSH-vits), the largest of the camps. Auschwitz consisted of three main camps. All were labor camps, and one included a killing center. Because Auschwitz was at a junction where several railways converged, the camp served as a convenient place for the Nazis to transport prisoners from all across Europe. In 1944, for example, Nazis transferred more than 400,000 Hungarian Jews there.

When prisoners first arrived, a doctor would review them, sending certain groups of people to their death, including pregnant women, young children, the elderly, the disabled, and the ill. Most of these people were killed immediately in specially prepared gas chambers, where they were told they would simply be taking a shower. Then the victims' bodies were burned in **crematoria**, or ovens. Those who were in good physical shape were put to work, often in factories in the area. When the laborers could no longer work due to malnutrition, illness, or exhaustion, the Nazis sent them to the gas chambers. An estimated 1.1 million Jews died at Auschwitz, including those who had been subjected to terrible medical "experiments" performed by the camp's chief doctor, Josef Mengele.

Even when the end of the war in Europe—and the end of the Third Reich—was in sight, the killings at Auschwitz and other death camps continued. But as the Soviets and other Allies advanced across eastern Europe, the Nazis who ran the camps abandoned them and fled. First, however, they tried to destroy any evidence of what had happened in the camps. They dismantled the barracks where prisoners had lived, burned down buildings that housed crematoria, and destroyed warehouses containing prisoners' clothing and personal items. Nonetheless, plenty of evidence remained of the murders that had been committed in the camps. In all, about 6 million Jews died in the **Holocaust**, which is what the systematic genocide carried out by the Nazis came to be called.

1. **READING CHECK** What was the "final solution"?

2. **MAKE INFERENCES** Why do you think the Nazis forced Jews to wear a yellow Star of David?

3. **DRAW CONCLUSIONS** In what ways did the initial restrictions placed on the civil and political rights of the Jews impact the events of the holocaust?

REFUGEES AND JUSTICE

When American troops discovered the concentration camps and their starved, tortured inmates, they could scarcely believe what they saw. For the first time, many of the soldiers understood what they'd been fighting for.

PLIGHT OF THE REFUGEES

While most Americans were unaware of the existence of the Nazi concentration camps, the Allied leaders of the United States, Britain, and the Soviet Union did know about them. In December 1942, Roosevelt, Churchill, and Stalin issued a declaration officially recognizing the mass murder of European Jews and vowing to bring those responsible to justice. Even so, the Allies did not make bombing death camps and the railroad tracks that carried the prisoners a priority. Thousands of Jews fleeing Europe were admitted to the United States, but many thousands more were turned away. The U.S. State Department claimed that some of the refugees could be spies and therefore posed a national security risk.

Finally, pressured by American Jewish organizations and officials in his own government, President Roosevelt created the **War Refugee Board** in January 1944 to rescue Jews. In its most ambitious effort, the board helped finance the work of Swedish diplomat **Raoul Wallenberg** to save tens of

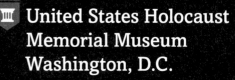

United States Holocaust Memorial Museum Washington, D.C.

When Masha Kessler and her 17-year-old daughter, Esther, arrived at the Kaiserwald concentration camp in the northern European country of Latvia, one of the two Polish women was issued this striped uniform coat. The rectangular patch at the top of the coat once contained the prisoner's ID number, and the yellow triangle beneath the patch indicated the prisoner was Jewish. Prior to their transfer to Kaiserwald, the mother and daughter had been forced to live in a Jewish ghetto. The pair worked as slave laborers in several concentration camps before Soviet troops liberated them in January 1945. Masha or Esther continued to wear the coat throughout their imprisonment in the camps. The Holocaust Memorial Museum displays this coat and other artifacts worn by Holocaust victims in their permanent collection.

thousands of Hungarian Jews from the death camps. Wallenberg traveled to Nazi-occupied Hungary and set up hospitals, soup kitchens, and safe houses for Jews in Budapest. He and his colleagues also distributed certificates of protection and Swedish passports to the Jews. During World War II, Sweden remained neutral, which meant the Nazis could not legally harm citizens holding a Swedish passport.

THE NUREMBERG TRIALS

The world learned about the extent of Nazi **atrocities**, or extremely cruel and shocking acts of violence, when the International Military Tribunal charged and tried former Nazi officials, military officers, industrialists, and others as war criminals. A **tribunal** is a court with authority over a specific matter. The series of trials, known as the **Nuremberg trials**, took place in Nuremberg, Germany, beginning in 1945. The tribunal determined that defendants could be charged with any of the following: crimes against peace, for having waged a war of aggression; crimes against humanity, for having exterminated groups of people; and war crimes, for having violated common and agreed-upon laws of war. Members of the tribunal represented the United States, Great Britain, the Soviet Union, and France and had the authority to determine the guilt of any individual or group. As evidence, the prosecution presented Nazi propaganda films, footage filmed at concentration camps by Allied troops, and ghastly artifacts taken from the camps. Survivors of the camps also testified, describing what they had witnessed and experienced.

Trials for 22 major Nazi war criminals were held in 1945 and 1946. Several of the leading figures in the party could not be tried, however. Hitler and two of his top officers, Heinrich Himmler and Joseph Goebbels, committed suicide before they could be brought to justice. Most of those charged did not deny or apologize for their actions. In their defense, many said they were "just following orders." On October 1, 1946, the tribunals issued their verdicts. While the tribunals acquitted some of the major war criminals and sent others to prison, they sentenced 12 to death by hanging. One of the 12 was Hermann Goering, whom Hitler had designated as his successor. However, Goering evaded execution by committing suicide. He swallowed a tablet of cyanide, which he had hidden in his cell, the day before he was to hang.

The Nuremberg trials attempted to bring Nazi war criminals to justice. But for many of those who

PRIMARY SOURCE

In 1986, Elie Wiesel was awarded the Nobel Peace Prize. In this excerpt from his acceptance speech, Wiesel explains our role in the face of suffering and oppression.

There is much to be done, there is much that can be done. One person—a Raoul Wallenberg . . . one person of integrity, can make a difference, a difference of life and death. As long as one dissident is in prison, our freedom will not be true. As long as one child is hungry, our lives will be filled with anguish and shame. What all these victims need above all is to know that they are not alone; that we are not forgetting them, that when their voices are stifled we shall lend them ours, that while their freedom depends on ours, the quality of our freedom depends on theirs.

—from Elie Wiesel's Nobel Peace Prize acceptance speech, December 10, 1986

survived the Nazi atrocities, their experiences would continue to haunt them throughout their lives. Some survivors, including the Romanian-born writer **Elie Wiesel**, wanted to bring the horrors of the Holocaust to the world's attention. Wiesel was 15 years old when he was sent to Auschwitz along with his parents and sister. He was later transferred to Buchenwald. After the war, Wiesel wrote *Night*, an account of the violence and abuse he experienced and witnessed in the camps. He did not want the world to forget what happened.

Holocaust museums created after the war have the same mission. By telling the stories of the victims and survivors, these museums show that those affected were not numbers but real people. The museums also stress the responsibility of citizens to speak out against hatred and prejudice to help prevent genocide from happening again.

HISTORICAL THINKING

1. **READING CHECK** What did Raoul Wallenberg do to try to save Hungarian Jews in Budapest?

2. **MAKE INFERENCES** Why do you think it was important to bring Nazi war criminals to trial instead of simply executing them?

3. **DRAW CONCLUSIONS** What did Wiesel mean when he said, "their [the victims'] freedom depends on ours, the quality of our freedom depends on theirs"?

VOCABULARY

Use each of the following vocabulary words in a sentence that shows an understanding of the term's meaning.

1. atomic bomb
   The atomic bomb caused firestorms and released radioactivity in Hiroshima and Nagasaki, resulting in thousands of casualties.

2. wage discrimination

3. Holocaust

4. infamy

5. ration

6. concentration camp

7. kamikaze

8. internment camp

READING STRATEGY
DETERMINE CHRONOLOGY

When you determine chronology, you place events in the order in which they occurred and note correlations between events. Use a time line like this one to order the key events in America's involvement in World War II. Then answer the question.

1941
Attack on Pearl Harbor

1942

1943

1944

1945

9. What events in 1945 led the United States to drop two atomic bombs on Japan?

MAIN IDEAS

Answer the following questions. Support your answers with evidence from the chapter.

10. Why did President Roosevelt order General MacArthur to leave the Philippines? **LESSON 1.1**

11. How did the experience of war impact California demographically, economically, socially, and politically? **LESSON 1.2**

12. What advantages did American-built Sherman tanks have over German panzers? **LESSON 2.1**

13. What unique impact did James Doolittle's raid on Tokyo have on Americans and the Japanese? **LESSON 2.2**

14. What postwar plans for Europe did Roosevelt, Churchill, and Stalin draw up at the Yalta Conference? **LESSON 3.1**

15. How did America win the war in the Pacific? **LESSON 3.2**

16. How did Roosevelt respond to Hitler's atrocities against Jewish people? **LESSON 4.2**

HISTORICAL THINKING

Answer the following questions. Support your answers with evidence from the chapter.

17. **MAKE INFERENCES** Why do you think Norman Rockwell chose to illustrate the four freedoms from Roosevelt's speech as scenes from everyday life?

18. **SYNTHESIZE** How did World War II serve to advance movements for equality at home and abroad?

19. **DRAW CONCLUSIONS** How did the American government change because of World War II?

20. **COMPARE AND CONTRAST** How was the war mobilized and fought differently in the Atlantic versus the Pacific?

21. **FORM AND SUPPORT OPINIONS** Do you think President Roosevelt and the Allies should have bombed death camps and railroads in Poland, or were they right to prioritize ending the war quickly? Explain your answer.

INTERPRET VISUALS

In 1942, the U.S. War Production Board published this poster to encourage Americans to contribute scrap—in this case, discarded pieces of metal, rubber, and clothing—to the war effort. Study the poster, and then answer the questions that follow.

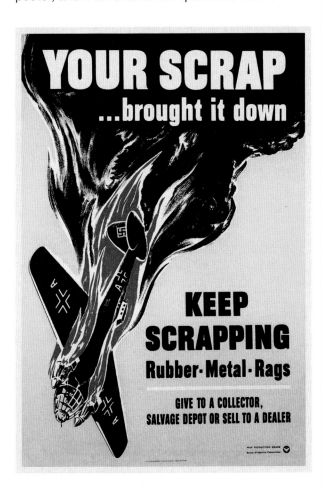

22. According to the poster, what did contributions of scrap bring down?

23. Why might the poster have inspired Americans to contribute scrap?

ANALYZE SOURCES

Lawson Inada's collection *Only What We Could Carry* provides firsthand accounts of the Japanese American experience during World War II, including oral histories of Japanese servicemen. The collection includes *Citizen 13660* by Miné Okubo, a Japanese American who was relocated during the war. In this excerpt from *Citizen 13660*, Okubo describes the train ride from the assembly center near San Francisco to the internment camp.

> The trip was a nightmare that lasted two nights and a day. The train creaked with age. It was covered with dust, and as the gaslights failed to function properly we traveled in complete darkness most of the night. All the shades were drawn and we were not allowed to look out of the windows. Many became train sick and vomited. The children cried from restlessness.

24. What details does Okubo use to convey the frightening journey?

CONNECT TO YOUR LIFE

25. **ARGUMENT** Before the attack on Pearl Harbor, many Americans did not want to get involved in World War II. Do you think the United States was ultimately right to go to war? Or do you believe that war is never justified? Write a paragraph in which you make an argument for or against going to war.

TIPS

- State your position about whether the country was right to go to war.

- Explain what, if any, circumstances make war justifiable.

- Use information from the chapter to help support your ideas.

- Address any counterarguments.

- Conclude your argument with a sentence summarizing your position.

THE COLD WAR AND KOREA 1945–1960

HISTORICAL THINKING What impact did communism have on the United States and the rest of the world?

CRITICAL VIEWING The Korean War Veterans Memorial on the National Mall in Washington, D.C., dedicated in 1995, includes 19 stainless steel figures representing all branches of the U.S. armed forces. The ponchos they are wearing indicate the extreme weather conditions the soldiers faced in Korea. How do the statues convey the tension and uncertainty the soldiers experienced?

"Peace must be built upon **power.**"
—President Harry S. Truman

MAIN IDEA After World War II, the United States and its allies set out to rebuild Europe and promote lasting peace through greater international cooperation.

EUROPE REBUILDS

When a powerful storm destroys buildings, people rebuild and try to make them stronger. Following the war, the United States and its allies worked to rebuild war-torn Europe and to strengthen international cooperation in order to keep the horrors of World War II from happening again.

THE UNITED NATIONS

In the autumn of 1945, the world sighed with relief. The guns were silent. Peace had arrived. As World War II ended, the Allies turned their attention to building a lasting peace. As you have read, early in the war, a number of nations signed on to the Atlantic Charter, which promoted the ideals of democracy and mutual respect among nations. The Allies acted on these ideals to create the **United Nations (UN)**, a global organization promoting cooperation among nations and working together to resolve conflicts peacefully. On October 24, 1945, the required 28 nations had ratified the organization's charter, and the United Nations became a reality. By the end of the year, it had a total of 52 member nations.

While the main focus of the United Nations was to promote international peace, it also worked proactively to help promote economic development, social progress, and human rights around the world. Officials created a number of smaller organizations within the UN to support these goals. The **United Nations Educational, Scientific, and Cultural Organization (UNESCO)** was created in 1945 to rebuild schools, libraries, and museums that had been destroyed during World War II. The **UN Commission on Human Rights**, established in 1946, aimed to protect fundamental human rights and freedoms around the world. And in 1948, the United Nations established the **World Health Organization (WHO)** to promote health worldwide.

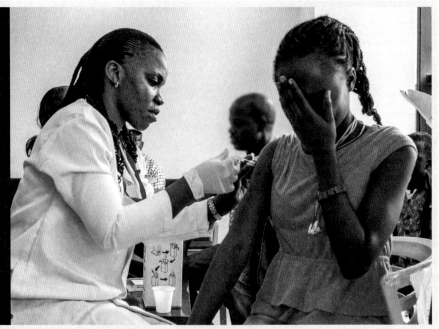

A GLOBAL PERSPECTIVE

In 2016, the World Health Organization worked with local authorities in Angola and the Democratic Republic of the Congo (DRC) to vaccinate 30 million citizens against yellow fever.

In this photo, a nurse vaccinates a young woman at a clinic in Kinshasa, the capital of the DRC. Yellow fever causes severe flu symptoms and in some cases can be fatal. Nearly 1,000 cases of the disease had been confirmed in the 2 countries before the end of the outbreak was declared in July 2016.

In addition to establishing a much-needed structure of organizations to rebuild and promote peace, the United Nations also formally documented basic human rights. In 1948, the UN adopted its **Universal Declaration of Human Rights**, which set out the fundamental rights of all people of all nations. These rights include freedom of thought and religion as well as freedom of expression and the right to assemble peacefully.

Several other organizations were created after the war to help battle-scarred nations recover economically. Proposed in 1944, the **International Monetary Fund** was officially established in 1945 to standardize worldwide financial relations and rates of exchange between countries. Its purpose is to safeguard and stabilize the global monetary system. The **World Bank** was founded in 1944 to provide financial support to countries that needed to rebuild after World War II. The **General Agreement on Tariffs and Trade (GATT)** was launched in 1947 and created rules for world trade.

In addition to working toward a lasting peace, the United States and its allies also sought to make any future wars more humane and just. In 1949, a number of nations agreed to the **Geneva Conventions**. This was the collective name of a revised set of three earlier treaties establishing rules for the humane treatment of prisoners of war as well as wounded or sick soldiers. Nations created and agreed to a fourth treaty that called for fair treatment and protection of civilians living in and around war zones.

THE MARSHALL PLAN

Across Europe, from Germany to Poland and the Soviet Union, the destruction from World War II was immense. Rail lines lay in ruin, roads were impassable, and major parts of cities were piles of rubble. Economies were no longer functioning, and the threat of mass starvation hung over the continent. In contrast, the United States had emerged from the war as the world's strongest economic and military power. The United States was determined to rebuild Europe and keep its economy from collapsing.

In June 1947, U.S. Secretary of State George C. Marshall proposed a massive financial aid plan he called the **European Recovery Program**. Marshall assured Europeans that it was a helping hand and not a way for the United States to control the continent. "Our policy is not directed against any country or doctrine," Marshall said, "but against hunger, poverty, desperation, and fear." Most Americans agreed and broke from their isolationist past. As citizens of the

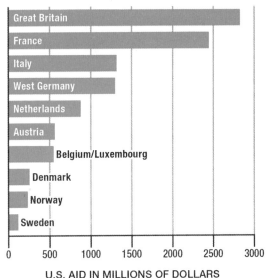

The Marshall Plan

U.S. AID IN MILLIONS OF DOLLARS

Source: Nicholas Crafts (2011), "The Marshall Plan: A Reality Check"

wealthiest and most powerful nation, they accepted the idea that they had some responsibility to keep the peace and help countries rebuild. Congress granted the billions of dollars needed to fund the proposal, which became known as the "**Marshall Plan**," and committed more than 10 percent of the U.S. federal budget to restore Europe's economic health.

As the Marshall Plan came together, the nations of Europe, including the Soviet Union, met to assess their common needs. But the Soviets soon walked out. They objected to giving critical Soviet economic information to outsiders. The Soviets also believed that accepting aid from capitalist countries might undermine their communist system. With the Soviets out, the Marshall Plan targeted mainly Western Europe. In the end, the program proved to be a tremendous success. It helped to rebuild Britain, Germany, and France and restore economic confidence to many European nations. Helping rebuild Europe also increased American trade and investment in Europe, creating new markets for U.S. goods.

HISTORICAL THINKING

1. **READING CHECK** What are the main goals of the United Nations?

2. **DRAW CONCLUSIONS** What might the Soviet Union's response to the Marshall Plan meeting have indicated about the potential for tension with the United States?

3. **INTERPRET GRAPHS** In total, how much did the Marshall Plan give to the top three aid recipients?

THE SOVIET THREAT

Did you ever work with someone you didn't like in order to win a game or complete a project? The United States and the Soviet Union put aside their differences to help win World War II—but then their differences re-emerged and ushered in a new struggle.

THE DIVISION OF EUROPE

The Allies had fought hard together to defeat Nazi Germany and Imperial Japan, and the Soviet Union had been essential to that effort. Soon, however, relations between the Soviets and the West began to decline. As you have read, President Franklin Roosevelt, Soviet Premier Joseph Stalin, and British Prime Minister Winston Churchill met at Yalta in 1945 to make plans for postwar Europe. The leaders had difficulty reaching any agreements. Underlying the rift was a vast difference between the political and economic structures of the United States and Soviet Union.

The disagreement was based on differing visions of government and economic policy. The United States and Great Britain wanted capitalist democratic governments established throughout Europe. Capitalism is an economic system in which private individuals or groups own the resources and produce goods for a profit. In contrast, Stalin wanted the Soviet Union to dominate the internal affairs of its Eastern European neighbors, controlling them under a communist regime, where all economic resources are owned by the state. In addition, the Soviets wanted to spread communism to other nations. The fundamental differences between communism and capitalism would shape the relationship between the United States and the Soviet Union for decades to come.

By the war's end, Soviet forces had occupied much of Eastern Europe, creating suspicion of communism among Western countries. Instead of withdrawing, the Soviet Army stayed, and Stalin installed communist rule throughout the region.

СЛАВА РУССКОМУ НАРОДУ—
НАРОДУ-БОГАТЫРЮ, НАРОДУ-СОЗИДАТЕЛЮ!

"Glory to the Russian people—the *bogatyr* people, the creator people!" is the message on this Soviet propaganda poster created by Viktor Ivanov in 1947. The man in front is a Russian engineer, a symbol of Soviet postwar industrial growth, and the towering figure standing behind him is a *bogatyr*, a Russian medieval hero. The intention of the poster is to motivate the working masses, the new "heroes" of Soviet nationalism.

By 1947, Stalin had created a ring of communist "satellite states" around the Soviet Union that became known as the **Eastern Bloc**. These Soviet-style communist governments suppressed political opposition, using the brutal methods employed by Stalin and his Soviet secret police. When the slightest stirrings of political independence arose in Eastern Europe, Soviet officials removed key people from power, imprisoned opponents, and in some instances, executed perceived "rebels."

The defeated nation of Germany was a special case. In the summer of 1945, the victors—the United States, Great Britain, France, and the Soviet Union—split Germany into four allied **occupation zones**. The eastern part of Germany became an occupation zone ruled by the Soviet Union. The western part was split into three occupation zones, with the United States, Great Britain, and France each controlling a zone. Berlin, Germany's capital, was entirely within the Soviet occupation zone, but it was governed by a joint agency of all four nations.

In 1946, the Americans and British combined their two sections of Berlin into a single section: West Berlin. In May 1949, the occupation zones of Germany controlled by the United States, Britain, and France merged into a single zone and, on May 23, this zone became the sovereign nation of the **Federal Republic of Germany**, or West Germany. The Soviets reacted to the formation of West Germany by creating the **German Democratic Republic**, or East Germany, in October 1949.

CONTAINMENT AND THE TRUMAN DOCTRINE

While visiting the United States in 1946, former British prime minister Winston Churchill addressed the growing concern over Soviet expansion. Speaking at Westminster College in Missouri, Churchill summed up the division of Europe. "From Stettin in the Baltic to Trieste in the Adriatic," he declared, "an **iron curtain** has descended across the Continent." The term "iron curtain" became shorthand for the divide in Europe between Western capitalist and Eastern communist countries. Churchill insisted the Soviets must be dealt with from a position of strength, and the United States must take a leading role in preventing the further expansion of communism.

By the time Churchill had spoken, the United States was already mapping out a plan for confronting the Soviets. The plan's architect was George F. Kennan, a foreign service officer stationed at the U.S. embassy in Moscow. In early 1946, Kennan laid out the doctrine of **containment**, or control of Soviet influence, that would shape American foreign policy for the next 40 years. Under containment, the

Division of Europe, 1949

United States would focus on keeping communism from expanding. American forces, Kennan said, would employ "the adroit [skillful] and vigilant [watchful] application of counterforce at a series of constantly shifting geographical and political points, corresponding to the shift and maneuvers of Soviet policy." President Truman firmly supported the policy of containment and its goal of blocking the Soviets from spreading communism to other countries. "Unless Russia is faced with an iron fist and strong language, another war is in the making," Truman predicted. "I am tired of babying the Soviets."

In 1947, the United States acted on its containment policy as it entered a conflict in the Mediterranean region. The Soviet Union was threatening to take land in Turkey, while in Greece, communist-led guerrillas were battling the government in a bloody civil war. Great Britain, which controlled the area, warned the United States that Britain could no longer afford to offer military and economic aid to Greece and Turkey. In response, Truman told Congress that "Great Britain finds itself under the necessity of reducing or liquidating its commitments in several parts of the world." He then proposed that the United States provide economic and military aid to all countries threatened by a communist takeover. This proposal became known as the **Truman Doctrine**. The president asked for and received from Congress $400 million in aid for Greece and Turkey.

The world had now entered an era of U.S.-Soviet conflict known as the **Cold War** that would last from the late 1940s to 1991. It was termed the "cold" war because the United States and Soviet Union would never engage in open warfare against each other. Instead, each country would try to weaken the other's influence around the world, and each country would take sides in a number of smaller wars. In the end, the Cold War would be a massive ideological and geopolitical struggle with consequences rippling across the globe.

HISTORICAL THINKING

1. **READING CHECK** Why is the decades-long struggle between the United States and Soviet Union referred to as the "Cold War"?

2. **INTERPRET MAPS** What does the map show about Berlin in 1949?

3. **COMPARE AND CONTRAST** Following WW II, how did the economic policies of Western capitalist and Soviet communist countries differ from each other?

4. **MAKE CONNECTIONS** What is the doctrine of containment, and how was it applied?

THE BERLIN AIRLIFT

The Soviet Union resented having a democratic West Berlin in the middle of its occupation zone. In June 1948, the Soviets began a blockade of the city, cutting off land access and hoping to starve out the British and Americans. Unwilling to use military force to end the blockade, the Western allies devised another way to get food, fuel, and other supplies to West Berlin.

In what became known as the Berlin Airlift, allied cargo planes used open air corridors over the Soviet occupation zone to drop the supplies into West Berlin. By the spring of 1949, it was clear that the Soviet blockade had failed, and it was lifted by the middle of May.

While on their way to school in 1948, West Berlin children and adults turned to watch an inbound U.S. C-47 cargo plane heading for Tempelhof Airport with food and other supplies.

THE COLD WAR BEGINS

The years following the end of World War II saw the onset of the Cold War, as the United States and the Soviet Union battled each other for global dominance.

The notion of an "Iron Curtain" across Europe symbolized the Cold War and the deep division between the free West and the communist world. Not surprisingly, it was a favorite subject of cartoonists. British cartoonist Leslie Illingworth sketched this cartoon the day after Winston Churchill's famous speech in Missouri in 1946. He depicts Churchill peeking under a curtain that carries a message signed by "Joe," a reference to Soviet leader Joseph Stalin. The cartoon also features several symbols of the division of Europe.

CRITICAL VIEWING Look closely at the cartoon. Which symbols of the division of East and West does the cartoonist include?

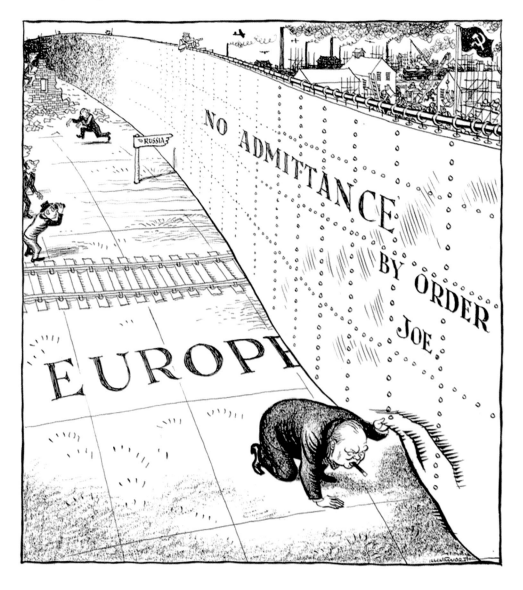

DOCUMENT ONE

Primary Source: Speech
from Winston Churchill's speech, delivered at Westminster College in Fulton, Missouri, March 5, 1946

In this famous speech, Churchill condemned the Soviet Union's policies in Europe and coined the phrase "Iron Curtain." The speech ends with a strong plea for a unified international front against communist expansion.

CONSTRUCTED RESPONSE A metaphor is a figure of speech that directly compares two unlike things. What does the metaphor "iron curtain" help you understand about the situation Churchill describes in his speech?

An *iron curtain* has descended across the Continent. Behind that line lie all the capitals of the ancient states of Central and Eastern Europe. Warsaw, Berlin, Prague, Vienna, Budapest, Belgrade, Bucharest and Sofia, all these famous cities and the populations around them lie in what I must call the Soviet sphere, and all are subject . . . not only to Soviet influence but to a very high and, in some cases, increasing measure of control from Moscow.

DOCUMENT TWO

Primary Source: Speech
from President Harry S. Truman's speech, delivered March 12, 1947, before a joint session of Congress

How should the United States react to the advance of communism in Europe? In a dramatic speech to a joint session of Congress, President Truman asked Congress to appropriate money to stop communist aggression in Greece and Turkey. The president first articulated the Truman Doctrine in this speech.

CONSTRUCTED RESPONSE Truman's speech is considered the opening "shot" of the Cold War. Why do you think it is regarded as such?

At the present moment in world history nearly every nation must choose between alternative ways of life. The choice is too often not a free one. . . . I believe that it must be the policy of the United States to support free peoples who are resisting attempted subjugation [control] by armed minorities or by outside pressures. I believe that we must assist free peoples to work out their own destinies in their own way. I believe that our help should be primarily through economic and financial aid which is essential to economic stability and orderly political processes.

DOCUMENT THREE

Secondary Source: Newspaper Article
from "Truman Acts to Save Nations From Red Rule,"
by Felix Belair, Jr., March 12, 1947, the *New York Times*

The *New York Times* journalist Felix Belair covered the speech in which President Truman announced the Truman Doctrine.

CONSTRUCTED RESPONSE What are two important points the newspaper reporter has gathered from Truman's speech?

President Truman outlined a new foreign policy for the United States. He proposed that this country intervene wherever necessary throughout the world to prevent the subjection of free peoples to Communist-inspired totalitarian regimes. . . . Although the President refrained from mentioning the Soviet Union by name, there could be no mistaking his identification of the Communist state as the source of much of the unrest throughout the world.

SYNTHESIZE & WRITE

1. **REVIEW** Review what you have learned about the events that led to the Cold War and the division of Europe.

2. **RECALL** On your own paper, write the main differences between the views of Stalin and other Soviet leaders and the views of Western leaders toward the postwar situation.

3. **CONSTRUCT** Construct a topic sentence that answers this question: How did President Truman respond to the advance of communism in Europe?

4. **WRITE** Using evidence from this chapter and the documents, write an informative paragraph that supports your topic sentence in Step 3. Include information about Truman's and Churchill's views of the Soviet Union.

MAIN IDEA After the 1948 election, President Truman proposed a progressive plan that extended the New Deal.

TRUMAN'S FAIR DEAL

Imagine being a soldier returning home after fighting on the front lines of World War II. You have no job waiting for you. What do you do? Can you count on the government to help you?

THE POSTWAR ECONOMY

In addition to the foreign policy challenges of the impending Cold War, President Truman's domestic challenges proved demanding as well. When millions of soldiers came back from overseas, ready to resume their lives as civilians, the U.S. economy struggled to accommodate them. With no more military orders to fill, factories closed, causing widespread layoffs. There was little work for returning soldiers. In addition, home construction had been on hold during the war, which caused a major housing shortage for veterans and their families. Homelessness spiked in major cities—Chicago had more than 100,000 homeless veterans and Washington, D.C., had 25,000.

Fortunately, the United States was entering a period where both the Democrats and Republicans saw the benefit of working together to solve many of the nation's problems. They agreed that the welfare state that began during the New Deal should be continued and even expanded. Legislators supported the development of a national security system to fight communism within the country. And they believed a strong central government with a powerful executive branch could help achieve these goals. Historian Godfrey Hodgson called this agreement between parties the **liberal consensus**.

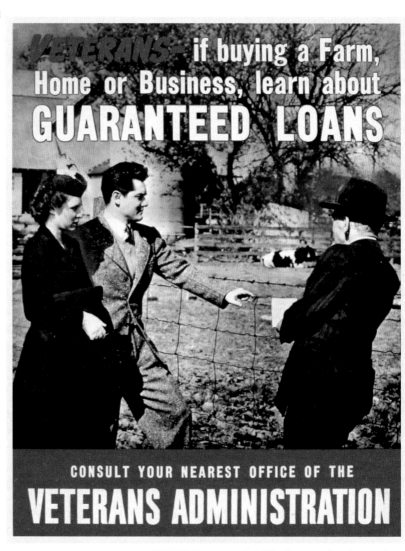

CRITICAL VIEWING The longest lasting and most popular feature of the GI Bill was the guaranteed loan for veterans. How might the poster above encourage a World War II veteran and his family to apply for a loan?

For example, in 1944 both parties in Congress worked together to pass the Servicemen's Readjustment Act, commonly known as the **GI Bill**. "GI," short for "Government Issue," is a military term that refers to U.S. armed forces. The GI Bill provided long-term, low-interest loans to veterans; funds to help pay college tuition; and a $2,000 bonus toward the purchase of a new home. As a result, millions of new homes popped up around the country, and newly educated veterans joined the nation's growing **white-collar**, or professional, workforce.

Not all domestic efforts went so smoothly. In June 1946, Truman lifted the price controls on consumer goods previously imposed during the war to prevent inflation, even though he feared the cost of food and other necessities would skyrocket without the controls. They did. In just weeks, the cost of meat doubled. Faced with higher prices and no increase in wages, unions across the country began to strike.

The United Auto Workers went on strike for 113 days, demanding a pay increase. Large railroad and mine workers' unions also went on strike for higher pay, bringing U.S. transportation and energy industries to a standstill. Although the strikes were resolved, Congress passed the **Taft-Hartley Act** in 1947 to limit strikes in the future. The act allowed the president to impose an 80-day federal injunction to temporarily stop strikes that threatened national safety or health and required unions to give their employers a 60-day notice before staging a strike. Truman vetoed it, but Congress overrode his veto.

TRUMAN'S PLAN

Truman also faced the problem of racial conflict in the United States after the war, and he took a strong stand for civil rights. He authorized a special task force to investigate racial discrimination in the country. The task force recommended the desegregation of the armed forces, the creation of a civil rights division in the federal government, and the end of segregation and lynching in the United States. After Congress failed to pass any civil rights laws, Truman ordered the armed forces to be desegregated in 1948.

As the 1948 election approached, President Truman was on shaky ground. His stance on racial equality had caused a group of southern Democrats to split from the party, demanding "complete segregation of the races." He had a rocky relationship with other members of Congress as well, some of whom urged him not to run for re-election. And he faced a strong Republican opponent, New York Governor **Thomas E. Dewey**.

PRIMARY SOURCE

We cannot afford to float along ceaselessly on a postwar boom until it collapses. It is not enough merely to prepare to weather a recession if it comes. Instead, government and business must work together constantly to achieve more and more jobs and more and more production—which mean more and more prosperity for all the people.

—from President Harry Truman's State of the Union speech in reference to the "Fair Deal," 1949

As the election neared, Dewey held the lead in opinion polls and was widely predicted to become the next president. However, Truman launched a vigorous campaign, traveling by train across the country attacking the "do-nothing" Congress. In a surprising upset, Truman won the election. The *Chicago Tribune* newspaper even ran the mistaken headline "Dewey Defeats Truman."

At his inauguration on January 20, 1949, Truman introduced a plan he called the **Fair Deal**, after Roosevelt's New Deal. The Fair Deal included such progressive ideas as expanding Social Security, increasing the minimum wage, continuing subsidies to support crop prices, instituting national health care, and passing an anti-discrimination law. He also called for expanding the Tennessee Valley Authority and providing funds for **rural electrification** in farm communities that did not yet have electricity.

The Fair Deal was a mixed success. By the end of his term, Truman had managed to expand Social Security and raise the minimum wage, but many of his other proposals were blocked by a conservative Congress. Also, the national debt grew in order to cover the government programs that boosted the postwar economy. In turn, the federal government had to pay higher interest rates on that debt, although neither the vital programs nor the nation's economy were in jeopardy. Still, the Fair Deal set the stage for future administrations to push a progressive agenda with the help of the liberal consensus.

HISTORICAL THINKING

1. **READING CHECK** What did Truman propose in the Fair Deal, and how did Congress respond?

2. **MAKE GENERALIZATIONS** How did the GI Bill improve the lives of soldiers returning from the war?

3. **IDENTIFY MAIN IDEAS AND DETAILS** What were the goals of the liberal consensus?

MAIN IDEA The United States and the Soviet Union established themselves as opposing superpowers as they built up their arms and formed protective alliances.

ESCALATING TENSIONS

One of the benefits of being part of a group of friends is a feeling of security and knowing that people "have your back." As the Cold War began, nations joined sides with either the United States or the Soviet Union, seeking that same feeling of protection in a world of new dangers.

THE SOVIETS UNVEIL THE BOMB

On August 29, 1949, a little more than four years after the United States dropped the first atomic bomb on Hiroshima, the Soviet Union stunned the world by conducting a test explosion of its own atomic bomb. Americans were shocked. Few believed the Soviets could have developed such a weapon. After all, the Soviet Union was considered a backward nation struggling to rebuild its destroyed infrastructure— roads, buildings, and public utilities—after the war. A number of officials accused the Soviets of espionage, or obtaining the bomb plans through theft or spying.

The development of the Soviet bomb set off a nuclear **arms race** between the United States and the Soviet Union that would last for decades. As the two countries continued their competitive buildup of nuclear weapons, the odds that they might use them kept rising. However, the complete destructive potential of both stockpiles ultimately acted as a deterrent to using them.

The onset of the arms race led to rapid growth for the U.S. defense industry. Factories geared up to design and build planes, rockets, and satellites. Southern California, in particular, became the booming center of the U.S. **aerospace industry**. The availability of land and a favorable climate made southern California an attractive location, and more than half of the nation's 25 largest aerospace companies would

NATO and the Warsaw Pact 1955

Sources: NATO and U.S. State Department

NATO
Warsaw Pact

■ NATO
■ Eastern Bloc
■ Soviet Union

Nuclear Stockpiles 1945–1991

NUMBER OF NUCLEAR WEAPONS

40,000
30,000
20,000
10,000
0

United States   Soviet Union

1945 1950 1955 1960 1965 1970 1975 1980 1985 1990

Source: Hans M. Kristensen & Robert S. Norris, "Global nuclear weapons inventories, 1945–2013," 2013

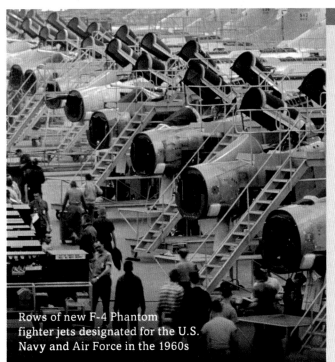

Rows of new F-4 Phantom fighter jets designated for the U.S. Navy and Air Force in the 1960s

PRIMARY SOURCE

Many years after the arms race began, President Dwight D. Eisenhower (elected in 1952) gave a speech in which he warned against the close relationship that had grown between the military and the aerospace industry, a relationship he called the **military-industrial complex**.

In the councils of government, we must guard against the acquisition of unwarranted influence, whether sought or unsought, by the military-industrial complex. The potential for the disastrous rise of misplaced power exists and will persist. . . . Only an alert and knowledgeable citizenry can compel the proper meshing of the huge industrial and military machinery of defense with our peaceful methods and goals, so that security and liberty may prosper together.

—from President Dwight D. Eisenhower's Farewell Address, 1961

come to reside there. Between 1952 and 1962, the U.S. government funneled more than $50 billion into California, twice the amount received by any other state. For decades, the aerospace industry would be a major driving force of the California economy.

CREATING ALLIANCES

In addition to stockpiling arms, the United States and the Soviet Union formed alliances to keep each other in check. In 1949, the United States, Canada, and 10 Western European nations formed the **North Atlantic Treaty Organization (NATO)**. Member nations agreed to aid each other should one of the countries be attacked. To counter NATO, the Soviets created the **Warsaw Pact**, a collective defense treaty of communist countries that included the Soviet Union, Albania, Poland, Romania, Hungary, East Germany, Czechoslovakia, and Bulgaria. Similar to NATO, the Warsaw Pact stated that the member countries would defend each other against attack. Several years later, the United States would help establish a similar alliance among Asian countries, known as the **Southeast Asia Treaty Organization (SEATO)**.

As the United States built global alliances, the nation also moved to strengthen its own security and defense. In 1947, lawmakers passed the National Security Act, which unified all of the armed forces under a single **Department of Defense.** The act also created the **National Security Council (NSC)** to gather and provide foreign policy information to the president. In addition, the act established the **Central Intelligence Agency (CIA)** to collect classified information overseas and uncover what other nations were doing behind the scenes. The CIA was similar to wartime intelligence agencies that had since been disbanded.

In 1950, Secretary of State Dean Acheson wrote a secret document known as National Security Council Paper 68 (NSC68), which called for a steep increase in peacetime military spending—from $13 billion to $50 billion per year. It also called for the construction of a "thermonuclear device," a **hydrogen bomb**, that would be even more powerful than the atomic bomb. Truman never showed NSC68 to Congress, but when the document was declassified, or made public, in 1975, it provided a look at how U.S. defense policy was shaped.

HISTORICAL THINKING

1. **READING CHECK** How was the establishment of international alliances in the 1950s tied to the arms race?

2. **ANALYZE CAUSE AND EFFECT** How did the development of a Soviet atomic bomb affect the economy of southern California?

3. **INTERPRET GRAPHS** During which decade did the Soviets begin to surpass the United States in number of nuclear weapons?

COLD WAR AROUND THE GLOBE

Have you ever seen a video of hundreds of dominoes falling in a chain reaction? During the Cold War, some feared that might happen with countries: if one became communist, its neighbors might quickly follow.

THE CHINESE REVOLUTION

As the United States and its allies confronted the Soviet Union, another communist power was emerging—China. As you have read, communist forces had been active in China since the 1920s. By the 1930s, the Chinese Communist Party (CCP), led by Mao Zedong, was battling Chiang Kai-shek and his Chinese Nationalist Party, which ruled the country.

When World War II broke out, the two sides joined together to help defeat Japan. After the war, however, their civil war resumed. On paper, Chiang and his forces had better resources. But Chiang's government had grown increasingly corrupt, ineffective, and unpopular during World War II. Meanwhile, Mao had become an inspiring leader. He attracted many people, and his Communist Party gained a reputation for supporting the common man. Chiang responded to communist attacks with increased violence and repression, which only made him more unpopular.

Despite strong U.S. support for Chiang in the Chinese civil war, the tide turned in favor of Mao's communist army, now called the People's Liberation Army (PLA). The PLA captured the city of Beijing in January 1949 and occupied, or took over, Nanjing and Shanghai soon after. In late 1949, Mao claimed victory. He announced the formation of the **People's Republic of China** and declared his communist solidarity with the Soviet Union.

Chiang and his remaining forces fled to the island of Taiwan, where they set up a **government-in-exile**, or a government that has been deposed and attempts to rule from another land. Chiang claimed to lead the only legitimate Chinese government. The United States strongly backed this claim. Now, mainland China, once a loyal U.S. ally, had become a clear enemy to the United States. With the world starkly divided into American and Soviet spheres of influence, or areas

🏛 **The Andy Warhol Museum Pittsburgh, Pennsylvania**

The 5-foot wide by 7-foot tall image of Mao by artist Andy Warhol suggests the enormous scale of the images of communist leaders publicly displayed in their countries. Warhol made hundreds of silk screens of Mao, each altered in a different way by adding paint. The Mao series of work comments on communist propaganda and popular culture in the United States. Warhol was a leading practitioner of pop art.

Andy Warhol, "Mao", © 2017 The Andy Warhol Foundation for the Visual Arts, Inc. / Artists Rights Society (ARS), New York

In 1945, Ho Chi Minh declared Vietnam's independence from France using rhetoric from the French Declaration of the Rights of Man and the Citizen and from the American Declaration of Independence.

The Declaration of the French Revolution made in 1791 on the Rights of Man and the Citizen also states: 'All men are born free and with equal rights, and must always remain free and have equal rights.' Nevertheless for more than 80 years, the French imperialists . . . have built more prisons than schools. They have mercilessly slain our patriots; they have drowned our uprisings in rivers of blood. They have . . . impoverished our people, and devastated our land. They have robbed us of our rice fields, our mines, our forests.

—from Declaration of Independence of the Democratic Republic of Vietnam, by Ho Chi Minh, 1945

Southeast Asia, 1954

of authority, China's shift was seen as a serious loss for the West. A debate raged in Washington about who was to blame for "losing China" to communism. Opponents of President Truman portrayed Mao's victory as an "avoidable catastrophe" that the president failed to prevent by focusing too much on Eastern Europe and not enough on China.

FROM CHINA TO SOUTHEAST ASIA

The policy of containment, as you have read, was based on a fear that communism would spread. Western leaders reinforced this idea with the **domino theory**. They argued that just like rows of dominoes knocking each other down, communist countries—especially those in Asia—would "knock over" their neighbors and make them communist as well.

After World War II, the French controlled much of Southeast Asia, including Vietnam, Laos, and Cambodia, a region known as Indochina. In Vietnam, France soon faced a revolt led by communist leader **Ho Chi Minh**. Ho led a group known as the Viet Minh. In September 1945, the Viet Minh announced their independence from France, seized control of the northern part of the country, and declared the **Democratic Republic of Vietnam (North Vietnam)** with Ho as president.

Financial backing and military supplies from the United States helped France secure control of the southern region and set up the **State of Vietnam (South Vietnam)**. For the next five years, France fought the

Viet Minh, who were supported by the Soviet Union and China, for control of Vietnam. Ho and his troops realized it was impossible to win large-scale battles against the French. Instead, they conducted a guerrilla war in the countryside, attacking the French and then retreating into Vietnam's mountains and jungles.

In March 1954, the Viet Minh defeated a large French force at the **Battle of Dien Bien Phu**. The two sides negotiated a peace agreement that officially divided Vietnam into two countries: communist North Vietnam and democratic South Vietnam. However, the situation remained unstable and battles continued to erupt. By the end of the 1950s, the United States would increase its direct involvement in the Vietnam conflict. But before that, the United States focused on stopping the spread of communism in another Asian country—Korea.

HISTORICAL THINKING

1. **READING CHECK** Why did the United States support Chiang's Chinese government-in-exile?

2. **INTERPRET MAPS** What war advantage did North Vietnam have, considering its location next to China?

3. **DRAW CONCLUSIONS** How might breaking Vietnam into two separate countries lead to conflict later on? Use evidence from the text to support your prediction.

4. **FORM AND SUPPORT OPINIONS** Does it make sense to compare countries to game pieces that might fall in a chain reaction as the domino theory did? Why or why not?

THE KOREAN WAR

Did you ever become involved in an argument or debate between two people because you wanted to support a friend or because you strongly supported one side? As the Cold War heated up, the United States became involved in a far-off civil war in order to halt the spread of communism.

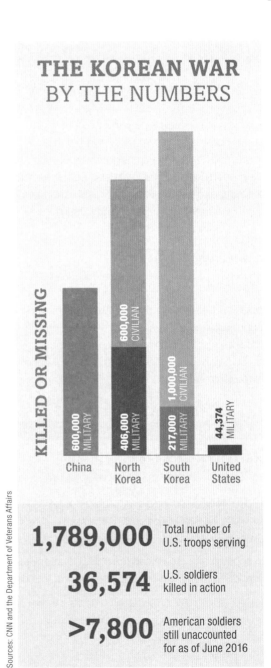

THE KOREAN WAR BY THE NUMBERS

KILLED OR MISSING

China: 600,000 MILITARY
North Korea: 406,000 MILITARY, 600,000 CIVILIAN
South Korea: 217,000 MILITARY, 1,000,000 CIVILIAN
United States: 44,374 MILITARY

1,789,000 Total number of U.S. troops serving

36,574 U.S. soldiers killed in action

>7,800 American soldiers still unaccounted for as of June 2016

Sources: CNN and the Department of Veterans Affairs

WAR ERUPTS IN KOREA

The nation of Korea lies on a peninsula that borders northeastern China. Japan had ruled the land since the late 1800s. In 1945, after Japan's defeat in World War II, the Allies took control. They divided the Korean Peninsula roughly in half at the **38th parallel**, which is 38 degrees latitude north of the equator. Soviet troops controlled North Korea, while American-backed troops controlled the Republic of Korea, also called South Korea. With Soviet backing, a communist government was set up in North Korea, while the United States helped establish democratic rule in the south. Both sides claimed to be the legitimate ruler of the entire peninsula, and skirmishes along the border were common. In 1948, the United Nations moved to unify the country through national elections. But the Soviets refused to let UN officials into North Korea, preventing the elections from taking place.

On June 25, 1950, North Korean troops crossed the 38th parallel and invaded South Korea, taking everyone by surprise. It was clear that, although North Korea was the immediate aggressor, it attacked with the approval of the Soviet Union. This situation—where a major power starts a war in which it does not become directly involved—is called a **proxy war**. A proxy is a person or nation that acts as a substitute for or on behalf of another.

President Truman viewed the invasion as a test of his containment policy aimed at preventing the Soviets from spreading communism further. At Truman's urging, the United Nations condemned the attack and ordered North Korea to withdraw. North Korea refused, and the UN dispatched a multinational military force to South Korea. Meanwhile, Truman ordered American troops stationed in Japan to provide additional military support to the UN forces, including those U.S. troops already stationed on the Korean peninsula. He also sent an American naval fleet into the waters between China and Taiwan.

The Korean War, 1950–1954

June 25, 1950
CHINA · Chongjin · Yalu · NORTH KOREA · Pyongyang · Sea of Japan · 38°N · Seoul · Incheon · SOUTH KOREA · Yellow Sea · Pusan
N W E S
← North Korean advance
← United Nations advance

Aug. 1–Sept. 14, 1950
CHINA · Chongjin · Yalu · NORTH KOREA · Pyongyang · Sea of Japan · 38°N · Seoul · Incheon · SOUTH KOREA · Yellow Sea · Pusan

Sept. 15–Nov. 25, 1950
CHINA · Chongjin · Yalu · NORTH KOREA · Pyongyang · Sea of Japan · 38°N · Seoul · Incheon · SOUTH KOREA · Yellow Sea · Pusan

July 27, 1953
CHINA · Chongjin · Yalu · NORTH KOREA · Pyongyang · Sea of Japan · 38°N · Seoul · Incheon · SOUTH KOREA · Yellow Sea · Pusan
■ North Korea
■ South Korea and UN

A BACK-AND-FORTH BATTLE

North Korean forces had moved swiftly, and within weeks they had captured the South Korean capital of Seoul (sohl). The army continued to push south. By the end of July 1950, North Korea had pushed UN troops to the southern tip of the peninsula, into a small region around the city of Pusan. The defenders, however, dug in and fought off one furious attack after another as they waited for reinforcements.

As North Korea seemed poised to win, U.S. commander General Douglas MacArthur executed a bold plan. He sent UN and U.S. troops by sea to the port of **Incheon**, 150 miles behind North Korean lines. MacArthur intended to surprise and overwhelm the enemy by attacking from the rear. It worked. With their communications cut and under heavy bombardment, the North Koreans fled back north across the 38th parallel. Sensing an opening, MacArthur chased the enemy over the border, deep into North Korea. Surrounded and under siege, the North Koreans pressed for peace and a return to the old border at the 38th parallel. The United States and South Korea, however, had set their sights on controlling all of Korea. Then China stepped in.

CHINA JOINS THE WAR

In November 1950, China staged a massive attack across its border into Korea. While the Chinese had initially stayed out of the conflict, they were not about to let their fellow communists in North Korea suffer a defeat. More than 300,000 Chinese troops overwhelmed American and South Korean forces.

MacArthur, who had assured President Truman the Chinese would not enter the fight, now admitted, "We face an entirely new war." Scores of troops retreated to the south by sea. Meanwhile, several U.S. Marine and Army divisions trapped inland battled ferociously to escape. U.S. and UN forces withdrew south of the 38th parallel, and in January 1951, abandoned Seoul for a second time. After several months of intense fighting, the retreating forces held their ground just south of Seoul along the 37th parallel. MacArthur launched attack after attack, slowly pushing the Chinese and North Koreans back up the peninsula and eventually back over the 38th parallel.

TRUMAN FIRES MACARTHUR

China's entry into the war caused tensions between Truman and MacArthur. The general wanted to strike China with nuclear weapons, but President Truman strongly rejected the idea. Any attempt to widen the war, Truman reasoned, would alarm other UN partners and perhaps provoke the Soviets into starting a larger, more deadly war.

MacArthur, however, refused to be silent. He sent a letter to Congress criticizing Truman's refusal to meet force "with maximum counterforce" and ended with his oft-quoted phrase: "There is no substitute for victory." MacArthur also leaked information to the press, warning of a crushing defeat for UN forces if nuclear bombs were not used. On his own, MacArthur issued a warning to China, threatening to expand the war into Chinese territory. Truman was furious. In April 1951, the President

With deep regret I have concluded that General of the Army Douglas MacArthur is unable to give his wholehearted support to the policies of the United States Government and of the United Nations in matters pertaining to his official duties. In view of the specific responsibilities imposed upon me by the Constitution of the United States and the added responsibility which has been entrusted to me by the United Nations, I have decided that I must make a change of command in the Far East. I have, therefore, relieved General MacArthur of his commands and have designated Lt. Gen. Matthew B. Ridgway as his successor.

—from a statement by President Harry Truman, April 11, 1951

removed MacArthur from his post, accusing him of insubordination, or refusal to obey orders. Truman replaced MacArthur with General Matthew Ridgway.

MacArthur returned to the United States to public acclaim as a hero who symbolized old military values in a world complicated by the threat of nuclear war. Letters poured into the White House, and the vast majority—21 to 1—were against his firing. Angry groups of citizens even burned President Truman in effigy. An effigy is a crude model of a person, made to be damaged in protest. MacArthur gave a farewell address to a joint session of Congress. His closing words were: "Old soldiers never die; they just fade away. And like the old soldier of that ballad, I now close my military career and just fade away—an old soldier who tried to do his duty as God gave him the light to see that duty."

THE KOREAN WAR ENDS

As the Truman-MacArthur drama unfolded on the home front, the war in Korea settled into a standoff. By spring of 1951, both sides seemed willing to accept the prewar border of the 38th parallel. Truce talks began that summer but dragged on for two more years due to continuous disagreements. In July 1953, both sides finally signed a truce that stopped the fighting without formally ending the war.

The truce called for both sides to pull back from the battle line and designated the space between them along the 38th parallel as a **demilitarized zone**. No army could enter the zone without breaking the truce. The demilitarized zone, often referred to as the DMZ, still stretches across the entire width of the Korean Peninsula—a 148-mile border—from which hundreds

of thousands of troops remain ready for conflict to erupt. South Korean troops, joined by U.S. troops, face North Korean troops across this fenced and guarded wasteland, which has now become a haven for vegetation and wildlife.

The toll from the first "hot" conflict of the Cold War was high, resulting in hundreds of thousands of lives lost, hundreds of cities and villages destroyed, and a ruined countryside, but it did not change the postwar division of Korea into two countries. War is always brutal, but the devastation of the

North Korea today remains a communist-ruled country and is isolated from much of the rest of the world. In this 2012 photo, North Korean soldiers carry a large portrait of late leader Kim Il Sung in a military parade in Kim Il Sung square in Pyongyang, the capital city of North Korea. North Korea follows a policy of "Songun Chong'chi," or "Military First," and its army of more than 1 million is one of the largest in the world.

Korean War is unparalleled. The demilitarized zone continues to separate families and stifle the culture of a once united nation. But in defining their Korean identity, many South Koreans see themselves as a united community. North Korea presents itself as a united country, but its people have experienced long famines and much poverty. The armies still poised on either side of the DMZ ready to fight at any moment keep the two countries and the rest of the world on edge. After the North Korean government tested nuclear missiles in March 2013, South Korean officials called the act "an unforgiveable threat to the Korean peninsula's peace and safety."

HISTORICAL THINKING

1. **READING CHECK** What were the two major turning points in the Korean War?

2. **EVALUATE** North Korea was the Soviet Union's proxy in the Korean War. Was South Korea a proxy for the United States? Explain your answer.

3. **INTERPRET MAPS** According to the map, how did the war affect territory controlled by each side?

4. **FORM AND SUPPORT OPINIONS** Was President Truman right to fire MacArthur? Explain your opinion.

THE RED SCARE CONTINUES

Everyone knows fear can be contagious, and there was plenty of fear to go around in the years following World War II. Many people were afraid communism could gain a foothold in the United States, and that fear led to a period of suspicion and accusations, some of which implicated ordinary, innocent Americans.

A SECOND RED SCARE

As you have read, fear of communism seized America following World War I in what became known as the Red Scare. After World War II, a second Red Scare swept the nation. Americans watched with alarm as the Soviet Union imposed its communist rule across Eastern Europe and successfully tested an atomic bomb. In Asia, Mao Zedong's communist army toppled the pro-American government of Chiang Kai-shek in China, and the United States sent troops overseas to battle communist forces in Korea. As communism appeared to be on the march everywhere, Americans started to look for signs of the enemy at home, even among their friends and neighbors.

Congress led the attack on suspected communists through its **House Un-American Activities Committee (HUAC)**. The committee had originally been established to investigate Nazi propaganda in the United States in the 1930s. After World War II, HUAC began targeting suspected communists. Officials used the **Alien Registration Act**, also called the Smith Act, to prosecute alleged communist activity. The 1940 act, written in part by Democratic congressman Howard W. Smith, made it illegal to discuss overthrowing the government and required immigrants to register with authorities. Fewer than 200 people were charged under the legislation. When civil rights organizations spoke out against such practices, they too were targeted as possible communist sympathizers.

The 1956 Hollywood movie *Invasion of the Body Snatchers* tells the story of aliens who take over the bodies of humans. Many viewed the film as a commentary on the nation's postwar, anticommunist hysteria. The official movie poster released by the studio, Allied Artists Pictures, highlights the fear of the postwar years.

THE HOLLYWOOD TEN

In 1947, HUAC launched a highly publicized anticommunist investigation into the American motion picture industry. The committee accused ten screenwriters and film directors of creating pro-communist films and materials. Committee members issued the writers and directors a subpoena, or formal request to appear before them. During their hearings, the writers and directors refused to answer questions about their political beliefs and associations. Judges charged the "**Hollywood Ten**," as they became known, with contempt of Congress and sent them to jail. In addition, the group was blacklisted in the entertainment industry, which meant no one was willing to do any further work with them.

In the years that followed, many people found themselves in communism-related Supreme Court cases. The film industry became so linked to communism that its labor union, the Screen Actors Guild (SAG), required its members to take a **loyalty oath**, a sworn statement that they did not belong to various organizations including those identified as communist. Some universities, school districts, and school boards also started requiring their members to take loyalty oaths. In 1950, as part of a newly enacted state law, leaders of the University of California required its employees to take a loyalty oath and reject radical beliefs. A number of university professors lost their positions when they refused to sign loyalty oaths. In 1952, the California Supreme Court ruled in favor of the professors, but not until 1967 did federal courts rule the law unconstitutional.

SPY CASES GRIP THE NATION

The growing fear of communism at home sparked two prominent spy cases that captivated Americans. In 1948, American writer **Whittaker Chambers** testified before HUAC and claimed to have once been part of a "communist cell" in Washington, D.C. Chambers added that the cell included **Alger Hiss**, a former government official who had advised President Roosevelt in foreign affairs. Hiss denied the allegations in testimony before HUAC. When Chambers repeated the charge on a national radio broadcast, Hiss sued him for libel, the crime of making unsubstantiated negative claims about someone.

Chambers struck back by producing dozens of classified State Department documents from the 1930s that suggested Hiss was a spy for the Russians. The evidence included photographs and summaries of confidential reports Hiss had written in longhand or typed on a unique typewriter he once owned. **Richard M. Nixon**, a young California congressman, made a name for himself by pushing hard for Hiss's indictment, or formal charge of a criminal offense. Hiss could not be charged with espionage, as the alleged crime occurred too long ago. Instead, a federal grand jury indicted him for perjury, or lying, before HUAC. Hiss's first trial ended in a hung jury, or a jury that can't agree on a verdict. His second trial ended with a guilty verdict and a jail sentence for Hiss.

Another stunning trial involved **Julius and Ethel Rosenberg**, a New York couple who were active in the Communist Party. The case began in 1950, when the FBI discovered a spy network of American and British communists who were passing the Soviets information about U.S. atomic bomb development. After authorities arrested a German-born nuclear physicist for espionage, they discovered that Julius and Ethel Rosenberg were part of the same network of spies.

The Rosenbergs were arrested and convicted, in part on the testimony of Ethel Rosenberg's brother, David Greenglass, an engineer working on the Manhattan Project, which developed the American atomic bomb. A number of people viewed the Rosenbergs as innocent victims of anticommunist hysteria. However, numerous appeals and pleas for clemency, or mercy, failed. In 1953, the Rosenbergs were executed for treason.

Decades later, after the fall of the Soviet Union, information concerning the case was made public, including a number of radio messages. These messages were gathered and decrypted by the Venona Project, a code-breaking operation run by the U.S. Army. The messages, known as the Venona Papers, bolstered HUAC's claims of a communist threat in the United States. For years, the Rosenbergs' sons worked to prove their parents' innocence. By 2016, new evidence confirmed their father's guilt, but cast doubt on their mother's involvement.

HISTORICAL THINKING

1. **READING CHECK** What international events sparked the second Red Scare?

2. **DESCRIBE** Who were the prime targets of the House Un-American Activities Committee, and why were they targeted?

3. **MAKE INFERENCES** Why do you think the Screen Actors Guild agreed to blacklist members of its own union?

MAIN IDEA A U.S. Senator named Joe McCarthy emerged as the leading figure in the hunt for suspected communists, creating an atmosphere of hysteria and fear in the United States.

THE RISE OF MCCARTHYISM

Have you ever been afraid to speak your mind out of fear that others will attack you or accuse you of something? That is the way many people felt during Senator Joseph McCarthy's hunt for communists within the U.S. government during the early 1950s.

McCARTHY'S LIST OF COMMUNISTS

On a bleak February evening in 1950, Senator **Joseph R. McCarthy**, a little-known politician from Wisconsin, delivered a speech to a Republican women's club in Wheeling, West Virginia. The topic of the speech was communist subversion in the federal government. **Subversion** is the act of secretly undermining something in an attempt to destroy it. "I have here in my hand," McCarthy told his audience, "a list of 205 Communists that were made known to the secretary of state and who are still working and shaping the policy of the State Department." The message was clear. The United States was losing the Cold War to the evil forces of communism because the U.S. government was filled with "traitors."

Among the politicians who targeted suspected communists at home during the Cold War, none stood out more than Joe McCarthy. Wisconsin's junior senator was an erratic, or unpredictable, politician, known for his reckless ambition and rowdy behavior. He knew little about communists in government or anywhere else. But as he spoke out about alleged sympathizers of communism within the U.S. government, the public listened. McCarthy had struck a nerve in a country growing more anxious about Soviet aggression and communist expansion. As the nation searched for explanations, McCarthy provided a simple answer. Disloyal Americans, especially those working in Washington, D.C., were the real enemy.

PRIMARY SOURCES

In an attack on President Truman's foreign policy in February 1950, Senator Joseph McCarthy claimed to have a list of hundreds of communists employed by the federal government, but he never publicly revealed any of those names. In June 1950, Senator Margaret Chase Smith went before the Senate to deliver a personal rebuttal to McCarthyism in her "Declaration of Conscience."

While I cannot take the time to name [them], I have in my hand 205 cases of individuals who would appear to be either card carrying members or certainly loyal to the Communist Party, but who nevertheless are still helping to shape our foreign policy.

One thing to remember in discussing the Communists in our government is that we are not dealing with spies who get thirty pieces of silver to steal the blueprints of a new weapon. We are dealing with a far more sinister type of activity because it permits the enemy to guide and shape our policy.

—from a speech in West Virginia by Senator
  Joseph R. McCarthy, 1950

The United States Senate has long enjoyed worldwide respect as the greatest deliberative body in the world. But recently that deliberative character has too often been debased to the level of a forum of hate and character assassination sheltered by the shield of congressional immunity.

The American people are sick and tired of being afraid to speak their minds lest they be politically smeared as "Communists" or "Fascists" by their opponents. Freedom of speech is not what it used to be in America. It has been so abused by some that it is not exercised by others.

—from a speech in the Senate by Senator
  Margaret Chase Smith, 1950

Senator Joseph McCarthy points to a map while questioning Joseph Welch, the lawyer for the army in Senate committee hearings in 1954. McCarthy's accusations of communist infiltration of the army led to diminishing support for his investigations.

RECKLESS ACCUSATIONS

McCarthy's charges of treason in high places made him an instant celebrity. Prominent Republicans, sensing the political benefits of the "communist issue," embraced his attacks, which became known as **McCarthyism**. As he gained fame, McCarthy's assertions grew bolder. He called former secretary of state George C. Marshall a traitor, mocked the current secretary of state, Dean Acheson, as the "Red Dean of fashion," and described President Truman as a drunkard, saying that he should be impeached. Yet Republican colleagues continued to encourage McCarthy, who they thought could turn public distrust into votes for their party.

During the 1952 national elections, Republicans won control of Congress. McCarthy became chairman of the Senate Subcommittee of Investigations. He used the power of his committee to force government officials to testify and defend their loyalty. Among those he targeted were homosexuals in government positions who might have access to classified information, whom he claimed were vulnerable to blackmail. In what became known as the Lavender Scare, federal agencies fired many employees suspected of being homosexuals. The wave of discrimination didn't end there. Throughout the nation, suspected lesbians and gay men were targeted for surveillance and persecution, and many were forced out of career positions in state and local government, education, and even private industry.

Academics—specifically, faculty members at the nation's most prestigious colleges and universities—were also targeted as dangerous communist influences by McCarthy and his fellow committee members. Professors at Harvard, the University of Chicago, Johns Hopkins, Sarah Lawrence College, and other centers of higher learning were called to testify before the committee. Fortunately, most of these schools supported their faculty and refused to take action against any accused employees.

MCCARTHY'S FALL

Eventually, McCarthy went too far. In 1954, his committee attempted to uncover suspected communists within the ranks of the army. During televised hearings, the senator repeatedly bullied respected army officials, including General Ralph W. Zwicker, whom McCarthy declared was "unfit to wear the uniform" of the U.S. Army. Even President Eisenhower had seen enough. McCarthy quickly lost his credibility. The public turned away from him, and the Senate openly criticized him for bringing it into "dishonor and disrepute." The darkest days of McCarthyism soon ended, but the effects of the "witch hunts" and the alarm over communism followed the country into the next decade.

HISTORICAL THINKING

1. **READING CHECK** How did Joseph McCarthy increase suspicion of government officials?

2. **SYNTHESIZE** How might McCarthy's investigations have affected academic freedom in U.S. colleges?

3. **ANALYZE LANGUAGE USE** What did Senator Smith mean when she said that freedom of speech had "been so abused by some that it is not exercised by others"?

VOCABULARY

Write a paragraph to answer each question. Use all the words that appear below each question in your paragraph.

1. How were American politics and culture shaped by the Cold War?

    subversion   hydrogen bomb
    domino theory   containment
    McCarthyism

2. What effect did the Cold War have on jobs in business and government sectors?

    aerospace industry   white-collar
    arms race   GI Bill

READING STRATEGY
SYNTHESIZE

When you synthesize, you identify the most important information in a text, look for evidence that connects the facts, and think about what you already know about the topic. Then you use the evidence, explanations, and your prior knowledge to form an overall understanding of what you have read. Use the chart below to help you synthesize the information presented in this chapter. Then answer the question.

The Roots of McCarthyism

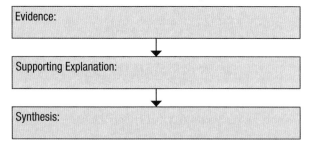

Evidence:

↓

Supporting Explanation:

↓

Synthesis:

3. How did world events following the Allied victory in World War II lead to distrust and suspicion within the United States?

MAIN IDEAS

Answer the following questions. Support your answers with evidence from the chapter.

4. Name two organizations formed by the United Nations in the 1940s and the purposes of those organizations. **LESSON 1.1**

5. How did American foreign policy shift after World War II? **LESSON 1.2**

6. What caused the arms race between the United States and the Soviet Union? **LESSON 2.1**

7. How was the Chinese Communist Party able to win the support of the Chinese people following World War II? **LESSON 2.2**

8. Why did President Truman remove General Douglas MacArthur from command of the American troops in Korea? **LESSON 2.3**

9. How were the Alger Hiss and the Rosenberg spy cases similar and different? **LESSON 3.1**

10. What brought about the end of Joseph McCarthy's investigation of communist influence in the U.S. government? **LESSON 3.2**

HISTORICAL THINKING

Answer the following questions. Support your answers with evidence from the chapter.

11. **IDENTIFY MAIN IDEAS AND DETAILS** How did the United Nations originate, and what purpose was it intended to serve?

12. **DRAW CONCLUSIONS** How did the Cold War and fear of communism affect ordinary Americans?

13. **ANALYZE CAUSE AND EFFECT** What triggered the larger conflict in Korea?

14. **ANALYZE LANGUAGE USE** Why did the historian Godfrey Hodgson refer to the postwar interaction of Republicans and Democrats as a "liberal consensus"?

15. **SUMMARIZE** What threats did the United States face from the expansion of communism throughout Eastern Europe and parts of Asia?

16. **MAKE INFERENCES** Why do you think the National Security Council Paper 68 called for an increase in military spending?

17. **FORM AND SUPPORT OPINIONS** How did the Cold War affect American politics?

Look carefully at this comic book cover created during the Cold War. Then answer the questions that follow.

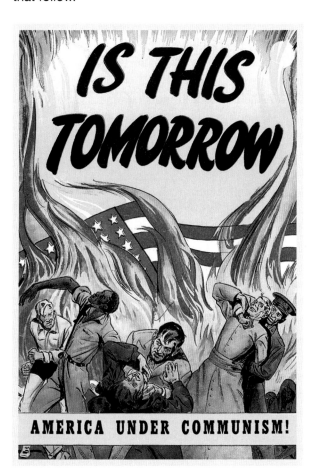

18. What elements in the image convey the fear that arose from the Cold War?

19. Is the message of this image based on opinion or fact? Explain your response.

Not everyone trusted Senator Joseph McCarthy or believed his accusations. The excerpt below is from a letter President Truman wrote in 1950, but never sent, in response to a telegram he had received from the senator.

> This is the first time in my experience . . . that I ever heard of a Senator trying to discredit his own Government before the world. Your telegram is not only not true and an insolent approach to a situation that should have been worked out between man and man—but it shows conclusively that you are not even fit to have a hand in the operation of the Government of the United States.

20. Based on the excerpt, how would you describe the president's attitude toward McCarthy's accusations?

21. **NARRATIVE** You have considered how the Cold War affected ordinary American citizens between 1945 and 1960. Judging a person's response to historical events is often easier than knowing how you might behave in the same situation without the advantage of hindsight. Write a story in which you are a main character and explore what you may have thought or done in the midst of the Cold War as events occurred.

TIPS

- Focus on one or two historical events that present a conflict for you and describe them.

- Identify your character's thoughts and feelings as world events unfolded.

- Use vivid language to describe the location of the story and the other characters in it.

- Include realistic dialogue in your story.

- Use two or three vocabulary terms from the chapter in your narrative.

- End the narrative by stating a moral, or a lesson one or more of the characters learned.

HISTORICAL THINKING How did the prosperity of the post–World War II period shape American society?

Young couples dance to music at the Harlem Cafe in Greenville, South Carolina, in 1956, while others look over the song list in the coin-operated jukebox. American photographer Margaret Bourke-White took this photo as she traveled through the South.

"I don't care what people say, **rock and roll is here to stay.**"

—Danny and the Juniors

THE BIRTH OF ROCK AND ROLL

CRITICAL VIEWING Rock and roll pioneer Chuck Berry performs before an enthusiastic audience in 1966. What do you observe about the demographics of the crowd?

It's the rhythm that gets to the kids— they're starved for music they can dance to, after all those years of crooners.

—disc jockey Alan Freed, 1956

Transistor radio c. 1960

Since the dawn of humanity,

there have been teenagers. The word *teenager*, however, didn't come into existence until sometime during World War II. At the time, there was nothing new about young people coming of age and seeking ways to rebel against society's norms. In the 1920s' Jazz Age, youths in their twenties defined themselves through music, clothing, and behavior that their elders found scandalous. In the 1940s and 1950s, the rebels were a little younger—high-school age—but they too sought their own social identity. And, like the jazz fans of the 1920s, they were looking for a new kind of music to serve as the soundtrack to their rebellion.

As the 1950s dawned, the tunes playing on America's pop radio stations weren't exactly exciting to a teenage audience. A record producer of the era later recalled, "Big fiddle-faddle orchestras . . . played lush mood music for relaxing, cocktails, and vacationing in far-away places." Such singers as Frank Sinatra and Bing Crosby—known as "crooners" because of their deep voices and smooth, romantic styles—dominated the airwaves, appealing to mainly white audiences.

American teenagers, however, were looking for something different in the way of entertainment, and they had the money to spend on it in the prosperous postwar economy. Teens also had access to new technology that made it easier to buy and listen to music independently from their parents.

Transistor radios like the one shown above were small, portable units, unlike the large console radios that squatted somberly in a family's living room. Advancements in recording technology allowed teens to buy inexpensive "singles," small vinyl records that featured just one song on each side.

While the crooners serenaded white listeners, many African Americans were drawn to "race records," songs with strong, syncopated beats and a sound directly derived from jazz and the blues. Around 1950, the term *race records* was replaced by the more accurate—and less offensive—*rhythm and blues*, or R & B.

One record store owner in Cleveland, Ohio, noticed his white teenage customers purchasing R & B records in large numbers. When he shared this information with local disc jockey Alan Freed, a rock and roll phenomenon was born. Freed debuted *The Moondog Show* on WJW radio in June 1951 in an exuberant, unheard-of style. As the records spun, Freed would leave his microphone on and accompany the music with cries of "Ho, now!" and "Go! Go! Gogogogogogogo!" while pounding madly on a phone book he kept in the studio. Music critic Ed Ward later wrote, "It was just what a very large number of teenagers had been waiting all their lives to hear." Freed is credited with first using the term *rock and roll* to describe the music that was emerging from R & B in the 1950s.

Guitar wizard Les Paul plays in the New York City nightclub called Fat Tuesday's.

LES PAUL

New technologies helped create the distinctive sounds of rock and roll both onstage and in the recording studios. One of rock's most influential early innovators was Les Paul, an inventor and popular, well-respected guitarist.

Paul was a pioneer in the use of overdubbing—recording a performance, and then replaying it and layering additional instruments or voices onto the recording. Using overdubbing, Paul sped up the sound of his guitar to create new and unusual effects. In 1952, he invented the eight-track tape recorder, which facilitated overdubbing and became standard in the recording industry. Today, music recording has gone digital, but the complex, layered sounds listeners are accustomed to hearing owe much to Paul's experiments.

Paul is perhaps best known for the solid-body electric guitar he designed, which was also released in 1952. He had worked for years to perfect an electric guitar that could sound and sustain a note without distortions. Paul's was not the first solid-body guitar on the market; the Fender Broadcaster had been introduced in 1948. However, the Les Paul Standard, sold by the Gibson guitar company, quickly rose in popularity and was adopted by many legendary rock guitarists.

Throughout his inventing career, Paul remained an accomplished, Grammy-winning performer. He was inducted into the Rock and Roll Hall of Fame in 1988 and continued both tinkering and performing until his death in 2009.

1968 Prototype Gibson Les Paul Custom Recording Model

1952 Gibson Les Paul Goldtop

Freed moved to New York in 1954 and began to organize R & B concerts that drew enthusiastic audiences of both white and African-American teens. He drew criticism from those who considered rock and roll obscene and from those who objected to people of different races mixing socially, but his popularity expanded throughout the 1950s.

Who were the artists making the new music that enthralled American teens and horrified many of their elders? In the early 1950s, most of the hit-makers were male, with roots in R & B or country and western music. Bill Haley, for example, started his career playing in a country band called the Saddlemen, but he loved the blues and experimented with combining many musical traditions. In 1953, the Saddlemen became Bill Haley & His Comets. In 1954, they released the single "Rock Around the Clock," which was featured in the 1955 film *Blackboard Jungle* and became a wildly successful anthem for the new rock generation, selling a record-setting 6 million copies.

Meanwhile, in Memphis, Tennessee, record producer Sam Phillips was frustrated because he was recording tracks by talented black musicians, but white radio stations would not give them airtime.

"If I could find a white man with the Negro sound and Negro feel, I could make a million dollars," he told his assistant. Enter Elvis Presley, soon to become a rock star of unprecedented fame and teen idol to millions worldwide.

Presley's signature sound was strongly influenced by the African-American blues and gospel singers he had listened to in his youth, and he gratefully acknowledged their contributions throughout his career. In addition to having a versatile singing voice, Presley was handsome and charismatic, had a dazzling smile, and performed energetic, provocative dance moves. Presley once remarked, "Rock and roll music, if you like it, if you feel it, you can't help but move to it. That's what happens to me. I can't help it." Not everyone agreed that Presley's way of moving was a good thing. When he appeared on a popular television variety show, he was filmed from the waist up because his hip shimmy was considered too suggestive for viewers. One Catholic cardinal accused Presley of promoting a "creed of dishonesty, violence, lust, and degeneration" among teens. Presley's best-selling singles of the 1950s include "Hound Dog," "Jailhouse Rock," "Heartbreak Hotel," "Love Me Tender," and "Don't Be Cruel."

Rock and roll singer Elvis Presley leans toward his screaming fans during an outdoor concert around 1957.

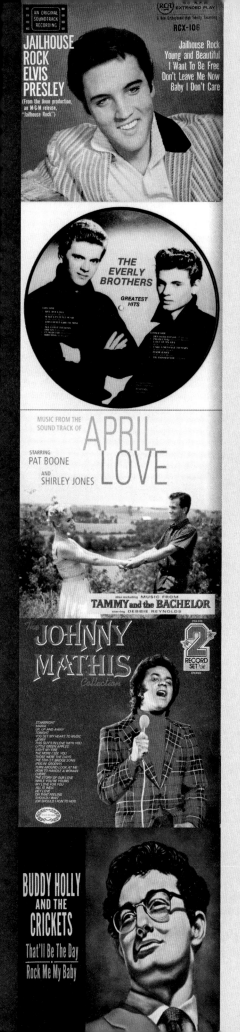

TOP OF THE LIST

In the 1950s, *Billboard* was a magazine that tracked the popularity of individual musicians and songs, publishing weekly charts of top sellers. From 1950 through 1954, the number one songs on the *Billboard* charts were mostly swing songs and ballads, with frequent appearances by such crooners as Tony Bennett and Frank Sinatra. Les Paul and his wife Mary Ford appeared on the 1953 list with a slow song called "Vaya Con Dios" (May God Be With You).

In July 1955, "Rock Around the Clock" by Bill Haley and His Comets took the number one spot, opening the door for rock and roll to dominate the charts. Chuck Berry and Little Richard also had hit records in 1955, and by 1957, rock and roll musicians were regular top sellers.

Excerpt from *Billboard's* Top 50 Best Sellers in Stores, November 18, 1957

Position In List	TITLE	ARTIST
1	JAILHOUSE ROCK	Elvis Presley
2	WAKE UP LITTLE SUSIE	The Everly Brothers
3	YOU SEND ME	Sam Cooke
4	SILHOUETTES	The Rays
5	BE-BOP BABY	Ricky Nelson
6	LITTLE BITTY PRETTY ONE	Thurston Harris
7	MY SPECIAL ANGEL	Bobby Helms
8	APRIL LOVE	Pat Boone
9	CHANCES ARE	Johnny Mathis
10	HONEYCOMB	Jimmie Rodgers
15	KEEP A KNOCKIN'	Little Richard
19	ROCK AND ROLL MUSIC	Chuck Berry
25	PEGGY SUE	Buddy Holly
30	WAIT AND SEE	Fats Domino
39	WHOLE LOTTA SHAKIN' GOIN' ON	Jerry Lee Lewis
40	THAT'LL BE THE DAY	The Crickets (Buddy Holly)

Joel Whitburn's Top Pop Playlists 1955–1969, 2014

While performing with his band in 1956, rock and roll star Little Richard props his foot on top of the piano, a signature move.

COVERING UP

Today, when a song has potentially offensive lyrics, radio stations play it with the problematic words edited out. In the 1950s, a cover artist would record the song with alterations to make it appealing to different markets. Many R & B hits, for example, were recorded in "sanitized" versions that were more acceptable to the decision-makers at pop radio stations. It was not uncommon for several versions of a hit song to be in circulation at the same time.

Pat Boone was one of the most successful of the cover artists, with an enthusiastic following of mostly white teenagers and a string of hit songs. His clean-cut, wholesome image presented a contrast to the raucous and raw performances of Elvis Presley, Little Richard, and other early rockers. In 1956, rock and roll music reached a milestone when Little Richard's sensual recordings of "Long Tall Sally" and "Rip It Up" outsold Pat Boone's covers of the same tunes. Parents and conservative radio station owners may have preferred the white cover artist's cleaned-up version, but the younger generation had voted with their dollars.

Rock and roll is the most brutal, ugly, degenerate, vicious form of expression—lewd, sly, in plain fact, dirt. —singer Frank Sinatra, 1957

Several African-American stars also rose to fame on the rock and roll tide. Little Richard burst onto the scene with a flamboyant splash and was one of the first African-American rock and roll musicians to play to integrated audiences. A brilliant pianist, Little Richard fixed his audiences with an intense, wide-eyed gaze and astonished them with irrepressible dance moves, sometimes planting a foot on top of the piano as he played. In the words of music writer Donald Clarke, "In two minutes [Little Richard] used as much energy as an all-night party." Little Richard's hit songs "Tutti Frutti" and "Good Golly Miss Molly" were hugely popular, but because his lyrics were suggestive, he received relatively little airplay.

Chuck Berry, another African-American musician, was an early master of the instrument that came to define the sound of rock and roll—the electric guitar. His dexterous playing and unforgettable guitar licks, or short patterns of notes, influenced generations of players. Berry engaged his listeners with songs that told a story. His first hit, "Maybellene," narrated the comic miseries of a man chasing after his unfaithful girlfriend. "Sweet Little Sixteen" spoke directly to the teenagers in his audience.

By the end of the 1950s, some people felt, and perhaps hoped, rock and roll was a fad that would quickly fade away. Instead, it not only endured but evolved into a musical scene more diverse than even Alan Freed might have imagined. Later rock stars have acknowledged the debt they owe to the musicians who pioneered the genre. In fact, singer-songwriter John Lennon of the Beatles, one of the best-selling rock bands of all time, introduced Chuck Berry on a 1972 television show by saying, "If you had to give rock and roll another name, you might call it Chuck Berry."

THINK ABOUT IT

How did the introduction of rock and roll serve as a means for social change?

THE DAY THE MUSIC DIED

Ritchie Valens, the first Latino rock and roll star, added a distinctive Mexican flavor to the R & B beat of his songs. Born in California, the Mexican American singer had a number of hits in his short career, including "Donna," which reached number two on the pop charts in 1959. Today, he is best remembered for "La Bamba," a Mexican folk tune with a rock and roll beat. Since its first release in 1958, the song has been recorded by several bands, including Los Lobos.

While still a teenager, Valens appeared on national television and on Alan Freed's radio show. In 1959, Valens went on tour with a group of fellow rock sensations, including Buddy Holly, whose 1957 song "That'll Be the Day" had reached number one on the charts in both the United States and Great Britain. On February 3, Valens, Holly, and J. P. "the Big Bopper" Richardson boarded a small plane for their next stop on the tour. The plane crashed near Clear Lake, Iowa, killing everyone aboard. Valens was just 17 years old, and Holly just 22. In 1971, singer Don McLean wrote a popular song about the crash and called it "American Pie." In the song, McLean referred to the tragedy as "the day the music died."

A self-taught musician, Ritchie Valens joined his first band at age 16.

MASON CITY GLOBE-GAZETTE
"The Newspaper That Makes All North Iowans Neighbors"

VOL. 97   Associated Press and United Press International Full-Lease Wires   MASON CITY, IOWA, WEDNESDAY, FEBRUARY 4, 1959   (5c a copy)—This paper contains ad Sections—Section One   No. 106

Rock 'n' Roll Idols Among Lake Crash Dead

Plane Piloted by Clear Lake Man Plows Into Field

Four persons, three identified as nationally famous rock 'n' roll singers, died early Tuesday in a plane crash five miles north of Clear Lake.

The three singers were Buddy Holly, 22, Texas, Ritchie Valens, 21, Los Angeles, and J. P. Richardson, 24, of Louisiana, known professionally as the "Big Bopper."

Also killed was the pilot of the plane, Roger Peterson, 21, Clear Lake.

The entertainers had appeared at the Surf Ballroom Monday night and were to appear at Fargo, N.D., Tuesday night.

Other members of the troupe which appeared at Clear Lake left after the show by chartered bus for Fargo. They are Dion and the Belmonts, Frankie Sardo and the Crickets, of which Holly was the singing star.

APPARENTLY HOLLY, Valens and Richardson decided to fly in order to arrive ahead of the troupe and make advance preparations.

The single-engine, four-place Beechcraft Bonanza left the Mason City Municipal airport shortly after 1 a. m. It crashed about seven miles northwest of the air...

Russ Hold   **Iowa's Right-to-Work Law**   '3 Reasons'

Bodies of two victims (arrows) lie near the demolished plane in stubble field

An Iowa newspaper reports the plane crash that killed a local pilot and musicians Ritchie Valens, Buddy Holly, and J. P. Richardson on February 3, 1959.

EISENHOWER AS PRESIDENT

Have you ever found it hard to choose sides in a political debate? Dwight D. Eisenhower didn't fit neatly on either the Democratic or the Republican side. But when he ran for president, he had to choose.

THE ELECTION OF EISENHOWER

The Cold War affected not only the nation's foreign policy but also the lives of everyday Americans. The United States enjoyed great prosperity and stability in the post–World War II period, made possible in part by the growth of industries that provided the technology needed to fight the Cold War. Not all Americans shared in the general prosperity, however. Minorities continued to face discrimination that made it more difficult to achieve the American dream of a secure job, a comfortable home, and a healthy family.

As the Cold War continued, Americans turned to a strong general to lead the country's government and maintain stability.

In preparation for the 1952 presidential election, Democrats and Republicans searched for candidates to nominate. Both parties approached the same person—General Dwight D. Eisenhower, a celebrated World War II general and former commander of NATO forces. Until this time, Eisenhower had never declared allegiance to a particular political party.

In this photograph from September 1956, President Eisenhower (left) escorts Vice President Nixon (right) to the airplane that would take Nixon on a campaign tour for their re-election.

In January 1952, he chose to run for president as a Republican, probably to distance himself from Truman and the Democratic Party, which had been losing popularity.

The Republican Party had problems as well. The party was split between moderates and conservatives, who fought each other for control. Eisenhower, a moderate, had to face off against a conservative Republican leader, Ohio senator Robert A. Taft. Eisenhower's fame as a dynamic leader won him the nomination and unified the party. The Democrats nominated the governor of Illinois, **Adlai Stevenson**. While Stevenson was a distinguished diplomat and had helped found the United Nations, he lacked the popularity that bolstered Eisenhower's election campaign.

Eisenhower did not wage a typical Republican campaign. He supported many of Truman's Fair Deal programs, which conservative Republicans threatened to revoke, and he vowed to support the U.S. soldiers who were fighting in the Korean War. But he purposefully left out specific details about his goals as president. He stated he was "pro-business" and practiced "modern Republicanism," which he defined as economic conservatism paired with social liberalism. Eisenhower and his running mate, Richard Nixon, beat Stevenson in a landslide, 442 electoral votes to 89.

Eisenhower immediately assigned several business leaders to his Cabinet. He chose the former president of General Motors, Charles E. Wilson, to serve as secretary of defense and a former steel company president, George Humphrey, to serve as secretary of the treasury. In 1953, he appointed Oveta Culp Hobby, the first commander of the Woman's Army Corps (WACs), to run the newly created Department of Health, Education, and Welfare. Eisenhower took measures to continue Social Security and unemployment insurance but otherwise cut government spending whenever he could. And due to the liberal consensus, which you have read about, Congress was usually willing to follow his lead.

PROSPERITY UNDER EISENHOWER

Postwar prosperity continued through the 1950s for the majority of Americans. This ongoing economic success was due largely to the position of the United States as a dominant world power, which enabled the nation to negotiate advantageous trade deals worldwide, and its embrace of **consumerism**. According to the theory of consumerism, the economy flourishes when people buy, or consume, a lot of goods and services.

The country's new role as a world leader meant the United States had to be on the cutting edge of technology. Military defense, electronics, and aerospace industries, essential to fighting the Cold War, flourished. Many of these industries were located in the **Sunbelt**, the southern region of the country that enjoys warm weather year-round. As a result, people from the **Frostbelt**, the north-central and northeastern region that has cold winters, migrated to Georgia, Florida, Texas, and California, where manufacturing jobs were on the rise.

Labor unions grew stronger and helped expand the middle class by ensuring that their members, who worked in these booming industries, received competitive pay, health insurance, paid vacations, and retirement benefits. Additionally, the number of service-sector, white-collar, and professional-sector jobs in business and government increased.

The growing middle class had more money to spend on consumer goods, such as food and automobiles. New industries developed to meet consumers' demands. Railroad, bank, and meatpacking companies created **agribusiness**—or the commercial business of agriculture—by buying up small family farms and creating huge, efficient factory farms. The companies converted the relatively humble occupation of farming into lucrative businesses. They opened supermarkets that offered middle-class shoppers a much wider variety of foods than was available at small corner markets.

As more people bought cars, the demand for highways and gasoline grew. Oil companies expanded their exploration programs and refineries and quickly became dominant businesses. Gas stations and auto repair shops flourished.

The growth of industries had some negative effects, however. Throughout the 1950s and into the 1960s, industrial waste products polluted the air and the lakes and rivers of major cities. **Smog**, a noxious combination of fog and smoke from factories, began to blanket such cities as Gary, Indiana, and Pittsburgh, Pennsylvania. The beaches of Lake Erie, the smallest and shallowest of the Great Lakes, were often covered in dead fish, killed by industrial pollutants that poisoned the water.

COLD WAR DEVELOPMENTS

Just as he supported many of Truman's domestic policies, Eisenhower also supported Truman's containment policy, aimed at preventing the spread of communism in the world. However, Eisenhower believed he could prevent any communist advance

WORLD EVENTS, 1953–1956

February 1953
President Eisenhower appoints Allen Dulles, the brother of Secretary of State John Foster Dulles, to head the CIA.

July 27, 1953
China signs a truce establishing North and South Korea, thus ending the Korean War.

June 18, 1954
The CIA stages a coup in Guatemala, replacing the recently elected president with a military dictator who supports United States' interests.

1953 | **1954**

January 20, 1953
Dwight D. Eisenhower is sworn in as the 34th president of the United States. *(Campaign button of Dwight "Ike" Eisenhower, 1952)*

August 19, 1953
The United States restores the shah of Iran to power after his prime minister had successfully overthrown him a few days before. *(Reza Shah Pahlavi's honor guard salutes him upon his return to Iran in 1953.)*

PRIMARY SOURCE

As the threat of nuclear war loomed in 1953, President Eisenhower addressed the United Nations about his nuclear deterrence policy.

I know that the American people share my deep belief that if a danger exists in the world, it is a danger shared by all—and equally, that if hope exists in the mind of one nation, that hope should be shared by all. . . . Atomic bombs today are more than 25 times as powerful as the weapons with which the atomic age dawned, while hydrogen weapons are in the ranges of millions of tons of TNT equivalent. . . . But the dread secret, and the fearful engines of atomic might, are not ours alone.

—from President Eisenhower's "Atoms for Peace" address to the United Nations, December 8, 1953

by using the threat of a nuclear attack rather than by mobilizing an army. Eisenhower's plan was called **nuclear deterrence**. It involved placing enough nuclear weapons in numerous safe places to guarantee that an enemy could not destroy all the weapons at once. Supposedly, nations would not risk war because both sides would be annihilated. Nuclear deterrence resulted in a world constantly on the brink, or the edge, of nuclear war. Secretary of State **John Foster Dulles** called this tension "**brinkmanship**," claiming that "the ability to get to the verge without getting into the war is the necessary art." Critics of nuclear deterrence claimed it was too dangerous. Still, the production of nuclear warheads increased, while the number of soldiers in service decreased and overall defense spending was actually cut by 20 percent between 1953 and 1955.

Meanwhile, the importance of strategic military bases in Hawaii and Alaska helped move these two U.S. territories toward full statehood. Near the end of Eisenhower's terms of office, in 1959, first Alaska and then Hawaii became the 49th and 50th states.

U.S. INVOLVEMENT OVERSEAS

As part of his containment program, Eisenhower gave the Central Intelligence Agency (CIA) new authority to investigate communism in other countries. In 1953, Eisenhower appointed **Allen Dulles** to head the CIA. Under Dulles, the CIA practiced **covert action**, gathering intelligence and secretly getting involved in the politics and internal affairs of other nations. In opposing communism, the United States came to support some authoritarian and corrupt governments.

For example, in 1953 in Iran, a new, duly elected government led by Prime Minister **Mohammad Mossadegh** (MOH-sah-dehk) deposed

July 26, 1956
President Nasser takes control of the Suez Canal in Egypt. *(Container ship in the modern Suez Canal)*

November 4, 1956
Soviets crush the Hungarian revolt.

November 6, 1956
Eisenhower is re-elected to a second term as president.

1955

1956

October 23, 1956
Hungarian citizens revolt against Soviet troops in Budapest. *(Hungarians burn a portrait of Stalin in 1956.)*

November 6, 1956
Egypt, Israel, Britain, and France sign a cease-fire in the Suez Canal conflict. *(United Nations peacekeeping troops in Port Said, Egypt, in 1956)*

the shah, or king, named **Reza Shah Pahlavi** (rih-ZAH shah PAH-luh-vee). The U.S. government feared Mossadegh was a communist. Eisenhower did not want a communist heading the country from which the United States received most of its oil, so he commanded the CIA to work with the secret services of other nations to topple Mossadegh and return the shah to power. In exchange, the shah's government granted American companies 40 percent of Iran's oil production. Reacting to similar communist suspicions, in 1954 the CIA ousted the newly elected president of Guatemala, **Jacobo Árbenz Guzmán**, and replaced him with a military dictator who protected American business interests in that Central American nation.

In 1956, two major world events captured Americans' attention. In Budapest, Hungary, citizens revolted against the communists that governed their country. Street battles soon escalated into all-out war. The Soviet Union sent troops to help the Hungarian government. Eisenhower refused to send American troops for fear of triggering a war between the United States and the Soviet Union. Soviet troops crushed the revolt within a month.

In Egypt, President **Gamal Abdel Nasser** seized control of the **Suez Canal**, the British-controlled waterway that lay between Africa and Asia, connecting the Red and Mediterranean seas. Two months later, Israeli troops advanced on Egypt,

followed by French and British paratroopers who worked together to retake the canal. Tensions heightened when the Soviet Union threatened nuclear war on Western Europe if Israel, Britain, and France did not withdraw from Egypt. A cease-fire resolved the situation, but the canal remained a source of conflict.

Meanwhile, the Cold War continued. As you've read, the Truman Doctrine supported free people and nations resisting communist takeovers. Although Eisenhower had failed to live up to this doctrine in Hungary, he continued to funnel money and American soldiers to Turkey and Greece, the **bulwarks**, or protective defenses, against Soviet expansion into the Middle East and Africa.

HISTORICAL THINKING

1. **READING CHECK** Which of Truman's domestic policies did President Eisenhower continue?

2. **DESCRIBE** How did technological development affect society and the economy in the United States during the 1950s?

3. **INTERPRET TIME LINES** How did the United States interfere in foreign governments during Eisenhower's first term in office?

4. **EVALUATE** What were some advantages of Eisenhower's nuclear deterrence plan?

AMERICAN SOCIETY

If you had more money than you needed, what would you do with it? Would you save it? Spend it? Share it? Many Americans had this choice to make as they confronted social changes during the Cold War years.

THE COLD WAR'S EFFECTS

The Cold War shaped the daily lives of Americans in numerous ways. Its economic effects were especially significant. To fight the Cold War, the government made heavy investments in the defense and aerospace industries, which became major American employers in such states as California and Missouri. In addition, millions of veterans took advantage of the GI Bill of Rights and received a college education. Many of them then contributed to building the nation's technology industries. Thus, the livelihoods of many Americans depended on Cold War government investments and goals.

A growing group of educated, white-collar Americans strengthened the nation's industrial base, earned more money, and enjoyed a steady increase in their standard of living. With their new affluence, these Americans began to consume more goods and services, adding to the general prosperity.

PRESSURES ON AMERICAN WOMEN

It happened after World War I, and again after World War II. After each war, employers pressured the women who had stepped in to keep industries and businesses running during the wars, to leave their jobs and make room for the returning soldiers. Between 1945 and 1947, more than 2 million women dropped out of the workforce, either by choice or by force. Women were also pressured to drop out of college to make room for men. The graduation rate for college women fell from 40 percent during the war to 25 percent by 1950.

Married and single women generally returned to domesticity, or home life. Many women, especially those who enjoyed working or were college-educated, found the transition from self-sufficiency to dependence on male breadwinners difficult and disappointing. Those who remained in the workforce, often out of financial necessity, were typically paid 53 percent less than men performing similar tasks.

The return of soldiers after World War II brought other changes as well. Americans were longing for life to return to normal after years of war. As you have read, the GI Bill helped many veterans of the war obtain college educations, improving their career prospects and earning potential. Provisions of the law also encouraged home-ownership, another cornerstone of increasing affluence and financial stability, through downpayment and mortage rate assistance. And as families were being reunited, many more couples were marrying and starting new families.

Immediately following World War II, the U.S. marriage rate spiked dramatically before leveling off slightly, which you can see in the graph on the next page. Americans were also entering into marriage at younger ages than prior to the war. The high marriage rate, in turn, led to a situation that changed the nation in profound ways.

THE BABY BOOM

More marriages, paired with increased economic optimism, led to a 20-year surge in the number of babies born in the United States, a phenomenon called the **baby boom**. American birth rates began to climb following the war, reaching more than 4 million births in 1954, a figure that held relatively steady until the mid-1960s.

It wasn't only that there were more couples having children during the baby-boom years; perhaps due to confidence in the economy and their ability to provide for their families, couples were having more children as well. An estimated 75 million Americans were born between 1946 and 1964, and by 1965, around 40 percent of Americans were younger than 20 years old.

Manufacturers and advertisers zeroed in on the growing market in children's products. Clothing, specialized foods, and toys were promoted directly to children during televised cartoons and other programming. Baby boomers, as this generation came to be called, are still a prime target of advertisers nearly a lifetime later.

Due to their sheer numbers, baby boomers have affected the national culture throughout their lives. They spearheaded the social changes and antiwar activism of the 1960s. Today, as they move into retirement, they are putting a strain on the Social Security system. Perhaps the baby boom's major impact, however, has been to spur on consumerism in every decade from the 1950s to the present.

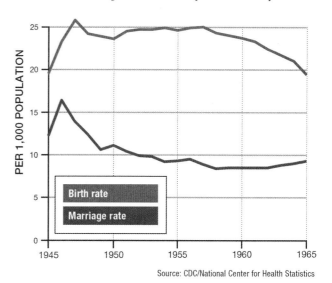

Birth and Marriage Rates in the Baby Boom Era (1945–1965)

PER 1,000 POPULATION

Birth rate
Marriage rate

1945   1950   1955   1960   1965

Source: CDC/National Center for Health Statistics

In 1958, nurses deliver a group of infants to their mothers in a hospital dormitory room. During the baby boom, a shortage of rooms for mothers and babies overwhelmed hospitals, which were designed for fewer births. In addition, home births declined and hospital births rose from 37 percent of all births in 1935 to 88 percent in 1950. The baby boom led to a growth in hospitals and a dramatic increase in the demand for many products and services.

Customers listen as a salesperson points out the new features of a television set at an appliance store in Silver Spring, Maryland, in 1950.

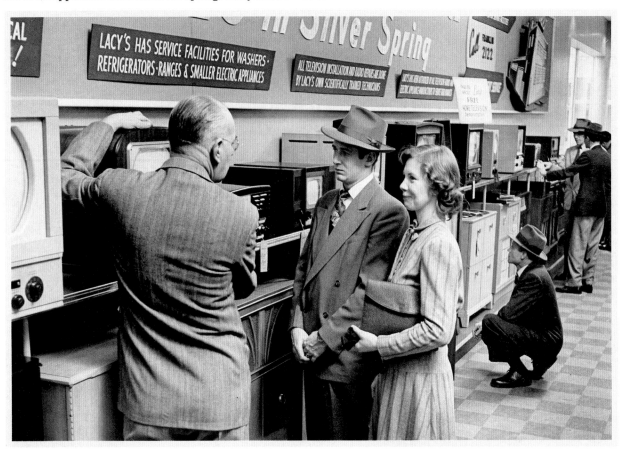

THE CONSUMER SOCIETY

During the Cold War years, many Americans had more money to spend and more goods to buy. Thanks to strong labor unions negotiating for regular working hours and personal time off, they also had more free time in which to shop. Consumer spending was now considered a patriotic way to build the nation's economy. Between 1946 and 1950, this new **consumer society** purchased over 21 million automobiles, 20 million refrigerators, 5.5 million electric stoves, and more than 2 million dishwashers. Shopping became an important part of the American lifestyle.

The consumer society was supported by easy access to credit—buying now and paying later, in installments. In 1950, a financial company called Diners Club issued the first credit cards in the United States. Department stores soon followed, offering charge accounts with easy payment plans.

Televisions became a popular item to charge to credit accounts. By the 1950s, televisions were no longer a luxury item that only upper-class families could afford. Most American homes had a TV; in fact, stores were selling millions of televisions every year.

Television provided advertisers easy access to millions of consumers. Enticing television commercials promoted shiny new appliances and unique gadgets guaranteed to make life easier for Americans. Much of this advertising was directed specifically at women. Commercials told women they could be more efficient and effective wives and mothers if they owned the newest washing machine, dishwasher, and vacuum. In addition to encouraging consumer spending, these advertisements also reinforced women's traditional domestic roles.

MEDICINE, SCIENCE, AND EDUCATION

The Cold War years also featured major advances in medicine, science, and education. One of the most important medical breakthroughs was the development of a vaccine against polio, an infectious, crippling disease. Between the late 1940s and early 1950s, doctors had reported 35,000 new cases of the disease in the United States. In 1952, the nation experienced its worst polio outbreak—58,000 cases. Three years later, in 1955, **Jonas Salk**, an American physician and medical researcher, introduced the **Salk vaccine**. The incidence of polio quickly fell, and the disease is no longer a threat in the United States.

A young girl looks apprehensively at the needle before receiving a lifesaving Salk polio vaccine in the 1950s. Health departments and schools vigorously publicized the free vaccination program with public service posters, newspaper ads, and radio announcements. An oral vaccine developed by Alfred Sabin was also developed in the 1950s and given in drops placed on a sugar cube.

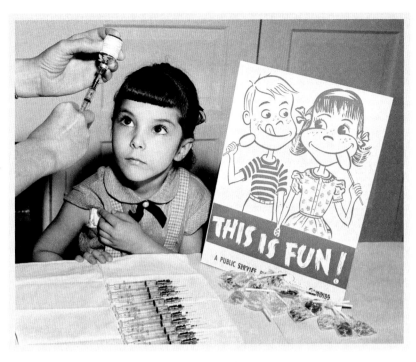

In the late 1940s, three American physicists invented the **transistor**, an electronic device used to control the flow of electricity in electronic equipment. Transistors became available for public purchase during the 1950s and were commonly used in small, portable radios and hearing aids. Today, transistors are components of the microchips found in computers and many other electronic devices.

One of the first commercial computers designed for processing business data was the **Universal Automatic Computer (UNIVAC)**. Developed in the late 1940s, the room-size UNIVAC was put into use by various businesses and organizations. For example, the **Bureau of the Census**, the government agency that counts the nation's population, used the UNIVAC to count and record part of the 1950 population.

Scientists also explored ways to produce cheaper energy to meet the nation's growing energy demands. Using the same science behind the atomic bomb, scientists working in the United States developed a way to capture the heat released during nuclear fission, which is the reaction that occurs when atoms split apart. The steam from this heat can be used to turn turbine blades to power generators and make electricity. The energy created from this process is called **nuclear power**. In 1957, the first large-scale American nuclear power plant started operating in Shippingport, Pennsylvania.

Advances in the sciences were not limited to earthbound endeavors. Scientists studied planetary satellites, or bodies in space that orbit other bodies of a larger size. On October 4, 1957, the Soviet Union sent the first mechanical, or human-made, satellite, called *Sputnik 1*, into space to orbit Earth. Americans worried that such satellites might enable the Soviets

to direct nuclear missiles toward the United States. President Eisenhower responded by establishing the **National Aeronautics and Space Administration (NASA)**, which oversees the U.S. space program. NASA worked to match and exceed the Soviets' accomplishments in space exploration.

After being caught off guard by *Sputnik*, the American public demanded improvements to their educational systems. Eisenhower responded by signing the National Defense Education Act (NDEA) into law on September 2, 1958. The purpose of NDEA was to improve schools through government funding, encourage students to attend college, and promote education in science, engineering, math, and foreign languages. In California, educators used NDEA funding to reorganize the state's higher education system. The **California Master Plan**, adopted in 1960, joined the state's universities and community colleges into one accessible and affordable system governed by a framework that promoted academic excellence.

HISTORICAL THINKING

1. **READING CHECK** How did the Cold War affect the lives of ordinary Americans?

2. **ANALYZE CAUSE AND EFFECT** Explain how the return of World War II veterans had complex effects on women in the workforce, and identify the types of data that could be used in determining these effects.

3. **IDENTIFY MAIN IDEAS AND DETAILS** What factors contributed to the development of a consumer society in the United States?

SUBURBS SURROUND CITIES

Where would you most like to live—in a city, suburb, small town, or rural area? During the Cold War years, many Americans chose to move to suburbs. Why might the suburbs have appealed to them?

MOVING TO THE SUBURBS

As populations were increasing in Sunbelt states in response to the expansion of aerospace and other industries in the region, another major demographic change was also taking place. **Suburbanization**, or a population shift from cities to outlying communities, was rapidly transforming the American landscape.

In 1950, about 1.7 million new houses were built in the United States, and more than 80 percent were built in suburbs. A home in the suburbs offered relief from crowded cities. Suburbs often had larger homes, better schools, and lower crime rates. By 1950, more than 18 million people, or 1 in every 8 Americans, had moved from cities to suburbs.

The GI Bill, which offered loans to World War II veterans to purchase houses, helped make suburbanization possible. So did two federal government agencies. The **Veterans Administration (VA)**, which serves the needs of veterans, and the **Federal Housing Administration (FHA)**, which provides financing for housing, worked together to manage the GI Bill program. From 1944 to 1952, the government issued nearly 2.4 million low-interest home loans as a benefit of the GI Bill, accelerating the movement of families to the suburbs.

All over the country, veterans paid building contractors to construct affordable, single-family homes. **William Levitt**, a New York contractor, purchased several thousand acres of farmland in Hempstead, New York, 25 miles east of Manhattan, for the mass production of private homes. Levitt based his building operation on Henry Ford's assembly lines. His company manufactured precut building materials in his factories, delivered them using his trucking company, and assembled the homes using his builders. On the construction site, each worker performed a single task, such as framing or pouring concrete, to complete each house. Levitt's builders constructed as many as 180 houses in a week. When completed in 1951, **Levittown, Long Island**, boasted 17,000 houses plus dozens of parks, ball fields, swimming pools, churches, and shopping areas for its 82,000 residents.

Levitt's system of mass-produced neighborhoods was duplicated across the country. Linking Cold War thinking and home ownership, Levitt declared, "No man who owns his own house and lot can be a communist."

Meanwhile, new expressways improved access between suburbs and cities. President Eisenhower viewed road improvement as vital to the national defense during the Cold War. When he signed the **Federal-Aid Highway Act of 1956**, launching one of the greatest public works projects in history, he stated, "In case of atomic attack on our key cities, the road net must permit quick evacuation of target areas." Better roads would also benefit the economy by creating jobs, making it easier and cheaper for industries to transport goods, and allowing Americans to live farther away from their workplaces. In fact, state and local governments often covered the entire cost of highway segments in response to local commuting demand. The resulting **Interstate Highway System** linked towns, cities, and suburbs nationwide with limited access, multilane highways.

IMPACT OF SUBURBANIZATION

Suburbanization dramatically transformed American culture. The American dream of owning one's home became a reality for millions. The first house sold in Levittown, Long Island, came with a free television and appliances, prompting Levitt to call it "the best house in the U.S."

But social observers criticized these developments, mocking the uniform design of the "little boxes." Far more troubling was the **homogeneity**, or sameness, of the residents. Many mass-produced neighborhoods, or **subdivisions**, refused to admit minorities, especially African Americans. Levittown's standard sales contract stated that homes could not be "used or occupied by any person other than members of the Caucasian race." Nearly 10 years after the U.S. Supreme Court ruled in 1948 against such discrimination, not a single African American lived in Levittown. Social observers also deplored the homogeneity of the suburbanites' lives. The men commuted from their uniformly designed houses to work in offices that were also mostly alike, and the women cleaned house, cooked, and raised children.

Suburbanization and discrimination changed the makeup of American cities. African Americans and the less wealthy remained in the cities, where making a living became more difficult. Many businesses and factories also moved to the suburbs, taking jobs and services with them. Fewer residents and businesses meant lower revenues for city or local governments, but as taxes were raised to cover the shortfall, even more people moved to the suburbs. In just a few years, many American cities lost a large portion of their upper- and middle-class residents.

Suburbanization also affected rural communities and natural environments. The relentless demand for subdivisions and the expansion of interstate highways pressured farmers near cities to sell their land. In 1930, more than 30 million Americans lived on farms. By 1960, that number had fallen to 15.6 million, and nearly one in three Americans lived in a suburb. Suburbs and highways also disrupted wildlife habitats, a process that continues to this day.

HISTORICAL THINKING

1. **READING CHECK** What motivated many Americans to move to suburbs during the Cold War years?

2. **MAKE INFERENCES** What did William Levitt mean when he said "No man who owns his own house and lot can be a communist"?

3. **IDENTIFY PROBLEMS AND SOLUTIONS** What do you consider the greatest problem to have resulted from the growth of suburbs?

CRITICAL VIEWING An aerial photograph taken in 1954 reveals the sprawling Levittown, Long Island, suburb that had once been farmland. What elements in this photograph support the criticism that suburban developments featured too much uniformity, or sameness?

AUTOMOBILE MANIA

Can you imagine never using a car? If not, you're in step with the majority of Americans who rely on cars for transportation at least part, if not most, of the time. That dependence developed during the 1950s.

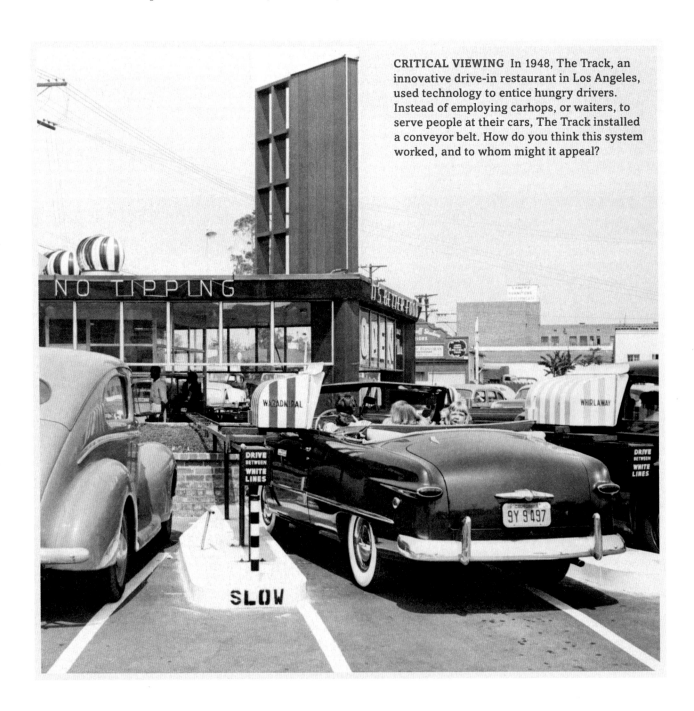

CRITICAL VIEWING In 1948, The Track, an innovative drive-in restaurant in Los Angeles, used technology to entice hungry drivers. Instead of employing carhops, or waiters, to serve people at their cars, The Track installed a conveyor belt. How do you think this system worked, and to whom might it appeal?

GROWING RELIANCE ON AUTOMOBILES

The growth of suburbs during the Cold War years made Americans more dependent on automobiles. Many workers had to commute from the suburbs to jobs in the city each day. As the demand for automobiles increased, American production quadrupled from 2 million cars in 1946 to 8 million in 1955. Between 1945 and 1960, new technologies cut by half the time it took to manufacture a car. As a result, the nation's gross national product (GNP), the total value of goods and services produced during a year, skyrocketed from $212 billion to $503 billion. The business of making cars became the most important contributor to the U.S. economy.

During the Cold War years, the automobile industry employed a large percentage of the country's population. By 1960, one out of six Americans earned paychecks by contributing to the production of cars, either directly by assembling vehicles or indirectly by working for a company that supplied automotive parts and equipment. Factory employees rolled out close to 58 million new cars during the 1950s.

The United Automobile Workers (UAW), an industrial union representing automotive workers, had grown in size and become a powerful force in the automotive industry by the 1950s. The UAW, in partnership with other labor unions, successfully organized strikes for better wages and benefits and negotiated paid vacation days, pensions, and medical care for union members.

A CAR CULTURE

The growth of the car culture rapidly transformed the American landscape. Entire industries blossomed along the increasing network of roads and highways lined with gas stations. Restaurants adjusted their operations so drivers could buy food "to go" or even eat meals without leaving their cars. One of the first restaurant owners to adopt this "fast food" model was Ray Kroc. He opened the first McDonald's restaurant in 1955 in Des Plaines, Illinois, a suburb of Chicago. Motor hotels, or motels, were built along busy roads to accommodate the growing number of travelers taking road trips. The American car culture also prompted the development of drive-in movie theaters and shopping malls. All these businesses added to **suburban sprawl**, or the spread of suburban developments over more and more land.

As the car culture spread, the economies of the United States and other Western nations became increasingly dependent on oil, which is the source of gasoline, diesel fuel, and many other products.

ROUTE 66

Completed in 1926, this famous highway ran 2,448 miles between Chicago and Los Angeles. Over the years, Route 66 became a symbol of the open roads in the United States. Okies, or migrant farm workers from Oklahoma, used it during the Great Depression to travel west, seeking a better life in California. Families traveled the highway to visit the American heartland, the canyons and deserts of the Southwest, and the Pacific Ocean. Some stores and restaurants along the route are now historic landmarks. But Eisenhower's Interstate Highway System threatened its existence in the 1950s. Many travelers chose the newer, more direct highways over the often meandering Route 66.

Between 1945 and 1960, U.S. oil production rose by nearly 50 percent, and annual oil imports increased from 74 million to 371 million barrels. The need for oil—not only to power automobiles but also to meet other energy needs—would affect American foreign and domestic policy for decades to come.

The large number of gas-guzzling cars on American roads led to rising air pollution in cities. By 1966, motor vehicles contributed more than 60 percent of the pollutants discharged into the nation's air, amounting to 86 million tons out of 146 million tons. In 1955, the U.S. Congress passed the Air Pollution Control Act, the first law to address air pollution. The act was amended in 1963 to provide funding to study the effects of automobile exhaust on people's health.

Other environmental problems resulted from the extraction, refining, and transportation of oil. During the 1960s and beyond, oil spills and the dumping of oil wastes damaged wildlife habitats and polluted streams, lakes, and other bodies of water.

HISTORICAL THINKING

1. **READING CHECK** Why did many Americans become dependent on automobiles during the Cold War years?

2. **MAKE INFERENCES** How might the need for oil affect American foreign policy?

3. **ANALYZE ENVIRONMENTAL CONCEPTS** How did its increased oil production help the United States, and what environmental problems were caused by Americans' growing dependence on oil?

1950s hot rod

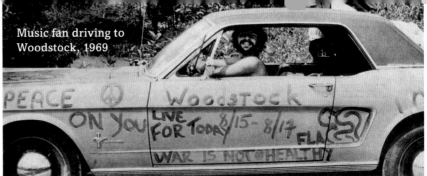

Music fan driving to Woodstock, 1969

THROUGH THE LENS

CARS & AMERICAN CULTURE

It's surprising that a brutish industrial-age machine has maintained its status as a cultural icon amid the buzz of technology in the digital age. Decades ago, owning a car was about horsepower, status, and youthful rebellion. Cars inspired movies, songs, and literature. They were a driver's ticket to the freedom and glory of the open road. Do you think concerns about pollution, gridlock, and gas prices will cause the American car obsession to subside?

American World War II soldier in a seagoing Jeep, Europe, c. 1946

Tail fins on a 1959 Cadillac Eldorado

Architect Frank Lloyd Wright's 1930 Cord L-29

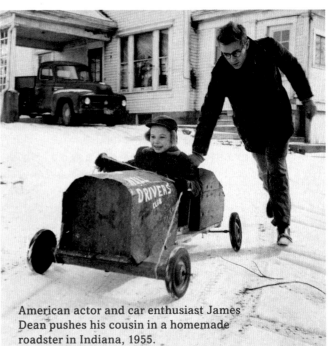

American actor and car enthusiast James Dean pushes his cousin in a homemade roadster in Indiana, 1955.

Dressed in their Sunday best, boys strike a serious pose on the hood of a car in a Chicago South Side neighborhood, 1941.

ILLINOIS 1941
922 933

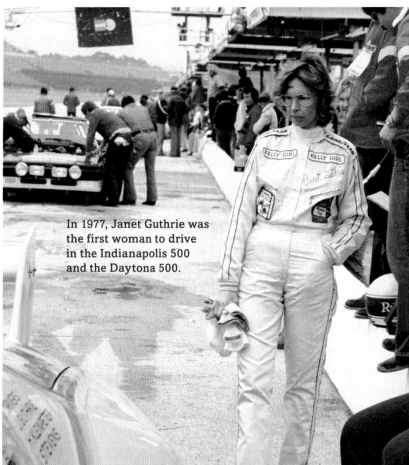

In 1977, Janet Guthrie was the first woman to drive in the Indianapolis 500 and the Daytona 500.

Electric vehicle charging at a Detroit, Michigan, auto show

CULTURE OF THE FIFTIES

The next time you're watching your favorite TV show or listening to your favorite music, consider that much of what we now consider American pop culture came into being during the 1950s.

THE GOLDEN AGE OF TELEVISION

You have read about the important role television played in American consumer culture, both as an item for consumers to purchase and as a way for advertisers to sell their products. In 1948, less than one percent of American households could boast of owning a TV set. Back then, television's fuzzy black-and-white images were anything but "must-see." The first televised baseball game was filmed using only one camera. The first TV actors sweated under hot lights and wore black lipstick and green makeup just to show up on screen. But by 1959, more than 83 percent of homes in the United States had one or more televisions.

Television evolved by modeling itself on another medium—radio. In the 1930s and 1940s, radio offered a variety of entertainment to more than 60 percent of U.S. households and was available in nearly 2 million cars. Some radio programs were so popular that many movie theaters did not bother opening for the evening until after the top programs had aired. Early television programs just couldn't compete with the witty dialogue and skillfully achieved sound effects of radio, but television continued to improve.

Among the major changes in television technology was the introduction of color in 1950. In the early 1950s, special cables were used to link both coasts, marking a significant change in communication and allowing millions of viewers to watch the same program simultaneously. In 1949, a TV set appeared for the first time in the Sears department store catalog. Its price was $149.95. Only a year later, Americans were buying 20,000 television sets a day.

By 1954, three national television networks—ABC, CBS, and NBC—were broadcasting regularly. These networks were also the major radio broadcasters, and they boasted better technology and greater talent than their competitors. They also had two other advantages. Their profits from radio broadcasting enabled them to invest in new television programming. They could also move their most popular radio programs, including *Jack Benny, Burns & Allen*, and *Amos 'n' Andy*, over to television.

Television in the 1950s introduced or reinvented many genres, including variety shows, quiz shows, informational programming, and high-quality dramas. Among the most popular genres was the **situation comedy**, or sitcom, a weekly series that featured a familiar setting and a group of characters who faced amusing problems. These shows reflected traditional elements of American society, often with a twist. For example, on the popular sitcom *I Love Lucy*, the title character was a woman who stayed at home while her husband, Ricky, worked as a musician. Money was never an issue for the couple and their young son, and no one stayed angry for long. The show's humor came from crazy schemes Lucy developed to make her life more interesting. *I Love Lucy* introduced techniques that revolutionized the television industry, including taping in front of a live studio audience and using multiple cameras to film scenes from different angles. The show became so popular that more people tuned in to watch *I Love Lucy* on January 19, 1953—a staggering 44 million—than would watch President Eisenhower's inauguration the following day.

Though racial minorities rarely appeared in the 1950s sitcoms, they did play major—if stereotypical—roles in several popular shows. The most popular was *Amos 'n' Andy*, an adaptation of a radio comedy created by two white men and featuring an all-black cast. The NAACP angrily denounced *Amos 'n' Andy*

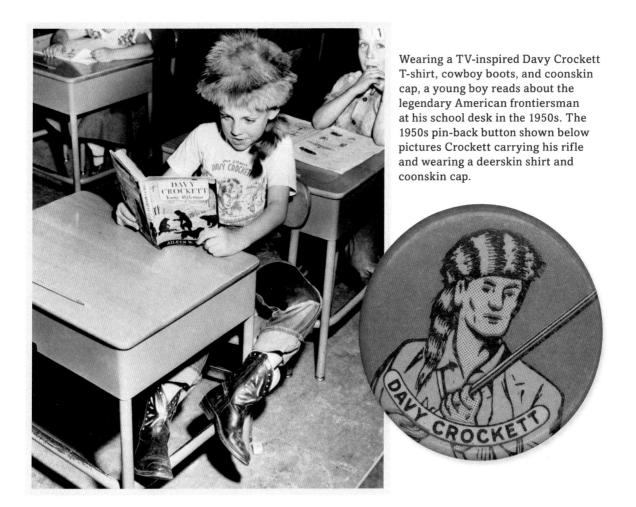

Wearing a TV-inspired Davy Crockett T-shirt, cowboy boots, and coonskin cap, a young boy reads about the legendary American frontiersman at his school desk in the 1950s. The 1950s pin-back button shown below pictures Crockett carrying his rifle and wearing a deerskin shirt and coonskin cap.

for portraying blacks as "clowns" and "crooks," but others praised the performers for transforming racist stereotypes into humor that authentically portrayed the African-American experience.

By the mid-1950s, TV networks were mining the riches of children's programming. American film producer Walt Disney struck gold with his three-part series about the historical American frontiersman Davy Crockett, which aired nationally in December 1954. In the months that followed, millions of schoolchildren began wearing coonskin caps just like the one Crockett wore on the program. Stores soon began selling other Davy Crockett merchandise, including shirts, blankets, toothbrushes, and lunch boxes. One department store chain sold 20,000 surplus tents in less than a week simply by printing "Davy Crockett" on a flap.

Television and marketing businesspeople noted the new media's power to sell products. Important advertisers started sponsoring entire programs. The television industry expanded with each new program, providing work for hundreds of performers and technicians at a time and taking business away from the motion picture industry. By the mid-1950s, the "golden age" of television was in full swing.

A NEW KIND OF MUSIC

In the 1950s, a distinctive teenage culture emerged, rooted in the prosperity and population boom that followed World War II. While the threat of nuclear war was ever-present, teenagers had little experience of the grim events of the previous two decades. They were raised in relative affluence, surrounded by ads that ignored the traditional value of thrift. Fewer were employed than in prewar years, but close to half had summer jobs, and many had their own money. By 1956, teenagers bought $9 billion worth of products a year; a typical teen spent as much on entertainment as the average family had spent in 1941.

Many teens chose to spend their money on the popular music of the time. Known as **rock and roll**, this musical genre grew out of rhythm and blues, the music brought north by African-American musicians during the Great Migration. Most rock and roll songs were originally written or performed by African-American artists. Because African-American music was not considered appropriate for white audiences, music studio executives rerecorded versions of these songs using white "cover artists" so that white radio stations would play them.

The wildly popular Elvis Presley (1935–1977) sings and dances at the Olympia Theater in Miami, Florida, in 1956. Presley had an exceptional vocal range.

That situation began to change in 1951, after an American disc jockey named **Alan Freed** learned that white teens in Cleveland were buying up records featuring African-American rhythm and blues artists. Freed began playing the hard-edged music on the air. Suddenly, teens could discover new music just by turning a radio dial.

In 1955, African-American rhythm and blues artist **Chuck Berry** (1926–2017) recorded one of the first rock and roll songs, "Maybellene," which quickly became a hit. Berry followed up with "Roll Over Beethoven" (1956), "Rock and Roll Music" (1957), and "Johnny B. Goode" (1958). A rock and roll pioneer, Berry played guitar in an infectious, rhythmic style and wrote songs about cool cars and dances to appeal to teenagers. Berry's showmanship on stage—playing guitar between his legs and behind his head and performing a movement called the "duckwalk"—influenced many rock and roll guitarists.

In 1955, a 21-year-old truck driver from Memphis named **Elvis Presley** exploded onto the popular music scene. Born in rural Mississippi, Presley grew up singing country music, gospel, and blues. Tall and handsome with long sideburns and slicked-back hair, he was a riveting performer. His music was strongly rooted in the southern music of his childhood.

Presley quickly became a national sensation. In less than a year, he recorded 8 number one songs and 6 of the all-time top 25 records of music company RCA. However, Presley had many critics, including teachers and members of the clergy, who complained that his unique way of dancing and shaking his hips proved that rock and roll posed a moral danger to the country's youth. This criticism only increased Presley's popularity among young people.

In 1956, rock and roll reached a milestone when an African-American singer named **Little Richard** outsold tamer versions of his songs that had been rerecorded by Pat Boone, a leading white cover artist. The success of Little Richard and other rock and roll musicians led major record companies to start recording more of the genre, performed by both black and white musicians. Music sales tripled during the 1950s, aided by such technological advances as portable transistor radios and vinyl records.

THE BEAT GENERATION

While rock and roll was changing the American music scene, another youth rebellion transformed American writing. The **Beat Generation** was a group of young writers and poets in San Francisco and New York City who attacked the values and beliefs of mainstream American society. They called themselves "beat" because they were tired of living in the homogenous, or uniform, society they felt was taking hold in the United States. They despised politics, consumerism, and technology, and they valued creative expression.

Poet **Allen Ginsberg** expressed the Beats' disgust for the conventions of the time in his long, free verse poem "Howl" (1955). Its opening line—"I saw the best minds of my generation destroyed by madness"—sets a mood of anger and despair. Ginsberg's work demonstrated his belief that a mass audience could relate to an individual's thoughts and experiences, no matter how outside the norm they might be.

The Beats equated happiness and creativity with total freedom of expression. Their model of authentic living was Dean Moriarty, the hero of *On the Road* (1957) by Beat author **Jack Kerouac**. Loosely based on an actual road trip that Kerouac and some friends took, the book tells of the cross-country adventures of a group of young Americans trying to escape from middle-class life. *On the Road* became a national best seller and a cult book on college campuses. Like Presley, Little Richard, and Ginsberg, Kerouac appealed to the young people dissatisfied with conventional American culture of the 1950s.

HISTORICAL THINKING

1. **READING CHECK** What forms of entertainment that developed in the 1950s became part of mainstream American culture?

2. **ANALYZE CAUSE AND EFFECT** How did racism affect television programming in the 1950s?

3. **MAKE CONNECTIONS** How do you think the historical story of rock and roll influenced social trends in today's popular music?

NATIONAL BASEBALL HALL OF FAME AND MUSEUM COOPERSTOWN, NEW YORK

The National Baseball Hall of Fame and Museum in Cooperstown, New York, celebrates and preserves the history of America's favorite pastime. Dedicated on June 12, 1939, the museum houses the bronze plaques of more than 300 inductees elected to the Hall of Fame, the sport's highest honor. Exhibits feature trophies, baseballs, gloves, jerseys, and other artifacts associated with legendary players and managers, from Ted Williams to Ken Griffey, Jr. The museum also tells the history of African Americans in baseball—as well as the story of women in the game. Each year, about 300,000 visitors tour the museum to relive the greatest moments in baseball history and learn more about the heroes of the sport.

Lou Gehrig's Trophy

Lou Gehrig is one of the most respected players in baseball history. Called the "Iron Horse" for playing 2,130 consecutive games without a break, Gehrig was forced to retire when he was diagnosed in 1939 with an incurable, fatal disease. On July 4, 1939, the Yankees held an appreciation day at Yankee Stadium to honor him and present him with the trophy shown here. To a packed stadium, Gehrig delivered his famous farewell speech, calling himself "the luckiest man on the face of the earth."

The names of Gehrig's teammates and a poem honoring Gehrig are inscribed on the trophy.

Hank Aaron's Plaque

Each year, baseball writers vote on candidates for induction into the National Baseball Hall of Fame. In addition, a special committee periodically elects inductees. A bronze plaque is made for each inductee, like this one for Hank Aaron, identifying the person's accomplishments. Aaron reigned as baseball's home run king from 1974 until 2007, when his career record of 755 home runs was surpassed by Barry Bonds of the San Francisco Giants.

Which other major league players served in the World Wars? Do research to find out.

Hank Greenberg's Baseball and ID Card

One of the best hitters in baseball, Henry "Hank" Greenberg won two Most Valuable Player awards with the Detroit Tigers before his career was interrupted by World War II. Like many other major league players, Greenberg served in the war from 1941 to 1945. His War Department ID card appears above. When Greenberg returned to the major leagues in 1945, he helped the Tigers win the World Series by driving in 7 runs in 7 games. The next year, he led the American League in home runs and RBIs.

"I love that baseball is timeless. I love that it's traditional, but that it has adapted over the years. . . . **There's nothing better than sitting at a ballgame.**"

—Jeff Idelson, President, National Baseball Hall of Fame and Museum

Catcher's mitts lack individual fingers, like mittens, and have heavy padding.

Yogi Berra's Mitt

A colorful baseball icon, New York Yankees catcher Yogi Berra was a 10-time World Series champion. He used this mitt to catch a perfect game thrown by pitcher Don Larsen in the World Series on October 8, 1956. The game was played at Yankee Stadium in New York City against the Brooklyn Dodgers. In a perfect game, a pitcher allows no hits or walks through at least 9 innings. A perfect game is a rare accomplishment. In major league history through 2016, only 23 pitchers had achieved the feat.

URBAN AND RURAL POVERTY

If you don't experience something yourself, you may find it hard to imagine it even exists. In the 1950s, middle-class suburbanites lived sheltered from the poverty that plagued inner cities and rural areas.

PERSISTENT POVERTY

The 1950s were a prosperous time for the United States as a whole, but the nation's wealth was not distributed equally. While the total amount of wealth in the country increased, the economic gap between the wealthy and the poor remained the same. In the late 1950s, the **poverty rate**, or the percentage of the population living in poverty, was 22.4 percent, which amounted to about 39.5 million people.

American journalists and writers of the early 1960s worked to expose the pervasive poverty in the United States. In 1960, journalist Edward R. Murrow revealed the harsh living conditions of migrant farm workers in a nationally aired documentary for CBS, *Harvest of Shame*. Television viewers witnessed families who could barely afford food for themselves as they harvested crops for the wealthiest, best-fed

country in the world. In the book *The Other America*, published in 1962, author Michael Harrington portrayed the persistence of poverty among such groups as the working poor, the elderly, and the mentally ill. The book became required reading in college courses and prompted government officials to address some of the problems it had exposed.

URBAN POVERTY

As you have read, many middle-class Americans and businesses moved to the suburbs in the 1950s. This population shift lowered the taxes collected by cities, decreased municipal budgets, and influenced the racial concentrations in cities. Those departing for new homes in the suburbs were mostly white, while those who remained in the cities were more often members of minority groups. This difference was due both to economic factors and to discriminatory practices that prevented members of minorities from moving to largely white suburban neighborhoods.

President Truman's Fair Deal had included the American Housing Act of 1949. The act provided mortgage assistance for Americans buying homes and began the process of **urban renewal**, which involved clearing slums to replace them with large, publicly funded housing projects. Federal and state government urban renewal programs continued into the 1960s. Although the original intent of the plan was good, the huge projects destroyed existing communities, were too large to manage efficiently, and often isolated the residents from affordable services. Instead of alleviating problems, many of the housing projects became centers of despair and unemployment. Out-of-wedlock births increased, as did criminal activity and drug abuse. By the late 1960s, the urban renewal effort was largely deemed a failure.

PRIMARY SOURCE

The American city has been transformed. The poor still inhabit the miserable housing in the central area, but they are increasingly isolated from contact with, or sight of, anybody else. Middle-class women coming in from Suburbia on a rare trip may catch the merest glimpse of the other America on the way to an evening at the theater, but their children are segregated in suburban schools. The business or professional man may drive along the fringes of slums in a car or bus, but it is not an important experience to him. The failures, the unskilled, the disabled, the aged, and the minorities are right there, across the tracks, where they have always been. But hardly anyone else is.

— from *The Other America*,
  by Michael Harrington, 1962

American photographer Wayne Miller took this photograph of tenements in Chicago in 1948 as part of a project documenting the lives of African Americans who were left out of the postwar economic boom.

RURAL POVERTY

Poverty in the United States was not confined to the inner cities in the 1950s. As you have read, suburbanization affected rural areas as well. The loss of farmland, the rise of agribusiness, and increased mechanization meant fewer farming jobs. Many rural communities slowly declined, especially as young people left in search of job opportunities.

Some rural areas were extremely poor. **Appalachia**, a part of the Appalachian Mountain region that stretches from northern Alabama to southern New York, had one of the most severe poverty rates in the United States in the late 1950s and early 1960s. In 1960, when the overall United States poverty rate was 22 percent, the poverty rate in Appalachia averaged more than 31 percent.

Appalachia was mountainous and hard to farm, but it had an abundance of coal. With little else to sustain the local economy, the region became dependent on coal mining. But mining was hard, dirty, and dangerous work. It stripped forests and polluted the air, land, and water, contributing to a variety of environmental problems. By the mid-20th century, the introduction of machinery that could do the

work of many miners in a much shorter time frame put many miners out of work. Logging provided some temporary jobs, but the process scarred the Appalachian landscape.

Over time, efforts to reduce poverty in many places in the United States were successful, but Appalachia saw little economic improvement. In a decade, the region had lost 1.5 percent of its jobs, even as the nation's total employment grew by 17 percent. Its rugged landscape was unattractive to most industries, and re-education and job training programs were well intentioned but ineffective. Between 1945 and 1965, approximately 3.5 million people left Appalachia, seeking better lives and work opportunities in larger cities in the Midwest.

HISTORICAL THINKING

1. **READING CHECK** How did suburbanization contribute to urban and rural poverty in the 1950s?

2. **ANALYZE CAUSE AND EFFECT** Why did many urban renewal projects of the 1950s and 1960s fail?

3. **IDENTIFY PROBLEMS AND SOLUTIONS** Why did attempts to reverse Appalachian poverty fail?

MAIN IDEA Many Native Americans and Mexican Americans struggled against poverty and discrimination during the 1950s.

NATIVE AMERICANS AND MEXICAN AMERICANS

The 1950s were great years to be a white, middle-class American. But if you were Native American or Mexican American, it was a different story.

DEMANDING A PLACE AS CITIZENS

In the years following World War II, Native Americans, many of whom had volunteered and fought bravely during the war, found themselves shut out of both the postwar economic boom and the political system. On reservations, they faced high rates of poverty and unemployment, poor access to government assistance and services, and inadequate schools. Many Native Americans did not even have the right to vote, despite the fact that, in 1924, Congress had granted citizenship to all Native Americans born within the United States. In addition, for decades, the federal government's policy toward Native Americans' sovereignty, or self-government, was inconsistent.

Some states refused to grant suffrage to Native Americans. The states took the position that Native Americans living on reservations were not citizens of the state, but rather citizens of their individual tribes or nations. Native Americans turned to the courts.

In 1948, Miguel Trujillo, a U.S. Marine war veteran and member of the Isleta Pueblo in New Mexico, was denied when he attempted to register to vote. He filed suit against the registrar and the state. A panel of three federal judges ruled in *Trujillo* v. *Garley* that the portion of New Mexico's constitution that prohibited Native American reservation residents from voting violated the 14th and 15th amendments of the U.S. Constitution.

Their decision backed up a similar case, *Harrison and Austin* v. *Laveen*, which had been brought by two Mojave-Apache men in Arizona that same year. These two cases effectively granted all Native American citizens the right to vote throughout the United States; however, Maine did not officially grant this right until 1953, and Utah held out until 1957.

Another major issue in the postwar era was poor government management of reservations. The Meriam Report, a government study released in 1928, had documented the problems and suggested specific reforms. The Indian Reorganization Act, passed in 1934, was an attempt to address the problems. The act sought to decrease federal control of Native American affairs and to encourage Native American self-government. It ended the government practice—adopted with the Dawes Act in 1887—of selling off the best reservation lands to white land speculators and homesteaders. It recognized the authority of tribal governments and promoted their self-government by urging them to adopt constitutions drafted by the Bureau of Indian Affairs.

But the reorganization was not a success. The act did not give Native Americans full control over their lands and governments. Instead, the reservations remained under the management of the Bureau of Indian Affairs, and little progress was made in solving the problems detailed in the Meriam Report.

Hoping to restore their tribal sovereignty and take control of their own future, Native Americans from 50 tribes and associations met in Denver, Colorado, to establish the National Congress of American Indians in 1944. In one year, membership rose to about 800 tribes and nations, representing nearly every Native American group in the United States. The organization began working to protect treaty rights, maintain Native American traditions, and push for self-determination and self-government.

Protester George Pletnikoff, Jr., a member of the Unangax̂ (Aleut) tribe, helps train protesters in nonviolent methods.

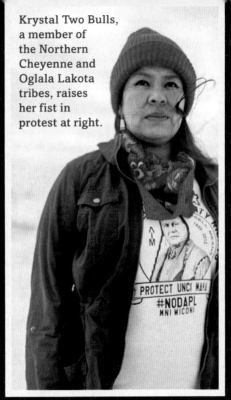

Krystal Two Bulls, a member of the Northern Cheyenne and Oglala Lakota tribes, raises her fist in protest at right.

Nailed to a signpost at the main protest camp are the names of participating tribes and the distances to their homelands.

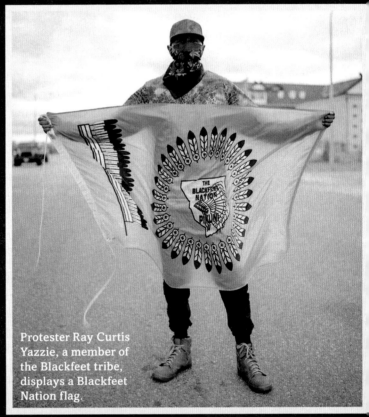

Protester Ray Curtis Yazzie, a member of the Blackfeet tribe, displays a Blackfeet Nation flag.

STANDING ROCK PROTEST

The struggle by Native Americans to protect their rights has continued into the 21st century. Beginning in April 2016, the Standing Rock Sioux led a 10-month protest in North Dakota against construction of the Dakota Access oil pipeline, designed to travel along the Missouri River and connect North Dakota oil fields with pipeline networks in Illinois. Seeking to protect their freshwater source and the diverse environmental regions crossed by the pipeline from potential oil leaks, the Standing Rock Sioux were joined by people from hundreds of indigenous tribes, including those shown above. In late February 2017, police cleared the main protest camp, following an executive order by President Donald Trump to advance approval of the pipeline's construction.

MORE FAILED POLICIES

In 1943, a year before the National Congress of American Indians began to organize, the U.S. Senate decided to investigate living conditions on Native American reservations. They found serious problems: poverty, racism, abuse by police officers, and alarming rates of alcoholism and suicide.

Under President Eisenhower, the federal government decided to remove Native Americans from reservations and encourage them to assimilate into mainstream society. And so began the disastrous government program known as the **termination policy**. In 1953, Congress set a goal to "as rapidly as possible make Indians within the territorial limits of the United States subject to the same laws and entitled to the same privileges and responsibilities as are applicable to other citizens of the United States." Under this policy, the government terminated all benefits and services to reservations, withdrawing its responsibility to maintain reservations and ending the limited sovereignty of individual tribes and nations.

Among the first tribes to be terminated were the Agua Caliente, who owned the land around Palm Springs, California, and the Klamath, whose land in Oregon was rich in lumber. The federal government took over their lands, as well as the land belonging to 107 other tribes between 1953 and 1964. Much of the land was sold to non-Native Americans.

Under this policy, Native Americans were expected to assimilate quickly into the mainstream of American society. To aid in this process, the Bureau of Indian Affairs set up a relocation program to move Native Americans from reservations to cities, where they were expected to find higher-paying jobs. The bureau set up relocation centers in Los Angeles, San Francisco, San Jose, Denver, Dallas, Cincinnati, Cleveland, St. Louis, and Chicago to help Native Americans find work, housing, and community resources. But not everyone found employment, and adjustment was difficult. Families were often separated, and tribal affiliations severed. In addition, a large number of Native Americans remained in poverty, and alcoholism continued to be a problem among many relocated populations.

Ultimately, the termination policy and the relocation program were failures. Federal termination efforts ended in 1963, and some of the affected tribes have been successful in regaining their lands through a number of lawsuits. The relocation era lasted for nearly two more decades, with as many as 750,000 Native Americans migrating to cities between 1950 and 1980.

THE THREAT OF DEPORTATION

During President Truman's eight years in office, from 1945 to 1953, about 127,000 undocumented immigrants were deported and more than 3.2 million left in fear of deportation. In 1954, under President Eisenhower, the government responded to an economic recession and a large U.S. labor pool with a program called "Operation Wetback," a reference to an offensive name for Mexicans who crossed the Rio Grande illegally. Intended to deport undocumented workers, the program mistreated many Mexicans and indiscriminately deported U.S. citizens as well. Officially, 2.1 million people of Mexican descent were deported through this aggressive, military-like campaign between 1954 and 1958.

MEXICAN AMERICAN WORKERS

In the 1950s and 1960s, the Latino population in the United States was relatively small. In 1960, about 6 million Latinos lived in the country. Many had first entered the United States to take part in the Bracero Program, an organized labor program that invited Mexican agricultural workers to replace U.S. farmworkers who were serving in World War II.

The government extended the Bracero Program after the war, and the number of braceros entering the United States increased. Most of the workers arrived from Mexico, but some came from Jamaica and the Bahamas. When the program was terminated in 1964, nearly 5 million worker contracts had been issued. Although President Truman had signed legislation to protect the rights of legal migrant workers in the United States, he also proposed legislation to stop employers from hiring undocumented immigrants. Congress did not approve it.

After the Bracero Program ended, many workers maintained connections with friends and families by continuing to cross the border informally and to return at will. Still others, knowing they would find fewer opportunities back at home, remained in the United States illegally after they were no longer in the program. Businesses were happy to hire these workers, paying them even lower wages than other migrant laborers. These low-paid workers contributed much to the economy of California and the Southwest, yet they lived in poverty and faced the constant threat of deportation.

THE LONGORIA INCIDENT

Even though they aided the United States during World War II, Mexican Americans faced

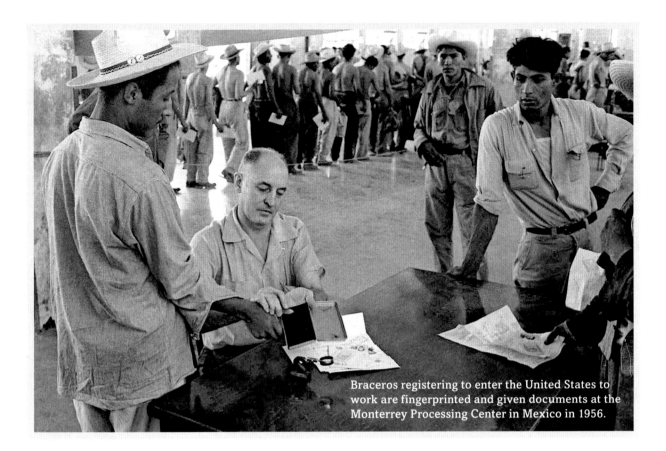

Braceros registering to enter the United States to work are fingerprinted and given documents at the Monterrey Processing Center in Mexico in 1956.

discrimination in the Southwest and elsewhere in the nation, whether they were citizens or undocumented immigrants. The Longoria incident was a prime example. Felix Longoria, a Mexican American war hero, was killed in the Philippines during World War II. When his body was returned to his family in 1948, his widow attempted to hold a wake in his honor at the only funeral home in Three Rivers, Texas. The owner of the funeral home refused her, saying, "The whites wouldn't like it."

The incident became front-page news across the country. **Dr. Hector P. Garcia**, a Mexican American and the president of the American GI Forum, a Latino veterans' civil rights organization, gathered more than 1,000 people to protest. He also sent a telegram directly to influential Texas senator **Lyndon B. Johnson**, who would later rise to the presidency. By the next afternoon, Johnson replied with an offer to bury Private Longoria at Arlington National Cemetery. The funeral was held there on February 16, 1949. The incident inspired many Mexican Americans to unify in their quest for civil rights and equal opportunities.

As early as the 1920s, Mexican Americans had organized to address discrimination. The **League of United Latin American Citizens (LULAC)**, formed in 1929, was one such organization. In 1945, LULAC sued the segregated Orange County, California, school system for openly discriminating against

Latino children. LULAC also protested the Longoria incident. In the 1960s, the organization actively supported the United Farm Workers, a labor union representing California farmworkers, most of whom were Latino. LULAC grew in the following decades, and today it provides college scholarships and other kinds of support to the Latino community.

Inspired by the agendas, strategies, and effectiveness of the civil rights movement elsewhere in the country, another Mexican American organization, the **Unity League,** was launched in California in 1947. The league campaigned against blatant acts of discrimination in housing, cemeteries, theaters, schools, and public administration. The league won lawsuits in the 1950s in cases involving segregation in schools and public swimming pools.

HISTORICAL THINKING

1. **READING CHECK** What kinds of discrimination did Native Americans and Mexican Americans face during the 1950s?

2. **IDENTIFY MAIN IDEAS AND DETAILS** Why did the United States open its borders to Mexican workers during World War II?

3. **IDENTIFY PROBLEMS AND SOLUTIONS** What actions did Mexican Americans take to gain civil rights during the 1950s?

VOCABULARY

Use each of the following vocabulary terms in a sentence that shows an understanding of the term's meaning.

1. suburbanization
   As a result of suburbanization, subdivisions replaced large tracts of land.

2. nuclear deterrence

3. brinkmanship

4. consumer society

5. suburban sprawl

6. situation comedy

7. urban renewal

8. poverty rate

9. termination policy

READING STRATEGY
MAKE INFERENCES

Complete a graphic organizer like the one below to make an inference about the postwar effects of the GI Bill of Rights. Tell what you know about the subject in the "I Know" section. Write your inference in the "And So" section. Then answer the question that follows the graphic organizer.

Make Inferences

I Read
Millions of veterans gained a college education through the GI Bill of Rights, and many became employed in technology industries.

I Know	And So

10. Why might some Americans today idealize the 1950s?

MAIN IDEAS

Answer the following questions. Support your answers with evidence from the chapter.

11. How did Eisenhower present his political ideas during his campaign for president in 1952? **LESSON 1.1**

12. How did women's wages compare with men's wages after the end of World War II and during the 1950s? **LESSON 1.2**

13. How was the system used to build houses in Levittown similar to production on an assembly line? **LESSON 1.3**

14. In what ways did Americans' obsession with cars affect other industries during the 1950s? **LESSON 2.1**

15. What aspects of American life did the Beat poets rebel against? **LESSON 2.3**

16. Why did Appalachia suffer from a high poverty rate in the 1950s? **LESSON 3.1**

17. How did Dr. Hector P. Garcia help resolve the Longoria incident? **LESSON 3.2**

HISTORICAL THINKING

Answer the following questions. Support your answers with evidence from the chapter.

18. **EVALUATE** What were some drawbacks of Eisenhower's nuclear deterrence plan?

19. **MAKE CONNECTIONS** What effects of the suburbanization of the 1950s do you notice in your life today?

20. **IDENTIFY** What were some long-lasting effects of the Bracero Program?

21. **FORM AND SUPPORT OPINIONS** Based on the results of the urban renewal projects of the 1950s and 1960s, what advice would you give an urban planner who wants to replace decaying neighborhoods in a city?

22. **MAKE INFERENCES** How do you think voters in Guatemala reacted when the United States ousted their elected president in 1954?

23. **DETERMINE CHRONOLOGY** What sequence of events led the federal government to establish the termination policy and relocation programs for Native Americans?

INTERPRET VISUALS

With the baby boom in full swing in the 1950s, toy manufacturers had a ready market for their products. Study the toy advertisement and answer the questions that follow.

24. What is the manufacturer's purpose in offering a space man and jet rocket for free?

25. What does it tell you about the growing consumer society that the manufacturers chose a space rocket as the perfect toy to offer kids?

ANALYZE SOURCES

In the 1950s, William H. Whyte, a magazine editor, wrote a book about the culture of large corporate organizations and the suburbs where the employees—the "organization men"—lived. He found the suburbs alarming rather than blissful.

> At Levittown, Pennsylvania, residents are very much aware of who has what "modification" of the basic ranch-house design, and one house on which the owner mounted a small gargoyle became so famous a sight that many residents used to drive out of their way to show it to visitors. People have a sharp eye for interior amenities also, and the acquisition of an automatic dryer . . . or any other divergence from the norm is always cause for notice. Those who lack such amenities, conversely, are also noted.
>
> —from *The Organization Man*, by William Whyte, 1956

26. What is Whyte implying about people's values and attitudes in the suburbs?

CONNECT TO YOUR LIFE

27. **EXPLANATORY** You have read about American life and culture during the 1950s. Some historians think the postwar era laid the foundation for our current American identity. Review the chapter and research the lives of teenagers in the 1950s. Then write a short essay comparing their lives and experiences with yours.

TIPS

- Use a Venn Diagram or a T-Chart to make notes about similarities and differences between your experiences and those of a teenager in the 1950s.

- Choose two or three of the most interesting items on your chart to write about.

- Conduct an Internet or library search to find more information on the topic.

- Use two or three vocabulary words from the chapter in your essay.

- End the essay with a generalization about the similarities and differences.

NATIONAL GEOGRAPHIC | CONNECTION

America's Propaganda Machine

BY BECKY LITTLE

Adapted from "Inside America's Shocking WWII Propaganda Machine," by Becky Little, news.nationalgeographic.com, December 2016

The United States was about six months into World War II when it founded the Office of War Information (OWI). Its mission: to disseminate political propaganda. The office spread its messages through print, radio, and film. But perhaps its most striking legacy is its posters with bright colors and sensational language. They encouraged Americans to ration their food, buy war bonds, and basically perform everyday tasks in support of the war effort. In one, a woman carrying her groceries is compared to soldiers carrying weapons. The poster implies that by walking instead of driving she is doing her patriotic duty. By not driving, people extended the lives of their cars and reduced the use of rubber and metal, which were instead needed to make tanks and weapons for the war.

LOOSE LIPS SINK SHIPS

Both the Allies and the Axis powers feared that leaked information could undermine their troops. With that in mind, the OWI produced posters urging people to keep sensitive information to themselves so enemies wouldn't overhear it. According to Stephen G. Hyslop, co-author of the National Geographic book *The Secret History of World War II*, the OWI struggled to find the best way to convey this message. As an example, he points to a poster that depicts a mysterious figure in a German helmet and warns "He's Watching You."

"The point of the poster is it's a German soldier" who could overhear what you say, Hyslop explains, but its message was too subtle. Consequently, the United States began to favor posters that got right to the point. In one of these, a woman's image appears alongside the words "WANTED! FOR MURDER. Her careless talk costs lives." This very clear message was still a bit strange. Most civilians didn't have access to sensitive military information, yet the images telling them to zip their lips were pretty aggressive and sometimes created the feeling of "Are the authorities on my side or are they after me?"

The OWI's propaganda was made for people at home and abroad, and it was always clear that these messages came from the U.S. government. However, the United States had another propaganda arm that produced messages specifically for the enemy and made it look like this propaganda was coming from inside the enemy's country.

ATTACKING ENEMY MORALE

Creating propaganda that hid or misrepresented its source wasn't only done by the United States. Germany transmitted radio messages to France, Britain, and other countries that appeared to originate from inside those nations.

The American Office of Strategic Services (OSS) responded with its own "black propaganda," as the practice was known. One mission, called Operation Cornflakes, involved dropping mailbags into Germany containing fake newspapers that looked as if they were made by Nazi resisters. Some of the mail had stamps with a picture of a deathly, skeletal-looking Hitler with the words *Futsches Reich* ("Ruined Empire").

The Allies also transmitted radio messages that appeared to come from inside Germany. This was an easier way to get information into the country than by dropping mailbags, Hyslop says.

Three-quarters of a century later, technological advances have made it even easier to sneak information into a country. As an example, Hyslop points to Russia's use of the Internet to spread propaganda during the 2016 U.S. election. Could future history books about our current era be illustrated with Internet political memes, just as today's history books are with propaganda posters? It's not unthinkable.

For more from National Geographic, check out "Dogs at War" online.

UNIT INQUIRY: Persuade an Audience

In this unit, you learned about a watershed event in which the United States became a major actor on the global stage: World War II. The Second World War placed tremendous demands on Americans, both those who fought abroad and those who remained at home. In public speeches and informal talks, Franklin Roosevelt and other leaders of the time worked to inspire citizens to make huge personal sacrifices in support of the war effort. How important were the rhetorical skills of the major leaders of this period? What kinds of persuasive language and appeals did they use? As you read quotes from their addresses, think about the way in which they crafted their messages to reach people's minds and hearts.

ASSIGNMENT

Choose an audience of the World War II era—such as newly enlisted soldiers, factory workers, farmers, or high school students—and write a speech persuading them to contribute to the war effort in a specific way. For example, you might research victory gardens and encourage high school students to plant one at their school to supplement the nation's food supply. Be prepared to present your speech to the class.

Plan Think about the reasons that success in World War II was vital to Americans and the way that Allied leaders like Roosevelt and Churchill inspired people to go all out to win the war. Then consider your audience and the contribution you're asking them to make. You might want to use a graphic organizer to outline your argument.

Produce Use your outline to write a persuasive speech that will inspire your audience to support the war effort in the way you've identified. Incorporate persuasive language and appeals directed specifically to your audience. Use words and phrases that clarify the relationship between your reasons and evidence. Provide a concluding statement that supports your argument.

Present Share your speech with the class. You might consider one of these options:

- Record a "fireside chat" audiotape. Play the audiotape in class, and then play a portion of one of Roosevelt's fireside chats. Invite students to compare and contrast your oratory style with Roosevelt's style.

- Create notes of your speech, then practice the speech and deliver it to the class. Ask students to identify the persuasive techniques you used and rate their effectiveness.

 NATIONAL GEOGRAPHIC | LEARNING FRAMEWORK ACTIVITY

Write About a Cold War Advance

SKILLS Observation, Communication

KNOWLEDGE Our Human Story

Major advances in medicine, science, and technology occurred during the Cold War years. Identify and research a Cold War development that improved Americans' lives, like the use of nuclear power as an energy source, or the development of new vaccines or commercial computers. Write a narrative incorporating real or imagined experiences during the Cold War, focusing on how the advancement affected a particular character's life. Use dialogue, description, and reflection to express the importance of the advancement on society.

Debate the Origins of the Cold War

ATTITUDE Curiosity

SKILL Collaboration

Work with a small group to research the major debates among historians concerning the origins of the Cold War. Read excerpts from *Origins of the Cold War* by Arthur M. Schlesinger, Jr., and excerpts from *The Tragedy of American Diplomacy* by William A. Williams. Evaluate each historian's use of evidence, looking for sound generalizations or misleading oversimplifications. Choose a creative way to present both sides of the argument, and have a class debate about the roles the United States and the Soviet Union played in the start of the Cold War.

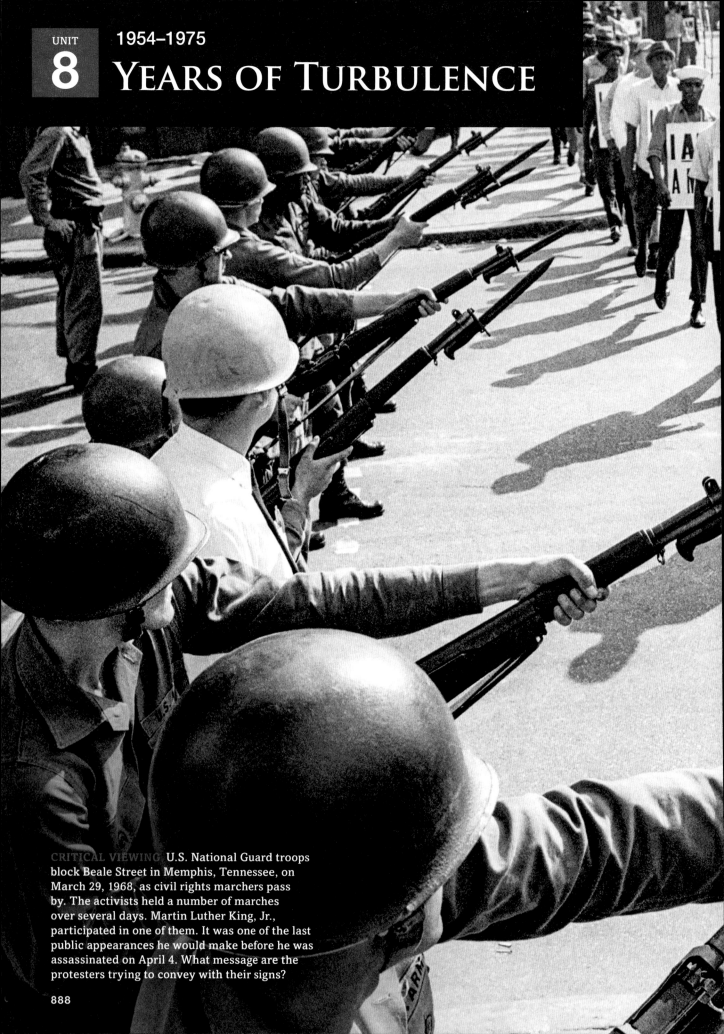

CRITICAL VIEWING U.S. National Guard troops block Beale Street in Memphis, Tennessee, on March 29, 1968, as civil rights marchers pass by. The activists held a number of marches over several days. Martin Luther King, Jr., participated in one of them. It was one of the last public appearances he would make before he was assassinated on April 4. What message are the protesters trying to convey with their signs?

889

YEARS OF TURBULENCE

THE UNITED STATES

KENNEDY FOR PRESIDENT

1964
After a North Vietnamese torpedo boat allegedly fires on an American destroyer in Southeast Asia's Gulf of Tonkin, the United States greatly expands its role in the Vietnam War.

1960
John F. Kennedy is elected president.
(Kennedy campaign button)

1955
African Americans in Montgomery, Alabama, boycott the city's buses shortly after Rosa Parks is arrested for refusing to give up her seat on one of them to a white man.
(bus Rosa Parks was riding when she refused to give up her seat)

1963
Martin Luther King, Jr., leads the March on Washington and delivers his "I Have a Dream" speech; Kennedy is assassinated, and Lyndon Johnson assumes the presidency.

1954
The ruling in *Brown* v. *Board of Education of Topeka, Kansas*, ends the legal segregation of public schools.

1960

1950

1954 ASIA
After the overthrow of France, Vietnam is divided into North Vietnam and South Vietnam.

1959 AMERICAS
Fidel Castro becomes the communist leader of Cuba.

"THIS HURTS ME MORE THAN IT HURTS YOU!"

THE WORLD

1957 AFRICA
Ghana gains its independence from Britain. *(Ghana's Independence Arch)*

1962 EUROPE
The Soviet Union places missiles in Cuba, triggering the Cuban Missile Crisis. *(political cartoon depicting Soviet leader Nikita Khrushchev as a dentist pulling out Fidel Castro's teeth, which are shaped like missiles)*

HISTORICAL THINKING

DETERMINE CHRONOLOGY What happened two years after the United States withdrew from Vietnam?

1965
Johnson sends the first U.S. ground troops to Vietnam.
(radio used during Vietnam War)

1972
The American Indian Movement occupies the Bureau of Indian Affairs to protest broken treaties; the Equal Rights Amendment for women passes Congress but fails to be ratified.

1966
César Chávez leads a march to Sacramento, California's capital, to protest the low wages and poor working conditions of the state's farmworkers.

1969
American astronauts are the first to land and walk on the moon.

1973
The United States pulls its troops from Vietnam, ending its involvement in the war in Southeast Asia.

1968
Martin Luther King, Jr., is assassinated at the age of 39; Richard Nixon is elected president.

1975

1970

1975 ASIA
South Vietnam falls to the communists, ending the civil war in Vietnam.

1967 AFRICA
Civil war breaks out in Nigeria after the Republic of Biafra secedes from the African nation.
(flag of Biafra)

1968 ASIA
North Vietnamese forces launch the Tet Offensive and attack many cities and towns in South Vietnam.
(Troops battle in Saigon following the Tet Offensive.)

THE CIVIL RIGHTS MOVEMENT

1954–1964

HISTORICAL THINKING How did the civil rights movement redefine American identity?

In 1963, the African American Student Nonviolent Coordinating Committee (SNCC) staged a sit-in to protest racial segregation at two Toddle House restaurants in Atlanta, Georgia.

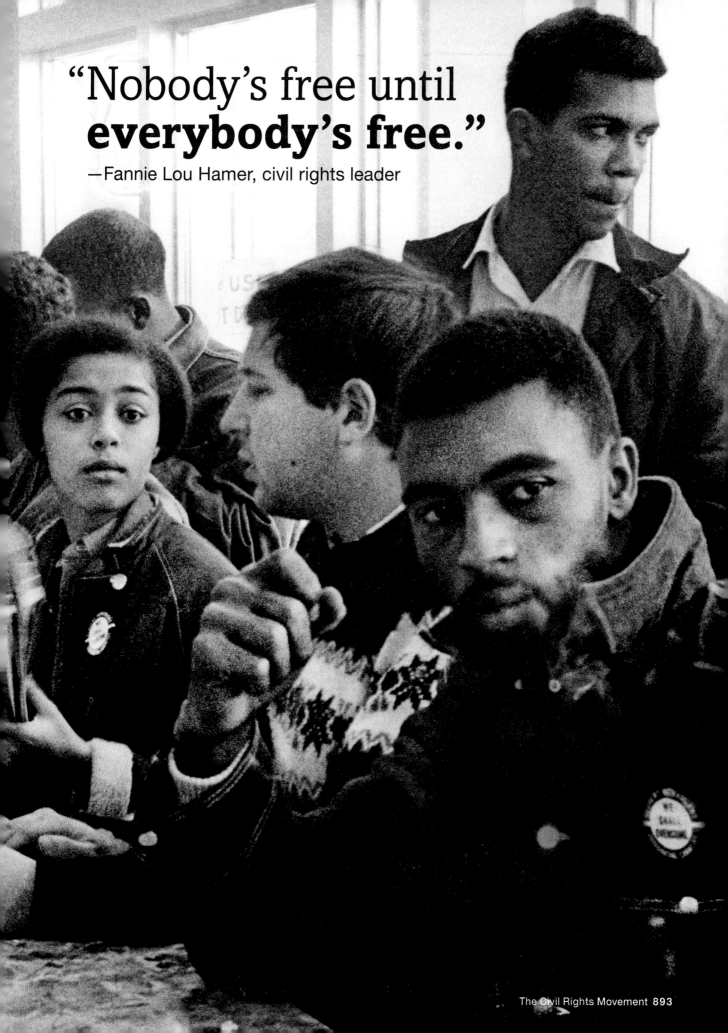

"Nobody's free until **everybody's free.**"
—Fannie Lou Hamer, civil rights leader

CIVIL RIGHTS STORIES

On June 26, 2015, the White House was lit with rainbow colors to mark a civil rights milestone: the U.S. Supreme Court's ruling to legalize same-sex marriage.

The struggle for civil rights in the 1950s and 1960s evokes powerful images in the minds of Americans: Dr. Martin Luther King, Jr., delivering his "I Have a Dream" speech; young African-American children facing angry crowds of protesters trying to keep them out of school; citizens marching to demand equal voting rights or school desegregation. These images represent the long and ongoing process of establishing and defending civil rights for all citizens. This American Story highlights the stories of some of the key people, places, and events in the civil rights movements, from the 1930s to the present day.

THE MARCH ON WASHINGTON

One familiar image from the civil rights movement shows Dr. Martin Luther King, Jr., standing on the steps of the Lincoln Memorial in Washington, D.C., delivering his most famous speech to a crowd of more than 200,000 people. It was a day of true unity—civil rights organizations, religious leaders, and men and women of all races came together to protest the inequalities African Americans still faced even 100 years after Abraham Lincoln's Emancipation Proclamation.

The 1963 March on Washington for Jobs and Freedom was not the first-ever march to the capital planned to support the rights of African Americans. You may recall that in 1941, A. Philip Randolph proposed a march on Washington to protest racial discrimination in the context of federal jobs. Randolph canceled the march, however, when President Franklin D. Roosevelt issued an executive order barring discrimination in the growing defense industry.

In 1963, President John F. Kennedy proposed a sweeping civil rights bill, but it was mired in a divided Congress. In an attempt to demonstrate public support for the bill and encourage Congress to act, Randolph and other civil rights leaders decided it was time to organize an even larger march on Washington. About 100,000 participants were expected to flood the city. Organizations such as the National Association for the Advancement of Colored People (NAACP) and the Southern Christian Leadership Conference planned the event, encouraging African Americans and whites from all states to come to Washington in a display of unified support for equal rights. And on August 28, 1963, around 200,000 people gathered peacefully in front of the Lincoln Memorial.

At the 1963 march, a multiracial crowd listened to songs by popular performers, prayers by prominent clergymen, and speeches by activists, including Dr. Martin Luther King, Jr.

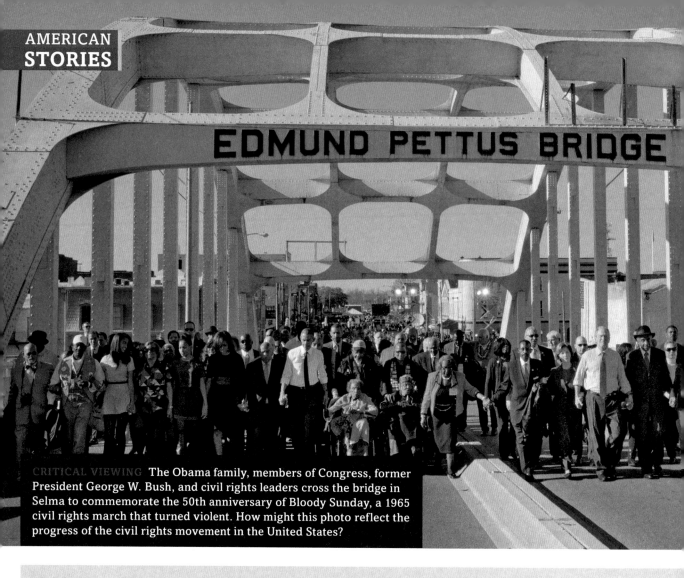

EDMUND PETTUS BRIDGE

CRITICAL VIEWING The Obama family, members of Congress, former President George W. Bush, and civil rights leaders cross the bridge in Selma to commemorate the 50th anniversary of Bloody Sunday, a 1965 civil rights march that turned violent. How might this photo reflect the progress of the civil rights movement in the United States?

COLLABORATING TO DESEGREGATE EDUCATION

As you will read in greater detail later in this chapter, well into the 1950s, many parts of the United States, especially the South, had racially segregated schools. School segregation had been made legal in 1896 by the *Plessy* v. *Ferguson* court case, which held that having separate public facilities for African Americans and whites was constitutional as long as the facilities were equal to each other.

For many decades, African-American and white civil rights lawyers worked together to challenge this "separate but equal" ruling. In 1930, the NAACP hired Nathan Margold, a white lawyer from New York. Margold conducted a study and found that African-American and white schools were not funded equally. This violated the equal protection rights provided for by the 14th Amendment. He recommended suing segregated public schools.

In 1934, Charles H. Houston, a prominent African-American lawyer, began directing the NAACP's

legal campaign against segregation and focused on higher education programs. One case involved African-American student Lloyd Gaines who was denied admission to the University of Missouri's law school because of his race. At the time, no law school in the state accepted African-American students. Although Gaines was offered a scholarship to attend a school out of state, he sued the university with the help of Houston, who argued that the state must either admit Gaines or provide an equal facility in Missouri. The courts agreed.

Through numerous other cases and victories, the NAACP's lawyers worked to protect civil rights. By the 1950s, a young African-American lawyer named Thurgood Marshall made it his mission to end segregation. He won many cases, preparing him for a historic legal battle in Topeka, Kansas.

In Kansas, segregation still existed in public schools. Linda Brown was denied enrollment in

The Edmund Pettus Bridge

Some places will forever remain in the national consciousness as symbols of the fight for African-American civil rights in the 1950s and 1960s. One such place is the Edmund Pettus Bridge in Selma, Alabama. Completed in 1940, the bridge was named after a Confederate general and leader of the racist Ku Klux Klan in Alabama.

On March 7, 1965, a group of 600 protesters set out from Selma on a march to the state capital of Montgomery, to protest restrictions on voting rights for African Americans. On the Edmund Pettus Bridge just outside of town, local law enforcement officers waited with clubs and tear gas. They attacked the demonstrators and forced them back into Selma in an outbreak of violence that came to be known as Bloody Sunday. The marchers tried again on March 9 and were again turned away at the bridge. On March 21, after a federal judge had ruled in favor of the protesters' right to march along a public highway in order to "petition . . . government for redress of grievances," a new Selma-to-Montgomery march began. This time, 3,200 people set out from Selma and 25,000 arrived in the state capital. You will read more about these three marches in the next chapter.

Today, the Edmund Pettus Bridge is part of the Selma to Montgomery National Historic Trail administered by the National Park Service. On March 7, 2015, President Barack Obama and his family joined thousands of Americans at the bridge to commemorate the courage of the Bloody Sunday protesters. Among the 2015 marchers were some who had been present on Bloody Sunday, including Representative John Lewis of Georgia and Amelia Boynton Robinson, one of the original march's organizers.

the all-white school in her neighborhood. She had to walk more than a mile, cross a dangerous railroad yard, and then take a bus, to attend a school that accepted African Americans. Represented by Thurgood Marshall, the Brown family and other families decided to sue the school system, and in 1954, they won what would become one of the most important Supreme Court cases of all time, *Brown v. Board of Education of Topeka*.

While the landmark Brown ruling legally ended segregation, it did not erase it from the United States. Today, few schools and neighborhoods are truly racially integrated.

THINK ABOUT IT

Why might it have been advantageous for African-American and white lawyers to collaborate on cases to end racial discrimination in schools?

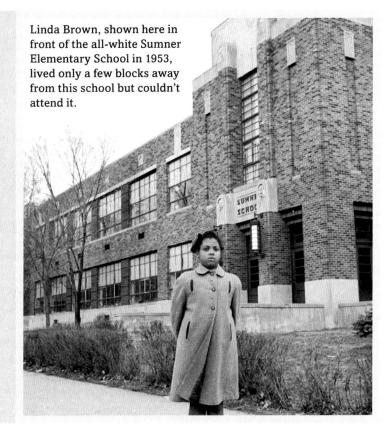

Linda Brown, shown here in front of the all-white Sumner Elementary School in 1953, lived only a few blocks away from this school but couldn't attend it.

THE RIGHTS OF THE DISABLED

In 1990, the Americans With Disabilities Act (ADA), a bipartisan effort, was passed by Congress and signed into law by President George H. W. Bush. It banned job discrimination against people with disabilities and required buildings, businesses, and public transportation to be accessible to all. "The ADA was a response to an appalling problem: widespread, systemic, inhumane discrimination against people with disabilities," explains Robert Burgdorf, Jr., a disability rights legal advocate.

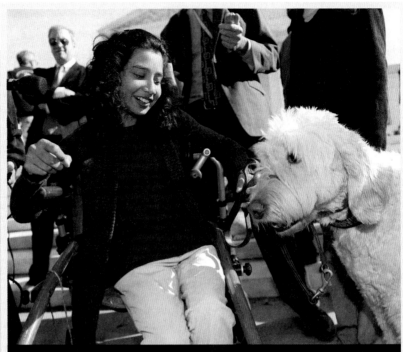

Ehlena Fry, 12, of Michigan, sits with her service dog Wonder outside the Supreme Court in Washington, D.C. Fry, who has cerebral palsy, is fighting to bring Wonder to school with her for assistance.

In 1971, according to Burgdorf, a "judge described people with disabilities as 'the most discriminated [against] minority in our nation.'" He was not alone in believing this. State-run residential treatment centers were "primitive and often unsanitary, dangerous, overcrowded and inhumane," states Burgdorf. Many children with disabilities were routinely prevented from attending public schools and therefore did not have access to an adequate education. Very few public transportation systems or private vehicles accommodated the disabled, making taxis, buses, trains, and ferries virtually unusable by people with physical impairments. Accessibility aids, such as flat entrances, ramps, sidewalk curb cuts, or Braille elevator signs, were not included in parks, stores, and office buildings.

Additionally, individuals with disabilities were often excluded from rights most Americans count on, from applying for a driver's license, to voting, to running for public office. In some states, people with developmental disabilities could not legally marry or enter into a contract. Even cities, such as Columbus, Ohio, and Chicago, practiced discrimination by enacting "ugly laws" to keep people whose physical conditions were perceived as "unpleasant" from public places.

Crucial victories in the courts during the 1970s and 1980s led to gains for people with disabilities in the fight for equal access to public schools and improved conditions in live-in facilities. As activists and protesters tackled the unfair treatment of individuals with disabilities, the courts ruled against discrimination in housing, transportation, voting, contracts, and medical services.

Since its passage, the ADA has had a positive impact on the lives of people with disabilities and their families. Accessible entrances, now the norm rather than the exception, assist those with mobility limitations as they enter buildings, cross streets, and visit public parks. Conveniently located parking spaces for people with disabilities are set aside in garages and parking lots to give people better access to public and private buildings. Mass transit accessibility in cities has also progressed, even if improvements to public transportation systems under the ADA have occurred more slowly and less consistently than many would like.

Yet not all equality issues for people with disabilities have been resolved, and people see tremendous disparities in how the ADA is enforced among business owners, school districts, and communities. In fact, according to Burgdorf, "Some . . . have taken an I-won't-do-anything-until-I'm-sued attitude toward the obligations imposed on them" by the act. Although there are many battles yet to be fought, the passing of the ADA was an inarguably significant milestone for ensuring equal rights for the disabled.

MARRIAGE LEGISLATION

The question of marriage as a civil rights issue for same-sex couples garnered much attention in the 2010s, but the legal struggle began decades earlier. In 1970, Jack Baker and Michael McConnell applied for a marriage license in Minneapolis, Minnesota. When the men were refused a license, they took the case to court. Baker, a lawyer, made the case that prohibiting same-sex marriage was unconstitutional and a form of discrimination. He drew parallels to the 1967 case *Loving* v. *Virginia*, in which the Supreme Court ruled that it was unconstitutional to forbid interracial marriage. When Baker and McConnell's case was sent to the Supreme Court in 1972, however, the court refused to hear it.

The next legal test for same-sex marriage rights took place in Hawaii in 1996. There, a judge ruled that the state had no reason to prevent same-sex couples from marrying. A national backlash soon followed. Congress passed and President Bill Clinton signed the Defense of Marriage Act (DOMA), which defined marriage as existing solely between a man and a woman in federal law. Several states, Hawaii among them, enacted constitutional amendments prohibiting same-sex marriage.

With the majority of both legislators and public opinion against same-sex marriage, gay activists and their supporters began a long campaign to change the minds of individual Americans. They also worked to bring the question to courtrooms and ballot boxes throughout the country. Gay marriage advocacy groups launched extensive advertising campaigns and engaged lobbyists to meet with lawmakers. Over time and despite staunch opposition, their efforts began to pay off. In 2004, the Massachusetts Supreme Court ruled in favor of same-sex marriage, and this time, the ruling was not reversed by a constitutional amendment. By 2011, the majority of the public supported same-sex marriage.

In 2015, when the United States Supreme Court agreed to rule on the issue it had turned down in 1972, gay marriage was legal in 36 states. On June 26, 2015, the nation's highest court ruled that the Constitution guarantees the right to marriage for same-sex couples in all 50 states. In the decision, Justice Anthony Kennedy wrote, "Their hope is not to be condemned to live in loneliness, excluded from one of civilization's oldest institutions. They ask for equal dignity in the eyes of the law. The Constitution grants them that right."

In what ways were the campaigns for same-sex marriage and other civil rights campaigns similar and different?

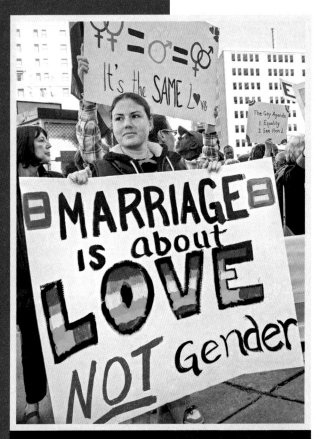

Legislation aside, same-sex marriage remains a hotly debated topic. Some believe all individuals deserve the right to be married, regardless of gender or sexual orientation (above). Others only support marriages between a man and a woman (below). The issue has become highly politicized in the United States.

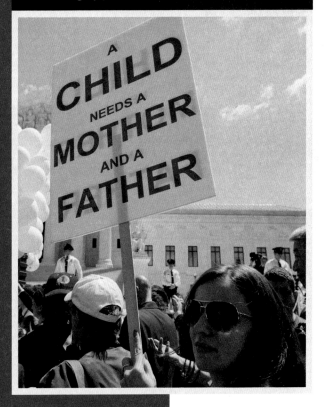

THE NATIONAL MUSEUM OF AFRICAN AMERICAN HISTORY AND CULTURE

On September 24, 2016, the Smithsonian Institution in Washington, D.C., opened a new museum. Standing alongside the other Smithsonian buildings on the National Mall, the National Museum of African American History and Culture (NMAAHC) offers a unique perspective on U.S. history, civil rights, and national identity. "This museum will tell the American story through the lens of African-American history and culture," explained Lonnie G. Bunch, III, the NMAAHC's Founding Director. "This is America's Story and this museum is for all Americans."

The galleries on the lower levels of the NMAAHC display collections of original artifacts that recount African-American history from the earliest years of the country to the present day. The dark times of slavery are represented by the manacles, whips, and other items used by slaveholders to control the enslaved. The museum also gives a voice to enslaved Americans by displaying items they created to express themselves. One such object is an embroidered pillowcase given by an enslaved mother to her nine-year-old daughter when the girl was sold. The pre-emancipation collection also includes Harriet Tubman's hymn book and Frederick Douglass's cane.

PRIMARY SOURCE

At the opening of the National Museum of African American History and Culture in Washington, D.C., President Barack Obama struck a hopeful note in a speech about the need for continuing progress on civil rights and the museum's role in the quest for equality.

This national museum helps to tell a richer and fuller story of who we are. . . . Hopefully this museum can help us talk to each other. And more importantly, listen to each other. And most importantly, see each other—Black and White and Latino and Native American, and Asian American—see how our stories are bound together. And bound together with women in America, and workers in America, and entrepreneurs in America, and LGBT Americans.

—President Barack Obama, September 24, 2016

CRITICAL VIEWING At the 2016 museum dedication, President Barack Obama praised the coexistence of "protest and love of country" and referenced recent examples of racial tension in the U.S. Which other individuals do you recognize in the photo below, and why might it have been significant that they attended this event?

Other collections in the historical galleries illustrate Reconstruction and the civil rights movement. More recent events such as the 2008 election of the first African-American president of the United States and the 2012 Olympic successes of African-American gymnast Gabby Douglas are also celebrated.

The Culture and Community galleries of the museum focus on the diverse African-American communities within the United States. Exhibits highlight achievements in the arts and sports, and ongoing efforts to bring about positive social change.

In 1963, a bomb exploded at the predominantly African-American 16th Street Baptist Church in Birmingham, Alabama, killing four young girls. This stained glass rosette from that church is part of the NMAAHC collection.

THE CIVIL RIGHTS MOVEMENT'S NEW ERA

The civil rights movement of the 1950s and 1960s achieved notable advancements for African Americans, such as desegregation and bans on many forms of discrimination. Yet many issues remain, such as poverty and lack of jobs in African-American neighborhoods, and the disproportionate numbers of African Americans who are jailed.

Present-day organizations such as Black Lives Matter (BLM) utilize social media and public protests to make their voices heard. BLM began in July 2013, after a white man named George Zimmerman was acquitted of the shooting death of black teenager Trayvon Martin. Alicia Garza wrote in a Facebook post, "I continue to be surprised at how little Black lives matter." Patrice Cullors, a friend of Garza's, was struck by that sentence and created the hashtag #BlackLivesMatter. Another friend built a social-media platform around the hashtag.

Many Americans became aware of Black Lives Matter in 2014, after a black teenager named Michael Brown was shot and killed by a white police officer in Ferguson, Missouri. People from all parts of the country used the platform to express their outrage and to plan protests in Ferguson and other cities. BLM groups continue to stage protests following other police shootings of African Americans and to strongly advocate for reform.

Black Lives Matter is sometimes described as "not your grandfather's civil rights movement." For one thing, social media was not an option years ago. And unlike groups such as the Student Nonviolent Coordinating Committee, which had centralized leadership, Black Lives Matter chapters operate independently to plan local events. BLM also pursues civil rights for women and the LGBTQ community, while earlier civil rights groups often marginalized female leaders and put men at the forefront.

Some believe that Black Lives Matter's methods are most effective for today's civil rights issues. Others feel modern civil rights groups should more closely follow the structures and techniques that succeeded in the 1950s and 1960s.

Photojournalist Eli Reed's book *Black in America* includes this 1999 photo of members of the Minority Achievement Committee at Shaker Heights High School in Ohio. Reed captures the diversity of the African-American experience, the consequences of prejudice, and the continuing efforts to secure a better life for all.

MAIN IDEA After World War II, the Truman administration, the NAACP, and African-American authors helped bring civil rights to the forefront of American society.

PROGRESS AFTER THE WAR

The struggle for civil rights in America spans many decades, many presidents, and across many states, and it continues today. Change has come slowly. But with each court ruling and protest, more people have seen the need for all Americans to have the same rights. This chapter highlights some of the key events and people who have inspired racially based social changes throughout the mid-20th century in America.

CHANGE DRIVEN BY THE PEOPLE

In many ways, World War II changed race relations in the United States and gave momentum to the civil rights movement. Millions of African Americans, Native Americans, and Mexican Americans had contributed to the U.S. war effort through military service or work in the defense industry. Having served their country in a war often framed as being against two racist empires (Germany and Japan), they were determined to claim their rights as guaranteed by the Constitution. Minority groups began fighting against laws that prevented them from voting and kept their children from attending public schools. Some Native American veterans filed lawsuits challenging these practices. Furthermore, many minorities did not want to lose the economic foothold they had gained from their wartime jobs.

Individuals engaged in **grassroots activism** to bring about the equality they desired. Grassroots activism refers to political movements driven by people who individually do not have much power, but who, working together, can be very effective. Churches in the rural South and urban North played important roles in the grassroots diffusion of the civil rights movement. Church leaders stressed the value of equality and communal support, which inspired church members to make sacrifices for racial justice. Groups also used churches as meeting places. The NAACP, a grassroots group, began with 60 members in 1909. By 1946, it had 600,000 members and was working to persuade Congress to pass federal anti-lynching laws. NAACP leaders, including **Walter White**, **Thurgood Marshall**, and the writer James Weldon Johnson, organized lawsuits against people accused of civil rights violations and used those cases to command the public's attention.

A. Philip Randolph and **Bayard Rustin** were also notable civil rights leaders. As you've read, Randolph, a journalist and labor organizer, established the country's first African-American trade union, the Brotherhood of Sleeping Car

PRIMARY SOURCES

Today, the American people enjoy more freedom and opportunity than ever before. Never in our history has there been better reason to hope for the complete realization of the ideals of liberty and equality.

We shall not, however, finally achieve the ideals for which this Nation was founded so long as any American suffers discrimination as a result of his race, or religion, or color, or the land of origin of his forefathers.

—from "Special Message to the Congress on Civil Rights," by President Harry S. Truman, February 2, 1948

Mr. Speaker, not since the first gun was fired on Fort Sumter . . . has any message of any President of these glorious United States provoked so much controversy . . . as did President Truman's so-called civil-rights message. Not only did that message provoke serious racial controversies, but it raised anew the issue of the rights of the sovereign States as against a strong centralized government and drove a devastating wedge into the unity of the Democratic Party at a time when that party was riding high on a wave of popularity in the entire country.

—from Mississippi Representative William M. Colmer's response to President Truman's "Special Message to Congress on Civil Rights," April 8, 1948

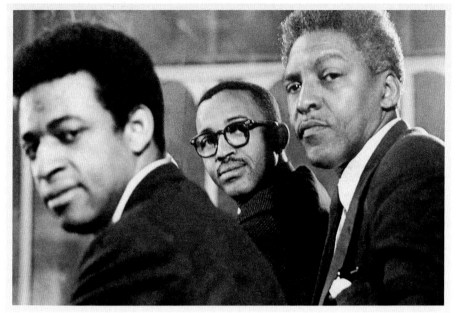

At a press conference in New York City in 1964 (from left) Norman Hill, Frederick D. Jones, and Bayard Rustin called for New York City to desegregate its public schools or face a series of coordinated boycotts. The three civil rights leaders were lifelong anti-violence activists who orchestrated demonstrations and boycotts and negotiated with government officials.

Porters. Rustin became a leader in movements for civil rights and nonviolence beginning in the 1940s and for gay rights in the 1950s. He would eventually become a close advisor to Dr. Martin Luther King, Jr. In 1941, Randolph and Rustin threatened to lead tens of thousands of people in a march on Washington, D.C., to protest employment discrimination in the federal government. President Franklin D. Roosevelt averted the march by issuing an executive order prohibiting discriminatory hiring in government jobs. The order also established the Fair Employment Practices Committee, whose mission was to investigate violations of the new policy.

In 1942, civil rights activist **James Farmer** helped to found the interracial **Congress of Racial Equality (CORE)**. The organization fought discrimination through nonviolent acts of protest. It would play a crucial role in future decades of the civil rights movement. Activist and NAACP member **Mary Church Terrell** led the antidiscrimination struggle in deeply segregated Washington, D.C. In 1950, she entered a restaurant and ordered lunch, knowing the owners would refuse to serve her. In a lawsuit, she cited laws from the 1870s that guaranteed equal rights to African Americans in all "places of public accommodation." Her case reached the Supreme Court, which ruled unanimously in her favor.

TRUMAN'S SUPPORT FOR CIVIL RIGHTS

After Franklin D. Roosevelt's death in 1945, his vice president Harry Truman became the 33rd president. Truman was the grandchild of slave owners and had grown up in a segregated town in Missouri. But Truman proved to be a strong supporter of

civil rights. In 1946, he established the **President's Committee on Civil Rights (PCCR)**. Its mission was to protect all Americans' civil rights. The PCCR report, "To Secure These Rights," detailed widespread discrimination and recommended 34 immediate actions, including desegregating the U.S. military. Truman sent to Congress a plan for stronger civil rights statutes, better protection of the right to vote, and federal protection against lynching. But Republicans and conservative southern Democrats blocked the plan.

At the 1948 Democratic National Convention, Senate candidate Hubert Humphrey implored his fellow Democrats to strongly support the civil rights movement. Moderates, including aides to Truman, favored a weaker stance on civil rights, fearing the loss of votes in the South. In the end, Humphrey got his way. Shortly after the convention, Truman abolished segregation in the U.S. military and prohibited discriminatory hiring practices in the federal civil service. When Americans cast their ballots in 1948, Truman won re-election, thanks in part to the support of African-American voters.

HISTORICAL THINKING

1. **READING CHECK** How did World War II stimulate the civil rights movement?

2. **DRAW CONCLUSIONS** How can grassroots activism cause change? Use examples from the text.

3. **SYNTHESIZE** How does Truman's message to Congress and William Colmer's response reflect the idea that change is complicated?

RESISTANCE THROUGH THE ARTS

Looking at a painting, listening to a song from another culture, and reading a book can help us understand how another person views the world. With that idea in mind, artists, musicians, and writers use their art to influence public opinion.

FREEDOM THROUGH ART AND SONG

The civil rights movement wasn't limited to nonviolent student and political organizations or the leadership of individual activists, such as Martin Luther King, Jr. Other forms of social advocacy sprang up around the country, notably in its art and music scenes. Activists took ideas from earlier artists and musicians and incorporated them into their own works as a way to express the connections between generations of African-American creativity.

The folk-inspired style of artist **William H. Johnson**, who painted from roughly 1920 to 1945, showed scenes of African-American soldiers and people doing everyday activities. His expressionistic subjects and use of bright colors are reflected in the paintings of **Jacob Lawrence** and **Charles Henry Alston**, artists working at the beginning of the civil rights movement.

Some artists working in the 1960s saw the civil unrest happening around them and found ways to incorporate their passion and solidarity with the protesters into their art. The subject matter of many African-American artists became more political. For example, artist **Norman Lewis** chose to use red, white, and blue in his work. Sculptor **Elizabeth Catlett** posed her figures in defiant positions, with crossed arms or a fist to the sky.

Musicians also built public awareness about civil rights. In 1939, jazz singer **Billie Holiday** recorded "Strange Fruit," a song about lynching in the South. It was the first time a popular African-American singer had spoken out against racism through music. She inspired other

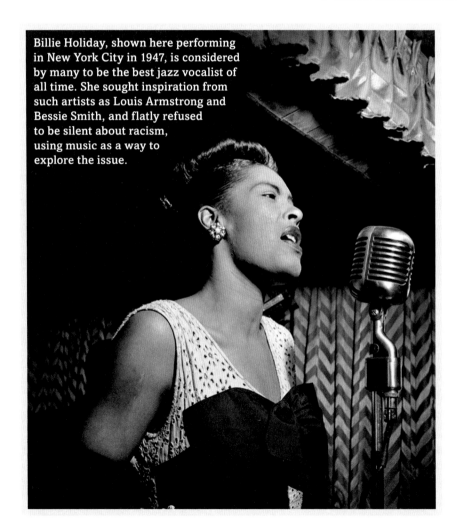

Billie Holiday, shown here performing in New York City in 1947, is considered by many to be the best jazz vocalist of all time. She sought inspiration from such artists as Louis Armstrong and Bessie Smith, and flatly refused to be silent about racism, using music as a way to explore the issue.

Recipient of the 1953 National Book Award for fiction, Ralph Ellison wrote *Invisible Man* in an experimental style, hoping to portray a truth about the human condition, race, and identity.

I am an invisible man. No, I am not a spook like those who haunted Edgar Allan Poe; nor am I one of your Hollywood-movie ectoplasms [ghosts]. I am a man of substance, of flesh and bone, fiber and liquids—and I might even be said to possess a mind. I am invisible, understand, simply because people refuse to see me.

—from *Invisible Man* by Ralph Ellison, 1952

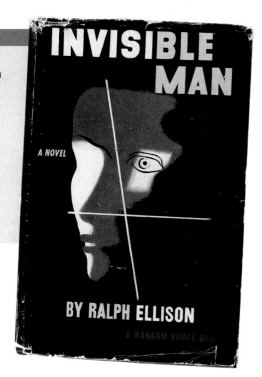

singers to do so as well. Throughout her career, jazz singer **Nina Simone** performed songs protesting lynching, segregation, and the Vietnam War. **Harry Belafonte**, a singer famous for a style of Caribbean music called calypso, was a social activist who donated time and money to civil rights efforts.

Many African-American musicians incorporated the spirituals and gospel songs that arose out of the slavery era to help fuel the civil rights movement. African-American folk singer **Odetta** taught her audiences the lyrics to spirituals as a way to unite the protesters. Odetta knew the old work songs, such as "We Shall Overcome" and "Go Tell It on the Mountain," from her childhood in Birmingham, Alabama. The spirituals inspired white folk singers, including Pete Seeger, **Bob Dylan**, and **Joan Baez**, to perform them at concerts and raise money and popular support for the civil rights cause.

Other activist musicians fought racism not with the words they sang but through the concert halls where they performed. In 1955, Marian Anderson became the first African-American opera singer to perform at New York's Metropolitan Opera. People flocked to hear the well-respected artist. "Men as well as women were dabbing at their eyes," reported the *New York Times*. Anderson's success at the Met was considered an important step toward racial equality because she proved African-American artists could draw large and diverse crowds.

THE POWER OF THE WRITTEN WORD

African-American authors bolstered the civil rights movement with words. In his 1940 novel *Native Son*, **Richard Wright** explored poverty and oppression in the lives of African Americans. Another novel, *Invisible Man* by **Ralph Ellison**, told of an unnamed African-American civil rights worker who moves from the South to New York City to escape segregation. The civil rights worker in the

novel feels **dehumanized**, no longer regarded as a person, after he encounters racism in the city.

Playwright **Lorraine Hansberry** examined racial harassment as experienced by a working-class African-American family in the groundbreaking 1959 play *A Raisin in the Sun*. The character Beneatha decides to wear her hair in the natural style of people living in Africa, instead of in the straightened style of white women. Her decision symbolized a shift in African-American identity because Beneatha embraced her African heritage.

Civil-rights activist and influential African-American author **James Baldwin** released a book of two essays in 1963 called *The Fire Next Time*. In the book, he uses his personal experiences to explain what it was like to live in the United States as an African American. "[White people] have had to believe for many years, and for innumerable reasons, that black men are inferior to white men," he wrote. "Many of them, indeed, know better, but, as you will discover, people find it very difficult to act on what they know."

1. **READING CHECK** How did artists raise awareness of the civil rights movement among the public?

2. **ANALYZE LANGUAGE USE** What does Ralph Ellison mean when he writes, "I am an invisible man"?

3. **MAKE INFERENCES** How might spirituals and gospel songs from the slavery era help fuel the civil rights movement?

CHALLENGING SCHOOL SEGREGATION

Third-grader Linda Brown lived just a short walk from an elementary school in Topeka, Kansas. But because she was an African American, she was forced to walk to a school farther from her home. This injustice became the focus of a landmark civil rights case.

CHALLENGING "SEPARATE BUT EQUAL"

In the 1940s, civil rights activists such as Thurgood Marshall and **William Hastie** began to mount legal attacks on *Plessy* v. *Ferguson*, the 1896 case that established the doctrine of "separate but equal." Marshall was chief of the NAACP's Legal Defense and Education Fund, a group of lawyers who pursued inequality and segregation lawsuits against educational institutions. In 1946, a federal lawsuit known as ***Mendez v. Westminster*** successfully challenged "separate but equal." Five Mexican American families sued their local school board in California for forcing their children to attend schools for Mexican students only. The court ruled in favor of the families, declaring that the segregation of Mexican American, Native American, and Asian American students was unconstitutional. This case provided a basis for further challenges.

On September 4, 1957, 15-year-old Elizabeth Eckford was followed by an angry mob as she tried to enter Central High School. Eckford was one of the Little Rock Nine, a group of African-American students who desegregated the school in Little Rock, Arkansas.

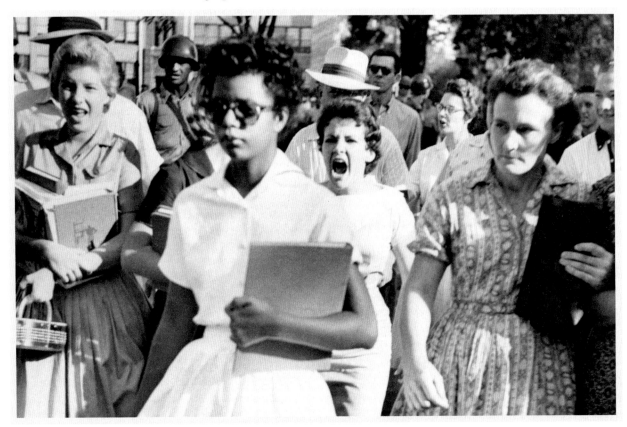

In 1946, Thurgood Marshall took the case of Heman Marion Sweatt, an African American seeking admission to the University of Texas School of Law. The university rejected Sweatt because of his race, but to comply with the "separate but equal" doctrine, it established a law school solely for African Americans. In 1950, the U.S. Supreme Court ruled in **Sweatt v. Painter** that the university must admit Sweatt to the original law school under the 14th Amendment. That same day, the Supreme Court ruled against segregation in **McLaurin v. Oklahoma State Regents**. Because of these decisions, college classes throughout the nation were to be integrated, meaning they would have to allow the free association of people of all races and ethnicities.

By 1953, five civil rights lawsuits had reached the Supreme Court, including **Brown v. Board of Education of Topeka**. That year, President Eisenhower had appointed **Earl Warren** as the court's Chief Justice, even though Warren's political views were more liberal than his own.

BROWN v. BOARD OF EDUCATION

Remember that *Brown v. Board of Education* centered on a Kansas law permitting cities to segregate their public schools. The case began when a team of six NAACP lawyers—five black, one white—represented the Reverend Oliver Brown in suing the Topeka school board. The lawyers argued that Brown's 8-year-old daughter should not have to attend a segregated school 21 blocks from her home when a white public school was much closer. One of the lawyers' strategies was to present social science studies showing that segregated schools had a negative effect on the self-esteem of African-American children, especially that of girls.

Eventually, the Supreme Court agreed to hear the case. The African-American and white lawyers collaborated on finding documented evidence of unequal education in several states. In a unanimous decision delivered on May 17, 1954, the Supreme Court ruled that the doctrine of "separate but equal" had no place in public education. Chief Justice Warren wrote, "Separate educational facilities are inherently [essentially] unequal." The court ordered the speedy integration of the nation's public schools. Because of the decision, the definition of *equal rights* included the equal opportunity for education and inspired a new generation of civil rights activists.

Many white southerners were outraged and reacted violently to **desegregation** efforts, or stopping the

PRIMARY SOURCE

Segregation of white and colored children in public schools has a detrimental effect upon the colored children. The impact is greater when it has the sanction of the law, for the policy of separating the races is usually interpreted as denoting the inferiority of the negro group. A sense of inferiority affects the motivation of a child to learn. Segregation with the sanction of law, therefore, has a tendency to [retard] the educational and mental development of negro children and to deprive them of some of the benefits they would receive in a racial[ly] integrated school system.

—from *Brown* v. *Board of Education of Topeka,* Supreme Court Decision, May 17, 1954

practice of separating groups of people in public spaces. To them, the ruling was an example of the federal government misusing its power. President Eisenhower was quiet about the issue. When asked directly about the *Brown* decision, he replied: "The Supreme Court has spoken . . . and I will obey."

In 1956, about 100 members of Congress from former Confederate states issued a document called "The Southern Manifesto on Integration." Vowing to use "all lawful means" to resist the *Brown* decision and court-ordered integration, they claimed *Brown* was a misinterpretation of the 14th Amendment and that the government was forcing states to carry out a law no one had voted for.

In 1957, this conflict over federal authority and states' rights erupted in Little Rock, Arkansas, when nine African-American students who tried to integrate a local high school were denied access to the school by the governor, the National Guard, and local citizens. President Eisenhower finally sent federal troops to escort the **Little Rock Nine** to their classes and to restore order. That month, he signed the **Civil Rights Act of 1957**, which protected the voting rights of African Americans. To remedy the act's shortcomings, he later signed the **Civil Rights Act of 1960**. Neither act proved to be effective.

HISTORICAL THINKING

1. **READING CHECK** How did many white southerners, including those in Congress, react to desegregation?

2. **ANALYZE CAUSE AND EFFECT** How did the court decisions in *Mendez*, *Sweatt*, and *McLaurin* affect the Brown ruling?

THURGOOD MARSHALL 1908–1993

"To protest against injustice is the foundation of all our
American democracy."—Thurgood Marshall

Fighting for justice and the rights of others became Thurgood Marshall's life's work. In his first case as a lawyer, he helped defend Donald Murray, a young African American who had been denied admission to the University of Maryland School of Law in 1935 because of his race. The case hit home. In 1930, Marshall himself had been refused entry to the school because he was black. He took on the Murray case to battle against the school's blatant discrimination and won. The young man became the first African American admitted to the law school.

CIVIL RIGHTS LAWYER

Instead of Maryland's law school, Marshall attended the Howard University School of Law in Washington, D.C., the oldest historically black law school in the United States. There he found a mentor in Charles Hamilton Houston, the school's vice-dean from 1929 to 1935 and an early civil rights lawyer. After graduating in 1933 from Howard—*cum laude*, or "with distinction"—Marshall eventually followed Houston to New York City. In time, Marshall became the chief counsel of the NAACP Legal Defense and Education Fund, a position he held for 21 years.

During his career at the NAACP, Marshall took on cases involving segregation and discrimination and, as you know, helped to successfully overturn the entire legal basis of "separate but equal." Sometimes his work took him to the Deep South where he experienced firsthand the racism his clients suffered. After winning one case in Tennessee, Marshall was nearly lynched. Many of his cases went to the Supreme Court, including the one for which he is

In his early years as chief counsel of the NAACP, Marshall successfully challenged the practice in several southern states of holding "white primaries" and preventing African Americans from voting.

most famous, *Brown* v. *Board of Education*. Of the 32 cases he argued before the Court, Marshall won 29. In fact, over his career, he won more Supreme Court cases than any other lawyer in American history.

Those who witnessed him in action said that Marshall's oratorical style was not flowery and emotional. Rather, he spoke eloquently and with great dignity, often addressing the moral and social implications of a case. Most of all, he conveyed his deep respect for the law and the Constitution, which he had been forced to memorize as punishment for

Marshall is sworn in as U.S. solicitor general while his family (front left) and Johnson (behind left) look on. The solicitor general is often called the 10th justice because he or she works closely with Supreme Court justices.

misbehaving when he was a high school student in Baltimore. When asked by a journalist why he had become a lawyer, Marshall (who had once wanted to be a dentist) replied that he didn't know. "The nearest I can get," he said, "is that my dad, my brother, and I had the most violent arguments you ever heard about anything. I guess we argued five out of seven nights at the dinner table."

JUDGE AND JUSTICE

In recognition of his brilliance, Marshall was appointed to high-level judicial positions during the 1960s. In 1961, President John Kennedy nominated him to the U.S. Court of Appeals. Four years later, President Lyndon Johnson made Marshall the first African-American U.S. solicitor general, the lawyer representing the federal government before the Supreme Court. Finally, in 1967, Johnson appointed Marshall as a justice on the Court, claiming that it was "the right thing to do, the right time to do it, the right man and the right place." And so the great-grandson of a slave became the first African American on the Supreme Court.

During Marshall's first years there, the Court, headed by Chief Justice Earl Warren, was decidedly liberal. Most of the justices agreed on such issues as racial discrimination and immigration. However, after Johnson, a Democrat, left the White House, Republican presidents picked the next eight justices. When President Richard Nixon made Warren Burger

chief justice in 1969, the Court became more ideologically conservative, and Marshall grew more and more marginalized. As the Court's rulings chipped away at abortion rights, limited affirmative action laws, and reinstated the death penalty, Marshall voiced his disagreement with these decisions in forceful dissents.

Marshall retired from the Supreme Court in 1991 and was replaced by Clarence Thomas, a conservative African American. Though Marshall was less celebrated than Martin Luther King, Jr., and Malcolm X—an African-American civil rights activist in the 1960s—he arguably had the greatest impact on the civil rights movement of the three. As one obituary declared after Marshall died in 1993, "We make movies about Malcolm X, we get a holiday to honor Dr. Martin Luther King, but every day we live with the legacy of Justice Thurgood Marshall."

HISTORICAL THINKING

1. **READING CHECK** What was particularly meaningful about Marshall's first case?

2. **MAKE INFERENCES** Why do you think it was important to Marshall to express his disagreement with some of the Supreme Court decisions made under Warren Burger?

3. **DRAW CONCLUSIONS** What did the writer of the obituary mean by the statement: "every day we live with the legacy of Justice Thurgood Marshall"?

MAIN IDEA A yearlong bus boycott by African Americans in Montgomery, Alabama, led to a landmark Supreme Court decision against segregation on city buses.

WOMEN TAKE A STAND

Sometimes people have to break the rules to prove a point. A woman stepped onto a city bus in Montgomery, Alabama, one fateful evening in 1955 to do just that. Her action sparked a national debate over civil rights.

A BOYCOTT BEGINS

A year and a half after the Supreme Court's ruling in *Brown* v. *Board of Education*, its decision continued to rock the nation. Meanwhile, in Montgomery, Alabama, another major civil rights development was taking shape.

Segregation and discrimination were firmly established and strictly enforced in Montgomery, "the cradle of the Confederacy." African Americans were expected to tip their hats to whites, stand in the presence of whites unless told to sit, and address whites with titles of respect. City buses were segregated, and the first four rows of seats were reserved for whites, according to a Montgomery ordinance. African Americans had to pay their fares in the front, then get off the bus and enter the designated "colored section" through the rear door. They could also sit in the middle rows of the bus, but they had to relinquish their seat to white passengers when the front section filled up.

One regular bus rider was **Rosa Parks**, an African-American woman and longtime civil rights activist who worked as an assistant tailor at a downtown Montgomery department store. She also served as secretary for the Montgomery chapter of the NAACP, which she had joined in 1943. In the summer of 1955, the 42-year-old Parks traveled to the Highlander Folk School in Tennessee for a two-week interracial conference focused on leadership in the struggle against segregation. She later revealed that through this experience, she "gained strength to persevere in my work for freedom, not just for [African Americans] but for all oppressed people."

Rosa Parks holds up the identification number in her booking photo after being arrested during the Montgomery Bus Boycott in 1956.

PRIMARY SOURCE

Four months after refusing to give up her bus seat, Rosa Parks spoke to an interviewer about that fateful evening.

I felt that I was not being treated right, and that I had a right to retain the seat that I had taken as a passenger on the bus. The time had just come when I had been pushed as far as I could stand to be pushed, I suppose. They placed me under arrest. No, I wasn't frightened at all. I don't know why I wasn't, but I didn't feel afraid. I had decided that I would have to know once and for all what rights I had as a human being and a citizen, even in Montgomery, Alabama.

—from a transcript of a radio interview with Rosa Parks, April 1956

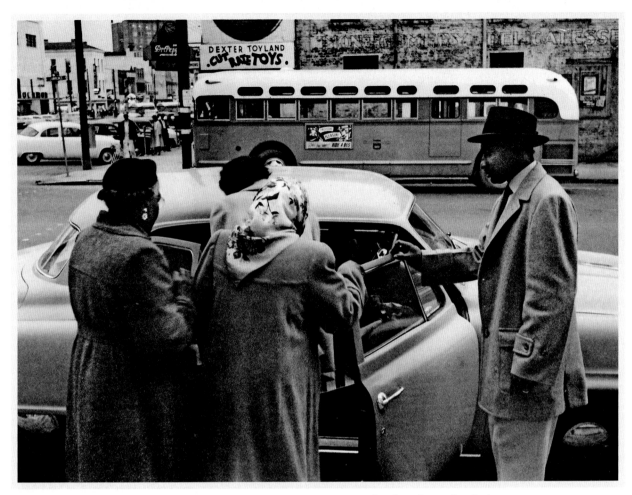

During the Montgomery Bus Boycott, many people chose to carpool rather than take the bus, as shown in this 1956 photo. The empty bus in the background is a sign of the boycott's success.

Earlier in 1955, other African-American women had refused to give up their bus seats in Montgomery. In March, 15-year-old Claudette Colvin was arrested after refusing to give up her seat in the black section of the bus for a white woman. "It's my constitutional right to sit here as much as that lady. I paid my fare!" she yelled as the policemen dragged her off the bus. Rosa Parks was one of the volunteers who raised money for Colvin's court hearing, but in addition to segregation violations, police charged Colvin with assaulting the officers, so civil rights activists decided not to pursue her case. In October, police arrested 18-year-old Mary Louise Smith for violating the same segregation policies. Civil rights leaders deemed Smith an unsympathetic plaintiff because she was poor and young.

Knowing that the NAACP was looking for a lead plaintiff in a case to test Montgomery's segregated bus law, Parks boarded a bus on December 1, 1955. She took a seat in the middle section of the mostly empty bus, but after a few stops, the white section of the bus filled up. When more white passengers stepped aboard, the driver asked Parks and three

other African-American passengers sitting in the same row to move to the back of the bus, where they would have had to stand. The others reluctantly complied, but Parks refused to give up her seat. The driver called the police, who arrested Parks for violating the ordinance.

Parks's civil disobedience, or act of purposely breaking a law in protest, and her arrest galvanized Montgomery's African-American community. **Jo Ann Robinson**, the president of a local political group called the Women's Political Council, organized volunteers who distributed 50,000 flyers declaring a one-day boycott of the city's buses. The initial **Montgomery Bus Boycott** was so successful that Robinson and other civil rights leaders decided to extend it to a long-term campaign. Activists, including Robinson's Women's Political Council and members of the NAACP, joined with a group of local ministers at the Holy Street Baptist Church to form the Montgomery Improvement Association (MIA). For its president, the MIA chose an eloquent, energetic young minister named **Martin Luther King, Jr.**, who had just arrived in Montgomery the previous year.

THE MURDER OF EMMETT TILL

While some women fought for civil rights through activism, staging and engaging in boycotts and marches, others took very personal stands that led to national action. In August of 1955, Mamie Till-Mobley sent her 14-year-old son Emmett on a train to visit relatives in Mississippi. A few days after Emmett had left his home in Chicago, Mrs. Till-Mobley received a phone call. Two white men had killed her child. The men claimed Emmett had flirted with a white woman in a local grocery store. They beat Till, shot him, and hung a 75-pound metal fan around his neck to keep his body hidden at the bottom of the Tallahatchie River.

A jury quickly released the white men. It wasn't until 2008 that the woman who claimed Till had physically and verbally attacked her admitted that she had made up those accusations.

Mrs. Till-Mobley brought Emmett's body back home to Chicago. The condition of Emmett's maimed body would usually call for a closed casket, but Mrs. Till-Mobley insisted on keeping his casket open during the funeral. "Let the people see what I've seen," she said. *Jet* magazine published photos of Mrs. Till-Mobley mourning over her son's body and forced the American public to witness the glaring brutality of racism in their country. Till's casket is now at the Smithsonian National Museum of African American History and Culture in Washington, D.C.

An undated photograph shows the young Emmett Till before his murder in 1955.

Mamie Till-Mobley mourns for her son as she leans against his glass-covered coffin. Following Emmett's funeral, she helped form a campaign for justice and civil rights.

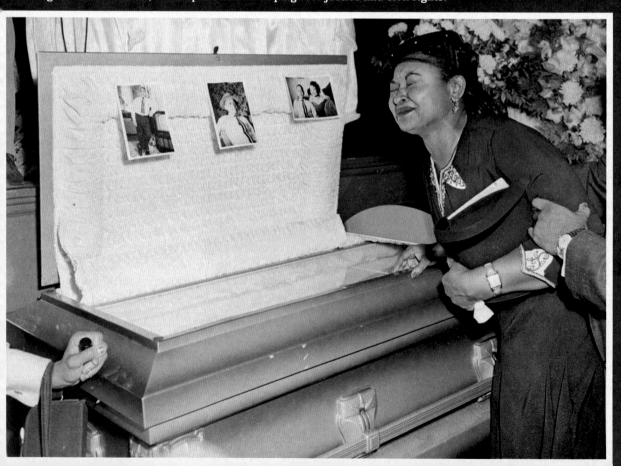

THE BOYCOTT GAINS MOMENTUM

Boycott organizers knew their protest would be effective because African Americans accounted for roughly three-quarters of Montgomery's bus ridership. Losing most of these riders would have harsh economic consequences for the city's bus company. The organizers also knew that since few African Americans owned cars, the boycott would be difficult to sustain. However, the community was determined to keep the protest going. Friends, coworkers, and neighbors formed carpools to get people to their jobs and other destinations. Churches hosted boycott-related meetings and raised money for fuel, and African-American-owned garages did auto repair work free of charge. Many people rode bicycles or simply walked.

Days stretched into weeks, weeks into months, and still the boycott continued. It pushed the bus company to the brink of bankruptcy and dealt a severe financial blow to white-owned businesses in downtown Montgomery. Some whites retaliated by firing or threatening to fire African-American workers, and others threw bombs into churches and homes, including King's home.

On June 5, 1956, a federal district court, citing the *Brown* v. *Board of Education* decision as precedent, ruled that Alabama state statutes and Montgomery city ordinances requiring segregation on buses were unconstitutional. The Supreme Court affirmed this ruling on November 13 of that year, and on December 20, a U.S. marshal delivered a court order to Montgomery City Hall requiring the integration of the city's buses. King immediately called off the boycott and urged African Americans to begin riding the buses again the following day. The 381-day boycott had demonstrated both the power of collective action and the possibility of social change.

Coretta and Martin Luther King, Jr., leave the courthouse after his arrest for conspiring to boycott Montgomery city buses in 1956.

HISTORICAL THINKING

1. **READING CHECK** How did the African-American community work together to sustain the bus boycott?

2. **DESCRIBE** How might historical events have taken a different direction if Claudette Colvin, Mary Louise Smith, and Rosa Parks had not taken a stand?

3. **MAKE INFERENCES** What personal traits do you think Rosa Parks and other civil rights activists must have had in order to work for the freedom of all people?

MARTIN LUTHER KING, JR., AND A GROWING MOVEMENT

When he was 15 years old, Martin Luther King, Jr., left the segregated South for the first time and spent the summer in Connecticut. Seeing African Americans and whites eating in the same restaurants, shopping in the same stores, and worshiping in the same churches shaped his vision of what the United States could be: a multiracial, peaceful society.

THE EMERGENCE OF DR. KING

King was born on January 15, 1929, in Atlanta, Georgia. His parents were college educated, and the family lived in a middle-class neighborhood known for its thriving African-American businesses and churches. His father was a pastor at the highly regarded Ebenezer Baptist Church, a position his maternal grandfather had also held.

In 1944, King graduated from high school and entered Atlanta's Morehouse College. His studies there focused on medicine and law, but by the time of his graduation, he had decided to follow the example of his father and join the ministry. His spiritual and intellectual mentor, Morehouse president Benjamin Mays, also influenced his decision. Mays was not only an influential educator and minister, but also a strong voice for racial equality. King enrolled at the liberal-leaning Crozer Theological Seminary in Pennsylvania and graduated three years later with a bachelor's degree in divinity. He then earned a doctoral degree in theology from Boston University.

While completing his studies, King accepted a position in Montgomery, Alabama, as pastor at Dexter Avenue

WAITING ROOM FOR WHITES ONLY BY ORDER OF POLICE DEPT.

Official signs enforcing segregated seating were common, particularly across the South, during the first half of the 20th century.

Baptist Church. The following year, in 1955, he led the Montgomery Bus Boycott, which helped bring an end to segregation on the city's buses. In the wake of that successful protest, King joined with other African-American ministers and civil rights activists to form the **Southern Christian Leadership Conference (SCLC)** in 1957. This organization, whose strength came from the leadership of African-American churches, promoted racial justice through peaceful means and provided assistance and guidance to local protest groups.

King was convinced that nonviolent civil disobedience was the best way for African Americans to fight injustice and bring about social change. His philosophical and religious dedication to nonviolence took shape while he was in the seminary where his studies exposed him to the teachings of **Mohandas Gandhi**. A lawyer, politician, writer, and civil rights activist, Gandhi advocated peaceful protest and noncooperation in the struggle against colonial injustice in India. Through this approach, Gandhi had helped free his country from British imperial rule. King applied Gandhi's use of nonviolent methods throughout his career as a civil rights activist.

A MASS MOVEMENT FORMS

The Supreme Court's *Brown* v. *Board of Education* decision and the success of the Montgomery Bus Boycott profoundly altered race relations in the United States. Thanks to the extraordinary courage of ordinary African-American men, women, and children who joined the battle, the call for civil rights transformed into a mass movement that included Americans of all races.

Developments in North Carolina in 1960 ushered in a new phase in the movement. On February 1, four African-American college students entered a Woolworth's store and restaurant in Greensboro, took seats at the lunch counter marked "For Whites Only," and politely attempted to order lunch. The waitstaff refused to serve them and the manager asked them to leave, but they stayed until closing time. The next day, they returned with 25 fellow students. On the third day, the number of student protesters rose to 63, and by the fifth day it exceeded 300.

News outlets around the country reported the story, and soon more people in many other cities were staging **sit-ins**, coordinated protests in which people occupy seats or floor space in places that are the targets of protest. There also were other "ins." African-American churches organized kneel-ins at segregated churches and wade-ins at segregated pools. These protests were remarkably effective. In the following months, segregation began to yield to integration in cities across the South. On July 25, nearly six months after the first day of the Greensboro sit-in, the four original protesters were finally served at the Woolworth's lunch counter.

The success of the sit-ins and similar nonviolent protests inspired a group of African-American students to create their own political organization, the **Student Nonviolent Coordinating Committee (SNCC)**. A cofounder of SCLC, **Ella Baker**, had become frustrated with its cautious approach and hierarchical nature, so she left that organization to become an advisor to SNCC. Baker had also served as a national director for the NAACP and had co-founded an organization called In Friendship, which raised money to fight Jim Crow laws in the South. While serving at SCLC, Baker helped to organize a "prayer pilgrimage" to Washington, D.C., and an ambitious voter registration campaign called the Crusade for Citizenship.

North Carolina A&T College students (left to right) Ronald Martin, Robert Patterson, and Mark Martin joined the second day of the sit-in at the Greensboro lunch counter.

Barely escaping alive from their burning bus, a group of Freedom Riders waits on the roadside outside Anniston, Alabama. The 13 men and women who set out on an interstate trip to test desegregation laws were assaulted by Ku Klux Klan members before they were rescued several hours later. News of this and other vicious attacks led hundreds of people to join the Freedom Riders throughout 1961.

Another prominent leader of SNCC was a woman named **Fannie Lou Hamer**. Hamer had been born into poverty and oppression in the Mississippi Delta, the 20th child of sharecropper parents, and her education had ended at the 6th-grade level. Her background made her later accomplishments all the more remarkable.

As a SNCC field secretary whose job was to assist in building membership, Hamer fought to end segregation and protect the rights of African Americans. Angered that Mississippi's conservative, white-dominated Democratic Party did not allow African Americans to participate in meetings, she helped to establish the **Mississippi Freedom Democratic Party**, a grassroots political group established as an alternative to the larger, more conservative state arm of the Democratic Party. The Mississippi Freedom Democratic Party was dedicated to encouraging African-American voter registration. Hamer earned the respect of many, and in 1964, she delivered a powerful speech at a Democratic National Convention about the intimidation and violence that African Americans in her state faced when they attempted to register to vote. Because of their strong leadership, Baker and Hamer joined Rosa Parks as influential women in the civil rights movement.

THE FREEDOM RIDERS

In November 1960, **John F. Kennedy** was elected president of the United States. (Read more about Kennedy's election and presidency in the next chapter.) Although he was more sympathetic to the civil rights cause than Eisenhower had been, Kennedy wanted change to come slowly, without the mass protests and violent incidents that had made headlines around the world. He worried, too, that White House support for immediate desegregation would cost him the goodwill of powerful southern Democrats in Congress.

In December 1960, the Supreme Court had ruled in a case called *Boynton* v. *Virginia*, finding that racial segregation was illegal in bus terminals, restrooms, and other facilities serving passengers traveling across state lines. Shortly thereafter, CORE, which you read about earlier in this chapter, announced plans to test that court decision to see if local police were upholding the law. CORE's stated objective was "to provoke the southern authorities into arresting us and thereby prod the Justice Department into enforcing the law of the land."

In May 1961, seven African-American and six white "**Freedom Riders**" left Washington, D.C., on two buses bound for New Orleans. At stops along the way, they ignored "white" and "colored" signs that hung by the restrooms, lunch counters, and waiting rooms in defiance of federal law. Trouble erupted in Anniston, Alabama, when white segregationists firebombed one of the buses. As the passengers

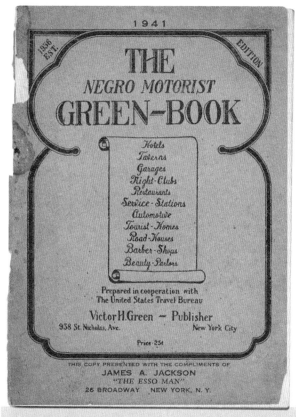

THE GREEN BOOK

In 1936, publisher Victor Green saw the need for a national guide for African-American travelers. Titled *The Negro Motorist Green Book*, the book listed restaurants, rooming houses, barbers, and tourist activities that welcomed African Americans in the time of segregation, particularly in areas with strict Jim Crow laws. Unlike most book publishers, Green looked forward to the time when his Green Book was not necessary. "That is when we as a race will have equal opportunities and privileges in the United States," he wrote in an introduction to his book.

escaped, a mob beat them with fists and clubs. Riders on the second bus suffered a similar attack in Birmingham. Local police in these and other cities made little effort to stop the attacks. The continuing violence finally compelled Attorney General **Robert F. Kennedy**, who was President Kennedy's younger brother and close aide, to send U.S. marshals to protect the riders. CORE, with assistance from SNCC, continued to organize freedom rides until September of that year, when the federal government banned interstate buses and trains from using any terminal that segregated people by race.

Meanwhile, another key development in the civil rights movement unfolded in Mississippi. After repeatedly being denied admission to the all-white University of Mississippi, an African-American student named James Meredith filed a discrimination lawsuit against the university. Supported by the NAACP, Meredith took his case all the way to the Supreme Court, which ruled in his favor. When he attempted to register at the university, however, state troopers, acting on the orders of Mississippi governor Ross Barnett, turned him away. U.S. marshals accompanied Meredith during several more attempts to register, but large numbers of protesters and state troopers blocked him. Riots broke out as the situation escalated. After the federal government sent hundreds of agents to the scene, Meredith was finally able to register and attend classes as the university's first African-American student.

This period in Mississippi's civil rights movement is memorably captured in *Coming of Age in Mississippi*, an autobiography by activist and writer Anne Moody. With bracing honesty, she tells of growing up desperately poor in rural southern Mississippi, of the brutal racism that she and her family faced, and of fighting for the rights of African Americans.

HISTORICAL THINKING

1. **READING CHECK** What legal action did the federal government take in response to the Freedom Rides?

2. **FORM AND SUPPORT OPINIONS** Do you think nonviolent civil disobedience proved to be a good strategy for bringing about social change? Support your opinion with evidence from the text.

3. **MAKE INFERENCES** Why do you think Fannie Lou Hamer focused her efforts on African-American voter registration?

4. **ANALYZE CAUSE AND EFFECT** What caused the sit-in protest in Greensboro, and what effect did the protest have on the larger civil rights movement?

MAIN IDEA In 1963, a brutal police response to peaceful protests in Birmingham, Alabama, prompted President John F. Kennedy to propose strong new civil rights legislation.

PROTESTS IN BIRMINGHAM

In Kelly Ingram Park in Birmingham, Alabama, vicious police dogs lunge at peaceful protesters. Children cower before a powerful water cannon. Church ministers kneel in prayer. These scenes, depicted in sculptures, tell of a dark time in the city's history.

CONFRONTATION IN BIRMINGHAM

In December 1962, three months after James Meredith's lawsuit to be admitted into the University of Mississippi was successful, President Kennedy received a telegraph from Dr. Martin Luther King, Jr., with this message: "A virtual reign of terror is still alive in Birmingham, Alabama. It is by far the worst big city in race relations in the United States."

The previous day, Birmingham's Bethel Baptist Church had been bombed for the third time in 6 years. For 15 years, white segregationists had committed numerous other acts of intimidation and violence against African Americans, including the 1961 attack on the Freedom Riders. The police, under the command of **Eugene T. "Bull" Connor**, the Commissioner of Public Safety, strictly enforced segregation ordinances. Connor was an active white segregationist with close ties to the Ku Klux Klan.

The following spring, King and other leaders of SCLC developed plans for an all-out campaign to confront segregation in Birmingham. They scheduled the campaign to coincide with the busy Easter shopping season. The organizers kicked off the campaign in early April 1963 with mass meetings, lunch-counter sit-ins, a boycott of downtown merchants, and marches, each intended to provoke confrontation and sympathy for the civil rights cause. As days passed, more people joined in the protests, and the police made more arrests.

"LETTER FROM BIRMINGHAM CITY JAIL"

On April 12, 1963, King himself was arrested. That same day, the *Birmingham News* published a letter from eight white ministers titled "A Call for Unity." The ministers appealed to African Americans to withdraw their support for the demonstrations, and they denounced King and others for inciting hatred and violence. From his jail cell, King responded with what would become known as his "Letter from Birmingham City Jail." The letter eloquently rebutted the ministers' arguments and defended the morality of nonviolent civil disobedience. King was released from jail after eight days of **solitary confinement**, being locked in an enclosed cell alone.

As support for the protests began to fade, King and the other organizers seized upon the idea of bringing local students into the campaign in order to re-energize it. On May 2, more than 1,000 students, some as young as 6, marched from the 16th Street Baptist Church to City Hall. Police arrested and held 969 students, among others, packing the city's jails.

Abandoning restraint, Bull Connor ordered the police and fire departments to use police dogs and high-pressure fire hoses to break up the protest. News outlets across the United States and around the world carried shocking images of Birmingham police officers striking peaceful protestors with batons, vicious dogs attacking children and adults alike, and officials blasting people with powerful fire hoses.

On May 10, the campaign's organizers announced that they had worked out an agreement with Birmingham city leaders to end the public demonstrations. The agreement established specific steps and a timetable for ending segregation in Birmingham's public facilities and for creating an employment program for African Americans.

Once again Alabama was headlined in national newspapers when, on June 11, 1963, its segregationist governor **George Wallace**, flanked

By 1963, major news media sent reporters and photographers to cover the unfolding civil rights demonstrations that targeted the segregated city of Birmingham, Alabama. As the Birmingham fire department turned high velocity water hoses on peaceful demonstrators, a photographer recorded one of the assaults that shocked Americans.

by state troopers, physically blocked two African-American students from registering at the University of Alabama in Tuscaloosa. President Kennedy and Attorney General Robert Kennedy responded to Wallace's symbolic action by authorizing the Alabama National Guard to physically remove the governor and by allowing the students to register.

On national television that evening, President Kennedy delivered an impassioned speech on civil rights. He spoke of the "moral crisis" facing the country and declared that "The events in Birmingham . . . have so increased the cries for equality that no city or state or legislative body can prudently choose to ignore them." Just hours after the broadcast, a white segregationist in Mississippi shot and killed civil rights activist **Medgar Evers** in front of his home.

The following week, Kennedy expanded the role of the federal government as a guarantor of civil rights by sending Congress a proposal for a civil rights bill that was far stronger than the civil rights bills that had passed in 1957 and 1960. In fact, it was the most sweeping civil rights bill since Reconstruction.

The turmoil in Alabama had a powerful impact on race relations in the United States, as well as on the perception of how protesters were being treated. Many white Americans had been indifferent to the plight of African Americans. But because the violence and brutality in Birmingham was widely televised, most Americans, no matter what their backgrounds, were horrified by the violence. They began to pay attention to and support the civil rights movement.

HISTORICAL THINKING

1. **READING CHECK** What was the goal of the Birmingham campaign, and what caused the organizers to end the campaign?

2. **EXPLAIN** How did the television footage of police officers attacking protesters contribute to the diffusion of the civil rights movement?

3. **FORM AND SUPPORT OPINIONS** What effect do you think President Kennedy's address about the events in Birmingham had on the nation?

4. **IDENTIFY** What was the role of Martin Luther King, Jr., in the Birmingham protests?

DEMANDING REFORM

African-American civil rights activists worked through the nation's judicial and legislative systems to win the rights of full citizenship, but they also turned to nonviolent protest to raise awareness of their cause and win support for their movement. Sometimes that meant paying a legal cost.

CRITICAL VIEWING In 1967, four years after he wrote "Letter from Birmingham City Jail," Martin Luther King, Jr., returned to the Alabama jail to complete serving his sentence for participating in the 1963 civil rights demonstration. In 10 years, King was arrested more than 10 times for conducting peaceful protests. Why do you think this photo of King in an Alabama jail cell has become a symbol of the civil rights movement?

DOCUMENT ONE

Primary Source: Speech
from *Speech at the March on Washington*, by John Lewis, August 28, 1963

John Lewis, the son of Alabama sharecroppers, helped organize the March on Washington for Jobs and Freedom and was its youngest speaker. His speech focused on the need for civil rights legislation that would address how the economy affected African Americans and the nation's poor and homeless.

CONSTRUCTED RESPONSE What does Lewis mean when he says "we will not and cannot be patient"?

We march today for jobs and freedom, but we have nothing to be proud of. While we stand here, there are sharecroppers in the Delta of Mississippi who are out in the fields working for less than three dollars a day, twelve hours a day.

We must have legislation that will protect the Mississippi sharecropper who is put off of his farm because he dares to register to vote. We need a bill that will ensure the equality of a maid who earns five dollars a week in a home of a family whose total income is $100,000 a year. . . . For we cannot stop, and we will not and cannot be patient.

DOCUMENT TWO

Primary Source: Newspaper Article
from "A Call for Unity," by eight Alabama clergymen, April 12, 1963

During the campaign in Birmingham, as you have learned, local newspapers printed a letter titled "A Call for Unity," which was signed by eight white religious leaders. The men agreed that segregation was wrong, but believed King's tactics were "unwise and untimely."

CONSTRUCTED RESPONSE What evidence in the text suggests the clergymen are sympathetic to the protesters?

We are now confronted by a series of demonstrations by some of our Negro citizens, directed and led in part by outsiders. We recognize the natural impatience of people who feel that their hopes are slow in being realized. But we are convinced that these demonstrations are unwise and untimely.

DOCUMENT THREE

Primary Source: Letter
from "Letter from Birmingham City Jail," by Martin Luther King, Jr., April 16, 1963

In this excerpt from the letter he wrote in response to "A Call for Unity," King addresses the ministers' assertion that the demonstrations were "directed and led in part by outsiders."

CONSTRUCTED RESPONSE What is King's response to the label of "outsider"?

I cannot sit idly by in Atlanta and not be concerned about what happens in Birmingham. Injustice anywhere is a threat to justice everywhere. We are caught in an inescapable network of mutuality, tied in a single garment of destiny. Whatever affects one directly affects all indirectly. Never again can we afford to live with the narrow, provincial "outside agitator" idea. Anyone who lives inside the United States can never be considered an outsider anywhere in this country.

SYNTHESIZE & WRITE

1. **REVIEW** Review what you have learned about the civil rights movement from the *Speech at the March on Washington*, the Birmingham campaign, and other strategies.

2. **RECALL** On your own paper, write the main idea expressed in each of these documents: John Lewis's speech, the "A Call for Unity" letter, and the "Letter from Birmingham City Jail."

3. **CONSTRUCT** Construct a topic sentence that supports this question: In what ways did the different forms of protest work together to bring about change?

4. **WRITE** Using evidence from this chapter and the documents, write an informative paragraph that supports your topic sentence in Step 3.

MAIN IDEA The 1963 March on Washington demonstrated the unity of the civil rights movement and featured one of the most famous speeches in American history.

THE MARCH ON WASHINGTON

Important speeches tend to include memorable and often-quoted words. Take, for example, Patrick Henry's "Give me liberty or give me death!" Without question, the most famous speech of Martin Luther King, Jr., became a rallying point for justice, freedom, and a better world.

JOBS AND FREEDOM

As you have read, in July 1963 President Kennedy sent Congress a proposal for a sweeping civil rights bill. Recent events in Birmingham and Tuscaloosa, Alabama, had convinced him of the urgent need for strong legislation protecting the rights of African Americans. The legislation faced stiff opposition in Congress, and the bill stalled there.

Meanwhile, plans were underway for a major rally in the nation's capital in support of civil rights and the civil rights bill. The demonstration took place on August 28, 1963, and was called the **March on Washington for Jobs and Freedom**. Its chief organizer was Bayard Rustin. Starting in 1941, Rustin and A. Philip Randolph had built an alliance of civil rights, labor, and religious organizations, bringing unity to the movement.

Rustin expected 100,000 people to take part in the 1963 March on Washington, but more than twice that number arrived. They came from every region of the country and every walk of life. Most were African American, but roughly one-fourth were white. After assembling on the grounds of the Washington Monument, the participants sang "We Shall Overcome" and marched down Constitution and Independence avenues. They ended at the Lincoln Memorial for the day's main program. It featured prayers, a performance by gospel singer **Mahalia Jackson**, and speeches by civil rights leaders.

DR. KING'S DREAM

The last and most highly anticipated speaker at the March on Washington was King. The eloquent and uplifting speech he delivered that afternoon is considered one of the greatest orations in American history. King began by reminding his listeners that although almost 100 years had passed since President Lincoln emancipated enslaved people, "the Negro is still sadly crippled by the manacles of segregation and the chains of discrimination. Now is the time," he proclaimed, "to rise from the dark and desolate valley of segregation to the sunlit path of racial justice." Putting aside his prepared notes, King spoke of his dream for a brighter future:

I have a dream that one day this nation will rise up and live out the true meaning of its creed: "We hold these truths to be self-evident, that all men are created equal."

I have a dream that my four little children will one day live in a nation where they will not be judged by the color of their skin but by the content of their character.

The March on Washington demonstrated the growing power and unity of the civil rights movement. Just weeks later, however, a horrific event in Alabama was a reminder of the gulf between King's dream and the harsh reality that African Americans still faced. On Sunday morning, September 15, a bomb planted by the Ku Klux Klan killed four young African-American girls at Birmingham's 16th Street Baptist Church.

In the fall of 1963, SNCC and CORE launched a **voter registration drive** in Mississippi to sign up as many eligible African-American voters as possible. Expanded in 1964, the program was called the Mississippi Summer Project, or **Freedom Summer**. More than 700 student volunteers, most of whom were white, came from colleges in the North

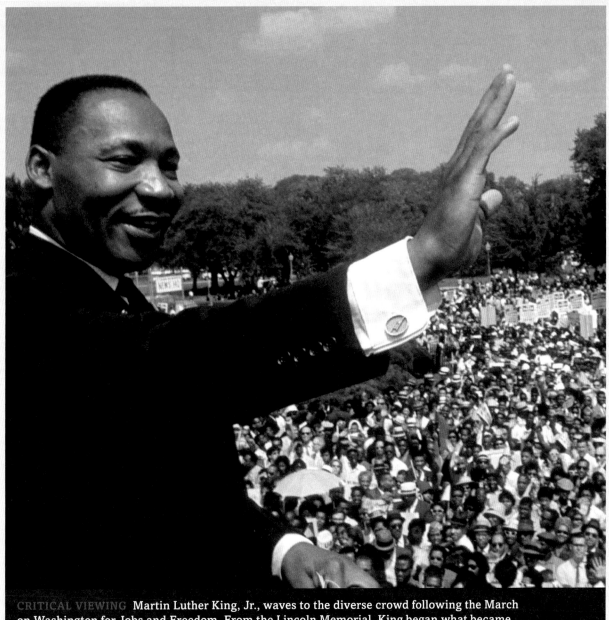

CRITICAL VIEWING Martin Luther King, Jr., waves to the diverse crowd following the March on Washington for Jobs and Freedom. From the Lincoln Memorial, King began what became known as his "I Have a Dream" speech. As he spoke, his friend, gospel singer Mahalia Jackson, eagerly called out to him "Tell them about the dream." From your view of King and the crowd in the photograph, what do you think was the effect of King's message about his dream?

to work with local civil rights organizations in Mississippi. On June 21, 1964, two white workers, Andrew Goodman and Michael Schwerner from New York, and one local African-American worker, James Chaney, disappeared after investigating the burning of an African-American church. Six weeks later, acting on a tip, authorities uncovered the bodies of the workers. All three had been shot at close range. It was clear that the nonviolent civil rights movement still faced dangerous opposition.

HISTORICAL THINKING

1. **READING CHECK** In what ways did the March on Washington demonstrate the power and unity of the civil rights movement?

2. **MAKE GENERALIZATIONS** How does the fact that students volunteered to travel to Mississippi after the violence of the Birmingham campaign speak to larger developments in the civil rights movement?

3. **ANALYZE LANGUAGE USE** What was the impact of King's deliberate repetition of the phrase "I have a dream" in his speech?

CHAPTER 25 · THE CIVIL RIGHTS MOVEMENT REVIEW

VOCABULARY

Use each of the following vocabulary terms in a sentence that shows an understanding of the term's meaning.

1. **desegregation**
   The Supreme Court ruled against "separate but equal" education, which led to the desegregation of public schools.

2. **Freedom Riders**

3. **sit-in**

4. **grassroots activism**

5. **dehumanize**

6. **solitary confinement**

READING STRATEGY
MAKE INFERENCES

Texts don't always spell out exactly how an event affected the lives of those who lived through it or the outcomes of other related events. Sometimes a reader needs to evaluate the information in the text to infer these effects and outcomes. Use a chart like the one below to make inferences about ways Americans reacted to key events in the civil rights movement. Then answer the question.

The Civil Rights Movement

Key Events	American Reactions	Inferences

7. How did the civil rights movement redefine American identity?

MAIN IDEAS

Answer the following questions. Support your answers with evidence from the chapter.

8. How did the issue of civil rights divide Democrats at their 1948 convention? **LESSON 1.1**

9. By writing about his own experience of living in the United States as an African-American man, what did James Baldwin hope to accomplish? **LESSON 1.2**

10. How did the definition of equal rights change after the Supreme Court issued the *Brown* decision? **LESSON 1.3**

11. How did the Montgomery African-American community react to the arrest of Rosa Parks, and what was the arrest's effect? **LESSON 2.1**

12. In what ways do the teachings of Gandhi still affect the civil rights movement today? **LESSON 2.2**

13. What impact did the Greensboro sit-in have across the South? **LESSON 2.2**

14. How did Dr. King respond to the letter titled "A Call for Unity" written by white ministers in Birmingham? **LESSON 2.3**

15. How was the March on Washington a key event in the evolution of the civil rights movement? **LESSON 2.5**

HISTORICAL THINKING

Answer the following questions. Support your answers with evidence from the chapter.

16. **IDENTIFY PROBLEMS AND SOLUTIONS** What was the role of various civil rights organizations in influencing public opinion and achieving civil rights legislation?

17. **DESCRIBE** Who were some of the leaders of the civil rights movement, and what were their contributions?

18. **SYNTHESIZE** Why was the civil rights movement able to gain momentum during the 1950s and into the 1960s?

19. **EVALUATE** What were the goals and strategies of the civil rights movement, and how did change affect those goals?

20. **DRAW CONCLUSIONS** Describe the strategy civil rights lawyers used to end segregation in education.

INTERPRET VISUALS

Pulitzer Prize-winning cartoonist Bill Mauldin drew this cartoon in 1960, six years after the Supreme Court's *Brown* v. *Board of Education* decision and five years after the court ordered that desegregation of public schools should proceed "with all deliberate speed."

INCH BY INCH

21. What point is the cartoonist making about segregation in schools?

22. What details from the cartoon support this point of view?

ANALYZE SOURCES

In his January 1963 inaugural speech, Alabama governor George Wallace defied the civil rights movement and federal efforts to end discrimination and segregation in his state.

Today I have stood, where once Jefferson Davis stood, and took an oath to my people. It is very appropriate then that from this Cradle of the Confederacy, this very Heart of the Great Anglo-Saxon Southland, that today we sound the drum for freedom as have our generations of forebears before us done, time and time again down through history. Let us rise to the call of freedom-loving blood that is in us and send our answer to the tyranny that clanks its chains upon the South. In the name of the greatest people that have ever trod this earth, I draw the line in the dust and toss the gauntlet before the feet of tyranny and I say: segregation today, segregation tomorrow, segregation forever.

23. What is Wallace referring to when he says "the tyranny that clanks its chains upon the South," and does this statement show bias?

CONNECT TO YOUR LIFE

24. **EXPOSITORY** The civil rights protesters you've read about risked their safety to achieve equal rights. Write a short paragraph describing a cause you would march for, and explain why the cause is important.

- List causes that are important to you, and if necessary, research them online.

- Decide which cause you listed is most important by evaluating how society would be affected if the cause were not supported.

- State your main idea clearly at the beginning of the paragraph.

- Provide a concluding sentence that summarizes the importance of the cause.

REFORM IN THE 1960S

1960–1968

HISTORICAL THINKING What challenges did Americans face during the 1960s?

In October 1960, three weeks before being elected the 35th president of the United States, Senator John F. Kennedy campaigned in a parade in New York City. Kennedy and his wife, Jacqueline, charmed voters with their friendliness and energy. The couple were known as Jack and Jackie.

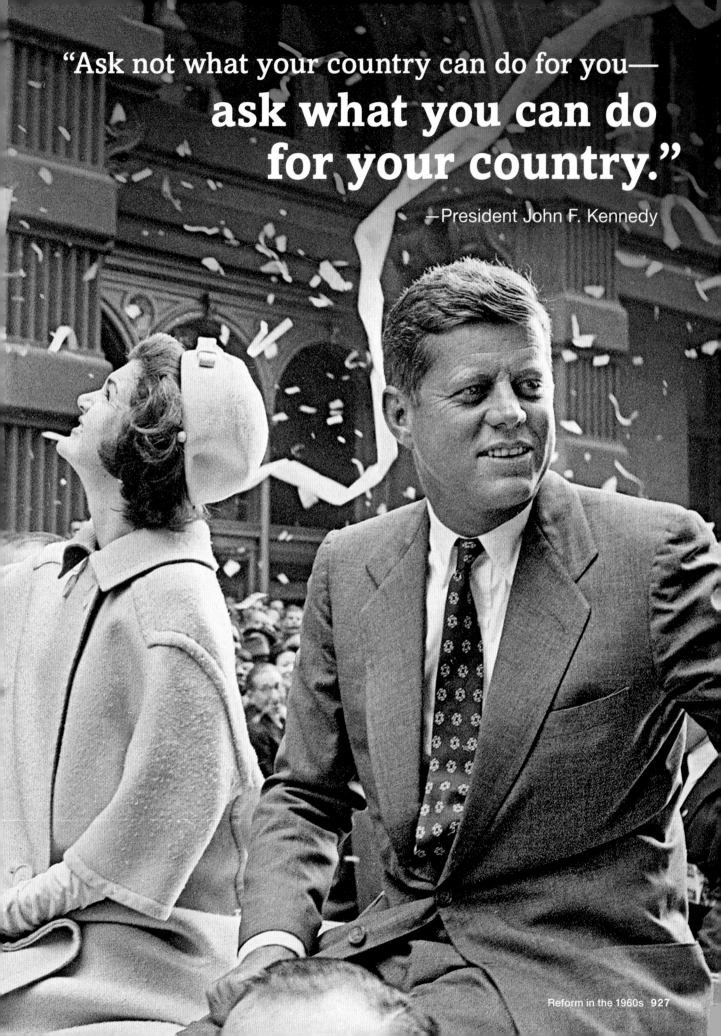

"Ask not what your country can do for you—
ask what you can do
for your country."

—President John F. Kennedy

KENNEDY'S EARLY CHALLENGES

When you commit to something, you know how important it is to follow through. In 1960, both presidential candidates promised to fight communism aggressively. John Kennedy won the election and had to act quickly on his commitment.

THE 1960 ELECTION

In the previous chapter, you read about John F. Kennedy's fight for the civil rights movement. Before that battle, he had fought hard to become president. In the 1960 election, both presidential candidates were tough, hard-driving campaigners. The Republicans ran Eisenhower's vice president Richard M. Nixon against then-Senator John Kennedy, the Democratic candidate. The men were the first two presidential candidates born in the 20th century, and both had entered Congress in 1946 after serving as junior naval officers during World War II.

But that was where the similarities ended. Nixon, 47, had grown up in modest circumstances. His Quaker parents ran a grocery store in Whittier, California, near Los Angeles, where Nixon worked as a boy. After his service in the Navy, Nixon's political rise was swift, helped by his strong stance against communism. Nixon then went on to win a U.S. Senate seat in 1950 after accusing his Democratic opponent, Helen Gahagan Douglas, of being "soft on communism." From 1953 to 1960, Nixon served as vice president, where he emerged as a vocal leader of the Republican Party.

John Kennedy, on the other hand, grew up in Boston, a child of wealth and privilege. A Catholic, Kennedy attended the finest private schools and graduated from Harvard University. Though he was elected to Congress in 1946 and to the Senate in 1952, Kennedy did not really stand out as a legislator. Nonetheless,

CRITICAL VIEWING On September 26, 1960, Kennedy and Nixon met in the first-ever televised presidential debate. What details in the photos convey how the two men might have come across to voters watching on television?

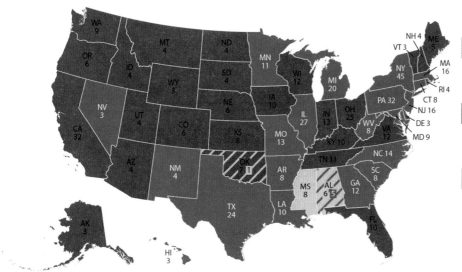

The 1960 Election

John F. Kennedy, Democrat
Electoral Vote: 303 votes, 56.5%
Popular Vote: 34,227,096, 49.7%

Richard M. Nixon, Republican
Electoral Vote: 219 votes, 40.75%
Popular Vote: 34,107,646, 49.6%

Harry Byrd, Democrat*
Electoral Vote: 15 votes, 2.75%
Popular Vote: 0, 0%

*Although he was not formally a candidate, electors in three states cast votes for Democratic Senator Harry Byrd.

he showed a desire to run for higher office. In 1956, he was nearly chosen to be the Democratic vice presidential candidate. Over the next four years, Kennedy traveled the country with his wife, Jacqueline, to build support for a 1960 presidential run. The couple drew crowds wherever they went.

For his running mate, Nixon chose Henry Cabot Lodge, Jr., a respected politician who served in the Senate and as U.S. ambassador to the United Nations. Like Kennedy, Lodge was from Massachusetts, and Nixon hoped his roots in the Northeast would help make the Republican ticket competitive in Kennedy's home region. Meanwhile, Kennedy surprised almost everyone by selecting Senator Lyndon Johnson, a longtime rival, as his running mate. Johnson was a Texan who held liberal political views. Kennedy felt Johnson, as a Texan, could help win votes in the conservative South without losing votes in the more liberal North.

Nixon campaigned largely on Eisenhower's record, reminding Americans that the United States was prosperous and at peace. Kennedy attacked that record without criticizing the popular Eisenhower directly. He portrayed the United States as reacting too slowly to a changing world and promised new leadership "to get the country moving once again." Kennedy had two main obstacles to overcome: a prejudice against Catholics that ran through U.S. history, and his inexperience—he was 43 years old. Kennedy addressed the religion issue in a powerful speech in the fall of 1960 in which he vowed to uphold the constitutional separation of church and state. He dispelled much doubt about his inexperience during a series of debates with Nixon.

For the first time in a presidential election, the debates were televised, which benefited Kennedy.

The first debate had the greatest impact, as more than 80 million Americans watched on television or listened by radio. Though both candidates spoke well, the handsome, well-groomed Kennedy radiated confidence and charm on the TV screen, while Nixon appeared awkward and ill at ease.

Kennedy won the election, but the popular vote was the closest since the presidential election of 1888. A difference of several thousand votes in Texas and Illinois, where there were charges of **voter fraud**, or illegal manipulation of ballots, would have given the election to Nixon.

TROUBLE IN CUBA

President Kennedy charged into office in 1961 with ambitious plans both at home and abroad, and with increased powers in response to the Cold War. He immediately had to focus on a growing foreign policy crisis. The threat of communism had emerged on the small island nation of Cuba, just 90 miles south of Florida. In 1959, a year before Kennedy's election, communist revolutionaries led by **Fidel Castro** had overthrown Fulgencio Batista, the dictator of Cuba. Castro seized control of most of the country's industries and drove out foreign investors. Those investors, many of whom were Americans, lost millions of dollars. Thousands of Cubans who had supported Batista fled to the United States, mostly to Florida. They settled largely around Miami, where they would help shape the culture and politics of the region for years to come.

Castro quickly joined the Soviet bloc, establishing economic and military ties with the Soviet Union. Americans responded with alarm, as they now faced an ally of the Soviet Union located just off their shores. Soviet leader **Nikita Khrushchev** (nih-KEE-tuh KROOsh-chehf) warned the United

States not to interfere with Cuba, promising to defend his new ally with nuclear weapons, if necessary. In response, the United States issued a trade embargo against Cuba.

THE BAY OF PIGS

As tensions grew between the United States and Cuba, Kennedy put into action a plan developed by the Eisenhower administration to overthrow Castro's government. The covert, or secret, plan called for anti-Castro exiles, trained and equipped by the CIA, to invade Cuba and trigger an anticommunist revolution. On April 17, 1961, 1,500 exiles waded ashore at the **Bay of Pigs**, on Cuba's southern coast. The attack fell apart almost immediately. The landing site contained sharp coral reefs and swampy terrain, making it hard to unload supplies and move out from the beaches. In addition, Cuban intelligence already knew of the plan from gossip among Cuban exiles in Miami. Cuban forces fired on the invaders as they came ashore. More than 100 of the anti-Castro exiles were killed, and most of the rest were captured.

The invasion was a humiliating defeat for the United States. American aggression in the region angered Cubans and other Latin Americans and drove Castro even closer to the Soviet Union. After reviewing the events with his advisors, Kennedy took a walk on the White House lawn. It was "the first time in my life," a friend recalled, "that I ever saw tears come to his eyes." Nonetheless, the president continued trying to overthrow Castro. During his administration, he approved a top-secret program, code-named Operation Mongoose, intended to topple the Cuban government and assassinate its leaders. U.S. officials also devised plans to destroy Cuba's vital sugar crop and even send a box of exploding cigars to Castro. The plans never materialized. In hindsight, one Kennedy aide called the overall effort against Cuba "an expensive and embarrassing failure."

THE BERLIN WALL

Shortly after the Bay of Pigs, Kennedy faced another communist challenge, this time in Europe. As you have read, following World War II, Germany was divided into democratic West Germany and communist East Germany. Berlin, the capital of Germany and its largest city, was located entirely within East Germany and itself was divided into three Western-occupied zones that made up West Berlin, and East Berlin, a Soviet-occupied zone. By the early 1960s, the division of Berlin was proving an embarrassment to Khrushchev. West Berlin thrived as a model of democracy and capitalism, while East

PRIMARY SOURCE

There are many people in the world who really don't understand, or say they don't, what is the great issue between the free world and the communist world. Let them come to Berlin. There are some who say that communism is the wave of the future. Let them come to Berlin. And there are some who say in Europe and elsewhere we can work with the communists. Let them come to Berlin. And there are even a few who say that it is true that communism is an evil system, but it permits us to make economic progress. Lass' sie nach Berlin kommen. *Let them come to Berlin.*

—from President John F. Kennedy's "Ich bin ein Berliner" speech, June 26, 1963

Berlin was communist. Each day, more than 1,000 refugees from East Berlin poured into West Berlin seeking a better life. As a result, East Germany was losing many skilled workers to the West.

In August 1961, East German officials constructed a wall of concrete that encircled West Berlin. Intended to stop the migration from East Berlin and from surrounding East Germany to West Berlin, the **Berlin Wall** stretched 27 miles and divided the city in two. It stopped the flow of refugees across the border and for decades would stand as a symbol of the division between the **Western bloc** and the **Soviet bloc** nations of Europe. The presence of the wall heightened the anxiety of the Cold War.

Kennedy chose not to challenge the building of the Berlin Wall, but he did make a historic visit to the site in June 1963. Thousands of West Berliners greeted him with flowers and confetti. In a brief speech to a crowd of 120,000 people, Kennedy praised the city and declared his solidarity with its citizens. "Today," he declared, "Ich bin ein Berliner (I am a Berliner)!"

HISTORICAL THINKING

1. **READING CHECK** Why did the United States launch the Bay of Pigs invasion? Why did the mission fail?

2. **EVALUATE** Using text evidence, explain how you think historical events influenced Kennedy's decision not to challenge the building of the Berlin Wall.

3. **DRAW CONCLUSIONS** What did the Berlin Wall seem to say about life under communism?

4. **INTERPRET MAPS** Examine the 1960 election map. Why would Nixon have won the election if he had won Illinois and Texas?

CRITICAL VIEWING Built around 1790, the Brandenburg Gate served as a monument at an entry point to the city of Berlin. When Berlin was divided, the gate was on the border, barely within East Berlin, as shown in the top photo from around 1965. In the 1981 photo below, a West Berlin policeman patrols in front of a sign that reads, "Caution: You are leaving West Berlin." What do the photos reveal about people's feelings about the division of East and West Berlin?

KENNEDY EMBRACES PROGRESS

"The Best and the Brightest" was the nickname some observers gave to John Fitzgerald Kennedy's administration. Young, well-educated, and full of new ideas, his team was eager to make its mark and continue moving the nation forward.

THE NEW FRONTIER

Kennedy's ambitious presidential agenda became known as the **New Frontier**, a reference to a new decade and new opportunities awaiting the nation. Kennedy believed that creative problem solving could help the United States win friends overseas, resolve economic challenges at home and abroad, and achieve scientific and technological feats only imagined by others.

Kennedy's administration shared the president's optimism and confidence in problem solving. The new secretary of state, Dean Rusk, came from the Rockefeller Foundation, while the new defense secretary, Robert McNamara, had resigned as president of the Ford Motor Company so he could help restructure the nation's armed forces. You might recall that Kennedy chose his younger brother Robert Kennedy to serve as his attorney general.

SUCCESS AND SETBACK

A key domestic priority for Kennedy and his team was re-energizing the U.S. economy. Economic growth in the Eisenhower years had been steady but increasingly slow. Real wages for an average family rose a remarkable 20 percent in the 1950s. However, a series of recessions toward the end of Eisenhower's second term prompted a drop in factory production and a rise in unemployment. By the time Kennedy took office, more Americans were out of work than at any other time since the end of World War II. In 1961, Kennedy devised an economic plan that called for a major tax cut for consumers and businesses. He hoped the tax cut would boost the economy by encouraging both individuals and businesses to spend more. The plan successfully achieved low unemployment, stable prices, and steady growth. He pushed through Congress increases in various Social Security benefits, including an increase in the minimum monthly retirement benefit from $33 to $40. Kennedy also asked for and received a raise in the minimum wage, from $1 to $1.25 an hour.

Congress did not support all of Kennedy's plans, however. It defeated a number of the president's proposals, including an effort to increase education spending for school construction and higher teacher salaries. For the most part, Kennedy moved cautiously in pushing his domestic agenda, including the push for civil rights, as you have read. Since he had won the election by a slim margin, he lacked the widespread popularity that might have enabled him to do more.

In addition, Republicans and conservative southern Democrats in Congress were largely opposed to expanding the power and reach of the federal government. Kennedy understood this, so he picked his battles carefully and only pushed on those proposals he thought were most critical. One of them was a civil rights bill designed to strengthen the weak bills that had passed in 1957 and 1960. The new bill would eventually pass and would become an important step toward achieving equal rights for all.

STRENGTHENING FRIENDSHIPS

President Kennedy bypassed Congress to implement one of his most famous and lasting programs. On March 1, 1961, Kennedy issued an executive order, or a legally binding directive from a president, to create the **Peace Corps** and named R. Sargent Shriver, the husband of Kennedy's sister Eunice, as its director. The first group of 51 Peace Corps volunteers arrived

A GLOBAL PERSPECTIVE The Peace Corps proved to be one of Kennedy's most successful and long-lasting endeavors. By 2016, the Peace Corps had sent more than 220,000 volunteers to 140 nations throughout the world. In Cambodia in 2014, a volunteer helps villagers develop safe and nutritious food practices, including managing gardens and preparing healthy meals.

in Accra, the capital of the African nation of Ghana, in August 1961, to serve as teachers. Within 6 years, the Peace Corps sent thousands of American volunteers to 55 underdeveloped nations, or nations with a low standard of living compared with other nations, to provide educational and technical assistance.

With a tiny budget, the Peace Corps became one of Kennedy's great triumphs, showcasing American idealism and know-how throughout the world. A geopolitical consequence of the Cold War, American leaders viewed the Peace Corps as not only a humanitarian program, but also a vital tool in the fight against communism. By spreading American goodwill and improving living conditions in underdeveloped nations, the president and others hoped the Peace Corps would help prevent countries from embracing communism.

With this same goal in mind—winning more allies and undermining communism—the Kennedy administration worked to strengthen its Latin American policy. During the 1940s and 1950s, the United States had focused primarily on assisting Europe and confronting the Soviet Union, resulting in a weakening of relationships with Latin American countries. After seeing Cuba turn communist, however, American leaders moved to improve relations with the larger Latin American world. In 1961, Kennedy persuaded Congress

With John Glenn standing beside him, President Kennedy (left) looks inside *Friendship 7* in 1962, after Glenn's historic mission to orbit the earth.

carefully selected seven men for the first class of American astronauts, or space travelers. These astronauts trained for nearly two years as part of Project Mercury. The scientists' primary goal for Project Mercury was to send a manned spacecraft into orbit around the earth. Doing so naturally entailed the astronauts returning to Earth unharmed, with their spacecraft intact. While in space and afterward, scientists closely monitored the physical effects of space travel on the astronauts' bodies, gathering data to improve safety and technology for future launches.

By the time Kennedy took office, both countries were making bold advances into space—and captivating the world. In April 1961, Soviet cosmonaut—the Russian term for *astronaut*—Yuri Gagarin orbited Earth in less than two hours. A month later, American Alan Shepard rocketed 300 miles from Cape Canaveral into space. In February 1962, American John Glenn achieved the historic feat of orbiting Earth three times aboard *Friendship 7* before splashing down in the Caribbean Sea. Glenn became a national hero, celebrated with ticker-tape parades and a televised address before a joint session of Congress.

Throughout the 1960s, astronauts were cheered as heroes and celebrities as the media closely followed space-race developments. The space race would have a huge impact on the world, producing dramatic scientific and technological advances with far-reaching applications in a surprisingly short amount of time.

to fund the **Alliance for Progress**, an aid program to improve education, health, and economic conditions in Latin America. During its first year alone, the program provided more than $1 billion in aid to various countries. The effort achieved mixed results. Some corrupt leaders misspent the money, and communism ultimately gained a foothold in some Latin American countries. In the end, however, houses, schools, electrical grids, roads, and hospitals were built, and children fed.

THE SPACE RACE

One of Kennedy's boldest proposals involved expansion of the space program. Shortly after taking office, the president declared the United States would put a man on the moon before the end of the decade, and he persuaded Congress to allocate between $7 billion and $9 billion for space research.

As with many of his other initiatives, the Cold War drove Kennedy's push for technological development in space travel. In addition to their arms race, the United States and Soviet Union engaged in a **space race**, or the Cold War rivalry between the United States and the Soviet Union to see who would dominate in its ability to travel in and collect data from space.

The competition had begun in the late 1950s, after the Soviets launched the first satellite, *Sputnik 1*, and President Eisenhower responded with the creation of NASA to advance space exploration. In 1959, NASA

HISTORICAL THINKING

1. **READING CHECK** What important roles did the Peace Corps serve in the context of the Cold War?

2. **DRAW CONCLUSIONS** Why might some people consider the Alliance for Progress a failure despite its successes?

3. **FORM AND SUPPORT OPINIONS** How was Kennedy both bold and cautious in promoting his presidential agenda? Support your opinion with evidence from the text.

4. **MAKE CONNECTIONS** What effects did the space race have on society and the economy?

Sputnik 1

THE **SPACE** RACE

SOVIET UNION

UNITED STATES

1957

OCT. 4 *Sputnik 1*, the first satellite, launches into orbit.

NOV. 3 *Sputnik 2* launches "space-dog" Laika, who died during the mission, into orbit.

DEC. 6 America attempts to launch the Vanguard TV3 satellite, but the rocket explodes on the launchpad.

1958

MAY 15 *Sputnik 3* is successfully launched, after a failed attempt in April of that year.

JAN. 31 *Explorer 1* becomes the first American satellite to reach orbit.

JULY 28 The National Aeronautics and Space Administration (NASA) is established.

1959

JAN. 4 *Luna 1* becomes the first satellite to reach heliocentric orbit.

SEPT. 14 *Luna 2* is the first man-made object to reach the moon.

FEB. 17 *Vanguard 1*, the first solar-powered satellite, is launched.

1960

AUG. 19 *Sputnik 5* launches "space-dogs" Strelka and Belka into orbit; they are the first living creatures to survive a space voyage.

APRIL 1 *TIROS 1*, the first weather observation satellite, is put into orbit.

1961

APRIL 12 Cosmonaut Yuri Gagarin becomes the first human in space.

MAY 5 Alan Shepard becomes the first American astronaut in space.

MAY 25 President Kennedy announces the United States will land a man on the moon by the end of the decade.

1962

APRIL 12 Cosmonaut Andriyan Nikolayev orbits Earth 64 times aboard *Vostok 3* to test the endurance of humans and spacecraft.

FEB. 20 Astronaut John Glenn becomes the first American to orbit Earth.

1963

JUNE 16 Cosmonaut Valentina Tereshkova becomes the first woman in space.

JULY 19 *X-15*, the first reusable piloted spacecraft, is launched. The craft goes on to complete 15 successful missions.

1964

OCT. 12 With 3 cosmonauts aboard, *Voskhod 1* becomes the first spacecraft to carry a multiperson crew into orbit.

AUG. 19 *Syncom 3*, the first satellite to achieve geostationary orbit, is launched.

1965

MARCH 18 Cosmonaut Alexey Leonov takes the first spacewalk.

JUNE 3 Astronaut Ed White becomes the first American to perform a spacewalk.

1966

FEB. 3 The *Luna 9* probe achieves the first soft landing on the moon, and sends back the first photographs from the moon's surface.

JUNE 2 *Surveyor 1* lands on the moon, sending back photos and data.

1967

OCT. 30 *Cosmos 186* and *Cosmos 188* are successfully docked in space via Earth-based remote control.

JAN. 27 Project Apollo is temporarily paused when astronauts Gus Grissom, Ed White, and Roger Chaffee are killed by a fire during prelaunch testing.

1968

SEPT. 15 *Zond 5* orbits the moon with worms, insects, and two tortoises aboard. It returns to Earth with all its "passengers" alive and healthy.

DEC. 21 *Apollo 8* launches; astronauts Frank Borman, James Lovell, and William Anders become the first humans to orbit the moon and return to Earth.

1969

JAN. 16 *Soyuz 4* and *Soyuz 5* dock in space and exchange crew members via spacewalk.

JULY 20 Astronauts Neil Armstrong and Buzz Aldrin are the first humans to walk on the moon, while Michael Collins pilots the capsule in moon orbit.

Astronaut Buzz Aldrin sets up an experiment on the lunar surface.

THE CUBAN MISSILE CRISIS

Do you remember a time when you were involved in a compromise—when each side gave up something to avoid a fight or some other negative outcome? In 1962, the United States and the Soviet Union engaged in a tense standoff, and only a compromise would be able to save the world from an impending nuclear war.

THE MISSILES OF OCTOBER

By 1962, Americans were in good spirits. A growing economy and Kennedy's optimism were inspiring the nation. But ongoing Cold War tensions between the United States and the Soviet Union continued to be a threat. In October 1962, those tensions erupted and would put the world at the brink of nuclear war.

The trouble began with rumors, confirmed by American U-2 spy plane photos, that the Soviets were establishing intermediate-range **ballistic missiles**, or rocket-propelled, self-guiding nuclear weapons, in Cuba. In the eyes of Cuban leader Fidel Castro, this was simply a means of defending his nation. As a communist country in the middle of the Western Hemisphere, Cuba felt increasingly isolated and under siege. The Kennedy administration had imposed an economic embargo on Cuba and arranged for Cuba's expulsion from the **Organization of American States (OAS)**, an alliance of Western Hemisphere nations established in 1948, whose purpose is to keep peace among the nations of North and South America. What's more, the United States had already attacked Cuba at the Bay of Pigs in early 1961. Whatever his reasons, Castro was stockpiling nuclear weapons capable of reaching dozens of American cities. U.S. leaders would not stand for such a threat.

A TENSE STANDOFF

Kennedy demanded the Soviets remove the missiles in Cuba. In addition, the president ordered a **naval quarantine**, or blockade of ports, of Cuba to stop the Soviets from delivering more missiles. On October 22, 1962, the president went on television to reassure an increasingly tense nation. The entire world watched anxiously as Soviet ships headed toward Cuba and the U.S. warships enforcing the quarantine. On October 26, Kennedy received a note from Soviet leader Nikita Khrushchev suggesting a settlement. "There is no intention to . . . doom the world to the catastrophe of thermonuclear war," he wrote. "Let us take measures to untie [the] knot."

Khrushchev promised to remove his missiles if the United States pledged never to invade Cuba. Before Kennedy could respond, he received a second note, demanding the United States also remove its missiles on the Soviet border with Turkey. Attorney General Robert Kennedy advised his brother to respond to the first note and ignore the second. On October 27, the president vowed not to invade Cuba if the Soviets removed the missiles. In private, Robert Kennedy assured the Soviets the United States would remove its missiles from Turkey in the near future.

On October 28, Khrushchev accepted the deal. In the end, he had miscalculated the stern American response to the placement of offensive missiles so close to U.S. shores. In fact, many of the president's advisors had recommended a military strike, but Kennedy rejected their advice. Secretary of State Dean Rusk summed up the feelings of everyone in the Kennedy administration: "We [were] eyeball to eyeball, and I think the other fellow just blinked." The **Cuban Missile Crisis**, as it came to be known, had ended, but it left a deep impression. For those two weeks, the world had seemed headed for nuclear war and the real possibility of annihilation for both sides.

PEACEFUL RESOLUTION

Throughout the 1950s, the U.S. government developed a civil defense system to keep American

Cuban Missile Crisis, 1962

- ▦ Range of medium-range ballistic missiles (1,000 miles)
- ▦ Range of intermediate-range ballistic missiles (2,000 miles)
- ◇ Soviet missile sites
- ⋯⋯ U.S. naval blockade
- ← Approaching Soviet ships

Range of intermediate-range ballistic missiles (2,000 miles)

Range of medium-range ballistic missiles (1,000 miles)

CANADA

Boston
New York
Washington, D.C.
Detroit
Chicago
Denver
UNITED STATES
Atlanta
Dallas
Houston
New Orleans
Miami
Havana
CUBA

ATLANTIC OCEAN

PACIFIC OCEAN

Gulf of Mexico

MEXICO

Tropic of Cancer

Caribbean Sea

0   100   200 miles
0   100   200 kilometers

Kidde Kokoon

CANNED FOOD

CANNED WATER

A year before the Cuban Missile Crisis, President Kennedy urged Americans to build fallout shelters for their homes. Promotional photos show the features of one model available commercially in 1955.

THE SECOND VATICAN COUNCIL

On October 11, 1962, 10 days before President Kennedy went on television to explain to the nation the crisis around the presence of Soviet missiles in Cuba, Pope John XXIII (the 23rd) announced the principles of the Second Vatican Council in Rome. The Council called for a new openness in the Catholic Church and for the Church to take a role in promoting peace and social justice worldwide.

As news of the crisis became known, a priest from the Vatican attending a conference on peace in Massachusetts suggested asking the pope to intervene. The White House approved the suggestion, and the pope broadcast a message on Vatican radio begging the two leaders to consider all of humanity and find a peaceful solution to the crisis.

The pope also sent a message personally to Khrushchev asking him to be "the man of peace." Khrushchev agreed to do so and ordered the missiles withdrawn. The Soviet leader was reported to say the pope's message was the only "gleam of hope" in the crisis. In 1963, partly in response to the crisis now past, the pope issued a statement calling for "Peace on Earth," reinforcing that principle of what came to be called Vatican II (2).

leaders and as many American civilians as possible safe in case of nuclear war. Civil defense plans were communicated throughout the nation, through signs in public places and a broadcast communications network that was established to keep people informed should an attack occur. Plans to build large-scale public shelters, however, were put forth and rejected. In their place were signs in public buildings indicating evacuation areas.

But the Cuban Missile Crisis frightened U.S. and Soviet leaders into changing their relationship from brinkmanship to one in which they would work together to manage tensions. The reality of mutual assured destruction seemed to inspire the leaders to consider more peaceful options. In July 1963, officials installed a direct telephone link, known as the "hotline," between the White House and the Kremlin, the residence and office of the Soviet leader. Shortly after, the United States and the Soviet Union joined other nations in agreeing to limits on future development of nuclear weapons. The United States and the Soviet Union began seeking ways to coexist peacefully. While no one denied that significant differences existed between them, the countries both mutually recognized that they could not risk the type of confrontation that could destroy civilization.

Nonetheless, the nation's civil defense system remains active in protecting citizens. When natural disasters such as hurricanes and floods strike, the people affected depend on clear communication and effective evacuation plans and routes. In addition, since the early years of the 21st century, concerns about terrorism have emerged, and civil defense practices appropriate to the new types of threats have been developed.

TRAGEDY IN DALLAS

By 1963, President Kennedy had positioned himself well to run for re-election. He had moved the country forward economically and had proved himself on the world stage. However, not all Americans were behind him. Kennedy's support for the growing civil rights movement particularly angered white southern Democrats. In an attempt to win southern votes, President and Jacqueline Kennedy traveled to Texas—the southern state with the most electoral votes—to campaign in late November 1963. On November 22, as the Kennedys' motorcade passed through Dealey Plaza in Dallas, shots rang out from a window on the sixth floor of a nearby building—a textbook depository, or warehouse, near the motorcade route. Kennedy suddenly slumped in his seat, shot in the head. The motorcade raced to Parkland Hospital, where doctors pronounced the president dead.

Within hours, the police arrested a 24-year-old suspect named **Lee Harvey Oswald**, whom witnesses identified as fleeing the book depository after Kennedy's assassination. Two days later, on November 24, as law enforcement officers were moving Oswald between jails, Dallas nightclub owner Jack Ruby stepped forward and shot and killed him. Ruby claimed he killed Oswald out of a sense of patriotism and extreme distress over Kennedy's death. Ruby died in prison four years later.

With the murder of the prime suspect in Kennedy's assassination, many people suspected the events were all part of a larger conspiracy. The federal government immediately assembled a special group led by Chief Justice Earl Warren to investigate. After spending almost a year sifting through every bit of evidence available on the murders, the **Warren Commission** report concluded that both Oswald and Ruby had acted alone. Despite this conclusion, alternative interpretations of this event are still debated as various theories of the assassination have been proposed. Some blame Fidel Castro, others the Mafia, the Ku Klux Klan, or the CIA. To some, the simple explanation that a deranged man had committed a senseless act of violence and met a violent end himself did not explain sufficiently the death of a president so young and full of life.

Such doubts reflected the depth of shock over Kennedy's assassination. Few other events in the

Three-year-old John Kennedy, Jr., salutes his father, President Kennedy, one last time at the president's funeral, November 25, 1963.

nation's history produced so much bewilderment and grief. Even Khrushchev felt a deep loss, calling Kennedy's death "a heavy blow to all people who hold dear the cause of peace and Soviet-American cooperation." Kennedy had seemed an ideal president: a charming, handsome war hero with a glamorous wife. The reality was different, of course. Kennedy's three years in office saw failures as well as successes, and after his death, evidence emerged of personal shortcomings that raised questions about his character. Still, Kennedy's final months were his most productive, and many supporters felt he would have accomplished even more in a second term.

HISTORICAL THINKING

1. **READING CHECK** What were the origins and geopolitical consequences of the Cuban Missile Crisis?

2. **DETERMINE CHRONOLOGY** Identify in order three major events that occurred between November 22 and November 24, 1963.

3. **INTERPRET MAPS** Based on the map, what part of the United States would be safe from a missile attack from Cuba?

JOHN FITZGERALD KENNEDY 1917–1963

"Let the word go forth from this time and place, to friend and foe alike, that the torch has been passed to a new generation of Americans."—John F. Kennedy

John F. Kennedy, who is often referred to by his initials, JFK, spoke these words at his inaugural address on January 20, 1961. The words were probably meant to energize his supporters and send a warning to his enemies. JFK heralded a new era of youth, vigor—one of his favorite words—and confidence. He embodied all three. Kennedy was the youngest U.S. president ever elected, and he seemed the picture of health. (He wasn't; more on that later.) His confidence was very likely a quality instilled by his family.

In September 1962, JFK addressed a crowd of 40,000 at Rice University in Houston, Texas, with his now-famous speech in which he boldly announced, "We choose to go to the moon."

THE KENNEDY CLAN

Kennedy, as you know, grew up amid great wealth in Boston, Massachusetts. His father, Joseph (Joe) Kennedy, Sr., was a highly successful businessman and held several political positions, including U.S. ambassador to Great Britain. However, Joe, Sr., always felt he had been prevented from achieving higher office as a result of the anti-Catholic animosity in the United States. He vowed his children would overcome that prejudice. Rose Kennedy, the family matriarch, was "the glue that always held the family together," as John once said about his mother. She devoted herself to her brood of four boys and five girls.

The brothers and sisters were close-knit but extremely competitive, especially in sports. Any visitor to the family's summer home in Hyannis Port on Cape Cod had to be ready to take part in a game of touch football. And the game could get rough. John's wife, Jacqueline (Jackie), once broke her ankle while playing—and she was pregnant at the time. After that, she refused to play touch football again. John threw himself into the family games, but the physical activity was often hard on him. He had been a sickly child and suffered from ill health all his life. Nevertheless, Joe, Sr., liked to pit John and his older brother, Joe, Jr., against each other. On a bicycle race organized by their father, the brothers collided, and John had to have 28 stitches. Joe, Sr., wanted his boys to be tough.

The entire Kennedy clan gathered for this 1935 photo taken at Hyannis Port. Seated from left to right: Patricia, Robert, Rose, John, Joseph, Sr., with Edward on his lap; standing from left to right: Joseph, Jr., Kathleen, Rosemary, Eunice (rear), Jean

During World War II, both brothers served in the U.S. Navy. As a lieutenant, John commanded a patrol torpedo boat, PT-109. One night, a Japanese destroyer rammed into the boat in the Pacific Ocean. Two crew members were killed, but 11 others survived the collision, including John. Despite suffering from a bad back, he swam for 4 hours to an island while tugging an injured man with him. They ending up swimming to yet another island in search of food and fresh water. There, John carved a message on a coconut shell and sent it with two scouts in a canoe to the Australian Coast Guard. John was awarded a medal for gallantry. Later, when someone asked Kennedy how he came to be a hero, he replied, "It was involuntary. They sank my boat."

Joe, Jr., flew combat missions over Europe in the war. Then he volunteered to take part in a secret and highly dangerous mission that involved flying a drone loaded with explosives to Normandy, France. The explosives unexpectedly detonated before Joe, Jr., could parachute out of the plane. His death at age 29 was the first in a series of tragedies that plagued the Kennedy family. Some called it a curse. Kathleen, the second-eldest daughter of the clan, died in a plane crash three years later. Before his son's death, Joe, Sr., had hoped to fulfill his political ambitions through Joe, Jr. Now he pinned his hopes on John.

THE CAMELOT PRESIDENCY

John Kennedy may have succeeded beyond his father's wildest dreams. During the 1,037 days of his presidency, as you know, JFK experienced both successes and failures. But he remained a charismatic leader throughout his time in office. His idealism inspired people to believe they really could make their country and the world a better place. The handsome president and his beautiful wife enchanted Americans, who followed their trips and social engagements on television and in the news with avid interest. Women admired Jackie and tried to imitate her sophisticated taste in fashion. When the first lady gave the first-ever televised tour of the White House in 1962 to show the restorations she'd had done, a record 56 million people tuned in to watch.

Americans were also charmed by JFK's wit, which he often directed toward himself. After naming his inexperienced 36-year-old brother, Robert, as attorney general, JFK joked, "I don't see anything wrong with giving Bobby a little legal experience before he goes out on his own to practice law." On a visit to Paris in 1961, as it became clear Jackie was the one the crowds had come out to see, he said, "I do not think it altogether inappropriate to introduce myself. I am the man who accompanied Jacqueline Kennedy to Paris, and I have enjoyed it."

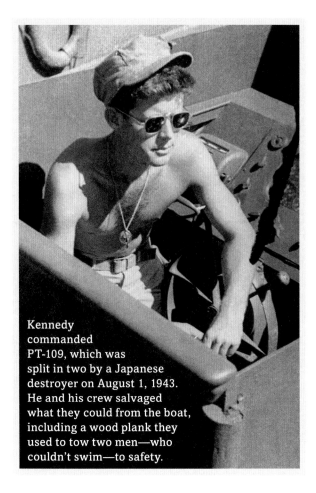

Kennedy commanded PT-109, which was split in two by a Japanese destroyer on August 1, 1943. He and his crew salvaged what they could from the boat, including a wood plank they used to tow two men—who couldn't swim—to safety.

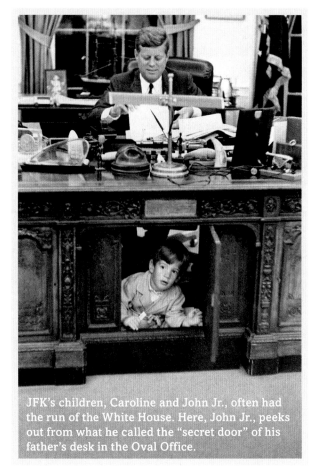

JFK's children, Caroline and John Jr., often had the run of the White House. Here, John Jr., peeks out from what he called the "secret door" of his father's desk in the Oval Office.

Kennedy's presidency would come to be called "Camelot," suggesting that it brought the romantic legend of King Arthur to life. But this characterization masks the anguish that lay beneath the surface. JFK had chronic back pain and suffered from a rare disorder called Addison's disease, which causes severe fatigue and muscle weakness. Jackie had her own pain while she endured her husband's unfaithfulness. Most tragically of all, they both mourned the death of their infant son, Patrick, who died 39 hours after his birth in August 1963.

TRAGEDY AND LOSS

Of course, just a few months later, John Kennedy himself would be dead. Widowed at 34, Jackie planned her late husband's funeral and modeled it on that of Abraham Lincoln. She had a horse-drawn wagon carry Kennedy's flag-draped casket to the White House. Then the mourners followed a riderless horse, with boots symbolically reversed in the stirrups, to the church where the service was to be held. Jackie's strength and dignity throughout the funeral helped the nation cope with its own sorrow.

At the Democratic National Convention held in August 1964, Robert Kennedy took the floor to introduce a short film on his brother's legacy.

But every time he tried to speak, the delegates erupted into applause. This went on for more than 20 minutes. Just about 4 years later, Robert would be cut down by an assassin's bullet, too. John Kennedy's son, John F. Kennedy, Jr., died in 1999 at age 38 in a plane crash. To many, the Kennedy family certainly seemed to be cursed.

In defiance of the curse, however, more than 50 years after his death, John Kennedy remained the most popular president of the post–World War II era. The young president's ideals still capture people's imaginations and hearts. As JFK once said, "A man may die, nations may rise and fall, but an idea lives on."

HISTORICAL THINKING

1. **READING CHECK** How was John Kennedy shaped by his early years?

2. **MAKE INFERENCES** What do the quotations by JFK in this lesson reveal about the man?

3. **ANALYZE CAUSE AND EFFECT** Describe the complex effects the death of Joseph Kennedy, Jr., had on JFK and the country.

4. **EVALUATE** What limitations might prevent you from determining the effects referred to in question 3?

People thronged the streets of Dallas to see JFK and Jackie riding in this limousine on November 22, 1963. John Connally, Jr., the governor of Texas, and his wife, Nellie, rode in the seat in front of them. Moments before JFK was shot, she said to Kennedy, "Mr. President, you certainly cannot say that Dallas does not love you."

President Kennedy's flag-draped coffin moves slowly past mourners on November 25, 1963. The president was buried in Arlington Cemetery, where an eternal flame marks his grave.

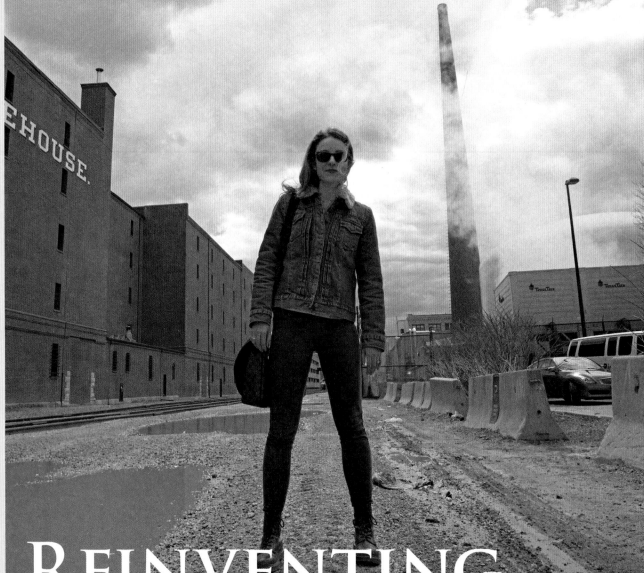

REINVENTING CLEAN ENERGY

"I think I can save the world with nuclear power."
—Leslie Dewan

Leslie Dewan stands out from the crowd—a visionary woman in a male-dominated field. With guidance and input from her female teachers and mentors, and with a nod to history and its lessons, Dewan is determined to develop a cleaner form of nuclear power that will reinvent the definition of clean energy. This carbon-free energy will power the world, and—as a side note—will greatly decrease the production of nuclear waste. It's ambitious, but if it can be done, this National Geographic Explorer will figure out how.

> ^
> As one of the only women in her graduate school classes at the Massachusetts Institute of Technology (MIT), Leslie Dewan, shown here on the MIT campus, learned to take the lead.

MAIN IDEA Leslie Dewan is developing a safer, cleaner alternative to traditional nuclear power.

A NEW SOURCE OF ENERGY

From the beginning of history, humans have used fire to generate power. In fact, as early as 2000 B.C., people burned coal for energy. They later discovered the usefulness of natural gas and petroleum. But as you know, fossil fuels like coal, oil, and natural gas are nonrenewable energy sources. Burning them is believed to have negative impacts on our planet, including air, land, and water pollution. Utilizing cleaner energy sources is a must for the environment.

In 1979, the Three Mile Island nuclear power station in Pennsylvania had the most serious accident in U.S. history. Luckily, the small amount of radioactive material released had no health effects on plant workers or the public.

Although fossil fuels are still widely in use, we now harness the power of the sun, wind, water, and geothermal sources more than ever before to generate power and electricity. Leslie Dewan, an MIT-trained nuclear engineer, National Geographic Explorer, and environmentalist, would like to add nuclear power to that list, but others disagree. The impact on people and the environment that resulted from nuclear disasters at power plants, including Three Mile Island in the United States, Chernobyl in the Ukraine, and Fukushima in Japan, leaves many uneasy. They feel nuclear power is just too dangerous.

Scientists first figured out how to generate nuclear power about 70 years ago. It was exciting at first, imagining nuclear-powered cars, planes, and weapons, and nuclear reactors to generate electricity. At that time, the focus was not on reducing carbon dioxide emissions, but on gaining energy independence from other countries.

As you have read, nuclear technology was used during the Cold War to create weapons of mass destruction. The Cuban Missile Crisis brought the world to the brink of nuclear war. After World War II, Americans were acutely aware of the destructive power of nuclear weapons, so the fear of "being nuked" during the Cold War led people to build bomb shelters and practice nuclear attack drills.

Decades later, highly publicized nuclear disasters gave people the impression that nuclear power was more dangerous than useful. Serious failures did occur, and they were disastrous—in the case of Chernobyl, a whole continent was affected. There were also serious concerns about technology and safety. In its rush to develop reactors, the United States built reactors similar to those designed for nuclear submarines instead of developing ones better suited for land. Nearly all of the reactors still in use in this country today are submarine-style reactors.

SAFER NUCLEAR REACTORS

That's where Dewan comes in. She's designing a safer, more efficient alternative to today's nuclear reactors, and says, "I want to come up with new technology that keeps the good elements of nuclear power but solves the bad aspects." Dewan and her colleague, Mark Massie, developed a new design for a molten salt reactor, initially intended for nuclear-powered airplanes. Ideally, their reactors would leave behind less than half as much nuclear waste as existing reactors, and produce enough energy to power the world for decades. Dewan hopes to develop a prototype by 2020 and a commercial reactor by the 2030s.

Currently, nuclear power provides 10 percent of the world's electricity and 45 percent of the world's fossil-free electricity. Dewan believes nuclear energy will move the world away from fossil fuels and offer dramatic reductions in carbon dioxide emissions. She notes, "I think the world needs nuclear power, alongside solar, wind, hydro, and geothermal, if we want to have any hope of reducing fossil fuel emissions and preventing global climate change."

HISTORICAL THINKING

1. **READING CHECK** What problem is Dewan attempting to solve with her development of new nuclear reactor technology?

2. **ANALYZE ENVIRONMENTAL CONCEPTS** How might nuclear technology affect the environment in both positive and negative ways?

EDIFICIO FORTUNA

THROUGH THE LENS

DAVID
GUTTENFELDER

In May 2016, **National Geographic photographer David Guttenfelder** set sail from Miami, Florida, on the first cruise ship to sail from the United States to Havana, Cuba, in nearly 50 years. His images capture Cuba's colorful culture and identity, but also its infrastructure, much of which hasn't been updated since the 1960s when the United States cut off ties. Guttenfelder's photos reveal how, in many ways, time has stood still on this island country until recently.

JOHNSON'S STRONG START

"All I have, I would gladly have given not to be standing here today," Lyndon Johnson said in his first address to Congress. But the job was his, and, while determined to carry on the work started by Kennedy, he still blazed his own path forward.

A SMOOTH TRANSITION

On the night of November 22, 1963, just hours after President Kennedy's assassination, Vice President Lyndon Johnson took the presidential oath of office aboard Air Force One. Lyndon Baines Johnson—popularly called LBJ—was born in a small house in the hills of south-central Texas in 1908. He belonged to a lower social class and an older political generation than Kennedy. And with his down-home style and earthy language, he seemed rather crude to the East Coast newscasters and journalists compared with the media-savvy Kennedy. Yet few people knew more than LBJ about how to get things done in Washington.

Lyndon Johnson was sworn in as president aboard Air Force One before it left Dallas, only 90 minutes after Kennedy was pronounced dead. Crowded into the plane's stateroom, and photographed by White House photographer Cecil Stoughton, were Johnson, Judge Sara Hughes, Jacqueline Kennedy, Johnson's wife Lady Bird, reporters, and Kennedy's staff.

Senator Richard Russell, Jr., a Democrat from Georgia, opposed civil rights legislation for decades and joined the Senate filibuster against the civil rights bill. Illinois senator Everett M. Dirksen, a Republican and a strong supporter of the bill, spoke out to end the long filibuster and debate and move it to a vote.

We will resist to the bitter end any measure or any movement which would have a tendency to bring about social equality and intermingling and amalgamation [mixture] of the races in our [Southern] states.

—from a speech by Senator Richard Russell, Jr., during the Senate filibuster, March 30, 1964

There is another reason why we dare not temporize with [delay] the issue which is before us. It is essentially moral in character. It must be resolved. It will not go away. Its time has come.

—from a speech in the Senate by minority leader Everett M. Dirksen, June 10, 1964

Johnson entered the White House with three decades of political experience in hand. After running the Texas division of the National Youth Administration, a New Deal program, he won a seat in Congress in 1937. By 1949, Johnson had become a master of Texas politics, and used all his savvy to win election to the U.S. Senate. Elected Senate majority leader in the 1950s, he worked with the Eisenhower White House to craft important legislation on defense spending, highway construction, and civil rights. Johnson proved to be such an effective Senate majority leader that some even referred to him as the "Master of the Senate."

He became president under tragic circumstances but moved quickly to restore public confidence through a smooth transition of power. Johnson told Congress, "The ideas and ideals which [Kennedy] so nobly represented must and will be translated into effective action." To provide continuity, he kept Kennedy's team largely intact, persuading Secretary of State Dean Rusk, Secretary of Defense Robert McNamara, and other key cabinet members to stay on.

THE CIVIL RIGHTS ACT

With his political expertise, Johnson was able to win early legislative victories. One of his first presidential acts was to work for the stalled tax cut Kennedy had supported. Like Kennedy, Johnson believed lower taxes would encourage economic growth and reduce unemployment. In February 1964, he signed a measure that cut taxes by $10 billion over the following two years. The economy responded. The GNP rose by 7 percent in 1964 and 8 percent in 1965. Unemployment fell below 5 percent for the first time since World War II. As Johnson predicted, the resulting economic growth also generated greater federal revenues.

Johnson also set about achieving some of Kennedy's civil rights goals. Both Kennedy and Johnson were supporters of civil rights and believed the federal government needed to create laws to help promote greater equality in the United States. As Senate majority leader, Johnson had steered the Civil Rights Acts of 1957 and 1960 through Congress. Just weeks after taking office, Johnson met with Martin Luther King, Jr., and other African-American leaders to assure them of his commitment to a stronger civil rights act—the one Kennedy had proposed in 1963.

At great political risk, Johnson immediately took up the battle for Kennedy's stalled bill. "No memorial oration or eulogy," Johnson said in a speech to Congress on November 27, 1963, "could more eloquently honor President Kennedy's memory than the earliest possible passage of the civil rights bill for which he fought so long." Johnson then successfully persuaded Congress to enact federal programs in civil rights, education, and social welfare.

In early 1964, the House of Representatives, by a vote of 290 to 130, approved Kennedy's civil rights bill, but it hit a wall in the Senate. Southern senators had formed a bloc to oppose the bill. They used the **filibuster**—a strategy in which a small group of senators take turns speaking and refuse to stop the debate or allow the bill to come to a vote—against it. A number of Democratic and Republican senators gathered **bipartisan** support to ultimately end what had grown to an 83-day filibuster. The Senate passed the bill, proving Congress's commitment to civil rights.

On July 2, President Johnson signed the **Civil Rights Act of 1964** into law. The seven-part act was one of the most comprehensive civil rights laws Congress had ever enacted. It expanded the role of the federal government in the fight for civil rights by enforcing desegregation in public schools and prohibiting discrimination in federally funded public programs and in such facilities as restaurants, parks, libraries, and movie theaters. The new law made discrimination in the workplace based on gender illegal, and it created the **Equal Employment Opportunity Commission (EEOC)** to monitor and protect workplace rights. The act prohibited employment discrimination based on race, creed, national origin, and gender. As a result of the Civil Rights Act, women and minorities who faced workplace discrimination could seek assistance from the EEOC.

RESISTANCE IN THE SOUTH

The Civil Rights Act of 1964 met with stiff resistance in the South. One of the most notable examples occurred in Atlanta, Georgia, within a few days of the act's signing. A segregationist restaurant owner named Lester Maddox refused to serve food to three African-American college students, calling them "dirty devils" and "dirty communists" and pointing a gun at them. Some of the white customers in the restaurant threatened the students with ax handles that Maddox kept on hand. A month later, Maddox decided to close his restaurant rather than obey a court order to desegregate it. Maddox went on to become governor of Georgia in 1966.

Dr. Martin Luther King, Jr., stands behind President Lyndon Johnson (seated) to witness the signing of the Civil Rights Act of 1964. Others in the room include Republican and Democratic representatives who voted for the most far-reaching civil rights legislation enacted since Reconstruction.

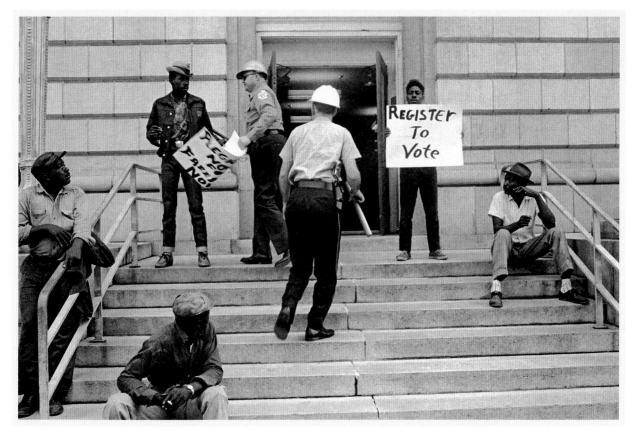

CRITICAL VIEWING In the South, African Americans were still being kept from voting even after the Civil Rights Act was passed. On September 7, 1963, SNCC organized more than 350 African Americans to come to register to vote at the county courthouse in Selma, Alabama. What appears to be taking place on the courthouse steps?

Voting rights gained additional protection in August 1964 when the states ratified the **24th Amendment**, which banned poll taxes. Southern states had required citizens to pay fixed voter registration fees, a strategy used to discourage African Americans from voting. With these landmark laws, the federal government re-established a commitment to providing people of all races, ethnicities, religious groups, and sexes with the rights of full citizenship.

December 1964 brought yet another victory for the civil rights movement. Dr. Martin Luther King, Jr., was awarded the Nobel Peace Prize for his leadership in the movement against discrimination and segregation and his commitment to nonviolence in the effort. In his acceptance speech, he said, "I refuse to accept the view that mankind is so tragically bound to the starless midnight of racism and war that the bright daybreak of peace and brotherhood can never become a reality."

King celebrated the 1964 Civil Rights Act as a tremendous advance in the struggle for racial equality, but believed it fell short in some areas, especially voting rights. The act restricted, but did not prohibit, literacy tests and other tricks white segregationists used to **disenfranchise** African Americans, or take away their right to vote. The tricks proved effective: in many areas of the Deep South, only a small percentage of the African-American population was registered to vote. King and other civil rights leaders chose establishing hard and fast voting rights as their next battle, while Johnson turned to other social and international issues.

HISTORICAL THINKING

1. **READING CHECK** Why did Johnson want members of Kennedy's Cabinet to stay in their current roles?

2. **COMPARE AND CONTRAST** Examine the primary source excerpts in this lesson. How do the senators' points of view differ on the issue of civil rights?

3. **DRAW CONCLUSIONS** How do you think Johnson's experiences in Congress may have helped him get legislation passed as president?

4. **DETERMINE CHRONOLOGY** How did the Civil Rights Act of 1964 build on previous legislation and civil rights activism?

THE GREAT SOCIETY

Do you know someone who can walk into a room and make his or her presence felt right away? To many people, that was President Lyndon Johnson. The president had energy and determination to spare, and he relied on it to work toward many lofty goals.

LANDSLIDE IN 1964

Lyndon Johnson achieved legislative success early on as he worked to accomplish some of Kennedy's goals. Johnson hoped to build on this momentum and enact his own sweeping presidential agenda. First, he would have to hold on to the presidency by winning the 1964 election. Johnson chose as his running mate Senator Hubert H. Humphrey of Minnesota, a likable leader nicknamed "the Happy Warrior," who shared Johnson's goals.

For Republicans, things did not line up so easily. By 1964, the party was facing deep divisions between moderates, who supported the civil rights movement and agreed with a limited expansion of government, and conservatives, who favored smaller government and the use of force to stop communism.

PRIMARY SOURCE

The Great Society is a place where every child can find knowledge to enrich his mind and to enlarge his talents. It is a place where the city of man serves not only the needs of the body and the demands of commerce but the desire for beauty and the hunger for community.

But most of all, the Great Society is not a safe harbor, a resting place, a final objective, a finished work. It is a challenge constantly renewed, beckoning us toward a destiny where the meaning of our lives matches the marvelous products of our labor.

—from a speech at the University of Michigan by President Lyndon B. Johnson, May 22, 1964

After intense debate, Republicans nominated conservative senator **Barry Goldwater** of Arizona for president and Representative William Miller of New York as his running mate. Goldwater's vision for the country couldn't have been further from those of Johnson and Kennedy. In the Senate, he had voted against Social Security increases, the Nuclear Test Ban Treaty of 1963, and the Civil Rights Act of 1964. In accepting the nomination, Goldwater promised a "spiritual awakening" for the United States. He declared: "Extremism in the defense of liberty is no vice. Moderation in the pursuit of justice is no virtue."

The Johnson campaign focused on some of Goldwater's most extreme views to portray him as a dangerous and unpredictable candidate. In one of the most famous television campaign commercials ever, a three-year-old child was shown counting the petals of a daisy, out of order. Her counting turned into an ominous male voice counting down to a launch. The girl disappeared as the viewer saw a missile being launched, followed by the blast and mushroom cloud of a nuclear explosion. The "Daisy" ad, the name by which it became known, implied that Goldwater would destroy innocent lives by leading the nation into a nuclear war. Viewers found the commercial so disturbing that it ran only once.

On Election Day, Johnson won 61 percent of the popular vote and 44 of the 50 states, which translated to 486 electoral votes. Johnson's lopsided margin of victory helped the Democrats increase their substantial majorities in both houses of Congress. Although the Republicans lost ground, the election returns showed that a new coalition was forming in their ranks. The party was gaining strength among middle-class white voters in the South and Southwest. Furthermore, Goldwater attracted thousands of young recruits determined to reshape the Republican Party along more conservative lines. For the growing number of Republicans, 1964 was a beginning rather than the end.

WAR ON POVERTY

President Johnson viewed his landslide victory as a mandate for change. He spoke of creating "a great society" for Americans, one free of poverty, ignorance, and discrimination, where the spirit of "true community" would prevail. Together, his sweeping set of programs became known as the

Great Society. The centerpiece of Johnson's agenda was what he called his **War on Poverty**—an all-out effort to address the persistence of poverty and create a decent standard of living for all Americans. Despite a strong economy, about 20 percent of the nation still lived in poverty in 1964. "We shall not rest until [this] war is won," Johnson insisted. "The richest nation on Earth can afford to win it. We cannot afford to lose it."

Some War on Poverty programs aimed to help children. **Head Start**, for example, was an educational program designed to better prepare low-income preschoolers for primary school. Title I of the

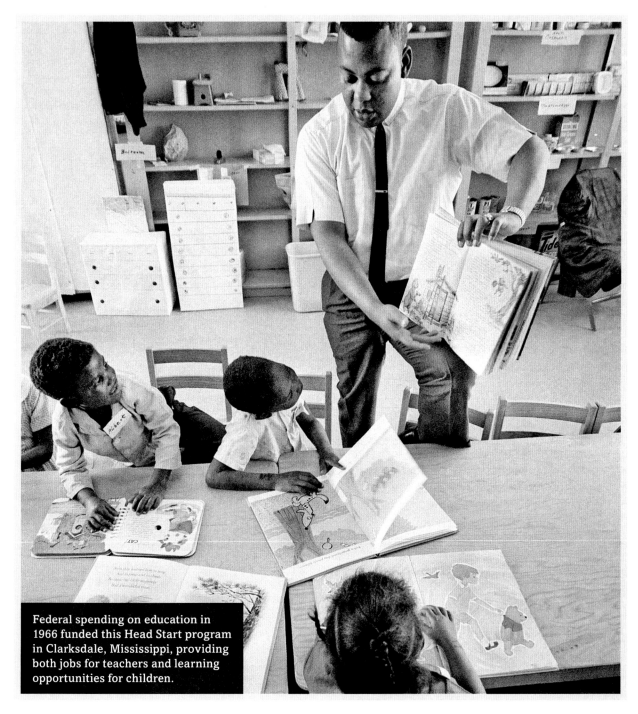

Federal spending on education in 1966 funded this Head Start program in Clarksdale, Mississippi, providing both jobs for teachers and learning opportunities for children.

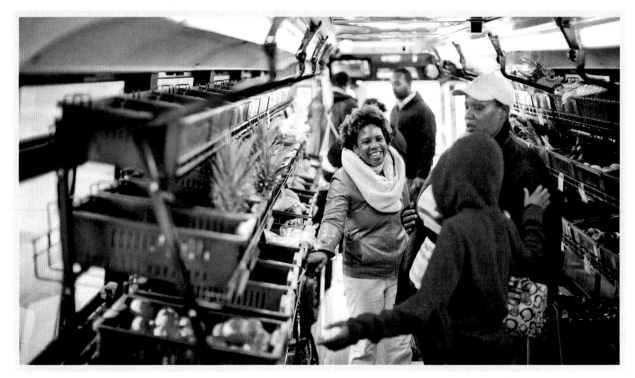

Food stamps help people pay for meals, but low-income neighborhoods often lack supermarkets with affordable healthy foods. In response, a nonprofit organization in Chicago has pioneered the use of buses to bring fresh produce to communities where there are no markets residents can reach easily.

Elementary and Secondary Education Act of 1965 provided extra federal funding to public schools that served a high percentage of low-income students. In addition, the Food Stamp program helped families afford nutritional meals. Johnson himself had experienced poverty and hunger as a child, and those memories drove his desire to help relieve the suffering of others.

As another part of his antipoverty effort, Johnson pushed the **Economic Opportunity Act** through Congress in 1964. The act established a range of programs aimed at creating jobs and battling poverty. The War on Poverty focused attention on community action, which led to an increase of minority participation in local affairs. Johnson named Peace Corps director R. Sargent Shriver to coordinate the numerous work programs created by the act. These work programs included the Job Corps, an education and training program for young people; the Neighborhood Youth Corps, which provided employment, job counseling, and additional education to low-income youth; and Volunteers in Service to America (VISTA), a domestic service program modeled on the Peace Corps.

Overall, the War on Poverty achieved considerable success. It did not eradicate poverty, and some critics have argued that it made impoverished people dependent on the federal government. Nonetheless, poverty declined dramatically in the late 1960s—the result of both the expanding economy and the federal programs aimed directly at alleviating poverty. By 1970, the number of Americans living below the poverty line had dropped from more than 40 million (about 20 percent of the population) to around 24 million (about 12 percent). Over the years, Congress continued to renew many of these anti-poverty programs, most of which are still in place today.

HEALTH CARE AND IMMIGRATION

In addition to tackling the issue of poverty, Johnson believed medical care for all was an essential part of the Great Society. When Johnson took office in 1963, a majority of older Americans, as well as the one-fifth of the nation living below the poverty line, were without health insurance. The American Medical Association (AMA) and private insurers strongly opposed the idea of lower-cost or even free health care, calling it "socialized medicine." The president, however, was determined. After months of intense lobbying, Congress passed landmark legislation that Johnson had requested to fund medical insurance for the neediest Americans. The legislation created two federal programs. **Medicare** provided federal health care assistance to the elderly. **Medicaid** extended medical coverage to welfare recipients.

IMMIGRATION AND CITIZENSHIP, 1960–2015

Source: Migration Policy Institute

Non-U.S. Citizens Granted Permanent-Resident Status by Year, 1963–2013

Immigrants' Regions of Origin

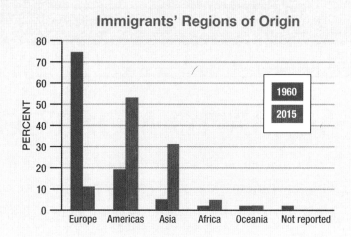

Both programs grew rapidly, reaching as many as 40 million Americans by 1970. Supporters pointed to statistics showing an increase in life expectancy and a drop in infant mortality as a result of the programs. However, opponents argued the programs led to high costs and gaps in coverage, while the quality of care patients received through the programs was low.

The Great Society also included an important new immigration law that went largely unnoticed at the time. In one bold sweep, the **Immigration Act of 1965** removed the national origins quotas as well as the ban on Asians, which dated back to 1924. Although it capped the number of immigrants allowed into the country at about 300,000 per year, the law permitted many foreign family members of American citizens to enter the United States without limit. Immigration from Asia and Latin America grew rapidly. By the mid-1970s, the majority of legal immigrants came from seven Asian and Latin American countries: Korea, Taiwan, India, the Philippines, Cuba, the Dominican Republic, and Mexico. The law had a dramatic impact on the **demographic composition** of the United States, which refers to the number and concentration of a variety of ethnic groups within the nation.

THE DOMINICAN INTERVENTION

The challenges faced by President Johnson and his administration were not confined to domestic issues, however. In 1965, the United States intervened in a civil war in the nearby **Dominican Republic**. The Dominican Republic lies slightly southeast of Cuba and shares the island of Hispaniola with the nation of Haiti.

Until he was assassinated in 1961, General **Rafael Trujillo** (troo-HEE-yoh) had ruled over the Dominican

Republic as a dictator for more than 30 years. Although a brutal leader, he opposed communism, earning U.S. support. His death created a power vacuum, and the government was unstable for several years. In 1965, civil war broke out. In April of that year, Johnson sent in thousands of U.S. Marines, who joined troops from the Organization of American States in an attempt to bring the chaotic situation under control. The official reason for Johnson's action, which became known as the **Dominican Intervention**, was to rescue Americans on the island. However, the actual reason for the intervention was to keep communism from spreading to other Caribbean nations.

The strategy worked. The troops put down the rebellion within a few weeks, and the OAS restored a democratically elected government to the Dominican Republic. While the outcome was positive, Johnson was widely criticized for using American military might to interfere in the government of another nation. This criticism grew as the United States became involved even more deeply in a fight against communism in Vietnam, half a world away.

HISTORICAL THINKING

1. **READING CHECK** What was the Great Society?

2. **ASK AND ANSWER QUESTIONS** Read about cost-benefit analysis in the online Financial Literacy Handbook. Generate a list of questions you could ask to help determine how society benefits economically from the reduction of poverty.

3. **INTERPRET GRAPHS** Which region of the world experienced the largest decrease in immigration to the United States from 1960 to 2015?

SELMA TO MONTGOMERY

For centuries, African Americans suffered cruel and violent oppression. That treatment continued as they marched for voting rights, but as support grew from around the country, glimmers of hope appeared.

MARCHING FOR EQUALITY

As you have read, Dr. Martin Luther King, Jr., viewed the 1964 Civil Rights Act as a victory for racial equality, but he felt it fell short in terms of voting rights. Securing equal voting rights for all, King and other civil rights leaders believed, was the next battle to wage. One place where the fight was already underway was Selma, Alabama, where in 1963 SNCC and other local activists had organized a "Freedom Day." Lines formed around the block as 350 African-American people appeared at the courthouse to register to vote. Facing strong white resistance, the activists asked King and SCLC for support.

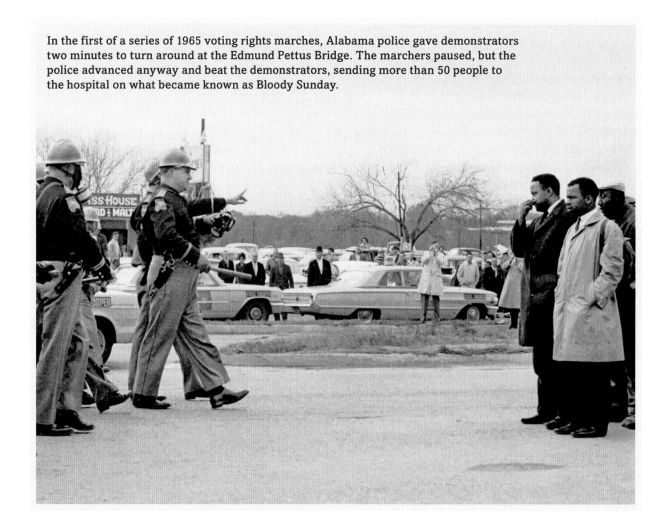

In the first of a series of 1965 voting rights marches, Alabama police gave demonstrators two minutes to turn around at the Edmund Pettus Bridge. The marchers paused, but the police advanced anyway and beat the demonstrators, sending more than 50 people to the hospital on what became known as Bloody Sunday.

Freedom Day led to the Selma voting rights campaign that began early in 1965. Local African Americans marched daily to the courthouse, where Sheriff Jim Clark—wearing a huge button bearing the single word *NEVER*—turned them away with force. Thousands were beaten with clubs, shocked with cattle prods, and arrested for attempting to register with the local election board.

On March 7, a day that would be remembered as **Bloody Sunday**, 700 people set out to walk 50 miles to the state capital on the first of 3 **Selma-to-Montgomery marches**. Leading the procession was a key organizer of the march, **John Lewis**, a representative of SNCC. Upon crossing the Edmund Pettus Bridge at the edge of Selma, Lewis and the marchers found their way blocked by a large contingent of Sheriff Clark's deputies and Alabama state police. When the peaceful marchers refused orders to disperse, the police attacked them with clubs, whips, and tear gas. The police officers forced the marchers to retreat while white onlookers cheered. Dozens of marchers were injured, and some required hospitalization. News crews captured the assault on film. That evening, television stations aired the shocking footage into millions of American homes, sparking national outrage and calls for government action to protect voting rights.

On March 9, a crowd of 2,000 people gathered with King for the second march. Roughly a third were religious leaders who had rushed to Selma to show their support. When they crossed the Edmund Pettus Bridge and again faced a roadblock, the marchers knelt in prayer. Then, instead of attempting to continue on to Montgomery, they turned back. That night in Selma, a group of white segregationists attacked three white Unitarian Universalist ministers who had participated in the march. One of the ministers, James Reeb, died from his injuries two days later.

On March 21, a third attempt at the march to Montgomery got underway, with King leading roughly 3,200 marchers out of Selma. Under the terms of a ruling by a federal judge, more than 1,800 members of the Alabama National Guard under federal command, as well as roughly 2,000 U.S. soldiers, federal marshals, and FBI agents, protected the marchers. The protesters walked about 12 miles each day and slept in fields along the highway at night. Their numbers grew along the way, and on the fifth day, 25,000 marchers arrived at the steps of the state capitol for a final rally.

VOTING RIGHTS ACT OF 1965

In early August 1965, less than five months after the Selma-to-Montgomery marches, Congress passed the **Voting Rights Act of 1965**, and President Johnson signed it into law. The act outlawed literacy tests and other discriminatory tactics used by segregationists to deny African Americans and other minorities the right to vote. It also required states with a history of voting discrimination to obtain approval from federal authorities for any changes, even minor ones, to their voting laws or practices. The act did not ban poll taxes, but it directed the U.S. attorney general to challenge their constitutionality wherever they were found to be in use in local and state elections.

It did not take long for the impact of this **landmark legislation**, or important and historic law, to be felt. By the end of 1965, as many as 250,000 new African-American voters had been registered, and within three years, the registration rate of African Americans in the South had climbed to more than 60 percent. Although challenged in the courts because it changed the relationship of the federal and state governments, the Supreme Court upheld the act's constitutionality in 1966 and in 1968. With the Civil Rights Act of 1964 and the Voting Rights Act of 1965, the civil rights movement had been the most important stimulus in moving the federal government to ensure and protect African-American civil rights, including voting rights.

The movement used grassroots activism to mobilize the government into defending those rights for all citizens. Through the efforts of grassroots organizations and the leadership of presidents Kennedy and Johnson, the civil rights movement made great strides in the 1960s in the South. Discrimination was most visible and dramatic there, but African Americans also faced obstacles in the North, where there was still much work to be done.

HISTORICAL THINKING

1. **READING CHECK** How did the passage of the Civil Rights Act of 1964 and the Voting Rights Act of 1965 affect the nation?

2. **MAKE CONNECTIONS** Describe the role of the government, citizens, and religious leaders in the civil rights movement.

3. **SYNTHESIZE** How did the Selma marches represent the role of civil rights advocates in ensuring the ability of African Americans to vote in elections?

MAIN IDEA Between 1956 and 1968, new African-American leaders emerged who favored militancy and separatism over nonviolence and integration, and King shifted the focus of the civil rights movement to the North.

NEW LEADERS AND CHALLENGES

By the mid-1960s, many African Americans were growing increasingly impatient with the slow pace of racial progress in the United States. Was it time to abandon the nonviolent tactics preached by King in favor of a more militant approach?

SEGREGATION OUTSIDE THE SOUTH

From its beginnings in the early 20th century, the civil rights movement had focused on the South, where African Americans faced blatant discrimination and *de jure* **segregation**—separation enforced by law. In other regions of the country, however, African Americans and other minorities also confronted discrimination, though it was perhaps less extreme than in the South. Northern states had not passed laws mandating racial separation, but it existed anyway. *De facto* **segregation**, or segregation that is present in society despite there being no laws to enforce it, greatly affected urban areas. Many African Americans lived in public housing where crime was rampant, public services were poor, and schools were inferior. Banks often refused home loans to African Americans who sought to buy houses outside their traditional neighborhoods. Many people self-segregated simply to avoid ugly conflicts. And yet conflicts arose and anger was building.

One catalyst for frustration was police targeting of and violence against African Americans. For instance, in August 1965, a white police officer pulled an African-American motorist over on suspicion of impaired driving in the predominantly African-American section of south central Los Angeles known as Watts. African-American drivers were often pulled over and cited for traffic infractions, founded or not. The incident escalated into an argument, which in turn sparked a riot. Rioters looted stores and burned down hundreds of buildings. When police officers clashed with the rioters, at least 34 people died and more than 1,000 were injured. The violent clashes between residents and police, which became known as the **Watts Riots**, continued for 6 days. The following year, similar conflicts rocked Chicago, Detroit, Cleveland, Newark, and other U.S. cities.

THE BLACK POWER MOVEMENT

At the time of these riots, King's leadership in the civil rights movement was coming under increasing criticism due to a split between generations. On one side were "old" civil rights groups, such as King's and the NAACP, which saw racial integration and nonviolent resistance as the keys to African-American advancement. On the other side were "new" movement groups, such as SNCC, who embraced more forceful and even violent strategies.

At a 1966 rally in Mississippi, an activist named **Stokely Carmichael** who had just served time in jail for peacefully protesting, set out to fire up the crowd by yelling about "Black Power." The phrase became a rallying cry for many younger African Americans. To some, it meant group strength and independent action. To the more radical **black separatists**—those like Carmichael who believed in the political and cultural division of African Americans and whites—it meant taking extreme measures to claim their rights and maintain their freedoms. The radicals felt that African Americans should work together to gain economic power in order to create a separate nation within the United States. As you have read, these ideas were central to black nationalism, a movement Marcus Garvey originally embraced in the early 20th century.

One of the most extreme of the "new" movement groups was the **Black Panther Party**, founded in Oakland, California, in 1966 by **Huey Newton** and **Bobby Seale**. Its original mission was to conduct heavily armed patrols to protect African-American neighborhoods from police brutality and harassment. It also began an effective free-lunch program for children, but as the party grew, it evolved into a revolutionary movement that fiercely opposed

THE ULTIMATE JUSTICE OF THE PEOPLE·

CRITICAL VIEWING Black Panther Party members hold a vigil outside a New York City courthouse on April 11, 1969, to protest the arrest of party members accused of criminal activities related to terrorism. The arrested men were acquitted more than one year later. Why do you think the photographer included the Abraham Lincoln quote "the ultimate justice of the people" in the photograph of the Black Panthers?

American society. The Black Panthers demanded that the government release all African Americans from prison and pay reparations for slavery. They won modest support for their community work but lost influence when a few members were jailed for committing crimes such as extortion, or obtaining money through forceful coercion, and drug-dealing. The Panthers became a feared enemy and primary target of local, state, and federal law enforcement. While they never received the mainstream support that the general civil rights movement did, their emphasis on racial pride, their celebration of black culture, and their powerful criticisms of racism continue to influence American culture today.

MALCOLM X AND THE NATION OF ISLAM

Newton and Seale had been strongly influenced by **Malcolm X**, one of the most controversial African-American activists of the 1960s. Malcolm X, born Malcolm Little and later known as el-Hajj Malik el-Shabazz, adopted the "X" to replace Little, the slave name imposed on his ancestors by their slave master. In the late 1940s, while serving in prison for robbery, Malcolm X became a member of the **Nation of Islam**, a religious black nationalist movement founded in Detroit in 1930. The organization preached a doctrine of self-help, moral discipline, and complete separation of the races. Members of the Nation of Islam, also called Black Muslims, were forbidden to smoke, drink alcohol, or eat pork.

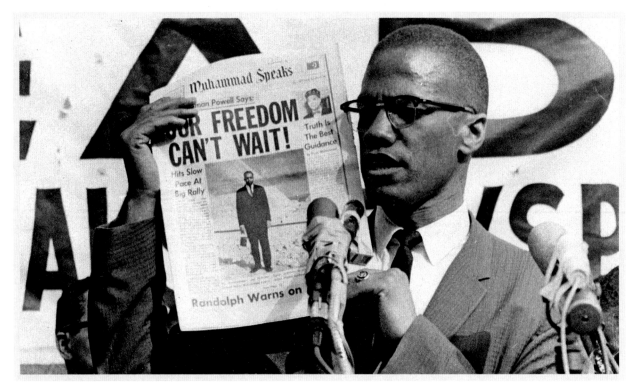

While at a New York City rally, Malcolm X held up the *Muhammad Speaks* newspaper, emphasizing his consistent message: "Our Freedom Can't Wait!"

Malcolm X quickly rose to a position of prominence within the Nation of Islam and helped it to achieve explosive growth. In fiery speeches, he denounced white American society for the injustices it inflicted on African Americans. He also scorned King's tactics of nonviolence and civil disobedience. He preached self-defense, saying that African Americans must protect themselves "by any means necessary" and that "killing is a two-way street." Malcolm X's intense philosophy made it easy to interpret the Nation of Islam's message as one of violence and hate.

In 1963, tensions developed between Malcolm X and **Elijah Muhammad**, the leader of the Nation of Islam, and in early 1964 Muhammad expelled Malcolm from the religion. After making a pilgrimage to the Muslim holy city of Mecca, Malcolm renounced some of the more extreme ideas he had espoused in the past, including racial separatism. Upon returning to the United States, Malcolm continued to speak out against racism and work for change, despite threats against his life from members of the Nation of Islam. In February 1965, they followed through with their threats, assassinating Malcolm X as he gave a speech in Harlem.

THE MOVEMENT MOVES NORTH

As rioting shook northern cities and the Black Power movement grew, Dr. King decided to take the civil rights movement to the North and broaden its scope. He focused his efforts on fighting poverty among African Americans and on opposing U.S. military involvement in the Vietnam War. Speaking in New York City in April 1967, he pointed out the contradiction of sending young African-American men 8,000 miles away "to guarantee liberties in Southeast Asia which they had not found in southwest Georgia and East Harlem."

On April 3, 1968, King led a peaceful march in Memphis in support of a strike by sanitation workers. The following day, while King was standing on the balcony of the Lorraine Motel, a white segregationist named James Earl Ray shot and killed him. The nation mourned the assassination of the civil rights movement's most famous leader. But King's words would have enduring effects on American life as his legacy continued with the work of other supporters, including President Johnson.

The rioting and segregation that had troubled King also troubled President Johnson. Johnson had established the National Advisory Commission on Civil Disorders in 1967, also known as the Kerner Commission, to study the causes of urban riots. He appointed Illinois governor Otto Kerner to lead it. In its report, the commission concluded that the United States was "moving toward two societies, one black, one white—separate and unequal." The report criticized the media for failing to cover the violent

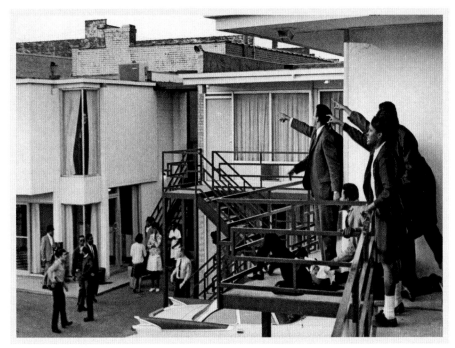

This iconic photograph by South African photographer Joseph Louw was taken immediately after Martin Luther King, Jr.'s assassination on April 4, 1968. King lies on the hotel balcony, bleeding from a neck wound, while aides point to the opposite rooftop where they had seen the shooter, James Earl Ray, fleeing after firing at King.

protests from the rioters' perspective and concluded by stating "the press has too long basked in a white world, looking out of it, if at all, with white men's eyes and a white perspective."

As you have read, Johnson's administration developed strategies for expanding the welfare state and providing a broader safety net for vulnerable Americans as part of his Great Society program. One of these strategies demonstrated the government's commitment to providing education to all Americans. You have read about the Elementary and Secondary Education Act, which Johnson signed into law in 1965. This act provided federal funding to ensure that all children regardless of race, ethnicity, religion, or sex received equal educational opportunities.

Still, schools remained unequal because of *de facto* segregation, so courts ordered **busing**, or transporting students of all races to schools outside their school districts or neighborhoods to assure integration and therefore equal opportunity. Busing sparked controversy and legal challenges. In the 1971 case *Swann v. Charlotte-Mecklenburg Board of Education*, the Supreme Court unanimously upheld busing programs. Three years later, however, in *Milliken v. Bradley* (1974), the Court struck down a plan to desegregate schools in Detroit by busing students between the predominantly African-American city and its predominantly white suburbs.

Supreme Court rulings continued to expand the government's role in supporting civil rights. In the 1967 case *Loving v. Virginia*, the Court cited a violation of the 14th Amendment when it overturned Virginia state laws prohibiting **miscegenation**, or marriage between people of different races. The Court's decision abolished anti-miscegenation laws around the country.

Another strategy of the Johnson administration was **affirmative action**, a government policy that institutes racial quotas to favor groups that suffer from discrimination. The goal of supporters of affirmative action was to improve educational and employment opportunities for all Americans. Like school busing, affirmative action ignited controversy and was challenged in court. In the 1978 case, *Regents of the University of California v. Bakke*, the Supreme Court ruled that affirmative action programs were constitutional in some circumstances but that quotas based solely on race were not.

HISTORICAL THINKING

1. **READING CHECK** In the 1960s, what were some of the challenges African Americans faced in the North?

2. **COMPARE AND CONTRAST** On which issues did the "old" and "new" civil rights activists disagree?

3. **INTERPRET VISUALS** In addition to the headline, what message do you think Malcolm X wanted to convey when he held up the newspaper?

4. **IDENTIFY MAIN IDEAS AND DETAILS** What were the Johnson administration's strategies for fighting segregation and poverty?

National Civil Rights Museum Memphis, Tennessee

The National Civil Rights Museum has a fascinating location: the grounds of the Lorraine Motel, where Dr. Martin Luther King, Jr., was assassinated in 1968 while staying in Memphis, Tennessee. Visitors reflect upon this important historical site while viewing the museum's impressive collection of historic objects, documents, and photographs spanning five centuries of African-American history—from the beginning of the resistance to slavery through the Civil War, Reconstruction, the rise of Jim Crow, and the civil rights movement. The National Civil Rights Museum's exhibits center around African-American history and the quest for racial equality in the United States, but also feature the culture of slavery and international human rights. The museum's mission is clear: to educate, inform, and inspire.

> The museum's four-acre site includes the Lorraine Motel (shown below) and its related buildings and the nearby Young and Morrow Building, from which James Earl Ray fired the shot that killed Dr. King.

Room 306

Dr. Martin Luther King, Jr., was a frequent guest at the Lorraine Motel in downtown Memphis. He stayed there in April 1968 while in town to support a strike by sanitation workers. On April 4, he spent the day at the motel with his brother and aides. When Dr. King stepped onto the balcony outside his room to talk to friends, he was shot in the neck from across the street. Motel owner Walter Bailey never rented room 306 again, turning it instead into a memorial. As part of the museum's collection, room 306 has been preserved exactly as it looked on that tragic night.

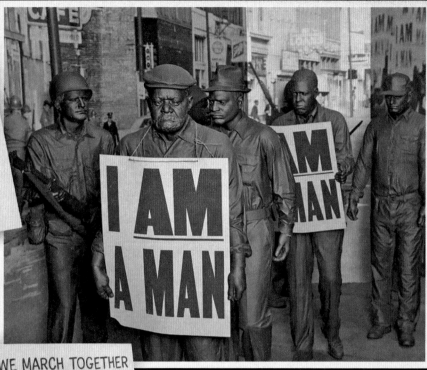

Protest signs from the
museum's 1963 March
on Washington exhibit

"I Am a Man" Exhibit

This museum exhibit tells the story of the 1968 sanitation strike that drew Dr. King to Memphis during what would become his final days. Represented in bronze statues, strikers holding iconic "I am a man" signs—designed to humanize the protesters—appear in front of National Guard troops, while footage from the strike is projected onto a garbage truck. The exhibit also features footage from Dr. King's famous "I've Been to the Mountaintop" speech, which he gave in Memphis the day before his assassination.

Black Panther Jacket

The museum's Black Power exhibit highlights the rise and fall of one of the most influential movements in civil rights history: the Black Panther Party.

The black leather jacket shown here was worn in the late 1960s by Cyril Innis, Jr., of the Corona, New York, chapter of the Black Panthers. The museum's collection also includes a beret and a crossed fist necklace worn by party members. Black Panther Party founders Huey P. Newton and Bobby Seale encouraged members to dress neatly in a uniform consisting of a light blue shirt under a black leather jacket, black pants and shoes, a black beret, and black gloves.

What impact do you think historical events such as the assassination of Dr. King and the fall of the Black Power movement had on the civil rights movement?

VOCABULARY

Use each of the terms below in a sentence that expresses an understanding about an event or topic from the chapter.

1. affirmative action

2. ballistic missiles

3. bipartisan

4. disenfranchise

5. *de facto* segregation

6. miscegenation

7. Medicare

8. New Frontier

9. space race

READING STRATEGY
DRAW CONCLUSIONS

Drawing conclusions can help a reader make connections and better understand the text. Complete the following chart to draw conclusions about how the domestic policies of Kennedy and Johnson affected the United States.

Text Clues	What I Know	My Conclusions
"optimism and confidence in problem solving"	Kennedy developed new programs and approaches.	Kennedy looked forward to the future in responding to problems.

10. How did Kennedy's and Johnson's domestic policies impact the United States?

MAIN IDEAS

Answer the following questions. Support your answers with evidence from the chapter.

11. What were Kennedy's first two challenges? **LESSON 1.1**

12. Why did the Soviet Union build the Berlin Wall? **LESSON 1.1**

13. What was the purpose of the international treaty the United States and the Soviet Union signed in 1963? **LESSON 1.2**

14. What event sparked the Cuban Missile Crisis? **LESSON 1.3**

15. What is the main function of the Equal Employment Opportunity Commission? **LESSON 2.1**

16. How did southern members of Congress try to kill the Civil Rights Act? **LESSON 2.1**

17. What was the collective name of Johnson's reform policies designed to relieve economic inequality in the United States? **LESSON 2.2**

18. What did the Immigration Act of 1965 eliminate? **LESSON 2.2**

19. How was the Civil Rights Act of 1964 different from previous civil rights legislation? **LESSON 2.3**

20. What was the goal of the Selma-to-Montgomery marches? **LESSON 2.3**

21. In what ways did Stokely Carmichael's phrase "Black Power" divide the civil rights movement? **LESSON 2.4**

HISTORICAL THINKING

Answer the following questions. Support your answers with evidence from the chapter.

22. **FORM AND SUPPORT OPINIONS** Using information from the chapter, explain whether and why you think a cost-benefit analysis would have supported continuing the Alliance for Progress program.

23. **ANALYZE CAUSE AND EFFECT** How did the Cuban Missile Crisis ultimately make the world safer, and how could events surrounding it have taken a different direction?

24. FORM AND SUPPORT OPINIONS Would you have agreed with senators supporting the Immigration Act of 1965 or with those opposing the bill? Write a brief paragraph explaining your response.

25. COMPARE AND CONTRAST How were the presidencies of Kennedy and Johnson similar and different in terms of their accomplishments, problems, and impact on larger social, economic, and political trends?

INTERPRET GRAPHS

Look closely at the graph below. Use information from the chapter and in the graph to answer the questions that follow.

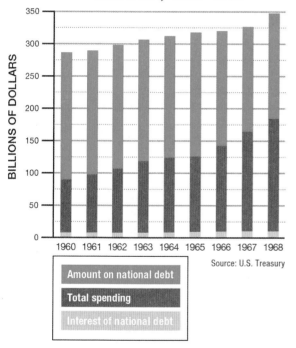

U.S. National Spending and Debt, 1960–1968

Source: U.S. Treasury

Amount on national debt

Total spending

Interest of national debt

26. Based on what you know about programs and issues during the Kennedy and Johnson administrations, how would you explain the trend in government spending shown in the graph?

27. According to the graph, how are changes in spending reflected in changes in the national debt, or the amount of money the government has borrowed, and in the interest on that debt?

ANALYZE SOURCES

The space race was both an idealistic vision and important to national security. Here, in interviews, two of the seven Mercury astronauts, Wally Schirra and Scott Carpenter, express different thoughts about the meaning of the effort.

> The challenge was that Kennedy had made a mess in Cuba at the Bay of Pigs, and he had to do something to look good. The . . . concept of going to the moon and back before the decade was out was quite a goal, which we all accepted, because we loved the man. —Wally Schirra, 2007
>
> I am so overjoyed that the competition has now [changed] into cooperation. Space is not an enterprise that belongs to the United States or to Russia or to China—it is a human endeavor. —Scott Carpenter, 2012

28. What different messages do Schirra and Carpenter convey about the American space program, and what evidence do you see of bias and prejudice in the historical interpretations of these individuals?

CONNECT TO YOUR LIFE

29. ARGUMENT Many people questioned President Kennedy's proposal to spend billions of dollars to put a man on the moon within 10 years. Suppose a president of the United States proposed to commit trillions of dollars to colonizing Mars within 10 years. Write a short argument stating reasons why you would or would not support such an endeavor.

TIPS

- Evaluate the consequences of Kennedy's plan and determine the lessons that were learned.

- Summarize your viewpoint and your reasoning clearly before you present your points in more depth.

- Use textual evidence from the chapter in supporting your argument.

- Include reasons why the United States should or should not invest in such a goal.

- Counter the strengths of the opposing viewpoint with your own position.

HISTORICAL THINKING How did the Vietnam War affect Americans at home and on the battlefield?

"I saw courage both in the Vietnam War and in the **struggle to stop it.**"

—John Kerry, Vietnam veteran
and former secretary of state

In this photo taken in 1971, U.S. soldiers maneuver their tanks through the rugged, mountainous terrain of Quang Tri Province. At the time of the Vietnam War, the South Vietnamese province bordered communist North Vietnam and was the site of several fierce battles. Vietnam's mountains, jungles, and dense forests posed a challenge for American troops throughout the war.

1.1

MAIN IDEA The United States supported the anticommunist government that arose in South Vietnam, but the South Vietnamese leader proved to be a tyrant.

THE COLD WAR IN THE THIRD WORLD

If you've ever fought for a cause you believed was just, you probably encountered some obstacles along the way. The United States would run into quite a few as it tried to halt the spread of communism in Southeast Asia.

After Ngo Dinh Diem formed South Vietnam and made himself its president in 1955, tribesmen from the country's mountains and plateaus came to pledge their loyalty to him. Here, President Diem (seated) receives gifts from the tribesmen.

CONFRONTING COMMUNISM IN ASIA

In the 1950s and 1960s, the U.S. government focused to a large extent on domestic policy, particularly on civil rights for African Americans. But foreign policy and events in Southeast Asia also claimed the attention of several presidents during this period, beginning with Dwight Eisenhower. Remember reading about the victory of Ho Chi Minh's communist forces against the French in the Southeast Asian country of Vietnam? After the decisive Battle of Dien Bien Phu in 1954, a peace agreement negotiated in Geneva, Switzerland, temporarily divided the country roughly in half.

According to the **Geneva Accords**, which detailed the terms of the agreement, Vietnam was split along the 17th parallel. Ho and the Viet Minh governed the northern part of the country, while the French colonial government remained in the south. The accords also called for free democratic elections in 1956, the withdrawal of the French from Indochina, and the reunification of Vietnam under a national government. In 1955, however, **Ngo Dinh Diem** (ungh-oh dihn zih-EHM), the prime minister of the southern part of the country, founded the Republic of Vietnam, or South Vietnam, and proclaimed himself its president. During Ho's anti-imperialist revolution against the French, Diem had lived for a time in the United States.

The United States fully backed Diem and his new government. Eisenhower embraced President Harry Truman's containment policy to prevent the spread of communism throughout Asia. To achieve that goal, Eisenhower believed that an anticommunist government had to be established in South Vietnam, which was considered a "third world" country. During the Cold War, a country that was not aligned with either the United States or the Soviet Union was called a **third world** country. Communist and democratic forces struggled to gain influence over third world countries. The United States used the Southeast Asia

Treaty Organization (SEATO) to justify its increasing involvement in Southeast Asia after the French conceded to the Vietnamese in 1956. You may recall that the United States and other countries, including France, Great Britain, Thailand, and the Philippines, formed SEATO in 1955 to help prevent communist expansion in Southeast Asia. The United States claimed Vietnam as a whole to be a territory that fell under SEATO protection.

DIEM'S GOVERNMENT

Diem had declared that he would uphold democratic principles as stipulated by the Geneva Accords. However, with Eisenhower's support and encouragement, he refused to allow free elections to take place in 1956. Instead, he ruled

This North Vietnamese poster shows two soldiers and a worker standing in front of the Thang Hoa Bridge. In 1945, the Viet Minh destroyed the bridge (nicknamed Ham Rong, or "Dragon's Jaw") to prevent the French from transporting arms across it. The bridge was rebuilt in 1957.

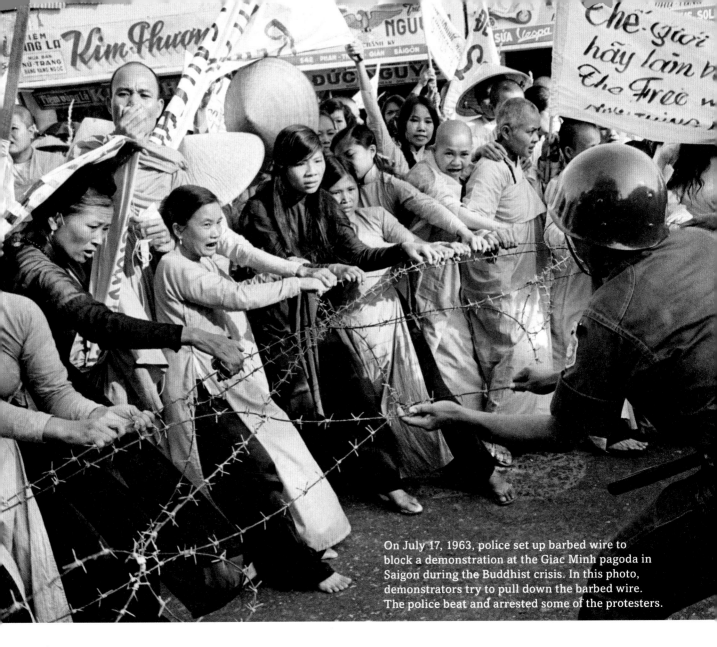

On July 17, 1963, police set up barbed wire to block a demonstration at the Giac Minh pagoda in Saigon during the Buddhist crisis. In this photo, demonstrators try to pull down the barbed wire. The police beat and arrested some of the protesters.

as an **autocrat**, a tyrant with absolute power, and appointed members of his own wealthy family to serve in the highest levels of his government. For example, Diem's younger brother was his chief advisor.

Furthermore, even though the majority of Vietnamese people were Buddhist, Diem, a Roman Catholic, strongly favored those of his own faith. He filled his government with Catholics and retained the anti-Buddhist laws the French had put in place. On the positive side, Diem provided refuge in his country for the hundreds of thousands of Vietnamese fleeing communist rule in the north. However, he dealt harshly with **insurgents**, or rebels, within his country who belonged to the National Liberation Front, or **Viet Cong**. These insurgents tried to spread communism among the South Vietnamese and wage war against Diem's government. Diem put his

younger brother in charge of a special army unit that tracked down communists and imprisoned or killed them. Even those who were only suspected of aiding the rebels—often with little or no evidence—were likely to meet the same fate.

Diem's heavy-handed tactics against the insurgents and his treatment of Buddhists made him increasingly unpopular among the people of South Vietnam. Nonetheless, presidents John Kennedy and Lyndon Johnson continued to support President Eisenhower's domino theory, formulated in 1954. As you may recall, this theory states that if one Southeast Asian country were to become communist, all the rest would follow like falling dominoes. Kennedy and Johnson used the domino theory to explain the presence of the U.S. military in South Vietnam.

THE BUDDHIST CRISIS

Eisenhower began to send military personnel and aid to South Vietnam in 1955. By the time Kennedy became president in January 1961, however, this aid effort had decreased. An anticommunist, Kennedy revitalized the effort and sent 500 Special Forces troops as military advisors to South Vietnam in May. Kennedy ignored the advice of French general Charles de Gaulle, who warned him that war in Vietnam would drag the United States into "a bottomless military and political swamp." The American president continued to send military advisors to South Vietnam until their numbers totaled about 16,000 in 1963.

Meanwhile, Diem's discrimination against Buddhists reached a critical point. On May 7, 1963, government forces angered Buddhists by tearing down the religious flags they hung on homes and buildings in the city of Hue (HWAY). Diem had passed a law against such displays, but up to that point, the law had not been enforced. In protest, a crowd of more than 3,000 Buddhists gathered the next day—on the Buddha's birthday—and marched to the center of town. Later that evening, as the protests continued, soldiers fired bullets and tossed grenades at the crowd, killing 8 people and seriously injuring another 4. Diem blamed the Buddhists for the violence.

Seeking nonviolent solutions, Buddhist clergy presented a list of demands to the government. They asked the government to grant Buddhists the right to display their flags, worship freely, and enjoy the same rights as Catholics. Some Buddhists also staged hunger strikes. Kennedy encouraged Diem to reform his policy toward the Buddhists, but Diem ignored his advice. Finally, in June, 500 monks and nuns gathered in Saigon, South Vietnam's capital. They watched while a monk immolated himself, or burned himself to death, to protest Diem's treatment of Buddhists. A photographer captured the event, drawing worldwide attention to the Buddhists' plight in South Vietnam.

Protests continued throughout the summer, and more Buddhist monks and nuns immolated themselves. Then, on August 21, Diem declared martial law, giving military forces, rather than the police, the authority to enforce order. That night, the military raided Buddhist pagodas in cities throughout South Vietnam. When monks and nuns used sticks and stones to resist the soldiers, many were arrested on charges of possessing weapons.

As the Buddhist crisis continued, the United States began to distance itself from Diem and withdraw its support from his government. When officers in the South Vietnamese Army approached U.S. officials about staging a **coup** (KOO), or an illegal overthrow of the government, the Americans stated they would do nothing to prevent it. According to some accounts, in fact, the U.S. officials even encouraged the action. As a result, Diem was arrested on November 1, 1963, and assassinated the next day.

Diem's death caused political instability in South Vietnam. A series of military leaders followed who, like Diem, never actually instituted a democratic government. As you know, President Kennedy was also assassinated in November 1963. Under President Johnson, U.S. engagement in South Vietnam increased. As in Korea, the United States conducted a proxy war in Vietnam.

HISTORICAL THINKING

1. **READING CHECK** Why did the United States back Ngo Dinh Diem's government?

2. **DRAW CONCLUSIONS** Why did Kennedy suspend financial aid to South Vietnam after the Buddhist pagoda raids?

3. **MAKE INFERENCES** Why do you think the U.S. government did nothing to prevent the coup against Diem?

4. **ANALYZE CAUSE AND EFFECT** What complex string of events led to the assassination of Diem?

GULF OF TONKIN

A challenge by one side in wartime often results in an increase in hostilities by the other side. That's exactly what happened when a perceived threat occurred in the waters off the coast of Vietnam.

Vietnam, 1964

UNOFFICIAL DECLARATION OF WAR

When Lyndon Johnson assumed the presidency after John Kennedy's assassination in 1963, he had little foreign policy experience. As a result, he chose to continue the former president's course of action in Southeast Asia. But he also decided to make Vietnam a priority. Determined not to lose South Vietnam to the communists, Johnson intensified the effort there. For example, he authorized the U.S. military to carry out covert operations in North Vietnam and gather information on communist activity. However, Johnson was opposed to sending American ground forces to Vietnam. As he said, "We are not about to send American boys nine or ten thousand miles away from home to do what Asian boys ought to be doing for themselves." Johnson insisted the ultimate responsibility for resolving the conflict lay with the Vietnamese.

Soon, though, several events made him re-evaluate his position. On August 2, 1964, the USS *Maddox* reported that it had been attacked by a North Vietnamese torpedo boat while patrolling off the coast of northern Vietnam in the Gulf of Tonkin. The U.S. destroyer fought off the attack, and the torpedo boat retreated. Then, on August 4, the *Maddox* and another destroyer, the USS *C. Turner Joy*, reported renewed unprovoked attacks. In response, Johnson ordered an air attack on North Vietnamese naval bases and put the **Gulf of Tonkin Resolution** before Congress. The resolution would give the president the power to take any action necessary to repel armed aggression and defend South Vietnam.

Congress passed the resolution within days. Although the resolution was not an official declaration of war against North Vietnam, it came to be considered as such. Almost immediately, however, some people questioned whether the second attack had actually occurred. After reviewing the often contradictory tape recordings from the incident, even Johnson said that the Vietnamese in the boats were probably just "sailors shooting at flying fish!" Others even believed the attack had been provoked by American forces. Nevertheless, the Johnson administration publicly stuck to its official line, claiming the Vietnamese had been the aggressors.

WAR EXPANDS

Johnson's secretary of defense, Robert McNamara, who strongly championed war, made many of the decisions related to the conflict in Vietnam. In fact, over the next few years, the war would come to be called "McNamara's War." As you may remember, McNamara had been part of Kennedy's Cabinet and continued to serve Johnson after the latter won re-election in November 1964. The secretary favored **escalation**, or

On March 8, 1965, about 3,500 Marines landed in Da Nang to protect its airbase. They were the first U.S. combat troops in South Vietnam. Although both the United States and South Vietnam had wanted the troops to come ashore without fanfare, the Marines were greeted by a cheering crowd.

an increase in intensity, of the war. Under McNamara's advice, Johnson increased the number of military advisors in Vietnam to 23,000 and ordered limited air raids on the Ho Chi Minh Trail, a series of connected paths linking North Vietnam with South Vietnam by way of neighboring Laos and Cambodia.

The war escalated further in February 1965. The Viet Cong attacked a U.S. air base at Pleiku (PLAY-koo), South Vietnam, killing eight Americans. Johnson

PRIMARY SOURCE

In a televised address on August 4, 1964, Johnson informed the nation about the attacks in the Gulf of Tonkin and the retaliation that would be taken against North Vietnam. In this excerpt from the address, the president paints a frightening picture of the situation.

Aggression by terror against the peaceful villagers of South Vietnam has now been joined by open aggression on the high seas against the United States of America. The determination of all Americans to carry out our full commitment to the people and to the government of South Vietnam will be redoubled [increased all the more] by this outrage. Yet our response, for the present, will be limited and fitting. We Americans know, although others appear to forget, the risks of spreading conflict. We still seek no wider war.

—from President Lyndon B. Johnson's report on the Gulf of Tonkin Incident, August 4, 1964

countered by initiating a sustained air bombing campaign of North Vietnam, known as Operation Rolling Thunder. The campaign involved a series of gradually intensified bombings designed to decrease the flow of supplies from North Vietnam to the Viet Cong and force the communists to negotiate a lasting peace. Operation Rolling Thunder would continue for more than three years. During this period, bombs dropped by air strikes on the Ho Chi Minh Trail and other targets in Southeast Asia would be twice the number of those dropped during World War II.

Soon after Rolling Thunder began, Johnson sent the first ground troops to South Vietnam—even though, as you know, he had vowed he would not do so. In the beginning, the troops were instructed to protect U.S. air bases, not to fight. But before long, American soldiers would be drawn into combat as the U.S. military embarked on an air and ground war that aimed to eliminate the communist threat from South Vietnam.

HISTORICAL THINKING

1. **READING CHECK** What authority did the Gulf of Tonkin Resolution give Johnson?

2. **EVALUATE** Identify examples of bias in Johnson's televised address used to sway the American people into thinking that retaliation against North Vietnam was justified.

3. **FORM AND SUPPORT OPINIONS** Do you think Johnson was right to escalate the war? Cite evidence from the text to support your opinion.

WAR STRATEGIES

Imagine running onto a field with a game plan in hand for playing a soccer match only to find you're actually playing baseball. Something like that happened to the U.S. military forces when they came to fight in Vietnam.

HEARTS AND MINDS

The United States employed two key strategies to win the war in Vietnam. First, it planned to use its superior military technology and weaponry to defeat the enemy through both air strikes and ground force operations. Second, it set out to gain the complete support of the South Vietnamese people—to win their hearts and minds. The United States particularly wanted their help in defeating the Viet Cong. But many South Vietnamese believed life under their U.S.-supported government was no better than life under the North Vietnamese communists.

The increasing influx of American troops arriving in South Vietnam did not help win the people's hearts and minds. General **William Westmoreland**,

CRITICAL VIEWING U.S. Army paratroopers wade across a river in the rain, searching for Viet Cong in a jungle area of South Vietnam in September 1965. Paratroopers are military personnel who parachute into a war zone. What details in the photo convey the conditions the soldiers had to deal with?

who had begun commanding the American forces in Vietnam in June 1964, persuaded leaders in Washington to increase the number of ground troops in Vietnam. By the end of 1965, nearly 185,000 American troops had landed. The American soldiers were originally supposed to train the South Vietnamese troops of the Army of the Republic of Vietnam (ARVN). The idea was that, once they were transformed into a strong fighting force, the ARVN would be equipped to combat the communists from the north. Unfortunately, many of the South Vietnamese troops—and their generals—were ineffectual. While some ARVN soldiers were well trained, disciplined, and dedicated to the cause, others were not. In some cases, they were reluctant to fight against those they considered their countrymen. As a result, American troops soon found themselves engaged in actual combat.

Still, Westmoreland hoped to weaken and wear down the North Vietnamese and Viet Cong through a **war of attrition**. The American general thought he could win the war by inflicting heavy losses on the enemy through fighting many small battles that would add up, ultimately, to victory. But the communists refused to back down, no matter how many casualties they suffered. They were engaged in what they considered a national struggle for independence. Men from the North and the South were willing to take the place of fallen soldiers and reoccupy areas that the Americans and ARVN had cleared. The communist forces in Vietnam also benefited from the weapons and other supplies they received from the Soviet Union and China.

A GUERRILLA WAR

General Westmoreland underestimated his enemy's determination. He and other military leaders were also not prepared for the type of war the Vietnamese fought. The United States was supremely ready to fight a conventional war against another industrialized country. But Vietnam was not industrialized, and the Viet Cong and others opposing U.S. forces engaged in unconventional warfare. Bands of trained and untrained Viet Cong soldiers fought a guerrilla war against the ARVN and the U.S. military. Their arsenal included guns, grenades, and **mortars**, or short range, muzzle-loaded cannons. They also manufactured their own bombs and set booby traps.

Helicopters like this one, nicknamed "Huey" for their early "HU-1" designation, were used to transport soldiers to and from war zones and airlift the wounded in Vietnam. Hueys carried U.S. troops to South Vietnam's Ia Drang Valley in November 1965, where the American soldiers engaged in the first major battle of the war with North Vietnamese forces.

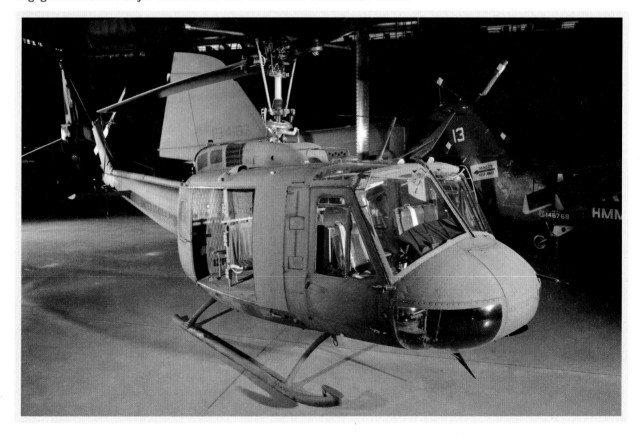

The war in Vietnam did not have official fronts and battles like conventional wars. More often, the Viet Cong launched ambushes and carried out hit-and-run attacks against the U.S. troops and the ARVN, taking off before they could be captured. And American soldiers couldn't always tell enemies apart from friends. The Vietnamese villagers who smiled in welcome when the soldiers arrived were sometimes hiding hand grenades ready to be tossed.

Fighting often took place in jungle terrain, where the dense foliage made it easy for the Viet Cong to camouflage both themselves and their bases. Often soldiers on both sides had to slog through swamps, submerged up to their waists in the mosquito-infested waters. In areas closer to Saigon, where the terrain provided less cover, the Viet Cong traveled through an extensive system of underground tunnels. Local villagers had helped build the tunnels, which stretched for thousands of miles and served not only as shelters where soldiers could retreat, but also as bases of operation.

As they launched their surprise attacks—sometimes firing from concealed bunkers within the tunnels—the Viet Cong entered and exited through well-hidden entryways. The tunnels contained chambers where the Viet Cong stored their weapons, water, and food, and even housed sleeping chambers and kitchens, enabling the soldiers to live in the tunnels for weeks at a time. American and South Vietnamese troops known as "tunnel rats" crawled through the narrow passages, searching for Viet Cong and setting off explosives in an attempt to collapse the tunnels. In the process, however, they had to be careful not to trigger any of the booby traps planted by the Viet Cong, such as bamboo spikes or trip wires that set off grenades.

Air shaft

Fighting bunker

Booby trap

Kitchen

Booby trap

Storeroom

Sleeping chambers

Storeroom

Well

Hospital

Viet Cong Tunnels

The Vietnamese dug tunnels all over South Vietnam, but the tunnels just northwest of Saigon—first excavated by the Viet Minh during the war with the French—were the most elaborate. Stretching nearly 150 miles, the tunnels were narrow, requiring the Viet Cong to crawl through them on their stomachs. The tunnels led to larger spaces including kitchens, a hospital, and a theater. Ventilation holes connected to air shafts were dug above the tunnels. The holes were ingeniously hidden, often at the base of a tree or beneath a termite mound.

SEARCH-AND-DESTROY MISSIONS

To combat the Viet Cong and North Vietnamese Army, General Westmoreland used search-and-destroy missions in villages and along the Ho Chi Minh Trail. First, low-flying helicopters sprayed an area with gunfire, and then ground troops moved in to search out enemies, destroy them, and get away quickly. Though these missions often resulted in the eradication of Viet Cong bases and the confiscation of their arms and supplies, such attacks could also devastate entire villages and kill hundreds of civilians.

To deal with the thick growth in the jungles that so effectively concealed the Viet Cong, the U.S. Air Force began spraying **Agent Orange**, a potent herbicide, or chemical substance used to kill vegetation. Agent Orange destroyed foliage, but doctors discovered later that the herbicide caused serious health issues, for both the Vietnamese and U.S. soldiers. American troops also frequently used napalm, a flammable jellied gasoline that, like Agent Orange, helped clear foliage and undergrowth. When it came into contact with skin, however, napalm caused severe burns, leaving some people with long-lasting injuries. Together, the search-and-destroy missions and use of chemical agents did little to win the hearts and minds of the South Vietnamese or turn them against the communists. The chemicals harmed many South Vietnamese civilians and burned their villages and farms.

The American cause wasn't helped by the rise to power of **Nguyen Cao Ky** (NWIHN KOW KAY), who became prime minister of South Vietnam following a military coup in 1965. The Vietnamese people viewed Ky, who prohibited criticism of his government and imprisoned his opponents, as an autocrat similar to Diem. The United States supported Ky, even though his corrupt regime was anything but democratic.

Meanwhile, by the end of 1965, great numbers of soldiers had deserted the ARVN, with many joining the North Vietnamese army. The Viet Cong had gained control, to some degree, of about 50 percent of the countryside in South Vietnam. As Westmoreland's war of attrition failed to discourage the communist forces in Vietnam, American casualties started to mount over the course of that first year of the war. Progress seemed elusive, and methods of calculating success were muddled and hard to measure. American troops fought bravely, but the stress of combat in Vietnam led many soldiers to suffer from low morale and depression. As the war dragged on, the conflict also became the subject of growing criticism at home.

In 1963, the Ca Mau Peninsula at the southern tip of South Vietnam was almost completely covered with forests. As a stronghold of the Viet Cong, this stretch of Ca Mau was heavily sprayed with Agent Orange and defoliated in 1968. This photo was taken four years later and, as you can see, the forests showed no signs of recovery.

HISTORICAL THINKING

1. **READING CHECK** How did the U.S. military hope to win the war in Vietnam?

2. **MAKE INFERENCES** Why do you think guerrilla warfare was so effective against American troops?

3. **ANALYZE ENVIRONMENTAL CONCEPTS** How did Agent Orange and napalm affect the natural systems and resources in the jungles of South Vietnam?

4. **DRAW CONCLUSIONS** How did the U.S. military strategy undermine the campaign to win the hearts and minds of the South Vietnamese?

GROWING OPPOSITION TO THE WAR

You're no doubt used to the 24/7 coverage of world events available on TV, the Internet, and social media. But in the 1960s, information wasn't so easily accessed. So when reports on the Vietnam War filled the television airwaves, people watched—and thought about what they saw.

THE TELEVISION WAR

The Vietnam War became the first in the nation's history to be broadcast regularly on television. Journalists and photographers covered the war from the jungles and battlefields of Vietnam and brought it into people's homes, night after night. As a result, the Vietnam War became known as the "television war" or "living-room war." Recording their accounts in the haze of war, American journalists reported on television what urban warfare and guerrilla fighting entailed. Film clips of fighting, bombings, and dead or wounded soldiers appeared on nightly newscasts. The public's daily exposure to the horrors of war kept people informed about events. In time, it would also begin to influence their opinion of the war.

However, despite what television reports revealed about casualties and conditions in Vietnam, government and military officials made announcements about the war's progress. The Johnson administration launched a "success

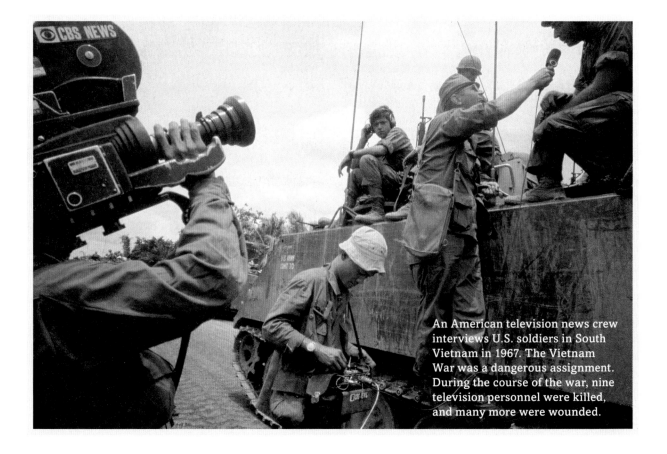

An American television news crew interviews U.S. soldiers in South Vietnam in 1967. The Vietnam War was a dangerous assignment. During the course of the war, nine television personnel were killed, and many more were wounded.

offensive," a campaign to convince the public that the United States was defeating the communists in Vietnam.

In 1967, General Westmoreland made three trips to the United States to promote this idea, appearing before Congress to present his positive assessments of the war. But Westmoreland manipulated the numbers of enemy losses and claimed that U.S. forces had won every battle. He told Congress that "your continued strong support is vital to the success of our mission . . . over the communist aggressor!" In truth, neither the bombing campaign nor the ground war in Vietnam was having any measurable effect on the enemy.

Americans became increasingly aware of the difference between the optimistic reports they heard from the government and what they saw for themselves on television. This contrast resulted in a **credibility gap**, an increasing skepticism about what the government told them about the war. In this context, Americans eventually started to call into question the principles upon which the war was being fought. Why, many wondered, was the United States involved in Vietnam at all?

Some members of Congress also began to take issue with the U.S. involvement in Vietnam. Senator George McGovern of South Dakota expressed his opposition in 1963. In 1966, Arkansas senator J. William Fulbright, chairman of the Senate Foreign Relations Committee, also voiced his opposition to the bombing of North Vietnam. That same year, Fulbright published a book called *The Arrogance of Power* in which he criticized the government's goal in Vietnam. He wrote, "We are trying to remake Vietnamese society, a task which certainly cannot be accomplished by force and which probably cannot be accomplished by any means available to outsiders. The objective may be desirable, but it is not feasible [practical]."

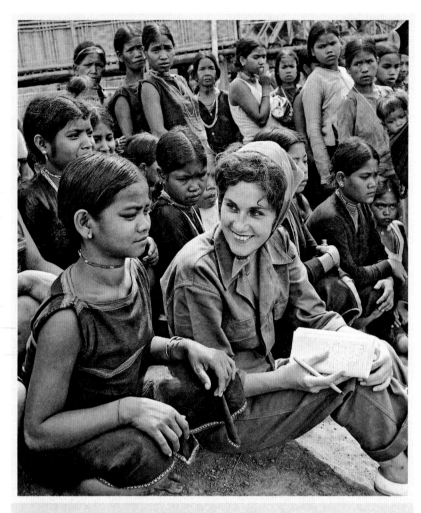

AMERICAN WOMEN IN VIETNAM

Women could not serve in combat during the conflict, but thousands of female members of the military took on other roles in Vietnam. The vast majority worked as nurses. The number and severity of war casualties—and the rate at which the wounded arrived to be treated—meant that the nurses had to make quick decisions about whom to treat first. They also had to determine the treatment on their own, without much advice from doctors, who were often busy with their own patients. Thousands of civilian women also worked in Vietnam, many of them serving with the American Red Cross or working as journalists, like the woman in this photo.

CONTROVERSY OVER THE DRAFT

While some people voiced their objection to the war, many others opposed the idea of conscription, commonly known as the draft. With the escalation of the war, more young men were needed to fight it. Hundreds of thousands of American men volunteered for or were drafted to serve in the war, which government and military leaders portrayed as an extension of broader Cold War struggles. The Selective Service System, a federal agency, administered the draft. On turning 18 years old, all young men were required to register with their local draft board, but some could be granted a **deferment**, or official permission to delay conscription. For example, men enrolled full-time in college could claim a student deferment for as long as they remained in school.

However, the agency did not always act fairly in its selection process. Draft board members could show favoritism to friends, family members, and others by granting their sons special deferments. Many of the men who received deferments also came from wealthy and educated families. As a result, most of the draftees came from poor and working-class families. A substantial percentage of these men belonged to minority groups. In the first few years of the war, once it became clear that American minorities were fighting and dying in numbers that were disproportionate to their representation in the country, many activist rights groups loudly protested the war. They objected to the war on the grounds that, to them, it represented one more form of oppression—oppression for minorities at home and abroad.

More moderate voices also spoke out against the war, including civil rights leader Martin Luther King, Jr., who called it "a white man's war, a black man's fight." Most famously, in a 1967 speech, King criticized the war both for its expense and for the large number of poor men of all races who were fighting it. He pointed out that the money the government spent on the war could have been used to fight poverty in the United States. He also objected to the devastation the war was bringing to the Vietnamese people and their land. The response to King's speech was largely negative. Newspaper editorials attacked him for his stance on the war. And even the NAACP criticized King for linking what the organization considered two separate issues: civil rights and the Vietnam War. However, King did not back down and continued to speak out against the war and the draft.

INCREASING PROTESTS

In 1964, other civil rights advocates began the **Free Speech Movement** in response to a ban on distributing political flyers at the University of California at Berkeley campus. When police arrested a student for handing out civil rights pamphlets and put him in their patrol car, other students sat down around the car to prevent it from being driven away. A young man named Mario Savio jumped on top of the car and addressed the crowd. Savio emerged as the movement's leader, and the students sitting around the police car passed around a hat to collect money to repair the vehicle. They wanted to show

that they were good citizens. The protest continued for more than 30 hours until authorities dropped the charges, and the student was released.

Then, on December 1, 1964, Savio and other movement leaders led a rally, exhorting students to take part in a sit-in at Sproul Hall, Berkeley's administration building. As a result, thousands of students occupied the building and remained there for many hours. Finally, the police moved in and arrested about 800 people. As the police ushered them away, some of the officers physically assaulted the students. Eventually, the university lifted its ban of on-campus political activity, and the Free Speech Movement declared victory.

The Free Speech Movement soon turned its focus on the Vietnam War. Students at Berkeley and other college campuses throughout the country organized protests against the war. These antiwar protests, provoked by the expansion of the war in Vietnam, reflected and contributed to a deep rift within American society and culture. Americans became divided into **hawks**, who supported the war, and **doves**, who opposed it.

Another movement, called the **New Left**, arose out of student activism. One New Left group, the **Students for a Democratic Society (SDS)**, originated at the University of Michigan at Ann Arbor in the early 1960s and soon spread to other colleges. The SDS promoted socialist principles and denounced racism, militarism, and in time, U.S. involvement in Vietnam. In April 1965, the SDS sponsored the first major antiwar rally in Washington, D.C.

PRIMARY SOURCE

Just before the 1964 sit-in, Mario Savio delivered a speech on the steps of Berkeley's Sproul Hall. In this excerpt from the speech, Savio refers to the university as a "machine" that may need to be actively stopped.

There's a time when the operation of the machine becomes so odious [hateful]—makes you so sick at heart—that you can't take part. You can't even passively take part. And you've got to put your bodies upon the gears and upon the wheels, upon the levers, upon all the apparatus, and you've got to make it stop. And you've got to indicate to the people who run it, to the people who own it that unless you're free, the machine will be prevented from working at all.

—from a speech in Berkeley, by Mario Savio, 1964

During the March on the Pentagon, this young woman offered a flower to the soldiers guarding the building with bayoneted M-14 rifles. At one point, a group of demonstrators tried to levitate, or lift, the Pentagon and used spells to drive "the evil war spirits" out of the Defense Department headquarters.

About two weeks earlier, President Johnson had pledged to continue military operations in Vietnam. The event drew tens of thousands of people calling for U.S. withdrawal from South Vietnam. Protesters picketed the White House and carried signs saying "No more war." At the Capitol, people delivered speeches, and performers such as activist and folksinger Joan Baez (BY-ehz) led the crowd in song.

While the 1965 protest rally was largely peaceful, the March on the Pentagon, which took place in the capital in October 1967, was far more confrontational. The demonstration, organized by the National Mobilization Committee to End the War in Vietnam—a coalition of antiwar groups—sought to shut down the Pentagon. By this point in the war, about 13,000 Americans had died in Vietnam, and more than half of the population disapproved of the president's handling of the war. An estimated 100,000 people rallied first at the Lincoln Memorial and then marched to the Pentagon. When the protesters arrived, they found about 2,500 troops and U.S. marshals guarding the Pentagon. Some of the protesters placed flowers in the barrels of the soldiers' rifles, but a small group of demonstrators managed to gain access to the building. Soldiers and marshals used tear gas and force to clear them out. In the end, nearly 700 people were arrested.

Despite the protests at home, the war in Vietnam continued. But in 1968, a military campaign launched by North Vietnam and the Viet Cong would mark a turning point in the war and the beginning of American withdrawal from the conflict.

HISTORICAL THINKING

1. **READING CHECK** Why was the Vietnam War called the "television war"?

2. **DRAW CONCLUSIONS** How did the war in Vietnam affect the larger trend toward equality at home?

3. **MAKE INFERENCES** Why did Mario Savio compare the University of California at Berkeley to a machine?

4. **FORM AND SUPPORT OPINIONS** Do you think peaceful antiwar protests in the 1960s were more effective than more confrontational protests? Why or why not?

THE TET OFFENSIVE

The element of surprise can be key in a battle. An attack by communist forces in South Vietnam surprised the U.S. military and stunned the American people, who began to cry "Enough!" in ever greater numbers.

A SURPRISE ATTACK

It all began on Tet, the celebration of the Lunar New Year and the most important holiday in Vietnam. In other years, hostilities on both sides of the war had been suspended during the holiday. But early on the morning of January 31, 1968, about 80,000 North Vietnamese and Viet Cong forces initiated a coordinated and unexpected attack on dozens of locations throughout South Vietnam. The sites of the **Tet Offensive** included cities and towns, military bases, General Westmoreland's headquarters, and even the U.S. embassy in Saigon. In launching their attack, communist forces hoped to provoke a popular uprising against U.S. and ARVN troops and persuade the United States to pull out of Vietnam.

A few months before the Tet Offensive, the communists had begun a campaign to distract the Americans and ARVN from the real targets. First, the communists attacked a couple of towns in South Vietnam, and then a U.S. Marine base located in the northwest corner of the country. Johnson and Westmoreland sent 50,000 troops to protect the besieged Marine base as well as other bases in the country. Once the troops had been diverted and the communists' true targets stood nearly undefended, the Tet Offensive began.

Initially, the communist forces scored a few successes, including invading the embassy grounds in Saigon, but the U.S. and ARVN troops soon defeated the communists there and managed to retake most of the other targeted locations. However, fighting in the city of Hue raged on for nearly a month. As you may remember, Hue was the site of a major Buddhist protest against Diem in 1963. Hue was also once the capital of Vietnam and the

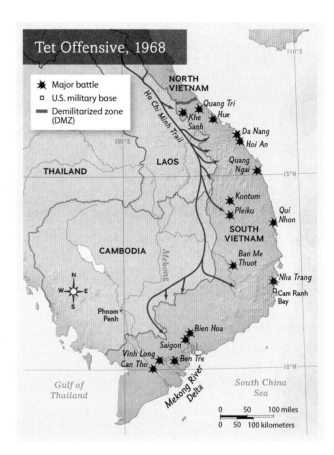

Tet Offensive, 1968

home of its emperor. It was a symbolic target for the communists and poorly defended. On the morning of the Tet Offensive, communist forces quickly seized control of the city. The U.S. and ARVN troops fought fiercely, going from house to house in the city to root out the communist occupiers before finally winning the Battle of Hue.

It would be one of the longest and bloodiest battles of the war. After taking control of the city, the Americans discovered mass graves filled

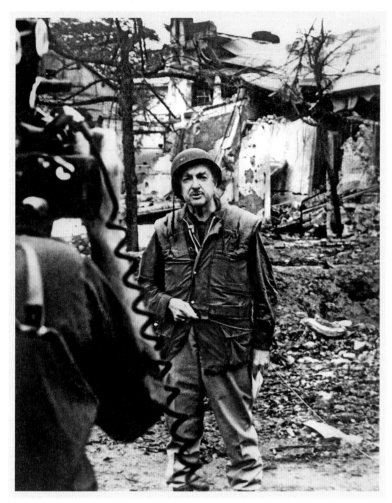

Journalist Walter Cronkite, popularly called "the most trusted man in America" for the integrity of his reporting, went to Vietnam to cover the aftermath of the Tet Offensive. For two weeks, he reported from battle sites, and his commentary influenced public opinion.

conflict. From Saigon, American broadcast journalist Walter Cronkite reported that the Tet Offensive made "more certain than ever that the bloody experience of Vietnam is to end in a stalemate." In other words, Cronkite believed neither side would be able to claim a clear victory.

In February 1968, Secretary of Defense Robert McNamara resigned from his position. He, too, had become disillusioned with the war and realized he had misjudged the resolve of the North Vietnamese. Like McNamara, the American public had grown weary of the war. They no longer believed the government's positive assessment of it or Westmoreland's optimistic claim after the Tet Offensive that there was now "light at the end of the tunnel."

Just a few weeks after Tet, General Westmoreland requested an additional 206,000 troops in Vietnam. About 550,000 American troops were already stationed there. Clark Clifford, who replaced McNamara as secretary of defense, advised Johnson to deny the request. He also recommended that the United States reduce its bombing raids over North Vietnam and take steps to end the war.

with thousands of Hue civilians murdered by the communists. Before the battle, the North Vietnamese and Viet Cong had executed those they believed were sympathetic to the American cause. The Battle of Hue also resulted in heavy losses, with about 5,000 dead on the communist side and around 500 on the American and South Vietnamese side. Thousands more died or were wounded in other battles of the Tet Offensive. The communists were defeated militarily, and they didn't win more South Vietnamese to their side, but they did score a strategic victory. Television crews had captured scenes of the fighting. To many viewers, it didn't look as though the United States was about to win the war, as the government had led them to believe.

DISILLUSIONMENT WITH THE WAR

After the Tet Offensive, an overwhelming number of Americans called for an end to the war. Few now really believed the United States was winning the

Johnson took Clifford's advice and refused to send Westmoreland all the troops he'd requested, approving only an additional 13,500 soldiers. The president also informed the South Vietnamese leadership that its army would have to assume a greater role in the fight. But to many Americans, Johnson's actions were too little, too late. After the Tet Offensive, his approval ratings dropped by more than 10 percentage points. The unpopular war had taken a severe toll on Johnson's presidency.

HISTORICAL THINKING

1. **READING CHECK** How did the communists devise and carry out their surprise attack?

2. **ANALYZE CAUSE AND EFFECT** What does the Tet Offensive—which North Vietnam lost—suggest about the complexity of historical causes and effects?

3. **DRAW CONCLUSIONS** Why was the Tet Offensive a major turning point in the war?

1968: Violence and Division

When Walter Cronkite said after the Tet Offensive that the war was mired in stalemate, Johnson reportedly said, "If I've lost Cronkite, I've lost Middle America." Soon, Johnson would make a decision that would rock the nation.

A DIVIDED DEMOCRATIC PARTY

Johnson's unpopularity among Middle America, or average middle-class Americans, weakened his chances in the 1968 presidential race. At the end of November 1967, Senator **Eugene McCarthy** of Minnesota announced he would seek the nomination of the Democratic Party. McCarthy opposed the Vietnam War and won strong support for his position, especially among young people. He also performed surprisingly well against Johnson in the first Democratic primary election in New Hampshire in March 1968. Johnson won the primary with 49 percent of the vote—but McCarthy was a close runner-up. He captured 42 percent of the vote. As you may know, in a primary election, voters in a particular state choose the candidate they'd like to see on the ballot in the general election.

Just a few days after the primary, John Kennedy's brother and former attorney general, Senator Robert Kennedy of New York, also joined the race. Kennedy had stated before that he would not run, but McCarthy's success in New Hampshire made

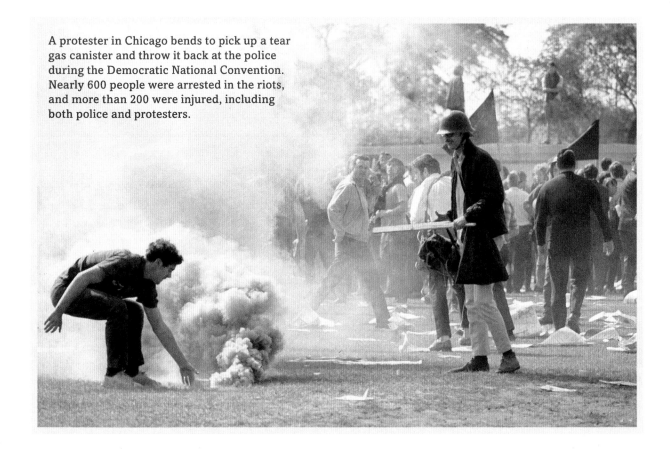

A protester in Chicago bends to pick up a tear gas canister and throw it back at the police during the Democratic National Convention. Nearly 600 people were arrested in the riots, and more than 200 were injured, including both police and protesters.

him change his mind. Like McCarthy, Kennedy ran as an antiwar candidate. Kennedy's decision to run upset some voters because they believed his candidacy might undermine McCarthy's campaign. Others, however, acknowledged that Kennedy, with his money and connections, had a better prospect of winning the Democratic nomination.

On March 31, faced with the likelihood of losing the primary in Wisconsin, Johnson dropped a bombshell by announcing that he would not seek a second term as president. During his televised address, Johnson also revealed his intentions to scale back the bombings in North Vietnam and engage in peace talks with the North Vietnamese. A few weeks later, Johnson's vice president, Hubert Humphrey, joined the race for president. Humphrey, who received Johnson's endorsement, decided against directly campaigning or running in the state primaries against McCarthy and Kennedy. Instead, he hoped to receive enough votes from the state delegations to win the nomination at the Democratic National Convention.

Meanwhile, peace talks began with the North Vietnamese in Paris, but negotiations were short-lived. The North Vietnamese demanded that Johnson scale back the bombing everywhere, not just in North Vietnam, but Johnson resisted. With the talks at an **impasse**, or standstill, heavy combat continued in South Vietnam throughout the spring of 1968. And American troops continued to fight and die in Southeast Asia.

VIOLENCE AND CHAOS

Less than a week after Johnson's startling announcement, Martin Luther King, Jr., was assassinated in Memphis, Tennessee. His violent death touched off a series of riots in more than 100 cities across the country, including Washington, D.C., Baltimore, San Francisco, and Chicago. Rioters set fires and looted stores. In some cities, officials called in the military to establish order. The police made thousands of arrests across the country, and dozens of people died. And the violence was just beginning. In fact, 1968 would become one of the most chaotic years in American history.

Throughout the turbulent spring, McCarthy and Kennedy continued battling in the primaries. Kennedy drew greater support from African Americans and Latinos, while McCarthy had more success with white college students. But on June 5, the contest between the two came to an abrupt and horrifying end. Only moments after Kennedy delivered a victory speech in Los Angeles celebrating his California primary win, an assassin shot him. Kennedy died the following day. For the second time in just two months, the nation was shocked and heartbroken over the death of a major national leader.

McCarthy remained in the race after Kennedy's assassination, but Hubert Humphrey was the strong favorite going into the Democratic National Convention, which was held in Chicago during the last week of August. Chicago mayor Richard J. Daley had prepared for the internal divisions among delegates inside the convention hall. He was also ready for any confrontations that might take place outside the hall. Daley had turned the convention center into a fortress, bulletproofing its doors and surrounding it with fencing and barbed wire. Police patrolled the area inside the fence, poised for the worst. And that's just what happened.

As many as 15,000 antiwar protesters flooded the city, intent on making their voices heard. The plan was for their protest to be peaceful but loud. Instead, violence erupted when protesters refused to leave a nearby park. The mayor sent about 27,000 police officers and members of the National Guard into the park to confront the crowds. There, the officers lobbed tear gas at the protesters and beat them with clubs. Clashes continued as protesters tried to approach the convention site. Innocent bystanders, including doctors and reporters, got caught in the mayhem. And once again, America watched the violence on television.

In the end, the delegates nominated Humphrey, who was backed by moderates in the Democratic Party. The young people who supported McCarthy felt betrayed. And they saw Humphrey's candidacy as a continuation of Johnson's pro-war policies. Disillusioned with American values, some young people would simply withdraw from traditional society and adopt an unconventional lifestyle.

HISTORICAL THINKING

1. **READING CHECK** What divided the Democratic Party in 1968?

2. **EVALUATE** How did the protests against the Vietnam War affect domestic issues and policies?

3. **MAKE INFERENCES** Given the social and political climate of 1968, how do you think Americans reacted to the images of the Democratic National Convention they saw on television?

THE COUNTERCULTURE

"Power to the people." "Don't trust anyone over 30." "Flower power." These are just a few of the slogans adopted by groups of young people who rejected middle-class values, the war, and what came to be called "the establishment."

ANTIESTABLISHMENT

From within the antiwar and rights protest movements of the New Left, a **counterculture** emerged, promoting a way of life that was in opposition with American society's established rules and behavior. Those who participated in the counterculture, often called "hippies," were frustrated with the war, politics, and discrimination in America. They believed that true equality and peace could only be realized through a revolution of cultural values.

Thus, hippies decided to "check out" from mainstream society as a way of rebelling against middle-class American values and seeking true happiness. They embraced pacifism and demonstrated against the conflict in Vietnam, declaring that waging war anywhere in the world was wrong. "Make love, not war" and "Give peace a chance" were popular hippie slogans. These members of the counterculture rebelled by calling into question Cold War values and even long-standing American principles.

The counterculture had its own distinctive style of music, dress, language, and films, all of which influenced mainstream social and cultural sensibilities. Both men and women in the counterculture typically let their hair grow long, dressed in tie-dyed shirts and bell-bottom pants, and adorned themselves with strings of beads.

They also had liberated attitudes toward sexuality and the use of psychedelic drugs, which produced hallucinations and an altered state of consciousness. In 1960, Harvard psychologist and researcher Timothy Leary had begun studying the effects of psychedelic drugs and became a folk hero of the counterculture. Leary promoted the use of such drugs with his slogan "Tune in, Turn On, Drop Out." Counterculture music used electronically distorted sounds to try to reproduce the experience of using these drugs. And films about the counterculture, such as *Easy Rider* and *Wild in the Streets,* were shown in theaters across the country.

To create a sense of family, some hippies formed communes, where they shared living arrangements, food, and possessions. Communes were often founded in rural areas where members longed to get "back to the land." They rejected the consumerism of modern life, grew their own food, and reconnected with nature. Many other members of the counterculture settled in urban areas, such as San Francisco's Haight-Ashbury neighborhood, where they lived in the company of like-minded hippies. More than 75,000 young people migrated to the neighborhood in 1967 alone.

WOODSTOCK NATION

Perhaps the high point of the counterculture came in August 1969 when the Woodstock Music Festival took place on a farm in Bethel, New York. Billed as "Three Days of Peace and Music," Woodstock drew a crowd of about 400,000 people—twice the number expected. They came to see some of the biggest musical acts of the day, including Jimi Hendrix, Janis Joplin, the Grateful Dead, and the Who. Many of these singers performed songs that were critical of the Vietnam War—to the delight of their audience.

The organizers of the festival had planned to use the profits from it to build a recording studio, but they were unprepared for the masses that thronged the festival. Unable to handle the crowds, the organizers let everyone in for free. Though plagued by rain, mud, and inadequate facilities for the audience, Woodstock was a great success and, remarkably, largely peaceful. Only two deaths occurred at the festival: one from an accident involving a tractor

In this photo, audience members at the Woodstock festival stand and perch on top of cars and buses to watch the show. The enormous crowds created a food shortage. When people in the area heard about the situation, they donated food, including 10,000 sandwiches. Others served rice, vegetables, and granola, which came to be associated with hippies. In an effort to feed everyone, thousands of cups of granola were passed through the audience.

and the other from a drug overdose. The term "Woodstock Nation" would be used to describe the youth counterculture of the 1960s.

By the end of the decade, however, the hippies' hopes for a world filled with peace and love were fading. The rampant drug use was taking its toll. Some of the musicians who had performed at the Woodstock festival had died from drug overdoses. Partly in response to the counterculture's drug abuse, the federal government declared a "war on drugs" in the early 1970s. Agencies were created to provide treatment for drug abusers and to establish federal and local task forces to fight the drug trade.

Meanwhile, many mainstream Americans, who had been scandalized by the counterculture and troubled by the protests, longed for an end to the unrest. They saw the counterculture's emphasis on "free love" and rejection of consumerism as a threat to the American

way of life. They feared that the drug culture was increasing crime in their communities. They wanted the nation to return to the way it was in the years of social conformity that followed World War II. They wanted a leader who could re-establish order and end the war in Vietnam. They believed they had found such a leader in former vice president Richard Nixon.

HISTORICAL THINKING

1. **READING CHECK** What values set members of the counterculture apart from members of traditional American society?

2. **MAKE INFERENCES** Why did the emergence of the counterculture coincide with the Vietnam War?

3. **MAKE CONNECTIONS** What characteristics of the counterculture described in the lesson do you see around you today? Explain the similarities.

VIETNAMIZATION UNDER NIXON

Many Americans wanted peace in Vietnam and on their streets. They thought Republican Richard Nixon could deliver on both.

AN HONORABLE PEACE

Republican Richard Nixon narrowly beat Democrat Hubert Humphrey in the presidential election, winning the popular vote by less than one percent. You may remember that Nixon was involved in the campaign against communism when he was a congressman in the 1940s. He also served for eight years as Dwight Eisenhower's vice president. To sway voters, Nixon had appealed to more conservative Americans—those who conformed to social norms, unlike the members of the counterculture. The social unrest the country had experienced made many people long for law and order. Nixon would later refer to these Americans as "the silent majority."

During his campaign, Nixon had promised he could bring about a quick victory in Vietnam, but he didn't provide any details. He also referred to seeking "an honorable peace." A reporter called this vague promise Nixon's "secret plan." Once Nixon assumed the presidency in January 1969, he and his National Security Advisor **Henry Kissinger** discussed what to do about Vietnam. They knew the United States could not win the war, but they didn't want to pull their forces out of South Vietnam, leaving it vulnerable to invasion from communist North Vietnam. And Nixon didn't want the war to destroy his presidency as it had Lyndon Johnson's. Soon he came up with a plan to end the war.

Nixon proposed a strategy called **Vietnamization**, which allowed for the gradual replacement of U.S. troops with ARVN troops. Under this plan, all American troops would be out of Vietnam by 1972. Nixon began the process of Vietnamization in June 1969 with the withdrawal of 25,000 U.S. troops. He announced more withdrawals that September. In April 1970, Nixon expressed his intention of pulling an additional 150,000 troops out of Vietnam within a year. General Creighton Abrams, who had replaced General Westmoreland as commander in Vietnam, expressed concern about the American troops' ability to train additional ARVN troops in such a short time, but Nixon was determined to follow through with his Vietnamization plan.

Nixon also proposed a change to the conscription process. During the early years of the war, the Selective Service had drafted any eligible man between the ages of 18 and 26, with the oldest men drafted first. This system was replaced with a draft lottery, which had last been used in 1942. On December 1, 1969, the Selective Service placed 366 plastic capsules—one for every day of the year, including February 29—into a

U.S. Troops in Vietnam, 1960–1972

NUMBER OF TROOPS, BY YEAR (IN THOUSANDS)

900   3,200

1960 1961 1962 1963 1964 1965 1966 1967 1968 1969 1970 1971 1972

Source: U.S. Department of Defense

Some men, like these protesters in New York's Central Park in 1967, publicly burned their draft classification cards to protest the draft and the Vietnam War.

jar and drew them out by hand. The first capsule drawn was September 14. This meant that all men born between 1944 and 1950 on that date were assigned the number 1 and would be the first to be considered for the draft. The drawing continued until all the dates had been assigned numbers. The higher your number, the less likely you would be chosen for **induction**, or being drafted into the military.

COVERUPS AND SECRETS

In the midst of what appeared to be positive news about the war, Americans learned about an incident in South Vietnam that had occurred the year before. In March 1968, U.S. troops led by Lieutenant William Calley entered the tiny village of My Lai (MEE LYE) in search of Viet Cong. The troops didn't find any Viet Cong, but they rounded up the unarmed civilians— mostly women, children, and elderly men—and brutally murdered them. Approximately 500 people died in the **My Lai Massacre**, almost the entire population of the village.

The U.S. Army covered up the mass killing, but a soldier who had heard of the massacre eventually spoke to the press, which broke the story to the public in November 1969. Outraged people from around the world demanded justice. In the end, only

Calley was punished for the incident. He was put under house arrest and released within four years.

Nixon also tried to keep some secrets of his own. The United States had suspected Vietnam's neighbors, Cambodia and Laos, of sheltering Vietnamese communists. The government also knew that communists transported supplies along the Ho Chi Minh Trail, which passed through those countries. General Abrams suggested carrying out heavy bombing raids on Cambodia and Laos to root out the communist forces, and Nixon and Kissinger agreed to the plan. The United States had conducted air attacks over Cambodia and Laos for several years, but Nixon chose to "carpet bomb" the countries, or attack them with large numbers of missiles.

By showing the communists in Vietnam the lengths to which he was willing to go, Nixon hoped to force them into negotiations. The secret bombing of Cambodia and Laos began in March 1969—not even Congress knew about it. But in May 1969, the *New York Times* reported on the attacks. Furious with the newspaper's revelation, Nixon had the FBI discover the source of the leak in the name of national security. In spite of the leak, the president continued carpet bombing Cambodia and Laos until 1973.

TRAGEDY AT KENT STATE

After several days of student protest at Kent State, classes resumed on May 4. When students gathered for an unauthorized demonstration that day, the National Guard fired

Then in April 1970, Nixon sent 20,000 U.S. and ARVN ground troops into Cambodia to find and destroy what he and the military thought were secret Viet Cong headquarters there. When the White House announced the Cambodian ground invasion, protests broke out. Some of the protests turned violent. On May 4, the National Guard shot into a crowd of student demonstrators at Kent State University in Ohio, killing four students and injuring several others. On May 15, at Jackson State, a predominantly black university in Mississippi, two African-American students were killed and 12 were injured following protests of U.S. policy in Cambodia and Vietnam and demonstrations against racial discrimination. Nixon pulled ground troops out of Cambodia in June.

The release in 1971 of what came to be known as the **Pentagon Papers** revealed more embarrassing secrets. In 1967, then Secretary of Defense Robert McNamara commissioned a study on U.S. activities and policies in Vietnam between 1947 and 1967. The 7,000-page work was never meant for the public eye. Daniel Ellsberg worked on the study and, at that time, was a strong supporter of the Vietnam War. As the war escalated, however, Ellsberg came to oppose it, and he turned the classified document over to the *New York Times*.

The Pentagon Papers revealed that U.S. involvement in Vietnam during the administrations of Truman, Eisenhower, Kennedy, and Johnson had been far greater than the American public had been led to believe. Although Nixon wasn't mentioned in the study, he was enraged by its publication. He considered the Pentagon Papers an attack on his presidency and his handling of the war. Nixon unsuccessfully used both legal and illegal means to incriminate Ellsberg.

THE END OF THE WAR

By 1972, only about 24,000 American troops remained in Vietnam as Nixon continued his gradual withdrawal plan. However, that spring, North Vietnam launched attacks on South Vietnam, prompting Nixon to bomb North Vietnam. Once again, he was trying to force North Vietnam to negotiate a peace agreement. The bombing continued into the next presidential election, which Nixon won in a landslide. In December, one month after Nixon's re-election, the United States dropped more bombs on the North Vietnamese cities of Hanoi and Haiphong than they had dropped in the previous two years. The bombing devastated North Vietnam, destroying harbors, railway lines, and factories.

PRIMARY SOURCE

On January 23, 1973, Nixon addressed the nation on television and radio, announcing an agreement to bring an end to the war in Vietnam. In this excerpt from his address, Nixon echoes the "honorable peace" he'd promised.

Your steadfastness in supporting our insistence on peace with honor has made peace with honor possible. Now that we have achieved an honorable agreement, let us be proud that America did not settle for a peace that would have betrayed our allies, that would have abandoned our prisoners of war, or that would have ended the war for us but would have continued the war for the 50 million people of Indochina. Let us be proud of . . . those who sacrificed, who gave their lives so that the people of South Vietnam might live in freedom and so that the world might live in peace.

—from an address by President Nixon, 1973

On January 27, 1973, North Vietnam, South Vietnam, and the United States negotiated an agreement calling for U.S. troop withdrawal from South Vietnam in exchange for the release of prisoners of war. But Nixon declared the United States would attack North Vietnam again if it committed acts of aggression against South Vietnam. About two months after the signing, the last American troops departed South Vietnam: U.S. involvement in the war was over.

In direct violation of the agreement they signed, the communists began planning their attack on South Vietnam in October 1974. North Vietnamese troops moved into the nation in March 1975. Congress denied requests to send emergency aid to South Vietnam. In late April, Saigon fell to the communists. With the communist victory, the Vietnam War was finally over, but its memory and legacy would haunt the United States for years to come.

HISTORICAL THINKING

1. **READING CHECK** What was Vietnamization?

2. **ANALYZE CAUSE AND EFFECT** What social and political developments occurred as a result of the Cambodian ground invasion?

3. **DRAW CONCLUSIONS** In his 1973 address, what did Nixon mean by "peace with honor"?

4. **FORM AND SUPPORT OPINIONS** Do you think the U.S. involvement in Vietnam was justified? Explain why or why not.

LEGACY OF THE WAR

Many American veterans came home to a country they hardly recognized and where they seemed to be regarded as living symbols of an unpopular war. It would be difficult for everyone to adjust to the post-war world.

CASUALTIES OF WAR

Before 2010, the Vietnam War was the longest conflict in U.S. history. It claimed the lives of almost 60,000 Americans and about 2 million Vietnamese. As agreed, about two weeks after they signed the January 1973 peace agreement, the North Vietnamese began releasing American prisoners of war, or POWs. The POW camps freed 120 prisoners every two weeks, with the sick and injured leaving first, followed by those who had been imprisoned the longest. Some soldiers had been prisoners for more than 8 years, during which time many endured torture and isolation. Prisoners referred to one of the worst prison camps as the "Hanoi Hilton," a sarcastic reference to a famous hotel chain. At this camp in North Vietnam's capital, American soldiers were tortured and interrogated for information. It took about two months for all of the nearly 600 POWs to return home.

In 1973, about 2,500 American troops remained missing in action, or MIA. The Vietnamese landscape, with its thick jungles and swamps, made it difficult to locate the soldiers' remains. The military could not search the area for missing or dead soldiers because the United States never occupied North Vietnam. Though some of those who were MIA later returned to the United States and others were discovered to have died in POW camps, 1,600 men were still designated MIA in 2015.

Once veterans returned from Vietnam, they faced a new set of problems. Unlike soldiers of other wars, Vietnam veterans were not given a hero's welcome when they came home. No parades or celebrations awaited them. The country was still deeply divided over the war. For the most part, Americans didn't

🏛 Vietnam Veterans Memorial Washington, D.C.

The Vietnam Veterans Memorial consists of three parts: The Three Soldiers statue, the Vietnam Women's Memorial, and the Vietnam Veterans Memorial Wall, which lists the names of all the servicemen and women who died in the war. Men and women who served in Vietnam sometimes leave mementos of their war experience in front of the three memorials—especially boots. The National Park Service collects these items and stores them. Many are put on display at the Smithsonian Museum of American History.

want to hear about the veterans' experiences in the war. At best, the returning soldiers were ignored; at worst, they were despised. While most veterans made a successful return to civilian life, some struggled with physical injuries, mental health problems, and drug addictions that had begun while they were in Vietnam.

Some of the physical problems veterans suffered from were due to exposure to Agent Orange. The herbicide contained dioxin, a toxic compound that could cause a host of problems, such as cancer and birth defects. The government was slow to acknowledge the relationship between exposure to Agent Orange and the various health problems soldiers reported.

Other veterans experienced **post-traumatic stress disorder (PTSD)**, a condition brought on by injury or psychological trauma. Symptoms of PTSD can include flashbacks—vivid, realistic memories of horrific events—sleeping disorders, and sudden, often irrational bursts of anger. When they didn't receive adequate support or treatment for their physical and emotional problems, many veterans turned to substance abuse, and some committed suicide. Long after the troops had returned home, the effects of their time in Vietnam lingered, sometimes for many years.

LESSONS OF WAR

Attitudes at home about the war often reflected peoples' political viewpoints. Conservatives fumed because the United States had lost the war, while liberals thought the country should never have waged the war. As one veteran said, "The left hated us for killing, and the right hated us for not killing enough." Over time, though, conservatives learned that Vietnam veterans had fought valiantly under very challenging circumstances, and liberals learned that the veterans, too, were victims of the war.

The American public also collectively realized that forcing democracy on an unstable country such as Vietnam was a recipe for disaster. As a result of the war, Americans became more critical of their government. In fact, the escalation of the Vietnam War and the secret bombings of Laos and Cambodia proved to be the culmination, or conclusion, of Cold War strategies. Ultimately, Vietnam caused Americans to question the underlying assumptions of the Cold War era and protest against their government's policies abroad.

In the 1990s, the United States began to normalize relations with Vietnam. In 1994, President William Clinton lifted a trade embargo that the United States had imposed on North Vietnam in 1964 and on the newly reunited Vietnam in 1975. Veterans' groups

After Saigon fell to North Vietnam in April 1975, the United States evacuated Americans and many South Vietnamese by helicopter. In this photo, U.S. Marines help a long line of South Vietnamese board a helicopter on a lawn near the U.S. Embassy, seen in the background at the left. The helicopters made many trips, but not all those desperate to leave could be evacuated.

initially opposed this decision. However, Clinton lifted the embargo largely due to Vietnam's cooperation in tracking down and supplying information about American MIAs. Finally, in 1995, Clinton re-established diplomatic relations with Vietnam. In 1997, he named Douglas Peterson, a former American POW who had been imprisoned in Vietnam for six years, as the country's ambassador from the United States. Today, Vietnam is still a communist nation, but it has also embraced elements of capitalism and has a growing economy.

POLITICAL AND SOCIAL CHANGE

The impact of the Vietnam War extended to the U.S. Constitution. The document mandated that citizens had to be 21 years old to vote. But during the war, some people began to support lowering the voting age to 18. Arguing in favor of the age reduction in 1970, Senator Edward Kennedy of Massachusetts pointed out that about one-third of the troops fighting in Vietnam—and about one-half of those who died— were under the age of 21. Kennedy said, "At the very least, the opportunity to vote should be granted in recognition of the risks an 18-year-old is obliged to assume when he is sent off to fight and perhaps die for his country." Senator Kennedy also pointed out that many other countries, including South Vietnam, gave 18-year-olds suffrage. The **26th Amendment**, which reduced the voting age to 18, was ratified in 1971.

Another important political change took place a couple of years later. In 1973, Congress passed the War Powers Resolution, also known as the War Powers Act. The act required the president to notify Congress about any American troops sent overseas within 48 hours of their deployment. After 60 days, the president had to obtain congressional approval for the troops to remain in a state of armed conflict or make a formal declaration of war. Legislators intended the act as a check on the president's power to send troops into battle without the consent of Congress. Many believed the act was also passed to avoid future Vietnams.

The reunification of Vietnam brought about social change to the United States in the form of a significant influx of Southeast Asian immigrants. When Saigon fell to the North Vietnamese in April 1975, crowds of South Vietnamese fled to the U.S. Embassy and other buildings in the city, hoping to escape the communist invasion. Though U.S. pilots managed to evacuate 7,000 South Vietnamese in less than 24 hours—making the effort the largest

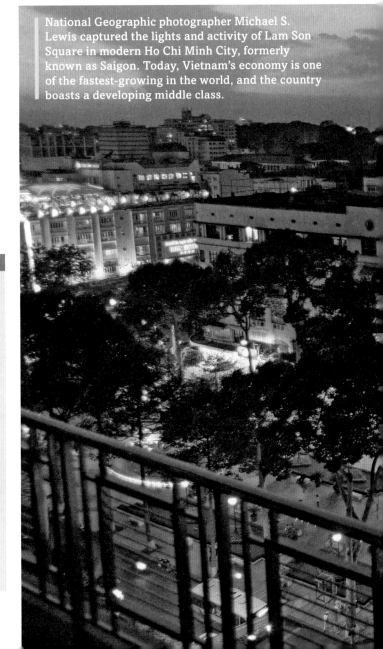

National Geographic photographer Michael S. Lewis captured the lights and activity of Lam Son Square in modern Ho Chi Minh City, formerly known as Saigon. Today, Vietnam's economy is one of the fastest-growing in the world, and the country boasts a developing middle class.

PRIMARY SOURCE

In 1975, John Tenhula began interviewing refugees from Vietnam, Cambodia, and Laos who immigrated to the United States. In this excerpt from an interview, Heng Mui, a South Vietnamese woman, talks about becoming an American citizen.

I became a citizen last year; I am now an American. I do not especially feel like an American, but I don't know if there is any special way I should feel. For some refugees, becoming an American is not an easy thing to do. It means you give up that final thing that is yours, your nationality. But after it happened, I never thought about it. There is something exciting about holding my new blue passport and knowing that I will vote next year for the president.

—from *Voices from Southeast Asia*, by John Tenhula, 1991

helicopter airlift in history—hundreds more were left behind in the embassy. About one month before the fall of Saigon, however, the U.S. government had ordered Operation Babylift. The government airlifted about 3,000 Vietnamese orphans from Saigon to the United States throughout April and placed them with adoptive parents.

Many Vietnamese, Cambodian, and Laotian refugees would arrive as immigrants to the United States in the coming decades, however. The greatest numbers of immigrants arrived between 1980 and 2000. Though the immigrant flow has since decreased, the Vietnamese still made up the sixth largest immigrant population in the United States as of 2014. Most settled in California, Texas, Washington, and Florida. Like other groups that have immigrated to the United States, the Vietnamese have become part of the country's rich diversity, and they now embrace their own American identities.

HISTORICAL THINKING

1. **READING CHECK** What problems did Vietnam veterans face when they returned home from the war?

2. **FORM AND SUPPORT OPINIONS** What do you think is the most important legacy of the Vietnam War? Support your opinion with evidence from the text.

3. **IDENTIFY** What domestic policies changed as a result of the Vietnam War?

4. **MAKE INFERENCES** Explain the meaning behind the Vietnam veteran's statement, "The left hated us for killing, and the right hated us for not killing enough," and describe how people's viewpoints toward Vietnam veterans could be so different.

VOCABULARY

Use each of the following vocabulary words in a sentence that shows an understanding of the term's meaning.

1. impasse
   Since neither side was willing to compromise, the negotiations reached an impasse.

2. hawk

3. post-traumatic stress disorder

4. coup

5. induction

6. escalation

7. deferment

8. counterculture

READING STRATEGY
FORM AND SUPPORT OPINIONS

When you form an opinion, you determine and assess the importance and significance of something. Your opinion is your personal judgment, not a fact, so you should support your opinion with examples and facts. Use a chart like this one to form and support an opinion about protesters during the Vietnam War. Then answer the question.

Role of Protesters		
Example/Fact	Example/Fact	Example/Fact
Opinion		

9. Do you think Vietnam War protesters played a positive or a negative role in the conflict?

MAIN IDEAS

Answer the following questions. Support your answers with evidence from the chapter.

10. Who were the Viet Cong? **LESSON 1.1**

11. Why was President Johnson initially opposed to sending American ground troops to Vietnam? **LESSON 1.2**

12. What was the purpose of General Westmoreland's war of attrition? **LESSON 2.1**

13. How did hawks and doves differ in their views of the war in Vietnam? **LESSON 2.2**

14. Why did the communists choose to begin their offensive on Tet? **LESSON 3.1**

15. Why did Johnson choose not to run for a second term as president? **LESSON 3.2**

16. What happened at My Lai? **LESSON 4.1**

17. What right did the 26th Amendment guarantee? **LESSON 4.2**

HISTORICAL THINKING

Answer the following questions. Support your answers with evidence from the chapter.

18. **ANALYZE CAUSE AND EFFECT** How did American journalists affect the war in Vietnam?

19. **EVALUATE** What did Martin Luther King, Jr., mean when he called the Vietnam War "a white man's war, a black man's fight"?

20. **MAKE INFERENCES** Why did the U.S. government present positive assessments of the war, even when it was going badly?

21. **DRAW CONCLUSIONS** How was the Tet Offensive a strategic victory for the communists in Vietnam?

22. **COMPARE AND CONTRAST** How was the war in Vietnam similar to and different from other Cold War struggles?

23. **ANALYZE CAUSE AND EFFECT** How did the Vietnam War cause Americans to question the assumptions behind Cold War policy?

24. **SUMMARIZE** What turned American public opinion against U.S. involvement in Vietnam?

25. **FORM AND SUPPORT OPINIONS** How do you think American society changed as a result of the Vietnam War?

26. **SYNTHESIZE** What combination of factors caused the United States to end its involvement in the Vietnam War?

27. **MAKE CONNECTIONS** What similarities do you detect between the Vietnam War and more recent conflicts in Southwest Asia?

INTERPRET GRAPHS

Study the graph below, which shows the Vietnamese immigrant populations in the United States between 1980 and 2010. Then answer the questions that follow.

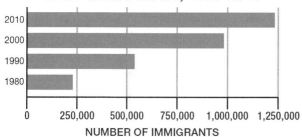

Vietnamese Immigrant Population in the United States, 1980–2010

NUMBER OF IMMIGRANTS

Sources: U.S. Census Bureau and American Community Surveys

28. Why do you think the number of Vietnamese immigrants more than quadrupled between 1980 and 2000?

29. How might Vietnam's growing economy explain why the number of immigrants coming to the United States had tapered off by 2010?

ANALYZE SOURCES

Tim O'Brien wrote about his experiences as a soldier in the Vietnam War. In this excerpt from his 1973 autobiographical story "If I Die in a Combat Zone," which appears in *The Vietnam Reader*, O'Brien discusses the summer he was drafted.

> The summer of 1968, the summer I turned into a soldier, was a good time for talking about war and peace. Eugene McCarthy was bringing quiet thought to the subject. Lyndon Johnson was almost forgotten. Robert Kennedy was dead but not quite forgotten; Richard Nixon looked like a loser. With all the tragedy and change that summer, it was fine weather for discussion. And, with all of this, there was an induction notice tucked into a corner of my billfold.

30. What details in the excerpt convey O'Brien's bias toward the politicians he names?

CONNECT TO YOUR LIFE

31. **ARGUMENT** Service in the armed forces today is voluntary. Do you think the draft should be reinstated? If so, do you think it should apply to both men and women? Write a paragraph in which you make an argument for or against the draft.

TIPS

- State your position on the draft.

- List arguments for and against the draft.

- Explain why you think either voluntary or required military service is more fair or just.

- Use information from the chapter to help support your ideas.

- Address the counterarguments you listed.

- Conclude your argument with a sentence summarizing your position.

CHAPTER 28
CHANGES IN SOCIETY 1960–1975

HISTORICAL THINKING How did new calls for equality and the space race impact American society?

AMERICAN **STORIES** | **One Giant Leap**

SECTION 1 **Latinos Organize**

SECTION 2 **Native Americans and Asian Americans**

SECTION 3 **Movements for Equality**

SECTION 4 **From Earth to the Moon**

AMERICAN **GALLERY** ONLINE | **The Women's Movement**

Taking a cue from Susan B. Anthony and the suffragists as well as the civil rights movement, women of the 1960s and 1970s used nonviolent resistance and marched for equal treatment. In the 21st century, women once more took to the streets for equality. More than 400,000 people joined the 2017 Women's March on Washington, D.C., declaring, "women's rights are human rights."

"**The fact that you can build and you can make nonviolent change through organization;** that's what I would want my legacy to be."

—Dolores Huerta, civil rights activist

ONE GIANT
LEAP

Astronauts Buzz Aldrin (shown here) and Neil Armstrong set up scientific experiments near their landing site on the moon. One of the experiments used seismometers powered by solar panels to measure lunar shock waves caused by seismic activity—moonquakes. It also measured the impact of meteoroids or other objects on the lunar surface.

On the evening of July 20, 1969, most Americans were fixated on a television screen, witnessing one of the greatest feats of engineering and technology in history: the first landing of a human on the moon. Years later in an interview, Neil Armstrong shared the credit for his lunar landing with a team of hundreds of thousands of men and women whose feet never left Earth, remarking, "Every guy that's setting up the tests, cranking the torque wrench, and so on, is saying—man or woman—'if anything goes wrong here, it's not going to be my fault.'"

Apollo 11
mission patch

THE SPACE RACE

Much of the technology needed to put Neil Armstrong and Buzz Aldrin on the moon was developed in a remarkably short span of time. One of the motivations for inventing that technology—competition—is as old as humanity.

As you have read, in 1957, the United States and the Soviet Union were engaged in a period of mutual distrust and hostility—the Cold War. Each country worried about the other developing more advanced weaponry or spying capabilities. When the Soviet Union launched *Sputnik* on October 4 of that year, Americans fretted that if the Soviets were more advanced in space technology, they might be ahead in weapons technology as well.

The American public was not reassured when, in December 1957, the U.S. Navy attempted to launch a satellite aboard a Vanguard rocket that caught fire upon take-off and crashed, earning the nickname "flopnik" from the press. A month later, however, the first U.S. satellite reached space atop a Jupiter rocket launched by the army. The space race between the Americans and Soviets was on.

HUMAN COMPUTERS

In May 1961, President Kennedy set out an ambitious goal in a speech before Congress, telling legislators, "I believe that this nation should commit itself to achieving the goal, before this decade is out, of landing a man on the moon and returning him safely to the earth." It was time to get to work.

Neil Armstrong's estimate of "hundreds of thousands" of people needed to place him on the moon was not an exaggeration. By one account, around 36,000 employees from NASA and 376,700 from universities or private industry worked on aspects of the lunar landing.

Armstrong was also correct to note that both men and women were involved in the massive effort. During the early years of space exploration, digital computers were not very advanced and could not perform the complex mathematics of placing a satellite, or a human being, in orbit or on the moon. That job fell to humans who held the job title of "computer" at NASA facilities such as Jet Propulsion Laboratory (JPL) in California and the Langley Research Center in Virginia. Most of the human computers were women.

Both Langley and JPL had started hiring female computers in the 1940s, before they became part of NASA, to calculate the trajectories of rockets and missiles being developed for World War II. Later, the women turned their superb math skills to plotting trajectories and calculating fuel loads for rockets that would carry satellites and humans into space.

The computers were a diverse group. At JPL, Helen Ling was an immigrant from China, and Janez Lawson was the first African American hired for a professional position at the laboratory. At Langley, many of the computers were African-American women who were forced to use a separate workspace and bathroom until the facility was officially desegregated in 1958.

As digital computers began to outpace humans' ability to perform calculations, the human computers became NASA's first programmers. In 1962, however, when preparing for his orbital flight, astronaut John Glenn was not ready to trust the new machines. He wanted Katherine Johnson, one of the African-American computers at Langley, to do the math. "Get the girl to do it," he said. "I want this human computer to check the output of the electronic computer, and if she says they're good, you know, I'm good to go."

On September 12, 1962, President John F. Kennedy gave a speech at Rice University about the quest for the moon. In it, he expressed his optimism and enthusiasm for the space program.

PRIMARY SOURCE

The exploration of space will go ahead, whether we join in it or not, and it is one of the great adventures of all time, and no nation which expects to be the leader of other nations can expect to stay behind in the race for space.

We mean to be a part of it—we mean to lead it. For the eyes of the world now look into space, to the moon and to the planets beyond, and we have vowed that we shall not see it governed by a hostile flag of conquest, but by a banner of freedom and peace. We have vowed that we shall not see space filled with weapons of mass destruction, but with instruments of knowledge and understanding.

Yet the vows of this Nation can only be fulfilled if we in this Nation are first, and, therefore, we intend to be first. In short, our leadership in science and in industry, our hopes for peace and security, our obligations to ourselves as well as others, all require us to make this effort, to solve these mysteries, to solve them for the good of all men, and to become the world's leading space-faring nation.

—from President John F. Kennedy's speech at Rice University, September 12, 1962

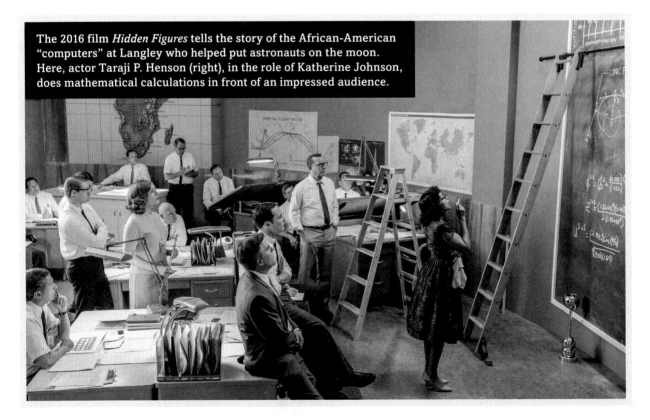

The 2016 film *Hidden Figures* tells the story of the African-American "computers" at Langley who helped put astronauts on the moon. Here, actor Taraji P. Henson (right), in the role of Katherine Johnson, does mathematical calculations in front of an impressed audience.

GOLD-PLATED SUN VISOR

PRESSURE-TIGHT INNER HELMET

MICROPHONE

BELLOWS FOR FLEXIBLE JOINT

EMERGENCY VALVE FOR PRESSURE AND VENTILATION

OXYGEN HOSE

PRESSURE GAUGE

POCKET FOR CONTINGENCY SAMPLE

LUNAR GLOVE

SELF-SEALING PATCH FOR EMERGENCY MEDICATION

21-LAYER FABRIC

1	NYLON
2	VINYL TUBING
3	LYCRA
4	NOMEX
5	NYLON COIL
6	NEOPRENE-COATED NYLON
7	NYLON
8	NEOPRENE-COATED NYLON
9	MYLAR
10	DACRON
11	MYLAR
12	DACRON
13	MYLAR
14	DACRON
15	MYLAR
16	DACRON
17	MYLAR
18	KAPTON
19	KAPTON
20	TEFLON-COATED GLASS FIBER
21	TEFLON

LUNAR OVERSHOE WITH TRACTOR-TREAD SOLE

OF SPACE SUITS AND GIRDLES

Before Sally Ride went into space aboard NASA's space shuttle in 1983, all American astronauts were men. And yet, the maker of the first space suits was best known for its popular lines of bras and girdles—attire not commonly associated with male pilots. The International Latex Corporation, known as Playtex, had experience and expertise in working with latex and other tough, stretchy fabrics—just the materials needed to make a space suit.

Skilled Playtex seamstresses had to meticulously assemble 21 layers of material into a space suit tailored to fit each astronaut. Neil Armstrong described the suit he wore on the moon as a "spacecraft," and it did indeed have to function as a one-man habitat, providing air and a constant temperature as he walked on the moon's inhospitable surface. In the 1970s, the division of Playtex that designed and made space suits split off to become a separate company called ILC Dover that continues to make space suits today.

How were the 1960s a period of rapid change? Explain your answer in the context of space technology, social values and norms, and politics.

TO THE MOON AND BACK

While the computers worked on the math, engineers and other specialists were laboring to develop the technology that could carry humans into space, keep them alive there, and bring them back to Earth. They invented a spacecraft called a command module that would launch atop a powerful Saturn V rocket, which would place it in orbit around the moon. A lunar module would detach from this spacecraft to land on the moon. For the return trip, the lunar module would blast off from the moon's surface to dock with the command module for the return to Earth. Every part of the rocket and modules had to be engineered to perfection. There would be no rescue if a key component malfunctioned in the airless cold of space.

Even packing food for the trip required enormous amounts of planning. NASA researchers had to consider what would happen to a sandwich in orbit. As author Mary Roach noted, "A crumb in zero gravity does not drop to the floor where it can be ignored and ground into the flooring until the janitor comes around." Instead, it can float into delicate equipment and cause real damage. Foods had to be devised that would be light, easily packed into tight spaces, and neat to eat. Sadly for the early astronauts, deliciousness wasn't a top requirement of space food.

When Neil Armstrong set foot on the moon, the United States won the space race. The prizes for winning, however, included benefits for all countries. Between 1969 and 1972, 12 astronauts walked on the lunar surface, gathering evidence that advanced our understanding of the solar system. These missions also spurred the growth of computer technology and led to numerous product advancements, from fireproof clothing to better navigation systems for airplanes.

THINK ABOUT IT

How did the space program affect the U.S. economy and society?

HOW TO PLANT A FLAG ON THE MOON

The American flag that was planted on the moon by the Apollo 11 astronauts symbolizes both a victory for the United States and the complexity of performing simple tasks without Earth's gravity.

Because there is no wind on the moon, but just enough gravity to pull a flag down into a droop, a special flagpole had to be designed with a hinged crossbar at the top from which the flag would hang. Next came the problem of how to transport the flagpole, as there was not enough room inside the lunar module. It had to be mounted on the outside of the vehicle in a specially engineered case that could withstand the 2,000-degree Fahrenheit heat produced by the module's descent engine.

Setting up the flag wearing gloves that limited their range of motion would be tricky for the astronauts once they reached the moon, so they conducted several practice sessions on Earth to make sure they could plant the flag while wearing space suits. As this photo reveals, all their planning and practice paid off.

EXPLORING ALTERNATIVE VIEWS

After the lunar landing, conspiracy theorists insisted the event was actually an elaborate hoax created by the U.S. government to appear to have beaten the Soviets to the moon. They claimed Armstrong and Aldrin acted out their space mission on a secret film set, citing evidence to support their theories.

One piece of so-called evidence is video footage of Aldrin planting a waving American flag on the moon. Conspiracy theorists claimed the moving flag reveals the presence of wind, which is impossible in space. NASA says Aldrin was twisting the flagpole to penetrate the lunar soil, causing the flag to wave.

Decades later, some still support the lunar landing conspiracy theory. Conduct research about the conspiracy theorists' alternative interpretation of the historic event. Analyze their evidence and consider why many experts and historians dispute it. **As you research, do the following:**

• Distinguish valid arguments from fallacious ones in the conspiracy theorists' historical interpretation.

• Identify any evidence of bias and/or prejudice in the conspiracy theorists' historical interpretation.

• Distinguish between sound generalizations and misleading oversimplifications in both the conspiracy theory and in the more widely accepted account of the lunar landing.

LIFE BEYOND EARTH?

National Geographic Explorer Kevin Hand wants to know if there is life beyond Earth. Working at JPL, the astrobiologist is helping to plan a NASA mission to Europa, a moon of Jupiter located about 600 million miles from Earth. In the 1990s, NASA's Galileo probe flew past the ice-covered moon and detected hints of a vast subsurface ocean. This led researchers to speculate about the possibility of life there. In 2013 and 2016, scientific teams using NASA's Hubble Space Telescope spotted what they believed were plumes of water erupting from beneath Europa's surface, raising hopes that a Europa probe might fly through a plume and analyze its chemistry.

To gain an understanding of the extreme conditions that might be found on other planets and their moons, Kevin Hand has explored such remote Earth locations as Alaska's north slope, Antarctica, and the depths of the ocean. "I'm trying to understand extremes of life here, so we can better assess and investigate habitable environments on alien worlds like Europa," he says.

Hand is as concerned about life on Earth as he is about possible life on a distant moon. He founded Cosmos Education, a foundation that helps educate and empower some of Africa's poorest children through science, health, and environmental education. "When I think about the desire to connect with life elsewhere in the universe," he reflects, "it gives me an incredible sense of the fragility of life here on Earth and how crucial it is to protect our collective home."

National Geographic's Kevin Hand prepares to deploy a rover beneath the ice of Alaska's Sukok Lake.

MISSIONS TO MARS

For some, the obvious next step in space exploration is Mars. NASA is exploring the possibility of sending astronauts to Mars and has already landed several unmanned vehicles on the planet. In September 2016, Elon Musk, owner of the private space contractor SpaceX, announced his goal to land a spaceship with humans aboard on Mars within a decade, establish a colony there, and ensure that humanity becomes a "multiplanetary species." Many are skeptical Musk can make this dream a reality in the foreseeable future, but his goals prove Mars exerts a strong pull on human imagination.

SpaceX's Falcon 9 rocket makes its first successful upright landing on a droneship in April 2016, 200 miles offshore in the Atlantic Ocean after launching from Cape Canaveral, Florida.

In the meantime, NASA missions are studying the sun and our solar system, expanding our understanding of the universe, and developing technology that also benefits humans on Earth. Whether we reach Mars in a decade or a century, it seems certain that our drive to explore space will continue to expand human knowledge and lead to new technologies we can only imagine today.

LATINO LIVES IN THE UNITED STATES

Once an idea takes hold, it tends to spread. The advances of the African-American civil rights movement encouraged other minority groups to mount their own campaigns for legislative and judicial recognition of their civil rights.

LATINOS IN THE 1950s AND 1960s

As you have read, the term *Latino* refers to someone whose heritage is Latin American. In the mid-20th century, the Latino population of the United States consisted of three main groups. The largest group of Latinos were Mexican Americans, who began coming to the United States in significant numbers during World War II as part of the Bracero Program, a government program created to fill the nation's need for agricultural workers. Most Mexican Americans settled in California and the Southwest. Cuban Americans, many of whom fled Cuba after communist leader Fidel Castro seized power, settled mainly in Florida. And about 900,000 Puerto Ricans lived in the United States at that time, the vast majority of them in New York City.

By 1960, almost 6 million Latinos lived in the United States. Within the next 10 years, the population had increased to over 9 million Latinos. Immigration rose largely because of the Immigration Act of 1965, which raised immigration quotas and eased restrictions on settling in the United States.

World War II generated opportunities for Mexican Americans, along with others, to serve on the battlefield and to support the war effort in a variety of ways. However, in the years following the war, Mexican Americans, like other minority groups, continued to face discrimination and bias. In 1948, the **American GI Forum (AGIF),** a newly formed Hispanic veterans' group, and other Mexican American organizations, such as the Unity League and the League of United Latin American Citizens (LULAC), mobilized during the postwar years to fight for Latinos' civil rights.

Aided by these organizations, Latinos pushed for greater equality in education. In 1948, organizers challenged the segregation of Latino children in Bastrop, Texas, and three other Texas school districts in the case *Delgado* v. *Bastrop Independent School District*. The suit maintained that the children were being separated and provided with substandard facilities because of their race and without any legal or educational basis. The court agreed and ordered an end to the segregation. This case was similar to *Mendez* v. *Westminster*, which, as you have read, preceded *Brown* v. *Board of Education* and paved the way to ending public school segregation nationwide.

Latinos also succeeded in advancing their legal rights, including a significant victory in the 1954 case *Hernandez* v. *Texas*. Supporters of farmworker Pete Hernandez sued the state of Texas after Hernandez was convicted of murder by an all-white jury. For many years, counties in Texas—including the county where Hernandez was tried—systematically kept Mexican Americans from serving as jurors. The Latino attorneys representing Hernandez argued that, because the jury had not been made up of Hernandez's **peers**, or equals, their client had been denied equal protection under the law as guaranteed by the 14th Amendment. The case, *Hernandez* v. *Texas*, went all the way to the U.S. Supreme Court. The Court ruled unanimously in favor of Hernandez, stating that the 14th Amendment guaranteed protection not only on the basis of race, but also on the basis of ethnicity. *Hernandez* v. *Texas* set a precedent, or a basic legal standard, for many of the civil rights cases that followed.

The *Arte de las Americas* mural runs along busy Calle Ocho, or Southwest 8th Street, in the Little Havana neighborhood, the heart of Cuban American life in Miami, Florida. Among the cultural icons portrayed on the wall are musicians, including world-famous salsa singer Celia Cruz.

A STRUGGLE FOR MANY

As Latinos pushed for greater civil rights, some made strides in achieving success. A number of Latinos joined the middle class. They also made notable achievements in the scientific fields. Latino biochemist Severo Ochoa received the Nobel Prize in medicine in 1959 for his research into the enzymes associated with DNA and RNA. Luis Alvarez received the Nobel Prize in physics in 1968 for his research into the basics of particle physics. Baseball star Roberto Clemente thrilled fans throughout the 1960s, while Cuban-born Desi Arnaz earned fame on the hit show *I Love Lucy* and became a successful television actor and producer.

For the vast majority of Latinos, however, success was a distant dream. In fact, life for the many Mexican American migrant workers was a struggle. Although migrant farm labor was vital to the success of the agricultural economy, in the mid-20th century migrant workers were not treated as the important human resource they were. They were paid poorly, earning an average of about $1,500 a year when the median U.S. income was about $6,200. They worked long hours with few breaks, and most lived in shacks, if they had housing at all. Because migrants continuously moved from farm to farm, most migrant children only occasionally attended school, and some received no education at all. And because they were poor and not well represented, farmworkers had been unable to organize or form a union, although they had been trying to improve their conditions since the end of World War II. Building upon the civil rights efforts of African Americans, a new generation of Latino leaders began an organized campaign to achieve greater equality and rights for farmworkers.

HISTORICAL THINKING

1. **READING CHECK** How did the Immigration Act of 1965 change the process for immigrating to the United States and transform American society?

2. **MAKE INFERENCES** How would serving in World War II affect the expectations of Latinos returning to the United States after the war?

3. **EVALUATE** How did the living and working conditions of migrant farmworkers make it difficult for them to demand greater equality and rights?

PANTONE® 58-7 C

PANTONE® 323-1 C

PANTONE® 51-6 C

1.2

THROUGH THE LENS

ANGÉLICA DASS

Humanæ, by the Brazilian artist Angélica Dass, is a photographic work intended to illustrate our similarities as global citizens. By identifying people with a Pantone color based on the actual color of their skin rather than by their nationality, gender, race, social class, or religion, Dass challenges us to think about how we see one another. Her portraits have been exhibited worldwide in museums and as public art installations.

PANTONE® 77-9 C

PANTONE® 58-6 C

PANTONE® 66-5 C

PANTONE® 97-7 C

PANTONE® 317-5 C

PANTONE® 58-7 C

PANTONE® 99-9 C

PANTONE® 321-6 C

PANTONE® 95-9 C

PANTONE® 62-6 C

PANTONE® 116-5 C

PANTONE® 7522 C

PANTONE® 92-9 C

PANTONE® 319-2 C

PANTONE® 57-7 C

PANTONE® 322-1 C

PANTONE® 71-5 C

PANTONE® 53-7 C

MINORITY WORKERS FIGHT FOR EQUALITY

Do you remember a time you felt ignored or treated unfairly? This was how a large number of Mexican American and Filipino American farmworkers felt during the 1960s. Latino and Filipino leaders joined forces to organize a historic campaign to win more rights for workers by drawing on strategies diffused from the African-American civil rights movement.

ORGANIZING FARMWORKERS

César Chávez was born in Yuma, Arizona, in 1927. His family owned a ranch and a grocery store, but they lost their property during the Great Depression. They moved to California, where they became migrant farmworkers. After serving two years in the U.S. Navy during World War II, Chávez returned to the fields. In 1952, Chávez became involved in the **Community Service Organization (CSO)**, a Latino civil rights group. He spoke on behalf of workers' rights and helped organize Latinos to register and vote in their local elections. In 1958, Chávez became director of the CSO.

During his time at the CSO, Chávez met **Dolores Huerta**. Huerta was born in New Mexico and moved at the age of three with her mother to Stockton, California, soon after her parents divorced. Growing up, Huerta was bright, talented, and a good student, but she often experienced discrimination because she was a Latina. After college, she became a teacher in an impoverished farming community. The difficult living situations of so many of her students— the children of migrant workers—inspired her to become an activist.

Chávez and Huerta quickly realized that they shared a common goal of helping better the lives and wages of farmworkers. Chávez left the CSO and formed the Farm Workers Association (FWA) while Huerta left to form the Agricultural Workers Association (AWA). In 1962, they merged their organizations to form the **National Farm Workers Association (NFWA)**. Their goal was to unionize farmworkers and help them seek better wages and more rights. The two activists were a powerful combination—Huerta was usually the negotiator and Chávez, an inspirational speaker and recruiter.

THE GRAPE BOYCOTT

Chávez and Huerta were dedicated to nonviolent protest. Chávez admired the work of Mohandas Gandhi and Martin Luther King, Jr., both of whom used nonviolent means—including boycotts and marches—to protest prejudice and injustice. These methods took time to deliver results, and Chávez knew that patience and cooperation were essential to success. In September 1965, Chávez and the NFWA joined a strike started by the **Agricultural Workers Organizing Committee (AWOC)**, made up largely of Filipino American grape packers in Delano, California. These farmworkers, led by labor leader **Larry Itliong**, were protesting a pay cut and demanding to be paid the legal minimum wage. On September 16, Mexican Independence Day, NFWA grape pickers walked out in solidarity with the AWOC strikers. It would be the beginning of *La Causa*, a five-year struggle to win a fair wage for the farm laborers.

Chávez organized a nationwide boycott of any grapes that did not bear a union label. To help build recognition for the strikers and the boycott, Chávez and Huerta led a peaceful 340-mile march from Delano, California, to the state capitol at Sacramento in March 1966. They began with only 100 people.

THE GREAT GRAPE STRIKE

For years, attempts to organize farmworkers were defeated, often by growers who had played one race against the other. But change began in 1965, when Larry Itliong and 1,000 mostly Filipino grape laborers walked off their jobs, demanding better pay. Within days, Itliong asked Dolores Huerta and César Chávez of the NFWA to join the strike. Dismayed at some growers' brutal treatment of the strikers, Chávez, Huerta, and 1,200 Latino farmworkers joined the strike. By working together, these three leaders brought new life to the nonviolent fight to gain equality for all farmworkers.

Dolores Huerta

César Chávez

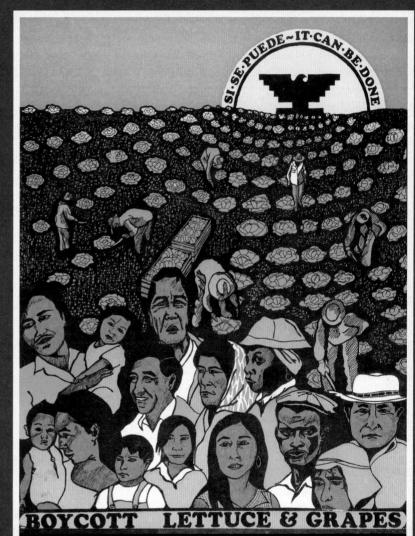

A boycott poster depicts farm-labor families gathered before a lettuce field as the setting sun displays the United Farm Workers symbol and its motto in Spanish and English. Immediately after the grape strike settlement, the UFW led a nationwide boycott of non-union lettuce to help improve lettuce pickers' wages and living conditions.

Larry Itliong

"We, as Filipinos, are not alone anymore. We have brothers among the Mexicans and the Blacks and in the conscience of the American people." —Larry Itliong

They finished the trek with more than 1,000. The pilgrimage drew national attention to the situation farmworkers faced. A few months later, in August, the NFWA and AWOC merged and became the United Farm Workers Organizing Committee, which later became the **United Farm Workers (UFW)**, a full-fledged union.

The union's combined strength enabled it to expand its protest movement and target all California grape growers. The UFW organized strikes and picket lines at farms across the state. Other unions offered their support. In the San Francisco Bay Area, for example, longshoremen refused to load grapes onto ships, instead leaving tons of grapes to rot on the docks. Meanwhile, a growing number of consumers in North America supported the workers by refusing to buy grapes. The campaign did not always go smoothly, and at one point Chávez went on a 24-day water-only fast to protest against some of his own union members who were advocating more violent forms of opposition. As grape growers watched their profits decline, they eventually gave in to the UFW. In 1970, the boycott ended as growers agreed to a collective bargaining agreement with at least 10,000 laborers, as well as better wages, union recognition, a health clinic, a health plan, and a credit union.

FIGHTING FOR CHICANO RIGHTS

As Latino civil rights efforts gained greater attention, a growing number of Mexican Americans in California and the Southwest began raising their voices. Throughout the 1960s, scores of activists and young people mobilized to protest a variety of issues—including the Vietnam War, police brutality,

---

PRIMARY SOURCE

I am Joaquín,
Lost in a world of confusion,
Caught up in a whirl of a gringo society,
Confused by the rules,
Scorned by attitudes,
Suppressed by manipulation,
And destroyed by modern society.
My fathers
  have lost the economic battle
and won
  the struggle of cultural survival.

—from the epic poem *I Am Joaquín*, by Rodolfo "Corky" Gonzales, 1967

What do you think the poet means when he says "My fathers have lost the economic battle and won the struggle of cultural survival"?

---

and economic and social inequalities—as well as to promote cultural pride. Many activists began identifying with the term "Chicano," another name for Mexican American, and their different protests and campaigns became known collectively as the **Chicano Civil Rights Movement**, or "El Movimiento."

A leading voice in the movement was **Rodolfo "Corky" Gonzales**, a poet and activist in Denver who called on Chicanos to take greater control over their own destinies. He argued that the white establishment could not provide adequate education, economic stability, or social acceptance, and that Chicanos should look for alternatives. Under his leadership, Denver's Chicano community developed its own school, newspaper, and credit bureau, and it continued to fight for better economic and housing opportunities. Gonzales became the voice of the Chicano movement when his epic poem *I Am Joaquín* became widely read. It is an elegant statement of the complex history of Mexican Americans and their lives in the United States.

Gonzales also convened the first Chicano Youth Liberation Conference in Denver in 1969, which was attended by many activists and artists. At the conference, attendees drafted the *El Plan Espiritual de Aztlán*, more commonly known as **El Plan de Aztlán**. This **manifesto**, or declaration, called for a new nationalism among Chicanos. It spoke to the dream of gaining back the land Mexico surrendered to the United States—including California and much of the Southwest—in the Treaty of Guadalupe Hidalgo in 1848.

In California, Chicano students became increasingly engaged in El Movimiento. In 1968, approximately 15,000 high school students protested racial discrimination and low-quality education by walking out of their classrooms in five East Los Angeles high schools in a series of protests they called "blowouts." At that time, schools in Los Angeles received funding based on how many students attended per day. By walking out of their homerooms before attendance was taken, the students made their point both actively and financially. Although the blowouts did not bring about immediate change, they empowered the Chicano community and built unity and solidarity for the cause. Chicano activists also drafted the **El Plan de Santa Bárbara: A Chicano Plan for Higher Education**, a document that called for the creation of Chicano Studies programs throughout the California state college system. In a victory for the Chicano movement, state officials adopted the plan in April 1969.

©Herald-Examiner Collection/Los Angeles Public Library

THE LOS ANGELES BLOWOUTS
During a walkout at Belmont High School in East Los Angeles, police in riot gear handcuff a member of the Brown Berets (left) and a press photographer (right). The **Brown Berets**, a group within the Chicano movement, arose in East Los Angeles in 1968 to agitate for the Chicano community. A militant group modeled on the Black Panthers, they focused on educational and employment opportunities and against police harassment and brutality. They also established a free clinic and supported the creation of urban Chicano art and murals. Following the blowouts across East Los Angeles, 13 of the activist leaders were arrested and charged with "conspiring to disrupt education," which was punishable by up to 66 years in jail. The charges were dropped for violating the Bill of Rights, but only after 2 years of legal battles.

As part of their fight for greater equality and rights, some Chicano activists publicly protested the Vietnam War, claiming that a disproportionately high number of Mexican Americans were being drafted, wounded, and killed in the conflict. Across the country, Chicanos engaged in a series of antiwar protests, which became known as the Chicano Moratorium. This movement culminated in a major protest in Los Angeles in August 1970. The protest proceeded peacefully enough, as more than 30,000 people marched through East Los Angeles. Although it inspired more Hispanics to become involved in the movement for Chicano rights, it ended in tragedy as protesters were met with a heavy-handed police response. In the resulting violence, three people were killed.

In Texas in 1968, the **Mexican American Legal Defense Education Fund (MALDEF)** was founded specifically to protect and promote Latino civil rights. Modeled on the NAACP's Legal Defense Fund and LULAC, the organization's role was to provide the legal expertise for the grassroots Latino community. Throughout the 1960s, Chicanos increased their political activity, and by the end of the decade they had organized their own political party. José Angel Gutiérrez, later an attorney and college professor,

founded the **La Raza Unida Party** in response to many Chicanos' dissatisfaction with the mainstream political parties. La Raza Unida promoted Chicano nationalism and was most influential in Texas and southern California. The party experienced its greatest successes at the local level in southwest Texas, where its members won seats on a number of city councils and school boards. But the party failed to gain widespread support, and by the late 1970s, it had faded away. However, Hispanic Americans around the country would continue to organize politically and work to promote their causes at the local, state, and national levels of government.

HISTORICAL THINKING

1. **READING CHECK** What were the goals of the National Farm Workers Association?

2. **DRAW CONCLUSIONS** Why was the cooperation of Chávez, Huerta, and Itliong vital to maintaining a five-year, nonviolent strike and boycott?

3. **ANALYZE CAUSE AND EFFECT** What were some of the actions that finally forced the grape growers to agree on a fair contract with farmworkers?

4. **MAKE GENERALIZATIONS** Why did Chicanos protest the war in Vietnam as a civil rights issue?

NATIVE AMERICANS MOBILIZE

What are the things you like most about where you live? Why do you consider your neighborhood a special place? Many Native Americans considered their ancient homelands special and sacred. They did not want to move from their lands. Instead, they wanted greater rights and opportunities to improve their living conditions.

THE DECLARATION OF PURPOSE

In the 1960s, Native Americans were one of the nation's smallest minority groups, but collectively, they continued to suffer greatly. Many lived in poverty and faced discrimination and neglect from the nation at large.

As you have read, the U.S. government enacted the termination policy in the early 1950s in an effort to better assimilate Native Americans into mainstream society. Officials ended federal support for reservations—many of which had become isolated, poverty-stricken places—and tried to urge Native American families to move to the cities, where more jobs were available. The effort was largely a failure.

Many Native Americans did not wish to assimilate. Instead, they began to seek greater rights and opportunities as they insisted on preserving their distinct culture and staying on their land. **Ben Nighthorse Campbell**, a member of the Northern Cheyenne tribe and later a U.S. senator from Colorado, spoke for many Native Americans in criticizing the

PRIMARY SOURCE

After the American Indian Chicago Conference, President Kennedy met with delegates from 90 Native American tribes, including (from left) Eleanor Red Fawn Smooth, Mohawk and Cherokee Nations, Connecticut; Calvin W. McGhee, Atmore, Alabama, representing the Creek Nation east of the Mississippi; and Kathitha Addison, of the Narragansett Nation. They spoke on the lawn of the White House, where Kennedy acknowledged the plight of Native Americans and promised his support.

I hope that this visit here, which is more than ceremonial, will be a reminder to all Americans of the number of Indians whose housing is inadequate, whose education is inadequate, whose employment is inadequate, whose health is inadequate, whose security and old age is inadequate—a very useful reminder that there is still a good deal of unfinished business.

—John F. Kennedy, August 15, 1962

termination policy. "If you can't change them [Native Americans], absorb them until they simply disappear into the mainstream culture," he declared with irony. "In Washington's infinite wisdom, it was decided that tribes should no longer be tribes, never mind that they had been tribes for thousands of years."

Rather than assimilate, Native Americans pushed to preserve their identity and demanded greater support from the federal government in helping them improve their lives. In 1961, some 700 Native Americans from 64 tribes met in Chicago to draft a common agenda and call to action. During the weeklong conference, the group created the **Declaration of Indian Purpose**, a document listing the major issues facing Native Americans and calling for a policy of greater self-determination. "We, the Indian People, must be governed in a democratic manner with a right to choose our own way of life," the statement declared. "We believe we have the responsibility of preserving our precious heritage." The declaration urged the federal government to move away from its termination policy and instead help Native Americans to better thrive on their own. "What we ask of America," the declaration stated, "is that the nature of our situation be recognized and made the basis of policy and action."

SLOW PROGRESS

By the early 1960s, U.S. officials began pulling back from the termination policy and instead promoted greater self-determination for Native Americans. Activists found sympathetic supporters in both President Kennedy and President Johnson. Kennedy secured funding to build adequate public housing on a prominent Native American reservation, and he worked during his short time as president to set the groundwork for later legislation promoting greater rights and federal support for Native Americans.

When Lyndon Johnson assumed the presidency after Kennedy's death, he pledged to help Native Americans as part of his War on Poverty. As you have read, this program sought to create a decent standard of living for all Americans. Early in his term Johnson stated, "Both in terms of statistics and in terms of human welfare, it is a fact that America's first citizens, our Indian people, suffer more from poverty than any other group in America." In 1968, Johnson gave a speech titled "The Forgotten American" to Congress, in which he stressed the need to raise Native American living standards to the same level as that of other American citizens. He said that Native Americans should be able to

live wherever they pleased, whether it was on a reservation or in a city, and that any Native American policy should stress self-help, self-development, and self-determination for the minority group. "For two centuries," Johnson told Congress, "he [the Native American] has been an alien in his own land."

Despite such commitment at the highest level, progress proved slow. Among Native Americans, younger activists began to express frustration—both with the federal government and their own tribal leaders—over what they viewed as too little action and too few results. A group of younger leaders eventually broke away and formed the **National Indian Youth Council (NIYC)**. The NIYC included members of diverse tribes, yet they shared the same agenda: to draw greater attention to the cause of Native Americans through stronger mobilization and protest. The NIYC charter, or founding document, declared, "We, the younger generation, at this time in the history of the American Indian, find it expedient [practical] to band together on a national scale in meeting the challenges facing our Indian people."

NIYC priorities included reclaiming Native American hunting and fishing rights on their traditional lands. Diffusing the African-American civil rights movement model of sit-ins, NIYC held "fish-ins" by occupying areas around rivers and disrupting the commercial fishing activity there. Members of the group also protested at museums that displayed sacred artifacts taken from their tribes. They challenged movies and other media to present more honest portrayals of Native Americans and asked colleges and universities to create Indian Studies programs. These efforts revealed a younger generation of Native Americans ready to advance its agenda through bolder protest strategies. In the years ahead, they would engage in even more disruptive and confrontational tactics in their quest to gain greater rights.

HISTORICAL THINKING

1. **READING CHECK** What was the thinking behind the Declaration of Purpose?

2. **ANALYZE LANGUAGE USE** Why do you think President Kennedy kept repeating the word "inadequate" in the primary source quotation?

3. **EVALUATE** Why did young Native American leaders start the National Indian Youth Council?

4. **COMPARE AND CONTRAST** How were the federal policies and actions toward Native Americans in the 1960s different from those of the past, and why?

MAIN IDEA In their fight for greater rights, some Native Americans moved away from peaceful demonstrations and turned to more confrontational protests.

NATIVE AMERICAN ACTIVISM

The advances of the African-American civil rights movement helped breathe new life into Native Americans' fight for their own rights, but the way forward proved to be more difficult. Native Americans were few in number and saw little public attention paid to their cause. As a result, they began taking more extreme measures to make their voices heard.

THE AMERICAN INDIAN MOVEMENT

In 1968, a group of Native American activists in Minneapolis founded the **American Indian Movement (AIM)**. The group's founders, including **George Mitchell, Dennis Banks**, and others, were members of the Ojibwe (oh-JIHB-way) tribe. Their goal was to help fellow Native Americans displaced during the years of the termination policy and to call attention to their substandard living conditions. AIM established urban centers where Native Americans could meet to give and receive help finding jobs, housing, and transportation. The organization grew and set up chapters in Cleveland, Chicago, Milwaukee, Denver, and San Francisco.

As AIM expanded, its leaders' strategies took an increasingly active and **militant**, or forceful, turn in promoting Native American rights. In November 1969, AIM members occupied the abandoned federal prison on Alcatraz Island in San Francisco Bay as a protest against the city's refusal to let Native Americans use the site as a cultural and heritage center. AIM initially received an outpouring of support in the form of donated funds, food, and clothing, but the protest eventually lost momentum and effectiveness. The occupiers included a number of local college students who returned to school and were replaced by people less interested in the cause than in living rent-free. By June 1971, the number of occupiers had dwindled, and U.S. marshals removed them from the island.

A "Remember Wounded Knee" embroidered patch from the American Indian Movement

A year later, a week before the 1972 presidential election, AIM organized the "Trail of Broken Treaties," a march on Washington, D.C., involving about 1,000 protesters. It ended with the occupation of the **Bureau of Indian Affairs (BIA)** headquarters. AIM protesters seized large numbers of files from the BIA offices and caused more than $2 million in damage to the building. They also presented President Nixon with 20 demands for immediate action. Government officials eventually negotiated a peaceful end to the occupation.

Meanwhile, in Minnesota, AIM leaders helped parents establish Native American "survival schools" to avoid the biases of local child welfare and legal systems. As the schools multiplied, they engaged adults and students with issues of Native American language, culture, spirituality, and identity.

PROTESTS AT WOUNDED KNEE

In February 1973, AIM engaged in what would become one of its best-known and most violent protests. About 200 members of the Oglala Lakota tribe along with AIM leaders seized and occupied the town of Wounded Knee, South Dakota, on the Pine Ridge Reservation. The occupiers were protesting the failure to impeach tribal president Richard Wilson, whom they accused of corruption and abuse of opponents. They were also protesting the U.S. government's failure to fulfill promises made in treaties with Native Americans, and they

CRITICAL VIEWING In 1969, the members of various Native American tribes held a vigil, or watchful protest, on the dock at Alcatraz Island as other members negotiated with the U.S. government over the island's fate. What alterations were made to the sign behind the occupiers, and what do you think was the purpose of the alterations?

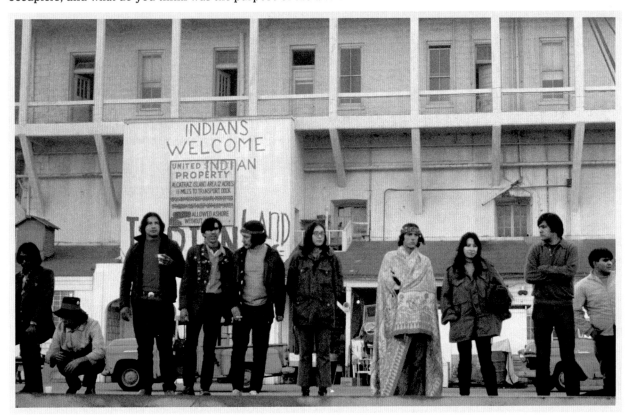

demanded the reopening of treaty negotiations. The activists chose the site of the 1890 Wounded Knee Massacre, where federal troops had killed more than 150 Lakota. A tense standoff ensued for 71 days, in which two AIM members were shot and killed and a U.S. marshal was shot and paralyzed. Ultimately, a truce was negotiated and federal officers agreed to review a number of treaties made with Native Americans. Dennis Banks and another prominent AIM leader, **Russell Means**, were charged with crimes for their role in the event, but the charges were later dismissed.

Despite their largely symbolic protests, the strategies and effectiveness of Native Americans led to some gains. In 1975, Congress passed the **Indian Self-Determination and Educational Assistance Act**, which boosted funds for Native American education and gave Native Americans greater control in administering local programs. In 1978, Congress passed the **Indian Religious Freedom Act**, which allowed Native Americans to practice their traditional religions freely. Native Americans also gained greater representation within the Bureau of Indian Affairs, a federal organization they had long criticized for not being fully attentive to their needs.

In addition, Native Americans used the courts to accomplish what protests could not. They sued state and federal governments to force compliance with old treaties that had been ignored and took legal action to win back numerous land and water rights. The Pueblo in New Mexico, for example, regained rights to their land, as did several tribes in Maine. Court decisions also enabled Native Americans to receive millions of dollars for their land claims, while other rulings allowed Native Americans to impose taxes on businesses on their reservations and take greater control of their economic futures.

HISTORICAL THINKING

1. **READING CHECK** Why did the American Indian Movement take more drastic actions than other civil rights movements?

2. **ANALYZE CAUSE AND EFFECT** What effect did the passage of the Indian Self-Determination and Education Assistance Act have on the Native American community?

3. **DRAW CONCLUSIONS** How effective were the lawsuits brought by Native Americans to establish their basic civil rights? Support your response with evidence from the text.

ASIAN AMERICAN CIVIL RIGHTS

Asia, the world's largest continent, encompasses many diverse countries and cultures. As a result, the term "Asian American" refers to all Americans of Asian origin. They share a desire for equal opportunities in the United States.

DISCRIMINATION AGAINST ASIAN AMERICANS

Like other groups seeking equal civil rights, the story of Asian Americans has been one of exclusion, discrimination, and the gradual gaining of rights and respect. The decision by Congress to pass the Chinese Exclusion Act in 1882 was based largely on complaints that Chinese immigrants were taking labor union jobs. The measure denied any Chinese person the opportunity to immigrate to the United States. The Immigration Act of 1924 expanded the law and excluded all Asians. It wasn't until World War II, when the United States and China became allies, that restrictions against Chinese immigration were eased. During the war, as you learned, it was

Japanese Americans who suffered discrimination, and worse. Thousands of Japanese Americans were confined to internment camps based on fears they were disloyal and dangerous.

Internment robbed many Japanese Americans of their homes, land, and livelihoods, and racist discrimination made it hard for many of them to recover their property. For example, in California, an Alien Land Law passed in 1913 prohibited Asian immigrants who were noncitizens—usually because of immigration restrictions—from owning agricultural land. Kajiro Oyama had moved to the United States as a teenager. In 1934, he bought six acres of farmland, registering the property in the name of his son, Fred,

Protesters surrounded the San Francisco State College administration building, demonstrating against alleged racism and political harassment by college administrators.

who had been born in the United States and thus was an American citizen. During World War II, the Oyama family took part in a "voluntary evacuation," relocating to Utah rather than being forced into an internment camp. When they returned to California after the war, they found that their farm had been seized. With the help of the **Japanese American Citizens League**, Kajiro sued to get his land back. *Oyama* v. *California* reached the U.S. Supreme Court, which ruled in 1948 that Fred Oyama's rights as an American citizen had been violated. The Oyama family retained ownership of the land, but the Court did not overturn the Alien Land Law until 1952.

Other Asian American groups also endured discrimination. As you have read, Filipino Americans worked largely as farm laborers and collaborated with Latino workers to push for better pay and more rights. Pacific Islanders struggled in their relations with the United States. The natives of Guam became Americans overnight when the United States acquired their island after winning the Spanish-American War in 1898. But Americans did little to acknowledge and support the island's culture. Similarly, when the United States annexed the Hawaiian Islands in 1898, land was taken from native Hawaiians and their culture suffered from the imposition of American values in the territory.

PROGRESS ON CIVIL RIGHTS

As a result of the Immigration Act of 1965, which raised quotas on immigrants from outside Europe, the number of Asian Americans grew steadily through the second half of the 20th century. In the 1950s, Asians represented 6 percent of all immigrants to the United States, and by 1980, that number had climbed to 42 percent. Like other groups that had to fight for their civil rights, Asian Americans and Pacific Islanders also vary widely in their backgrounds and cultures, and as they grew in numbers, they united to fight for greater rights and recognition.

In 1968, students at the University of California, Berkeley, started the **Asian American Political Alliance (AAPA)** to advocate on behalf of Asian Americans. The group fought for many issues, from improved housing for poor Asians to use of the term "Asian American" rather than widely used derogatory terms. That same year, Asian American students went on strike at San Francisco State College (renamed San Francisco State University in 1974). Forming a coalition with other student groups, including the Black Student Union and the Third World Liberation Front (a group that included Native Americans, African Americans, and Latinos),

PRIMARY SOURCE

Born on a U.S. military base in Japan in 1948, Merilynne Hamano Quon came to adulthood in the turbulent 1960s. As an activist, she drew on her own experiences of racism as well as on those of her parents and grandparents during World War II.

While American society saw Japanese Americans as the model minority, many in the Japanese American community suffered quietly, on their own, with problems that could be traced directly back to racism and what happened in our community during World War II. My mother's mother died while sharecropping in Utah after her father "voluntarily" evacuated his family to Utah during World War II.

—from a memoir by Merilynne Hamano Quon in *Asian Americans: The Movement and the Moment*

the students demanded establishment of an Ethnic Studies program. The strike lasted five months until the university acquiesced, agreeing to add the program. In 1969, students and activists in Seattle, Washington, founded the **Asian Coalition for Equality (ACE)**, which protested police brutality and worked to desegregate the region's industries and open up clubs and organizations to minorities.

Meanwhile, Japanese Americans began pressuring the federal government to issue an apology for the World War II internment camps. In 1976, the government responded. President Gerald Ford signed **Proclamation 4417**, formally apologizing for the internment program. Twelve years later, President Reagan signed the **Civil Liberties Act of 1988**, which paid each living internee $20,000 in reparations for what they had experienced in the camps. Today, some 18 million Asian Americans and Pacific Islanders live in the United States. That is about 5.8 percent of the country's population. Their population continues to grow, and while they continue to face prejudice, they also continue to achieve success and help to shape and build the American identity.

HISTORICAL THINKING

1. **READING CHECK** What kinds of discrimination have Asian Americans faced?

2. **IDENTIFY** What were the reasons given for American immigration policies, and how did bias or prejudice contribute to the policies' transformation of society?

3. **COMPARE AND CONTRAST** How are Asian Americans similar to and different from other groups seeking equal rights?

New Voices for Women

Did you ever expect a streak of good fortune to continue, and then it didn't? After World War II, the professional opportunities American women had grown accustomed to decreased, and women were strongly discouraged from working outside the home.

THE WOMEN'S MOVEMENT REAWAKENS

Like other groups, women had done their fair share during World War II. They worked in factories and served in the military, although they were not officially allowed to fight in combat. Yet, as you have read, after the war many women found themselves back in the midst of domestic life. They were often discouraged from pursuing careers, and those still in the workforce generally received lower pay than men doing the same jobs.

Even so, in the post-war years the nation made some attempts to address the problem of limited opportunities for women. In 1961, President Kennedy created the **President's Commission on the Status of Women**, a 20-member committee chaired by Eleanor Roosevelt, that developed recommendations for overcoming employment discrimination and establishing services "which will enable women to continue their role as wives and mothers while making a maximum contribution to the world around them." The committee recommended paid maternity leave, affordable child care, and equal employment opportunities. Its report led to the **Equal Pay Act of 1963**, which prohibited wage discrimination based on sex. Two years later, in 1965, President Johnson established the Equal Employment Opportunity Commission (EEOC) to help give women greater security in the workplace.

The EEOC, for example, declared that employers who fired a woman for such acts as getting married or having a baby were in violation of federal law.

Despite these actions, progress for women was slow. Just like other groups, women realized they could not rely solely on the federal government. They would have to push for greater equality themselves. Like their predecessors in the early 1900s, women in the 1960s began to mobilize. In the eyes of many, the effort began with the publication of a groundbreaking book.

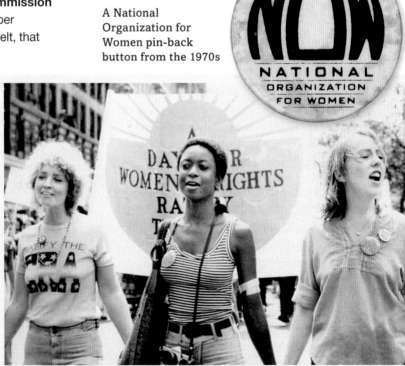

A National Organization for Women pin-back button from the 1970s

In 1970s' New York City, three young women donned Equal Rights Amendment (ERA) buttons to march for the ERA and celebrate a day for women's rights.

Its author was **Betty Friedan**, a graduate of Smith College who worked as a reporter. When Friedan and her husband Carl were expecting their second child, she lost her job, so she stayed home to raise her children. But she experienced a growing sense of restlessness and frustration with the limits imposed on her by society. She talked to other Smith graduates and discovered that many felt the same way.

Friedan compiled what she learned into a book called *The Feminine Mystique*. The word *mystique* means "an air of mystery," and in this context, referred to the silent unhappiness, or "problem that had no name," that many women dealt with. Published in 1963, *The Feminine Mystique* challenged the assumption that all women wanted to be mothers and homemakers. The book encouraged women to seek their own paths.

Response to the book was overwhelming, and it became a bestseller. Women across the country began voicing their dissatisfaction and their demands. The idea of "choice," implicit in the book, captured what many women wanted: the opportunity to make choices that weren't limited to domestic roles or by other people. While the book's ideas may seem less controversial now than they did in 1963, *The Feminine Mystique* is still considered one of the most influential books of its time. Inspired, women wanted their contributions and importance acknowledged, and began working to promote the ideals of **feminism**, or greater political, economic, social, and cultural rights for women. **Gloria Steinem** was another writer and feminist who used communication to unite women in the fight for equality. In 1971, she and several other feminists founded *Ms.*, a successful magazine that focused on life and politics from women's perspectives.

FEMINISM IN ACTION

The civil rights movements of the 1960s helped fuel women's push for greater equality. Women were obviously inspired by the efforts of African Americans and other minorities in their quest for equality, and many women became part of and worked hard for civil rights causes. Ironically, however, many women who joined the larger civil rights movements reported feeling like second-class citizens, restricted to unimportant tasks and largely kept out of any policy decisions. Just as in their personal lives, women found that their contributions were not as highly valued as those of men. It was clear that in order to achieve success in their quest for equality, women needed to form their own movement and promote their agenda.

In 1966, Friedan and other women leaders gathered together to form the **National Organization for**

PRIMARY SOURCE

The problem lay buried, unspoken, for many years in the minds of American women. It was a strange stirring, a sense of dissatisfaction, a yearning that women suffered in the middle of the twentieth century in the United States. Each suburban wife struggled with it alone. As she made the beds, shopped for groceries, matched slipcover material, ate peanut butter sandwiches with her children, chauffeured Cub Scouts and Brownies, lay beside her husband at night—she was afraid to ask even of herself the silent question—"Is this all?"

—from *The Feminine Mystique,* by Betty Friedan, 1963

What information in the source leads you to understand why Friedan and others decided to form a women's rights organization?

Women (NOW). This grassroots association of activist feminists included not only straight women and lesbians, but also men. NOW's goals extended beyond fair pay: it wanted to guarantee women's access to health care, including reproductive rights, affordable child care, and the passage of equal rights legislation at the state and national levels. Similar to the NAACP, NOW pursued legal equality for women in the public sphere. The group lobbied Congress to pass laws emphasizing equality for women, raised awareness about women's issues, and reached out to women in all walks of life to promote feminism.

Led by NOW, feminists pushed for significant changes in society, and while their fight ahead would be a difficult one, they would achieve a number of groundbreaking victories. A major victory for women occurred in 1968 when **Shirley Chisholm** was elected the first African-American Congresswoman. She represented her Brooklyn, New York, district for seven terms, building a reputation as a "people's politician" and "Fighting Shirley" from her advocacy for inner-city poor people.

HISTORICAL THINKING

1. **READING CHECK** Why did women want a larger role in society?

2. **DRAW CONCLUSIONS** Why was *The Feminine Mystique* so much more controversial when it first appeared than it is today?

3. **ANALYZE CAUSE AND EFFECT** What lesson did women learn from their early participation in the civil rights movements of the 1960s?

WOMEN SEEK EQUALITY

The fight for equality sometimes proceeds at an uneven rate, with breakthroughs and advances alternating with long periods where progress is difficult or impossible. Half a century after securing the right to vote, women were still struggling for fair wages, attention to women's health issues, and an end to discrimination based on gender.

BATTLES FOR GENDER EQUALITY

NOW leaders and women activists pushed for a number of reforms. One area they focused on was long-standing **gender bias**, or the preference for one gender over another, against women in education. In particular, activists targeted the area of women's sports, which schools and colleges viewed as an afterthought. Women's teams often received little funding and support. As a result, women had fewer opportunities to earn scholarships or play collegiate sports. Feminists pushed for federal legislation banning gender discrimination in education. In 1972, Congress passed a law known collectively as the **Education Amendments**. One section, **Title IX**, prohibited federally funded schools from discriminating against girls and women in nearly all areas, from admissions to athletics. Title IX helped to bolster women's athletics as well as to give women and girls the chance to obtain athletic and academic scholarships formerly reserved only for men.

Women also made advances on social and cultural fronts. Throughout the 1970s, feminists promoted women's health clinics and opened shelters for victims of domestic abuse. They tackled day-to-day sexism with the mantra "the personal is political"— meaning they were willing to fight against laws that restricted their personal and private lives.

One such area was women's health, particularly reproductive rights. When the Food and Drug Administration approved the use of an oral birth control pill in 1960, women finally had access to a discreet, extremely effective contraceptive, or means of preventing pregnancy. But some states still made it difficult for women to use birth control. In Connecticut, birth control had been outlawed in 1879. Women's groups claimed the law unconstitutionally denied women a right to privacy. The case, ***Griswold v. Connecticut***, went to the U.S. Supreme Court. In a victory for women, the Court agreed, ruling in 1965 that a ban on contraceptives violated privacy rights. The debate over forms of birth control continued, especially among Catholics. In the Second Vatican Council (Vatican II), held in 1962, the Church had an impact on civil rights and other human rights movements by encouraging its members to participate in them. But the Church was less supportive of women's rights when, in 1968, it condemned "artificial" birth control, defying a growing consensus among its parishioners.

In 1973, feminists achieved victory for a woman's right to make personal choices again, in a landmark case that remains controversial even today: ***Roe v. Wade***. During the 1950s and 1960s, abortion, or the purposeful termination of a pregnancy, was illegal in most states. Two Texas attorneys sued on behalf of "Jane Roe," an unnamed defendant, arguing that the inability to obtain a safe abortion violated Roe's constitutional right to privacy. The Supreme Court agreed, saying that a woman's decision to end her pregnancy lay within the "zone of privacy" that is protected by the Constitution. Since this decision, *Roe* v. *Wade* has been a target of conservatives, who argue against it on religious and moral grounds. For those who agree with the Court's decision, it supports a woman's right to make choices about her own reproductive health and to choose when and if to have children.

University of Tennessee Head Coach Pat Summitt (left) and guard Shanna Zolman (5) evaluate the play during a basketball game in 2004. Summitt retired from coaching at Tennessee having achieved the highest National Collegiate Athletic Association (NCCA) overall win record at that time of 1,098–208. The passage of Title IX gave many hardworking and talented women like Coach Summitt and her players the opportunity to compete at exceptionally high levels.

EQUAL RIGHTS AMENDMENT

Another primary goal of the women's movement was the long-overdue passage of the Equal Rights Amendment (ERA) to the Constitution, which would guarantee protection from gender-based discrimination or even from **misogyny**, a hatred of women. As you learned, the ERA was proposed in 1923, three years after the 19th Amendment granted women the right to vote. The ERA lacked support among several groups and stalled for years on Capitol Hill. Finally, in 1972, Congress passed the ERA and sent it to the states for ratification, with 38 states (three-quarters) needed to ratify, or vote "yes," and make the amendment part of the Constitution.

A coalition of fundamentalist religious groups, states' rights advocates, and political conservatives opposed the ERA. They claimed that it would have unintended consequences, such as forcing women into combat and destroying conventional marriage. Among women leaders opposing the ERA was **Phyllis Schlafly**, a lawyer and activist, who argued that the ERA would subject women to the military draft and force them to lose federal benefits they received as "dependents." The ERA's opponents eventually helped to defeat the measure and keep it from becoming law. It had been ratified by 35 states—3 states short of approval.

By the end of the 1970s, women's lives had changed dramatically. Their career options had grown and were no longer limited to traditional professions, such as nurse, secretary, or teacher. More women's health-care clinics, rape crisis centers, and shelters for domestic abuse victims were available. More women enrolled in medical and law schools. Colleges once closed to women, including the U.S. military academies, opened their doors to female students. The changing roles of women in society, especially as more women entered the labor force, were accompanied by changing family structures.

HISTORICAL THINKING

1. **READING CHECK** How did Title IX benefit college-bound women?

2. **ANALYZE LANGUAGE USE** What did feminists mean by the phrase "the personal is political"?

3. **MAKE GENERALIZATIONS** In what ways did the legal cases won by feminists help change the roles of women in society?

STONEWALL NATIONAL MONUMENT NEW YORK CITY

The mid-20th century saw the beginning of a broader struggle for equal rights for the **lesbian, gay, bisexual, transgender, and queer (LGBTQ)** community, which endured prejudice and discrimination. Not only was homosexuality against the law at that time, it was also classified as a mental illness. Emboldened by the civil rights movements, members of the LGBTQ community began seeking legal and political changes. By the mid-1970s, laws criminalizing homosexuality were repealed by 17 states.

The Stonewall Inn was a popular gathering place for LGBTQ individuals in the 1960s. On June 28, 1969, police raided Stonewall. Patrons refused to line up and show their identification, sparking several days of rioting in the New York neighborhood of Greenwich Village. This event, which is now known as the Stonewall Uprising, became the first major step in the modern LGBTQ rights movement. On June 24, 2016, President Barack Obama announced the Stonewall National Monument at this historic site. This American Place represents the first national monument focused on LGBTQ history.

CRITICAL VIEWING Designated the birthplace of the modern LGBTQ rights movement, the Stonewall Inn still maintains its local neighborhood identity. By the mid-1970s, the LGBTQ community had gained momentum in its quest for equality, but discrimination based on sexual orientation and gender identity continues today. Examine this photograph of the Stonewall Inn. How does a gathering place such as this one help unify a cause or community?

THE SPACE RACE CONTINUES

As the United States grappled with civil unrest and struggles for equality at home, the Cold War with the Soviet Union continued. Throughout the 1960s, the two nations battled for supremacy in space. During a time of turmoil, Americans found common ground in cheering on the U.S. space program's goal of putting a man on the moon.

THE DREAM OF SPACE TRAVEL

Life in the United States during the 1950s and 1960s came with an undercurrent of fear. The United States was at odds with the world's only other superpower, the Soviet Union. The two nations struggled with an uneasy and fragile peace. As you have read, one night in 1957, Americans got a fright: orbiting over their heads was a piece of Soviet machinery called *Sputnik 1*, the first artificial satellite ever launched into orbit. It was not just the satellite orbiting over their heads that concerned Americans. It was also the fact that *Sputnik* had been launched into orbit by a powerful rocket.

Rockets had been invented by the Chinese in the 13th century, and they have been used for fireworks and in warfare ever since. But modern rocket science really began in Germany during World War II. After the war, some of Germany's leading scientists surrendered to American forces and were brought to the United States, while others were recruited into the Soviet Union's rocket program. Among those who immigrated to the United States was **Wernher von Braun**, who had developed the powerful V-2 rocket for Hitler. Although his role in producing this rocket during the war is controversial, Von Braun's real desire

The 363-foot-tall Saturn V rocket launches the Apollo 11 spacecraft toward the moon in 1969.

was to design a rocket that would travel into space, and working for the United States gave him that opportunity.

When NASA was set up in 1958, it combined a number of different, individual organizations that had been working on space-age rocket research, including von Braun's team at the Army Ballistic Missile Agency in Huntsville, Alabama. The United States was not about to allow the Soviet Union to gain an advantage in rocket research, so the new agency had 8,000 employees and a budget of $100 million. The space race had begun, and, as you have read, in 1961 President Kennedy set a remarkable goal: the United States would land a man on the moon by the end of the decade.

With this ambitious challenge, NASA got to work. The location of many NASA facilities was determined by political influence. For example, Houston, Texas, was chosen as the location for the Johnson Space Center largely because Lyndon Johnson, then vice president, was from Texas. NASA's first major launch site, however, was in **Cape Canaveral**, Florida, and it offered two chief advantages, neither of them political. First, all rocket launches would be directed eastward, over the Atlantic Ocean, which was a safety precaution in case of any rocket malfunction. Second, Cape Canaveral was closer to the Equator than other possible launch sites. By launching rockets eastward from a site near the Equator, NASA could take advantage of Earth's eastward rotation in lifting the rocket into orbit.

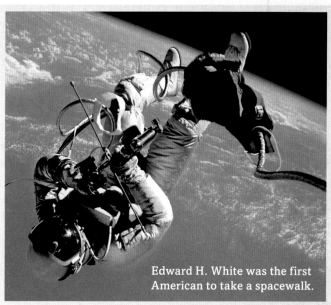
Edward H. White was the first American to take a spacewalk.

FROM GEMINI TO APOLLO

The early efforts in the space race focused on sending astronauts deeper and deeper into orbit and safely bringing them back. The first manned space flights were known as Project Mercury. They culminated with American astronaut John Glenn orbiting Earth three times before touching down in the Caribbean Sea. A second astronaut program, Project Gemini, built on what NASA had learned during Mercury's six flights. In a significant step forward, the Gemini space capsules carried two astronauts instead of one. A highlight of the Gemini mission was the first successful American **spacewalk**, in which an astronaut, Edward H. White, ventured outside the spacecraft on June 3, 1965.

From there, NASA initiated its Apollo program, which set its sights on taking the final crucial steps to achieving a moon landing. The earlier Mercury and Gemini programs had solved many of the major challenges involved with launching humans safely into space, from surviving in extreme conditions to returning safely to Earth. NASA now focused its efforts on developing the procedures and equipment that would make a moon orbit and landing possible.

Early on in the Apollo program, however, tragedy struck. On January 27, 1967, during a launch pad test, the Apollo 1 capsule caught fire, trapping three astronauts inside. Virgil "Gus" Grissom, Roger Chaffee, and Edward H. White—the first American to ever walk in space—died in the accident. In the aftermath of this tragedy, NASA conducted an investigation to discover the cause of the fire. The recommendations the investigators made in their report led to engineering and design improvements to the space capsule as well as advances in quality control, manufacturing, and testing procedures. Despite the horrific event, the space program pushed on.

HISTORICAL THINKING

1. **READING CHECK** What were Wernher von Braun's qualifications for working on the American space program?

2. **COMPARE AND CONTRAST** How were the goals of the Mercury and Gemini programs different from those of Apollo?

3. **DESCRIBE** Describe the effects of America's space program on society and the economy. Use evidence from the text to support your response.

4. **ANALYZE CAUSE AND EFFECT** How did NASA respond to the launch pad tragedy that killed three Apollo astronauts?

"One Giant Leap for Mankind"

Have you ever looked up at the moon and imagined what it would be like to walk on its surface, gazing back at Earth? People had been wondering about this for thousands of years, but it wasn't until 1969 that the technology, and the will to attempt such a challenge, allowed it to become reality.

THE U.S. MOON MISSION

In the years after the tragic loss of the Apollo 1 crew, the United States continued making steady progress toward its moon landing goal. NASA developed a rocket, the Saturn V, which officials believed would be powerful enough to set the astronauts on a course that would send them all the way to the moon. It also developed a command **module**, or unit, called *Columbia*, and a lunar module, nicknamed *Eagle*, that astronaut Michael Collins later described as "the weirdest looking contraption I have ever seen in the sky." Collins was one of the three men chosen as the crew of **Apollo 11**, the mission that would shoot for the moon. Collins piloted *Columbia*. **Neil Armstrong** was mission commander, and **Edwin "Buzz" Aldrin** was *Eagle's* pilot.

Dawn on July 16, 1969, was clear and sunny at Cape Kennedy. (Cape Canaveral's name was changed to Cape Kennedy in 1963 after the president's assassination, but it would revert to its original name in 1973.) At 9:32 a.m., Armstrong, Aldrin, and Collins took off in the nose of a massive Saturn V rocket. Spectators cheered as the rocket, wreathed in fire and smoke, rose into the sky. Twelve minutes later, the crew was in orbit and headed toward the moon. The trip took three days. As they approached the moon, Armstrong and Aldrin climbed into *Eagle*, disengaged from *Columbia*,

and headed for the moon's surface. Collins stayed behind, piloting *Columbia*. At 4:18 p.m. eastern daylight time on July 20, with just 30 seconds' worth of fuel left, *Eagle* landed on the moon. Armstrong radioed the news back to Earth: "Houston, Tranquility Base here. The *Eagle* has landed."

People at Mission Control in Houston roared in glee and applauded as they watched the landing. For the first time, human beings were on the surface of another celestial body. Kennedy's dream had been realized: Americans were on the moon before any other nation. Armstrong exited *Eagle*, climbed down its ladder, and

APOLLO 11

The Saturn V rocket launched Apollo 11 to the moon in stages. Each stage was discarded as its fuel was spent, until three module spacecraft remained. The escape launch at the top was available to pull the command module *Columbia* to safety in case of a malfunction during the early stages of the launch.

Lunar Spacecraft

Launch Escape Tower

Third Stage

Second Stage

First Stage

Service Module

Command Module *Columbia*

Command Service Module (CSM)

Lunar Module *Eagle* (LM)

Ascent stage

Descent stage

The National Air and Space Museum, Washington, D.C.

The *Columbia*, the Apollo 11 command module, was the living quarters of the three-person crew during the first manned lunar landing mission in July 1969. This command module, no. 107, was one of three parts of the complete Apollo spacecraft and was the only part of the spacecraft to return to Earth, transporting the three astronauts aboard. Its furnishings included a heating unit, water supply, pressure-suit connectors, scientific equipment, and even a vacuum cleaner! The module and its travel ring, or transporting cradle, weighs over 13,600 pounds.

became the first person to walk on the moon. "That's one small step for [a] man, one giant leap for mankind," he radioed back to Earth, where 500 million people—about 14 percent of the world's population—received his words and images broadcast from 238,900 miles away. Together, Aldrin and Armstrong explored and collected samples. "Magnificent desolation" is how Aldrin described the lunar surface.

After two and a half hours, they placed a plaque on the moon memorializing their visit, which described them not as Americans, but as "men of Earth" who came in peace. They also left an American flag, medallions in memory of the Apollo 1 crew and for 2 Russian cosmonauts, and a silicon disk engraved with goodwill wishes from 78 nations. Then they returned to *Eagle,* which was a two-part module: one for descending to the lunar surface, and one for taking off from the surface. Each part of the module had its own fuel supply. The ascent module blasted off, using the descent module as a launching pad, to meet up with Collins and *Columbia*. Upon their return to Earth (after a few days in quarantine), the astronauts were given a huge parade in New York City and were celebrated around the world.

OTHER LUNAR LANDINGS

Five more Apollo missions landed astronauts on the moon between 1969 and 1972. The soil and rock samples the Apollo astronauts brought back from the moon were a treasure trove of information. Scientists confirmed that no life existed on the moon and that its mineral composition was similar to Earth's. The moon is very ancient; its youngest rocks are about the same age as the oldest Earth rocks. These lunar rocks are still being studied.

One of the later Apollo missions, Apollo 13, never reached the moon. Launched on April 11, 1970, it was

200,000 miles from Earth when all water, electrical power, propulsion, and oxygen in the command module were lost. The crew retreated to the lunar module, which kept them alive while the damaged ship did a lunar flyby and headed back to Earth. The men drank only six ounces of water a day as Apollo 13 limped home. All three crewmembers survived. Investigators eventually determined that exposed wires on a fan shorted out, setting the insulation on fire, and causing an oxygen tank to explode.

After the Apollo program ended, NASA's focus shifted away from the moon. Starting in the 1980s, it developed the space shuttle, an orbiter that could be used repeatedly for missions. NASA also began admitting women to the astronaut program. On June 18, 1983, **Sally Ride** became the first American woman to fly in space on a space shuttle mission.

Together, the nations of the world, led by the United States and Russia (the former Soviet Union), began building the International Space Station. Scientists on the space station conduct experiments to learn about how outer space affects living things and study the cosmos without visual interference from Earth's atmosphere. NASA continues to send unmanned probes to explore Mars, Jupiter, Saturn, their moons, and the outer reaches of our solar system.

HISTORICAL THINKING

1. **READING CHECK** What was the major accomplishment of NASA's Apollo program?

2. **ANALYZE CAUSE AND EFFECT** Why do you think NASA has moved away from manned space missions?

3. **ASK AND ANSWER QUESTIONS** What questions do you still have about NASA's technological developments, and where can you find the answers?

VOCABULARY

Use each of the following vocabulary words in a sentence that shows an understanding of the term's meaning.

1. **peer**
   His new teammates considered him a peer because his skills were equal to theirs.

2. misogyny

3. manifesto

4. militant

5. module

6. feminism

7. gender bias

8. spacewalk

READING STRATEGY
ANALYZE CAUSE AND EFFECT

Use a graphic organizer like the one below to describe the civil rights movements, their effect on American society, and how they were influenced by the African-American civil rights movement.

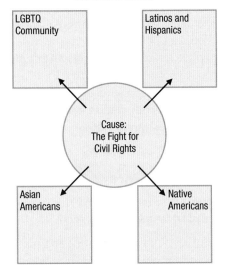

Cause and Effect

9. How did various groups experiencing discrimination fight for equality and civil rights in the 1960s?

MAIN IDEAS

Answer the following questions. Support your answers with evidence from the chapter.

10. What factors led to the Latino rights movement? **LESSON 1.1**

11. Why did Larry Itliong ask the Mexican American farmworkers to join the Filipino grape laborers' strike? **LESSON 1.3**

12. What governmental decision made the creation of the Native American Declaration of Purpose necessary? **LESSON 2.1**

13. What was the American Indian Movement (AIM)? **LESSON 2.2**

14. What were the goals of the National Organization for Women (NOW)? **LESSON 3.1**

15. How did Title IX make schools and sports more fair for women? **LESSON 3.2**

16. How did the technology NASA developed for the Apollo program build on lessons learned from Project Gemini? **LESSON 4.1**

17. What did Neil Armstrong mean when he said, "That's one small step for [a] man, one giant leap for mankind"? **LESSON 4.2**

HISTORICAL THINKING

Answer the following questions. Support your answers with evidence from the chapter.

18. **ANALYZE CAUSE AND EFFECT** Was *The Feminine Mystique* a cause or an effect of the women's movement, or both, and what limitations might prevent you from determining this?

19. **MAKE GENERALIZATIONS** Why is the designation of the Stonewall Inn as a National Monument important for the LGBTQ community?

20. **DRAW CONCLUSIONS** Which strategies undertaken by Native Americans in pursuit of their civil rights were similar to those strategies undertaken by African Americans, and how effective were they?

21. **FORM AND SUPPORT OPINIONS** Which civil rights movement in this chapter do you think made the greatest strides during this time period?

INTERPRET VISUALS

Physicist and astronaut Sally Ride monitors the control panel from the pilot's seat on the space shuttle. Ride took her first space flight in 1983 as a mission specialist.

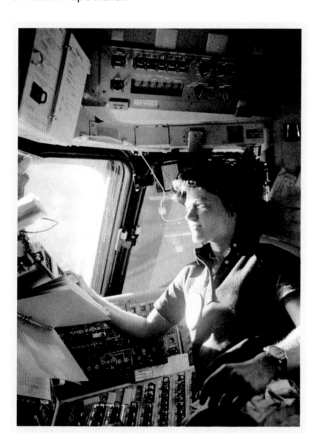

22. **DRAW CONCLUSIONS** What kind of training do you think Ride, or any other astronaut, would need to perform this job in the space shuttle?

23. **MAKE INFERENCES** Why would an astronaut need the large windows shown here, rather than the smaller ones in early capsules?

ANALYZE SOURCES

César Chávez led farmworkers in many protests.

"The consumer boycott is the only open door in the dark corridor of nothingness down which farm workers have had to walk for many years. It is a gate of hope through which they expect to find the sunlight of a better life for themselves and their families."

—César Chávez, as quoted in *Why We Fight: The Origins, Nature, and Management of Human Conflict*, by David Churchman, 2013

24. Based on the quotation, why do you think Chávez chose boycotts as an effective strategy for achieving equality?

CONNECT TO YOUR LIFE

25. **EXPOSITORY** Talk to family members or other adults you know about one of the civil rights movements described in this chapter. What does the adult remember about it? Ask him or her to explain in what ways civil rights for different groups of Americans have changed or remained unchanged over time. Have these movements made your life today different from what it would have been in the 1960s or 1970s? In a paragraph explain how these movements have affected your life today.

TIPS

- Use information from the chapter to craft your questions before you conduct any of your interviews.

- Ask the people you interview for concrete details from their memories and experiences.

- Compare your life today with the life described by the adults in your interviews.

- Conclude by drawing from your experiences and feelings to explain why you think these movements had an overall positive or negative impact on American society.

- Use two or three vocabulary terms from the chapter in your response.

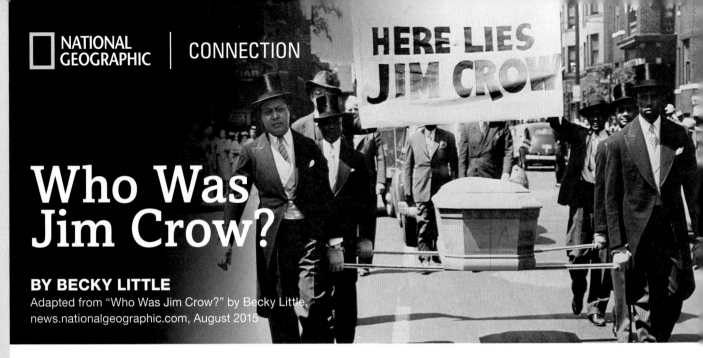

NATIONAL GEOGRAPHIC | CONNECTION

Who Was Jim Crow?

BY BECKY LITTLE

Adapted from "Who Was Jim Crow?" by Becky Little, news.nationalgeographic.com, August 2015

In 1944, the Detroit chapter of the National Association for the Advancement of Colored People (NAACP) held a mock funeral for him. In 1963, participants in the March on Washington for Jobs and Freedom symbolically buried him. Racial discrimination existed all over the United States in the 20th century, but it had a special name in the South—Jim Crow.

President Lyndon B. Johnson tried to bury Jim Crow by signing the Voting Rights Act of 1965 into law. The Voting Rights Act and its predecessor, the Civil Rights Act of 1964, fought racial discrimination by banning segregation in public accommodations and outlawing the poll taxes and tests that were used to stop African Americans from voting.

Today, we still use "Jim Crow" to describe that system of segregation and discrimination in the South. But the system's namesake isn't actually Southern. Jim Crow came from the North.

Thomas Dartmouth Rice, a white man, was born in New York City in 1808. He devoted himself to the theater in his 20s. In the early 1830s, he began performing the act that would make him famous: He painted his face black and did a song and dance he claimed were inspired by an African-American slave. The act was called "Jump, Jim Crow" (or "Jumping Jim Crow").

Rice's routine was a hit in New York City, one of many places in the North where working-class whites could see blackface minstrelsy, which was quickly becoming a dominant form of theater and a leading source for popular music in America. Rice took his act on tour. As his popularity grew, his stage name seeped into the culture. Jim Crow became a name that was applied to African Americans in general. "So much so," says Eric Lott, professor at the City University of New York Graduate Center, "that by the time of Harriet Beecher Stowe's *Uncle Tom's Cabin*, which was 20 years later in 1852," one character refers to another as Jim Crow.

Regardless of whether the term Jim Crow existed before Rice took it to the stage, his act helped popularize it as a derogatory term for African Americans. To call someone Jim Crow wasn't just to point out his or her skin color: it was to reduce that person to the kind of caricature that Rice performed on stage.

After the Civil War, southern states passed laws that discriminated against newly freed African Americans. As early as the 1890s, these laws had gained a nickname. In 1899, a North Carolina newspaper published an article subtitled "How 'Capt. Tilley' of the A. & N.C. Road Enforces the Jim Crow Law."

Experts aren't sure how a racist show in the North came to embody racist laws in the South. But they can speculate. Since the term originated in blackface minstrelsy, Lott says that it's almost "perversely accurate . . . that it should come to be the name for official segregation and state-sponsored racism."

"I think probably in the popular white mind, it was just used because that's just how they referred to black people," he says.

"Sometimes in history a movie comes out or a book comes out and it just changes the language . . . and you can point at it," says David Pilgrim, director of the Jim Crow Museum and vice president for Diversity and Inclusion at Ferris State University.

"And in just this case," he says, "I think it just evolved. And I think it was from many sources."

However it happened, the new meaning stuck. Blackface minstrelsy's popularity faded, and Thomas Rice is barely remembered. Most people today don't know his name. But everybody knows the name Jim Crow.

For more from National Geographic, check out "Before Stonewall" online.

UNIT INQUIRY: Design a Museum Exhibit

In this unit, you learned about a turbulent period in American life. The assassinations of three national leaders and a divisive war shattered the hopeful visions of progress proposed in the New Frontier and the Great Society. Protest movements by numerous groups—African Americans, Native Americans, Latinos, women, and antiwar activists—divided the nation and often turned violent. How did the popular culture of the time reflect this great turmoil? Which songs best express the mood of the time? What works of art and literature capture the confusion of those years? How did clothing and hairstyles become protest statements?

ASSIGNMENT

Design a museum exhibit that answers this question: How did popular culture reflect the turbulence of the time period? You might explore popular culture in general or focus on a particular aspect of it, such as music, art, literature, movies, or fashion. Be prepared to present your design to the class.

Plan First choose the subject of your exhibit and identify its main idea or theme. Then research your subject and compile a list of primary sources in diverse formats, such as songs, photographs, works of art, or newspaper articles, that will form your exhibit. You'll use these objects to tell your story. You might use a graphic organizer to outline your theme and arrange your primary sources.

Theme

Produce Create a title for your exhibit and write an introduction of one or more paragraphs. Then write a caption for each primary source in your exhibit, providing identifying information and explaining the object's significance.

Present Share your exhibit design with the class. You might consider one of these options:

- Use a computer program to create a virtual museum exhibit and post it on a website that your classmates can access. Invite viewers to share their reactions to the exhibit.

- Create a museum board model for display in the classroom. After viewing one another's displays, hold a class discussion comparing the popular culture of the period with the popular culture of the current time. Discuss how you would characterize the contemporary culture.

NATIONAL GEOGRAPHIC | **LEARNING FRAMEWORK ACTIVITIES**

Write a Letter

ATTITUDE Responsibility

KNOWLEDGE New Frontiers

Write a letter, addressed to your classmates or to the president of the United States, outlining a "New Frontier" or "Great Society" challenge that you think your generation should tackle. Explain your vision of progress, how you would implement it, and how it will improve people's lives. Compare your ideas with those of either President Kennedy or President Johnson. Share your letter with your classmates, and discuss the ideas and visions presented for the future.

Create a Song

KNOWLEDGE Our Human Story

SKILLS Collaboration, Communication

If you have musical skills, collaborate with one or more partners to compose a song that captures a current conflict in American society, perhaps in the lives of American youth. Consider various styles of music, such as rap, pop, country, folk, and rock. Choose a style and a theme, and play around with lyrics and melody until a song develops. Practice the song and perform it for the class. Discuss how it relates to the conflict. Ask for feedback, inviting suggestions for changes to the lyrics or music.

CRITICAL VIEWING The High Line, an elevated public park built on an old, unused freight rail line, extends between the buildings of Manhattan's West Side. Benches give visitors a peaceful place to rest above the busy New York City streets, and plants, grasses, and trees recall the wild landscape that once ran along the abandoned railway. How might the High Line serve as an example of a solution to a modern urban challenge?

THE UNITED STATES

1974
Nixon resigns his presidency in the wake of the Watergate scandal, and Vice President Gerald Ford becomes president.
(official presidential portrait of Ford)

1986
The space shuttle *Challenger* explodes soon after takeoff, killing all on board.
(The shuttle launches from Cape Canaveral.)

1980
Ronald Reagan is elected president, ushering in a new conservative movement.

1998
President William Clinton is impeached but is acquitted of all charges.

1970

1990

1975 ASIA
Saigon falls, and Vietnam is reunified under a communist government.

1980

1991 EUROPE
The Soviet Union breaks up, and the Cold War comes to an end.

1979 ASIA
Islamic militants hold 52 American hostages in Iran following the overthrow of the ruling monarchy.

THE WORLD

1989 EUROPE
The Berlin Wall falls, paving the way to the reunification of Germany a year later. *(Crowds celebrate on top of the wall.)*

1994 AFRICA
Voters take part in South Africa's first democratic elections and elect Nelson Mandela as president.

OBAMA ⬤ BIDEN

BARACKOBAMA.COM

HISTORICAL THINKING

DETERMINE CHRONOLOGY Which world event may have occurred in response to the 2001 attacks on the United States?

2008
Barack Obama becomes the first African-American president. *(2012 campaign sticker)*

2016
Donald Trump is elected president. *(cap featuring Trump's 2016 campaign slogan)*

2007
The Great Recession begins, which leads to widespread unemployment and a collapse in housing prices.

2005
Hurricane Katrina hits New Orleans, Louisiana, and devastates the city.

2001
On September 11, a series of attacks by militants associated with the Islamic terrorist group al Qaeda kill more than 3,000 people. *(security guard badge recovered from the ruins of the World Trade Center)*

2000

2010

2020

2008 AMERICAS
Fidel Castro resigns after leading Cuba for 49 years, and his brother Raúl succeeds him.

2015 EUROPE
The Islamic State in Iraq and Syria (ISIS) claims responsibility for a terrorist attack in Paris.

SADDAM HUSAYN AL-TIKRITI
President

2003 ASIA
The United States and Britain launch an attack on Iraq. *(Saddam Hussein on a playing card given to coalition forces)*

2010 AFRICA
The Arab Spring movement begins in Tunisia. *(Protesters stand on an army tank in Cairo, Egypt, in 2011.)*

PRESIDENTIAL SUCCESSES AND FAILURES
1968–1980

HISTORICAL THINKING What policies and challenges characterized the presidencies of Nixon, Ford, and Carter?

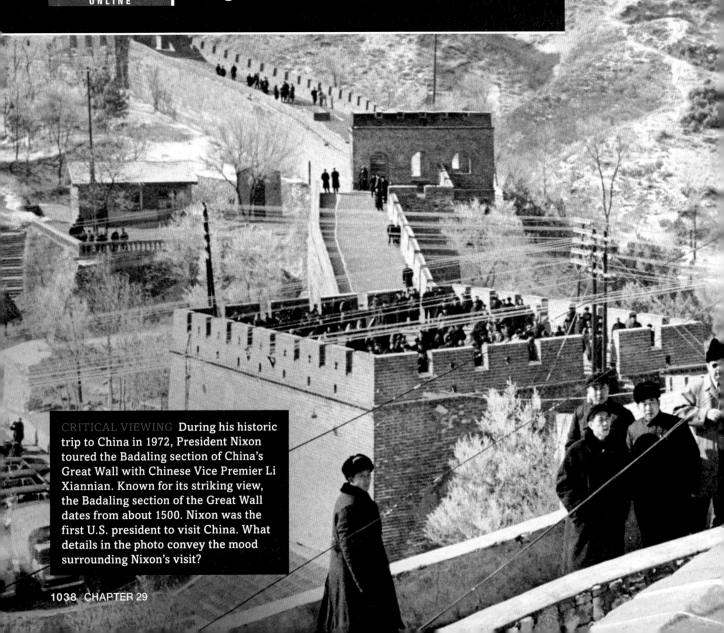

CRITICAL VIEWING During his historic trip to China in 1972, President Nixon toured the Badaling section of China's Great Wall with Chinese Vice Premier Li Xiannian. Known for its striking view, the Badaling section of the Great Wall dates from about 1500. Nixon was the first U.S. president to visit China. What details in the photo convey the mood surrounding Nixon's visit?

"What is most important is that **we have an open world.**"

—President Richard M. Nixon

NIXON'S COMEBACK

Have you ever achieved something important because you refused to give up and simply kept trying? Despite setbacks, Richard Nixon did not give up his quest for the presidency, and in 1968, his perseverance paid off.

NIXON'S RISE, FALL, AND RISE

In the months leading up to the 1968 election, many Americans were anxious about the state of the country. The assassinations of Martin Luther King, Jr., and Robert Kennedy, ongoing demonstrations against the Vietnam War, and changing cultural values left people feeling the country was out of control.

Richard Nixon was a familiar name to most Americans, having served as President Eisenhower's vice president from 1953 to 1961. The son of Quaker parents living in California, Nixon had excelled in academics and debate. After law school, he took a government job, which he left to serve in the U.S. Navy during World War II. After the war, Republican Party leaders suggested he run for a Congressional seat in California, which he won. Nixon appeared to be a rising star in the party.

As a member of Congress, Nixon gained a reputation for being tough on communism. His participation in the trial of Alger Hiss, a suspected Russian spy, in 1949 helped him win a seat in the U.S. Senate in 1950. Just two years later, Dwight Eisenhower chose Nixon as his vice-presidential running mate. However, trouble emerged during the campaign when some critics accused Nixon of accepting an $18,000 campaign contribution and using it for his personal benefit. To silence these critics, Nixon went on national television and admitted to accepting one personal gift from a supporter—a dog, whom his young daughter named Checkers. The speech won over the public.

After serving eight years as Eisenhower's loyal vice president, Nixon seemed destined to win the White House in 1960. As you have read, however, he narrowly lost that election to John F. Kennedy. Two years later, he lost the California governor's race. Many observers thought Nixon's political career was over. In fact, after his defeat, a bitter Nixon told reporters, "You won't have Nixon to kick around anymore."

PRIMARY SOURCE

After being accused of spending campaign money on private expenses, Richard Nixon addressed the nation, claiming that the only gift he had received was a dog named Checkers.

We did get something, a gift, after the election. A man down in Texas heard . . . that our two youngsters would like to have a dog, and, believe it or not . . . we got a message from Union Station in Baltimore, saying they had a package for us. It was a little cocker spaniel dog . . . black and white, spotted, and our little girl Tricia, the six year old, named it Checkers. And you know, the kids, like all kids, loved the dog, and . . . we are going to keep it.

—from Richard Nixon's "Checkers" speech, September 23, 1952

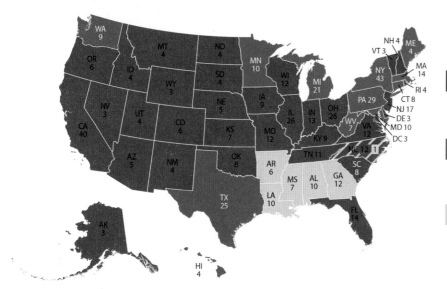

The 1968 Election

Richard Nixon, Republican
Electoral Vote: 301 votes, 55.9%

Popular Vote: 31,785,480 votes, 43.4%

Hubert Humphrey, Democrat
Electoral Vote: 191 votes, 35.5%

Popular Vote: 31,275,166 votes, 42.7%

George Wallace, Independent
Electoral Vote: 46 votes, 8.4%

Popular Vote: 9,906,473 votes, 13.5%

With no political office to keep him in California, Nixon moved to New York City, where he practiced law and successfully rebuilt his reputation by assisting Republican candidates in their campaigns. Despite his election failures, he was regarded as a knowledgeable and experienced politician. After the Republicans lost the 1964 national election, their leaders turned to Nixon, hoping he could regain the White House in 1968. They felt voters were dissatisfied with reform-minded Democrats. Nixon chose Governor **Spiro T. Agnew** of Maryland as his running mate. Agnew was a moderate who supported civil rights but advocated a tough stance on crime. Nixon hoped Agnew would increase the ticket's appeal to both moderate and conservative voters.

THE 1968 ELECTION

The year 1968 marked the beginning of a swing toward conservatism that would last for several decades. Many Americans were upset with the excesses of the 1960s, including the counterculture, illegal drug use, and rising crime rates in cities. In his campaign, Nixon tapped into these feelings of insecurity and appealed to what he called the **silent majority**, those who are not actively involved in politics and do not voice their political opinions publicly. At this time, the silent majority consisted of moderate voters who wanted the United States to take a more stable and conservative course.

At the Republican National Convention, Nixon promised to make law and order his top priority at home and to bring "peace with honor" to Vietnam. The Democrats, on the other hand, were divided over the war in Vietnam, and antiwar protesters were upset with the nomination of Vice President Hubert Humphrey as the Democratic candidate. Demonstrations turned violent outside the Democratic National Convention in Chicago when police officers clashed with protesters. The clashes gave Nixon an advantage with voters who wanted a more peaceful country.

To attract even more voters, Nixon's campaign also targeted people in the southern states who historically voted for Democrats. His southern strategy appealed to white southerners who were disappointed with Democratic support of the civil rights movement. If Nixon could turn these southern states Republican, he stood an excellent chance of winning the election.

However, for the first time since 1948, there was a serious third-party candidate: former Alabama governor George Wallace. Wallace was a segregationist, and now he based his platform on his opposition to civil rights. Wallace proved popular among the white southern voters Nixon had hoped to attract. While these voters rejected Humphrey's support of civil rights, they also did not favor Nixon, who was neither pro-civil rights nor a segregationist. Wallace ended up winning five southern states, but Nixon still won the election.

HISTORICAL THINKING

1. **READING CHECK** Why did some experts believe that Richard Nixon's political career was over by the early 1960s?

2. **ANALYZE CAUSE AND EFFECT** Describe the complex cause-and-effect relationship between the political situation in the country, Nixon's campaign platform, and his victory in the 1968 presidential election.

3. **INTERPRET MAPS** What effect did Wallace's third-party candidacy have on the 1968 election?

NIXON'S NEW FEDERALISM

Some presidents are easy to categorize as being either conservative, moderate, or liberal. But Richard Nixon is difficult to pigeonhole. His actions covered the entire political spectrum.

NIXON'S DOMESTIC POLICIES

President Nixon advocated a number of reforms in welfare policy, civil rights, and other areas. In 1970, he requested a bill be introduced in Congress called the **Family Assistance Plan (FAP)**. The plan provided direct cash payments to those in need, while requiring participants to work or receive job training. Conservative members of Congress opposed the idea of the government supporting unemployed people. Liberal Congress members thought the minimum household income in order to qualify for Nixon's plan was too low. Because of these and other dissenting views, Congress never passed the FAP.

Also in 1970, Nixon signed amendments that renewed the Voting Rights Act of 1965, which protected African-American voters at the polls by prohibiting literacy tests. Even though African Americans had the right to vote, many still experienced discrimination and intimidation at polling stations, which kept a number of them away from the polls. After Nixon's renewal of the act, the number of African-American voters fully participating in the election process increased. Nixon also issued an executive order supporting affirmative action, which aimed to improve job opportunities for minorities. However, many white citizens opposed the order, believing it was a form of reverse racism, or prejudice against white people.

Nixon supported other progressive reforms. For example, he approved legislation that provided automatic cost-of-living adjustments for Social Security recipients. He also signed the bill that established the **Occupational Safety and Health Administration (OSHA)**, which enforces workplace safety standards.

Although he supported some progressive measures, Nixon believed the federal government had assumed too much responsibility for social problems. In 1972, Nixon signed legislation to return some of the authority of the federal government to state and local governments. He created a five-year revenue sharing plan, which required the federal government to collect taxes and then distribute the money directly to state and local governments. The system allowed those governments to allocate, or give out, money to the programs that benefited their constituents most. Nixon called his tax plan the **New Federalism**.

SCHOOL DESEGREGATION

By 1971, Nixon had the rare opportunity to appoint four Supreme Court justices. In 1969, he chose **Warren E. Burger**, a moderate Republican, as chief justice. His other three appointees were conservatives. Some politicians were concerned that Nixon's conservative appointments would shift the Supreme Court radically to the right, but the Burger Court proved more independent than expected.

PRIMARY SOURCE

The Voting Rights Act of 1965 has opened participation in the political process. In the 5 years since its enactment, close to 1 million Negroes have been registered to vote for the first time and more than 400 Negro officials have been elected to local and State offices. These are more than election statistics; they are statistics of hope and dramatic evidence that the American system works. They stand as an answer to those who claim that there is no recourse except to the streets.

—from Richard Nixon's Voting Rights Act Amendments signing speech, 1970

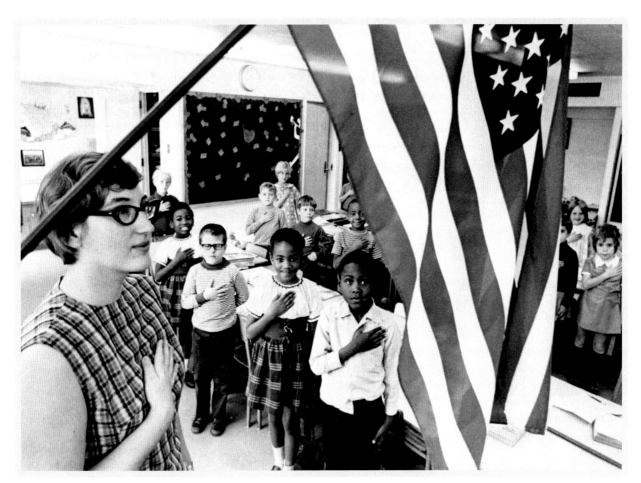

In 1970, two Cincinnati school districts agreed to a busing plan in which African-American children from one district would attend the predominantly white schools of the other. Second graders in one of the newly merged schools say the Pledge of Allegiance together to begin their school day.

Nixon stated that he opposed school segregation, which the Court had found unconstitutional in 1954. However, in one case, his administration won a request in a lower court to allow 33 Mississippi school districts to postpone their school desegregation plans. In a 1969 ruling, the Burger Court overturned the lower court ruling and ordered the immediate desegregration of the Mississippi school districts.

However, the Burger Court went on to issue mixed decisions on the use of forced busing to eliminate *de facto* segregation. *De facto* segregation of schools still existed because children attended neighborhood schools, and neighborhoods were not integrated. In 1964, an African-American couple in Charlotte, North Carolina, Vera and Darius Swann, tried to enroll their son in an integrated public school. The Swanns lived in the attendance area of a school in which all the students were African American, but the integrated school was actually closer to their home. The Swanns' request was denied, and the NAACP brought the case to a federal court on their behalf.

In 1969, the court ruled in favor of the Swanns and went further by requiring the Charlotte-Mecklenburg school district to implement a busing program to integrate its schools. As you have read, in the landmark case of *Swann* v. *Charlotte-Mecklenburg Board of Education*, the Supreme Court upheld the lower court's ruling. The ruling also granted the federal courts broad powers in ordering and overseeing school desegregation.

The *Swann* ruling changed, however, in 1974 after the Court's decision on *Milliken* v. *Bradley*. In that case, the NAACP had sued the state of Michigan for failure to desegregate Detroit-area schools. Most African-American families lived in the city, so a desegregation plan would require busing students to suburban areas, which would be similar to the plan in Charlotte. In *Milliken*, however, the Court ruled that the federal government could not force the local government to bus students across school districts' boundaries. The decision shifted most of the responsibility for carrying out integration back to local communities.

NIXON'S FOREIGN POLICY

Nixon preferred to focus on foreign policy, where presidents sometimes have a more immediate and direct impact than they do on domestic affairs. As you have learned, Henry Kissinger was Nixon's national security advisor and secretary of state, and he aided the president in many diplomatic achievements. Nixon and Kissinger believed in a foreign policy based on realism, as opposed to idealism. They thought national interests, rather than such ideals as freedom and human rights, should dictate foreign policy. In Latin America and the Middle East, for example, they supported dictatorships that furthered U.S. interests.

One of Nixon's first moves as president was to take advantage of the growing divide between communist China and the Soviet Union. Nixon wanted a closer relationship with China for several reasons. He wanted to promote trade with China. He also hoped China, as an ally of North Vietnam, would help the United States achieve a peace settlement in Vietnam. In addition, a close relationship with China would strengthen the United States' bargaining position with the Soviet Union, who feared any alliance between the United States and China.

No American president had visited China or even officially talked with Chinese leaders since China became a communist state in 1949, partly because Nixon and other anti-communist leaders had opposed any contact. Nixon broke this taboo on February 22, 1972, becoming the first American president to visit China. The trip ended with a joint statement that promised closer relations between the two countries in trade, travel, and cultural exchange. Three months later, the president traveled to Moscow for a summit meeting with Soviet leader Leonid Brezhnev (LEHY-uh-nihd BREZH-nehf). Nixon believed that his successful trip to China, coupled with a declining Soviet economy, would make the Soviets more likely to strike serious deals with the United States on arms control and trade. Both countries possessed huge numbers of nuclear weapons that cost billions of dollars and increased the chances of nuclear war. In addition, the Soviets desperately needed grain, heavy equipment, and technical assistance. American farmers and manufacturers were eager to market these goods and services to the Soviet Union.

On May 22, 1972, the United States and the Soviet Union signed an agreement arising out of the **Strategic Arms Limitation Talks**. The agreement

President Nixon (center) already knew how to use chopsticks when he sat down with Premier Chou En-Lai (left) and Communist Party leader Chang Chun-Chiao (right) at a banquet in honor of his visit to China in 1972. Before the trip, Nixon had taken lessons on how to properly use chopsticks, hoping to make a good impression on his hosts.

TOWARD ENERGY INDEPENDENCE

Americans were already aware of the benefits of using less petroleum before the 1973 war between Israel and Egypt and Syria. Although the oil embargo of 1973 was short-lived, it served as a wakeup call that the United States was in a vulnerable position regarding its energy needs.

The Arab countries in OPEC that participated in the embargo provided only a small percentage of all the oil imported, but a decrease in supply of more than a million barrels a day still made a difference. Spurred on by the environmental movement and the development of new technologies, the United States began to work toward energy independence. While petroleum imports increased through the 1980s and 1990s, new sources of energy were being developed. These energy sources included shale oil, natural gas, and such renewables as wind and solar power. Experts think energy independence by 2035 may be an attainable goal for the United States.

Petroleum Imports, 1970–2015

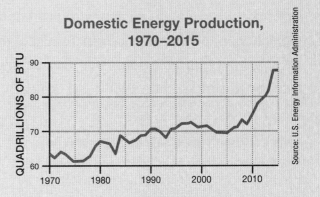

Domestic Energy Production, 1970–2015

Source: U.S. Energy Information Administration

became known as **SALT I**, and it limited the number of long-range offensive missiles both countries could possess. The two countries also signed an agreement to stop the production of **antiballistic missiles (ABMs)**—missiles designed to destroy other bomb-carrying missiles before they hit the ground—for the next five years. ABMs were a problem because their possession by one side or the other provided an advantage and increased the temptation for those owning them to attack first with their own weapons. Henry Kissinger helped negotiate these treaties, which taken together represented a breakthrough in Soviet-American relations. The Moscow summit provided a solid foundation for **détente** (day-TAHNT), or an easing of tension between countries.

Despite these successes, Nixon continued to face foreign policy challenges in the Middle East. War broke out in the Middle East on the Jewish holiday of Yom Kippur, October 6, 1973. Egypt and Syria attacked the predominantly Jewish country of Israel on two fronts. The United States supported Israel, a longtime ally, by airlifting vital military supplies. These supplies proved essential in helping Israel drive back the attack. The Yom Kippur War lasted less than three weeks and ended when United Nations officials negotiated a cease-fire.

To protest American support of Israel, certain Middle Eastern countries in the **Organization of Petroleum Exporting Countries (OPEC)**, a multinational organization that sets petroleum prices and policies, began an embargo, or official ban, on exports of oil to the United States. While Americans accounted for barely 6 percent of the world's population in 1974, they used more than 30 percent of the world's oil. Between 1968 and 1973, the United States' consumption of imported oil had tripled. The embargo created an immediate panic. It forced Americans to reduce their energy use and wait in long lines to buy high-priced gas for their cars. The oil embargo ended in April 1974, but oil costs continued to rise because OPEC had tripled its prices.

HISTORICAL THINKING

1. **READING CHECK** What was the New Federalism?

2. **SYNTHESIZE** Explain the connections between Nixon's trip to China and larger political and economic developments during his administration.

3. **MAKE INFERENCES** What did Nixon mean when he said that the increase in the number of African-American elected officials and registered voters was evidence that the American system worked?

4. **INTERPRET GRAPHS** How does the overall trend in petroleum imports from 1970 to 2015 compare with that of domestic energy production, and what significant change in the relationship between the two occurred in 2005?

PROTECTING THE ENVIRONMENT

Consider what you do each day to protect the environment. Perhaps you recycle old school papers or drink from a reusable water bottle. The idea of taking responsibility for how your everyday behavior affects the environment gained traction during the late 1960s and the early 1970s.

THE ENVIRONMENTAL MOVEMENT

Americans have long been concerned about the negative effects of human activities on the environment. Near the beginning of the 20th century, conservationists such as John Muir and Theodore Roosevelt took action to protect natural places from human destruction. In the 1950s, activists protested the negative environmental effects of nuclear weapons development and testing and of nuclear energy production.

In the 1960s, American scientists published environmental articles and books that raised public awareness and gave rise to the modern environmental movement. American marine biologist **Rachel Carson** published *Silent Spring* in 1962, bringing concerns about pollution into the spotlight. After years of research, Carson showed how a common pesticide called **DDT** entered the food chain. Farmers sprayed DDT on their crops to kill insects, but the contaminated food ended up killing animals, especially birds, and harming people. If the contamination of the food supply continued, Carson warned, it could lead to a world in which all life would be endangered.

Stanford University biologist **Paul Ehrlich** warned about the global consequences of human population growth in *The Population Bomb* (1968). Ehrlich argued that the global food supply would not be able to support the increasing number of people on Earth. He predicted that the world would experience wide-scale hunger by the 1970s. Ehrlich's predictions did not come true, partly because of a dramatic increase in agricultural production, but he continued to promote the need to curb global population growth.

PRIMARY SOURCE

Rachel Carson (above) was a biologist whose gift for writing enabled her to explain environmental science to the public. She sounded an alarm about environmental pollution in her book *Silent Spring*.

The most alarming of all man's assaults upon the environment is the contamination of air, earth, rivers, and sea with dangerous and even lethal materials. This pollution is for the most part irrecoverable; the chain of evil it initiates not only in the world that must support life but in living tissues is for the most part irreversible. In this now universal contamination of the environment, chemicals are the sinister and little-recognized partners of radiation in changing the very nature of the world—the very nature of its life.

—from *Silent Spring*, by Rachel Carson, 1962

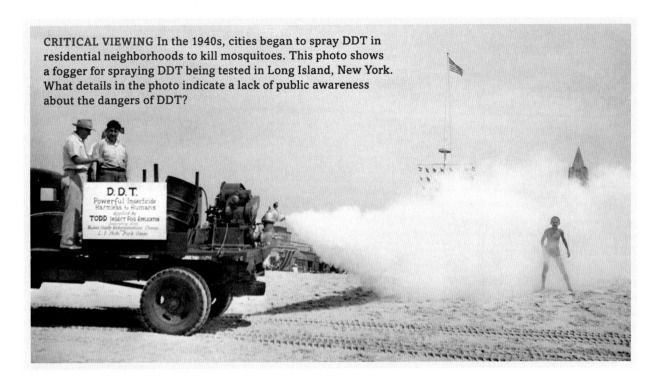

CRITICAL VIEWING In the 1940s, cities began to spray DDT in residential neighborhoods to kill mosquitoes. This photo shows a fogger for spraying DDT being tested in Long Island, New York. What details in the photo indicate a lack of public awareness about the dangers of DDT?

During Nixon's presidency, environmental problems often covered the front pages of newspapers. In June 1969, the Cuyahoga River in Cleveland, Ohio, caught fire due to the dumping of industrial waste. Lake Erie was declared "dead," or lacking in any aquatic life, due to pollution. Smog blanketed major cities, such as New York City and Los Angeles. Biologists warned that the national symbol of the United States, the bald eagle, faced extinction due to habitat destruction, illegal hunting, and DDT contamination. The environmental problems were so severe that people around the country began to push for more effective conservation measures.

On April 22, 1970, U.S. Senator Gaylord Nelson and Harvard graduate student Denis Hayes organized the first Earth Day, a celebration to raise awareness about the environmental movement and to educate people on the importance of conservation. Around the country, nearly 20 million people participated. The largest gatherings were in Washington, D.C., and New York City, where conservationists took to the streets to show their support of the movement.

LEGISLATION AND ORGANIZATIONS

Responding to these growing concerns, President Nixon worked with Congress to pass laws to preserve and protect the environment. The **National Environmental Policy Act (NEPA)** was the first law of its kind when it was enacted on January 1, 1970. It required the federal government to consider the environmental impact of any new federally funded construction project. The following year, Nixon created the **Environmental Protection Agency (EPA)** to ensure enforcement of environmental laws. The **Clean Air Act** of 1970 set strict national guidelines to reduce emissions from vehicles and factories and help curb smog. In 1972, Congress passed amendments to the 1948 Federal Water Pollution Control Act, which then became known as the **Clean Water Act**. The amendments allotted $25 billion for the cleanup of polluted lakes and rivers. This costly effort proved effective in bringing polluted waters, such as the Cuyahoga River, back to life. In 1973, Congress passed the **Endangered Species Act** to keep rare plant and animal species from dying out.

The courts also played a role as environmental groups brought lawsuits against various businesses to stop them from polluting. In a 1966 case brought on behalf of all the citizens of Suffolk County in Long Island, New York, the Suffolk County Supreme Court awarded relief in the form of a ban on DDT use in the county. The case was supported by scientists who documented for the court the nearly irreparable environmental damage resulting from use of the pesticide. Interest in the group's success arose across the nation, and in 1967, Charles Wurster and nine other scientists involved in the suit formed the **Environmental Defense Fund (EDF)** to work on a variety of environmental issues. The EDF's efforts led to a New York statewide ban on DDT in 1971 and a nationwide ban by the EPA in 1972. In 1970, a group of law students and attorneys founded the **National Resources Defense Council (NRDC)**.

Yellowstone National Park, Wyoming

Minerva Terrace, part of Mammoth Hot Springs in Yellowstone National Park, consists of a series of multi-colored terraces composed of calcium carbonate deposited by hot springs. Microorganisms tint the terrace rock various colors. Minerva Terrace is one of the many spectacular natural features of Yellowstone, the world's first national park.

This stunning photograph of Minerva Terrace was taken by National Geographic photographer Frans Lanting. By capturing the magnificence of the natural world, National Geographic photographers help people understand the importance of protecting Earth and its diversity.

The EDF and the NRDC were the first nonprofit environmental groups focused initially on bringing about environmental change by filing research-based lawsuits against polluting companies and agencies.

Some conservation organizations that had existed for many years experienced a newfound popularity and purpose as a result of the environmental movement of the late 1960s and the 1970s. The **Sierra Club**, founded in 1892 by naturalist John Muir, was largely responsible for the preservation of lands in the West, including Yosemite National Park in California. By the 1970s, the Sierra Club had become a leading lobbyist group and environmental protection advocate, fighting to protect natural areas from industrial and agricultural development. The club helped protect California's redwood forests as well as wilderness areas in Alaska.

The Sierra Club often joined with other environmental groups to achieve common goals. One of these groups was the **Wilderness Society**, which was founded in 1935 to fight for the protection of America's wild natural areas. Since its founding, the Wilderness Society has succeeded in preserving some 110 million acres of land across 44 states. In 1969, David Brower, a former leader of the Sierra Club, formed the **League of Conservation Voters** to organize support for pro-environmental political candidates and policies.

CONTROVERSY ON REGULATION

The new environmental laws passed in the 1970s restricted business operations and land use. Some corporations and conservative politicians began to criticize what they viewed as **overregulation**, or excessive control and oversight, by the EPA and other federal agencies. They claimed that the regulations limited profits, job creation, and economic progress.

In the early 1970s, for example, officials with the Tennessee Valley Authority (TVA) were attempting to expand construction of a dam along the Little Tennessee River. The dam promised to extend hydroelectric power over a large region. In 1973, researchers discovered a previously unknown species of fish, called the snail darter, in the Little Tennessee River area. Scientists warned that the dam could destroy the snail darter's natural habitat, and thus potentially destroy the entire population of this rare creature. In 1975, government officials listed the snail darter as protected under the Endangered Species Act. After several years of back and forth decisions in the courts, the U.S. Supreme Court ruled in 1978 that the dam would violate the law protecting the snail darter. The Court ordered a halt to construction of the dam. Eventually, Tennessee officials persuaded Congress to pass a law specifically allowing completion of the dam. As a result, the snail darter became extinct in the Little Tennessee River region. However, thanks to relocation efforts, the snail darter was able to survive in other areas.

Meanwhile, the amount of federally protected land was growing. In 1978, Congress passed a law expanding the size of California's Redwood National and State Parks, much to the disappointment of some leaders in the logging industry. Federal officials also expanded the protection of lands in Alaska, where many oil companies wanted to drill in such wilderness areas as the Arctic National Wildlife Range. The range was renamed the **Arctic National Wildlife Refuge** to highlight its protected status. By the end of the 1970s, new legislation more than doubled the size of the national park system, protecting millions of acres of land and thousands of plant and animal species, but at the same time upsetting some business leaders.

The mid-1970s saw the rise of a movement called the **Sagebrush Rebellion**, led by a group of landowners, miners, loggers, and ranchers in certain western states who resented federal laws limiting the extraction of natural resources on federally protected lands. As supporters of property rights, or the right to use property as the owner sees fit, they wanted more local control and even ownership of federal lands so they could use the lands for their benefit. The rebellion continued into the early 1980s and inspired similar movements in later years to reclaim western lands from federal control.

HISTORICAL THINKING

1. **READING CHECK** What environmental problems resulted from human modifications of landscapes in the 1960s and 1970s?

2. **COMPARE AND CONTRAST** How was the environmental movement similar to and different from other activist movements of the 1960s and 1970s?

3. **FORM AND SUPPORT OPINIONS** Do you think the U.S. government should own land and control how it is used? Give reasons for your opinion.

4. **ANALYZE ENVIRONMENTAL CONCEPTS** How might the quality of life in the United States be different today if the modern environmental movement had not developed?

Canadian-born National Geographic photographer and marine biologist Paul Nicklen documents both the beauty and the plight of the world's oceans and Arctic regions for a global audience. His personal mission is to use his emotional, evocative, and inspiring photographs to ignite conversations about the future of our planet's natural wonders and to promote conservation.

THE WATERGATE SCANDAL

Have you ever wanted something so badly you were willing to do almost anything to get it? Unfortunately, Richard Nixon wanted to remain president so badly that he was willing to break the law and compromise his entire administration.

NIXON'S BID FOR RE-ELECTION

By the end of his first term, President Nixon had built a strong record, especially in foreign affairs. He had successfully negotiated foreign policy agreements with China and the Soviet Union. He also had made progress in the Vietnam War peace talks.

The Republican Party nominated Nixon and his vice president, Spiro Agnew, for re-election, and they did so enthusiastically. Statisticians and journalists favored Nixon to win handily against any of the 11 Democratic primary candidates who were vying for their party's nomination.

Despite all his accomplishments, Nixon worried about the election. Not only did he want to maintain the presidency, he wanted his party to take control of Congress. To this end, some of his supporters founded a political action group called the **Committee to Re-Elect the President (CRP)** in the

Washington Post reporters Carl Bernstein (left) and Bob Woodward received anonymous tips linking the Watergate break-in to the White House. In 2005, it was revealed that the source had been a deputy director of the FBI.

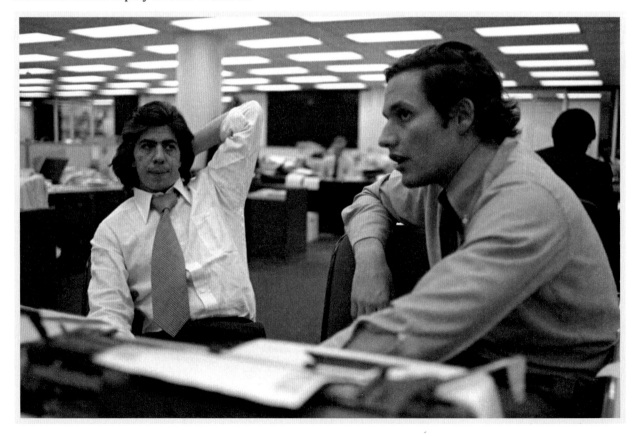

spring of 1971. Nixon's opponents mocked him by referring to the CRP as "CREEP." Attorney General **John Mitchell** resigned his cabinet position to lead the committee.

Mitchell and other CRP members resorted to what came to be known as "dirty tricks" to ruin the chances of the strongest contenders for the Democratic presidential nomination. For example, one CRP member sent a forged letter to a newspaper in New Hampshire that accused the Democratic primary favorite, Senator Edmund Muskie of Maine, of using an ethnic slur to refer to French Canadians.

CRP's dirty tricks may have worked. In July 1972, the Democratic Party chose an underdog as its nominee, South Dakota Senator **George McGovern**. McGovern was a staunch opponent of the Vietnam War, but otherwise his platform was vague. His relative inexperience in politics, compared to Nixon's broad experience, made him a weak candidate.

THE WATERGATE BREAK-IN

On June 17, 1972, just weeks before McGovern won the Democratic nomination, a security guard on his rounds of the Watergate building complex in Washington, D.C., noticed a piece of tape that prevented a door from locking. That door was the entrance to the Democratic National Headquarters. The security guard called the police, who surprised and arrested five men in possession of burglary tools, cameras, film, tear gas guns, and surveillance equipment. Among the burglars was **James W. McCord, Jr.**, the security director for CRP. The next day a second CRP member and a former presidential aide were named as accomplices in the burglary. Journalists called the incident the **Watergate break-in**.

In response to news of the break-in, President Nixon assured the public that no one "presently employed" in his administration was involved "in this very bizarre incident." At first, few people paid much attention to the crime. But over the next several months, *Washington Post* reporters **Bob Woodward** and **Carl Bernstein** slowly began to uncover the connection between the break-in and top government officials closely connected to the White House.

Months passed, and the election campaigns continued. The Watergate break-in had little effect on the outcome of the November 1972 election because the journalists were still investigating the incident. Nixon won the presidency by a landslide, but the Democratic Party, much to Nixon's disappointment, kept control of Congress.

THE WATERGATE TRIALS

Woodward and Bernstein continued to publish reports through the end of 1972 describing the dirty tricks that CRP members had played to sabotage Nixon's opponents. In January 1973, the same month as Nixon's inauguration, the trial of the Watergate burglars began with Judge **John Sirica** presiding.

At the time, Nixon's public approval rating was very high, at 68 percent, but it fell sharply as the journalists continued to uncover information about the break-in. The *Post's* reports led Judge Sirica to suspect a **cover-up**, or an attempt to hide the truth. He did not believe that the burglars had acted without the knowledge of either the CRP or the president. In January, four of the Watergate burglars pled guilty to minor charges of theft and **wiretapping**, or placing a device on a telephone in order to secretly listen to conversations. McCord, who had pled not guilty, was convicted of conspiracy along with the other two offenses.

In March 1973, McCord wrote a letter to Judge Sirica implicating Nixon in the cover-up of the Watergate burglary. McCord's letter resulted in the dismissal or the resignation of several of Nixon's chief advisors, including White House counsel John Dean, chief of staff H. R. Haldeman, and chief domestic advisor John Ehrlichman. Nixon continued to deny any involvement in Watergate. He claimed that he had been too busy running the nation to keep up with the activities of his re-election campaign staff. Many Americans—and most Republican leaders—believed Nixon. Representative **Gerald R. Ford** of Michigan declared, "I have the greatest confidence in the president and am absolutely positive he had nothing to do with this mess."

Nonetheless, the Senate formed the **Watergate Committee** in May 1973. The special committee, chaired by North Carolina senator **Sam Ervin**, heard sworn testimonies from present and former Nixon aides. The aides described crimes committed before the 1972 election that were intended to undermine the president's opponents. Additionally, a former aide to the president revealed that Nixon had been secretly tape-recording his conversations in the White House's Oval Office since 1971.

In May 1973, Attorney General **Elliot Richardson** appointed Harvard Law School professor **Archibald Cox** as a special prosecutor in the Watergate case. Cox, Judge Sirica, and committee chairman Ervin demanded to hear the relevant Oval Office tapes. However, Nixon withheld them, claiming **executive privilege**, the principle that the president may withhold certain information from Congress in the nation's interest. Cox presented the White House with a subpoena demanding the tapes, which Nixon's lawyers asked Sirica to block. Sirica ordered the tapes to be turned over. Now the White House was in a battle with the courts as well as with the Watergate Committee, provoking a constitutional crisis.

At the same time, Vice President Spiro Agnew was enmeshed in his own separate scandal. Beginning in April 1973, the U.S. Justice Department had been investigating allegations that Agnew had accepted

PRIMARY SOURCE

As a member of the committee given the task of deciding Nixon's fate, Representative Barbara Jordan asserted that a failure to impeach Nixon went directly against the Constitution.

The President has engaged in a series of public statements and actions designed to thwart the lawful investigation by government prosecutors. Moreover, the President has made public announcements and assertions . . . which the evidence will show he knew to be false. If the impeachment provision in the Constitution of the United States will not reach the offenses charged here, then perhaps that 18th-century Constitution should be abandoned to a 20th-century paper shredder.

—from a speech delivered by Representative Barbara Jordan, House Judiciary Committee, during Watergate hearings, July 25, 1974

illegal payoffs from building contractors while he was governor of Maryland from 1967 to 1969. Initially, Agnew denied the charges. Then, on October 10, 1973, he pleaded no contest in court to income tax evasion, and he resigned as vice president.

On October 20, Nixon ordered Attorney General Richardson to fire Cox, but Richardson refused. Nixon retaliated by firing Richardson. With Richardson gone, the attorney general's second-in-command, Solicitor General Robert Bork, fired Cox and replaced him with a lawyer named Leon Jaworski. These dramatic developments, known as the "Saturday Night Massacre," prompted the House Judiciary Committee to consider hearings for impeachment, or formal charges brought against a public official for misconduct while in office. At this point, the White House turned over some, but not all, of the tapes. In December 1973, Congress confirmed Nixon's choice of Gerald Ford to replace Agnew as vice president.

THE TAPES AND THE RESIGNATION

In March 1974, Nixon's chief advisors, who had resigned or were dismissed as a result of McCord's letter to Judge Sirica, were indicted for crimes. In July, prosecutor Jaworski ordered Nixon to release 64 additional tapes of his conversations in the Oval Office. Rather than release the tapes, Nixon handed over more than 1,000 pages of edited transcripts. Jaworski appealed to the Supreme Court. In *United States* v. *Nixon*, the Supreme Court ruled unanimously that the tapes did not fall under the

CRITICAL VIEWING On August 9, 1974, the day after announcing his resignation, Nixon boarded the Marine One helicopter that took him from the White House lawn to Andrews Air Force Base for his flight to his home in southern California. What attitude does Nixon convey in his body language?

protection of executive privilege and that Nixon must surrender them. By this point, Nixon had lost the trust of most American citizens. A Gallup poll taken just months earlier showed Nixon's public approval rating had dropped from 68 to 27 percent.

Also in July 1974, the House Judiciary Committee began debating charges of presidential impeachment before a national television audience. One member of the committee was Representative **Barbara Jordan** of Texas, who became famous for her powerful speeches. Three days after the Supreme Court ordered Nixon to hand over the Oval Office tapes, the committee approved three charges: obstruction of justice, abuse of power, and contempt of Congress. On August 5, the president released the tapes, one of which had an 18-minute gap of silence. The gap led many people to believe that something may have been erased. Although investigators could not prove Nixon knew of the burglary before it occurred, the tapes confirmed that he played an active role in the attempt to cover up the burglary. He offered money to the burglars to keep quiet about their role in the crime. He developed a plan for the CIA to block the FBI's investigation. Ultimately, Nixon was charged with obstruction of justice and abuse of power.

Nixon's impeachment seemed certain. Rather than risk further disgrace, on August 8, 1974, Nixon resigned, becoming the first president to do so. In a tearful farewell to his staff the next morning, he offered advice he himself had ignored. "Always remember," he said, "those who hate you don't win unless you hate them. And then you destroy yourself." Vice President Gerald Ford was sworn in as president shortly after noon on the same day.

Nixon's involvement in Watergate deepened a public distrust of government that had grown during the Vietnam War years. The scandal also demonstrated the dangers of an imperial, or overly powerful, presidency and sent the Congress into constitutional crisis mode. Fortunately, the Constitution's system of checks and balances allowed the judicial and legislative branches to rein in the executive branch. For his part, however, Nixon, who died in 1994 at the age of 81, never directly admitted his guilt in the matter.

HISTORICAL THINKING

1. **READING CHECK** What was Nixon's involvement in the Watergate scandal?

2. **DRAW CONCLUSIONS** Do Representative Jordan's comments indicate bias on her part, or does she present valid arguments? Explain your answer.

3. **SYNTHESIZE** What role did the characteristics of power in Washington, D.C., play in the actions and resignation of Nixon?

4. **EVALUATE** Within the context of the Watergate scandal, identify what you believe to be a valid argument that was used as well as a fallacious argument used to analyze events. Explain your choices.

FORD SUCCEEDS NIXON

Americans felt betrayed by the Watergate scandal. Their president left office barely apologizing for the chaos he had caused and without admitting his guilt. They hoped the man who took his place would prove more trustworthy.

THE WATERGATE LEGACY

When Vice President Agnew resigned in 1973, Gerald Ford rose from Congressional representative to vice president—the first selected under the **25th Amendment**. Ratified under President Johnson in 1967, the amendment calls for the president to nominate and Congress to approve a replacement for the vice president when necessary. On August 9, 1974, the day after President Nixon resigned and less than a year after being confirmed as vice president, Ford became the 38th president of the United States. The American people had a president they had never voted for—another first.

In his 25 years in Congress, Ford had developed a reputation for honesty and openness, traits Americans were looking for in their president. During his vice-presidential confirmation hearing in 1973, Ford had stated he would not give Nixon a presidential pardon. A president has the constitutional right to grant a pardon to anyone. A pardon excuses a person from punishment for a crime. In September 1974, Ford reversed his position and pardoned Nixon for all crimes he "may have committed" during his term in office. Ford's pardon ended any further criminal investigation into Nixon's actions as president.

Ford hoped the pardon would finally allow Americans to move forward and put the Watergate scandal behind them. However, many Americans wanted justice and felt that Ford had betrayed them. As a result, Ford's public approval rating plummeted from 72 percent to 49 percent.

ECONOMIC TROUBLES

Ford inherited an ailing economy that worsened over the course of his presidency. The economy slowed almost to a standstill, a situation called **economic stagnation**. The stagnation was due to years of slow economic growth and high unemployment rates. At the same time, energy costs kept rising, pushing up the inflation rate, or the annual percent increase in the prices of goods and services. Economists called this unusual combination of stagnation and inflation "**stagflation**."

Ford was at odds with the Democratic Congress over economic policies. He did not want to increase the federal deficit, and so he defied Congress's plan to lower taxes and increase government spending. Instead, in October 1974, Ford proposed a plan that involved a tax hike and a reduction in government spending. To get Americans on board with his plan, he initiated a campaign called Whip Inflation Now (WIN), in which he asked citizens to voluntarily limit their spending and consumption through thriftiness.

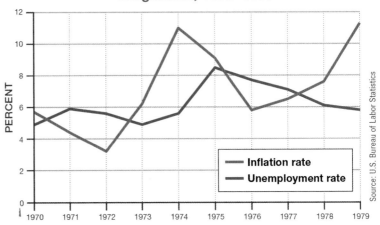

Stagflation, 1970–1979

Source: U.S. Bureau of Labor Statistics

In January 1975, he offered a new plan that called for a modest tax cut and a reduction in government spending. Congress approved this plan, but only after adding more tax cuts and raising government spending. In his battle with Congress, Ford vetoed more than 60 bills. Congress overrode the president's veto on several bills, increasing Social Security benefits, funding public works projects, and raising the minimum wage. Ford also battled Congress over energy policy, which had arisen as an issue under Nixon.

FOREIGN POLICY

In addition to an ailing economy, Ford also inherited the ongoing conflict in Vietnam and its many geopolitical consequences. As you have read, the United States withdrew combat troops from Vietnam in 1973 but kept

President Ford inherited from his predecessor the issue of U.S. dependence on foreign oil. In 1975, to promote conservation and energy independence, Ford imposed an import fee on oil. He hoped the fee would spur consumers to use less energy and so decrease demand for OPEC oil. Here Ford discusses his plan with the press outside the White House.

an embassy in South Vietnam. However, fighting between the North and South Vietnamese had continued. The South Vietnamese army was no match for the combined North Vietnamese and Viet Cong forces. In October 1974, the leaders of communist North Vietnam prepared their final plans for the conquest of South Vietnam.

In March 1975, the North Vietnamese launched a massive assault, overwhelming South Vietnamese forces near the demilitarized zone (DMZ). As North Vietnamese troops rapidly advanced toward Saigon, the capital of South Vietnam, chaos and panic gripped the city. Thousands of soldiers left their units, and masses of civilians crowded the highways, trying to flee. Ignoring a plea from President Ford, the U.S. Congress refused to extend emergency aid to South Vietnam. A few U.S. forces remained in the city, and they worked to evacuate as many Americans and South Vietnamese as they could. On April 30, 1975, the North Vietnamese took control of Saigon and reunited North and South Vietnam into one communist-led nation. With the fall of Saigon, American efforts to stop the spread of communism in Southeast Asia failed, raising concerns about the limits of U.S. military power.

Communism also spread to neighboring Cambodia with the rise of a rebel guerilla force called the **Khmer Rouge** (kuh-MEHR ROOZH). After a civil war, a brutal communist regime took over Cambodia in 1975. The Khmer Rouge carried out a massive genocide against the Cambodian people. Not wanting to become involved in another war in Southeast Asia, the United States took no military action. By the time the regime was overthrown four years later, the Khmer Rouge had killed almost 2 million people—one-fourth of the nation's population.

Ford continued Nixon's policy of détente with the Soviet Union and signed the Helsinki Accords, or the Helsinki Final Act, in 1975. In this agreement, the 35 signing nations, including the United States and the Soviet Union, agreed to resolve conflicts peacefully, cooperate economically and scientifically, and respect human rights.

HISTORICAL THINKING

1. **READING CHECK** What challenges did President Ford inherit from President Nixon?

2. **ASK AND ANSWER QUESTIONS** What questions do you have about the fall of Saigon, and how can you find the answers to your questions?

3. **INTERPRET GRAPHS** In terms of the economic behavior of the United States, what was the trend in inflation while unemployment was falling from 1975 to 1979?

CARTER AND THE ENERGY CRISIS

If you're like most people, you probably wouldn't want to be considered an "outsider." But for a presidential candidate, it's sometimes an advantage, particularly if voters don't trust the "insiders."

THE OUTSIDER PRESIDENT

Gerald Ford dreamed of winning the White House in his own right, but he faced a serious challenge in 1976—conservative California governor **Ronald Reagan**. In his primary campaign, Reagan portrayed Ford as a weak president who was unable to control a Democratic Congress or to confront the Soviet Union. Reagan campaigned effectively, but Ford managed a narrow primary victory and became the Republican presidential nominee.

Because Ford appeared vulnerable in 1976, the Democratic race for president attracted a number of candidates. Among them was a little-known politician named **James Earl (Jimmy) Carter, Jr.** Although he was not taken seriously at first, Carter presented the right image for the post-Watergate era. He was a deeply religious man who promised voters, "I will never lie to you." And he was not part of the Washington political establishment, which many Americans had come to distrust.

Born in Plains, Georgia, in 1924, Carter graduated from the U.S. Naval Academy and spent seven years as a naval officer. He returned to Plains to run the family's farm supply and peanut business. As his company prospered, he turned to politics, becoming the governor of Georgia in 1970. Known as a "new South" politician, Carter supported progressive causes and civil rights, which appealed to African-American voters. At the Democratic National Convention, delegates chose Carter as their presidential nominee, and he went on to win the 1976 presidential race against Ford.

Carter won praise for some of his early actions in office, including the appointment of popular civil rights leader **Andrew Young, Jr.**, as U.S. ambassador to the United Nations. Young had been a close associate of Dr. Martin Luther King, Jr., and was elected to Congress in 1972. Carter also supported the creation of the **Department of Education** to coordinate federal education policy. Previously, numerous federal offices had handled education-related issues. Through Carter's efforts, Congress approved the consolidation of these efforts into one cabinet-level department in 1979. Carter was also a strong supporter of affirmative action in federal government hiring. As you have read, affirmative action was challenged and upheld by the Supreme Court in the 1978 case of *Regents of the University of California* v. *Bakke*.

Carter often found himself at odds with Congress, however. Many Congressional representatives considered Carter difficult to work with. A relationship of dislike and distrust developed as Congress voted down bill after bill that Carter proposed. In return, Carter vetoed many of the bills that Congress had approved.

THE ENERGY CRISIS

Like Presidents Nixon and Ford, Carter had to battle an ongoing energy crisis. Since the 1973 oil embargo, the United States had faced rising prices for oil, declining domestic supplies, and growing energy needs. To address the crisis, Carter presented Congress with his plan for the National Energy Program in April 1977. This environmental policy emphasized reducing the demand for energy through conservation. It also called for decreased dependence on foreign oil and increased use of domestic coal as well as the development of alternative energy sources, such as solar, wind, and nuclear power. In promoting his program, Carter appealed to Americans to reduce their consumption of oil and gas.

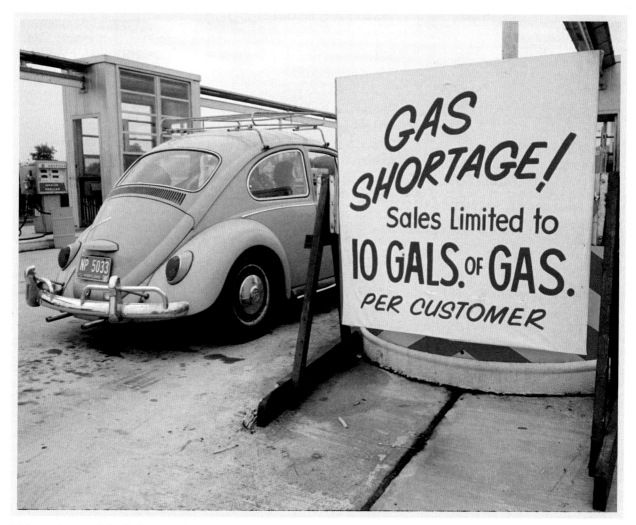

Rising prices and declining supplies of oil in the 1970s resulted in long lines and rationing at gas stations such as this one in Connecticut. States, cities, and individual gas stations themselves imposed limits on gas purchases.

Carter's plan ran into immediate opposition from oil companies, the auto industry, and others who supported the increased production of oil and the removal of restrictions on oil pricing. Nonetheless, in October 1977, President Carter established the **Department of Energy** to oversee federal energy policy and programs. In November 1978, he signed five energy bills into law.

Carter's push for alternative energy sources experienced a setback in 1979. A mechanical failure at the Three Mile Island nuclear power plant in Pennsylvania threatened the East Coast with a possible radiation leak. Even though power plant workers avoided a crisis, the incident raised awareness of the great risks associated with nuclear power.

In early 1979, a public uprising in Iran, as well as a strike by oilfield workers, disrupted the oil supply from that country. In late 1979, two OPEC nations decided to raise oil prices. The oil shortage and price increases led to a high rate of inflation in the United States. The events underscored the need for new sources of energy to build energy independence. But in the meantime, angry and frustrated Americans blamed Carter.

In a nationally televised speech, Carter prefaced his proposals for solving the energy crisis by describing a "crisis of confidence" gripping the nation. He claimed that many Americans no longer believed in a great future for the nation. In what came to be called the "malaise" (muh-LAYZ) speech, Carter portrayed Americans as suffering from low morale. The word *malaise* means "a general feeling of illness or unease." In the days following his speech, Carter's approval rating increased, but then negative reviews came out in the press. Carter's speech ultimately undermined confidence in his leadership. Many Americans felt that Carter blamed them, instead of his own lack of leadership, for the state of the country.

It's clear that the true problems of our nation are much deeper—deeper than gasoline lines or energy shortages, deeper even than inflation or recession.

The threat is nearly invisible in ordinary ways. It is a crisis of confidence. It is a crisis that strikes at the very heart and soul and spirit of our national will. We can see this crisis in the growing doubt about the meaning of our own lives and in the loss of a unity of purpose for our nation.

The erosion of our confidence in the future is threatening to destroy the social and the political fabric of America.

—from the "malaise" speech by President Carter, July 15, 1979

CARTER'S FOREIGN POLICY

In foreign affairs, Carter centered his policies on human rights. He believed the United States should promote human rights throughout the world, including rights to food, housing, and education as well as civil and political rights. He also believed all people had the right to bodily integrity, or ownership of one's self, which provides freedom from slavery, torture, and unlawful imprisonment. Addressing human rights violations in Latin America, Carter withdrew American support for a military dictatorship in Chile, cut off aid to a repressive regime in Nicaragua, and encouraged the governments of Brazil and Argentina to take steps toward establishing democracy.

Despite having little previous experience in foreign affairs, President Carter proved to be a successful diplomat. Shortly after taking office, he prioritized resolving a long-standing issue with the country of Panama. As you've read, Theodore Roosevelt negotiated for the United States to have control of the Panama Canal Zone in 1904. Over the years, tension grew between the United States and Panama over the issue of canal ownership. In 1977, President Carter and Omar Torrijos (OH-mahr toh-REE-hohs), the dictator of Panama, negotiated two treaties. The first treaty allowed the U.S. military to use the canal for defense. The second treaty outlined the

CRITICAL VIEWING President Carter (center), Egyptian president Anwar Sadat (left), and Israeli prime minister Mehanchem Begin shake hands together to celebrate the signing of the 1979 treaty that ended 31 years of war between Egypt and Israel. What does the photo convey about the mood of this moment?

process of transferring ownership of the Panama Canal Zone from the United States back to Panama. Both treaties provoked fierce national debate in the Senate for more than six months, but they were eventually ratified. The treaties greatly improved relations between the United States and Latin America.

Carter's greatest foreign policy achievement involved the Middle East, however. In 1977, Egyptian President **Anwar Sadat** (AHN-wahr suh-DAHT) stunned the Arab world by visiting Israel to explore the possibility of peace talks with Prime Minister **Menachem Begin** (muh-NAH-khuhm BAY-gihn). Egypt and Israel had been enemies for many years and seemed at an impasse. Their discussions were friendly but unproductive, as neither man seemed willing to take the political risks that peace demanded.

Carter invited Sadat and Begin to join him at the presidential retreat at Camp David in Maryland in September 1978 to negotiate a peace agreement. The **Camp David Accords** led to a historic treaty the following year. Egypt agreed to recognize the state of Israel, previously unthinkable for an Arab nation. Israel agreed to return the Sinai Peninsula, which it had acquired in the 1967 Six-Day War, to Egypt.

Carter also worked to improve foreign relations with the Soviet Union by building upon the SALT I treaty you have read about. A new round of talks, **SALT II**, had begun in 1972, when Nixon was president. For seven years, negotiators refined the language of the treaty. In 1979, President Carter and General Secretary Leonid Brezhnev of the Soviet Union signed the SALT II Treaty, which limited the number of weapons each nation could have and restricted their deployment. When the U.S. Senate received the treaty for ratification, Republicans and conservative Democrats opposed the deal and wrote a letter to Carter in December 1979 explaining, "Ratification of a SALT II Treaty will not reverse trends in the military balance adverse to the United States." Days later, the Soviets invaded neighboring Afghanistan, which resulted in Carter withdrawing the

Israel and the Sinai Peninsula, 1978

Territories occupied by Israel
Territory Israel returned to Egypt

SALT II treaty from consideration and organizing an international boycott of the 1980 Summer Olympics to be held in Moscow. The Soviet invasion was intended to stop a revolt by Islamic fundamentalists against the pro-Soviet regime that ruled the country. The United States then supported and equipped the Afghan fighters, contributing to massive casualties for the Soviet troops. The invasion worsened the tensions between the United States and the Soviet Union.

HISTORICAL THINKING

1. **READING CHECK** How did President Carter plan to address the energy crisis?

2. **IDENTIFY MAIN IDEAS AND DETAILS** Describe the main features of U.S. Middle East policy and outline its strategic, political, and economic objectives.

3. **MAKE INFERENCES** Why were the Camp David Accords historically important?

4. **INTERPRET MAPS** After returning the Sinai Peninsula to Egypt, what territories did Israel still occupy?

HOSTAGES IN IRAN

On a visit to Iran in 1977, President Carter described the Middle Eastern nation as "an island of stability in one of the most troubled areas in the world." He did not know that within two years upheaval in Iran would threaten his own presidency.

TURMOIL IN THE PERSIAN GULF

Today, the United States and the world face an ongoing threat to peace due to uprisings and violent unrest in the Middle East, but the anti-American, anti-Western sentiments of many people in the region are nothing new. In the 1970s, Iran was vital to American interests as both an oil supplier and a political ally against communist influences in the Middle East. But the United States' relationship with Iran changed dramatically in 1979.

In 1953, President Eisenhower approved a CIA operation to return the shah of Iran, Reza Shah Pahlavi, to power by overthrowing the democratically elected prime minister Mohammed Mossadegh.

Eisenhower feared that Mossadegh's rise to power would affect American access to oil supplies in the Middle East.

Many Iranians resented the United States for directly interfering with their government by returning the shah to power. They also opposed the shah's dictatorial rule. In January 1979, protesters launched the Iranian Revolution, also referred to as the Islamic Revolution, under the leadership of **Ayatollah Ruhollah Khomeini** (ah-yuh-TOH-luh roo-HOH-luh koh-MAY-nee). An exiled religious leader. Khomeini aimed to turn Iran into an **Islamic republic**, or a state governed by Islamic law. The shah fled Iran, initially for Egypt, as Khomeini returned to the

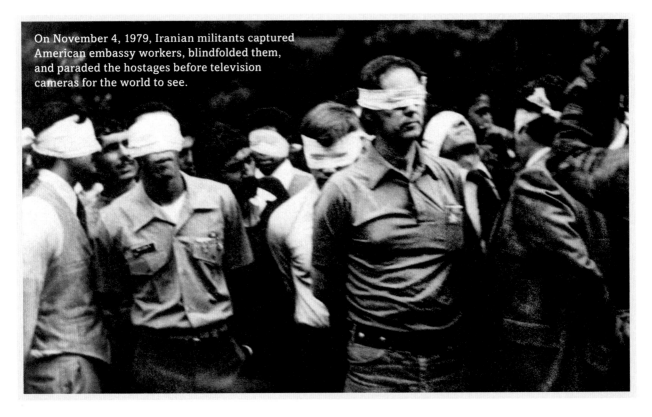

On November 4, 1979, Iranian militants captured American embassy workers, blindfolded them, and paraded the hostages before television cameras for the world to see.

country and took power. As a result of perceived corruption in the shah's relationship with the United States, the new leadership opposed Western influence. One of Khomeini's first moves was to end oil shipments to the United States, which he called "the Great Satan." Then other OPEC countries raised their oil prices. In the United States, long lines reappeared at gas stations, and the price of gas reached a dollar per gallon—the most expensive it had ever been.

The wreckage of an American helicopter and the plane it crashed into lie in the Iranian desert. The collision occurred during a failed mission in April 1980 to rescue American hostages held in Iran.

THE HOSTAGE CRISIS

In October 1979, President Carter allowed the deposed shah to enter the United States to receive cancer treatments. This decision, which Carter viewed as a simple humanitarian gesture, angered many Iranians. On November 4, militant students in **Tehran**, the capital of Iran, stormed the American embassy and took 66 Americans as hostages, or prisoners held to force another party to do what the holder of the prisoners wants. The world watched as the blindfolded hostages were paraded before television cameras. The militants demanded the United States return the shah to Iran for trial in exchange for the release of the American hostages. Otherwise, the prisoners would be tried and possibly executed as spies.

Carter refused to return the shah to Iran. Diplomats from the United States and other countries tried to negotiate the release of the hostages but failed. The militants ignored Carter's attempts to settle the crisis through the United Nations. A painful standoff ensued.

Many Americans believed the Iran hostage crisis demonstrated that the United States' prestige and power were declining in the world. Television networks flashed nightly pictures of the hostages on humiliating public display in Tehran while crowds shouted "Death to Carter" and "Down with the United States." Americans appeared helpless and discouraged as they faced daunting challenges abroad.

DEATH IN THE DESERT

As the hostage crisis continued, President Carter consulted with the families of the hostages and mobilized his administration to find a diplomatic solution. Finally, desperate to save the Americans, Carter ordered a secret military mission to free them by force. The result was disastrous. In April 1980, two American helicopters involved in the secret rescue mission were disabled by mechanical problems in the Iranian desert. Another helicopter hit a U.S. cargo plane, killing eight members of the mission. Not only did the soldiers fail to free the hostages, they never even made it to Tehran. The Iranians proudly displayed the burned corpses of the helicopter crash victims before the television cameras.

Carter's credibility as a leader plummeted because most Americans blamed him for the failed mission. The 1980 presidential election was approaching, and Carter's chances for re-election did not look good.

HISTORICAL THINKING

1. **READING CHECK** What was the purpose of the Iranian Revolution of 1979?

2. **SYNTHESIZE** Describe the strategies President Carter used to address the hostage crisis in the Middle East, and explain how they related to political and economic interests.

3. **MAKE PREDICTIONS** If President Carter had made different choices during the hostage crisis, how might they have led to an alternative outcome to this historical event?

4. **ANALYZE VISUALS** What message about American power do the two photos on these pages convey?

VOCABULARY

Use each of the following vocabulary words in a sentence that shows an understanding of the term's meaning.

1. silent majority

   Nixon hoped to appeal to the silent majority, rather than to those Americans protesting on the streets.

2. détente

3. DDT

4. overregulation

5. wiretapping

6. stagflation

7. malaise

8. Islamic republic

READING STRATEGY
IDENTIFY MAIN IDEAS AND DETAILS

Use a graphic organizer like the one below to identify the supporting details about the impact of the Watergate scandal. Then answer the question.

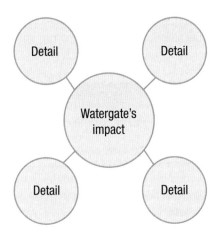

9. What impact did the Watergate scandal have on Nixon's presidency?

MAIN IDEAS

Answer the following questions. Support your answers with evidence from the chapter.

10. What group of Americans made up Nixon's silent majority? **LESSON 1.1**

11. What were some of the Burger Court's rulings on forced busing to achieve integration? **LESSON 1.2**

12. Why did Nixon create the Environmental Protection Agency? **LESSON 1.3**

13. What conflict arose between environmentalists and property rights advocates in the 1970s? **LESSON 1.3**

14. How did the Watergate scandal provoke a constitutional crisis? **LESSON 1.5**

15. How did the Vietnam War come to an end, and what were the results? **LESSON 2.1**

16. What were the results of the Camp David Accords? **LESSON 2.2**

17. What event initiated the Iran hostage crisis? **LESSON 2.3**

HISTORICAL THINKING

Answer the following questions. Support your answers with evidence from the chapter.

18. **DRAW CONCLUSIONS** What did George Wallace's presidential campaign reveal about changing voting patterns in the United States?

19. **MAKE CONNECTIONS** What aspects of Carter's energy policy are still emphasized today?

20. **EVALUATE** What were some of Nixon's notable achievements as president?

21. **FORM AND SUPPORT OPINIONS** What is your opinion of President Ford's pardon of Richard Nixon? Give reasons for your answer.

22. **SYNTHESIZE** How did events in the 1970s reflect a more global and interconnected economy?

23. **COMPARE AND CONTRAST** How did national policies on integration in public schools change during the 1970s?

INTERPRET GRAPHS

This graph shows the percent change in world oil prices, U.S. gas prices, sales of Japanese-made cars in the United States, and all car sales in the United States from 1978 to 1982. The base year is 1978. A positive percent change represents an increase from the base, while a negative percent change represents a decrease. Study the graph and answer the questions that follow.

**Gas Prices and Car Sales
in the United States, 1978–1982**

Sources: Inflationdata.com, CQPress, U.S. International Trade Commission

24. Based on the graph and what you know about Japanese-made cars, what is a possible cause of the increase in the sales of these cars in 1979?

25. What limitations exist in assigning exact cause-and-effect relationships to the factors shown on the graph? In other words, why is it difficult to say for sure that one factor causes another?

ANALYZE SOURCES

American nature writer Edward Abbey based his book *Desert Solitaire* (1968) on his experiences working as a park ranger in Utah. Abbey's writing, though sometimes controversial, expressed his deep-seated love of the American West. Read this excerpt from *Desert Solitaire* and answer the question that follows.

> No, wilderness is not a luxury but a necessity of the human spirit, and as vital to our lives as water and good bread. A civilization which destroys what little remains of the wild, the spare, the original, is cutting itself off from its origins and betraying the principle of civilization itself.

26. What is your opinion of the reasons Abbey gives for the need to practice environmental conservation?

CONNECT TO YOUR LIFE

27. **EXPLANATORY** President Nixon enacted various measures to address environmental problems in the United States. Choose a region of the United States and identify an environmental issue there. Write an essay in which you describe the policies that address that issue, and explain how these policies affect your life.

TIPS

- Research the physical and human characteristics of the region you've chosen as well as policies that address the environmental issue you've identified.

- Create a topic sentence that introduces the region and issue you've chosen.

- Develop your topic by describing relevant policies on this issue and explaining their effects on your life.

- Use two or three vocabulary words from the chapter in your essay.

- End your essay with a general statement about the impact of environmental protections.

THE CONSERVATIVE REVOLUTION 1980–1992

HISTORICAL THINKING What major changes occurred in the United States during Ronald Reagan's presidency?

CRITICAL VIEWING *Portrait of President Ronald Reagan in the Oval Office* was taken by American photographer Arnold Newman in 1981, the year Reagan took office. What does the photo convey about the former actor and California governor's attitude toward his new job?

"The business of our nation goes forward."

—President Ronald Reagan

ROOTS OF THE CONSERVATIVE MOVEMENT

The Republican Party had suffered two major blows in the 1960s and 1970s: the failed 1964 candidacy of Barry Goldwater and Richard Nixon's Watergate scandal. For the 1980 election, the party was looking for an upbeat nominee with the charisma to charm both Republicans and Democrats dissatisfied with Carter's presidency.

A CONSERVATIVE MOVEMENT ARISES

With the nation enduring economic and foreign policy difficulties, Jimmy Carter faced a difficult bid for re-election in 1980. Carter and his fellow Democrats faced another challenge as well—the steady rise of a conservative movement in the country. Several Republican presidential candidates competed for the nomination in 1980. Two notable politicians in the running were former CIA director **George H.W. Bush** and moderate Republican congressman **John B. Anderson** from Illinois. But the favorite to win the nomination was Ronald Reagan, the

popular California governor and former movie star. Since delivering a well-received speech endorsing Barry Goldwater for president in 1964, Reagan had emerged as a conservative leader.

The conservative movement began in the late 1960s when numerous grassroots organizations, such as the American Conservative Union (ACU) and Young Americans for Freedom, began working together to promote their ideals. **Conservatives** support traditional policies in economic and social legislation and are more likely to favor established systems of government over progressive ideas

Three teleprompters broadcast Pastor Joel Osteen's Sunday service to about 25,000 people at the Lakewood Church in Houston, Texas. The rise in religious fundamentalism during the 1980s led to the creation of today's megachurches, or very large non-Catholic Christian churches.

or radical changes. During this time, a number of conservative **think tanks** emerged: groups of experts who conduct research and discuss issues in order to craft potential solutions to social and economic problems. Conservative politicians used the data that think tanks generated to inform their decisions about legislation. Prominent conservative think tanks still active today include the **American Enterprise Institute** and the **Heritage Foundation**. Conservative think tanks, lobbyists, and politicians shared the goal of shaping a compelling message to attract voter support. They hoped to gain more influence throughout the nation and in Washington.

CONSERVATIVE BELIEFS

In general, conservatives favored making the government smaller, decreasing taxes, and deregulating industries. They opposed greater federal regulation of the economy. They argued that if people and businesses had more freedom to make their own economic choices, their purchasing power would stimulate greater growth and a better standard of living for all. Conservatives favored less taxation, arguing that allowing consumers and businesses to keep more of their wages and profits would spur greater investment and growth. In addition, because of their belief that individualism is superior to government action, conservatives opposed government social programs, including many of President Johnson's Great Society welfare reforms, claiming they required high taxation and massive spending by the federal government. As American patriots, however, they did believe in government spending to support a robust, well-funded military.

Many conservatives, but not all, drove a large social agenda that was deeply rooted in religion. This agenda was hotly debated by those who felt that allowing religious views to shape political policies violated the separation of church and state. Still, the 1970s and 1980s were a time of renewed interest in Christian values, much like the First and Second Great Awakenings of the 18th and 19th centuries. Instead of giving powerful sermons in tents, however, the conservative movement built part of its base and conveyed its message through evangelical churches, televangelism, and other media outlets. The Reverend **Jerry Falwell**, a Baptist minister from Virginia, started a grassroots organization called the **Moral Majority**. The organization was made up of Christian fundamentalists, or people who believe in the literal interpretation of the Bible, and evangelists, or people who believe it is their duty to spread their religious faith and win converts. According to Falwell,

the purpose of the Moral Majority was to press the government into supporting social programs that promoted what they termed "traditional family values." Falwell and his followers spoke out against what they saw as the evils of society: abortion, out-of-wedlock births, homosexuality, the teaching of evolution in schools, and increased drug use among Americans. They also condemned what they perceived as the resulting breakdown of the American family.

Television programs, magazines, and newspapers featured Falwell regularly. The organization's message became so popular that Pat Robertson, one of Falwell's supporters and a fundamentalist Christian preacher, created a television network to feature the views of prominent members of the Moral Majority. The ideas of the Moral Majority spread throughout American politics as well. Conservative politicians spoke out against abortion and the *Roe* v. *Wade* decision (1973), which made abortion legal under certain circumstances. They demanded that Congress restrict access to abortion, publicly protesting outside abortion clinics and organizing large "Right to Life" demonstrations.

Many religious conservatives also spoke out against Darwin's theory of evolution, an idea they deemed blasphemous, or ungodly, because it contradicted the creation account in the Bible. The growing gay rights and feminist movements as well as the rise in out-of-wedlock births received criticism because the Moral Majority believed these things threatened the traditional definition of family—a married man and woman, and their children. Throughout the late 1970s, and especially in the South and the West, conservatives were becoming a growing and powerful political force.

HISTORICAL THINKING

1. **READING CHECK** What were the conservatives' views on the federal government?

2. **DESCRIBE** What was the main goal of the conservative movement?

3. **MAKE GENERALIZATIONS** The Moral Majority was concerned about the effects of which social changes and movements on the American family, and why?

GROWTH OF THE SUNBELT

Have you ever moved from one part of the country to another, or do you know friends or family members who have? In the decades following World War II, many Americans migrated from the northern part of the country to the South and West—a demographic shift that changed the nation's political landscape.

DEMOGRAPHIC SHIFTS

As you have read, after World War II, the United States experienced a widespread demographic shift as families moved from cities and farms to suburbs. In addition, a large number of Americans began moving from the nation's Frostbelt—the Northeast, the Great Lakes region, and the Midwest—to the nation's southern and western states, a region that became known as the Sunbelt. Population booms occurred in states such as Texas, Florida, and California. In fact, migration to the Sunbelt helped California become the most populous state in the country by 1962. And the migration continued for the next few decades.

Low taxes were one of the primary draws to the Sunbelt for both people and businesses. Taxes had steadily increased in the large cities of the North to help support aging infrastructure and social programs, such as the War on Poverty. In contrast, there were smaller populations and less infrastructure to support across the Sunbelt. Furthermore, land in the Sunbelt states cost a fraction of what it did in the crowded Northeast. Businesses could build

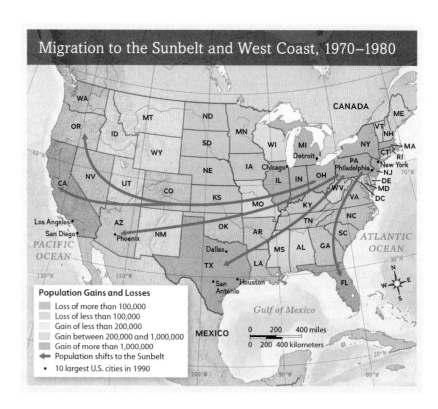

Migration to the Sunbelt and West Coast, 1970–1980

Population Gains and Losses
- Loss of more than 100,000
- Loss of less than 100,000
- Gain of less than 200,000
- Gain between 200,000 and 1,000,000
- Gain of more than 1,000,000
- ← Population shifts to the Sunbelt
- • 10 largest U.S. cities in 1990

AIR-CONDITIONING AND THE SUNBELT

People first started using mechanical air conditioners in the early 20th century, but air-conditioning units did not become a practical appliance in most homes until after World War II. Innovations during the war made them more portable and less expensive. Air conditioners made it possible for people living in the American South and West to escape the dangerous summer heat. As a result, more people moved to the Sunbelt. With the increased population came increased political representation for Sunbelt states, including Florida, Georgia, Texas, California, Arizona, and New Mexico.

new factories for much less than it cost to update their old facilities in the North. And the warmer weather meant less wear-and-tear on buildings and equipment—another cost saver for businesses. As a result, a number of companies closed their Frostbelt factories and moved south or west. Soon some northern industrial cities became known collectively as the **Rustbelt**, a reference to the way that abandoned tools and machines corrode and rust.

In addition to attracting businesses, the Sunbelt drew many senior citizens. Due to improvements in medicine, life spans in the United States were steadily increasing. Payouts from pensions and Social Security also gave people greater financial security later in life. Healthier and more secure, many elderly Americans chose to enjoy their retirement years in warmer climates.

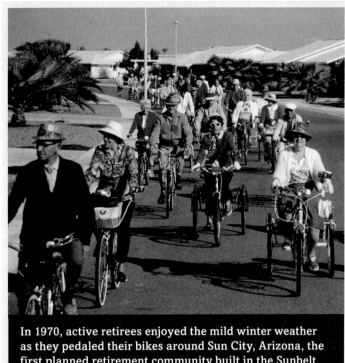

In 1970, active retirees enjoyed the mild winter weather as they pedaled their bikes around Sun City, Arizona, the first planned retirement community built in the Sunbelt.

POLITICAL IMPACT OF THE SUNBELT

Traditionally, the southern and western regions of the United States have been more politically conservative than the Northeast and upper Midwest. As you have read, the South became even more conservative following the Civil Rights Act of 1964. Many southern Democrats were opposed to civil rights legislation. In the wake of the historic act, a number of southern Democrats switched to the Republican Party as a protest against their more progressive northern counterparts. The influx of new residents strengthened the region's conservatism. Business owners and workers, especially those who flocked to the defense and energy industries in the Sunbelt, tended to be politically conservative. So did many senior citizens. As a result, cities and towns across the Sunbelt grew increasingly conservative during the 1960s and 1970s.

Places such as Orange County, California, located just south of Los Angeles, became centers of conservative thought. In the years leading up to the 1980 election, residents of Orange County sponsored anticommunism events for school students and eagerly backed conservative presidential candidate Barry Goldwater in his 1964 bid. They also spearheaded local and state initiatives against women's reproductive rights, public obscenity, and taxation. In particular, they targeted rising property taxes. Much like the people involved in the Sagebrush Rebellion, Orange County residents and other Sunbelt conservatives distrusted big government and liberal legislators.

With every new resident who migrated to the region, the Sunbelt's political power expanded. As you have learned, a state's population determines the number of representatives it sends to the House of Representatives. The migration to the South and West helped the Sunbelt states gain seats in Congress even as the Rustbelt states were losing them. The shift in population also affected each state's designated number of electoral votes, or votes cast by the representatives who elect the president and the vice president. The combination of conservative northerners' migration to the Sunbelt and southern politicians moving away from the Democratic Party eventually made the South and West strongholds for the Republican Party. The phenomenon became a significant factor in the 1980 presidential election.

HISTORICAL THINKING

1. **READING CHECK** What is the connection between the Sunbelt migration and the rise of the conservative movement?

2. **DESCRIBE** What government and economic factors drew businesses to the Sunbelt?

3. **ANALYZE CAUSE AND EFFECT** How did the Sunbelt migration affect northeastern and upper midwestern states both politically and economically?

4. **INTERPRET MAPS** Which areas of the country experienced the least significant population shift?

ELECTION OF RONALD REAGAN

Can a movie actor or entertainer be a good president? What traits and experiences would work in his or her favor, and which ones would work against such a candidate? During the late 1970s, former actor Ronald Reagan leveraged his strong communication skills and his conservative beliefs to reach the highest office in the land.

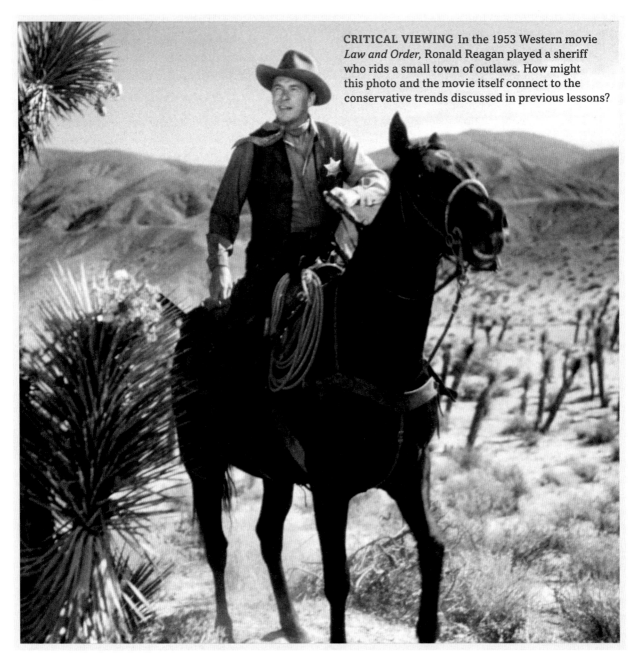

CRITICAL VIEWING In the 1953 Western movie *Law and Order,* Ronald Reagan played a sheriff who rids a small town of outlaws. How might this photo and the movie itself connect to the conservative trends discussed in previous lessons?

THE RISE OF REAGAN

As the 1980 election loomed, the conservative movement found a strong messenger for their cause in California politician Ronald Reagan. Reagan grew up in Illinois and moved to Iowa shortly after graduating from college to work as a sports broadcaster. While on a business trip to California, he auditioned for Hollywood producers, who liked his presence on camera and hired him to act in films. Reagan was cast in 53 roles and, in 1947, became president of the Screen Actors Guild, the union for film actors. During his leadership of the union, his political views shifted. Reagan had been a New Deal Democrat, but the FBI investigations of communist activity in the movie industry led him to adopt more conservative beliefs. During this time, he met Nancy Davis, a film actor whom he would marry in 1952.

From 1954 to 1962, Reagan was a spokesman for the General Electric (GE) company. He was charismatic, and his years in front of the camera had made him a seasoned communicator. Reagan hosted GE's television program, *General Electric Theater*, and toured the country for the company, giving speeches about the dangers of communism, big government, and high taxes. The job prepared him for a televised speech he gave in support of Republican leader Barry Goldwater in 1964. As you've read, that speech caught the attention of California politicians, who later asked Reagan if he was interested in being governor. He ran for governor in 1966 and won. After serving two terms, Reagan moved on to the national scene. In 1976, he challenged incumbent president Gerald Ford in the Republican presidential primary. Reagan narrowly lost, but his strong national showing positioned him well for the future.

THE ELECTION OF 1980

That future came four years later, when Reagan became the Republican candidate in the 1980 presidential election. His opponent, President Jimmy Carter, was seeking a second term. With the ongoing hostage crisis in Iran, a gas shortage, and a struggling economy, many voters in both parties saw President Carter as an ineffective leader. Carter won the Democratic nomination, but only after a strong challenge from U.S. Senator Ted Kennedy of Massachusetts. The race also featured a third-party candidate, Congressman John B. Anderson, a Republican from Illinois, who had run in the Republican primaries in the hope of securing the party's nomination. Arguing that Reagan was too conservative, Anderson ran as an independent candidate and promoted himself as an alternative to the two traditional parties.

The campaign, however, ultimately pitted Reagan against Carter. As the two candidates prepared for their single televised debate, popularity polls had them tied. During the debate in late October 1980, Carter described Reagan as a dangerous and unreliable political extremist, citing Reagan's plans to repeal the minimum wage, gut social **safety-net programs** that were helping people in poverty, and promote a nuclear arms buildup in the Middle East. Reagan focused on the nation's faltering economy, asking viewers: "Are you better off now than you were four years ago?" referring to when Carter took office. Reagan bet that when Americans thought about gas shortages and rising unemployment, most would answer, "No."

He was right. In November 1980, Reagan won the election in a landslide. Voters cast nearly 44 million ballots for Reagan and 35 million for Carter. John Anderson received 5.7 million votes, a strong showing for a third-party candidate. The Republicans also regained control of the Senate, picking up 12 seats from the Democrats. Reagan won by uniting the growing population of fiscal and social conservatives and by winning over a number of working-class Democrats worried about the economy and jobs. With Ronald Reagan's victory, a new era of conservatism was about to begin.

HISTORICAL THINKING

1. **READING CHECK** What made Ronald Reagan a good choice to lead the conservative movement of the 1980s?

2. **FORM AND SUPPORT OPINIONS** Was President Carter's warning about Ronald Reagan a good argument in support of his re-election? Support your opinion with evidence from the text.

3. **IDENTIFY** In his address to the nation on the economy, how did President Reagan propose to reduce unemployment and inflation?

REDUCING GOVERNMENT

Change is hard—especially when you're in the habit of doing things a certain way. The United States had spent four years under Democratic leadership and was now facing the challenge of shifting to a conservative Republican administration.

THE REAGAN ERA BEGINS

The Reagan administration led a resurgence of the Republican Party with a focus on three key areas that restructured the scope of the federal government. The first was to establish a smaller government by decreasing taxes on individuals and businesses and deregulating industries. The second was to advocate conservative social values, including supporting legislation to outlaw abortion, promoting heterosexual marriage, opposing ratification of the Equal Rights Amendment, and championing individual accomplishment as opposed to funding social safety-net programs.

Also troubled by a rise in out-of-wedlock births and drug abuse, conservatives hoped to affect these and their other social concerns by supporting faith-based **cultural advocacy**, or exerting influence on politicians and social institutions to advance a particular religious belief system—in this case, conservative Christianity. The third area of the administration's focus was to expand the military while managing the Cold War. In all of these areas, the Reagan administration achieved both successes and setbacks.

The first months of Reagan's term were eventful and established the new president as a strong leader. After 444 days in captivity, the U.S. hostages in Iran were released as Reagan took office, a significant victory for the president. In February, his proposed economic program of tax and spending cuts was well received. Then, on March 30, 1981, a would-be assassin named John W. Hinckley, Jr., shot Reagan and his press secretary, James Brady, as the president and his advisors were leaving the Washington Hilton Hotel in Washington, D.C. The president recovered completely, and his courage and good humor during the crisis increased his popularity.

That summer, Reagan took decisive action during a strike by some 13,000 members of the Professional Air Traffic Controllers Organization (PATCO). As government employees, the controllers could not legally strike, and Reagan gave them 48 hours to return to work or lose their jobs. Most of them refused, and they were fired. While some citizens considered Reagan's actions to be extreme, much of the public backed the president. A Gallup poll taken shortly afterward showed that 59 percent of the American people supported firing the striking air traffic controllers.

The risk Reagan took in breaking the PATCO strike paid off for his administration immediately: he achieved a reputation for being a tough negotiator, both domestically and internationally, and particularly with the Soviet Union. The long-term consequences were less positive, though. To restore the air traffic control system to its pre-strike condition cost billions of dollars (an amount much higher than that requested from the strikers for pay increases and revised safety procedures) and took several years. In addition, air travel decreased during that time, thus affecting the earnings of airlines and related travel industries as well.

REAGANOMICS

An urgent focus for the Reagan administration was reviving the stalled U.S. economy and addressing the persistence of poverty. Reagan called for decreasing taxes on individuals and corporations, a strategy his administration termed **supply-side economics**.

Reagan administration officials believed that lower taxes would encourage consumers and businesses to spend and invest the money they kept, thus stimulating the economy and leading to job growth. Critics referred to the plan as "trickle-down economics," arguing that it aided the wealthiest Americans most, while only a small amount of job growth and wealth would "trickle down" to the neediest groups. In addition to tax cuts, Reagan called for an increase in military spending. To offset the loss of tax revenue and cover those increases in spending, Reagan proposed significant cuts to social programs, including public education, low-income housing, and Medicaid.

As Reagan worked to implement his policies, the economy worsened. During the early 1980s, unemployment rose to nine million, while thousands of businesses failed and many people lost their homes. The president's popularity plummeted, and Republicans lost seats in the House in the 1982 midterm elections. By the end of 1983, however, the economy began to turn around. Unemployment dropped and so did inflation. The economic growth continued, and Reagan's supporters would eventually cheer what they called "the longest peacetime expansion in American history."

Critics, however, argued that tax cuts continued to benefit mainly the rich and that under Reagan, **income inequality**, or a large gap between what the poorest and the richest citizens earn, had grown wider. Opponents also criticized the administration's continued military spending. While many of Reagan's supporters credited his increased defense spending as part of the reason for the eventual collapse of the Soviet Union, military spending played a big role in tripling the national debt by the end of Reagan's second term.

DEREGULATION

Another campaign promise Reagan sought to fulfill was his pledge to reduce government regulations on American industry. The Carter administration had already begun to eliminate government regulations on the airlines, as well as on the railroad and trucking industries. Reagan, however, felt that these moves didn't go far enough. He initiated a program of **deregulation**, or removing rules and limitations, on a large scale. Among his first targets were environmental regulations.

His choice for secretary of the interior, **James Watt**, was a fierce opponent of environmental protection. Watt proposed a number of changes that outraged environmentalists, including leasing federal lands for oil and gas exploration and reducing funding to national parks. Watt was one of Reagan's most controversial cabinet appointees, and his brief tenure as secretary of the interior was marked not only by his environmentally damaging proposals but also by his frequent insulting remarks, which did not endear him either to Congress or the American people. Watt resigned in October 1983, just as the Senate was drafting a resolution to have him removed from office.

Anne Gorsuch, tapped to direct the Environmental Protection Agency (EPA), was another of Reagan's controversial cabinet picks. During her two years as EPA director, she cut the EPA budget by 22 percent and made moves that critics claimed weakened the Clean Air and Clean Water Acts. In 1982, Congress demanded that the EPA turn over records for the Superfund program, which was responsible for the cleanup of toxic waste sites. Few of the sites designated for cleanup were actually being cleaned up, and Gorsuch and her agency were accused of mismanagement. When she refused to turn over the records, she was forced to resign.

Of President Reagan's efforts at deregulation, the one that may have had the most long-lasting impact was the lifting of regulations on the savings and loan (S&L) industry. The original S&Ls were small banks designed to help people buy homes at a time when most banks did not issue relatively small loans and mortgages. By the early 1980s, inflation and interest rates were high enough that S&Ls were hurting, and the mortgages they held began to lose value. The government's reaction was to deregulate the S&L industry, which then expanded rapidly.

At the same time, the Reagan administration reduced the number of bank examiners, which contributed to less oversight and fewer inspections of the S&L industry. In addition, the S&Ls carried federal deposit insurance that guaranteed they would be bailed out if they lost money. Those two conditions gave S&L operators a false sense of security and led many of them to plunge into risky and often illegal ventures. In 1983 and 1984, banks and S&L businesses made bad loans, created poorly financed companies, and hired corrupt employees who looted their firms. The reckoning for these actions would not come until 1989, after Reagan had left office, when the S&L industry suffered a catastrophic collapse, leaving taxpayers with the $500 billion bill for reimbursing depositors at the failed institutions. In all, over 1,000 people involved in the banking scandal were prosecuted, and many went to jail.

TROUBLE AT THE EPA
The federal Superfund program was established within the EPA to protect the public and the country's natural resources by cleaning up large contaminated toxic waste sites. In 1982, however, the agency's regulatory actions dropped by about 60 percent, and few highly polluted sites were added to the Superfund list. Of the $700 million in fines owed by corporate polluters of water, land, and air, only $40 million was collected, which left the Superfund budget more reliant on taxpayer funds than on fines collected from polluters during the 1980s.

RESHAPING THE SUPREME COURT
President Reagan also moved the Supreme Court in a more conservative direction. Upon the retirement of Justice Potter Stewart in 1981, Reagan nominated **Sandra Day O'Connor** as his replacement. A moderate conservative, her nomination had

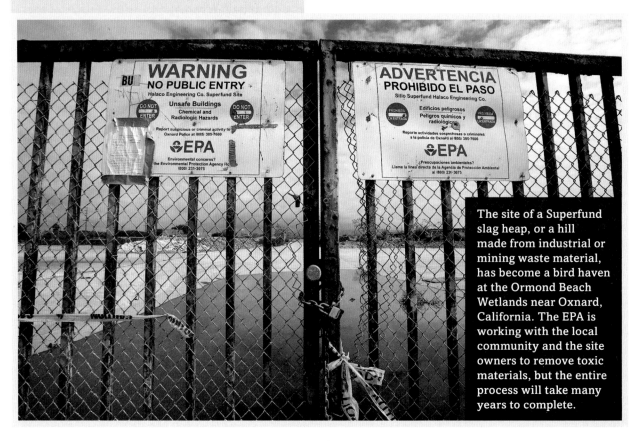

The site of a Superfund slag heap, or a hill made from industrial or mining waste material, has become a bird haven at the Ormond Beach Wetlands near Oxnard, California. The EPA is working with the local community and the site owners to remove toxic materials, but the entire process will take many years to complete.

widespread support from both conservatives and liberals. She made history as the first woman justice to serve on the Supreme Court, a symbol of the changing roles of women in society.

The president would not have another opportunity to appoint a justice until Chief Justice Warren Burger resigned in 1986. Reagan elevated Justice William Rehnquist, a conservative, to replace Burger as Chief Justice and named a conservative federal appeals court judge, Antonin Scalia, to fill the seat Rehnquist had vacated. Scalia was a strong proponent of **originalism**, the belief that when interpreting the Constitution, the courts should refer to what it meant when it was originally adopted, not to what it might mean from a present-day perspective. If people wanted to change the law, he thought, they should use the democratic process and do so through legislation. Scholars and justices who disagreed with Scalia categorized originalism as a **static**, or unchanging, doctrine that does not allow the law to change with the times. While Justice Scalia helped to make the idea of originalism more widespread within academic and popular culture, he was often unable to get other justices to agree in applying it to court cases.

In 1987, after the Democrats had regained control of the Senate, Justice Lewis Powell resigned, and President Reagan nominated Robert Bork, another conservative appeals court judge, to replace him. Bork had written extensively on many divisive legal issues before becoming a judge, and Senate Democrats and many women and civil rights organizations opposed him. They said he was outside the mainstream of American judicial thinking. The Senate rejected Bork's nomination, but the contentious process had a lasting impact on future Supreme Court nominations. Anthony Kennedy was nominated for the seat and confirmed to the Court early in 1988. Perceived as being balanced and fair in his judicial rulings and writings, he received bipartisan support.

An oil painting of Associate Justice of the Supreme Court Sandra Day O'Connor dressed in her judicial robes hangs in the National Portrait Gallery, Washington, D.C. The painting is by Jean Marcellino.

Yes, I will bring the understanding of a woman to the Court, but I doubt that alone will affect my decisions. I think the important thing about my appointment is not that I will decide cases as a woman, but that I am a woman who will get to decide cases.

—Sandra Day O'Connor, quoted in "Sandra Day O'Connor, Warm, Witty, and Wise," by Pam Hait, *Ladies' Home Journal*, 1982

HISTORICAL THINKING

1. **READING CHECK** How was supply-side economics supposed to revive the economy and decrease poverty?

2. **ANALYZE ENVIRONMENTAL CONCEPTS** What human practices of the past led to the designation of Superfund sites for cleanup processes?

3. **MAKE GENERALIZATIONS** What were some of the consequences of President Reagan's deregulation of the savings and loan industry?

4. **ANALYZE LANGUAGE USE** Why did Sandra Day O'Connor make the distinction that it was important that she was "a woman who will get to decide cases"?

REAGAN'S FOREIGN POLICY

Think of something you strongly believe in. President Reagan was a strong anticommunist who believed in standing up to the Soviets around the world. This belief would serve as the foundation of U.S. foreign policy during the 1980s.

ANTICOMMUNIST POLICIES

Ronald Reagan's tough stance against communism had long been a part of his image. As president, he vowed to fight the spread of communism around the world. He increased military spending, advocating a policy of "peace through strength."

The Reagan administration put its anticommunist stance into action around the world with results of success as well as failure. When the Soviet Union invaded Afghanistan in 1979 to support a Soviet-backed government, the Carter administration had sent military aid to the anti-Soviet guerillas. Reagan increased the aid, hoping the guerillas could use it to force a Soviet withdrawal.

Reagan also moved against communism in Latin America. The United States invaded the small Caribbean island of Grenada in 1983 after a communist government seized power. Within two days, the Marines had subdued the communist forces and helped establish a new anticommunist government. The United States also took action in Nicaragua after a pro-Soviet group known as the **Sandinistas** seized power and attempted to shape Nicaragua's government along communist lines. In response, the Reagan administration began secretly arming an anti-Sandinista guerilla force known as the **Contras**. The Contras waged a civil war with the Sandinistas throughout the 1980s from the headquarters they established in Honduras, directly north of Nicaragua.

Two days before the invasion of Grenada, tragedy struck the American military half a world away. On October 23, 1983, a suicide bomber drove a truck bomb into a barracks, or sleeping quarters, for marines in Beirut, Lebanon. The tremendous explosion had the force of 12,000 pounds of TNT. It destroyed the barracks and killed 241 marines. They had been deployed as peacekeepers during a cease-fire in the hostilities between Lebanese Christians and Muslims, a move that was controversial among Reagan's military advisors, who believed the situation was too unstable to be contained.

Back home, some people accused the president of using the invasion of a tiny, nonthreatening Caribbean country as a distraction from the reckless political blunders that had put those 241 marines in Lebanon in harm's way. The planning done before the October 23 bombing proved that the invasion wasn't merely a reaction to the event. When Reagan ran for re-election in 1984, however, it was clear that the invasion of Grenada had offered the president a public relations boost that helped to distract voters from the Beirut bombing.

IRAN AND SOUTH AFRICA

Congress eventually learned of the secret funding of the Contras and banned further aid to the group in 1984. Two years later, a news story reported that the United States had sold military equipment to Iran—a country that supported international terrorism—as part of an effort to gain the release of the American hostages taken prisoner there in the late 1970s. This contradicted Reagan's claim that the United States would never negotiate with terrorists, but the Reagan administration was afraid of political fallout from another hostage situation. Less than a month later, a follow-up news story revealed that $48 million from the weapons sale to Iran had been turned over to the Contras, which became known as the **Iran-Contra scandal**. Reagan fired the two men most responsible for the scandal: head of the National Security Council

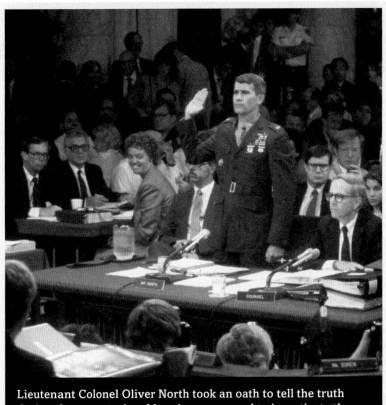

Lieutenant Colonel Oliver North took an oath to tell the truth during the congressional hearings convened to investigate the Iran-Contra scandal.

But Reagan's policy led South Africa to continue its segregation, and violence erupted. Ironically, Reagan's policy also tarnished American ideals and, ironically, hampered U.S. efforts abroad as the "good guy" in its competition with the Soviet Union. Finally, in 1986, the Senate overrode Reagan's veto of sanctions against South Africa.

THE STRATEGIC DEFENSE INITIATIVE

Meanwhile, tension between the Soviet Union and the United States continued to escalate. In 1983, several false alarms about imminent missile strikes by both sides cast doubt on the effectiveness of the doctrine of mutual assured destruction. And, while neither side overreacted, the arms race between the Soviet Union and the United States had reached its highest point, with the accumulation of more than 69,000 global nuclear weapons.

John Poindexter and one of his aides, Lieutenant Colonel Oliver North of the U.S. Marine Corps. The president appointed John Tower, a former Texas senator, to head a commission to investigate the scandal. Poindexter and North were tried and convicted of lying to Congress and obstruction of justice, among other charges.

President Reagan took full responsibility for the arms-for-hostages deal, but he claimed he knew nothing about the diversion of funds to the Contras. Still, a number of people, including some members of Congress, doubted him. Reagan's popularity declined, but only temporarily. A federal appeals court eventually overturned the convictions of Poindexter and North.

Reagan's strong anticommunist policy also became controversial when he allied the United States with the government of South African prime minister P. W. Botha. The repressive South African regime supported a system of **apartheid**, or extreme official racial segregation. Seeing Botha as a leader who would join him in preventing the spread of communism, Reagan proposed that moderates in the South African government would eventually end apartheid. He vetoed sanctions the U.S. Congress wanted to place on South Africa for its apartheid.

In this atmosphere, Reagan proposed his most ambitious plan for addressing Soviet power: to put a missile defense system in orbit around Earth. Dubbed the **Strategic Defense Initiative (SDI)**, it would use lasers and other technologies to destroy Soviet missiles before they reached their targets. Popularly referred to as "Star Wars," after the movie series, this idea met with many critics who argued that the "other technologies" used to blow the missiles out of the sky didn't even exist yet. They feared that the technical challenges of such a project might swallow the entire defense budget. Ultimately, the proposed SDI technology became too complex and expensive, and the program was never realized.

HISTORICAL THINKING

1. **READING CHECK** How did President Reagan try to achieve his policy of "peace through strength"?

2. **DRAW CONCLUSIONS** Why did some people believe that the invasion of Grenada was a distraction from the bombing in Lebanon?

3. **COMPARE AND CONTRAST** How was U.S. involvement in Nicaragua different from U.S. involvement in Grenada?

4. **MAKE INFERENCES** Why did no president after Reagan continue the Strategic Defense Initiative?

SOCIAL CHANGES AND TENSIONS

Consider how much computers, smartphones, and tablets are part of your daily life. The 1980s saw a wave of advances in technology—including computer technology—that began to change many aspects of how people lived.

NEW TECHNOLOGIES

Away from the political arena, the 1980s was a time of significant technological progress. In 1981, a communications company called International Business Machines (IBM) announced its plan to sell **personal computers**, small computers for home use. The announcement caused two computer software writers, Bill Gates and Paul Allen, to develop their own graphical user interface system, or GUI, that would appeal to a wide audience by helping people understand how to use the computer. They built their system using a simpler version of a computer language called BASIC. From there, Gates and Allen developed other software programs for their Microsoft company, such as spreadsheets and Microsoft Windows, an operating system that manages computer memory and function.

Apple, a competing company founded in 1976 by Steve Jobs and Steve Wozniak in a garage in Cupertino, California, also developed a GUI and, eventually, a version of a personal computer, named the Apple Macintosh, now known as the Mac. These innovations quickly transformed the personal computer from a novelty item to a common household device. Soon, people would be able to use their computers to publish books, track finances, make travel reservations, and play games.

CRITICAL VIEWING Desktop computers like the one below were among the earliest computers sold in the 1970s in America. This one came with a cassette drive and a tape player attached. It was popular in schools that had just begun teaching computer technology. Although the screen looks like a movable monitor, it was actually an attached built-in display. The computer sold new for about $700. Which of its elements can you identify, and how is the computer similar to or different from the computers you use?

After January 1983, sales of personal computers rose to more than half a million per year. New software companies sprang up all over the country, especially in California and Massachusetts. The California tech corridor would become known as "Silicon Valley" for the local resource, silica, used to make silicon computer chips.

Massachusetts companies were able to recruit computer talent from the pool of expertise at MIT, the Massachusetts Institute of Technology. Eventually computers needed to be connected so that people in different cities could collaborate on the same projects. The Pentagon offered its network of computers to computer users and researchers to exchange messages. Other networks in the United States and around the world connected throughout the late 1970s and early 1980s, and this supernetwork became known as the **Internet**, the global system of interconnected computer networks.

At the same time, television technology was expanding. Cable television, a system in which televisions receive transmissions through wires instead of air waves like radios do, had been around since the late 1940s. Its original purpose was to provide television reception to people who lived in geographically isolated communities. By the early 1980s, cable television could provide improved picture and sound quality and offer viewers throughout the whole nation a wide variety of channels. Suddenly every American with cable access could tune in to the same television networks, which contributed to shared cultural experiences. Teenagers watched their favorite bands play in music videos broadcast by MTV. Cable News Network (CNN) reported national news all day, every day.

Meanwhile, NASA continued to make strides with its shuttle program in the 1980s. Unfortunately, a catastrophe temporarily set back its efforts. On January 28, 1986, NASA launched the spacecraft *Challenger* from its facility at Cape Canaveral, Florida. Seconds later, however, it disintegrated in midair in a fiery explosion, killing the seven astronauts onboard. One of the astronauts was Christa McAuliffe, a high school teacher from Concord, New Hampshire, who had been selected from thousands of applicants to be the first private citizen in space. An investigation later determined

TEACHER AND ASTRONAUT
Christa McAuliffe was the first candidate accepted for the NASA Teacher in Space Project in 1985. She received her astronaut training and became a payload specialist on board the orbiter *Challenger* when it launched on January 28, 1986. McAuliffe had prepared a science lesson plan for students who would have tuned in to the *Challenger* for the live and taped lessons. After McAuliffe died in the *Challenger* explosion, many of her students told how she had challenged them and inspired them to enter the field of education.

that a damaged rocket booster was to blame for the tragedy. After the investigation, NASA scientists made changes to space shuttles to improve safety conditions, but the shock of the tragedy temporarily stopped work on the space program.

CHANGES IN THE AMERICAN FAMILY

Technology wasn't the only thing changing in the 1980s. The decade saw dramatic shifts in the dynamics of American families. For instance, the number of women giving birth out of wedlock had risen steadily since the 1970s, a social trend that contributed to the 6.7 million increase of single-parent households in the country from 1970 to 1992.

In 1996, the AIDS Memorial Quilt (left) made its fifth appearance on the National Mall in Washington, D.C. The quilt held 37,440 panels, or blocks, covering the entire grassy stretch of lawn on the Mall. What do the individual panels (above) tell you about the people they memorialize and the people who made them?

AMERICAN PLACES
The National Mall, Washington, D.C.

The most familiar part of the National Mall is a broad grassy area stretching for almost two miles between the U.S. Capitol Building and the Lincoln Memorial. Americans have historically held rallies and protests here, watched presidential inaugurations, and displayed challenging exhibits, such as the AIDS Memorial Quilt. The Mall is also the gateway to presidential and American memorials and a growing number of museums that house art, cultural artifacts, and unique architecture. An estimated 25 million people visit the Mall each year, free of charge.

Nearly 2,300 American elm trees line the Mall, and more than 26 miles of sidewalks and 8 miles of bike trails extend throughout the surrounding area, officially called the National Mall and Memorial

Parks. This larger area encompasses the White House, museums, lush gardens, and the Tidal Basin, where the Cherry Blossom Festival is held each spring. The more than 9,000 trees that cover the larger Mall area not only provide shade and landscaped scenery but also remove about 492 tons of air pollution from Washington, D.C.

The National Mall was originally designed in 1791 by Pierre L'Enfant to be the city's grandest avenue. But it wasn't until 1902 that a commissioned report to Congress advised a restoration, development, and extension of L'Enfant's proposal. The result, with continued modern, sustainable alterations, is the National Mall of today.

Divorce rates reached their highest levels ever in the early 1980s. And women were entering the workforce in record numbers: 67 percent of married women were working in 1986 compared with 26 percent in 1950.

American families were also facing challenges in education. In 1983, a government committee released a document called *A Nation at Risk* on the status of public schools in the United States. The committee's findings were grim. American schools were experiencing low state test scores and high turnover rates among teachers. As many as 23 million American adults could not read or write. The report stated, "If an unfriendly foreign power had attempted to impose on America the mediocre educational performance that exists today, we might well have viewed it as an act of war." *A Nation at Risk* called for massive reform to retain the best teachers and to raise students' academic performances.

One of the most famous educational reforms of the 1980s began in a school in Oakland, California. First Lady Nancy Reagan was addressing an elementary school about the perils of drug use and abuse. A student stood up and asked Mrs. Reagan what students should say if someone asks them to try drugs or alcohol. Mrs. Reagan responded, "Just say no." That advice became a national catchphrase, and schools around the country formed clubs that aimed to teach students how to resist peer pressure. Ultimately, data showed that the programs were not successful.

THE CHALLENGE OF HIV/AIDS

Beginning in the early 1980s, a new disease caused by the **human immunodeficiency virus (HIV)** was attacking its victims' immune systems. In the United States, most of the first victims of HIV were members of the gay community, where the incidence of infection was particularly high. In some patients, the virus destroyed so much of the immune system, the infected person's body could no longer fight off the most common ailments. The last stage of HIV was known as **acquired immunodeficiency syndrome (AIDS)**. Not all HIV patients advanced to this often-deadly stage.

As the 1980s progressed, more HIV/AIDS patients were identified, mostly in large American cities such as New York City and San Francisco. Little was known about the disease then, so panic and confusion rose in the nation and around the world.

In 1985, after the New York City school system reported a child with AIDS attending one of its 622 elementary schools, a large number of parents kept their children home out of fear of the virus. This made the gay community and especially those who contracted the virus an even greater target for discrimination.

Eventually, scientists determined that the virus spread through the exchange of certain body fluids, including fluids exchanged during sexual contact. Infected pregnant mothers could pass the disease to their children in the womb. Drug users contracted the virus if they shared contaminated needles, and some hospital patients were stricken after receiving infected blood during transfusions.

In an effort to stop the epidemic, many HIV/AIDS activists promoted safer sex practices, provided clean needles to intravenous drug users, and generated greater awareness about the disease. The Reagan administration as well as leading conservatives resisted such actions. They argued that poor "lifestyle" choices put people at risk for the disease, and they urged a greater adherence to "traditional family values." By 1989, at least 100,000 Americans had contracted HIV/AIDS and thousands of people had died from the disease. The number of deaths rose until the mid-1990s when new drugs were introduced to manage the virus's symptoms.

In 1985, activist Cleve Jones launched the Names Project, enlisting families and friends of people with AIDS to create quilted panels in an effort to keep alive the memory of the thousands who had died. When first displayed in 1987, the quilt covered an area larger than a football field. Since the disease first appeared, 600,000 to 700,000 Americans have died from AIDS.

HISTORICAL THINKING

1. **READING CHECK** What social tensions were caused by changing demographics in the United States during the 1980s?

2. **IDENTIFY** How have personal computers changed the lives of Americans?

3. **MAKE PREDICTIONS** What might have happened if the Reagan administration had chosen to support the educational programs HIV/AIDS activists had suggested?

4. **DESCRIBE** In what ways did women's roles change in society during the 1980s?

MAIN IDEA In the 1980s, economic dissatisfaction and increasing demands for freedom led to the collapse of the Soviet Union and the fall of communism throughout Eastern Europe.

COLLAPSE OF THE SOVIET UNION

The fall of the Soviet Union and the end of communism in Eastern Europe was surely something people believed they would never witness in their lifetimes. And then it happened.

A WEAKENED SOVIET EMPIRE

Since the aftermath of World War II, the opposing doctrines of the capitalist United States and the communist Soviet Union had generated conflicts that had an impact on the entire world. In 1980, Ronald Reagan took office as president, hoping to promote free-market relations and anticommunist policies throughout the world.

By 1984, the U.S. economy had revived and was growing. This helped Ronald Reagan win a convincing re-election. What also helped was Reagan's strong anticommunist stance, which a majority of Americans favored. As Reagan pursued his anticommunist foreign policy into his second term, the Soviet Union was experiencing a period of inner turmoil. By the mid-1980s, the Soviet Union was struggling with a deteriorating economy and an unpopular war against anticommunist rebels in Afghanistan.

In 1985, the Soviet **Politburo**, the ruling committee of the Communist Party and thus the nation, agreed on a new leader, **Mikhail Gorbachev** (mih-KYL GOR-buh-chof). Younger than most of the aging Communist Party leaders, Gorbachev brought energy and new ideas to the nation. Hoping that increasing freedom of ideas and speech would lead to a stronger nation, he instituted the policy of *glasnost*, or "openness." For the first time in decades, churches were allowed to open, some political prisoners were released, and journalists were given some freedom to criticize officials.

Central planning, which directed all aspects of Soviet business, farming, and manufacturing, continued to be an inefficient way to govern such a massive country, and people had no economic incentive to

pursue innovation. The Soviet Union's economy had stagnated. In addition, in 1979, the Soviet Union had invaded Afghanistan, hoping to intervene on behalf of the country's communist government against anticommunist Muslim rebels. This decision led to a decade-long hostile occupation of Afghanistan, in which thousands of Soviet soldiers died. The conflict drained an enormous amount of money from the Soviet treasury.

Gorbachev reformed the economy more directly through his policy of ***perestroika*** (peh-ruh-STROY-kuh), or economic restructuring. Loosening the nation's strict control over the economy, he gave more freedom to local officials to make decisions. Some people were even allowed to open small businesses. Gorbachev was not trying to overturn communism with his reforms. Rather, he hoped that these changes would lead to a more efficient, more innovative, and wealthier nation. The country's economy remained stalled, however. And the people used their increased freedom to speak up about their dissatisfactions.

Meanwhile, President Reagan had been building a massive military program, the largest in U.S. peacetime history. He also took an aggressive position against the Soviets' hold on Eastern Bloc countries. On June 12, 1987, he delivered a speech in West Berlin about the evils of communism. He stood not far from the Berlin Wall, a symbol of communist rule. He declared, "Mr. Gorbachev, tear down this wall!" That admonition became an iconic moment, marking the peak of the conflict between the two nations. The Soviet Union's economy was too weak to compete with a U.S. military buildup, so Gorbachev began working on a diplomatic program aimed at controlling nuclear arms.

On December 9, 1987, he met with Reagan to sign the Intermediate-Range Nuclear Forces (INF) Treaty, which banned both nations from owning certain kinds of nuclear missiles.

As Soviet power dwindled, Reagan reached the end of his second presidential term. His vice president, George H.W. Bush, ran against Michael Dukakis, the former Democratic governor of Massachusetts. Bush was elected president in 1988 by a large margin of electoral and popular votes. Formerly ambassador to the United Nations and director of the Central Intelligence Agency, Bush had extensive foreign policy experience and was poised to continue the nation's strong stance against the Soviet Union.

END OF THE SOVIET UNION

Gorbachev's economic policies had not energized the Soviet Union as much as he had hoped. He withdrew troops from Afghanistan in 1989, but the Soviet intervention there had been costly and damaging for national morale. *Glasnost*, which had been meant to spur innovation, had encouraged rebellious voices. While Russia was the largest republic in the Soviet Union, non-Russians held the ethnic majority in many of the other Soviet republics, and they wanted freedom from Soviet rule. In 1990, the Baltic republic of Lithuania declared its independence from the union. Worried that other republics would follow its lead, Gorbachev ordered a military assault in 1991 on unarmed citizens in Lithuania's capital.

Soviet General Secretary Mikhail Gorbachev and President Ronald Reagan strolled on the South Lawn of the White House during the Washington Summit on December 10, 1987. Two days before, they had signed the Intermediate-Range Nuclear Forces Treaty.

This assault further damaged Gorbachev's reputation in the Soviet Union. **Boris Yeltsin**, a member of parliament and the newly elected president of the Russian Republic, emerged as a rival to Gorbachev's overarching power. Though he assisted Gorbachev in leading the country, he was a vocal critic of Gorbachev's policies.

On August 18, 1991, conservative members of the Communist Party attempted a coup to overthrow Gorbachev, fearing that their power was diminishing. Tanks and other military vehicles rolled into Moscow, but the party **hardliners**, or staunch Soviet communists, were shocked to find that the people no longer feared such shows of government force.

Despite his disagreements with Gorbachev, Yeltsin jumped onto a tank and rejected the coup, to cheers from the crowd and support from President Bush and other world leaders. Shortly after, the hardliners ordered the military to attack the Soviet parliament, but military leaders refused. The Communist Party and the Politburo had lost. The Russian parliament voted to dissolve them completely. As communist rule collapsed, many of the Soviet republics, such as Estonia and Latvia, declared their independence. Though Gorbachev pushed for unity, the momentum for independence was too great. On December 25, 1991, the Soviet Union ceased to exist, and the former republics of the Union of Soviet Socialist Republics (U.S.S.R.) became independent countries.

As in the Soviet Union, democratic movements arose across the globe during the late 1980s and early 1990s. In China, a solitary demonstrator stands in the way of Chinese army tanks as they roll along the Avenue of Eternal Peace in Beijing. For weeks during the spring of 1989, people had demonstrated in the nearby Tiananmen Square (below) for freedom of speech and the press.

FREEDOM IN CENTRAL AND EASTERN EUROPE

Even before the Soviet Union collapsed, communist rule had fallen throughout Eastern Europe. The reforms instituted by Gorbachev had included granting greater freedom to the Soviet-controlled Eastern Bloc countries. This inspired those countries, starting with Poland, to push for even greater control of their economic and political futures. In 1988, Polish workers, angry at a faltering economy, went on a countrywide strike. Poland's military leaders agreed to legalize a workers' union and cooperate with them, which eventually led to other national reforms and the country's first free elections in 1989 and 1990. The Polish people voted union leader Lech Walesa (LEHK vuh-WEHN-suh) the country's new president in 1990.

In Hungary, reformers were inspired by Poland's drastic transformation. Hungarian leaders adopted policies that moved the country toward a free-market economy and free elections. In 1989, radical reformers took over the Communist Party congress and voted to dissolve the party itself. Czechoslovakia also enjoyed a peaceful transition to democracy. Watching the developments elsewhere, the Czech public marched peacefully against the nation's Communist Party. Massive protests forced the dissolution of the party in 1989. A newly formed parliament elected playwright and activist Václav Havel (VAHT-slav HAH-vehl) president. Romania also saw the fall of communism in 1989, though not without bloodshed. After dictator Nicolae Ceausescu (NIHK-oh-ly chow-CHEHS-kew) ordered the killing of hundreds of peaceful protestors, the Romanian army sided with the uprising against him. Ceausescu and his wife were arrested and executed, and Romania started to hold free elections in 1990.

Meanwhile, people in East Germany organized massive protests for greater freedom. Then, on November 9, 1989, the Berlin Wall was opened. An East German official had mistakenly issued an order to let people cross to West Germany. A series of contradictory instructions followed. Meanwhile, East German crowds at the wall grew by thousands. In an attempt to restore stability, the government first let a few people cross the border and then more. Soon, thousands of people from East and West Germany descended on the scene in joyous celebration. East Germans made it clear that they rejected the Communist Party and wanted reunification with West Germany. About a year later, Germany became one country again, and the Berlin Wall was torn down.

FREEDOM SPREADS

In addition to the spectacular fall of the Soviet Union, the world witnessed other successful freedom movements during this time. In 1989, the newly elected president of South Africa, F. W. de Klerk, began to dismantle apartheid. He lifted restrictions on the media and civil rights groups and ended the plan to force black people to live in separate homelands. In 1990, he freed civil rights leader Nelson Mandela, who had spent 27 years in prison for anti-apartheid activities. The following few years were filled with negotiations led by Mandela and de Klerk to finally end the practice of apartheid and establish the country's first multi-ethnic government. In 1994, Mandela was elected president of South Africa.

Free elections were held in Chile in 1989, ending the military dictatorship that had ruled since 1973. In Nicaragua, the long conflict between the ruling Sandinistas and the rebel Contras, which had sparked the Iran-Contra scandal in the United States, ended when a coalition of anti-Sandinista political parties finally won the national election.

As a wave of activism for democracy rose in China, the nation's communist government stood firm. In 1987, Chinese Communist Party general secretary Hu Yaobang was forced to resign largely for encouraging democratic reforms. When Hu died in 1989, he became a symbol of political democracy. That spring, students demonstrated against the government in **Tiananmen Square**, a large public space in Beijing. Thousands of students protested peacefully and started a hunger strike, gaining support from around the world. On June 4, the military rolled tanks into the square, opening fire and killing hundreds. Despite the democratic movements across the globe, repressive regimes still prevailed in a number of countries, and international tensions still ran high.

HISTORICAL THINKING

1. **READING CHECK** What were Mikhail Gorbachev's policies of *glasnost* and *perestroika*?

2. **MAKE CONNECTIONS** What larger political trends in Eastern Europe were reflected in the opening of the Berlin Wall?

3. **ANALYZE CAUSE AND EFFECT** How did changes in the Soviet Union lead to the fall of communism in other Eastern Bloc countries?

4. **MAKE INFERENCES** How did Mikhail Gorbachev's policies hurt his own reputation after the Soviet invasion of Lithuania in 1989?

🏛 THE NEWSEUM WASHINGTON, D.C.

Located between the White House and the U.S. Capitol, the interactive Newseum promotes, explains, and defends free expression and the five freedoms of the First Amendment: religion, speech, press, assembly, and petition. The museum's goal is to serve as a neutral forum for fostering open discussions. It engages visitors in the central debates of our time, including the future of investigative journalism, the tensions between national security and privacy, and the role of religious freedom.

The Newseum's 7 levels of interactive exhibits include 15 galleries and 15 theaters. Among the most memorable exhibits are the 9/11 Gallery, which features the broadcast antenna from the top of the World Trade Center and the Pulitzer Prize Photographs Gallery, displaying photographs from every Pulitzer Prize-winning entry since 1942. The Newseum also traces the evolution of electronic communication from the birth of radio to the technologies of the present and the future.

The Berlin Wall Gallery

At the center of the Newseum's Berlin Wall Gallery stand eight 12-foot-high concrete sections of the Berlin Wall—the largest display of unaltered portions of the wall outside of Germany. A three-story East German guard tower that stood near Checkpoint Charlie, Berlin's best-known East-West crossing point, stands nearby. The gallery tells the story of how news and information helped topple a closed and oppressive society, signaling the end of the Cold War.

Documenting the Kennedy Assassination

Before President John F. Kennedy even reached the Dallas hospital after being shot on November 22, 1963, 58-year-old Russian immigrant Abraham Zapruder knew the president was dead. He had watched the assassination unfold through the viewfinder of his 8-millimeter Bell and Howell home movie camera and had unknowingly created one of history's most famous films.

Abraham Zapruder's camera as well as an ID belonging to White House correspondent Sid Davis are part of the Newseum's traveling exhibit devoted to the assassination of President Kennedy.

How does a museum like the Newseum show the connections between historical events and larger social and political trends and developments?

"I am dedicated to keeping the Newseum at the cutting edge of national and international conversations about **the meaning of—and threats to—freedom.**"

—Jeffrey Herbst, Newseum President and CEO

The 9/11 Gallery

Exploring an event like 9/11 through artifacts, such as the newspaper headlines shown here, documentary films, and first-person accounts from journalists who covered the story, has a profound impact on Newseum visitors in this gallery.

Along with police and firefighters, journalists ran toward danger on September 11, 2001. Among the 2,749 people who lost their lives in New York City that day were photojournalist Bill Biggart, who was killed in the collapse of one of the World Trade Center towers, and 6 broadcast engineers who died at their posts at the top of the 110-story complex.

News organizations faced extraordinary challenges that day. From the Pentagon to New York City to Shanksville, Pennsylvania, shocking news broke minute by minute, and journalists scrambled to cover the stories.

THE END OF THE COLD WAR

As the general secretary of the Communist Party of the U.S.S.R., Mikhail Gorbachev took office in 1985 with ideas for reform. U.S. President Ronald Reagan had had a few years to develop his foreign policy plan by then, and he had made a commitment to fighting communist forces around the world. Though the two leaders had competing ideologies, they were willing to work with each other to decrease tensions between their countries.

On November 9, 1989, East German officials opened the border between East and West Berlin. That weekend, more than 2 million Berliners flowed across the border, breaking down the concrete and barbed wire barrier that had divided them for 28 years. This photo was taken from the West Berlin side of the wall.

CRITICAL VIEWING Examine the scene in the photo and compare the activity in the foreground on the west side of the Berlin Wall to that in the background on the east side of the wall. How would you describe the scene on both sides of the wall?

DOCUMENT ONE

Primary Source: Article
from *Pravda,* April 24, 1985, by Mikhail Gorbachev

Soon after being appointed general secretary of the Communist Party, Mikhail Gorbachev wrote a newspaper article addressing the country's economic problems. Here, he explains his new ideas of *glasnost* and *perestroika* and how he thinks that restructuring the economy can help the Soviet Union become stronger.

CONSTRUCTED RESPONSE How did Gorbachev's ideas for reform signal a move toward free-market economics?

The main question now is: How, and at what cost, will the country be able to achieve accelerated economic development? Examining this question in the Politburo [a committee made up of the Soviet Union's main policy makers], we have unanimously reached the conclusion that there are real possibilities for this. The task of accelerating growth rates, substantially accelerating them, is completely feasible. We must more boldly advance along the path of expanding the rights of enterprises and their independence, introduce economic accountability and, on this basis, increase the responsibility and stake of labor collectives in the final results of work.

DOCUMENT TWO

Primary Source: Speech
from President Ronald Reagan's speech in West Berlin, June 12, 1987

President Reagan's speech at the Berlin Wall was amplified so that people in East Berlin could hear it as well. He addressed the recent changes in the Soviet Union and wondered where they would lead.

CONSTRUCTED RESPONSE Why did Reagan use the Berlin Wall as a symbol as he addressed changes in the Soviet Union?

Now the Soviets themselves may, in a limited way, be coming to understand the importance of freedom. Are these the beginnings of profound changes in the Soviet state? Or are they token gestures, intended to raise false hopes in the West, or to strengthen the Soviet system without changing it? There is one sign the Soviets can make that would be unmistakable, that would advance dramatically the cause of freedom and peace. General Secretary Gorbachev, if you seek peace, if you seek prosperity for the Soviet Union and Eastern Europe, if you seek liberalization: Come here to this gate! Mr. Gorbachev, open this gate! Mr. Gorbachev, tear down this wall!

DOCUMENT THREE

Primary Source: Speech
from President George H.W. Bush's address to the nation, December 25, 1991

President George H.W. Bush addressed the citizens of the United States on Christmas, announcing the resignation of Mikhail Gorbachev and, essentially, the end of the Cold War.

CONSTRUCTED RESPONSE How did President Bush view Gorbachev's role in the dissolution of the Cold War?

New, independent nations have emerged out of the wreckage of the Soviet empire. Last weekend, these former republics formed a Commonwealth of Independent States. This act marks the end of the old Soviet Union, signified today by Mikhail Gorbachev's decision to resign. Mikhail Gorbachev's revolutionary policies transformed the Soviet Union. His policies permitted the peoples of Russia and the other republics to cast aside decades of oppression and establish the foundations of freedom. The United States applauds and supports the historic choice for freedom by the new states of the Commonwealth. We congratulate them on the peaceful and democratic path they have chosen, and for their careful attention to nuclear control and safety during this transition.

SYNTHESIZE & WRITE

1. **REVIEW** Review what you have learned about the events that led to the end of the Cold War.

2. **RECALL** On your own paper, write details about American and Soviet leaders' actions during the 1980s.

3. **CONSTRUCT** Construct a topic sentence that explains President Reagan's and Mikhail Gorbachev's roles in ending the Cold War.

4. **WRITE** Using evidence from the chapter and these documents, write an informative paragraph that supports your topic sentence in Step 3.

GEORGE H.W. BUSH AND THE PERSIAN GULF WAR

Have you ever had to challenge assumptions that you have held for a long time? What was difficult about it? After decades of sparring with the Soviet Union during the Cold War, the United States faced threats from a new location, which required very different strategies.

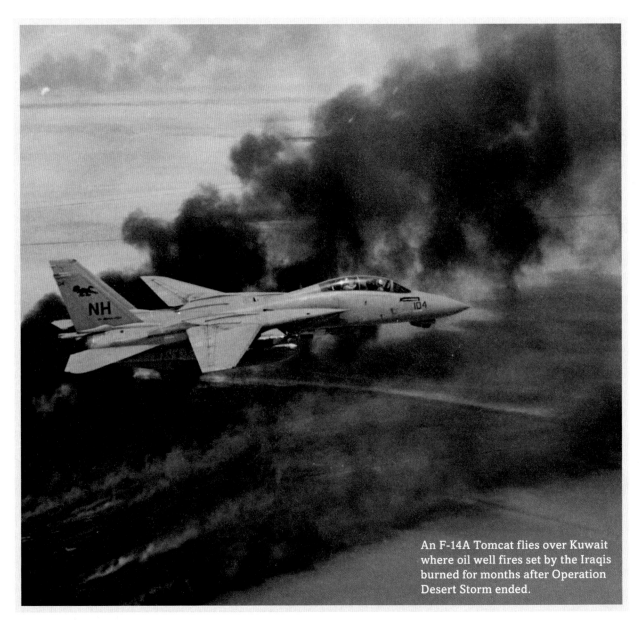

An F-14A Tomcat flies over Kuwait where oil well fires set by the Iraqis burned for months after Operation Desert Storm ended.

CONFLICT IN THE MIDDLE EAST

After the Soviet Union collapsed, President Bush was in the position to use his years of experience handling international conflict to assist the former Warsaw Pact countries as they adjusted to democracy. While hope grew in Europe, tensions were about to boil over in Southwest Asia, more commonly known as the Middle East.

In the 1980s, the Southwest Asian countries of Iran and Iraq both had authoritarian governments. Since the Iranian Revolution of 1979, Iran had operated as a **theocracy**, or a nation governed by the principles of a single religion. Its leaders were fundamentalist Muslim clerics, or religious leaders. Meanwhile, in Iraq, a member of the Ba'th political party, **Saddam Hussein**, helped his party orchestrate a coup against the country's prime minister. By 1979, Hussein had forced out Iraq's sick and aging president, Ahmad Hasan al-Bakr, and he began a long, tyrannical reign. A brutal dictator, Hussein extinguished any voices of dissent, operating a secret police force that arrested and tortured his enemies.

In 1980, Iran and Iraq went to war. Hussein's goal was to conquer the other countries around the Persian Gulf and preside as the leader over a single, oil-rich Arab nation. In 1980, he attempted an invasion of neighboring Iran's oil fields, leading to the Iran-Iraq War. Religious tensions also played a role in the conflict. Dominated by different branches of Islam, the two countries were often at odds with each other over their beliefs and traditions, especially as they intersected with political and government practices and goals. Hussein was a member of the **Sunni** (SOO-nee) denomination, while Iran was controlled by the **Shi'ite** (SHE-ite) sect. The war between the two countries raged until 1988, when both sides, depleted of funds and resources, agreed to a hostile ceasefire, or an agreement in which the problems being fought over remain unchanged or unresolved, but the parties to the conflict agree to stop fighting while peace plans are made.

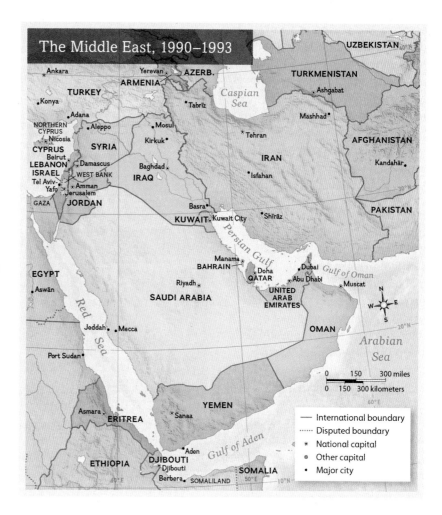

The Middle East, 1990–1993

International boundary
Disputed boundary
National capital
Other capital
Major city

OPERATION DESERT STORM

In August 1990, Hussein ordered Iraqi troops to invade another neighboring country, **Kuwait**, in order to take over the small nation's vast oil resources. The conflict, which later became known as the **Persian Gulf War**, expanded to include a buildup of international troops in nearby countries. The presence of Iraq in Kuwait was a major concern for the rest of the world, especially since world leaders suspected that Hussein planned next to attack Saudi Arabia, the world's largest oil producer.

In response, President Bush increased the number of American troops stationed in Saudi Arabia to 400,000, hoping to deter Iraq with a show of force. In addition, the United Nations called for an international ban on trade with Iraq, but neither action deterred Hussein. President Bush then worked with other NATO countries to form a military coalition against Hussein. On January 16, 1991, the coalition moved into Kuwait to force Iraqi troops out.

The coalition effort, called **Operation Desert Storm**, ended quickly. In six weeks it drove Iraq out of Kuwait. The coalition's success was partly owed to modern technology that was used for the first time in a war. Microchips and digital advances were used in precision-guided munitions that relied on laser guidance systems to increase the effectiveness of aerial bombings. On the ground, microcomputers, laser rangefinders, and guided-missile systems were incorporated in new tanks, helicopters, and weapons.

Bush did not pursue Hussein to remove him from power. The goal of Operation Desert Storm had been to drive the Iraqis out of a country they had invaded. To send military troops into Iraq itself would be considered an act of aggression and would put NATO troops at risk. Allowing Hussein to stay in power, however, set the stage for later conflict.

THE CHALLENGE OF ACHIEVING PEACE

Much like Saddam Hussein, **Manuel Noriega** of Panama had developed a troubled relationship with the United States as he turned from a CIA informer to a criminal liability. Noriega had brutally gained control of Panama and engaged in drug trafficking and racketeering throughout the 1980s. In 1988, the Senate subcommittee on terrorism, narcotics, and international operations declared that Noriega "represents one of the most serious foreign policy failures for the United States."

Americans intervened in Panama in 1989, when President Bush ordered an invasion to depose and capture the dictator. Though the United States was successful, many people around the world criticized its involvement in foreign governments. President Bush was aware of this growing criticism, and during the conflict with Iraq, he presented to Congress and the nation his ideas for achieving peace through cooperation, in what he called a **New World Order**. His emphasis was on ensuring that nations relied on the rule of law, multinational cooperation, and collective security through the United Nations as the Cold War ended.

BUSH'S DOMESTIC POLICIES

President Bush's four years in office were heavily associated with the intervention of the United States in the Persian Gulf. Many items on his domestic

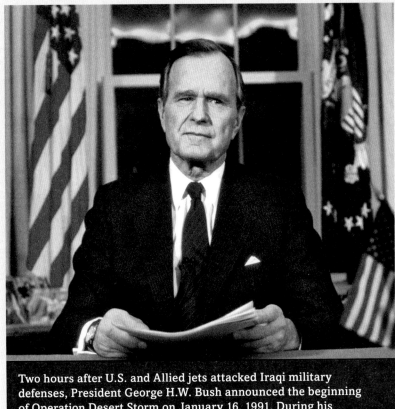

Two hours after U.S. and Allied jets attacked Iraqi military defenses, President George H.W. Bush announced the beginning of Operation Desert Storm on January 16, 1991. During his televised speech, Bush explained that a coalition of 28 nations had "exhausted all reasonable efforts to reach a peaceful resolution."

agenda still managed to stand out, however. When the liberal-leaning Supreme Court justice William J. Brennan announced his retirement in 1990, President Bush appointed the little-known New Hampshire judge David H. Souter to replace him.

During Souter's first year on the Court, he joined Justice William Rehnquist in several conservative rulings. Then, in 1991, the retirement of Supreme Court justice Thurgood Marshall allowed President Bush to appoint a new justice to the high Court. He nominated **Clarence Thomas**, a federal judge who had held several offices under the Reagan administration. Senate hearings for his appointment to the Court erupted in controversy, however, when law professor Anita Hill testified that Thomas had sexually harassed her when she had worked for him. Despite the contentious hearings, which the nation watched live on television, the Senate eventually approved Thomas's appointment with a vote of 52 to 48.

Republican appointees to the Court held eight seats and seemed ready to move the Court to the right, rolling back rulings on civil rights, abortion, and religion. But Justice Souter surprised conservatives by often voting with the Democrats' appointees and liberal justices. Souter's record on the Court

In the following remarks, President Bush introduced the Americans with Disabilities Act that guaranteed civil rights to people with disabilities.

This act is powerful in its simplicity. It will ensure that people with disabilities are given the basic guarantees for which they have worked so long and so hard . . . specifically, first the ADA ensures that employers covered by the act cannot discriminate against qualified individuals with disabilities. Second, the ADA ensures access to public accommodations such as restaurants, hotels, shopping centers, and offices. And third, the ADA ensures expanded access to transportation services. And fourth, the ADA ensures equivalent telephone services for people with speech or hearing impediments.

—from George H.W. Bush's remarks on the signing of the Americans with Disabilities Act, July 26, 1990

disappointed many conservatives and contributed to their growing dissatisfaction with President Bush.

However, President Bush kept a campaign promise and signed significant civil rights legislation for people with disabilities. For years, the disability rights movement had been working to show that the exclusion and segregation of people with disabilities was discrimination. Following the example of the civil rights movement, activists conducted sit-ins at federal buildings, obstructed public transportation, marched in the streets, and took their case to the courts and Congress. Legal changes began in the 1970s, but the most comprehensive civil rights legislation wasn't passed until 1990 when President Bush signed the **Americans with Disabilities Act**, which had passed Congress with bipartisan support.

Another major piece of legislation signed by President Bush was also the result of activism that began in the mid-20th century. In the 1980s, Americans became aware that rainfall made acidic by industrial pollution could travel from the pollution source to other areas, often damaging forests and lakes. In 1989, Bush proposed revisions to the Clean Air Act, specifically targeting acid rain, urban air pollution, and toxic air emissions. The revisions also improved pollution enforcement authority. The bill passed by large votes in both the House of Representatives and the Senate in 1990.

The United States had stopped developing and testing nuclear weapons by the early 1990s. Growing efforts made throughout the 1980s by activists as part of the "nuclear freeze" movement had brought attention and pressure to both the Reagan and Bush administrations to change U.S. nuclear policies. Though complete nuclear disarmament was not achieved, the United States significantly reduced its nuclear weapons. President Bush also signed the Radiation Exposure Compensation Act, which gave partial restitution to people, mostly in western states, who contracted cancer and other diseases as a result of their exposure to atmospheric nuclear testing undertaken during the Cold War or from their employment in the uranium industry.

Bush ran for re-election in 1992, but he was haunted by a campaign promise he had made four years earlier. In 1988, during his speech at the Republican National Convention, he had declared, "Read my lips: no new taxes." His words proved memorable to the American people. But when he took office in 1989, the federal budget debt was about $2.8 trillion, almost three times what it had been in 1980. Unemployment rose, and gas prices spiked during the Gulf War conflicts. Ultimately, the United States faced a recession. The budget deficit was quickly growing, and it limited the president's ability to increase domestic spending. In 1990, President Bush found that he needed to compromise with Congress on a plan of **deficit reduction** that included budget cuts and tax increases to rein in spending and improve the economy.

As Bush explained to the nation why he felt this plan was necessary, people were reminded of his famous pledge to avoid new taxes. Even other Republicans were quick to bring up the broken promise. Despite bipartisan attempts at deficit reduction, people were dissatisfied with the economy by the end of Bush's term. A moderate Democrat, **William Jefferson "Bill" Clinton**, was readying himself to take on the challenge of running for the presidency.

HISTORICAL THINKING

1. **READING CHECK** What were the main criticisms of George H.W. Bush's economic policies?

2. **IDENTIFY MAIN IDEAS AND DETAILS** How did the United States government have to shift its foreign policy during Bush's presidency?

3. **ANALYZE CAUSE AND EFFECT** What was the main cause of the Persian Gulf War?

4. **SUMMARIZE** What impact did President Bush's revisions to the Clean Air Act have on protecting the environment?

VOCABULARY

Use each of the following vocabulary words in a sentence that shows an understanding of the term's meaning.

1. conservative
   A person who supports traditional social or economic policies is a conservative.

2. think tank

3. safety net

4. supply-side economics

5. deregulation

6. originalism

7. income inequality

8. apartheid

9. deficit reduction

READING STRATEGY
ANALYZE CAUSE AND EFFECT

When you identify causes and effects, you determine how events affect later events. Complete the following chart to identify causes and effects related to Ronald Reagan's presidency. Then answer the question.

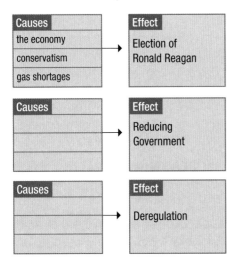

Causes		Effect
the economy	→	Election of Ronald Reagan
conservatism		
gas shortages		

Causes		Effect
	→	Reducing Government

Causes		Effect
	→	Deregulation

10. What were some of the most influential policies enacted during Reagan's presidency, and how did they affect the nation?

MAIN IDEAS

Answer the following questions. Support your answers with evidence from the chapter.

11. How did the conservative movement respond to Johnson's Great Society programs? **LESSON 1.1**

12. What aspects of post–World War II life in the United States contributed to Sunbelt migration? **LESSON 1.2**

13. What was the significance of Reagan asking the American people if they were better off under Carter's presidency? **LESSON 1.3**

14. Why did the government deregulate the savings and loan industry? **LESSON 2.1**

15. What was the Iran-Contra scandal? **LESSON 2.2**

16. How did the Reagan administration address the increased use of drugs in the United States? **LESSON 2.3**

17. How did the collapse of communism after the fall of the Soviet Union affect countries in Central and Eastern Europe? **LESSON 3.1**

18. What international challenges did President George H.W. Bush face during his term? **LESSON 3.4**

HISTORICAL THINKING

Answer the following questions. Support your answers with evidence from the chapter.

19. **COMPARE AND CONTRAST** In what ways did President Reagan's position on the size of government differ from President Carter's?

20. **MAKE CONNECTIONS** The early years of the HIV/AIDS epidemic were confusing and people were fearful. What other events in American history caused similar anxiety?

21. **DETERMINE CHRONOLOGY** What evidence reveals that the invasion of Grenada was not planned as a distraction from the bombing in Beirut, Lebanon, that killed 241 U.S. marines?

22. **ANALYZE CAUSE AND EFFECT** Why did the Soviet Politburo select Mikhail Gorbachev to become general secretary in 1985?

23. **FORM AND SUPPORT OPINIONS** Do you think President Reagan was right to fire air traffic controllers during the PATCO strike? Support your opinion with evidence from the text.

24. **IDENTIFY PROBLEMS AND SOLUTIONS** What regional environmental problems did President George H.W. Bush address in legislation?

INTERPRET VISUALS

Look closely at this photo of American medical students who were studying at a university in Grenada when the U.S. military invaded to oust the communist government. Then answer the questions that follow.

25. Why do you think the expressions of the students and that of the soldier appear to convey different emotional states?

26. What details in the photograph help you understand how U.S. intervention in Grenada increased Reagan's popularity among American voters?

ANALYZE SOURCES

Read the excerpt from Ronald Reagan's Farewell Address, January 11, 1989, at the end of his presidency. Then answer the question that follows.

> And in all of that time I won a nickname, "The Great Communicator." I wasn't a great communicator, but I communicated great things, and they didn't spring full bloom from my brow, they came from the heart of a great nation—from our experience, our wisdom, and our belief in the principles that have guided us for two centuries. They called it the Reagan revolution. Well, I'll accept that, but for me it always seemed more like the great rediscovery, a rediscovery of our values and our common sense.

27. How does the excerpt above help demonstrate why President Reagan was considered "The Great Communicator"?

CONNECT TO YOUR LIFE

28. **EXPLANATORY** Think about the challenges, achievements, and shortcomings faced by President Ronald Reagan. Then consider the challenges, achievements, and shortcomings of the current U.S. president. In a short essay, explain how the role of president has changed and stayed the same from Ronald Reagan's two terms to the present day.

TIPS

- Research legitimate biographical and news sources about the current president. List the challenges, accomplishments, and missteps, if any, faced by the president while in office.

- Read through the chapter for text evidence of Reagan's accomplishments, challenges, and missteps, and list them.

- Chart similarities and differences in a Venn diagram or another graphic organizer.

- Use your findings to craft a solid thesis statement. Write a paragraph containing at least three sentences and three vocabulary words from the chapter in your response.

HISTORICAL THINKING What does it mean to be an American in the 21st century?

In 2016, Spanish architect Santiago Calatrava designed this structure, called the Oculus, to soar over the World Trade Center Transportation Hub in New York City. The structure and transit hub form part of the redevelopment of the World Trade Center site, which was destroyed in the September 11, 2001, terrorist attacks. Each year on the anniversary of the attacks, the skylight, or oculus, at the top of Calatrava's structure will be opened to fill the huge space below with light.

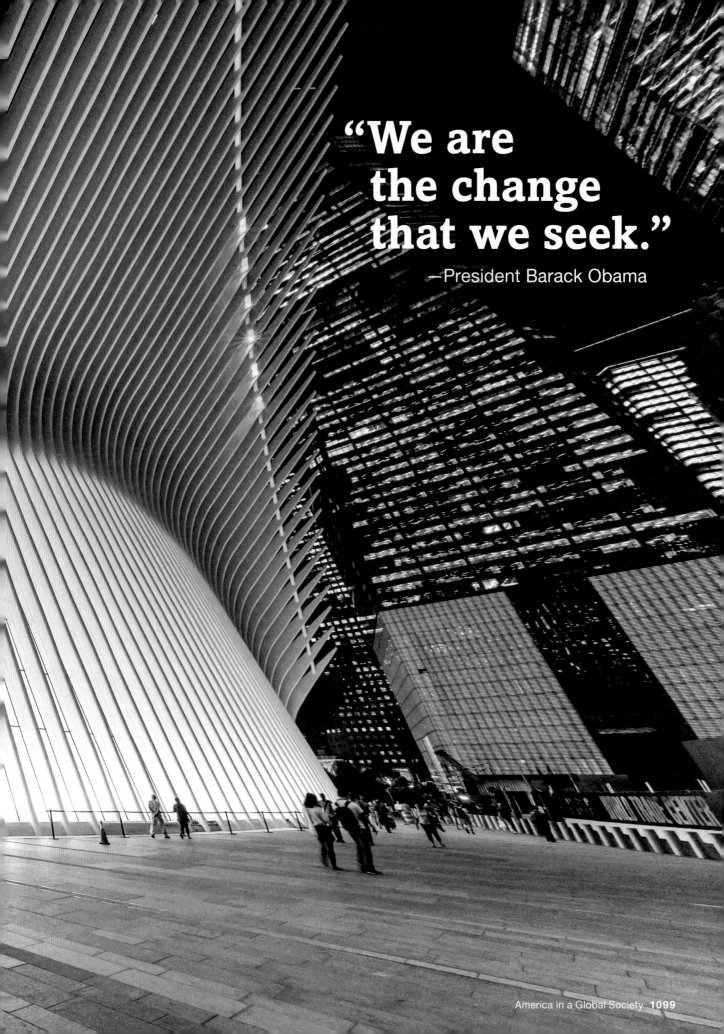

"We are
the change
that we seek."

—President Barack Obama

THE FIRST ENVIRONMENTALISTS

Protesters march on the Standing Rock Indian Reservation in North Dakota in 2016, attempting to halt the construction of a pipeline along the northern edge of the reservation.

In 1971, an organization called Keep America Beautiful launched an anti-pollution advertising campaign that quickly went viral. Billboards, magazine ads, and television commercials featured a solemn-faced Native American man in traditional clothing. As he regarded a landscape littered with garbage, a single tear trickled down his weathered cheek. The image (right), accompanied by slogans such as "Pollution hurts all of us," became instantly recognizable. The "Crying Indian" campaign was hugely successful in enlisting Americans to join the crusade against pollution.

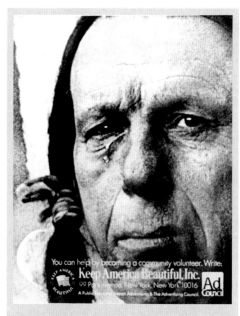

IRON EYES CODY

The story of the "Crying Indian" from the Keep America Beautiful ad campaign contains some curious twists relating to perceptions of Native American identity. The craggy-faced man featured in the ads was an actor named Iron Eyes Cody who had played Native Americans in movies since the 1920s. Sometime after the famous ad campaign, however, it was revealed that Iron Eyes Cody was not of Cherokee and Cree ancestry, as he claimed. In fact, he was a Sicilian American, born in Louisiana with the name Espera Oscar de Corti.

It would be easy to dismiss Cody as a mockery or cheap fake, but he took his pseudo-Native American identity very seriously. He married a Native American woman, adopted two Native American sons, and followed Native American practices and beliefs during his entire adult life. He also vigorously supported numerous Native American causes. In 1995, the Hollywood Native American community honored him for his work, although some were angered by Cody's very public appropriation of Native American identity through actions and beliefs rather than birth.

This signature image also effectively illustrates a long-held stereotype of Native Americans as simple hunters or farmers living in harmony with nature, leaving no trace—the first American environmentalists. While some may consider this portrayal as flattering, it may also be an oversimplification. Native Americans have been using natural resources in a variety of sophisticated, evolving ways since long before the first Europeans arrived. Native American groups are as diverse as the nationalities found on any continent, and their complex relationships with nature reflect that diversity.

PRE-CONTACT

The term "pre-contact" is sometimes used to refer to Native Americans during the time before their first encounters with European explorers and settlers. Scholars believe that most pre-contact groups shared a broadly similar worldview incorporating the ideas that animals, plants, and the earth itself harbored sacred spirits, and that humans could ask the spirits to influence the weather, harvests, or the results of an upcoming battle. However, the cultures and survival practices of the tribes varied widely to suit the diverse North American geography. Some groups did indeed leave little trace on the land, while others took an active role in molding the ecosystems that surrounded them. Historian Louis S. Warren wrote, "To claim that Indians lived without affecting nature is akin to saying that they lived without touching anything, that they were a people without a history."

Different groups manipulated their environments in different ways to suit their needs. The Choctaw, Iroquois, and Pawnee, for example, cleared forests to create fields for farming. When those fields were no longer fertile, the tribes would abandon them and clear new land. When land was abundant, this practice could continue for a long time but led to deforestation and stress on local species. There is evidence that certain tribes may have even caused their own downfall by overusing local resources. Some researchers believe the Ancestral Puebloans who once lived in southeastern Utah disappeared from their villages in the 13th century because they had depleted the wood in the region by burning it for fuel.

Fire was a powerful tool groups used to shape an ecosystem to their advantage. For example, some groups used fire to help create open prairies where large game animals such as bison, deer, elk, and antelope could graze. Fires were sometimes used in hunts to force animals into small open areas where they could be easily hunted. Burning was also used to clear ground for crops or drive out pests.

But many pre-contact groups actively practiced conservation techniques to protect the species they relied upon. The Algonquian lived along the Atlantic Coast and divided hunting territories among families. Each family would hunt its land according to systems the group had developed to maintain the game supply. In the Pacific Northwest, some Native American tribes trapped salmon swimming up rivers to spawn, but were also careful to let enough fish escape and lay their eggs so that the supply would be maintained from year to year.

THE PRESENT DAY

For years after European settlers arrived, Native Americans continued to use many of their pre-contact techniques for living within and managing ecosystems. As the groups were relocated and pushed onto reservations in the 19th century, however, most of these systems were disrupted. In the centuries since the first European contact, Native Americans have faced the challenge of adapting to new environments and maintaining their cultures in a changing, sometimes hostile world. Climate change may pose one of the most severe threats to some groups, particularly in Alaska, where melting ice and permafrost are profoundly affecting species including polar bears and caribou.

Native American groups remain at the forefront of conservation efforts, and many tribes are uniquely positioned to protect wild lands. According to one study, "many tribal lands still represent some of the largest intact habitats . . . in North America," and more than 81,236 square miles of land in the lower 48 states and 62,500 square miles of land in Alaska are controlled by Native American tribes. "Much of this land is relatively undisturbed, providing a significant amount of rare and important fish and wildlife habitat," the authors of the study claim.

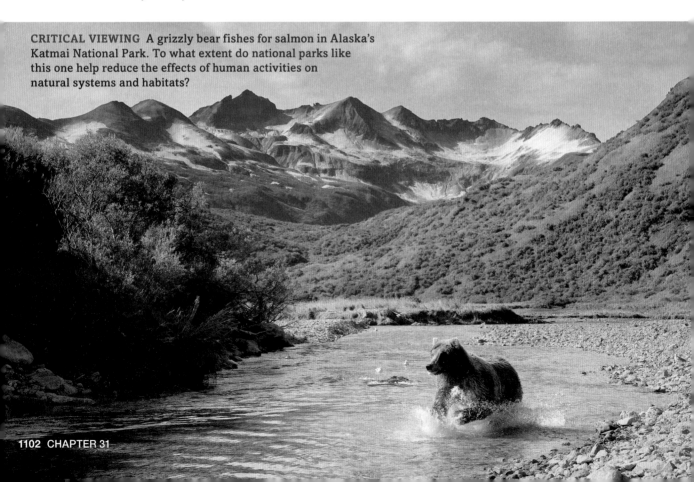

CRITICAL VIEWING A grizzly bear fishes for salmon in Alaska's Katmai National Park. To what extent do national parks like this one help reduce the effects of human activities on natural systems and habitats?

Examples abound of Native American tribes working to restore habitats and species. One of the most publicly recognized Native American conservation efforts is the fight to restore the American bison. Historically, the bison had provided a living for numerous tribes on the Great Plains and was important to the tribes' cultural and religious lives. By 1884, as a result of overhunting, only 325 wild bison remained in the United States. Today, organizations such as the Intertribal Buffalo Council (ITBC) work to reintroduce American bison to tribal lands in South Dakota, Montana, Oklahoma, and New Mexico. Currently, the ITBC has 58 member tribes, including the Lakota, Crow, Blackfeet, Ho Chunk, and Choctaw. In 2016, ITBC controlled a herd of more than 15,000 bison spread across 19 states. Emphasizing the cultural and environmental importance of bison, the ITBC asserts, "To re-establish healthy buffalo populations on tribal lands is to re-establish hope for Indian people."

Still, it would be shortsighted to view Native Americans' relationship with the environment as one-dimensional. Like all Americans, Native Americans need to make a living, coping with the demands of modern life while maintaining cultural traditions. In some cases, that means balancing conservation with the use of natural resources to earn money. Members of the Hoopa Valley Tribe in California, for example, have a strong belief in conservation and powerful cultural and religious ties to the species that populate their wooded land. At the same time, cutting and selling trees for timber is necessary for the tribe's economy. Thus, the Hoopa have developed ways to maintain a sustainable logging industry while protecting the forest habitat. Similarly, on the Great Plains, some groups harvest and sell bison meat as a healthier alternative to beef and also work to preserve the wild herds.

Occasionally, tribes' traditional practices bring them into conflict with environmental organizations. The Makah Indians in Washington State had been whaling for more than 1,000 years when they stopped in 1929, in the face of a declining whale population. In 1999, they resumed hunting, having been authorized by the government to take five whales a year. The Makah argue that whaling is central to their culture and traditions. They also point to the Treaty of Neah Bay, signed in 1855, which granted whaling rights to the Makah in exchange for tribal lands.

THE GREAT LAW OF PEACE

The Iroquois Confederacy was bound by a constitution that had existed for centuries before the first Europeans arrived. In the present day, it is known by different names, including the Great Law of Peace. In pre-contact times, the constitution was transmitted by oral tradition.

One passage in the constitution has, in recent years, been used to form the basis of an idea called seven-generation sustainability, or the seventh-generation principle. The concept, supported by many environmentalists and other scientists, is that humans should make decisions about natural resources with the fate of our seventh-generation descendants in mind. Today's decisions, in other words, should lead to healthy, sustainable ecosystems for many generations to come.

PRIMARY SOURCE

In all of your deliberations in the Confederate Council, in your efforts at lawmaking, in all your official acts, self-interest shall be cast into oblivion. Cast not over your shoulder behind you the warnings of the nephews and nieces should they chide you for any error or wrong you may do, but return to the way of the Great Law which is just and right. Look and listen for the welfare of the whole people and have always in view not only the present but also the coming generations, even those whose faces are yet beneath the surface of the ground—the unborn of the future Nation.

—from the Constitution of the Iroquois Nations

Environmentalists argue that certain gray whale groups are nearly depleted, and whaling by the Makah could threaten their dwindling numbers. Some also criticize the Makah for using modern technology, in addition to traditional tools, to kill whales.

In 2000, former Tribal Council Chairman Ben Johnson summed up the frustration many Native Americans feel about stereotypes that would simplify Native American culture and freeze it in time. "Times change and we have to change with the times," he said. "[People] want us to be back in the primitive times. We just want to practice our culture."

THE DAKOTA ACCESS PIPELINE

In 2016, an environmental protest placed the Standing Rock Sioux tribe in headlines across the country. The Sioux were fighting the construction of the Dakota Access Pipeline (DAPL) beneath the Missouri River on land that is adjacent to the Standing Rock Reservation in North Dakota. The DAPL is a 1,170-mile-long underground pipeline intended to transport oil from fields in North Dakota to southern Illinois, where it can be shipped to refineries. The $3.7 billion project is financed by a private company.

The Standing Rock Sioux object to the pipeline on both cultural and environmental grounds. They claim construction will disrupt sacred tribal burial sites and believe that if the DAPL suffers an oil spill, it will permanently contaminate the Missouri River, the reservation's principal source of water. Protesters claim the land through which the pipeline runs is in fact Sioux land, deeded to them in the Treaty of Fort Laramie in 1851. Since 1851, the government has taken much of the land, but the treaty was never nullified.

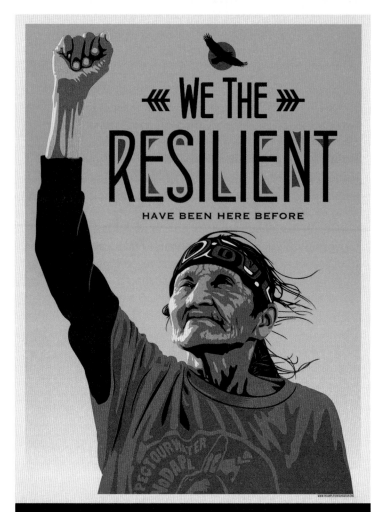

In 2016, artist-activists collaborated with photographers to create a series of images, including this one by Ernesto Yerena, that capture the shared humanity of our diverse America.

In spring of 2016, tribe members set up a camp on the reservation in North Dakota and publicized their mission statement, stating: "Our goal is to peacefully and prayerfully defend our rights, and rise up as one to sustain Mother Earth and her inhabitants." Protests staged from the camp were largely peaceful, although some clashes with police did occur. Environmentalists, celebrities, and others joined the Standing Rock Sioux in their protests. Many others used donations or social media to express their support. For example, in November 2016, when the rumor circulated that police officers were using Facebook check-ins to track the locations of protesters, more than 1 million people across the United States "checked in" at the Standing Rock Reservation.

On the other side of the issue, many Americans favor the construction of the DAPL, which some claim has created thousands of jobs—the reason the pipeline is supported by several labor unions. Others believe transporting oil through a pipeline is much safer than using trucks, tankers, and trains.

Experts debate the relative safety of moving oil through pipelines, and a major leak discovered in 2016 in an older North Dakota pipeline added to safety concerns about the new one.

At the end of 2016, the matter of the Dakota Access Pipeline was still unsettled. In November 2016, the Army Corps of Engineers, which must approve the project, determined "additional discussion and analysis are warranted in light of the history of the Great Sioux Nation's dispossessions of lands, the importance of Lake Oahe to the Tribe, our government-to-government relationship, and the statute governing easements through government property." In December, the Army denied a permit to complete the project and said it would continue its environmental impact study.

ANALYZE ENVIRONMENTAL CONCEPTS

What decisions have Native American groups faced in terms of resources and natural systems, and how did those factors influence the groups' actions?

RESTORING THE RIO GRANDE

In September 2016, National Geographic Freshwater Fellow Sandra Postel reported on an innovative collaboration between Native American tribes and Audubon New Mexico, a conservation society, to restore flow to the Rio Grande. Even though the Rio Grande is the second largest river in the Southwest, parts of it dry up in the summer as water is diverted for irrigation and other purposes. This is alarming to water conservationists like Postel because the Rio Grande supports numerous native fish and birds, including some listed as threatened or endangered.

Seeking to restore some of the river's flow, Audubon New Mexico asked Native American groups in the Middle Rio Grande Valley to contribute a portion of the water they receive from the river through allocations. In exchange, Audubon committed to use the water for the river's benefit and to seek funding to restore river habitats on tribal lands. The Sandia, Isleta, Santa Ana, and Cochiti Pueblos agreed, transferring over 130 million gallons of water to Audubon New Mexico. With contributions from another user, the total water donation came to more than 260 million gallons.

National Geographic Freshwater Fellow (2009–2015) Sandra Postel

The water was stored in a reservoir and released at strategic locations during the summer of 2016. At the same time, the Pueblos and Audubon New Mexico worked to plant trees and restore habitats along the river's banks. Postel praised the partnership between Native American groups and an environmental organization to save the threatened Rio Grande. "River by river," she wrote, "the movement of water stewardship and restoration we are working to build is growing."

CRITICAL VIEWING Why is cooperation among tribes and outside agencies important in achieving environmental goals such as the restoration of the Rio Grande, shown below?

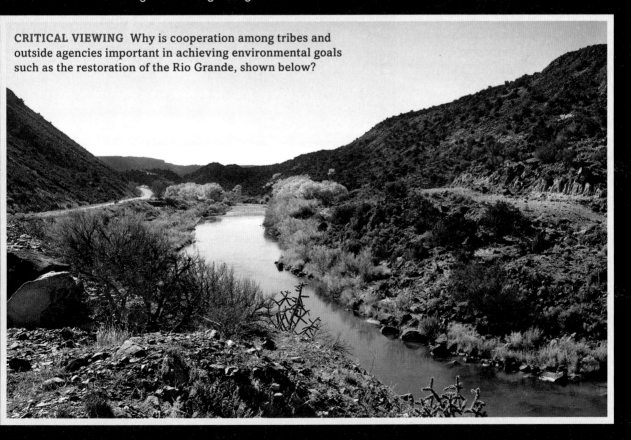

MAIN IDEA During his first term as president, Bill Clinton pursued domestic and social reforms and faced growing opposition from Republicans.

MODERATE REFORM UNDER BILL CLINTON

In 1963, a 16-year-old boy named Bill Clinton visited the White House and shook hands with President John F. Kennedy. Afterward, the boy told his friends that he would have Kennedy's job someday. Three decades later, Clinton became the country's 42nd president.

THE 1992 ELECTION

In February of 1992, President George H.W. Bush announced plans to run for a second term on the Republican Party ticket. A year earlier, he might have seemed unbeatable. However, as you have read, his approval rating had dropped sharply as the result of an economic recession.

Arkansas governor Bill Clinton emerged on the Democratic side as Bush's challenger in the presidential election. For his vice-presidential running mate, Clinton went against political wisdom by selecting another southerner: Senator Al Gore of Tennessee, who had championed many environmental issues in Congress. Clinton campaigned as a "New Democrat," or a moderate member of the party who supported more conservative economic policies than many other Democrats.

As governor, Clinton boasted a strong record in education, civil rights, and economic growth in Arkansas. His critics attacked his character, however, claiming that Clinton, a married man, had had extramarital affairs and

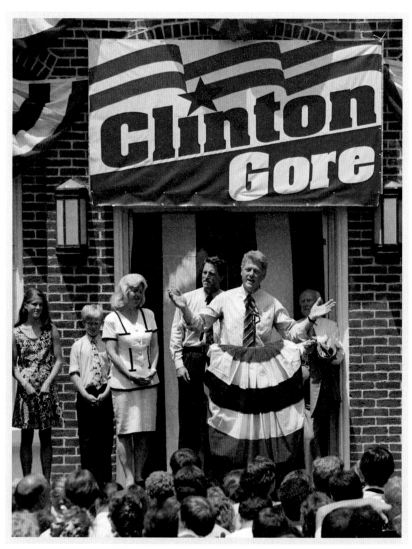

Clinton addresses a rally in front of the courthouse in Carthage, Tennessee, during the 1992 campaign. Gore, along with his wife and children, stand behind Clinton. Growing up, Gore spent his summers working on his family's farm in Carthage.

evaded the draft during the Vietnam War. The legality of some of his business dealings was also questioned.

Disappointed by the Bush-Clinton matchup, many voters—especially Republicans—wanted an alternative. They got one when a Texas computer billionaire named **H. Ross Perot** threw his hat into the ring. Plainspoken and tough-talking, Perot argued that professional politicians lacked the will to tackle the country's most difficult problems. His popularity soared, and he briefly moved ahead of Bush and Clinton in the polls. However, with the Republican base split between Bush and Perot, Clinton won on election day.

DOMESTIC REFORMS

Upon taking office, President Clinton focused on domestic policy. To slash the massive federal budget deficit he had inherited from his predecessor, Clinton proposed an economic package that combined tax increases and spending cuts. He lobbied hard to win support for the plan, and in August 1993, it squeaked through Congress. Other initiatives of the early Clinton administration included the expansion of federal support for housing and nutritional programs aimed at assisting low-income families and addressing the persistence of poverty.

Clinton's most ambitious domestic goal was to overhaul the country's health care system to ensure that all Americans had access to quality, affordable care. Nearly 40 million Americans at that time lacked health insurance, and the costs of medical care were rising at an alarming rate. Just days into his presidency, Clinton created a **task force**, or group organized for a special mission, to reform the health care system. He appointed his wife, Hillary Clinton, to lead it. Mrs. Clinton, an accomplished lawyer, had advocated for children and education as first lady of Arkansas. During the 1992 campaign, Clinton had told the public that, with his election, they would get "two for the price of one," meaning that his wife would play an active role in his administration.

By September 1993, Mrs. Clinton and the task force had developed a proposal called the Health Security Act, which called for universal health coverage, managed care, and a restructured health insurance industry. The proposal met with fierce opposition from insurance companies, small-business organizations, the American Medical Association, and Congress. The "Clinton Health Plan," as it was known, failed to be adopted.

Among Clinton's domestic reforms was the Brady Handgun Violence Prevention Act, passed by Congress in 1993. James Brady (left), President Ronald Reagan's press secretary, was shot in the head and left partially paralyzed in the assassination attempt against the president in 1981. After the shooting, Brady and his wife worked tirelessly to promote handgun legislation. The act helped block the sale of an estimated one million guns to dangerous criminals.

SOCIAL CHANGES

President Clinton also dealt with important social issues. In fact, the first bill he signed into law was the Family and Medical Leave Act, which Bush had vetoed twice. Designed to help employees balance work and family life, the act allowed workers to take up to 12 weeks of unpaid, job-protected leave each year to care for newborn or newly adopted children or seriously ill family members.

The growing activism and prominence of LGBTQ (lesbian, gay, bisexual, transgender, and queer) groups resulted in further social change. In 1974, a politician and LGBTQ activist named Elaine Noble had won election to the Massachusetts House of Representatives, becoming the first openly lesbian or gay person ever elected to a state legislature. Three years later, voters in San Francisco elected a popular community leader and openly gay activist named **Harvey Milk** to the city's Board of Supervisors.

In 1992, the year Clinton was elected, the AIDS epidemic remained one of the most critical issues affecting the LGBT community. That year, AIDS became the number one cause of death for

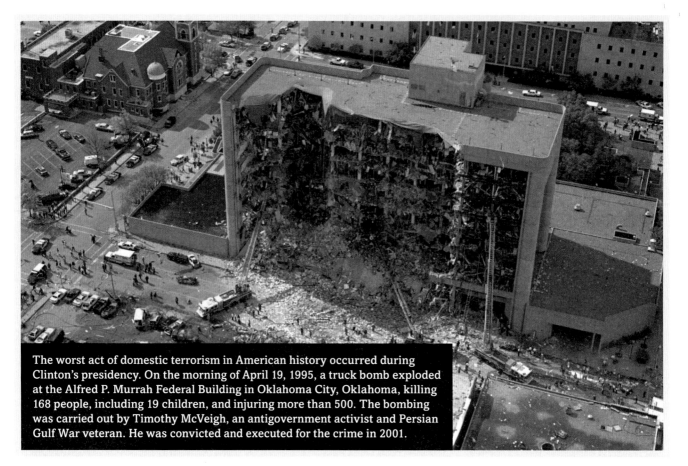

The worst act of domestic terrorism in American history occurred during Clinton's presidency. On the morning of April 19, 1995, a truck bomb exploded at the Alfred P. Murrah Federal Building in Oklahoma City, Oklahoma, killing 168 people, including 19 children, and injuring more than 500. The bombing was carried out by Timothy McVeigh, an antigovernment activist and Persian Gulf War veteran. He was convicted and executed for the crime in 2001.

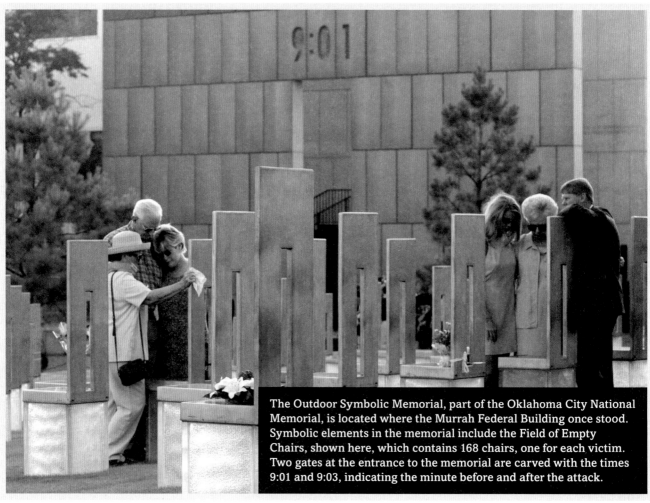

The Outdoor Symbolic Memorial, part of the Oklahoma City National Memorial, is located where the Murrah Federal Building once stood. Symbolic elements in the memorial include the Field of Empty Chairs, shown here, which contains 168 chairs, one for each victim. Two gates at the entrance to the memorial are carved with the times 9:01 and 9:03, indicating the minute before and after the attack.

American men between the ages of 25 and 44. A disproportionate number of the disease's victims were gay men. The Clinton administration responded to the crisis by establishing the Presidential Advisory Council on HIV/AIDS and by dramatically increasing government funding for AIDS research, prevention, and treatment.

Clinton was the first major presidential candidate to court the gay vote. Shortly after taking office, he reaffirmed a controversial campaign vow to overturn the U.S. military's longstanding ban on homosexuals. Top military leaders wanted to keep the ban, as did many members of Congress, including Senator Sam Nunn of Georgia, the powerful chairman of the Senate Armed Services Committee.

In July 1993, Clinton announced a compromise policy that came to be known as "Don't Ask, Don't Tell." Under the new policy, homosexuals would be allowed to serve in the military as long as they kept their sexual orientation to themselves. But Clinton's support for gay rights had limits. In 1996, he took a stand against same-sex marriage by signing the **Defense of Marriage Act (DOMA)**. This law defined marriage as "a legal union between one man and one woman," and it denied same-sex couples the federal benefits, privileges, and recognition that opposite-sex couples received. Clinton's stand left many of his gay supporters feeling betrayed.

THE REPUBLICAN REVOLUTION

Meanwhile, Republican opponents began to investigate the Clintons' purchase in the late 1970s of a real estate development in Arkansas known as **Whitewater** and charged the couple with financial wrongdoing. In early 1994, the U.S. attorney general appointed a special prosecutor to look into their role in what came to be known as the Whitewater scandal. The resulting inquiry spanned about 6 years and cost more than $50 million, but investigators failed to find sufficient evidence to charge the Clintons with any crime.

The president's rivals had greater success when they challenged him politically. In the 1992 election, Democrats had retained their majorities in both houses of Congress. This political landscape shifted dramatically in 1994, however, after the midterm congressional elections. The Republicans won a sweeping victory, gaining control of both the Senate and the House of Representatives for the first time in four decades. **Newton "Newt" Gingrich**, a congressman from Georgia, became Speaker of the House. Before the elections, Gingrich had co-authored a document called a **Contract with America**, which promised tax cuts for the middle class, strong anticrime legislation, and constitutional amendments requiring a balanced budget and term limits for members of Congress.

When Congress reconvened in January 1995, the House Republicans immediately began to push the legislation detailed in the contract through Congress. Some of the measures eventually passed into law, including a major welfare reform law called the Personal Responsibility and Work Opportunity Reconciliation Act of 1996. This legislation required welfare recipients to work after receiving benefits for two years, limited the time they could stay on welfare, and shifted much of the responsibility for social welfare administration from the federal government to the states. Critics argued that the act destroyed the safety net that protected the country's neediest and most vulnerable citizens. Still, many of the measures proposed by the House were rejected by the Senate or vetoed by Clinton.

The 1994 midterm elections seemed to make Clinton's re-election in 1996 unlikely, but missteps on the part of Republicans in 1995 helped the president regain popularity. One of these errors occurred toward the end of the year when the White House and Congress became deadlocked over the federal budget. Rather than negotiate, Gingrich and other members of the GOP majority in the House shut down the government. They hoped this action would pressure the White House into agreeing with their position. The strategy backfired when the public blamed the Republicans for the budget impasse. By early January 1996, the government had resumed normal operations.

HISTORICAL THINKING

1. **READING CHECK** How did H. Ross Perot's candidacy affect the 1992 presidential election?

2. **ANALYZE CAUSE AND EFFECT** Describe the causes that may have led to the Republicans gaining control of both the Senate and House of Representatives in 1994.

3. **EXPLAIN** How did the government respond to social changes during the Clinton administration? Provide examples from the text.

4. **DRAW CONCLUSIONS** How did the persistence of poverty influence the social policies of President Clinton?

GLOBALIZATION AND IMMIGRATION

"Nothing is permanent except change." In the 1990s, this saying might have rung truer than ever. The world was shrinking, and everything seemed to be in a state of flux. What would all this change mean for Americans?

GLOBALIZED BUSINESS

During the Clinton presidency, **globalization**, or the faster and freer flow of people, resources, goods, and ideas across national borders, had a powerful effect on the United States. Through trade, investments, migration, and the rapid sharing of information, countries and people around the world became increasingly interconnected.

Globalization had a profound impact on U.S. manufacturing. Many American companies began moving their operations to Mexico, where lower labor costs meant they could produce goods for less money. In time, some companies moved their operations from Mexico to China and then to smaller nations such as Bangladesh, to take advantage of even lower labor costs. These shifts resulted in falling prices for many goods that Americans consumed. However, producing these goods outside of the United States also led to **job dislocations**, or the movement of jobs to other places. These dislocations caused many Americans to lose their jobs.

Some American businesses, including computer software, retail, and automobile companies, have fared well in the globalized world. These industries established research centers and factories abroad and expanded their businesses in European, Asian, and African markets. American industrial leaders also recruited the best and the brightest from around the world to work in their companies.

THE UNITED STATES AND MEXICO

The growth of world trade in the second half of the 20th century came largely as a result of international trade agreements. In 1947, as you may recall,

23 countries signed the General Agreement on Tariffs and Trade (GATT), whose purpose was to reduce tariffs and other trade barriers so that countries could trade more freely with one another. In 1994, the World Trade Organization (WTO) replaced GATT. The WTO strives to set and enforce rules for trade, resolve trade disputes, ensure that developing countries benefit from the growth in international trade, and continue to support free trade.

The success of the European Economic Community—which, as you know, formed in 1958—prompted leaders in North America to consider creating a similar union. In 1988, the United States and Canada signed a free-trade pact that called for the elimination of most trade barriers. Then, in 1992, the United States, Canada, and Mexico ceremonially signed the **North American Free Trade Agreement (NAFTA)**. In the United States, George H.W. Bush had proposed and led the fight for the agreement during his presidency. NAFTA played a central role in fostering close relationships among the three countries and created the world's largest trading bloc.

The economic ties between the United States and Mexico had begun to deepen after the Cold War ended. These ties were strengthened by manufacturing plants called *maquiladoras* (mah-kee-luh-DOOR-uhz), which were established along the border between the United States and Mexico in the 1960s. A **maquiladora** is a plant located in an export-processing zone. A plant in this zone imports materials and then uses them to manufacture products for export. The plants allow

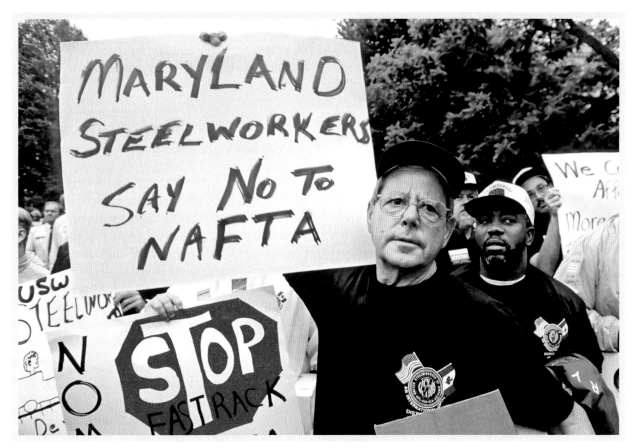

Many American workers and labor unions united in their opposition to NAFTA. When a bill was proposed in 1997 that would require Congress to vote yes or no on a trade agreement submitted by a president within 90 days, these Maryland steelworkers protested. The legislation was defeated.

U.S. companies to take advantage of low labor costs in Mexico. In addition, maquiladoras operate as **free-enterprise zones**, which allow the suspension of both Mexican and U.S. tax and custom laws. As a result, goods flowed between the two countries at freer and faster rates from the 1980s through the 2000s.

In the early 1990s, Mexico prepared for **integration**, or the process of joining economic forces, with the United States and Canada under NAFTA by instituting a series of economic reforms. One of these called for communally owned farms in the southern Mexico state of Chiapas to be privatized, or transferred from public to private ownership. In response, an armed uprising called the **Chiapas Rebellion** took place in 1994. The rebellion was launched by a revolutionary force made up of local, rural people called Zapatistas (zah-puh-TEES-tuhz). They called for "a world in which many worlds fit," not a mono, or single, world with no space for them. Their response was an example of **disintegration**, or the endurance of nationalist, tribalist, and separatist alternatives to globalization.

Implementation of NAFTA was and continues to be controversial on both sides of the border. In the United States, critics feared the agreement would cause the country to lose even more manufacturing jobs to Mexico. And although it is true that the United States did lose some jobs, the loss was not as large as some critics had predicted. Still, tensions remain on issues related to economic regulation, labor conditions, increased immigration from Mexico, and damage to the environment. However, on the plus side, trade between the United States and Mexico has grown dramatically since NAFTA. A huge increase in exports bolstered Mexico's economy, and a similar increase in imports gave Mexican consumers access to lower-priced, better-quality goods. The borderland between the United States and Mexico is the scene of dynamic interactions in work, commerce, and culture.

NEW IMMIGRATION PATTERNS

As you've read, many critics of NAFTA were concerned that the agreement would result in a rise in the number of Mexican immigrants. The Immigration Act of 1965 had already liberalized country-of-origin policies by opening the United States to people of all nationalities. The act emphasized family reunification by giving special preference to relatives of immigrants who were already citizens of the United States. The new policy soon brought about major demographic and social changes. The U.S. population became increasingly diverse as immigration increased and newcomers arrived from all parts of the world. Immigration from Mexico jumped dramatically, from approximately 575,000 Mexicans in 1960 to more than 4 million in 1990.

As legal immigration to the United States increased, so did illegal immigration. Many of the people who crossed the border illegally—without proper documentation—came from Mexico or Central America in search of work and a better future. Illegal immigration emerged as a major issue in the 1990s, especially in states along the U.S.-Mexico border. Many people felt that these undocumented immigrants took jobs away from Americans, caused crime rates to rise, and took advantage of the country's social services without paying taxes. In 1996, Congress addressed the flood of illegal immigrants by allocating funds for increased border security.

People in some states bordering Mexico also took steps against illegal immigration. For example, in 1994, California voters approved **Proposition 187**, a controversial ballot measure that denied illegal immigrants state services such as public education

During the 1994 Chiapas Rebellion against NAFTA, a man known as "Subcomandante Marcos" (shown below wearing a black mask) led the Zapatistas. His army, consisting mostly of poor Maya farmers, briefly occupied several towns before agreeing to a truce with the Mexican government.

Vendors at the Little Saigon Night Market in Westminster, California, grill fresh fish and other street food in this 2015 photo. These open-air stalls are common in Vietnam, and immigrants brought the tradition to the United States. Night markets have sprung up across the country.

and health care. All but one provision of Proposition 187 was blocked by federal courts throughout the 1990s, but other anti-immigrant measures soon followed. **Proposition 209**, which won approval in 1996, prohibited state-supported affirmative action that was intended to help minority groups suffering from discrimination. Two years later came **Proposition 227**, which banned bilingual education in California's public schools.

Major world events also affected immigration patterns in the last decades of the 20th century. As you've learned, the end of the Vietnam War in 1975 brought hundreds of thousands of refugees from Vietnam and neighboring Southeast Asian countries to the United States. Immigration from Vietnam continued to grow as relatives sought to join family members who had arrived earlier. Similarly, the 1979 Islamic Revolution in Iran drove a large influx of Iranians to U.S. shores.

The United States has always been made up of people from many different cultures. However, the growing diversity of the U.S. population led to debate over the concept of multiculturalism. In the early 1990s, conservatives accused liberals of using multiculturalism to divide society into conflicting groups, limit free speech on campuses by suppressing conservative views, and reject traditional Western culture. Liberals countered that multiculturalism was necessary to tackle problems that arise as our society becomes more diverse.

As Clinton dealt with globalization and immigration, he also concentrated on seeking a second term as president. He would be aided in achieving this goal by the country's strong economy. Clinton's second four years, however, would not be smooth sailing.

HISTORICAL THINKING

1. **READING CHECK** Why did some American companies move to Mexico, China, and Bangladesh?

2. **COMPARE AND CONTRAST** What have been some of the advantages and disadvantages of NAFTA?

3. **FORM AND SUPPORT OPINIONS** Based on what you have read in this lesson, do you think globalization is a good thing? Support your opinion with evidence from the text.

4. **SUMMARIZE** How did the federal government and California voters respond to international migration in the 1990s?

ECONOMIC BOOM AND SCANDALS

Websites, blogs, Wi-Fi, and social media are part of everyday life today, but before the technology boom of the 1990s, they were all but unknown. They all have to do with the Internet, which fueled major cultural changes and big economic growth.

SECOND-TERM ACCOMPLISHMENTS

After Clinton defeated Republican candidate Robert Dole and Reform Party candidate H. Ross Perot in the 1996 election, the nation's economy continued to improve. Unemployment fell from 5.4 to 4.9 percent in 1997, and by 2000, it had dropped to 4 percent—the lowest level in three decades. The stock market soared to record levels, and inflation fell. In 1998, the president presented the first balanced budget since 1969. The federal government took in more money than it spent in 1998 and in each of the next three years, allowing for a rare budget surplus. With Americans enjoying plentiful jobs and stable prices, a sense of optimism swept the nation and kept Clinton's job approval ratings around 60 percent.

One of the main forces driving this strong economic growth was the rise of the Internet and the rapid development of companies that took advantage of this revolutionary new mode of information-sharing. The result was a "dot-com" boom in the stock market, named for the suffix of most corporate web pages. Investors poured money into the stocks of Internet-related companies, and entrepreneurs who started popular social media and commercial websites became millionaires almost overnight. The center of this rapid growth in technology was California's Silicon Valley where, as you know, the personal computer was developed.

In his second term, as in his first, Clinton pursued an agenda of moderate domestic reforms. Addressing Americans' concerns about the soaring costs of higher education, for example, he proposed and signed a bill calling for tax breaks, tuition grants, and scholarships to help working-

and middle-class families pay for college. In foreign policy matters, Clinton led efforts to expand the North Atlantic Treaty Organization (NATO) by bringing in former communist countries in Eastern Europe. In 1995, during his first term, Clinton had worked to bring about a cease-fire among warring Serbs, Croats, and Bosnians in the Balkans, a mountainous region in Eastern Europe that was once part of Yugoslavia. In 1999, Clinton authorized NATO to carry out air strikes against Serbia to end its mass killing of ethnic Albanians in the Serbian province of Kosovo. Clinton's administration also played an important role in implementing the **Oslo Accords**, which were aimed at ending the decades-long conflict between the Israelis and Palestinians.

The Dot-Com Boom, 1995–2004

Source: Federal Reserve Bank of St. Louis

* The NASDAQ is a stock market of stocks that are traded electronically. The index expresses stocks' values with respect to a 1971 base index of 100.

CLINTON'S IMPEACHMENT

While Clinton achieved many political successes during his second term, a serious scandal arose that threatened to end his presidency. In 1994, a former Arkansas state employee named Paula Jones had filed a sexual harassment suit against Clinton, accusing him of unwanted sexual advances. Kenneth Starr, the special prosecutor in charge of the Whitewater inquiry, expanded his investigation to include the Paula Jones case, even though there was no connection between the two. In late 1997, stories began to surface about another sexual relationship, this one between Clinton and a young female White House intern named Monica Lewinsky. Lawyers for Jones subpoenaed Lewinsky as a witness, but in a sworn statement, she denied any relationship with the president. When Clinton testified under oath in the case, he, too, denied the relationship.

However, Starr eventually uncovered strong evidence of sexual encounters between Clinton and Lewinsky. Faced with this evidence, the president testified before a grand jury in August 1998 and admitted to having had "inappropriate intimate contact" with her. The following month, Starr submitted a report to Congress that identified 11 possible grounds on which the president could be impeached, or formally charged with "treason, bribery, or other high crimes and misdemeanors." Impeachment is limited to the president, vice president, and other civil officers of the United States. An official convicted of the charge is removed from office.

According to the Constitution, the House of Representatives votes to impeach an official, while the Senate tries the case. In December 1998, the Republican-controlled House voted largely along party lines to bring two charges against Clinton. The first alleged the president had committed **perjury**, or had lied under oath. The second claimed he had obstructed justice by attempting to hide his relationship with the intern and encouraging her to lie in her sworn statement. The only other president ever to be impeached was Andrew Johnson in 1868.

In January 1999, Clinton's impeachment trial began. After just four weeks of testimony, the Senate voted to acquit Clinton of both charges, having failed to obtain the two-thirds majority needed for conviction. He remained in office, but the scandals and trial damaged his reputation with the American people. As a result, concern over candidates' moral character would have a big impact on the election of 2000.

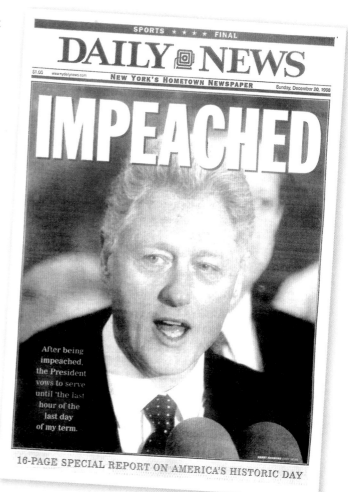

The *New York Daily News* ran this special edition of its newspaper on December 20 1998, the day after the House voted to impeach Clinton. Before his acquittal, the president told the American people that he was "profoundly sorry for all I have done wrong in words and deeds."

HISTORICAL THINKING

1. **READING CHECK** What were some of the indicators of the strong economy during Clinton's second term, and how did the Internet play a role?

2. **MAKE INFERENCES** What might the Republicans in Congress have hoped to gain by impeaching President Clinton?

3. **FORM AND SUPPORT OPINIONS** Do you think Clinton's presidency was a success or a failure? Explain your opinion.

4. **INTERPRET GRAPHS** What stock market trend began just after 2000, and what impact did this probably have on Internet-related companies?

THE CONTESTED ELECTION OF 2000

Most elections are decided easily: the candidate receiving the most votes is the winner. But as Americans learned in 2000, sometimes U.S. presidential elections are not so straightforward.

THE 2000 CAMPAIGN

During Clinton's impeachment trial, many leading political figures were already looking ahead to the 2000 presidential election—particularly among Republicans. They knew Clinton's scandals had weakened the Democratic Party. By early July 1999, nine Republicans had announced their candidacy. After a long primary battle, the Republican Party nominated Texas governor **George W. Bush**, the eldest son of former president George H.W. Bush.

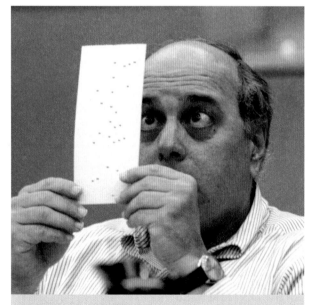

HANGING CHADS

Many Florida voters used punch-card ballots in the 2000 presidential election. However, a number of voters failed to punch a hole in their card, leaving a fragment of paper, called a "hanging chad," attached. Election officials, like the one shown here, studied the ballots, trying to determine the voter's intent in each instance.

Bush embraced what he called **compassionate conservatism**, a political philosophy that blended traditional conservative ideas about economic policies with a concern for disadvantaged people. He echoed Ronald Reagan's populist stand in the 1980s. Like Reagan, Bush criticized establishment elites and supported a smaller, contracted government and advocated for social programs that promoted traditional family values. He also vowed to restore executive power, which he felt Congress had weakened.

As his vice president, Bush chose Richard Cheney, who had served as secretary of defense under George H.W. Bush. Politically, Cheney was a neoconservative. A **neoconservative**, or "neocon," is someone who strongly supports a free-market economy with few regulations and believes the United States should use its influence and military power to actively promote its ideals and national interests around the world. For example, neocons shared the view that Saddam Hussein, the autocratic president of Iraq, was a destabilizing influence in Southwest Asia (often referred to as the Middle East), one of the world's most troubled regions. Neocons regretted that George H.W. Bush had not removed Hussein from power during the 1990–91 Persian Gulf War. They also believed strongly in what they called **American exceptionalism**—the idea that the United States is superior to other nations due to its history and ideology. As such, neocons claimed the country had a mission to spread democracy and change the world.

On the Democratic side, Vice President Al Gore easily won his party's nomination. In the minds of many Americans, however, Gore had been tarnished by the scandals of the Clinton presidency, and many

The 2000 Election

Al Gore, Democrat

Electoral Vote: 266 votes, 49.4%

Popular Vote: 50,992,335 votes, 48.4%

George W. Bush, Republican

Electoral Vote: 271 votes, 50.4%

Popular Vote: 50,455,156 votes, 47.9%

Ralph Nader, Green

Popular Vote: 2,882,738 votes, 2.7%

The 2000 election was one of the closest in modern U.S. history. In this photo, candidate Bush shakes hands with supporters at a campaign rally.

voters thought he was arrogant. In televised debates with Bush, Gore sighed, rolled his eyes, and seemed to talk down to his opponent. Ralph Nader ran as the candidate of the Green Party, which supported nonviolence, environmentalism, and social justice. During his candidacy, Nader promoted universal health care and spoke out against the power of big business. Because he drew much of his support from young, liberal, politically independent voters, some people would later claim that Nader took votes away from Gore and cost the vice president the election.

BUSH v. GORE

On election day, the voting was very close in many states. By the end of the night, with final and projected counts still being reported, Gore led in the popular vote. Still, neither candidate had yet gained the 270 electoral votes needed to win the election. It became clear that Florida, with 25 electoral votes, would determine the next president.

Shortly after 2 a.m., news outlets began declaring that Bush had won Florida and, therefore, the election. Gore called Bush to concede, or accept, defeat but soon took back his concession when he learned the count in Florida was much closer than had been previously reported. Bush led by fewer than 600 votes, and the gap continued to narrow as the counting continued. Furthermore, Gore's aides had noted irregularities and compromised ballots at polling places in several Democratic counties.

The slimness of the margin called for the application of a Florida law, which required a statewide recount by machine. The recount reduced Bush's

lead to 327. Some counties then initiated manual recounts, although the legality of these recounts was challenged in court. The Gore and Bush camps exchanged charges of fraud, manipulation, and the exercise of excessive political pressure throughout November.

In early December, the Florida Supreme Court ordered a manual statewide recount of the roughly 45,000 undervotes—ballots that had not been counted by the voting machines because the voter's intent was unclear. Days later, lawyers for both sides argued the **Bush v. Gore** case before the U.S. Supreme Court. In a decision that many commentators considered both hasty and biased toward Republicans, the Court declared the Florida Supreme Court's recount order unconstitutional. As a result, Bush became the president-elect. Although Gore had won the nationwide popular vote by more than 500,000 votes, he accepted the outcome as final and conceded the election.

HISTORICAL THINKING

1. **READING CHECK** How could the election of 2000 have taken other directions?

2. **ANALYZE CAUSE AND EFFECT** What impact did the closeness of the election and its controversial results have on the American people and on Bush's authority as president?

3. **FORM AND SUPPORT OPINIONS** Based on past elections, including the 2000 election, do you think American voters should directly elect the president, or do you think the current system is fine as it is? Explain your answer.

SEPTEMBER 11, 2001

A list of the darkest dates in U.S. history would certainly include April 12, 1861, the day the Civil War broke out, and December 7, 1941, when Japanese warplanes attacked Pearl Harbor. It would also include September 11, 2001, the day of the deadliest terrorist attacks ever on American soil.

UNDER ATTACK

As Americans went about their normal routines on the morning of Tuesday, September 11, 2001, news outlets reported an odd event in New York City. At 8:46 a.m., an airplane crashed into one of the twin 110-story towers of the World Trade Center in the city's downtown financial district. Smoke and flames billowed out of a gaping hole near the top of the north tower, and firefighters and police officers rushed to the scene. At first, many people assumed the crash had been an accident. Seventeen minutes later, however, people around the country looked on in disbelief as news cameras filmed another large jetliner slamming into the south tower. There could no longer be any question: the United States was under attack by terrorists.

The Federal Aviation Administration (FAA) immediately ordered all takeoffs to be halted at U.S. airports. Airplanes in the air were directed to land at the nearest airport. Minutes after the FAA issued this order, another plane crashed into the Pentagon, the headquarters of the U.S. Department of Defense, near Washington, D.C. Soon news came that a fourth airplane had crashed. This one was not flown into a building, however. It plunged into a field in a rural area of southwestern Pennsylvania. Passengers onboard the plane had struggled with the terrorists and prevented the aircraft from hitting its intended target, believed to have been the White House or the U.S. Capitol Building.

The attacks ended with the fourth crash, but there were more horrors to come. Around 10 a.m., as emergency responders worked desperately to evacuate the World Trade Center and battle the fires that engulfed it, the south tower collapsed. The collapse created a thick cloud of dust in the air that spread outward in every direction. Less than a half hour later, the north tower collapsed. The site of the collapsed towers became known as Ground Zero. In the hours after the attack, people with missing loved ones began gathering at the site, hoping desperately for good news. "Missing" posters soon covered walls, lampposts, and store windows in the area.

Over the next few days, authorities pieced together the story of the attacks. Nineteen terrorists, divided into groups of four or five, had boarded four

🏛 National September 11 Memorial Museum, New York City

The New York firefighter who wore this helmet on 9/11 was last seen carrying a woman from the north tower lobby when the building collapsed on top of them. His helmet, partially melted by the heat in the tower after it was hit, is one of thousands of artifacts on display in the museum.

The day after the attack on the World Trade Center, firefighters, city workers, members of the National Guard, and others began searching the wreckage for the bodies of victims, as well as any possible survivors.

commercial airplanes—two in Boston, one in Newark, New Jersey, and one in Washington, D.C. All four planes were originally scheduled to fly to the West Coast, so they were carrying full fuel tanks. After takeoff, the terrorists seized control of each airplane, perhaps using box cutters as weapons. They then piloted the planes toward targets selected for their symbolic significance. On the fourth airplane, however, the passengers and crew had learned about the other plane crashes and, as you've read, fought back.

Authorities believed the terrorists were linked to **al Qaeda** (al KY-duh), an Islamic extremist organization founded in the late 1980s. A Saudi Arabian militant named **Osama bin Laden** led this group from his base in Afghanistan. There, al Qaeda was protected and supported by the **Taliban**, an ultraconservative Islamic group that had gained control of much of the country. Determined to bring an end to U.S. influence in Southwest Asia, bin Laden employed **terrorism**, or the use of violent acts and threats to achieve a political goal, as his principal tactic. He had masterminded other attacks against the United States, including the 1998 bombing of U.S. embassies in Kenya and Tanzania, which left 224 people dead, and the 2000 bombing in Yemen of a U.S. warship called the U.S.S. *Cole*, which killed 17 sailors. The September 11, 2001, attacks were far deadlier. About 2,750 people were killed in New York City alone. The death toll at the Pentagon was 184, and the plane crash in Pennsylvania claimed 40 lives.

THE NATION UNITES

The September 11 attacks left Americans feeling profoundly sad, angry, and vulnerable. But the attacks also drew Americans together. In his first months in office, George W. Bush had governed a deeply divided populace. Increasingly, Americans saw their country as split between Democrats and Republicans. The public was also divided over the tax cuts passed by the president and the Republican-controlled Congress. Democrats claimed the tax cuts mainly benefited the wealthy.

However, 9/11, as the day of the terrorist attacks came to be called, inspired strong feelings of patriotism that united all Americans. The night of the attacks, Bush addressed the country saying, "These [terrorist] acts shattered steel, but they cannot dent the steel of American resolve." Many Americans displayed the flag or wore flag pins. People in countries around the world also condemned the attacks and expressed their solidarity with the United States. On September 12, a French newspaper declared, "We are all Americans."

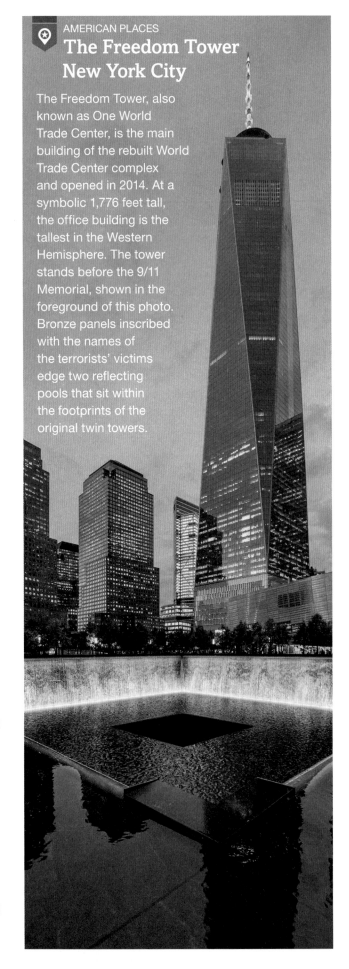

AMERICAN PLACES
The Freedom Tower
New York City

The Freedom Tower, also known as One World Trade Center, is the main building of the rebuilt World Trade Center complex and opened in 2014. At a symbolic 1,776 feet tall, the office building is the tallest in the Western Hemisphere. The tower stands before the 9/11 Memorial, shown in the foreground of this photo. Bronze panels inscribed with the names of the terrorists' victims edge two reflecting pools that sit within the footprints of the original twin towers.

Stories of heroism, sacrifice, and resilience during and after the attacks also drew people together. Many of the stories involved firefighters, police, and other first responders who had rushed bravely into the burning towers of the World Trade Center and led countless people to safety. But when the towers collapsed, more than 400 of the responders lost their own lives. Thousands more later developed severe health problems related to the smoke and toxic dust they inhaled. The collapse of the twin towers released dust containing high levels of lead, mercury, asbestos, and other harmful substances.

The mayor of New York City, Rudy Giuliani, also emerged as a hero. The calm, courage, and humanity he showed after the attacks helped comfort distressed New Yorkers. He spoke with many rescue workers and grieving families and, as victims were buried, attended as many as five funerals a day.

THE AFTERMATH

In the wake of the attacks, U.S. foreign policy, especially on the Middle East, underwent great change. The Bush administration shifted its focus from rival superpowers Russia and China to the connections between terrorist groups such as al Qaeda and **rogue states** . These states included countries, such as Iraq, Iran, and North Korea, that were perceived to violate international law and threaten world peace. Government officials suspected some rogue states of possessing **weapons of mass destruction (WMD)** , or weapons that use nuclear, chemical, or biological substances to harm large numbers of people.

Domestically, the attacks led to a dramatic increase in governmental vigilance. New laws passed during the Bush administration strengthened border and airport security and tightened screening of international travelers. The **USA Patriot Act** greatly expanded the government's powers to conduct surveillance on its own citizens. The act allowed federal agencies to tap the phones of those suspected of terrorist activity. Critics argued that the new policies focusing on national security and defense impinged upon Americans' civil liberties, especially freedom of speech and protection from unreasonable search and seizure.

The attacks also resulted in a rise in hate crimes against Muslims. Although the attacks had been carried out by an Islamic extremist group, some Americans blamed all Muslims for 9/11. Hate crimes were also carried out against those believed to be Muslims—notably Sikhs. Within days of the attacks,

PRIMARY SOURCE

In a speech to Congress after the 9/11 attacks, Bush addressed Muslims everywhere. Note that the term *Allah* used in the speech is an Arabic word Muslims use to refer to God.

I also want to speak tonight directly to Muslims throughout the world. We respect your faith. It's practiced freely by many millions of Americans and by millions more in countries that America counts as friends. Its teachings are good and peaceful, and those who commit evil in the name of Allah blaspheme [insult] the name of Allah. The terrorists are traitors to their own faith, trying, in effect, to hijack Islam itself. The enemy of America is not our many Muslim friends. It is not our many Arab friends. Our enemy is a radical network of terrorists and every government that supports them.

—from George W. Bush's presidential address to Congress, September 20, 2001

a Sikh gas station owner in Arizona, who had just donated $75 to help 9/11 victims, was shot by a man who had announced his intention to kill Muslims.

Following September 11, the Bush administration embraced the idea of taking pre-emptive, or preventive, military action against countries that harbored or actively supported terrorist groups. In a nationally broadcast speech before Congress 10 days after the attacks, Bush promised a "war on terror." Addressing the leaders of the Taliban, he made a non-negotiable demand: "Deliver to United States authorities all the leaders of al Qaeda who hide in your land." Bush went on to say that if the Taliban refused to hand over the terrorists, the Islamic group would "share in their fate." The president soon took steps to make good on this threat.

HISTORICAL THINKING

1. **READING CHECK** How did foreign and domestic policies change after the 9/11 attacks?

2. **MAKE INFERENCES** Al Qaeda chose its targets for their symbolic value. What do you think the World Trade Center symbolized?

3. **FORM AND SUPPORT OPINIONS** Does the Patriot Act protect U.S. citizens or violate their civil liberties? Research both arguments to formulate a response.

4. **MAKE CONNECTIONS** How do the events leading up to and following 9/11 relate to the U.S. Middle East policy at the time? Use information from this chapter and other sources to explain.

THE WAR ON TERROR

It was a high-stakes game of hide-and-seek. Osama bin Laden, leader of al Qaeda, was believed to be hiding out somewhere in the mountains of Afghanistan. The U.S. government was determined to find him.

WAR AGAINST THE TALIBAN

Less than a month after September 11, President Bush put his war on terror in motion. The first phase of the war focused on the Southwest Asian country of Afghanistan, which, as you know, was largely controlled by the Taliban. Since the mid-1990s, the group had instituted policies based on a strict interpretation of *shari'a*, or Islamic law, over the Afghani people. These laws enforced the unequal treatment of women and harsh punishments for crimes such as theft. When the Taliban refused to hand over suspected terrorists—and, in particular, Osama bin Laden—the United States initiated Operation Enduring Freedom on October 7, 2001.

The war began with U.S. and British air strikes launched against Taliban and al Qaeda targets in Afghanistan. Within weeks, both the United States and Britain also began sending ground troops to Afghanistan. Soon, other countries, including France and Germany, joined the coalition, while other allies provided intelligence and the use of their military bases. These nations believed the United States had the right to strike those who had supported and sheltered the 9/11 terrorists. By December, the multinational coalition had driven the Taliban out of power. U.S. intelligence services then began an exhaustive but unsuccessful search for bin Laden.

Afghanistan held democratic elections and passed a new constitution, but fighting in the country continued. Taliban insurgents, or rebels, reorganized and took up arms against the coalition forces. More troops went to fight in Afghanistan as the war dragged on and crossed into neighboring Pakistan. Finally, in May 2011, the U.S. military located bin Laden in a compound in Pakistan and killed the al Qaeda leader. Major U.S. combat operations in Afghanistan officially ended in December 2014. It became the longest war the United States had ever fought.

WAR IN IRAQ

While U.S. troops were engaged in Afghanistan, the Bush administration also focused its efforts on Iraq and ousting its brutal president, Saddam Hussein. The Bush administration claimed that Hussein's regime was linked to al Qaeda. Officials also believed Iraq possessed weapons of mass destruction (WMD)

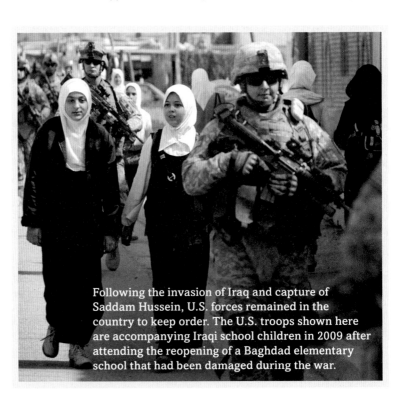

Following the invasion of Iraq and capture of Saddam Hussein, U.S. forces remained in the country to keep order. The U.S. troops shown here are accompanying Iraqi school children in 2009 after attending the reopening of a Baghdad elementary school that had been damaged during the war.

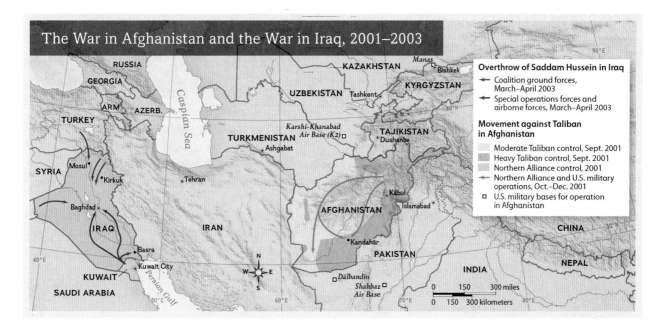

The War in Afghanistan and the War in Iraq, 2001–2003

Overthrow of Saddam Hussein in Iraq
- ← Coalition ground forces, March–April 2003
- ← Special operations forces and airborne forces, March–April 2003

Movement against Taliban in Afghanistan
- Moderate Taliban control, Sept. 2001
- Heavy Taliban control, Sept. 2001
- Northern Alliance control, 2001
- ← Northern Alliance and U.S. military operations, Oct.–Dec. 2001
- □ U.S. military bases for operation in Afghanistan

that could be used against the United States. In November 2002, the United Nations demanded that Iraq allow weapons inspectors to search for WMD. The inspectors failed to find any such weapons, but the Bush administration remained skeptical. Vice President Cheney and other neocons didn't trust the Iraqi government. They had called for Hussein's elimination since the Persian Gulf War in 1990.

On March 19, 2003, coalition forces, again led by the United States and Britain, launched strikes against government and military targets in Iraq. This time, though, few other countries joined the coalition. Days later, ground troops invaded the country. Within a few weeks, they had defeated the Iraqi army and brought an end to Saddam Hussein's rule. Hussein himself went into hiding, but he was eventually captured, tried in an Iraqi court, and executed.

After Iraq's defeat, inspectors continued to search for WMD, but none were ever found. Further, no links were uncovered between Hussein's regime and al Qaeda. Many Americans became angry after learning the Bush administration had led the United States into war based on faulty intelligence.

Meanwhile, the United States and Britain occupied Iraq and began rebuilding the country and preparing its people for a democratic form of government. But democracy never really took hold in Iraq. Government corruption and a civil war between the country's two main religious groups, the Sunni Muslims and the Shi'ite Muslims, prevented Iraq from becoming the stable state the United States had envisioned.

The war in Iraq was a major issue in the 2004 presidential election. Bush faced a strong challenge from the Democratic Party's nominee, Senator John Kerry of Massachusetts. Bush won a narrow victory, but his second term got off to a rocky start. As the violence continued in Iraq and more American soldiers died, Bush's approval rating fell. It dropped even further following his mismanagement of the Hurricane Katrina relief effort in August 2005, when the storm flooded low-lying areas of New Orleans where the city's poor and minority populations lived. Tens of thousands of people were left stranded on the tops of buildings, and more than 1,500 died. These factors helped the Democrats gain control of both houses of Congress in the 2006 elections and allowed Democrat Nancy Pelosi of California to become the first female Speaker of the House.

In January 2007, President Bush announced plans for a **surge**, or quick increase, in the number of U.S. troops in Iraq to halt the ongoing fighting and restore security. The United States sent roughly 30,000 additional troops to Iraq, bringing total troop strength to about 170,000, but still the war continued. Soon, however, Bush was forced to shift his focus from Iraq to a crisis at home that threatened the United States with economic collapse.

HISTORICAL THINKING

1. **READING CHECK** What U.S. interests led to the war in Afghanistan?

2. **SYNTHESIZE** How did U.S. involvement in the wars in Afghanistan and Iraq demonstrate neoconservative views?

3. **INTERPRET MAPS** Why were some of the U.S. military bases for operations in Afghanistan located outside of that country?

NEW ORLEANS, LOUISIANA

Built in a bowl-shaped geographic depression, much of New Orleans lies below sea level. When Hurricane Katrina, the most destructive storm in U.S. history, struck the Gulf Coast on August 29, 2005, it sent a storm surge barreling toward the low-lying city. The floodwaters demolished New Orleans' ineffective levee system, flooding the streets and leaving most of the city underwater. Nearly 2,000 people died in the city and along the Gulf Coast, and more than 1 million lost their homes.

Stranded and desperate for aid that was slow to come, the people of New Orleans felt abandoned by President George W. Bush and the government agencies tasked with providing support during disasters. According to the *New York Times*, "New Orleans became a global symbol of American dysfunction and government negligence. At every level and in every duty, from engineering to social policy to basic logistics, there were revelations of malfunction and failure before, during and after Katrina."

CRITICAL VIEWING What does this 2015 photo of New Orleans' Lower Ninth Ward reveal about its recovery from Katrina and the neighborhood's relationship with the Mississippi River?

Fortunately, New Orleans has slowly rebounded. Neighborhoods destroyed by flooding, like the Lower Ninth Ward (opposite page), are being rebuilt, and billions of dollars in federal aid have funded new schools and hospitals, replacing some that were in dire need of an overhaul before Katrina even hit. Many residents have also returned—although local demographics have changed dramatically. In 2013, nearly 100,000 fewer African Americans lived in New Orleans than in 2000. Population shifts are common in port towns, but for a city challenged by racial and class inequalities throughout history, the fallout from Katrina has been especially hard to overcome.

While the economic and social impact of the hurricane may affect New Orleans long after the restoration of the city is complete, its music, culture, and character remain strong and dynamic. The bustling, vibrant French Quarter (shown below), filled with music and colorful historic buildings, celebrates the city's distinctive Creole culture and is as unique, diverse, and rich in history as ever. Hundreds of thousands of people flock to New Orleans' legendary Mardi Gras festivities, boosting the city's continued rebuilding efforts with tourism dollars and establishing New Orleans as an example of the strength and resilience of great American cities.

CRITICAL VIEWING On Bourbon Street in New Orleans' French Quarter, you might suddenly find yourself marching in a second line parade, made up of people who follow the band just to enjoy the music. What do you observe about the physical and human characteristics of the city from the photos in this lesson, and how might those characteristics have been impacted by Hurricane Katrina?

THE GREAT RECESSION

We all know that bubbles burst pretty quickly. In the first years of the 21st century, a housing bubble developed, fueled by the high demand for new homes. When the bubble burst, it had terrible consequences for the country's economy.

HOUSING MARKET RISE AND FALL

The housing market crash was many years in the making. Banks and other lenders had begun to adopt unwise economic policies and lending strategies—mostly related to home-buying—in the 1980s and 1990s. These practices continued into the first decade of the 2000s, setting the stage for the economic problems that developed in 2007, toward the end of George W. Bush's second term.

Owning a home is a big part of the American dream, but rates of homeownership are usually significantly lower among minorities and people with low incomes. Spurred by their own business interests and by affordable-housing goals established by the federal government, lenders took steps to increase the pool of potential home buyers. They relaxed down-payment and employment-history requirements and began to offer more **subprime mortgages**, or home loans to buyers with poor credit history. To entice people to buy, banks also offered loans with low initial interest rates, called adjustable-rate mortgages. After a certain period of time, though, the interest rates on these loans would be raised, increasing the borrowers' payments— often to amounts few could afford.

Although subprime mortgages were risky, banks felt comfortable offering them because they could sell many of the mortgages to two government-sponsored enterprises: Fannie Mae (the Federal National Mortgage Association) and Freddie Mac (the Federal Home Loan Mortgage Corporation). Wall Street investment banks bundled groups of mortgages into what they called "managed packages" and sold them on the international financial market as profitable but highly unstable investments. An **investment bank** is a financial institution that purchases and sells stocks and bonds and helps other companies raise capital and manage their assets.

As demand for housing increased, prices rose dramatically. The widespread belief was that rising prices would cause the real estate to increase significantly in value. But then the bubble burst in 2007, and housing prices fell. Increasing numbers of subprime mortgage holders found they could not afford their loan payments. To make matters worse, they could not sell their homes. There were too many homes up for sale at the same time, and demand was low. Housing prices tumbled. Many of these homes went into foreclosure—that is, the banks took possession of them because the buyers could no longer make their house payments. Millions of families lost their homes to foreclosure. The housing market crash triggered a severe recession that, because of globalization, spread quickly around the world. Japan and many countries in Europe were hit especially hard due to their strong financial and

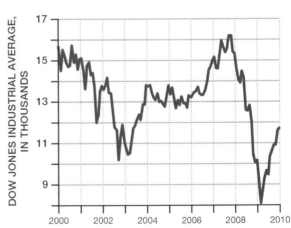

Stock Market Index, 2000–2010

DOW JONES INDUSTRIAL AVERAGE, IN THOUSANDS

Source: Federal Reserve Bank of St. Louis

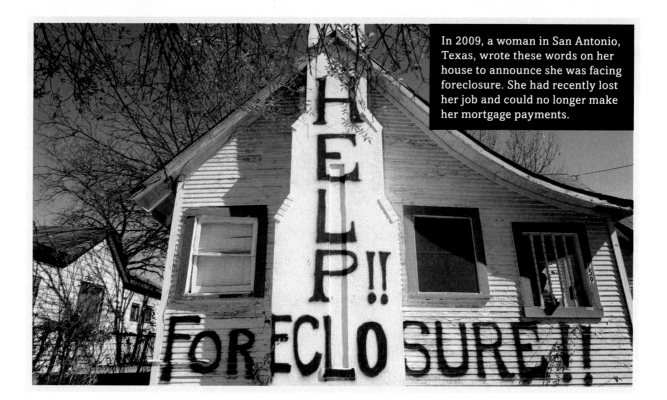

In 2009, a woman in San Antonio, Texas, wrote these words on her house to announce she was facing foreclosure. She had recently lost her job and could no longer make her mortgage payments.

trade ties to the United States. Echoing the Great Depression of the 1930s, the downturn became known as the **Great Recession**.

LOOMING ECONOMIC COLLAPSE

The Great Recession grew steadily worse in 2008. Many small banks went bankrupt, and other banks severely limited their lending. Wall Street financial institutions that had invested heavily in managed packages tied to subprime mortgages suffered huge losses. Plunging real estate prices meant that Americans could no longer finance major purchases such as cars by borrowing against the value of their homes. As a result, the recession also devastated the American automobile industry. A reduction in spending by wary consumers hurt many other industries, including those related to travel, construction, and home furnishings. Many companies were forced to make cuts, and millions of people lost their jobs. As government revenues shrank, cities and states also cut their budgets and laid off workers. As a result, the unemployment rate climbed to around 10 percent.

The terrible state of the economy raised the concern that some investment banks were "too big to fail." And if they did, many economists believed the country's entire financial system would collapse. But after some powerful firms did go bankrupt, Congress passed the Emergency Economic Stabilization Act (EESA) of 2008. This act, which Bush signed into

law in October, provided the Treasury Department with up to $700 billion to buy mortgages and other "troubled assets," or unstable investments, from banks. The legislation also established the Troubled Asset Relief Program (TARP), designed to help individuals and businesses secure bank loans. But much of this money was used to save large investment banks. The costly **bailout** spurred widespread resentment. Some critics blamed the recession on the greed of the banks and argued that the government should have let them fail.

While the bailout was being debated, the stock market plunged on September 29. The crash erased much of the savings ordinary Americans had been counting on. The recession affected almost everyone. And with so many people unemployed and in debt, the recession and the persistence of poverty became the main issues of the 2008 presidential election.

HISTORICAL THINKING

1. **READING CHECK** Why were lenders eager to offer subprime mortgages to potential buyers?

2. **FORM AND SUPPORT OPINIONS** Who do you think played the biggest role in the housing market crash: home buyers, mortgage companies, or investment banks? Explain.

3. **INTERPRET GRAPHS** How many points did the stock market plunge between 2008 and 2009?

THE ELECTION OF 2008

At the beginning of 2008, an atmosphere of gloom hung over the United States. The Great Recession was worsening, and the war in Iraq was dragging into its sixth year. As the 2008 election approached, many Americans were ready for a change.

HISTORY IS MADE

With George W. Bush's approval rating around 30 percent, Democrats felt they had the advantage over Republicans in 2008. The early Democratic favorite was New York senator Hillary Clinton, wife of former president William Clinton. She faced a strong challenge, however, from Senator **Barack Obama** of Illinois. A historic outcome was guaranteed. If Clinton won, she would become the first female nominated for president by a major party. If Obama won, he would become the first African American nominated by a major party.

On election night, November 4, 2008, President-elect Barack Obama delivered his victory speech before 240,000 people gathered in Chicago's Grant Park. With his family beside him, Obama said, "If there is anyone out there who still doubts that America is a place where all things are possible; who still wonders if the dream of our founders is alive in our time; who still questions the power of our democracy, tonight is your answer."

Ceding many of the most populated states to Clinton, Obama focused his efforts on winning as many convention delegates as he could in less populous states. The strategy worked. Even though Clinton won the popular vote in the primaries, Obama secured more convention delegates and thus became the Democratic nominee. For his vice-presidential running mate, he chose Senator Joe Biden of Delaware.

On the Republican side, the leading candidates in the primary elections included former Massachusetts governor Mitt Romney, former Arkansas governor Mike Huckabee, and Senator John McCain of Arizona. McCain eventually secured the Republican nomination, winning all but one of the final 21 primaries. For his running mate, he chose Alaska governor Sarah Palin, who was not well known outside her home state. Her controversial remarks, however, quickly brought her a great deal of public attention. The outspoken Palin drew large crowds to her campaign speeches.

Both presidential candidates addressed the financial crisis facing the nation. But while McCain seemed uncertain about what measures he would take, Obama's focused, confident response to the crisis won over many voters. With his message of hope and change, Obama won the election in November with relative ease and became the first African-American president in the country's 232-year history.

OBAMA'S PRIORITIES

One of Obama's top priorities as president was to lead the country out of the Great Recession. Soon after taking office, he signed into law the American Recovery and Reinvestment Act, which authorized $787 billion in government spending as an **economic stimulus**, or a measure aimed at promoting and enabling financial recovery and growth. The act was designed to save existing jobs and to create new ones. Obama and the federal government also bailed out the auto industry, providing $80 billion to the three major U.S. automakers to prevent them from failing. By the end of Obama's two terms as president, the unemployment rate had dropped to 5 percent, and the auto industry had recovered— and repaid the bailout money.

Initiating comprehensive health care reform was another of Obama's goals. Like Bill Clinton, the new president sought to extend the scope of the government and provide health care insurance for all U.S. citizens. In a speech to Congress in September 2009, he pointed out that more than 30 million Americans lacked health insurance. He also spoke of rising health care costs, unethical insurance practices and claims, and the heavy burden government programs such as Medicare and Medicaid put on taxpayers. The House passed a health care bill in early November, and on Christmas Eve, the Senate passed its own version of the bill.

A development in Massachusetts, however, threatened to doom the legislation. Scott Brown, a conservative Republican, won a special election to fill the vacancy created by the death of Democratic Senator Edward Kennedy, the brother of John and Robert Kennedy. By picking up a seat in the Senate, Republicans gained the ability to block legislation through the use of filibusters. Congressional Democrats, meanwhile, retreated from their commitment to health care reform.

Prospects for passage of the president's initiative seemed bleak. However, the determination of Speaker of the House Nancy Pelosi and Obama's persistence helped secure the passage of a health care package in March 2010. The bill that Obama signed into law was called the **Patient Protection and Affordable Care Act (PPACA)**, but it became popularly known as Obamacare. Although Republicans tried to block it through legislation and in the federal courts, the act had provided health insurance coverage to nearly 20 million Americans by 2016.

Passage of the Affordable Care Act and other progressive bills inspired the rise of a conservative populist movement known as the **Tea Party**. It was not a formal organization but rather a loose confederation of individuals and groups united by their antigovernment, antitax, and anti-immigration views. Most of those in the grassroots movement were Republicans who hoped to influence the direction of the party. Energized by the fast-growing Tea Party, Republicans gained 6 seats in the Senate and took control of the House by picking up 63 seats there in the 2010 midterm elections. As a result, Obama would face strong opposition to many of his initiatives during the rest of his time in office.

HISTORICAL THINKING

1. **READING CHECK** What factors helped Obama win the 2008 presidential election?

2. **EVALUATE** How did President Obama seek to address U.S. poverty and economic problems?

3. **MAKE INFERENCES** How do you think most members of the Tea Party felt about the economic stimulus legislation and Obamacare?

Barack Hussein Obama II 1961–
Michelle LaVaughn Robinson Obama 1964–

"If you were going to list the 100 most popular things that I have done as president, being married to Michelle Obama is number one."—Barack Obama

The president probably wasn't exaggerating. When Barack Obama's approval numbers were at their lowest in 2013—due to controversies over both his domestic and foreign policies—his wife, Michelle, still drew adoring crowds wherever she appeared in public. Initially reluctant to embrace Washington and relinquish her own career, Michelle threw her full support behind her husband when he first ran for the presidency. Barack and Michelle entered the White House as a team, but their path to its door could hardly have been more different.

EARLY LIVES

Barack Obama had an unsettled childhood. His parents met as students at the University of Hawaii. His mother, Ann Dunham, was a white American from Kansas. His father, Barack Obama, Sr., was a black African from Kenya. The couple divorced when their child was two years old, and Barack had very little contact with his father after that. His mother later married an Indonesian, and the family lived in Indonesia for a time. Then, when Barack was 10, his mother sent him to live with his grandparents in Hawaii. She eventually returned to Hawaii and her parents' home after divorcing her second husband. Barack's parents died when he was a young man: his father in 1982, his mother in 1995.

By contrast, Michelle Obama grew up in a stable, close-knit family. Her parents, Marian and Fraser

The Obamas stroll along the Colonnade of the White House in 2010. In his final speech, the president told his wife, "You have made me proud, and you have made the country proud."

Robinson, raised their children in a small house in Chicago. Michelle and her brother, Craig, slept in the living room and strung up a sheet to divide the space and provide some privacy. Education was a priority in the Robinson home, and both children did well in school. Michelle would later say, "I liked being smart. I thought being smart was cooler than anything in the world."

Barack Obama pursued education as well. After graduating from Columbia University in New York City and working as a community organizer in Chicago, he enrolled in Harvard Law School in 1988. After his first year at Harvard, he interned at a law firm in Chicago. His supervisor was Michelle Robinson, and he was immediately attracted to her. At first, Michelle resisted his advances, but eventually the pair fell in love. They married in 1992. Meanwhile, Barack completed his law degree at Harvard. Soon he decided to enter politics.

POTUS and FLOTUS

Running as a Democrat, Obama won an Illinois state senate seat in 1996. Then, in 2004, he was elected to the U.S. Senate representing Illinois. That same year he gave the keynote speech at the Democratic National Convention to endorse presidential candidate John Kerry. However, the speech is best remembered for launching Obama onto the national stage and paving the way for his successful presidential run in 2008. In his speech, he delivered a message of unity that resonated with many Americans: "There's not a liberal America and a conservative America—there's the United States of America. There's not a black America and white America and Latino America and Asian America; there's the United States of America." Because of speeches like this, Obama is considered one of the most powerful orators of his generation.

As you know, Obama faced a host of political issues when he became president of the United States (POTUS), but he also endured challenges to the legitimacy of his presidency. Members of the so-called "birther movement" claimed the president had not been born in the United States and so was ineligible to hold the office. Some birthers also asserted that Obama was Muslim, a charge designed to suggest the president was somehow "un-American." Despite concrete evidence disproving birther allegations—his Hawaiian birth certificate, for example—the contentions dogged Obama throughout his presidency.

While lies swirled during his presidency, Obama depended on Michelle—his "rock," as he called her—to help keep him grounded. Levelheaded and funny, Michelle was not part of what Obama called the

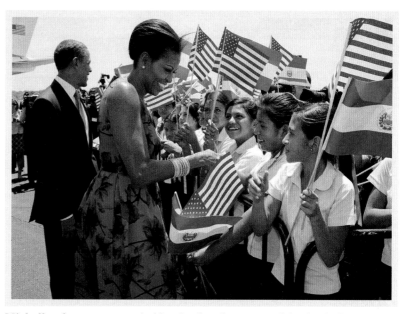

Michelle often accompanied her husband on state visits, including this trip in March 2011 to the Central American country of El Salvador. Here, shortly after their arrival in the country's capital of San Salvador, the POTUS and FLOTUS greet school children waving American flags.

"silliness of Washington." As first lady of the United States (FLOTUS), Michelle undertook an initiative called "Let's Move" to get kids to exercise and eat healthy foods. She and the POTUS also protected the privacy of their daughters, Malia and Sasha, as they grew up in the White House.

At the end of his second term, Obama delivered a farewell address in Chicago. After encouraging Americans not to take their democracy for granted, he said: "I do have one final ask of you as your president—the same thing I asked when you took a chance on me eight years ago. I am asking you to believe. Not in my ability to bring about change—but in yours." And in her final speech, Michelle Obama had a special message, based on her own experience, for young Americans: "Empower yourself with a good education. Then get out there and use that education to build a country worthy of your boundless promise. Lead by example with hope: never fear."

HISTORICAL THINKING

1. **READING CHECK** How did Barack and Michelle Obama's early lives differ?

2. **MAKE INFERENCES** What does Barack Obama's speech at the Democratic National Convention suggest about politics in the country at that time?

3. **EVALUATE** What false charges were leveled against President Obama, and what did those who alleged them hope to accomplish?

CIVIL RIGHTS IN THE 21ST CENTURY

To oppressed people around the world, the United States symbolizes freedom and opportunity. Some Americans, however, are still denied their full rights as citizens. The fight for these rights goes on.

ADVANCES AND SETBACKS FOR WOMEN

Women have made great strides in gaining their civil rights in recent decades. In business, some have broken through the "glass ceiling"—an invisible barrier of attitudes and prejudices that prevents women and minorities from advancing to high-level positions. In 1998, for instance, Meg Whitman was named president and chief executive officer of a major online auction company. The following year, Carly Fiorina was appointed head of a giant software and computer services company. Women continue to increase their representation in politics as well. Since 1990, about half of the 50 states have elected female governors. In 2007, as you've learned, Congresswoman Nancy Pelosi became the first female Speaker of the House. And in 2016, women held about 20 percent of the seats in Congress.

Nevertheless, little progress has been made in other areas. For decades, women have been demanding equal pay for equal work. They make up about half of the American workforce and are the main wage-earners in roughly 4 of every 10 families. Yet white women are paid about 20 percent less than men, African-American women earn around 35 percent less, and Latinas make about 40 percent less.

As more women have moved into the workforce, access to affordable, quality childcare has also posed a significant problem, especially for low-income women. Although traditional ideas about the family structure and gender roles in society are changing, the primary responsibility for taking care of children is still more often assumed by women than by men. This means that women face a greater challenge in balancing work and family commitments. In a 2015 survey, the majority of women said that being a working parent made it harder for them to advance in their career.

Legal access to abortion was one of the most divisive issues in the United States in the second half of the 20th century, and it remains so in the 21st. Despite being challenged many times, the landmark 1973 Supreme Court ruling in *Roe* v. *Wade*, which legalized abortion nationwide, has never been overturned. The Department of Health and Human Services, at both the federal and state levels, has provided family planning and pregnancy prevention and care programs. However, some lawmakers have tried to cut off the funding for such programs. In addition, many states have passed laws restricting women's access to abortion.

JUSTICE FOR ALL

As you know, the civil rights movement of the 1950s and 1960s achieved major breakthroughs in the struggle to end segregation and discrimination against African Americans. Activists have continued to fight for further progress, but full racial equality

THE AMERICANS WITH DISABILITIES ACT

In 1990, President George H.W. Bush signed the Americans with Disabilities Act (ADA), which granted civil rights for Americans with a disability, defined as "a physical or mental impairment that substantially limits one or more major life activities." Amendments were added to the ADA in 2008 that broadened the definition of "disability" and protected more people. Considered one of America's most comprehensive pieces of civil rights legislation, the ADA prevents discrimination in employment and guarantees access to public services, accommodations, and transportation.

has remained elusive. Many African Americans continue to live in segregated city neighborhoods where schools, housing, and public services are inferior. Public housing funded by federal and state governments has contributed to keeping these neighborhoods segregated. In addition, federal, state, and local laws that had ended in the late 20th century still impact racial segregation today. These laws include those that designated white neighborhoods as residential areas and black neighborhoods as commercial areas, and those that prohibited the sale of property to African Americans.

Crime rates in segregated neighborhoods are higher, and drug abuse and out-of-wedlock births are more prevalent. Prison sentences for many of the crimes are also longer. For example, blacks convicted of drug offenses serve substantially more time in prison than do whites convicted of similar offenses. Local law enforcement often focuses on urban areas and, in particular, low-income communities. Blacks are also less likely than whites to graduate from high school and attend college. They suffer higher rates of unemployment and poverty. And although their incomes have risen, their pay is still, on average, far below those of whites.

In the 21st century, increasing charges of local police brutality against African Americans have been leveled. In some instances, police officers have used excessive force and sometimes shot and killed unarmed African Americans. One of the most widely publicized of these shootings occurred in Ferguson, Missouri, a predominantly African-American suburb of St. Louis. As you read in the American Story on civil rights, in 2014, a white Ferguson police officer shot and killed an unarmed black teenager named Michael Brown, touching off angry protests that continued for weeks. Remember that in the wake of this event and others like it, **Black Lives Matter** rose to national prominence. Activists in the movement organized protests to draw attention to unwarranted police violence toward African Americans and to demand justice for victims of this violence.

The movement polarized Americans. Some people believed it increased the violence. At a Black Lives Matter protest in Dallas, Texas, in July 2016, a sniper opened fire on police officers, killing five of them. A week and a half later, another gunman ambushed and killed three police officers in Baton Rouge, Louisiana. The African-American men who carried out the shootings were killed by the police.

In December 2014, Black Lives Matter supporters marched in New York City to take part in a "Justice for All" demonstration. A similar march took place in Washington, D.C. Protesters called for an end to racial profiling and police violence and demanded change in the justice system.

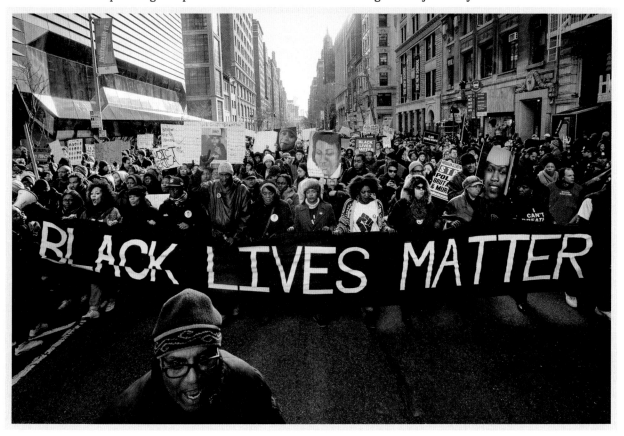

The incidents increased racial tensions and led some to accuse Black Lives Matter of encouraging violence against police. However, white citizens also directed racially charged violence against African Americans. In June 2015, Dylann Roof, a self-proclaimed white supremacist, massacred nine African-American worshipers attending a prayer meeting at the Emanuel African Methodist Episcopal Church in Charleston, South Carolina. When arrested, Roof claimed he wanted to start a race war.

SOCIAL LEGISLATION

In the American Story on civil rights, you also read about the LGBTQ community's struggle to achieve marriage equality. **Marriage equality** is the legal right of gays and lesbians to marry their partners and have the same privileges that married heterosexual couples enjoy. However, even after same-sex marriage became legal in 2015, other issues arose that challenged the LGBTQ community's civil rights. One of these involved the right of transgender individuals to use the public restroom that corresponds to their gender identity rather than their gender at birth. In 2013, California became the first state to pass a law guaranteeing this right for transgender students in public schools. The law allowed them to use whichever restroom they wanted. Over the next few years, other states passed similar laws. Then, in 2016, President Obama issued guidelines to all school districts in the country, detailing the steps they should take to make sure their students were not discriminated against. The guidelines included allowing students to use the restroom of their choice.

Supporters of transgender laws suffered a number of setbacks in 2017. The federal government withdrew its position on bathroom protections for transgender students and declared the issue was one of states' rights. Soon after this declaration, North Carolina, which had passed a bathroom bill in 2016, repealed the measure after just a year. In Virginia, a transgender high school student named Gavin Grimm sought to ban discrimination based on gender identity at his school, where separate facilities had

The U.S. Border Patrol apprehended these Central American women and children after they crossed the Rio Grande and illegally entered Texas in 2014. The law at that time required such refugees to appear at a hearing before an immigration judge.

been set aside for him alone. Grimm took his case to the Supreme Court, but it would not hear the case.

MEXICAN IMMIGRATION

American civil rights leaders in the 21st century consider immigration a civil rights issue because they claim that many immigrants are not given a chance to succeed economically—especially those from Mexico. By the 2000s, the status of Mexican Americans and Mexican immigrants became a national political discussion. The wave of immigration from Mexico—in particular, the estimated 6 million who entered the United States illegally, or without documentation—worried and angered many Americans. Some claimed these immigrants hurt the economy by taking jobs from American citizens, driving down wages, avoiding paying taxes, and putting pressure on social service agencies. Many economists dismissed such claims, stating that immigrants actually benefit the economy by taking jobs Americans don't want, paying their share of taxes, and buying products and services.

After the September 11, 2001, terrorist attacks, fear for national security led Congress to provide for increased border enforcement. And so, in 2006, President George W. Bush signed into law the Secure Fence Act, authorizing the construction of 700 miles of fencing along the U.S.-Mexico border. Still, the influx of immigrants continued. Meanwhile, a bill called the Development, Relief, and Education for Alien Minors (Dream) Act was proposed by a coalition of both Democrats and Republicans in 2001 but failed to pass. The act would have provided children brought to the United States illegally the opportunity to seek legal residency in the country. Proponents continued to urge passage of the act, but time and again the legislation died in Congress due to a lack of consensus, or agreement. Finally, President Obama created the **Deferred Action for Childhood Arrivals (DACA)** program in 2012. The program allowed the children of illegal immigrants who came to the United States before 2007 to defer deportation and apply for work permits in the country for a two-year renewable period. Applicants had to undergo a thorough background check every two years. In 2012, about 800,000 young people—who came to be known as "Dreamers"—enrolled in DACA.

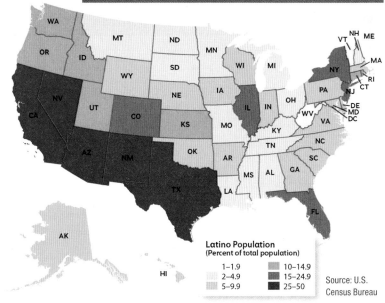

Percentages of Latino Populations, 2010

Latino Population
(Percent of total population)
- 1–1.9
- 2–4.9
- 5–9.9
- 10–14.9
- 15–24.9
- 25–50

Source: U.S. Census Bureau

Obama also sought to enforce border security. In 2014, he issued an executive order that strengthened the border between Texas and Mexico. However, the order also offered temporary legal status to millions of illegal immigrants. After issuing the order, Obama emphasized that the efforts of immigration authorities would be focused on punishing "Felons, not families. Criminals, not children. Gang members, not a mom who's working hard to provide for her kids." Republican leaders and many American citizens were angered by the order, claiming that the president's actions would lead to more illegal immigration, not less. During his presidency, Obama wrestled with many other issues that divided Americans, including one that scientists said affected the entire planet: climate change.

HISTORICAL THINKING

1. **READING CHECK** How have beliefs about women's roles changed, and how have they stayed the same?

2. **FORM AND SUPPORT OPINIONS** Since the civil rights movement, do you think African Americans have continued to make significant gains in achieving equality? Explain your answer.

3. **MAKE INFERENCES** Why do you think DACA applicants were called "Dreamers"?

4. **INTERPRET MAPS** Which states had the largest percentages of Latino populations in the country in 2010, and why do you think that was so?

ENVIRONMENTAL CHALLENGES

You've probably heard scientists and politicians talk about climate change and global warming. They're not the same thing, but the two terms are related. The vast majority of scientists believe global warming is driving climate change.

CLIMATE CHANGE OR GLOBAL WARMING?

Climate change is a gradual shift in Earth's overall climate. Throughout its history, Earth has undergone many climate changes. Global warming, on the other hand, is a term used by many scientists to describe the rapid warming of Earth's surface observed over the last century. These scientists believe this warming is causing climate change and is largely due to human activities. Experts say that the heavy use of nonrenewable fossil fuels, including coal, oil, and natural gas, contributes to rising temperatures. Burning these energy sources releases **greenhouse gases**, such as carbon dioxide and methane. The greenhouse gas emissions trap the sun's heat and warm Earth's surface, causing its temperature to rise. This warming is called the **greenhouse effect**.

Scientists believe the greenhouse effect began to significantly increase around 1750 with the Industrial Revolution, when people began burning more fossil fuels to run factories. Consumption of these fuels has intensified during the last 250 years or so, with the introduction of trains, automobiles, and airplanes. As

a result, since the beginning of the 20th century, the average temperature of the globe has risen 1.4° F. That number may seem small, but a change of even one degree is cause for concern.

Researchers believe they have already detected evidence of the impact of this seemingly small rise in global temperature. The vast ice sheets that cover Antarctica and Greenland, for example, have begun to melt and shrink. And oceans are warming, causing sea ice to melt and sea levels to rise. Scientists say these changes are already destroying habitats and changing ecosystems. Earth's warming may also result in more intense hurricanes and typhoons, which in turn could lead to high casualty tolls and damage to coastlines and other geographic features.

COMBATING GLOBAL WARMING

The majority of scientists believe that global warming will continue unless greenhouse gas emissions are dramatically reduced. Such a reduction will not be easy to achieve, however. In 1988, as concern about global warming was growing, the United Nations and the World Meteorological Organization took a step toward addressing the problem by creating the **Intergovernmental Panel on Climate Change (IPCC)**. The panel is made up of top climate experts from around the world. Its mission is to assess "the scientific, technical, and socioeconomic information relevant to understanding the scientific basis of risk of human-induced climate change." The panel's reports help world leaders set climate policies.

International action on climate change was undertaken in 1997 with a treaty called the **Kyoto Protocol**, which committed countries to reducing greenhouse gas emissions to below 1990 levels. Eventually, nearly 200 countries implemented the treaty, but the United States—which at the time was

AN INCONVENIENT TRUTH

In this 2006 documentary film, former vice president Al Gore seeks to educate the public about global warming. Throughout the film, Gore uses photos, graphs, and flow charts to make his case that global warming is real and caused by human activities. Stressing that global warming is a moral issue rather than a political one, Gore encourages his audience to take steps to combat it. He says, "We have everything that we need to reduce carbon emissions, everything but political will. But in America, the will to act is a renewable resource."

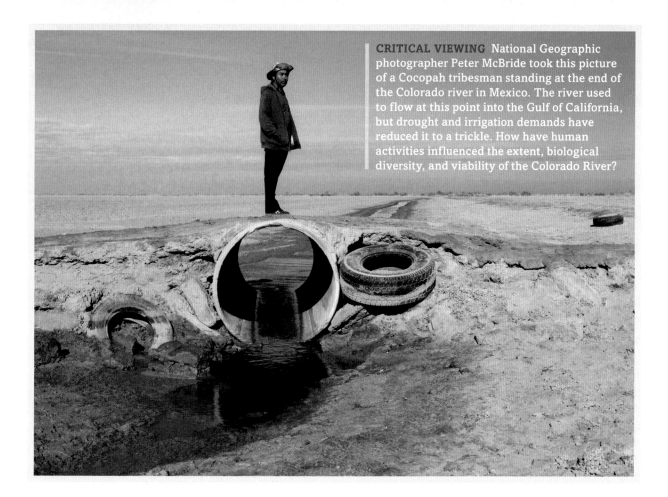

CRITICAL VIEWING National Geographic photographer Peter McBride took this picture of a Cocopah tribesman standing at the end of the Colorado river in Mexico. The river used to flow at this point into the Gulf of California, but drought and irrigation demands have reduced it to a trickle. How have human activities influenced the extent, biological diversity, and viability of the Colorado River?

the world's largest emitter of these gases—was not among them. President George W. Bush, who was skeptical about what caused climate change, opposed the treaty, arguing that it would "harm our economy and hurt our workers." He also objected to the fact that developing countries were exempt from complying with the treaty.

Since then, however, the United States has made efforts to reduce emissions by moving toward the use of more renewable energy sources, such as solar, wind, and geothermal power. In 2009, President Obama allocated billions of dollars to promote renewable and clean energy programs. In 2016, the country's first offshore wind farm was completed in the Atlantic Ocean near Rhode Island's Block Island, and federal agencies announced a plan to accelerate the development of additional offshore wind energy.

Obama and the U.S. Environmental Protection Agency unveiled the Clean Power Plan in 2015. The president called the plan "the single most important step America has ever taken in the fight against global climate change." It established nationwide standards aimed at greatly reducing carbon dioxide emissions from power plants.

In 2016, the United States made its most ambitious commitment to date toward dealing with global warming by ratifying the Kyoto Protocol's successor, a climate treaty known as the **Paris Agreement**. The goal of the agreement was to prevent Earth from warming more than 2°C, or approximately 3.6°F. Scientists believe that allowing Earth to warm beyond that limit would result in destructive and dangerous climate change. It remains to be seen whether the countries that signed the agreement will meet the pledge—and even if they do, whether their efforts will help protect the environment.

HISTORICAL THINKING

1. **READING CHECK** What controversies are associated with the concept of climate change and with environmental conservation?

2. **ANALYZE ENVIRONMENTAL CONCEPTS** How might our consumption of natural resources, such as coal, oil, and natural gas, influence the geographic extent, composition, biological diversity, and viability of natural systems?

3. **DESCRIBE** How has the human modification of landscapes contributed to global warming, and what types of environmental policies have resulted from it?

GLOBALIZING AMERICAN SOCIETY

Not so long ago, Americans found satisfying, well-paid work in automobile plants and steel factories. In our global economy, those days seem to be over.

ECONOMY AND ENVIRONMENT

Beginning in the 1970s and continuing through recent times, U.S. economic production has shifted away from heavy industry and toward the service sector. The **service sector** provides services rather than goods and includes jobs in banking, education, retail, and health care. This de-industrialization has altered the daily lives of many working- and middle-class American families.

Over the past 30 years, the gaps in income between top earners and middle- and working-class earners have become wider and more pronounced. Working-class wages have stagnated as higher-paying unionized blue collar factory jobs have been outsourced and replaced with minimum-wage paying service sector jobs. The stagnant or decreasing wealth of working- and middle-class Americans has been compounded by changes in tax structures and safety-net programs. It has also been amplified by higher costs for education, child care, and housing. In the early 2010s, a populist movement called Occupy Wall Street sought to bring attention to the income gap through protests and demonstrations. Some members of the movement tried to provide solutions through education or organization.

Part of the reason for the decreasing income of many Americans is globalization and the rise of **multinational corporations**, or companies that have offices and factories in multiple countries. In the first 15 years of the 21st century, the United States lost an estimated 5 million manufacturing jobs. Many of these jobs were outsourced to Mexico or China, where wages are much lower than in the United States.

In many ways, the globalized economy has had a broad, negative impact on the environment. The rapid industrialization of countries with lax environmental standards, such as China, Mexico, and India, has resulted in severe air, water, and soil pollution. Globalization has also led to a tremendous increase in deforestation. Around the world, people have cleared vast tracts of forest so that the land can be developed for homes or factories or used as farmland or pasture for grazing cattle. Because trees absorb carbon dioxide through the process of photosynthesis, the loss of immense numbers of them is a major factor in global warming. Even the use of large, standardized containers to ship goods all over the world has played a role in increasing the levels of carbon dioxide released into the air.

SOCIAL IMPACT

The way we work has become globalized, and so has the way we communicate, thanks to new media. **New media** refers to digital products and services that provide content through the Internet, and it has fundamentally changed the way people work, learn, interact socially, and spend their leisure time. Today, texting, instant messaging, and social networking allow fast and easy communication among people around the world. Much of this is done with smartphones, which combine communication and software applications into one handheld device. The technology enables people all over the world to connect with one another and share ideas and information instantaneously. As a result, culture sometimes forms around shared ideas or interests, rather than in a physical location.

Globalization has even affected what the world eats. Multinational fast food chains have popped up all over the planet. In just about any country, you can find some of your favorite restaurants. Some fear this will create a universal food culture, one in which people in all parts of the world eat the same things rather than the traditional foods of their culture. A universal food culture could result in the loss of regional cuisines and a wide range of crop varieties.

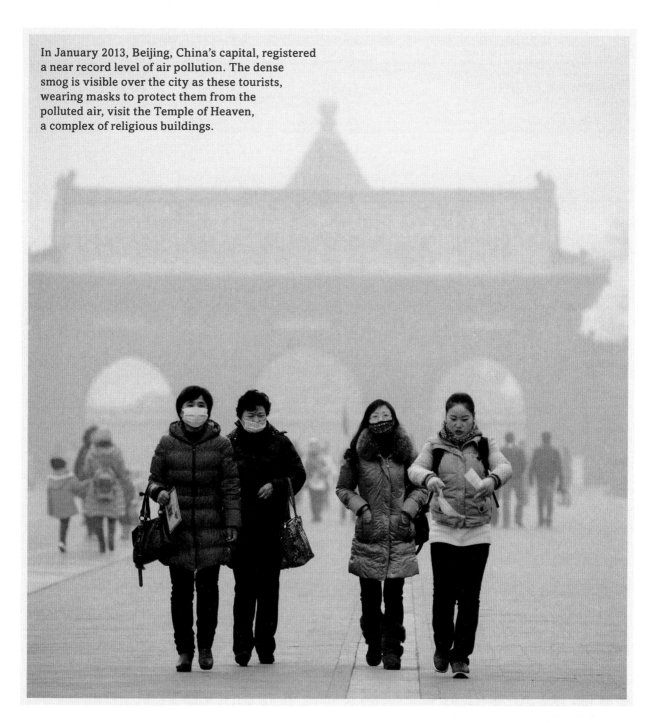

In January 2013, Beijing, China's capital, registered a near record level of air pollution. The dense smog is visible over the city as these tourists, wearing masks to protect them from the polluted air, visit the Temple of Heaven, a complex of religious buildings.

Foods from other countries are also imported to the United States. But because food production in some of these countries lacks safety standards, some Americans worry about possible contamination and public health issues. Many are also concerned about the explosion of genetically modified (GM) foods. **Genetically modified foods** are grown from plants that have been changed in a way that does not occur naturally, often through the introduction of a gene from a different organism. Plants are sometimes modified in this way to make them disease-resistant and to increase crop yields. While the practice is controversial, GM foods may provide a sustainable way to feed the world's population.

HISTORICAL THINKING

1. **READING CHECK** Why did the wealth gap between top earners and the majority of Americans grow between the 1970s and 2010s?

2. **ANALYZE ENVIRONMENTAL CONCEPTS** How have global industrialization and the modification of landscapes affected natural systems around the world?

3. **ANALYZE CAUSE AND EFFECT** How do you think the aspects of globalization discussed in the lesson might define U.S. environmental policy issues?

4. **EVALUATE** What are some of the advantages and disadvantages of new media?

USING FOOD WASTE TO FEED THE WORLD

"We want to catalyze a food-waste revolution one person, one town, one country at a time."—Tristram Stuart

Tristram Stuart has an ambitious goal in mind: to create a healthy planet with zero hunger. He knows it can be done. After all, one-third of all food produced on Earth ends up in landfills and garbage heaps, and the impact extends far beyond the dinner plate. Growing food and raising animals takes its toll on the land. Water and other precious resources are wasted, trees are cut down. Pollution is greatly increased. Stuart is starting a food-waste revolution, and he urges you to join him: to eat less, buy less, waste less.

^
National Geographic Explorer, author, and campaigner Tristram Stuart is also a renowned activist fighting against worldwide food waste at a farmer's market near you.

MAIN IDEA Tristram Stuart is creating a food-waste revolution to stop hunger and save our planet.

WASTED FOOD

For thousands of years, pigs have been fed what their human owners didn't need. In fact, National Geographic Explorer Tristram Stuart says that's the exact reason pigs were domesticated—to recycle human food scraps. So when Stuart raised pigs as a teen, he fed them leftovers from his school cafeteria and local stores—good-quality leftovers that would otherwise have been discarded. But most pigs are now fed soy, wheat, and corn—foods that could nourish hungry people.

Food waste is a big problem, and it goes well beyond the pigs. As Stuart attests, "About a third of all food globally is wasted in the same world in which 1 billion people don't have enough to eat." From the moment he became aware of this global epidemic, Stuart hasn't looked back. He has written two best-selling books and has spoken to people around the world about curbing food waste. "I'd seen bins full of food being trucked off to landfill sites. And I thought, surely there is something more sensible to do with food than waste it."

What's unfortunate is that the food being thrown away is not rotten at all—it's good, fresh food that may not meet strict grocery store regulations of size, shape, or appearance. Before Stuart intervened, as much as 40 percent of these "ugly" fruits and vegetables were left in fields to rot around the world—even in countries where millions suffer from malnutrition.

This immense waste extends beyond produce. Bakeries throw away the ends of bread, edible parts of animals are discarded, fish that are too small are dumped back in the sea. In addition, harvesting food that ends up getting thrown away creates pollution, wastes water, and greatly impacts the land.

ADDRESSING A GLOBAL ISSUE

To demonstrate just how much actually gets wasted, Stuart and his organization, Feedback, set up an initiative called Feeding the 5,000. Food that would have been discarded is cooked up by local chefs and served to the community—for free. This public event first took place in London in 2009 and has since expanded to many locations around the world, including New York City in 2016. The goal is to create awareness while calling on individuals and

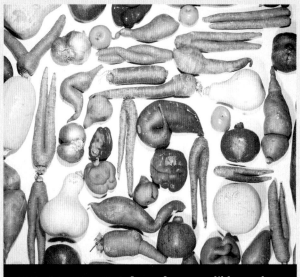

CRITICAL VIEWING Imperfect yet edible produce like this typically gets rejected by stores and consumers. Why might shoppers pass up food like this, contributing to potential food waste?

companies to strategize more responsible ways to waste less—whether by buying less or by planning better—so that everything purchased is consumed.

Food waste is a global issue, and its solution is one that we must all take part in. Stuart recognizes that it is nearly impossible to have a world with zero waste. However, he draws attention to the burdens that our wastefulness is putting on Earth. "We are reaching the ecological limits that our planet can bear. And when we chop down forests—as we are every day to grow more and more food—when we extract water from depleting water reserves, when we emit fossil fuel emissions in the quest to grow more and more food and then we throw away so much of it—we have to start thinking about what we can start saving."

Through his books and public campaigns—including Gleaning Network, which coordinates the collection of produce that would normally have been left to rot—Tristram Stuart is on a mission to end food waste and save the world, 5,000 meals at a time.

HISTORICAL THINKING

1. **READING CHECK** What do Tristram Stuart's Feeding the 5,000 events aim to accomplish and inspire among their participants?

2. **ANALYZE CAUSE AND EFFECT** How does a global issue like hunger relate to the physical and human characteristics of places and regions?

3. **DRAW CONCLUSIONS** How can you and your family contribute to Stuart's mission to end food waste and improve the world?

AN INTERCONNECTED WORLD

During the 20th century, the United States became so powerful and dominant that historians began speaking of "the American century." How will the country's role change in the interconnected world of the 21st century?

PURSUING A MORE HOPEFUL WORLD

During his terms in office, President Obama favored a diplomatic approach in shaping U.S. relations with other countries. In 2009, the president began working to improve relations with Cuba. The two countries had been at odds since Fidel Castro seized power in Cuba in 1959 and established a communist dictatorship there. Then in 2008, with his health declining, Castro handed over power to his brother Raúl, who soon began to institute reforms. The following year, Obama lifted restrictions on travel to Cuba from the United States, and in 2015, the two countries restored diplomatic ties. In March 2016, Obama became the first sitting U.S. president to visit Cuba in nearly 90 years. Fidel Castro died at the age of 90 in November 2016.

Obama also attempted to improve relations between the United States and Iran. The two countries had been adversaries since the 1979 Iranian Revolution, which brought an anti-American Muslim cleric, or religious leader, to power. Tensions between the two countries increased early in the 21st century when the United States accused Iran of secretly developing a nuclear weapons program. As a result, the United States imposed harsh economic sanctions on Iran. In 2012, diplomats representing the two nations began discussing the nuclear issue and struck a deal in 2015. Iran promised to use its nuclear research for peaceful purposes and to provide inspectors greater access to the program, and the United States agreed to lift its sanctions. Obama said the agreement marked "one more chapter in our

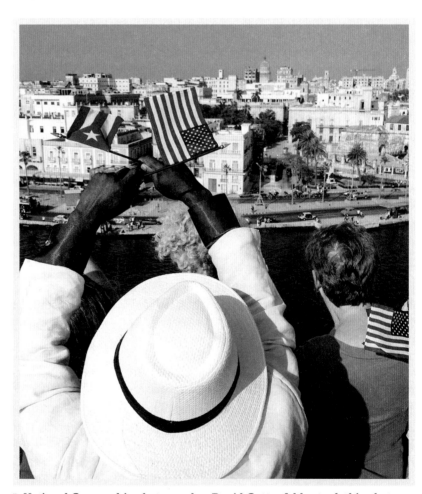

National Geographic photographer David Guttenfelder took this photo of a passenger waving the American and Cuban flags as his ship arrived in Havana, Cuba's capital, in May 2016. The vessel was one of the first cruise ships to travel from the United States to Cuba in decades.

pursuit of a safer, more helpful and more hopeful world." However, the deal drew criticism from many Americans who did not believe Iran would keep its promise.

GLOBAL TERRORISM

No deals can be made with terrorists, however. Terrorist groups have emerged as major threats to world security. Foremost among these groups is al Qaeda, which you have read about. During the ongoing war on terror, President Obama ordered American soldiers to hunt down and kill al Qaeda leaders, including Osama bin Laden, the mastermind of the September 11, 2001, terror attacks. Nevertheless, the group has survived and continues to commit acts of terrorism.

Another terrorist organization called the **Islamic State in Iraq and Syria (ISIS)** may be more dangerous than al Qaeda. ISIS is a militant extremist group that has taken control of large areas of Syria and Iraq. The group first gained widespread attention in early 2014 when its forces seized control of cities and territories in Iraq and Syria, which was being torn apart by a bloody civil war. In the summer of 2015, ISIS destroyed ancient buildings and artifacts in and around the Syrian city of Palmyra. Leaders of the group claimed the ancient Greek and Roman ruins had no value because they weren't made by Muslims. The rest of the world condemned this misguided attack on our common heritage. In the end, however, terrorism can't destroy the enduring record of human life on Earth.

Europe also came under attack. In November 2015, ISIS members carried out terrorist attacks in Paris, killing roughly 130 people. Five months later, the militant Muslim group claimed credit for killing more than 30 people in Brussels, Belgium. Some of the men who carried out the attacks were born and raised in Europe. ISIS and other terrorist groups have been able to recruit new members through the Internet. Their message of inclusion appeals to many economically disadvantaged and alienated people—particularly young men—around the world.

The fighting in Syria and Iraq displaced millions of people and contributed to a worldwide refugee crisis. By 2015, about 4 million refugees had fled from Syria. In the United States, the question of whether or not to accept Syrian refugees sparked intense debate. Opponents expressed fear that some of the refugees might carry out terrorist attacks on U.S. soil.

ISIS in Asia and Africa, 2017

Yet as the leader of the world's democratic societies, the United States has long been a magnet for people all over the world who yearn for a life of freedom and opportunity—and political stability. Under our democratic political system, the United States has achieved a level of freedom and economic prosperity that has made it a model for other nations.

As you know, Americans' rights and freedoms are the result of a carefully defined set of political principles embodied in the Constitution. But these freedoms are imperfect. For example, even though Americans elected an African-American president in 2008, poverty, incarceration, and lower life-expectancy rates continue to afflict communities of color at rates that are far higher than those of white communities. Still, the enduring significance of the United States lies in its free political system, its pluralistic nature, and its promise of opportunity. The country has demonstrated the strength and dynamism of a racially, religiously, and culturally diverse people. Our democratic political system depends on them—as educated citizens—to survive and prosper.

HISTORICAL THINKING

1. **READING CHECK** What steps did President Obama take to improve relations with Cuba?

2. **SYNTHESIZE** How has globalization helped encourage the rise of terrorist groups?

3. **FORM AND SUPPORT OPINIONS** Do you think the United States should pursue diplomatic solutions to problems with other countries, or use force? Explain your answer.

THE ELECTION OF 2016

In 2016, American voters were presented with two historic major party candidates. One was a wealthy businessman and TV personality with no political experience. The other was a woman with more than a decade of experience in both the legislative and executive branches. The outcome surprised many.

A POPULIST PREVAILS

As you have read, populists such as William Jennings Bryan and H. Ross Perot launched unsuccessful presidential bids in the past. In 2016, after emerging from a crowded field of candidates to become the Republican nominee, **Donald J. Trump** ran a populist campaign in which he claimed that only he, with his business expertise, could solve the nation's problems. Unlike his populist predecessors, Trump won the 2016 election, defeating Democratic nominee Hillary Rodham Clinton.

Clinton had served as U.S. Senator from New York and as President Obama's secretary of state. She was the wife of former president Bill Clinton. Trump, on the other hand, had never run for or served in public office prior to 2016. A real-estate developer and reality TV celebrity, Trump was extremely outspoken in his views, political and otherwise. He chose **Mike Pence**, the governor of Indiana, as his running mate. Clinton's running mate was Tim Kaine, a senator from Virginia.

While Clinton ran a traditional campaign based on issues and proposed solutions, Trump's populist campaign was fueled by his message: The interests of the United States should be placed above those of other nations. His lively rallies attracted the support of traditional Republicans and a number of independent voters. His promises to build a wall along the entire length of the border with Mexico, deport undocumented immigrants, and ban foreign Muslims from entering the United States appealed to nativists. He pledged to repeal the Affordable Care Act, put an end to NAFTA, and bring a quick end to international terrorism.

During the campaign, U.S. intelligence agencies and the Department of Justice gathered evidence that Russia had engaged in a complex, high-tech effort to disrupt the nation's electoral process. According to the Department of Homeland Security, Russian hackers attempted to access voter databases in 21 states and succeeded in breaching the systems of three states. There was no evidence these efforts affected the actual vote. Russian operatives also spread misinformation and negative "news" about Clinton on social media and hacked into both parties' email systems, leaking information that tended to be primarily unfavorable to Clinton and the Democrats.

On Election Day, Trump won a narrow majority of voters in a number of **swing states**, or states where

Donald Trump and Hillary Clinton take the stage for their second of three 2016 presidential debates. The debate was held at Washington University in St. Louis, Missouri, on October 9.

The 2016 Election

Donald J. Trump, Republican

Electoral Vote: 306 votes, 56.9%

Popular Vote: 62,979,636 votes, 46.1%

Hillary Rodham Clinton, Democrat

Electoral Vote: 232 votes, 43.1%

Popular Vote: 65,844,610 votes, 48.2%

Write-Ins & Others

7,804,213 votes, 5.7%

the election might go to either party. Even though almost 3 million more Americans cast their votes for Clinton, Trump won the electoral vote 306 to 232.

In 2017, Congress overwhelmingly voted to add new sanctions to those already in place to address Russia's cyberattacks during the election. The unusual election also raised suspicion that Trump's campaign had **colluded**, or conspired, with the Russians. Even though Trump denied the allegations, the Department of Justice appointed a special prosecutor, **Robert Mueller**, to investigate. As of early 2018, the investigation was still ongoing, while Trump declined to impose the additional sanctions on Russia. He claimed existing sanctions were effective enough.

TRUMP'S FIRST YEAR

Trump began his presidency by issuing a number of executive orders, including a controversial directive banning people from seven specific, primarily Muslim, nations from entering the United States. Enforcement of the order began as many travelers were already on their way to the United States, causing widespread confusion at airports. Federal courts initially blocked this order, stating it was unconstitutional. Parts of the ban were reinstated and the government issued new versions of the ban in 2017. These were also contested in federal courts.

Trump attempted to secure funding for the construction of a border wall early in his term, but Congress approved only a small portion of the money required. He also ordered a sharp increase in the number of **Immigration and Customs Enforcement (ICE)** agents, raising the deportation rate of undocumented immigrants. In September 2017, President Trump chose to end the DACA program,

handing Congress the responsibility of passing an act to protect the Dreamers. Otherwise, these immigrants would face deportation to the place of their birth. Trump also insisted that Congress should pass tougher immigration laws and fund the border wall.

Congress failed to repeal the Affordable Care Act, but a clause in its Tax Cuts and Jobs Act, which passed in December 2017, ended the individual mandate, an important funding measure requiring Americans not covered by an insurance plan to pay a tax. This threatened the affordability and the future of the ACA. The tax bill lowered tax rates for individuals temporarily and corporations permanently but took no steps to make up the lost revenue caused by these cuts. Some economists believed this new tax plan would result in a sharp rise to the national debt.

On the international front, Trump ended U.S. involvement in the **Trans-Pacific Partnership (TPP)**, a trade agreement with Asia. He also threatened to leave NAFTA, although he ultimately decided to try to renegotiate it. To the dismay of many nations, Trump withdrew the United States from the Paris Agreement on climate change. Together with his pledge to promote the use of coal and other fossil fuels, as opposed to cleaner energy sources, Trump's actions have put the United States at odds with many of its allies.

HISTORICAL THINKING

1. **READING CHECK** How did the swing states affect the 2016 election?

2. **DETERMINE WORD MEANINGS** How did Trump fit the definition of a populist?

3. **EVALUATE** How effective was Trump in meeting his campaign promises during his first year as president?

African migrants wait to be rescued from their rubber boat in the Mediterranean Sea in 2014. Many countries patrol international waters to rescue refugees and transfer them safely to shore in Europe, where more than 1.3 million applied for asylum in 2015 alone.

CRITICAL VIEWING Addario captured this photo of refugees from Egypt, Syria, and other countries being examined and treated by medical personnel from Doctors Without Borders. What role do relief organizations play in the refugee crisis? Do online research to support your answer.

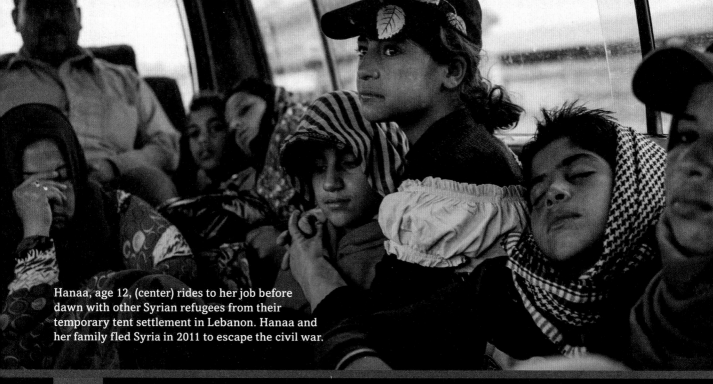

Hanaa, age 12, (center) rides to her job before dawn with other Syrian refugees from their temporary tent settlement in Lebanon. Hanaa and her family fled Syria in 2011 to escape the civil war.

4.7

THROUGH THE LENS

LYNSEY ADDARIO

After studying international relations in college, Lynsey Addario had a thought: photojournalism could be a marriage between international relations and art, telling stories with pictures. Fast-forward a few years, and Addario is one of National Geographic's most accomplished conflict photographers. Refugees are a primary focus of her work. "My philosophy has always been that I'm there for the people I'm covering," says Addario. "I'm just a messenger documenting whatever is going on and bringing their message to people in power who may be able to do something about it."

Children like Hanaa from the Bekaa Valley refugee settlement work alongside adults on Lebanese farms, picking cucumbers for about $5 per day. The education of many refugee children gets put on hold while they stay in settlement camps.

VOCABULARY

For each of the following vocabulary terms, write a sentence in which you use the term correctly.

1. globalization
   Globalization, which has allowed for the faster and freer flow of people and goods across national borders, has powerfully affected the United States.

2. free-enterprise zone

3. compassionate conservatism

4. neoconservative

5. rogue state

6. bailout

7. service sector

8. marriage equality

9. greenhouse gas

10. new media

READING STRATEGY
FORM AND SUPPORT OPINIONS

When you form an opinion, you determine and assess the importance and significance of an issue. Your opinion is your personal judgment, not a fact, so you should support your opinion with examples and facts. Use a chart like this one to form and support an opinion about issues in the 21st century. Then answer the question.

Example/Fact	Example/Fact	Example/Fact

Opinion

11. What do you think is the most critical issue facing the United States in the 21st century?

MAIN IDEAS

Answer the following questions. Support your answers with evidence from the chapter.

12. What was the Contract with America?
    LESSON 1.1

13. How did globalization affect U.S. manufacturing jobs during the 1990s?
    LESSON 1.2

14. How might bias have played into the outcome of the 2000 presidential election? **LESSON 2.1**

15. Why did President George W. Bush order the invasion of Iraq? **LESSON 2.3**

16. What impact did the Great Recession have on American industries and the employment rate?
    LESSON 3.1

17. What were Obama's priorities when he became president? **LESSON 3.2**

18. What evidence of global warming have scientists detected? **LESSON 4.2**

19. What are genetically modified foods?
    LESSON 4.3

20. Why were many voters surprised by the outcome of the 2016 election? **LESSON 4.6**

HISTORICAL THINKING

Answer the following questions. Support your answers with evidence from the chapter.

21. **COMPARE AND CONTRAST** Why is the United States more diverse now than it was in the middle of the 20th century?

22. **DRAW CONCLUSIONS** How have shifts in foreign policy and immigration affected America's national identity from the 1980s through recent times?

23. **MAKE INFERENCES** How do you think Muslims in the United States may have been regarded by some other Americans after September 11, 2001?

24. **EVALUATE** How has the role of the federal government—and especially the presidency—changed from the 1970s through more recent times?

25. **SYNTHESIZE** What does globalization mean, and how has it affected Americans?

26. **FORM AND SUPPORT OPINIONS** Do you think groups such as Black Lives Matter and Occupy Wall Street are ultimately effective? Why or why not?

27. **ANALYZE ENVIRONMENTAL CONCEPTS** How has deforestation affected the natural system of photosynthesis and increased global warming?

INTERPRET GRAPHS

Study the graphs below, which show the relative populations of ethnic groups in the United States between 1950 and 2010. Then answer the questions that follow.

U.S. Ethnic Population, 1950–2010

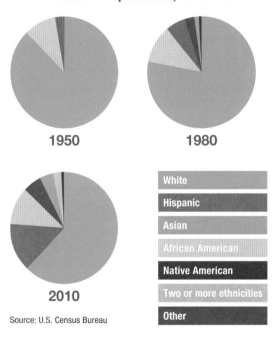

1950

1980

2010

White

Hispanic

Asian

African American

Native American

Two or more ethnicities

Other

Source: U.S. Census Bureau

28. How did the composition of the United States shift between 1950 and 1980?

29. What additional shifts occurred between 1980 and 2010?

ANALYZE SOURCES

In this excerpt from an address to the nation on immigration that President Obama delivered on November 20, 2014, he explains why he welcomes immigrants to the United States.

> My fellow Americans, we are and always will be a nation of immigrants. We were strangers once, too. And whether our forebears were strangers who crossed the Atlantic, or the Pacific, or the Rio Grande, we are here only because this country welcomed them in, and taught them that to be an American is about something more than what we look like, or what our last names are, or how we worship. What makes us Americans is our shared commitment to an ideal—that all of us are created equal, and all of us have the chance to make of our lives what we will.

30. What vision of the United States does Obama describe in his address?

CONNECT TO YOUR LIFE

31. **EXPLANATORY** Grassroots movements such as the Tea Party, Occupy Wall Street, and Black Lives Matter formed in the early 21st century. Why do you think such movements form, and why are people drawn to them? Write a paragraph in which you explain the connection between such groups and larger issues.

TIPS

- State the purpose of grassroots movements in a main idea statement.

- Describe the social, economic, and political factors that may be involved in the movements' formation.

- Explain what people who join the movements hope to get out of them.

- Use information from the chapter to help support your ideas.

- Conclude your paragraph with a sentence summarizing your ideas.

NATIONAL GEOGRAPHIC | CONNECTION

U.S. Climate Refugees Race Against Time

BY CAROLYN VAN HOUTEN

Adapted from "The First Official Climate Refugees in the U.S. Race Against Time," by Carolyn van Houten, news.nationalgeographic.com, May 2016

A shot rings out across what remains of Isle de Jean Charles as the sun drops behind the gnarled skeletons of what once were massive oak trees. Rifle in hand, Howard Brunet, 14, looks down at the rabbit he shot. His sister Juliette, 13, leaps down the stairs to retrieve the body. Next comes rabbit stew. It's a normal evening at the Brunet household. The kids are tough. The water forces them to be.

Since 1955, the Isle de Jean Charles band of the Biloxi-Chitimacha-Choctaw tribe has lost 98 percent of its land to the encroaching Gulf waters. Of the 22,400-acre island that stood at that time, only several hundred acres remain. The island is located deep in the southern bayous of Louisiana, about 15 miles (24 kilometers) from the Gulf of Mexico. As the land has eroded, the tribe's identity, food, and culture have slowly eroded with it.

In response, in 2016, the Department of Housing and Urban Development awarded the tribe $48 million to relocate. But moving isn't a simple solution. The tribe is receiving funding, but the fight to save their culture is not over. The federal grant will help save the tribe from the eroding landscape, but addressing the effects of cultural erosion is far more difficult. "Once our island goes, the core of our tribe is lost," says Chantel Comardelle, the deputy tribal chief's daughter. "We've lost our whole culture—that is what is on the line."

For generations, the Biloxi-Chitimacha-Choctaw have sustained themselves off of the island's natural resources. But today, residents say the land loss has made that untenable. The land is disappearing into the Gulf of Mexico because of a combination of coastal erosion, rising sea levels, lack of soil renewal, and shifting soil due to dredging for oil and gas pipeline placement. The soil that remains is nutrient depleted due to saltwater intrusion enabled by eroding marshes.

As the effects of climate change transform coastal communities around the world, the people of Isle de Jean Charles will be only 60 of the estimated 200 million people globally who could be displaced by 2050 because of climate change.

The only way into or out of Isle de Jean Charles is on Island Road. In 1953, the year the road was built, land and thick marsh surrounded the road. But erosion is eating away at it. Every time a strong storm heads toward the island, residents have to decide whether they will evacuate. Once the storm arrives, the road out of the island will be flooded. The water has overtaken many structures that were once a part of the community. Many of the tribal members who remain on the island can't afford any other option. Most of those who have left the island remain in the tribe but are spread throughout Louisiana.

"The tribe has physically and culturally been torn apart with the scattering of members," states the resettlement proposal submitted to the Department of Housing and Urban Development. "A new settlement offers an opportunity for the tribe to rebuild their homes and secure their culture on safe ground."

The resettlement proposal argues that Isle de Jean Charles is an excellent test case for deciding how to best relocate people threatened by climate change. The plan aims to move families to a culturally appropriate community. Because tribe members have already lost so much of their land and their tribal heritage to the water, relocation is crucial not just for their personal safety but also for the longevity of their culture and traditions.

"At one time, water was our life, and now it's almost our enemy because it is driving us out, but it still gives us life," Comardelle says. "It's a double-edged sword. It's our life and our death."

For more from National Geographic, check out "Shell Shock" online.

UNIT INQUIRY: Conduct Oral History Interviews

In this unit, you learned about recent American history, which includes events that your parents and many adults alive today have witnessed. You'll have no difficulty finding adults who watched TV news reports of the Watergate investigation and of President Nixon leaving the White House after resigning. These adults have vivid, emotional memories of the 9/11 terrorist attacks on the World Trade Center in New York City and on the Pentagon in Washington, D.C. What can you learn from these adults about the way average Americans reacted to such events? How has life in the United States changed over the course of their lives? What is better about life today? What is worse?

ASSIGNMENT

Conduct oral history interviews with people who were adults in the years after 1970. Find out how they and other Americans reacted to major events that occurred between 1970 and 2010. Be prepared to present your findings to the class.

Plan Review the major events covered in this unit and choose a couple to focus on. Compose a list of questions about those events and about changes in the United States between 1970 and 2010. You might use a graphic organizer to help you formulate your questions or to take notes. Then identify three adults and ask if they would be willing to be interviewed.

Produce Decide if you want to take notes during your interviews or make an audio or video recording. Then schedule and conduct the interviews. In your notes or at the beginning of a recording, be sure to identify each interviewee by name and birthdate.

Present Share your interviews with the class. You might consider one of these options:

- If you made audio or video recordings, write and record an introduction to them. Then edit your recordings and produce a final version to play for the class. (You have created your own primary source.)

- Either transcribe your interviews or write a summary of what you learned from them and distribute your written account to the class.

- Prepare and deliver an oral report of the highlights of your interviews.

Check out the History Notebook for another oral history project.

Who? _____

What? _____

Where? _____

When? _____

Why? _____
_____
_____

NATIONAL GEOGRAPHIC | LEARNING FRAMEWORK ACTIVITIES

Create a History Game

ATTITUDE Curiosity

SKILLS Communication, Collaboration

Perhaps you've played board games that require you to answer questions about literature, science, popular culture, and other subjects. Work with a partner to create a history game modeled on such board games. Using the information in this unit, write 50 questions that can be answered in a word or phrase. Use the questions as the basis of a board game, and play the game with a group of classmates. As an alternative, create a crossword puzzle using key words and names from the unit. Give the puzzle to a classmate to solve.

Form a Political Party

ATTITUDES Responsibility, Empowerment

KNOWLEDGE Our Human Story

You've read about the beliefs, policies, and agendas of a number of American political parties during this course. Now form a political party that represents your beliefs. Decide on a name for your party, and write a platform and a description of the programs you'd like to institute. Tell how your party differs from the Democratic and Republican parties in the United States. Identify groups of Americans who would be likely to support your party. Give an oral presentation in which you describe your political party to the class.

AMERICA THROUGH THE DECADES

A picture is worth a thousand words. You've probably heard that before—now see if you agree. Each image in this photo essay represents one of the decades you have learned about, starting with the 1900s and going through the 2010s. Test your knowledge of American history by identifying each photograph according to its decade while you consider the historical events, important people, and social and cultural movements you have studied.

STUDENT REFERENCES

CITIZENSHIP HANDBOOK ...R2

U.S. CAPITOL, WASHINGTON, D.C.

CITIZENSHIP
HANDBOOK

This Citizenship Handbook will help you take an in-depth look at our nation's two most important documents: the Declaration of Independence and the U.S. Constitution, which contains the Bill of Rights. The handbook includes notes to help you understand the formal language and difficult concepts contained in the more than 225-year-old documents. The handbook also provides background information and historical context to better help you understand the thinking and motivations of the Framers. At the end of the handbook, you will read about citizenship and the rights and responsibilities that come along with it. You will also find out how you can build and practice citizenship skills in the classroom and beyond.

The Charters of Freedom, as the Declaration of Independence, U.S. Constitution, and Bill of Rights are collectively known, are housed in the National Archives Museum in Washington, D.C.

DECLARATION OF INDEPENDENCE

Introduction

The American colonists wrote the Declaration of Independence in 1776 to formally call for their separation and independence from Britain. Up until then, colonists who were legally British citizens had lived in relative isolation from the king's authority and largely governed themselves. They modeled their colonial governments on Parliament, Britain's legislative body, by forming elected assemblies similar to the House of Commons. Unlike the British legislature, however, elected officials in colonial assemblies lived in the areas they represented. The colonists believed representatives who lived among those who elected them would better understand local interests and needs. At the same time, the colonists had no representatives in Parliament and sometimes resented what they felt to be unfair treatment by Britain.

ROAD TO REVOLUTION

The colonists' resentment grew after they fought alongside the British in the French and Indian War. The Americans had joined the fight so they could expand their settlements westward into Native American territory. But after Britain won the war against the French in 1763, British king George III wanted to keep the peace. To do so, he believed he needed to limit contact between the Native Americans and the colonists. As a result, the British government issued the Proclamation of 1763, which stated that colonists could not settle west of the Appalachian Mountains.

Furthermore, victory in the war had left Britain with overwhelming debt. To help pay it down, King George introduced a series of taxes against the colonists, including customs duties, the Sugar Act of 1764, and the Stamp Act of 1765, which taxed printed materials in the colonies. The Stamp Act was the first direct tax Britain had imposed on the colonists.

The American colonists protested the British legislation with shouts of "No taxation without representation." Angry colonists formed secret groups, such as the Sons of Liberty, and organized demonstrations and boycotts of British goods. As tensions continued to rise, violence erupted. In 1770, the Boston Massacre resulted in the deaths of five colonists at the hands of British soldiers. Three years later, colonists demonstrated their anger over a law on the sale of tea by staging the Boston Tea Party in Boston Harbor.

Finally, in 1775, feelings on both sides reached the boiling point. After British troops learned the colonists had stored weapons in Concord, Massachusetts, the troops marched to the town.

Colonial militiamen rushed to face down the British soldiers in nearby Lexington. During the clash, shots rang out at what would later be called the first battle of the American Revolution.

BREAK WITH BRITAIN

American leaders had convened a conference of colonial delegates to respond to British taxation in 1774. At this conference in Philadelphia, known as the First Continental Congress, some delegates had called for the colonies to separate completely from Britain. By 1775, the Second Continental Congress was prepared to take action. The Congress raised an army and formed a committee to write an official document to declare independence from Britain. This "Committee of Five" included Thomas Jefferson, John Adams, Benjamin Franklin, Roger Sherman, and Robert Livingston. Jefferson, the youngest member of the Congress at 33, was chosen to be the principal author of the Declaration of Independence.

Enlightenment thinkers such as John Locke influenced the ideological origins of the American Revolution and the Declaration. Locke argued that humans were born free and equal and that a leader could rule only with the consent of the people. Jefferson was also inspired by the Enlightenment philosophy of unalienable, or natural, rights. The Founding Fathers considered that these rights were "divinely bestowed," or God-given. Unalienable rights, Jefferson insisted, could not be taken away.

On July 4, 1776, the delegates to the Continental Congress adopted the Declaration of Independence. In 1782, seven years after the first shots were fired, the American Revolution officially ended. The American colonists had fought for and won their freedom and independence from Britain.

THE DECLARATION OF INDEPENDENCE

IN CONGRESS, JULY 4, 1776

The Declaration of Independence begins by explaining why the colonists at the Continental Congress want to break away from Britain and become independent. Jefferson and the other Founding Fathers believed it was necessary to explain their motivations.

The unanimous Declaration of the thirteen united States of America, When in the Course of human events, it becomes necessary for one people to dissolve the political bands which have connected them with another, and to assume among the powers of the earth, the separate and equal station to which the Laws of Nature and of Nature's God entitle them, a decent respect to the opinions of mankind requires that they should declare the causes which impel them to the separation.

Here, Jefferson states that people are born equal and have rights, including life, liberty, and the pursuit of happiness, that should be safeguarded by the government. John Locke's idea that government is based on the consent of the people is also established. Jefferson claims that when a government takes away the people's rights, they must overthrow the government. But this step should not be taken lightly.

We hold these truths to be self-evident, that all men are created equal, that they are endowed by their Creator with certain unalienable Rights, that among these are Life, Liberty and the pursuit of Happiness.—That to secure these rights, Governments are instituted among Men, deriving their just powers from the consent of the governed, —That whenever any Form of Government becomes destructive of these ends, it is the Right of the People to alter or to abolish it, and to institute new Government, laying its foundation on such principles and organizing its powers in such form, as to them shall seem most likely to effect their Safety and Happiness. Prudence, indeed, will dictate that Governments long established should not be changed for light and transient causes; and accordingly all experience hath shown, that mankind are more disposed to suffer, while evils are sufferable, than to right themselves by abolishing the forms to which they are accustomed. But when a long train of abuses and usurpations, pursuing invariably the same Object evinces a design to reduce them under absolute Despotism, it is their right, it is their duty, to throw off such Government, and to provide new Guards for their future security.—Such has been the patient sufferance of these Colonies; and such is now the necessity which constrains them to alter their former Systems of Government. The history of the present King of Great Britain is a history of repeated injuries and usurpations, all having in direct object the establishment of an absolute Tyranny over these States. To prove this, let Facts be submitted to a candid world.

The Declaration goes on to explain exactly what King George has done by listing the colonists' grievances against him.

HISTORICAL THINKING Why do you think Jefferson lists the colonists' grievances against the king?

The king has failed to approve or disapprove laws needed by the people. At the time, colonial laws had to be approved by the king. Britain could also veto colonial legislation.

He has refused his Assent to Laws, the most wholesome and necessary for the public good.

He has forbidden his Governors to pass Laws of immediate and pressing importance, unless suspended in their operation till his Assent should be obtained; and when so suspended, he has utterly neglected to attend to them. He has refused to pass other Laws for the accommodation of large districts of people, unless those people would relinquish the right of Representation in the Legislature, a right inestimable to them and formidable to tyrants only.

The king has ordered his royal governors to block colonial legislation. He has claimed that unless people in the colonies give up the right to have representatives in their own government in America, he will not pass laws those people need.

He has called together legislative bodies at places unusual, uncomfortable, and distant from the depository of their public Records, for the sole purpose of fatiguing them into compliance with his measures.

The king has dissolved many colonial lawmaking bodies because they stood up against laws that threatened the rights of Americans. By 1776, many colonial assemblies had been dissolved.

He has dissolved Representative Houses repeatedly, for opposing with manly firmness his invasions on the rights of the people.

He has refused for a long time, after such dissolutions, to cause others to be elected; whereby the Legislative powers, incapable of Annihilation, have returned to the People at large for their exercise; the State remaining in the mean time exposed to all the dangers of invasion from without, and convulsions within.

After the legislatures were dissolved, some colonies had no laws to protect them. Citizens often created special assemblies to maintain some form of government.

He has endeavored to prevent the population of these States; for that purpose obstructing the Laws for Naturalization of Foreigners; refusing to pass others to encourage their migrations hither, and raising the conditions of new Appropriations of Lands.

He has obstructed the Administration of Justice, by refusing his Assent to Laws for establishing Judiciary powers.

Some colonial legislatures tried to establish courts, but the king dismissed them. Judges have also been appointed who favored the king's interests.

He has made Judges dependent on his Will alone, for the tenure of their offices, and the amount and payment of their salaries.

He has erected a multitude of New Offices, and sent hither swarms of Officers to harass our people, and eat out their substance.

He has kept among us, in times of peace, Standing Armies without the Consent of our legislatures.

The king has sent soldiers to America without the consent of colonial legislatures. He has made his soldiers more powerful than the colonists.

He has affected to render the Military independent of and superior to the Civil power.

DECLARATION OF INDEPENDENCE

The king has allowed others to pass and enforce new laws in the colonies that the colonists consider to be invalid ("pretended").

He has combined with others to subject us to a jurisdiction foreign to our constitution, and unacknowledged by our laws; giving his Assent to their Acts of pretended Legislation:

For Quartering large bodies of armed troops among us:

For protecting them, by a mock Trial, from punishment for any Murders which they should commit on the Inhabitants of these States:

For cutting off our Trade with all parts of the world:

For imposing Taxes on us without our Consent:

For depriving us in many cases, of the benefits of Trial by Jury:

For transporting us beyond Seas to be tried for pretended offences

Jefferson introduces acts of Parliament the colonists considered to be unconstitutional. For example:

• making sure that soldiers who kill colonists are given a fake trial and not held accountable for murder;

• stopping American trade with other countries;

• taxing without permission;

• often refusing the right of trial by jury;

• sending colonists far away to be tried in courts for things they have not done;

• abolishing laws made by the colonies;

• stopping lawmaking groups in America and declaring that only the British government can make laws for people in America.

For abolishing the free System of English Laws in a neighboring Province, establishing therein an Arbitrary government, and enlarging its Boundaries so as to render it at once an example and fit instrument for introducing the same absolute rule into these Colonies:

For taking away our Charters, abolishing our most valuable Laws, and altering fundamentally the Forms of our Governments:

For suspending our own Legislatures, and declaring themselves invested with power to legislate for us in all cases whatsoever.

The colonists claim that the king has essentially given up, or abdicated, his power to govern them. Now the king refuses to protect the colonists and has started a war against them.

He has abdicated Government here, by declaring us out of his Protection and waging War against us.

He has plundered our seas, ravaged our Coasts, burnt our towns, and destroyed the lives of our people.

The king is sending foreign soldiers to fight and suppress the colonists—an act of barbarism unworthy of a civilized nation.

He is at this time transporting large Armies of foreign Mercenaries to complete the works of death, desolation and tyranny, already begun with circumstances of Cruelty & perfidy scarcely paralleled in the most barbarous ages, and totally unworthy the Head of a civilized nation.

He has constrained our fellow Citizens taken Captive on the high Seas to bear Arms against their Country, to become the executioners of their friends and Brethren, or to fall themselves by their Hands.

He has excited domestic insurrections amongst us, and has endeavored to bring on the inhabitants of our frontiers, the merciless Indian Savages, whose known rule of warfare, is an undistinguished destruction of all ages, sexes and conditions.

He has encouraged Native Americans to attack the colonists.

In every stage of these Oppressions We have Petitioned for Redress in the most humble terms: Our repeated Petitions have been answered only by repeated injury. A Prince whose character is thus marked by every act which may define a Tyrant, is unfit to be the ruler of a free people.

The colonists have repeatedly and unsuccessfully made formal requests for this behavior to stop. However, the king has become a tyrant.

Nor have We been wanting in attentions to our British brethren. We have warned them from time to time of attempts by their legislature to extend an unwarrantable jurisdiction over us. We have reminded them of the circumstances of our emigration and settlement here. We have appealed to their native justice and magnanimity, and we have conjured them by the ties of our common kindred to disavow these usurpations, which, would inevitably interrupt our connections and correspondence. They too have been deaf to the voice of justice and of consanguinity. We must, therefore, acquiesce in the necessity, which denounces our Separation, and hold them, as we hold the rest of mankind, Enemies in War, in Peace Friends.

We have appealed to the British people, pointing out the injustice of our treatment and our close ties to them ("consanguinity"), but they have ignored us. We have no choice but to consider them our enemies.

We, therefore, the Representatives of the united States of America, in General Congress, Assembled, appealing to the Supreme Judge of the world for the rectitude of our intentions, do, in the Name, and by Authority of the good People of these Colonies, solemnly publish and declare, That these United Colonies are, and of Right ought to be Free and Independent States; that they are Absolved from all Allegiance to the British Crown, and that all political connection between them and the State of Great Britain, is and ought to be totally dissolved; and that as Free and Independent States, they have full Power to levy War, conclude Peace, contract Alliances, establish Commerce, and to do all other Acts and Things which Independent States may of right do. And for the support of this Declaration, with a firm reliance on the protection of divine Providence, we mutually pledge to each other our Lives, our Fortunes and our sacred Honor.

For all these reasons, Jefferson declares that the United Colonies are free and independent states with no further allegiance to Britain. As free and independent states, they can declare war, negotiate peace, make agreements to work with other countries, establish commerce, and participate in all other activities allowed by independent states.

CONSTITUTION OF THE UNITED STATES

Introduction

In 1787, delegates at the Constitutional Convention in Philadelphia engaged in debates for four months as they drafted the Constitution. Among other issues, they debated how the legislative branch should work, how to elect the president, and whether enslaved people should be included in a state's population. After agreeing to a series of compromises, the Framers signed the U.S. Constitution, which, once ratified by the states, became the supreme law of the land in the United States. Considering the size and complexity of the United States today and its position as a world power, the U.S. Constitution is relatively simple. It consists of a Preamble, 7 articles, and currently 27 amendments, based on the 7 key principles below.

1. Popular Sovereignty The phrase means "the authority of the people." The opening words of the Constitution, "We the people" emphasize the idea that people together create a social contract in which they agree to be governed. Government authority is derived from the citizens, who determine how much power the government should have and what rules it must follow.

2. Republicanism This is a form of representational democracy. In a republic, citizens have the power and authority to make decisions as to how they are governed. Citizens elect representatives, who then have the power to write and enforce laws. Most Americans today use the terms *representational democracy* and *republicanism* interchangeably.

3. Federalism Federalism is a form of government in which power is distributed among several levels of government. A federalist system features a strong central government, but states do not lose all rights and power. States pursue and protect their interests as they see fit, while working together as a nation. In American federalism, the federal government's powers are enumerated, or listed. The states have powers that are reserved, or unwritten. Concurrent powers are powers shared by the federal and state governments.

4. Separation of Powers To reduce the potential for abuse of power and to prevent one branch from becoming too powerful, government was divided into three branches: the legislative branch (Congress, consisting of the Senate and the House of Representatives), which writes laws; the executive branch (led by the president), which enforces the laws written by Congress; and the judicial branch (made up of the U.S. Supreme Court and additional lower federal courts), which interprets and applies the laws.

5. Checks and Balances Each branch of government can limit the power of the other two, and so exert a check on the others. As with separation of powers, a system of checks and balances helps prevent one branch from becoming too powerful. For example, the judicial branch can declare a law passed by Congress to be unconstitutional. The president can veto a law written by Congress, but Congress can override the presidential veto. Congress can confirm or reject the president's nominees to his cabinet and the courts.

6. Limited Government The Articles of Confederation had failed because the central government was too weak and lacked the authority to tax or regulate trade. A stronger, stable central government was needed, but the Framers did not want to give it too much power or allow it to abuse what power it had. This principle of limited government seeks to protect rights by restricting the power of the central government. The Framers explicitly outlined the powers of the federal government and set additional limits in the Bill of Rights and other amendments.

7. Individual Rights Amendments, or changes and additions to the Constitution, have become part of the U.S. Constitution over the years. The first 10 amendments, known as the Bill of Rights, were added in 1791. These amendments address many individual rights, such as freedom of religion, freedom of speech, and the right to trial by jury. The Bill of Rights also places strict limits on what the federal government can do. The Bill of Rights was added to the Constitution to ensure that all states would accept and ratify this new plan for government.

THE CONSTITUTION

Preamble We the People of the United States, in Order to form a more perfect Union, establish Justice, insure domestic Tranquility, provide for the common defense, promote the general Welfare, and secure the Blessings of Liberty to ourselves and our Posterity, do ordain and establish this Constitution for the United States of America.

Article I Legislative Branch

SECTION 1: CONGRESS

All legislative Powers herein granted shall be vested in a Congress of the United States, which shall consist of a Senate and House of Representatives.

SECTION 2: THE HOUSE OF REPRESENTATIVES

1 The House of Representatives shall be composed of Members chosen every second Year by the People of the several States, and the Electors in each State shall have the Qualifications requisite for Electors of the most numerous Branch of the State Legislature.

2 No Person shall be a Representative who shall not have attained to the Age of twenty five Years, and been seven Years a Citizen of the United States, and who shall not, when elected, be an Inhabitant of that State in which he shall be chosen.

3 *Representatives and direct Taxes shall be apportioned among the several States which may be included within this Union, according to their respective Numbers, which shall be determined by adding to the whole Number of free Persons, including those bound to Service for a Term of Years, and excluding Indians not taxed, three fifths of all other Persons.* The actual Enumeration shall be made within three Years after the first Meeting of the Congress of the United States, and within every subsequent Term of ten Years, in such Manner as they shall by Law direct. The Number of Representatives shall not exceed one for every thirty Thousand, but each State shall have at Least one Representative; and until such enumeration shall be made, the State of New Hampshire shall be entitled to choose three, Massachusetts eight, Rhode-Island and Providence Plantations one, Connecticut five, New-York six, New Jersey four, Pennsylvania eight, Delaware one, Maryland six, Virginia ten, North Carolina five, South Carolina five, and Georgia three.

4 When vacancies happen in the Representation from any State, the Executive Authority thereof shall issue Writs of Election to fill such Vacancies.

5 The House of Representatives shall choose their Speaker and other Officers; and shall have the sole Power of Impeachment.

PREAMBLE
UNDERSTANDING THE CONSTITUTION The Preamble to the Constitution outlines the goals of the U.S. government. With the words, "We the People," the Framers establish that the Constitution's authority comes from the people of the United States.

ARTICLE I
UNDERSTANDING THE CONSTITUTION Sections 1 and 2 The Constitution establishes a bicameral, or two-house, Congress. Representatives in the House serve the members of their districts and are elected every two years. The House provides one of the most direct and effective ways in which citizens can participate in the political process. Constituents can contact their representatives by mail, email, and phone, and by visiting their lawmakers' offices. Representatives must be responsive to the needs and interests of their constituents or face losing their seats.

UNDERSTANDING THE CONSTITUTION 2.3 The number of seats in the House is based on each state's population. Populous states have more representatives than less-populated states.

HISTORICAL THINKING How might changes in a state's population affect its political power?

UNDERSTANDING THE CONSTITUTION 2.5 The Speaker of the House presides over sessions of Congress, but the Constitution says nothing about further responsibilities of the Speaker or those of other officers.

UNDERSTANDING THE CONSTITUTION 3.1 Section 3 describes the Senate. Originally, state legislatures chose the senators. With the passage of the 17th Amendment in 1913, senators were elected by voters, which made the process of selecting these federal officials more democratic.

UNDERSTANDING THE CONSTITUTION 3.2 The terms of senators are staggered. One class of senators begins its term in an even-numbered year, the next class begins two years later, and the third class begins two years after that.

As president of the Senate, Vice President Richard Cheney is shown here presiding over the daily proceedings of the legislative body in 2009. House Speaker Nancy Pelosi stands beside him.

UNDERSTANDING THE CONSTITUTION 3.6 The House of Representatives has the power to bring impeachment charges, but the Senate conducts the trial and determines if the individual is to be removed from office. The president, vice president, all civil officers, and federal judges can be impeached.

HISTORICAL THINKING Do you think the power to impeach is essential to the system of checks and balances? Explain why or why not.

SECTION 3: THE SENATE

1 The Senate of the United States shall be composed of two Senators from each State, chosen by the Legislature thereof, for six Years; and each Senator shall have one Vote.

2 Immediately after they shall be assembled in Consequence of the first Election, they shall be divided as equally as may be into three Classes. The Seats of the Senators of the first Class shall be vacated at the Expiration of the second Year, of the second Class at the Expiration of the fourth Year, and of the third Class at the Expiration of the sixth Year, so that one third may be chosen every second Year; and if Vacancies happen by Resignation, or otherwise, during the Recess of the Legislature of any State, the Executive thereof may make temporary Appointments until the next Meeting of the Legislature, which shall then fill such Vacancies.

3 No Person shall be a Senator who shall not have attained to the Age of thirty Years, and been nine Years a Citizen of the United States, and who shall not, when elected, be an Inhabitant of that State for which he shall be chosen.

4 The Vice President of the United States shall be President of the Senate, but shall have no Vote, unless they be equally divided.

5 The Senate shall choose their other Officers, and also a President pro tempore, in the Absence of the Vice President, or when he shall exercise the Office of President of the United States.

6 The Senate shall have the sole Power to try all Impeachments. When sitting for that Purpose, they shall be on Oath or Affirmation. When the President of the United States is tried, the Chief Justice shall preside: And no Person shall be convicted without the Concurrence of two thirds of the Members present.

7 Judgment in Cases of Impeachment shall not extend further than to removal from Office, and disqualification to hold and enjoy any Office of honor, Trust or Profit under the United States: but the Party convicted shall nevertheless be liable and subject to Indictment, Trial, Judgment and Punishment, according to Law.

SECTION 4: CONGRESSIONAL ELECTIONS

1 The Times, Places and Manner of holding Elections for Senators and Representatives, shall be prescribed in each State by the Legislature thereof; but the Congress may at any time by Law make or alter such Regulations, except as to the Places of choosing Senators.

2 *The Congress shall assemble at least once in every Year, and such Meeting shall be on the first Monday in December, unless they shall by Law appoint a different Day.*

SECTION 5: RULES

1 Each House shall be the Judge of the Elections, Returns and Qualifications of its own Members, and a Majority of each shall constitute a Quorum to do Business; but a smaller Number may adjourn from day to day, and may be authorized to compel the Attendance of absent Members, in such Manner, and under such Penalties as each House may provide.

2 Each House may determine the Rules of its Proceedings, punish its Members for disorderly Behavior, and, with the Concurrence of two thirds, expel a Member.

3 Each House shall keep a Journal of its Proceedings, and from time to time publish the same, excepting such Parts as may in their Judgment require Secrecy; and the Yeas and Nays of the Members of either House on any question shall, at the Desire of one fifth of those Present, be entered on the Journal.

4 Neither House, during the Session of Congress, shall, without the Consent of the other, adjourn for more than three days, nor to any other Place than that in which the two Houses shall be sitting.

SECTION 6: PAY AND EXPENSES

1 The Senators and Representatives shall receive a Compensation for their Services, to be ascertained by Law, and paid out of the Treasury of the United States. They shall in all Cases, except Treason, Felony and Breach of the Peace, be privileged from Arrest during their Attendance at the Session of their respective Houses, and in going to and returning from the same; and for any Speech or Debate in either House, they shall not be questioned in any other Place.

2 No Senator or Representative shall, during the Time for which he was elected, be appointed to any civil Office under the Authority of the United States, which shall have been created, or the Emoluments whereof shall have been increased during such time; and no Person holding any Office under the United States, shall be a Member of either House during his Continuance in Office.

SECTION 7: PASSING LAWS

1 All Bills for raising Revenue shall originate in the House of Representatives; but the Senate may propose or concur with Amendments as on other Bills.

2 Every Bill which shall have passed the House of Representatives and the Senate, shall, before it become a Law, be presented to the President of the United States; If he approve he shall sign it, but if not he shall return it, with his Objections to that House in which it shall have originated, who shall enter the Objections at large on their Journal, and proceed to reconsider it. If after such Reconsideration two thirds of that House shall agree to pass the Bill, it shall be sent, together with

UNDERSTANDING THE CONSTITUTION Section 5 This section empowers each house of Congress to make its own rules. The House and Senate have developed different rules over the years that affect how they operate. For example, only members of the Senate can engage in a filibuster, which allows a senator to speak in the chamber as long as it may take to block a piece of legislation. The filibuster gives the minority party in the Senate some power to block or slow the passage of legislation.

UNDERSTANDING THE CONSTITUTION 7.2

How a Bill Becomes a Law in Congress

A The first step in the legislative process is the introduction of a bill to Congress. Although anyone can write a bill or request certain legislation, only a member of Congress can introduce a bill.

B The bill is debated and usually revised. Congressional committees and their subcommittees are the key groups that move bills through the process. Once out of committee, the full House or Senate votes on the bill.

C Each house reviews, debates, and amends the bill, often resulting in different versions. A committee made up of members from both houses then works to resolve differences and create one final version of the bill.

D If both houses accept the compromises, Congress sends the bill to the president.

E The president can either sign the bill—and it becomes law—or veto the bill, which prevents the bill from becoming law. Congress can, however, override the veto with a vote of two-thirds of the members present in each house, in which case the bill becomes law.

the Objections, to the other House, by which it shall likewise be reconsidered, and if approved by two thirds of that House, it shall become a Law. But in all such Cases the Votes of both Houses shall be determined by yeas and Nays, and the Names of the Persons voting for and against the Bill shall be entered on the Journal of each House respectively. If any Bill shall not be returned by the President within ten Days (Sundays excepted) after it shall have been presented to him, the Same shall be a Law, in like Manner as if he had signed it, unless the Congress by their Adjournment prevent its Return, in which Case it shall not be a Law.

3 Every Order, Resolution, or Vote to which the Concurrence of the Senate and House of Representatives may be necessary (except on a question of Adjournment) shall be presented to the President of the United States; and before the Same shall take Effect, shall be approved by him, or being disapproved by him, shall be re-passed by two thirds of the Senate and House of Representatives, according to the Rules and Limitations prescribed in the Case of a Bill.

SECTION 8: POWERS OF CONGRESS

1 The Congress shall have Power To lay and collect Taxes, Duties, Imposts and Excises, to pay the Debts and provide for the common Defense and general Welfare of the United States; but all Duties, Imposts and Excises shall be uniform throughout the United States;

2 To borrow Money on the credit of the United States;

3 To regulate Commerce with foreign Nations, and among the several States, and with the Indian Tribes;

4 To establish an uniform Rule of Naturalization, and uniform Laws on the subject of Bankruptcies throughout the United States;

5 To coin Money, regulate the Value thereof, and of foreign Coin, and fix the Standard of Weights and Measures;

6 To provide for the Punishment of counterfeiting the Securities and current Coin of the United States;

7 To establish Post Offices and post Roads;

8 To promote the Progress of Science and useful Arts, by securing for limited Times to Authors and Inventors the exclusive Right to their respective Writings and Discoveries;

9 To constitute Tribunals inferior to the supreme Court;

10 To define and punish Piracies and Felonies committed on the high Seas, and Offences against the Law of Nations;

11 To declare War, grant Letters of Marque and Reprisal, and make Rules concerning Captures on Land and Water;

UNDERSTANDING THE CONSTITUTION Section 8 Section 8 begins with a list of 17 enumerated powers given to Congress, which cannot be modified by the states. The Constitution includes little detail as to how some of these powers should be carried out. The authority to collect taxes—perhaps the most important power granted to Congress—is often referred to as the "power of the purse."

HISTORICAL THINKING Why do you think the authority to collect taxes is an important power?

UNDERSTANDING THE CONSTITUTION 8.3 This clause is generally referred to as the commerce clause. Regulating commerce with foreign nations means controlling imports and exports to provide maximum benefit for U.S. businesses and consumers. Regulating commerce between states means maintaining a common market among the states, with no restrictions.

HISTORICAL THINKING Without the commerce clause, what kinds of disputes might arise between states engaged in interstate commerce?

12 To raise and support Armies, but no Appropriation of Money to that Use shall be for a longer Term than two Years;

13 To provide and maintain a Navy;

14 To make Rules for the Government and Regulation of the land and naval Forces;

15 To provide for calling forth the Militia to execute the Laws of the Union, suppress Insurrections and repel Invasions;

16 To provide for organizing, arming, and disciplining, the Militia, and for governing such Part of them as may be employed in the Service of the United States, reserving to the States respectively, the Appointment of the Officers, and the Authority of training the Militia according to the discipline prescribed by Congress;

17 To exercise exclusive Legislation in all Cases whatsoever, over such District (not exceeding ten Miles square) as may, by Cession of particular States, and the Acceptance of Congress, become the Seat of the Government of the United States, and to exercise like Authority over all Places purchased by the Consent of the Legislature of the State in which the Same shall be, for the Erection of Forts, Magazines, Arsenals, dock-Yards, and other needful Buildings;—And

18 To make all Laws which shall be necessary and proper for carrying into Execution the foregoing Powers, and all other Powers vested by this Constitution in the Government of the United States, or in any Department or Officer thereof.

SECTION 9: RESTRICTIONS ON CONGRESS

1 *The Migration or Importation of such Persons as any of the States now existing shall think proper to admit, shall not be prohibited by the Congress prior to the Year one thousand eight hundred and eight, but a Tax or duty may be imposed on such Importation, not exceeding ten dollars for each Person.*

2 The Privilege of the Writ of Habeas Corpus shall not be suspended, unless when in Cases of Rebellion or Invasion the public Safety may require it.

3 No Bill of Attainder or ex post facto Law shall be passed.

4 *No Capitation, or other direct, Tax shall be laid, unless in Proportion to the Census or Enumeration herein before directed to be taken.*

5 No Tax or Duty shall be laid on Articles exported from any State.

6 No Preference shall be given by any Regulation of Commerce or Revenue to the Ports of one State over those of another: nor shall Vessels bound to, or from, one State, be obliged to enter, clear, or pay Duties in another.

UNDERSTANDING THE CONSTITUTION Section 8 The last of the enumerated powers has been referred to as the "elastic clause" or the "necessary and proper clause." This clause allows Congress "to make all laws which shall be necessary and proper" to support its duties and responsibilities. It is called the "elastic clause" because it allows Congress to expand its authority and handle issues that might not have been anticipated. The vagueness of the phrase "necessary and proper" has created controversy. The Supreme Court provided some guidance in the 1819 case of *McCulloch* v. *Maryland* when it gave Congress wide authority to determine what is "necessary and proper."

UNDERSTANDING THE CONSTITUTION Section 9 Section 9 lists specific areas in which Congress may not legislate.

UNDERSTANDING THE CONSTITUTION 9.4 A "capitation tax" is a tax charged on an individual.

UNDERSTANDING THE CONSTITUTION 9.6 Congress cannot pass laws that favor commerce in one state over that in another. For example, Congress cannot pass a law requiring shipping to go through a particular state's port.

7 No Money shall be drawn from the Treasury, but in Consequence of Appropriations made by Law; and a regular Statement and Account of the Receipts and Expenditures of all public Money shall be published from time to time.

8 No Title of Nobility shall be granted by the United States: And no Person holding any Office of Profit or Trust under them, shall, without the Consent of the Congress, accept of any present, Emolument, Office, or Title, of any kind whatever, from any King, Prince, or foreign State.

SECTION 10: LIMITING THE AUTHORITY OF STATES

1 No State shall enter into any Treaty, Alliance, or Confederation; grant Letters of Marque and Reprisal; coin Money; emit Bills of Credit; make any Thing but gold and silver Coin a Tender in Payment of Debts; pass any Bill of Attainder, ex post facto Law, or Law impairing the Obligation of Contracts, or grant any Title of Nobility.

2 No State shall, without the Consent of the Congress, lay any Imposts or Duties on Imports or Exports, except what may be absolutely necessary for executing its inspection Laws: and the net Produce of all Duties and Imposts, laid by any State on Imports or Exports, shall be for the Use of the Treasury of the United States; and all such Laws shall be subject to the Revision and Control of the Congress.

3 No State shall, without the Consent of Congress, lay any Duty of Tonnage, keep Troops, or Ships of War in time of Peace, enter into any Agreement or Compact with another State, or with a foreign Power, or engage in War, unless actually invaded, or in such imminent Danger as will not admit of delay.

Article II The Executive Branch

SECTION 1: ELECTING THE PRESIDENT

1 The executive Power shall be vested in a President of the United States of America. He shall hold his Office during the Term of four Years, and, together with the Vice President, chosen for the same Term, be elected, as follows

2 Each State shall appoint, in such Manner as the Legislature thereof may direct, a Number of Electors, equal to the whole Number of Senators and Representatives to which the State may be entitled in the Congress: but no Senator or Representative, or Person holding an Office of Trust or Profit under the United States, shall be appointed an Elector.

3 *The Electors shall meet in their respective States, and vote by Ballot for two Persons, of whom one at least shall not be an Inhabitant of the same State with themselves. And they shall make a List of all the Persons voted for, and of the Number of Votes for each; which List they shall sign and certify, and transmit sealed to the Seat of the Government of the United States, directed to the President of the Senate. The President of the Senate shall, in the Presence of the Senate and House of Representatives, open all the Certificates, and the Votes shall then be counted. The Person having the greatest Number of Votes shall be the President, if such Number be a Majority of the whole Number of Electors appointed; and if there be more than one who have such Majority, and have an equal Number of Votes, then the House of Representatives shall immediately choose by Ballot one of them for President; and if no Person have a Majority, then from the five highest on the List the said House shall in like Manner choose the President. But in choosing the President, the Votes shall be taken by States, the Representation from each State having one Vote; A quorum for this Purpose shall consist of a Member or Members from two thirds of the States, and a Majority of all the States shall be necessary to a Choice. In every Case, after the Choice of the President, the Person having the greatest Number of Votes of the Electors shall be the Vice President. But if there should remain two or more who have equal Votes, the Senate shall choose from them by Ballot the Vice President.*

4 The Congress may determine the Time of choosing the Electors, and the Day on which they shall give their Votes; which Day shall be the same throughout the United States.

5 No Person except a natural born Citizen, or a Citizen of the United States, at the time of the Adoption of this Constitution, shall be eligible to the Office of President; neither shall any Person be eligible to that Office who shall not have attained to the Age of thirty five Years, and been fourteen Years a Resident within the United States.

6 *In Case of the Removal of the President from Office, or of his Death, Resignation, or Inability to discharge the Powers and Duties of the said Office, the Same shall devolve on the Vice President, and the Congress may by Law provide for the Case of Removal, Death, Resignation or Inability, both of the President and Vice President, declaring what Officer shall then act as President, and such Officer shall act accordingly, until the Disability be removed, or a President shall be elected.*

7 The President shall, at stated Times, receive for his Services, a Compensation, which shall neither be increased nor diminished during the Period for which he shall have been elected, and he shall not receive within that Period any other Emolument from the United States, or any of them.

UNDERSTANDING THE CONSTITUTION 1.3 The italicized text refers to how vice presidents were originally elected. In the presidential election of 1800, the top two vote winners (Thomas Jefferson and Aaron Burr) received the same number of electoral votes. The selection of the president then fell to the House of Representatives, which chose Jefferson. Today, presidential candidates select a running mate, and voters cast a single vote for the entire ticket.

UNDERSTANDING THE CONSTITUTION 1.4 The Constitution does not stipulate when federal elections are to be held. Congress determined in 1792 that federal elections should be held in November. In 1845, it established election day as the Tuesday following the first Monday in November in years divisible by four.

UNDERSTANDING THE CONSTITUTION 1.8 Beginning with George Washington, every president has taken the oath of office as it appears in the Constitution.

UNDERSTANDING THE CONSTITUTION Section 2 Section 2 outlines the president's authority. Among other duties, the president serves as commander in chief of the armed forces, has the power to make treaties, and can appoint ambassadors and Supreme Court justices. However, the powers of the presidency increased during the Great Depression, World War II, and the Cold War. For example, although the Constitution states that only Congress can declare war, President Harry Truman began an undeclared war against North Korea in the Cold War.

HISTORICAL THINKING Do you think a president is justified to exceed constitutional powers in some situations? Why or why not?

In this photo, President Barack Obama delivers his annual State of the Union address to Congress in 2016. To fulfill the rule in Section 3 on keeping Congress informed "from time to time," presidents present this address every year except in the first year of a new president's term.

UNDERSTANDING THE CONSTITUTION Section 4 In the phrase "high crimes and misdemeanors," the word *high* does not mean "more serious" but rather refers to highly placed public officials.

8 Before he enter on the Execution of his Office, he shall take the following Oath or Affirmation:—"I do solemnly swear (or affirm) that I will faithfully execute the Office of President of the United States, and will to the best of my Ability, preserve, protect and defend the Constitution of the United States."

SECTION 2: EXECUTIVE POWERS

1 The President shall be Commander in Chief of the Army and Navy of the United States, and of the Militia of the several States, when called into the actual Service of the United States; he may require the Opinion, in writing, of the principal Officer in each of the executive Departments, upon any Subject relating to the Duties of their respective Offices, and he shall have Power to grant Reprieves and Pardons for Offences against the United States, except in Cases of Impeachment.

2 He shall have Power, by and with the Advice and Consent of the Senate, to make Treaties, provided two thirds of the Senators present concur; and he shall nominate, and by and with the Advice and Consent of the Senate, shall appoint Ambassadors, other public Ministers and Consuls, Judges of the supreme Court, and all other Officers of the United States, whose Appointments are not herein otherwise provided for, and which shall be established by Law: but the Congress may by Law vest the Appointment of such inferior Officers, as they think proper, in the President alone, in the Courts of Law, or in the Heads of Departments.

3 The President shall have Power to fill up all Vacancies that may happen during the Recess of the Senate, by granting Commissions which shall expire at the End of their next Session.

SECTION 3: THE PRESIDENT AND CONGRESS

He shall from time to time give to the Congress Information of the State of the Union, and recommend to their Consideration such Measures as he shall judge necessary and expedient; he may, on extraordinary Occasions, convene both Houses, or either of them, and in Case of Disagreement between them, with Respect to the Time of Adjournment, he may adjourn them to such Time as he shall think proper; he shall receive Ambassadors and other public Ministers; he shall take Care that the Laws be faithfully executed, and shall Commission all the Officers of the United States.

SECTION 4: IMPEACHMENT

The President, Vice President and all civil Officers of the United States, shall be removed from Office on Impeachment for, and Conviction of, Treason, Bribery, or other high Crimes and Misdemeanors.

Article III The Judiciary Branch

SECTION 1: SUPREME COURT AND LOWER COURTS

The judicial Power of the United States, shall be vested in one supreme Court, and in such inferior Courts as the Congress may from time to time ordain and establish. The Judges, both of the supreme and inferior Courts, shall hold their Offices during good Behavior, and shall, at stated Times, receive for their Services, a Compensation, which shall not be diminished during their Continuance in Office.

The Supreme Court justices posed for this photo in 2017. In the top row, from left to right, are Elena Kagan, Samuel Alito, Jr., Sonia Sotomayor, and Neil Gorsuch. In the bottom row, from left to right, are Ruth Bader Ginsburg, Anthony Kennedy, John Roberts, Jr. (chief justice), Clarence Thomas, and Stephen Breyer.

SECTION 2: AUTHORITY OF THE SUPREME COURT

1 The judicial Power shall extend to all Cases, in Law and Equity, arising under this Constitution, the Laws of the United States, and Treaties made, or which shall be made, under their Authority;—to all Cases affecting Ambassadors, other public Ministers and Consuls;—to all Cases of admiralty and maritime Jurisdiction;—to Controversies to which the United States shall be a Party;—*to Controversies between two or more States;—between a State and Citizens of another State;—between Citizens of different States;—between Citizens of the same State claiming Lands under Grants of different States, and between a State, or the Citizens thereof, and foreign States, Citizens or Subjects.*

2 In all Cases affecting Ambassadors, other public Ministers and Consuls, and those in which a State shall be Party, the supreme Court shall have original Jurisdiction. In all the other Cases before mentioned, the supreme Court shall have appellate Jurisdiction, both as to Law and Fact, with such Exceptions, and under such Regulations as the Congress shall make.

3 The Trial of all Crimes, except in Cases of Impeachment, shall be by Jury; and such Trial shall be held in the State where the said Crimes shall have been committed; but when not committed within any State, the Trial shall be at such Place or Places as the Congress may by Law have directed.

SECTION 3: TREASON

1 Treason against the United States, shall consist only in levying War against them, or in adhering to their Enemies, giving them Aid and Comfort. No Person shall be convicted of Treason unless on the Testimony of two Witnesses to the same overt Act, or on Confession in open Court.

2 The Congress shall have Power to declare the Punishment of Treason, but no Attainder of Treason shall work Corruption of Blood, or Forfeiture except during the Life of the Person attainted.

ARTICLE III
UNDERSTANDING THE CONSTITUTION Section 1 Article III Section 1 establishes the federal court system. The Supreme Court of the United States is the highest court in the land and the only part of the federal judiciary specifically required by the Constitution. Lower courts were established by Congress by the Judiciary Act of 1789.

UNDERSTANDING THE CONSTITUTION Section 2 The italicized portion in 2.1 was changed in 1795 by the 11th Amendment. The last part of 2.2 describes the Supreme Court as the final appeals court. As a result of the landmark 1803 case *Marbury* v. *Madison*, the Court is often asked to rule on the constitutionality of a law.

UNDERSTANDING THE CONSTITUTION Section 3 Treason is the only crime specifically defined in the Constitution. Between 1954 and 2016, one person was charged with treason for collaborating in the production of propaganda videos for the terrorist group al Qaeda. Protesting or opposing U.S. government actions or policies, however, is protected by the free speech clause in Amendment 1.

Article IV States and Citizens

SECTION 1: MUTUAL RESPECT AMONG STATES

Full Faith and Credit shall be given in each State to the public
Acts, Records, and judicial Proceedings of every other State. And
the Congress may by general Laws prescribe the Manner in which
such Acts, Records and Proceedings shall be proved, and the
Effect thereof.

SECTION 2: CITIZENS OF STATES AND OF THE UNITED STATES

1 The Citizens of each State shall be entitled to all Privileges and
Immunities of Citizens in the several States.

2 A Person charged in any State with Treason, Felony, or other
Crime, who shall flee from Justice, and be found in another State,
shall on Demand of the executive Authority of the State from
which he fled, be delivered up, to be removed to the State having
Jurisdiction of the Crime.

3 *No Person held to Service or Labor in one State, under the Laws
thereof, escaping into another, shall, in Consequence of any Law
or Regulation therein, be discharged from such Service or Labor,
but shall be delivered up on Claim of the Party to whom such
Service or Labor may be due.*

SECTION 3: NEW STATES

1 New States may be admitted by the Congress into this Union;
but no new State shall be formed or erected within the Jurisdiction
of any other State; nor any State be formed by the Junction of
two or more States, or Parts of States, without the Consent of the
Legislatures of the States concerned as well as of the Congress.

2 The Congress shall have Power to dispose of and make all
needful Rules and Regulations respecting the Territory or other
Property belonging to the United States; and nothing in this
Constitution shall be so construed as to Prejudice any Claims of
the United States, or of any particular State.

SECTION 4: PROTECTION OF STATES BY THE UNITED STATES

The United States shall guarantee to every State in this Union a
Republican Form of Government, and shall protect each of them
against Invasion; and on Application of the Legislature, or of the
Executive (when the Legislature cannot be convened), against
domestic Violence.

Article V Amending the Constitution

1 The Congress, whenever two thirds of both Houses shall deem it necessary, shall propose Amendments to this Constitution, or, on the Application of the Legislatures of two thirds of the several States, shall call a Convention for proposing Amendments, which, in either Case, shall be valid to all Intents and Purposes, as Part of this Constitution, when ratified by the Legislatures of three fourths of the several States, or by Conventions in three fourths thereof, as the one or the other Mode of Ratification may be proposed by the Congress.

2 Provided that no Amendment which may be made prior to the Year One thousand eight hundred and eight shall in any Manner affect the first and fourth Clauses in the Ninth Section of the first Article; and that no State, without its Consent, shall be deprived of its equal Suffrage in the Senate.

Article VI The Supreme Law of the Land

1 All Debts contracted and Engagements entered into, before the Adoption of this Constitution, shall be as valid against the United States under this Constitution, as under the Confederation.

2 This Constitution, and the Laws of the United States which shall be made in Pursuance thereof; and all Treaties made, or which shall be made, under the Authority of the United States, shall be the supreme Law of the Land; and the Judges in every State shall be bound thereby, any Thing in the Constitution or Laws of any State to the Contrary notwithstanding.

3 The Senators and Representatives before mentioned, and the Members of the several State Legislatures, and all executive and judicial Officers, both of the United States and of the several States, shall be bound by Oath or Affirmation, to support this Constitution; but no religious Test shall ever be required as a Qualification to any Office or public Trust under the United States.

ARTICLE V
UNDERSTANDING THE CONSTITUTION Article V This article describes the process for amending the Constitution but states that the first and fourth clauses in Article 1's ninth section cannot be amended before 1808. These clauses refer to the importation of slaves and to a tax charged on an individual. The Framers realized that the Constitution would need to be amended at some point, but they made the amendment process extremely difficult. According to U.S. Senate records, approximately 11,699 bills have been proposed as amendments to the Constitution. However, as of 2017, only 27 amendments had been added to the Constitution.

HISTORICAL THINKING Do you think the amendment process should be made easier? Explain why or why not.

ARTICLE VI
UNDERSTANDING THE CONSTITUTION Article VI Paragraph 2 is known as the "supremacy clause." The clause establishes the Constitution and all federal laws and treaties as the supreme law of the land. When state law is in conflict with federal law, federal law prevails. The Supreme Court has used the supremacy clause to ensure that federal law pre-empts, or takes priority over, state law. This is known as the doctrine of pre-emption.

Today, "the people" referred to in the Constitution includes all adult U.S. citizens.

ARTICLE VII
UNDERSTANDING THE CONSTITUTION Article 7 The Framers clearly stated in Article 7 that the Constitution required the approval of only 9 states, not the entire 13. This contrasted with the Articles of Confederation, which required the consent of all 13 states. In addition, the Framers decided to hold a special ratification convention in each state. Delegates to these conventions were chosen by the state's citizens.

On June 21, 1788, New Hampshire became the 9th state to ratify the Constitution and make it the law of the United States. However, the Framers knew that the new nation's survival depended on the populous and wealthy states of Virginia and New York, which were slow to ratify. After lengthy debates, first Virginia and then New York approved the measure, becoming the 11th and 12th states to ratify the Constitution. Rhode Island was the only obstacle to unanimous approval. It officially joined the United States only after being warned that it would be treated like a foreign government if it did not.

HISTORICAL THINKING Why did the Framers call for ratification conventions in the 13 states?

Article VII Ratification

The Ratification of the Conventions of nine States, shall be sufficient for the Establishment of this Constitution between the States so ratifying the Same.

[Here appears some text noting corrections that were made on the original copy of the document.]

Done in Convention by the Unanimous Consent of the States present the Seventeenth Day of September in the Year of our Lord one thousand seven hundred and Eighty seven and of the Independence of the United States of America the Twelfth In witness whereof We have hereunto subscribed our Names,

G°. Washington
President and deputy from Virginia

Massachusetts
Nathaniel Gorham
Rufus King

New York
Alexander Hamilton

Delaware
George Read
Gunning Bedford, Jr.
John Dickinson
Richard Bassett
Jacob Broom

Virginia
John Blair
James Madison, Jr.

Pennsylvania
Benjamin Franklin
Thomas Mifflin
Robert Morris
George Clymer
Thomas Fitzsimons
Jared Ingersoll
James Wilson
Gouverneur Morris

New Hampshire
John Langdon
Nicholas Gilman

New Jersey
William Livingston
David Brearley
William Paterson
Jonathan Dayton

Connecticut
William Samuel Johnson
Roger Sherman

North Carolina
William Blount
Richard Dobbs Spaight
Hugh Williamson

South Carolina
John Rutledge
Charles Cotesworth Pinckney
Charles Pinckney
Pierce Butler

Maryland
James McHenry
Daniel of St. Thomas Jenifer
Daniel Carroll

Georgia
William Few
Abraham Baldwin

THE BILL OF RIGHTS AND AMENDMENTS 11–27

Introduction

Individual rights are fundamental to liberty. The Magna Carta, the charter of English liberties granted in 1215, helped inspire the Bill of Rights. Those who sailed to North America from Britain had enjoyed the freedoms granted to them under both the Magna Carta and the English Bill of Rights. They believed they were entitled to these same rights when they settled their colonies.

No one argued whether Americans should have these rights, but there was debate as to whether it was necessary and advisable to include them in the Constitution. At first, James Madison didn't believe the rights needed to be included. He argued that state constitutions already offered the explicit protection of individual liberties. Stating the rights in the Constitution might actually have the effect of limiting them. However, in 1787, Thomas Jefferson wrote to Madison, "[A] bill of rights is what the people are entitled to against every government on earth, general or particular, and what no just government should refuse." After long discussion among the Framers, Madison changed his mind. He drafted 19 amendments. On December 15, 1791, 10 of them were ratified, and the Bill of Rights was added to the Constitution.

The following is a transcription of the Bill of Rights. Over time, as you'll see, more amendments were added to the Constitution to address issues that arose as the nation grew and changed.

The Preamble to the Bill of Rights

Congress of the United States begun and held at the City of New York, on Wednesday the fourth of March, one thousand seven hundred and eighty nine.

THE Conventions of a number of the States, having at the time of their adopting the Constitution, expressed a desire, in order to prevent misconstruction or abuse of its powers, that further declaratory and restrictive clauses should be added: And as extending the ground of public confidence in the Government, will best ensure the beneficient ends of its institution.

RESOLVED by the Senate and House of Representatives of the United States of America, in Congress assembled, two thirds of both Houses concurring, that the following Articles be proposed to the Legislatures of the several States, as amendments to the Constitution of the United States, all, or any of which Articles, when ratified by three fourths of the said Legislatures, to be valid to all intents and purposes, as part of the said Constitution; viz.

UNDERSTANDING THE PREAMBLE *Viz* is Latin for "that is to say" or "namely."

UNDERSTANDING AMENDMENT 1

Amendment 1 protects the free exercise of religious liberty by prohibiting the government from establishing a church, endorsing a particular religion, or favoring one set of religious beliefs over another. Thomas Jefferson's 1786 Statute for Religious Freedom, which he wrote for the Virginia legislature, influenced the protection of religious freedom. In his statute, Jefferson also called for the separation of church and state. This idea is contained—although not explicitly—in the "establishment" clause. The Framers debated the wording of the clause and finally adopted that shown here.

UNDERSTANDING AMENDMENT 2

This amendment has been debated for decades. Many Americans believe the amendment ensures the right to possess guns. Others think gun ownership should be controlled. In 2008, the Supreme Court ruled in *District of Columbia* v. *Heller* that Amendment 2 guarantees the right to possess a firearm for self-defense and hunting. There has been debate as to whether the amendment protects ownership of any type of weapon, however.

HISTORICAL THINKING Do you think gun ownership should be controlled? Why or why not?

ARTICLES in addition to, and Amendment of the Constitution of the United States of America, proposed by Congress, and ratified by the Legislatures of the several States, pursuant to the fifth Article of the original Constitution.

Amendment 1 (1791)

Congress shall make no law respecting an establishment of religion, or prohibiting the free exercise thereof; or abridging the freedom of speech, or of the press; or the right of the people peaceably to assemble, and to petition the Government for a redress of grievances.

Amendment 2 (1791)

A well regulated Militia, being necessary to the security of a free State, the right of the people to keep and bear Arms, shall not be infringed.

Amendment 3 (1791)

No Soldier shall, in time of peace be quartered in any house, without the consent of the Owner, nor in time of war, but in a manner to be prescribed by law.

Amendment 4 (1791)

The right of the people to be secure in their persons, houses, papers, and effects, against unreasonable searches and seizures, shall not be violated, and no Warrants shall issue, but upon probable cause, supported by Oath or affirmation, and particularly describing the place to be searched, and the persons or things to be seized.

Amendment 5 (1791)

No person shall be held to answer for a capital, or otherwise infamous crime, unless on a presentment or indictment of a Grand Jury, except in cases arising in the land or naval forces, or in the Militia, when in actual service in time of War or public danger; nor shall any person be subject for the same offence to be twice put in jeopardy of life or limb; nor shall be compelled in any criminal case to be a witness against himself, nor be deprived of life, liberty, or property, without due process of law; nor shall private property be taken for public use, without just compensation.

Amendment 6 (1791)

In all criminal prosecutions, the accused shall enjoy the right to a speedy and public trial, by an impartial jury of the State and district wherein the crime shall have been committed, which district shall have been previously ascertained by law, and to be informed of the nature and cause of the accusation; to be confronted with the witnesses against him; to have compulsory process for obtaining witnesses in his favor, and to have the Assistance of Counsel for his defence.

Amendment 7 (1791)

In Suits at common law, where the value in controversy shall exceed twenty dollars, the right of trial by jury shall be preserved, and no fact tried by a jury, shall be otherwise re-examined in any Court of the United States, than according to the rules of the common law.

Amendment 8 (1791)

Excessive bail shall not be required, nor excessive fines imposed, nor cruel and unusual punishments inflicted.

Amendment 9 (1791)

The enumeration in the Constitution, of certain rights, shall not be construed to deny or disparage others retained by the people.

Amendment 10 (1791)

The powers not delegated to the United States by the Constitution, nor prohibited by it to the States, are reserved to the States respectively, or to the people.

UNDERSTANDING AMENDMENTS 4–6 These three amendments protect people who are suspected of a crime or are being tried for one.

Amendment 4 says that police must have "probable cause" (a good reason) before they can seize someone's possessions. It also protects people from unreasonable searches by government officials.

Amendment 5 protects those accused of crimes. The Due Process Clause was the basis for the defense of Fred Korematsu, an American citizen and and the son of Japanese parents, who refused to obey President Franklin Roosevelt's executive order and report to an internment camp during World War II. Under Roosevelt's order, Korematsu's lawyers argued, Japanese Americans were "deprived of life, liberty, or property, without due process of law." The case, *Fred Korematsu* v. *United States of America*, finally went to the Supreme Court, which upheld Korematsu's removal to an internment camp.

Amendment 6 guarantees a speedy public trial to those accused of a crime.

HISTORICAL THINKING Why do you suppose the Supreme Court upheld Roosevelt's executive order?

UNDERSTANDING AMENDMENTS 9 and 10 Amendment 9 prevents the government from denying rights that are not listed in the Bill of Rights. These are called "unenumerated" rights and include the right to travel and to vote.

The Framers added Amendment 10 to better define the balance of power between the states and the federal government. Each state is given the power to make laws that are not covered by the Constitution.

Amendment 11 (1798)

[**Note:** Article 3, Section 2, of the Constitution was modified by the 11th Amendment.]

The Judicial power of the United States shall not be construed to extend to any suit in law or equity, commenced or prosecuted against one of the United States by Citizens of another State, or by Citizens or Subjects of any Foreign State.

Amendment 12 (1804)

[**Note:** Part of Article 2, Section 1, of the Constitution was replaced by the 12th Amendment.]

The Electors shall meet in their respective states and vote by ballot for President and Vice-President, one of whom, at least, shall not be an inhabitant of the same state with themselves; they shall name in their ballots the person voted for as President, and in distinct ballots the person voted for as Vice-President, and they shall make distinct lists of all persons voted for as President, and of all persons voted for as Vice-President, and of the number of votes for each, which lists they shall sign and certify, and transmit sealed to the seat of the government of the United States, directed to the President of the Senate; —the President of the Senate shall, in the presence of the Senate and House of Representatives, open all the certificates and the votes shall then be counted; —The person having the greatest number of votes for President, shall be the President, if such number be a majority of the whole number of Electors appointed; and if no person have such majority, then from the persons having the highest numbers not exceeding three on the list of those voted for as President, the House of Representatives shall choose immediately, by ballot, the President. But in choosing the President, the votes shall be taken by states, the representation from each state having one vote; a quorum for this purpose shall consist of a member or members from two-thirds of the states, and a majority of all the states shall be necessary to a choice. *And if the House of Representatives shall not choose a President whenever the right of choice shall devolve upon them, before the fourth day of March next following, then the Vice-President shall act as President, as in case of the death or other constitutional disability of the President.* The person having the greatest number of votes as Vice-President, shall be the Vice-President, if such number be a majority of the whole number of Electors appointed, and if no person have a majority, then from the two highest numbers on the list, the Senate shall choose the Vice-President; a quorum for the purpose shall consist of two-thirds of the whole number of Senators, and a majority of the whole number shall be necessary to a choice. But no person constitutionally ineligible to the office of President shall be eligible to that of Vice-President of the United States.

UNDERSTANDING AMENDMENT 12 Amendment 12 established the electoral college. As you know, prior to its passage, the presidential candidate who received the most electoral votes won the presidency. The candidate with the second most votes became the vice president. The amendment changed this system by allowing the delegates of each party to choose its nominees for both president and vice president.

The electoral college was challenged in 2000 and 2016, when the candidates who won the popular vote (Al Gore in 2000 and Hillary Clinton in 2016) lost the elections to George W. Bush and Donald Trump, respectively.

HISTORICAL THINKING Do you think the electoral college should be abolished? Why or why not?

Amendment 13 (1865)

[Note: A portion of Article 4, Section 2, of the Constitution was superseded by the 13th Amendment.]

SECTION 1: Neither slavery nor involuntary servitude, except as a punishment for crime whereof the party shall have been duly convicted, shall exist within the United States, or any place subject to their jurisdiction.

SECTION 2: Congress shall have power to enforce this article by appropriate legislation.

Amendment 14 (1868)

[Note: Article 1, Section 2, of the Constitution was modified by Section 2 of the 14th Amendment.]

SECTION 1: All persons born or naturalized in the United States, and subject to the jurisdiction thereof, are citizens of the United States and of the State wherein they reside. No State shall make or enforce any law which shall abridge the privileges or immunities of citizens of the United States; nor shall any State deprive any person of life, liberty, or property, without due process of law; nor deny to any person within its jurisdiction the equal protection of the laws.

SECTION 2: Representatives shall be apportioned among the several States according to their respective numbers, counting the whole number of persons in each State, excluding Indians not taxed. But when the right to vote at any election for the choice of electors for President and Vice-President of the United States, Representatives in Congress, the Executive and Judicial officers of a State, or the members of the *Legislature thereof, is denied to any of the male inhabitants of such State, being twenty-one years of age, and citizens of the United States,* or in any way abridged, except for participation in rebellion, or other crime, the basis of representation therein shall be reduced in the proportion which the number of such male citizens shall bear to the whole number of male citizens twenty-one years of age in such State.

SECTION 3: No person shall be a Senator or Representative in Congress, or elector of President and Vice-President, or hold any office, civil or military, under the United States, or under any State, who, having previously taken an oath, as a member of Congress, or as an officer of the United States, or as a member of any State legislature, or as an executive or judicial officer of any State, to support the Constitution of the United States, shall have engaged in insurrection or rebellion against the same, or given aid or comfort to the enemies thereof. But Congress may by a vote of two-thirds of each House, remove such disability.

UNDERSTANDING AMENDMENTS 13–15 Amendments 13–15 are often referred to as the "civil war" or "reconstruction" amendments because they were created in the aftermath of the war. These post-Civil War amendments laid the foundation for the legal phase of the 20th-century civil rights movement.

UNDERSTANDING AMENDMENT 13 This amendment outlawed slavery.

UNDERSTANDING AMENDMENT 14 Section 1 This section defines citizenship and ensures that all citizens enjoy the same rights and the same protections by the law. The amendment has been continually reinterpreted and applied to different contexts by the courts. For example, sometimes it has been employed as a protection for workers and other times as a protection for corporations. In the 1877 case, *Munn* v. *Illinois*, the Supreme Court upheld the idea that a corporation and its business activities were protected by the 14th Amendment.

UNDERSTANDING AMENDMENT 14 Section 2 This section overrides the three-fifths clause in Article I. As a result of this amendment, each citizen is counted as a whole person. Section 2 also calls for reducing the number of representatives of a state if it denies some citizens the right to vote.

SECTION 4: The validity of the public debt of the United States, authorized by law, including debts incurred for payment of pensions and bounties for services in suppressing insurrection or rebellion, shall not be questioned. But neither the United States nor any State shall assume or pay any debt or obligation incurred in aid of insurrection or rebellion against the United States, or any claim for the loss or emancipation of any slave; but all such debts, obligations and claims shall be held illegal and void.

SECTION 5: The Congress shall have the power to enforce, by appropriate legislation, the provisions of this article.

Amendment 15 (1870)

SECTION 1: The right of citizens of the United States to vote shall not be denied or abridged by the United States or by any State on account of race, color, or previous condition of servitude—

SECTION 2: The Congress shall have the power to enforce this article by appropriate legislation.

UNDERSTANDING AMENDMENT 15
The 15th Amendment prohibits federal and state governments from limiting or denying an individual's ability to vote because of "race, color, or previous conditions of servitude." Section 2 of the amendment gives Congress the authority to enforce the amendment by passing federal laws that guarantee voting rights. Note that the amendment granted African-American men voting rights but not women of any race. In addition, some states imposed literacy tests, white primaries, poll taxes, and other barriers to keep African Americans from voting. Almost 100 years would pass before African Americans secured stronger protections through federal legislation and the 24th Amendment.

HISTORICAL THINKING Why might some states have made it difficult for African-American men to vote?

In this illustration, a group of men who helped bring about the 15th Amendment, including Abraham Lincoln, Hiram Revels, and Frederick Douglass, watch as President Ulysses S. Grant signs the amendment.

UNDERSTANDING AMENDMENT 16
The 16th Amendment was the first of four "Progressive" amendments. During the Progressive Era (1890–1920), many Americans worked to reform government. Seeking to reduce tariffs and still provide revenue for the federal government, progressives pushed for this amendment, which established an income tax.

Amendment 16 (1913)

[**Note:** Article 1, Section 9, of the Constitution was modified by the 16th Amendment.]

The Congress shall have power to lay and collect taxes on incomes, from whatever source derived, without apportionment among the several States, and without regard to any census or enumeration.

Amendment 17 (1913)

[**Note:** Article 1, Section 3, of the Constitution was modified by the 17th Amendment.]

The Senate of the United States shall be composed of two Senators from each State, elected by the people thereof, for six years; and each Senator shall have one vote. The electors in each State shall have the qualifications requisite for electors of the most numerous branch of the State legislatures.

When vacancies happen in the representation of any State in the Senate, the executive authority of such State shall issue writs of election to fill such vacancies: Provided, That the legislature of any State may empower the executive thereof to make temporary appointments until the people fill the vacancies by election as the legislature may direct.

This amendment shall not be so construed as to affect the election or term of any Senator chosen before it becomes valid as part of the Constitution.

Amendment 18 (1919)

Repealed by the 21st Amendment.

SECTION 1: *After one year from the ratification of this article the manufacture, sale, or transportation of intoxicating liquors within, the importation thereof into, or the exportation thereof from the United States and all territory subject to the jurisdiction thereof for beverage purposes is hereby prohibited.*

SECTION 2: *The Congress and the several States shall have concurrent power to enforce this article by appropriate legislation.*

SECTION 3: *This article shall be inoperative unless it shall have been ratified as an amendment to the Constitution by the legislatures of the several States, as provided in the Constitution, within seven years from the date of the submission hereof to the States by the Congress.*

UNDERSTANDING AMENDMENT 17
The 17th Amendment changed the process by which Senators are elected. Through the popular election of senators, the amendment made the process more democratic.

UNDERSTANDING AMENDMENT 18
Known as the Prohibition Amendment, the 18th Amendment prohibited the production, sale, or transportation of alcoholic beverages in the United States. Many of those who supported the amendment also supported the temperance movement, which advocated for the control of alcohol consumption. Many progressives viewed alcohol abuse as a significant social problem. Congress passed the Volstead Act in 1919, which gave the U.S. Treasury Department the power to enforce Prohibition.

HISTORICAL THINKING In what way was Amendment 18 different from the preceding amendments?

Philadelphia's Director of Public Safety, Smedley Butler, smashes casks of beer in 1924 to enforce Prohibition.

Following the passage of the 19th Amendment, the women shown here voted for the first time in a 1920 election in New York City.

UNDERSTANDING AMENDMENT 19
Although many states had granted some voting privileges to women before 1920, the 19th Amendment extended equal voting rights to all women in the country. In the 1800s, women's rights leaders such as Elizabeth Cady Stanton and Susan B. Anthony dedicated their lives to securing political and social equality for women. Their actions helped inspire and launch another movement in the 1960s, which called for further rights for women and offered differing perspectives on the roles of women.

HISTORICAL THINKING Why does the amendment specify that women's right to vote "shall not be denied or abridged by the United States or by any state"?

UNDERSTANDING AMENDMENT 20
This amendment is often called the "Lame Duck Amendment." In government, a lame duck is an elected official whose term in office is about to end. So, for instance, a president who has already served two terms is a lame duck. Officials who have not won re-election are also considered lame ducks. Congress has little incentive to work with a lame duck president.

Amendment 19 (1920)

The right of citizens of the United States to vote shall not be denied or abridged by the United States or by any State on account of sex.

Congress shall have power to enforce this article by appropriate legislation.

Amendment 20 (1933)

[**Note:** Article 1, Section 4, of the Constitution was modified by Section 2 of the 20th Amendment. In addition, a portion of the 12th Amendment was superseded by Section 3.]

SECTION 1: The terms of the President and the Vice President shall end at noon on the 20th day of January, and the terms of Senators and Representatives at noon on the 3d day of January, of the years in which such terms would have ended if this article had not been ratified; and the terms of their successors shall then begin.

SECTION 2: The Congress shall assemble at least once in every year, and such meeting shall begin at noon on the 3d day of January, unless they shall by law appoint a different day.

SECTION 3: If, at the time fixed for the beginning of the term of the President, the President elect shall have died, the Vice President elect shall become President. If a President shall not have been chosen before the time fixed for the beginning of his term, or if the President elect shall have failed to qualify, then the Vice President elect shall act as President until a President shall have qualified; and the Congress may by law provide for the case wherein neither a President elect nor a Vice President elect shall have qualified, declaring who shall then act as President, or the manner in which one who is to act shall be selected, and such person shall act accordingly until a President or Vice President shall have qualified.

SECTION 4: The Congress may by law provide for the case of the death of any of the persons from whom the House of Representatives may choose a President whenever the right of choice shall have devolved upon them, and for the case of the death of any of the persons from whom the Senate may choose a Vice President whenever the right of choice shall have devolved upon them.

SECTION 5: Sections 1 and 2 shall take effect on the 15th day of October following the ratification of this article.

SECTION 6: This article shall be inoperative unless it shall have been ratified as an amendment to the Constitution by the legislatures of three-fourths of the several States within seven years from the date of its submission.

Amendment 21 (1933)

SECTION 1: The eighteenth article of amendment to the Constitution of the United States is hereby repealed.

SECTION 2: The transportation or importation into any State, Territory, or possession of the United States for delivery or use therein of intoxicating liquors, in violation of the laws thereof, is hereby prohibited.

SECTION 3: This article shall be inoperative unless it shall have been ratified as an amendment to the Constitution by conventions in the several States, as provided in the Constitution, within seven years from the date of the submission hereof to the States by the Congress.

Amendment 22 (1951)

SECTION 1: No person shall be elected to the office of the President more than twice, and no person who has held the office of President, or acted as President, for more than two years of a term to which some other person was elected President shall be elected to the office of the President more than once. But this Article shall not apply to any person holding the office of President when this Article was proposed by the Congress, and shall not prevent any person who may be holding the office of President, or acting as President, during the term within which this Article becomes operative from holding the office of President or acting as President during the remainder of such term.

SECTION 2: This article shall be inoperative unless it shall have been ratified as an amendment to the Constitution by the legislatures of three-fourths of the several States within seven years from the date of its submission to the States by the Congress.

UNDERSTANDING AMENDMENT 21
Amendment 21 repealed Amendment 18 and ended Prohibition. Amendment 21 is the only amendment that was ratified by state conventions rather than state legislatures. Section 2 of the amendment returned the regulation of alcohol to the states, giving them significant control of alcohol within and across their borders. Consequently, alcohol laws vary throughout the states. States also have the power to establish the legal drinking age within their borders. In an effort to prohibit the sale of alcohol to minors, the federal government provides federal funds only to states who set the legal drinking age at 21. All 50 states have done so.

HISTORICAL THINKING What potential problems or issues might arise when states have different laws regulating people of the same age?

UNDERSTANDING AMENDMENT 22
Democrat Franklin D. Roosevelt served three terms as president of the United States and was elected to a fourth term shortly before he died in 1945. George Washington had declined to run for a third term. All presidents before Roosevelt followed this unwritten custom and served no more than two terms. Within months of Roosevelt's death, Republicans in Congress presented the 22nd Amendment for consideration.

HISTORICAL THINKING Do you think a president should be able to serve for more than two terms? Explain your answer.

UNDERSTANDING AMENDMENT 23

The District of Columbia is the official seat of the U.S. government, but it is a federal territory, not a state, and has only a nonvoting representative in Congress. Washington, D.C., began as a small community, but by 1960, more than 760,000 people who paid federal taxes and could be drafted into the military lived there. The states ratified Amendment 23 in 1961 to allow residents of the District to vote in presidential elections. The District of Columbia has three electoral votes.

UNDERSTANDING AMENDMENT 24

This amendment abolished poll taxes and election fees charged by states to keep low-income and mostly African-American citizens from voting. The successful push to get the amendment passed was in part based on the support and demands of the civil rights movement. The amendment gave African Americans greater access to the political process. As written, Amendment 24 prohibits poll taxes only in federal elections. The Voting Rights Act of 1965 and a 1966 Supreme Court decision banned poll taxes in state elections as well.

HISTORICAL THINKING Why do you think the amendment refers to the "right of citizens of the United States to vote," rather than name specific minority groups?

Amendment 23 (1961)

SECTION 1: The District constituting the seat of Government of the United States shall appoint in such manner as the Congress may direct:

A number of electors of President and Vice President equal to the whole number of Senators and Representatives in Congress to which the District would be entitled if it were a State, but in no event more than the least populous State; they shall be in addition to those appointed by the States, but they shall be considered, for the purposes of the election of President and Vice President, to be electors appointed by a State; and they shall meet in the District and perform such duties as provided by the twelfth article of amendment.

SECTION 2: The Congress shall have power to enforce this article by appropriate legislation.

Amendment 24 (1964)

SECTION 1: The right of citizens of the United States to vote in any primary or other election for President or Vice President, for electors for President or Vice President, or for Senator or Representative in Congress, shall not be denied or abridged by the United States or any State by reason of failure to pay any poll tax or other tax.

SECTION 2: The Congress shall have power to enforce this article by appropriate legislation.

Amendment 25 (1967)

[Note: Article 2, Section 1, of the Constitution was affected by the 25th Amendment.]

SECTION 1: In case of the removal of the President from office or of his death or resignation, the Vice President shall become President.

SECTION 2: Whenever there is a vacancy in the office of the Vice President, the President shall nominate a Vice President who shall take office upon confirmation by a majority vote of both Houses of Congress.

SECTION 3: Whenever the President transmits to the President pro tempore of the Senate and the Speaker of the House of Representatives his written declaration that he is unable to discharge the powers and duties of his office, and until he transmits to them a written declaration to the contrary, such powers and duties shall be discharged by the Vice President as Acting President.

SECTION 4: Whenever the Vice President and a majority of either the principal officers of the executive departments or of such other body as Congress may by law provide, transmit to the President pro tempore of the Senate and the Speaker of the House of Representatives their written declaration that the President is unable to discharge the powers and duties of his office, the Vice President shall immediately assume the powers and duties of the office as Acting President.

Thereafter, when the President transmits to the President pro tempore of the Senate and the Speaker of the House of Representatives his written declaration that no inability exists, he shall resume the powers and duties of his office unless the Vice President and a majority of either the principal officers of the executive department or of such other body as Congress may by law provide, transmit within four days to the President pro tempore of the Senate and the Speaker of the House of Representatives their written declaration that the President is unable to discharge the powers and duties of his office. Thereupon Congress shall decide the issue, assembling within forty-eight hours for that purpose if not in session. If the Congress, within twenty-one days after receipt of the latter written declaration, or, if Congress is not in session, within twenty-one days after Congress is required to assemble, determines by two-thirds vote of both Houses that the President is unable to discharge the powers and duties of his office, the Vice President shall continue to discharge the same as Acting President; otherwise, the President shall resume the powers and duties of his office.

UNDERSTANDING AMENDMENT 25
The 25th Amendment was ratified in 1967 to establish procedures to follow if a president becomes disabled while in office. The amendment was proposed after the assassination of President John F. Kennedy in 1963. Following his death, many questioned what would have happened if he had survived the shooting but been unable to govern. Eight presidents have died and one resigned while in office. In addition, seven vice presidents have died while in office and two have resigned. This amendment provides for an orderly transfer of power.

HISTORICAL THINKING Why is there a plan of succession for the presidency?

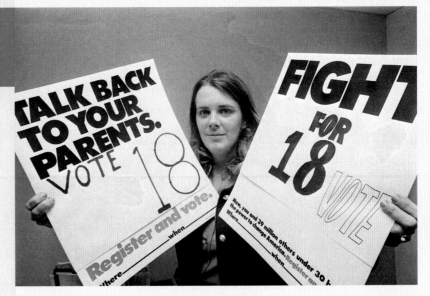

Pat Keefer, a leader in advocating for the youth vote in the early 1970s, holds signs urging 18-year olds to vote.

UNDERSTANDING AMENDMENT 26

Amendment 26 continued the Constitution's expansion of voting rights. In 1954, President Dwight Eisenhower proposed lowering the voting age to 18 years. The movement acquired new momentum in the late 1960s during the Vietnam War. People began to question why 18-year-old men could be drafted to serve in the military but could not vote.

HISTORICAL THINKING Do you think the voting age should be reduced even more? Explain your answer.

UNDERSTANDING AMENDMENT 27

Amendment 27 defers any congressional pay raise to the next election cycle. The amendment was first proposed in 1789 by James Madison. However, it was ratified more than 200 years later, thanks to a college student's research project. In his research, the student found that a proposed amendment remains pending, no matter how much time passes before action is taken on it. The student decided to see if he could get the amendment passed and found that he was able to gather enough support to do so.

Amendment 26 (1971)

[**Note:** Amendment 14, Section 2, of the Constitution was modified by Section 1 of the 26th Amendment.]

SECTION 1: The right of citizens of the United States, who are eighteen years of age or older, to vote shall not be denied or abridged by the United States or by any State on account of age.

SECTION 2: The Congress shall have power to enforce this article by appropriate legislation.

Amendment 27 (1992)

No law, varying the compensation for the services of the Senators and Representatives, shall take effect, until an election of Representatives shall have intervened.

Citizenship and You

For many high school students, getting to a job, meeting with friends, and participating in activities require some source of transportation. Many young adults borrow a car from their parents to get around. To continue to enjoy this privilege, you have to handle responsibilities and prove you are dependable. You have to obey the rules of the road and be a careful, alert driver. Similarly, our responsibilities to our communities, states, and nation balance the rights we receive as citizens. Let's examine some aspects of American citizenship—of being a full member of a country in exchange for certain responsibilities.

STRUGGLE FOR EQUAL RIGHTS

As you have learned by studying the U.S. Constitution and Bill of Rights, privileges and rights such as citizenship and voting have been contested, reshaped, and amended during our country's history. Beginning with freedoms and rights cherished and protected in the Constitution by the Framers, Americans from all walks of life have struggled to expand their own rights and those of others. People gained rights they had been denied through the efforts of the civil rights movement, including the right to participate in government, the right to free expression—in all its forms—and the right to equal treatment under the law. Federal, state, and local governments have responded to these social changes with more equitable laws. For example, in response to demands by the LGBT community, the

Supreme Court legalized same-sex marriage in 2015. The efforts and sacrifices of rights activists have helped move all Americans forward in our continuing struggle to become a more perfect union—a struggle that continues today.

WE THE PEOPLE

What role do rules play in your life? Have you ever considered what your life would be like if there were no rules? Imagine arriving at school on the first day of your senior year of high school. You discover that there are no schedules. No one knows where to go, what classes to attend, which locker to use. No one understands the processes and procedures that allow a school to operate efficiently.

This is similar to what would happen in a government without clear rules—or laws—that define the rights and responsibilities of citizens. Order, organization, equality, and safety would all be threatened without laws and established procedures and processes. The most concrete example of our society's rules are our laws, and the most fundamental duty of an American citizen is to obey them.

Is it fair that a government makes laws that people must follow? As you learned while studying the Constitution, the United States is a representative democracy, as demonstrated by the phrase "We the people." Your exploration of the Constitution has revealed that the American people hold the power to shape the government and determine its practices. When our government and representatives act in ways that oppose our rules and ideals, we have the means to point the country in the right direction. Americans work to be *good citizens* by obeying laws, *participatory citizens* by voting and serving on juries, and *socially-just citizens* by standing up for the rights of others.

Individuals act as participatory citizens by exercising their right to vote in local, state, and federal elections.

THINK ABOUT IT

SUMMARIZE Why are rules and laws important, and what would happen without them?

The Rights and Responsibilities of Citizens

Our Constitution defines many of the rights we enjoy as Americans. These rights apply to all citizens, regardless of whether they were born here or immigrated from another country. Knowing your rights can help you better understand the responsibilities that come with being a citizen, and help you determine what you must do to support and protect those rights. Responsibilities include doing what is right, showing good character, and acting in an ethical manner. As you read, think about specific actions you already perform and other steps you might take to be a good, participatory, and socially just citizen.

AMERICAN CITIZENSHIP

Some residents of the United States are citizens because they were born in the country. They are native-born citizens. Others came legally from foreign countries to live in the United States. Our democratic principles have fostered high levels of freedom, political stability, and economic prosperity. These features have attracted people to our nation for hundreds of years. In addition, our political and economic systems have become models for other nations throughout the world. People looking for opportunity and freedom are drawn to our country.

A person who has immigrated to the United States and desires to become a legal citizen goes through a process called **naturalization**. Individuals may qualify for naturalization if they are at least 18 years old and have been a permanent resident in the United States for at least 5 years (or 3 years if they are married to a U.S. citizen). They must learn the laws, rights, and responsibilities of American citizenship.

Following a successful interview with government officials, a prospective citizen must pass a citizenship test. After completing all the steps in this process, a new citizen is sworn in during a naturalization ceremony. As you know, the United States is a country of immigrants. Throughout our country's history, immigrants have helped build our nation, strengthen our economy, and enhance our society. It is a proud day when they become U.S. citizens.

For both native and naturalized citizens, being an American means much more than just living in the United States. After all, Americans living in foreign countries are still citizens of the United States. They are always connected to the United States and other Americans because of their citizenship. Citizenship also encompasses elements of the American tradition, which includes a shared history, customs, and political and cultural beliefs and values. These values include freedom, liberty, and equality—those principles Thomas Jefferson described in the Declaration of Independence.

Rights of Citizens
Right to freedom of religion
Right to freedom of speech (with some limits)
Right to freedom of the press
Right to assemble
Right to trial by jury (in specific types of cases)
Right to vote
Right to buy and sell property
Right to freely travel across the country and to leave and return to the country

RESTRICTIONS ON RIGHTS

By now, you're probably familiar with the basic rights of citizens as guaranteed in the Constitution. These rights also carry responsibilities and are subject to interpretation by the courts. For example, Amendment 1 guarantees the right to free speech—to state one's views or ideas without fear of punishment. Nonetheless, an employer or teacher, for example, can limit speech to what is appropriate in the circumstances. Speech intended to cause harm to others is not protected. For example, crying "Fire!" in a crowded theater when there is no fire is not protected by the right to free speech. The person's "speech" could cause harm to others. The Supreme Court has also placed limits on speech intended to motivate an individual to break the law. Threats of violence are also restricted.

New citizens are sworn in at a naturalization ceremony on July 4, 2016, in Seattle, Washington.

TWO TYPES OF RESPONSIBILITIES

American citizens have two different types of responsibilities: civic and personal. **Civic responsibilities** include voting, paying taxes, and serving on juries. Some of these responsibilities are duties: actions required by law. For example, all citizens must obey laws, pay taxes, and perform jury duty when notified. Neglecting these duties may result in legal penalties. Males over the age of 18 must register with the government in case they are needed for military service.

Personal responsibilities are not required, but they contribute to a more civil society. These include respecting others and their rights, helping in the community, standing up for others, and staying informed about important issues. Personal responsibilities are not as clearly defined as civic duties. They are, however, vital to maintaining an effective government and just society.

All American citizens over the age of 18 have the right to vote. Many people take that right for granted but don't bother to exercise it. Perhaps they don't consider the fact that the right to vote is a privilege that is not granted to people in some countries. These people have no say in how they are governed. Voters also have a responsibility to become informed about issues. They have an obligation to use reliable sources to learn about candidates and their positions on issues. Informed voters can then analyze the credibility of a candidate's claims.

BEING A RESPONSIBLE CITIZEN

When you think of your personal responsibilities as a citizen, consider the choices you make in terms of your actions. Being a responsible citizen means behaving in ways that are right, moral, and just, and acting in a way that benefits you and those around you. Considering the rights of all people, not just the rights of a select few, will help you be a personally responsible citizen.

Citizens have many personal responsibilities, such as being open-minded, respecting the opinions of others, and showing respect for the beliefs and individuality of people with different backgrounds. People of any age can take on personal responsibilities by doing community service projects, standing up for the rights of others, and respecting all people regardless of ethnicity, nationality, gender identity, sexual orientation, or beliefs. Tolerance for others is an important part of being an American citizen.

Tolerance of differences is essential in a democracy, especially one that is as diverse as the United States. Responsible citizens are also willing to give time, effort, and money to improve their communities. Living up to these personal responsibilities helps citizens contribute to an environment of respect and caring and one that protects and promotes the health and welfare of everyone. Responsible citizens work to contribute to the common good.

THINK ABOUT IT

EXPLAIN How does taking on personal responsibilities as a citizen contribute to the common good?

Building and Practicing Citizenship Skills

Building citizenship skills is like learning to play an instrument. It takes hard work and repetition, but the rewards make the effort worth it. Some citizenship skills, such as helping raise voter participation, will require you to seek out specific opportunities. Others, such as refusing to tolerate unjust behavior, can be exercised whenever appropriate situations arise. Citizenship affords many rights and requires many responsibilities. Enjoying these rights and responsibilities is the reward of being a good citizen.

The following chart includes ways you can build and apply citizenship skills in the classroom and in your community to become an active participant in our democracy. Study the chart and check out the Active Citizenship for the Environment Activities in this program's online resources. Then brainstorm more ways you can be a good, participatory, and socially just citizen and put them to practice.

After a gunman terrorized her Parkland, Florida high school on February 14, 2018, killing 17 people and injuring many others, Emma González transformed from a high school student into an activist and gun control advocate. As an engaged citizen, González lobbies for changes to gun legislation, and participates in peaceful protests such as the March For Our Lives, which was held on March 24, 2018, in hundreds of U.S. cities.

THINK ABOUT IT

DESCRIBE What opportunities for active citizenship appeal to you? Explain what you could do to be involved and engaged in your community and country.

ACTIVE CITIZENSHIP

Responsibilities	Citizenship Projects: Ways to Promote Civic Engagement
Become engaged.	• Get information from reliable, unbiased sources. • Ask questions of others who are well informed. • Attend or organize peaceful public demonstrations about issues important to you. • Register to vote, encourage others to vote, and consider becoming an election judge or poll watcher. • Serve your country and your fellow citizens through the military or by participating in organizations such as AmeriCorps, AmeriCorps VISTA, and the Peace Corps. • Participate in citizen journalism by reporting information accurately through blogs, news sites, and social media.

Responsibilities	Citizenship Projects: Ways to Promote Civic Engagement
Do historical research.	• Conduct oral histories with family or community members to better understand historical trends. • Interview citizens who served in the military, took part in social justice movements, or were involved in bringing about social change in schools or the workplace. • Research how you and your classmates can participate in National History Day at a state or national level.
Participate in the democratic process.	• Ask a teacher to organize a trip to a local courtroom to see the legal system in action. • Contact a local political candidate whose ideas you support to see how you might help with his or her campaign. • With the help of a parent or teacher, seek opportunities to witness a naturalization ceremony.
Lobby for change.	• Form a lobbying committee with other students to influence legislation or public policy. • Establish a goal for your lobbying campaign. • Identify whom to lobby. (Who are the people who can help you accomplish your goal?) • Find information and statistics to support your goal. • Get public support for your cause. You might consider gathering signatures on a petition or creating flyers to publicize your campaign. • Present your case to the appropriate individuals.
Volunteer in your community.	• Determine how your skills and interests could help someone else. • Talk with your parents, teachers, and friends to learn what types of volunteer services your community needs. • Make volunteering a regular part of your life. You could consider serving food to the homeless, collecting clothing or canned goods to help a local shelter, cleaning or restoring a local park or playground, or tutoring students who are struggling with their school work.
Pay taxes.	• Read more about your local and state taxes, and what the revenue is used for. • Recognize that you are already paying sales taxes when you purchase many items.
Express political opinions.	• Write a letter or an email to a newspaper editor about an issue that concerns you.
Obey the law.	• Become familiar with the laws in your state, city, and town that apply to people your age.
Stand up for the rights of others.	• Work to stop the discrimination of all people. • Write articles and blog posts about the importance of protecting and supporting the rights of people of different races, religions, and sexual orientations.
Listen to the opinions of others. Discuss differences of opinion in a kind and civil manner.	• When friends or acquaintances express opinions that differ from yours, politely explain why you disagree, if you do.
Respect the value of individuals. Respect differences among people.	• Enjoy and appreciate the differences among people from various backgrounds. • Make friends with people who are different from you. • Volunteer in your community to interact with and help others.
Accept responsibility for your actions.	• If someone asks about a mistake you have made, tell the truth. • Ask what you might do to make up for the mistake.

VOCABULARY WORDS BY CHAPTER

VOCABULARY WORDS BY CHAPTER

GLOSSARY

A

49th parallel *n.* (for-tee-NYNTH PAIR-uh-lehl) the line of latitude established at 49 degrees north latitude; the fixed border between the United States and Canada established with Britain in 1818 (page 236)

abolitionist *n.* (a-buh-LIH-shuhn-ihst) a person who wants to end slavery (page 223)

acquired immunodeficiency syndrome (AIDS) *n.* (uh-KWYRD ih-MYOO-noh-dih-FIH-shun-see SIHN-drohm) the final stage of a virus that attacks the system in the human body that fights off illnesses (page 1083)

active defense *n.* (ACK-tihv DEE-fehns) a policy allowing U.S. warships to defend against attacks by German submarines on ships in shipping traffic lanes in the Atlantic Ocean (page 771)

adversary *n.* (AD-vur-sehr-ee) an enemy, an opponent (page 145)

aerospace industry *n.* (AIR-oh-spayss IHN-duhs-tree) the business of building airplanes, spacecraft, and other vehicles that travel in the air (page 834)

affirmative action *n.* (uh-FUR-muh-tihv AK-shuhn) a government policy that institutes racial quotas to favor groups that suffer from discrimination (page 961)

African diaspora *n.* (A-frih-kuhn dy-AS-puh-ruh) the removal of Africans from their homelands to the Americas (page 49)

Agent Orange *n.* (AY-juhnt OR-ihnj) a potent herbicide used to kill vegetation (page 977)

agrarian *adj.* (ah-GRAIR-ee-ehn) related to agriculture or farming (page 182)

agribusiness *n.* (A-gruh-bihz-nuhs) the commercial business of agriculture (page 859)

Agricultural Revolution *n.* (AHG-rih-kuhl-chuhr-uhl REV-oh-luh-shuhn) the transition in human history from hunting and gathering food to planting crops and raising animals (page 4)

Allied Powers *n.* (AHL-ayhd POHW-uhrs) Several countries, including France and Great Britain, working together to oppose the Axis Powers of Germany, Italy, and Japan during World War II (page 755)

allotment *n.* (uh-LOT-muhnt) a portion; specifically, a piece of land given to a Native American for farming (page 484)

American Anti-Imperialist League *n.* (uh-MAIR-uh-kuhn AN-ty ihm-PIHR-ee-uhl-ist LEEG) an organization that formed in 1898 to oppose the United States' annexation of the Philippines (page 581)

American Civil Liberties Union (ACLU) *n.* (uh-MAIR-uh-kuhn SIH-vuhl LIH-bur-teez YOON-yuhn) an organization, formed in 1920, dedicated to defending the individual rights and freedoms of all Americans (page 643)

American exceptionalism *n.* (uh-MAIR-uh-kuhn ek-SEHP-shuhn-uh-lih-zuhm) the idea that the United States is superior to other countries due to its history and ideology (page 1116)

American Expeditionary Forces (AEF) *n.* (uh-MAIR-uh-kuhn ehk-spuh-DIH-shuhn-air-ee FORS-uhz) the corps of American soldiers sent to fight in Europe during World War I (page 608)

American System *n.* (uh-MAIR-uh-kuhn SIHS-tuhm) a policy of promoting the U.S. industrial system through the use of tariffs, federal subsidies to build roads and other public works, and a national bank to control currency (page 227)

Americanization *n.* (uh-mair-uh-kan-ih-ZAY-shuhn) an effort to immerse immigrants in what some people defined as American culture and transform them into "true" Americans (page 518)

amnesty *n.* (AM-nuh-stee) the pardon of a large group of individuals by a government or other authority (page 434)

amphibious assault *n.* (am-FIH-bee-uhs uh-SAWLT) an attack that uses naval support to protect military forces invading by land and air (page 801)

amphibious force *n.* (am-FIH-bee-uhs FAWRS) a military unit consisting of troops attacking from both land and sea or air simultaneously (page 331)

amphibious landing craft *n.* (am-FIH-bee-uhs LAN-ding KRAFT) boats used to convey soldiers and equipment from the sea to the shore during military attacks (page 804)

Anaconda Plan *n.* (a-nuh-KAHN-duh PLAN) a military strategy during the Civil War in which the North planned to set up a blockade around the southern coast to ruin the South's economy and secure ports on the Mississippi River; much as a huge snake, such as an anaconda, crushes its prey (page 393)

anarchism *n.* (AN-ahr-kih-zuhm) the idea that governments are not necessary and that all social and political cooperation should be voluntary (page 515)

annexation *n.* (a-nehk-SAY-shuhn) the adding of a territory to a country (page 323)

Anti-Defamation League (ADL) *n.* (AN-ty deh-fuh-MAY-shun LEEG) an international Jewish service organization founded to combat anti-Semitism, religious and racial intolerance, and all forms of organized discrimination based on stereotypical beliefs (page 643)

anti-Semitism *n.* (AN-ty SEHM-ih-tih-zuhm) discrimination, prejudice, and hostility against the Jewish people (page 524)

antiaircraft gun *n.* (AN-ty-AIR-kraft GUHN) a piece of heavy artillery modified so that it can be pointed skyward at enemy planes (page 612)

antiballistic missile (ABM) *n.* (AN-ty-buh-LIHS-tihk MIH-suhl) a missile designed to destroy a bomb-carrying missile before it hits its target (page 1045)

antifederalist *n.* (an-tee-FEH-duh-ruh-lihst) a person who opposed the U.S. Constitution of 1787 because of its emphasis on a strong national government (page 162)

apartheid *n.* (uh-PAHR-tayt) the legal separation of the races in South Africa (page 1079)

appeasement *n.* (uh-PEEZ-muhnt) a policy of making political compromises in order to avoid conflict (page 761)

aqueduct *n.* (A-kwuh-duhkt) a structure that carries a canal or water system over a river or ravine; a water bridge (page 228)

aquifer *n.* (AH-kwuh-fur) a geologic formation below Earth's surface that can hold a large groundwater reservoir (page 474)

archipelago *n.* (ahr-kuh-PEH-luh-go) a chain of islands (page 572)

armistice *n.* (AHR-muh-stuhss) an agreement between opposing sides in a conflict to stop fighting (page 625)

arms race *n.* (AHRMZ RAYSS) a political situation in which rival countries try to gather or produce the most military weapons (page 834)

arsenal *n.* (AHRS-uh-nuhl) a place where weapons and other military equipment are stored (page 117)

Articles of Confederation *n.* (AHR-TIH-kuhls UHV kuhn-feh-duh-RAY-shuhn) a set of laws adopted by the United States in 1777 that established each state in the Union as a republic; replaced by the U.S. Constitution in 1789 (page 126)

artifact *n.* (AHR-tif-ackt) an item made by a human that has historical or cultural meaning (page 342)

assassination *n.* (uh-SA-suh-nay-shuhn) an act of murder committed for political reasons (page 427)

assembly line *n.* (uh-SEHM-blee LYN) a method of manufacturing in which the work passes from one worker to another, each of whom has a specific, specialized task (page 651)

assimilate *v.* (uh-SIHM-uhl-ate) to take on the qualities and similarities and way of life of another culture (page 260)

Atlantic Charter *n.* (aht-LAHN-tick CHAHR-tuhr) a charter that lists eight principles for a better world, composed during a meeting between President Franklin Roosevelt and British Prime Minister Winston Churchill in August 1941 (page 770)

atomic bomb *n.* (uh-TAH-mihk BAHM) a type of nuclear bomb whose violent explosion is triggered by splitting atoms, which releases intense heat and radioactivity (page 810)

atrocity *n.* (uh-TRAH-suh-tee) an extremely cruel and shocking act of violence (page 819)

attorney general *n.* (uh-TUR-NEE JEN-ruhl) a member of the president's Cabinet, whose primary roles are to represent the United States before the Supreme Court and act as head of the Department of Justice (page 179)

autocrat *n.* (AW-tuh-krat) a tyrant with absolute power (page 970)

Axis Powers *n.* (ACK-sihs POHW-uhrs) Germany, Italy, and Japan, which formed an alliance together at the start of World War II (page 755)

B

baby boom *n.* (BAY-bee BOOM) a significant increase in the birthrate (page 862)

back-to-Africa movement *n.* (BAK TOO A-frih-kuh MOOV-muhnt) a movement headed by Marcus Garvey that encouraged African Americans to leave the United States and return to Africa (page 665)

backcountry *n.* (BAK-kuhn-tree) the western part of the Southern Colonies just east of the Appalachian Mountains (page 78)

bailout *n.* (BAYL-owt) during the Great Recession, the act of buying mortgages and unstable investments from banks (page 1127)

ballistic missile *n.* (buh-LIHS-tihk MIH-suhl) a nuclear weapon that is propelled by a rocket and guided using a GPS system (page 936)

bank holiday *n.* (BANGK HAH-luh-day) a day or period when banks are closed by government order (page 716)

bankruptcy *n.* (BANGK-ruhpt-see) the state of lacking sufficient funds to pay one's debts; business failure (page 229)

barrage *n.* (buh-RAHJ) heavy artillery fire concentrated on a single line or area (page 416)

battery *n.* (BA-tuh-ree) a group of artillery pieces such as cannons (page 410)

belligerent *n.* (buh-LIH-juh-ruhnt) a country fighting in a war (page 768)

GLOSSARY

Bering Land Bridge *n.* (BAIR-ingh LAND BRIJ) a piece of land between Alaska and Siberia that was above sea level 13,000 years ago, allowing early humans to cross into North America (page 2)

besiege *v.* (bih-SEEZH) to surround using military force (page 45)

Bessemer process *n.* (BEH-seh-mur PRAH-sehs) a process in which workers use forced air to remove impurities such as carbon from iron, which transforms the iron into steel (page 503)

bicameral legislature *n.* (BY-KA-muh-ruhl LEH-jeh-slay-chur) a government body responsible for making laws, made up of two separate houses (e.g. the Senate and the House of Representatives of the U.S. Congress) (page 158)

Bill of Rights *n.* (BIHL UHV RYTS) the first 10 amendments to the U.S. Constitution; a list of guarantees to which every person in a country is entitled (page 165)

bipartisan *adj.* (by-PAHR-tuh-zuhn) relating to both parties in a two-party system (page 949)

black separatist *n.* (BLAK SEH-puh-ruh-tihst) a radical African-American activist who believes the only way to achieve equality and justice in the United States is to separate culturally and economically from whites (page 958)

Bleeding Kansas *n.* (BLEE-dihng KAN-zuhs) the nickname given to the Kansas Territory in the wake of a number of clashes between proslavery and antislavery supporters in 1856 (page 371)

Bonus Army *n.* (BOH-nuhs AHR-mee) the thousands of veterans, determined to collect promised cash bonuses early, who came to Washington during the summer of 1932 to listen to Congress debate the bonus proposal (page 701)

boomtown *n.* (BOOM-town) a town that experiences a great population increase in only a short time period (page 335)

bootlegger *n.* (BOOT-leh-gur) an individual who made, transported, or supplied alcohol illegally to saloons or "speakeasies" where city dwellers congregated in the evenings (page 646)

border state *n.* (BOR-dur STAYT) at the time of the Civil War, a state that bordered both Union and Confederate states, namely Maryland, Kentucky, Delaware, Missouri, and West Virginia (page 391)

Boston Massacre *n.* (BAW-stuhn MA-sih-kur) the 1770 incident in which British soldiers fired on locals who had been taunting them (page 114)

Boston Tea Party *n.* (BAW-stuhn TEE PAHR-tee) the 1773 incident in which the Sons of Liberty boarded British ships and dumped their cargo of tea in protest of British taxes on the colonists (page 114)

Boxer Rebellion *n.* (BAHK-sur rih-BEL-yuhn) a 1900 political uprising in northern China against foreigners in the country (page 574)

boycott *n.* (BOY-kaht) a form of protest that involves refusing to puchase goods or services (page 111)

Bracero Program *n.* (brah-SEH-roh PROH-gram) a program designed to import Mexican laborers to replace native-born agricultural and transportation industry workers who were mobilizing for World War II (page 788)

brain trust *n.* (BRAYN TRUHST) a group of experts who advised President Franklin Roosevelt during the Great Depression (page 716)

breadwinner *n.* (BREHD-wih-nur) a member of a household who contributes to the family's income (page 734)

brinkmanship *n.* (BRIHNGK-muhn-ship) the practice of pushing a conflict to the edge of violence without getting into a war, usually as a tactic to gain a favorable outcome (page 860)

broadside *n.* (BRAWD-syd) a single sheet of printed information (page 139)

bulwark *n.* (BUHL-wurk) something that provides protection or defense (page 861)

busing *n.* (BUH-sing) transporting students of all races to schools outside their neighborhoods or school districts to assure integration and provide equal opportunities in education (page 961)

C

Cabinet *n.* (KAB-niht) the heads of the departments that assist the U.S. president (page 178)

capital *n.* (KA-puh-tuhl) money and other assets needed to start and fund a business (page 219)

capitalism *n.* (KAP-ih-tuh-lih-zuhm) an economic system in which private individuals or groups own the resources and produce goods for a profit (page 642)

caravan *n.* (KEHR-uh-van) a group of people and animals traveling together, usually for trade (page 25)

caravel *n.* (KEHR-ah-vehl) a small, fast ship used by Spanish and Portuguese explorers (page 28)

carpetbagger *n* (KAHR-puht-ba-gur) a northerner who went South after the Civil War, often looking to make a living from the Reconstruction government or to gain power through involvement in the politics of the South (page 439)

cartographer *n.* (kahr-TAH-gruh-fuhr) a mapmaker (page 28)

cavalry *n.* (KA-vuhl-ree) army troops who fight on horseback (page 395)

census *n.* (SEHN-suhs) a formal count of the population of a country (page 179)

charter *n.* (CHAHR-tur) a document that establishes the main goal of an endeavor (page 50)

chattel slavery *n.* (CHA-tuhl SLAY-veh-ree) a system of permanent bondage in which enslaved people have no human rights and are classified as goods (page 30)

checks and balances *n.* (CHEHKS AND BA-luhn-suhz) the system established by the U.S. Constitution that gives each of the branches of government the power to limit the power of the other two (page 160)

chiefdom *n.* (CHEEF-duhm) a large community of people ruled by a chief (page 4)

Children's Bureau *n.* (CHIHL-druhnz BYUR-oh) a U.S. government agency that was created in 1912 and is focused on improving the lives of children and families (page 554)

circumnavigate *v.* (sur-cuhm-NA-vuh-gayt) to go around something instead of through it (page 30)

civic republicanism *n.* (SIH-vihk rih-PUH-blih-kuh-nih-zuhm) the tradition of political thought that stresses individual freedom, active citizenship, and support for the common good (page 180)

civic responsibility *n.* (SIH-vihk rih-SPAWN-suh-BIHL-uh-tee) responsibility that is either required or essential that people perform, such as voting, paying taxes, and serving on juries (page R35)

civil case *n.* (SIH-vuhl KAYS) a legal dispute between two or more individuals or organizations, often involving contract issues or other business problems (page 179)

civil disobedience *n.* (SIH-vuhl dihs-uh-BEE-dee-uhnts) the nonviolent disobeying of laws as a form of protest (page 282)

civil liberties *n.* (SIH-vuhl LIH-bur-teez) individual rights protected by law from government interference (page 610)

coalition *n.* (koh-uh-LIH-shuhn) an alliance of people, parties, or states focused on a common goal (page 241)

collateral *n.* (kuh-LA-tuh-ruhl) secondary property pledged by a borrower as security to protect the lender's interests (page 435)

collective bargaining *n.* (kuh-LEHK-tihv BAHR-guhn-ihng) negotiation between an employer and union leaders on behalf of all union members (page 728)

collude *v.* (kuh-LOOD) to conspire (page 1145)

Columbian Exchange *n.* (kuh-LUM-bee-uhn ehks-CHAYNJ) the exchange of plants, animals, microbes, people, and ideas between the Americas, Europe, and Africa that began after Columbus's first voyage to the Western Hemisphere (page 31)

commission government *n.* (kuh-MIH-shuhn GUH-vur-muhnt) a form of city government in which voters elect a small number of officials called commissioners, each of whom heads a city department (page 560)

committee of correspondence *n.* (kuh-MIH-tee UHV KAWR-uh-spahn-duhnts) in the Revolutionary era, a group of colonists whose duty it was to spread news about protests against the British (page 114)

Committee on Public Information (CPI) *n.* (kuh-MIH-tee ON PUH-blihk ihn-fur-MAY-shuhn) a committee established during World War I to counter possible dissent and raise the country's enthusiasm for the war (page 610)

commodity *n.* (kuh-MAH-duh-tee) a trade good (page 48)

common school *n.* (KAH-muhn SKOOL) a colonial elementary school (page 74)

common school movement *n.* (KAH-muhn SKOOL MOOV-mehnt) an educational reform movement in the 1830s that promoted free public schools funded by property taxes and managed by local governments (page 278)

communism *n.* (KAHM-yuh-nih-zuhm) a form of government in which all the means of production and transportation are owned by the state (page 625)

compassionate conservatism *n.* (kuhm-PAH-shuh-nuht kuhn-SUR-vuh-tih-zuhm) a political philosophy that blends traditional conservative ideas about economic policies with a concern for disadvantaged people (page 1116)

Compromise of 1877 *n.* (KAHM-pruh-myz UHV 1877) a deal in which Democrats agreed to make Rutherford B. Hayes president if Republicans ended Reconstruction and pulled federal troops out of the South (page 453)

concentration camp *n.* (kahnt-suhn-TRAY-shuhn KAMP) a place where prisoners of war or members of persecuted minorities are confined; in World War II, the camps where Jews and others were held and murdered by the Nazis (page 814)

Conestoga wagon *n.* (kah-nuh-STOH-guh WA-guhn) a kind of wagon, made by German settlers in North America, that could carry heavy loads (page 78)

Confederacy *n.* (kon-FED-ur-uh-see) the 11 southern states that seceded from the Union to form their own nation, the Confederate States of America (page 379)

confiscate *v.* (KON-fuh-skayt) to take by governmental act (page 408)

conquistador *n.* (kon-KEES-tuh-dohr) a Spanish conqueror who sought gold and other riches in the Americas (page 44)

conscientious objector *n.* (KAHN-shee-ehnt-shuhs ahb-JEHK-tur) a person who refuses to fight in a war for religious reasons (page 610)

conscription *n.* (kuhn-SKRIHP-shuhn) the requirement to enlist for service in a country's armed forces (page 407)

conservation *n.* (kahn-sur-VAY-shuhn) the management and protection of natural resources (page 562)

conservative *n.* (kuhn-SUR-vuh-tihv) a member of a political party who believes in traditional values, social structure, and gradual change in policies (page 1068)

constituency *n.* (kuhn-STIH-chu-uhn-see) a group of citizens who has elected, or is entitled to elect, a representative to the government (page 663)

constitutional republic *n.* (kahn-stuh-TOO-shuh-nuhl rih-PUH-blihk) a government in which the representatives gain their authority from the consent of the governed as determined by a written constitution (page 158)

consumer society *n.* (kuhn-SOO-mur suh-SY-uh-tee) a society in which shopping and buying goods has become an important part of people's lifestyles (page 864)

consumerism *n.* (kuhn-SOO-muh-rih-zuhm) a theory stating that the economy flourishes when people buy, or consume, a lot of goods and services (page 859)

containment *n.* (kuhn-TAYN-muhnt) a U.S. security policy during the Cold War in which military action was used to stop the Soviet Union from spreading communism (page 827)

context *n.* (KAHN-text) the circumstances and setting in which an object is located, which gives an understanding of how an object is used (page 342)

contiguous *adj.* (kuhn-TIH-gyuh-wuhs) connected (page 331)

contingent *n.* (kuhn-TIHN-juhnt) a small group that represents a larger group (page 415)

contraband *n.* (KON-truh-band) during the Civil War, an enslaved African American living in the South who was captured by Union troops and treated as enemy property during the U.S. Civil War (page 404)

cooperative *n.* (koh-AH-pruh-tihv) an organization run and funded by its members (page 477)

Copperhead *n.* (KAH-pur-hehd) a negative nickname for Democrats who opposed emancipation of enslaved people and the draft (page 404)

corporation *n.* (kor-puh-RAY-shuhn) a company or group that acts legally as a single unit to run a business (page 227)

cotton gin *n.* (KAH-tuhn JIHN) a machine that separates the cotton seeds and hulls from the cotton boll (tuft of cotton) (page 222)

counterculture *n.* (kown-tur-KUHL-chur) a movement in the 1960s that promoted a way of life in opposition to American society's established rules and behavior (page 986)

coup *n.* (KOO) an illegal overthrow of the government (page 971)

court-packing plan *n.* (KORT PA-king PLAN) President Franklin Roosevelt's controversial plan to increase the number of justices on the Supreme Court from nine to fifteen by adding six justices who shared his progressive views (page 730)

cover-up *n.* (KUH-vur UHP) an attempt to hide the truth from the public (page 1054)

covert action *n.* (KOH-vurt AK-shuhn) an activity performed secretly to influence the political, economic, or military situation in another country (page 860)

credibility gap *n.* (kreh-dih-BIHL-uh-tee GAP) an increasing skepticism among Americans about government reports on the Vietnam War (page 979)

credit *n.* (KREH-diht) the privilege of purchasing something or borrowing money and paying the purchase price or money back over time (page 156)

crematorium *n.* (kree-muh-TOR-ee-uhm) a furnace or oven used to burn human or animal remains; in World War II, the ovens used by Nazis to burn their victims' bodies (page 817)

criminal case *n.* (KRIH-muh-nuhl KAYS) a legal dispute in which the government accuses a person or group of breaking the law and endangering society (page 179)

Crittenden Plan *n.* (KRIHT-uhn-duhn PLAN) a proposal that stated the federal government would have no power to abolish slavery in the states where it already existed; it proposed reestablishing and extending the Missouri Compromise line to the Pacific Ocean (page 378)

Crusades *n.* (kroo-SAYDZ) military expeditions of the Roman Catholic Church to take back holy lands in the Middle East from Muslim control, 1096–1291 (page 21)

Cuban Missile Crisis *n.* (KYOO-buhn MIH-suhl CRY-suhs) a political showdown in 1962 between the United States and the Soviet Union caused by the presence of Soviet nuclear weapons in Cuba (page 936)

cult of domesticity *n.* (KUHLT UHV doh-mehs-TIH-suh-tee) an opinion about women common during the 19th century in the middle and upper classes that women should marry, stay at home to care for the family household and children, and act as the moral center of the household (page 292)

cultural advocacy *n.* (KUHLCH-ruhl AD-vuh-kuh-see) a political strategy in which members of a religion influence politicians and social institutions in an effort to promote their beliefs (page 1074)

cultural diffusion *n.* (KUHLCH-ruhl di-FYOO-zhuhn) the spreading of traditions and ways of living from one place to another (page 49)

currency *n.* (KUR-uhn-see) money that is in circulation to be used for buying and selling goods and services; paper money (page 156)

D

D-day *n.* (DEE DAY) the day, June 6, 1944, in World War II when Allied forces invaded northern France by landing on beaches at Normandy (page 804)

dark horse *n.* (DARK HAWRS) a little-known candidate whose nomination is unexpected and usually the result of a compromise between factions (page 326)

DDT *n.* (DEE-DEE-TEE) a pesticide, now banned in the United States and many other countries, that was found to be harmful to animals and to cause long-term contamination of the environment (page 1046)

de facto segregation *n.* (dih FAK-toh seh-grih-GAY-shuhn) segregation that is present in society even though no laws enforce it (page 958)

de jure segregation *n.* (dee JUR-ee seh-grih-GAY-shuhn) segregation enforced by law (page 958)

debt peonage *n.* (DEHT PEE-uh-nihj) a form of labor in which a person works just to pay off a debt (page 444)

Declaration of Independence *n.* (deh-kluh-RAY-shun UHV ihn-duh-PEHN-duhns) the document declaring U.S. independence from Great Britain, adopted July 4, 1776 (page 125)

defensive war *n.* (dih-FEHN-sihv WOR) a war to protect one's own land, on familiar ground, from outside attackers (page 391)

deferment *n.* (dih-FUR-muhnt) an official permission to delay conscription (page 980)

deficit *n.* (DEH-fuh-suht) a negative monetary balance that occurs when expenditures exceed income (page 716)

deficit reduction *n.* (DEH-fuh-suht rih-DUHK-shun) the steps taken by a government to pay off debt (page 1095)

deficit spending *n.* (DEH-fuh-suht SPEHND-ihng) the act of spending more money than the government receives from taxes (page 742)

deflation *n.* (dee-FLAY-shuhn) a decrease in the prices of goods and services (page 513)

dehumanize *v.* (dee-HYOO-mahn-ize) to treat people as if they are not human beings (page 905)

demilitarized zone *n.* (dee-MIH-luh-tuh-ryzd ZOHN) an area in which military personel and weapons are not allowed (page 840)

demobilization *n.* (dih-moh-buh-ly-ZAY-shuhn) the release of soldiers from military duty (page 791)

demographic composition *n.* (dem-uh-GRA-fihk kahm-puh-ZIH-shuhn) the make-up of the population of a specific area based on ethnicity (page 955)

department store *n.* (dee-PAHRT-mehnt STOHR) large store that provides a wide variety of merchandise organized into different departments but all under one roof (page 531)

deploy *v.* (dih-PLOY) to send into military action (page 131)

deport *v.* (dih-PORT) to forcibly remove from the country, or to pressure to leave (page 691)

depression *n.* (dee-PREH-shuhn) a severe and longterm economic decline characterized by a number of business failures, reduced industrial output, and high unemployment (page 152)

depth charge *n.* (DEHPTH CHAHRJ) an underwater bomb that is programmed to explode at a certain depth (page 799)

deregulation *n.* (dee-reh-gyuh-LAY-shun) the act of repealing laws on a large scale; usually related to a particular industry (page 1075)

desegregation *n.* (dee-seh-grih-GAY-shuhn) the process of ending a policy that forces the separation of groups of people in public spaces (page 907)

détente *n.* (day-TAHNT) an easing of tensions and an improvement in relations between countries (page 1045)

dime novel *n.* (DYM NAH-vuhl) popular fiction that sold for 10 cents a book in the late 18th and early 19th centuries (page 489)

direct primary *n.* (duh-REKT PRY-mair-ee) a preliminary election in which voters choose the party candidates to run in a later election for public office (page 561)

GLOSSARY

disenfranchise *v.* (dihs-ihn-FRAN-chyz) to deprive someone of a legal right or privilege, such as the right to vote (page 951)

disintegration *n.* (dihs-ihn-tuh-GRAY-shuhn) the endurance of nationalist, tribalist, and separatist alternatives to globalization (page 1111)

disposable income *n.* (dih-SPOH-zuh-buhl IHN-kuhm) spending money (page 685)

dissenter *n.* (dih-SEHN-tur) a person who disagrees with a majority belief or position (page 56)

dividend *n.* (DIH-vuh-dehnd) money paid regularly to shareholders of a company from the company's profits or reserves (page 183)

doctrine of nullification *n.* (DAHK-truhn UHV nuh-luh-fuh-KAY-shuhn) a doctrine that said a state could nullify, or reject, a federal law they felt was unconstitutional, held by some southern politicians before the Civil War (page 258)

domesticate *v.* (duh-MEHS-tih-kayt) to raise plants and animals for human benefit and consumption (page 15)

domestication *n.* (duh-mehs-TIH-kay-shuhn) the practice of raising animals and growing plants for human benefit (page 4)

domino theory *n.* (DAH-muh-noh THEER-ee) an idea during the Cold War that countries that neighbor communist countries are more likely to fall to communism (page 837)

dove *n.* (DUHV) a person who opposes war (page 980)

Dow Jones Industrial Average *n.* (DAU JOHNZ ihn-DUH-stree-uhl A-vuh-rihj) an index of the stock of leading companies, tracked daily and used as a measure of general stock market trends (page 686)

draft *n.* (DRAFT) a mandatory term of military service (page 407)

Dred Scott decision *n.* (DRED SKAHT dih-SIH-zhuhn) a Supreme Court decision that African Americans held no rights as citizens and that the Missouri Compromise of 1820 was unconstitutional; Dred Scott, the escaped slave at the center of the case, was returned to slavery (page 372)

dry farming *n.* (DRY FAHR-mihng) agricultural techniques used in areas with little rainfall (page 471)

dual sovereignty *n.* (DOO-uhl SAH-vuh-ruhn-tee) the concept that state governments have certain powers the federal government cannot overrule (page 158)

Dust Bowl *n.* (DUHST BOHL) areas of Kansas, Colorado, Oklahoma, Texas, and New Mexico that, during the 1930s, suffered ecological devastation and turned into a barren desert (page 695)

duty *n.* (DOO-tee) a tax on imports (page 110)

E

earthworks *n.* (URTH-wurks) human-made land modifications (page 122)

economic planning *n.* (eh-kuh-NAH-mihk PLAN-ihng) management of the economy by the federal government (page 719)

economic stagnation *n.* (eh-kuh-NAH-mihk stahg-NAY-shuhn) a period of little or no economic growth (page 1056)

economic stimulus *n.* (eh-kuh-NAH-mihk STIHM-yuh-luhs) a measure aimed at promoting and enabling financial recovery and growth (page 1129)

egalitarianism *n.* (ih-gal-uh-TAIR-ee-uhn-ih-zuhm) a belief in the equality of all people, especially in their political, economic, and social concerns (page 152)

electoral college *n.* (ee-lehk-TAWR-uhl KAH-lihj) the group that elects the U.S. president; each state receives as many electors as it has congressional representatives and senators combined (page 160)

emancipation *n.* (ih-man-suh-PAY-shuhn) the act of freeing the enslaved (page 288)

Emancipation Proclamation *n.* (ih-man-suh-PAY-shuhn prah-kluh-MAY-shuhn) an 1863 document issued by Abraham Lincoln that declared all slaves living in Confederate-held territory during the American Civil War to be free (page 405)

embargo *n.* (ihm-BAHR-goh) a ban against engaging in commerce with specified countries (page 198)

empresario *n.* (ehm-pruh-SAH-ree-oh) an agent who entered into a contract with New Spain or, later, the Mexican government, to recruit Americans to settle the land that is now Texas (page 321)

encomienda *n.* (ehn-koh-mee-EHN-duh) a system in Spain's American colonies in which wealthy settlers were given plots of land and allowed to enslave the people who lived there (page 47)

enemy alien *n.* (EH-nuh-mee AY-lyuhn) someone whose loyalty to the nation in which the person lives is suspect (page 794)

enfranchisement *n.* (ihn-FRAN-chyz-muhnt) the granting of the rights of citizenship, especially the right to vote (page 555)

Enlightenment *n.* (ihn-LY-tuhn-muhnt) an intellectual movement that emphasized the use of reason to examine previously accepted beliefs (page 88)

entrepreneur *n.* (ahn-truh-pruh-NUR) a person who starts, manages, and is responsible for a business (page 335)

envoy *n.* (AHN-voy) an ambassador (page 187)

escalation *n.* (ehs-kuh-LAY-shuhn) an increase in intensity (page 972)

espionage *n.* (EH-spee-uh-nahj) the practice of spying to obtain information (page 139)

estuary *n.* (EHS-chuh-wair-ee) the area at the mouth of a river where fresh water and sea water mix (page 194)

eugenics *n.* (yoo-JEH-nihks) the belief that some races were superior to others and that breeding should be controlled so that populations of superior races increase (page 644)

evangelist *n.* (ih-VAN-juh-lihst) a preacher who enthusiastically urges believers to experience a spiritual rebirth and accept Jesus as their personal savior (page 277)

excise tax *n.* (EHK-syz TAKS) a tax levied on one particular product (page 182)

executive branch *n.* (ihg-ZEH-kyuh-tihv BRANCH) the section of the U.S. government headed by the president; responsible for enforcing the law (page 158)

executive order *n.* (ihg-ZEH-kyuh-tihv OR-dur) a directive issued by a president that has the force of law (page 795)

executive privilege *n.* (ihg-ZEH-kyuh-tihv PRIHV-lij) the principle that in the nation's interest, the president may withhold certain information from Congress (page 1054)

exemption *n.* (ihg-ZEHMP-shuhn) a release from obligations (page 408)

Exoduster *n.* (EKS-oh-duhs-tur) an African American who migrated from the South to the Great Plains after Reconstruction had failed (page 470)

expansionism *n.* (ihk-SPAN-shuh-nih-zuhm) a policy or practice of increasing a country's territory (page 572)

exploitative *adj.* (ehks-PLOY-tuh-tihv) unfairly and often abusively using people for profit or other advantage (page 221)

exposé *n.* (ehk-spoh-ZAY) a work of writing that publicizes a scandal or injustice (page 553)

F

fascism *n.* (FA-shih-zuhm) a political movement based on extreme nationalism, militarism, and racism promoting the superiority of a particular people over all others (page 699)

federalism *n.* (FEH-duh-ruh-lih-zuhm) a system of government in which power is shared between national and state or provincial governments (page 158)

federalist *n.* (FEH-duh-ruh-lihst) a person who supported the U.S. Constitution of 1787 as it was written during the process of ratification (page 162)

feminism *n.* (FEH-muh-nih-zuhm) the idea that women are equal to men socially and politically (page 1021)

feudalism *n.* (FEW-dahl-izm) a political and social system in which a vassal receives protection from a lord in exchange for obedience and service (page 20)

filibuster *n.* (FIH-luh-buhs-tur) a political strategy in which a small group of legislators take turns speaking and refuse to stop the debate or allow a bill to come to a vote (page 949)

financier *n.* (fih-nuhn-SIHR) a person who lends or manages money for a business or undertaking (page 137)

fireside chat *n.* (FY-ur-syd CHAT) one of a series of radio broadcasts that President Franklin Roosevelt made to the nation throughout his presidency (page 716)

First Hundred Days *n.* (FURST HUHN-druhd DAYZ) President Franklin Roosevelt's first 100 days in office, during which he produced 15 laws that formed the basis of the New Deal (page 716)

flanking maneuver *n.* (FLAYNG-kihng muh-NOO-vuhr) a military movement of troops around the side of an enemy line in the hope of gaining an advantage (page 411)

flapper *n.* (FLA-pur) a young woman in the 1920s who embraced a freer style of dress and the use of cosmetics (page 660)

forage *v.* (FOR-ihj) to search for plants (page 480)

foreclosure *n.* (fohr-KLOH-zhur) the action of a bank taking possession of a property because the buyer can no longer make payments (page 156)

forty-niner *n.* (FAWR-tee-NY-nur) one of the thousands of prospective miners who traveled to California seeking gold in 1849 (page 335)

Fourteen Points *n.* (FOR-teen PAWIHNTS) President Woodrow Wilson's proposed program for peace at the end of World War I (page 623)

Framer *n.* (FRAYM-ur) one of the delegates sent by the states to create the Constitution of the United States (page 157)

franchise *n.* (FRAN-chyz) a constitutional right, especially the right to vote (page 555)

free silver movement *n.* (FREE SIHL-vur MOOV-mehnt) a monetary system that would allow private citizens to mint their silver into U.S. coins (page 477)

free-enterprise zone *n.* (FREE EHN-tur-pryz ZOHN) an area that allows the suspension of both tax and custom laws (page 1111)

freedman *n.* (FREED-man) a formerly enslaved person (page 404)

Freedmen's Bureau *n.* (FREED-muhns BYOOR-oh) the Bureau of Refugees, Freedmen, and Abandoned Lands, created by Congress in 1865 to help former slaves, as well as poor white southerners (page 446)

Freedom Riders *n.* (FREE-duhm RY-durz) interracial groups who rode buses in the South and ignored "white" and "colored" signs when they stopped at restrooms and lunch counters so that a series of federal court decisions declaring segregation illegal in facilities serving travelers would not be ignored by white officials (page 917)

front *n.* (FRUHNT) a battle line between armies (page 401)

Frostbelt *n.* (FRAHST-behlt) the north-central and northeastern regions of the United States, which have cold winters (page 859)

fugitive slave clause *n.* (FYOO-juh-tihv SLAYV KLAWZ) a provision in Article 4 of the U.S. Constitution that prevented free states from emancipating enslaved workers who had escaped from their masters in other states (page 161)

fundamentalism *n.* (FUHN-duh-mehn-tah-lih-zuhm) a movement that promoted the idea that every word of the Bible was the literal truth (page 647)

G

gag rule *n.* (GAG ROOL) a series of regulations adopted by Congress in the 1830s and 1840s to prevent the discussion or consideration of antislavery petitions brought to Congress; any regulation that prohibits legislative or public discussion of a specific subject (page 291)

garrison *n.* (GAIR-uh-suhn) a defense force of soldiers (page 132)

gender bias *n.* (JEHN-dur BY-uhs) the preference for one gender over another (page 1022)

genetically modified food *n.* (juh-NEH-tik-lee MAH-duh-fyd FOOD) food grown from plants that have been changed in a way that does not occur naturally (page 1139)

genocide *n.* (JEH-nuh-syd) the deliberate murder of a large number of people belonging to a specific racial, cultural, or political group (page 483)

Gestapo *n.* (guh-SHTAH-poh) Nazi secret police force (page 754)

Ghost Dance *n.* (GOHST DANSS) a ceremonial dance performed by some Native Americans who believed the dance would summon a deliverer who would restore their world (page 484)

GI Bill *n.* (JEE I BIHL) a government program started in 1944 that helped veterans returning from World War II buy homes and attend college (page 833)

glacial period *n.* (GLAY-shuhl PEER-ee-uhd) a period of time in history during which huge sheets of ice covered much of Earth (page 1)

glacial till *n.* (GLAY-shuhl TIHL) a deposit of unsorted sediment that may include silt, sand, clay, rock, and other materials dropped and left behind by retreating glaciers (page 238)

glasnost *n.* (GLAZ-nohst) a government policy of open communication in the former Soviet Union (page 1084)

globalization *n.* (gloh-buh-luh-ZAY-shuhn) the faster and freer flow of people, resources, goods, and ideas across national borders (page 1110)

gold standard *n.* (GOHLD STAN-durd) a monetary system in which a nation's currency is backed by gold (page 477)

government-in-exile *n.* (GUH-vur-muhnt IHN EHG-zyl) a government that has been deposed and attempts to rule from another land (page 836)

grandfather clause *n.* (GRAHND-fah-thur KLAWZ) a part of a law that excludes certain people and things because of conditions that existed before the law was passed (page 535)

grassroots activism *n.* (GRAS-roots AK-tih-vih-zuhm) political movements driven by people who individually do not have much power, but who, working together, can be very effective (page 902)

Great Awakening *n.* (GRAYT uh-WAY-kuhn-ing) a series of Protestant religious revivals that swept across the American colonies (page 90)

Great Depression *n.* (GRAYT dee-PREH-shuhn) a worldwide economic downturn in the 1930s, marked by poverty and high unemployment (page 687)

Great Migration *n.* (GRAYT my-GRAY-shuhn) a massive movement of African Americans who left the South for cities in the North, beginning in 1910 (page 619)

greenback *n.* (GREEN-bak) paper currency issued by the Union, replacing the notes of individual banks (page 393)

greenhouse effect *n.* (GREEN-hows uh-FEHKT) the warming of Earth's surface caused when greenhouse gas emissions trap the sun's heat (page 1136)

greenhouse gas *n.* (GREEN-hows GAS) a gas such as carbon dioxide or methane (page 1136)

gross national product (GNP) *n.* (GROHS NA-shuh-nuhl PRAH-duhkt) the total goods and services produced by the nation plus the income earned by its citizens (page 687)

guerrilla tactic *n.* (guh-RIH-luh TAK-tihk) an unconventional method of warfare, such as sneak attacks and sabotage, used by independent military groups (page 117)

H

hacienda *n.* (hah-see-EHN-duh) a large plantation in a Spanish-speaking colony (page 47)

hardliner *n.* (HAHRD-ly-nur) a person, usually within a political or special-interest group, who strictly supports a set of ideas or policies (page 1085)

Harlem Renaissance *n.* (HAHR-luhm reh-nuh-SAHNTS) a cultural movement that originated in Harlem in the 1920s and promoted African-American writers, artists, and musicians (page 666)

hawk *n.* (HAWK) a person who supports war (page 980)

Haymarket Riot *n.* (HAY-mahr-kuht RY-uht) a violent confrontation between workers and police on May 4, 1886, which began as a protest against police conduct during a strike at a factory of the McCormick Company in Chicago, Illinois (page 515)

heretic *n.* (HAIR-uh-tihk) a person who holds beliefs different from the teachings of the Catholic Church (page 54)

Hessian *n.* (HEH-shuhn) a German soldier hired by the British to fight during the American Revolution (page 123)

Holocaust *n.* (HOH-luh-cawst) the mass slaughter by the Nazis of six million Jews and others during World War II (page 817)

homogeneity *n.* (hoh-muh-juh-NAY-uh-tee) the state of being the same or similar (page 867)

Hooverville *n.* (HOO-vur-vil) a makeshift village for homeless Americans, usually at the edge of a city with shelters made of cardboard, scrap metal, or whatever was cheap and available (page 698)

horizontal integration *n.* (hor-uh-ZAHN-tuhl ihn-tuh-GRAY-shuhn) purchasing other companies that offer the same goods and services in order to reduce the number of competitors and achieve control within an industry (page 503)

human immunodeficiency virus (HIV) *n.* (HYOO-muhn ih-MYOO-noh-dih-FIH-shun-see VY-ruhs) a virus that attacks the system in the human body that fights off illnesses (page 1083)

humanism *n.* (HYOO-muh-nih-zhum) a movement that focuses on the importance of the individual (page 21)

hunter-gatherer *n.* (HUHN-tuhr GAHTH-uhr-uhr) a human who hunts animals and gathers wild plants to eat (page 3)

hydraulic mining *n.* (hy-DRAW-lik MY-nihng) a process of uncovering precious minerals by using pressurized water to remove soil (page 472)

hydrogen bomb *n.* (HY-druh-juhn BAHM) a nuclear weapon that explodes due to compacted gases inside (page 835)

I

ice age *n.* (AISS AJ) a period of time in history during which huge sheets of ice covered much of Earth (page 1)

impasse *n.* (IHM-pass) a situation in which no progress is possible (page 985)

impeachment *n.* (ihm-PEECH-muhnt) formal charges brought against a public official for misconduct in office (page 160)

imperialism *n.* (ihm-PIHR-ee-uh-lih-zuhm) a policy or practice of exerting control over weaker nations or territories (page 572)

impressment *n.* (ihm-PREHS-muhnt) the act of forcing people into military or naval service (page 186)

inauguration *n.* (uh-NAW-gyuh-ray-shun) the swearing-in ceremony that marks the beginning of a presidency (page 178)

income inequality *n.* (IHN-kuhm ih-nih-KWAH-luh-tee) an economic phenomenon in which a large gap exists between what the poorest and the richest citizens in a nation earn (page 1075)

income tax *n.* (IHN-kuhm TAKS) a tax that is based on the amount a person earns (page 571)

indentured servant *n.* (ihn-DEHN-churd SUR-vuhnt) a person under contract to work, usually without pay, in exchange for free passage to the colonies (page 51)

Indian Removal Act *n.* (IHN-dee-uhn rih-MOO-vuhl AKT) a law that ended the U.S. government's earlier policy of respecting the rights of Native Americans to remain on their land (page 260)

Indian Territory *n.* (IHN-dee-uhn TAIR-uh-tawr-ee) the area of land in present-day Oklahoma and parts of Kansas and Nebraska to which Native Americans were forced to migrate (page 260)

induction *n.* (ihn-DUHK-shun) the act of being drafted into the military (page 989)

indulgence *n.* (in-DUHL-juhnts) the release from punishment for sins, sold by papal officials (page 22)

Industrial Revolution *n.* (ihn-DUH-stree-uhl rehv-uh-LOO-shuhn) an era in which widespread production by machinery replaced goods made by hand (page 219)

infamy *n.* (IHN-fuh-me) the state of being known for committing an extremely shameful or evil act (page 784)

infantry *n.* (IHN-fuhn-tree) foot soldiers (page 395)

GLOSSARY

inflation *n.* (ihn-FLAY-shuhn) a decrease in the value of money that causes an increase in the price of goods and services (page 137)

influenza *n.* (ihn-floo-EHN-zuh) an acute and highly contagious illness commonly called "the flu" (page 621)

infrastructure *n.* (IHN-fruh-struhk-chur) the basic systems of a society including roads, bridges, sewers, and electricity (page 17)

initiative *n.* (ih-NIH-shuh-tihv) a procedure by which citizens can propose new laws to be voted on by the public or by the legislature (page 561)

injunction *n.* (ihn-JUHNGK-shuhn) court orders that demand or forbid certain actions (page 700)

insurgent *n.* (ihn-SUR-juhnt) a rebel or revolutionary (page 970)

insurrection *n.* (ihn-suh-REHK-shuhn) a violent rebellion against a government or political authority (page 330)

integrate *v.* (IHN-tuh-grayt) to bring into society as equals (page 435)

integration *n.* (ihn-tuh-GRAY-shuhn) the process of joining economic forces (page 1111)

interchangeable part *n.* (ihn-tur-CHAYN-juh-buhl PAHRT) a part of a mechanism that can be substituted for another identical one (page 219)

intermediary *n.* (ihn-tur-MEE-dee-ehr-ee) someone who helps disputing sides negotiate and come to an agreement (page 187)

interned *v.* (ihn-TURND) confined in prisons or camps for military or political reasons during wartime (page 794)

Internet *n.* (IHN-tur-neht) the worldwide network of computers (page 1081)

internment camp *n.* (ihn-TURN-muhnt KAMP) a prison camp to hold enemy aliens and other prisoners of war during wartime (page 795)

interstate commerce *n.* (IHN-tur-stayt KAH-murs) the sale, purchase, or trade of goods; transportation of people, money, or goods; and navigation of waters between different states (page 161)

Interstate Highway System *n.* (IHN-tur-stayt HY-way SIHS-tuhm) the network of highways launched by President Eisenhower in 1956 to span the United States and connect states and major cities (page 866)

investment bank *n.* (ihn-VEHST-muhnt BANK) a financial institution that purchases and sells stocks and bonds and helps companies raise capital and manage their assets (page 1126)

iron curtain *n.* (I-urn KUR-tuhn) the military and political divide in Europe between Western capitalist and Eastern communist countries (page 827)

ironclad *n.* (I-urn-klahd) a ship armored with iron plates to protect it from cannon fire (page 399)

irregular *n.* (ih-REH-gyuh-lur) a soldier who fights for an army on and off instead of committing to a set length of time of military service (page 142)

Islamic republic *n.* (IZ-lahm-ik RE-puhb-lik) a state either incorporating or based entirely on Islamic law (page 1062)

island hopping *n.* (I-luhnd HAH-pihng) a strategy that involves capturing and setting up military bases on island groups one island at a time (page 803)

isolationism *n.* (I-soh-LAY-shuh-nih-zuhm) a policy in which a nation stays out of the affairs of other nations (page 572)

isthmus *n.* (IHS-muhs) a narrow strip of land connecting two larger land areas (page 583)

J

Jacksonian democracy *n.* (jak-SOH-nee-uhn dih-MAH-kruh-see) a political movement that celebrated the common man and defended the will of the people, named for President Andrew Jackson (page 253)

jazz *n.* (JAZ) a style of music originating among African-American musicians that contains lively rhythms, sounds from a variety of instruments, and improvisation (page 654)

Jim Crow laws *n.* (JIHM KROH LAWZ) laws established after the Reconstruction period that enforced racial segregation across the southern states (page 535)

job dislocation *n.* JAHB dihs-loh-KAY-shuhn) the movement of jobs to other places (page 1110)

joint-stock company *n.* (JOYNT STAHK KUHM-puh-nee) a company whose shareholders own stock in the company (page 50)

judicial branch *n.* (joo-DIH-shuhl BRANCH) the section of the U.S. government that includes the courts and legal system, led by the Supreme Court; responsible for interpreting the law (page 158)

judicial review *n.* (joo-DIH-shuhl rih-VYOO) the power to invalidate any law the Supreme Court deems unconstitutional, even if it has been passed by Congress and signed into law by the president (page 189)

K

kamikaze *n.* (kah-mih-KAH-zee) one of a group of Japanese suicide bomber pilots who crashed their planes, loaded with explosives, into American ships (page 808)

Kellogg-Briand Pact *n.* (KEH-lawg bree-AHN PAKT) a multinational agreement from 1928 in which the signing countries agreed to reject war (page 685)

kitchen cabinet *n.* (KIH-chuhn KAB-niht) a group of unofficial advisors to Andrew Jackson (page 255)

L

labor union *n.* (LAY-bur YOON-yuhn) groups of workers who band together to achieve better pay, safer working conditions, and other benefits (page 279)

laissez-faire economics *n.* (leh-say FAIR eh-kuh-NAH-mihks) a policy that calls for less government involvement in economic affairs, so that businesses choose how they will operate, with little or no oversight (page 513)

lame duck *n.* (LAYM DUHK) an outgoing elected official soon to be replaced by a successor (page 715)

landmark decision *n.* (lahnd-MARK dih-SIH-zhuhn) a legal case that settles important questions about new or existing laws (page 235)

landmark legislation *n.* (lahnd-MARK lehj-iss-LAY-shun) an important and historic law (page 957)

League of Nations *n.* (LEEG UHV NAY-shuhnz) President Woodrow Wilson's plan proposed after World War I for a general assembly of countries that would stabilize relations among countries and help preserve peace (page 626)

legislative branch *n.* (LEH-jeh-slay-tihv BRANCH) the section of the U.S. government led by Congress; responsible for making the law (page 158)

libel *n.* (LY-buhl) the crime of publishing negative claims about someone without evidence (page 93)

liberal consensus *n.* (LIH-buh-ruhl kuhn-SEHN-suhs) the agreement between the Democrats and Republicans in Congress made after World War II to continue welfare, develop a national security system, and strengthen the executive branch of government (page 832)

Liberty Bond *n.* (LIH-bur-tee BAHND) a government bond sold to individuals to help support U.S. involvement in World War I (page 608)

lien *n.* (LEEN) a legal claim to a person's property and income if debts aren't paid (page 443)

literacy test *n.* (LIH-tur-uh-see TEST) a test of one's ability to read and write (page 451)

local color *n.* (LOH-kuhl KUH-lur) a writing style that expresses the style and characteristics of a region (page 490)

lock *n.* (LAHK) a confined section of water used to raise or lower ships (page 227)

lode *n.* (LOHD) vein of ore (page 472)

Long March *n.* (LOHNGH MAHRCH) a 6,000-mile journey by Chinese communists to relocate the communist revolutionary base from southeast China to central China (page 765)

long-staple cotton *n.* (LAWNG STAY-puhl KAH-tuhn) a type of cotton that produces long fibers suitable for the manufacture of fine cloth and lace; it grows best in just a few climates and soils (page 222)

loose constructionist *n.* (LOOS kuhn-STRUHK-shuh-nihst) someone who interprets the U.S. Constitution as giving expansive powers to Congress and the president (page 182)

Louisiana Purchase *n.* (loo-ee-zee-A-nuh PUR-chuhs) an 1803 treaty in which the United States purchased a large area of land between the Mississippi River and the Rocky Mountains from France (page 190)

Loyalist *n.* (LOY-uh-lihst) an American colonist who supported Britain during the American Revolution (page 111)

loyalty oath *n.* (LOY-uhl-tee OHTH) a sworn statement confirming a person does not belong and has never belonged to various organizations including those identified as communist (page 843)

lynch *v.* (LIHNCH) to hang someone illegally by mob action (page 409)

M

machine gun *n.* (muh-SHEEN GUHN) a gun designed to fire hundreds of bullets per minute (page 612)

malaise *n.* (muh-LAYZ) a general feeling of illness or unease (page 1059)

mandate *n.* (MAN-dayt) the authority to carry out a course of action, given to a representative by voters (page 269)

manifest destiny *n.* (MAN-uh-fehst DEHS-tuh-nee) the belief that Americans were intended to settle all the land between the Atlantic and Pacific coasts (page 314)

manifesto *n.* (man-uh-FEHS-toh) a written declaration of intent (page 1012)

manor system *n.* (MA-nur SIHS-tuhm) an economic system in which peasants are bound to a lord and work his land, or manor, in exchange for food and shelter (page 20)

maquiladora *n.* (mah-kee-luh-DOR-uh) a manufacturing plant located in an export-processing zone (page 1110)

margin *n.* (MAHR-juhn) money borrowed from a bank in order to pay for an investment, such as stocks (page 686)

maritime *adj.* (MAR-uh-tym) related to the sea (page 72)

market revolution *n.* (MAHR-kuht rehv-uh-LOO-shuhn) the transition from a pre-industrial economy to a market-oriented, capitalist economy (page 226)

marriage equality *n.* (MEHR-ihj ih-KWAH-luh-tee) the legal right of gays and lesbians to marry their partners and have the same privileges that married heterosexual couples enjoy (page 1134)

Marshall Plan *n.* (MAHR-shuhl PLAN) a U.S. economic aid program to restore economic stability to Western Europe after World War II (page 825)

martial law *n.* (MAHR-shuhl LAW) law applied to an occupied society and enforced by the military (page 117)

mass market *n.* (MAS MAHR-kuht) a large number of consumers to whom manufacturers can sell goods that are manufactured in mass quantities (page 651)

mass media *n.* (MAS MEE-dee-uh) forms of communication such as radio, film, and musical recordings with the potential to reach large audiences (page 696)

mass production *n.* (MAS pruh-DUHK-shuhn) the use of machinery to make goods in large quantities (page 219)

material record *n.* (muh-TEEHR-ee-uhl REK-uhrd) the buildings and objects that survive from a previous era (page 342)

McCarthyism *n.* (muh-KAHR-thee-ih-zuhm) the practice of accusing people of being traitors to their country without offering proof (page 845)

Medicaid *n.* (MEH-dih-kayd) a U.S. government program started in 1965 that gives medical insurance to impoverished people (page 954)

Medicare *n.* (MEH-dih-kair) a U.S. government program started in 1965 that gives medical insurance to elderly people (page 954)

mercantilism *n.* (MUHR-kuhn-teel-ih-zuhm) an economic policy that gives a country sole ownership of the trade occurring in its colonies (page 23)

mercenary *n.* (MUR-suh-nair-ee) a soldier who is paid to fight for a country other than his or her own (page 123)

merger *n.* (MUR-jur) the act of incorporating two or more businesses into one (page 563)

Middle Passage *n.* (MIH-duhl PA-sihj) the long trip across the Atlantic Ocean in which enslaved Africans were brought to the Americas; the second leg of the triangular trade route (page 49)

midnight judge *n.* (MIHD-nyt JUHJ) one of a group of judges commissioned by President John Adams the night before he left office (page 189)

militant *adj.* (MIH-luh-tuhnt) overly aggressive in achieving a goal (page 1016)

militarism *n.* (MIH-luh-tuh-rih-zuhm) the belief that a government must create a strong military and be prepared to use it to achieve the country's goals (page 600)

military-industrial complex *n.* (mih-luh-tair-EE ihn-DUS-tree-uhl CAHM-plehks) a country's military establishment and industries producing arms or other military materials (page 835)

minuteman *n.* (MIH-nuht-man) an American colonial militia member who was ready to join in combat at a moment's notice (page 117)

miscegenation *n.* (MIH-sehj-ehn-a-shuhn) marriage between people of different races (page 961)

misogyny *n.* (MISS-ah-jihn-ee) a dislike, contempt for, or hatred of women; prejudice against women (page 1023)

Missouri Compromise *n.* (mih-ZUR-ee KAHM-pruh-myz) an agreement that stated the people of Missouri could own slaves and be admitted to the Union along with Maine, a free state (page 240)

mobilization *n.* (moh-buh-luh-ZAY-shuhn) the act of assembling and organizing military forces (page 741)

mobilize *v.* (MOH-buh-lyz) to organize and prepare troops for war (page 125)

modernism *n.* (MAH-dur-nih-zuhm) a modern artistic and literary style, featuring a hard, realistic tone and a tendency to reject or avoid artistic and literary practices of the past (page 658)

module *n.* (MAH-jool) a segment of a spacecraft that can function on its own (page 1028)

monoculture *n.* (mahn-oh-KUHL-chuhr) the practice of growing a single crop (page 509)

monopoly *n.* (muh-NAH-puh-lee) the complete and exclusive control of an industry by one company (page 226)

Montgomery Bus Boycott *n.* (mahnt-GUH-muh-ree BUHS BOY-kaht) a mass protest, sparked by the arrest of Rosa Parks, against the racial segregation practices of the public bus system in Montgomery, Alabama (page 911)

moral diplomacy *n.* (MOR-uhl duh-PLOH-muh-see) the concept that the United States should drastically reduce its intervention in the affairs of other countries (page 604)

morphine *n.* (MOR-feen) a powerful painkiller (page 429)

mortar *n.* (MOR-tur) a short-range, muzzle-loaded cannon (page 975)

mountain men *n.* (MOWN-tuhn MEHN) the American trappers, fur traders, and explorers who began to explore and move west (page 314)

mountain pass *n.* (MOWN-tuhn PAS) a passageway through a mountain range that is lower than the surrounding peaks (page 337)

muckrakers *n.* (MUHK-ray-kurs) investigative journalists of the early 1900s who exposed misconduct by powerful organizations or people (page 505)

multinational corporation *n.* (muhl-tee-NA-shuh-nuhl kor-puh-RAY-shuhn) a company that has offices and factories in multiple countries (page 1138)

Munich Agreement *n.* (MYOO-nihk uh-GREE-muhnt) an agreement Hitler made with the rulers of Great Britain, France, and Italy, declaring that Germany had the right to seize the Sudetenland, a portion of Czechoslovakia (page 761)

N

napalm *n.* (NAY-pahlm) a thick flammable, jellylike substance used in bombs to cause and spread fires (page 786)

nation-state *n.* (NAY-shuhn STAYT) a country with an independent government and a population united by a shared culture, language, and national pride; a political unit in which people have a common culture and identity (page 23)

National Socialism *n.* (NA-shuh-nuhl SOH-shuh-lih-zuhm) the political doctrine of the Nazi Party in Germany, which promoted the superiority of Germany and the German people, rejected communism, and carried anti-Semitism—hatred of Jewish people—to extreme levels (page 724)

nationalism *n.* (NA-shuh-nuh-lih-zuhm) a strong sense of loyalty to one's country and belief in its superiority to others (page 145)

nativist *n.* (NAY-tih-vihst) someone who opposes immigration and favors the interests of native-born citizens (page 369)

naturalization *n.* (NACH-uh-ruh-lih-ZAY-shuhn) the process of becoming a U.S. citizen for people who are not native-born citizens (page R34)

naval quarantine *n.* (NAY-vuhl KWAWR-uhn-teen) a blockade imposed on the ports of another country (page 936)

Nazi Party *n.* (NAHT-see PAHR-tee) a political party that was led by Adolf Hitler and used force to exert complete control over Germany from 1933 to 1945 (page 724)

neoconservative *n.* (nee-oh-kuhn-SUR-vuh-tihv) a person who strongly supports a free-market economy and believes the United States should actively promote its ideals around the world (page 1116)

New Deal *n.* (NOO DEEL) the laws, agencies, and programs initiated by President Franklin Roosevelt and his administration in response to the Great Depression of the 1930s (page 717)

New Federalism *n.* (NOO FEH-duh-ruh-lih-zuhm) a plan by President Richard Nixon to turn the control of some federal programs over to the states (page 1042)

New Frontier *n.* (NOO fruhn-TEER) a U.S. political strategy in 1960 in which President Kennedy stressed creative problem solving, foreign diplomacy, and technological advancements to overcome the country's problems (page 932)

new media *n.* (NOO MEE-dee-uh) digital products and services that provide content through the Internet (page 1138)

nomadic *adj.* (noh-MA-dihk) roaming across land without a fixed pattern of movement, sometimes following animal herds (page 16)

nonaggression pact *n.* (nahn-uh-GREH-shuhn PAKT) an agreement made in 1939 between Nazi Germany and the Soviet Union, declaring that they would not take military action against each other for the next 10 years (page 761)

nuclear deterrence *n.* (NOO-klee-ur dih-TUR-unts) a strategy of using nuclear weapons as a threat to ward off an enemy attack (page 860)

nuclear power *n.* (NOO-klee-ur POW-ur) energy that is created by either splitting or fusing the nuclei of atoms (page 865)

nullification *n.* (nuh-luh-fuh-KAY-shuhn) the act of taking away legal or binding force; in the case of American history, the attempt of a state government to veto a federal law that it deems unconstitutional (page 187)

O

occupation zone *n.* (AH-kyoo-pay-shuhn ZOHN) an area of a country in which a foreign military takes control (page 827)

offensive war *n.* (uh-FEHN-sihv WOR) a war fought mostly on the enemy's land (page 391)

omnibus bill *n.* (AHM-nih-buhs BIHL) a proposed law within one bill that may address many unrelated topics (page 362)

GLOSSARY

Open Door Policy *n.* (OH-puhn DOHR PAH-luh-see) an American proposal that aimed to establish equal access to ports among countries trading with China in 1900 (page 574)

ordinance *n.* (AWR-duh-nuhns) a law or authoritative regulation (page 154)

originalism *n.* (OH-rihj-ihn-uh-lih-zuhm) a belief system used to interpret the U.S. Constitution from the point of view of the intent of the document when it was originally written (page 1077)

overregulation *n.* (oh-vur-reh-gyuh-LAY-shuhn) excessive rules and regulations (page 1049)

overseer *n.* (OH-vur-see-ur) a supervisor (page 81)

P

pacifism *n.* (PA-suh-fih-zuhm) the belief that war is morally wrong (page 60)

Pan-Africanism *n.* (PAN A-frih-kuh-nih-zuhm) a movement in the early 1900s that sought to unify people of African descent (page 665)

pandemic *n.* (pan-DEH-mihk) the sudden outbreak of a disease that spreads over a wide geographic area (page 621)

Panic of 1837 *n.* (PA-nihk UHV 1837) the widespread fear of a failing economy that caused the beginning of a U.S. economic recession that lasted until 1840 (page 270)

Panic of 1873 *n.* (PA-nihk UHV 1873) an economic crisis triggered by bank and railroad failures (page 453)

panzer *n.* (PAHN-zur) a thickly armored German tank with impressive firepower used during World War II (page 799)

parent company *n.* (PAIR-uhnt KUHM-puh-nee) a company that controls all or part of other, smaller companies (page 509)

Parliament *n.* (PAHR-luh-muhnt) the legislative body of England, and, later, Great Britain (page 93)

patent *n.* (PA-tuhnt) a document that gives the bearer exclusive rights to make and sell an invention (page 226)

Patriot *n.* (PAY-tree-uht) an American colonist who supported the right of the American colonies to govern themselves (page 111)

peer *n.* (PEER) a person of the same age, rank, or social status as another (page 1006)

penicillin *n.* (peh-nuh-SIH-luhn) an antibiotic, or bacteria killer, made from mold and used to treat infections and disease (page 786)

penitentiary *n.* (peh-nuh-TEHN-chuh-ree) a state or federal prison whose stated goal was to rehabilitate criminals (page 278)

pension fund *n.* (PEHN-shuhn FUHND) a pool of money used to pay people a small, established income after they retire (page 722)

perestroika *n.* (peh-ruh-STROY-kuh) a government policy of reform in the former Soviet Union (page 1084)

perjury *n.* (PUR-juh-ree) the act of lying under oath (page 1115)

personal computer *n.* (PURS-uh-nuhl kuhm-PYOO-tur) an electronic device that processes data and is specifically designed for home use (page 1080)

personal responsibility *n.* (PURS-uh-nuhl rih-SPAWN-suh-BIHL-uh-tee) responsibility that is not required but that contributes to a more civil society, such as respecting and standing up for others' rights, helping in the community, and staying informed (page R35)

phonograph *n.* (FOH-nuh-graf) a machine that reproduces sounds from a record (page 509)

picket line *n.* (PIH-kuht LYN) a group of strikers who form a barrier to keep scabs, or strikebreakers, from entering a building to work in their place (page 729)

Piedmont *n.* (PEED-mont) a relatively flat area between the Appalachian Mountains and the coastal plain (page 78)

placer mining *n.* (PLAH-sur MY-nihng) mining techniques involving the use of lightweight tools to pan for gold in rivers and streams (page 472)

planned scarcity *n.* (PLAND SKEHR-suh-tee) the economic theory that lowering the supply of a product will increase demand for it and raise its price (page 718)

Pleistocene epoch *n.* (PLEIS-to-seen EH-puhk) a period in the history of Earth in which large animals and plants existed and glaciers covered Earth (page 1)

polio *n.* (POH-lee-oh) an infectious disease that sometimes causes muscle weakness or paralysis (page 715)

Politburo *n.* (PAW-luht-byoor-oh) the main ruling government committee that made policy decisions in the Communist Party; often refers to those of China or the former Soviet Union (page 1084)

political machine *n.* (poh-LIH-tih-kuhl muh-SHEEN) a political organization in which one person or a small group is able to maintain control over a city or a state (page 532)

poll tax *n.* (POHL TAKS) a fee charged when people register to vote (page 451)

pontoon *n.* (pahn-TOON) a portable, cylindrical float used to build a temporary bridge (page 403)

popular sovereignty *n.* (PAH-pyuh-lur SAHV-run-tee) the idea that the residents of a region or nation decide an issue by voting (page 362)

populism *n.* (PAH-pyuh-lih-zuhm) the belief that ordinary people should control government (page 477)

populist *n.* (PAH-pyuh-lihst) a politician who claims to represent the concerns of ordinary people (page 724)

portage *n.* (POHR-tihj) the act of carrying boats or goods between bodies of water or around obstructions on a waterway (page 193)

posse *n.* (PAH-see) group of armed men formed to capture an outlaw (page 488)

post-traumatic stress disorder (PTSD) *n.* (POHST truh-MAH-tihk STREHS dihs-AWR-dur) a condition brought on by injury or psychological trauma (page 993)

potlatch *n.* (PAHT-lach) a gift-giving ceremony practiced by the Kwakiutl and Haida Native American tribes (page 15)

poverty rate *n.* (PAH-vur-tee RAYT) the percentage of the population living in poverty (page 878)

prairie schooner *n.* (PRAIR-ee SKOO-nur) a horse-drawn wagon with a white canvas cover; used for traveling long distances in the early 19th century (page 319)

preamble *n.* (PREE-am-buhl) a short written introduction before a constitution or statute (page 125)

precedent *n.* (PREH-suh-duhnt) an example; a previous determination in a court case that sets a standard for comparison with similar new cases (page 154)

Presidential Reconstruction *n.* (preh-zuh-DEHN-shuhl ree-kuhn-STRUHK-shuhn) a policy that stated Confederate states must take loyalty oaths to the Union, ratify the 13th Amendment, and create new governments with new constitutions before they could rejoin the Union (page 436)

presidio *n.* (prih-SEE-dee-oh) a military post or settlement (page 330)

privateer *n.* (pry-vuh-TEER) an armed but privately owned ship that acts under the authority of a government to participate in warfare; or a sailor on such a ship (page 137)

Proclamation of 1763 *n.* (prah-kluh-MAY-shuhn UHV 1763) a law requiring colonists to stay east of a line drawn on a map along the crest of the Appalachian Mountains (page 99)

profiteering *n.* (prah-fih-TEER-ihng) the act of charging high prices for items in high demand and short supply to make more money (page 137)

Progressive Era *n.* (pruh-GREH-sihv EHR-uh) a period from about 1890 to 1920 in which reformers sought to correct many social, economic, and political inequalities and injustices in the United States (page 552)

progressivism *n.* (pruh-GREH-sih-vih-zuhm) reform movement from 1890 to 1920 that sought to make state and national politics more democratic and government more efficient (page 533)

prohibition *n.* (proh-uh-BIH-shuhn) the act of outlawing the production, distribution, and sale of alcohol (page 557)

Prohibition *n.* (proh-uh-BIH-shuhn) the constitutional ban on the sale of alcoholic beverages that was in effect between 1920 and 1933 (page 619)

promissory note *n.* (PRAH-muh-sawr-ee NOHT) a written agreement to pay a person or business back by a specified date (page 393)

propaganda *n.* (prah-puh-GAN-duh) misleading ideas and information that are spread in order to influence people's opinions or advance an organization or party's ideas (page 526)

proprietor *n.* (pruh-PRY-uh-tuhr) a person with ownership of a colony, including the right to manage and distribute land and to establish government (page 62)

prospector *n.* (PRAH-spek-tur) a person who searches in the earth for valuable resources, such as gems or precious metals (page 334)

protectorate *n.* (pruh-TEHK-tuh-ruht) a country that is partly governed by a more powerful country (page 572)

Protestant Reformation *n.* (PRAH-tuh-stuhnt reh-fuhr-MAY-shuhn) the religious movement to reform Christianity that occurred in Western Europe in the 1500s (page 23)

provision *n.* (pruh-VIH-zhuhn) a legal condition that anticipates a future need (page 145)

proviso *n.* (pruh-VY-zoh) a condition attached to a legal document or legislation (page 360)

proxy war *n.* (PRAHK-see WOR) a series of battles that are provoked by a nation that does not participate in the fighting (page 838)

purge *n.* (PUHRJ) removing or eliminating something (page 764)

push-pull factor *n.* (PUSH PUL FAK-tur) a reason why people migrate; "push" factors cause them to leave; "pull" factors make them come to a place (page 518)

Q

quinine *n.* (KWHY-nyn) a substance made from the bark of a tree that is an effective remedy for malaria (page 31)

R

radical *n.* (RA-dih-kuhl) a person who wants an extreme change or holds an extreme political position (page 185)

Radical Reconstruction *n.* (RA-dih-kuhl ree-kuhn-STRUHK-shuhn) the name given to the Republicans' plan in passing the Reconstruction Acts of 1867 (page 439)

Radical Republican *n.* (RA-dih-kuhl rih-PUH-blih-kuhn) an abolitionist member of the U.S. Congress who supported African-American rights (page 404)

rancho *n.* (RAN-choh) land granted by Mexico to settlers in the form of a large estate in what is now California (page 333)

ratify *v.* (RA-tuh-fy) to approve, formally, by vote (page 127)

ration *v.* (RA-shuhn) to control the supply of goods made available to the public, especially in wartime (page 788)

rearmament *n.* (ree-AHR-muh-muhnt) the effort of a nation to rebuild a stockpile of weapons to replace those that are out-of-date or have been taken away (page 754)

recall *n.* (REE-kawl) a procedure by which citizens can vote to remove an elected public official from office (page 561)

recession *n.* (rih-SEH-shuhn) a relatively short-lasting slowdown in economic growth, often part of a normal business cycle (page 359)

Reconstruction *n.* (ree-kuhn-STRUHK-shuhn) the effort to rebuild and reunite the United States following the Civil War (page 427)

Red Scare *n.* (REHD SKAIR) a period in 1919 and 1920 when the federal government targeted suspected communists, anarchists, and radicals (page 642)

referendum *n.* (reh-fuh-REN-duhm) an election where the people vote directly on specific measures (page 533)

refugee *n.* (REH-fyoo-jee) a person seeking shelter and protection from political persecution (page 759)

Renaissance *n.* (reh-nuh-SAHNTS) meaning "rebirth," a period in the 1300–1500s in which culture and the arts flourished (page 21)

reparations *n.* (reh-puh-RAY-shunz) money paid to the victors by the losing side in a war (page 575)

repatriation *n.* (ree-PAY-tree-ay-shuhn) returning or being returned to the country of one's origin or citizenship (page 691)

republican motherhood *n.* (rih-PUH-blih-kuhn MUH-thur-hud) the idea that women should raise their children to be good citizens who participate actively in the government (page 180)

republicanism *n.* (rih-PUH-blih-kuh-nih-zuhm) the belief that a government's power comes from its citizens and the representatives they choose to make their laws (page 152)

reservation *n.* (reh-zur-VAY-shuhn) an area of land designated for and managed by a particular Native American tribe (page 480)

reservoir *n.* (REH-zuh-vwahr) a large, contained body of water that can be tapped (page 474)

robber barons *n.* (RAHB-ur BA-ruhns) railroad industry leaders such as Cornelius Vanderbilt and Jay Gould who became renowned for their ruthless methods against competitors (page 503)

rock and roll *n.* (RAHK AND ROHL) a form of music, derived from rhythm and blues, that became popular in the 1950s (page 873)

rogue state *n.* (ROHG STAYT) a country perceived to violate international law and threaten world peace (page 1121)

Romanticism *n.* (roh-MAN-tuh-sih-zuhm) a philosophical, literary, and artistic movement in the 19th century that emphasized imagination, emotion, and action (page 281)

Rome-Berlin Axis *n.* (ROHM-buhr-LIHN ACK-sihs) an agreement formed between Germany and Italy in 1936 (page 755)

rule of law *n.* (ROOL UHV LAW) the idea that people and institutions are required to follow the regulations set forth by the government (page 120)

rural electrification *n.* (RUR-uhl ih-LEHK-truh-fuh-kay-shuhn) a government program that ran power lines through rural communities (page 833)

Rustbelt *n.* (RUHST-behlt) the area in the northeastern and midwestern United States in which manufacturing has diminished significantly (page 1071)

S

sack of Lawrence *n.* (SAK UHV LAWR-uhns) a term describing a violent attack in May 1856 in Lawrence, Kansas, in which proslavery advocates ransacked the town and destroyed homes and businesses (page 371)

safety-net programs *n.* (SAFE-tee NEHT PROH-grams) a collection of programs provided by the state or federal government designed to prevent people from falling deeper into poverty (page 1073)

salutary neglect *n.* (SAL-yuh-tair-ee nih-GLEKT) the policy of the British government to not strictly enforce its colonial policies (page 93)

salvation *n.* (sal-VAY-shuhn) the act of being forgiven by one's deity (god) for one's wrongdoings or sins (page 90)

sanitation *n.* (sa-nuh-TAY-shuhn) measures such as sewers to protect public health (page 532)

savanna *n.* (su-VA-nuh) an area of lush tropical grasslands (page 26)

scabs *n.* (SKABS) nonunion workers willing to cross strike lines in order to work (page 515)

scalawag *n.* (SKA-lih-wag) an unworthy person; term used to refer to white southerners who acted to support Reconstruction for personal gain after the Civil War (page 440)

scapegoat *n.* (SKAYP-goht) an individual or group blamed for the mistakes or faults of others (page 409)

Schlieffen Plan *n.* (SHLEE-fuhn PLAN) a German plan (1905–1906) to make a rapid conquest of France, followed by a march on Russia (page 602)

scientific management *n.* (sy-uhn-TIH-fihk MA-nihj-muhnt) a management method that relies on experimental studies to identify the most efficient way to execute tasks in a factory or other workplace (page 570)

secession *n.* (seh-SEH-shuhn) the act of formally withdrawing from an organization, a nation, or any other group in order to be independent (page 191)

Second Great Awakening *n.* (SEHKund GRAYT uh-WAYK-ning) an American Protestant movement based on revival meetings and a direct and emotional relationship with God (page 276)

Second New Deal *n.* (SEHK-und NOO DEEL) a second set of New Deal programs, which President Franklin Roosevelt presented to Congress after the 1934 midterm elections (page 722)

sectionalism *n.* (SEHK-shuh-nuh-lih-zuhm) a loyalty to whichever section or region of the country one is from, rather than to the nation as a whole (page 239)

sedition *n.* (sih-DIH-shuhn) the criminal act of trying to persuade individuals to undermine the government (page 187)

segregation *n.* (seh-grih-GAY-shuhn) the separation of different groups of people, usually based on race (page 535)

Seneca Falls Convention *n.* (SEH-nihkuh FAWLS kuhn-VEHN-shuhn) an 1848 women's rights convention organized by Elizabeth Cady Stanton and Lucretia Mott in Seneca Falls, New York (page 294)

separate but equal *n.* (SEHP-uh-reht BUHT EE-kwuhl) a policy that allowed businesses and institutions to segregate African Americans from whites as long as the facilities or services provided were about equal (page 536)

separation of powers *n.* (seh-puh-RAY-shuhn UHV POW-urz) the division of governmental power among the three branches of U.S. government: the executive branch, the judicial branch, and the legislative branch (page 158)

separatist *n.* (SEH-prah-tihst) a person who wished to leave the Church of England (page 56)

service sector *n.* (SUR-vuhss SEHK-tur) the part of the economy that provides services rather than goods (page 1138)

shaft mining *n.* (SHAFT MY-nihng) mining technique in which a vertical channel is blasted into a mountain and people are lowered down the shaft to mine (page 472)

sharecropping *n.* (SHAIR-krahp-ihng) an agricultural system in which a farmer raises crops for a landowner in return for part of the money made from selling the crops (page 443)

short-staple cotton *n.* (SHORT STAY-puhl KAH-tuhn) a coarse, easy-to-cultivate type of cotton with short fibers; it is suited for growing in a wide range of climates and soils (page 222)

silent majority *n.* (SY-luhnt muh-JOR-uh-tee) a term used by Richard Nixon in the late 1960s to describe a large group of moderate voters who did not publicly express their political opinions (page 1041)

sit-down strike *n.* (SIHT DAUN STRYK) a strike in which the workers do not walk out, but rather stay at their place of employment and refuse to do any work (page 731)

sit-in *n.* (SIHT IHN) an organized protest where people sit down and refuse to leave (page 915)

situation comedy *n.* (sih-chuh-WAY-shuhn KAH-muh-dee) a weekly series that features a familiar setting and a group of characters who face amusing problems (page 872)

slash-and-burn agriculture *n.* (SLASH AND BURN A-grih-kuhl-chur) a method of clearing fields for planting that involves cutting and setting fire to existing trees and plants (page 16)

slave codes *n.* (BLAK KOHDZ) laws adopted by the colonies beginning in 1660 that limited the rights of enslaved African Americans with varying degrees of severity, depending on the colony (page 67)

sluice *n.* (SLOOS) an inclined wooden trough used in mining to strain water from gold (page 472)

smallpox *n.* (SMAWL-pawks) a deadly virus that causes a high fever and small blisters on the skin (page 45)

smog *n.* (SMAHG) a noxious combination of fog and smoke from factories (page 859)

GLOSSARY

Social Darwinism *n.* (SOH-shuhl DAHR-wuh-nih-zuhm) 19th-century philosophy that argued that human social history could be understood as a struggle between the wealthy and poor, with the strongest and the fittest invariably triumphing (page 503)

social justice *n.* (SOH-shuhl JUH-stuhs) the fair distribution of opportunities and privileges, including for racial equality (page 448)

Social Security *n.* (SOH-shuhl sih-KYOOR-ih-tee) a government program that provides income to the elderly, disabled, and unemployed (page 570)

socialism *n.* (SOH-shuh-lih-zuhm) a system of government in which the community or government controls economic resources (page 517)

solitary confinement *n.* (SAHL-it-tar-ee cuhn-FINE-ment) a form of punishment, isolating a prisoner from contact with other people (page 918)

sovereignty *n.* (SAH-vuh-ruhn-tee) the power to govern (page 152)

space race *n.* (SPAYS RAYS) the competition between the United States and the Soviet Union to be the first to travel outside Earth's atmosphere (page 934)

spacewalk *n.* (SPAYS-wawk) any period of time when an astronaut ventures outside the spacecraft (page 1027)

speakeasy *n.* (SPEEK-ee-zee) an illegal drinking club where people secretly gathered in the evenings during Prohibition (page 646)

specie *n.* (SPEE-shee) coined money; often refers to silver or gold coins (page 156)

speculation *n.* (speh-kyuh-LAY-shuhn) taking on a business risk, such as buying stocks on margin even though there is no guarantee that they will increase in value (page 686)

speculator *n.* (SPEH-kyuh-lay-tur) someone who invests in property or stocks, hoping to make a profit (page 155)

sphere of influence *n.* (SFEER UHV IHN-floo-ents) the claim by a country to exclusive control over a foreign area or territory (page 574)

spoils system *n.* (SPOY-uhlz SIHS-tuhm) the practice of rewarding political backers with government jobs; also known as the patronage system (page 241)

stagflation *n.* (stag-FLAY-shuhn) an economic condition in which stagnation, or slow economic growth, is accompanied by inflation, or rising prices (page 1056)

stalactite *n.* (stuh-LAK-tyt) a column of minerals that hangs from the roof of a cave (page 648)

stalagmite *n.* (stuh-LAG-myt) a column of minerals that form upward from the floor of a cave (page 648)

stalemate *n.* (STAYL-mayt) a situation in which neither side in a conflict can claim victory (page 141)

static *adj.* (stat-IK) having the quality of not moving or changing (page 1077)

steppe *n.* (STEP) a vast, grassy plain (page 24)

stewardship *n.* (STOO-uhrd-shihp) the responsible management of someone or something entrusted to one's care (page 287)

stock market *n.* (STAHK MAHR-kuht) the buying and selling of shares in companies (page 685)

Stono Rebellion *n.* (STOH-noh rih-BEL-yuhn) a 1739 revolt by enslaved Africans against their owners (page 83)

streetcar *n.* (STREET-kahr) a vehicle that runs on rails through city streets and carries passengers (page 531)

strict constructionist *n.* (STRIHKT kuhn-STRUHK-shuh-nihst) someone who interprets the U.S. Constitution as honoring the rights of states over federal power (page 182)

subdivision *n.* (SUHB-duh-vih-zhuhn) a tract of land that has been divided into smaller lots on which houses are built (page 867)

subprime mortgage *n.* (SUHB-prym MOR-gihj) home loan issued to buyers with poor credit history (page 1126)

subsidiary *n.* (suhb-SIH-dee-ehr-ee) a secondary business (page 509)

subsidy *n.* (SUHB-suh-dee) a government grant for improvements or support of commerce (page 227)

subsistence farming *n.* (suhb-SIHS-tuhnts FAHR-ming) the practice of producing enough food for a farmer and his or her family but not enough to sell for profit (page 72)

subtreasury system *n.* (suhb-TREH-zhuh-ree SIHS-tuhm) a system proposed by which farmers would store their crops in silos until prices rose and the government would lend the farmer money to buy new seeds for the next year's crops (page 477)

suburb *n.* (SUH-burb) a community near or on the outskirts of a city (page 531)

suburban sprawl *n.* (suh-BUR-buhn SPRAWL) the spread of housing developments over more and more suburban and rural land (page 869)

suburbanization *n.* (suh-bur-buh-nuh-ZAY-shuhn) a population shift from cities to outlying communities (page 866)

subversion *n.* (suhb-VUR-zhuhn) an act of destabilizing a major social or political system in an attempt to destroy it (page 844)

suffrage *n.* (SUH-frihj) the right to vote (page 152)

suffragist *n.* (SUHF-rih-jihst) a person who supports women's right to vote (page 295)

Sunbelt *n.* (SUHN-behlt) the southern and southwestern regions of the United States, which have mild winters (page 859)

supply-side economics *n.* (suh-PLY SYD eh-kuh-NAH-mihks) a financial theory in which tax rates are lowered for businesses and investors in the hope of boosting production and trade in the country (page 1074)

surge *n.* (SURJ) a sudden increase (page 1123)

swing state *n.* (SWIHNGH STAYT) a state where the election may be won by either party (page 1144)

syllabary *n.* (SIH-luh-bair-ee) a set of written symbols or characters used to represent a word's syllables (page 260)

syndicate *n.* (SIHN-dih-kuht) a group of criminals who control organized criminal activities (page 568)

T

tank *n.* (TANGK) an armored, heavily armed vehicle that uses treads instead of wheels (page 612)

tariff *n.* (TAIR-uhf) a tax on imports and exports (page 227)

Tariff of Abominations *n.* (TAIR-uhf UHV uh-bah-muh-NAY-shuhns) the term used by southerners to refer to the Tariff of 1828 because it stirred feelings of disgust and hatred (page 256)

task force *n.* (TASK FORS) a group of people organized for a special mission (page 1107)

telegraph *n.* (TEHL-uh-graf) a device that transmits messages along connected wires to communicate over long distances (page 508)

temperance movement *n.* (TEHM-pur-uhns MOOV-mehnt) a 19th-century reform movement that encouraged the reduction or elimination of alcoholic beverage consumption (page 277)

tenant farmer *n.* (TEH-nuhnt FAHR-muhr) a farmer who works land owned by someone else and who pays rent for it either in cash or with produce (page 443)

tenement *n.* (TEH-nuh-muhnt) a large building that rents rooms and apartments, and which is usually overcrowded and badly maintained (page 524)

termination policy *n.* (tur-muh-NAY-shuhn PAH-luh-see) a policy enacted under President Eisenhower that removed Native Americans from reservations, while the government ended the limited sovereignty of individual tribes and nations (page 882)

terrorism *n.* (TEHR-ur-ih-zuhm) the use of violent acts and threats to achieve a political goal (page 1120)

theocracy *n.* (thee-AH-kruh-see) a government ruled by a religious leader or religious leaders (page 1093)

think tank *n.* (THIHNK TAYNK) a group of experts who conduct research and discuss issues in order to craft potential solutions to social and economic problems (page 1069)

Third Reich *n.* (THURD RYK) name used by the Nazi party to describe the time when Adolph Hitler believed he was creating a third German empire (page 754)

third world *adj.* (THURD WURLD) during the Cold War, a country that was not aligned with either the United States or the Soviet Union (page 969)

topography *n.* (tuh-PAH-gruh-fee) the arrangement of the physical features of a landscape (page 336)

total war *n.* (TOH-tuhl WOR) a war in which all rules and laws of war are ignored and all resources are used for defeating the enemy (page 422)

totalitarian *adj.* (toh-ta-luh-TAIR-ee-uhn) relating to a government that is headed by a dictator and requires complete obedience to the state (page 724)

trading pool *n.* (TRAYD-ihng POOL) groups formed to buy and sell large amounts of stocks (page 688)

Trail of Tears *n.* (TRAYL UHV TEERS) the route the Cherokee and other Native Americans took during their forced migration from the southeastern United States to Oklahoma (page 265)

trans-Saharan *adj.* (tran-suh-HAHR-uhn) across the Sahara (page 25)

transcendentalism *n.* (tran-sehn-DEHN-tuh-li-zuhm) an intellectual and social movement of the 1830s and 1840s that called for rising above society's expectations (page 281)

transcontinental railroad *n.* (trans-kahn-tuh-NEHN-tuhl RAYL-rohd) a railroad that runs across a continent (page 336)

transistor *n.* (tran-ZIHS-tur) an electronic device used to control the flow of electricity in electronic equipment (page 865)

Treaty of Versailles *n.* TREE-tee UHV vur-SY) the treaty that officially brought World War I to a close (page 626)

trench warfare *n.* (TREHNCH WOR-fair) a type of warfare in which long ditches dug deep in the ground provide protection for soldiers (page 407)

triangular trade *n.* (try-ANG-yuh-lur TRAYD) a transatlantic trade network formed by Europe, West Africa, and the Americas (page 48)

tribunal *n.* (try-BYOO-nuhl) a court of justice with authority over a specific matter (page 819)

trust *n.* (TRUHST) a company managed by members of a board rather than by owners or stockholders (page 505)

trustbuster *n.* (TRUHST-buhst-ur) a person who seeks to break up business trusts, or monopolies, especially a federal official who enforces antitrust laws (page 564)

trustee *n.* (truhs-TEE) a person who has powers to administer a colony or other institution for the purpose of supporting that institution, and not for personal gain (page 65)

tundra *n.* (TUHN-druh) the flat treeless land found in arctic and subarctic regions (page 14)

turnpike *n.* (TURN-pyk) a road on which tolls are charged to allow travelers to pass (page 227)

U

U-boat *n.* (YOO BOHT) a German submarine (page 606)

Underground Railroad *n.* (uhn-dur-GROWND RAYL-rohd) a network of people who worked together to help African Americans escape from slavery from the southern United States to the northern states or to Canada before the Civil War (page 364)

underwrite *v.* (UHN-dur-ryt) to take on the financial responsibilities—including the risks—of a set of assets (page 698)

unorganized territory *n.* (uhn-AWR-guh-nyzd TAIR-uh-tawr-ee) lands governed by the federal government but not belonging to any state (page 240)

urban renewal *n.* (UR-buhn rih-NOO-uhl) a program that involves clearing slums and replacing them with large, publicly funded housing projects (page 878)

utopian community *n.* (yu-TOH-pee-uhn kuh-MYOO-nuh-nee) a group of people who live together cooperatively to form an ideal society (page 282)

V

vaquero *n.* (vah-KAIR-oh) a cowboy, especially in Spanish-settled North America (page 320)

vaudeville *n.* (VAWD-vihl) theatrical show that involved singing and dancing acts (page 530)

vertical integration *n.* (VUR-tih-kuhl ihn-tuh-GRAY-shuhn) a procedure in which a company takes control of all phases of production from start to finish (page 503)

veteran *n.* (VEH-tuh-ruhn) a person who has served in the military (page 429)

viceroyalty *n.* (VYS-roy-uhl-tee) a territory governed by a governor of Spain's colonies in the Americas who represented the Spanish king and queen (page 47)

Vietnamization *n.* (vee-eht-nuh-muh-ZAY-shun) a military strategy that allowed for the gradual replacement of U.S. troops with South Vietnamese troops during the Vietnam War (page 988)

voter fraud *n.* (VOH-tur FRAWD) illegal manipulation of ballots to help win an election (page 929)

voter intimidation *n.* (VOH-tur ihn-tih-muh-DAY-shuhn) actions, often violent, taken to frighten and deter people from voting and often specifically aimed at African Americans, immigrants, or people a powerful group does not agree with. (page 445)

voter registration drive *n.* (VOH-tur reh-juh-STRAY-shuhn DRYV) an effort by groups or government to sign up as many eligible voters in a targeted area as possible (page 922)

voting bloc *n.* (VOHT-ihng BLOK) a large group of citizens who share a common concern and tend to vote the same in elections (page 736)

W

wage discrimination *n.* (WAYJ dihs-krih-muh-NAY-shuhn) the act of lowering pay for the same job based on gender, race, or ethnicity (page 790)

wage economy *n.* (WAYJ ih-KAH-nuhmee) an economy in which people are paid for their work (page 447)

war bond *n.* (WOR BAHND) a debt security issued by the government to help finance military expenses during wartime (page 153)

War Hawk *n.* (WOR HAWK) a person who approves of and encourages war; an American who favored war with Great Britain in 1812 (page 199)

War Industries Board (WIB) *n.* (WOR IHN-duh-streez BAWRD) a board that oversaw manufacturing in the United States during World War I (page 608)

war of attrition *n.* (WOR UHV uh-TRIH-shun) a military strategy in which an army wears another down by conducting many small battles over a long period of time (page 975)

Watergate break-in *n.* (WAH-tur-gayt BRAYK IHN) a break-in at the Democratic National Headquarters in the Watergate complex in Washington, D.C., in 1972 by burglars associated with President Richard Nixon's re-election committee (page 1053)

weapons of mass destruction (WMD) *n.* (WEH-puhnz UHV MAS dih-STRUHK-shuhn) weapons that use nuclear, chemical, or biological substances to harm large numbers of people (page 1121)

welfare capitalism *n.* (WEHL-fair KA-puh-tuh-lih-zuhm) a business practice in which companies offer workers extra benefits, including recreational facilities, benefit plans, and profit-sharing opportunities (page 653)

welfare state *n.* (WEHL-fair STAYT) a system in which the government provides for the health and well-being of its citizens (page 742)

Whig Party *n.* (WIHG PAHR-tee) a political party formed to oppose the policies of Andrew Jackson, who the party believed had exceeded his power as president (page 269)

white-collar *adj.* (HWYT-KAH-lur) relating to the class of people whose jobs typically take place in an office or professional environment and don't involve manual labor (page 833)

wiretapping *v.* (WY-urh-tap-ihng) placing a device on a telephone in order to secretly listen to conversations (page 1054)

workers' compensation *n.* (WUR-kurz kahm-puhn-SAY-shuhn) insurance for employees injured while on the job, providing assistance for medical care and loss of income (page 513)

writ of assistance *n.* (RIHT UHV uh-SIHS-tuhns) a legal document giving authorities the right to enter and search a home or business (page 112)

writ of *habeus corpus* *n.* (RIHT UHV HAY-bee-uhs COR-puhs) a law that allows prisoners to petition to a judge if they believe they have been arrested unlawfully (page 391)

Y

yellow journalism *n.* (YEH-loh JUR-nuh-lih-zuhm) a type of journalism that stresses sensationalism over facts (page 577)

Z

Zimmermann Telegram *n.* (ZIH-mur-muhn TEH-luh-gram) a secret German telegram sent to the German ambassador in Mexico laying out a plan to ally with Mexico (page 607)

ACADEMIC VOCABULARY

acquiesce *v.* (a-kwee-EHS) to agree, especially after an argument (page 1019)

affluence *n.* (A-floo-ehns) wealth, prosperity (page 862)

agitator *n.* (A-juh-TAY-tuhr) someone who stirs up anger and rebellion (page 484)

allegory *n.* (A-luh-gawr-ee) a story in which objects or people stand for abstract or spiritual ideas (page 21)

allocate *v.* (A-luh-kayt) to give out, to distribute (page 1042)

amenity *n.* (uh-MEH-nih-tee) a benefit that promotes comfort and ease of use or lifestyle (page 516)

arable *adj.* (A-ruh-buhl) fertile, as soil for agriculture (page 78)

artisan *n.* (AHR-tuh-zuhn) craftsperson (page 27)

autonomy *n.* (aw-TAH-nuh-mee) independence; freedom to act on one's own (page 167)

blacklist *v.* (BLAK-lihst) to put one or more people on a list indicating they are to be shunned or punished (page 843)

blasphemous *adj.* (BLAS-fuh-muhs) ungodly, sacrilegious (page 1069)

boll *n.* (BOHL) cotton seed pod (page 222)

brackish *adj.* (BRA-kihsh) partially salty (page 50)

brevity *n.* (BRE-vuh-tee) shortness; the quality of being quick and to the point (page 425)

burgeon *v.* (BUR-juhn) to expand; to grow (page 79)

card *v.* (KARD) to prepare cotton fibers for spinning by cleaning, combing out tangles, and gathering fibers together (page 220)

charisma *n.* (kuh-RIHZ-muh) charm, often connected with magnetic leadership ability (page 187)

clandestine *adj.* (klan-DEHS-tuhn) secret (page 330)

clemency *n.* (KLEH-mehn-see) mercy, leniency (page 843)

coerce *v.* (coh-URS) to make someone do something by use of force, threat, or trickery (page 738)

cohesion *n.* (coh-HEE-zhuhn) unity, tight organization (page 801)

comply *v.* (uhm-PLY) to meet the terms of, to obey (page 907)

conclusive *adj.* (kuhn-KLOO-sihv) final (page 401)

contraband *n.* KAHN-truh-band smuggled goods (page 112)

covenant *n.* (KUHV-nuhnt) binding promise (page 95)

culmination *n.* (kuhl-muh-NAY-shuhn) the conclusion, the finale (page 993)

default *v.* (dee-FAWLT) to fail to pay, as a debt (page 152)

depository *n.* (dih-PAH-suh-tor-ee) a warehouse, a place where items are stored (page 939)

devout *adj.* (dih-VOWT) religiously faithful (page 277)

disproportionate *adj.* (dihs-pruh-POR-shuh-nuht) unequal, unbalanced, usually weighed to the larger part (page 1109)

diversify *v.* (dih-VUR-sih-fy) to expand one's options (page 476)

diversity *n.* (duh-VUR-suh-tee) variety (page 77)

domestic *adj.* (duh-MEHS-tihk) household (as type of chores or duties) (page 67)

effigy *n.* (EH-fuh-jee) a dummy representing a person, particularly a famous person (often a politician) who is hated or reviled (page 111)

eke *v.* (eek) to obtain with great effort (page 472)

empathize *v.* (EM-puh-thyz) to feel an emotional connection with another (page 365)

eradicate *v.* (ih-RA-duh-kayt) to wipe out, to destroy utterly (page 562)

erratic *adj.* (ih-RA-tihk) unpredictable, inconsistent (page 844)

exodus *n.* (EHK-suh-duhs) departure (usually of many people at once) (page 21)

exorbitant *adj.* (ihg-ZOR-buh-tuhnt) excessive, overpriced (page 472)

expedient *adj.* (ehk-SPEE-dee-uhnt) convenient, practical (page 1015)

extortion *n.* (ecks-TOR-shuhn) the act of obtaining something—usually money or information—through forceful coercion; blackmail (page 959)

frugality *n.* (froo-GA-luh-tee) thriftiness (page 189)

ghetto *n.* (GEH-toh) a section of a city in which certain groups, usually Jews, are required to live; more recently, a section of a city where certain minority groups live, usually due to poverty (page 815)

herbicide *n.* (UR-buh-syd) a chemical substance used to kill plants (page 977)

hieroglyphic *adj.* (hy-uh-ruh-GLIH-fihk) picture-based (as in a writing form) (page 17)

homogenous *adj.* (hoh-MAH-juh-nuhs) uniform, equal, consistent, standardized (page 875)

hostage *n.* (HAH-stihj) someone who is held prisoner to force another party to follow the demands of those who hold him or her (page 1062)

hypothesis *n.* (hy-PAH-thuh-suhs) specific idea to be tested through the scientific method (page 88)

illicit *adj.* (ih-LIH-suht) illegal, unlawful (page 655)

immolate *v.* (IH-muh-layt) to destroy by setting on fire (page 971)

incorporate *v.* (ihn-COR-puh-rayt) to blend, to unite (page 905)

influx *n.* (IHN-fluhks) an arrival, an entry (as of immigrants) (page 518)

insubordination *n.* (ihn-suh-bor-dih-NAY-shuhn) disobedience, rebelliousness (page 568)

interventionist *n.* (ihn-tur-VEHN-shuh-nishst) someone who supports getting involved, as in a war (page 762)

invincible *adj.* (ihn-VIHN-suh-buhl) impossible to conquer, indestructible (page 557)

jurisdiction *n.* (jur-uhs-DIHK-shuhn) legal power (page 364)

laudable *adj.* (LAW-duh-buhl) praiseworthy (page 658)

lease *v.* (lees) to either sign or provide a contract that gives rights to land or facilities for a certain amount of time at an agreed upon rent (page 579)

lucrative *adj.* (LOO-kruh-tihv) moneymaking, profitable, well-paid (page 76)

mudslinging *n.* (MUHD-slihng-ing) nasty personal attacks (usually on a political opponent) (page 253)

mystique *n.* (mih-STEEK) an air of mystery, or the unknown, that surrounds a person, thing, or idea (page 1021)

normalcy *n.* (NOR-muhl-see) a condition or situation that is typical, usual, or expected, such as the general social, political, and economic conditions of a nation (page 629)

notorious *adj.* (noh-TOR-ee-uhs) famous for having a bad reputation, dishonorable (page 646)

noxious *adj.* (NAHK-zhuhs) foul, offensive, digusting (page 532)

obstruction *n.* (uhb-STRUHK-shuhn) something that blocks a path or an action (page 1055)

oratorical *adj.* (or-uh-TOR-ih-kuhl) having to do with speechmaking (page 908)

philanthropic *adj.* (fih-lahn-THRAW-pihk) charitable (page 505)

pluralism *n.* (PLUR-uh-lih-zuhm) the coexistence of different cultural groups within a single larger civilization (page 518)

pragmatism *n.* (PRAG-muh-tihzm) practicality, rationality (page 716)

pre-emptive *adj.* (pree-EHMP-tihv) preventive, defensive (page 1121)

privatize *v.* (PRY-vuh-tyz) to transfer from public to private control (page 111)

prominence *n.* (PRAH-muh-nuhnts) the state of being important or noticeable (page 253)

proponent *n.* (pruh-POH-nuhnt) a supporter, an advocate (page 518)

protagonist *n.* (proh-TA-guh-nihst) the main character of a work of fiction (page 489)

quota *n.* (KWOH-tuh) a proportional amount, percentage, or share, often in reference to proportion of members of minority or gender groups allotted for a particular benefit (page 691)

redress *n.* (rih-DREHS) compensation for wrongdoing (page 795)

relinquish *v.* (rih-LIHNG-kwihsh) to give up; to surrender (page 327)

renounce *v.* (rih-NOWNTS) to reject, to give up (page 685)

repressive *adj.* (rih-PREH-sihv) oppressive, brutally authoritarian (page 1079)

rescind *v.* (ree-SIHND) to withdraw; to take back (page 113)

scurrilous *adj.* (SKUR-uh-luhs) insulting, slanderous, scandalous (page 610)

solidarity *n.* (saw-luh-DAIR-uh-tee) unity of purpose (page 516)

subjugation *n.* (suhb-jih-GAY-shuhn) the act of bringing a group of people under control by force (page 831)

subordinate *adj.* (suh-BAWR-duh-nuht) lesser (page 298)

subpoena *n.* (suh-PEE-nuh) a legal demand to appear before a court, judge, or government committee (page 843)

subversive *adj.* (suhb-VUR-sihv) rebellious (page 58)

superfluous *adj.* (suh-PUR-floo-uhs) unnecessary (page 164)

unanimous *adj.* (yoo-NA-nuh-muhs) undisputed, with all votes the same (page 907)

unicameral *adj.* (yoo-nih-KA-mur-uhl) having one chamber, as a legislature with only one house of lawmakers (page 158)

warlord *n.* (WOR-lord) a local military leader who holds great power in his limited region (page 765)

GLOSARIO

A

abolicionista *s.* persona que quiere acabar con la esclavitud (página 223)

acción afirmativa *s.* política gubernamental que establece cuotas raciales para favorecer a los grupos que han sufrido discriminación (página 961)

activismo comunitario *s.* movimiento político impulsado por personas que individualmente no tienen mucho poder, pero que trabajando juntos logran obtener resultados (página 902)

acto de hábeas corpus *s.* ley que permite a los prisioneros reclamar una audiencia ante un juez si consideran que han sido arrestados ilegalmente (página 391)

acueducto *s.* estructura que transporta agua o un sistema de aguas (página 228)

Acuerdos de Múnich *s.* acuerdos que realizó Hitler con los gobernantes de Gran Bretaña, Francia e Italia, declarando que Alemania tenía el derecho de apoderarse de la región de los Sudetes, que formaba parte de Checoslovaquia (página 761)

acuífero *s.* formación geológica debajo de la superficie de la tierra que puede albergar un gran depósito de agua subterránea (página 474)

adjudicación *s.* lote de tierra entregado a un indígena para su cultivo (página 484)

administración *s.* manejo responsable de alguien o algo confiado a nuestro cuidado (página 287)

administrador *s.* persona con el poder de administrar una colonia o una institución con el único propósito de ayudar y sin recibir retribución (página 65)

adversario *s.* enemigo; oponente (página 145)

Agente Naranja *s.* herbicida potente usado para matar la vegetación (página 977)

agrario *adj.* relativo a la agricultura y siembra (página 182)

agricultura de subsistencia *s.* modo de producir suficientes alimentos para el granjero y su familia, pero no para la venta (página 72)

agricultura de tala y quema *s.* método de despejar los campos para sembrar cultivos que consiste en cortar y quemar los árboles y las plantas existentes (página 16)

agroindustria *s.* el negocio comercial de la agricultura (página 859)

aislacionismo *s.* política en la cual una nación permanece fuera de los asuntos de otras naciones (página 572)

algodón de punta corta *s.* tipo de algodón grueso de fibras cortas y fácil de cultivar que se podía cultivar en una amplia variedad de climas y suelos (página 222)

algodón de punta larga *s.* tipo de algodón que produce fibras largas útiles en la producción de prendas finas; crece en pocos climas y suelos (página 222)

Aliados *s.* varios países, entre ellos Francia y gran Bretaña, que lucharon juntos para oponerse a las Potencias del Eje de Alemania, Italia y Japón (página 755)

alimentos genéticamente modificados *s.* alimentos producidos a partir de plantas que han sido modificadas de una manera que no ocurre naturalmente (página 1139)

allanamiento de Watergate *s.* allanamiento en la sede nacional del Partido Demócrata dentro del complejo de Watergate en Washington, D.C., en 1972 por ladrones asociados con el comité para la reelección del presidente Richard Nixon (página 1053)

amarillismo *s.* tipo de periodismo que hace hincapié en el sensacionalismo en lugar de los hechos (página 577)

americanización *s.* proceso de inmersión dirigido hacia los inmigrantes para que aprendieran lo que algunos definen como la cultura estadounidense y así transformarlos en "verdaderos" estadounidenses (página 518)

ametralladora *s.* pistola diseñada para disparar cientos de balas por minuto (página 612)

amnistía *s.* perdón que concede un gobierno u otra autoridad a un grupo de personas (página 434)

anarquía *s.* concepto que postula que los gobiernos no son necesarios y que toda la cooperación social y política debe ser voluntaria (página 515)

anexionarse *v.* tomar posesión de un territorio o país (página 323)

antifederalista *s.* persona que se oponía a la Constitución de EE. UU. de 1787 porque el énfasis de esta era un gobierno nacional poderoso (página 162)

antisemitismo *s.* discriminación, prejuicio y hostilidad contra el pueblo judío (página 524)

apaciguamiento *s.* política de hacer compromisos para evitar conflictos (página 761)

aparcería *s.* sistema agrícola en donde los jornaleros levantan la cosecha de un terrateniente a cambio de recibir una parte de la venta de dichas cosechas (página 443)

aparcero *s.* agricultor que trabaja la tierra de un terrateniente y, a cambio de provisiones y refugio, entrega la mayor parte de sus cultivos al terrateniente (página 443)

apartheid *s.* separación legal entre las razas en Sudáfrica (página 1079)

aplazamiento *s.* permiso oficial para demorar el reclutamiento (página 980)

arancel de las abominaciones *s.* término usado por los sureños para referirse al arancel de 1828 porque lo consideraban odioso y opresivo (página 256)

archipiélago *s.* conjunto de islas (página 572)

armas de destrucción masiva (ADM) *s.* armas que usan material nuclear, químico o biológico para causar un inmenso daño a un gran número de personas (página 1121)

armisticio *s.* acuerdo entre dos fuerzas en conflicto para detener el combate (página 625)

arsenal *s.* lugar donde se almacenan armas y otros equipos militares (página 117)

artefacto *s.* artículo hecho por un ser humano que tiene un significado histórico o cultural (página 342)

artículo investigativo *s.* escrito que revela un escándalo o una injusticia (página 553)

Artículos de la Confederación *s.* conjunto de leyes adoptado por los Estados Unidos en 1777, que establecía cada estado de la Unión como una república, reemplazado por la Constitución en 1789 (página 126)

artillería antiaérea *s.* arma pesada modificada para poder ser dirigida hacia el cielo y disparar contra aviones enemigos (página 612)

asegurar *v.* asumir las responsabilidades financieras, incluidos los riesgos, de un conjunto de activos (página 698)

asimilar *v.* asumir las cualidades de otra cultura, así como su modo de vida (página 260)

atrocidad *s.* acto de crueldad y violencia extremas (página 819)

autócrata *s.* gobernante que tiene poder absoluto; tirano (página 970)

B

backcountry *s.* la zona oeste de las Colonias del Sur justo al este de los montes Apalaches (página 78)

baluarte *s.* algo que proporciona protección o defensa (página 861)

bancarrota *s.* estado en cual se carece de fondos para asumir las deudas; fracaso empresarial (página 229)

banco de inversión *s.* institución financiera que compra y vende acciones y bonos y ayuda a las empresas a recaudar capital y administrar sus activos (página 1126)

bar clandestino *s.* un local ilegal donde las personas se reunían en secreto para consumir alcohol durante la Prohibición (página 646)

batería *s.* grupo de piezas de artillería, como cañones (página 410)

beligerante *s.* país que está en guerra (página 768)

bimetalismo *s.* sistema monetario que permitiría a los ciudadanos acuñar moneda estadounidense con plata de su propiedad (página 477)

bipartidista *adj.* relativo a ambas partes en un sistema de dos partidos políticos (página 949)

bloque electoral *s.* grupo grande de ciudadanos que comparten ideologías y tienden a votar por igual en las elecciones (página 736)

boicot *s.* forma de protesta que rechaza la compra de bienes o servicios (página 111)

boicot de autobuses de Montgomery *s.* protesta masiva, provocada por el arresto de Rosa Parks, en contra de las prácticas de segregación racial del sistema de autobuses públicos en Montgomery, Alabama (página 911)

bolsa de valores *s.* marco en el cual se realiza la compra y venta de acciones de sociedades y empresas (página 685)

bomba atómica *s.* un tipo de bomba cuya violenta explosión es provocada por la división de los átomos, lo cual libera un intenso calor y radioactividad (página 810)

bomba de hidrógeno *s.* arma nuclear que explota debido a los gases compactados dentro (página 835)

bombardeo *s.* fuego de artillería pesada dirigido hacia un objetivo o área específicos (página 416)

bono de guerra *s.* título de deuda emitido por el gobierno para ayudar a financiar los gastos militares durante una guerra (página 153)

bono de la libertad *s.* bono del gobierno vendido a ciudadanos para ayudar a apoyar la participación de los Estados Unidos en la Primera Guerra Mundial (página 608)

GLOSARIO

Brain Trust *s.* grupo de expertos que asesoró al presidente Franklin Roosevelt durante la Gran Depresión (página 716)

brecha de credibilidad *s.* creciente escepticismo de los estadounidenses acerca de los informes gubernamentales sobre la guerra de Vietnam (página 979)

bribones *(scalawags)* *s.* término para describir después de la Guerra Civil, a aquellos blancos sureños que apoyaron la Reconstrucción únicamente por intereses económicos (página 440)

C

caballería *s.* tropas de un ejército que luchan montadas a caballo (página 395)

caballo negro *s.* candidato poco conocido cuya nominación inesperada es usualmente el resultado de un compromiso entre facciones (página 326)

Cabeza de Cobre *s.* apodo peyorativo para designar a los miembros del Partido Demócrata que en los estados de la Unión se oponían a la emancipación de los esclavos y al reclutamiento (página 404)

cacicazgo *s.* comunidad de personas regida por un cacique o jefe (página 4)

callejón sin salida *s.* situación en la que no es posible progresar (página 985)

caminata espacial *s.* cualquier período de tiempo en el que un astronauta sale de la nave espacial (página 1027)

Camino de Lágrimas *s.* ruta que los cheroquis y otras tribus norteamericanas tomaron durante su migración forzada desde el sureste de los Estados Unidos hacia Oklahoma (página 265)

campaña de registro electoral *s.* esfuerzo realizado por grupos independientes o por el gobierno para inscribir la mayor cantidad posible de votantes en un área determinada (página 922)

campo de concentración *s.* lugar donde se encuentran confinados prisioneros de guerra o miembros de minorías perseguidas; en la Segunda Guerra Mundial, los campos donde judíos y otros fueron detenidos y asesinados por los nazis (página 814)

campo de internamiento *s.* campo de prisioneros para detener a extranjeros enemigos y otros prisioneros de guerra durante la guerra (página 795)

capataz *s.* supervisor (página 81)

capital *s.* dinero y otros bienes necesarios para fundar y emprender una empresa (página 219)

capitalismo benefactor *s.* práctica empresarial en la que las empresas ofrecen a los trabajadores beneficios adicionales, incluyendo instalaciones recreativas, cobertura médica y oportunidades de participación en las ganancias (página 653)

capitalismo *s.* sistema económico donde las entidades privadas, por oposición al gobierno, son propietarias de negocios que administran con fines de lucro (página 642)

carabela *s.* barco pequeño y rápido usado por los exploradores españoles y portugueses (página 28)

caravana *s.* grupo de personas y animales que viajan juntos, usualmente para comerciar (página 25)

carga de profundidad *s.* bomba submarina que está programada para explotar a cierta profundidad (página 799)

carrera de armamentos *s.* situación política en la que países rivales tratan de acumular o producir la mayor cantidad de armas militares (página 834)

carrera espacial *s.* competencia entre los Estados Unidos y la Unión Soviética para ser el primero en realizar un viaje fuera de la atmósfera terrestre (página 934)

carreta Conestoga *s.* tipo de carreta diseñada por colonos alemanes en Norteamérica para llevar cargas pesadas (página 78)

carreta cubierta *s.* vehículo cubierto con una lona blanca y tirado por caballos que se usó para recorrer grandes distancias en el siglo XIX (página 319)

Carta del Atlántico *s.* un documento que enlista ocho principios para un mundo mejor, redactado durante la reunión entre el presidente Franklin Roosevelt y el primer ministro británico Winston Churchill en 1941 (página 770)

Carta *s.* documento de tipo histórico en el cual se establece el objetivo principal de un proyecto o un empeño (página 50)

cartógrafo *s.* persona que hace mapas (página 28)

casa de vecindad *s.* edificio grande que alquila habitaciones y apartamentos, y que suele estar abarrotado y mal mantenido (página 524)

caso civil *s.* disputa legal entre dos o más individuos u organizaciones que involucra a menudo asuntos contractuales o de negocios (página 179)

caso criminal *s.* disputa legal en la cual el gobierno acusa a una persona o grupo de romper la ley y ser una amenaza para la sociedad (página 179)

caso Dred Scott *s.* decisión de la Corte Suprema que dictaminó que los afroamericanos no tenían derechos como ciudadanos y que invalidó el Compromiso de Missouri de 1820; Dred Scott, el esclavo en cuestión, fue devuelto a la esclavitud (página 372)

caso histórico *s.* caso legal que sienta un precedente para leyes nuevas o ya existentes (página 235)

cateador *s.* persona que busca en la tierra recursos minerales valiosos, especialmente piedras y metales preciosos (página 334)

Catorce Puntos *s.* programa propuesto por el presidente Woodrow Wilson para establecer la paz al final de la Primera Guerra Mundial (página 623)

cazador y recolector *s.* ser humano que caza animales y recolecta plantas silvestres para alimentarse (página 3)

censo *s.* conteo formal de la población de un país o una región (página 179)

chivo expiatorio *s.* individuo o grupo culpado por los errores o las faltas de otros (página 409)

circunnavegar *v.* viajar por completo alrededor de la Tierra (página 30)

ciudad en auge *s.* ciudad cuya población aumenta repentinamente y en grandes cantidades (página 335)

cláusula de esclavo fugitivo *s.* disposición del Artículo 4 de la Constitución de EE. UU. que prohíbe a los estados libres la liberación de trabajadores esclavos que se hayan escapado de sus amos en otros estados (página 161)

cláusula de exención *s.* parte de una ley que excluye a ciertas personas y cosas debido a condiciones previas a su promulgación (página 535)

cláusula *s.* condición adjunta a un documento legal o ley (página 360)

clientelismo *s.* práctica que recompensa a los partidarios políticos con puestos en el gobierno (página 241)

coalición *s.* alianza de personas, partidos o estados centrada en un objetivo común (página 241)

códigos de esclavos *s.* leyes adoptadas en las colonias a principios de 1600 que regían los derechos de los esclavos afroamericanos con diferentes grados de severidad según la colonia (página 67)

colateral *s.* segunda propiedad ofrecida como seguro al solicitar un préstamo, y que protege los intereses del prestamista (página 435)

colega *s.* persona de la misma edad, rango o estatus social que otra (página 1006)

Colegio electoral *s.* grupo que elige al presidente de los EE. UU.; cada estado tiene un número de electores igual al número de sus representantes y senadores en el Congreso (página 160)

coludir *v.* conspirar o armar un complot para hacer daño a otros (página 1145)

combativo *adj.* extremadamente agresivo en la búsqueda de un objetivo (página 1016)

comercio interestatal *s.* la compra, venta o intercambio de bienes; transporte de personas, dinero o bienes entre los diferentes estados (página 161)

comercio triangular *s.* red transatlántica de comercio formada por Europa, África Occidental y las Américas (página 48)

comité de correspondencia *s.* en la época de la independencia, grupo de colonos cuyo deber era hacer correr la voz para la organización de protestas contra los británicos (página 114)

Comité de Información Pública (CPI) *s.* comité establecido durante la Primera Guerra Mundial para contrarrestar la posible disensión y estimular el entusiasmo del país por la guerra (página 610)

comité de vigilancia *s.* grupo de hombres armados reunidos para capturar a un proscrito (página 488)

complejo industrial-militar *s.* dirigencia militar de un país y las industrias que producen armas u otros materiales bélicos (página 835)

composición demográfica *s.* composición de la población de un área específica basada en la etnicidad (página 955)

Compra de Louisiana *s.* tratado entre Francia y los Estados Unidos, por el cual fue comprada una gran extensión de tierras entre el río Mississippi y las montañas Rocosas (página 190)

Compromiso de 1877 *s.* acuerdo mediante el cual el Partido Demócrata se comprometió a reconocer a Rutherford B. Hayes como presidente a cambio de que los Republicanos concluyeran la Reconstrucción y retiraran a las tropas federales del Sur (página 453)

Compromiso de Missouri *s.* acuerdo que estableció que Missouri podía tener esclavos y a su vez ser admitido a la Unión junto con Maine, un estado libre (página 240)

computadora personal *s.* dispositivo electrónico que procesa datos y está específicamente diseñado para el uso doméstico (página 1080)

comunidad utópica *s.* grupo de personas que viven juntas y cooperan para formar una sociedad ideal (página 282)

comunismo *s.* forma de gobierno en la que todos los medios de producción y transporte son propiedad del estado (página 625)

Confederación *s.* los 11 estados que se separaron de la Unión para formar su propia nación: los Estados Confederados de América (página 379)

confinamiento solitario *s.* forma de castigo en la que se aísla a un prisionero del contacto con otras personas (página 918)

confiscar *v.* acto de tomar posesión de una propiedad por parte del gobierno (página 408)

conquistador *s.* explorador español que buscaba oro y otras riquezas en las Américas (página 44)

consenso liberal *s.* acuerdo entre demócratas y republicanos en el Congreso, pactado después de la Segunda Guerra Mundial, para continuar las prestaciones sociales, desarrollar un sistema de seguridad nacional y fortalecer el poder ejecutivo (página 832)

conservador *s.* miembro de un partido político que cree en los valores tradicionales, la estructura social y el cambio gradual en las políticas (página 1068)

conservadurismo compasivo *s.* filosofía política que combinaba las ideas conservadoras tradicionales sobre las políticas económicas con una preocupación por las personas desfavorecidas (página 1116)

consumismo *s.* teoría que sostiene que la economía florece cuando la gente compra o consume muchos bienes y servicios (página 859)

contención nuclear *s.* estrategia de usar las armas nucleares como amenaza para evitar un ataque enemigo (página 860)

contención *s.* política de seguridad estadounidense durante la Guerra Fría en la que se utilizó la acción militar para impedir que la unión soviética propagara el comunismo (página 827)

contexto *s.* las circunstancias y el entorno en el que se encuentra un objeto que ayudan a comprender cómo se utiliza un objeto (página 342)

contiguo *adj.* conectado; junto (página 331)

contingente *s.* pequeño grupo de personas que representa a uno más grande (página 415)

contrabandista *s.* individuo que fabricaba, transportaba o suministraba alcohol ilegalmente a tabernas o "bares clandestinos" donde los habitantes se congregaban por las tardes (página 646)

contracultura *s.* movimiento de los años sesenta que promovió un modo de vida que estaba en oposición a las reglas y el comportamiento establecidos por la sociedad estadounidense (página 986)

contrato colectivo *s.* negociación entre un empleador y un sindicato (página 728)

Convención de Seneca Falls *s.* convención por los derechos de la mujer, organizada por Elizabeth Cady Stanton y Lucretia Mott en Seneca Falls, Nueva York, en 1848 (página 294)

Conversación junto a la chimenea *s.* serie de emisiones de radio que el presidente Franklin Roosevelt hizo a la nación durante su presidencia (página 716)

cooperativa *s.* organización dirigida y financiada por sus miembros (página 477)

corporación *s.* empresas o grupos de personas que invierten en un negocio y luego comparten sus beneficios (página 227)

corsario *s.* buque mercante privado autorizado por un gobierno para perseguir a las embarcaciones enemigas siguiendo las leyes de guerra, o un marinero a bordo ese tipo de barco (página 137)

cortina de hierro *s.* división militar y política en Europa entre los países capitalistas occidentales y los países comunistas orientales (página 827)

crédito *s.* privilegio para comprar algo o pedir prestado dinero, devolviendo el dinero con el tiempo (página 156)

crematorio *s.* horno utilizado para quemar restos humanos o animales; en la Segunda Guerra Mundial , los hornos utilizados por los nazis para quemar los cuerpos de sus víctimas (página 817)

Crisis de los Misiles en Cuba *s.* enfrentamiento político de 1962 entre los Estados Unidos y la Unión Soviética causado por la presencia de armas nucleares en Cuba (página 936)

Crusadas *s.* expediciones militares patrocinadas por la Iglesia Católica para recuperar la llamada "tierra santa" del dominio musulmán en Oriente Medio, 1096–1291 (página 21)

cuarentena naval *s.* un bloqueo impuesto a los puertos de otro país (página 936)

cuartel *s.* edificio militar utilizado para alojar a los soldados (página 132)

cuerpo especial *s.* un grupo de personas organizadas para una misión especial (página 1107)

cultivo en seco *s.* conjunto de técnicas agrícolas utilizadas en zonas con escasa precipitación (página 471)

culto a la domesticidad *s.* concepto que durante el siglo XIX planteaba que las mujeres de clases media y alta debían casarse y permanecer en la casa al cuidado de los hijos, y el deber de constituirse en el eje moral del hogar (página 292)

D

Danza de los Espíritus *s.* danza ceremonial realizada por algunos indígenas con la esperanza de que esta convocaría a un libertador que restauraría su mundo (página 484)

darwinismo social *s.* filosofía del siglo XIX que sostenía que la historia social humana podía entenderse como una lucha entre los ricos y los pobres, con los más fuertes y los más aptos invariablemente triunfando (página 503)

DDT *s.* insecticida, actualmente prohibido en los Estados Unidos y muchos otros países, que resultó ser perjudicial para los animales

y causar contaminación a largo plazo del medio ambiente (página 1046)

de cuello blanco *adj.* relacionado con la clase de personas cuyos trabajos suelen tener lugar en una oficina o entorno profesional y no implican trabajo manual (página 833)

Declaración de Derechos *s.* las diez primeras enmiendas a la Constitución de EE. UU.; lista de garantías a las que tienen derecho todas las personas del país (página 165)

Declaración de Independencia *s.* documento que declara la independencia de los Estados Unidos de Gran Bretaña, emitido el 4 de julio de 1776 (página 125)

defensa activa *s.* política que permite a los buques de guerra de los Estados Unidos defenderse contra los ataques de submarinos alemanes sobre buques en tránsito dentro del océano Atlántico (página 771)

déficit *s.* saldo monetario negativo que ocurre cuando los gastos exceden los ingresos (página 716)

deflación *s.* disminución en los precios de bienes y servicios (página 513)

democracia jacksoniana *s.* movimiento político que honraba al hombre común y defendía la voluntad del pueblo; su nombre deriva de Andrew Jackson (página 253)

deportar *v.* expulsar por la fuerza del país, o presionar para que esto se haga (página 691)

depresión *s.* deterioro económico severo y a largo plazo, caracterizado por una serie de fracasos empresariales, reducción de la producción industrial y elevado desempleo (página 152)

derechos civiles *s.* derechos individuales protegidos por la ley contra el abuso gubernamental (página 610)

desagravio *s.* dinero pagado para compensar por daños hechos (página 575)

desegregación *s.* proceso mediante el cual se pone fin a una política que obliga a la separación de grupos de personas en espacios públicos (página 907)

deshumanizar *v.* tratar a las personas como si no fueran seres humanos (página 905)

desigualdad económica *s.* fenómeno económico en el que existe una gran brecha entre lo que ganan los ciudadanos más pobres y los más ricos de una nación (página 1075)

desintegración *s.* resistencia por parte de alternativas nacionalistas, tribales y separatistas a la globalización (página 1111)

desmotadora de algodón *s.* máquina que separa las fibras de algodón de sus semillas y vainas (página 222)

desmovilización *s.* liberación de soldados del servicio militar (página 791)

desobediencia civil *s.* desobediencia no violenta de las leyes como forma de protesta (página 282)

desplegar *v.* el envío de tropas en una operación militar (página 131)

desregulación *s.* acto de derogar a gran escala algunas leyes, generalmente relacionadas con una industria en particular (página 1075)

destino manifiesto *s.* creencia de que era el destino de los estadounidenses colonizar toda la tierra entre las costas atlántica y pacífica (página 314)

GLOSARIO

détente *s.* distención y mejoramiento de relaciones entre dos países (página 1045)

Día-D *s.* 6 de junio de 1944, día en el que los Aliados invadieron el norte de Francia durante la Segunda Guerra Mundial, desembarcando en las playas de Normandía (página 804)

diáspora africana *s.* el traslado de africanos de su lugar natal a las Américas (página 49)

difusión cultural *s.* la propagación de las tradiciones y maneras de vivir de un lugar a otro (página 49)

diplomacia moral *s.* concepto de que los Estados Unidos debería reducir drásticamente su intervención en los asuntos de otros países (página 604)

discriminación salarial *s.* el acto de recibir un sueldo más bajo por el mismo trabajo debido al género, la raza o el origen étnico (página 790)

discriminación sexual *s.* preferencia por un género sobre otro (página 1022)

disidente *s.* persona que está en desacuerdo con la mayoría de una posición o creencia (página 56)

dislocación de empleo *s.* movimiento de los trabajos a otros lugares (página 1110)

dividendo *s.* dinero pagado con regularidad a los accionistas de una compañía y que proviene de los ingresos y reservas de la misma compañía (página 183)

doble soberanía *s.* sistema en el cual los gobiernos de los estados tienen ciertos poderes que el gobierno federal no puede desautorizar (página 158)

doctrina de anulación *s.* doctrina que decía que un estado podía anular o rechazar una ley federal si creía que era inconstitucional, apoyada por un político sureño antes de la Guerra Civil (página 258)

domesticación *s.* práctica de criar animales y cultivar plantas para el beneficio humano (página 4)

domesticar *v.* criar animales y cultivar plantas para el beneficio humano (página 15)

Dust Bowl *s.* áreas de Kansas, Colorado, Oklahoma, Texas y Nuevo México que, durante la década de 1930, sufrieron devastación ecológica y se convirtieron en un desierto árido (página 695)

E

ecologismo *s.* gestión y protección de los recursos naturales (página 562)

economía de la oferta *s.* teoría financiera en la que las tasas de impuestos se reducen para las empresas y los inversionistas con la esperanza de impulsar la producción y el comercio en el país (página 1074)

economía *laissez-faire* *s.* política que exige menos participación del gobierno en los asuntos económicos, para que las empresas escojan cómo operar, con poca o ninguna supervisión (página 513)

economía salarial *s.* economía en la que una persona recibe un pago regular por su trabajo (página 447)

efecto invernadero *s.* calentamiento de la superficie de la Tierra que ocurre cuando las emisiones de gases de efecto invernadero atrapan el calor del Sol (página 1136)

Eje Roma-Berlín *s.* acuerdo entre Alemania e Italia firmado en 1936 (página 755)

ejecución hipotecaria *s.* acción que realiza un banco para tomar posesión de una propiedad porque el comprador ya no puede hacer los pagos de la hipoteca (página 156)

Ejército del Bono *s.* grupo de miles de veteranos de guerra, decididos a cobrar los bonos en efectivo que les habían sido prometidos, que acudieron a Washington, D.C., durante el verano de 1932 para escuchar el debate del Congreso sobre la propuesta de bonificación (página 701)

el Sangriento Kansas *s.* nombre dado en 1856 al Territorio de Kansas debido al gran número de enfrentamientos entre tropas antiesclavistas y esclavistas (página 371)

elección primaria directa *s.* elección preliminar en la cual los votantes eligen a los candidatos de su partido que luego se postularán a elecciones para cargos públicos (página 561)

electorado *s.* grupo de ciudadanos que ha elegido o tiene derecho a elegir un representante para el gobierno (página 663)

electrificación rural *s.* programa gubernamental que trajo electricidad a las comunidades rurales (página 833)

emancipación *s.* fin de la esclavitud (página 288)

embalse *s.* gran cuerpo de agua que puede ser aprovechada (página 474)

embarcaciones de desembarco anfibio *s.* botes o barcazas usadas para transportar soldados y equipamiento militar desde el mar a la costa durante ataques militares (página 804)

embargo *s.* prohibición de comerciar con determinados países (página 198)

empoderamiento *s.* concesión de derechos de ciudadanía, especialmente del derecho al voto (página 555)

emprendedor *s.* persona que inicia, administra y es responsable de un negocio (página 335)

empresario *s.* agente que tenía un contrato con el gobierno mexicano para reclutar Americanos y poblar los territorios de Nueva España, antes de que fueran parte de los EE.UU. (página 321)

encomienda *s.* sistema de España en sus colonias en América, en el cual colonos ricos recibían terrenos y se les permitía esclavizar a las personas que allí vivían (página 47)

encubrimiento *s.* intento de esconder la verdad del público (página 1054)

energía nuclear *s.* energía que se crea dividiendo o fusionando los núcleos de átomos (página 865)

enviado *s.* embajador (página 187)

era glacial *s.* período de tiempo en la historia durante el cual enormes capas de hielo cubrieron gran parte de la Tierra (página 1)

Era Progresista *s.* período de 1890 a 1920 en el que los reformadores trataron de corregir muchas desigualdades e injusticias sociales, económicas y políticas en los Estados Unidos (página 552)

escasez planificada *s.* teoría económica de que bajar la oferta de un producto aumentará su demanda y por lo tanto su precio (página 718)

esclavitud como propiedad personal *s.* sistema según el cual las personas esclavizadas no tienen ningún derecho humano y se clasifican como bienes (página 30)

esclavos de contrabando *s.* esclavos afroamericanos del Sur que durante la Guerra Civil eran capturados por tropas de la Unión y tratados como propiedad enemiga (página 404)

escuela común *s.* escuela colonial (página 74)

esfera de influencia *s.* afirmación de un país al control exclusivo de una zona o territorio extranjero (página 574)

esmog *s.* combinación nociva de niebla y humo de fábricas (página 859)

especulación *s.* asumir un riesgo empresarial, como comprar acciones con reserva, sin garantía de que aumenten en valor (página 686)

especulación *s.* aumento en los precios de los artículos escasos y de gran demanda con la intención de ganar más dinero (página 137)

especulador *s.* alguien que invierte en propiedades y acciones para obtener ganancias (página 155)

espionaje *s.* la actividad de espiar (página 139)

estado benefactor *s.* sistema en el que el gobierno proporciona los servicios de salud y beneficios a sus ciudadanos (página 742)

estado bisagra *s.* estado en el que puede triunfar cualquier partido político (página 1144)

Estado de derecho (rule of law) *s.* concepto según el cual las personas e instituciones deben acatar las regulaciones establecidas por el gobierno (página 120)

estado fronterizo *s.* estado que durante la Guerra Civil limitaba tanto con los estados de la Unión como con los estados Confederados, específicamente Maryland, Kentucky, Delaware, Missouri y Virginia Occidental (página 391)

estado paria *s.* país percibido como violador del derecho internacional y que amenaza la paz mundial (página 1121)

estalactita *s.* columna de minerales que cuelga del techo de una cueva (página 648)

estalagmita *s.* columna de minerales que se forma hacia arriba desde el suelo de una cueva (página 648)

estancamiento económico *s.* período de poco o ningún crecimiento económico (página 1056)

estanflación *s.* condición económica con estancamiento, o crecimiento económico lento, acompañado de inflación, o aumento de los precios (página 1056)

estático *adj.* tener la cualidad que no moverse ni cambiar (página 1077)

estepa *s.* planicie amplia y cubierta de hierbas (página 24)

estímulo económico *s.* medida destinada a promover y permitir la recuperación y el crecimiento financieros (página 1129)

estuario *s.* lugar donde un río se junta en su desembocadura con el agua salada del mar (página 194)

eugenesia *s.* creencia de que algunas razas son superiores a otras y que la reproducción humana debe ser controlada para que aumenten las poblaciones de razas superiores (página 644)

evangelista *s.* predicador entusiasta que urge a los creyentes a aceptar a Jesús como su salvador (página 277)

excavaciones *s.* modificaciones a la tierra hechas por la mano del hombre (página 122)

exceso de regulación *s.* conjunto de reglas excesivas (página 1049)

exclusa *s.* espacio cerrado de agua que se usa para subir o bajar embarcaciones (página 227)

exención *s.* librar de obligaciones a alguien (página 408)

exoduster *s.* afroamericano que emigró del Sur a las Grandes Llanuras después de que la Reconstrucción había fracasado (página 470)

expansión urbana *s.* desarrollo de proyectos de vivienda en áreas cada vez más suburbanas y rurales (página 869)

expansionismo *s.* política o práctica de ampliar el territorio de un país (página 572)

explosión de natalidad *s.* aumento significativo en la tasa de natalidad (página 862)

explotar *v.* aprovecharse de personas o recursos, por lo general con fines de lucro (página 221)

extranjero enemigo *adj.* persona cuya lealtad a la nación en la que vive es poco fiable (página 794)

F

factor de expulsión o atracción *s.* una razón por la cual las personas emigran; los factores de "expulsión" hace que se vayan; los factores de "atracción" hace que vengan de un lugar (página 518)

fascismo *s.* movimiento político basado en el nacionalismo extremo, el militarismo y el racismo, que promueve la superioridad de un pueblo en particular sobre todos los demás (página 699)

federalismo *s.* apoyo al gobierno en el cual el poder es compartido entre el gobierno nacional central y los estados o provincias (página 158)

federalista *s.* persona que apoyaba la Constitución de EE. UU. de 1787 según se redactó durante el proceso de ratificación (página 162)

feminismo *s.* principio de que las mujeres son iguales a los hombres social y políticamente (página 1021)

feriado bancario *s.* día o período de tiempo en el que los bancos están cerrados por orden del gobierno (página 716)

ferrocarril transcontinental *s.* ferrocarril que opera a lo largo de un continente (página 336)

feudalismo *s.* sistema político y social en el que un vasallo recibe protección de un señor feudal a cambio de prestarle obediencia y servicio (página 20)

financista *s.* persona que presta o maneja dinero para un negocio u emprendimiento (página 137)

fiscal general *s.* miembro del Gabinete del presidente, cuyo papel principal es representar a los EE. UU. ante la Corte Suprema (página 179)

flanquear *s.* movimiento de tropas hacia un lado de la línea enemiga para tomar ventaja (página 411)

flapper *s.* mujer joven en la década de 1920 que adoptó un estilo más libre de vestir y el uso de cosméticos (página 660)

fondo de pensiones *s.* reserva de dinero usada para pagar a una persona un pequeño ingreso establecido después de jubilarse (página 722)

fonógrafo *s.* máquina que reproduce sonidos de un disco (página 509)

forrajear *v.* buscar plantas para comer (página 480)

forty-niner **(buscador de oro)** *s.* uno de los miles de futuros mineros que viajaron a California a buscar oro en 1849 (página 335)

Framers **(autores de la Constitución)** *s.* término histórico para los delegados en la Convención Constitucional de 1787, quienes ayudaron a crear y redactar la Constitución de los Estados Unidos (página 157)

fraude electoral *s.* manipulación ilegal de boletas para ganar una elección (página 929)

frente *s.* línea de batalla entre dos ejércitos (página 401)

Frostbelt *s.* región del centro-norte y noreste de los Estados Unidos, que tiene inviernos fríos (página 859)

fuerza anfibia *s.* unidad militar compuesta por aviones y barcos que atacan simultáneamente (página 331)

Fuerzas Expedicionarias Estadounidenses (AEF) *s.* cuerpo de soldados estadounidenses enviados a luchar en Europa durante la Primera Guerra Mundial (página 608)

fundamentalismo *s.* movimiento que promulgó la idea de que cada palabra de la Biblia debía ser tomada literalmente (página 647)

fusión *s.* acto de incorporar dos o más negocios en uno (página 563)

G

G.I. Bill *s.* programa del gobierno iniciado en 1944 que ayudó a los veteranos que regresaban de la Segunda Guerra Mundial a comprar casas y asistir a la universidad (página 833)

Gabinete *s.* los jefes de los departamentos que asisten al presidente de los EE. UU. (página 178)

gas de efecto invernadero *s.* gas como el dióxido de carbono o metano (página 1136)

gastar públicamente déficit *v.* gastar más dinero del que el gobierno recibe por impuestos (página 742)

genocidio *s.* asesinato intencional de un gran número de personas pertenecientes a determinado grupo racial, cultural o político (página 483)

Gestapo *s.* policía secreta nazi (página 754)

glasnost *s.* política gubernamental de comunicación abierta en la ex Unión Soviética (página 1084)

globalización *s.* flujo más rápido y libre de personas, recursos, bienes e ideas a lo largo de las fronteras entre países (página 1110)

gobierno en exilio *s.* gobierno que ha sido depuesto e intenta gobernar desde otro país (página 836)

gobierno por comisión *s.* forma de gobierno citadino en la que los votantes eligen un pequeño número de funcionarios llamados comisionados, cada uno de los cuales dirige un departamento de la ciudad (página 560)

golpe de estadp0 *s.* derrocamiento ilegal del gobierno (página 971)

Gran Depresión *s.* una recesión económica mundial en la década de 1930, marcada por la pobreza y el alto desempleo (página 687)

Gran Despertar *s.* serie de avivamientos religiosos protestantes que se extendieron por las colonias en Norteamérica (página 90)

Gran Migración *s.* movimiento masivo de afroamericanos que se fueron del Sur para las ciudades del norte, comenzando en 1910 (página 619)

gravamen *s.* reclamación legal sobre los bienes e ingresos de una persona si no se pagan deudas (página 443)

grupo de comercio *s.* grupo formado para comprar y vender grandes cantidades de acciones

grupo de comercio *s.* grupos que se forman para manipular la compra y venta de acciones (página 688)

guerra de desgaste *s.* una estrategia militar en la que un ejército lleva a otro abajo conduciendo muchas pequeñas batallas durante un largo período de tiempo (página 975)

guerra de guerrillas *s.* guerra en la que pequeños grupos móviles de fuerzas anómalas usan tácticas de ataque y huida para luchar contra fuerzas militares convencionales (página 117)

guerra de trincheras *s.* tipo de guerra en la que se excavan largas y profundas zanjas en el suelo para proteger a los soldados (página 407)

guerra defensiva *s.* guerra que se libra en terreno conocido para defender la tierra propia de un ataque externo (página 391)

guerra ofensiva *s.* guerra que se libra principalmente en terreno enemigo (página 391)

guerra sin cuartel *s.* guerra en la cual se ignoran todos los convenios bélicos y se usan todos los recursos para vencer al enemigo (página 422)

guerra subsidiaria *s.* conjunto de batallas provocadas por una nación que luego no participa en la lucha (página 838)

H

hacienda *s.* plantación grande en una colonia española (página 47)

Halcón de Guerra *s.* persona partidaria de la guerra; estadounidense que estaba a favor de la guerra contra Gran Bretaña en 1812 (página 199)

halcón *s.* persona que apoya la guerra (página 980)

helero *s.* depósito de una mezcla de sedimentos que puede incluir cieno, arcilla, arena, rocas y otros materiales que dejan los glaciares en retroceso (página 238)

hereje *s.* persona que tiene creencias diferentes a las enseñanzas de la Iglesia Católica (página 54)

hesianos *s.* soldados alemanes contratados por los británicos para luchar durante la Guerra de Independencia (página 123)

hipotecas de alto riesgo *s.* préstamos hipotecarios otorgados a compradores que tenían un historial de crédito pobre (página 1126)

hito legislativo *s.* una legislación importante e histórica (página 957)

GLOSARIO

Holocausto *s.* la matanza masiva por parte de los nazis de seis millones de judíos y otros durante la Segunda Guerra Mundial (página 817)

hombre de paja *s.* funcionario electo que está por finalizar su mandado y será reemplazado por un sucesor (página 715)

hombres de montaña *s.* cazadores y comerciantes de pieles conocidos como tramperos que contribuyeron con la exploración del Oeste (página 314)

homogeneidad *s.* estado de similitud o igualdad (página 867)

Hooverville *s.* un grupo de viviendas improvisadas para dar albergue a gente sin techo, hechas con restos de cartón, placas metálicas u otros materiales baratos, que se construyeron durante la Gran Depresión y fueron bautizadas con el nombre del presidente Herbert Hoover (página 698)

huelga de brazos caídos *s.* huelga en la que los trabajadores no se van del lugar trabajo, sino que permanecen ahí sin realizar labor alguna (página 731)

humanismo *s.* movimiento basado en la importancia del individuo (página 21)

I

igualdad matrimonial *s.* derecho legal de las personas homosexuales a casarse con sus parejas y tener los mismos privilegios que disfrutan las parejas heterosexuales casadas (página 1134)

igualitarismo *s.* creencia de que todas las personas son iguales, especialmente en sus interese políticos, económicos y sociales (página 152)

Ilustración *s.* movimiento intelectual caracterizado por el uso de la razón para revisar creencias aceptadas anteriormente (página 88)

imperialismo *s.* política o práctica de ejercer control sobre naciones o territorios más débiles (página 572)

impuesto electoral *s.* impuesto cobrado en el momento de registrarse para votar (página 451)

impuesto sobre la renta *s.* impuesto que se basa en la cantidad de dinero que gana una persona (página 571)

impuesto sobre ventas *s.* impuesto que grava un artículo en particular (página 182)

inauguración *s.* ceremonia de juramento que enmarca el comienzo de un periodo presidencial (página 178)

indemnización laboral *s.* seguro que cubre a los empleados lesionados en el trabajo y que ofrece asistencia médica y compensación por la falta de ingresos (página 513)

índice bursátil Dow Jones *s.* índice de las acciones de empresas líderes, que tiene seguimiento diario y es utilizado como medida de las tendencias generales del mercado bursátil (página 686)

índice de pobreza *s.* porcentaje de la población que vive en la pobreza (página 878)

indiferencia saludable *s.* política del gobierno británico que evitaba que sus leyes en las colonias se cumplieran estrictamente (página 93)

indulgencia *s.* perdón de los pecados que vendían los oficiales papales (página 22)

industria aeroespacial *s.* negocio comercial relacionado a la construcción de aviones, naves espaciales y otros vehículos que vuelan (página 834)

infamia *s.* acción de maldad o vileza extrema (página 784)

infantería *s.* tropas de soldados a pie (página 395)

inflación *s.* disminución en el valor de una moneda que causa el aumento en el precio de bienes y servicios (página 137)

influenza *s.* enfermedad aguda y altamente contagiosa comúnmente llamada "gripe" (página 621)

infraestructura *s.* sistemas físicos básicos de una sociedad, incluyendo carreteras, puentes, alcantarillas y electricidad (página 17)

iniciativa *s.* procedimiento mediante el cual los ciudadanos pueden proponer nuevas leyes para ser votadas por el público o por los legisladores (página 561)

injuria *s.* delito de hacer declaraciones negativas verbales o escritas sobre alguien sin evidencia (página 93)

insurgente *s.* rebelde o revolucionario (página 970)

insurrección *s.* rebelión violenta contra un gobierno o una autoridad política (página 330)

integración horizontal *s.* compra por parte de una compañía de otras que ofrecen los mismos bienes y servicios para reducir el número de competidores y lograr el dominio de una industria (página 503)

integración *s.* proceso mediante el cual se juntan recursos económicos (página 1111)

integración vertical *s.* procedimiento en el que una empresa toma el control de todas las etapas de producción (página 503)

integrado *adj.* que permite la libre asociación de personas de diferentes razas o grupos étnicos (página 435)

intensificación *s.* aumento en la intensidad durante una guerra (página 972)

intercambio colombino *s.* intercambio de plantas, animales, microbios, personas e ideas entre Europa y las Américas después del primer viaje de Colón al Hemisferio Occidental (página 31)

interdicto *s.* orden judicial que exige o prohíbe ciertas acciones (página 700)

intermediario *s.* alguien que ayuda a dos partes en disputa a llegar a un acuerdo (página 187)

internar *v.* confinar a una prisión o campo por razones militares o políticas durante la guerra (página 794)

Internet *s.* red mundial de ordenadores (página 1081)

interpretación estricta *s.* un entendimiento de la Constitución en el cual la Constitución debe ser seguida estrictamente como fue redactada (página 182)

interpretación flexible *s.* un entendimiento de la Constitución que le da al Congreso y al presidente amplios poderes (página 182)

intervención telefónica *s.* la colocación de un dispositivo en un teléfono para poder escuchar en secreto las conversaciones ajenas (página 1054)

intimidación del votante *s.* acciones a menudo violentas con la intención de atemorizar a los votantes; con frecuencia dirigidas a afroamericanos, inmigrantes o a personas con quienes un grupo de poder no está de acuerdo (página 445)

intransigente *s.* persona que generalmente pertenece a un grupo político o de intereses especiales y que apoya de manera estricta y dura un conjunto de ideas o políticas (página 1085)

ironclad (barco blindado) *s.* barco revestido con planchas de hierro para protegerlo del fuego de los cañones (página 399)

irregular *s.* soldado que combate intermitentemente en un ej (página 142)

istmo *s.* estrecha franja de tierra que conecta dos áreas de tierra más grandes (página 583)

J

jazz *s.* estilo de música que se originó entre los músicos afroamericanos y que contiene ritmos vivos, sonidos de una variedad de instrumentos y mucha improvisación (página 654)

jueces de medianoche *s.* grupo de jueces nombrados por el presidente John Adams una noche antes de terminar su mandato de gobierno (página 189)

juicio político *s.* cargos formales presentados contra un funcionario público por mala conducta en el cargo (página 160)

Junta Militar de Industrias (WIB) *s.* consejo que supervisó la industria de manufactura dentro de los Estados Unidos durante la Primera Guerra Mundial (página 608)

juramento de lealtad *s.* declaración jurada que confirma que una persona no pertenece y nunca ha pertenecido a determinadas organizaciones, por ejemplo, aquellas identificadas como comunistas (página 843)

justicia social *s.* régimen caracterizado por una justa distribución de las oportunidades y los privilegios, incluyendo la igualdad racial (página 448)

K

kamikaze *s.* miembro de un grupo de pilotos japoneses que estrellaban su avión, cargado con explosivos, en los barcos estadounidenses (página 808)

kitchen cabinet *s.* grupo de asesores no oficiales de Andrew Jackson (página 255)

L

la Reforma *s.* movimiento religioso protestante basado en la necesidad de reformar la cristiandad en Europa Oriental en el siglo XVI (página 23)

laboratorio de ideas *s.* grupo de expertos que realizan investigaciones y discuten temas para elaborar soluciones potenciales a problemas sociales y económicos (página 1069)

Larga Marcha *s.* viaje de 6.000 millas realizado por los comunistas chinos para trasladar la base revolucionaria comunista del sureste al centro de China (página 765)

leal a Gran Bretaña *s.* colono que apoyaba a Gran Bretaña en la Guerra de Independencia (página 111)

legislatura bicameral *s.* órgano del gobierno conformado por dos cámaras separadas que tiene la facultad de hacer leyes (ej. el Senado y la Cámara de Representantes) (página 158)

leva *s.* reclutamiento forzoso en las fuerzas militares (página 186)

Ley de Desalojo de los Indígenas *s.* ley que terminó con una ley anterior de los EE. UU. que respetaba los derechos de los indígenas norteamericanos a permanecer en sus tierras (página 260)

ley marcial *s.* ley que se impone a un país ocupado por parte de las fuerzas al mando (página 117)

ley mordaza *s.* serie de medidas adoptadas por el Congreso entre 1830 y 1840 para evitar la discusión y consideración de políticas antiesclavistas; cualquier medida que prohíbe discusión legal o pública sobre un tema específico (página 291)

Leyes de Jim Crow *s.* leyes establecidas después de la Reconstrucción que imponían la segregación racial a lo largo de los estados sureños (página 535)

liberto *s.* condición del esclavo liberado (página 404)

Liga antidifamación (ADL) *s.* organización judía internacional de servicio fundada para combatir el antisemitismo, la intolerancia religiosa y racial, y todas las formas de discriminación organizada basadas en estereotipos (página 643)

Liga estadounidense antiimperialista *s.* organización formada en 1898 para oponerse a la anexión de las Filipinas por los Estados Unidos (página 581)

linchar *v.* ejecución ilegal por parte de una turba (página 409)

línea de ensamblaje *s.* sistema en el cual cada trabajador se coloca en determinado lugar, y el proceso de producción pasa de una función a otra, en línea recta, hasta que un producto se ensambla por completo (página 651)

M

macartismo *s.* la práctica de acusar a la gente de ser traidores a su país sin ofrecer pruebas (página 845)

mafia *s.* grupo de delincuentes que controlan actividades criminales organizadas (página 568)

magnates ladrones *s.* líderes de la industria ferroviaria, como Cornelius Vanderbilt y Jay Gould, que se hicieron famosos por sus métodos despiadados en contra de sus competidores (página 503)

magnicidio *v.* el asesinato de una persona muy importante por su cargo o poder (página 427)

malestar *s.* sensación general de enfermedad (página 1059)

mandato *s.* autoridad para llevar a cabo alguna acción, otorgado a un representante por los votantes (página 269)

manejo científico *s.* gestión basada en estudios experimentales para identificar la forma más eficiente de ejecutar tareas en una fábrica u otro lugar de trabajo (página 570)

manifiesto *s.* declaración de intenciones por escrito (página 1012)

maquiladora *s.* planta de manufactura ubicada en una zona de exportación (página 1110)

maquinaria política *s.* organización política en la que una persona o un grupo pequeño es capaz de mantener el control sobre una ciudad o un estado (página 532)

margen *s.* diferencia que representa el porcentaje por el cual se gana o se pierde algo, como en una elección (página 686)

marítimo *adj.* relativo al mar (página 72)

Masacre de Boston *s.* incidente en 1779, en el cual soldados británicos dispararon contra personas locales que los estaban insultando (página 114)

maternidad republicana *s.* la idea de que las mujeres debían criar a los hijos para ser buenos ciudadanos que participaran activamente en el gobierno (página 180)

mayoría silenciosa *s.* término usado por Richard Nixon a finales de los años sesenta para describir a un gran grupo de votantes moderados que no expresaban públicamente sus opiniones políticas (página 1041)

Medicaid *s.* programa del gobierno de los Estados unidos iniciado en 1965 para ofrecer cobertura médica a la gente pobre (página 954)

Medicare *s.* programa del gobierno de los Estados Unidos iniciado en 1965 para ofrecer cobertura médica a personas de edad avanzada (página 954)

medios de comunicación de masas *s.* formas de comunicación como la radio, el cine y las grabaciones musicales que tienen el potencial de alcanzar grandes audiencias (página 696)

medios de comunicación modernos *s.* productos y servicios digitales que proporcionan contenido a través de internet (página 1138)

mercado masivo *s.* enorme número de consumidores a quienes los fabricantes venden mercancías producidas en cantidades industriales (página 651)

mercantilismo *s.* política económica que le da a un país la propiedad exclusiva del comercio en sus colonias (página 23)

mercenario *s.* soldado al que se le paga para luchar por un país que no es el suyo (página 123)

mestizaje *s.* matrimonio entre personas de diferentes razas (página 961)

militarismo *s.* creencia de que un gobierno debe desarrollar un ejército fuerte y estar preparado para usarlo para alcanzar sus objetivos (página 600)

minería aluvial *s.* técnicas mineras que incluyen el uso de herramientas ligeras para encontrar oro en ríos y arroyos (página 472)

minería hidráulica *s.* proceso de descubrimiento de minerales preciosos mediante el uso de agua a presión para eliminar el suelo (página 472)

minería subterránea *s.* técnica minera en la que se abre un túnel vertical en una montaña para que los mineros bajen hacia la mina (página 472)

minuteman *s.* miliciano colonial listo para entrar en combate al instante (página 117)

misil antibalístico (ABM) *s.* misil diseñado para destruir un misil portador de bomba antes de que este alcance su objetivo (página 1045)

misil balístico *s.* arma nuclear propulsada por un cohete y guiada por un sistema GPS (página 936)

misoginia *s.* aversión, desprecio u odio hacia las mujeres; prejuicio contra las mujeres (página 1023)

modernismo *s.* estilo artístico y literario moderno, con tono duro y realista y una tendencia a rechazar o evitar las prácticas artísticas y literarias del pasado (página 658)

módulo *s.* segmento de una nave espacial que puede funcionar de manera independiente (página 1028)

moneda *s.* dinero en circulación para la compra de bienes y servicios (página 156)

monedas *s.* cambio; relacionado a menudo con monedas de plata y oro (página 156)

monocultivo *s.* la práctica de cultivo único de una especie vegetal (página 509)

monopolio *s.* control total de una industria o el mercado de un servicio o producto (página 226)

morfina *s.* potente analgésico (página 429)

mortero *s.* cañón de corto alcance cuya carga se inserta por la boca (página 975)

Motín del Té *s.* incidente en 1773, en el cual los Hijos de la Libertad subieron a bordo de barcos británicos y botaron al mar los cargamentos de té en protesta por los impuestos británicos a los colonos (página 114)

movilización militar *s.* acto de reunir y organizar fuerzas militares (página 741)

movilizar *v.* organizar y preparar tropas para la guerra (página 125)

movimiento de escuelas comunes *s.* movimiento de reforma a la educación en la década de 1830 para promover escuelas públicas gratuitas financiadas por la recolección de impuestos a la propiedad y manejadas por los gobiernos locales (página 278)

movimiento de retorno a África *s.* movimiento encabezado por Marcus Garvey, quien alentó a los afroamericanos a abandonar los Estados Unidos y regresar a África (página 665)

movimiento por la moderación *s.* movimiento social y político del siglo XIX y principios del siglo XX que animaba a las personas a limitar su consumo de alcohol o abstenerse del alcohol por completo (página 277)

muckrakers *s.* periodistas de investigación de principios del siglo XX que revelaron las conductas indebidas de organizaciones o personas poderosas (página 505)

multinacional *s.* empresa que tiene oficinas y fábricas en varios países (página 1138)

N

nación-estado *s.* país con un gobierno independiente cuyos habitantes comparten cultura, lenguaje y orgullo nacional; unidad política con una cultura e identidad en común (página 23)

nacionalismo *s.* fuerte sentido de lealtad al país al que uno pertenece y la creencia en la superioridad del mismo los demás países (página 145)

nacionalsocialismo *s.* doctrina política del partido nazi en Alemania, que promovió la superioridad de Alemania y del pueblo alemán, rechazó el comunismo y llevó el antisemitismo (el odio al del pueblo judío) a niveles extremos (página 724)

napalm *s.* substancia espesa, inflamable y gelatinosa usada en bombas para causar y propagar incendios (página 786)

nativista *s.* persona que se opone a la inmigración y quiere proteger los intereses de la población nativa (página 369)

naturalización *s.* proceso mediante el cual una persona que no nació en los Estados Unidos se convierte en ciudadana (página R34)

neoconservador *s.* persona que apoya firmemente una economía de libre mercado y cree que los Estados Unidos debe promover activamente sus ideales en todo el mundo (página 1116)

New Deal *s.* leyes, organismos y programas iniciados por el presidente Franklin Roosevelt y su administración en respuesta a la Gran Depresión de la década de 1930 (página 717)

nómada *adj.* persona que recorre una extensión de tierra sin un patrón fijo de movimiento, algunas veces siguiendo las manadas de animales (página 16)

novela de diez centavos *s.* publicación de literatura popular que se vendía por 10 centavos a finales del siglo XVIII y principios del XIX (página 489)

Nueva Frontera *s.* estrategia política de los Estados Unidos en 1960, en la que el presidente Kennedy enfatizó la resolución creativa de problemas, la diplomacia extranjera y los avances tecnológicos para superar los problemas del país (página 932)

Nuevo Federalismo *s.* plan del presidente Richard Nixon para transferir el control de algunos programas federales a los estados (página 1042)

nulificar *s.* anular o negar algo, especialmente en términos legales; en la historia de EE. UU. se entiende como el intento del gobierno estatal de vetar una ley federal que considera inconstitucional (página 187)

O

objetor de conciencia *s.* persona que se niega a luchar en una guerra por razones religiosas (página 610)

obstrucción *s.* estrategia política en la que un pequeño grupo de legisladores se turnan para hablar y evitar así que finalice un debate o que un proyecto de ley sea sometido a votación (página 949)

Oficina de Libertos *s.* Oficina para Refugiados, Hombres Libres y Tierras Abandonadas, creada por el Congreso en 1865 para brindar ayuda a los afroamericanos que habían sido esclavos, así como a los sureños blancos más pobres (página 446)

Oficina de Protección al Menor *s.* agencia gubernamental estadounidense creada en 1912 para mejorar la vida de los niños y sus familias (página 554)

oleada *s.* aumento repentino (página 1123)

operación anfibia *s.* ataque que utiliza el apoyo naval para proteger a las fuerzas militares que invaden por tierra y por aire (página 801)

operación encubierta *s.* actividad realizada secretamente para influir en la situación política, económica o militar en otro país (página 860)

orden de asistencia *s.* documento legal que daba a las autoridades el derecho de entrar y registrar una casa o negocio (página 112)

orden ejecutiva *s.* directiva emitida por un presidente que tiene fuerza de ley (página 795)

ordenanza *s.* mandato, decreto o ley oficial (página 154)

originalismo *s.* sistema de creencias utilizado para interpretar la constitución de los Estados Unidos desde el punto de vista de la intención del documento cuando fue escrito originalmente (página 1077)

P

pacifismo *s.* creencia de que la guerra es moralmente incorrecta (página 60)

Pacto de Briand-Kellogg *s.* acuerdo multinacional de 1928 en el que los países firmantes aceptaron rechazar la guerra (página 685)

pagaré *s.* acuerdo por escrito que especifica una fecha de pago (página 393)

país de tercer mundo *s.* durante la Guerra Fría, cualquier país que no estaba alineado ni con los Estados Unidos ni con la Unión Soviética (página 969)

paloma *s.* persona que se opone a la guerra (página 980)

pan-africanismo *s.* movimiento de principios del siglo XX que procuró unificar a la gente de ascendencia africana (página 665)

pandemia *s.* el brote repentino de una enfermedad que se extiende sobre una amplia área geográfica (página 621)

Pánico de 1837 *s.* episodio de temor por una caída de la economía, que causó el comienzo de una recesión económica en los EE. UU. hasta 1840 (página 270)

Pánico de 1873 *s.* crisis económica desencadenada por la quiebra de algunos bancos y empresas ferroviarias (página 453)

panzer *s.* tanque alemán fuertemente blindado y que poseía gran potencia de fuego, utilizado durante la Segunda Guerra Mundial (página 799)

paralelo 49 *s.* línea de latitud establecida a los 49 grados de latitud norte; frontera entre los EE. UU. y Canadá demarcada por los británicos en 1888 (página 236)

Parlamento *s.* cámara legislativa de Inglaterra, y después de Gran Bretaña (página 93)

parte intercambiable *s.* parte de un mecanismo que puede ser sustituida por otra (página 219)

Partido de los Whigs *s.* partido político que se opuso a las políticas de Andrew Jackson, de quien consideraban que tenía demasiado poder (página 269)

Partido Nazi *s.* partido político dirigido por Adolfo Hitler y que mediante la fuerza ejerció control total sobre Alemania de 1933 a 1945 (página 724)

pasaje medio *s.* el largo viaje a través del océano Atlántico durante el cual los africanos esclavizados eran llevados a las Américas; segunda etapa de la ruta del comercio triangular (página 49)

Pasajeros de la libertad *s.* grupos interraciales que viajaban en autobuses por el Sur, haciendo caso omiso a las leyes de segregación cuando usaban los baños públicos y los cafés, para así asegurar que las decisiones judiciales federales que habían establecido como ilegal la segregación en lugares de atención públicos para viajeros fuesen cumplidas por los funcionarios blancos (página 917)

paso de montaña *s.* ruta para atravesar una montaña que evita escalar los picos altos (página 337)

patente *s.* licencia que otorga a un inventor derechos exclusivos para usar, vender o hacer una invención durante un número específico de años (página 226)

patriota *s.* colono que apoyaba el derecho de las colonias en Norteamérica a gobernarse a sí mismas (página 111)

patrón oro *s.* sistema monetario en el que la moneda de una nación está respaldada por oro (página 477)

penicilina *s.* antibiótico hecho de moho y utilizado para tratar infecciones y enfermedades (página 786)

penitenciaría *s.* prisión federal o estatal cuyo objetivo es la rehabilitación de los criminales (página 278)

perestroika *s.* política gubernamental de reforma en la antigua Unión Soviética (página 1084)

período glacial *s.* período de tiempo en la historia durante el cual enormes capas de hielo cubrieron gran parte de la Tierra (página 1)

perjurio *s.* acto de mentir bajo juramento (página 1115)

pesos y contrapesos *s.* sistema establecido en la Constitución de EE. UU. que da a cada una de las ramas del gobierno el poder para controlar a las otras dos (página 160)

piedemonte *s.* área relativamente plana entre los montes Apalaches y la planicie costera (página 78)

piquete *s.* grupo de huelguistas que forman una barrera para evitar que los rompehuelgas entren en un edificio para trabajar en su lugar (página 729)

Plan Anaconda *s.* estrategia militar durante la Guerra Civil, en la cual el Norte planeó un bloqueo alrededor de las costas sureñas para arruinar la economía del Sur y tomar los puertos en el Mississippi; al igual que una enorme serpiente, como la anaconda, estrangula a su presa (página 393)

Plan de Crittenden *s.* propuesta que establecía que el gobierno federal no tuviera poderes para abolir la esclavitud en los estados donde ya existía; reestablecía y extendía el límite del Compromiso de Missouri hasta el océano Pacífico (página 378)

Plan de desbordamiento de la corte *s.* controvertido plan del presidente Franklin Roosevelt para aumentar el número de jueces de la Corte Suprema de nueve a quince, sumando seis jueces que compartían sus valores progresistas (página 730)

Plan Marshall *s.* programa de ayuda económica de los Estados Unidos para restablecer la estabilidad económica en Europa occidental después de la Segunda Guerra Mundial (página 825)

Plan Schlieffen *s.* plan alemán para conquistar rápidamente a Francia entre 1905 y 1906, seguido por un ataque a Rusia (página 602)

planificación económica *s.* administración de la economía por el gobierno federal (página 719)

Pleistoceno *s.* era de la historia de la Tierra en la que vivieron grandes animales y plantas y los glaciares cubrieron la tierra (página 1)

poder ejecutivo *s.* rama del gobierno de EE. UU. presidida por el presidente; responsable de que se cumpla la ley (página 158)

poder judicial *s.* rama del gobierno de EE. UU., que incluye las cortes o tribunales y el sistema legal, presidida por la Corte Suprema; responsable de interpretar las leyes (página 158)

poder legislativo *s.* rama del gobierno de EE. UU. presidida por el Congreso; responsable de hacer las leyes (página 158)

polio *s.* enfermedad infecciosa que a veces causa debilidad muscular o parálisis (página 715)

politburó *s.* principal comité gubernamental que tomó decisiones políticas en el partido comunista; a menudo se refiere al comité de China o la antigua Unión Soviética (página 1084)

Política De Puertas Abiertas *s.* propuesta estadounidense que pretendía establecer la igualdad de acceso a los puertos de los países que comerciaban con china en 1900 (página 574)

política de riesgo calculado *s.* la práctica de llevar un conflicto hasta el borde de la violencia sin caer en una guerra, usualmente una táctica para obtener un resultado favorable (página 860)

política de terminación *s.* política promulgada bajo el presidente Eisenhower que sacó a los indígenas de sus reservas a la vez que el gobierno ponía fin a la limitada soberanía de las tribus y pueblos (página 882)

pontón *s.* flotador cilíndrico portable, que se usaba para construir un puente temporal (página 403)

populismo *s.* creencia de que la gente común debe controlar el gobierno (página 477)

populista *s.* político que dice representar las preocupaciones de la gente común (página 724)

portear *v.* acto de cargar embarcaciones o bienes entre cuerpos de agua o alrededor de obstrucciones en una vía fluvial (página 193)

Potencias del Eje *s.* Alemania, Italia y Japón, que formaron una alianza a comienzos de la Segunda Guerra Mundial (página 755)

potlatch *s.* ceremonia de entrega de obsequios practicada por las tribus indígenas norteamericanas kwakiutl y haida (página 15)

preámbulo *s.* texto corto que se escribe como introducción a una constitución o un estatuto (página 125)

precedente *s.* determinación previa en un caso judicial para establecer una comparación con casos nuevos similares (página 154)

presidio *s.* cárcel o asentamiento militar (página 330)

presión cultural *s.* estrategia política en la que los miembros de una religión influyen en los políticos y las instituciones sociales en un esfuerzo por promover sus creencias (página 1074)

Primeros Cien Días *s.* los primeros 100 días del presidente Franklin Roosevelt en el gobierno, durante los cuales promulgó 15 leyes que formaron la base del New Deal (página 716)

privación *v.* acción de negar a alguien un derecho legal o un privilegio (página 951)

privilegio ejecutivo *s.* principio que sostiene que, para proteger los intereses de la nación, el Presidente puede no divulgar cierta información al Congreso (página 1054)

privilegio estadounidense *s.* la idea de que los Estados Unidos es superior a otros países debido a su historia e ideología (página 1116)

Procedimiento Bessemer *s.* proceso en el que se utiliza aire forzado para eliminar impurezas del hierro, como el carbono, transformando así el hierro en acero (página 503)

Proclamación de 1763 *s.* ley que establecía que los colonos debían mantenerse al este de una línea dibujada en un mapa, a lo largo de la cima de los montes Apalaches (página 99)

Proclamación de Emancipación *s.* documento de 1863, emitido por Abraham Lincoln, que abolió la esclavitud en los estados gobernados por la Confederación durante la Guerra Civil de los Estados Unidos (página 405)

producción masiva *s.* uso de maquinaria para producir mercancías en grandes cantidades (página 219)

producto básico *s.* un bien de intercambio; mercancía (página 48)

producto nacional bruto (PNB) *s.* total de bienes y servicios producidos por un país, más los ingresos obtenidos por sus ciudadanos (página 687)

Programa Bracero *s.* programa diseñado para importar obreros mexicanos para reemplazar a los trabajadores agrícolas y de transporte estadounidenses que eran reclutados para la Segunda Guerra Mundial (página 788)

progresismo *s.* reforma entre 1890 y 1920 que buscaba hacer más democráticas las políticas estatales y nacionales y hacer más eficiente el gobierno (página 533)

prohibición *s.* el acto de prohibir la producción, distribución y venta de alcohol (página 557)

Prohibición *s.* prohibición constitucional de la venta de bebidas alcohólicas, vigente entre 1920 y 1933 (página 619)

propaganda *s.* información difundida para influenciar las opiniones o promover la ideas de un partido o una organización (página 526)

propietario *s.* dueño de una colonia, que tenía el derecho a manejar y distribuir tierras y a establecer un gobierno (página 62)

protectorado *s.* país que es gobernado en parte por un país más poderoso (página 572)

provisión legal *s.* condición legal que establece una necesidad a futuro (página 145)

Proyecto de ley sobre ajustes distintos *s.* propuesta dentro de un proyecto de ley que podría abarcar temas no relacionados (página 362)

prueba de alfabetización *s.* un examen mediante el cual se mide la capacidad de leer y escribir (página 451)

puente de Beringia *s.* pedazo de tierra entre Alaska y Siberia que estaba por encima del nivel del mar hace 13.000 años y que permitió a los primeros humanos cruzar hacia Norteamérica (página 2)

punto muerto *s.* situación en la que ninguna de las partes en un conflicto puede afirmar la victoria (página 141)

purga *s.* eliminación de algo (página 764)

Q

quinina *s.* sustancia hecha de la corteza de un árbol que es un remedio eficaz contra la malaria (página 31)

R

racionar *v.* control de los suministros a la población, especialmente en tiempos de guerra (página 788)

radical *s.* persona que quiere un cambio extremo o tiene una posición política extrema (página 185)

rancho *s.* terreno cedido por México a los colonos, en forma de grandes fincas, en lo que hoy es California (página 333)

ratificar *v.* aprobar formalmente mediante el voto (página 127)

rearmamento *s.* el esfuerzo de una nación para reaprovisionar su arsenal y reemplazar aquellas que están desfasadas o han sido eliminadas (página 754)

rebelión de los bóxer *s.* levantamiento político de 1900 en el norte de China contra los extranjeros en el país (página 574)

rebelión del Stono *s.* revuelta de esclavos africanos en contra de sus dueños ocurrida en 1793 (página 83)

recesión *s.* desaceleración relativamente breve del crecimiento económico, a menudo parte de un ciclo económico normal (página 359)

reclutamiento *s.* acto de ser ingresado en el ejército (página 407)

reclutamiento *s.* acto de ser llamado a prestar servicio militar (página 989)

Reconstrucción Presidencial *s.* política impulsada para obligar a los estados confederados a ratificar la Decimotercera Enmienda y a formar nuevos gobiernos, regidos por nuevas constituciones, como condición para poder reintegrarse a la Unión (página 436)

Reconstrucción Radical *s.* nombre dado al plan del Partido Republicano que buscaba aprobar las Leyes de Reconstrucción de 1867 (página 439)

Reconstrucción *s.* etapa posterior a la Guerra de Secesión caracterizada por el anhelo de reunificar a los Estados Unidos de América (página 427)

redes de seguridad *s.* conjunto de programas proporcionados por el gobierno estatal o federal diseñados para evitar que la gente permanezca en la pobreza (página 1073)

reducción del déficit *s.* medidas adoptadas por un gobierno para pagar una deuda (página 1095)

referendo *s.* una elección donde el pueblo vota directamente sobre medidas específicas (página 533)

refugiado *s.* persona que huye a otro país para escapar de un peligro o una persecución (página 759)

regionalismo *s.* lealtad a cualquier sección o región del país de donde una persona es, en vez de a la nación como tal (página 239)

registro material *s.* edificaciones y objetos que sobreviven de épocas anteriores (página 342)

Renacimiento *s.* período entre 1300 y 1500 en que florecieron la cultura y las artes (página 21)

GLOSARIO

Renacimiento de Harlem *s.* movimiento cultural que se originó en Harlem en la década de 1920 y dio a conocer a muchos escritores, artistas y músicos afroamericanos (página 666)

renovación urbana *s.* programa que consiste en rehabilitar los barrios pobres y construir grandes proyectos de vivienda financiados con fondos públicos (página 878)

renta disponible *s.* dinero del que se dispone para gastos (página 685)

repatriación *s.* el acto de devolver a un ciudadano a su país de origen (página 691)

república constitucional *s.* gobierno en el cual los gobernantes obtienen el poder de parte de sus gobernados según lo determina una Constitución escrita (página 158)

República islámica *s.* estado o país que incorpora o se basa enteramente en la ley islámica (página 1062)

republicanismo cívico *s.* pensamiento político que enfatiza la libertad individual, el activismo ciudadano y el respeto del bien común (página 180)

republicanismo *s.* gobierno en el que la gente elige a sus representantes para crear las leyes (página 152)

republicano radical *s.* miembro del Congreso de los Estados Unidos que apoyaba los derechos de los afroamericanos (página 404)

rescate financiero *s.* durante la Gran Recesión, el acto de comprar hipotecas e inversiones inestables de los bancos (página 1127)

reserva *s.* área de tierra designada y administrada por una tribu indígena (página 480)

responsabilidad cívica *s.* obligación requerida o necesaria por parte de la población, como votar, pagar impuestos y formar parte de los jurados (página R35)

responsabilidad personal *s.* responsabilidad que no es regulada pero que contribuye a una sociedad más civil, como respetar y defender los derechos de los demás, ayudar en la comunidad y mantenerse informado (página R35)

reverso verde *(greenback)* *s.* papel moneda emitido por la Unión para crear una moneda nacional (página 393)

revisión judicial *s.* poder de la Corte Suprema para invalidar cualquier ley que considere inconstitucional, incluso si fue aprobada por el Congreso o firmada por el presidente (página 189)

revocatoria *s.* proceso mediante el cual los ciudadanos pueden votar para sacar del poder a un funcionario público (página 561)

Revolución agrícola *s.* transición en la historia humana de la caza y la recolección de alimentos a la siembra de cultivos y la cría de animales (página 4)

revolución del mercado *s.* transición de una economía preindustrial a una economía capitalista, o sea orientada hacia el mercado (página 226)

Revolución industrial *s.* época en que la producción de bienes hechos con máquinas reemplazó de manera generalizada a los productos hechos a mano (página 219)

Revuelta de Haymarket *s.* enfrentamiento violento entre los trabajadores y la policía el 4 de mayo de 1886, que comenzó como una protesta contra la conducta policial durante una huelga en una fábrica de la compañía McCormick, en Chicago, Illinoiss (página 515)

rock and roll *s.* estilo musical derivado del rhythm and blues, que se popularizó en la década de 1950 (página 873)

Romanticismo *s.* movimiento artístico, literario y filosófico del siglo XIX que enfatizaba en la imaginación, la emoción y la acción (página 281)

rompehuelgas *s.* trabajadores no sindicalizados dispuestos a desafiar los piquetes para trabajar (página 515)

rustbelt *s.* el área en el Noreste y Medio Oeste de los Estados Unidos en la que la industria manufacturera ha disminuido significativamente (página 1071)

S

sabana *s.* área de praderas tropicales exuberantes (página 26)

saetín *s.* canal de madera inclinado utilizado en la minería para separar el agua del oro (página 472)

salto de rana *s.* estrategia en la que se capturan grupos de islas una por una para establecer en ellas bases militares (página 803)

salvación *s.* acto de ser perdonado por una deidad (Dios) por los pecados cometidos (página 90)

saneamiento *s.* medidas como las alcantarillas para proteger la salud pública (página 532)

saqueo de Lawrence *s.* término para describir el violento ataque de 1856 a Lawrence, Kansas, en el cual personas a favor del esclavismo arrasaron la ciudad destruyendo casas y negocios (página 371)

secesión *s.* acto de separación formal de una nación o de un territorio para ser independiente (página 191)

sector de servicios *s.* parte de la economía que proporciona servicios en lugar de bienes (página 1138)

sedición *s.* acto criminal de tratar de persuadir a las personas para rebelarse o menoscabar el gobierno (página 187)

segregación *de facto* *s.* segregación presente en la sociedad a pesar de que no hay leyes que la impongan (página 958)

segregación *de jure* *s.* segregación impuesta por la ley (página 958)

segregación *s.* separación de diferentes grupos de personas, generalmente basada en la raza (página 535)

Segundo Gran Despertar *s.* movimiento protestante estadounidense basado en las reuniones de reavivamiento y en una relación directa y emocional con Dios (página 276)

Segundo *New Deal* *s.* segundo conjunto de programas del New Deal, que el presidente Franklin Roosevelt presentó al Congreso después de las elecciones del Congreso de 1934 (página 722)

seguridad social *s.* programa gubernamental que proporciona ingresos a los ancianos, discapacitados y desempleados (página 570)

sentada *s.* protesta organizada donde la gente se sienta y se niega a irse (página 915)

separación de poderes *s.* división de poderes gubernamentales entre las tres ramas del gobierno de los EE. UU.: el poder ejecutivo, el poder judicial y el poder legislativo (página 158)

separados pero iguales *s.* política que permitió a las empresas e instituciones segregar a los afroamericanos de los blancos, siempre y cuando las instalaciones o servicios proporcionados fueran casi iguales (página 536)

separatista negro *s.* activista afroamericano radical que creía que la única manera de lograr la igualdad y la justicia en los Estados Unidos era separarse cultural y económicamente de los blancos (página 958)

separatista *s.* persona que quería dejar la Iglesia de Inglaterra (página 56)

servicio militar *s.* obligación de alistarse para el servicio en las fuerzas armadas de un país (página 407)

servidumbre por mora *s.* tipo de servidumbre en la cual una persona trabaja únicamente para pagar una deuda (página 444)

silabario *s.* grupo de símbolos o caracteres usados para representar las sílabas de una palabra (página 260)

sindicato de trabajadores *s.* grupos de trabajadores que se unen para lograr mejores salarios, condiciones de trabajo más seguras y otros beneficios (página 279)

síndrome de inmunodeficiencia adquirida (SIDA) *s.* etapa final de un virus que ataca al sistema del cuerpo humano que combate las enfermedades (página 1083)

sirviente ligado por contrato *s.* persona obligada por contrato a trabajar, generalmente sin paga, a cambio de un boleto gratis a las colonias (página 51)

Sistema americano *s.* política para promover el sistema industrial de los EE. UU. mediante aranceles, subsidios federales para construir carreteras y otras obras públicas y un banco nacional para controlar la moneda (página 227)

Sistema de carreteras interestatales *s.* red de autopistas inaugurada por el presidente Eisenhower en 1956 para poder atravesar los Estados Unidos y conectar entre sí estados y grandes ciudades (página 866)

sistema de señorío *s.* sistema que consistía en que los campesinos trabajaban la tierra de un señor feudal a cambio de protección militar (página 20)

sistema de sub-tesorería *s.* propuesta mediante la cual los agricultores almacenarían sus cultivos en silos hasta que los precios subieran, mientras que el gobierno les prestaría dinero para comprar semillas para los cultivos del siguiente año (página 477)

sitio *s.* táctica militar que consiste en rodear una ciudad (página 45)

soberanía popular *s.* idea de que los residentes de una región o país deciden sobre un tema mediante el voto (página 362)

soberanía *s.* libertad de control por parte de potencias externas (página 152)

socialismo *s.* sistema de gobierno en el que la comunidad o el gobierno controla los recursos económicos (página 517)

sociedad de consumo *s.* sociedad en la que la compra de bienes y productos se ha convertido en una parte muy importante del estilo de vida de las personas (página 864)

Sociedad de las Naciones *s.* plan que propuso el presidente Woodrow Wilson después de la Primera Guerra Mundial, en el que habría una asamblea general de países para estabilizar las relaciones entre sí y ayudar a preservar la paz (página 626)

sociedad fiduciaria *s.* empresa administrada por miembros de una junta directiva en lugar de por propietarios o accionistas (página 505)

sociedad mayor *s.* compañía que tiene el control total o parcial de otras empresas más pequeñas (página 509)

sociedad por acciones *s.* compañía cuyos accionistas poseen un número determinado de acciones (página 50)

sostén de familia *s.* miembro de la familia que contribuye más a los ingresos del hogar (página 734)

subdivisión *s.* parcela de terreno que ha sido dividida en lotes más pequeños en los que se construyen casas (página 867)

subsidio *s.* fondo del gobierno para mejoras y apoyo al comercio (página 227)

suburbanización *s.* asentamiento de la población de las ciudades en comunidades de la periferia (página 866)

suburbio *s.* comunidad cerca o en las afueras de una ciudad (página 531)

subversión *s.* acto de desestabilización de un sistema social o político importante en un intento por destruirlo (página 844)

sucursal *s.* negocio secundario (página 509)

sufragio femenino *s.* derecho de las mujeres al voto (página 152)

sufragio *s.* derecho constitucional, especialmente el derecho al voto (página 555)

sufragista *s.* persona que apoya el derecho de las mujeres a votar (página 295)

sunbelt *s.* las regiones del sur y suroeste de los Estados Unidos, que tienen inviernos templados (página 859)

T

tanque *s.* vehículo blindado y fuertemente armado que usaba bandas de rodadura en lugar de ruedas (página 612)

tarifa arancelaria *s.* impuesto a las importaciones y exportaciones (página 227)

telecomedia *s.* serie televisiva semanal que cuenta con un entorno familiar y un grupo de personajes que se enfrentan a problemas divertidos (página 872)

telégrafo *s.* dispositivo que transmite mensajes a lo largo de cables conectados, para comunicarse a largas distancias (página 508)

telegrama Zimmermann *s.* un telegrama secreto alemán enviado al embajador alemán en México, exponiendo un plan para la alianza con México (página 607)

Temor Rojo *s.* período en 1919 y 1920 en el que el gobierno federal acosó a presuntos comunistas, anarquistas y radicales (página 642)

teocracia *s.* gobierno liderado por uno o más líderes religiosos (página 1093)

teoría del dominó *s.* una idea de la Guerra Fría que sostenía que los países cercanos a un vecino comunista son más propensos a adoptar ese régimen (página 837)

Tercer Reich *s.* nombre utilizado por el Partido Nazi para describir la época en que Adolf Hitler creía que estaba creando un tercer imperio alemán (página 754)

Territorio Indígena *s.* área de tierra, en lo que hoy es Oklahoma y parte de Kansas y Nebraska, a la cual fueron obligados a migrar los indígenas norteamericanos (página 260)

territorio no organizado *s.* tierras bajo el gobierno federal pero que no le pertenecían a ningún estado (página 240)

terrorismo *s.* el uso de actos violentos y amenazas para lograr un objetivo político (página 1120)

tienda por departamentos *s.* tienda grande que ofrece una amplia variedad de mercancías, organizadas en diferentes departamentos, pero todos bajo un mismo techo (página 531)

topografía *s.* el estudio y reconocimiento de las características físicas de un terreno (página 336)

totalitario *adj.* relativo a un gobierno que está encabezado por un dictador y que requiere completa obediencia al estado (página 724)

transahariano *adj.* que cruza el Sahara (página 25)

transistor *s.* dispositivo electrónico utilizado para controlar el flujo de electricidad en equipos electrónicos (página 865)

transporte escolar de minorías *s.* transporte de estudiantes de diferentes razas a escuelas fuera de sus vecindarios o distritos escolares para asegurar la integración y proporcionar igualdad de oportunidades en la educación (página 961)

tranvía *s.* vehículo que corre sobre rieles por las calles de la ciudad y transporta pasajeros (página 531)

trascendentalismo *s.* movimiento intelectual y social en las décadas de 1830 y 1840 que pedía ir más allá de lo que la sociedad esperaba de cada uno (página 281)

trastorno por estrés postraumático (TEPT) *s.* condición causada por lesión o trauma psicológico (página 993)

Tratado de no Agresión *s.* acuerdo hecho en 1939 entre la Alemania nazi y la Unión Soviética, declarando que no tomarían acción militar el uno contra el otro durante los siguientes 10 años (página 761)

Tratado de Versalles *s.* tratado que oficialmente puso fin a la Primera Guerra Mundial (página 626)

Tren Clandestino *s.* red de personas que trabajaron juntas para ayudar a los afroamericanos a escapar de la esclavitud en los estados sureños de los EE. UU. hacia los estados del Norte y Canadá antes de la Guerra Civil (página 364)

tribunal *s.* corte de justicia con autoridad sobre un asunto específico (página 819)

trustbuster *s.* persona que busca deshacer las sociedades fiduciarias o los monopolios, especialmente un funcionario federal que hace cumplir las leyes antimonopolio (página 564)

tundra *s.* terreno plano y sin árboles de las regiones ártica y subártica (página 14)

turnpike *s.* carretera en la que se pagan peajes para transitar (página 227)

U

U-boat *s.* submarino alemán (página 606)

Unión Estadounidense por las Libertades Civiles (ACLU) *s.* organización formada en 1920, dedicada a defender los derechos y las libertades individuales de todos los estadounidenses (página 643)

V

valijeros *s.* blancos norteños que se desplazaron al sur tras la Guerra Civil, a menudo buscando oportunidades durante el periodo de Reconstrucción o en busca de poder político (página 439)

vaquero *s.* nombre dado al trabajador de las haciendas ganaderas en tierras de los EE. UU. colonizadas por españoles (página 320)

veta *s.* filón mineral (página 472)

veterano *s.* persona que sirvió en el ejército (página 429)

vietnamización *s.* estrategia militar que permitió la sustitución gradual de tropas estadounidenses por tropas sur vietnamitas durante la guerra de Vietnam (página 988)

virrey *s.* gobernador de las colonias españolas en las Américas que representaba al Rey y la Reina de España (página 47)

viruela *s.* virus mortal que causa fiebre alta y pequeñas ampollas en la piel (página 45)

virus de la inmunodeficiencia humana (VIH) *s.* virus que ataca al sistema del cuerpo humano que combate las enfermedades (página 1083)

visión regional *s.* estilo de escritura que expresa las características de una región (página 490)

vodevil *s.* espectáculo teatral que incluía canto y danza (página 530)

volante *s.* hoja o pedazo de papel con información que se reparte en la calle (página 139)

Z

zona de libre empresa *s.* área que permite la suspensión de leyes fiscales y de aduanas (página 1111)

zona de ocupación *s.* área de un país en la que el ejército de otro país toma el control (página 827)

zona desmilitarizada *s.* área en la que se prohíbe la presencia de personal y armas militares (página 840)

afluencia *s.* arribo, entrada en masa (de inmigrantes) (página 518)

agitador *s.* alguien que llama a la rebelión o la desobediencia (página 484)

alegoría *s.* una historia en la que personas y objetos representan ideas abstractas o espirituales (página 21)

arable *adj.* fértil, como el suelo para la agricultura (página 78)

arrendar *v.* firmar o proporcionar un contrato que otorgue derechos a tierras o a propiedades por un tiempo en base a un alquiler acordado (página 579)

artesano *s.* persona que fabrica objetos manualmente (página 27)

asentir *v.* consentir, estar de acuerdo con alguien luego de un debate o discusión (página 1019)

autonomía *s.* independencia; libertad de actuar según sus propios principios (página 167)

blasfemo *adj.* que va contra Dios, sacrílego (página 1069)

bolita de algodón *s.* cápsula que contiene la semilla del algodón (página 222)

brevedad *s.* corta extensión o duración de una cosa (página 425)

cardar *v.* preparar las fibras del algodón para su limpieza, peinando los nudos y juntando las fibras sueltas (página 220)

carisma *s.* agradable y de carácter atractivo, frecuentemente relacionado con la capacidad de atracción de un líder (página 187)

citación *s.* exigencia legal de presentarse a corte, ante un juez o comité del gobierno (página 843)

clandestino *adj.* secreto (página 330)

clemencia *s.* misericordia, capacidad de perdonar (página 843)

coerción *s.* presión ejercida sobre alguien mediante la amenaza o el engaño (página 738)

cohesión *s.* que muestra unidad y buena organización (página 801)

comodidad *s.* un beneficio generado a partir de servicios para mejorar la forma de vida (página 516)

cumplir *v.* satisfacer los términos de un acuerdo, obedecer (página 907)

conclusivo *adj.* final (página 401)

contrabando *s.* bienes que se comercian de manera ilegal (página 112)

conveniente *adj.* oportuno (página 1015)

culminación *s.* la conclusión, el final de algo (página 993)

cuota *s.* proporción, porcentaje o participación, a menudo en referencia a la proporción de grupos minoritarios o de género que obtienen algún beneficio en particular (página 691)

depósito *s.* un almacén, lugar donde se guardan cosas (página 939)

desistir *v.* ceder; renunciar (página 327)

desproporcionado *adj.* desigual, desequilibrado, generalmente en comparación a la mayoría (página 1109)

devoto *adj.* entregado a su fe religiosa (página 277)

difamación *s.* ataque al carácter de otra persona (generalmente un rival político) (página 253)

distribuir *v.* repartir (página 1042)

diversidad *s.* variedad (página 77)

diversificar *v.* ampliar las opciones (página 476)

doméstico *adj.* relativo a las tareas del hogar (página 67)

efigie *s.* imagen o representación de una persona (por lo general un político) odiado o repudiado por el pueblo (página 111)

erradicar *v.* eliminar, destruir por completo (página 562)

errático *adj.* impredecible, inconsistente (página 844)

éxodo *s.* emigración (generalmente de muchas personas a la vez) (página 21)

exorbitante *adj.* excesivo, caro (página 472)

extorsión *s.* acto de obtener algo, generalmente dinero o información, mediante el uso de coacción; chantaje (página 959)

filantrópico *adj.* caritativo, bondadoso (página 505)

florecer *v.* expandirse; crecer (página 79)

frugalidad *s.* templanza, moderación en algo (página 189)

gueto *s.* sección de una ciudad en la cual ciertos grupos, generalmente judíos, estaban obligados a vivir; en uso moderno se refiere a la sección de una ciudad donde viven ciertos grupos minoritarios, generalmente debido a la pobreza (página 815)

herbicida *s.* sustancia química que se usa para matar plantas (página 977)

hipótesis *s.* idea específica que debe ser comprobada a través del método científico (página 88)

homogéneo *adj* uniforme, igual, coherente, estandarizado (página 875)

ilícito *adj.* ilegal (página 655)

incorporar *v.* unir (página 905)

incumplimiento de pago *s.* que se ha dejado de pagar una deuda, moroso (página 152)

injurioso *adj.* insultante, calumnioso, escandaloso (página 610)

inmolar *v.* destruir mediante el fuego (página 971)

insubordinación *s.* desobediencia, rebeldía (página 568)

intervencionista *adj.* persona cuya tendencia es involucrarse en algo, como en una guerra (página 762)

invencible *adj.* imposible de vencer, indestructible (página 557)

jeroglífico *adj.* representación pictórica de una historia (página 17)

jurisdicción *s.* que tiene poder legal sobre algo (página 364)

laudable *adj.* meritorio, digno de reconocimiento (página 658)

lucrativo *adj.* que genera ganancia, bien remunerado o pagado (página 76)

mística *s.* aire de misterio que rodea a una persona, cosa o idea (página 1021)

nocivo *adj.* ofensivo, desagradable (página 532)

normalidad *s.* condición o situación típica, usual o esperada, como las condiciones sociales, políticas y económicas generales de una nación (página 629)

notorio *adj.* famoso por tener mala reputación (página 646)

obstrución *s.* estrategia política en la que un pequeño grupo de legisladores se turnan para hablar y evitar así que finalice un debate o que un proyecto de ley sea sometido a votación (página 1055)

opulencia *s.* riqueza, prosperidad (página 862)

oratoria *adj.* relacionado al discurso (página 908)

partidario *s.* defensor, seguidor de una causa o idea (página 518)

pluralismo *s.* coexistencia de diferentes grupos culturales dentro de una civilización (página 518)

poner en la lista negra *v.* poner a una o más personas en una lista indicando que deben ser rechazadas o castigadas (página 843)

pragmatismo *s.* utilidad, sentido práctico (página 716)

preventivo *adj.* prioritario, defensivo (página 1121)

privatizar *v.* transferir del control público al privado (página 111)

prominente *s.* cualidad de ser importante o notable (página 253)

protagonista *s.* personaje principal de una obra de ficción (página 489)

rectificar *v.* compensar por un daño (página 795)

rehén *s.* persona detenida para obligar a alguien a cumplir las demandas de quienes han detenido a esa persona (página 1062)

represivo *adj.* opresivo, cruelmente autoritario (página 1079)

rescindir *v.* anular (página 113)

salobre *adj.* un poco salado (página 50)

señor de la guerra *s.* líder de una milicia local que ejerce un gran poder en esa limitada región (página 765)

simpatizar *v.* sentir una conexión emocional con otra persona (página 365)

solidaridad *s.* unidad por una causa (página 516)

subordinado *adj.* que pertenece a algo mayor (página 298)

subsistir a duras penas *v.* obtener algo luego de un gran esfuerzo (página 472)

subversivo *adj.* rebelde (página 58)

subyugación *s.* acto de controlar a un grupo de personas mediante el uso de la fuerza (página 831)

superfluo *adj.* innecesario (página 164)

tratado *s.* promesa vinculante (página 95)

unánime *adj.* indiscutible, que ha obtenido todos los votos (página 907)

unicameral *adj.* formado por una sola cámara, como el poder legislativo que solo tiene una cámara de representantes (página 158)

INDEX

INDEX

INDEX

INDEX

INDEX

INDEX

INDEX

INDEX

INDEX

SKILLS INDEX

ACKNOWLEDGMENTS

NATIONAL GEOGRAPHIC | CENGAGE
L E A R N I N G

National Geographic Learning gratefully acknowledges the contributions of the following National Geographic Explorers and affiliates to our program:

Sam Abell, National Geographic Photographer
Lynsey Addario, National Geographic Photographer
Robert Ballard, National Geographic Explorer-in-Residence
Ari Beser, Fulbright-National Geographic Fellow
Jimmy Chin, National Geographic Photographer
Kevin Crisman, National Geographic Explorer
Jason De León, National Geographic Explorer
Leslie Dewan, National Geographic Explorer
Jeffrey Gusky, National Geographic Photographer
David Guttenfelder, National Geographic Photographer
Kevin Hand, National Geographic Explorer
Fredrik Hiebert, National Geographic Archaeologist-in-Residence
Kathryn Keane, Vice President, National Geographic Exhibitions
Bill Kelso, National Geographic Explorer
Michael Nichols, National Geographic Photographer
Paul Nicklen, National Geographic Photographer
Sarah Parcak, National Geographic Fellow
William Parkinson, National Geographic Explorer
Sandra Postel, National Geographic Freshwater Fellow (2009–2015)
Robert Reid, National Geographic Digital Nomad
Andrés Ruzo, National Geographic Explorer
Tristram Stuart, National Geographic Explorer

Photographic Credits

Front cover, Title, Copyright (tl) Tetra Images/Getty Images. (tr) Andy Sacks/Getty Images. (cl) ©Rosalia Torres/Brandon Torres-Weiner. (c) ©Bettmann/Getty Images. (cr) pidjoe/Getty Images. (bl1) Joel Sartore/National Geographic Creative. (bl2) David Hiser/National Geographic Creative. (bc) Amos Chapple/Getty Images. (br) Library of Congress, LC-DIG-ds-07422. **Back Cover** SpaceX.

iii (bl) Mark Thiessen/National Geographic. (bc) Mary Lynne Ashley Photography/National Geographic Learning. (br) National Geographic Learning. **iv** (tl) KMK/National Geographic Creative. (tr) Robert Reid/National Geographic Creative. (cl) Brian Nelson/National Geographic Learning. (cr) Courtesy of Andres Ruzo/National Geographic Learning. **v** (tl) ©Kari Wehrs. (tcl) MARK THIESSEN/National Geographic Creative. (tcr) Ari Beser. (tr) ©Kevin Crisman/National Geographic. (cl) ©Jason DeLeon. (c1) ©Lynn Johnson/National Geographic Creative. (c2) ©Mark Thiessen/National Geographic Creative. (cr) MLADEN ANTONOV/Getty Images. (bl1) ©freddieclaire. (bc1) ©Mark Thiessen/National Geographic Creative. (bc2) HOGUE KAT KEENE /National Geographic Creative. (bl2) Roberto Ricciuti/Getty Images. (bc2) MIKEY SCHAEFER/National Geographic Creative. (bc3) ©Jeff Gusky. (bcr1) Nick Nichols/National Geographic Creative. (bcr2) DAVID GUTTENFELDER /National Geographic Creative. (br) Christina Mitermeier/National Geographic Creative. **vi-vii** (spread) Paul Chesley/National Geographic Creative. **vii** (tl) Michael Marquand/Getty Images. (tr) ©Daniella Nowitz/National Geographic Creative. (c) ©US Capitol. **viii-ix** (spread) ©Jez Coulson/Insight-Visual. **ix** (tl) debra millet/Alamy Stock Photo. (tr) aimintang/Getty Images. (c) Richard Wong/Alamy Stock Photo. **x-xi** The Oregon Trail, 1869 (oil on canvas)/Bierstadt, Albert (1830-1902)/BUTLER INSTITUTE OF AMERICAN ART/Butler Institute of American Art, Youngstown, OH, USA/Bridgeman Images. **xi** (t) joe daniel price/Getty Images. (cl) Nativestock.com/Marilyn Angel Wynn/Alamy Stock Photo. (cr) JamesTung/Getty Images. **xii-xiii** (spread) Library of Congress, Prints & Photographs Division, LC-DIG-cwpb-05505. **xiii** (tl) Hulton Archive/Getty Images. (tr) Marc Hoberman/Getty Images. (cl) ©Jason Demek/500px. (cr) Library of Congress Prints and Photographs Division[LC-DIG-cwpb-02660]. **xiv-xv** (spread) Library of Congress, Prints & Photographs Division, LC-D401-13643. **xv** (tl) ©The Field Museum, Image No. GN91795_07Ad. (tr) Library of Congress, Prints & Photographs Division, LC-DIG-ppmsca-24362. (cl) ©Anthony Barboza/Getty Images. (cr) PETE MCBRIDE/National Geographic Creative. **xvi-xvii** (spread) Allentown Art Museum; Purchase: Leigh Schadt and Edwin Schadt Art Museum Trust, 2012. (2012.09). **xvii** (tl) swim ink 2 llc/Getty Images. (tr) Buyenlarge/Getty

Images. (cl) New York Times Co./Getty Images. (cr) New York Times Co./Getty Images. **xviii-xix** (spread)©Robert Capa/International Center of Photography/Magnum Photos. **xix** (tl) Library of Congress, Prints & Photographs Division, Reproduction number LC-DIG-fsac-1a35369 (digital file from original transparency) LC-USW361-137 (color film copy slide). (tr) ANDREW CABALLERO-REYNOLDS/Getty Images. (cr) Yale Joel/Getty Images. **xx-xxi** (spread) Bettmann/Getty Images. **xxi** (tl) Courtesy of NASA. (tr) ©NASA. (cl) Keystone-France/Getty Images. (cr) ZUMA Press, Inc./Alamy Stock Photo. **xxii-xxiii** (spread) DIANE COOK, LEN JENSHEL/National Geographic Creative. **xxiv** (tl) ©Lynsey Addario/Reportage/Getty Images. (cl) Wathiq Khuzaie/Getty Images. (tr) PETE MCBRIDE /National Geographic Creative. **xxv** (tr) ©freddieclaire. (b) ©Danny Lyon/Magnum Photos. **xxvi** (tl) Buyenlarge/Getty Images. (bl) Source: Library of Congress, Prints & Photographs Division, LC-DIG-ppmsca-54230. **0-1** (spread) ©Mapping Specialists/National Geographic Learning. (background) Daniel Gomes Lacerda / EyeEm/Getty Images. **2** ©Levi Stroud/Michigan News. **3** ©David Coventry/National Geographic Creative. **4** IRA BLOCK/National Geographic Creative. **5** (tl) Philippe Psaila/Science Source. (t) Nicolle Rager Fuller, National Science Foundation. **6** (tr) Werner Forman/Getty Images. (cr) IRA BLOCK/National Geographic Creative. (cr) Paul Chesley/National Geographic Creative. (br) ©Werner Forman Archive/Heritage Image Partnership Ltd/Alamy Stock Photo. **7** (tr) ©National Museum of the American Indian, Smithsonian Institution 5/4385. (cr) Werner Forman/Getty Images. (bc) ©musée du quai Branly - Jacques Chirac, Dist. RMN-Grand Palais/Art Resource, NY. (br) Human effigy vessel, Late Mississippian period, 1300-1500 (ceramic)/Mississippian culture (c.800-1500)/DIRK BAKKER PHOTOGRAPHY/Private Collection/Bridgeman Images. (bl) IRA BLOCK/National Geographic Creative. **8-9** Paul Chesley/National Geographic Creative. **10** (c) Science & Society Picture Library/Getty Images. (tr) Robert Clark/National Geographic Creative. (b) Alexanderclayton/Getty Images. **11** (tl) Kean Collection/Getty Images. (cr) Scottish pistol marked to the 1st Battalion of the 42nd Regiment of Foot/DON TROIANI COLLECTION/Private Collection/Bridgeman Images. (bl) John Warburton Lee/SuperStock. (br) Imagno/Getty Images. **12-13** (spread) Richard Ellis/Alamy Stock Photo. **14** (b) Peter Horree/Alamy Stock Photo. **16** (b) Michael Marquand/Getty Images. **17** (tr) Kenneth Garrett/National Geographic Society/BANCO CENTRAL DE RESERVA DEL PERÚ, Lima, Perú. **18** (t) ©freddieclaire. **19** (tr) ©Sarah Parcak/Digital Globe. **20** (b) Science Source. **21** (t) Woman Holding a Balance, c.1664 (oil on canvas)/Vermeer, Jan (Johannes) (1632-75)/National Gallery of Art, Washington DC, USA/Bridgeman Images. **22** (b) Two folios from the Gutenberg Bible, printed in the workshop of Johannes Gutenberg, 1455 (parchment)/German School, (15th century)/BILDARCHIV STEFFENS (FIRST ACCOUNT)/Universitatsbibliothek, Gottingen, Germany/Bridgeman Images. **25** (t) Jorge Santos/Getty Images. **26** (t) ©Jimmy Chin/National Geographic. **28** (b) DEA/W. BUSS/Getty Images. **30** (tr) Erich Lessing/Art Resource, NY. **32** (b) Glasshouse Images/Alamy Stock Photo. **35** (tr) Abraham Cresques/Getty Images. **36-37** (spread) Kevin Fleming/Getty Images. **38-39** (spread) Ira Block/National Geographic. **40** (b) MANNIE GARCIA/Getty Images. **41** (cr) ©Ira Block/National Geographic Creative. **42** (tr) ©Ira Block/National Geographic Creative. (bl) john norman/Alamy Stock Photo. **43** (tr) ©Historic Jamestowne. (cl) IRA BLOCK/National Geographic. (cr) ©Historic Jamestowne. (br) Pamphlet encouraging colonists to go to Virginia in America, published in 1609 (colour litho)/English School/PETER NEWARK'S PICTURES/Private Collection/Bridgeman Images. **44** (b) Lebrecht Music and Arts Photo Library/Alamy Stock Photo. **47** (t) canimag/AGE Fotostock. **48** (t) Library of Congress Prints and Photographs Division [LC-USZ62-44000]. **50** (b) ©Daniella Nowitz/National Geographic Creative. **51** (tr) Pocahontas (c.1595-1617) 1616 (oil on canvas)/English School, (17th century)/PETER NEWARK'S PICTURES/Private Collection/Bridgeman Images. **52** (t) MLADEN ANTONOV/Getty Images. **53** (tl) ©Art Resource, NY. (tr) ©National Geographic. **55** (t) Bildarchiv Preussischer Kulturbesitz/Art Resource, NY. **56** (b) Tom Croke/Alamy Stock Photo. **57** (tr) Head of Squanto (wood)/American School, (17th century)/Private Collection/Bridgeman Images. **59** (t) North Wind Picture Archives/Alamy Stock Photo. **61** (t) US Capitol. **63** (t) ©2010 robinharrison. **64** (bl) Indigo (colour litho)/PURIX VERLAG/Bridgeman Images. (br) American Folk Art Museum/Art Resource, NY. **65** (tr) Richard Ellis/Alamy Stock Photo. **66** (bl) Collection of the Smithsonian National Museum of African American History and Culture, Gift of Oprah Winfrey. (br) ©Courtesy, Georgia Archives, Vanishing Georgia Collection, sap093. **70-71** (spread) Sean Pavone/Alamy Stock Photo. **72** (br) Hemis/Alamy Stock Photo. **73** (t) Richard Cavalleri/Shutterstock.com. **74** (c) Pictorial Press Ltd/Alamy Stock Photo. **75** (t) ©Chris Randall. **77** (t) Everett - Art/Shutterstock.com. **78** (b) National Museum of American History, Kenneth E. Behring Center. **80** (b) Bloomberg/Getty Images. **81** (tr) Bloomberg/Getty Images. **83** (t) The Trustees of the British Museum/Art Resource. (b) USA: 'The Old Plantation' (Slaves Dancing on a South Carolina Plantation), watercolour on paper, attributed to John Rose, c. 1785-95. Abby Aldrich Rockefeller Folk Art Museum, Williamsburg, Virginia, USA/PICTURES FROM HISTORY/Bridgeman Images. **84** (c) British Library Board / Robana/Art Resource, NY. **85** (tr) British Library Board/Robana/Art Resource, NY. **86** (b) (c) ©2015 Elsa Hahne/Whitney Plantation. **87** (t) (c) (b) ©2015 Elsa Hahne/Whitney

Plantation. **88** (c) Print Collector/Getty Images. **89** (tr) Barry Winiker/Getty Images. **91** (t) George Whitefield preaching/Collet, John (c.1725-80)/Private Collection/Bridgeman Images. **92** (b) AP Images/Dan Kitwood. **94** (b) Philip Scalia / Alamy Stock Photo. **95** (t) Library of Congress Prints and Photographs Division. **97** (tl) Library of Congress Prints & Photographs Division, [LC-USZC4-5315]. **99** (t) Pontiac (1720-69) 1763 (oil on canvas)/Stanley, John Mix (1814-72)/PETER NEWARK'S PICTURES/Private Collection/Bridgeman Images. **102** NYC Department of Records. **104-105** ©Jez Coulson/Insight-Visual. **106** (tl) Boston Tea Party tea leaves in a glass bottle, collected by T.M. Harris, Dorchester Neck, December 1773/American School, (18th century)/MASSACHUSETTS HISTORICAL SOCIETY/Massachusetts Historical Society, Boston, MA, USA/Bridgeman Images. (tr) George Ostertag/AGE Fotostock. (b) Best View Stock/Alamy Stock Photo. **107** (tl) George Washington Inaugural button circa 1789/DON TROIANI COLLECTION/Private Collection/Bridgeman Images. (tr) Ira Block/National geographic. (b) DEA/A. DAGLI ORTI/Getty Images. **108-109** (spread) ©Brian Jannsen Photography. **110** (b) Teapot 'Stamp Act Repeal'd', Cockhill Pit Factory, 1766 (lead-glazed earthenware)/English School, (18th century)/PEABODY ESSEX MUSEUM/Peabody Essex Museum, Salem, Massachusetts, USA/Bridgeman Images. **111** (tl) Colonists under Liberty Tree (colour litho)/American School, (18th century)/PETER NEWARK'S PICTURES/Private Collection/Bridgeman Images. **112** (b) Mrs James Warren (Mercy Otis) c.1763 (oil on canvas)/Copley, John Singleton (1738-1815)/MUSEUM OF FINE ARTS, BOSTON/Museum of Fine Arts, Boston, Massachusetts, USA/Bridgeman Images. **113** (t) Art Resource, NY. **115** (t) Michael Blanchard Photography/Boston Tea Party Ships & Museum. **116** (b) The Metropolitan Museum of Art. Image source: Art Resource, NY. **118-119** (spread) Steve Dunwell/age fotostock/Superstock. **121** (t) Library and Archive of Quebec. (b) debra millet/Alamy Stock Photo. **123** (t) Brunswick drum captured at the Battle of Bennington/DON TROIANI COLLECTION/Massachusetts State Archives, Boston, MA., USA/Bridgeman Images. **124** (cr) DEA PICTURE LIBRARY/Getty Images. **125** (b) Drafting the Declaration of Independence (oil on canvas)/Chappel, Alonzo (1828-87)/HECKSCHER MUSEUM OF ART/The Heckscher Museum of Art, Huntington, NY, USA/Bridgeman Images. **126-127** (t) Drafting the Declaration of Independence (oil on canvas)/Chappel, Alonzo (1828-87)/HECKSCHER MUSEUM OF ART/The Heckscher Museum of Art, Huntington, NY, USA/Bridgeman Images. **128** (b) Buyenlarge/Getty Images. **130** (bl) (br) Museum of the American Revolution. **133** (b) Washington Crossing the Delaware River, 25th December 1776, 1851 (oil on canvas) (copy of an original painted in 1848)/Leutze, Emanuel Gottlieb (1816-68)/Metropolitan Museum of Art, New York, USA/Bridgeman Images. **135** (t) Battle of Saratoga, the British General John Burgoyne surrendering to the American General, Horatio Gates, October 17, 1777, c.1822-32 (oil on canvas)/Trumbull, John (1756-1843)/Yale University Art Gallery, New Haven, CT, USA/Bridgeman Images. **136** (t) aimintang/Getty Images. (c) The New York Historical Society/Getty Images. **139** (tr) Universal History Archive/Getty Images. **140** (c) RMN-Grand Palais/Art Resource, NY. **141** (tr) Smith Collection/Gado/Getty Images. **142-143** (t) ©Swamp Fox Murals Trail Society, Manning, Clarendon County, SC, www.swampfoxtrail.com. **144** (b) Architect of the Capitol. **146** (bl) ©Mount Vernon Ladie's Association. (br) Courtesy of Mount Vernon Ladies' Association. Photograph by Mark Finkenstaedt. **147** (t) ©Mount Vernon Ladie's Association. (cr) Courtesy of Mount Vernon Ladies' Association. Photograph by Gavin Ashworth. (bl) ©Mount Vernon Ladie's Association. **150-151** (spread) kickstand/Getty Images. **152** (c) Everett Collection Inc/Alamy Stock Photo. **153** (tl) Fine Art/Getty Images. **155** (t) N.C. Wyeth's painting Daniel Boone—The Home Seeker: Cumberland Val ley (c. 1940) ©Copyright 2018 National Museum of American Illustration™, Newport RI Photos courtesy Archives of the American Illustrators Gallery™ NYC. **156** (c) IllustratedHistory/Alamy Stock Photo. **157** (t) Library of Congress. Exchange and Gift Division/Smithsonian. **159** (l) Library of Congress, Prints & Photographs Division, Reproduction number LC-DIG-det-4a26389 (digital file from original). (c) Classic Image/Alamy Stock Photo. (r) Everett Collection Historical/Alamy Stock Photo. **160** (b) A Slave Sale notice published in a newspaper in Charleston, South Carolina, 1766 (print)/American School, (18th century)/PETER NEWARK'S PICTURES/Private Collection/Bridgeman Images. **162** (bl) John Jay, 1786 (oil on canvas)/Wright of Derby, Joseph (1734-97)/NEW YORK HISTORICAL SOCIETY/Collection of the New-York Historical Society, USA/Bridgeman Images. (br) Patrick Henry, 1851 (oil on canvas)/Sully, Thomas (1783-1872)/VIRGINIA HISTORICAL SOCIETY/Virginia Historical Society, Richmond, Virginia, USA/Bridgeman Images. **165** (t) The Signing of the Constitution of the United States in 1787, 1940 (oil on canvas)/Christy, Howard Chandler (1873-1952)/Hall of Representatives, Washington D.C., USA/Bridgeman Images. **166** (b) UniversalImagesGroup/Getty Images. **169** (bl) Bequest of Susan W. Tyler, 1979/The Metropolitan Museum of Art. **170-171** (spread) ©Cameron Davidson. **172** ©Courtesy National Gallery of Art, Washington. **174** (tr) Portrait of Thomas Jefferson, 1805 (oil on canvas)/Peale, Rembrandt (1778-1860)/NEW YORK HISTORICAL SOCIETY/Collection of the New-York Historical Society, USA/Bridgeman Images. (bl) Fine Art/Getty Images. **175** (c) Cephas Picture Library/Alamy Stock Photo. **176** (t) Benjamin Franklin (1706-1790), c.1779 (oil on canvas)/Duplessis, Joseph Siffred (1725-1802)/NORTH CAROLINA MUSEUM OF ART/North Carolina Museum of Art, Raleigh, USA/Bridgeman Images. **177** (tr) Science & Society Picture Library/Getty Images. (cl) Library of CongressCover page o/CQ/Roll Call/Washington D.C. USA. (cr) Benjamin Franklin Drawing Electricity from the Sky, c.1816 (oil on canvas)/West, Benjamin (1738-1820)/PHILADELPHIA MUSEUM OF ART/Philadelphia Museum of Art, Pennsylvania, PA, USA/Bridgeman Images.

(br) Photo by Peter Harholdt, 2004. **178** (br) First in War, First in Peace and First in the Hearts of His Countrymen (colour litho)/American School, (19th century)/NEW YORK HISTORICAL SOCIETY/Collection of the New-York Historical Society, USA/Bridgeman Images. **180** (br) The Copley Family, 1776/77 (oil on canvas)/Copley, John Singleton (1738-1815)/National Gallery of Art, Washington DC, USA/Bridgeman Images. **183** (t) Sara Krulwich/The New York Times/Redux. **185** (b) DEA/G. DAGLI ORTI/Getty Images. **186** (b) Justin Sullivan/Getty Images. **188** (b) Rudy Sulgan/Getty Images. **191** (tr) "A Deed of the Pen", Louisiana Purchase Exposition, March-Two-Step by the Composer of "Hiawatha" Whitney-Warner Pub-Co. Detroit, New York, 1904 (colour litho)/American School, (20th century)/SMITHSONIAN INSTITUTION/Smithsonian Libraries, Washington DC, USA/Bridgeman Images. **192** (cl) (cr) James E. Russell/National Geographic Creative. **193** (t) Richard Wong/Alamy Stock Photo. **194** (tl) ©American Philosophical Society. **195** (tr) Division of Political History, National Museum of American History, Smithsonian Institution. **196** (c) GROVE, DAVID (ARTIST)/National Geographic Creative. **197** (tr) Sacagawea with Lewis and Clark during their expedition of 1804-06 (colour litho)/Wyeth, Newell Convers (1882-1945)/PETER NEWARK'S PICTURES/Private Collection/Bridgeman Images. **199** (t) Library of congress Prints and Photographs Division [LC-DIG-pga-01891]. **200** (br) Smithsonian's National Museum of American History. **201** (tr) ©2004 White House Historical Association. **203** (bl) The Miriam and Ira D. Wallach Division of Art, Prints and Photographs: Photography Collection, The New York Public Library. "Repairing the Star Spangled Banner" The New York Public Library Digital Collections. 1860 - 1920. **204-205** National Geographic. **206-207** The Oregon Trail, 1869 (oil on canvas)/Bierstadt, Albert (1830-1902)/BUTLER INSTITUTE OF AMERICAN ART/Butler Institute of American Art, Youngstown, OH, USA/Bridgeman Images. **208** (tr) Dorling Kindersley ltd/Alamy Stock Photo. (tl) Cream Jug, 1825-1840 (lead glass)/Boston & Sandwich Glass Company (fl.1825-1888) (attr.to)/MUSEUM OF FINE ARTS, HOUSTON/Museum of Fine Arts, Houston, Texas, USA/Bridgeman Images. (b) PATRICK KOVARIK/Getty Images. **209** (tl) Mexican War Veteran's Medal/DON TROIANI COLLECTION/Private Collection/Bridgeman Images. (tr) ©Smithsonian National Museum of American History. (b) Bernie Epstein/Alamy Stock Photo. **210-211** (spread) ©Walter Scriptunas II. **212-213** (spread) ©Valentin Valkov/500px. **214** (t) Buyenlarge/Buyenlarge/Superstock. (br) OlegSam/Shutterstock.com. **215** (tr) Science History Images/Alamy Stock Photo. (cl) Science & Society Picture Library/Getty Images. (bl) Pro3DArtt/Shutterstock.com. (bc1) Alex Kosev/Shutterstock.com. (bc2) Glowimages/Getty Images. (br) Tom Vickers/Splash News/Ventura/CA/United States. **216** (t) Division of Work & Industry, National Museum of American History, Smithsonian Institution. (br) Ruth Black/Shutterstock.com. **217** (tr) United States Patent and Trademark Office. (b) StockPhotosArt/Shutterstock.com. (bc) ©Artville. (br) Mark Herreid/Shutterstock.com. **218** (b) Courtesy: Everett Col/AGE Fotostock. **219** (t) Everett Collection Historical / Alamy Stock Photo. **220** (b) Bettmann/Getty Images. **222** (br) Hauling The Whole Weeks Picking, c.1842 (w/c on paper)/Brown, William Henry (1808-83)/HISTORIC NEW ORLEANS COLLECTION/The Historic New Orleans Collection/Bridgeman Images. **223** (cr) ©From the Collections of The Henry Ford/Henry Ford Museum. (b) Hauling The Whole Weeks Picking, c.1842 (w/c on paper)/Brown, William Henry (1808-83)/HISTORIC NEW ORLEANS COLLECTION/The Historic New Orleans Collection/Bridgeman Images. **224** (b) I. Liveoak/Alamy Stock Photo. **225** (t) North Wind Picture Archives/Alamy Stock Photo. **227** (t) ©SSPL/Science Museum/Art Resource, NY. **228** (t) Art Resource, NY. **229** (tl) ©Frank E. Sadowski Jr., webmaster: The Erie Canal (http://www.eriecanal.com). **230** (t) National Geographic Creative. **231** (tr) Peter Rindlisbacher/Oklahoma Historical Society. **232-233** (spread) JamesTung/Getty Images. **235** (t) Carlos Barria/Reuters. **237** (tr) DEA PICTURE LIBRARY/Getty Images. **238** (b) George Eastman House/Getty Images. **240** (b) Andy Murphy/Alamy Stock Photo. **241** (tr) Bettmann/Getty Images. **244-245** (spread) Panther Media GmbH/Alamy Stock Photo. **246-247** (Spread) Jeff Greenberg/Getty Images. **248** (tr) Nativestock.com/Marilyn Angel Wynn/Alamy Stock Photo. (b) John Berkey/National Geographic Creative. **250** National Anthropological Archives, Smithsonian Insitution [217-2217_01]. **250** National Anthropological Archives, Smithsonian Insitution [217-2217_01]. **250** Accession Number: 1979.395The Cherokee Female Seminary. **251** AP Images. **252** Battle of New Orleans, 1856 (oil on canvas)/Carte, Dennis Malone (1827-81)/HISTORIC NEW ORLEANS COLLECTION/The Historic New Orleans Collection/Bridgeman Images. **255** Louis S. Glanzman, image courtesy the White House Historical Association. **257** Richard Ellis/Alamy Stock Photo. **258** Mark Summerfield/Alamy Stock Photo. **261** The New York Times/Alyssa Schukar/Redux Picture. **262** Portrait of Osceola (1804-38) (oil on canvas)/Catlin, George (1796-1872)/SUPERSTOCK INC./Private Collection/Bridgeman Images. **263** National Museum of the American Indian, Smithsonian Institution. http://www.AmericanIndian.si.edu. **264** Ed Lallo/Getty Images. **266** (cr) From the collection of Gilcrease Museum, Tulsa, Oklahoma. (cl) From the collection of Gilcrease Museum, Tulsa, Oklahoma. (b) From the collection of Gilcrease Museum, Tulsa, Oklahoma. **267** (tl) Antelope Head with Pedernal, c.1... O'Keeffe ,Georgia (1887-1986) Credit: Private Collection Photo Christie's Images/Bridgeman Images. (tr) From the collection of Gilcrease Museum, Tulsa, Oklahoma. (b) From the collection of Gilcrease Museum, Tulsa, Oklahoma. **268** (bl) Universal Images Group North America LLC/Alamy Stock Photo.(br) National Museum of American History, Kenneth E. Behring Center. **269** World History Archive/Alamy Stock Photo. **271** The Frent Collection/Getty Images. **273** Niday Picture Library/Alamy Stock Photo. **274-275** (Spread) Fontny/Stockimo/Alamy Stock Photo. **276** Harry T. Peters 'America on Stone' Collection, National Museum of American

History, Smithsonian Institution. **277** Library of Congress-Prints&Photographs Division/LC-DIG-pga-04983. **278** MPI/Getty Images. **279** Bettmann/Getty Images. **280** Illustration for Rip Van Winkle (colour litho)/Wyeth, Newell Convers (1882-1945) (after)/LOOK AND LEARN (M IMAGES)/Private Collection/Bridgeman Images. **281** Hulton Archive/Getty Images. **282** Sunset in the Rockies (oil on canvas)/Bierstadt, Albert (1830-1902)/CHRISTIES IMAGES/Private Collection/Bridgeman Images. **283** Field Museum Library/Getty Images. **284-285** (spread) ©Lydia Schrandt/500px. **286** Charlotte Observer/Getty Images. **287** National Museum of African American History and Culture, Smithsonian Institution, Accession: 2008.10.4. **288** (bl) Encyclopaedia Britannica/Getty Images. (br) The Liberator Commenced...' William Lloyd Garrison abolitionist banner, 1831 (oil on silk)/American School, (19th century)/MASSACHUSETTS HISTORICAL SOCIETY/Massachusetts Historical Society, Boston, MA, USA/Bridgeman Images. **289** (tl) GL Archive/Alamy Stock Photo. (tr) ©Libraray of Congress. **290** Libraray of Congress. **291** Snap Stills/REX/Shutterstock.com. **292** Walter Oleksy/Alamy Stock Photo. **293** Epics/Getty Images. **294** George Pimentel/Getty Images. **295** MPI/Getty Images. **296** Bettmann/Getty Images. **297** MPI/Getty Images. **298** Courtesy of Smithsonian Institution, National Postal Museum. **301** Smithsonian American Art Museum, Washington, DC/Art Resource, NY. **302-303** (spread) Arron Huey/National Geographic. **304-305** (spread) Elias Funez/ZUMA Press/Modesto/California/U.S. **307** Chuck Place/Alamy Stock Photo. **308** Shannon Finney/Getty Images. **309** Smithsonian American Art Museum. Gift of Eugene Iredale and Julia Yoo. **311** (b) ©Richard Barnes. (t) ©Michael Wells. **312-313** (spread) Niday Picture Library/Alamy Stock Photo. **313** (br) Ruslan Semichev/Shutterstock.com. **315** Universal History Archive/Getty Images. **316-317** (spread) MICHAEL NICHOLS/National Geographic Creative. **317** (tr) Nick Nichols/National Geographic Creative. **318** Fort Laramie, 1858-60 (w/c on paper), Miller, Alfred Jacob (1810-74) / Walters Art Museum, Baltimore, USA/Bridgeman Images. **319** From the Collections of The Henry Ford. **321** National Portrait Gallery, Smithsonian Institution / Art Resource, NY. **322** (br1) joe daniel price/Getty Images. (br2) UniversalImagesGroup/Getty Images. **323** (br) ©State Preservation Board, Austin, Texas. (bl) ©Star of the Republic Museum. **324** (cl) (br) ©Mexic-Arte Museum. **325** (tl) (cr) (br) ©Mexic-Arte Museum. **326** The Frent Collection/Getty Images. **328-329** (spread) Blaine Harrington III/Getty Images. **331** Niday Picture Library/Alamy Stock Photo. **332** Junipero Serra (1713-1784). Spanish Franciscan friar./PRISMA ARCHIVO FOTOGRAFICO (TARKER)/Gallery of the Illustrious sons, Majorca, Spain/Bridgeman Images. **334** Courtesy of the California History Room, California State Library, Sacramento, California. **336** scorton/Alamy Stock Photo. **339** The Independent Gold Hunter, 1849 (colour litho)/American School, (19th century)/PETER NEWARK'S PICTURES/Private Collection/Bridgeman Images. **340** Stock Montage/Getty Images. **342** (tl) Wynne Brewer/National Geographic Learning. (b) John Elk III/Getty Images. **343** (t) TED S. WARREN/Getty Images. (b) IRA BLOCK/National Geographic Creative. **344** (cl) Courtesy of the Burke Museum of Natural History and Culture, catalog number 1991-58/6. (cr) IRA BLOCK/National Geographic Creative. **345** (cr) Collection 9/11 Memorial Museum, Gift of the Weinberg family in memory of our beloved Michael, Photograph by Michael Hnatov. (bc) IRA BLOCK/National Geographic Creative. **346-347** Library of Congress, Prints & Photographs Division, LC-DIG-ds-05505. **348** (tc) Library of Congress, Prints & Photographs Division, LC-DIG-pga-02797. (cr) NPS. (b) Radek Borovka/Shutterstock. **349** (tl) Hat insignia of Colonel Stovall Tilton/DON TROIANI COLLECTION/Private Collection/Bridgeman Images. (tc) ©Smithsonian National Museum of American History. (bl) INTERFOTO/Alamy Stock Photo. **350-351** Hemis/Alamy Stock Photo. **352** Abraham Lincoln (1809-65) 1860 (b/w photo)/Hesler, Alexander (1823-95)/PETER NEWARK'S PICTURES/Private Collection/Bridgeman Images. **354** (t) Liszt Collection/Newscom. (b) Source: Library of Congress, Prints & Photographs Division, LC-USZC4-6189. **355** Buyenlarge/Getty Images. **356** Getty Images. **357** Abraham Lincoln Presidential Library & Museum. **359** Smithsonian. **360** Gilcrease Museum. **362** Chicago History Museum, ICHi-05242. **363** ©Pictorial Press Ltd/Alamy Stock Photo. **364** Chronicle/Alamy Stock Photo. **365**.ARS, NY, Photo: The Jacob and Gwendolyn Lawrence Foundation /Art Resource, NY. **366** Source: Library of Congress, Prints & Photographs Division, LC-DIG-ppmsca-32303663. **367** The Jacob and Gwendolyn Lawrence Foundation/Art Resource, NY. **369** American 'Know-Nothing' Party Cartoon, 1854 (engraving)/American School, (19th century)/PETER NEWARK'S PICTURES/Private Collection/Bridgeman Images. **370** John Brown, 1859 (colour litho)/Balling, Ole Peter Hansen (1823-1906)/PETER NEWARK'S PICTURES/Private Collection/Bridgeman Images. **371** Hulton Archive/Getty Images. **372** Missouri Historical Society. **374-375** ©Kenneth Garrett. **376** George L. and Mary E. Compton/National Museum of American History, Kenneth E. Behring Center. **379** ©Jason Demek/500px. **381** Collection of the New-York Historical Society, USA/The Bridgeman Art Library. **382-383** (spread) ©Kenneth Garrett Photography. **384-385** (Spread) Buyenlarge/Getty Images. **386** (br) Source: The Library of Congress. (bl) Matt McIntosh, courtesy of NOAA's Monitor National Marine Sanctuary . **387** Source: The Library of Congress. **388** The USS 'Monitor' fighting the CSS 'Merrimack' at the Battle of Hampton Roads during the American Civil War, 9th March 1862 (colour litho)/American School, (19th century)/PETER NEWARK'S PICTURES/Private Collection/Bridgeman Images. **389** ©Ira Block/National Geographic Creative. **392** Scott's Great Snake, 1861 (hand-coloured engraving)/Elliott, J. B. (fl.1861)/Collection of the New-York Historical Society, USA/Bridgeman Images. (tl) WorldPhotos/Alamy Stock Photo. (tr) US Ten Dollar note known as a greenback 1863/DON TROIANI COLLECTION/Museum of Connecticut History, Hartford, CT., USA/

Bridgeman Images. **394** Kenneth Garrett Photography. **396-397** (spread) ©Kenneth Garrett. **398** Library of Congress Prints and Photographs Division Washington, D.C.[LC-USZ62-1770]. **399** Buyenlarge/Superstock. **401** ©Confederate Memorial Hall Museum. **402** Source: Library of Congress Prints and Photographs Division/LC-DIG-ppmsca-33279. **403** IanDagnall Computing/Alamy Stock Photo. **405** (tl) MPI/Getty Images. (tr) National Museum of African American History and Culture, Smithsonian Institution. **406** Kenneth Garrett. **407** MPI/Getty Images. **408** Fotosearch/Getty Images. **409** Moviestore/REX/Shutterstock.com. **411** MPI/Archive Photos/Getty Images. **412** (t) Sam Abell/National Geographic Creative. (bl) ©Kari Wehrs. **413** Sam Abell/National Geographic Creative. **414** Source: The Library of Congress- Prints & Photographs/LC-USZ62-3794. **415** Maurice Savage/Alamy Stock Photo. **416** David Monette/Alamy Stock Photo. **418** (c) (b) National Civil War Museum. **419** (tl) (cl) (br) National Civil War Museum. **420** Justin Sullivan/Getty Images. **421** National Museum of American History. **422** GL Archive/Alamy Stock Photo. **423** The Protected Art Archive/Alamy Stock Photo. **424** Abraham Lincoln, Proclamation of Freedom, 1863/UNIVERSAL IMAGES GROUP/Bridgeman Images. **427** TOM LOVELL/National Geographic Creative. **428** (t) Bettmann/Getty Images. (b) Library of Congress Prints and Photographs Division [LC-USZC4-5341]. **432-433** Howard University. **434** GL Archive/Alamy Stock Photo. **435** Arlington National Cemetery. **436** ©CORBIS/Corbis via Getty Images. **440** Bettmann/Getty Images. **441** JUNG YEON-JE/Getty Images. **442** Library of Congress Prints and Photographs Division[LC-DIG-cwpb-02660]. **443** Lightfoot/Getty Images. **444** Source: Detroit Publishing Company LC-DIG-det-4a13398. **445** MPI/Getty Images. **446** ©The Art Archive/REX/National Archives Washington DC/Mathew Brady. **447** Sunday morning in Virginia, 1877 (oil on canvas)/Homer, Winslow (1836-1910)/CINCINNATI ART MUSEUM/Cincinnati Art Museum, Ohio, USA/Bridgeman Images. **448** 'The First Vote' for black voters in the South during state elections of 1867 (colour litho)/Waud, Alfred Rudolph (1828-91) (after)/PETER NEWARK'S PICTURES/Private Collection/Bridgeman Images. **449** Library of Congress Prints & Photographs Division [LC-DIG-ppmsca-17564]. **450** National Museum of American History. **451** Library of Congress Prints and Photographs Division[LC-DIG-ppmsca-34808]. **452** The Rush from the New York Stock Exchange on September 18, 1873, from 'A History of the Last Quarter Century' by E. Benjamin Andrews, published in Scribner's Magazine, July 1895 (oil on canvas)/Pyle, Howard (1853-1911)/DELAWARE ART MUSEUM/Delaware Art Museum, Wilmington, USA/Bridgeman Images. **454** Library of Congress Prints and Photographs Division [LC-DIG-ppmsca-15783]. **456** Library of Congress, Prints & Photographs Division, LC-DIG-ppmsca-21452. **458-459** (spread) The Library of Congress. **460** (tr) Collection of the Smithsonian National Museum of African American History and Culture; Gift of the Descendants of Garfield Logan, In Honor of Philip Henry Logan. (cl) DEA PICTURE LIBRARY/Getty Images. (br) Nick Norman/National Geographic Creative. **461** (tl) Gift of Mr. James Harvey Young, Division of Medicine & Science, National Museum of American History, Smithsonian Institution. (c) David Frent/Getty Images. (br) Steve Speller/Alamy Stock Photo. **462-463** (spread) Jim Brandenberg/Minden/SuperStock. **464-465** (spread)Columbia Pictures/Courtesy Everett Co/Everett Collection. **466** Transcendental Graphics/Getty Images. **467** The Library of Congress. **468** Silver Screen Collection/Getty Images. **469** (tr) AF archive/Alamy Stock Photo. (br) ©National Museum of American History/Smithsonian Institution. **471** Pioneer Family Portrait, Custer County, Nebraska, 1888 (b/w photo)/UNIVERSAL IMAGES GROUP/Bridgeman Images. **473** A Mexican Vaquero, 1890 (oil on canvas)/Remington, Frederic (1861-1909)/ART INSTITUTE OF CHICAGO/The Art Institute of Chicago, IL, USA/Bridgeman Images. **474** Library of Congress, Prints & Photographs Division, LC-DIG-fsa-8b27566. **475** Randy Olson/National Geographic Creative. **476** Jake Lyell/Alamy Stock Photo. **478-479**(spread) Rick Herrmann/500px. **482** ANAND VARMA/National Geographic Creative. **483** Library of Congress, Prints & Photographs Division, Reproduction number LC-USZ62-49148. **485**(t) ©National Museum of the American Indian/Smithsonian Institution. (cr) ©National Museum of the American Indian/Smithsonian Institution. **486**(cr) ©The Field Museum, Image No. GN91795_07Ad. (b) ©The Field Museum, Image No. GN91795_07Ad, Photographer John Weinstein. **487** (tl) ©The Field Museum, Image No. A114986d_009B, Cat. No. 15781, PhotographerJohn Weinstein. (cr) ©The Field Museum, Image No. A108351c, Cat. No. 19166, Photographer Ron Testa. (bl) ©The Field Museum, Image No. A110026c, Cat. No. 56174, Photographer Ron Testa. **489**Library of Congress Prints and Photographs Division [LC-DIG-ppmsca-24362]. **490** Pictorial Press Ltd/Alamy Stock Photo. **491** This image was obtained from the Smithsonian Institution. The image or its contents may be protected by international copyright laws. **493** Library of Congress Printed Ephemera Collection. **494-495**(spread) Bettmann/Getty Images. **496-497**(spread)Bill Pugliano/Getty Images. **498** The Library of Congress. **499** Everett Collection Inc/Alamy Stock Photo. **500** STEVE RAYMER/National Geographic Creative. **501** Marcie Goodale/National Geographic Learning. **504** Keith Levit/Axiom Photographic/Design Pics/Superstock. **506** (cr) ©California State Railroad Museum Library. (bl) ©California State Railroad Museum Library. **507** (tr) LeighSmithImages/Alamy Stock Photo. (cl) ©California State Railroad Museum Library. (br) ©California State Railroad Museum Library. **508** ullstein bild/Getty Images. **511** (t) Anthony Barboza/Getty Images. (br) Graphic Arts Collection, National Museum of American History, Smithsonian Institution. **512** National Archives and Records Administration. **515** Front cover of booklet entitled' The Chicago Riot: A record of the terrible scenes of May 4', 1886 by Paul C. Hull, 1886 (colour litho)/Williams, True (19th Century)/CHICAGO HISTORY

MUSEUM/©Chicago History Museum, USA/Bridgeman Images. **517** ©Lorenzo Dow Turner papers, Anacostia Community MuseumArchives, Smithsonian Institution, gift of Lois Turner Williams. **519** (tl) (tr)(bl) (br) ©Jordan J. Lloyd/Dynamichrome. **520** National Geographic Learning. **521** ©Courtesy of California State Parks. Image 231-18-9. **522** (tl) Courtesy of California State Parks, Image 231-18-87. (tc) Courtesy of California State Parks, Image 231-18-76. (tr) (b) The Library of Congress. **523** (t) The Library of Congress. (cl) DAVID BOWMAN/National Geographic Creative. (br) The Library of Congress. (bl)Jose Azel/Aurora Photos. **525** (t) Lewis W. Hine/George Eastman House/Getty Images. (br) ©The University of Chicago Map Collection. **526** ©The Ohio State University Billy Ireland Cartoon Library & Museum. **527** ©Riverside Metropolitan Museum, Harada Family Archival Collection. **528** Bettmann/Getty Images. **529** (tc) Wallace Kirkland/Getty Images. (tr) ©*Courtesy of Jane Addams Hull-House Museum.* **530** Library of Congress, Prints & Photographs Division, Reproduction number LC-USZC4-6075. **531** Museum of the City of New York/The Art Archive at Art Resource, NY. **532** Chicago History Museum/Archive Photos/Getty Images. **534** Courtesy Sal Bigone/McIntyre-Sullivan Family History Site. **535** Universal Images Group/Art Resource, NY. **536** Library of Congress, Prints and Photographs Division [LC-USZC2-1058]. **538** Smithsonian American Art Museum, Washington, DC/Art Resource, NY. **541** National Geographic Learning. **542-543** (spread) Gary Crabbe/Enlightened Images/Alamy Stock Photo. **545** National Archives and Records Administration. **547** (br) ©From the Collections of The Henry Ford. (bl) ©The New York Public Library Digital Collections. **548** (t) National Archives and Records Administration. (b) National Geographic Learning. **549** INTERFOTO/Alamy Stock Photo. **550** The Library of Congress. **551** AFP/Getty Images. **552** George Rinhart/Getty Images. **555** AP Images. **556** Library of Congress, Prints & Photographs Division, Reproduction number LC-USZ62-683. **558** (br1) "Votes for Men", cover of 'Life' magazine, 15 September 1910 (litho)/O'Malley, Power (b.1909)/TOPHAM PICTURE SOURCE/Private Collection/Bridgeman Images. (br2) NEW YORK HISTORICAL SOCIETY/Collection of the New-York Historical Society, USA/Bridgeman Images. **559** ©From the Collections of The Henry Ford. **560** Niday Picture Library/Alamy Stock Photo. **562** ©Division of Political History/National Museum of American History. **563** Bettmann/Getty Images. **564** Library of Congress, Prints & Photographs Division, Reproduction number LC-DIG-ppmsca-36413. **566-567** (spread)PETE MCBRIDE/National Geographic Creative. **569** Everett Collection Inc /Alamy Stock Photo. **570** ullstein bild/Getty Images. **573** DESIGN PICS INC/National Geographic Creative. **575** China: Official portrait of Empress Dowager Cixi (1835-1908) by court photographer Yu Xunling, c. 1895/Yu Xunling (c.1880–1943)/PICTURES FROM HISTORY/Bridgeman Images. **576** Destruction of the U.S. Battleship Maine in Havana Harbor, February 15th, 1898 (colour litho)/Kurz and Allison (fl.1880-98)/NEW YORK HISTORICAL SOCIETY/Collection of the New-York Historical Society, USA/Bridgeman Images. **578** Buyenlarge/Getty Images. **580** Damir Sagol/Reuters. **582** Bettmann/Getty Images. **585** ©National Geographic Learning. **586** Michael & Patricia Fogden/Minden Pictures/Superstock. **588-589** (spread) Allentown Art Museum; Purchase: Leigh Schadt and Edwin Schadt Art Museum Trust, 2012. (2012.09). **590** (tr) Car Culture/Getty Images. (cl) Library of Congress, Prints & Photographs Division, LC-DIG-ppmsc-03521 . (bc) Akademie/Alamy Stock Photo. **591** (tl) Fotosearch/Getty Images. (tr) Carol Highsmith Library of Congress, Prints & Photographs Division, LC-DIG-ppmsc-03521. (br) Eddie Gerald/Alamy Stock Photo. **592-593** (spread) Buyenlarge/UIG/AGE Fotostock. **594** Bettmann/Getty Images. **595** National Geographic Learning. **596** MPI/Getty Images. **597** DeAgostini/ Superstock. **599** (tr) MARK THIESSEN/National Geographic Creative. (b) ©Ken Marschall. **602** Precision Graphics/National Geographic Learning. **603** Popperfoto/Getty Images. **604** Bettmann/Getty Images. **605** National Geographic Learning. **606** Bygone Collection/Alamy Stock Photo. **609** (tl) FPG/Getty Images. (tr) Bettmann/Getty Images. **611** (cr) ©The National World War I Museum. (bl) Library of Congress, Prints & Photographs Division, Reproduction number LC-USZC4-4455 (color film copy transparency) LC-USZCN4-25 (color film copy neg.). (br) swim ink 2 llc/Getty Images. **612** PhotoDisc. **613** (tl) (tr) (cl) (cr) Lachina/National Geographic Learning. (b) Artville. **614** ©National Portrait Gallery, Smithsonian Institution. **615** Buyenlarge/Getty Images. **616** (tc)(bl)(br) ©Jeffrey Gusky. **617** (tl) (tr) (cr) (b) ©Jeffrey Gusky. **618** The Migration Series, Panel No. 1: During World War I there was a great migration north by southern African Americans, 1940-41 (casein tempera on hardboard)/Lawrence, Jacob (1917-2000)/PHILLIPS COLLECTION/The Phillips Collection, Washington, D.C., USA/Bridgeman Images. **619** David Frent/Getty Images. **620** Bettmann/Getty Images. **621** National Geographic Learning. **624** (t) Rick Herrmann/500px. (b) Neil Hall/Reuters. **626** Hulton Archive/Getty Images. **628** Bettmann/Getty Images. **629** ©University of Washington Libraries, Special Collections, [A. Curtis 37055]. (tc) ©University of Washington. **631** PARIS PIERCE/Alamy Stock Photo. **632-633** (spread) AF archive/Alamy Stock Photo. **634-635** Robert Holmes/Alamy Stock Photo. **636** Nightlife, 1943 (oil on canvas)/Motley Jr., Archibald J. (1891-1981)/ART INSTITUTE OF CHICAGO/The Art Institute of Chicago, IL, USA/Bridgeman Images. **637** (t)The Estate of David Gahr/Premium Archive/Getty Images. (bl) INTERFOTO/Alamy Stock Photo. **638** (bl) ©National Museum of African American History and Culture. (br) ©National Geographic Learning. **639** ClassicStock/Alamy Stock Photo. **640** Dosfotos/Getty Images. **641** (tr) Everett Collection Historical/Alamy Stock Photo. (cr) EVERETT COLLECTION, INC. (br) Michael Ochs Archives/Getty Images. **642** Library of Congress Prints and Photographs Division Washington, D.C. **643** National Geographic Learning. **645** (t)(cr) ©Courtesy of the Syracuse University Art Collection. **646** Image Asset Management/

AGE Fotostock. **647** GL Archive/Alamy Stock Photo. **649** (tl) National Geographic Learning. (b) National Geographic Learning. **650** (l) Mary Evans/Jazz Age Club Collection/AGE Fotostock. (br)Mary Evans Picture Li/AGE Fotostock. **652** Bettmann/Getty Images. **654** Pictorial Press Ltd/AlamyStock Photo. **655** Blank Archives/Getty Images. **656** (bl) Glasshouse Images/Alamy Stock Photo. (br) Herbert Dorfman/Getty Images. **657** Richard T. Nowitz/Getty Images. **658** Division of Culture & the Arts, National Museum of American History, Behring Center, Smithsonian Institution. **659** Photo by Eric Long,Smithsonian National Air and Space Museum. **660** Kirn Vintage Stock/Getty Images. **661** Hulton Deutsch/Corbis Premium Historical/Getty Images. **662** Governor Nellie Ross, c. 1925 (b/w photo)/Bain, George Grantham (1865-1944)/Private Collection/Bridgeman Images. **665** Bettmann/Getty Images. **666** State Archives of Florida/Florida Memory/Alamy Stock Photo. **667** The Jacob and Gwendolyn Lawrence Foundation/Art Resource, NY. **668** Photo Researchers, Inc/Alamy Stock Photo. **670** Robert W. Kelley/Getty Images. **671** (tr) (cr) (br) ©National Geographic Learning. **673**Universal History Archive/Getty Images. **674-675** (spread) Library of Congress, Prints & Photographs Division, Reproduction number LC-DIG-ppmsca-15611. **676-677** (spread) The Library of Congress. **678** The Library of Congress. **679** Library of Congress Prints and Photographs Division Washington, D.C. **680** Artepics/Alamy Stock Photo. **682** The Library of Congress. **683** (tl) (tr) (b) The Library of Congress. **684** Everett Collection Inc/Alamy Stock Photo. **686** Everett Collection Inc/Alamy Stock Photo. **690** New York Times Co./Getty Images. **692-693** (spread) ©Jimmy Chin Photography. **693** (tr) MIKEY SCHAEFER/National Geographic Creative. **694** Everett Collection Inc/Alamy Stock Photo. **696** National Air and Space Museum. **697** Eric Schaal/Getty Images. **699** Bettmann/Getty Images. **700** Everett Collection Inc/Alamy Stock Photo. **703** (bl) Photo Researchers/Getty Images. (tr) California Industrial Scenes fresco Image Missing in RP. **704-705** (spread)FrancoisGalland/Getty Images. **706** Universal History Archive/Getty Images. **707** ©National Baseball Hall of Fame Library. **708** (bl)PhotoQuest/Getty Images. (bc) ©National Baseball Hall of Fame. **709** ©Ronald Gabriel Baseball Memorabilia Collection, 1912-2009, Archives Center, National Museum of American History. **710** Transcendental Graphics/Getty Images. **711** (t) National Baseball Hall of Fame Library/MLB Photos/Getty Images. (br) Transcendental Graphics/Getty Images. **712** TASOS KATOPODIS/Getty Images. **713** Ron Vesely/Getty Images. **714** (bc) Bettmann/Getty Images. (br) Blank Archives/Getty Images. **716** ©Division of Political History, National Museum of American History, Smithsonian Institution. **717** Stock Montage/Getty Images. **718** AP Images. **719** David Frent/Getty Images. **720** Historical/Getty Images. **723** (tl) Library of Congress, Prints & Photographs Division, Reproduction number LC-USZC2-854. (tr) Library of Congress, Prints & Photographs Division, Reproduction number LC-USZC2-987. (bl) Library of Congress, Prints & Photographs Division, Reproduction number LC-USZC2-1174. (br) Library of Congress, Prints & Photographs Division, Reproduction number LC-USZC2-5653. **724** Bettmann/Getty Images. **726** (cr) ©Image Courtesy of Milwaukee Public Museum, negative number #H49639-34a. (bl) ©Image Courtesy of Milwaukee Public Museum. **727** (tl) ©Image Courtesy of Milwaukee Public Museum, negative number #H49624-24a. (tr) ©Image Courtesy of Milwaukee Public Museum. (b) ©Image Courtesy of Milwaukee Public Museum, negative number #H49629-35a. **727** MARK RALSTON/Getty Images. **730** Bettmann/Getty Images. **731** Bloomberg/Getty Images. **732-733** (spread) Tom Till/SuperStock. **734** Bettmann/Getty Images. **736** Bettmann/Getty Images. **737** David Frent/Getty Images. **738** National Geographic Learning. **739** Library of Congress, Prints & Photographs Division, Reproduction number LC-USZC2-936. **741** Bettmann/Getty Images. **743** Kerrick James/Getty Images. **745** ©Billy Warren/The Buffalo News. **746** ©Jeffrey Gusky. **748-749** Robert Capa/International Center of Photography/Magnum Photos. **750** (tr) LOS ALAMOS NATIONAL LABORATORY/SCIENCE PHOTO LIBRARY/Getty Images. (cl) American Stock Archive/Getty Images. (bl) 7maru/Getty Images. (br) Keren Su/Getty Images. **751** (tc) schlol/Getty Images. (cr) United States coin image from the United States Mint. (br) Everett Collection Historical/Alamy Stock Photo. **752-753** (spread) Hulton Deutsch/Getty Images. **755** Print Collector/Getty Images. **756** Guernica, 1937 (oil on canvas)/Picasso, Pablo (1881-1973)/MuseoNacional Centro de Arte Reina Sofia, Madrid, Spain/Bridgeman Images. **757** Universal ImagesGroup/Getty Images. **759** Eric TSCHAEN/REA/Redux. **761** SZ Photo/Scherl/The Image Works. **763** Paul Popper/Popperfoto/Getty Images. **764** FototecaStoricaNazionale./Getty Images. **766-767** (spread) VCG/Getty Images. **769** Fox Photos/Getty Images. **771** Franklin D. Roosevelt Presidential Library & Museum/National Archives. **773** Bettmann/Getty Images. **774-775** Everett Collection Inc/Alamy Stock Photo. **776-777** Everett Collection Inc/Alamy Stock Photo. **779** (bl) AP Images/Dean Hanson. (br) Lyn Alweis/Getty Images. **780** Science & Society Picture Library/Getty Images. **781** Weinstein Company/Everett Collection. **783** Pictorial Press Ltd/Alamy Stock Photo. **784-785** Library of Congress, Prints & Photographs Division, Reproduction number LC-USW33-038539-ZC. **787** Library of Congress, Prints & Photographs Division, Reproduction number LC-DIG-ppmsca-13259 (digital file from original neg.). **788** Bettmann/Getty Images. **789** Bettmann/Getty Images. **791** Peter Stackpole/Getty Images. **792** Photo 12/Alamy Stock Photo. ©Printed by permission of the Norman Rockwell Family AgencyCopyright ©1942 the Norman Rockwell Family Entities. **793** Library of Congress. **794** Library of Congress, Prints & Photographs Division, Reproduction number LC-DIG-ppprs-00368. **795** Manzanar National Historic Site/NPS. **796** ©Japanese American National Museum, Gift of IbukiHibi Lee (96. 601. 8). **797** (cl) Japanese American National Museum, Gift of June HoshidaHonma, Sandra Hoshida and Carole HoshidaKanada (97. 106. 1EN). (tr) Japanese American National

Museum, Gift of June HoshidaHonma, Sandra Hoshida and Carole HoshidaKanada (97. 106. 1EN). (br) Japanese American National Museum, Gift of Jack and Peggy Iwata (93. 102. 127). (tc) Japanese American National Museum, Gift of June HoshidaHonma, Sandra Hoshida and Carole HoshidaKanada (97. 106. 1EN). (cr) Japanese American National Museum, Gift of June HoshidaHonma, Sandra Hoshida and Carole HoshidaKanada (97. 106. 2CA). **800** Thomas D. McAvoy/Getty Images. **801** Historical/Getty Images. **802** ANDREW CABALLERO-REYNOLDS/Getty Images. **803** ©Aviation History Collection/Alamy Stock Photo. **805** Hulton Archive/Getty Images. **806** LAPI/Getty Images. **807** Library of Congress, Prints & Photographs Division, Reproduction number LC-USZ62-7449. **810** Photo Researchers, Inc/Alamy Stock Photo. **811** Alfred Eisenstaedt/Pix Inc./Time & Life Pictures/Masters/Getty Images. **812** (tc) ©Courtesy of the Beser family. **813** KIMIMASA MAYAMA/Newscom/European Pressphoto Agency/HIROSHIMA/HIROSHIMA/JAPAN. **814** ©United States Holocaust Memorial Museum. **815** National Archives/Getty Images. **816** Historical/Getty Images. **817** Anne Frank Fonds Basel/Premium Archive/Getty Images. **818** ©United States Holocaust Memorial Museum. **821**GalerieBilderwelt/Hulton Archive/Getty Images. **823-824** (spread) Cameron Davidson/Getty Images. **824** ©WHO/E. Soteras Jalil. **826** Heritage Images/Getty Images. **828-829** (spread) Walter Sanders/Getty Images. **830** ©Leslie Illingworth Associated Newspaper/Solo Syndication, London. **832** National Archives. **835** BRUCE DALE/National Geographic Creative. **836** ©The Andy Warhol Museum, Pittsburgh; Founding Collection, Contribution Dia Center for the Arts©The Andy Warhol Foundation for the Visual Arts, Inc. **840-841** (spread) Bobby Yip/REUTERS. **840-841** (spread) AFP/Getty Images. **842** Movie Poster Image Art/Getty Images. **845** (tc) Everett Collection Inc/Alamy Stock Photo. **847** Universal History Archive/Getty Images. **848-849** (spread) Margaret Bourke-White/Getty Images. **850-851** Tony Frank/Sygma/Getty Images. **852**INTERFOTO/Alamy Stock Photo. **853** (r) KevorkDjansezian/Getty Images. (tl) New York Daily News Archive/Getty Images. **854** Hulton Archive/Getty Images. **855** (tl) The Advertising Archives/Alamy Stock Photo. (cl) Apic/Getty Images. (c) C12/Corbis. (cl) CBW/Alamy Stock Photo. (bl) Marc Tielemans/Alamy Stock Photo. **856** Michael Ochs Archives/Getty Images. **857** (tr) RB/Getty Images. (b) ZUMA Press, Inc./Alamy Stock Photo. **858** Everett Collection/AGE Fotostock. **860** (tl) ©Collection of the New-York Historical Society. (tr) Bettmann/Getty Images. **861** (tl) Frederic Neema/Getty Images. (cl) Hulton Deutsch/Getty Images. (cr) Popperfoto/Getty Images. **863** Yale Joel/Getty Images. **864** PhotoQuest/Getty Images. **865** ClassicStock/AlamyStock Photo. **867** Everett Collection Inc/Alamy Stock Photo. **868** Bettmann/Getty Images. **869** vincent noel/Shutterstock.com. **870** (tl) Wayne Miller/Magnum Photos. (tr) Three Lions/Getty Images. (cc) David M. McAvoy/Getty Images. (cr) Car Culture/Getty Images. (bl) Carol M. Highsmith/The Library of Congress. (br) Dennis Stock/Magnum Photos. **871** (t) Corbis Premium Historical/Getty Images. (bl) ZUMA Press, Inc./Alamy Stock Photo. (br) Bryan Mitchell/Getty Images. **873** (tl) Bettmann/Getty Images. (tr) Blank Archives/Getty Images. **874** Charles Trainor/Getty Images. **876** (b) (cr) ©National Baseball Hall of Fame. **877** (tl)(tr)(br) ©National Baseball Hall of Fame. **879** ©Wayne Miller/Magnum Photos. **881** (tl)(tc) (tr) (bl) (br) Erika Larsen/National Geographic Creative. **883** ©Leonard Nadel/National Museum of American History/Kenneth E. Behring Center. **885** Buyenlarge/Getty Images. **886** Bettmann/Getty Images. **888-889** (spread) Bettmann/Getty Images. **890** (t) Independent Picture Service/Alamy Stock Photo. (c) Ian Dagnall/Alamy Stock Photo. (bl) Ulrich Doering/Alamy Stock Photo. (br) Library of Congress, Prints & Photographs Division, Reproduction number LC-DIG-ppmsc-07978. **891** (t) Gary Ombler/Getty Images. (c) New York Daily News Archive/Getty Images. (bl) Pacific Press/Getty Images. (br) Bettmann/Getty Images. **892-893** (spread) Danny Lyon/Magnum Photos. **894-895** AP Images/Pablo Martinez Monsivais. **895** Leonard Freed/Magnum Photos. **896-897** AP Images/Jacquelyn Martin. **897** (bl) Carl Iwasaki/Getty Images. **898** AP Images/Molly Riley. **899** (t) Jim West/Alamy Stock Photo. (b) B Christopher/Alamy stock photo. **900** David Hume Kennerly/Getty Images. **901** (t) ©National Museum of African American History and Culture, Gift of the Family of Rev. Norman C. "Jim" Jimerson and Melva Brooks Jimerson. (b) Eli Reed/Magnum Photos. **903** Arthur Brower/Getty Images. **904** The Library of Congress- Prints & Photographs Online Catalog. **905** 'Invisible Man' by Ralph Ellison (1914-94) published by Random House, New York, 1952/American School, (20th century)/CHRISTIES IMAGES/Private Collection/Bridgeman Images. **906** Bettmann/Getty Images. **908** Cornell Capa/Getty Images. **909** Bettmann/Getty Images. **910** UniversalImagesGroup/Getty Images. **911** Don Cravens/Getty Images. **912** (t) (b) AP Images. **913** Bettmann/Getty Images. **914** ©Smithsonian National Museum of African American History and Culture. **915** Bettmann/Getty Images. **916** Underwood Archives/Getty Images. **917** ©Collection of the Smithsonian National Museum of African American History and Culture. **919** AP Images/BILL HUDSON. **920** Wyatt Tee Walker/CSU Archives/Everett Collection. **923** Francis Miller/Getty Images. **925** Copyright 1960, St. Louis Post-Dispatch/Library of Congress [LC-DIG-ppmsca-05522]. **926-927** (spread) Bettmann/Getty Images. **928** (bl) (br) Bettmann/Getty Images. **931** (t) Historical/Getty Images. (b) Ulrich Baumgarten/Getty Images. **933** Photo Courtesy of Peace Corps. **934** Everett Collection Inc/Alamy Stock Photo. **935** (t) (b) NASA. **937** (bl) Underwood Archives/Getty Images. (br) Bettmann/Getty Images. **938** Art Rickerby/Getty Images. **939** Bettmann/Getty Images. **940** Bettmann/Getty Images. **942** (tl) Bachrach/Getty Images. **942** (tl) Historical/Getty Images. (tr) Bettmann/Getty Images. **943** (t) Bettmann/Getty Images. (b) Everett Collection Historical/Alamy Stock Photo. **944** Lynn Johnson/National Geographic Creative. **945** Phil Degginger/Alamy Stock Photo. **946-947** (spread) DAVID GUTTENFELDER/National

Geographic Creative. **948** Keystone-France/Getty Images. **950** UniversalImagesGroup/Getty Images. **951** Danny Lyon/Magnum Photos. **953** AP Images/Charles Kelly. **954** ©Bob Stefko. **956** ©Copyright held by Spider Martin/The Spider Martin Civil Rights Collection. NARA. **959** David Fenton/Getty Images. **960** AP Images/Anonymous. **961** Joseph Louw/Getty Images. **962** (cr) Brooks Kraft/Getty Images. (br) National Geographic Learning. **963** (tr) National Geographic Learning. (tcr) Ian Dagnall/Alamy Stock Photo. (cl) Paul Briden/Alamy Stock Photo. (br) Raymond Boyd/Getty Images. **966-967** (spread) BrunoBarbey/Magnum Photos. **968** AP Images. **969** Vietnam: Communist propaganda poster: 'Victorious Ham Rong'/PICTURES FROM HISTORY/Bridgeman Images. **970** AP Images/HORST FAAS. **973** AP Images. **974** AP Images/HENRI HUET. **975** ©National Air and Space Museum. **977** Ian Berry/Magnum Photos. **978** tim page/Getty Images. **979** AP Images/Anonymous. **981** Marc Riboud/Magnum Photos. **983** CBS Photo Archive/Getty Images. **984** Julian Wasser/Getty Images. **987** John Dominis/Getty Images. **989** BurtGlinn/Magnum Photos. **990** John Filo/Getty Images. **992** Photograph courtesy of the National Mall and Memorial Parks, National Park Service. **993**Juan Valdez/National Geographic Learning. **994-995** (spread) MICHAEL S. LEWIS/National Geographic Creative. **998-999** (spread) ©Aaron Huey. **1000-1001** Courtesy of NASA. **1001** ©Smithsonian National Air and Space Museum. **1002** EVERETT COLLECTION, INC. **1003** ©Smithsonian National Air and Space Museum. **1004** NASA. **1005** (t) MARK THIESSEN/National Geographic Creative. (b) NASA/Getty Images. **1007** ZUMA Press, Inc./Alamy Stock Photo. **1008** (bg) ©AngélicaDass. (c) ©KattiaZanetta. **1009** ©AngélicaDass. **1011** (tl) Cathy Murphy/Getty Images. (cl)Tim Graham/Getty Images. (r) Library of Congress Prints and Photographs Division Washington [LC-DIG-ds-03091] With permission from CWLU Herstory Project. (bl) National Geographic Learning. **1013** ©Los Angeles Public Library. **1014** Bettmann/Getty Images. **1016** ©Minnesota Historical Society. **1017** Bob Kreisel / Alamy Stock Photo. **1018** Bettmann/Getty Images. **1020** (cr) Blank Archives/Getty Images. (br) ©Library of Congress Prints and Photographs Division Washington, D.C. (br) Blank Archives/Getty Images. **1023** NCAA Photos/Getty Images. **1024-1025** istock.com/jcarillet. **1026** Ralph Morse/The LIFE Picture Collection/Getty Images. **1027** Science & Society Picture Library/Getty Images. **1028** Kenneth Batelman/National Geographic Learning. **1029** ©National Air and Space Museum. **1031** NASA. **1032** Historical/Getty Images. **1034-1035** DIANE COOK, LEN JENSHEL/National Geographic Creative. **1036** (tr)Bettmann/Getty Images. (cl) Universal History Archive/Getty Images. (b) Tom Stoddart Archive/Contributor. **1037** (tl)Universal History Archive/Getty Images. (tr) Bettmann/Getty Images. (b) Tom Stoddart Archive/Contributor. (br) Dennis Tarnay, Jr./Alamy Stock Photo. (cl) MICKE Sebastien/Getty Images. (cr) JEFF KOWALSKY/European Pressphoto Agency/Newscom. (bl)Mark Stewart/Camera Press/Redux. (br) Peter Macdiarmid/Getty Images. **1039-1040** (spread)Bettmann/Getty Images. **1040** George Silk/Getty Images. **1043** Bettmann/Getty Images. **1044** Bettmann/Getty Images. **1046** George Rinhart/Getty Images. **1047** Bettmann/Getty Images. **1048** FransLanting/FransLanting Stock/National Geographic Creative. **1050-1051** (spread) PAUL NICKLEN/National Geographic Creative. **1051** Christina Mitermeier/National Geographic Creative. **1052** AP Images. **1053** ©National Archives. **1055** Bettmann/Getty Images. **1057** Library of Congress Prints and Photographs Division Washington, D.C. **1059** Owen Franken/Getty Images. **1060** Government Press Office. **1062** Bettmann/Getty Images. **1063** Bettmann/Getty Images. **1066-1067** (spread) Arnold Newman/Getty Images. **1068** Timothy Fadek/Getty Images. **1071** Ralph Crane/Getty Images. **1072** Entertainment Pictures/Alamy Stock Photo. **1075** Diana Walker/Getty Images. **1076** Al Seib/Getty Images. **1077** National Portrait Gallery, Smithsonian Institution/Art Resource, NY. **1079**Terry Ashe/Getty Images. **1080** Retro Ark/Alamy Stock Photo. **1081** Encyclopaedia Britannica/Getty Images. **1082** (t) ZUMA Press, Inc./Alamy Stock Photo. (tr)Richard Ellis/Alamy Stock Photo. **1085** AP Images/Boris Yurchenko. **1086** (t) Bettmann/Getty Images. (b) David Turnley/Getty Images. **1088** Rolf Adlercreutz/Alamy Stock Photo. **1089** (tcr) BRENDAN SMIALOWSKI/Getty Images. (tr) BRENDAN SMIALOWSKI/Getty Images. (b) Alex Wong/Getty Images. **1090** AP Images/LIONEL CIRONNEAU. **1092** Historical/Getty Images. **1094** jean-Louis Atlan/Contributor. **1097** DOD Photo/Alamy Stock Photo. **1098-1099** (spread) Michael Lee/Getty Images. **1100** Alyssa Schukar/The New York Times/Redux. **1101** Everett Collection Inc/Alamy Stock Photo. **1102** MatthiasBreiter/Minden Pictures. **1104** ©Amplifier Foundation. **1105** (tr) Mark Thiessen/National Geographic Creative. (b)Robert Alexander/Getty Images. **1106** AP Images/Cliff Schiappa. **1107** AP Images/GREG GIBSON. **1108** (t)AP Images/Anonymous. (b) Joe Raedle/Getty Images. **1111** Richard Ellis/Alamy Stock Photo. **1112** GERARDO MAGALLON/Getty Images. **1113** AP Images/Cliff Schiappa. **1115** New York Daily News Archive/Getty Images. **1116** Robert King/Getty Images. **1117** Brooks Kraft/Getty Images. **1118** Collection 9/11 Memorial Museum, Gift of the Weinberg family in memory of our beloved Michael, Photograph by Michael Hnatov. **1119** Everett Collection Historical/Alamy Stock Photo. **1120** Siegfried Layda/Getty Images. **1122** WathiqKhuzaie/Getty Images. **1124-1125** (spread) The Washington Post/Getty Images. **1125** Poolservice/Getty Images. **1127** AP Images/Eric Gay. **1128** The Washington Post/Getty Images. **1130** ©Official White House Photo by Pete Souza. **1131** ©Official White House Photo by Pete Souza. **1133** AP Images/John Minchillo. **1134** Bloomberg/Getty Images. **1137** PETE MCBRIDE /National Geographic Creative. **1139** Lou Linwei/Alamy Stock Photo. **1140** Kat Keene Hogue/National Geographic Creative. **1141** BRIAN FINKE/National Geographic Creative. **1142** DAVID GUTTENFELDER/National Geographic creative. **1144** MANDEL NGAN/Getty Images. **1146** (t)(b) LynseyAddario/Reportage/Getty Images. **1147** (t)

LynseyAddario/Reportage/Getty Images. (cr) Roberto Ricciuti/Getty Images. (b) LynseyAddario/Reportage/Getty Images. **1150** CAROLYN VAN HOUTEN/National Geographic Creative. **1152** (tl) AP Images/Uncredited. (tr) Pictorial Press Ltd/Alamy Stock Photo. (cl) J. R. EYERMAN/Getty Images. (bl) GalerieBilderwelt/Getty Images. (br) The Library of Congress. **1153** (tl) Bruno Barbey/Magnum. (tr) Historical/Getty Images. (cl) Bettmann/Getty Images. (cr) Spencer Platt/Getty Images. (bl) Ebet Roberts/ Redferns/Getty Images. (cr) The Library of Congress. (br) Jonathan Bachman/Reuters. **R0-R1** Danita Delimont/Getty Images. **R2** Kumar Sriskandan/Alamy Stock Photo.**R10** Chip Somodevilla/Getty Images. **R16** Mark Wilson/Getty Images. **R17** Jonathan Ernst/Reuters. **R19** National Archives. **R26** Everett Collection Inc/Alamy Stock Photo. **R27** Underwood Archives/Getty Images. **R28** Underwood Archives/Getty Images. **R32** Bettmann/Getty Images. **R33** Blend Images-Hill Street Studios/Getty Images. **R35** David Ryder/Reuters. **R36** RHONA WISE/Getty Images.

Illustration and Map Credits

Unless otherwise indicated, all illustrations were created by Lachina and all maps were created by Mapping Specialists.

Text Credits

Pg. 921 "Letter from Birmingham City Jail," by Dr. Martin Luther King Jr. April 16, 1963. Reprinted by arrangement with The Heirs to the Estate of Martin Luther King Jr., c/o Writers House as agent for the proprietor New Nork, NY. ©1963 Dr. Martin Luther King Jr. ©Renewed 1991 Loretta Scott King.

Pg. 922 "I Have a Dream," by Dr. Martin Luther King Jr. Reprinted by arrangement with The Heirs to the Estate of Martin Luther King Jr., c/o Writers House as agent for the proprietor New Nork, NY. ©1963 Martin Luther King Jr. ©Renewed 1991 Coretta Scott King.